september

brabners chaffe street
bristows (for september interviews)
cadwalader, wickersham & taft
field fisher waterhouse
herbert smith
hewitson becke + shaw
hill dickinson
keoghs
laytons
leboeuf, lamb, greene & macrae
lovells
mcdermott, will & emery
prettys
shadbolt & co
taylor vinters
thring townsend
wedlake bell

1 training contract application deadline:
fenners

30 training contract application deadline:
cleary, gottlieb, steen & hamilton
cumberland ellis peirs
hodge jones & allen (for 2004)
taylor walton
travers smith braithwaite

31 training contract application deadline:
gouldens
teacher stern selby

The Law Society's Guide to Good Practice requires law firms not to interview students for training contracts before 1st September in the final year of undergraduate study. For the full regulations see www.lawsoc.org.uk

april

15 vacation scheme application deadline:
- penningtons (summer)

30 vacation scheme application deadline:
- fenners
- hill dickinson
- taylor walton
- ward hadaway

> Why not spend a part of your vacation at a law firm or undertaking a mini-pupillage?

june

30 training contract application deadline:
- henmans
- hugh james

july

24 training contract application deadline:
- freshfields bruckhaus deringer (non-law grads)

25 training contract application deadline:
- sidley austin brown & wood

27 training contract application deadline:
- watson, farley & williams

28 training contract application deadline:
- baker & mckenzie (law)
- olswang

31 training contract application deadline:
- addleshaw booth & co
- ashurst morris crisp
- barlow lyde & gilbert
- berwin leighton paisner
- bevan ashford
- bird & bird
- blake lapthorn
- bond pearce
- boyes turner
- brachers
- browne jacobson
- campbell hooper
- capsticks
- charles russell
- cms cameron mckenna
- cobbetts
- coffin mew & clover
- coudert brothers
- covington & burling
- cripps harries hall
- dechert
- d j freeman
- dickinson dees
- dla
- edwards geldard
- eversheds
- farrer & co
- finers stephens innocent
- fladgate fielder
- forbes
- freethcartwright
- gateley wareing
- goodman derrick
- halliwell landau
- hammond suddards edge
- harbottle & lewis
- holman fenwick & willan
- howes percival
- ince & co
- irwin mitchell
- klegal
- landwell
- lawrence graham
- lee bolton & lee
- lewis silkin
- linnells
- lupton fawcett
- macfarlanes
- manches
- martineau johnson
- masons
- mayer, brown, rowe & maw
- mccormicks
- mcdermott, will & emery
- mishcon de reya
- morgan cole
- nabarro nathanson
- nicholson graham & jones
- osborne clarke
- pinsent curtis biddle
- pritchard englefield
- radcliffeslebrasseur
- reed smith warner cranston
- richards butler
- russell jones & walker
- salans
- shearman & sterling
- shoosmiths
- sj berwin
- spechly bircham
- stephenson harwood
- theodore goddard
- thomson snell & passmore
- walker morris
- ward hadaway
- weightman vizards
- weil, gotshal & manges
- white & case
- withers
- wragge & co

august

1 training contract application deadline:
- beachcroft wansbroughs
- norton rose
- pannone & partners
- payne hicks beach
- trowers & hamlins

2 training contract application deadline:
- dwf

8 training contract application deadline:
- burges salmon
- denton wilde sapte
- russell-cooke
- taylor wessing

15 training contract application deadline:
- arnold & porter
- clyde & co
- mills & reeve
- penningtons
- reynolds porter chamberlain
- simmons & simmons

16 training contract application deadline:
- lester aldridge
- tlt solicitors

21 training contract application deadline:
- wiggin & co

24 training contract application deadline:
- freshfields bruckhaus deringer (law grads)

31 training contract application deadline:
- allen & overy (law students)

CALENDAR OF EVENTS

february

5 university of nottingham law fair

7 **vacation scheme application deadline:**
slaughter and may
withers

12 university of sheffield law fair

14 **vacation scheme application deadline:**
addleshaw booth & co
arnold & porter
bird & bird
freshfields bruckhaus deringer
gateley wareing
holman fenwick & willan
ince & co
lovells (easter and summer)
speechly bircham
weil, gotshal & manges

chambers student guide essay competition deadline

15 **vacation scheme application deadline:**
penningtons (easter)
richards butler

17 university of hull law fair

18 **training contract application deadline:**
baker & mckenzie (non-law)

19 university of wales, swansea law fair

21 **vacation scheme application deadline:**
burges salmon
klegal
masons
simmons & simmons
stephenson harwood
taylor wessing

28 **training contract application deadline:**
allen & overy (cpe candidates)
davenport lyons (for 2004)

vacation scheme application deadline:
barlow lyde & gilbert
berwin leighton paisner
bristows (easter and summer)
capsticks
clyde & co
covington & burling
d j freeman
dechert
dickinson dees
dla
edwards geldard
field fisher waterhouse
gouldens (easter and summer)
hammond suddards edge
macfarlanes
mccormicks
nabarro nathanson
pannone & partners
pinsent curtis biddle
reynolds porter chamberlain
shoosmiths
theodore goddard
walker morris
wedlake bell
white & case

march

1 **vacation scheme application deadline:**
irwin mitchell
mills & reeve
olswang
trowers & hamlins

2 **vacation scheme application deadline:**
watson, farley & williams

10 **vacation scheme application deadline:**
nicholson graham & jones

14 **vacation scheme application deadline:**
denton wilde sapte

17 **vacation scheme application deadline:**
mishcon de reya

28 **vacation scheme application deadline:**
radcliffeslebrasseur

30 **vacation scheme application deadline:**
finers stephensons innocent

31 **training contract application deadline:**
mace & jones (for 2004)

vacation scheme application deadline:
bevan ashford
bond pearce
foot anstey sargent
halliwell landau
laytons
lester aldridge
morgan cole
taylor vinters

CHAMBERS AND PARTNERS
STUDENT GUIDE:

2002

november

1 vacation scheme application deadline:
norton rose (christmas)

5 university of leicester law fair

6 university of east anglia law fair

8 vacation scheme application deadline:
clifford chance (christmas)

12 university of bristol law fair

13 university of bristol law fair (continued)

14 university of manchester law fair

15 university of st andrews law fair

vacation scheme application deadline:
lovells (christmas)

16 oxford university law fair

18 university of leeds law fair

19 university of liverpool law fair

20 queen mary, university of london law fair
queen's university, belfast law fair
university of reading law fair

21 city university law fair
university of southampton careers evening

22 vacation scheme application deadline:
herbert smith (christmas)

25 university of newcastle law fair

26 university of durham law fair
university of warwick law fair

27 university of birmingham law fair

29 vacation scheme application deadline:
bristows (christmas)

december

2 university college london law fair

3 university college london law fair (continued)

5 university of cambridge law event

6 university of cambridge law event (continued)

31 training contract application deadline:
dmh (for 2004)

2003

january

22 university of exeter law fair

27 king's college, london law fair

28 king's college, london law fair (continued)

30 northumbria university law fair

31 training contract application deadline:
bristows (for february interviews)

vacation scheme application deadline:
allen & overy
ashurst morris crisp
baker & mckenzie
clifford chance
dmh
eversheds
farrer & co
herbert smith (easter and summer)
lawrence graham
manches
norton rose (summer)
osborne clarke
reed smith warner cranston
sj berwin
travers smith braithwaite
wragge & co

Keep an eye out for events organised by your student law society, law faculty or careers service

Published by Chambers and Partners Publishing
(a division of Orbach & Chambers Ltd)
Saville House, 23 Long Lane, London EC1A 9HL
Tel: (020) 7606 1300 Fax: (020) 7600 3191
email: info@ChambersandPartners.co.uk
www.ChambersandPartners.com

Our thanks to the many students, trainees, pupils, solicitors, barristers, graduate recruitment personnel and careers officers who assisted us in our research. Also to Chambers and Partners recruitment team for their knowledge and assistance and to the researchers of the Chambers Guide to the UK Legal Profession 2002-2003 and Chambers Global 2002-2003 from which all firm rankings are drawn.

Copyright © 2002 Michael Chambers and
Orbach & Chambers Ltd
ISBN: 0-85514-305-3

Publisher: Michael Chambers
Managing Editor: Fiona Boxall
Editor: Anna Williams
Writers: Rob Wainwright, James Plummer, Ian Malone, Juliette Seddon, Amy Clemitshaw, David Nicholls
Database Team: Nigel Birch, Derek Wright
A-Z Team: Nicola Cowan, Alex Ballantine
Production: Laurie Griggs
Business Development Manager: Brad D. Sirott
Business Development Team: Richard Ramsay, Neil Murphy, Sarah Lovell, Janis Witicki
Proofreaders: Frances Worlock, Rita Perry, Sarah Reardon

Printed by: Polestar Wheatons Limited

CONTENTS

starting out

choices

contacts
useful numbers, addresses and websites to get
you started   6

solicitor or barrister?
we help you make that all
important first decision   8

CPE/PgDL
who needs to do it and where is it offered   13

funding
how to get funding for the CPE/PgDL, LPC, BVC
and pupillage   15

cvs and application forms
some very useful do's and don'ts   17

i wish i'd done more at university
top tips on how to make a good impression   19

solicitors section

solicitors timetable
what to do and when to do it   22

vacation schemes
fancy spending your vacation with a top law firm?
the full skinny on who's offering what   23

preferred universities and lpc providers
we found out which unis and LPC courses law firms
really rate   28

the lpc
how to choose a law school plus law society
assessment grades   30

lpc providers – the inside story
what law school students and graduates really
think about their colleges   32

applications and selection
making sense of it all and how to avoid being
a pushover during group excercises   41

applications and selection table
open days and interviews – who does what and
how many training contracts are they offering?   43

what the top firms are looking for
which buttons you should be aiming to press   49

what you are looking for – salaries table
the hard cash plus law school sponsorship   51

paralegal questions
answers to the most commonly asked questions   60

qualifying in other jurisdictions
new york, australia and scotland – how to
qualify in each   62

prospects for newly qualifieds
it seems a long time away, but you should be
thinking about it now   64

becoming an english solicitor
qualifying in the UK from abroad   66

barristers section

barristers timetable
what to do and when to
do it   68

thinking of the bar?
an introduction to the
sometimes mystifying
world of the bar   69

the bvc
what students really think of the eight bar schools   72

money, money, money...
how to get your hands on the £3 million
available from the inns of court   77

the inns of court
which one do you join?   79

www.ChambersandPartners.com

mini-pupillages
are they really necessary and how do you get one? **82**

getting pupillage
OLPAS is a year old. we examine the agony and the ecstasy of securing pupillage **83**

practice areas at the bar
chancery, commercial, common law, criminal, employment, family, public law **72**

specialist practice areas

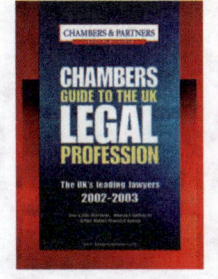

what you should know about the main areas of law and a guide to who does them best. information about the top firms hot off the press from the *Chambers Guide to the UK Legal Profession 2002-2003*. banking, competition, construction, corporate, crime, employment, environmental, family, IP, litigation, media, personal injury, private client, property, public interest, shipping, sports, tax, TMT **97**

international firms...international locations

leading international firms
the big-hitters from *Chambers Global 2002-2003* **174**

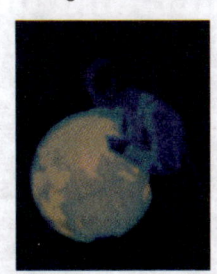

top ten trainee get-aways
postcards from near, far and the edge **175**

who goes there?
if you're after an overseas seat, check our table to find out which firms are where **183**

the true picture

it's bigger than ever this year so put down that firm brochure and get the true picture here. we interviewed hundreds of trainees and newly qualified solicitors at our top 120 firms and asked them to tell us about their training contracts in their own words... and they did!

introduction
how we research plus what's new at law firms in 2002 **186**

our 120 firms table
120 english and welsh firms chosen by size of trainee populations **188**

the true picture reports
frank, detailed and uncut! **191**

A-Zs

the phone numbers, addresses and e-mails you need to make your applications. plus loads of really useful facts and figures on the top law firms. all in simple easy to follow A-Z format

universities and law schools A-Z	442
barristers A-Z	453
solicitors A-Z	457

www.ChambersandPartners.com

ESSAY COMPETITION
PRIZE £3,000

Subject: Is the law, compared to science and the liberal arts, too narrow a subject to inflict on undergraduates?

Open to those studying law at undergraduate, postgraduate and vocational level.
Closing date 14th February 2003
For competition rules check out the Student Guide website
www.ChambersandPartners.com

STARTING OUT

contacts	6
solicitor or barrister?	8
CPE/PgDL	13
funding	14
cvs and application forms	17
i wish i'd done more at university	19
solicitors timetable	22
vacation schemes	23
preferred universities and LPC providers	28
LPC	30
applications and selections	41
what the top firms are looking for	49
what you are looking for (salaries table)	51
paralegal questions	60
overseas qualifications	62
prospects for NQs	64
becoming an english solicitor	66
barristers timetable	68
thinking of the bar?	69
BVC	72
money, money, money... and the inns of court	77
pupillage – minis, getting it and after	82
practice areas at the bar	86

CONTACTS

The Law Society:	114 Chancery Lane, London WC2A 1PL Tel: 020 7242 1222 Email: info-services@lawsociety.org.uk www.lawsoc.org.uk
Legal Education and Training Department:	Tel: 0870 606 2555 Email: legaled@lawsociety.org.uk www.training.lawsociety.org.uk
Trainee Solicitors Group:	The Law Society 114 Chancery Lane, London WC2A 1PL Tel: 020 7320 5794 Email: info@tsg.org www.tsg.org.uk
The Bar Council:	3 Bedford Row, London WC1R 4DB Tel: 020 7242 0082 www.barcouncil.org
Education and Training Department:	2/3 Cursitor Street, London EC4A 1NE Tel: 020 7440 4000 www.legaleducation.org.uk
Gray's Inn, Education Department:	8 South Square. Gray's Inn, London WC1R 5ET Tel: 020 7458 7900 www.graysinn.org.uk
Inner Temple, Education & Training Department:	Treasurer's Office, Inner Temple, London EC4Y 7HL Tel: 020 7797 8250 www.innertemple.org.uk
Lincoln's Inn, Students' Department:	Treasury Office, Lincoln's Inn, London WC2A 3TL Tel: 020 7405 0138 www.lincolnsinn.org.uk
Middle Temple, Students' Department:	Treasury Office, Middle Temple, London EC4Y 9AT Tel: 0207 427 4800 www.middletemple.org.uk
Career Development Loans:	Freepost, Warrington WA4 6FB Tel: (freephone) 0800 585505 www.lifelonglearning.co.uk/cdl
Government Legal Service:	Recruitment Team GLS Secretariat, Queen Anne's Chambers, 28 Broadway, London SW1H 9JS Tel: 020 7210 3574/3304/3386 E-mail: recruit@gls.gsi.gov.uk www.gls.gov.uk
Crown Prosecution Service:	50 Ludgate Hill, London EC4M 7EX Tel: 020 7796 8053 www.cps.gov.uk

CONTACTS

The Law Centres Federation:	Duchess House, 18-19 Warren Street, London W1T 5LR Tel: 020 7387 8570 Email: info@lawcentres.org.uk
Institute of Chartered Secretaries and Administrators:	16 Park Crescent, London W1B 1AH Tel: 020 7580 4741 www.icsa.org.uk
The Institute of Legal Executives:	Kempston Manor, Kempston, Bedfordshire MK42 7AB Tel: 01234 841000 Email: info@ilex.org.uk www.ilex.org.uk
Chartered Institute of Patent Agents:	Staple Inn Buildings, High Holborn, London WC1V 7PZ Tel: 020 7405 9450 Email: mail@cipa.org.uk www.cipa.org.uk
Institute of Trade Mark Attorneys:	Canterbury House, 2-6 Sydenham Road, Croydon, Surrey CR0 9XE Tel: 020 8686 2052 www.itma.org.uk
Free Representation Unit:	Fourth Floor, Peer House, 8-14 Verulam Street, London WC1X 8LZ Tel: 020 7831 0692 www.fru.org.uk
The Law Commission:	Conquest House, 37-38 John Street, Theobalds Road, London WC1N 2BQ Tel: 020 7453 1220 Email: secretary@lawcommission.gsi.gov.uk www.lawcom.gov.uk
Citizens Advice Bureaux:	Head Office, Myddleton House, 115-123 Pentonville Road, London N1 9LZ Tel: 020 7833 2181 www.nacab.org.uk
Legal Services Commission:	Head office, 85 Gray's Inn Road, London WC1X 8TX Tel: 020 7759 0000 www.legalservices.gov.uk
CPE Central Applications Board:	P.O. Box No. 84, Guildford, Surrey GU3 1YX Tel: 01483 451080 www.lawcabs.ac.uk
LPC Central Applications Board:	P.O. Box No. 84, Guildford, Surrey GU3 1YX Tel: 01483 301282 www.lawcabs.ac.uk
Online Pupillage Application System:	Helpline: 01491 828918 Email: olpas@gti.co.uk www.olpas.gti.co.uk

solicitor or barrister?

Commercial law firms commonly offer training contracts two years before they start, so your decision as to which branch of the profession to follow needs to be made earlier than you might prefer. Unless you're intending to take a year or two out, it won't be possible to wait until you finish your law degree before picking a profession. We hope that this guide will help you to decide what type of career you want and how to go about achieving it.

Your decision should be based on two things - the nature of the work and the likelihood that you will be successful in your chosen career. We'll discuss both.

barrister

Opting for the Bar will automatically put you in line for a stream of raised eyebrows and words in your shell-like urging you to think carefully about your choice. In the wake of such cautionary advice, many wannabe barristers join the majority of aspiring lawyers and take the solicitor route. There's a tacit acceptance by most students that it's easier to become a solicitor as the Bar embraces only the best of candidates. But how do you know if you should step up to the start line and put yourself forward as one of the best?

To choose the Bar half-heartedly is unwise, but it's equally unwise to throw away a long-held dream. Match your passion with realism when you decide if the Bar is for you. In spite of the dismal success rates for those seeking a long-term career at the Bar, good chambers are desperate for high-calibre candidates and are concerned that the City law firms will snap up the brightest young talent.

If your academic record and inter-personal skills are excellent, the next step will be to make sure your preconceptions of a career at the Bar are accurate. Don't just rely on your image of Rumpole of the Bailey or the roles portrayed in *This Life* and *North Square*.

A barrister sets himself apart from a solicitor by the services he provides. His two main functions are advocacy and specialist opinion. If advocacy is what draws you to the law, the Bar is an obvious place for you but it is no longer the only place. The gradual erosion of the Bar's monopoly on advocacy has been hastened by the Access to Justice Act 1999. The basic principle is that appropriately qualified solicitors must have equal rights of audience. If you want to read more on this topic turn to the **Litigation** practice area section in the second part of this book. Even as a barrister, the amount of advocacy you'll undertake will depend on the area of law in which you specialise. Read the **Practice areas at the Bar** section on pages 86 to 95. If you choose an advocacy-heavy area of practice though, you'll need to develop a sophisticated, persuasive, clear and concise style. If you've always hated mooting, are you reading the right section of this book?

But advocacy is not the be all and end all. The smart young barrister will specialise and secure career success by offering genuine expertise in a particular field. There will always be a demand from solicitors for a second legal opinion on complex cases and often advocacy will play no part in the service a barrister provides.

When researching the Bar sections of *Chambers UK*, our colleagues get plenty of feedback from solicitors and lay clients as to why they respect various leading barristers. Not every barrister excels in every aspect of the job, but they all have at least one aspect in which they are superb. Some are magnificent on their feet in court and those who can modify their performance appropriately for judges, witnesses and (where relevant) jury are especially valued. Some barristers may not be the smoothest or silkiest of advocates, but their knowledge of the law and the industry sector for which they work is unparalleled.

Solicitors frequently describe such barristers as not just bright but *"fearfully bright."* In today's legal profession solicitors are continually asking themselves "Why buy a dog if I can bark myself?" Well, if the dog can bark better...

The Bar Council's own website states that the following skills are prerequisite:
- **academic ability**
- **written and oral communication skills**
- **numeracy skills**
- **interpersonal skills**
- **personal effectiveness**
- **IT skills**
- **professional responsibility**
- **a commitment to continuing professional development**

As a barrister, your working environment will be completely different to that of your solicitor peers. You'll be self-employed for a start and that means you'll have to pay rent in chambers, VAT on your earnings and organise your own tax returns. You'll also be the master of your own destiny. Establishing a client base and keeping it will become a priority, although the majority of barristers work in sets or groups of barristers, sharing premises called chambers. Chambers will provide a support network and the opportunity to share the services of professional managers called clerks. But you'll not be sharing your fees with fellow members of your set. Notions of partnership are absent. You'll rise or fall on your own merits.

Seeking out funding for Bar school will be an important task. Rich parents will prove enormously useful, but face it, you don't all have them. Before you start looking at your family in a completely different (and less than loving) light, read the **Funding** section on pages 14 to 15 and **Money, money, money...** on page 77.

If you haven't been warned before then take this as the first in a long line of warnings. The young Bar is feeling the pinch at the moment with dwindling fees, increased competition from solicitors and fewer cases reaching court. For every three graduates who commence the BVC, only one will find a lasting career at the Bar. Those graduates preparing to take the BVC have reconciled themselves to the fact that to have a serious stab at a career at the Bar, they must be prepared to spend a couple of years attempting to secure pupillage. On the plus side, if things do not go quite according to plan, do remember that the BVC is a valuable qualification.

solicitor

The majority of you will choose to qualify as a solicitor. Unless you plan to take a year out for travel or other experience, for those seeking to train in a commercial firm (as opposed to a high street practice) the decision making process should start in the second year of a three-year law degree or the final year of a non-law degree. This is because the larger commercial firms generally offer training contracts two years prior to their commencement. Your choice of training contract is crucial, as it will determine your finances, your geography and your experiences.

After finishing your degree, law school awaits. If you have a law degree then you'll do time for just one year on the Legal Practice Course (LPC). Those with a non-law degree must complete the one-year CPE/PgDL before being eligible to take the LPC. The larger and more commercial firms will offer scholarships to cover course fees and some maintenance for the LPC and (if necessary) the CPE/PgDL. Some firms will require you to attend one of the three law schools that offer the City LPC. It's a course designed to cater for the corporate and finance work of these firms.

The client base and work on offer at a particular firm will determine the experience you gain and your future marketability as a lawyer. Selecting the right firm for you is a crucial decision. In addition to finding out about the size and location of a firm and the work they handle, you should research the firm's reputation and learn about its culture. At Chambers and Partners, we've made it our business to know who does what, how well they do it and what it might be like working at a particular firm. In the **Practice Areas** section of this book, you'll find tables drawn from the research of *Chambers UK*. These tables will help you work out which firms have the best reputations for different areas of work. An enormous amount of information is available in *Chambers UK*, including details of the top clients and deals of law firms as well as their reputation. All this information is available on our website: www.chambersandpartners.com and copies of the book should be available in your university careers office. If you want to throw your research net even wider, you can find out about a firm's international work and reputation in *Chambers Global* and shortly in a new publication called *Chambers US*.

We've profiled 120 of the leading firms in England and Wales in the **True Picture**, giving you a taster of life on the inside as a trainee. This section seeks to give you an indication of the kind of firm that might suit you and the kind of work you can expect to receive when you get there. Law firms come in all shapes and sizes. Do your research, do a bit of navel-gazing and work out what's best for you.

Magic Circle: Slaughter and May, Clifford Chance, Freshfields, Allen & Overy and Linklaters. These are seen by many as the elite and are high paying, hard working and very corporate and finance oriented. The prestige that attaches to a magic circle training is undeniable and, to that end, there are many students who'd consider going nowhere else. Whether this is because of the advice they are given by course directors, careers advisors, friends already at these firms or plain herd mentality, the fact is that these firms do have the pick of the best and offer a superb training. Their size and big-money deals will not appeal to all students and it's important that those who'd fare better in a smaller environment feel able to make an alternative choice.

London - commercial: The top 10 City of London firms will offer around 1,000 training contracts between them in 2002, representing around 20% of all training contracts registered by the Law Society. At trainee level there's not a huge difference between the magic circle and firms such as Lovells, Herbert Smith and others of their ilk. In these largest commercial firms, work is almost entirely focused around business law, although a tiny number retain specialists in family law and private client. Hours are often long, but the money is very good. Expect high-profile and challenging work. Expect to be pushed and, at times, be prepared to give 110%. If you are working against a deadline on a deal then you will be expected to stay until it is finished. This can mean working through the night and coming in at weekends from time to time.

To get into one of the top firms you will need a consistently excellent academic record, from A-Levels through to your first- and second-year exam results or final degree. Unfortunately you'll need to go right to the back of a very long queue if you failed to gain at least a 2:1. Recruitment personnel in City firms are also keen to ensure that prospective trainees possess commercial awareness. In other words, understanding what businesses want, how they work and what lawyers can do to help them. You need to show that you have an interest in law, an interest in business and an interest in the firm you are going to. If you can't… there's something wrong with your decision.

Regionals: The City of London may be the beating heart of big, blue-chip international business, but there's more to life than an EC postcode. Out in the regions firms such as Dickinson Dees, Burges Salmon and Wragge & Co – to name but a few – offer top-notch clients and some international work. While some regional firms might as well be top London firms, which just happen to be based in the regions, others focus on regional clients and work.

Regional firms can be every bit as difficult to get into as their City rivals. In some cases you are statistically more likely to get into a magic circle firm, as the ratio of vacancies to applications can be much better at the bigger practices. If the magic circle has refused you, don't assume you'll walk into a top regional firm ... they are unimpressed by sloppy-seconds applications. If you are applying to join a firm in Bristol, for example, and have studied and lived in London all your life, be prepared to be asked why you want to move to the area. The last thing firms want is to spend a fortune on training only for newly qualified lawyers to swan off to jobs in the City. Recruitment personnel at the top regional practices are looking for exactly the same abilities and experience as the top City firms.

Salaries are lower outside London, in some cases significantly so, but the cost of living is much more reasonable than in the capital. You will also benefit from less frenetic hours than the largest City-based practices. Regional firms have a reputation for (generally) being a bit friendlier, a bit calmer and a bit more human than the City. As you will see in the *True Picture*, however, it is all about finding a firm, which has an atmosphere to suit you.

Nationals: There's a breed of firm called the national firm. These organisations have offices in a number of UK cities. Eversheds has the greatest number of offices (11); DLA, Hammond Suddards Edge, Addleshaw Booth and Pinsent Curtis Biddle each have a handful. A London office is the norm, with others commonly in Birmingham, Leeds and Manchester. Each of the nationals have a different approach to recruitment and whether or not trainees move around the country, so make sure you know the policy adopted by your chosen firm.

Niche: Particularly in London, but to a degree elsewhere in the country, there are a variety of niche firms to choose from. Construction, entertainment, IP, insurance litigation, family... the list goes on. If you are absolutely certain that you want to specialise in a particular practice area (particularly if you have already worked in the relevant industry) a niche firm is a sound choice. Be aware that many firms described as niche practices actually offer much more besides.

High Street: Practices range from larger, long-established firms in large town centres to sole practitioners working above shops in the suburbs. These firms act for clients on legal aid, individuals funding themselves and local businesses. Staple work includes matrimonial, landlord and tenant, personal injury, employment, family, wills and probate, and crime. It's increasingly likely that firms have an additional specialism in small-ticket commercial work for local businesses.

Be prepared to earn considerably less than those in commercial practice – commonly, trainees are paid at the Law Society's minimum salary level – £13,000pa for the provinces and £14,600pa for inner London. The hours can be unsociable if you find yourself working in crime, but in this kind of firm you will get to handle clients and real work from a very early stage and you'll grow up fast! You'll also have an opportunity to see how the law actually affects individuals and the community in which you practice. The largest firms may take on four or five trainees a year while the smallest will recruit as and when trainees are needed. Unlike commercial firms, most do not recruit two years in advance and most do not sponsor students through the LPC.

government

Although the vast majority of training contracts are in private practice, there are opportunities in local and central government.

Government Legal Service: About 30 training positions are available with the Government Legal Service every year. The majority are in London with the occasional one in Manchester. Positions are available for both trainee solicitors and pupil barristers and, according to Peter Beecroft, Recruitment Manager for the Service, the split was roughly evenly between the two types last year. *"We don't mind which branch of the profession they wish to pursue, it's their good mind, communication skills and commitment to become a good Government lawyer we're after."*

Various departments take trainees/pupils every year, namely Customs & Excise, Inland Revenue, the DTI, the Department for Work & Pensions/Department of Health, the Treasury Solicitor's Department, the Home Office, Department for Environment, Food and Rural Affairs, the Lord Chancellor's Department and the Office of the Deputy Prime Minister/Department for Transport. Some departments take one trainee; others up to half a dozen. Legal teams vary in size from a single lawyer in some of the smaller bodies to up to 300 in larger departments and agencies, in particular the Treasury Solicitor's Department and the Lord Chancellor's Department. Successful candidates are asked to nominate the area in which they would like to work.

Trainee solicitor 'seats' are allocated after discussion with trainees. *"If they're in a large department, they might be able to get all the experience they need,"* says Peter, adding that they may be trained in more than one department if that is needed to give them the right experience. The training involves a variety of work, concerned with both public and private law, including *"learning about litigation, working on government contracts and giving advice to ministers or administrators generally."* However, trainees are unlikely to work on the drafting of legislation, although *"maybe they would observe the process from the fringe."*

For pupil barristers, some departments follow the traditional 'two-six' system, whereby six months are spent in a barristers Chambers and the other six within the GLS. Other departments have adopted the newer 'four-four-four' system: starting in their government department, going out to a barristers chambers and then returning to their department.

The first stage in securing training with the GLS is to contact its recruitment team, rather than the departments themselves. The GLS recruits two years before the pupillage/training contract begins and all vacancies are advertised in the national press and on the GLS website. Sponsorship for the LPC/BVC is available. A vacation scheme offers two- or three-week work placements.

Local government: Around the country there are hundreds of local authority legal departments, some of which will offer training contracts. The variety of work and experience to be gained is certainly wide and for many there's real appeal in working for a public sector organisation that's closely involved with their local environment and community. For further information on a career in local government try **www.lgcareers.com.**

other

The Crown Prosecution service and a small number of law centres offer training contracts, as do certain large companies and banks. For information on in-house legal teams registered to take trainees check the Law Society's website.

CPE/PgDL

If you've not studied for a law degree but have decided on a career at the Bar or as a solicitor, you'll need to take the Common Professional Exam (CPE) or its equivalent, a Postgraduate Diploma in Law (PgDL).

who's it open to?

The standard qualification requirement is a degree from a university in the UK or the Republic of Ireland. If your degree is from an overseas university you'll need to apply to the Law Society or to the General Council of the Bar for a Certificate of Academic Standing. This certificate is also required if, in the absence of a degree, you wish to apply on the basis of other professional qualifications (eg a Diploma in Magisterial Law). If your degree has a legal component, you should investigate exemption from certain aspects of the CPE.

The CPE can be done on a one-year full-time or two-year part-time basis. The full-time course stacks up to a notional 1,620 hours or 45 hours of lectures, tutorials, private study and research in each week of the course. To ascertain the exact course content, obtain brochures for a number of colleges that interest you. Each will start off with an introductory course on the English Legal System and basic legal research skills, followed by:

- Law of Contract
- Law of Tort
- Criminal Law
- Public Law
- Land Law
- Equity & Trusts
- Law of the European Union
- One other area of legal study.

There are now around 30 CPE/PgDL providers to choose from. How do you make the right choice? Unlike the LPC course, there are no formal assessments made by the Law Society. You might consider the LPC performance assessments to be of relevance, particularly if you intend to stay at the same institution for your LPC. These assessment reports are worth reading as they are quite detailed about a school's strengths and weaknesses.

Some students use the CPE to maximise their chances of getting onto a popular LPC course. BPP is oversubscribed as an LPC provider and the majority of its places on the LPC are allocated to students who will train at one of eight City law firms. BPP also guarantees a place to those who did their CPE at BPP.

Certain colleges - Nottingham Law School and City University, for example - are over-subscribed by virtue of their reputation for academic excellence. City Uni is seen to offer a top-notch and academically rigorous CPE course and is a favourite amongst many aspiring barristers. It comes as no surprise that City has now tied up with the Inns of Court School of Law. The College of Law receives the largest number of applications and, across its five branches, it offers the greatest number of places. For a full list of all course providers and full details on how to apply, log on to the CPE/PgDL Applications Board website at **www.lawcabs.ac.uk**. The board also publishes a booklet called *A Guide to CPE/Postgraduate Diploma in Law Courses*.

Location and price will naturally be important. Prices for full-time courses hover between £3,000 and £6,000. For students who feel most at home in cyberspace, the University of Huddersfield offers an internet-based PgDL course by way of distance learning.

funding

The essay competition we ran in conjunction with last year's *Student Guide* asked the question: "Do lawyers deserve what they earn?" It brought a flood of responses, many detailing the impoverished state into which law students sink. It's one thing dreaming about a fat wallet, but how do you actually find the cash to see you through law school and on towards the filthy lucre?

grants

Some local authority grants may be available. Our advice is to apply as early as possible, but don't hold your breath. Discretionary awards will be means-tested in relation to your own and, if relevant, your parent's income. Make sure you understand the criteria on which awards are made and establish whether or not you should be judged as a mature or independent student. Local authorities differ in their classification of applicants. Get started by checking out the Department for Education and Skills' web page **www.dfes.gov.uk/studentsupport**.

hardship awards and charities

Do ask your law school if any such funds exist and find out if you qualify. Find out from your local authority or local libraries if there are local charities or trusts that might be a source of funds.

bank loans

Some retail banks will offer special packages to post-graduate students. Certain banks go the extra mile for CPE/PgDL, LPC and BVC students (you may have seen Nat West at student law fairs) and there are some pretty good rates and repayment terms available; commonly, interest rates hover around 1% above base rate. Check out what your own bank is offering and then find out about some of the deals on offer from others. Ask your law school to tell you if they have negotiated a special package with a particular bank. For example, College of Law students can get special terms from NatWest. Although students might be carrying up to £12,000 of existing student loans plus overdrafts and credit card debts, banks are still willing to lend. It's crucial that you take the time to sit down with your bank and work out just how much you're going to have to pay back and when. Don't cripple yourself financially by maxing out on the loans. Ash Khan of NatWest has years of experience advising law students on their finances. His advise is to watch your expenditure carefully and draw down funds on a planned monthly basis.

Officially Lloyds TSB offers a Further Education Loan of up to £10,000, but applications can be made for more in certain cases. Barclays on the other hand offers £25,000 to law students over two years (especially helpful if you are taking the CPE). The interest rate is 2.5% above base rate with repayments beginning nine months after the course ends. 'Course' also includes pupillage so repayments can be delayed for some time.

career development loans

These are available through Barclays Bank, the Clydesdale, the Co-Operative, and the Royal Bank of Scotland on behalf of the DfES. The maximum loan is £8,000 and for the year of study and one month afterwards the Government pays the interest. It's not available if you receive a government grant or sponsorship from an employer. All you need to know is set out at **www.lifelonglearning.co.uk/cdl**.

the folks, part-time jobs and benefits

If your family can keep you afloat or lend you the money, this is obviously the cheapest option. But remember to be nice to them and work hard. The official line from law schools is that the courses they offer on a full-time basis are exactly that - full-time. If you intend to hold down a job and study, consider whether you should be studying part-time over two years rather than full-time over one. Many students find employment for a few hours a week or during vacations and colleges accept this as a necessity. Be realistic as to what you can achieve. Sadly, no state benefits are available to those on the CPE/PgDL, LPC or BVC. Remember to scoop up all the travel and other discounts on offer to students though.

solicitors

Law firm sponsorship: If you're aiming for commercial practice, you may be fortunate enough to have the offer of a training contract before you start the LPC, and your firm may stump up the cash for the course fees and a modest maintenance grant. Sponsorship is quite often available for the CPE/PgDL too. The **Salaries Table** on pages 51 to 59 details the law school funding on offer from leading firms.

Of course, many CPE and LPC students start the academic year without a training contract offer. For them it's a gamble as to whether they will then get any financial assistance or indeed whether they will get a training contract offer at all. There's no easy solution to this problem of having to commit to course fees before you know whether it will all be worth it in the end.

Law Society bursary scheme: The society grants a few awards and loans to CPE/PgDL and LPC students. Application forms are available from 1 March from the Law Society's Legal Education Department. The closing date is 10 May prior to the start of the course. Successful applicants will need to show they suffer from genuine hardship and prove outstanding achievement or dedication. A few scholarships are available for ethnic minority students. Contact the ethnic minorities careers officer at the society.

barristers

Scholarships and awards: Between them, the four Inns of Court distribute over £3 million a year in funding to those studying for the BVC, the CPE/PgDL and during pupillage. Some awards are merit-based; others take financial hardship into account. Students can only apply to one Inn for an award, and our interviews with pupils and junior tenants confirmed that the volume and size of awards is a key factor in choosing an Inn. Some opt for a few larger awards whilst others offer a greater number of more modest ones. Check out the separate funding section for barristers called **Money, money, money...** on page 79 and the **Table of scholarships from the Inns** on page 78.

The Bar Council has its own trust, which offers pupils interest-free loans up to a maximum of £5,000. There's a February deadline for applications. See the Bar Council's website **www.legaleducation.org.uk** for more info.

Pupillage awards and earnings: Very few sets provide any financial assistance for the CPE or the BVC but, thankfully, the tide has turned on pupillage funding. From the start of 2003 chambers must fund all pupillages. During the first six months a minimum award of £5,000 must be paid, and in the second six, all pupils must be guaranteed minimum earnings of £5,000. In addition, pupils must be paid for certain travel expenses and fees for compulsory courses. The practice of "devilling" - earning money by carrying out work for more senior members of chambers - is a feature at some sets, so you may earn more. At the top end of the commercial and Chancery Bar there are massive awards available. Often part of these awards can be drawn down early during the BVC year so the high-fliers should have few problems. Thankfully, the award for the first six months is tax-free and only when a pupil starts earning in the second six does tax kick in. It's no surprise that these are in place to entice the most talented applicants. Consult the *Pupillage and Awards Handbook* and the Olpas website for full information on what the different chambers are offering.

Professions

Do you need to finance your way through the CPE, LPC or BVC ?

Do you have a Relationship Bank Manager who understands the Legal Profession and can advise you on the options available ?

We are a specialist Branch, whose client base is completely legal. To discuss our Professional Trainee Loan Scheme, please write to:

Law Courts, Temple Bar Legal Centre
PO Box 11052
217 Strand
London WC2R 1AR

or contact Alan Mills, Senior Business Manager
Telephone: 020 7353 7664

Remember to mention the Chambers Student Guide

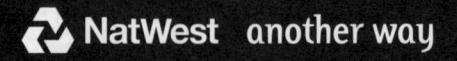

NatWest another way

Written quotations available on request. National Westminster Bank Plc. Registered Office: 135 Bishopsgate, London EC2M 3UR. Registered Number: 929027 England.

cvs and application forms

When deciding whether to interview candidates, most large employers will spend only a couple of minutes per CV making a first cut from the hundreds or thousands of applications they receive. A well-drafted CV or application form is essential.

There is no winning formula for writing a CV, but there are guidelines you should follow. Adhere to these principles and you won't be criticised for the way in which you present yourself.

- Limit your CV to two or three pages at most. US-style one-page documents work well as a summary but need supporting documentation so this might not be the best approach.
- Clarity and presentation are everything. Recruiters are looking for evidence of your ability to communicate well. Choose a clear font and use good quality white or cream paper. Typographical errors spell disaster and indicate that either you don't care or you simply can't get it right.
- Stay clear of borders, graphics and swirly fonts. These make a CV difficult to read and come across as gimmicky.
- The layout should be self-evident to the reader. At a glance they should know exactly where to find a specific piece of information.
- The things that most impress you about yourself may be of very little relevance to the reader. If you're mad keen on surfing then mention it as a hobby. However, this information belongs at the end of the CV in a brief section about your interests. Don't give top billing to your victory in the under-16 longboard competition at Fistral Beach six years ago. You're not applying for a life-guard's job.
- Read the firm's brochure and recruitment materials for hints as to the type of information/person it's looking for.
- Get feedback from family, friends, careers advisors and your tutors – these people will be happy to help you.
- Somewhere between an honest CV and one that contains outright lies is the CV that embellishes certain aspects of your experience. Don't be tempted to give false information; you will merely lay yourself open to being caught out. Similarly, don't be tempted to portray yourself as someone you are not. If you sang in the chorus line of the sixth form panto just the once, don't sell yourself as a chorister – the recruitment partner may wish to discuss Bach. Whilst he won't care that you can't sing, he will care that you tried to deceive him.
- If you have held posts of responsibility then stress these. Involvement in a variety of activities shows that you are a well-rounded person. Recruiters like active all-rounders and those who show initiative.
- Once it's finalised, read through your CV. If you don't recognise yourself then take another look at it and figure out what's gone wrong. A bureau can prepare your CV for you but will they capture the essence of who you are?

Some key 'don'ts':
- Don't attach a photograph.
- Don't bind your CV. It may stand out for the wrong reasons (the one that is difficult to photocopy or fit into an envelope).
- Don't leave gaps in your academic/job history. State when travelling, unemployed or taking a career break, etc.
- Don't fall into the trap of using worn-out clichés such as 'a highly motivated team player with excellent communication skills'. By saying this you say nothing. Demonstrate by example.
- Don't assume that recruiters will share your inter-

ests or your religious/moral/social concerns. Don't define yourself by them.
- Don't feel obliged to indicate your marital status or ethnic background on your CV. However, separate forms asking for details of your gender, ethnic or cultural background and any disabilities are often included with standard application forms. These should state specifically that the information is for the employer's statistical monitoring to ensure that it is adhering to its equal opportunities policy. Recruiters should separate this information from the application form before shortlisting candidates for interview.

Regarding application forms, recruiters stress the following:
- Don't send in a messy form. Unbelievably, some do arrive crumpled, coffee-ringed or with ink smudges.
- Excessive crossings out or miles of correction fluid don't impress. Using more than one pen to complete the form is off-putting. Always make a copy of the form and complete the copy first. Once you are satisfied, take your time in filling in the original.
- Some sections of the form have enormous significance. Recruiters look closely at the sections that give them clues as to what sort of person you are. It's make or break on these sections, so get them right. Those awful open-ended questions are designed to enable you to illustrate whether or not you have the qualities that make a good solicitor. They differ from form to form so don't just regurgitate a standard response, assuming that it will suit each firm. There might be two or three separate issues to be covered in the answer to a single question, so analyse it until you've spotted exactly what needs to be addressed.
- When asked why you chose the firm, don't just regurgitate the messages in the firm's recruitment material. The last thing recruiters want to see is a chewed-up version of their own words. What really attracted you to the firm? Did you meet people at a law fair? Does the firm handle exactly the areas of work that you want to experience? Is it the size of the firm, its location, or its client base? Maybe you just liked what we wrote about it in the *True Picture*.

Finally, pace yourself with your applications. If you end up doing 20 in two days the quality will suffer. Prepare a schedule or wallchart to map your progress and get applications in early. If you apply close to a deadline your application will be dealt with at a time when recruiters are very busy (and possibly very stressed!).

i wish i'd done more at university

The sooner you start planning your strategy for achieving your career ambitions, the better. This doesn't mean you have to become a bore or ruin your social life, just think ahead and ask yourself what sort of life you might want in four or five years' time.

don't cruise

At the risk of stating the obvious, performing below your academic potential is suicidal. You may not think those first- and second-year exam marks count but they do. If your CV is required before your final degree result is available, recruiters will look at the existing measures of your academic achievement. Your brilliance is irrelevant if you can't prove it. The message you'll send out by listing poor results is that you're either not capable of achieving better or you're simply not prepared to work that hard.

on a plate

Law firms and chambers try to woo the best students through presentations, careers evenings and sponsorship of events. True, the cash and manpower thrown at the students of some universities (Oxford, Cambridge, Bristol and some redbricks) is huge, while others will receive the modest attentions of local firms. Whether lavish or basic, social or serious, attend the events and gather what you can from them. Make contacts. These events are normally open to all students, not just those studying law. You'd be mad to miss out… that episode of *Eastenders* can surely wait until the omnibus on Sunday! For details, keep a close watch on your university careers service website or noticeboard, and monitor all events and info put together by the law faculty and/or student law society. For dates of the major university law fairs, see the calendar at the front of this book. Set some time aside during the holidays to undertake mini-pupillages or vacation schemes.

no comment

If you're aiming for commercial law then start keeping an eye on the financial and business news; this is step one in acquiring 'commercial awareness' - a trait that the majority of law firms bang on about and one that is so often missing in the students they recruit. Do you really want to have to go on a crash course on business definitions and corporate profiles just before you start attending interviews? It is much better to pick things up gradually over the course of your degree by paying attention to relevant stories as they happen. Think about reading the *FT* once or twice a week. Hang on, stop groaning - you're the one who wants to be a highly paid commercial lawyer! If you prep a bit now, the transition to work will be so much easier.

get involved

Joining an organisation or society that works in or promotes your chosen area of interest will keep you up to date with changes and demonstrate your commitment to the area. Barristers chambers and law firms do value such practical experience. Some of the top human rights chambers and criminal law firms see this sort of experience and commitment as being just as important as academic qualifications. Your student law society may already have links to organisations, otherwise, the internet is the easiest place to start searching for ideas.

www.knowuk.co.uk is a directory of voluntary agencies in the UK. Local Law Centres can be tracked down through www.lawcentres.org.uk. For human rights and civil liberties, www.justice.org.uk and www.amnesty.org are obvious places to start and these sites have good links to similar organisations. Many of these organisations do internships or welcome volunteers. Think about doing an evening or a day a week while on the BVC or LPC. The International Secretariat of Amnesty International runs a volunteer programme based in London. They recruit volunteers for a minimum of eight weeks full-time or three months part-time. Alternatively, you could contact the organisation directly in the country you want to work in.

Katharine Fortin volunteered for the AIRE Centre (Advice on Individual Rights in Europe) – **www.aire-centre.org**. She found herself working with people of different nationalities and backgrounds. A number of BVC and LPC students assist in the centre in London's Red Lion Square one day a week. *"Everyone is motivated by an interest in either European Community law or European human rights law,"* Katharine explained. Her duties include dealing with enquiries received by post or manning the advice line. Unless the answer can be given simply, she researches the problem before writing a legal opinion. The organisation also offers three-month internships on a voluntary basis.

When filling in application forms, many students draw a blank on what to write in the sections asking about activities and interests, positions of responsibility and achievements. There are endless opportunities to participate in student activities, be they sporting, cultural, social or political. A few examples of your readiness to get involved in things are essential. But a word of warning: make sure your quest to become president of something doesn't cause your academic life to suffer.

Your application needs to appear rounded and impressive. Many graduates complain, *"I wish I had done more at university."* If it is not too late, don't become one of them.

SOLICITORS

SOLICITORS TIMETABLE

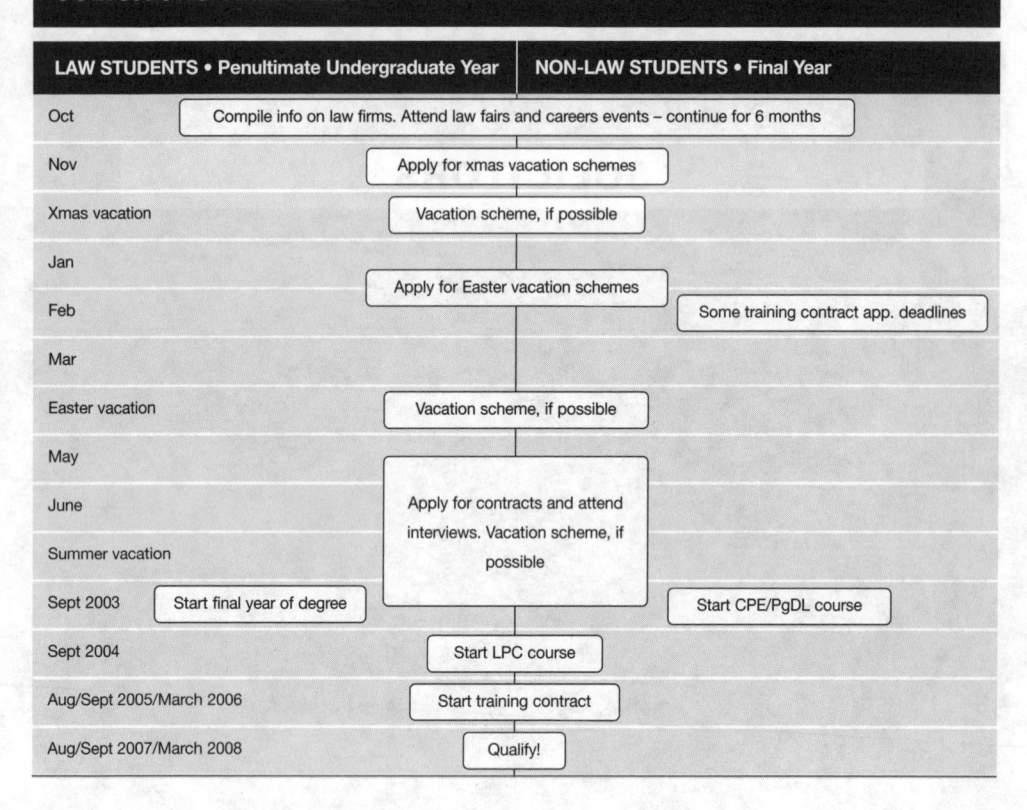

	LAW STUDENTS • Penultimate Undergraduate Year	NON-LAW STUDENTS • Final Year
Oct	Compile info on law firms. Attend law fairs and careers events – continue for 6 months	
Nov	Apply for xmas vacation schemes	
Xmas vacation	Vacation scheme, if possible	
Jan		
	Apply for Easter vacation schemes	
Feb		Some training contract app. deadlines
Mar		
Easter vacation	Vacation scheme, if possible	
May		
June	Apply for contracts and attend interviews. Vacation scheme, if possible	
Summer vacation		
Sept 2003	Start final year of degree	Start CPE/PgDL course
Sept 2004	Start LPC course	
Aug/Sept 2005/March 2006	Start training contract	
Aug/Sept 2007/March 2008	Qualify!	

Notes

1 It is important to check application closing dates for each firm as these will vary.
2 Some firms will only accept applications for vacation schemes from penultimate year students whether law or non-law. See A-Z pages for further information.
3 Some firms require very early applications from non-law graduates. See A-Z pages for further information.
4 The timetable refers primarily to those firms that recruit two years in advance. Smaller firms often recruit just one year in advance or for immediate vacancies.

vacation schemes

A vacation scheme is an excellent way of getting a feel for the law in practice and working out if you're suited to becoming a solicitor. Competition for places is stiff so don't be too disheartened if you miss out, but if you are successful, don't waste the opportunity.

Is a vac scheme a legal version of Big Brother? Yes and no. If you get a place, take comfort from the fact that you will have already impressed the firm on paper and possibly even been through an interview equally as tough as a training contract interview. You start from a position of strength, so just show enthusiasm, a willingness to learn and try not to mess up. It should be an enjoyable experience, which allows you to find out what the firm does and whether you like the place and the people. You can only get so much of an idea from brochures, law fairs or an interview or open day so this is a great opportunity. Regard it as a very long house viewing where you are the buyer, but do remember that you are being scrutinised. Don't make a fool of yourself like one student on a magic circle vac scheme who got so drunk one lunchtime that he spent the afternoon throwing up in the office.

Our *True Picture* interviewees often speak of how the trainee social scene picks up during the vac scheme 'season' and the party budget goes through the roof. In this respect, vac schemes are not always an accurate measure of the training experience. But you'll have ample opportunity to get to know people at the firm, how they work and what they work on. Pay attention. Some firms will make a huge effort to keep you occupied, not just with work, but also with presentations, group exercises and social events.

Other firms don't put in as much effort, as is clear from the words of a student: *"I felt like I was just passing through; there was no real work to get my teeth into and again and again I would be standing in a lift with 15 people whose names I did not know, feeling like a spare part."* If there's a particular type of work you want to experience, ask the firm if you can spend time in that department. *"Speak to people, that is the most important thing,"* advised one trainee. It's not just the lawyers you'll get to talk to; students pool information too, but use your own judgement - it's going to be your career.

Vac schemes are great but there's more to life! If your CV indicates you trudged around numerous firms in your holidays it could suggest a lack of initiative on your part. One recruiter said, *"We're more interested in applicants who've used their initiative and got some alternative experience through involvement in industry or travel. The schemes are mainly there so the firm can get a close look at you, and you can have a close look at the firm; they don't really make you a better applicant as such."* However, some firms do place great weight on their own scheme. Bond Pearce, for example, describes its scheme as *"an integral part of the recruitment process,"* drawing attention to this on its application form. The bottom line: whilst a vac scheme puts you ahead at that specific firm, it is unlikely to count for much elsewhere.

Every year we speak to disorganised students who miss application deadlines, so get your application in early. Finally, **Law Society guidelines state that no training contract interviews may take place or offers be made until 1 September in the final year of undergraduate study.**

VACATION SCHEMES

FIRM NAME	NUMBER OF PLACES	DURATION	REMUN-ERATION	2003 DEADLINE
Addleshaw Booth & Co	40	2 weeks	Not known	14 February 2003
Allen & Overy	90 in London, Brussels, Frankfurt & Paris	3 weeks	£250 p.w.	31 January 2003
Arnold & Porter	Yes	Not known	Not known	14 February 2003
Ashurst Morris Crisp	Easter (graduates & final year non-law); Summer (penultimate year law)	Easter: 2 weeks Summer: 3 weeks	£250 p.w.	31 January 2003
Baker & McKenzie	London: 30 International: 3-5*	3 weeks *6-12 weeks in Lon/o'seas office	£250 p.w	31 January 2003
Barlow Lyde & Gilbert	Yes plus open days and drop in days	Not known	Not known	28 February 2003
Berwin Leighton Paisner	180 Easter open day places leading to one of 60 summer placements	1 week	Not known	28 February 2003
Bevan Ashford	80	Not known	Not known	31 March 2003
Bird & Bird	24	3 weeks	£220 p.w.	14 February 2003
Bond Pearce	Yes	Not known	Not known	31 March 2003
Bristows	Yes	Christmas/Easter: 1 week summer: 2 weeks	200 p.w.	Christmas: 29 November 2002 Easter/summer: 28 February 2003
Burges Salmon	32	2 weeks	£150 p.w.	21 February 2003
Capsticks	Yes	2 weeks	Not known	28th February 2003
Clarks	Yes	Not known	Not known	Not known
Clyde & Co	Easter open days; summer placements	2 weeks	Not known	28 February 2003
Clifford Chance	Yes - Christmas, Easter and summer	2 weeks	£270 p.w.	Christmas: 8 Nov 2002 Easter/Summer: 31 Jan 2003
CMS Cameron McKenna	55	2 weeks	£225 p.w.	Not known
Cobbetts	24	Not known	Not known	Not known
Coffin Mew & Clover	Open week in July	Not known	Not known	Not known
Covington & Burling	16	Not known	Not known	28 February 2003
D J Freeman	18	3 weeks	£200 p.w.	28 February 2003
Davenport Lyons	10	2 weeks	£175 p.w.	Jan 2003
Dechert	16 plus 20-30 open days at both Easter and summer	2 weeks	Min. £225 p.w.	OD: 4 April 2003 & 2 July 2003 Vac scheme: 28 February 2003

STARTING OUT — VACATION SCHEMES TABLE

VACATION SCHEMES

FIRM NAME	NUMBER OF PLACES	DURATION	REMUNERATION	2003 DEADLINE
Denton Wilde Sapte	Approx. 50 information weeks/open days	Not known	Not known	14 March 2003
Dickinson Dees	36	1 week	£125 p.w.	28 February 2003
DLA	200	1 week	£210 p.w (Lon) £155 p.w (Ors)	28 February 2003
DMH	Yes	1-2 weeks	Unpaid	31 January 2003
DWF	Open days	n/a	n/a	Not known
Eversheds	130	2 weeks	Regional variations	31 January 2003
Farrer & Co	18	Easter: 2 weeks; summer: 3 weeks	£220 p.w.	31 January 2003
Fenners	6	2 weeks	competitive rates	30 April 2003
Field Fisher Waterhouse	Yes	Not known	Not known	1 February to 28 February 2003
Finers Stephens Innocent	12	2 weeks	Not known	30 March 2003
Foot Anstey Sargent	Yes	Not known	Not known	31 March 2003
Freshfields Bruckhaus Deringer	100	2 weeks	£500 total	14 February 2003 (apply asap after 1 December 2002)
Gateley Wareing	12	2 weeks	Not known	14 February 2003
Gouldens	16 Christmas: non-law 16 Easter: non-law 40 summer: law	2 weeks	£250 p.w.	Christmas: 31 October 2002 Easter/summer: 28 February 2003
Halliwell Landau	24	2 weeks	£100 p.w.	31 March 2003
Hammond Suddards Edge	60	3 weeks	£230 p.w. (Lon) £180 p.w. (Ors)	28 February 2003
Herbert Smith	115 (Christmas: non-law; Easter/summer: law and non-law)	Not known	Not known	Christmas: 22 November 2002 Easter/summer: 31 January 2003
Hewitson Becke + Shaw	Yes	1 week	Not known	Not known
Hill Dickinson	Yes	1 week	Not known	30th April 2003
Holman Fenwick & Willan	16	2 weeks	£250 p.w.	1 January to 14 February 2003
Howes Percival	Yes	Not known	Not known	Not known
Hugh James	Yes	Not known	Not known	Not known
Ince & Co	21	2 weeks	£250 p.w.	14 February 2003
Irwin Mitchell	50	1 week	£75 p.w.	1st March 2003
KLegal	12	5 weeks	£250 p.w.	21 February 2003

VACATION SCHEMES

FIRM NAME	NUMBER OF PLACES	DURATION	REMUN-ERATION	2003 DEADLINE
Knight & Sons	Yes	Not known	Not known	Xmas: 31 Oct 2002 Easter: 28 Feb 2003 summer: 30 April 2003
KLegal	12	5 weeks	£250 p.w.	21 February 2003
Knight & Sons	Yes	Not known	Not known	Xmas: 31 Oct 2002 Easter: 28 Feb 2003 summer: 30 April 2003
Lawrence Graham	40 Easter & summer	2 weeks	£225 p.w.	31 January 2003
Laytons	6	1 week	Not known	31 March 2003
Lester Aldridge	8	2 weeks	£75 p.w.	31 March 2003
Linklaters	120 Christmas, Easter and summer (some overseas)	Not known	£250 p.w.	Not known
Linnells	Yes	Not known	Not known	Not known
Lovells	90 Christmas, Easter and summer	Not known	Not known	Xmas: 15 Nov 2002 Easter/summer: 14 February 2003
Macfarlanes	40	2 weeks	£250 p.w.	1 January to 28 February 2003
Manches	Aprox. 24	1 week	Under review	31 January 2003
Masons	Approx 18 in London, approx 5 in Manchester	2 weeks	Not known	21 February 2003
Mayer, Brown, Rowe & Maw	25 Easter and summer	2 weeks	Not known	Not known
McCormicks	Yes	Not known	Not known	28 February 2003
Mills & Reeve	Yes	2 weeks	Not known	1 March 2003
Mishcon de Reya	12	2 weeks	£200 p.w.	17 March 2003
Morgan Cole	6 open days	n/a	n/a	31 March 2003
Nabarro Nathanson	60	3 weeks	Not known	28 February 2003
Nicholson Graham & Jones	8	2 weeks	£210 p.w.	10 March 2003
Norton Rose	15 Christmas 45 summer 5 or 6 six open days	2 weeks 3 weeks	£250 p.w.	1 November 2002 31 January 2003
Olswang	Yes	2 weeks	£250 p.w.	1 March 2003
Osborne Clarke	25-30 Easter and summer	1 week	£175-200 p.w.	31 January 2003
Pannone & Partners	50	1 week	None	28 February 2003
Penningtons	London: 60 Easter open day places + some summer vac places	Not known	Expenses	Days: 15 February 2003; vac scheme: 15 April 2003
Pinsent Curtis Biddle	90	2 weeks	Not known	28 February 2003
Prettys	One day placements	n/a	n/a	Not known

VACATION SCHEMES

FIRM NAME	NUMBER OF PLACES	DURATION	REMUNERATION	2003 DEADLINE
RadcliffesLeBrasseur	20	2 weeks	£200 p.w.	28 March 2003
Reed Smith Warner Cranston	12	4 weeks (Lon) 2 weeks (Mids)	£800 (Lon) £300 (Mids)	31 January 2003
Reynolds Porter Chamberlain	12	2 weeks	£200 p.w.	28 February 2003
Richards Butler	20 in London plus overseas placements	3 weeks	£200 p.w.	15 February 2003
Shadbolt & Co	6	2 weeks	£170 p.w.	16 March 2003
Shoosmiths	30	2 weeks	£155 p.w.	28 February 2003
Simmons & Simmons	40-50	2-4 weeks	£250 p.w.	21 February 2003
SJ Berwin	60	2 weeks	£225 p.w.	31 January 2003
Slaughter and May	60 (penult. year of degree)	2 weeks	£250 p.w.	7 February 2003
Speechly Bircham	12	3 weeks	£250 p.w.	14 February 2003
Steele & Co	Yes	Not known	Not known	Not known
Stephenson Harwood	16	2 weeks	£250 p.w.	21 February 2003
Taylor Vinters	Yes	1 week	Not known	31 March 2003
Taylor Walton	8	Up to 4 weeks	To be agreed	30 April 2003
Taylor Wessing	28	2 weeks	£200 p.w.	21 February 2003
Teacher Stern Selby	Possibly	Not known	Not known	Not known
Theodore Goddard	20 in summer + 70 Easter open day places	2 weeks	£200 p.w.	28 February 2003
TLT Solicitors	8	1 week	Not known	Not known
Travers Smith Braithwaite	60 summer + Christmas & Easter	2 weeks	£250	31 January 2003
Trowers & Hamlins	25-30 plus open days	2 weeks	£200 p.w.	1 March 2003
Walker Morris	45	1 week	£150 p.w.	28 February 2003
Ward Hadaway	Yes	1 week	Not known	30 April 2003
Watson, Farley & Williams	30	2 weeks	£200 p.w.	2 March 2003
Wedlake Bell	6	3 weeks	£150 pw	28 February 2003
Weil, Gotshal & Manges	12	Not known	Not known	14 February 2003
White & Case	40-50	2 weeks	£250 p.w.	28 February 2003
Withers LLP	6 Easter and 24 summer	2 weeks	Not known	7 February 2003
Wragge & Co	Easter and summer	Not known	Not known	31 January 2003

preferred universities and lpc providers surveys

preferred universities

During the summer of 2002 we conducted a survey among law firms in England and Wales, asking them to identify the universities from which they preferred to recruit trainees. 135 firms of all sizes and types and from all areas of the country responded and 72% of them confirmed that they had no preference.

Bristol University has just eclipsed Oxford this year as the university producing the graduates most widely sought by law firms. Cambridge, Durham and Nottingham were only slightly behind. We attribute the different scores at the top end of the table to the preferences of a just a few firms. For example, two firms in the south of England mentioned Oxford and not Cambridge in their responses, accounting for the two-point difference between those two universities.

A number of universities showed a marked increase on the scores they attained in our last survey of two years ago. Some doubled their earlier score. Worthy of particular mention are UCL, Kings College, London and LSE, and the Universities of Sheffield, Leeds and Leicester. A number of universities were mentioned for the first time.

43% of large London firms (more then 200 lawyers) stated preferences for particular universities (as opposed to 28% of our respondents as a whole.) Of the national, multi-site firms some 40% listed preferences. There is some evidence of regional bias, most notably from firms in the Midlands, the North and the South West.

Our conclusions: More firms are abandoning the concept of 'approved lists' of universities and those that remain selective are casting their nets wider than in the past.

Scores from our 2000 survey are shown in brackets

PREFERRED UNIVERSITIES	
No preference	94 (84)
Bristol	28 (32)
Oxford	27 (30)
Cambridge	25 (30)
Durham	25 (23)
Nottingham	24 (25)
Exeter	19 (22)
Kings College, London	19 (9)
UCL	19 (10)
Manchester	18 (14)
Sheffield	18 (9)
Warwick	18 (15)
Birmingham	17 (21)
Leeds	16 (8)
LSE	14 (5)
Southampton	14 (13)
Leicester	12 (2)
Newcastle	9 (5)
Cardiff	7 (3)
Edinburgh	6 (5)
Liverpool	6 (3)
London (any college)	6 (10)
Reading	6 (1)
St Andrews	4 (1)
York	4 (-)
Bath	3 (-)
Glasgow	3 (-)
Imperial College, London	3 (-)
'Top 20 universities'	3 (-)
UEA	3 (1)
Essex	2 (-)
'Established universities'	2 (-)
Queens Belfast	2 (-)

PREFERRED UNIVERSITIES (CONTINUED)	
SOAS	2 (-)
UWE	2 (2)
City	1 (-)
Coventry	1 (-)
Hull,	1 (-)
Keele	1 (-)
Loughborough	1 (-)
Northumbria	1 (-)
Nottingham Trent	1 (3)
Oxford Brookes	1 (-)
QMU, London	1 (-)
Sheffield Hallam	1 (-)
Trinity, Dublin	1 (-)

Scores from our 2000 survey are shown in brackets

preferred lpc providers

The firms that responded to our preferred universities survey also told us which institutions were their preferred providers of the LPC. 70% of our respondents had no preference, but 30% opted for one or more providers.

At first glance, Nottingham Trent appears to be the clear winner, with BPP, The College of Law (all branches) and Oxford Institute just off the pace. However, when individual COL branches' scores are added in to the picture, Guildford attains 23 'votes' and Store Street and Chester 21 each. BPP's standing has improved from our survey of two years ago and has overtaken Oxford.

35.5% of large London firms (more than 200 lawyers) stated preferences. This is explained, in part, by the existence of the City LPC course and the fact that it is only taught at Nottingham, BPP and Oxford. Examining the preferences of these 27 large London firms as a group, it is clear that (after adding all references to College of Law branches together) there is little difference between the attitudes of these firms towards Nottingham, BPP, Oxford and COL.

Additionally, these larger London firms account for six out of the eight 'votes' given to UWE.

Our conclusions: The majority of law firms are unconcerned as to which LPC provider their recruits choose. Many firms now appreciate that the three City LPC providers are to all intents and purposes 'off limits' to their future trainees. The College of Law's popularity endures.

PREFERRED LPC PROVIDERS	
Any approved	94 (84)
Nottingham Trent	24 (38)
BPP Law School	21 (16)
The College of Law (any)	20 (29)
Oxford Institute	19 (20)
UWE	8 (12)
'Institutions rated as excellent or very good by the Law Society'	4 (-)
Exeter	3 (5)
Guildford (College of Law)	3 (2)
Sheffield	3 (3)
Cardiff	2 (3)
Manchester Metropolitan	2 (-)
COL Chester	1 (-)
COL Store Street	1 (-)
De Montfort	1 (-)
Liverpool John Moores	1 (-)
London (any)	1 (2)
London Guildhall (now London Metropolitan)	1 (-)
University of Westminster	1 (-)

Scores from our 2000 survey are shown in brackets

the legal practice course

The Legal Practice Course (LPC) is the one-year vocational training course that all prospective solicitors are required to undertake. The LPC aims to provide students with the skills they will need to survive as a solicitor in practice. The course is a long way away from undergraduate legal study, which has its focus on theory and academic legal issues.

The LPC varies slightly between different course providers as they design their own courses, but broadly its content is divided into compulsory subjects, legal skills and electives. **Compulsory subjects** cover the knowledge areas deemed fundamental to practice as a solicitor. They will certainly include litigation, conveyancing and business law. **Legal skills** are those that you will need on a daily basis as a solicitor. Eg – interviewing, drafting, advocacy and IT. You will choose two or three **elective** subjects suited to the kind of practice you hope to move into. Those offered at the College of Law include:

- acquisitions and group structures, commercial law (commercial contracts, competition law, intellectual property) corporate finance, commercial litigation.
- commercial property, media and entertainment law, employment law and practice, personal injury and clinical negligence, litigation, family law and practice, welfare benefits and immigration law, private client: wills, trusts and estate planning.

how do you choose a law school?

When the LPC was introduced in 1993, the College of Law had a monopoly but there are now 26 institutions offering the course. If you have secured a training contract at one of eight 'consortium' firms (Allen & Overy, Clifford Chance, Freshfields Bruckhaus Deringer, Herbert Smith, Linklaters, Lovells, Norton Rose and Slaughter and May), then ten years on, your choice of where you study will be almost as limited as in 1993. Your firm will send you to BPP Law School, Nottingham Law School or the Oxford Institute of Legal Practice to do a special 'City' LPC.

LAW SOCIETY'S ASSESSMENT GRADES	
Anglia Polytechnic University	Good
Bournemouth University	Good
BPP Law School	Very Good
Bristol Institute of Legal Practice at UWE	Excellent
Cardiff Law School	Excellent
College of Law at Birmingham	Very Good
College of Law at Chester	Very Good
College of Law at Guildford	Very Good
College of Law at London	Very Good
College of Law at York	Very Good
De Montfort University	Good
Inns of Court School of Law	Very Good
Leeds Metropolitan University	Satisfactory
Liverpool John Moores University	Good
London Metropolitan University (formerly London Guildhall and The University of North London)	Good
Manchester Metropolitan University	Good
Nottingham Law School	Excellent
Oxford Institute of Legal Practice	Very Good
Staffordshire University	Very Good
Thames Valley University	Good
University of Central England at Birmingham	Satisfactory
University of Central Lancashire	Very Good
University of Exeter	Good
University of Glamorgan	Good
University of Hertfordshire (p/t)	Good
University of Huddersfield	Good
University of Northumbria	Good
University of Sheffield	Very Good
University of Westminster	Very Good
University of Wolverhampton	Good

The rest of you do have a choice of where to study and can seek some guidance from the Law Society's assessment of the performance of each of the LPC providers. With some effort, reviews and ratings can be found on the Law Society's website: **www.lawsociety.org.uk**.

Electives: Work out what kind of firm you are going to or hope to train with and match its practice with the electives on offer at the different LPC providers. The City LPC providers offer a range of electives suitable to high-value corporate work, but there are a number of electives, which are not offered by them - media, e-commerce, consumer law and IP, for example.

Money matters: Fees range from just over £5,000 to just over £8,000. Living expenses need to be taken into account on top of this, which may make living at home with the olds an attractive proposition and your choice of provider an obvious one.

Timetabling: Some institutions are more flexible with their timetabling than others, allowing you to fit in other commitments. For example, the College of Law offers morning or afternoon classes. If you commute, train fares may be cheaper for afternoon classes.

Size matters: At smaller institutions it's easier to build up close relationships with fellow students and staff, rather then being a blob on a conveyor belt. But, some students prefer anonymity and to be left to get on with it as long as they have good quality teaching. Look at your choice of firm – do you see a pattern?

Career support: Some institutions stand out as having strong links with the profession, arranging work experience or mentoring schemes with local firms. This is useful if you intend to train with a smaller firm and start your LPC without a training contract.

Social scene: Not an insignificant feature of the LPC. The social life on smaller courses tends to be tighter. We are told that you should expect everyone to turn into pumpkins after classes at London providers.

Assessment style: Certain providers have moved away from open book exams in favour of only allowing statute books and practitioner texts. At some, coursework takes place under supervision (in up to five-hour epic sittings) rather than as take-home assignments.

Your classmates: At City LPC providers many students are conscious of a divide between those going to consortium firms and those who aren't. Students headed for high street firms are few and far between at these schools. You may pick a course because the other students are following a similar career path or because there will be a cross-section.

Pass rates: These should be published each autumn on the Law Society's website following retakes. Be aware that there is no single examining body and different institutions have different exam methods. The results cannot be used as any sort of definitive guide as to which LPC courses are better than others.

the city lpc

The course is now in its second year so a flock of fledgling trainees is out in practice brandishing its newly acquired skills set.

Those training at a consortium firm, will have to attend one of the three City LPC providers. In addition, they will have no choice over 'electives', but will be required to take private acquisitions, debt finance and equity finance. Having ranked the three institutions in order of preference, they may find themselves in a ballot for the most popular institution. If they've done a CPE at one of the three, there seems to be an unofficial guarantee of a place on its LPC, irrespective of where the firm billets them.

If headed for the City but not to a consortium firm, rather than simply jumping on the bandwagon, you should consider both City and 'non-City' providers. There are some perceived advantages to non-City providers: You may find a wider range of electives, securing a place should be easier and fees may be cheaper. Nigel Savage, chief executive of the College of Law advises, *"There is bound to be an element of 'Everyone else is doing it and so should I', but think of what sort of practice you want to be in."*

lpc providers – the inside story

For this section we have gathered together the opinions of the hundreds of trainees interviewed for the *True Picture* and sought out the views of current students. We have chosen to profile the 11 LPC providers that take 100 or more students and have also been rated either 'Excellent' or 'Very Good' by the Law Society. We've also interviewed the LPC course directors (or similar) at these 11. Remember, all the institutions have websites, publish prospectuses and hold open days. There is plenty of information out there.

bpp law school, london
number of places: 432 full-time, 72 part-time

BPP is the London provider of the City LPC. Last year it moved into a swanky, new, glass-fronted building and went all hi-tech with funky computers in the library. BPP is a commercial venture that appreciates the need to operate at the leading edge of its market. Most students have a training contract at one of the eight consortium firms or have already done a CPE at BPP. If you don't qualify for a place on these grounds, be aware that last year 1,800 applications were received for the remaining 50 places. The 50 lucky winners either had law degrees, or were going to other City firms such as Ashurst Morris Crisp, Simmons & Simmons or Macfarlanes. Having said this, Carl Lygo, chief executive of BPP, stresses *"There are other courses as good as this in London so don't feel like a reject if you don't get on it."*

The course is rated 'Very Good' and, in line with the other City LPC providers, it emphasises the use of 'black letter' law and primary sources. Indeed, this emphasis is set to increase even further. As the vast majority of students are destined for City firms, it is unsurprising that corporate electives are undertaken by almost all. Private acquisitions, debt finance and equity finance are the most popular, with 85%-95% of students taking at least one of these. As for personal injury, just 3% of students opted for this in 2001/2. BPP is also one of the few institutions offering an advanced criminal litigation elective.

The compulsory parts of the course are focused very much on City practice. Carl stresses that students not going to City firms should not feel like second-tier students. *"We've worked to hard to try to make sure they're not."* The careers service is geared up to helping the 15% of students who start the course without a training contract and BPP enlisted the help of specialist firms when designing the non-commercial electives. The only noticeable disadvantage that a non-City student may face is that the timetable for the non-commercial electives and exams is less accommodating than for the commercial subjects. Even Carl suggests, *"If you're not doing commercial law, go elsewhere."* The non-consortium firm students that we spoke to didn't seem to feel second-tier, but agreed that it would be an odd choice of LPC if you didn't intend to go into commercial practice.

Expect to work hard at BPP. The new course is *"more intensive – and it won't necessarily let up,"* according to Carl. Students agree: *"It was a lot of work, rather than difficult work."* Last year 22% of students had a First and practically everyone else had a 2.1, but students do come from a wide range of good universities. Whilst the calibre of teaching is generally very good, the efforts of some tutors were described as variable. *"Our conveyancing tutor had an encyclopaedic knowledge of land law and practice, but [a.n.other] tutor looked like she'd cry if you took the crib sheet away."*

The social life suffers a bit from everyone living so far apart, but students can usually be found in the surrounding pubs of an evening (and sometimes between sessions). At the beginning of the year the law school generously subsidises a group dinner/bonding session for each tutor group.

apply if:
- You have a tc with a consortium firm
- You are going into City practice
- You are a genius and want to be with your City-firm friends

bristol institute of legal practice at uwe

number of students: 320 full-time, 80 part time

The institute at UWE prides itself on offering perhaps the widest range of electives of any LPC provider (13 at the moment). Coupled with its 'Excellent' rating, this is a competitive course to get onto. UWE has just taken over the De Montfort LPC previously offered at Bristol Uni and this has increased application numbers even further but the number of places has also risen. The structure of the UWE course underwent few changes in 2001/2. These were mainly limited to an increase in the emphasis on company financing in the compulsory BLP course and, in turn, this perhaps reflects the university's confidence in the quality of its course. Tutors only teach what they have practised and the style of teaching focuses much more on three-hour small group sessions than lectures. The idea is to reflect a morning or an afternoon in the office.

We gleaned a few statistics from Steven Dinning, LPC programmes director, to gauge what kind of electives students opt for. *"We have roughly 150 students doing employment, and commercial law and commercial litigation are popular. Around 90 students do M&A, and around 60 take commercial property and family options. 40 students do criminal, 30 corporate finance and 20 private client. This is reflective of where they're going to train."*

Some 40% of students on the full-time course have a training contract before starting and by the February following the end of the course, 90% have found legal employment. The course mostly attracts students aiming for large and medium-sized firms in Bristol and London. Steven adds, *"There is still a strong local presence with students going to smaller firms – it's a broad church."* To be offered a place you must be able to give a convincing reason as to why you want to study in Bristol. This may be family commitments, financial considerations or an undergrad degree at one of the city's universities. It is sensible to put UWE as first choice on the LawCABs application form. Good academics will count for a lot and are likely to override any need for a link to Bristol. The standard of applicant is generally high and most students have a 2.1 or better. *"There are no guaranteed places, though our CPE students always fit the criteria."*

We'll also add that student comment was glowing. Apparently *"UWE doesn't have the reputation it deserves,"* said one satisfied student. From another we learned that a year at UWE is *"very enjoyable and valuable."* Bristol is a city made for students.

apply if:
- You have great academics
- You love Bristol
- You want a wide range of electives to choose from

cardiff law school

number of places: 160 full-time

Cardiff is a top-notch school. Students choose the course for its 'Excellent' rating from the Law Society and the fact that Cardiff is now a great city with a thriving social scene. Not everyone wants to be one of several hundred and those in charge at Cardiff feel that the relatively small student intake produces a close working relationship between staff and students.

The range of electives is broad, with corporate and commercial subjects strong enough to support those going to large City and national firms and subjects that are suitable for those going to private client or niche firms. Most importantly Ian Brookfield, LPC course leader, categorically states, "*We have never not run an elective.*" The school has strong links with the profession so that each elective is taught partly, or wholly, by a practitioner rather than a full-time lecturer. Students praise the tutors for the wealth of experience they bring from practice. And there's more support from local firms: each student without a training contract is guaranteed a work placement during the year. These are provided especially for Cardiff LPC students and are not just tacked on to the usual vacation schemes run by the firms.

Many students are destined for Welsh firms but others will head of elsewhere and to all sizes of firm. The kind of work students intend to do is reflected in the most popular electives. Employment is the top choice every year as it is seen as suitable to both commercial and private client practice. Commercial property and family are also favourites. Students say, "*The work is based on group work. They tried their best to make it interesting and fun.*" There were no major changes in the course structure in 2001/2. Ian told us, "*We don't want to sound like we're complacent. The course is continually reviewed and changes are put in place. Trainees won't be thrown by things I was totally thrown by when I went into practice.*"

Roughly 40% of students have a training contract before they start and these tend to be with larger firms. The proportion rises to 60% by the end of the course, and by the following Christmas most of those who want legal employment have found it. The selection criteria require a 2.2 but the majority of students have a 2.1 or above. If your degree is from Cardiff University and you put the law school first in order of preference on your application form, you are pretty much guaranteed a place.

apply if:
- You want a top-rated but smaller institution
- You want to become absorbed into Cardiff's social scene and professional community
- You want a wide range of electives to choose from

the college of law

number of places: 3,552 full-time, 408 part-time

The College of Law is the largest LPC provider, with five branches in England. All five branches have attained a 'Very Good' rating from the Law Society. The college has changed the structure of its LPC so students now have a choice within the compulsories. This is a feature unique to the college. All students do the same conveyancing and litigation courses, but have a choice in Business Law & Practice (BLP), electing for either a corporate slant or a general commercial slant. The law and procedure is common to both but the case studies differ, using a plc for the former and a private company for the latter. The other big change on this course is a greater emphasis on legal research, drafting and 'black letter' law.

All this sounds rather like the City LPC, but chief executive, Nigel Savage, stresses that the COL retains its accessibility to all. "*It is a national law school providing a corporate course, but we can't become exclusive.*" Students at the Store Street branch have traditionally been destined for large commercial firms, but this now excludes the eight consortium firms. In 2001/2 we estimated that around 25% of Store Street students were likely to be going to hardcore City firms as roughly this proportion was taking the corporate BLP option.

The college's selling point is that it can cater for a range of needs and Nigel believes that this is because the COL has retained its independence. It is certainly reflected in the broad spectrum of electives on offer and apparently exactly the same course is taught with consistency all over the country. Whichever branch you pick, it seems you won't go wrong, and all credit to the college for achieving a 'Very Good' rating at its new Birmingham branch within three months of opening. Worth noting are the extra-curricular activities, such as student Advice Centres, while the legendary COL manuals and materials continue to win the hearts of students, who commonly refer to them long after starting in practice.

Students have encountered similar experiences at different locations as regards the course itself. The big differences between the branches are social life, types of student and expense.

store street, london
number of students: 1,248 full-time, 192 part-time

If you like big crowds then this is the place to go. Overall, the standard of teaching is well regarded by students though it seems to vary *"from really inspiring to rather mediocre."* The social life bears all the symptoms of Londonitis: *"It's difficult to co-ordinate as everyone lives so far apart."* Store Street itself is *"quite big – there's no community spirit,"* thought some. In the interests of balance, we should say that other students reported a great social life so it perhaps depends on how much effort you make. There are also two schools of thought as to whether or not an LPC year in the costly capital is a good idea. *"The year cushioned the move to London before starting work,"* said one student, but another stated, *"I would go elsewhere, based on what others told me – they enjoyed their time more."*

birmingham
number of students: 336 full-time, 40 part-time

It's been difficult to get feedback as the course was only run for the first time this year. The few reports we received were favourable and we hope to report in more detail next year. The location of the college in the old jewellery quarter is excellent and the involvement of local firms has added value to the course.

chester
number of students: 600 full-time, 56 part-time

"Fantastic place, boring course" and *"helpful lecturers and nice drinking holes"* is how most of the ex-students we spoke to summed up the Chester experience. On teaching: *"Some tutors were very good while others were heavily reliant on the course's printed materials."* Students are destined for top firms right through to small, high street practices. *"The college was a good size"* and *"The campus is lovely – nice, modern buildings, playing fields and a garden, plus a big car park, which gets very busy as most people drive. There's a really nice common room and the canteen food is OK."* The social life very much depends on your group. Thursdays tend to be the night out – *"It's student night, so cheap and cheerful."*

guildford
number of students: 720 full-time, 80 part-time

The leafy greenery of Braboeuf Manor is, for many students, infinitely preferable to the hassle and grime of London. According to a student who'd sampled both venues, the quality of teaching is the same in both. Guildford has had something of a reputation for being a bit 'jolly hockey sticks', evidenced by *"lots of flash cars in the car park,"* yet this could change now that some of these students will be forsaking the college for the City LPC. Time will tell. The campus boasts *"a good canteen, a tennis court and a country setting. Unfortunately it's up hill from the station!"* Guildford is a fairly pricey place to live but benefits from its proximity to London, which is just as well as *"the nightlife is not amazing but OK."*

york
number of students: 532 full-time, 40 part-time

York is rather like a nursery school for Leeds' firms. Most students have studied in northern universities or will be going on to train in the region. This is a great place to make friends. On IT/information resources, the consensus seems to be *"not bad, but a bit sparse on computers."* On sports facilities there's a big thumbs up. York is a *"nice little town"* and the college has *"a good mix of students and a good location"* (it's next to the race course and within smelling distance of a chocolate factory). The quintessentially studenty social scene is a whirl of *"endless, endless house parties and a dreadful disco in The Willow."*

apply if:
- You're looking for a broad range of electives
- You want a respected qualification and the chance to do pro bono work
- You like the sound of one of the COL's five locations

inns of court school of law (icsl)
number of students: 100 full-time

ICSL is better known as the largest provider of the BVC. The LPC has only been running for two years but has already gained a 'Very Good' rating from the Law Society, which particularly stressed the standard of teaching. The BVC caters for a huge number of students, but the LPC takes on fewer than most London providers. Paul Aber, LPC director, stresses that this gives the course an *"intimate feel"* as groups can be kept as small as possible (a maximum of 16 in small group sessions and only 8 per group in the 'skills' sessions). Students can expect to receive plenty of feedback on their work.

The teaching materials attempt to replicate practice with students working in teams. A range of methods is used to try to vary the work and IT is used in every classroom. As with the City LPC, there's a heavy emphasis on black letter law. The commercial focus suits students going to both small and large City firms and there are electives covering more specialised areas for those going to niche firms. The most popular electives are employment and advanced civil litigation with the majority of students taking these subjects. Around a quarter of students take one or other of corporate finance, e-commerce, M&A, family or immigration.

Paul wasn't able to pin down one type of student, but believes they all chose the course for its size, teaching and commercial focus. Students end up in a range of different firms, from the midsize in London through national firms to smaller regional and high street practices.

The course is oversubscribed so it is wise to put ICSL as first choice if you want a place there. It looks for those with a 2.1 or better, or those with interesting work experience.

apply if:
- You want a large London school but a smaller course
- You are going into commercial practice
- Your barrister mates are there

manchester metropolitan university
number of places: 168 full-time, 48 part-time

The LPC at MMU is a local affair. Staff are encouraged to continue working in private practice while teaching and this means they are bang up to date with current trends and links with local firms are good. Students tend to have studied at one of Manchester's universities or have come back to live at home, either for good or before moving away to start their training contract.

Manchester is a vibrant city and that atmosphere seems to have seeped into the course. Sallie Spilsbury, LPC director, tells us, *"When students come to open days they say they like the way the teaching team is relatively small and approachable. It's a relatively young teaching team so it looks a nice place to study."* Added to this is a comparatively broad range of electives for the size of the place. This year a media elective has been added and another unusual offering is consumer law. Popular choices include employment, commercial law, personal injury and family. It's a real mixed bag.

Around a third of students are destined for commercial firms in the North West and beyond. The remainder go to high street firms. Sallie said, *"We've got good feedback from students going to places like Nabarros, showing that we can viably teach commercial electives."*

The majority of students don't have a training

contract when they start, but by the September following the end of the course most are fixed up because high street firms commonly recruit just two or three months in advance. A number of local firms approach the university offering vacancies. The entry requirements are a 2.2 or higher with places guaranteed for MMU's CPE students. Manchester boasts a 'Very Good' assessment rating.

apply if:
- You want to study in a young and friendly atmosphere
- You and Manchester are inseparable
- You are looking for electives suited to smaller commercial or high street practice

nottingham law school
number of students: 650 full-time, 90 part-time

Super-school Nottingham carries a prized 'Excellent' assessment rating and offers the City LPC. It reserves up to half of its places for students with training contracts at the eight consortium firms. The new City LPC course structure focuses on research and writing skills and basic law - the skills that firms say have been lacking in trainees in past years. None of the law on the LPC is new, just the context in which it crops up. Expect to come out the other end with skills that can be usefully transferred into City practice. Having said this, Bob White, director of graduate development, hopes that *"our documentation, reputation and so on say we aren't a corporate factory."* A noble aspiration, but do the facts support this claim? With so many students going to the eight consortium firms, and a reputation for offering such a good LPC, Nottingham is heavily oversubscribed. This has pushed up admission standards so that AAB at A level and a good 2.1 are par for the course on the LawCABs forms Nottingham receives. The majority of students are headed for the corporate/commercial sphere. A quick look at the electives offered substantiates this view; they cover most aspects of commercial practice, but little outside that.

According to Bob, there is an element of *"non-corporate pride"* amongst those students not headed for the City. In fact, some 100 students were offered a place on the condition that they would not take the three corporate electives. The upshot of this is that those most likely to be offered a place at Nottingham are consortium firm trainees and students at the other end of the spectrum who are steering clear of corporate work. For those in between only the brightest will stand a chance of getting an offer. As Bob puts it, *"We have plenty of room for quality students."* Last year, students who didn't already have a training contract before starting their LPC were considered for a non-corporate place. The law school had not finalised its selection procedure when we contacted them but stated that it will continue to make sure that not all 650 students are destined for the City.

Students find the course focused and well structured, knowing exactly what they have to do and when. *"It's pretty military style,"* one said. Support is good and there's widespread praise for the school in the way that it has lived up to its reputation and students' expectations. From those not doing the corporate electives, there seems to be some disappointment that the compulsories had to change in one particular direction. *"I feel that what I have to do is dictated by the big eight. It puts more pressure on us."* Some even feel there is a divide between the corporate and non-corporate students. Another student found *"the sort of people on the course were very London biased and tended not to mix with the provincials."* On the whole, however, impressions are good; *"I've definitely come a long way from my law degree. I now have much more of an idea of what a solicitor does!"*

apply if:
- You are training at one of the consortium firms
- You have a brilliant academic record
- You are looking for commercial electives

oxford institute of legal practice
number of students: 294 full-time

Another of the three City LPC providers, Oxford carries a 'Very Good' assessment rating. But is it just a smaller version of BPP and Nottingham? In some ways, yes… the buzzwords of 'black letter law' and 'corporate/commercial focus' cropped up in our research. In practice, after a year at Oxford, you'll know a heck of a lot more about contract law, be better able to interpret statutes and have a good awareness of professional conduct and ethical issues in the context of a corporate firm. Last year nearly three-quarters of students were heading for corporate firms but not all were going to consortium firms. Nick Johnson, director of the institute, admits, *"There's a danger (in the compulsories) of non-corporate students feeling outnumbered."* One student we spoke to said they hadn't even met a student who wasn't going to a City firm. Nick continues, *"But in the second half of the course they feel they have special attention."* This second half is when the electives play a greater part and non-corporate electives are undertaken by smaller groups of students.

An amazing 92% of students had a training contract before starting the course last year. Many students want to extend their undergraduate lives in Oxford; others want to sample the ivory towers experience for the first time. Studying at the Institute brings you membership of the university, its libraries, sports teams and even college rowing regattas. Think bicycles, punting, Pimms and the Bodleian Library on tap, but the LPC itself is a far cry from lofty academia. The institute is located in an office building and attempts to offer an office-like environment.

Students with a commendation in the CPE from Oxford Brookes are guaranteed a place on this course, as are students directed there by the consortium firms. The institute is also interested in teaching students who are not going to City firms and may even go as far as reserving places for these students, so it is worth making clear on the LawCABs form if you are interested in PI, family or private client but would still like to study in Oxford.

Student feedback suggested the standard of tutors was mixed but particularly good for BLP. In the summer of 2002, stories circulated with regard to students being upset by lower than expected pass rates. Depending on who we spoke to, fingers were pointed at the tough 'closed book' exam method, and both teaching staff and students themselves. The truth is out there somewhere.

apply if:
- You have a consortium firm training contract
- Oxford inspires you
- You want a smaller school

university of sheffield
number of students: 120 full-time

Sheffield recently underwent a marketing drive to raise its profile. Consequently applications increased and the course was oversubscribed for 2001/2. But what do they have to shout about? Sheffield's hallmarks are a 'Very Good' assessment from the Law Society, intimacy, quality teaching and a broad range of electives.

There are only 120 places on this course so *"everybody knows everyone and tutors know all the students."* If this is the kind of environment that suits you then read on. 80% of teaching is focused around small group sessions (maximum 18 students). Even at the open day, the emphasis is on meeting the tutors and getting to know who will teach you.

Clare Firth, director of the LPC, says the course isn't focused on a particular type of legal practice; *"The aim is to cover the whole range of firms."* A few readjustments have been made to the compulsory parts of the course to revise basic contract law, to place more reliance on primary sources and to introduce a commercial context into the conveyancing course. As for the electives, this is one of the few institutions offering an advanced criminal litigation course; it culminates in a mock trial at Sheffield Magistrates' Court. Two new electives were added for 2002/3: M&A has split from the corporate finance elective and personal injury and clinical negligence have branched off in their own right from the advanced civil litigation course.

Usually the most popular electives are advanced civil litigation, employment and commercial law. Students move on to all kinds of firms, from one- to two-partner outfits to large City practices. Roughly a third of students have a training contract before they begin, rising to around two-thirds by the end of the course. Just over half of students have a 2.1 or First. A commitment or link to the region must be demonstrated on the LawCABs application form and the law school should ideally be placed as first choice. Sheffield law graduates or LLM graduates are guaranteed a place if they put Sheffield first or second in order of preference.

Students enjoy their year in Sheffield. *"On the positive side I had a lot of fun and the teaching was good; on the negative side, I realise now that there are some things you pick up more effectively on the job rather than being taught in the classroom."*

apply if:
- You want to study in a lively northern city
- You especially want to take a criminal elective
- You want to be a part of a smaller student body

staffordshire university
number of students: 100 full-time, part-time 25

The LPC is the bridge between studentdom and solicitorhood and it is evident that this philosophy is at the forefront of the teaching at Staffordshire. Rosemary Evans, LPC director, enthused on this point: *"We feel we are giving up-to-the-minute tuition on how it is in the office. It's how we know it happens. The focus is on what you can expect to see in practice."* This goes for most areas of practice. Family, employment and personal injury are usually popular electives but in 2001/2 commercial law took the top slot. Staffordshire provides an equal number of commercial and private client electives including new courses on immigration, corporate finance and M&A.

A high proportion of students go on to train in the Midlands and its environs, mostly Birmingham, Wolverhampton and north to Manchester. Students aren't necessarily destined for large corporate and commercial firms, and neither has the structure of the course shifted to a strong corporate emphasis, but many do seem to have been influenced by the current trend for taking commercial electives. If you haven't got a training contract at the start of this course, Staffordshire's mentoring scheme will assist. Each student is paired off with a practitioner for the year, during which time they visit him or her in the office. *"We find that quite a number of students pick up a job as a result, if not with that firm then with a firm where their mentor has heard of a vacancy."*

This course is well priced as LPCs go, particularly given its 'Very Good' rating. Many students are local or took their degree at the university, and the majority intend to remain in the region. This is reflected in the selection criteria. Rosemary says, *"The key thing is putting us as first choice."* This will effectively guarantee you a place but expect to be interviewed if your degree is lower than a 2.1. Just one other thing… while touring the Midlands we noted that the university is in a greenfield location. It struck us that a car would be very handy.

apply if:
- You intend to work in the Midlands
- You are funding yourself and want value for money
- You want good support in securing a training contract

university of westminster

number of students: full-time:120, part-time 64

What marks Westminster out from most London providers is its size. Robert Abbey, LPC director, stresses the benefits of remaining small. *"I would hate for the description 'a bit like a factory' to be used for our institution."* He firmly believes that students benefit from the close relationships that build up between staff and students.

Westminster stands out on the London scene in other ways too. For a start the fees come in at around £6,500 – a good price for a 'Very Good' rating from the Law Society. The student body is made up of those from a range of different backgrounds but seems slightly more mature than most because many students have done the PgDL/CPE or have simply come to study later in life. The university's PgDL is regarded as a very important feeder to the LPC and places are kept secure for these applicants. Students take up training contracts with a wide range of high street or smaller commercial firms, in London and beyond. These kinds of firms do not tend to recruit two years ahead so students tend to pick up training contracts during the course rather than before it.

Student choices of electives are split between the commercial and the private client side. The popularity of the employment course endures and there was a good uptake of commercial conveyancing, commercial litigation and immigration electives last year. Though the course does not profess to cater specifically to any particular type of practice, one student headed for private practice found the content of compulsories *"overly leans towards business,"* but *"the electives were more socially relevant."*

The school is situated in a vibrant area of London near Oxford Circus. It makes good use of its location by fostering links with nearby firms and many of the staff retain links with practice. Practitioners teach on the electives and are particularly involved with the new immigration elective. Local firms sponsor electives by giving prizes or work experience.

apply if:
- You are looking for value for money
- You love London town
- You want a smaller school offering plenty of individual attention

applications and selection

Students applying for training contracts are likely to face an assault course of group exercises, written tests and day-long assessments before they secure a job. Here are a few pointers to help guide you through the process.

making the application

The vast majority of firms will work to a timetable for applications and interviews, so make sure you don't miss the boat! The application deadlines for the largest firms can be found on the calendar inside the cover of this book. Some, notably Slaughter and May, recruit all year round while other, smaller firms recruit as and when a vacancy crops up.

When filling in application forms, do make sure that you answer all the questions and that you answer them fully. Graduate recruitment officers tell us that students make basic mistakes every year. It won't say much for your analytical skills if you appear to be unable to understand an application form. If you have a query it is perfectly acceptable to call graduate recruitment at the firm and ask for clarification, but obviously you can't expect them to fill the form in for you! Be very careful if sending applications online. At least one firm suffered a technical glitch and 'lost' a bunch of vac scheme applications last year.

Some firms will make life easier for applicants by simply requesting a CV and covering letter. Make sure that you include all relevant information in your CV. Andrew Hearn, graduate recruitment partner at London firm Dechert, points out that *"if you have something important to say, make sure it is in the application and not just in your covering letter."* Not all selection panel members will see your covering letter. For guidance on drafting a CV, see pages 17 to 18.

assessment days

With the current full-on approach to graduate selection, it's never been more important to get a good night's sleep before an assessment day. An assessment day means just that: a whole day. You are continuously assessed from the moment you stutter your name at reception through spilling coronation chicken down your front at the buffet lunch to the point where you wander out of the office at 5pm. The days when you could drink three cups of coffee, chat to a partner for half an hour and then fall asleep on the train home, smug in the knowledge you had got the job, are long gone.

A typical assessment day consists of one or two written tests, at least one group exercise, one or two interviews and perhaps a presentation to a group of partners. Firms place varying degrees of emphasis on the different elements. For some the interview is crucial, while for others group exercises are of primary importance. If possible, try to find out in advance (from current trainees perhaps). The day will commonly end with a drinks party, but don't relax too much – you're being assessed there too.

group exercises

When it comes to group exercises, the most obvious answer is to be yourself. You might feel more at ease with the people you're grouped with at one firm than you do at another. You might also feel more comfortable with the task you're asked to do at one firm rather than others. The quality of your performance rests partly on chance, although practice may improve it. Bob Llewellin, training director with Burges Salmon, says, *"It's important not to be a pushover – say something. But it doesn't help to be bombastic."* If your arguments aren't accepted by the group don't worry – you might have been asked to argue an unwinnable case. Recruiters are looking to see if you're a team player, whether you listen to other people's ideas, whether you can compromise, and whether you keep an eye on key factors, such as time and budget. One (successful) candidate said *"I was told in the interview afterwards that the assessors had been impressed that I had noticed time was running out when the others were still arguing over who should be spokesperson."*

Remember, recruiters are looking for all kinds of people – the more measured, thoughtful types as well as the outgoing team leaders. Though these events always bring out the actor in people, it won't help to reinvent your personality for the occasion.

written tests

These tend to be of two types. Reasoning/personality tests are usually presented in multiple-choice format. Though a minimum standard is required, you won't get the job simply on mental agility. On many assessment days the tests will be marked and returned to the assessors before you leave or even before your interview. As you cannot prepare for these tests, the best advice is to stay calm, work quickly but effectively and keep an eye on the clock.

In scenario-based written exercises, candidates may be asked to note the issues and propose some solutions in a particular situation. Your answer will be required in a particular form (ie letter, fax, report). In some exercises you may be asked to rewrite something into 'plain English'. Although spotting legal issues is sometimes an important part of the 'situation' exercises, the assessors will not want a detailed analysis of the case law, stuffed full of quotes from Lord Denning. Instead they'll want sensible, practical, business-aware comments on the problem. Non-law students need not worry about their lack of legal knowledge as this will be taken into account.

presentations

Two candidates at a City law firm were put together and asked to prepare a joint presentation to be given to a partner. To our source the task did not seem that difficult. After all, the scenario was quite fun and the other candidate easy to get on with. It was only when making the presentation that he realised the other candidate wouldn't let him get a word in. She even covered his areas in her speech. Halfway through the presentation it became obvious from his expression that the partner was not impressed by her attitude to her co-presenter. Result: she did not get an offer and he did. She had failed to realise just how crucial it is to not only show your mental agility and oratory skills, but how well you work with others.

a friendly chat?

If the day involves a session with trainees, be careful, particularly if it is one-to-one. They are not just there to answer your questions! They will be asked for feedback on you (do not believe them if they say otherwise) and will often be your harshest critics. So don't look at it as a chance to slag off your interviewer or confess that you don't really want to be a lawyer, but your parents have forced you into it. Lunch can also be a particularly stressful affair. Trying to eat tagliatelle with a fork whilst simultaneously drinking a glass of wine and making small talk with a senior partner can be more taxing than any reasoning test. Red wine on the carpet will not go down well.

In many firms, the recruitment process is a polished, highly professional procedure and the City firms in particular waste no time in letting successful and unsuccessful applicants know their fate. In many cases, candidates hear that day, especially if the firm wants them. Around the time of interviews and assessment days, graduate recruitment offices are a frenzy of activity. If the partners give the green light to make an offer to an applicant then it's action stations to get them signed up before another firm does. Don't be pressurised into saying yes before you are ready. Law Society guidlines to firms state that no time limit for acceptance of a training contract offer should expire before 1 November in the final year of a law degree or the CPE.

APPLICATIONS AND SELECTION

FIRM NAME	METHOD OF APPLICATION	SELECTION PROCESS	DEGREE CLASS	NUMBER OF CONTRACTS	NUMBER OF APPLICATIONS
Addleshaw Booth & Co	See website	Interview, assessment centre	2:1	40	2,300
Allen & Overy	Application form & online	Interview	2:1	120	4,000
Arnold & Porter	Application form	Interviews & assessment exercise	2:1	3-5	Not known
Ashurst Morris Crisp	Online	1 interview with assistant & another with 2 partners	2:1	50	2,500
B P Collins	Handwritten letter & CV	Screening interview & selection day	Not known	4	Not known
Baker & McKenzie	Letter & application form	Oral presentation, interview with 2 partners & meet a trainee	2:1	30	2,000
Barlow Lyde & Gilbert	Application form & covering letter	Interview day	Not known	16-18	2,000
Beachcroft Wansbroughs	Application form	Assessment centre & panel interview	2:1 preferred	25-30	Not known
Berwin Leighton Paisner	Application form	Assessment day & partner interview	2:1	35	2,000
Bevan Ashford	Application form & covering letter	Not known	2:1	25	Not known
Bird & Bird	Online application form	Assessment morning	2:1	14	1,500
Blake Lapthorn	Application form	Interview + presentation/group exercise	2:1	5-7	500
Bond Pearce	Application form, CV	Interviews & vacation placement scheme	Not known	10-15	500
Boyes Turner	Letter & CV	2 interviews & 1 week work placement	2:2	4	Not known
Brabners Chaffe Street	Application form	Interview & assessment day	2:1/post-grad	Not known	Not known
Brachers	Handwritten letter & CV	Interview day with partners	2:1	6	400
Bristows	Application form	2 interviews	2.1 preferred	Up to 10	3,500
Browne Jacobson	CV & covering letter	Assessment centre	2:1	8	1,500
Burges Salmon	Application form	Not known	2:1	20-25	1,500
Cadwalader, Wickersham & Taft	CV & covering letter	2 interviews	2:1	4-6	500
Campbell Hooper	CV & covering letter.	Interviews	2:1	3-4	c.1500
Capsticks	Application form	Summer placement then interview with Training Principal & partners	2:1 or above	6-8	c. 200
Charles Russell	Handwritten letter & app form	Assessment day	2:1	10-12	Approx 2,000
Clarks	Application form or letter & CV	Open day/interview; second interview & written tests	Usually 2:1 or above	5-6	5-600

APPLICATIONS AND SELECTION

FIRM NAME	METHOD OF APPLICATION	SELECTION PROCESS	DEGREE CLASS	NUMBER OF CONTRACTS	NUMBER OF APPLICATIONS
Cleary, Gottlieb, Steen & Hamilton	Letter & CV	2 interviews	2:1	Up to 4	Not known
Clifford Chance	Application form. (online)	Assessment day: interview + group exercise & verbal reasoning test	2:1	130	2,000
Clyde & Co	Application form & covering letter	1 interview with GR & another with 2 partners	2:1	20	3,000+
CMS Cameron McKenna	Online application form	Initial interview followed by assessment centre	2:1	80	1,500
Cobbetts	Application form (online or paper)	Half-day assessments	2:1	12-14	700
Coffin Mew & Clover	CV & covering letter	Interview	2:1 (a few exceptions)	4-5	400+
Coudert Brothers	Letter & CV	2 interviews with partners	2:1	4	Not known
Covington & Burling	Application form & covering letter	2 interviews	2:1	4	Not known
Cripps Harries Hall	Handwritten letter & form	1 interview with managing partner & head of HR	2.1	8	Up to 750
Cumberland Ellis Peirs	Letter & covering CV	2 interviews with partners	2:1	2	300
D J Freeman	Application form	Interview	2:1	12-15	800
Davenport Lyons	CV & covering letter	Interviews	2:1	5	1,500
Dawsons	Letter + app form or CV	Not known	2:1 & As/Bs at A-Level	Not known	Not known
Dechert	Application form	Communication exercises & interviews	2:1	20	Over 1,500
Denton Wilde Sapte	Application form	First interview; selection test; second interview	2:1	45	2,000
Devonshires	Online application form	Not known	2:1 and higher	6	400
Dickinson Dees	Application form & letter	Interview & in-tray exercise	2:1	15	700
DLA	Application form	1st interview, 2nd interview & assessment afternoon	2:1	85+	2,000
DMH	CV & covering letter	Not known	2:1	4-6	400
DWF	Letter & CV or application form	Two-stage interview/selection process	2:1 preferred	8	c.1000
Edwards Geldard	Application form	Interview	2:1 desirable	12	400
Eversheds	Application form	Selection day: group & written exercises, presentations & interview	2:1	100	4,000
Farrer & Co	Application form & covering letter	Interviews with GR manager and partners	2:1	6-8	1,500
Fenners	Handwritten letter & CV	2 interviews with partners	2:1	2	1,200
Field Fisher Waterhouse	Application form & covering letter	Interview	2:1	10-12	2,000

APPLICATIONS AND SELECTION

FIRM NAME	METHOD OF APPLICATION	SELECTION PROCESS	DEGREE CLASS	NUMBER OF CONTRACTS	NUMBER OF APPLICATIONS
Finers Stephens Innocent	CV & covering letter	2 interviews with the training partners	2:1	4	500
Fladgate Fielder	Application form & covering letter	Selection morning including interview & other exercises	2:1	3	500
Foot Anstey Sargent	Letter & CV or online form	Interview & assessment day	Not known	8	Not known
Forbes	Handwritten letter & CV	Interview with partners	2:1	3	350
Forsters	Application form	1st interview (HR manager & GR ptnr); 2nd (2 partners)	Not known	Not known	Not known
Freethcartwright	Application form	Interview & selection day	Not known	Not known	Not known
Freshfields Bruckhaus Deringer	Application form	1 interview with 2 partners & written test	2:1	100	c.2,500
Gateley Wareing	Not known	Not known	2:1 & 3 B's at A-level	6	Not known
Goodman Derrick	CV & covering letter	2 interviews	2:1 min	3/4	900
Gouldens	CV & letter online	2 interviews with partners	2:1	20	2,000
Halliwell Landau	CV & application form (online)	Open days or summer placements	2:1	10	1000
Hammond Suddards Edge	Online application form	2 interviews	2:1	40	2,000
Harbottle & Lewis	CV & letter	Interview	2:1	3	800
Harbottle & Lewis	CV & letter	Interview	2:1	3	800
Henmans	Application form	Interview with HR manager & partners	Not known	3	450
Herbert Smith	Application form	Interview	2:1	100	1,750
Hewitson Becke + Shaw	Application form	Interview	2:1 min	15	1,400
Hill Dickinson	CV & photograph with letter	Assessment day	Not known	Not known	Not known
Hodge Jones & Allen	Application form	Interview & selection tests	2:1 preferred	Not known	Not known
Holman Fenwick & Willan	Handwritten letter & CV	2 interviews with partners & written exercise	2:1	8	1,200
Howes Percival	Letter, CV & application form	Assess. centre & 2nd int'vw w. training p'pal & ptnr	2:1	6	300
Hugh James	Application form	Assessment day	2:2	7	350
Ince & Co	Letter & CV	1 interview with HR, 1 with 2 partners & written test	2:1	8	2,500
Irwin Mitchell	Application form & covering letter	Assessment centre and interview; second interview	Not known	15	1,000
Keoghs	CV & covering letter	Two-stage interview	2:1	4	800
KLegal	Online application	2 interviews & assessment exercises	2:1	30	c.750

APPLICATIONS AND SELECTION

FIRM NAME	METHOD OF APPLICATION	SELECTION PROCESS	DEGREE CLASS	NUMBER OF CONTRACTS	NUMBER OF APPLICATIONS
Knight & Sons	CV & handwritten letter	Not known	2:1	3/4	Not known
Landwell	Application form	Not known	2:1	8	Not known
Lawrence Graham	Application form	Interview	2:1	18	1,000
Laytons	Application form	2 interviews	1 or 2:1	8	2,000
LeBoeuf, Lamb, Greene & MacRae	CV & covering letter	2 interviews	Not known	4	1,000
Lee Bolton & Lee	Letter & CV	Panel interview	2:1	2	800
Lester Aldridge	Letter, CV & application form	Interview by a panel of partners	2:1	5	300
Lewis Silkin	Application form	Assessment day: interview with 2 partners & analytical exercise	2:1	6	1,000
Linklaters	Application form	2 interviews (same day)	2:1	150	2,500
Linnells	Cover letter & application form	Assessment centre & interviews with HR, training manager & 2 partners	2:1	3	2,000
Lovells	Online application form	Assessment day: critical thinking test, group exercise, interview	2:1	75	1,500
Lupton Fawcett	Application form & handwritten letter	Interviews & assessment days	2:1 preferred	4	300
Mace & Jones	Covering letter & CV	Interview with partners	2:1	9	1,500
Macfarlanes	Online application	Assessment day	2:1	25	1,500
Manches	Application form	Interview with 2 partners. 2nd interview & assessments.	2:1	10	1,000
Martineau Johnson	Online application form	Half-day assessment centre	2:1	14	500
Masons	Online application form	Assessment day & an interview	2:1	18	1,800
Mayer, Brown, Rowe & Maw	Online application form	Selection workshop: interview, business analysis exercise & group exercise	2:1	25-30	1,000
McCormicks	Application form	Selection day & interview with Training Partner	2:1	4	1,000
McDermott, Will & Emery	CV & covering letter	Not known	Not known	Not known	Not known
Mills & Reeve	Application form	One day assessment centre	2:1	20-25	Approx. 500
Mishcon de Reya	Application form	Not known	2:1	8	800+
Morgan Cole	Apply online	Assessment centre & interview	2.1 preferred	Not known	Not known
Nabarro Nathanson	Application form	Interview & assessment day	2:1	30	1,500
Nicholson Graham & Jones	Application form	Interview & assessment	2:1	10	1,000

APPLICATIONS AND SELECTION

FIRM NAME	METHOD OF APPLICATION	SELECTION PROCESS	DEGREE CLASS	NUMBER OF CONTRACTS	NUMBER OF APPLICATIONS
Norton Rose	Application form	Interview & group exercise	2:1	80-90	2,500+
Olswang	CV & covering letter	Business case scenario, interview, psychometric test	2:1	Up to 20	1,500
Osborne Clarke	Application form	Individual interviews, group exercises, selection testing	2:1 preferred	25-30	1,000-1,200
Pannone & Partners	Application form & CV	Interviews (2nd interview comprises tour of firm & lunch)	2:2	8	650
Payne Hicks Beach	Handwritten letter & CV	Interview	2:1	3	1,000
Penningtons	Covering letter, CV & application form	Interview with a partner and director of studies	2:1	10/11	2,000
Pinsent Curtis Biddle	Online application form	Assessment centre including interview	2:1	35	2,000
Prettys	Application letter & CV	Not known	2:1 preferred Good A- levels	4/5	Not known
Pritchard Englefield	Application form	Interview	Generally 2:1	3	300-400
RadcliffesLeBrasseur	CV & covering letter or application form	2 interviews with partners	2:1	6	1,000
Reed Smith Warner Cranston	Application form & covering letter	Assessment day: 2 interviews, aptitude test & presentation	2:1	6	1,000
Reynolds Porter Chamberlain	Handwritten covering letter & application form	Assessment day	2.1	10	1,200
Richards Butler	Online application form	Selection exercise & interview	2:1	20	2000
Russell Jones & Walker	Application form	Not known	2:1	10	1,000
Russell-Cooke	CV & covering letter	First & second interviews.	2:1	4	500
Salans	Handwritten letter & CV	2 interviews with partners	2:1	3 or 4	500+
Shadbolt & Co	Application form	Interview & written assessment	2:1	4	200
Shearman & Sterling	Application form	Interviews	2:1	6	Not known
Shoosmiths	Application form	Half-day selection centre	2:1	10	1,000
Sidley Austin Brown & Wood	Covering letter & application form	Interviews	2:1	6-8	500
Simmons & Simmons	App form, CV & letter (or online)	Assessment day: interview & written & document exercises	2:1	50-60	2,700
SJ Berwin	Check website	2 interviews	2:1	40	3,000
Slaughter and May	Covering letter & CV	Interview	2:1	Approx 85	2,500+
Speechly Bircham	Application form	Interview	2:1	5	1,000
Steele & Co	Online or CV & covering letter	Interview	2:1	6	300-400

APPLICATIONS AND SELECTION

FIRM NAME	METHOD OF APPLICATION	SELECTION PROCESS	DEGREE CLASS	NUMBER OF CONTRACTS	NUMBER OF APPLICATIONS
Stephenson Harwood	Application form	Interview with 2 partners	2:1	16-18	Not known
Tarlo Lyons	Application form	2 interviews with partners & skills assessment	2:1	3	500
Taylor Vinters	Application form	Single interview with one partner & HR Manager	2:2	5	300
Taylor Walton	CV & covering letter	First & second interviews	2:1 or above	Not known	Not known
Taylor Wessing	Application form	2 interviews, 1 with a partner	2:1	25	1,600
Teacher Stern Selby	Letter & application form	2 interviews	2:1 (not absolute)	6	1,000
Theodore Goddard	Online application form	Initial interview followed by second interview	2:1+	20	3000
Thomson Snell & Passmore	Handwritten letter & app form	1 interview with Training Partner and 1 other partner	2:1	4	Approx. 500
Thring Townsend	Application form	Assessment centre	2:1 or mature with experience	6	300
TLT Solicitors	Application form	Assessment day	n/a	8	750
Travers Smith Braithwaite	Handwritten letter & CV	Interviews	2:1	25	1,800
Trowers & Hamlins	Letter, application form & CV	Interview(s), essay & practical test	2:1+	12-15	1,600
Walker Morris	Application form	Telephone & face-to-face interviews	2:1	15	Approx. 600
Ward Hadaway	Application form & handwritten letter	Interview	2:1	10	400
Watson, Farley & Williams	Online application	Assessment centre & interview	2:1 min. and 24 UCAS points	12	1,000
Wedlake Bell	CV & covering letter	Interviews	2:1	4 or 6	800
Weightman Vizards	Application form	Not known	Not known	Not known	Not known
Weil, Gotshal & Manges	Application form	Not known	2:1	12	Not known
White & Case	Online application	Interview	2:1	20-25	1,500
Wiggin & Co	CV	2 interviews	2:1	3	300
Withers LLP	Application form & covering letter	2 interviews	2:1	12	1,500
Wragge & Co	Online or application form	Telephone discussion & assessment day	2:1	25	1,300

what the top firms are looking for

The obvious – great academics, communication skills, a well-organised approach and attention to detail. In a nutshell, recruiters want to know if you are right for the law and if the law is right for you.

languages
Language skills put you ahead at firms with overseas offices or existing business with the particular countries that speak your second language. Coudert Brothers says, "*In view of the international nature of the firm's work and clients, language skills are an advantage, but not essential.*" Pritchard Englefield is more specific. "*Normally only high academic achievers with a second European language (especially German and French) are considered.*"

law or non-law degree?
For most firms, a non-law degree is no drawback. Clyde & Co confirms, "*Non-law graduates are welcome, especially those with modern languages or science degrees.*" Macfarlanes seeks candidates from "*Any degree discipline.*" These firms are not alone but a few only want law graduates. For example, Cleary, Gottlieb, Steen & Hamilton states that it wants those with "*at least a 2.1 law degree from a top UK university.*" This is because it requires trainees to sit the New York Bar exam, which can only be taken if you have a degree in law.

class of degree
Leading commercial firms almost always require a 2:1 or better. There are exceptions, but such firms receive many hundreds of applications from candidates with at least a 2:1. Their policy is not an indication that they prefer those with a 2:2, just that they are prepared to be open minded on the subject. Pritchard Englefield confirms that "*exceptional subsequent education or experience*" can sometimes make up for a 2:2. We are regularly approached by students who tell us that they narrowly missed a 2:1 and wonder how to get this information over to recruiters. If there are valid reasons why your degree class does not reflect your capabilities then obtain a letter to that effect from your tutor and attach it to your application.

your university
The better regarded your university, the greater your chances of securing the job of your dreams. Oxbridge and leading redbrick universities are still favoured by many firms but there's good news in the results of our preferred universities poll on page 28.

local connections
These definitely count at many regional firms. The reason why firms look for local ties (family or an education in the area) is that on qualification you are more likely to stay with them rather than rushing off to London or the nearest big city. Forbes in Blackburn seeks "*high calibre recruits with strong local connections,*" while Manchester's Pannone & Partners looks for those with "*a connection with the North West.*"

previous careers
The *True Picture* flags up a number of firms that appreciate that those with first careers often make great lawyers. They already know what work is all about; many bring client contacts with them, and a number find themselves on a fast track through to partnership. The following industry sectors and careers are particularly popular: shipping, insurance, pharmaceuticals, medical professionals, engineers, surveyors, accountants, IT and the armed forces. Here's what some of the law firms said on the matter. Addleshaw Booth welcomes applications from "*mature students who may be considering a change of direction.*" Richards Butler says, "*Candidates from diverse backgrounds are welcome, including mature stu-*

dents with commercial experience and management skills," while Holman Fenwick & Willan welcomes those with *"a scientific or maritime background."*

personality

You should definitely have one. Many firms ask for creative problem solvers, others request those with a sense of humour and enthusiasm. Not every firm has a particular blueprint in mind and there are firms that stress that they look for a range of different characters. Newcastle's Dickinson Dees simply wants those *"able to fit into a team."* By reading the *True Picture* you should get a feel for the firms you are most likely to fit into. Remember, some firms will not be right for you, just as you will not be right for them.

commercial awareness

They all seem to be after it, but they're not expecting Sir John Harvey-Jones to turn up on their doorstep! Deborah Dalgleish, head of UK graduate recruitment at Freshfields Bruckhaus Deringer told us, *"We are not necessarily looking for someone who has commercial awareness as such. We don't expect it. Applicants aren't experienced enough. What we need to see is evidence that they have the ability to develop commercial awareness. This might be indicated by an applicant who has operated outside their comfort zone, pushed themselves or taken a sensible calculated risk."* This kind of experience could be gained during part-time employment, during a gap year, or at university. Slaughter and May *"does not expect applicants to know much of commercial life"* as it expects you to have been busy with academic work and extra-curricular activities. There are some clear messages from the firms in their own literature. Hodge Jones & Allen, for example, states that candidates should have *"a proven commitment to and/or experience of working in Legal Aid/Advice sectors."* Sometimes it's more vague: Farrer & Co says those who *"break the mould – as shown by their initiative for organisation, leadership, exploration, or enterprise – are far more likely to get an interview than the erudite, but otherwise unimpressive student."*

smells like team spirit

Most firms want applicants to demonstrate an ability to work with others in a team. A popular question on application forms and at interview could be along the lines of: 'Describe a situation where you had to work effectively as a member of a team…' Do try and come up with something!

interests and travel

You need to demonstrate that there's a little bit more to you than the next candidate. Recruiters look at how you spend your free time and whether you are a team player or a loner. Andrew Hearn, graduate recruitment partner at Dechert, told us, *"Everyone socialises with friends; not everyone has pursued that particular hobby or filled that particular role at university."* Deborah told us how firms are unimpressed by applicants who don't seem to have gone out and obtained this kind of experience. *"We are interested in applicants who might have a wide range of different experiences. We don't prescribe anything specific. Applicants who have not been involved in anything, especially at university, aren't doing themselves any favours."* And don't think for a minute that taking time out to travel is a bad thing. The majority of firms hold the opinion that travel broadens the mind and provides valuable life experience.

the right balance

Sell yourself to the firm but don't go over the top. Andrew gave the example of an applicant who, when asked if he had any questions of his own for the panel, dashed off the poser: *"How do you see the twin forces of globalisation and information technology shaping the future of your firm?"* Not necessarily the most relevant of questions for a potential trainee solicitor! Andrew also stresses the need to be polite to everyone you meet at the firm. One promising applicant was crossed off the list after he behaved arrogantly towards the administrator who took him to the interview room. Recruiters understand that you might be nervous. They do not expect you to be rude.

SALARIES AND BENEFITS

FIRM NAME	1ST YEAR SALARY	2ND YEAR SALARY	SPONSORSHIP/ AWARDS	OTHER BENEFITS	QUALIFICATION SALARY
Addleshaw Booth & Co	£20,000-20,500 (Manch/Leeds) £28,000-28,500 (London)	£21,000-21,500 (Manch/Leeds) £29,000-29,500 (London)	CPE & LPC: fees + maintenance of £2,500 & £4,500 respectively	Corporate gym m'ship, STL, subsd restaurant	£32,000 (Manch/Leeds) £48,000 (London)
Allen & Overy	£28,000	£32,000	CPE & LPC: fees + £5,000 p.a. maintenance (£4,500 outside London, Oxford & Guildford)	Pte healthcare scheme, PMI, STL, subsd restaurant, gym m'ship, 6 weeks unpaid leave on qual	£50,000
Arnold & Porter	Minimum £30,000	Not known	CPE & LPC: sponsorship	PHI, STL, life ass	£59,000
Ashurst Morris Crisp	£28,000-29,000	£31,000-32,000	CPE & LPC: fees + £5,000 p.a. maintenance (£4,500 outside London & Guildford), £500 LPC distinction award, language tuition bursaries	PHI, pension, life ass, STL, gym m'ship	£48,000
B P Collins	£17,000	£18,000	LPC: 50% costs refunded once trainee starts contract	Not known	Not known
Baker & McKenzie	£28,000 + £3,000 'golden hello'	£32,000	CPE & LPC: fees + £5000 p.a. maintenance + laptop or £2,000 for LPC	PHI, life ins, PMI, group personal pension, subsd gym m'ship, STL, subsd staff restaurant/bar	£50,000-£52,000
Barlow Lyde & Gilbert	£28,000	£30,000	CPE & LPC: fees + maintenance	Not known	£47,000
Beachcroft Wansbroughs	£24,750 (London) £17,500 (regions)	£26,750 (London) £19,500 (regions)	LPC fees + £3,000 bursary	Flexible scheme (buy & sell benefits, inc. holiday, pension, pte healthcare)	Not known
Berwin Leighton Paisner	£28,000	£32,000	CPE & LPC: fees + £4,500 p.a. maintenance	Flexible package inc. PHI, PMI, subsd conveyancing, subsd gym m'ship	£48,000
Bevan Ashford	Not known	Not known	LPC: yes CPE: sometimes	Not known	Not known
Bird & Bird	£26,500	£28,500	CPE & LPC: fees + £3,500 p.a. maintenance	BUPA, STL, subsd sports club m'ship, life cover, PHI, pension	£46,000
Blake Lapthorn	£16,000	£18,000	LPC: fees up to £6,000 + £4,000 bursary	Not known	£28,500
Bond Pearce	Depending on location, up to £16,250	Not available	LPC: financial assistance	Not known	Depending on location, up to £28,000
Boyes Turner	£17,000	£18,000	LPC: £3,000 interest-free loan	Pension, life ass	Not known
Brabners Chaffe Street	Not known	Not known	LPC: partial sponsorship possible	Not known	Not known

Notes: PHI = Permanent Health Insurance; STL = Season Travel Ticket Loan; PMI = Private Medical Insurance

SALARIES AND BENEFITS

FIRM NAME	1ST YEAR SALARY	2ND YEAR SALARY	SPONSORSHIP/ AWARDS	OTHER BENEFITS	QUALIFICATION SALARY
Brachers	£16,000	£17,500	LPC/CPE: £6,000 discretionary award.	Not known	£27,500-£30,000
Bristows	£26,000	£28,000	CPE & LPC: fees + £5,000 p.a. maintenance	Pension, life ass & health ins	£43,000
Browne Jacobson	£18,000	Not known	CPE & LPC: funding	Not known	Regional variations
Burges Salmon	£20,000	£21,000	CPE & LPC: fees + maintenance £4,500 for LPC only (£2,500 p.a. if studying both)	Annual bonus, pension, mobile phone	£34,000
Cadwalader, Wickersham & Taft	£30,000	£33,600	CPE & LPC: fees + £4,500 p.a maintenance	PHI, STL, BUPA (dental & health), life ass	£65,000
Campbell Hooper	£21,000-22,000	£23,000-24,500	LPC & CPE: fees	PMI, pension, life ass, PHI, STL	Not known
Capsticks	Not known	Not known	CPE & LPC: scholarship contributions	Bonus, pension, PHI, death in service, STL	£40,000
Charles Russell	£27,000	£29,500	London: CPE & LPC fees + £4,500 p.a. maintenance Chelt/Guildford: one off LPC grants	BUPA immediately, PHI & life ass after 6 months	£45,000
Clarks	£17,000	£18,500	Not known	Pension, free conveyancing	Not known
Cleary, Gottlieb, Steen & Hamilton	£33,000	£39,000	LPC: fees + £4,500 maintenance	Pension, health ins, long-term disability ins, health club, employee assistance programme	Not known
Clifford Chance	£28,500	£32,000	CPE & LPC: fees + £5,000 p.a. maintenance (Lon/Guild/Oxf), £4,500 p.a. (elsewhere), prizes for first class degree & LPC distinction	Interest-free loan, pte health ins, subsd restaurant, fitness centre, life ass, occupational health service, PHI	£50,000
Clyde & Co	£27,000	£30,000	CPE & LPC: fees + maintenance (provided where no LEA funding)	Subsd sports club, STL, staff restaurant, weekly free bar	£46,000
CMS Cameron McKenna	£28,000	£32,000	CPE & LPC: fees + £5,000 p.a. maintenance (Lon/Guild/Oxf), £4,500 (elsewhere)	Not known	£50,000
Cobbetts	Competitive	Competitive	CPE & LPC: grant available	Social club, LA Fitness pool & gym	Not known
Coffin Mew & Clover	Competitive	Competitive	CPE & LPC: discussed with candidates	Not known	£24,500
Coudert Brothers	£28,000	£32,000	CPE & LPC: fees + £4,000 p.a. maintenance (discretionary)	Pension, health ins, subsd gym m'ship, STL, pte med & dental care	Not known
Covington & Burling	£28,000	£32,000	CPE & LPC: fees + £5,000 p.a. maintenance	Pension, PHI, pte health cover, life ass, STL	Not known

Notes: PHI = Permanent Health Insurance; STL = Season Travel Ticket Loan; PMI = Private Medical Insurance

SALARIES AND BENEFITS

FIRM NAME	1ST YEAR SALARY	2ND YEAR SALARY	SPONSORSHIP/ AWARDS	OTHER BENEFITS	QUALIFICATION SALARY
Cripps Harries Hall	£16,000	£18,000	LPC fees: 50% interest free loan, 50% bursary (discretionary)	Not known	£30,000
Cumberland Ellis Peirs	Not known	Not known	None	STL, luncheon vouchers	Not known
D J Freeman	£26,000-27,000	£28,000-29,000	CPE & LPC funding	Subsd staff restaurant, BUPA after 3 months, social & sporting	£48,000
Davenport Lyons	£25,500	£27,500	Not normally	STL, client intro bonus, contrib to gym m'ship, discretionary bonus	Not known
Dechert	£28,000	£32,000	CPE & LPC: fees + £4,500 p.a. maintenance (where no LEA grant)	PHI, life ass, subsd gym m'ship, STL	c.£50,000
Denton Wilde Sapte	£27,000-28,000	£30,000-31,000	CPE & LPC: fees + £4,500 p.a. maintenance (£5,000 in London)	Meal allowance, pte health cover, STL, subsd sports club m'ship, PHI, life ass	£48,000 (£50,000 after 6 months)
Devonshires	Market rate	Market rate	LPC: funding considered	STL, healthcare scheme, subsd health-club m'ship	Negotiable
Dickinson Dees	£18,000	£19,500	CPE & LPC: fees + £4,000 interest free loan	Not known	£30,000
DLA	£28,000 (London) £20,000 (regions) £16,000 (Scotland)	£31,000 (London) £22,000 (regions) £18,000 (Scotland)	CPE & LPC: fees + maintenance	Contributory pension, health ins, life ass, sports & social facilities, car scheme	£48,000 (London) £33,000 (Birmingham) £32,500 (other English) £30,000 (Scotland)
DMH	£16,500	£19,000	Not known	Not known	£28,000
DWF	£16,750	Not known	LPC: fees	Life ass, pension	Not known
Edwards Geldard	£15,500	£16,500	LPC: £5,000 CPE: £2,000	Life ass at 3 x salary	Not known
Eversheds	£28,000 (London)	£31,000 (London)	CPE & LPC: fees + maintenance	Regional variations	£48,000 (London)
Farrer & Co	£26,000	£28,000	CPE & LPC: fees + £4,500 p.a. maintenance	Health & life ins, subsd gym m'ship, STL	£40,000
Fenners	Market for City	Market for City	CPE & LPC: discussed with candidates	Health ins, STL	Market for City
Field Fisher Waterhouse	£26,000	£29,120	CPE & LPC: fees + maintenance	STL, PMI, life ass	£45,000
Finers Stephens Innocent	Highly competitive	Highly competitive	LPC & CPE: fees	Pension, PMI, life ins, long-term disability ins, subsd gym m'ship, STL	Highly competitive

Notes: PHI = Permanent Health Insurance; STL = Season Travel Ticket Loan; PMI = Private Medical Insurance

SALARIES AND BENEFITS

FIRM NAME	1ST YEAR SALARY	2ND YEAR SALARY	SPONSORSHIP/ AWARDS	OTHER BENEFITS	QUALIFICATION SALARY
Fladgate Fielder	£23,000	£25,000	Not known	Pension, PHI, life ass, STL, sports club loan, bonus scheme	Not known
Foot Anstey Sargent	Not known	Not known	Not known	Contributory pension	£27,825
Forsters	£24,000	£26,000	None	STL, PHI, life ins, subsd gym m'ship	£41,000
Freethcartwright	£15,500	Not known	Not known	Not known	Not known
Freshfields Bruckhaus Deringer	£28,000	£32,000	CPE & LPC: fees + £5,000 p.a. maintenance (Lon/Oxf), £4,500 p.a. (elsewhere)	Life ass, PHI, group personal pension, interest-free loan, STL, PMI, subsd staff restaurant, gym	£50,000
Gateley Wareing	£17,500	£19,500	LPC: fees + £3,500 maintenance CPE: fees	Bonus scheme (up to 10% of salary)	£31,000
Goodman Derrick	£23,000	£24,500	LPC fees + maintenance	Med health ins, STL, pension	Not known
Gouldens	£32,000	£36,000	CPE & LPC: fees + £5,000 p.a. maintenance	BUPA, STL, subsd sports club m'ship, group life cover	£55,000
Halliwell Landau	£19,500	£20,500	CPE & LPC: fees	Subsd gym m'ship	£26,000-28,000
Hammond Suddards Edge	£20,500	£23,000	CPE & LPC fees paid & maintenance grant of £4,500 p.a.	Subsd accom (all locations), flexible benefits scheme (choose from range)	£47,500 (London) £33,000-34,000 (other)
Harbottle & Lewis	£23,500	£24,500	LPC: fees + interest-free loan	Lunch, STL	£41,000
Henmans	£15,500	£17,000	Not known	Not known	£26,000
Herbert Smith	£28,500	£32,000	CPE & LPC: fees + £5,000 p.a. maintenance	Profit share, PHI, PMI, STL, life ass, gym, group personal accident ins, matched contrib. pension	£50,000
Hewitson Becke + Shaw	£17,000	£18,000	None	Not known	Not known
Hill Dickinson	£16,500	£18,000	LPC fees (further funding/ maintenance under review)	Not known	Not known
Hodge Jones & Allen	Not known	Not known	Not known	Pension, life ass, PHI	Not known
Holman Fenwick & Willan	£28,000	£30,000	CPE & LPC: fees + £5,000 p.a. maintenance	PMI, PHI, accident ins, subsd gym m'ship, STL	£50,000
Howes Percival	£18,750	£20,000	LPC funding	Contributory pension, pte health ins, accommodation let to trainees	Not known

Notes: PHI = Permanent Health Insurance; STL = Season Travel Ticket Loan; PMI = Private Medical Insurance

SALARIES AND BENEFITS

FIRM NAME	1ST YEAR SALARY	2ND YEAR SALARY	SPONSORSHIP/ AWARDS	OTHER BENEFITS	QUALIFICATION SALARY
Hugh James	Competitive	Competitive	Not known	Contribution to stakeholder pension	Not known
Ince & Co	£27,000	£30,000	LPC: fees + £4,750 grant (London), £4,000 (elsewhere), CPE: discretionary	STL, corporate health cover, PHI, contributory pension	£47,000
Irwin Mitchell	£17,000 (outside London)	£19,000 (outside London)	CPE & LPC: fees + £3,000 p.a. maintenance	Not known	Not known
Keoghs	Not known	Not known	Not known	Not known	£26,500
KLegal	£28,000	£32,000	CPE & LPC: fees + £4,500 p.a. maintenance	Flextra (flexible scheme inc. life ass, pension, lunch allowance, holidays)	£50,000
Knight & Sons	Not known	Not known	Interest free loans may be available	Subsd gym m'ship	Not known
Landwell	Market rate	Market rate	CPE & LPC: fees + maintenance	Not known	Not known
Lawrence Graham	£28,000	£32,000	CPE & LPC: fees + £4,000 p.a. maintenance	STL, on-site gym	£48,000
Laytons	Market rate	Market rate	CPE & LPC: funding available	Not known	Market rate
LeBoeuf, Lamb, Greene & MacRae	£33,000	£37,000	CPE & LPC: fees + £4,500 p.a. maintenance	PMI, STL, subsd restaurant	£65,000
Lee Bolton & Lee	£19,000	£20,000	LPC: contribution	STL, discretionary bonus	£29,000
Lester Aldridge	£16,500	£18,000	Discretionary	Life ass, pension	£29,000
Lewis Silkin	£26,000	£28,000	LPC: fees	Life ass, critical illness cover, health ins, STL, pension	£42,000
Linklaters	£28,500	£32,000	CPE & LPC: fees + £4,500-£5,000 p.a. maintenance. Personal development programme: 20% of salary for constructive time off after LPC or on qual	PPP med ins, life ass, pension, STL, in-house gym, Holmes Place corp. m'ship, in-house dentist, doctor & physio, subsd restaurant	£50,000 + bonus
Linnells	£16,000	£17,000	£30,000	Med cover, social event subsidies, discounted legal services	£30,000
Lovells	£28,000	£32,000	CPE & LPC: fees + £5,000 p.a. maintenance (Lon/Guild/Oxf), £4,500 p.a.(elsewhere), £500 bonus & £1,000 salary advance on joining, £500 prize for first class degree	PPP med ins, life ass, PHI, STL, staff restaurant, in-house dentist, doctor & physio, local retail discounts	£50,000

Notes: PHI = Permanent Health Insurance; STL = Season Travel Ticket Loan; PMI = Private Medical Insurance

SALARIES AND BENEFITS

FIRM NAME	1ST YEAR SALARY	2ND YEAR SALARY	SPONSORSHIP/ AWARDS	OTHER BENEFITS	QUALIFICATION SALARY
Lupton Fawcett	Competitive	Competitive	LPC: interest-free loan	Health ins, STL	Competitive
Mace & Jones	£13,000	£13,500	Not known	Not known	Negotiable
Macfarlanes	£28,000	£32,000	CPE & LPC: fees + £5,000 p.a. maintenance (Lon/Guild/Oxf) £4,500 (elsewhere), prizes for LPC distinction or commendation	STL, pension, PHI*, PMI*; subsd conveyancing/ health club/gym m'ship/restaurant, subscriptions to City of London Law Soc/TSG *After 12 months	
Manches	£26,500 (London)	£30,000 (London)	CPE & LPC: fees + £4,000 p.a. maintenance	STL, BUPA after 6 months, PHI, life ins, pension after 3 months	£40,250 (London)
Martineau Johnson	£18,000	£19,500	LPC: fees + £3,000 maintenance CPE: discretionary interest free loan	Pension, pte health, life ass, PHI, travel loans, critical illness cover, Denplan, gym m'ship, conveyancing; will drafting, professional subscriptions	£33,000
Masons	Starts £26,000- (London) (varies between offices)	Rises to £30,000 (London) (varies between offices)	CPE & LPC: fees + maintenance	Life ass, pte health care (all offices) Subsd restaurant & STL (London)	£47,000 (London)
Mayer, Brown, Rowe & Maw	£28,000	Not known	CPE & LPC: + £4,500 p.a. maintenance (£5,000 for Lon/Guild)	STL, subsd sports club m'ship, pte health scheme	£50,000
McCormicks	Highly competitive	Highly competitive	Not known	Not known	Highly competitive
McDermott, Will & Emery	£30,000	Not known	CPE & LPC: fees + maintenance	Pte med & dental ins, life ass, PHI, STL, subisidised gym m'ship, employee assistance programme	Not known
Mills & Reeve	£17,000	£18,000	LPC: fees + maintenance CPE: funding discretionary	Life ass, contributory pension	£31,500-32,500
Mishcon de Reya	£25,000	£27,000	CPE & LPC: fees + bursary	Med cover, subsd gym m'ship, STL, PHI, life ass, pension	Not known
Morgan Cole	Competitive	Competitive	CPE & LPC: fees + maintenance	Not known	Not known
Nabarro Nathanson	£28,000 (London/ Reading) £20,000 (Sheffield)	£32,000 (London/Readi ng) £22,000 (Sheffield)	CPE & LPC: fees + £5,000 p.a. maintenance (Lon/Guild), £4,500 (elsewhere)	PMI, pension, STL, subsd restaurant, subsd corporate gym m'ship	£48,000 (London) £31,000 (Sheffield)
Nicholson Graham & Jones	£28,000	£31,000	CPE & LPC: fees + £4,000 p.a. maintenance	Life ass, STL, subsd gym m'ship, BUPA	£48,000

Notes: PHI = Permanent Health Insurance; STL = Season Travel Ticket Loan; PMI = Private Medical Insurance

SALARIES AND BENEFITS

FIRM NAME	1ST YEAR SALARY	2ND YEAR SALARY	SPONSORSHIP/ AWARDS	OTHER BENEFITS	QUALIFICATION SALARY
Norton Rose	£28,500	£32,000	CPE & LPC: fees + maintenance, £1,000 travel scholarship	£800 loan on arrival, life ass, pte health ins, STL, subsd gym m'ship, 4 weeks unpaid leave on qual	£50,000
Olswang	£26,500	£30,000	CPE & LPC: fees + maintenance	After 6 months: pension, med cover, life cover, dental scheme, STL, subsd gym m'ship. After 12 months: PHI	£46,000
Osborne Clarke	£25,000 (London/TV) £19,000 (Bristol)	Not known	CPE & LPC: fees + £3,000 p.a. maintenance	Pension contributions, pte healthcare cover, STL, PHI, group life ass	£47,500 (London) £43,000 (TV) £34,000 (Bristol)
Pannone & Partners	£17,000	£19,000	LPC: fees	Not known	£29,000
Payne Hicks Beach	£25,000	£27,500	CPE & LPC: fees	STL, life ass, PHI, pension	£43,000
Penningtons	£24,500 (London)	£26,500 (London)	LPC: funding + award for commendation or distinction	Subsd sports & social club, life ass, pte med, STL	£38,000 (London)
Pinsent Curtis Biddle	£28,000	£30,000	CPE & LPC: fees + maintenance (CPE: £3,000, LPC: £5,000)	Not known	Approx £48,000
Prettys	Not known	Not known	Discretionary	Not known	Not known
Pritchard Englefield	£20,750	£21,250	LPC: fees	Some subsd training, luncheon vouchers	Approx £30,000
RadcliffesLeBrasseur	£23,500 (London) £15,000 (Leeds)	£26,000 (London) £16,500 (Leeds)	LPC: fees + £4,000 maintenance	Health ins, STL, life ass, PHI	£38,000
Reed Smith Warner Cranston	£27,000	£31,000	CPE & LPC: fees + maintenance + interest-free loan	BUPA, STL, life ass, PHI, pension contributions	£48,000
Reynolds Porter Chamberlain	£27,000	£29,000	CPE & LPC: fees + £4,000 p.a. maintenance	Bonus, PMI, income protection, STL, subsd gym m'ship	£45,000
Richards Butler	£28,000	£31,000	CPE & LPC: fees + £5,000 p.a. maintenance	Bonus, life ins, BUPA, STL, subsd staff restaurant, conveyancing allowance	£48,000 + bonus
Russell Jones & Walker	Approx £20,000	Approx £21,500	LPC: interest-free loan	STL, pension, pte healthcare or gym m'ship, group life ass	Approx £32,000 (London)
Russell-Cooke	£20,500	£22,000	LPC: possibly fees	Not known	Market
Salans	£24,500	£25,500	LPC: fees	Pte healthcare, pension, STL	Variable

Notes: PHI = Permanent Health Insurance; STL = Season Travel Ticket Loan; PMI = Private Medical Insurance

SALARIES AND BENEFITS

FIRM NAME	1ST YEAR SALARY	2ND YEAR SALARY	SPONSORSHIP/ AWARDS	OTHER BENEFITS	QUALIFICATION SALARY
Shadbolt & Co	£21,000	£25,000	LPC: partly payable when trainee starts work	PHI, death in service, pref rates on pte med care, annual bonus, STL	£35,000
Shearman & Sterling	£30,000	£34,000	CPE & LPC: fees + £4,500 p.a. maintenance	Not known	£55,000
Shoosmiths	£17,000	£18,000	LPC: £12,500 split between fees & maintenance	Life ass, pension after 3 months, various staff discounts	Market rate
Sidley Austin Brown & Wood	£28,500	£32,000	CPE & LPC: fees + maintenance	Healthcare, disability cover, life ass, contrib to gym m'ship, STL	Not known
SJ Berwin	£28,000	£32,000	CPE & LPC: fees + £4,500 p.a. maintenance (£5,000 in London)	Corporate sports m'ship, free lunch, health ins	£50,000
Slaughter and May	£29,000	£32,500	CPE & LPC: fees + maintenance	BUPA, STL, pension, subsd health club m'ship, 24-hour accident cover	£50,000
Speechly Bircham	£26,000-27,000	£28,000-29,000	CPE & LPC: fees + £4,000 p.a. maintenance (£4,500 in Lon/Guild)	STL, PMI, life ass	£45,000
Steele & Co	Not known	Not known	Not known	Pension, accident ins, legal services, STL, gym m'ship loan	Not known
Stephenson Harwood	£26,000	£29,000	CPE & LPC: fees + maintenance	Subsd health club m'ship, pte health ins, BUPA, STL	£48,000
Tarlo Lyons	£24,000 (on average)	£26,000 (on average)	LPC: fees	Bonus, pte health scheme, pension plan, subsd health club m'ship	£42,000
Taylor Vinters	£16,000	£17,650	Not known	PMI, life ins, pension	£31,500
Taylor Wessing	£26,000	£29,000	CPE & LPC: fees + £4,000 p.a. maintenance	Pte med care, PHI, STL, subsd staff restaurant, pension	£48,000
Teacher Stern Selby	£23,000	Not known	LPC: funding possible	Not known	£33,000
Theodore Goddard	£27,500	£30,000	CPE & LPC: fees + £4,500 p.a. maintenance (Lon/S.E.), £4,000 (elsewhere)	Pension, bonus, PHI, PMI, subsd health club m'ship, restaurant	£48,000
Thomson Snell & Passmore	£15,750	£16,750	LPC: grant & interest free loan	Not known	£24,750
Thring Townsend	£13,500	£17,000	Not known	Life ass. After 12 months: pension, PMI	£25,000-30,000
TLT Solicitors	Not known	Not known	LPC: fees + maintenance	Pension, subsd health ins, subsd sports & health club m'ship, life ass	Market rate

Notes: PHI = Permanent Health Insurance; STL = Season Travel Ticket Loan; PMI = Private Medical Insurance

SALARIES AND BENEFITS

FIRM NAME	1ST YEAR SALARY	2ND YEAR SALARY	SPONSORSHIP/ AWARDS	OTHER BENEFITS	QUALIFICATION SALARY
Travers Smith Braithwaite	£28,000	£32,000	LPC & CPE: fees + £4,500-5,000 p.a. maintenance	Pte health ins, permanent sickness cover, life ass, STL, refreshment credit, subsd sports club m'ship	£50,000
Trowers & Hamlins	£25,500	£27,250	CPE & LPC: fees + £4,250–£4,500 p.a. maintenance	STL, pte health care after 6 months, employee assistance programme, bonus, death in service	£43,500
Walker Morris	£20,000	£22,000	CPE & LPC fees + maintenance (£3,500 p.a. CPE & LPC or £4,000 LPC only)	Not known	£32,000
Ward Hadaway	£17,000	£18,000	LPC: fees + £2,000 int-free loan	death in service insurance, pension	Min £27,500
Watson, Farley & Williams	£28,500	£32,500	CPE & LPC: fees £4,500 p.a. maintenance (£4,000 outside London)	Life ass, PHI, BUPA, STL, pension, subsd gym m'ship	Min £50,000
Wedlake Bell	Not known	Not known	LPC & CPE: fees + £2,500 p.a. maintenance (if no LEA grant)	Pension, STL, subsd gym m'ship. On qual: life ass, med ins & PHI	Not known
Weightman Vizards	Competitive	Competitive	CPE & LPC: fees	Pension, health cover, life ass	Not known
Weil, Gotshal & Manges	£35,000	Not known	CPE & LPC: fees + maintenance	Pension, PHI, pte health cover, life ass, subsd gym m'ship, STL	Not known
White & Case	£33,000-34,500	£36,000-37,500	CPE & LPC: fees + £5,500 p.a. maintenance, prize for LPC commendation or distinction	BUPA, gym m'ship contrib, life ins, pension, PHI, STL, bonus	£60,000
Wiggin & Co	£21,900	£28,000	CPE & LPC: fees + £3,000 p.a. maintenance	Life ass, pte health cover, pension scheme, PHI	£40,000
Withers LLP	£27,000	£29,500	CPE & LPC: fees + £4,500 p.a. maintenance, prize for CPE/LPC distinction or commendation	STL, PMI, life ass, Xmas bonus, subsd cafe	£45,000
Wragge & Co	£21,000	£24,000	CPE & LPC: fees + £4,500 p.a. maintenance, £1,000 int-free loan, prizes for first class degree & LPC distinction	Pension, life ass, PHI, travel schemes, travel desk, PMI, sports & social club, indep fin advice, Xmas gift	£33,000

Notes: PHI = Permanent Health Insurance; STL = Season Travel Ticket Loan; PMI = Private Medical Insurance

paralegal questions

Paralegals work as extra fee earners within firms. A qualified solicitor's time can be expensive and it is often more cost-effective for certain types of work to be completed by a paralegal. Many paralegals will have a law degree or the CPE/PgDL or even the LPC, and many will have some practical legal experience. However, it is not essential to have all the above. Whether you are looking at paralegal work as a career or want temporary work to gain experience and earn some money, you probably have a few questions. Chambers and Partners Recruitment's paralegal guru, Rebecca Saxby, gave us the following pointers.

how can agencies help me?

At Chambers and Partners Recruitment, we work with many of the top City law firms, high street practices and in-house legal departments. We assist them in recruiting paralegals for temporary vacancies, short-term contracts and permanent positions. We will spend time with you discussing your requirements over the telephone or invite you to come and meet us.

We have a number of positions available at any one time and regularly have new roles that we will consider you for and discuss with you. These vary enormously in terms of practice area and experience required. Generally, the candidates we register have six months' practical legal experience and have completed legal education.

if I have no practical legal experience, how can I go about getting some?

It can be difficult for us to assist you in finding a permanent role if you do not have any practical legal experience. The paralegal market is very competitive, but any additional experience or assets, such as fluency at business level in a foreign language or particularly impressive IT skills, could make you attractive to firms.

Undertaking vacation schemes, applying directly to law firms or working for a company that assists large firms on litigation cases will all provide you with the kind of experience that will help us to place you quickly.

can I work as a paralegal if I have not completed my LPC/BVC?

You can. It may prevent you from applying for certain roles; however, if you have some previous practical legal experience and your academic results to date are impressive, you will be able to secure work. It can work in your favour if you are pursuing a career in paralegal work, as firms will not have to be concerned about you hassling them for a training contract or leaving to train elsewhere.

if I undertake a number of short-term contracts in order to gain different work experiences, will this look unprofessional on my CV?

Not at all. If the roles you have taken are short-term and you have stayed for the duration of the contract, this will not be regarded negatively. It is perfectly acceptable to move between assignments on a regular basis, especially as many paralegal opportunities are short-term contracts.

can I apply to a firm for paralegal work that I have also applied to for a training contract?

The two applications are separate and are treated as such; therefore you can apply to the same firm for paralegal work.

can you get me a training contract?
As an agency we cannot assist you with finding a training contract; you must apply directly to law firms.

I am a qualified solicitor. I'd like to change specialisation. can I take a paralegal role to assist in my transition?
This is an option; however, in practice this is not usually feasible. There are a number of reasons why; firms would perceive you to be overqualified for the role and may question your ability as a solicitor if you are applying for a paralegal post. Additionally, the paralegal market is so competitive that firms will already have a wide choice of paralegals with relevant experience to fill any vacancy.

what could I expect from a career as a paralegal?
There are some interesting long-term roles for those who decide they do not want to qualify as a solicitor. We place candidates in managerial roles within paralegal departments, in professional support and know-how roles and as contract managers and legal assistants, particularly within in-house legal departments. All of these can be very rewarding and will pay a good salary.

what is the difference between a paralegal and a legal executive?
Quite often the two terms are interchanged. Paralegals usually have some practical legal experience and may or may not have completed the LPC, CPE or a law degree. Legal executives will be members or fellows of The Institute of Legal Executives (ILEX) and will study for the Institute's exams while gaining experience working in a solicitor's office or in-house legal department. If you would like more information on legal executives, please call our Legal Executive Consultant, Milo O' Connor, on 020 7606 8844 or refer to **www.ilex.org.uk**

I am legally qualified overseas and cannot work as a solicitor/barrister in this country. could I work as a paralegal?
Many firms and companies are more than happy to consider candidates with overseas qualifications; again, experience is the most important prerequisite. Paralegal work is the obvious choice if you are here for a short period of time or if you require employment before undertaking the Qualified Lawyers Transfer Test (QLTT). As an agency we place many overseas lawyers, particularly Australians, New Zealanders and South Africans. It is easier when the candidate has been trained in a common law jurisdiction similar to the one operating here. If English is the candidate's second language, they must be fluent in it. Fluency in a foreign language can be really useful too.

how much will i earn?
Each year Chambers and Partners Recruitment conducts a paralegal salary survey. For the most up to date results check out the Chambers and Partners student website:
www.chambersandpartners.com/chambersstudent

qualifying in other jurisdictions

Some lawyers go the extra mile and enhance their professional skill-set by becoming dual qualified. We looked at three of the most popular jurisdictions.

the US bar

The numbers of US firms in London and UK firms in the US have convinced some Americanophiles of the benefits of being dual qualified.

Matt Ziegler chose to qualify in the US rather than take the LPC & training contract route in the UK. After completing his degree in Law and Anthropology at the LSE he completed a master's degree in law at NYU. *"I liked New York so much I decided to stay. Doing the New York Bar exam followed on well from the end of the master's."* To complete his dual qualification, Matt will take the QLTT during 2002. His choice was not made on the basis that the NY Bar exam was the easy route. *"Actually it was a bit of a stinker; there's a lot of preparation involved. With 27 subjects to get to grips with, it involves a lot of logical thought as to how you are going to marshal the information."* The Bar Bri lecture programme was excellent, he thought, but it was a real culture shock. He had to forget everything he thought he knew about essay writing and adopt the US-preferred (but formulaic) Conclusions-Issues-Reasoning-Analysis-Conclusions (CIRAC) method.

Once he'd passed the exam and landed a job with Cleary, Gottlieb, Steen & Hamilton in London (the US visa enabling the master's year only gives the holder one further year in the US), Matt was able to practice as a qualified attorney. While he's taking advantage of the training contract programme at Clearys in London, he doesn't actually have to complete one. After taking the QLTT, he'll be fully dual qualified for English and US law. His colleague, Chris Jones, was encouraged to take the NY Bar exam by the firm. *"As a process it's tough,"* he says, *"The exam is peculiar and you have to approach it in the right way."* Both agreed that the Bar Bri course was invaluable and increased their prospects of passing. Chris concludes, *"Lots of NY law is pretty much the same as English law; they got it from us! Negligence, tort, contract – the framework is based on the common law system."*

To be eligible for the NY Bar exam you must hold a three-year full-time or four-year part-time LLB. A distance learning degree is unacceptable. Any eligibility queries should be addressed to the New York State Board of Law Examiners, Suite 202, 7 Executive Centre Drive, Albany, New York 12203-5915, USA.

Central Law Training is a UK organisation, offers a New York Bar lecture programme. The more popular option is a five-month lecture programme; the alternative is a home study course. Each leads up to the exams (twice yearly in February or July) in NY State. A California Bar programme is also offered, although it additionally requires 12 months experience in practice as a solicitor and is only available via the home study method. All lectures take place on Friday evenings and Saturdays (drinkers and socialites beware!) at the Café Royal on Regent Street.

Contact: Central Law Training, Tel: 0121 362 7703.
Website: www.centlaw.com

Holborn College offers an 11-week part-time course for the NY Bar exam. Lectures take place in west London on Friday evenings and weekends. A California Bar course is also offered.

Contact: Holborn College, Tel 0207 385 3377. **Website:** www.holborncollege.ac.uk

qualifying as an australian solicitor

Looking to swap your legal briefs for a pair of Billabong board shorts? Australia attracts overstressed northern hemisphere professionals seeking a lifestyle-driven career change. Its federal system supports several states with varying rules governing admission requirements.

The Legal Practitioners Admission Board (LPAB) is the admitting authority in New South Wales. English solicitors are required to apply to the LPAB for admission. Transfer requirements may necessitate further academic and practical legal training but exemptions often lighten the load. Once certified, a person is free to practise as a solicitor or barrister.

"Are you looking to swap your legal briefs for a pair of Billabong shorts?"

Brit Down Under, Helen Gregoriou, an assistant at Allens Arthur Robinson, told us how she made the change. Helen settled in Sydney, after responding to the firm's recruitment drive in London. She had no difficulties adjusting to practice or the legal system. *"It's based on English law and I have found it to be very similar. The major difference is style, ie the way a corporate transaction is negotiated… My requalification entailed applying to the LPAB for exemptions from legal and practical studies. They look at each application on its own merits and after assessment I had to take constitutional law, professional ethics and accounts. I studied all three by way of lectures. The latter two were open book exams and very similar to the English courses I had already taken during my training contract."* Helen told us that every Brit she knows has requalified. *"There is much more of an emphasis on further education/qualification in Australia, with many lawyers taking MAs, and the firm pays for this further study, which is an added bonus."*

Gareth Lewis moved to AAR's Melbourne office after training in London. He stressed just how portable a commercial/financial legal training is. *"The principles in those areas of the law apply the world over and so it is easy to translate skills learnt in London to practice in Australia. Transactions here have the same levels of complexity although there may be one less nought in the value."* Gareth explained, *"Whether or not you requalify is taken out of your hands if you intend remaining in Australia for any period of time. The Council of Legal Education in Victoria, for example, requires foreign lawyers to requalify within three years… It's a formal process that's more time-consuming than anything else."*

We nearly wept when Gareth told us how fabulous life could be down under. As a taster, he told us, *"We're renting an apartment 10 minutes on the tram from the office. It is a block from the beach, has a balcony with city views and a communal swimming pool, spa and gym. I wouldn't be able to do that in London without paying a high premium."* Both Helen and Gareth stressed that the legal market in Australia is just as varied, challenging and difficult as in the UK and involves its share of hard work. But there is a greater emphasis on *"finding a balance between work and a lifestyle."*

Contact: LPAB, Tel: 00 612 9392 0300. **Website:** www.lawlink.nsw.gov.au/lpab.nsf/pages/first
Contact: Law Institute Of Victoria, Tel: 00 613 9607 9311. **Website:** www.liv.asn.au
Contact: Queensland Law Society Inc., Tel: 00 617 3842 5888. **Website:** www.qls.com.au

qualifying in Scotland

Solicitors from England and Wales first need to be fully admitted to the Roll south of the border and a 'certificate of good standing' from the Law Society in London. There are no organised tuition programmes for the Intra-UK Transfer Test but Strathclyde University offers a correspondence course. Those preparing for the exam (three two-hour papers), held in Edinburgh, can find a detailed document as to the content of the exam and a reading list on the Law Society of Scotland's website.

Contact: The Law Society Of Scotland, Tel: 0131 226 7411. **Website:** www.lawscot.org.uk

prospects for newly qualifieds

The fortunes of newly qualified solicitors are determined to a great extent by the economy. Just two years ago, those qualifying found it much easier to secure exactly the type of position they were looking for. However, in the last 12 months the market has tightened considerably and the NQs of 2002 had a tougher time. We asked our colleagues at Chambers and Partners Recruitment to give us the lowdown on the NQ jobs market in autumn 2002. Here's what they had to say…

private practice

For newly qualified solicitors, the market is weaker than it was just a couple of years ago. *"There is good news, however: the majority of newly qualifieds are being offered suitable positions by their own firms,"* says Chambers' London consultant Paul Thomas. But the weaker state of the market is having some effect, particularly for those wanting jobs in more specialist areas of practice. *"Those qualifiers not offered a position in their first choice specialisation are finding it harder to move elsewhere. Similarly, it is more difficult to achieve the goal of many newly qualified solicitors – the move from a smaller firm to a larger firm, or from the regions to London,"* says Paul. Some newly qualifieds, it seems, may have to make compromises.

Good candidates from London looking to relocate to the regions are viewed well, although the number of regional firms looking for external candidates is lower than normal this year. Of those vacancies that have cropped up, many have been in property and private client work.

Huge salary hikes are a thing of the past and in many cases NQ earnings have remained static since last year (and a few have even fallen). It is likely that they will remain fairly static until the next positive shift in the recruitment market. A slowdown in business inevitably affects those with less experience.

Are there any lessons in all this for students commencing training contracts over the next few years? Certainly, yes. The first is to plan for qualification from the moment you join the firm; although in most cases the first seat is decided for you, you will be able to influence where you go next. If you want to be a corporate lawyer, try to back up a corporate seat with one, for example, in finance or banking, or even undertake a second seat in the same department.

The next thing to be aware of is timing. The third of four six-month seats is the most crucial time to be seen and heard by the partners you hope to work for after qualification. We suspect that some trainees will now be more careful about the timing of any client secondments or overseas postings, in the desire not to be away from the firm's main office when NQ vacancies are announced. Likewise, if your first seat was actually in your favourite department, use this time to remind people of your enthusiasm for that seat: perhaps attend seminars in that department or chat to the relevant partners/assistants in the pub or staff restaurant. Relationships are often key; doing a good and efficient job is not always enough, especially in large firms where there may be any number of equally talented trainees also after the job you want. When the decision time comes, you need someone who is going to speak up for you personally.

Above all: *"Don't burn your bridges at the firm you are training with – even if it isn't ideal; you may need their goodwill,"* advises Paul. *" If the market is strong when you qualify, we can place you almost anywhere. If it's tight, we can still find you a good position, but we may advise you to get an extra year's PQE to land the ideal job."*

industry and banking

It's easy to see the allure of the in-house culture – more predictable working hours, more opportunities to become involved in business decisions, and incentivised pay structures, which have the potential to translate into large bonuses or share options. But for some NQs, the lack of infrastructure and hands-on supervision may act as a deterrent.

Commonly most in-house positions are broad corporate/commercial roles, with an emphasis on negotiating commercial contracts, joint ventures and M&A activity. So if you're considering moving in-house, you'll benefit from a broad mix of commercial work during your training contract and would be well advised to qualify into a corporate or commercial department. In-house opportunities for litigators and property specialists are more limited, though positions do exist with a specialist slant, for example IP/IT or employment.

You can also consider positions within the banking sector. These are very well paid, but most banks are looking for those with some prior legal experience in banking and/or capital markets and successful applicants tend to come from the magic circle or other leading finance firms.

"*In any one year there aren't that many in-house jobs for newly qualifieds,*" says Stuart Morton of Chambers' in-house recruitment. "*Legal departments are relatively small and business people are relatively demanding, so there's not much time to train up junior lawyers.*" Also, positions are hard to plan for as they come up throughout the year when the need arises, not just in March/September when most training contracts end. "*The best advice is to position yourself well in a law firm and register with a reputable consultancy like Chambers, who will let you know when a suitable job arises – but be prepared for it to take a while,*" says Stuart.

Whether it's banking or industry, much of a candidate's success has to do with his or her attitude. "*Teams are small and employers are keen to find the right 'fit'. Personality will often take precedence over experience,*" advises Stuart. Commercial awareness is also a very important attribute and can be cultivated by keeping abreast of developments in industry-related and general financial publications, such as the *FT*. Candidates must, of course, be able to demonstrate an interest in and an understanding of the in-house legal environment. But, ultimately, there's no substitute for enthusiasm.

becoming an english solicitor

Since 2000 and the implementation of the European Lawyers Establishment Directive, EU lawyers have been able to requalify more or less automatically after three years' established practice of UK law in the United Kingdom.

Lawyers from Africa, the Caribbean, Asia and Australasia are among the main groups of non-EU lawyers seeking to add their name to the Roll of Solicitors of England and Wales by way of the QLTT (Qualified Lawyers Transfer Test). It's a Law Society-accredited conversion test that permits lawyers qualified in selected countries outside the UK and UK barristers to retrain and qualify as solicitors. The test covers four heads:

Property • Litigation • Principles of Common Law • Professional Conduct and Accounts.

The Law Society determines which heads candidates must pass, dependent on their primary professional qualification. If the existing qualification is in a common law jurisdiction, it is usually the latter two heads. There is normally a two-year experience requirement in addition to the test, although this may be reduced if the lawyer has completed a training in a common law jurisdiction. A full list of jurisdictions that fall under the umbrella of the Qualified Lawyers Transfer Regulations (QLTR) and the appropriate subjects and experience requirements are on the Law Society's website.

Barristers wishing to become solicitors must have gained the following previous experience in England, Wales or Northern Ireland within the last five years. Experience gained overseas may count if it occurred in a common law jurisdiction:

- Up to 12 months' pupillage certified as satisfactory by the pupilmaster;
- Any period spent in practice at the Bar;
- A period spent in legal employment in the office of a solicitor or lawyer in private practice;
- Legal employment with the CPS or with the Magistrates' Court/Court Service; and
- Any period spent in legal employment in the Civil Service, local government, a public authority, commerce or industry provided that the employment is in a legal department headed by a solicitor, barrister or lawyer of at least five years' standing.

The Transfer Casework Committee may consider certain other experience.

The Law Society initiated a review of the QLTT in 2000, but at the time of going to press, no results or proposals were available.

There are two official test providers offering the examination service and preparatory training and tuition courses. The Law Society refers enquiries to both the College of Law and BPP Law School.

the voice of experience

Kelly Tinkler qualified as a solicitor in Queensland and took the QLTT after coming to London. With only two of the four heads to sit, he thought the exam was *"quite practical"* and *"not that arduous,"* but acknowledged that a common law background helps enormously. Lawyers from civil law jurisdictions who take all four exams find the exam a tougher challenge and it's by no means a dead cert for them. The real benefit of weekend revision courses is in the study of past papers and the tips from tutors on how to best answer the exam questions. *"If you do the past papers you see a pattern emerging in the questions."*

Some foreign lawyers don't bother to take the QLTT, but *"it's worth doing, particularly if you're a litigator."* If you want to undertake advocacy in court then you must take the test. And, as Kelly says, *"Being qualified as an English solicitor never hurts when you eventually go back home!"*

BARRISTERS

BARRISTERS TIMETABLE

LAW STUDENTS • Penultimate Undergraduate Year | **NON-LAW STUDENTS • Final Year**

When	Action
Throughout the year	Think – do you want to be a barrister or a solicitor? Research chambers & mini pupillages. Attend law fairs
By the end of January	Apply for the CPE *(non-law students)*
By the end of April	Apply for a pupillage under the year early scheme on Olpas *(law students)*
May	Apply for a CPE scholarship from an Inn of Court. If successful, join that Inn *(non-law students)*
June to September	Do pre-CPE mini-pupillages *(non-law students)*
September/October 2003	Start final year of degree *(law students)* / Start CPE *(non-law students)*
November	By November apply through BVC Online for the BVC. Apply to an Inn of Court for a BVC scholarship
During final year/CPE	Apply for pupillage to non-OLPAS sets. Do mini-pupillages
April	Before 30th April apply for pupillage through OLPAS
June	Apply for Inn membership
September 2004	Start the BVC. Apply through the September tranche of OLPAS; make further pupillage applications to non-OLPAS sets
April	If unsuccessful last year, apply for pupillage before 30th April
June	Finish BVC
September	Apply for pupillage through OLPAS if you have yet to be successful
October 2005	Start pupillage
June	Be offered tenancy at your pupillage chambers or apply for it elsewhere
October 2006	Start tenancy
2026	Be appointed as one of Her Majesty's Counsel
2036	Be appointed to the High Court Bench

thinking of the bar?

barcode

If you're bamboozled by the various terms used at the Bar, relax. We've prepared a handy glossary of terms for you.

barrister – a member of the Bar of England and Wales; an advocate
bench – the judiciary
bencher – a senior member of an Inn of Court. Usually silks and judges, known as **masters of the bench**
brief – a case; the documents setting out instructions to a barrister
bvc online – the BVC online application system run by the Bar Council and GTI. CACH was the old disk-based application system for the BVC (the old term is likely to linger for some time)
call – the ceremony whereby you become a barrister
chambers – a group of barristers in independent practice who have joined together to share common costs of practice such as clerks' fees and building rents; the word refers both to the physical building and to the group of barristers
clerk – administrator/manager in chambers who organises work for barristers and organises diaries, payment of fees, etc.
counsel – a barrister
devilling – (paid) work done by a junior member of chambers for a more senior member
inns of court – Four ancient institutions, which alone have the power to 'make' barristers
junior – a barrister not yet appointed silk. Note: older juniors are known as **senior juniors**
mini-pupillage – a short period of work experience spent in chambers
olpas – the Online Pupillage Application System run by the Bar Council
pupil – essentially a 'trainee'; a barrister in pupillage
pupillage – the year of training undertaken after Bar school and before tenancy. It is divided into two consecutive six-month periods, hence **first six** and **second six**. These are commonly taken at the same set of chambers but may, especially in Chancery practice, be taken separately. The main distinction is that a pupil can start earning for himself during second six. Occasionally, and particularly in criminal practice (such is the difficulty of attaining tenancy), a pupil may have to take a **third six**.
pupilmaster – a senior barrister with whom a pupil sits and who teaches the pupil and gives him work
QC – Queen's Counsel; a silk
set – as in a 'set of chambers'
silk – one of Her Majesty's Counsel, appointed on the recommendation of the Lord Chancellor; so named after the silk robes they wear.
tenant/tenancy – a tenant is a barrister who is a member of chambers. Tenancy is essentially 'the job', that is, permission from chambers to join their set and work with them. This means you have to pay your fair share of the rent, hence the word.
treasury counsel – barristers appointed to work for the Government. They are graded on various panels and there are different lists for different areas of practice.

For years the doom and gloom merchants predicted the imminent demise of the Bar and urged bright young things to eschew heady lunacy and to become solicitors. But solicitors have been relatively slow in asserting their new rights of audience, and the Bar seems to have survived the great changes of the Government's three-pronged reform of the justice system. Lord Woolf's transformation of civil justice and Sir Robin Auld's recommendations for criminal justice reform are waking the Bar up to the need to modernise.

Although the Bar may have shrunk slightly, numbers appear to be stabilising (as are the number of pupillages on offer). The number of chambers may fall, but this is because the trend is to larger sets. There's still a need for barristers, both those who specialise in advocacy and those who can advocate in specialist areas of law. The overall effect is that there is even greater pressure on pupils and junior practitioners to specialise early, so we've discussed seven different areas of practice in more detail on pages 86 to 95.

what's it really like?

As a barrister in independent practice you will be self-employed. You will be responsible for how hard you work, when you work, paying your own tax, sick pay, holiday pay and arranging your own pension. There are no company perks, no free lunches, no hiding behind colleagues or bosses or sitting at your laptop pretending to work while nursing a hangover. In theory, it means that you can work as hard as you like and as often as you like. In practice, you will be a slave to your clerks - your lifeline to new work and an income. It is they who assess which member of chambers is best suited to handle a particular instruction received from a solicitor, so if you appear unwilling to take work, clerks will stop offering it to you and your practice could wither! Remember, in the early years, you have to do your utmost to build up your reputation and ensure your survival. It can be a cut-throat world out there.

Each set of chambers has a different ethos and this may affect how you work. A modern forward-looking set might be happy for you to work from home or to turn up in jeans, so long as you aren't meeting clients. A more traditional set might want you to be in chambers regardless of what work you have to do, to keep the hours of more senior members and to wear a suit at all times.

If you are a criminal barrister you may rarely see the inside of chambers, spending your days whizzing round the country arguing cases in court. You will also be paid considerably less than your Chancery colleagues, who may spend all day, every day in chambers, travelling only as far as the other side of the quad to take lunch in Hall at their Inn.

You might take more holidays than your solicitor and banker friends, but you'll have to spend those extra days battling with your tax returns! Although you'll have an accountant, you'll be responsible for paying your own tax, so you have to be sure you don't spend all your income as you earn it. And don't forget to file away all those little receipts - you never know when something might be tax-deductible. Such are the joys of the 'independent' life of the Bar.

jobs for the boys?

Think of a barrister and what do you see? A white, public-schooled and Oxbridge-educated, pinstripe-suited male. This is the age-old stereotype and it puts many students off. But is it the reality of those already at the Bar or the current generation of students passing through Bar school?

Whilst many barristers fit the stereotype, it is true to say that there is increasing diversity at the Bar. Twenty years ago there were very few ethnic minority or female barristers or Bar students. Now the male-female ratio at Bar school is 50-50 and in pupillage over 18% of places go to candidates from ethnic minorities. At the senior end of the Bar itself, these ratios are still out of balance, owing to the historical slowness with which women and ethnic minorities came to the Bar and with which the Bar opened itself to them. Of the 17 benchers elected in 2002, only one was female and none were of ethnic minority status. Although the Bar is shifting in the right direction, it will still be a very long time before we see a truly diversified and gender-balanced judiciary.

what you need to succeed

Academic strength is essential. You must have real intelligence and the ability to analyse things in great detail. If you're not bright, don't come to the Bar. Sadly, too many of our contacts said, *"We see far too* many students who don't have a hope in hell of getting pupillage." Academic strength is almost always judged by way of your academic record. As a general rule, without good A-levels, without a 2.1 degree class or better or without having been to an established or respected university, you will struggle to get pupillage. This is not to say that those with weak A-levels or a 2.2 (sometimes exceptionally a 3rd, but this requires special dispensation from the Bar Council), or those who have been to one of the newer universities, don't ever get pupillage. But rarely will those that meet with success be disadvantaged at all three measures, and they will almost always possess redeeming and desirable qualities (such as having read a master's degree or previous relevant industry experience), which make them stand out.

When chambers sift through hundreds of applications for pupillage, some suggest they may well just throw out those with anything less than a 2.1 or those without an old, established university on their CV, simply to cut down on the numbers. Others comment that procedures are more rigorous, and that they will tend to give greater weight to candidates from non-standard backgrounds because they have had 'further to come' than conventional candidates. One recruiter told us, *"An old university and a 2.1 all helps, but it is the personality which comes out at interview that is decisive."*

You won't make a good barrister or get pupillage just by being bright. A range of other skills (which to a certain degree may be taught) are also essential, not least the ability to advocate, the ability to think on your feet and interpersonal skills that allow you to relate to clients, solicitors, judges and juries. But above all, there's one characteristic that was mentioned over and over again by students, course directors, careers advisors and barristers – determination. Having stamina, tenacity and perseverance is crucial. You might be brilliant, but a career at the Bar won't fall in your lap. It is determination and a thick skin that will enable you to cope with setbacks and with the enormous financial strain under which you are likely to be placed. Some say that it goes beyond self-belief and confidence, and that it is arrogance which is needed. *"You must believe absolutely in yourself and then you will succeed."*

Many lament that such is the competition for pupillage and tenancy, and such are the financial and other difficulties to be surmounted, the best candidates are put off. Nevertheless, students from a whole host of backgrounds read for the Bar and become successful barristers. The idea that you must come from the 'right background' (whatever that may mean) seems to be dying, but some quirky statistics are hard to explain – one BVC course director confessed that *"Every single son and daughter of a judge or silk on our course has got pupillage."*

the bar vocational course

The BVC is a year's vocational training, which must be completed before you can be called to the Bar and start pupillage. There are currently eight institutions validated by the Bar Council to provide the course. All have to follow basic course components, and although the Bar Council tries to ensure that all the providers work to the same standard with comparable facilities, there are still variations between each course and each institution. It is worth taking time out to investigate each provider, to find out what barristers think of each one and to consider where would suit you best. With fees in the region of £7,000-£10,000, this decision should not be undertaken lightly.

course content

The BVC is not an academic course. It's based around practical exercises, usually in the form of a brief, which students prepare and then talk through in tutorials. Some courses follow the same half dozen cases throughout the year, from the initial claim or arrest to trial and then judgment and appeal. This focus on skills can be unsettling even for the brightest students. As one course director commented, *"The typical Oxbridge lot find it hard to do the practical stuff."* The general feeling is that most students find it *"conceptually easy, but hard work – there's a lot to do."* Others find it a walkover, complaining, *"The BVC is a complete waste of time."*

Obviously, advocacy is a key component of the course. Others include drafting and conferencing, as well as the *"very dull"* learning of procedure and evidence for the criminal and civil litigation exams. These are assessed through multiple-choice tests, which are not as easy as they sound. In fact, they can be *"rather harsh."*

The compulsory components are:
- Civil Litigation and Remedies
- Criminal Litigation and Sentencing
- Evidence
- Advocacy
- Conference Skills
- Negotiation
- Opinion Writing
- Drafting
- Case Preparation
- Legal Research
- Professional Ethics

In addition, students choose two optional subjects from a list of six, but the subjects on offer vary between the institutions. Options may include an element of pro bono work.

your fellow students

Like most areas of life, you'll find a complete cross section of students on the BVC, but, if anything, people seem larger than life and more colourful. On the one hand there are the crusty old lunatics who stagger around quoting Latin maxims, smoking pipes and wearing stiff collars. They'll probably get fitted out for wigs and gowns on the first day of school. On the other hand there are the Doc Marten- and dungaree-clad, dripping wet liberals, obsessed with human rights and equal opportunities. They join every committee going and are determined to never ever wear a wig and gown. Of course, most students are nothing like these caricatures, but you will meet all sorts, from the earnest bods who never leave the library to the brilliant high-flyers who never seem to work, from the child prodigies to the midlife crisis career-changers and the degenerate, profligate and idle.

what students think

Just as students vary, so do their comments on the BVC. We heard everything from *"I've had a fabulous time"* to *"It was the most dismal scholastic experience of my life."* One said, *"The course provided me with a solid foundation for pupillage,"* while another thought, *"We train in an uncompetitive nursery school environment. It's not the best introduction to a very competitive profession."* Agreeing with this sentiment, a further student added, *"You are not encouraged to think or be independent as you were at university or will be during pupillage."* One student even described the BVC as *"an exercise in learning how to drink red wine,"* although surely at £8,000 that's a fairly expensive learning experience.

Several students commented that they felt *"held back"* by the course and, worryingly, by fellow students. *"I certainly wouldn't recommend the mixed ability groups,"* one confided. Most felt that they were prepared for pupillage, but it was also recognised that *"pupillage is where the real training happens."* In general, there is a feeling that the course could be *"more focused and challenging,"* and many students are irritated that exercises seemed to only ever consist of personal injury or basic contractual matters.

how to choose a school

Students are influenced by a number of factors. Some opt for smaller institutions where they will receive more individual attention and benefit from the way *"the ethos of the Bar is generated."* Others base their decision on geography alone. Cost is the guiding light for many. At all schools, students are now given copies of the main practitioners' handbooks for civil and criminal procedure as well as the ICSL manuals (although these aren't always followed). They also get access to online information sources such as Butterworths and Law Online. The provincial providers have good relationships with their local Bars, whose members lead advocacy and practitioner classes.

When choosing a school, it is often worth considering whether it is attached to another institution. One affiliated to a university will benefit from large library collections, whereas private establishments may take time to build up such a collection. However, take comfort from the fact that the Bar Council checks all providers regularly, and all match up to its required standard. We interviewed course directors and students at each of the eight schools, and some of their comments follow.

bpp law school, london
number of places: 216 full-time, 48 part-time

"Innovative" BPP has an excellent reputation amongst both students and the profession. Known for its *"focused, professional and efficient approach,"* the school is also widely praised for its *"good teaching"* and *"new facilities."* It now offers a part-time course, which will increase accessibility. The vast majority of teaching is in tutorials, with less than 10% by way of lectures. Advocacy, conferencing and negotiation take place in intensive groups of six and the school now has seven mock courtrooms. As well as providing results of assessments throughout the course, the multiple-choice tests are taken in two stages, one at Christmas and the other at Easter. Optional subjects include international trade and intellectual property. Nearly half of the students are from overseas and BPP boasts one of the highest proportions of ethnic minority students. Its size presents a welcome alternative to the largest school, ICSL.

bristol institute of legal practice at uwe
number of places: 96 full-time

Previously UWE offered a combined course with Cardiff University, but 2002/3 sees Bristol and Cardiff going their separate ways for the first time. Commonly seen as *"the first choice after London,"* students here, as at most other provincial providers, do not restrict themselves to pupillage locally. Bristol provides each tutorial group with its own dedicated room, containing practitioners' books, a TV and computing facilities. This base room and the group are intended to *"operate like a set of chambers,"* engendering a peer group learning culture. We heard a few moans about the organisation of the course, including late exam results and late appearances by some staff (*"very unprofessional."*) Others speak in glowing terms, particularly concerning advocacy - *"The teachers are brilliant for this."*

The course includes two full placement weeks in a variety of situations, including the CPS, judge marshalling, the Courts Martial, and the ECJ. Amongst the optional subjects, students can take a course in Mercantile Court, which is of particular relevance to Bristol chambers. Like some other schools, there is a Bar dinner every year and six tutorial lunches. An important point to note is that most students and staff have to drive to UWE, which is reached up a narrow, single-track road; the only alternative is an infrequent and irregular bus service, which means that *"students and staff are often late."*

cardiff law school
number of places: 60 full-time

Now on its own after severing links with Bristol, Cardiff is making sure its BVC is distinctive. Thus, whereas Bristol teaches evidence as a separate part of the course, Cardiff combines it with the litigation elements. It also benefits from an especially close relationship with its local Bar, scheduling two weeks of the course during which every student spends five days with a barrister and five with a judge. One student told us this aspect of the course was of real appeal. The school also provides one of the highest levels of advocacy training, with three hours a week. However, these are for classes of 12 students, whereas most providers teach advocacy in classes of six. It also offers an ADR option for the final part of the course.

Although many students look for pupillage across the country, all but one of the local pupillages available last year went to Cardiff students. So if you've got a burning desire to wear your horsehair amongst the sheep wool, Cardiff looks to be your best bet.

the college of law, london
number of places: 120 full-time

Offering the smallest BVC course in London, the COL benefits from plenty of *"familiar faces"* and has a *"good feel."* The course has just relocated to the large Store Street campus (famed as the LPC factory), where it enjoys its own discrete, purpose-built set of rooms. Some fear it may lose the *"close family atmosphere"* of Chancery Lane, but others point out that BVC students will benefit from being in close proximity to LPC students who are, after all, their future clients. It is also something of the *"party provider,"* as it hosts a wide-ranging series of social events, which are well attended by staff and students. Karaoke evenings and quiz nights pop up alongside games of cricket and trips to rugby matches.

Opinions differ with regards to the standard of teaching. Some claim it is *"fantastic;"* others refer to it as *"varied."* The course progresses logically through the litigation process; however, some students think that this way of doing things causes the timetable to be rather uneven and feel the course is *"over-organised."* Some students indicated that the way in which assessments are spread throughout the course does not suit everyone, in that *"the work is constant and unending."* On the plus side, there's a healthy portion of pro bono work, especially amongst the options, and the civil and criminal trials (which come in the second half of the course) are judged by real judges and senior barristers who are happy to give feedback to students in practice skills sessions.

the inns of court school of law
number of places: 575 full-time, 75 part-time

Originally, there was only one institution at which you could do the BVC and that was ICSL. Because of this, some of the newer providers have found it hard to compete with the *"old monopoly provider."* Certainly, ICSL takes the largest number of students and many still see it as the 'IBM choice'. Typically we heard, *"I chose ICSL because it was the oldest."* But does older mean better? The school itself admits that a number of difficulties occurred when the competition arrived, and one candid outside (non-student) observer said, *"ICSL went down the pan a few years ago, but it's now pulling its socks up."* It is beginning to benefit from its recent affiliation with CPE supremo, City University, and it has recently undertaken a programme of building work.

Sheer numbers make the individual attention of smaller providers hard to achieve, and the negative attitude of many students perpetuates the problems. In terms of teaching staff, the school does offer a significant number from the early days of the BVC and they have considerable experience from which students should be able to benefit, if so inclined. The school also offers options not available at most other providers, such as immigration and competition law. Perhaps the complaint that sums up the students' feelings is that the course is run to get students to pass, not to fulfil their potential. We've refrained from setting out their comments, but it seems that the school attracts more of the type who see the BVC as a necessary evil and, accordingly, a culture of criticism has grown within the student body.

manchester metropolitan university
number of places: 100 full-time

MMU has a *"particularly good reputation"* among the city's law students, and many think they are on *"the best BVC in the country."* One or two reported in less glowing terms, indicating that the teaching can be *"something of a lottery."* The school benefits hugely from its 'Syndicate Room' group system, whereby each tutorial group has its own 'mini-chambers' with a small library and computing and video facilities. This is used as both common room and teaching room and is a *"fantastically good arrangement."* Students commented that it was good for both sharing ideas and making friends. The local Bar makes a valuable contribution, with practitioner classes and advocacy teaching. Senior barristers from Manchester and Liverpool also offer advice on professional conduct and careers, as well as attending a special Northern Bar dinner with the students. About half of all students intend to practise in the North with the rest going to London. Optional subjects include judicial review and family law.

university of northumbria, newcastle
number of places: 80 full-time + 20 LLB students

Northumbria offers a unique option, by which LLB students can undertake the BVC (or LPC) as a part of their degree course. It takes place on a part-time basis, and students are then exempt from further professional training once they finish their degree. Northumbria enjoys a *"flourishing"* practitioner programme, again owing to the wide support from the local Bar. Also, initiatives with the local police and other bodies mean that students can gain valuable experience cross-examining real police officers and expert witnesses. The university moved an entire courtroom from Morpeth so students can practise in the real thing. Options in the last term include landlord and tenant law, and work in the student law office, involving real cases that students take from scratch. Students aim to practise across the country and not just in the North East.

nottingham law school
number of places: 120 full-time

Nottingham has *"very high standards,"* and certainly it is seen to have a superior reputation for its LPC course. It's BVC comes highly recommended for its advocacy, especially as this takes place in the old Guildhall courtrooms. Students comment that it is *"well known for having good results and being sociable – no pompous types here."*

The course begins with seven briefs and these are handled throughout the year until trial in the summer. Just like real briefs, they even arrive tied in red ribbon! Teaching is in dedicated base rooms for each small group. Again, the local Bar is proactive in its involvement with the school and the commercial law option is delivered entirely by practitioners.

how much?

None of the providers make a profit from the course, and several subsidise the BVC with income from other courses, including the LPC. Designing the practical exercises on which the course is based, together with the high level of tutor input, all cause the costs to rocket. The provincial providers are noticeably cheaper than the London schools. In addition to the current fees listed in the table below, a £250 registration fee is payable to the Bar Council, as is a fee for using the BVC Online application system (currently in the region of £40).

BPP Law School www.bpp.com	£9,500
Bristol Institute of Legal Practice at UWE www.uwebristol.com/law/bvc	£7,150
Cardiff Law School www.cf.ac.uk/claws/cpls	£6,200
The College of Law www.lawcol.org.uk	£8,800
The Inns of Court School of Law www.icsl.ac.uk/bvc	£9,000
Manchester Metropolitan University www.prospectus.mmu.ac.uk	c. £7,000
The University of Northumbria at Newcastle www.unn.ac.uk	£6,920
Nottingham Law School www.nls.ntu.ac.uk	£7,935

Figures correct at the time of going to press

so what's the cach?

So you've picked a Bar school. How do you get a place? Up until 2002 the Bar Council ran a horrid application system known as CACH, whereby applications were made on computer disk. A new system called **BVC Online**, is due to kick off in autumn 2002. Like the Olpas system for pupillage applications, you need to have access to the internet.

In past years you were entitled to apply to three providers, ranked in order from first to third. It is likely that in future you may still apply to three providers, but the distinction between first, second and third will disappear. Out of all the schools, only Nottingham told us that it preferred to be put as first choice. The content of the application form is also unlikely to change radically, and will still require details of your academic background, work experience, mini-pupillages and other experiences that indicate your commitment to the Bar. If you have less than a 2:2, you will have to obtain special dispensation from the Bar Council.

Currently, all providers operate a transparent point scoring system. Prime considerations include your predicted or actual degree class, your academic reference and self-evaluation comments. Where possible, you should show an aptitude for advocacy beyond mooting and debating, legal experience and evidence of intellectual ability. Less weighty considerations include your A-level results, your ability to relate to all sections of society, reasons for your career choice and personal organisation skills.

Despite all of this, many students complained to us about the standard and ability of their fellow students. Even though most schools receive more applications than there are places and not everyone is accepted, *"There are a lot of people on the course who shouldn't be there."* This suggests that the scoring system is not sufficiently rigorous. The system is also greatly hindered by the fact that schools cannot interview applicants. It is not unusual to find *"students who are terrified of advocacy. Why are they training for a career as an advocate?"* Why, indeed.

money, money, money...

Why do you want to become a barrister? Do you have a love of the law and a passion for advocacy? Perhaps it's you desire to help the disadvantaged and oppressed? Or is it because you want to earn pots of money? While you rarely meet an experienced barrister who's poor, earnings do vary wildly. There is no guarantee that you will earn a fortune, or indeed anything like that, and even if you do find the cash rolls in, when will you have the time to spend it?

But the one thing that is certain is the sheer cost of getting there. We've already mentioned the cost of the BVC (page 77) and the CPE (page 13) but on top of these you will have to provide living expenses – often in London and therefore especially expensive. Likewise, although your pupillage will be funded in accordance with the Bar Council's new rules, £10,000 does not go far in your first year once you take off the cost of travelling to Magistrates' and County Courts halfway across England. And even if you make it to tenancy, those initial receipts will be sorely reduced by the hefty repayments on that fat loan you took out to pay for Bar School. You could end up with a worse lifestyle after starting work than when you were a student.

awards and scholarships

Bar school fees, books, Inn membership, dining fees, call fees, BVC Online fee, a wig and gown, suits, collars, shirts, shoes...it all adds up. Then there's rent and basic living expenses. It could easily swallow £20,000 that you simply don't have. There are several sources of financial assistance, and we've set out the main ones in the **Funding** section on pages 14 to 15. In addition to the range of loans from the High Street banks (which if used wisely need not be the most painful option), the Inns have several million pounds' worth of scholarships for the best students, details of which are set out in the following table. The procedure varies from Inn to Inn, but usually it's a simple application form and an interview. Gray's Inn requires at least a 2:1 degree; the others consider applications from those with at least a 2:2. There's no hard and fast policy on means testing, but you will have to answer questions about your finances and make a declaration of income. Scholarships would seem to be provided on merit first with means as a secondary consideration. Make your application look as impressive as possible. Being short-listed for interview is half the battle and if you are called to interview your chances of receiving an award are good. The selection panel looks for academic ability, the likelihood you'll make a good advocate and, importantly, a commitment to the Bar. The last thing they want is to give several thousand pounds to someone who will then drop out of the BVC and join the circus.

It is very unlikely that you will be tested on substantive legal matters, although you should definitely be ready to discuss topical legal issues or to talk through an area of law that interests you. In addition to this, expect to be quizzed on which area of law you want to go into and what skills you can bring to the Bar.

funding from chambers

Some students will be lucky enough to have gained a pupillage funded in excess of the Bar Council's recommended minimum of £10,000, and an increasing number of these high-paying sets allow their pupils to receive a drawdown of this award during the BVC.

SCHOLARSHIPS FROM THE INNS

NAME OF INN	FUNDS AVAIL.	CPE/BVC AWARDS	PUPILLAGE AWARDS	CONTACT DETAILS
Lincoln's Inn	£853,000	**CPE**: Up to 32 scholarships of up to £8,000 **BVC**: Up to 55 scholarships of between £5,000 and £15,000 each Up to 30 bursaries of up to £6,000 each 2 x £8,000 studentships 15 rooms in self contained flats **BVC/CPE**: Up to 100 awards for admission, call and dining	Up to 40 scholarships between £250 and £3,000 £3,000 for a place at European Court £3,000 for a place at European Court of Human Rights £10,000 bursary fund for overseas placements £2,000 for sundry prizes	Judith Fox Tel: 020 7405 0138 judith.fox@lincolnsinn.org.uk
Middle Temple	£700,000 + £66,000 subsidised accommodation	**CPE**: 20-30 of between £1000 and £8,000 **BVC**: 80 –100 of between £1,000 - £15,000 Subsidised accommodation for 23 students	Approx 25 awards of between £500 and £5,000	Students Department Tel: 020 7427 4800 student_enquiries@middletemple.org.uk
Gray's Inn	c. £650k+	**CPE**: £50,000 split into separate awards **BVC**: 9 x £15,000 max 12 x £12,500 max 42 x £7,000 max Up to 25 x admission fees (£85)	c. £60,000 split between various awards	Rachael Isaac, PA to Deputy Under Treasurer (Students) Tel: 020 7458 7900 rachael.Isaac@graysinn.org.uk
Inner Temple	£765,000	**CPE**: 1 x £12,500 5 x £10,000 **BVC**: 1 x £17,500 1 x £20,000 1 x £15,000 4 x £12,500 20 x £10,000 **BVC/CPE**: Up to 52 exhibitions of £6,000 – £10,000 50 x £160 for admission / call fees Various smaller scholarships and prizes £15,000 in disability grants Up to 15 Pegasus Scholarships to live and work abroad for 3-6 months	£14,000 available for internships	Clare Drewett Tel: 020 7797 8210 cdrewett@innertemple.org.uk

the inns of court

There are four ancient Inns of Court located around Holborn and Fleet Street in London – Lincoln's Inn, Inner Temple, Middle Temple and Gray's Inn – originally formed as societies to provide legal training for barristers. In addition, like the Oxbridge colleges to which they bear more than a passing similarity, their function included providing board and lodging for both barristers and students. These institutions alone have the power to 'make' a barrister in a ceremony known as Call. Successful BVC student barristers are called by the Treasurer to the 'Degree of the Utter Bar' with a few magic words and the wave of a wand...

the inns today

Their teaching function has largely been delegated to the eight BVC providers, but the Inns still provide some advocacy training in addition to fulfilling their ancient role as providers of hospitality for student barristers.

You must join an Inn by 30th June of the year in which your BVC commences. As well as passing the BVC, before you can be called it is necessary to 'keep term' at your Inn. This means you have to attend 12 qualifying sessions, but not so long ago students had to undertake 36. Largely, this means 'dining', but education days, introductory weekends and advocacy training all count as qualifying sessions.

dining – more than just dinner

Dining receives mixed reviews from students. *"Some think it is archaic, but others love it."* The best advice is to make the most of it. If you approach it negatively, it will be all the more arduous: *"There are always some who complain about it and don't get involved."* Others find it expensive, although at an average of £10 a dinner, this will hardly break the bank after the expenses of the BVC or buying a wig and gown, and remember, there are a large number of scholarships solely to cover the cost of dining. Dining is more than eating – the evening may include a concert, a debate or moot, or sometimes even a disco. At least once a term there is mixed dining (often at a 'Domus Dinner') when Bar, Bench and students sit together, and also a Guest Night, which tends to be popular. Simply sitting with your mates is *"of limited usefulness."* The point of dining is to reinforce the collegiate nature of the Inn and maintain social contact within the profession. Smart students use it as an opportunity to network.

Students usually have to wear gowns for dinner and will arrive in Hall first. Masters of the Bench arrive last and sit at High Table on the dais at one end of Hall. Before the food is served, grace will be said, sometimes in Latin. Students often sit in 'messes' of four, with the 'mess captain' having to serve the other three members. After dinner each member of the mess will toast the others.

mentoring

Each Inn runs a sponsorship scheme whereby students can be matched with a barrister who acts as a mentor, providing assistance and advice on pupillage applications, etc. Seen as useful contacts by some students, others do not find the system particularly helpful, especially if they've already secured pupillage. If you attend one of the provincial providers, make sure the Inn doesn't give you a London sponsor unless you request it. *"My sponsor was in London and I was in Manchester – not very clever."*

whose inn and who's not?

Broadly, the Inns are much of a muchness, but there are subtle differences, and it is a good idea to spend some time considering which would suit you best. After all (providing you are not disbarred), you'll be a member for life. Go and look around the Inns, meet the Education Department and talk to people. One student said, *"There's a chemistry between you and the place."* Students join for many different reasons – architecture, friends/family connections, the reputation of the chef, etc. All the Inns are friendly and assist their students, and although they try not to compete, we have managed to discern one or two differences…

lincoln's inn
Lincoln's Inn is the oldest and undoubtedly the most famous. Its Old Hall (once the out of term seat of the High Court of Chancery), is the opening setting of Dickens' *Bleak House*. It's fitting that *"those interested in full-blooded Chancery still tend to come here for historical reasons."* Its fame and popularity means Lincoln's Inn has the most students. Some believe it is thereby *"suffering,"* complaining that *"booking dining is a nightmare and you can't get called when you want."* Those with an eye to the future also note that *"being at the largest Inn means you have the slenderest chance of becoming a Bencher."* A victim of its own success? Maybe, but global fame means that Lincoln's has plenty of international students, ensuring a lively and *"enriching"* community. Students find it *"informal and friendly"* and it has *"a lot going on."* Others appreciate its *"amazing surroundings and atmosphere."* It maintains a visible profile in the provinces and keeps in touch with students, providing money for functions.

inner temple
Third in size for number of members, Inner Temple is known to students as the *"party Inn"* and is home to the famous Pegasus Bar to which they often retire after dinner to dance the night away. As a smaller Inn it is known to take a *"keen interest in student welfare,"* and it is easier to be more attentive to individuals. This *"really sociable Inn"* is *"definitely the warmest"* of the four. The *"wild"* Cumberland Lodge weekends are *"more fun than with the other Inns – Inner Temple really lets its hair down,"* with Benchers and barristers joining in the fun. It built a bright, light Hall after its mediaeval buildings were destroyed during WWII.

middle temple
The Inn has almost as many student members as Lincoln's Inn but doesn't attract the same criticisms. Its *"splendid"* sixteenth-century Hall is famous as the location for the first performance of Shakespeare's *Twelfth Night*. This thespian tradition continues today with the annual Middle Temple Revels in December – a student and barrister comic musical production. Similarly, the Inn may have anything from *"jazz to opera to steel bands"* after dinner. Like Inner Temple, it is known to be *"very lively,"* and after dinner *"everyone goes to the bar."*

gray's inn
The smallest Inn and *"more personal."* Despite plenty of music and drama, the emphasis is still *"very much on dining."* Only natural then that it should be known for *"good food and lots of port."* Perceptive students say the Inn *"must surely be in breach of some human rights' point"* by not allowing anyone to leave Hall during dinner – not even for the loo. Some think it is *"very traditional."* While dining, it is not unheard of for a student to *"get told to stand up and debate"* or perform a forfeit for a breach of etiquette. Some think this is *"a nightmare – so intimidating;"* others comment that it is *"fantastic – what a great way to improve your advocacy."* Applications for scholarships can be made online, but some complain that the Inn is *"not very organised."* *"Dining is fantastic on the night, but anarchic in organisation."* It seems to have a lower profile in the provinces. ICSL is within its precincts, so proximity to its libraries might influence some students to join.

a note on call and qualification
Being called to the Bar entitles you to call yourself a barrister but not to pass yourself off as one for business purposes without a practising certificate. This comes from the Bar Council once pupillage is completed. You can start pupillage before call, but must be called before you start your second six. However, you can be called without having a pupillage or indeed ever doing one!

THE HONOURABLE SOCIETIES

	LINCOLN'S INN	INNER TEMPLE	MIDDLE TEMPLE	GRAY'S INN
Contacts	Tel: 020 7405 1393 www.lincolnsinn.org.uk	Tel: 020 7797 8250 www.innertemple.org.uk	Tel: 020 7427 4800 www.middletemple.org.uk	Tel: 020 7458 7800 www.graysinn.org.uk
Architecture	Everything from the mediaeval Old Hall to the neo-Classical Stone Buildings to the Victorian gothic Great Hall	12th-century Temple Church stands opposite the modern Hall built after the original was destroyed in WWII; otherwise the Inn largely resembles a car park	Splendid Elizabethan Hall tucked down an intricate maze of alleys and narrow streets	Suffered serious war damage and is largely a 1950s red-brick creation, albeit with its ancient Hall and Chapel intact
Gardens	Small and shaded; always open	Stretching down to the Thames. Croquet may be played	Small but handy for the bar	Famous walks provide recreation for nearby ICSL students, but only open at lunchtimes
Style	Friendly, international and large	Sociable and hard-working	Musical and arty	Intimate, traditional and formal
Gastronomy	A new chef means good food; lunch served every day	Wine left over after dining; lunch served every day but suits must be worn	The construction of new kitchens augurs well; lunch served every day	The emphasis is on the port not the food; lunch served every day
Accommodation	For scholars, in the Inn	Not for students	For scholars, in the Inn and in Clapham	Not for students
Bar	Briefs – fairly dismal and quiet. Open for lunches and snacks during the day	The famous Pegasus Bar is soon to be refurbished	Brand new bar conveniently located beneath the library and adjacent to the gardens	Currently being renovated
Old Members	Mohammed Jinnah Lord Hailsham LC Lord Denning MR	Judge Jeffreys of the 'Bloody Assizes' M K Gandhi	Sir Walter Raleigh William Blackstone Charles Dickens	Sir Francis Bacon Lord Birkenhead LC
Current Members	Cherie Booth QC Tony Blair MP Lady Thatcher	Lord Irvine of Laing LC Dame Elizabeth Butler-Sloss P Jack Straw MP	Lord Phillips of Worth Maltravers MR Edward Garnier QC MP	Lord Lane Lord Bingham David Pannick QC
Points of Interest	Together with the Royal Navy, Lincoln's Inn takes the Loyal Toast seated	Temple Church	Shakespeare's *Twelfth Night* first performed here in 1602	Shakespeare's *Comedy of Errors* first performed here. Wooden screen in Hall made with timbers from the Armada
Scholarship Interview Process	Applicants are selected for 20-minute interview but there is only one round	CPE scholars normally expect automatic funding for BVC, but can apply for higher award. Scholarships awarded on merit and bursaries on merit and financial need	Every applicant will be interviewed	Must have an upper second class degree to be eligible for BVC scholarship

mini-pupillages

A mini-pupillage is a period of work experience - usually a week, sometimes less, rarely more - spent in a set of chambers. Some sets take an informal approach whereas others only offer assessed mini-pupillages. During an assessed mini-pupillage your performance is monitored and sometimes you are asked to hand in a piece of written work. Some sets require you to have undertaken a mini-pupillage at that set before they will even consider your pupillage application. Mini-pupillages are often more fiercely sought after than pupillage itself (and can be harder to obtain), so it is advisable to find out which sets have this requirement at least a year in advance. Very occasionally a set has been known to offer some form of remuneration during mini-pupillage, but the most you can realistically hope for is a free lunch courtesy of your mini-pupilmaster.

Not only is there no central source of information on mini-pupillages as there is for pupillages, but each set has its own application procedure. Usually a CV accompanied by a handwritten letter won't go far wrong, but some sets do have their own printed application forms.

what's the point?

Basically, they're **essential**. They serve two purposes – for you to get to know chambers and for chambers to get to know you. "*It is a huge advantage if a set knows you; you will get a pupillage over a person they have never seen; they will know you are committed.*" Myths perpetuate about how many you should undertake. Students have been known to do any number from two or three to a dozen. Whilst every pupillage application will be assisted by a modest number of mini-pupillages, chambers are quite likely to be put off if they see a huge number as it indicates a lack of direction. But some students suggest we recommend that "*the more you do, the better your chances of pupillage.*"

An application with no mini-pupillages may suggest that the student hasn't properly considered his chosen profession. One astonished student commented, "*Some people start Bar school without ever having done a mini-pupillage. It's like trying to be a chef without ever going into a kitchen!*" In short, you should do as many mini-pupillages as you feel you need to, and as soon as they stop being useful, stop doing them.

Initially mini-pupillages allow you to discover what life and work at the Bar is like and to find out about particular areas of law and how they differ in practice. "*It is a realistic insight into what you are getting yourself into, and into how long you spend waiting outside court.*" Later on, they allow you to find out about different sets of chambers in your chosen area of practice. Often two sets practising in the same area will have utterly different styles and atmospheres, one or other of which will not necessarily suit you.

a week hanging around croydon county court

Most students speak favourably about mini-pupillages, although they are also realistic, "*They are expensive – you're not earning and you have to bear the cost of travel and so on yourself.*" Experiences vary: "*Some are a waste of time! Some mini-pupilmasters just throw ten files at you and you spend all week reading them;*" others valued "*seeing those out-of-court moments (like conferences and negotiations) which the public wouldn't see.*"

getting pupillage

In 2001 the old PACH system for applying for pupillage was replaced by OLPAS. This new online system has generated far fewer complaints than PACH, but it has its faults. It's *"not a good system if you hate computers,"* but then you shouldn't be coming to the Bar if you're a technophobe. The Bar Council is of the opinion that online schemes increase the accessibility of the Bar, and unlike BVC Online, there's no fee to pay.

how olpas works

Every set of chambers and every employer offering pupillage is required by the Bar Council to advertise each pupillage on **www.olpas.co.uk**. Students can then peruse the website for details of pupillages, chambers, levels of funding and so on. Details are also reproduced in a *Pupillage and Awards Handbook*, published in March. OLPAS usually opens on the same day as the National Pupillage Fair at Lincoln's Inn.

Even if chambers are not participating in OLPAS, all pupillages are posted on the website. Check whether you apply to a set through OLPAS or through its own specified method.

OLPAS operates in two rounds. The first closing date is 30 April and the second is 30 September. Students may apply for pupillage in both rounds, but chambers can only offer pupillages in one round. You can apply for up to 12 pupillages in either round, making a total of 24 OLPAS applications per year. But don't forget the non-OLPAS sets: you can make as many applications as you like to these and their closing dates range throughout the year. Remember to make applications through OLPAS in the year before pupillage is to start. Thus, for pupillages starting in 2004, you must apply in April or September 2003.

The form requires details of your academic background, relevant work experience, motivation for being a barrister and referees. You complete the form just the once and it is sent automatically to all 12 sets. A section of the form enables you to address specific comments to each set of chambers directly.

For first-round applications, there are three months of interviews with chambers making offers from 31 July. In the second round there is only one month for interviews with offers allowed from 31 October. During this time, chambers and candidates communicate with each other by e-mail.

One disadvantage of the two-round system is that, if you are particularly keen to go to a set offering its pupillage in the second round, but you apply nevertheless during the first round to other sets and are then offered a pupillage, you have to take a gamble. Do you choose the pupillage you've been offered or do you reject the offer in order to give yourself a chance of going to the set you really want?

year early

OLPAS has enabled chambers to recruit pupils a year early in the hope that this will give more students the security of knowing that they had pupillage before committing to BVC fees. However, it seems that it is mostly high-flying commercial sets that have preferred this approach, owing to the fact that they are in direct competition with solicitors' firms for the very best candidates. Less remunerative crime and family sets tend to prefer students with greater experience and knowledge of the profession. Most sets want to know as much as possible about candidates to whom they make offers so it seems foolish to many to make early offers before even degree class is known for sure.

olpas agony

Although OLPAS is an improvement on PACH, over half of the students we interviewed experienced problems (*"it crashed nine times"*) or had negative comments. Most criticisim related to its online form – still a relatively novel method of making applications.

You, of course, will have the advantage over your predecessors by having experience of BVC Online.

Comments ranged from mediocre misery (*"filling it out was quite a pain"*) to exquisite agony (*"a lot of information can only be supplied from their drop-down menus – they think they've thought of everything, but they didn't have my degree or its classification and I couldn't address my referees correctly"*). Others felt *"under pressure to apply to 12 sets just to fill up the spaces."* The system was felt to have little scope for getting personality or style across. Some students feel that 'box checking' works against those who may have to explain poor results or a non-standard journey to the Bar. Some students whispered it was possible to make multiple applications, thereby greatly increasing your chance of pupillage. We put this to OLPAS and learned that although there have been no confirmed cases, the Bar Council intends to come down heavily on those who break the rules, bringing the miscreant's career at the Bar to a swift conclusion. Continuing on the theme of naughty behaviour, it is not uncommon for sets of chambers to give their preferred candidates an indication of their success before the July and October deadlines. Whilst this is in breach of the rules, what eager student would go running to complain to the Bar Council? If all this sounds bad, just imagine what the old PACH system must have been like…

non-olpas sets

Keep an eye open for sets not taking part in OLPAS. This information may be gleaned from the handbook and the website. Closing dates range throughout the year. Current students recommend you *"get forms in early – people who get them in at the deadline never seem to get interviews."* Some suggested that you should print your details onto application forms whenever possible – *"it shows you give a s**t"* – even if it is fiddly.

interviews

How do you survive this final step towards pupillage? First, don't worry: as one seasoned applicant said, *"If you are going to survive at the Bar, you are going to survive the interview."* If a chambers rejects you, it may be because you wouldn't have fitted into that set. It's important to get pupillage and tenancy in a set that is right for you – you may well spend the rest of your working life there.

Interviews range *"from whole day assessments to 20-minute 'get to know you' chats."* The best (and most obvious) advice is to be as well prepared as possible. Read the legal press and *The Times* on a Tuesday and develop opinions on current or controversial topics in the area of law that you are looking to move into.

Many chambers will set you exercises. These could be a simple legal problem, a topical issue to discuss or a general proposition to argue. An example of the latter, given by top human rights set Doughty Street Chambers, is: "Do you agree with the proposition women and children first?" You might receive the exercise shortly before your interview begins or a few days in advance. Make sure you prepare as well as you possibly can. If you are giving an oral answer then expect the panel to come back at you. Don't panic if it presents an argument or a case you have not heard before or did not anticipate. An important part of the interview is testing your ability to think on your feet. Stay calm and stick to your guns. The panel is neither looking for, nor does it expect, ready-packaged barristers. Many chambers will hold two rounds of interviews, whittling applicants down to a handful of hopefuls before making the final cut. Going through the selection process is a stressful and exhausting marathon. You need to be thick-skinned and must simply deal with the inevitable disappointments. Don't be disheartened if your first few interviews don't go quite according to plan. You will get much better with practice.

Chambers are looking for people who will fit in. They do not want robotic legal brains. Nor do they want cocky and arrogant students with no experience of life. Show your human side, conversational skills and (obviously in limited doses) sense of humour if you can.

pupillage and after...

So the great goose of the Bar has laid a golden egg, and it has fallen straight into your open lap... well done! But what is pupillage really like? It's the final period of training for the Bar, during which the pupil gains practical training under the supervision of his pupilmaster (or pupilmistress). It is divided into two parts. First, there is a non-practising six months during which pupils shadow their pupilmaster. This is followed by a practising six months during which pupils can undertake work in their own right and appear in court on their own. In addition, a number of compulsory professional training courses must be undertaken. Both sixes maybe taken in the same set or at two different sets.

Pupillage is demanding and competitive and has been known to reduce strong men to dribbling wrecks. The learning curve is steep and you will be assessed throughout. Filled with heart-in-the-mouth moments from start to finish pupillage will see you acquiring invaluable experience and you'll need to draw upon resources you never knew you had. Then at the end of the year it's crunch time. You may find yourself competing for tenancy with two or three other pupils at the same set. And if you luck out at your own set, you'll have to apply along with all the other unfortunates seeking tenancy elsewhere. Hard work... and fairly depressing. It is not unusual, especially in crime and family, for pupils to undertake a third six before tenancy becomes a realistic option.

If, ultimately, you decide the independent Bar is not for you, there are a number of other options open to you. You might consider working as a barrister employed by a firm of solicitors, or by a large corporation or bank, or for the Government, for example, in the CPS, GLS, Environment Agency or the Law Commission. Many opt to re-train as solicitors (although, as barristers, they are spared the ordeal of the LPC).

lies, damned lies and statistics...

Don't think of pupillage as some sort of holiday before the real world begins with tenancy. Tenancy itself is by no means guaranteed. The Bar Council's own statistics reveal much – a student starting the BVC has about a one in three chance of getting tenancy.

NUMBER OF:	1998-1999	1999-2000	2000-2001	2001-2002
BVC applicants	2,696	2,370	2,252	2,119
BVC enrolments	1,459	1,490	1,407	1,386
Students passing the BVC	1,238	1,206	1,082	n/a
Students getting first six	706	681	695	n/a
Students getting second six	694	704	699	n/a
Pupils getting tenancy	545	511	515	n/a

Bar Council statistics

practice areas at the bar

chancery

Chancery work is so named because cases are mostly heard in the Chancery Division of the High Court, as opposed to the Queen's Bench Division. In Chancery there is a strong emphasis on the application of the law and its principles, and its practitioners are viewed as 'lawyers' lawyers'. The tools of their trade are legal arguments and their skills lie in applying these tools to real situations. Typically, you'll build up a wide practice for the first few years, but then aim to develop a reputation for specific expertise, thus making you more attractive to clients. Leading Chancery barristers have a reputation for being expensive and maybe a 'cut above', but this is an area in which only the highest quality advice is viable.

type of work

Chancery is divided into 'traditional' (trusts, probate, real property, charities, mortgages, partnerships) and 'commercial' (company cases, shareholdings, banking, pensions, financial services, insolvency, media and IP, professional negligence). But the distinction between the two is blurring and most sets now do both types of work. There are some fine brains at the Chancery Bar and it produces highly respected QCs and judges, but don't labour under the illusion that it's all paperwork and lofty academia. You'll have plenty of opportunity to develop your advocacy style, although the volume of court work tends to be higher in other practice areas. After a few years you may develop an overseas practice – the offshore tax havens are notorious for providing plenty of high-value work.

At first, property and commercial cases will take you to County Courts up and down the country and you'll cut your teeth on mortgage-related actions, landlord and tenant work and winding up applications. As time goes on, and particularly in the bigger sets of chambers, you'll be brought in on some substantial cases as a first or second junior, for example a 10-day High Court trial on a matter relating to pensions, commercial trusts or professional negligence. It's a fairly fluid category of work in that Chancery barristers are increasingly taking on work that traditionally wouldn't have been seen as their preserve. For example, there are aspects of financial services, particularly pensions, which involve large trust funds.

skills needed

You need to be pretty bright to succeed within the Chancery Bar. As Joanne Wicks from Wilberforce Chambers says, *"The challenging intellectual nature of the work we do can't be over-emphasised."* It requires complex problem solving together with the application of hard legal principles and a rigorous examination of facts. More importantly, you must be an excellent communicator. Solicitors will sometimes come to you with extremely complex and puzzling cases. These must be pulled apart and analysed. You must adore research and get a buzz from getting to the crux of interesting and intellectual questions. You then need to be able to interpret and communicate these conceptual ideas to your client in a practical and business-like matter. And you need to be confident in your findings. Joanne states that *"clients don't really want to know the details of the 1882 Conveyancing Act, they want to know whether they're going to win or lose."*

One day you could be acting for a plc with an entire team from a big City firm behind it. The next day might bring you a high street solicitor and a little old lady who's been conned into signing her house over to the window cleaner. It is unlikely that either the solicitor or the little old lady will have any experience of High Court litigation, so you'll need to do a lot of hand-holding.

prospects

Most areas of the bar are extremely competitive, and Chancery is no different. Joanne says, *"We always get a lot of very good applicants for pupilage and I'm sure it's the same at other Chancery sets,"* but *"there's always space for good people, and it's an area where there is a demand for our services and money is being generated, so recruitment is happening."*

CHANCERY: COMMERCIAL • London

1
- Maitland Chambers (Lyndon-Stanford/Aldous)

2
- Serle Court (Lord Neill of Bladen QC)
- 3-4 South Square (Crystal/Alexander)
- 4 Stone Buildings (Philip Heslop QC)
- Wilberforce Chambers (Edward Nugee QC)

3
- New Square Chambers (Charles Purle QC)
- 24 Old Buildings (Mann/Steinfeld)
- 3 Stone Buildings (Geoffrey Vos QC)
- 11 Stone Buildings (Murray Rosen QC)

CHANCERY: TRADITIONAL • London

1
- Wilberforce Chambers (Edward Nugee QC)

2
- 5 Stone Buildings (Henry Harrod)

3
- Maitland Chambers (Lyndon-Stanford/Aldous)
- 11 New Square (Sonia Proudman QC)
- New Square Chambers (Charles Purle QC)
- 10 Old Square (Leolin Price QC)

Source: Chambers UK 2002-2003

commercial

In its purest sense, commercial work is dealt with in the Commercial Court or one of the County Court Business Courts. However, much of it is heard by the High Court (both Queen's Bench and Chancery Divisions) or dealt with by way of arbitration. There is an overlap of work with the Chancery Bar reflecting the fact that commercial work is an umbrella term and not a rigidly defined practice area. Alternative methods of dispute resolution are increasingly employed to conclude business disputes as they often enable commercial relationships to continue undamaged by full-blown litigation. The commercial Bar handles a broad range of business disputes for a variety of industry sectors. Some see industry specialisation as the way forward, but others prefer to remain generalists.

type of work

Instructions are generally paper- and fact-intensive, and may involve huge sums of money and multiple parties. There is a perception that commercial work involves written advice as opposed to court work. Top QC, Jeffrey Gruder from Essex Court Chambers, explains: *"Compared to criminal barristers who are in court every day, we do less court work. However, on some cases you may find yourself in court for months on end."* Around 90% of his work is contentious. Of course, the majority of disputes settle, which limits opportunities for trial work, but interlocutory applications and, increasingly, jurisdictional questions, take commercial barristers into court fairly regularly.

Jeffrey's work encompasses shipping, insurance, general commercial contracts of various kinds, banking, commodity dealing, and even arbitrations concerning patents. As he says, *"The fundamentals of what we do are contract and tort."* The area remains heavily based on common law, with domestic and European legislation also coming into play. The continuing trend towards globalisation means commercial barristers are advising more and more on cross-border issues, which encompass competition law, international public and trade law and conflicts of laws.

Juniors handle smaller specialist disputes, such as shipping or insurance claims, as well as general commercial claims, such as sale of goods matters. Jeffrey confirms that these cases *"wouldn't come into the Commercial Court in the narrow sense but are nevertheless* commercial in the wider sense." On larger commercial cases, young barristers assist QCs as second or third junior on one or other of the aspects of the case. Such disputes might be high in value, complexity and profile and enable the junior to observe quality silks in action, while making a valuable contribution in terms of case preparation and direction. They will also gain a working knowledge of the higher courts, although as second or third juniors it's unlikely there would be any opportunities for oral advocacy. The good news is that there's a steady flow of arbitrations and County Court hearings during the first few years and juniors can also gain valuable experience in interlocutory applications and through deployment in a range of tribunals.

skills needed

The ability to work fast under pressure and to meet deadlines is important – not just court deadlines, but those of clients too. As Andy George, a tenant at Blackstone Chambers, says, "*It can differ from Chancery work in that your clients come from a commercial environment and expect answers and ideas within a sometimes unreasonably short time.*" You need interpersonal skills that can be applied to all types of individual. Andy told us, "*During the course of an average day, my clients range from the East End rag trade to the City-based banking industry.*" Jeffrey thinks, "*You need an ability to learn how businesses work and an understanding of business problems.*" You also need to be on the same wavelength as your clients, and understand their needs and desires. A previous career in business may pay dividends but unlike, say patents, where a science qualification is almost mandatory, it's not vital to have had one – most haven't.

Illustrating the breadth of his practice, Jeffrey has an advanced knowledge of the shipping and insurance markets, but he also knows "*how recording companies deal with artists: what problems can arise and what the terms of the contracts are like.*" No doubt this gives him a better idea than most as to what Will and Gareth have gotten into!

prospects

Competition for pupilage at the commercial Bar is fought out by some of the very best candidates. Jeffrey feels that "*if you get a junior tenancy at one of the top seven or eight commercial chambers, then most solicitors will regard this as a pretty good recommendation and will give you a try. Unless something goes terribly wrong, you should then have a reasonable career. Whether it's going to be really good will depend on your ability and your commitment.*"

COMMERCIAL LITIGATION • London
1 **Brick Court Chambers** (Christopher Clarke QC)
Essex Court Chambers (Gordon Pollock QC)
One Essex Court (Anthony Grabiner QC)
Fountain Court (Anthony Boswood QC)
2 **Blackstone Chambers** (Baxendale/Flint)
3 Verulam Buildings (Symons/Jarvis)

Source: Chambers UK 2002-2003

common law

Common law comes from the precedents set in judicial decisions, rather than from statute. Most cases turn on principles of tort and contract and are dealt with in the Queen's Bench Division (QBD) of the High Court and the County Courts. Work blurs at the edges into both Chancery and commercial law.

type of work

A junior in a common law set could have a very mixed caseload as many such sets also handle crime, family, employment, civil actions against police and housing matters. In the early years, much of the work will involve drafting pleadings and attending hearings. These could relate to matters ranging from RTAs and consumer credit debts to criminal hearings. The opportunities for advocacy are fewer than at a criminal set, but greater than with Chancery or commercial. Tara Vindis, a tenant at 9 Gough Square, says, "*The work is fairly advocacy-based. Certainly junior tenants in my set are in court at least once and sometimes twice a day."* Typically, a junior might start early in chambers doing last minute preparation and then travel to court - perhaps a fifteen-minute stroll down the road or a long train ride to Bristol. It might be a two-day trial or a half-hour standard directions appointment.

It's challenging - you won't necessarily know what you'll be doing from one day to the next. It's likely to terrify those who like their days to be structured and planned to the nth degree. Barrister's clerks juggle the chambers' diary deciding who's best placed to handle matters and sometimes instructions arrive late in the day. It's not unusual to receive a brief at 5pm the night before going to court. But, as Tara says, *"It's rewarding in the sense that you've got a lot of opportunity to be in court and have client contact."*

The growth of ADR and mediation has reduced the number of cases available to the common law Bar. In addition, the Woolf reforms changed the adversarial nature of claims, such that many preliminary hearings simply no longer take place. The effect of legal aid cutbacks is that junior barristers are now being instructed in relation to more conditional fee agreements (CFA, or no win, no fee). In practice, cases with poor prospects lead to barristers doing work and spending time on matters where fees become unrecoverable. It's not all gloom and doom though. According to Tara, there's *"plenty of case management conference work to be had, for civil actions in general and PI matters in particular."* Solicitor advocates crop up reasonably frequently at directions hearings, but they are rarely seen on trials.

skills needed

You must be flexible and not mind rushing here, there and everywhere. You might have something come in at 2pm that needs to be done by 5pm. Or you might have spent all day preparing a case for court the next day and then be told at the last minute that it's all off. Could you handle these situations with good grace? You must be a quick learner with a good short-term memory for facts and a long-term one for the law.

This is particularly true during the early years when your practice will leapfrog between many different types of case. Perseverance is essential if you are to get to the stage where routine matters become familiar and straightforward and you can then specialise in a chosen area. Good people skills and an ability to adapt to a range of clients are both key. Tara makes the point that *"common law clients tend to be less high-flying than the clients in commercial sets."* Most won't be savvy company directors – they'll be ordinary people who just happen to have been involved in a traffic accident, tripped over or been sacked.

prospects

If work really is scarce in the early years, then you'll have to be impressive to secure your next instruction. Part of that will boil down to personality and how well you interact with clients. Common law sets will look closely at communication and people skills when recruiting pupils.

criminal

Rumpole... Kavanagh QC... even Judge John Deed manages to be a superb advocate (despite the fact that he's actually on the Bench!). But is the reality anywhere near as exciting as these fictional depictions? Maybe…

type of work

The first year or so will be a continual round of Magistrates' Court appearances on minor matters like motoring offences, committals to the Crown Court, sentencing, pleas in mitigation and directions hearings. Soon you'll progress to full trials, initially on smaller crimes such as common assault and the taking of motor vehicles, then graduating to ABH, robbery, indecent assault and possession of drugs with intent to supply. You may also get the opportunity to work with more senior barristers on matters such as white collar crime, kidnapping, rape or murder. Bear in mind that juniors are asked to do unappealing work at times and you will often be required to travel a great deal with papers you have had little or no time to prepare. And how will you cope when you arrive promptly for trial, but your witnesses are nowhere to be seen?

Following pupillage, you may apply to be included on the CPS List, entitling you to receive instructions to prosecute as well as defend individuals. Some juniors also advise on Criminal Injuries Compensation and do voluntary work for legal advice centres or organisations such as Victim Support, the Free Representation Unit and Justice.

On the whole, the criminal bar is not afflicted by a shortage of work. As Quentin Hunt, a junior at 2 Bedford Row, says, *"Crime is crime essentially. People will always commit crimes and people will always need criminal barristers. The work will always be there – it just depends on the Lord Chancellor's department how much we're paid."* David Spens QC from 6 King's Bench Walk speaks for most when he says, *"It's massively competitive. There's obviously competition from other barristers and down at the bottom end (ie the Magistrates' Courts) there are also solicitor advocates, who are making quite an impact on the defence side."* On the prosecution side, there are solicitors from the Crown Prosecution Services who are doing *"whole lists of cases,"* particularly in the Inner London Magistrates' Courts.

skills needed

As a criminal barrister, you really do need to know how to deal with people, particularly when conducting defence work. You will be dealing with defendants, the victims and witnesses of crimes, the juries that must reach verdicts, the solicitors instructing you, your opposing counsel and the professionals who administer justice. You'll encounter the whole spectrum of society: the real criminal underclass right through to aristocrats caught drink driving, so people skills are essential. Not everyone will be pleasant, not everyone will be sane. Not everyone will be an adult (in any sense of the word).

You need to be a good judge of character. You should also be comfortable with constantly being in the spotlight as an advocate. For Quentin, *"The best bit of the job is being in court every day doing lots of advocacy and lots of different cases."* If that's what you're looking for, then the criminal bar is ideal. The flip side of this is the fact that there's a lot of waiting around. You might arrive at a busy court at ten in the morning but not actually have your matter come up till three in the afternoon.

Hopefully, you'll be outgoing and personable as there's not much room for repressed academics at the criminal Bar, although you will have to keep on top of criminal evidence rules, which are ever changing. You also need to be able to express yourself clearly, particularly to lay people, and to be industrious in the sense of both managing detail and, at the same time, 'seeing the wood for the trees'.

CRIME • London

1 **2 Bedford Row** (William Clegg QC)
Doughty Street Chambers (Geoffrey Robertson QC)
Hollis Whiteman Chambers (Bevan/Whiteman)
6 King's Bench Walk (Roy Amlot QC)
3 Raymond Buildings (Clive Nicholls QC)
2 **23 Essex Street** (Michael Lawson QC)
Two Garden Court (Davies/Griffiths)
3 Gray's Inn Square (Rock Tansey QC)
2 Hare Court (Stephen Kramer QC)
18 Red Lion Court (Anthony Arlidge QC)
3 **7 Bedford Row** (David Farrer QC)
9-12 Bell Yard (D Anthony Evans QC)
Furnival Chambers (Andrew Mitchell QC)
2 Harcourt Buildings. Atkinson Bevan Chambers (Atkinson/Bevan)
Matrix Chambers
Tooks Court Chambers (Michael Mansfield QC)
2-4 Tudor Street (Richard Ferguson QC)
4 **10 King's Bench Walk** (David Nathan QC)
187 Fleet Street (Andrew Trollope QC)
5 Paper Buildings (Carey/Caplan)
3 Temple Gardens (Jonathan Goldberg QC)

Source: Chambers UK 2002-2003

prospects

The criminal Bar tends to award more pupillages than any other area. That said, Quentin told us that, of nine pupils at his chambers, only he and one other were given tenancy. Needless to say, competition remains fierce. Evidence of proven advocacy skill (if only from activities such as debating or mooting) would be advisable for anyone seeking a pupilage. David Spens describes criminal advocacy as being *"80% preparation, 10% luck and 10% performance on the day."* This emphasises two points well - you can't wing your cases and *"the charisma factor is the icing on the cake, and makes the difference between those who win and the also-rans."*

employment

Since 1997 the Labour government has passed a raft of new employment legislation. Couple this with the public's growing awareness of employment rights and the net effect is more cases, particularly in relation to discrimination. Great news for the employment Bar! Legal representation is not required in employment tribunals, however, many people have household contents insurance with a significant legal expenses component and cases are often of such complexity that specialist legal advice is advisable. Tom Coghlin from Cloisters Chambers believes that *"in a case where there's more than several thousand pounds at stake, you'd be silly not to engage a barrister to represent you."*

type of work

It's usual for juniors to undertake a mixture of employment cases and other areas of work, mainly commercial and civil matters. While the 'cab rank rule' applies (ie barristers will do whatever work comes through the door), most junior employment barristers handle roughly even amounts of work for applicants (often individual employees) and respondents (often HR managers representing the employer company). This is the case even though the specialist sets tend to have links to either applicant or respondent-oriented law firms. Bear in mind the fact that *"respondents generally pay better."*

With damages capped in all employment cases except those relating to discrimination, it rarely pays to get a senior barrister involved, so there's a good selection of work at the junior end. Straightforward tribunal work, such as unfair dismissals, discrimination cases and relatively low value contract claims are interspersed with more difficult work, such as whistle blowing and cases concerning trade union activities. Sarah Moor from Old Square Chambers says that acting for an applicant sometimes means *"you'll be up against a party who can afford a senior barrister, which of course is a useful learning opportunity for you."*

There's plenty of advocacy, particularly at the junior end. This marks it out from an area like commercial, which tends to involve more documents and drafting. Generally, you'll appear in the informal setting of an employment tribunal or the Employment Appeals Tribunal, as opposed to the courts, and you may have three or four different tribunals a week. David Craig from Devereux Chambers explains: *"Because there are no costs consequences in tribunals, a lot of people will go to trial. Even if they lose, they've only got their own costs to bear, not the other side's. If people had more to lose, they might be keener to settle."*

Employment barristers have been in competition with solicitor advocates for some time. Tom says, *"I normally expect to be against a barrister in the employment tribunal, but often I'm against a solicitor or a litigant in person."* David stressed the expense factor again: *"Barristers' brief fees tend to be considerably lower than solicitors' fees for preparing, travelling, waiting and appearing in court, particularly if City solicitors have been instructed."* Solicitor advocates are rare in the higher courts, but they may draft the pleadings themselves.

skills needed

Decent advocacy skills and an engaging personality will take you a long way. You'll come across all types in your work and it's important to interact well with them, be they High Court judges, tribunal members, union officials, high-flying execs or dinner ladies. In tribunal hearings, you'll need a gentle touch if you're against a litigant in person, *"otherwise you can come across as a bully!"* and you need to be less 'legalistic' in your language.

Perhaps more than most areas, you have to keep abreast of developments in the law. New directives, regulations and cases appear all the time and you'll be forever having your cases stayed while others with similar points are being heard on appeal. One disadvantage, according to Tom Coghlin, is that *"very often briefs are delivered at half past four the afternoon before trial, usually because solicitors are holding out till the last minute for a deal and don't want to incur the cost of instructing counsel until they absolutely have to."* Consequently, you may have little time to prepare a case for trial. It's in these situations where you realise how important it is to know all the relevant law *"so you don't have to be researching it at midnight the night before."*

prospects

The area is incredibly competitive and there are few pupillages available. Tom says that experience in almost any environment other than the Bar is a good thing. *"At the Bar you're neither an employer nor an employee, yet as an employment barrister you're arguing what is reasonable behaviour by an employer. How can you do this if you've never seen or been a manager yourself?"*

The best advice we can give is to make sure you can demonstrate your interest and commitment. Sarah says, *"It's most disappointing to see a very bright candidate with an excellent degree who can't put together a rational explanation as to why they want to do employment work – even if it's more theoretical than practical at that stage."* David recommends that you *"think about doing some employment cases for the Free Representation Unit. You act for applicants and run a case from start to finish, which will clue you up on the law and give you terrific advocacy experience."*

EMPLOYMENT • London

- **1** **11 King's Bench Walk Chambers** (Tabachnik/Goudie)
- **2** **Old Square Chambers** (John Hendy QC)
- **3** **Blackstone Chambers** (Baxendale/Flint)
  - **Cloisters** (Laura Cox QC)
  - **Littleton Chambers** (Michel Kallipetis QC)
- **4** **Devereux Chambers** (Colin Edelman QC)
  - **Matrix Chambers**

Source: Chambers UK 2002-2003

family

Feuding couples and bitter child custody battles - can you handle these? Family law is a demanding practice area for a barrister, who will only be involved in the most complex or combative cases.

Daniel Bentham, a tenant at Queen Elizabeth Building, told us, *"It's a relatively small niche at the Bar, but it accounts for a whole division of the High Court."* A large amount of court time in England & Wales is allotted to divorce, separation, adoption, child residence and contact orders, financial provision and domestic violence. However, there has been an increase in 'mediation' in an attempt to resolve disputes in a more efficient and less unsettling fashion. The family Bar had been concerned that this, and an increase in solicitor advocates, would lead to a downturn in work. With the exception of children's cases, in which solicitors have always been encouraged to do their own advocacy, work for the Bar appears to have continued largely unabated, although fees for publicly-funded work have been reduced.

type of work

Barristers cut their teeth on simple County Court matters, progressing to complex matters in the Family Division of the High Court. In the early years, there will be a lot of private law children work (disputes between parents), which will consist of minor appointments, directions hearings and timetabling. More substantive work, including final hearings, will follow. Public law children's work (care proceedings between local authorities and parents) tends to be publicly funded where the barrister is acting for the parents and is less lucrative for the barrister.

Ancillary relief work (financial arrangements) is often complex, so it helps to have a flair for things like pensions and shares and a good grounding in the basics of trusts and property. Specialising in matrimonial finance following marriage breakdown requires very different skills to children's work. That said, some barristers build up excellent reputations in both areas.

Daniel says, "*If you want to be an advocate, it's a pretty good place to be... I'm in court about three times a week, generally for small cases or applications rather than big trials.*" He does a lot of children's matters and directions hearings. A significant component of the work of Nick Anderson, a tenant at 1 King's Bench Walk, involves seeking injunctions in domestic violence cases. These issues can upset and anger, so be sure that long-term exposure will not affect your own well being.

The legislation affecting the area is comprehensive and well settled and there's also a large and flourishing body of case law (in the Family Law Reports). You must keep up with cases, but remind yourself that, while the basics remain the same in relation to the problems that couples and families experience, precedents are only useful to an extent. Unlike contracts, no two families are ever the same. The job is, therefore, more about negotiating general principles than strictly adhering to precedents.

skills needed

Whilst conflict is often deeply embedded in a case, the law requires an attempt at resolution through mediation. A tough adversarial approach is generally not appropriate and practitioners need to focus on client contact and genuine discussion. In children's cases, the paramount consideration is the child's best interests.

You can read the instructions or the brief, but often the case only comes alive when you meet the client. The ruling made or the settlement reached can have a massive impact on each of the lives touched by it and, consequently, it's vital that you find the appropriate course of action in each case and work with the solicitor in managing the case from an early stage. As Daniel says, "*A tactical, academic and practical approach to the matter needs to be combined with empathy for your client's situation – you don't want to come across as a legal machine.*" You need to stay objective, give clear-headed advice, but bear in mind that you are giving this advice to emotionally vulnerable clients.

Presentation and communication skills need to be tailored to different types of people. Nick told us, "*You will have clients ranging from a 17-year-old girl who's having her child taken into care, to a fairly well-off couple who are divorcing and dividing up their assets.*" He added, "*It's very much a job for those who enjoy working with people. Hopefully we're achieving some good rather than just making money by pushing paper around for faceless corporations.*"

prospects

It's a small area, so competition and standards are high. Even at specialist family sets, many pupils are not retained as tenants. Daniel says, "*Before you devote 25 years of your life to it, you should do some investigation – and mini-pupillages will mark you out as being committed to the area.*"

FAMILY/MATRIMONIAL • London
1 **One King's Bench Walk** (Anthony Hacking QC)
1 Hare Court (Bruce Blair QC)
Queen Elizabeth Building (Florence Baron QC)
2 **29 Bedford Row Chambers** (Nicholas Francis QC)
One Garden Court Family Law Chambers (Platt/Ball)
4 Paper Buildings (Lionel Swift QC)
3 **14 Gray's Inn Square** (Joanna Dodson QC)
Renaissance Chambers (Jubb/Setright)

Source: Chambers UK 2002-2003

public law

Public bodies operate within statutory constraints and their decisions may be challenged on a number of grounds. Have they considered the relevant facts in reaching their decisions? Have the officers acted strictly in accordance with the correct procedure? Did the body or officer have the authority to make the decision in the first place? Will they reveal to you how and why they have made a decision? If these questions interest you and you are passionate about principles of justice and the advancement of the law, read on.

type of work

While the breadth of public law work is huge, by far the most common matters are the judicial review of immigration decisions, which account for approximately half of the Administrative Court's case list. Such work features prominently in a junior barrister's practice. Those building up a local authority clientele may find themselves acting for a number of different departments on a range of work, which will often lean heavily towards decisions concerning planning, housing or environmental matters and education, health and children. A recent growth area has been community care matters, which concern the provision of social services by local authorities. For example, a single mother with two disabled children who is seeking more assistance and a larger council flat might bring an action against the council.

At the other end of the spectrum sit some high profile and contentious cases, such as that of 'Miss B', an irreversibly paralysed, woman who successfully pursued a claim in the High Court for the right to have her life-support machine switched off.

Very few sets limit themselves to public law cases; most will combine the work with general common law, competition, criminal or employment as second strings to their public law bow. Additionally, many sets that do not hold themselves out as public law specialists carry out judicial review work.

Andrew Blake, a tenant at 11 King's Bench Walk, makes the point that *"many sets link their public law work to their non-public law work."* For example, if a set does criminal work, its public law practice will often be in relation to prisons or breaches of procedure by police. Alternatively, if a set does commercial work, it might handle judicial reviews of DTI decisions.

Where an event is of great importance to society as a whole, or even just a segment of it, public inquiries are commissioned by the government and then operate independently. The Bloody Sunday Inquiry, the recent inquiry into Heathrow Terminal 5 and the Victoria Climbié Inquiry illustrate the different types of issue that come under scrutiny. All of these inquiries utilise the services of counsel, and sometimes multiple counsel. Bloody Sunday, for instance, involves 18 barristers.

The Human Rights Act has undoubtedly affected public law. *"In theory the HRA can influence any public law case,"* says Andrew. *"It's had a stealth impact in some ways, in that it doesn't have to be expressly referred to in order to have an impact on a case – it's already laid down a few general principles that are now standard considerations for any case."*

Initially, pupillage at a public law set will see you drafting opinions and shadowing your pupilmaster. In the second six you'll get the chance to undertake some advocacy. The nature of this may depend on the work of your chambers, but may include criminal work or applications for urgent injunctions. It's not usual for the most junior barristers to handle judicial review cases, although juniors will be led by QCs when complex or important matters make it to court. After a few years you should have built a practice with a good balance of advice and advocacy. You'll see an interesting array of cases which, given their nature, are often reported in the newspapers. Andrew said, *"One day I could be doing an education case about exclusion from school, the next day I could be doing a case involving a prison, or an environmental or planning matter."* If you subscribe to the theory that variety is the spice of life, this could well be the area for you.

Public international law appeals to many students, but openings are very limited. Issues of note include border disputes (eg between Nigeria and Cameroon), the Lockerbie air crash, the UK and Spanish governments' Pinochet extradition dispute, and the Irish and UK governments' Sea Tribunal concerning the effects of Sellafield. Traditionally it's been the preserve of academics – the leading names are predominantly sitting or ex-professors at the top universities, but also include Foreign Office veterans and the occasional pure barrister. Governments want tried and tested counsel and will expect those they instruct to be recognised, published authors. This is not an area of work you'll fall into by accident, nor is it one you're likely to get into until you're much more experienced. If the academic route is not for you, seek a pupillage at a leading public law set.

skills needed

The job is all about understanding red tape and wanting to battle through it. You have to really care about the fundamental laws by which we live. In order to have a successful practice, you must develop a comprehensive knowledge of administrative and constitutional law, and you need to be au fait with the inner workings of central and local government generally. In addition, familiarity with EU and international law is becoming increasingly important. You should remember, though, that the work won't always involve close contact with your lay client. In many cases, the client doesn't attend the hearing in person at all.

The Administrative Court is one of the most inundated branches of the High Court, so you'll need to develop an efficient style of advocacy. Long and dramatic performances are rarely well received; you must learn how to cut to the chase and deliver the pertinent information, draw on the relevant case law or statutory regulations and present your arguments promptly. An inquiring and analytical mind is essential.

prospects

"It's definitely a growing area, particularly in relation to judicial review," says Andrew. *"This is partly due to the HRA but it's also due to a growing awareness of the public of their ability to take legal action against government decisions – that the government should be and can be held accountable for their actions."* It's always been competitive and the introduction of the HRA has made it more so. *"Human rights is a very trendy area of law, and lots of people are intrigued by the idea of placing limits on what government or the police or any public body can do."* Andrew suggests focusing your studies on constitutional law subjects as one way of demonstrating your enthusiasm for the area. In addition, doing plenty of pro bono work in the early stages of your tenancy is an ideal way to get involved in public law matters.

ADMINISTRATIVE & PUBLIC LAW • London

1. Blackstone Chambers (Baxendale/Flint)
2. Matrix Chambers
3. 4 Breams Buildings (Christopher Lockhart-Mummery QC)
   Brick Court Chambers (Christopher Clarke QC)
   Doughty Street Chambers (Geoffrey Robertson QC)
   39 Essex Street (Nigel Pleming QC)
   11 King's Bench Walk Chambers (Tabachnik/Goudie)
4. 1 Crown Office Row (Robert Seabrook QC)
   Two Garden Court (Davies/Griffiths)

IMMIGRATION • London

1. Two Garden Court (Davies/Griffiths)
2. Doughty Street Chambers (Geoffrey Robertson QC)
   Matrix Chambers
3. 6 King's Bench Walk (Sibghat Kadri QC)
4. Blackstone Chambers (Baxendale/Flint)
   39 Essex Street (Nigel Pleming QC)
   Renaissance Chambers (Jubb/Setright)
   Tooks Court Chambers (Michael Mansfield QC)

PUBLIC INTERNATIONAL LAW • London

1. Blackstone Chambers (Baxendale/Flint)
   20 Essex Street (Iain Milligan QC)
2. Essex Court Chambers (Gordon Pollock QC)
   Matrix Chambers (Tim Owen QC)

Source: Chambers UK 2002-2003

The UK's leading law firms who does what and where

Available now in your careers service and at www.ChambersandPartners.com

The 2002-2003 edition of Chambers UK guide is the product of over 6,500 research interviews and the whole process is audited by the BMRB. The best law firms and practitioners are identified in over 60 areas of practice and across the UK. Your research won't be complete without it.

CHAMBERS & PARTNERS
LEGAL PUBLISHERS

CHAMBERS GUIDE TO THE UK LEGAL PROFESSION

The UK's leading lawyers
2002-2003

Over 6,500 interviews. Research audited by British Market Research Bureau

www.ChambersandPartners.com

SPECIALIST PRACTICE AREAS

banking & finance	98
competition	101
construction & projects	104
corporate	108
crime	112
employment	116
environmental law	120
family	123
IP	127
litigation/dispute resolution	131
media & entertainment	136
personal injury & clinical negligence	141
private client	147
property/real estate	151
public interest	156
shipping	161
sports	164
tax	167
TMT	170
international firms... international locations	174

banking and finance

banking: Work centres on commercial loan agreements – the documentation of lending money and arranging its signing and completion. The banking lawyer's work frequently overlaps with corporate finance work, particularly mergers and acquisitions.

capital markets: The issuance of 'debt' or 'equity' securities and related areas such as securitisation, repackaging and structured finance, plus the whole range of 'derivatives' products. If that's left you confused already, don't worry. **'debt'** relates to publicly tradeable financial instruments, which are listed on a stock exchange but traded off the exchange by bond traders. A company raises money by issuing bonds and a bank or group of banks will underwrite the issue. The bonds will pay interest until they are redeemable. **'equity'** is slightly sexier than debt. It's all about public offerings (including IPOs) of shares and company flotations. Because shares are riskier and more volatile than bonds, the returns are higher.

Both debt and equity transactions involve a company presenting itself to investors by way of a prospectus and documents recording the issue of security for cash. A typical capital markets transaction might involve, say, a company raising several million pounds sterling via the issue of a bond sold into Europe or a public offering of equity. The proceeds might then be swapped into dollars and perhaps used for the acquisition of another company. Lawyers will assist with the structuring of the deal and ensure compliance with securities laws.

type of work

Top-level banking and capital markets work is concentrated in the world financial centres – London, Frankfurt, New York, Hong Kong and Paris. The most complex transactions are handled by City law firms, whose clients tend to be international banks. At the biggest firms, lawyers are usually specialised. Out in the regions finance work is of a simpler and more domestic type for clients that are usually UK banks and building societies and the companies they lend to.

The demands on lawyers are intensive because of the cyclical nature of transaction management. A normal 50-hour week can rise to 75 or 100 hours as a deal nears completion, however, banking lawyers speak of the buzz of completing a deal. It's a major motivational force. Andrew O'Keeffe, a banking solicitor at Simmons & Simmons, describes most clients as *"very driven people but pretty decent. They expect high standards."* A capital markets lawyer working in-house in a large international bank echoed his sentiments on the buzz: *"My work is exciting, fast and snappy. I have to make decisions quickly and give on the spot advice to a wide variety of people – anyone from the corporate treasurer of a multinational to the mayor of the City of Moscow. I also like interacting with the traders on the floor."*

You need to be a bright spark to do well in finance law. Andrew tells us, *"You are faced with incredibly complex formulae in documents so the job is intellectually challenging."* Equally important is commercial awareness: *"We have to cater for the 'what if' scenario. Someone has a great idea and sells it to the banks. When we put the documentation together we are there to cater for the downside – anything that could possibly happen. You feel like a business advisor not a lawyer sometimes."* Andrew told us he'd recently had to become an expert on the Italian telecoms market. The bottom line: finance lawyers enable the work of most other commercial lawyers to reach fruition. As he says, *"Nothing moves without money. Money is the petrol in the engine that is the world economy. Banking lawyers are at the centre of things."*

It's widely accepted that banking and capital markets are not law-intensive areas of practice. They are not regulated heavily by case law and statutes. You won't be doing masses of research into black letter law but you will be researching market sectors. In this sense your career won't be stagnant. *"Things change and markets develop. 10 years ago there was no project finance."* Thankfully, the language isn't archaic and the more senior you get, the more time you spend managing deals and the less time you spend drafting. International travel will be part of your working life if you join a firm handling cross-border deals. Our in-house capital markets lawyer told us: *"I travel all over the world and find out about all manner of things. I've been to a Mexican tortilla factory and an Indonesian textile manufacturer to learn about the production of Rayon."*

a day in the life of…

9.30am: After short commute from trendy docklands apartment to rather grand office in EC2, check e-mails from NY counterparts and London clients with workaholic tendencies.

11.00am: E-postbag dealt with, call client to clarify instructions on financing of purchase of property portfolio. Draft set of new clauses into primary loan agreement following client's instructions.

1.00pm: Haul (expanding) belly and sense of guilt into office gym. (January is such a hateful month.)

2.15pm: Venezuelan oil pipeline project team meeting. Have sufficiently senior role on team to avoid any dogsbody tasks. Partner in charge praises my performance so far on drafting the loan agreement.

3.30pm: Venezuelan pipeline clients and other lawyers arrive. Our team batting for lenders. Negotiations tough but fair. Held own in negotiating controls that bank will have over borrower's business.

7.00pm: Meeting concludes. Send off latest draft of this morning's property loan document by courier. Faff around on e-mail to friends.

7.45pm: Depart for home clutching *FT*.

skills needed

…practical intelligence… analytical skills… interest in business and international finance… ability to dedicate to the task… accuracy and care… capacity to do routine work in the early days… love the rush of adrenalin… stamina… good interpersonal skills…

You must have confidence in yourself and be quite tough – sometimes people can be unpleasant in the way they negotiate with you. The full-on nature of the work will affect your personal life at times, so do make sure that the world of international finance and business interests you. To prime yourself for a career as a finance lawyer, read the business pages in your daily newspaper (ideally a salmon pink one!). Work experience in the finance sector will help you gain a better idea of how you'll take to this world. And, lastly, don't worry if you're not a mathematical wizard!

career options

This is a big money world and salaries in private practice and all related areas are high. Some deals keep you in the office from 9-7pm, some keep you there into the early hours of the morning and, through your choice of firm, you can gravitate towards the type of deal that suits you. In the top City firms, lawyers specialise to a high degree. For some this has real appeal; for others it's a turn off and they talk of the finance "factory firms." In smaller practices, lawyers are broader-based and enjoy a variety of deals, albeit lower profile. Read more about the leading banking/finance practices in *Chambers UK* and *Chambers Global*.

Some City solicitors view banking law as an ideal platform for a subsequent career in the financial markets, but if, when reading this book, you already know you want to become a banker, then become a banker, not a lawyer. It's really that simple.

Even at trainee level, secondments to international banks are available from City firms and can give a taster of things to come. Moves in-house at banks are common, especially in capital markets, where some find the job gets them *"one step closer to the business; thinking of deals and knocking ideas around."* There's less drafting and a lot of ad hoc queries from different parts of the bank. *"Some lawyers sit on trading floors; others set policies and help in deciding on risk."* Remember though, while the business of a law firm is law, the business of a bank is banking, and working as a lawyer in a bank, you have a back office function. For some, the ego needs to be pandered by a law firm partnership but others just appreciate the better hours in-house. Financial Services Regulation now employs ever-greater numbers of compliance lawyers. As credit risk departments and capital adequacy requirements become increasingly important so does the advisory role of these individuals.

LEADING FIRMS FROM CHAMBERS UK GUIDE 2002-2003

BANKING & FINANCE: LARGER DEALS — LONDON

1. Allen & Overy
   Clifford Chance
2. Linklaters
3. Freshfields Bruckhaus Deringer
4. Norton Rose
5. Ashurst Morris Crisp
   Lovells
   Shearman & Sterling
   Slaughter and May
6. Denton Wilde Sapte
   Herbert Smith
   White & Case

BANKING & FINANCE: MEDIUM DEALS — LONDON

1. Berwin Leighton Paisner
   CMS Cameron McKenna
   DLA
   Simmons & Simmons
2. Baker & McKenzie
   Macfarlanes
   Travers Smith Braithwaite
3. Gouldens
   Latham & Watkins
   SJ Berwin
   Taylor Wessing
   Watson, Farley & Williams
4. Dickson Minto WS
   Eversheds
   Theodore Goddard

BANKING & FINANCE — THE SOUTH & SOUTH WEST

1. Burges Salmon Bristol
   Osborne Clarke Bristol
2. Bond Pearce Bristol, Southampton
3. CMS Cameron McKenna Bristol
4. Blake Lapthorn Southampton

BANKING & FINANCE — MIDLANDS

1. Pinsent Curtis Biddle Birmingham
2. Eversheds Birmingham, Nottingham
3. Wragge & Co Birmingham
4. DLA Birmingham
   Gateley Wareing Birmingham
   Martineau Johnson Birmingham
5. Browne Jacobson Nottingham
6. Hammond Suddards Edge Birmingham

BANKING & FINANCE — EAST ANGLIA

1. Eversheds Cambridge, Norwich
   Mills & Reeve Cambridge, Norwich
2. Taylor Vinters Cambridge

BANKING & FINANCE — WALES

1. Eversheds Cardiff
2. Edwards Geldard Cardiff
   Morgan Cole Cardiff

BANKING & FINANCE — NORTH WEST

1. DLA Liverpool, Manchester
2. Eversheds Manchester
3. Addleshaw Booth & Co Manchester
   Halliwell Landau Manchester
4. Cobbetts Manchester
   DWF Liverpool, Manchester
   Hammond Suddards Edge Manchester
5. Kuit Steinart Levy Manchester

BANKING & FINANCE — YORKSHIRE

1. Addleshaw Booth & Co Leeds
2. DLA Leeds
   Hammond Suddards Edge Leeds
3. Eversheds Leeds
   Pinsent Curtis Biddle Leeds
   Walker Morris Leeds

BANKING & FINANCE — NORTH EAST

1. Dickinson Dees Newcastle upon Tyne
2. Eversheds Newcastle upon Tyne
   Ward Hadaway Newcastle upon Tyne
3. Robert Muckle Newcastle upon Tyne

competition

This section is devoted to domestic and European competition law. Previously, we've covered EU law in this section, but it no longer seems appropriate to discuss EU law as a separate entity. All lawyers, whatever their area of practice, must take responsibility for the EU laws that impact on their work. While you may study EU law as a separate subject at uni, you must not separate it out as such in practice.

The basic aim of the regulatory authorities is to ensure that markets function effectively on the basis of fair and open competition. Competition law in the UK is intrinsically tied to EU Articles 81 and 82 and their UK analogues – Chapters I and II of the Competition Act 1998. These address anti-competitive agreements (such as price-fixing cartels) and the abuse of dominant market positions (eg, by way of excessive or predatory pricing). It's easy to find examples of these types of behaviour. Recently there have been huge fines for the various household name producers of vitamins that clubbed together to keep prices high. The regulators make it their business to bust open these smoke-filled rooms deals. In addition to industry-wide enquiries (eg CDs, new cars, banking services, supermarkets), the behaviour of individual companies is scrutinised, particularly those who dominate their market and flex their commercial muscle so as to harm consumers.

Some competition lawyers specialise even further in areas such as anti-dumping (preventing companies exporting a product at a price lower than normally charged on its own home market) and State Aid (eg national governments propping up underperforming flag carrier airlines). Other lawyers specialise in particular industries such as electricity, gas, water, telecoms and media, each of which has an additional layer of sector-specific regulatory laws and a sector-specific regulator.

type of work

Competition work can be either contentious or non-contentious. The former commonly takes the form of merger control advice and clearance for both UK and European mergers, or structuring commercial agreements so as to comply with competition laws. It is fast moving, high profile work. Contentious work traditionally referred to High Court litigation which had a competition element, while work defending regulatory investigations (eg cartel investigations or industry investigations such as the recent Competition Commission inquiry into supermarkets) fell somewhere in between. Competition lawyers traditionally specialised in either contentious or non-contentious work, however, these days they have to be expert in both in order to be fully effective.

Domestic competition law brings practitioners into close contact with regulatory bodies. In the UK these include the Office of Fair Trading (OFT), the Competition Commission and industry-specific regulators, such as Oftel (soon to be folded into OFCOM, the new "umbrella regulator" for media and telecoms) and GEMA (gas and electricity). At EU level the relevant regulator is the European Commission.

There are examples of important M&A deals that failed to get clearance. In 2000 the EU regulators refused to allow a $20 billion tie-up between EMI and Time Warner's music subsidiary on the grounds that it would have placed 80% of Europe's record industry in the hands of just four global giants.

Competition law requires the lawyer to gain a thorough understanding of how industries and their markets operate. Rod Carlton, a competition partner at Freshfields Bruckhaus Deringer, couldn't stress this enough. For him, it's what appeals most about the work: over the last 10 years he's learnt a fair bit about retail, the music industry, pay TV, telecoms, public transport, cinema, newspapers and perfume. "*I've* never been bored by the job – quite the contrary," he told us. "*You analyse companies and sectors in order to understand why they do what they do. There's a comparison with what management consultants, such as McKinsey, do. We look at everything from the minutiae to the grand plans.*"

The lawyers we spoke to told us how the UK regulators had greater teeth and claws since the Competition Act 1998 had come into effect. Rod told us, "*The OFT now has more people, is more proactive and has greater powers to root out anti-competitive behaviour and impose stiffer sanctions. There's a much more contentious feel to the work.*"

Most competition firms have a Brussels office and are keen to send junior lawyers on placements there. Although some UK firms do the majority of active work on-site domestically, a presence in Belgium is useful for keeping eyes and ears open and maintaining close contact with the politicians and power brokers. Anti-dumping and trade law is one area of competition that remains very heavily Brussels-driven. For information on the firms with the best national and international competition practices, we recommend *Chambers UK* and *Chambers Global*.

a day in the life...

Dean Murray is an assistant at Newcastle firm Dickinson Dees. He told us about the OFT's habit of conducting 'dawn raids'. "*We might get a 9.30am call from the person in charge of a company or site that is about to be raided. Our dawn raid team (which can be up to 10 people – we take as many as there are investigators from the OFT) go to the premises and handle the raid.*" The team will try to get an idea of what the OFT is looking for. "*During the raid itself it's man-for-man marking almost. We make sure they are not looking at things they shouldn't, we take copies of whatever they take and make sure they don't ask questions that are out of order. Normally a raid goes on for most of the day. They are usually looking for evidence that something suspicious is going on, such as the existence of anti-competitive agreements. The event itself is exciting but the real work is only just beginning.*"

Back in the office, the team conducts its own investigation of the company's activities. The OFT will issue a 'Rule 14 Statement' detailing what the client is alleged to have done wrong. The lawyers will then make written and oral submissions about the statement and eventually the OFT's decision will be given. It can be appealed before the Competition Commission in London and then, if necessary, in the Court of Appeal. But not all OFT actions are fought all the way. Sometimes the lawyers find their clients are not whiter than white and will go for a leniency procedure, with the client holding its hands up to wrongdoing in the hope of getting a lower fine. Dawn raids are a rarity: not every day is as action-packed. Much of the average lawyer's time will be spent researching company and market information and drafting and reviewing merger notification documents. It's not a tick-the-box exercise though, as Rod told us, "*You start with a blank piece of paper each time; there are no standard forms to follow.*"

skills needed

...clever... clear, analytical mind... enquiring... good judgement and confident in relying on gut instincts... articulate, both orally and on paper... good mediation and lobbying skills... thoroughness... attention to detail... numeracy... decisiveness... linguistic ability... enthusiasm...

Diplomacy, common sense and an insatiable desire to understand business are prerequisite traits. Junior lawyers will spend most of their time working directly under the guidance of experienced partners and in the early years can't expect to fly too high or too far by themselves. Web research, 'market' research, talking to clients about their business, honing drafting skills and developing gut instinct are plenty to be getting on with. The work involves the exercise of advocacy skills, both written and oral. If you enjoy constructing an argument for an essay and then expressing it clearly, backing up your points with the necessary evidence, you're already on the right road. Academically gifted and skill-rich lawyers populate the area. Not only is there a lot of law to learn, the principles of economics and international trade have to become second nature.

The international nature of the work means overseas trips to learn about the practicalities of clients' businesses. Rod told us, *"I've been out to California to help plan a major merger… yet I've also been to Wimbledon to find out how holiday snaps are processed."*

career options

At the junior end, EU/competition can be difficult to break into, but don't be put off. The number of active firms and the size of competition departments are set to carry on growing with the increased activity of the OFT and plans to bring criminal sanctions in through the Enterprise Bill. The type of firm will determine the nature of the work available, with EU work more commonly going to London firms and domestic work being handled in the regions. A young lawyer must invest for future career success and, in time, the benefits of patience become clear. Rod told us, *"Clients are extremely grateful as your work makes a real difference. Competition lawyers, like tax and financial services lawyers, are regarded as premium advisors."*

Few competition lawyers leave private practice. Maybe they don't tire of the work or maybe it's because in-house jobs come up so rarely. Usually only global giants like Coca-Cola, Microsoft, Vodafone and Diageo can support a specialist team in-house. Some lawyers might turn gamekeeper and join the OFT or one of the UK sector regulators like Oftel. Dean talked of the OFT having emulated the US Dept. of Justice's *"revolving-door policy"* whereby lawyers move to the regulator, gain experience and go back out into private practice. It seems to benefit both sides. EU Commission jobs crop up and there are always opportunities to work in the foreign offices of UK firms.

LEADING FIRMS FROM CHAMBERS UK GUIDE 2002-2003

COMPETITION/ANTI-TRUST — LONDON
1. Freshfields Bruckhaus Deringer
   Herbert Smith
   Linklaters
   Slaughter and May
2. Lovells
   Simmons & Simmons
3. Allen & Overy
   Ashurst Morris Crisp
   Denton Wilde Sapte
   SJ Berwin
4. Baker & McKenzie
   Clifford Chance
   Norton Rose
5. Bristows
   CMS Cameron McKenna
   Eversheds
   Richards Butler
   Theodore Goddard

COMPETITION/ANTI-TRUST — SOUTH WEST
1. Burges Salmon Bristol
2. Bond Pearce Plymouth

COMPETITION/ANTI-TRUST — WALES
1. Edwards Geldard Cardiff
   Eversheds Cardiff
   Morgan Cole Cardiff

COMPETITION/ANTI-TRUST — MIDLANDS
1. Pinsent Curtis Biddle Birmingham
   Wragge & Co Birmingham
2. Eversheds Birmingham

COMPETITION/ANTI-TRUST — THE NORTH
1. Eversheds Leeds
2. Addleshaw Booth & Co Leeds
3. Pinsent Curtis Biddle Leeds
4. Dickinson Dees Newcastle upon Tyne

construction & projects

Once upon a time, construction lawyers drafted contracts for developers and construction companies. Buildings would go up, but often the parties fell into dispute. They'd call the lawyers back in to commence litigation that sometimes took years. Other parties, eg architects or subcontractors, would get caught up in the dispute, everyone spent huge amounts of money and working relationships ended up in tatters.

type of work

The main aspects to construction law: developing the contractual arrangements prior to building work and dispute resolution (when it all goes horribly wrong) are still the staple, but there's a different approach taken these days. Tom Pemberton, an assistant at Shadbolt & Co, talked about a new philosophy in construction – partnering – where all concerns try to achieve a common goal rather than sue the hide off each other. It seems to have had an effect: parties are increasingly 'working with' each other when things go wrong. For example, most contracts now contain a mandatory arbitration procedure to be adopted in case of dispute. Adjudication of disputes has become the industry norm and there's a swift 28 day timetable. Tom explains that it's only in the last few years since partnering concepts have become established that the old practice of recouping construction costs through claims has begun to die. Now, *"lawyers drafting contracts are really put under pressure. Clients don't want you to pick up too many points or cause too many headaches, but you do have to advise the client of where the risks lie."*

It's an unpretentious area of the law, according to Sally Davies, a partner at Mayer, Brown, Rowe & Maw. For the record, she thinks it's an area that's just as open to women as it is to the lads. Sally's gone into the contentious side of things and she recommends that you pick your team according to your natural inclination. *"Normally people have a natural bias for contentious or non-contentious work,"* so if you want to concentrate on one rather than the other, be aware that some firms like their construction lawyers to handle both aspects of the work. *Chambers UK* will give you more detail on the leading construction practices across the country.

skills needed

…pragmatism… attention to detail… excellent drafting… not a pushover… good judgement… down to earth attitude… feel comfortable with technical information… industry background a major boon… stamina… imagination… team worker… like socialising with clients…

Some pretty seminal legal decisions have arisen out of construction disputes – they deal with complex relationships between parties, which define the boundaries of contract and tort. You need to have an affinity with case law and be prepared to keep up to date with the reports as well as industry trends and thinking. But can you combine legal know how with practical advice and real imagination?

Sally says, *"You don't have to be frightened of dealing with a huge volume of documentation. You don't have to read it all but you do have to sift out the wheat from the chaff and home in on the detail... You feel a bit like a forensic investigator when you're going through documents, working out what's relevant and what's not."*

It's important that you get on with all sorts of people. Sally explains: *"You might be dealing with some real boffins – for example, geotechnical engineers and structural engineers who produce reports that you have to interpret. Some contractor and subcontractor clients are extremely down-to-earth; on the other hand, you have clients who are corporate types or in-house lawyers with whom you must speak on a more sophisticated level."* Some lawyers make a great name for themselves based partly on their social skills. We say this not to belittle their legal talents, but to stress the fact that, generally speaking, construction industry clients like to bond with their advisors. A lawyer who can put the client at ease and be 'one of the lads' (male or female) goes far.

Projects: Major projects are located worldwide and projects lawyers hail from every major jurisdiction. Be it an oil pipeline or a motorway, specialist construction lawyers work hand in hand with finance and corporate lawyers to enable projects to come to fruition. A few City firms and the largest US practices dominate the biggest international projects, but there's work for projects lawyers all over the UK.

PFI/PPP: In the UK, the Private Finance Initiative (PFI), a part of the Public Private Partnerships (PPP), is an important source of work. The objective of PFI is to introduce private funding and management into areas that were previously the domain of government, for example, the building and operation of hospitals. Over the last 15 years, the PFI/PPP sector has grown; once the preserve of City firms, lawyers from all over the country are getting involved.

type of work

Projects vary from oil and gas pipelines in far flung places to PFI prison facilities in Liverpool. The exact nature of the legal work depends on the type, size and location of the project and the firm's clients. Some consistently act for the project company – usually a special purpose company established to build, own and operate, say, a power station. Often the project company is a joint venture between a number of project sponsors who contribute equity to part-fund the project. Project sponsors could include the manufacturer of the gas turbines to be installed in the power station, the construction company that will erect the plant, and the power company that will buy the electricity produced. The company could also be partially owned by a government body or banks.

Other firms act for the project promoter – the organisation that commissions the project. It could be an NHS Trust that wants a new hospital or a foreign government that thinks a privately financed motorway would be a great idea. Then there are the firms that act purely on the finance side for banks, guarantors, export credit agencies, governments, and international funding agencies. Other categories of client include the contractors, operators, and so on. Each party requires its own legal representation.

Malcolm Austwick, a partner in Beachcroft Wansbroughs, explained just how long projects could go on for. After the initial tender process, in which bids are built up over a couple of years, the successful bidder is selected to manage the project. It then has to secure the finance, obtain the necessary planning permission and agree construction, service and employment contracts. Lawyers advising on any of these contracts must understand the big picture. They have to see how changing one contractual term will have a knock-on effect throughout the entire transaction. Only then does the physical construction phase begin.

"Because they're so complicated," says Malcolm, *"the only thing to do is to put in deadlines for the different stages. It's a real challenge putting together something so complicated."* There were few precedents in the early years, but now PFI/PPP is so widespread that many more boilerplate contracts are employed by the lawyers. Every project is unique, though.

skills needed

…prepared to travel/live overseas (international work)… all-round commercial awareness… patience… tact and diplomacy… strong client skills… good on contract and tort… good drafting… comfortable with long and complex documents… stamina…

If you enjoy the challenge of creating a scheme and figuring out all its possibilities and pitfalls, you're reading the right section of this book.

The ability to work well with a team of people, be they your own colleagues and clients or other lawyers and professionals, funders or subcontractors, is crucial. As projects go on for years, you need to build on-going relationships with all those involved in the matter.

career options

Nearly all international projects are governed (to varying degrees) by English or New York law, so experience in this field is internationally marketable. American law firms, in particular, are recruiting experienced English lawyers, which has forced up salaries to make international projects work one of the highest paid specialisms. Those who want to become solicitor advocates will find the opportunities are there; some will even find a niche in international arbitration.

The construction industry will, like any other, present opportunities for lawyers to work in-house. The role may be as a general corporate counsel or more specific as a litigator. Companies like Amec, Balfour Beatty, Sir Robert McAlpine and Carillion all have their own legal teams. Some lawyers join clients in a project management role.

LEADING FIRMS FROM CHAMBERS UK GUIDE 2002-2003

PROJECTS — LONDON
1. Allen & Overy
2. Clifford Chance
   Linklaters
3. Norton Rose
   Shearman & Sterling
4. Denton Wilde Sapte
   Freshfields Bruckhaus Deringer
5. Lovells
   Milbank, Tweed, Hadley & McCloy
   Slaughter and May
   White & Case
6. Ashurst Morris Crisp
   Baker & McKenzie
   CMS Cameron McKenna
   Herbert Smith
   Masons
   Simmons & Simmons

PFI — LONDON
1. Allen & Overy
   Clifford Chance
   Linklaters
2. Ashurst Morris Crisp
   Freshfields Bruckhaus Deringer
3. CMS Cameron McKenna
   Herbert Smith
   Lovells
4. Denton Wilde Sapte
   Masons
   Norton Rose
5. Berwin Leighton Paisner
   Simmons & Simmons
6. DLA
   Mayer, Brown, Rowe & Maw
   Slaughter and May
   Theodore Goddard
   Trowers & Hamlins

PROJECTS/PFI — THE SOUTH & WALES
1. Bevan Ashford Bristol
2. Burges Salmon Bristol
   Eversheds Cardiff
3. Masons Bristol
   Morgan Cole Cardiff

PROJECTS/PFI — MIDLANDS & EAST ANGLIA
1. Eversheds Nottingham
   Pinsent Curtis Biddle Birmingham
   Wragge & Co Birmingham
2. DLA Birmingham
   Mills & Reeve Cambridge

PROJECTS/PFI — THE NORTH
1. Addleshaw Booth & Co Leeds, Manchester
   Pinsent Curtis Biddle Leeds
2. Dickinson Dees Newcastle upon Tyne
3. DLA Leeds, Manchester
   Eversheds Leeds, Manchester
   Masons Leeds, Manchester
4. Nabarro Nathanson Sheffield

CONSTRUCTION
LONDON

1. Masons
2. CMS Cameron McKenna
   Shadbolt & Co
3. Berwin Leighton Paisner
   Fenwick Elliott
   Linklaters
   Mayer, Brown, Rowe & Maw
4. Allen & Overy
   Clifford Chance
   Freshfields Bruckhaus Deringer
   Herbert Smith
   Lovells
   Norton Rose
   Taylor Wessing
5. Ashurst Morris Crisp
   Denton Wilde Sapte
   Hammond Suddards Edge
   Kennedys
   Macfarlanes
   Nicholson Graham & Jones
   SJ Berwin
   Trowers & Hamlins
   Winward Fearon
6. Baker & McKenzie
   Beale and Company
   Berrymans Lace Mawer
   Campbell Hooper
   Davies Arnold Cooper
   Glovers
   Simmons & Simmons

CONSTRUCTION
THE SOUTH

1. Shadbolt & Co Reigate
2. Blake Lapthorn Portsmouth
   Cripps Harries Hall Tunbridge Wells

CONSTRUCTION
THAMES VALLEY

1. Clarks Reading
   Linnells Oxford
   Morgan Cole Oxford, Reading
6. Corbett & Co Teddington

CONSTRUCTION
SOUTH WEST

1. Masons Bristol
2. Bevan Ashford Bristol, Exeter
3. Beachcroft Wansbroughs Bristol
   Burges Salmon Bristol
4. Laytons Bristol
   Osborne Clarke Bristol
5. Bond Pearce Plymouth
   Veale Wasbrough Bristol

CONSTRUCTION
WALES

1. Eversheds Cardiff
   Hugh James Cardiff
   Morgan Cole Cardiff, Swansea

CONSTRUCTION
MIDLANDS

1. Wragge & Co Birmingham
2. Hammond Suddards Edge Birmingham
3. Gateley Wareing Birmingham
4. DLA Birmingham
   freethcartwright Nottingham
   Pinsent Curtis Biddle Birmingham
5. Browne Jacobson Nottingham
   Eversheds Birmingham, Nottingham
   Lee Crowder Birmingham
   Shoosmiths Northampton

CONSTRUCTION
EAST ANGLIA

1. Eversheds Cambridge, Ipswich, Norwich
   Mills & Reeve Cambridge
2. Hewitson Becke + Shaw Cambridge
   Greenwoods Peterborough

CONSTRUCTION
NORTH WEST

1. Masons Manchester
2. Hammond Suddards Edge Manchester
3. Mace & Jones Liverpool
4. Addleshaw Booth & Co Manchester
   DLA Liverpool, Manchester
   Halliwell Landau Manchester
   Hill Dickinson Liverpool
6. Elliotts Manchester
   Pannone & Partners Manchester

CONSTRUCTION
YORKSHIRE

1. Addleshaw Booth & Co Leeds
   Hammond Suddards Edge Leeds
2. Masons Leeds
3. DLA Leeds, Sheffield
4. Walker Morris Leeds
5. Eversheds Leeds
   Irwin Mitchell Leeds
   Nabarro Nathanson Sheffield
   Pinsent Curtis Biddle Leeds

CONSTRUCTION
NORTH EAST

1. Dickinson Dees Newcastle upon Tyne
   Eversheds Newcastle upon Tyne
   Watson Burton Newcastle upon Tyne

corporate

Corporate transactions are the lifeblood of commercial firms and experienced corporate lawyers are among the highest paid in the profession, earning seven-figure salaries in some instances.

type of work

Large City firms act for companies listed on stock exchanges, while smaller City and regional firms tend to advise leading regional private companies and a handful of the FTSE 250.

Mergers and acquisitions (M&A) and corporate restructurings are the core business and are interlinked with finance (banking and capital markets work), hence the umbrella term 'corporate finance'. Companies fund their acquisitions by a variety of means. They may restructure, disposing of certain assets not considered essential to their core business. If they are privately held, they may raise finance by 'going public' – offering shares to the public and institutional investors on any of the public stock exchanges. If they are already public companies, they may make a rights issue (offer of new shares). They may also raise money via debt, eg loans from the market (bonds) or from banks or other financial institutions. A complex, high-value deal may need to be financed by a combination of these methods.

Since the mid-80s private equity or venture capital has been a focus. At the top end of the work is the 'buyout', which might be as straightforward as the present management of a company raising capital to take control (an MBO). As the management wouldn't normally have the cash for the deal, the majority comes from venture capital companies like CVC, Cinven or Candover and/or banks. Sometimes the venture capital company will itself pinpoint the deal and take a controlling interest in the target company. At the other end of the scale are the 'development capital' deals where the management of a company might seek between, say, £250,000 and £20 million to start up or expand a company. Again, there are specialist funders: eg. 3i, Amadeus and JPMorgan Partners.

Irrespective of the type of corporate deal, there are three key phases to the work: negotiating and drafting the agreements, arranging the financing, and carrying out 'due diligence'. A private company sale commonly takes about three months to complete. Whereas a trainee can expect to be involved in one or two deals at a time, newly qualifieds can expect to be working on several at once. Due diligence is a time-consuming but necessary task to ensure the accuracy of information passed from the target to the bidder or from the company raising capital to the funder. If a target claims to be the largest baked beans canner in the country, then due diligence will reveal whether or not this is true and whether or not there is outstanding litigation or any other factors that could harm profitability after a takeover or buyout.

Private companies have few shareholders (owners), whereas stock exchange-listed companies can have millions. This makes the latter vulnerable to hostile takeover bids from rival companies seeking a controlling stake. To help public companies combat this threat, the City developed a detailed takeover code to govern both friendly and hostile M&A activity. Although voluntary, the code is universally followed. It sets a strict timetable for companies to make bids and respond to potential bidders and has guidelines for the treatment of shareholders. Lawyers need to know this code inside out.

a day in the life...

Michelle Thomas is a partner in Evershed's Cardiff office. She used to work at a magic circle firm and is able to contrast the types of deals the different firms handle. "*If you work outside the City you must be able to handle all types of transactions. In a large City firm you* might become very specialised, for example in IPOs or public takeovers. In a regional firm you might work on an IPO one day, be acting for the target of a public takeover the next and handle a private acquisition the next." If you work in a City megafirm a high proportion of the work will have an international flavour. If you want international work in the regions, judge a firm by its overseas offices, associations and client base.

There are other key differences between firms, most notably, hours and the increased chances of a junior lawyer getting close to the front-line action. The largest City firms handle the biggest transactions so, naturally, a trainee or junior assistant at one of these firms will not carry a huge amount of responsibility. As Michelle says, *"There will always be an element of tedium on any job. If you are a trainee working on a £2 billion deal, the reality is that you are not going to get much more responsibility than some research and managing a data room."* Essential yet administrative tasks on huge deals will hopefully be interspersed with greater responsibility on smaller transactions. Andrew Jolly, an assistant at Slaughter and May, feels that even as a very junior lawyer *"You're presented with a problem that you have to solve, either working within a team or working on your own. There's a good mix of independence and working with others."*

Team spirit is essential . Working three 20-hour days in a row may be rare but it does happen. Much has been said about killer hours in corporate, about 'all-nighters' and the loss of life and love in the quest for career progression. It's true that corporate departments tend to work the longest hours, but it's equally true that market conditions affect the time spent at work. Simon Beddow, a partner at Ashurst Morris Crisp, wonders if the hours are a little overstated. *"It's a fact of modern life that if you want to get on you have to put in the effort. The real strain comes when you are about 5-6 years PQE and you are really productive as lead fee earner behind a partner on two or three deals at any one time."*

skills needed...

...not for the faint-hearted... stamina… a touch of the glory-seeker…handling demanding and intelligent clients… comfortable with the several-zero price tag… good presentation skills... think on your feet... decisiveness... confidence… tact and clear communication skills... eye for detail... a good all-rounder...

Most corporate lawyers accept that there's a bit of brash ego-led behaviour around, but maybe that's inevitable when you've got highly motivated lawyers acting for equally motivated clients on big deals under tight deadlines. There is an element of showmanship and drama involved. Simon says, *"As the lawyer, you try and get everything organised in advance but there are always points at issue between the parties until the last moment. It may come down to a crunch meeting when it's all about who blinks first. When that's happened, the lawyer can document it, but until you know where everything will land, you can't finalise the deal."*

Some specialist lawyers contend that corporate lawyers' job's are all about doing deals and have very little to do with pure law. As a corporate lawyer you do have to be a jack of all trades. Merger control, IP/IT, employment, tax, etc. all need to be understood and the basics communicated to the client. OK, the corporate lawyer will call upon the skills of specialists, but they need to know when to do that.

Andrew highlighted certain essential skills: practical things and good old-fashioned common sense. *"You must have the ability to see through the rubbish and pick out important bits of information from a lot of documentation. Knowing which bits to focus on requires an analytical mind."* He certainly thinks that *"drafting skills are underrated – it's so important that what you draft is clear and understandable."* Lastly, Andrew thinks that *"general people skills – getting on with others,"* are vital. You'll spend a lot of time in meetings, much of it thrashing out points of agreement, but also making small talk with your client.

Those who excel in corporate work seem to thrive in pressured situations. Simon told us, *"You have to keep driving yourself when sometimes all you want to do is stop."* Deadlines are almost always genuine – eg. the end of an accounting year – and sometimes this means there aren't enough hours in a day. If you're going to have a problem with the working pattern, you should choose another area of law.

career options

Just a couple of years ago firms were keen to retain corporate lawyers that salaries rocketed. The market is considerably flatter in 2002 but activity will increase again perhaps with a new twist or flavour of deal.

Work in regional firms is usually of lower value, but can still be cross-border. The reward for working in a large commercial department of a smaller firm (both in the regions and in London) is involvement in clients' affairs at an earlier stage. Larger regional firms also provide the opportunity, like their City counterparts, for qualified lawyers to be seconded to major clients. A sound grounding in corporate finance makes an excellent springboard for working in industry. Many lawyers move in-house to major companies, tempted by decent hours and salaries.

Some lawyers join the banking world, either as an in-house lawyer or as a corporate finance exec or analyst. Those who have made the transition from lawyer to client seem to enjoy the dynamic pace of life and are glad to have shed the advisory role. Such moves generally occur early on, but high-profile moves of senior partners to investment banks do happen. Company secretarial positions suit senior lawyers with a taste for variety and responsibility. Our best advice to budding corporate lawyers is to keep up to date by making the *FT* your friend. You don't need to study it religiously, just make sure you know what the big stories are and have begun to understand the workings of corporate Britain. To find out more about the strengths of the different corporate law practices, read *Chambers UK* and *Chambers Global*.

LEADING FIRMS FROM CHAMBERS UK GUIDE 2002-2003

CORPORATE — THE SOUTH

[1] **Blake Lapthorn** Fareham, Ports, Soton
Bond Pearce Southampton
[2] **Shadbolt & Co** Reigate
Stevens & Bolton Guildford
[3] **asb law** Crawley
Brachers Maidstone
Clyde & Co Guildford
Cripps Harries Hall Tunbridge Wells
Lester Aldridge Bournemouth, Soton
Mundays Cobham
Paris Smith & Randall Southampton
Rawlison Butler Crawley
Thomas Eggar Chichester, Horsham, Reigate, Worthing
[4] **DMH** Brighton, Crawley
Shoosmiths Fareham
Thomson Snell & Passmore Tunbridge Wells
[5] **Coffin Mew & Clover** Southampton

CORPORATE — SOUTH WEST

[1] **Burges Salmon** Bristol
Osborne Clarke Bristol
[2] **Bevan Ashford** Bristol, Exeter
Bond Pearce Exeter, Plymouth
TLT Solicitors Bristol
[3] **Foot Anstey Sargent** Exeter, Plymouth
Michelmores Exeter
[4] **BPE** Cheltenham
Charles Russell Cheltenham
Clark Holt Swindon
Laytons Bristol
Lyons Davidson Bristol
Stephens & Scown Exeter, St Austell, Truro
Veale Wasbrough Bristol

CORPORATE — THAMES VALLEY

[1] **Osborne Clarke** Reading
[2] **Manches** Oxford
[3] **Brobeck Hale and Dorr** Oxford
Clarks Reading
Kimbells Milton Keynes
Nabarro Nathanson Reading
Pitmans Reading
Shoosmiths Reading

CORPORATE — EAST ANGLIA

[1] **Eversheds** Norwich
Mills & Reeve Cambridge, Norwich
[2] **Hewitson Becke + Shaw** Cambridge
Taylor Vinters Cambridge
Taylor Wessing Cambridge
[3] **Birketts** Ipswich
Prettys Ipswich
[4] **Greene & Greene** Bury St Edmunds
Greenwoods Peterborough

SPECIALIST PRACTICE AREAS — CORPORATE

CORPORATE: LARGER DEALS
LONDON

1. Freshfields Bruckhaus Deringer
   Linklaters
   Slaughter and May
2. Allen & Overy
   Clifford Chance
   Herbert Smith
3. Ashurst Morris Crisp
4. Lovells
   Macfarlanes
   Norton Rose
5. Simmons & Simmons

CORPORATE
WEST MIDLANDS

1. Wragge & Co Birmingham
2. Eversheds Birmingham
3. Hammond Suddards Edge B'ham
   Pinsent Curtis Biddle Birmingham
4. DLA Birmingham
   Gateley Wareing Birmingham
   Lee Crowder Birmingham
   Martineau Johnson Birmingham

CORPORATE
EAST MIDLANDS

1. Browne Jacobson Nottingham
   Eversheds Nottingham
2. Edwards Geldard Derby, Nottingham
   freethcartwright Nottingham
   Gateley Wareing Leicester, Nottingham
   Howes Percival Northampton
   Shoosmiths Northampton, Nottingham
3. Harvey Ingram Owston Leicester
   Hewitson Becke + Shaw Northampton

CORPORATE
NORTH EAST

1. Dickinson Dees Newcastle, Stockton
2. Ward Hadaway Newcastle upon Tyne
3. Eversheds Newcastle upon Tyne
4. Robert Muckle Newcastle upon Tyne
5. Watson Burton Newcastle upon Tyne

CORPORATE: MEDIUM DEALS
LONDON

1. CMS Cameron McKenna
   Travers Smith Braithwaite
2. Gouldens
   Mayer, Brown, Rowe & Maw
   SJ Berwin
   Weil, Gotshal & Manges
3. Baker & McKenzie
   Denton Wilde Sapte
4. Berwin Leighton Paisner
   Hammond Suddards Edge
   Taylor Wessing
   Theodore Goddard
5. Dechert
   DLA
   Eversheds
   Nabarro Nathanson
   Olswang
   Osborne Clarke
   Pinsent Curtis Biddle

CORPORATE
WALES

1. Morgan Cole Cardiff
2. Berry Smith Cardiff
   Edwards Geldard Cardiff
   Eversheds Cardiff
   M and A Solicitors Cardiff

CORPORATE
NORTH WEST

1. Addleshaw Booth & Co Manchester
   Eversheds Manchester
2. DLA Liverpool, Manchester
3. Halliwell Landau Manchester
4. Brabners Chaffe Street L'pool, Man
   Hammond Suddards Edge Man
5. Cobbetts Manchester
   DWF Liverpool, Manchester
   Pannone & Partners Manchester
   Kuit Steinart Levy Manchester
   Wacks Caller Manchester

CORPORATE: SMALLER DEALS
LONDON

1. Bird & Bird
   Memery Crystal
   Stephenson Harwood
2. DJ Freeman
   Field Fisher Waterhouse
   Lawrence Graham
   Reed Smith Warner Cranston
   Richards Butler
3. Harbottle & Lewis
   Lewis Silkin
   Nicholson Graham & Jones
4. Fox Williams
   Hobson Audley
   Howard Kennedy
   Marriott Harrison
5. Beachcroft Wansbroughs
   Charles Russell
   Coudert Brothers
   Manches
   Middleton Potts
   Steptoe & Johnson LLP
   Watson, Farley & Williams
   Wedlake Bell

CORPORATE
YORKSHIRE

1. Addleshaw Booth & Co Leeds
2. Eversheds Leeds
   Hammond Suddards Edge Leeds
3. DLA Leeds, Sheffield
4. Pinsent Curtis Biddle Leeds
   Walker Morris Leeds
5. Lupton Fawcett Leeds
   Rollits Hull, York
6. Andrew M Jackson Hull
   Cobbetts Leeds
   Gosschalks Hull
   Irwin Mitchell Leeds, Sheffield

crime

Forget gripping courtroom dramas in which cases are neatly wrapped up in an hour (including commercial breaks). What you'll be handling is real life.

Criminal lawyers act for defendants in Magistrates' Courts, Crown Courts and Courts Martial. However serious the charge, the basic process is the same; the difference is in the detail. Lesser offences are dealt with in the Magistrates' Courts where defendants are usually represented by solicitors. More serious cases are tried in the Crown Courts, where most clients still prefer to use a barrister. In addition to criminal law and procedure, lawyers need to be familiar with mental health, immigration and extradition issues, particularly in criminal fraud.

type of work

general crime: Most criminal lawyers live on a diet of 'everyday crime', giving plenty of opportunities for advocacy. Expect to visit police stations, prisons and Magistrates' Courts on a daily basis. Vanessa Lloyd of London firm Lewis Nedas told us about the early days of her career: "*I was quite often sent to prisons for instructions. I also got to sift through evidence, listen to tapes of interviews and visit crime scenes. You're dealing with clients face-to-face from the beginning; you're not just paper shuffling from behind your desk.*" Because the work is date-driven, cases have a quick turnover. Even murders are usually dealt with in under a year. Lawyers see the fruits of their labours relatively quickly, particularly those accredited to work as Duty Solicitors in the Magistrates' Courts.

The biggest issue facing criminal defence lawyers is the block contracting of criminal legal services. In 2001 the Legal Aid Board was replaced by the Legal Services Commission, which introduced a franchise system limiting the number of firms that handle publicly funded criminal defence. It's caused unease in the profession with concerns that everything will be done with an eye to costs, so reducing the system to a conveyor belt.

So-called 'top end' criminal firms like Burton Copeland and Kingsley Napley get a fair amount of private criminal work, usually through recommendations from existing clients or commercial law firms without a crime capability. Even some high street firms get a small amount of this private work. However, now that the means test for criminal legal aid has been removed, defendants no longer have to prove that they are poor enough. As Vanessa says, "*Now even a millionaire will qualify for 'legal aid'*," and so private client work in this field is increasingly rare.

These worries are compounded by the ongoing debate over trial mode. The government is keen to push ahead with plans to make a number of hybrid offences (triable by a magistrate or a jury at the defendant's discretion) 'summary offences', ie tried **only** in the Magistrates' Court. Civil liberties arguments aside, trials in the Magistrates' Court, which are without juries, will undoubtedly save on costs.

The Human Rights Act has impacted too. Stephen Gentle, a partner at Kingsley Napley, thinks it's made "*a cultural difference – people are more clued up and conscious of fairness in proceedings and evidence generally.*" Specific articles dealing with the right to privacy, the right to a fair trial and freedom of expression seem the most obviously applicable, but the full effects of the HRA are still unclear. It's an interesting time to become a criminal lawyer.

criminal fraud: Only firms on the Legal Services Commission's Serious Fraud panel may undertake this work. Stephen distinguishes it from general crime work: "*95% of all criminal trials are in the Magistrates' Court, but we only do cases in the Crown Courts, ie the other 5%. There are a large number of firms on the Serious Fraud Panel but there's only about four to five firms in London that do the really big fraud cases.*"

There's a whole other set of skills and knowledge you need to acquire. *"You actually need to learn about people's businesses in order to defend them properly. You don't need to know how an armed robber spends his day to be able to defend him."* As a result, *"it can be a much more intellectual exercise than blood and guts crime."*

a day in the life...

Criminal lawyers lead hectic lives. You might get into the office at 8.30am, having already spent some of the night at a police station. At 9.30am it's off to the Magistrates' Court for procedural and remand hearings or a plea in mitigation. After lunch on the hoof, you might be interviewing clients and conferring with counsel. There is still paperwork to deal with and you could be back in the police station tonight. Home at last but you'll have to spend some of your free time preparing for the next day in court.

While trainees used to be thrown in at the deep end, the Law Society has now introduced an accreditation process. Until accredited, they are no longer able to attend police station interviews by themselves, nor are they able to make Magistrates' Court appearances. Vanessa explained the police station accreditation process: *"You start off by going to watch a solicitor do a number of interviews, then a solicitor will watch you do it on your own. There are written and oral tests at the end of this. All up, it takes about a year to become accredited, during which time you can build up a portfolio of police station work."*

skills needed...

....an eye for detail... sharp and resolute on your feet... excellent people skills... empathy... good organisational and IT skills... 100% commitment... willing to work without huge financial reward....

Dealing with criminal clients can be challenging: they may come from deprived backgrounds with drink, drug and/or psychiatric problems. Vanessa says, *"This doesn't necessarily make them difficult to deal with – it just means you must be aware of any problems they have. Most clients appreciate that you're there to help them."* Michael Mackey, a partner at Burton Copeland in Manchester, explains, *"The relationship between a criminal lawyer and their clients is more dependent on fundamental trust than, say, for commercial or conveyancing clients. We deal with their liberty."* As Stephen says, *"For most clients, their predicament will be the worst thing that's ever happened to them... A bad result could mean 10 years away from their family, not watching their kids grow up."* There's a real camaraderie amongst criminal solicitors as they're always meeting peers in police stations and courts. Added to this, criminal lawyers are not up against each other; they're facing a 'common enemy', as it were, in the CPS.

Michael told us how important it is to be enthusiastic about your work as clients will be relying heavily on you for *"something which is very, very important to them."* You also have to be direct. If you mislead the client (especially if you are over-optimistic about their prospects) this leads to real problems for them... and you. Stephen agrees that you can't be frightened of giving unwelcome advice: *"If you tell a client they've got a good chance but you've read the case and they don't, they're not going to thank you when they get five years."*

In handling casework, there's also a certain element of detective work. When you speak with your client and sift through the evidence, you'll be looking for things the police have missed. In addition to your clients and the police, depending on the case, you'll be dealing with a number of expert witnesses – medical, forensic, ballistics, blood... You have to be a bit savvy and very questioning. If you're known for your gullibility, are you looking at the right career?

career options

If you're seeking a good criminal practice look at our parent publication, *Chambers UK*, or alternatively ask a Citizens Advice Bureau or your local Law Society which firms specialise in crime.

Training contracts at specialist criminal firms offering high-profile work are rare, but at general criminal firms there may be more openings. Under the new franchise system the idea is to take on as many cases as possible and so firms now need the personnel to bring in and handle the work. Some lawyers actively promote the idea of trying paralegal work for a while or outdoor clerking for solicitors or barristers. Additionally, work in the voluntary sector is a practical way of gaining a realistic view of people and real life. As Stephen says, *"You can't be starry-eyed when you start this job or you'll get your hands burnt very quickly."* The downside is the salary. As Vanessa says, *"Friends who qualified at the same time as me are now earning three times as much in the City, but if you want this job you're not looking to be a City solicitor!"* Michael adds, *"It's very demanding, very time-consuming and not as well paid, but I couldn't contemplate doing anything else."*

Good news: The Crown Prosecution Service has declared its intention to start recruiting trainees as well as qualified solicitors.

LEADING FIRMS FROM CHAMBERS UK GUIDE 2002-2003

CRIME
MIDLANDS

1. **Cartwright King** Nottingham
   Fletchers Nottingham
   The Johnson Partnership Nottingham
   The Smith Partnership Derby
2. **Glaisyers** Birmingham
   Nelsons Nottingham
   Varley Hadley Siddall Nottingham
3. **Banners Jones Middleton** Chesterfield
   Barrie Ward & Julian Griffiths Nottingham
   Bate Edmond Snape Coventry
   Bradley & Clarke Chesterfield
   Brethertons Rugby
   Elliot Mather Chesterfield
   Jonas Roy Bloom Birmingham
   Kieran Clarke Solicitors Chesterfield
   Parker & Grego Birmingham
   Purcell Parker Birmingham
   Tyndallwoods Birmingham
   Woodford-Robinson Northampton

CRIME
NORTH WEST

1. **Betesh Fox & Co** Manchester
   Burton Copeland Liverpool, Manchester
   Jones Maidment Wilson Manchester
   Maidments Manchester
   Tuckers Manchester
2. **Brian Koffman & Co** Manchester
   Cunninghams Manchester
   Draycott Browne Manchester
   Forbes Blackburn
   RM Broudie & Co Liverpool
3. **Cobleys** Salford
   Farleys Blackburn
   Garstangs Bolton
   Jackson & Canter Liverpool
   Kristina Harrison Solicitors Salford
   Russell & Russell Bolton
   The Berkson Globe Partnership Liverpool

CRIME
NORTH EAST

1. **David Gray Solicitors** Newcastle upon Tyne
   Grahame Stowe, Bateson Leeds
   Henry Hyams Leeds
   Irwin Mitchell Sheffield
   Sugaré & Co Leeds
2. **Howells** Sheffield
   Levi & Co Leeds
   The Max Gold Partnership Hull
   Williamsons Solicitors Hull

CRIME
EAST ANGLIA

1. **Belmores** Norwich
   Overbury Steward Eaton & Woolsey Norwich
   TMK Solicitors Southend-on-Sea
2. **Copleys** Huntingdon
   David Charnley & Co Romford
   Gepp & Sons Chelmsford
   Hatch Brenner Norwich
   Hunt & Coombs Peterborough
   Lucas & Wyllys Great Yarmouth
   Thanki Novy Taube Harlow

SPECIALIST PRACTICE AREAS — CRIME

CRIME
LONDON

1. Bindman & Partners
   Birnberg Peirce & Partners
   Edward Fail Bradshaw & Waterson
   Kingsley Napley
   Saunders & Co
   Taylor Nichol
2. Edwards Duthie
   Hallinan, Blackburn, Gittings & Nott
   Hickman & Rose
   Hodge Jones & Allen
   Powell Spencer & Partners
   Russell Jones & Walker
   Simons Muirhead & Burton
   Thanki Novy Taube
3. Andrew Keenan & Co
   Fisher Meredith
   Henry Milner & Co
   McCormacks
   Reynolds Dawson
   Russell-Cooke
   Tuckers
   TV Edwards
   Venters Solicitors
   Victor Lissack & Roscoe
   Whitelock & Storr
4. Burton Copeland
   Christian Fisher Khan
   Claude Hornby & Cox
   Dundons
   Iliffes Booth Bennett (IBB) Uxbridge
   Joy Merriam & Co
   Stokoe Partnership

CRIME
SOUTH WEST

1. Bobbetts Mackan Bristol
   Douglas & Partners Bristol
2. Nunn Rickard Solicitor Advocates Exeter
   Sansbury Campbell Bristol
   St James Solicitors Exeter
   Stones Exeter
3. Kelcey & Hall Bristol
   Wolferstans Plymouth

CRIME
WALES

1. Huttons Cardiff
   Martyn Prowel Solicitors Cardiff
2. Colin Jones Barry
   Gamlins Rhyl
   Graham Evans & Partners Swansea
   Robertsons Cardiff
   Spiro Grech & Harding-Roberts Solicitors Cardiff

FRAUD: CRIMINAL
LONDON

1. Burton Copeland
   Kingsley Napley
   Peters & Peters
2. Dechert
   Irwin Mitchell
3. Russell Jones & Walker
   Simons Muirhead & Burton
4. Claude Hornby & Cox
   Corker Binning Solicitors
   Garstangs
   Victor Lissack & Roscoe

FRAUD: CRIMINAL
SOUTH & SOUTH WEST

1. Bobbetts Mackan Bristol
2. Blake Lapthorn Fareham
   DMH Brighton
   Hodkinsons Locks Heath

FRAUD: CRIMINAL
WALES

1. Martyn Prowel Solicitors Cardiff
2. Huttons Cardiff
   Roy Morgan & Co Cardiff

FRAUD: CRIMINAL
MIDLANDS

1. Cartwright King Nottingham
   Nelsons Nottingham
2. Glaisyers Birmingham
3. Hammond Suddards Edge Birmingham
   Varley Hadley Siddall Nottingham

FRAUD: CRIMINAL
THE NORTH

1. Cooper Kenyon Burrows Manchester
2. Betesh Fox & Co Manchester
   DLA Manchester
   Irwin Mitchell Sheffield
   Pannone & Partners Manchester
3. Garstangs Bolton
4. Burton Copeland Manchester
   Russell Jones & Walker Manchester

employment law

Are you fascinated by human nature, curious about the forces at play in employer/employee relations and eager to be involved in cases provoking legislative and social changes affecting everyone who has ever had a job? Then think about employment law.

Specialist employment teams are normally divided along partisan lines. Commercial firms (corporate client base and higher fees) work for employers and highly paid senior executives. These departments are often combined with or allied to pensions law teams. The 'right on' firms act mainly for trade union clients and other individuals. Some have allied practices in claimant personal injury. Almost every high street practice, Citizens Advice Bureau and law centre purports to give employment advice to individuals. In fact, the practice area is now so law-intensive that even full-time specialists have a hard time keeping up with the almost weekly changes from the European and domestic courts.

type of work

The work of an employment lawyer is a rich and varied mix of advisory, pre-emptive, contractual and litigious work. Contentious matters are heard in employment tribunals, County Courts or the High Court. Some employment cases, which start in an employment tribunal, become test cases appealed to the higher courts and a few may even reach the Court of Appeal, House of Lords or even the European Court of Justice. In tribunals, employees ('applicants') may claim for redundancy pay, unfair dismissal, breach of contract, and sex, race and disability discrimination against their employers ('respondents'). Claims for breach of contract may also be made in the High Court or County Courts depending on the value of the claim. In January 2001, Julie Bower, a former City analyst won almost £1.5 million in a breach of contract case after the size of her bonus payment in 1998 was found to be derisory when compared to those earned by male colleagues and other aspects of her working environment were deemed to have been discriminatory.

Although the awards in most cases (save discrimination) will be capped at £53,000, the high value of some awards makes it easy to see why individuals are increasingly willing to bring claims and why employers defend them. Many firms (especially those outside the City) prefer their employment lawyers to handle most of their own advocacy and consequently this is one area of the law where the Ally McBeal experience is not a million miles from the truth. It's not a bad area for those who may have once thought about becoming a barrister.

The Government intends to widen the field in terms of discrimination. By 2005 we are likely to see anti-age discrimination laws, and legislation to prevent discrimination on the grounds of religion may come in even sooner. Given their experiences following the creation of laws against sex, race and disability discrimination, employment lawyers predict a wave of new claims from applicants following the introduction of these new laws. The employment lawyers we spoke to also reported an increase in work following recent legal requirements for workforce consultation prior to corporate disposals and large-scale redundancies. All of this is great news for budding employment lawyers.

Although acting for employees doesn't always put a lawyer on the side of the angels, those acting for trade unions and their members are often ideologically motivated. A lawyer may find himself representing thousands of union members in their campaigns to change working practices or the law on, say, pension rights for part-time workers. Employment law is, by its nature, highly politicised, regulating, as it does, the relationship between workers and employers. Dr John McMullen, the national head of employment law at Pinsent Curtis Biddle, which acts mainly for employers, emphasises this. "*It's one of the few subjects that can combine topical issues of politics, industrial relations and people alongside the intellectual disciplines studied at university.*"

Employment lawyers see themselves as somewhat different from corporate lawyers although they find themselves working closely with them on transactions, with employment advice increasingly becoming a vital ingredient in the deal. The hours are usually not as relentless as those experienced in the corporate departments though. Chris Goodwill, an employment partner at Clifford Chance, says, "*I'm glad you asked me and not my wife. The hours are absolutely fine and I've never missed a play or a film or a dinner or a Leeds match because of work. Can I uncross my fingers now?*" More seriously, he points out, "*The worst thing about an employment lawyer's hours is not so much the number of them, but the unpredictability of when they might have to be put in.*"

a day in the life of...

8.45am: Arrive at employment tribunal to greet white-faced HR director and head of IT from important corporate client. Client is defending an unfair dismissal claim brought by ex-employee sacked for downloading v. dodgy porn at work. Applicant is using somewhat teenage argument that 'everyone else was doing it', but has not managed to rally any colleagues in support of this.

10am: Explain to clients that the hearing will be relatively informal and the morning will be spent reading out their witness statements to the tribunal panel (which is supposed to be neutral – like Switzerland). Witnesses perform fabulously under my guidance and can't help thinking their performance is the result of own superb preparation of case.

1.30pm: After behaving like contortionists, tribunal panel stop bending over backwards to be helpful towards hapless (and unrepresented) ex-employee. He has no supporting witnesses and no way of proving his claim (of not being a sleazy, porn-obsessed time-waster). Suppress urge to do one-person Mexican wave as tribunal finds for my client.

2.30pm: Back in office. Scoff sandwich at desk (celebratory lunch with victorious client arranged for next week) and turn attention to phone messages. Return call to a client whose staff have got themselves into what is technically termed 'an intriguing pickle'. Following an office quiz night in a local bar, two teams had gone onto a club where some pretty steamy and v. public antics had ensued between drunk female employee and two male members of staff. Worried onlookers have reported the events. Employer now concerned that the participants may complain of sexual harassment (though who was harrassing who?). Consider whether events could be deemed to have taken place in the course employment and, if so, whether they amount to sexual harassment. Client calls back to say the participants are shame faced and can't remember much about it. Conclude it should be seen as high spirits out of work and suggest no disciplinary action be taken.

5pm: Call rather rambunctious partner in corporate department with advice on how TUPE regulations affect his client's acquisition of a rival's business. Persuade him that buyer can't just discontinue the seller's rather generous maternity scheme because "the place for women is at home with the babies." Put call on speakerphone so all nearby colleagues can appreciate just how impossible and mad (and loud) he is. Conclude that it is as much my dulcet tones as it is the soundness of advice that wins him over. Prepare memo summarising advice for the client.

7pm: Catch homeward bound train with good intention of perusing case updates...

skills needed

...being a people person... sensitivity and calmness... sense of humour... versatility... excellent communication and negotiation skills... a talent for advocacy... practicality... an ability to quickly assimilate changes in strategy and advice... knowing when to be tough... detailed knowledge of relevant law...

John points out, "*The law is so fast-moving that continuous education and development is vital for the employment law practitioner. Added to this, with dimensions of European law, discrimination, human rights, strikes and industrial action and dismissal disputes, no day is boring.*" Hilary O'Connor, a partner at SJ Berwin, agrees, "*A good memory is essential. However, in some cases the legal solution to a problem is not the cheapest or quickest solution for the client, so you need good business judgement and good instincts to know which one to choose. It is very people-oriented, so patience, tact, empathy and the ability to inspire confidence is essential.*" But it's not all about being warm and cuddly. Chris thinks that you have to be versatile in your approach to the work. "*An employment lawyer needs to be one part academic, one part agony aunt and one part hit man!*"

career options

Employment law is now one of the most popular areas of practice. The good news is that it's a growing field, but the bad news is that you'll meet with a lot of competition. Most commercial firms have at least a small, dedicated department and even the smallest high street firm will have clients seeking employment advice. Like most litigation, the volume of work increases in times of recession. As Hilary confirms, "*In times of recession we get instructions on redundancies and terminations. In times of economic strength there's more corporate-led advice needed.*" Chris agrees, saying, "*The chameleonic nature of the employment lawyer's work seems to add a bit of job security.*"

Very large employers, such as the Post Office and British Airways, have specialist employment lawyers within the in-house legal team, but more usually a move in-house would combine employment law with perhaps general commercial litigation. Experienced employment lawyers may apply to chair employment tribunals; many partners in leading employment practices combine their practice with part-time tribunal chairs. The last couple of years have also seen the rise of know-how lawyers, who handle no client work but are dedicated to keeping their colleagues up to date on changes in the law and draft client newsletters and standard forms of documents for use by their colleagues.

LEADING FIRMS FROM CHAMBERS UK GUIDE 2002-2003

EMPLOYMENT
■ NORTH EAST

[1] **Dickinson Dees** Newcastle upon Tyne
Eversheds Newcastle upon Tyne
Short Richardson & Forth Newcastle upon Tyne
Thompsons Newcastle upon Tyne
[2] **Crutes Law Firm** Newcastle upon Tyne
Jacksons Stockton on Tees
Samuel Phillips & Co Newcastle upon Tyne
Ward Hadaway Newcastle upon Tyne
Watson Burton Newcastle upon Tyne

EMPLOYMENT
■ NORTH WEST

[1] **Addleshaw Booth & Co** Manchester
Eversheds Manchester
Hammond Suddards Edge Manchester
[2] **DLA** Liverpool, Manchester
Mace & Jones Liverpool, Manchester
Whittles Manchester
[3] **Cobbetts** Manchester
Thompsons Liverpool, Manchester
[4] **DWF** Liverpool, Manchester
Halliwell Landau Manchester
Pannone & Partners Manchester

EMPLOYMENT
■ YORKSHIRE

[1] **Pinsent Curtis Biddle** Leeds
[2] **Hammond Suddards Edge** Leeds
[3] **Addleshaw Booth & Co** Leeds
DLA Leeds, Sheffield
[4] **Cobbetts** Leeds
Eversheds Leeds
Ford & Warren Leeds
Walker Morris Leeds
[5] **Irwin Mitchell** Sheffield
Nabarro Nathanson Sheffield
Rollits Hull

EMPLOYMENT: MAINLY RESPONDENT
■ LONDON

1. **Simmons & Simmons**
2. **Allen & Overy**
   - Baker & McKenzie
3. **Eversheds**
   - Fox Williams
   - Herbert Smith
   - Lewis Silkin
   - Lovells
   - Mayer, Brown, Rowe & Maw
4. **Charles Russell**
   - Clifford Chance
   - Dechert
   - Denton Wilde Sapte
   - Linklaters
   - McDermott, Will & Emery
   - Nabarro Nathanson
   - Olswang
   - Slaughter and May
5. **Beachcroft Wansbroughs**
   - Berwin Leighton Paisner
   - Boodle Hatfield
   - CMS Cameron McKenna
   - Doyle Clayton
   - Farrer & Co
   - Freshfields Bruckhaus Deringer
   - Hammond Suddards Edge
   - Macfarlanes
   - Norton Rose
   - Osborne Clarke
   - Salans
   - Speechly Bircham
   - Stephenson Harwood
   - Theodore Goddard
   - Travers Smith Braithwaite

EMPLOYMENT: MAINLY APPLICANT
■ LONDON

1. **Pattinson & Brewer**
   - Russell Jones & Walker
2. **Thompsons**
3. **Bindman & Partners**
   - Rowley Ashworth
4. **Lawfords**
5. **Irwin Mitchell**

EMPLOYMENT
■ THE SOUTH

1. **DMH** Crawley
2. **Blake Lapthorn** Portsmouth
3. **Bond Pearce** Southampton
   - Rawlison Butler Crawley
4. **asb law** Crawley
   - Brachers Maidstone
   - Cripps Harries Hall Tunbridge Wells
   - Paris Smith & Randall Southampton
   - Thomson Snell & Passmore Tunbridge Wells
5. **Lester Aldridge** Bournemouth, Southampton
   - Pattinson & Brewer Chatham
   - Stevens & Bolton Guildford

EMPLOYMENT
■ THAMES VALLEY

1. **Clarks** Reading
2. **Osborne Clarke** Reading
3. **Henmans** Oxford
   - Morgan Cole Oxford, Reading
   - Pitmans Reading
   - Underwoods Hemel Hempstead

EMPLOYMENT
■ WALES

1. **Eversheds** Cardiff
2. **Morgan Cole** Cardiff, Swansea
3. **Edwards Geldard** Cardiff
   - Hugh James Cardiff
4. **Palser Grossman** Cardiff Bay

EMPLOYMENT
■ SOUTH WEST

1. **Bevan Ashford** Bristol
   - Bond Pearce Plymouth
   - Burges Salmon Bristol
   - Osborne Clarke Bristol
2. **Pattinson & Brewer** Bristol
   - Thompsons Bristol
   - Thring Townsend Bath
3. **Burroughs Day** Bristol
   - TLT Solicitors Bristol
   - Veale Wasbrough Bristol
4. **Clarke Willmott & Clarke** Taunton
   - Michelmores Exeter
   - Stephens & Scown Exeter

EMPLOYMENT
■ MIDLANDS

1. **Eversheds** Birmingham, Nottingham
   - Wragge & Co Birmingham
2. **Hammond Suddards Edge** Birmingham
3. **Martineau Johnson** Birmingham
   - Pinsent Curtis Biddle Birmingham
4. **DLA** Birmingham
   - Shakespeares Birmingham
5. **Browne Jacobson** Nottingham
   - freethcartwright Nottingham
   - Higgs & Sons Brierley Hill

EMPLOYMENT
■ EAST ANGLIA

1. **Eversheds** Cambridge, Norwich
   - Hewitson Becke + Shaw Cambridge
   - Mills & Reeve Cambridge, Norwich
2. **Greenwoods** Peterborough
   - Steele & Co Norwich
   - Taylor Vinters Cambridge
3. **Prettys** Ipswich

SPECIALIST PRACTICE AREAS — EMPLOYMENT LAW

environmental law

While there are careers for tree-hugging, planet-saving heroes, these are unlikely to be in private practice. Most environmental lawyers work for corporate clients seeking damage limitation, pre-emptive advice and defence from prosecution. Additionally, there's a volume of corporate support work, ensuring environmental liability is fully understood and apportioned between corporate entities. As Caroline May, a partner at Hammond Suddards Edge, states, *"You don't have to be an environmentalist to be an environmental lawyer, but you do have to have a keen interest in environmental issues."*

type of work

Mike Nash, an associate at Simmons & Simmons, told us, *"Environmental law is a real Tardis. It looks small from the outside but get inside and it's gigantic."* Administrative law, property, planning, contract and corporate law, EU law, international law and, increasingly, human rights. This sounds like an interdisciplinary free-for-all, so picture the work grouped into three broad areas:

- transactional, project and property support;
- compliance and regulatory advice; and
- litigation (encompassing criminal and civil disputes, judicial reviews and statutory appeals).

The environmental lawyer's caseload will usually be split between contentious and non-contentious matters. Contentious work may involve defending clients from criminal prosecution for breach of regulations. Indeed, there's been an upturn in prosecutions since the authorities began to flex their muscles a couple of years ago. You might find yourself in the Magistrates' Court running an argument on abuse of process or you might be arguing that the regulator has interpreted the law incorrectly. On the civil side there are tortious claims ('toxic torts') brought by those who suffer loss as a result of environmental impact.

On the non-contentious side environmental lawyers have a vital role on the sale and purchase of businesses or land, drafting contractual provisions for the allocation of risk. There's also standalone work, such as advice to clients on the extent of their obligations under new EU regulations. These may cover issues such as waste, pollution control, water abstraction and nature conservation.

Environmental law is still relatively new and there's a substantial amount of research and interpretation of legislation to be done. A trainee can come into their own given that they might, almost by accident, become the team's expert on a new piece of legislation or EU directive. Increasingly, the Human Rights Act has an impact, particularly in terms of the right to peaceful enjoyment of property. Mike says, *"The HRA was primarily brought in to protect individuals, but many people don't realise that it also gives human rights to companies and can be used to protect those rights as well."*

a day in the life…

What about a typical day? Caroline stresses, *"No two days are alike. Today I've dealt with a health and safety prosecution; I've been meeting a client and then dealing with a regulator; I've been meeting with clients to get ongoing authorisation for compliance issues; I've been in court for criminal and civil litigation; and I've been talking to government ministers about contaminated land."* Phew! A mix of public, private, civil, criminal and general compliance work then. She added, *"A lot of environmental issues are mucky issues: waste and sludge and sewers and spills."* Sounds a bit grim. *"It can be, particularly if you've got to go wander around a riverbed in your wellies."* Mike has similar comments. *"Lawyers in this area actually go out and visit sites. Corporate lawyers for example may do a deal involving 100 sites yet never go near any of them."* His days are equally as varied. He might be in the office drafting a letter of advice or a warranty for a corporate sale and then get a call from a client saying, "The Environment Agency's arrived. Should we talk to them or hand over the documents they are asking for?" This is part of the appeal. *"If you're someone who enjoys an organised routine and a thoroughly methodical day, it's not really for you."*

Junior lawyers can find it a challenging area to get to grips with. There's a substantial body of environmental law to get your head around, plus corporate, property and litigation procedures. As environmental teams are quite small, junior lawyers probably get more responsibility than in many other areas. Mike points out, *"You often get bite-sized chunks of work. If there's a specific regulatory issue to advise on, for example, a relatively junior person can take responsibility for it rather than just be part of a larger project."*

skills needed

…deal with intellectual problems commercially… be an all-rounder… understand corporate structures… interest in environmental issues… a grasp of science… research, interpretation and presentation skills…

Mike says, *"It's a mix of the rarefied and absurdly practical. There are aspects of the job that are intellectually demanding, but the client doesn't want you to answer just for fun or do a dissertation for a year; they want you to weigh up the risks, decide whether they're acceptable and go with it."*

You're often giving regulatory advice over a number of years – it's not like a transaction where you do a deal and everyone goes home. You might be advising at board level in relation to strategic issues, but you'll also meet and deal with people on site visits, some of whom might have scientific or engineering backgrounds. In addition to engineering and manufacturing clients generally, those in the waste, chemicals, ports, energy, rail, construction, food and water industries will feature. We wondered if there was any industry sector that wasn't involved. Mike identified one: *"The dot.com world – there's no one spilling anything or impacting on the environment there. They leave us cold."* Brrrr!

career options

It's a popular and, therefore, competitive area. Just over a decade ago solicitors got pretty excited about the emerging work, but commercial reality has tempered attitudes. According to Caroline, *"City law firms thought environment law would be the next big thing and pumped masses of people into it, many of whom jumped out with equal speed when it became clear that it was still very much secondary – or even third – to banking and corporate finance work."* The market for new lawyers is merely *"trundling along about level"* but more students are studying the subject and thinking about it as a career. Mike told us: *"We always have more trainees wanting to specialise in it than we can take on."* Why is it so popular? Caroline thinks it may go back to the *"misguided notion that it's going to involve saving whales, seals and trees."*

The local authority route is an alternative to private practice. You'll handle regulatory work, planning issues, waste management and air pollution cases, and have a role in advising the authority on its own liability. In-house positions for environmental lawyers are few and far between in corporate Britain, howeverhat, organisations such as Greenpeace, Friends of the Earth and RSPB have in-house lawyers.

The Department for Environment, Food and Rural Affairs (DEFRA) employs over 80 lawyers, including trainees on GLS-funded schemes. Work covers litigation, drafting of subordinate legislation, straight advisory work and contract drafting. The Environment Agency for England and Wales has responsibility for protecting and enhancing the environment through regulation of those corporate activities which have the greatest potential to pollute. The legal workload is diverse and requires a number of different legal skills. The Agency is the prosecution body for environmental crime and a number of Agency lawyers are full-time prosecutors. In addition there's a large amount of other enforcement work. As well as this, lawyers are involved in advice work at either the policy or operational level, which spans guidance on new regulations to advising on a licence for a particular site. Agency policy lawyers work closely with government lawyers on implementing and drafting legislation. The scope of work covers water quality, waste management, Integrated Pollution Prevention and Control, contaminated land, water resources, flood defence, fisheries, navigation and conservation, as well as other areas such as Environmental Impact Assessment and information law. Oh… and another little matter — regulating the disposal of radioactive waste! 56 solicitors and two trainees, seven barristers and five legal execs work from Bristol and eight regional offices. Contact the relevant regional solicitor for more info.

LEADING FIRMS FROM CHAMBERS UK GUIDE 2002-2003

ENVIRONMENT — LONDON

1. **Freshfields Bruckhaus Deringer**
2. **Allen & Overy**
3. **Ashurst Morris Crisp**
   - Barlow Lyde & Gilbert
   - CMS Cameron McKenna
   - Linklaters
   - Mayer, Brown, Rowe & Maw
   - Simmons & Simmons
   - Slaughter and May
4. **Berwin Leighton Paisner**
   - Clifford Chance
   - Denton Wilde Sapte
   - Gouldens
   - Hammond Suddards Edge
   - Herbert Smith
   - Leigh, Day & Co
   - Nabarro Nathanson
   - Norton Rose
   - SJ Berwin
5. **Lawrence Graham**
   - Lovells
   - Nicholson Graham & Jones
6. **Stephenson Harwood**
   - Theodore Goddard
   - Trowers & Hamlins

ENVIRONMENT — THE SOUTH

1. **Bond Pearce** Southampton
2. **Blake Lapthorn** Portsmouth,
   - **Stevens & Bolton** Guildford
3. **Horsey Lightly Fynn** Newbury

ENVIRONMENT — SOUTH WEST

1. **Bond Pearce** Plymouth
   - **Burges Salmon** Bristol
   - **Osborne Clarke** Bristol
2. **Clarke Willmott & Clarke** Bristol, Taunton
3. **Bevan Ashford** Bristol
   - **Veale Wasbrough** Bristol

ENVIRONMENT — WALES

1. **Morgan Cole** Cardiff
2. **Edwards Geldard** Cardiff
   - **Eversheds** Cardiff
3. **Hugh James** Bargoed, Cardiff

ENVIRONMENT — MIDLANDS

1. **Wragge & Co** Birmingham
2. **Eversheds** Birmingham, Nottingham
   - **Pinsent Curtis Biddle** Birmingham
3. **Browne Jacobson** Birmingham, Nottingham
   - **Hammond Suddards Edge** Birmingham
   - **Kent Jones and Done** Stoke-on-Trent

ENVIRONMENT — EAST ANGLIA

1. **Mills & Reeve** Cambridge, Norwich
   - **Richard Buxton** Cambridge
2. **Eversheds** Norwich
   - **Hewitson Becke + Shaw** Cambridge

ENVIRONMENT — NORTH WEST

1. **Eversheds** Manchester
   - **Leigh, Day & Co** Manchester
2. **Addleshaw Booth & Co** Manchester
   - **Hammond Suddards Edge** Manchester
   - **Masons** Manchester
   - **Wake Dyne Lawton** Chester

ENVIRONMENT — NORTH EAST

1. **Eversheds** Leeds
2. **Nabarro Nathanson** Sheffield
3. **Addleshaw Booth & Co** Leeds
   - **DLA** Sheffield
4. **Dickinson Dees** Newcastle upon Tyne
   - **Hammond Suddards Edge** Leeds
   - **Pinsent Curtis Biddle** Leeds

family

Family lawyers deal with the fallout from marital breakdown and a wide range of issues concerning children. The work ranges from the restructuring of a client's finances and companies at the high-end of the private market, to issues of adoption, access and custody in the field of children's law, most of which falls in the public domain. Whether they were working in a high street firm alongside social services on a case involving child abuse, or from a 'boutique' firm trying to save a client's offshore investments, all the lawyers we spoke to echoed the sentiment that *"These are issues that really do matter; things that change the lives of individuals."* As a family lawyer you are in a position to help your client through one of life's most traumatic experiences and, with 40% of marriages ending in divorce these days, you're unlikely to be short of work.

type of work

Known for his ability to handle the more excitable client, Alex Carruthers, a partner in the newly established niche practice Hughes Fowler Carruthers, specialises in all aspects of matrimonial and family law at the top end of the market. Here you'll need to gain an understanding of tax, trusts, pensions and property issues and have *"an appreciation of money and how it works, combined with an insight into human nature."* While you may spend time crunching numbers, you must remember that there are feelings as well as finances at stake and never lose sight of the fact that *"You're going for the best overall deal, which involves money and emotions."*

Stephen Foster, head of family law at Lester Aldridge in Bournemouth, came to family law after practising commercial litigation in the City. With the area becoming increasingly technical, a sound knowledge of corporate law puts you at a distinct advantage. For Stephen, one of the main attractions of 'high-end' work is that it has become increasingly international and genuinely exciting. *"You're dealing with entrepreneurs who are positive people, full of drive and vigour. These are people for whom life poses no obstacles. It's a real buzz working with them."*

Work in the public arena is less glamorous and potentially more traumatic, since your cases are more likely to involve child abuse and domestic violence than trophy wives and offshore accounts. Michael Devlin, a partner at Stephensons in Salford, specialises in children's law and adoption issues. He specialised initially in criminal work and subsequently moved into family law. Typically a trainee will go into family law and then carve out a niche in an area like divorce or children's law within an established practice. As a family lawyer dealing with the general public, you will represent and work with local authorities, family members, children's guardians and, occasionally, children in their own right. This is a multidisciplinary area, so you'll have a lot of contact with social workers, psychologists, probation officers and medical professionals who are *"well qualified and committed to what they do."* Much of your time will be spent in court, with spare moments taken up with correspondence, client meetings or conferences. Michael warns that, while *"professional satisfaction is very high, the work is publicly funded so there are no fortunes to be made."* Setting yourself up as a high street family lawyer can be a commercially viable proposition however, just so long as you have a bit of nous and can build a strong following.

Family law may not be as intellectually rigorous as tax law or pensions but actually you do need to have a level of understanding of these areas. According to Michael, *"You shouldn't regard it as next door to being a social worker." "Strong academics make you stand out,"* but it is equally important to have a life outside the law. You need to have some experience of people, relationships and the ways of the world. Stephen's practice has recently taken on a new lawyer who used to run his own business and so is well positioned to understand the stresses and strains on their entrepreneurial clients.

There are increasing opportunities for advocacy as a family lawyer. Professional standards are generally considered to be high and *"there are not so many sharks and egos floating around. People tend to operate within the limits of openness, honesty and fairness."* The Human Rights Act has opened up new possibilities in the area of children's law and the proposed Adoption Act will also make big waves, if it comes into force. Since the 1991 Children's Act, the area has been very *"vibrant,"* and there have been continual case law developments.

a day in the life of…

One of the attractions of family law is that no two clients and no two days are ever the same. A typical day for a lawyer in high-end private practice might involve meeting with a client in a five star hotel to discuss the evolution of their companies and spending the afternoon in court up against a senior barrister, before heading back to the office for a three-hour phone call with an emotional client, which *"should really have lasted for 15 minutes."* A high street lawyer is likely to spend much of their time in court and in meetings with clients and the social services, with the beginning and end of the day taken up with correspondence. You won't be pulling all-nighters like your friends in City firms, but there's likely to be paperwork to take home in the evening.

As a junior lawyer in private practice you can expect to go to court with a partner, take notes and prepare bundles of case documentation. It's an easy area to become immersed in and it offers a good mixture of responsibility and interesting work. Stephen warns, however, that there is a steep learning curve for the newly qualified lawyer. You will immediately become exposed to difficult and complex issues. *"It could come as a shock to a 23-year-old who is naïve in the ways of the world to see how adults of their parents' age are behaving towards one another."*

skills needed

listening skills… life experience… professional distance… compassion… a real interest in human relations… wisdom… intelligence… numeracy… ability to remain non-confrontational… interest in advocacy… commercial acumen… non-judgemental…

According to Alex, those who are likely to succeed in this area will be gregarious and sensitive, and will combine a keen eye for detail with a real interest in people. *"We tend to be people people with big personalities."* Stephen looks out for *"intellectual voltage"* in those he recruits.

One of the key qualities that you need as a family lawyer is sensitivity, but *"this should not be mistaken for being soft."* What the client needs is firm and realistic advice. You must be interested in people and understand what motivates them. You must also be able to understand the psychodynamics of relationships and relationship breakdowns. *"Clients will often be driven by subconscious issues and so it is up to you to understand what people really want and to deliver it as far as possible."* Professional detachment is a must. Michael explains, *"You need to draw the line right from the start or else they could start thinking of you as a friend. You need to make it clear that you're not there to dance to whatever tune they're playing."*

career options

There are in-house positions with local authorities and some big charities, but in terms of hands-on, client-focused work, there is no substitute for private practice. High street opportunities abound for well-qualified and skilled applicants, but positions in commercial firms are far less common than 10 to 15 years ago as many of these firms shut down their family departments. High-end work is handled by a tight pool of firms, the best of which are identified and discussed in *Chambers UK*.

LEADING FIRMS FROM CHAMBERS UK GUIDE 2002-2003

SPECIALIST PRACTICE AREAS — FAMILY

FAMILY/MATRIMONIAL — LONDON

[1]
- Manches
- Withers LLP

[2]
- Alexiou Fisher Philipps
- Charles Russell
- Collyer-Bristow
- Hughes Fowler Carruthers
- Levison Meltzer Pigott
- Miles Preston & Co
- Payne Hicks Beach
- Sears Tooth

[3]
- Bindman & Partners
- Clintons
- Dawson Cornwell
- Goodman Ray
- Kingsley Napley
- Mishcon de Reya

[4]
- Farrer & Co
- Gordon Dadds
- International Family Law Chambers
- Reynolds Porter Chamberlain
- The Family Law Consortium

[5]
- Anthony Gold
- Barnett Sampson
- Cawdery Kaye Fireman & Taylor
- Dawsons
- Fisher Meredith
- Forsters
- Hodge Jones & Allen
- Osbornes
- Russell-Cooke
- Stephenson Harwood

FAMILY/MATRIMONIAL — THE SOUTH

[1]
- Lester Aldridge Bournemouth

[2]
- Brachers Maidstone
- Paris Smith & Randall Southampton
- Thomson Snell & Passmore Tunbridge Wells

[3]
- Blake Lapthorn Portsmouth
- Coffin Mew & Clover Portsmouth
- Cripps Harries Hall Tunbridge Wells
- Ellis Jones Bournemouth
- Horsey Lightly Fynn Newbury
- Max Barford & Co Tunbridge Wells

FAMILY/MATRIMONIAL — SOUTH WEST

[1]
- Burges Salmon Bristol
- Foot Anstey Sargent Plymouth
- TLT Solicitors Bristol
- Tozers Exeter, Plymouth, Torquay
- Wolferstans Plymouth

[2]
- Clarke Willmott & Clarke Bristol
- Gill Akaster Plymouth
- Ian Downing Family Law Practice Plymouth
- Stephens & Scown Exeter

[3]
- Hooper & Wollen Torquay
- Stone King Bath
- Stones Exeter
- Woollcombe Beer Watts Newton Abbot

[4]
- E David Brain & Co St Austell
- Ford Simey Exeter
- Hartnells Family Law Practice Exeter
- Veale Wasbrough Bristol
- Withy King Bath

FAMILY/MATRIMONIAL — THAMES VALLEY

[1]
- Blandy & Blandy Reading
- Manches Oxford

[2]
- Boodle Hatfield Oxford
- Darbys Oxford
- Henmans Oxford
- Iliffes Booth Bennett (IBB) Uxbridge
- Morgan Cole Oxford

FAMILY/MATRIMONIAL — WALES

[1]
- Hugh James Cardiff
- Larby Williams Cardiff
- Nicol Denvir & Purnell Cardiff

[2]
- Martyn Prowel Solicitors Cardiff
- Robertsons Cardiff
- Wendy Hopkins & Co Cardiff

[3]
- Harding Evans Newport
- Leo Abse & Cohen Cardiff

FAMILY/MATRIMONIAL — MIDLANDS

[1]
- Blair Allison & Co Birmingham
- Challinors Lyon Clark West Bromwich
- Rupert Bear Murray Davies Nottingham

[2]
- Nelsons Nottingham
- Tyndallwoods Birmingham

[3]
- Hadens Walsall
- Lanyon Bowdler Shrewsbury
- Wace Morgan Shrewsbury
- Young & Lee Birmingham

[4]
- Benussi & Co Birmingham
- Blythe Liggins Leamington Spa
- freethcartwright Nottingham

FAMILY/MATRIMONIAL
■ EAST ANGLIA

[1] **Mills & Reeve** Norwich
[2] **Buckle Mellows** Peterborough
Greenwoods Peterborough
Hunt & Coombs Peterborough
Silver Fitzgerald Cambridge
[4] **Cozens-Hardy & Jewson** Norwich
Hatch Brenner Norwich
Ward Gethin King's Lynn

FAMILY/MATRIMONIAL
■ NORTH EAST

[1] **Dickinson Dees** Newcastle upon Tyne
[2] **Sinton & Co** Newcastle upon Tyne
[3] **Hay & Kilner** Newcastle upon Tyne
Mincoffs Newcastle upon Tyne
Samuel Phillips & Co Newcastle upon Tyne
Ward Hadaway Newcastle upon Tyne
[4] **Askews** Redcar

FAMILY/MATRIMONIAL
■ YORKSHIRE

[1] **Addleshaw Booth & Co** Leeds
[2] **Gordons Cranswick Solicitors** Bradford
Grahame Stowe, Bateson Leeds
Irwin Mitchell Leeds, Sheffield
Jones Myers Gordon Leeds
[3] **Andrew M Jackson** Hull
Zermansky & Partners Leeds
[4] **Crombie Wilkinson** York
Kirbys Harrogate

FAMILY/MATRIMONIAL
■ NORTH WEST

[1] **Pannone & Partners** Manchester
[2] **Cobbetts** Manchester
Cuff Roberts Liverpool
Farleys Blackburn
[3] **Addleshaw Booth & Co** Manchester
Burnetts Carlisle
Green & Co Manchester
Jones Maidment Wilson Manchester
Laytons Manchester
Mace & Jones Knutsford, Liverpool
Stephensons Leigh
[4] **Morecroft Urquhart** Liverpool
Rowlands Manchester

intellectual property

Intellectual property law can be defined by its two halves: patent work (hard IP), ie the protection of inventions and processes; and non-patent work (soft IP), ie trademarks, design rights, copyright, passing off, anti-counterfeiting and confidential information. Both overlap with IT (information technology), telecommunications, broadcasting and internet work. The work often extends into Europe and beyond.

type of work

There are three main UK intellectual property rights providing owners with a complete monopoly. Patents protect new, industrially applicable inventions. They provide the proprietor with a monopoly to work the invention for a certain period. A registered trademark provides the owner with a limited monopoly to use that mark on certain goods or services. Finally, a registered design gives the owner an exclusive right to use the design. There are also more limited rights. For example, a work attracting copyright protection gives the owner of the copyright the right to prevent others copying the work.

IP clients include manufacturers and suppliers of hi-tech, engineering, pharmaceutical and agro-chemical products, leading brand owners, universities, scientific institutions and media clients. IP work can be contentious or non-contentious. Disputes usually revolve around arguments of infringement or the existence of one or more intangible property rights in an invention, a literary/artistic work, a trademark or a product, or whether any IP rights exist at all. Patent litigation, in particular, can be very complex indeed, with cases running for years – usually there's a lot at stake. Kerry Griffin, an assistant at Bird & Bird, told us, *"The larger contentious cases tend to be patent matters as the parties are often multinational companies and the financial consequences can be enormous; often the trademark infringement or cyber squatting cases settle out of court."* Carl Steele, an assistant at Taylor Wessing, sees how much effort is put into patent disputes. *"It's all-consuming. For example, two big drug companies going head-to-head – they need as much time as you can give them and will spend a lot of money for the best lawyers."*

Carl doesn't generally handle patent cases, preferring to concentrate on other IP work, especially trademarks. He thinks, *"Trademark issues can be conceptually as difficult as patents. Patent cases are all about understanding the science and framing a really good expert's report. Trademark cases often succeed and fail on the reactions of the public to a rival's trademark (which can be unpredictable to say the least!) and you really need to know your law. Copyright issues can also be horrendously complicated."* If one of his publisher clients wanted to buy the rights to a series of books, for example, Carl would have to review the 'title' or chain of ownership of copyright to these literary works – rather like reviewing the title to a piece of land.

Passing off disputes often focus on the get-up and packaging of a product. The Jif lemon case, which turned on the shape of the bottle, is a leading authority in this area. More recently, there's been Arsenal v Reed, in which the club tried to prevent a street trader selling unofficial club merchandise. The club was unsuccessful in both a registered trademark infringement action and in an action for passing off brought against Mr Reed.

The internet has also kept IP lawyers busy in the last few years. Cyber squatting (domain name disputes) have become commonplace, and there's little doubt that convergence in telecoms and IT will give rise to even more opportunities for the IP lawyer keen to work for clients in the technology sector.

a day in the life...

In some senses Carl's a jack of all trades. His work involves a multitude of things from advising on the results of basic trademark searches to trademark opposition work (stopping a rival registering a new mark), advising on a worldwide trademark filing strategy and drafting trademark-related agreements, for example sponsorship, endorsement and merchandising contracts. Then there's the excitement of the commencement or defence of trademark infringement procedings. These activities see him working either solo or with a small team of other IP specialists. On the other hand, there are times when he will be called upon to work as a part of a multi-disciplinary team on a large corporate transaction. For some companies a portfolio of intellectual property rights is one of the most valuable assets they own and even the humblest of companies will have IP issues to explore. Carl will have to advise on the IP warranties given or received by the parties to the transaction and perhaps check the title to the rights that are claimed.

Kerry can get caught up in mammoth pan-European pharmaceutical patent infringement cases (like the glaucoma drug litigation she's currently handling for a US pharmaceuticals client), or she can find herself handling a series of smaller non-contentious agreements – patent and trademark licences, Research & Development agreements, assignments of rights and material transfer agreements. Her workload is about 70/30 contentious/non-contentious. Sometimes the big disputes mean getting bogged down for months on end in the preparation of evidence and production of relevant documents (called disclosure), but there are also opportunities to carry out her own advocacy on small pre-trial points.

skills needed

Patent law...a basic understanding of science (minimum A-levels; ideally a degree)... aptitude for technical matters and concepts... well-organised... precise drafting...

General IP...curiosity for all things creative, artistic and technological... handle quirky/eccentric/artistic types... interest in the internet... up with consumer trends...

Carl and Kerry illustrate a crucial point very well. He has no science background and has found a career in areas of IP other than patents. On the other hand, Kerry, as a science graduate, has chosen an area of work in which only scientists tend to thrive. *"A lot of scientists who come into law don't like research – those days in a lab plating out bacteria – just horrendous! But with patent law they can use their science background and effectively get a kick-start to their career. As an IP lawyer you're right at front of scientific developments and you even get to talk to Nobel prizewinners – that's exciting."* She says that hopefully clients can talk to her in the same technical terms as if she were someone junior in their lab.

Drafting skills, precision and accuracy (or as some put it being *"picky"*) are absolutely crucial, particularly in patent work. It's all about getting beneath the surface of information and being dogged in your assessment of it. Kerry told us she sometimes has to play devil's advocate: *"As a non-expert you must examine the evidence and make sure it makes sense."* Time becomes your enemy. *"The trick is to be precise enough and get everything done in time. Things go incredibly rapidly – imagine having 99 CD-ROMs to look through for relevant documents or a witness statement to produce in less than 24 hours."*

With general IP you'll need to have a good sense of commercial strategy and branding issues and be innovative in the way you think. Ideas and public perceptions, images and symbols will be your stock-in-trade. Maybe in another life you'd have worked in an advertising agency.

Few students know much about IP when they begin their training contracts, which is why many large firms send newly qualifieds on a course in Bristol run by the Intellectual Property Lawyers Association. The residential course counts as half an MA and is taught by partners from major IP firms.

career options

If you choose the right firm you'll probably be able to do at least one IP seat during training. Carl says, "If you want to be a patent litigator you'd be well advised to join a specialist firm... but if you want to go for the publishing/music/ privacy/breach of confidence work then a West End firm may be a better option if you want to work with famous celebrities. Clients like that don't want to pay the fees of a big city corporate-oriented law firm. If you want a bit of everything, then go to a large commercial practice with a good IP/media department." Although IP lawyers in London will tell you that the capital is where it's at, there are other hot spots. The Thames Valley has a concentration of IT companies and Cambridge's 'Silicon Fen' has grown on the back of the hi-tech and biotech companies that have spun out of the university. *Chambers UK* identifies the leading IP practices in the UK and gives details of their particular specialisms and clients.

IP knowledge is valued outside private practice. Manufacturing, pharmaceutical and research companies employ patent specialists and there are in-house legal teams at all the large pharmaceutical companies, for example, Procter & Gamble, Reckitt Benckiser and Unilever. Non-patent lawyers find their way into the media world: all major publishers and television companies have in-house IP lawyers. Many broadcasting companies now employ lawyers in positions such as head of business and legal affairs. Additionally, firms of trademark agents and patent attorneys are often keen to recruit those with a legal training.

LEADING FIRMS FROM CHAMBERS UK GUIDE 2002-2003

INTELLECTUAL PROPERTY
PATENT LITIGATION ■ LONDON

1. Bird & Bird
   Bristows
2. Linklaters
   Simmons & Simmons
   Taylor Wessing
3. Herbert Smith
   Lovells
   Wragge & Co
4. Baker & McKenzie
   Clifford Chance
   Eversheds
   Roiter Zucker
5. Allen & Overy

INTELLECTUAL PROPERTY
■ THE SOUTH

1. Laytons Guildford
2. DMH Brighton
3. Blake Lapthorn Fareham
   Lester Aldridge Bournemouth

INTELLECTUAL PROPERTY
■ THAMES VALLEY

1. Willoughby & Partners Oxford
2. Nabarro Nathanson Reading
   Olswang Reading
   The Law Offices of Marcus J O'Leary Wokingham
3. Manches Oxford
4. Osborne Clarke Reading

INTELLECTUAL PROPERTY
■ SOUTH WEST

1. Osborne Clarke Bristol
2. Beachcroft Wansbroughs Bristol
   Bevan Ashford Bristol
   Burges Salmon Bristol
3. Humphreys & Co Bristol
4. Laytons Bristol

INTELLECTUAL PROPERTY
■ WALES

1. Edwards Geldard Cardiff
2. Eversheds Cardiff
3. Morgan Cole Cardiff

INTELLECTUAL PROPERTY
GENERAL ■ LONDON

1
- Bird & Bird
- Linklaters
- Taylor Wessing

2
- Bristows
- Simmons & Simmons

3
- Baker & McKenzie
- Lovells
- Willoughby & Partners
- Wragge & Co

4
- Allen & Overy
- Clifford Chance
- Denton Wilde Sapte
- Eversheds
- Herbert Smith
- Olswang
- Slaughter and May

5
- Ashurst Morris Crisp
- Field Fisher Waterhouse
- Freshfields Bruckhaus Deringer
- Gouldens
- Roiter Zucker
- Shook, Hardy & Bacon
- SJ Berwin

6
- Briffa
- Dechert
- Hammond Suddards Edge
- KLegal
- Mayer, Brown, Rowe & Maw

INTELLECTUAL PROPERTY
■ MIDLANDS

1
- Wragge & Co Birmingham

2
- Martineau Johnson Birmingham
- Pinsent Curtis Biddle Birmingham

3
- Browne Jacobson Nottingham
- Shoosmiths Northampton

4
- Eversheds Birmingham, Nottingham

INTELLECTUAL PROPERTY
■ EAST ANGLIA

1
- Eversheds Ipswich, Norwich
- Mills & Reeve Cambridge, Norwich

2
- Greenwoods Peterborough

INTELLECTUAL PROPERTY
■ NORTH WEST

1
- Addleshaw Booth & Co Manchester
- Halliwell Landau Manchester

2
- Eversheds Manchester
- Hill Dickinson Manchester

3
- DLA Manchester

4
- Hammond Suddards Edge Manchester
- Kuit Steinart Levy Manchester
- Taylors Blackburn

5
- Berg & Co Manchester
- Cobbetts Manchester
- Lawson Coppock & Hart Manchester

INTELLECTUAL PROPERTY
■ NORTH EAST

1
- Addleshaw Booth & Co Leeds
- Pinsent Curtis Biddle Leeds

2
- DLA Leeds
- Eversheds Leeds
- Hammond Suddards Edge Leeds

3
- Irwin Mitchell Leeds
- Walker Morris Leeds

4
- Dickinson Dees Newcastle upon Tyne
- Lupton Fawcett Leeds

litigation/dispute resolution

If you've ever watched *LA Law* or *Ally McBeal* you'd be forgiven for thinking that litigation is all about silver-tongued lawyers cross-examining thin-lipped corporate sharks in neat, hour-long disputes. Think again. Most disputes never reach trial – as a rule clients aren't interested in having their 'day in court'. Every litigator knows that, almost without exception, the best approach is to reach a commercial settlement quickly and cheaply.

Disputes are concluded in one of three ways: The first is through litigation itself – the issue and pursuit of court proceedings, which can be expensive and time-consuming. For this reason, contracts often provide for disputes between the parties to be referred to the second method, namely binding arbitrations, which are usually conducted by an expert in the subject matter where it is particularly specialised. Unlike court proceedings, arbitrations are confidential and are particularly common in the shipping, insurance and construction industries. The third method is Alternative Dispute Resolution (ADR). Although it can take various forms, the most common form of ADR is mediation. This involves structured negotiations between the parties, which are overseen and directed by an independent mediator. Less common forms of ADR include neutral evaluation, expert determination and conciliation. The parties retain the right to litigate if they find it impossible to reach an agreement.

type of work

General commercial litigators handle a variety of business disputes but most cases will be contractual, encompassing anything from a dispute over the sale of a multi-million pound business to an argument over the meaning of a term in a tenancy agreement. Such so-called generalists might also deal with negligence claims by companies against their professional advisors. Some litigators specialise in certain industry sectors, such as construction, shipping, insurance, property or media; however, the majority of skills will be common to all areas of commercial litigation as will the majority of procedures.

Quite simply, litigation is a process. Once a case has been commenced it follows a predetermined course laid down by the rules of court: statement of case, disclosure of documents, witness statements, various procedural applications and, in a small number of cases, trial. In a major case this process can take several years. The mutual disclosure of relevant documents can be a particularly protracted and expensive affair despite new rules, which came into force in April 1999, designed to limit this – namely the Woolf reforms to the civil justice system or Civil Procedure Rules (CPR). Managing this process is the litigator's primary role and this requires not only a mastery of the rules of court, but also a keen appreciation of tactics and detail.

Opportunities for litigators have increased in the last few years, which is to some extent due to the extension of High Court rights of audience to solicitors. Although solicitors were always entitled to draft statements of case – the formal documents setting out the claimant's claim and the defendant's response – and some even trained to act as advocates in High Court procedural hearings, they rarely did so. Instead such work was normally referred to barristers. However, this is now changing. While there hasn't been a flood of solicitor advocates into the High Court, the potential for savings in costs for the client is encouraging many firms to keep more advocacy in-house. This phenomenon is particularly marked in the large City firms. Lovells and Herbert Smith, for example, both have advocacy policies whereby solicitor advocates are used in most cases other than major hearings or full trials, while firms like Clifford Chance, Linklaters and Norton Rose are putting an increasing amount of their own solicitors through advocacy training programmes.

Looking more closely at Lovells, its litigators have been encouraged to attain higher rights of audience. The firm will go one step further in September 2002, when a three-day advocacy accreditation course will be included in the firm's annual foundation training course for newly qualified litigators. Lovells' partner Patrick Sherrington says, *"It's no more than the natural evolution of the legal market. As restrictive practices have disappeared, there has been a blurring of the edges as to what solicitors and barristers do."* Stephen Brown, the partner responsible for pensions and financial services dispute resolution at Mayer, Brown, Rowe & Maw, states *"We're very keen for our junior people to get higher rights and to do their own drafting. Both disciplines – advocacy and case preparation – are crucial to becoming good dispute resolvers."* The choice to bring in a barrister will be made on a case-by-case basis and will always be a question of what is in the client's best interests. As Patrick says, *"Certainly I'd be happy to appear in many different situations, but would I appear in a highly complex matter where the case would turn on intricate and specialist evidential rules and impeccable cross-examination skills honed over years of higher court advocacy? Of course not – I'd engage an experienced barrister."* It goes without saying that students who are aspiring litigators and are looking to become solicitor advocates should check firms' policies before applying, ie is becoming a solicitor advocate at the firm possible at all, purely optional, actively encouraged or mandatory?

a day in the life...

In a large City firm a qualified litigator may work on just a few big cases at a time. The caseload will probably be more varied in smaller litigation departments. Sarah Armstrong, an associate at Lovells, typically has three to four different cases on the go, all of which are at different stages of the litigation process. There's the factual investigation stage, whereby documents have been sent to her and she needs to work out the key facts. Then there's the stage of calling and meeting with counsel and clients, advising on developments and reviewing the case generally – tactical stuff. Next comes the advocacy element, where mediations, for example, can tie her up for one to two days at a time.

Sarah makes the point, *"We don't generally go to court all that much as we are dealing with fewer cases, but there are inevitably interlocutory hearings."* This raises an interesting question. When you're starting out as a litigator, is there much opportunity to do your own advocacy? Well, depending on the firm you're at, the potential is definitely there. The bigger and more valuable the cases your firm takes on, the more likely you are to be a 'cog in the machine' in terms of researching and helping with case preparation rather than be doing any advocacy yourself. However, as Sarah states, *"You've always got the chance to build up your advocacy experience on pro bono cases and other smaller cases and you can seize advocacy opportunities in the interlocutory stages of any case."* She also mentions the advocacy required in client meetings. Eh? *"You're explaining points to clients who don't necessarily want to hear the answer. This takes just as much skill – if not more – than when you're advocating in court or at a mediation."* Ah.

As a junior litigator or even a trainee in a firm that handles lower value cases, you'll frequently make undisputed court applications and ask for adjournments, which will enable you to practice your advocacy skills. You'll also be analysing an awful lot of documents, and, as a result, your research and legal analysis skills will develop quickly. The trickier task is then applying the law to all the facts.

skills needed

....drive... commercial awareness... be a tactician... natural toughness... enjoy formulating and articulating arguments… must like to win... assimilate information quickly… think laterally... good negotiator... thick-skinned but still sensitive to client's needs…

As well as being able to conceive ideas and arguments, you also need to communicate them to your client, counsel or, for junior lawyers, to the partner supervising you. In this respect, as Sarah says, "*The partners you're working with in the early years are really your clients in a way – you're building up their trust so that they'll then let you loose on real clients.*" Sarah's experience is in sharp contrast to the young litigator in firms that handle smaller value cases (eg personal injury claims) in which the activities carried out by megafirm partners would be done by juniors, and full responsiblity for a case is theirs from day one.

Good judgement, instinct and common sense are invaluable. Stephen adds, "*By the time you're one to two years into it people will be depending on you. I can only read so much of the material on each case and I have to depend on the assistants in my team to read and conclude what they do in terms of case preparation and strategy formulation.*"

Stephen also says, "*You can be the brightest person in the world, but if you can't handle criticism or pressure, or you muse indefinitely instead of making decisions, then you'll never make it as a litigator.*" His synopsis of litigation: "*It's about forming a view, thinking it through, making sure it's as watertight as possible and then having a good ding-dong with people.*" Couldn't have put it better ourselves!

Corporate clients see litigation as part of business risk; they take your advice and pay your fees and they can absorb whatever happens. For private individuals (such as minority shareholders) the impact of litigation on their lives shouldn't be underestimated – it can mean the difference between life going on and ruination. While this leads to important differences in handling the two types of client, both will be concerned with efficiency, good management and costs. It's important to develop good relationships with your clients so that they trust you to make decisions on their behalf. As Stephen says, "*Winning litigation for clients is not just an academic exercise – these are real people.*"

career options

Every commercial firm has a litigation department and some regard it as their primary practice area. The Law Society requires all trainees to undertake contentious work in their training contract and most know within the space of six months whether they click with litigation. We need say no more than that!

If you're looking to be a specialist litigator then experience in the relevant industry sector will help. However, when you're starting out it's probably best to focus on establishing a broad caseload. The consensus amongst our interviewees was that junior litigators should spend a few years – perhaps three to four – building up their general skills and then move into a specialist area. You'll be more marketable as a litigator if you've accumulated general skills from an early stage as this will ensure you'll be less vulnerable to market trends, particularly in recessionary times. That said, a career in a top-rated niche department or firm is not to be sniffed at.

In-house opportunities are not that common, although banks, insurance, construction and shipping companies sometimes employ specialist litigators. As a rule, only the very largest in-house departments need general commercial litigators. Stephen expresses his preference for private practice well: "*In-house you'll always be a bolt-on to the business, whereas in private practice you are the business.*"

LEADING FIRMS FROM CHAMBERS UK GUIDE 2002-2003

SPECIALIST PRACTICE AREAS

LITIGATION/DISPUTE RESOLUTION

LITIGATION: GENERAL COMMERCIAL (40+ LITIGATORS)
■ LONDON

1. **Herbert Smith**
2. **Clifford Chance**
   Freshfields Bruckhaus Deringer
   Lovells
3. **Allen & Overy**
4. **Linklaters**
5. **Ashurst Morris Crisp**
   Norton Rose
   Simmons & Simmons
   Slaughter and May
6. **Barlow Lyde & Gilbert**
   CMS Cameron McKenna
   Denton Wilde Sapte
   Richards Butler

LITIGATION: GENERAL COMMERCIAL (FEWER THAN 40 LITIGATORS)
■ LONDON

1. **Baker & McKenzie**
   SJ Berwin
2. **Dechert**
   Eversheds
   Gouldens
   Stephenson Harwood
3. **Clyde & Co**
   D J Freeman
   Nabarro Nathanson
   Nicholson Graham & Jones
4. **Berwin Leighton Paisner**
   Macfarlanes
   Mayer, Brown, Rowe & Maw
   Reynolds Porter Chamberlain
   Taylor Wessing
   Travers Smith Braithwaite
5. **Hammond Suddards Edge**
   Ince & Co
   Lawrence Graham
   Theodore Goddard
6. **Charles Russell**
   Lane & Partners
   Lewis Silkin
   Masons
   Memery Crystal
   Mishcon de Reya
   Pinsent Curtis Biddle
   Shook, Hardy & Bacon
   Watson, Farley & Williams
   White & Case

LITIGATION: GENERAL COMMERCIAL
■ THE SOUTH

1. **Blake Lapthorn** Fareham, Southampton
2. **Bond Pearce** Southampton
   Cripps Harries Hall Tunbridge Wells
   DMH Brighton
   Thomas Eggar Chichester, Reigate, Worthing
3. **asb law** Crawley, Maidstone
   Brachers Maidstone
   Clyde & Co Guildford
   Lester Aldridge Bournemouth
   Paris Smith & Randall Southampton
   Stevens & Bolton Guildford
4. **Barlows** Guildford
   Charles Russell Guildford
   Shoosmiths Fareham

LITIGATION: GENERAL COMMERCIAL
■ THAMES VALLEY

1. **Clarks** Reading
   Morgan Cole Oxford, Reading
   Nabarro Nathanson Reading
2. **Boyes Turner** Reading
   Pitmans Reading
   Shoosmiths Reading

LITIGATION: GENERAL COMMERCIAL
■ SOUTH WEST

1. **Burges Salmon** Bristol
   Osborne Clarke Bristol
2. **Beachcroft Wansbroughs** Bristol
   Bevan Ashford Bristol, Exeter
   Bond Pearce Bristol, Exeter, Plymouth
   Veale Wasbrough Bristol
3. **Clarke Willmott & Clarke** Bristol, Taunton
   Foot Anstey Sargent Exeter, Plymouth
   TLT Solicitors Bristol
4. **Laytons** Bristol
   Michelmores Exeter

LITIGATION: GENERAL COMMERCIAL
■ WALES

1. **Edwards Geldard** Cardiff
   Eversheds Cardiff
   Hugh James Cardiff
   Morgan Cole Cardiff, Swansea
2. **Palser Grossman** Cardiff Bay

LITIGATION: GENERAL COMMERCIAL
■ NORTH EAST

1. **Dickinson Dees** Newcastle upon Tyne
   Ward Hadaway Newcastle upon Tyne
2. **Eversheds** Newcastle upon Tyne
3. **Robert Muckle** Newcastle upon Tyne
   Watson Burton Newcastle upon Tyne
4. **Hay & Kilner** Newcastle upon Tyne

LITIGATION: GENERAL COMMERCIAL
■ MIDLANDS

1. **Wragge & Co** Birmingham
2. **Pinsent Curtis Biddle** Birmingham
3. **Eversheds** Birmingham, Nottingham
   Hammond Suddards Edge Birmingham
   Martineau Johnson Birmingham
4. **Browne Jacobson** Nottingham
   DLA Birmingham
   Gateley Wareing Birmingham
   Lee Crowder Birmingham
5. **Bell Lax Litigation** Birmingham
   Challinors Lyon Clark West Bromwich
   Freethcartwright Nottingham
   Kent Jones and Done Stoke-on-Trent
   Moran & Co Tamworth
   Shakespeares Birmingham
   Shoosmiths Northampton
   The Wilkes Partnership Birmingham

LITIGATION: GENERAL COMMERCIAL
■ EAST ANGLIA

1. **Eversheds** Cambridge, Norwich
   Mills & Reeve Cambridge, Norwich
2. **Hewitson Becke + Shaw** Cambridge
   Taylor Vinters Cambridge
3. **Greenwoods** Peterborough
   Prettys Ipswich
   Birketts Ipswich
   Steele & Co Norwich

LITIGATION: GENERAL COMMERCIAL
■ NORTH WEST

1. **DLA** Liverpool, Manchester
2. **Addleshaw Booth & Co** Manchester
   Eversheds Manchester
3. **Brabners Chaffe Street** Liverpool, Preston
   Cobbetts Manchester
   Halliwell Landau Manchester
   Hammond Suddards Edge Manchester
4. **Berg & Co** Manchester
   DWF Liverpool, Manchester
   Hill Dickinson Liverpool
   Wacks Caller Manchester
5. **Cuff Roberts** Liverpool
   Rowe Cohen Manchester
6. **Kershaw Abbott** Manchester
   Kuit Steinart Levy Manchester
   Mace & Jones Liverpool, Manchester
   Pannone & Partners Manchester

LITIGATION: GENERAL COMMERCIAL
■ YORKSHIRE

1. **Addleshaw Booth & Co** Leeds
   DLA Leeds, Sheffield
   Eversheds Leeds
   Hammond Suddards Edge Leeds
2. **Irwin Mitchell** Sheffield
   Pinsent Curtis Biddle Leeds
   Walker Morris Leeds
3. **Gordons Cranswick Solicitors** Bradford, Leeds
   Keeble Hawson Leeds
   Lupton Fawcett Leeds
   Rollits Hull
4. **Andrew M. Jackson** Hull
5. **Brooke North** Leeds
   Cobbetts Leeds
   Gosschalks Hull

SPECIALIST PRACTICE AREAS — LITIGATION/DISPUTE RESOLUTION

135

media and entertainment law

We have divided this section into three categories: advertising and marketing, defamation, and entertainment law.

advertising & marketing

Firms with advertising and marketing clients handle both 'pure' and general advertising law. 'Pure' advertising law focuses on the products or advertisements produced by clients, ensuring the content is legal and appropriate. General advertising law encompasses commercial contracts with suppliers, clients and the rest of the media, as well as corporate transactions, litigation and employment issues as they affect advertising clients.

type of work: Copy clearance lawyers advise clients on ad campaigns for all types of media – TV, radio, poster, internet, etc. Issues include comparative advertising (copy denigrating rivals), unauthorised references to living individuals and parodies of films or TV shows. A thorough understanding of defamation and intellectual property law is essential. Legislation such as the Lotteries and Amusement Act and the Consumer Protection Act feature and copy clearance work is further governed by regulatory codes such as those of the Advertising Standards Authority (ASA) and the Independent Television Commission (ITC). The lawyer must help the client to say exactly what it wants to say without falling foul of all of these regulations.

The lawyer may have to defend the client against allegations that their work has infringed the rights of third parties or advise whether an ad should be pulled. This "*can take some nerve,*" according to Brinsley Dresden, a partner at Lewis Silkin, and the action may well go "*right to the wire*" before the third party backs down (if they do at all). At times you may go on the offensive, helping clients to bring complaints about competitors' advertising to the ASA or the ITC. This may arise when a competitor is 'knocking copy' (making disparaging references to your client's products) or when a competitor is making claims that your client wouldn't be allowed to make.

Brinsley's clients are "*creative and lively individuals – well-educated, intelligent and demanding, but always good fun to deal with.*" They want fast and practical advice: "*You can't simply tell people 'no' because often they're committed to a course of action before they speak to you. Often you can only advise them on how to minimise the risks involved.*" Rarely is anything black and white; it's about risk management in grey areas and it's up to the lawyer to identify the risks and, if not eliminate them, manage them as best they can.

This is not a dry, document-intensive area of law. By all accounts advertising lawyers simply don't have the time to do hours of research. It's fast in and fast out, which keeps it fresh. "*It's great fun and very satisfying to advise on a TV commercial and then, when you're at home watching TV, suddenly there's your commercial. It's certainly immediate in terms of seeing the results of your labour.*"

There isn't a huge demand for these specialist advisors so competition is reasonably tough. While not essential, working in an ad agency prior to training could be helpful; you'll get to know the culture and you'll get to grips with how advertising is produced.

defamation

Until they bring back duelling, defamation laws will continue to be used to protect a person's honour and good name. Individuals and organisations can be defamed by written word, which constitutes libel, or by spoken word, which constitutes slander. The majority of actions undertaken in the field are for libel.

type of work: Non-contentious work includes pre-publication or pre-broadcast advice to authors, editors and TV companies. Contentious lawyers act for either claimants (individuals or companies alleging that publishers/broadcasters have damaged their reputation) or defendants. According to Jason McCue, a partner at H2O, *"The first decision to make is whether you want to act for claimants or defendants."* The work is quite different. It's mainly investigative work for defendants as *"there are only so many basic defences to a libel action,"* whereas for claimants *"you've got more control over shaping the action."*

Defamation hinges on questions of personal honour and the right to freedom of expression. Unlike most areas of law, these matter more to clients than money, and consequently clients may insist on their day in court even when they have a near-hopeless case. Principles can be expensive.

Clients range from high-profile politicians or pop stars to unknown businessmen. Client contact is likely to begin at junior level and many see it as critical to career progression to build up personal links with clients and in-house lawyers as quickly as possible. But there are important differences between various types of clients. Jason says, *"If you're dealing with a lawyer at a newspaper, rest assured they know what they're talking about – they've done it all before and know all the rules."* By contrast, a pop singer may know nothing about the process.

Certain high-profile libel matters (such as Neil Hamilton's ill-fated action against Mohamed Al Fayed) might make you think libel is all about trials. However, most libel lawyers have only one or two full trials a year. Like any other type of litigation, most cases settle before they get to the door of the court.

You definitely need to keep up with ever-shifting societal values and socio-political awareness is crucial, Jason explained. *"People are much more brand-conscious and media-aware these days"* and 'reputation management' is the new buzz phrase. Certain social issues are less clear-cut than they once were: *"There are more shades of grey."* For example, *"People used to sue if they were called gay – now they'll only sue if it's hypocritical. In the 60s many people saw nuclear power as dreadful and dangerous. Now you've got environmental organisations saying use it, it's better."*

Nothing is more embarrassing for a media lawyer than if a client rings up and says 'politician X has done something…' and you have to ask not only what party the politician belongs to but also who he or she actually is! You're expected to know these things and be au fait with the latest news and views; *"Otherwise, what right do you have to call yourself a media lawyer?"* In short, listen to the radio, watch the news, read newspapers… and *Hello!* Previous experience in the media will help, whether it's working on TV documentaries, on newspapers or as a press secretary to an MP. These jobs expose you to research tasks and a conception of *"what's going on in the world."* As Jason says, *"The law is easy to learn. Learning about the media industry can take a lifetime, but you can get a head start by working in it."*

And what of the Human Rights Act? *"It's now gone through its childhood and is starting to bite. It will continue to mature so it's important to come to grips with it. Lawyers weren't sure how it was going to work at first and didn't know what the courts were going to do. But now we have precedents and people are getting more cocky in using it."* Two of the biggies are Article 8 (the right to free speech) and Article 10 (the right to privacy – think Naomi Campbell getting out of bed and attempting to go head-to-head with *The Mirror* in court for only £3,500. *"You're dealing with people's deep, dark secrets – really intriguing stuff…"*

entertainment

Do you want to be in the world of money or the world of ideas? If you want the former, then become a corporate or banking lawyer. If you want something less institutionalised, entertainment law may just be for you. We have divided this section into film & broadcasting, music, theatre and publishing.

type of work: Clients of all types need contract, employment and litigation advice, and an understanding of commercial law is key to almost everything. Intellectual property is the other main legal discipline you'll need to apply.

film & broadcasting

Look at films or TV programmes as being like any other commercial product. You have to develop the product, finance it, produce it and then sell it. All of these elements require legal advice of one kind or another. The work is a combination of commercial contract law (with an element of banking and secured lending) and the law of copyright. The film lawyer would normally see the process through from start to finish. For just one film production you may have seven different types of finance, four producers and 58 separate agreements to deal with! At the other end of the scale, you might be asked to give swift and concise clearance and classification advice to the British Board of Film Classification.

music

Clients come from all sectors of the music industry, including record labels, production companies, managers and the artists themselves. Some firms lean more towards acting for talent, others for the record labels. Contract work is central to everything. High-profile litigation sometimes arises when there is a dispute over contract terms or ownership of rights in compositions. When band members split with each other or with their management, lawyers are brought in to fight their client's corner in the process of sorting out who is entitled to what. Whether they're specialising in contentious or non-contentious work, music lawyers have to be fully versed in all aspects of copyright as well as contract law. Specialist music firms may also advise on the incorporation and development of new record labels and joint venture agreements between larger and smaller labels.

theatre

There are a few practitioners in London who thrive off the theatrical world. Some work within broader media firms, others in niche outfits that attract clients by virtue of their own reputation. Clients include theatre and opera companies, producers, theatrical agents and actors. Theatre lawyers will spend a lot of time in contract negotiations for their clients; relationships between the constituent parties to a new production all need to be established and regulated through these contracts. A lawyer will usually find himself involved from the inception of the idea for a production right through to the opening curtain and beyond and, increasingly, lawyers will become involved in arrangements for the funding of a new production.

publishing

Work in this sector includes contractual, licensing, copyright and libel advice for newspapers and publishing houses. Most of this is carried out in-house or by libel lawyers, so there are only a few London firms that can be said to specialise in publishing law. An interest in language and literature is an obvious requirement. More and more work is for internet-based publications.

skills needed

...people skills... flexibility... understanding of basic psychology... same outlook and language as clients... understanding how creative people work... *"you need to do a lot of hand-holding"*... patience... prepared to immerse yourself in the industry... a thorough knowledge of contract and copyright law... creativity in problem solving... commercial aptitude... methodical nature... inquisitiveness...

In the early stage of your career you must learn quickly how the industry works; clients value experience. Abigail Paine, a senior associate at Harbottle & Lewis, explained that clients are creative people looking for commercial solutions. *"This isn't an area where you can just pull out a precedent and fill in the blanks – you actually need a lot of commercial acumen and you need to be innovative."* She also makes the point that *"you're very rarely instructed as to what to do, unlike in the big City* firms, where large corporate clients often structure the commercial deals themselves and then instruct lawyers to document them." Social skills are important: *"There's an awful lot of client development work... Entertainment lawyers at niche firms are expected to bring clients in... You need to be creative to do this. For example, I go to American film festivals every year and meet with US producers and financiers. I also go to the Cannes Film Festival."* In addition, she gets invited to the premieres of the films she's worked on. How utterly awful for her.

career options

It's not easy becoming an entertainment lawyer; there aren't many firms that do it and competition for training contracts is as stiff as it gets. There are two basic routes in – train at a niche entertainment firm or train at a large City firm with a specialism in entertainment. Abigail thinks it's more difficult to move to a City firm after training at an entertainment firm, as City firms are generally looking for someone with a wider commercial background in their training. However, at Harbottle & Lewis, *"We quite often take on people from bigger City firms at the six months to one year qualified level."* Remember though, it's an area in which many vacancies will come up by word of mouth. It really is a case of who you know.

Lawyers transfer between private practice and in-house jobs at media and entertainment organisations more readily than they did a few years ago. The money is generally perceived to be better in-house and the hours are considered more favourable – you don't need to go out looking for new clients, for example. In-house legal counsel can come from both specialist media firms and general commercial firms. A lack of stiffness and formality is characteristic of the entertainment industry generally, which often translates through to the working environment. Casual dress, less hierarchy and involvement in a fair degree of non-legal business management tasks can make for a refreshing contrast to the usual experience of a commercial lawyer.

Abigail worked in-house at the BBC for two years after she qualified, handling independent drama financing work. *"The people are more relaxed than in private practice, there's less pressure and you're never scared to ask things. You're given a lot more responsibility – I was the main lawyer involved in financing films with £3-4 million budgets, doing the work of a two-year qualified even though I had just completed a training contract!"* How did the vacancy come up? *"By word of mouth."* Naturally.

LEADING FIRMS FROM CHAMBERS UK GUIDE 2002-2003

DEFAMATION
■ THE REGIONS

1. **Foot Anstey Sargent** Exeter
   Wiggin & Co Cheltenham
2. **Brabners Chaffe Street** Liverpool
   Cobbetts Manchester
3. **Pannone & Partners** Manchester
   Wragge & Co Birmingham

MEDIA & ENTERTAINMENT
■ THE REGIONS

1. **Manches** Oxford
   McCormicks Leeds
   Wiggin & Co Cheltenham
2. **Eversheds** Leeds
   Morgan Cole Cardiff, Swansea

SPECIALIST PRACTICE AREAS — MEDIA AND ENTERTAINMENT LAW

ADVERTISING & MARKETING
LONDON

1. Lewis Silkin
   Macfarlanes
   Osborne Clarke
2. The Simkins Partnership
3. Hammond Suddards Edge
   Theodore Goddard
4. Lawrence Graham
   Olswang
   Taylor Wessing
5. Clifford Chance
   Mayer, Brown, Rowe & Maw
6. Baker & McKenzie
   CMS Cameron McKenna
   Harrison Curtis
   Lovells

DEFAMATION
LONDON

1. Davenport Lyons
   Farrer & Co
   Olswang
   Peter Carter-Ruck and Partners
   Schillings
2. D J Freeman
   David Price Solicitors & Advocates
   Reynolds Porter Chamberlain
   Theodore Goddard
3. Pinsent Curtis Biddle
   Russell Jones & Walker
4. Bindman & Partners
   Charles Russell
   Clifford Chance
   Goodman Derrick
   H2O
   Lovells
   Simons Muirhead & Burton
   Wiggin & Co
5. Finers Stephens Innocent
   Harbottle & Lewis
   Lee & Thompson
   Lewis Silkin
   Mishcon de Reya

MEDIA & ENTERTAINMENT: FILM FINANCE
LONDON

1. Richards Butler
   SJ Berwin
2. Davenport Lyons
   Denton Wilde Sapte
   Olswang
3. The Simkins Partnership
   Theodore Goddard

MEDIA & ENTERTAINMENT: FILM & TV PRODUCTION
LONDON

1. Olswang
2. Harbottle & Lewis
   Lee & Thompson
   Theodore Goddard
3. Davenport Lyons
   Richards Butler
   The Simkins Partnership
4. Denton Wilde Sapte
   Harrison Curtis
   Simons Muirhead & Burton
   SJ Berwin

MEDIA & ENTERTAINMENT: BROADCASTING
LONDON

1. Denton Wilde Sapte
   Olswang
2. Ashurst Morris Crisp
   Clifford Chance
3. Goodman Derrick
   Wiggin & Co
4. Allen & Overy
   DJ Freeman
   Davenport Lyons
   Field Fisher Waterhouse
   Harbottle & Lewis
   Herbert Smith
   Richards Butler
   SJ Berwin
   The Simkins Partnership
5. Lovells
   Travers Smith Braithwaite

MEDIA & ENTERTAINMENT: PUBLISHING
LONDON

1. Denton Wilde Sapte
2. Taylor Wessing
   The Simkins Partnership
3. Finers Stephens Innocent
   Harbottle & Lewis
   Lovells

MEDIA & ENTERTAINMENT: MUSIC
LONDON

1. Russells
2. Clintons
3. Lee & Thompson
4. Sheridans
   The Simkins Partnership
   Theodore Goddard
5. Bray & Krais
   Harbottle & Lewis
   Mishcon de Reya
6. Davenport Lyons
   Denton Wilde Sapte
   Eversheds
   Hamlins
   Harrison Curtis
   Marriott Harrison
   Searles
   Spraggon Stennett Brabyn

MEDIA & ENTERTAINMENT: THEATRE
LONDON

1. Clintons
   Tarlo Lyons
2. The Simkins Partnership
3. Bates, Wells & Braithwaite
   Campbell Hooper
   Harrison Curtis
4. Harbottle & Lewis
5. Theodore Goddard

personal injury & clinical negligence

PI and clinical negligence firms come in two flavours: claimant and defendant. Firms acting for defendants of personal injury claims act for insurance companies in the main and firms who defend clinical negligence claims represent health authorities, hospital trusts, other public bodies and insurers. Usually a firm with a strong defendant client base will not risk a conflict of interest by taking on claimant cases (which could be against its own client or a potential new client).

type of work

personal injury: PI cases can be small, such as pavement 'slippers and trippers' and whiplash claims arising from road traffic accidents (RTAs). At the other end of the scale are huge multi-party industrial disease claims against large companies. Deafness, diseases resulting from exposure to asbestos, Vibration White Finger (VWF) in miners... sadly there are plenty of examples.

'Lower end' (ie low value and high volume) PI work may be carried out by paralegals and trainees, while qualified solicitors at specialist firms take on more serious cases, such as major road accidents or accidents at work. Legal Aid is no longer available for PI cases, so almost all of the work is undertaken on a conditional fee agreement (CFA). This is what's called 'no win, no fee' and those of you who watch far too much daytime TV will all know the ads! No win, no fee involves stringent risk assessment by firms before they agree to take on a case, to ensure it has a good enough chance of winning. The new Civil Procedure Rules (CPR) have streamlined litigation procedure so that as much preparation and investigation of the claim as is possible takes place before trial. The aim is to promote greater transparency between the parties to ensure settlement is reached in many more cases.

These two changes effectively mean that PI work nowadays entails a lot of paperwork. This involves getting to grips with detailed medical reports, drafting witness statements and keeping clients updated on their case. It's not all paper pushing though. The work takes solicitors out of the office to see clients, some of whom may not be able to get out of the house because of their injuries, or perhaps to a conference with a barrister. They may also need to go and investigate the site of an accident or incident.

Defendant personal injury firms work on panels appointed by insurance companies. As the majority of insurance claims fall into the 'lower end' category, this kind of work is the daily staple of defendant firms. It's the higher value and often unusual claims which catch the public attention. Defendant firm Vizards Wyeth is currently acting for McDonald's handling a claim from a woman who spilt a cup of coffee on her knee!

clinical negligence: Quite simply, claimant clients are the victims of medical treatment that went wrong. Action taken on their behalf could be against a hospital or health authority for negligent treatment by one or more of their medical practitioners, or perhaps a pharmaceutical company arising out of the use of unsafe drugs. Additionally there are public enquiries, such as that into the Bristol heart babies, and cases which involve issues of patient confidentiality, mental health or consent to treatment, for instance where an abortion was performed very close to the legal time limit. The clients, while usually individual claimants, can be a part of a group action (eg MMR). Some firms have professional bodies as their clients. Welsh firm Hugh James, for instance, is on the panel of firms acting for the Royal College of Nursing in claims pertaining to back injuries and stress.

Claimant clinical negligence work necessitates

first and foremost building up a rapport with the client. Not only have they suffered great personal tragedy but they often mistrust professionals, having been let down by the one professional they feel they should most be able to trust – their doctor. As with PI, there's considerable paperwork required in preparation for trial and broadly the same client handling activities.

A significant change in this area is the streamlining of the number of firms who defend claims against the NHS. The National Health Service Litigation Authority (NHSLA) has appointed a panel of 16 firms to handle all its work. Capsticks is one of these firms and since April 2002 all of its clinical defence work has come from the NHSLA. According to Sarah Stanton, a partner at the firm, the NHSLA runs various schemes rather like an insurance company but is a part of the NHS and reports to the Department of Health. Consequently the NHSLA won't usually know the particular health professionals involved in the case in question. It is up to the solicitors to get the professionals' views on the case. *"The doctors and nurses involved in the case are witnesses and the solicitor has to make sure they understand the difference between being negligent and not. They often don't realise how much detail is required during the case."*

a day in the life...

Sarah will typically start her day with her postbag and a bit of general admin. She'll spend the greater part of the morning on 'heavy duty' paper work, such as drafting a witness statement or an advisory report to a client, although there's always a number of phone calls that interrupt the flow. The afternoon is filled with routine correspondence, chasing people for information, updating clients etc. and there may well be a meeting with the rest of her team to discuss one of their cases. Part of one day a week will be spent out of the office either at court or visiting witnesses - the doctors and nurses. Once or twice a month there will be an evening case conference with a barrister.

Life as a trainee is rewarding. Working under Sarah you would be *"fully involved... you can expect to be part of the team in a true sense and make a valuable contribution."* The standard trainee job is research, which may be into medical matters, duty of care, procedure or quantum (the level of damages the claimant should get). There is no escaping preparing trial bundles for any trainee in contentious work, but more interesting work might involve drafting instructions to an expert witness. Advocacy is also greatly encouraged for trainees so, if on a claimant case, you could expect to make an application to court, for instance to approve the level of damages to be made to a child claimant.

skills needed

...confidence in your own decisions... communication skills... good bedside manner... clear and logical thinker... sympathy for client... eye for detail... firm negotiator... interest in medical issues... interest in people... tact with professionals (they don't like being criticised!)... calm...organised...

Lawyers in this area, like any other, must have an eye for detail. More importantly, says Sarah, because the work involves wading through swathes of medical documents, you learn to expect the unexpected. *"A document can seem insignificant then it gets to trial and it's really significant."* A medical background is not necessary and although *"it helps in the early days, you do pick up the knowledge along the way."* That said, leading clinical negligence practices often have their fair share of former medical professionals. It's not an ideal practice area if you are squeamish as the facts of some cases can be harrowing. It can be an incredibly stressful area but does not provide the massive financial compensations of City firms. Simply put, money is not what motivates solicitors in this area.

Trainees learn to stand on their own two feet quickly. According to Stephen Webber, an assistant solicitor at Hugh James, the biggest difference between this kind of work and commercial work is that rather than having the partner make all the decisions, a trainee handling a PI caseload makes their own decisions on a daily basis.

It can be difficult remaining detached from the client when a case takes three or four years and the relationship becomes more intense as you near trial. To overcome this difficulty, *"you have to focus on proving the case and getting the best result"*. But a sense of great personal reward can come from the intensity of the relationship: *"the defendant is generally insured and can get the best advice – the claimant isn't and often doesn't understand the legal process. You can help them get justice using your professional training."* So for Stephen, *"it's a nice feeling handing over the cheque to a claimant who knows their house and kids are going to be secure."*

Ann Alexander, Managing Partner of Alexander Harris, loves her work most of all because she not only makes a difference to one person's life, but can also change the system. Since she took on and won a case involving patients who were awake but paralysed under anaesthetic, she says, *"there has been a complete rethink on training anaesthetists and preventing this happening again. They have developed a method of testing if people are awake. Things have changed in health care due to our work."*

career options

Sarah and Stephen trained in firms that carried out PI and clinical negligence work. Things were a bit different for Ann, who started off doing general high street contentious work, such as hearings in Magistrates' Courts and care proceedings. The reason she took on her first clinical negligence case is that she was recommended as a solicitor who would listen! The best start in this area is to gain a coveted training contract at one of the specialist firms. An alternative route in is applying for a paralegal position after your degree and LPC and to show the firm just what you can do. Alexander Harris and Hodge Jones & Allen recruit lots of their trainees from their paralegal departments, but still look for a 2.1, such is the competition for places.

After training there are few opportunities outside private practice. Some lawyers move in-house to the NHSLA or other defence organisations, such as the Medical Defence Union. Stephen Webber has diversified his work by taking on PI related cases with a human rights aspect.

LEADING FIRMS FROM CHAMBERS UK GUIDE 2002-2003

PERSONAL INJURY: MAINLY CLAIMANT — LONDON

1. **Irwin Mitchell**
   Leigh, Day & Co
   Russell Jones & Walker
2. **Evill and Coleman**
   Pattinson & Brewer
   Stewarts
   Thompsons
3. **Anthony Gold**
   Field Fisher Waterhouse
   Hodge Jones & Allen
   Rowley Ashworth
4. **Bolt Burdon**
   Levenes
   OH Parsons & Partners

PERSONAL INJURY: MAINLY DEFENDANT — LONDON

1. **Barlow Lyde & Gilbert**
   Beachcroft Wansbroughs
   Berrymans Lace Mawer
   Kennedys
2. **Vizards Wyeth**
3. **Badhams**
   Davies Arnold Cooper
   Hextalls

PERSONAL INJURY: MAINLY CLAIMANT — THE SOUTH

1. **Lamport Bassitt** Southampton
2. **George Ide, Phillips** Chichester
   Moore & Blatch Southampton
   Shoosmiths Basingstoke
   Thomson Snell & Passmore Tunbridge Wells
3. **Amery-Parkes** Basingstoke
   Blake Lapthorn Portsmouth
   Pattinson & Brewer Chatham
   Warner Goodman & Streat Fareham

PERSONAL INJURY: MAINLY DEFENDANT — THE SOUTH

1. **Beachcroft Wansbroughs** Winchester
   Berrymans Lace Mawer Southampton
   Bond Pearce Southampton
   Clarke Willmott & Clarke Southampton
2. **Davies Lavery** Maidstone
   Palser Grossman Southampton
   Vizards Wyeth Dartford

PERSONAL INJURY: MAINLY CLAIMANT — THAMES VALLEY

1. **Boyes Turner** Reading
   Osborne Morris & Morgan Leighton Buzzard
2. **Fennemores** Milton Keynes
   Harris Cartwright Slough
   Henmans Oxford

PERSONAL INJURY: MAINLY DEFENDANT — THAMES VALLEY

1. **Morgan Cole** Reading
2. **Henmans** Oxford

PERSONAL INJURY: MAINLY CLAIMANT — SOUTH WEST

1. **Bond Pearce** Bristol, Plymouth
   Veale Wasbrough Bristol
2. **Lyons Davidson** Bristol
   Russell Jones & Walker Bristol
   Thompsons Bristol
3. **Rowley Ashworth** Exeter

PERSONAL INJURY: MAINLY DEFENDANT — SOUTH WEST

1. **Beachcroft Wansbroughs** Bristol
2. **Bond Pearce** Bristol, Plymouth
   Cartwrights Insurance Partners Bristol
3. **Bevan Ashford** Bristol
   Palser Grossman Bristol
   Veitch Penny Exeter

PERSONAL INJURY: MAINLY CLAIMANT — WALES

1. **Hugh James** Cardiff, Merthyr Tydfil
   Leo Abse & Cohen Cardiff
2. **Thompsons** Cardiff
3. **Loosemores** Cardiff
   Russell Jones & Walker Cardiff

PERSONAL INJURY: MAINLY DEFENDANT — WALES

1. **Hugh James** Cardiff
   Morgan Cole Cardiff
2. **Palser Grossman** Cardiff Bay
3. **Dolmans** Cardiff

PERSONAL INJURY: MAINLY CLAIMANT
MIDLANDS

1. **Freethcartwright** Nottingham
   Irwin Mitchell Birmingham
   Rowley Ashworth Birmingham, Wolverhampton
   Thompsons Birmingham
2. **Barratt, Goff & Tomlinson** Nottingham
   Russell Jones & Walker Birmingham

PERSONAL INJURY: MAINLY DEFENDANT
MIDLANDS

1. **Beachcroft Wansbroughs** Birmingham
   Browne Jacobson Nottingham
   Buller Jeffries Birmingham
   Weightman Vizards Birmingham
2. **Everatt & Company** Evesham
3. **DLA** Birmingham
   Palser Grossman Birmingham

PERSONAL INJURY: MAINLY CLAIMANT
EAST ANGLIA

1. **Cunningham John** Thetford
2. **Morgan Jones & Pett** Great Yarmouth
   Taylor Vinters Cambridge
3. **Edwards Duthie** Ilford
   Leathes Prior Norwich

PERSONAL INJURY: MAINLY DEFENDANT
EAST ANGLIA

1. **Eversheds** Ipswich
2. **Mills & Reeve** Norwich
   Prettys Ipswich
3. **Edwards Duthie** Ilford
   Kennedys Brentwood

PERSONAL INJURY: MAINLY CLAIMANT
NORTH WEST

1. **Pannone & Partners** Manchester
2. **John Pickering & Partners** Oldham
   Leigh, Day & Co Manchester
   Russell Jones & Walker Manchester
   Thompsons Liverpool
3. **Donns Solicitors** Manchester
   Hugh Potter & Company Manchester
4. **Alexander Harris** Altrincham
   Linder Myers Manchester

PERSONAL INJURY: MAINLY DEFENDANT
NORTH WEST

1. **James Chapman & Co** Manchester
2. **Berrymans Lace Mawer** Liverpool, Manchester
   Halliwell Landau Manchester
   Keoghs Bolton
   Weightman Vizards Liverpool, Manchester
3. **Beachcroft Wansbroughs** Manchester
   Hill Dickinson Liverpool, Manchester

PERSONAL INJURY: MAINLY CLAIMANT
YORKSHIRE

1. **Irwin Mitchell** Sheffield
2. **Pattinson & Brewer** York
   Rowley Ashworth Leeds
   Russell Jones & Walker Leeds, Sheffield
3. **Bridge McFarland Solicitors** Grimsby
   Morrish & Co Leeds

PERSONAL INJURY: MAINLY DEFENDANT
YORKSHIRE

1. **Beachcroft Wansbroughs** Leeds
   DLA Bradford, Leeds, Sheffield
2. **Irwin Mitchell** Leeds
   Nabarro Nathanson Sheffield
   Keeble Hawson Leeds, Sheffield
   Langleys York
   Praxis Partners Leeds

PERSONAL INJURY: MAINLY CLAIMANT
NORTH EAST

1. **Thompsons** Newcastle upon Tyne
2. **Browell Smith & Co** Newcastle upon Tyne
   Marrons Newcastle upon Tyne
   Russell Jones & Walker Newcastle upon Tyne
3. **Hay & Kilner** Newcastle upon Tyne
4. **Beecham Peacock** Newcastle upon Tyne
   Gorman Hamilton Solicitors Newcastle upon Tyne

PERSONAL INJURY: MAINLY DEFENDANT
NORTH EAST

1. **Eversheds** Newcastle upon Tyne
   Hay & Kilner Newcastle upon Tyne
   Sinton & Co Newcastle upon Tyne
2. **Crutes Law Firm** Newcastle upon Tyne
   Jacksons Stockton on Tees

SPECIALIST PRACTICE AREAS — PERSONAL INJURY & CLINICAL

CLINICAL NEGLIGENCE: MAINLY CLAIMANT — LONDON
1. Leigh, Day & Co
2. Alexander Harris
   - Bindman & Partners
   - Charles Russell
   - Kingsley Napley
3. Evill and Coleman
   - Field Fisher Waterhouse
   - Parlett Kent
4. Irwin Mitchell
   - Russell Jones & Walker
   - Stewarts

CLINICAL NEGLIGENCE: MAINLY DEFENDANT — LONDON
1. Capsticks
2. Hempsons
3. Weightman Vizards
4. Bevan Ashford
   - RadcliffesLeBrasseur

CLINICAL NEGLIGENCE: MAINLY CLAIMANT — THE SOUTH
1. Blake Lapthorn Portsmouth, Southampton
2. Thomson Snell & Passmore Tunbridge Wells
3. Penningtons Basingstoke, Godalming
   - Wynne Baxter Brighton

CLINICAL NEGLIGENCE: MAINLY DEFENDANT — THE SOUTH
1. Beachcroft Wansbroughs Winchester
2. Brachers Maidstone

CLINICAL NEGLIGENCE: MAINLY CLAIMANT — THAMES VALLEY
1. Boyes Turner Reading
2. Osborne Morris & Morgan Leighton Buzzard
3. Harris Cartwright Slough

CLINICAL NEGLIGENCE: MAINLY CLAIMANT — SOUTH WEST
1. Barcan Woodward Bristol
   - Preston Goldburn Falmouth
2. Clarke Willmott & Clarke Bristol, Taunton
   - John Hodge & Co Weston-super-Mare
   - Withy King Bath
3. Over Taylor Biggs Exeter
   - Russell Jones & Walker Bristol
   - Wolferstans Plymouth
   - Woollcombe Beer Watts Newton Abbot

CLINICAL NEGLIGENCE: MAINLY DEFENDANT — SOUTH WEST
- Bevan Ashford Bristol
- Beachcroft Wansbroughs Bristol

CLINICAL NEGLIGENCE: MAINLY CLAIMANT — WALES
1. Huttons Cardiff
2. Hugh James Cardiff
   - John Collins & Partners Swansea
3. Edwards Geldard Cardiff
   - Russell Jones & Walker Cardiff

CLINICAL NEGLIGENCE: MAINLY CLAIMANT — MIDLANDS
1. freethcartwright Nottingham
   - Irwin Mitchell Birmingham
2. Anthony Collins Solicitors Birmingham
   - Challinors Lyon Clark Birmingham

CLINICAL NEGLIGENCE: MAINLY DEFENDANT — MIDLANDS
1. Bevan Ashford Birmingham
   - Browne Jacobson Birmingham, Nottingham
2. Weightman Vizards Birmingham

CLINICAL NEGLIGENCE: MAINLY CLAIMANT — EAST ANGLIA
1. Cunningham John Thetford
2. Gadsby Wicks Chelmsford
3. Attwater & Liell Harlow
   - Morgan Jones & Pett Great Yarmouth
   - Scrivenger Seabrook St Neots
4. Prettys Ipswich

CLINICAL NEGLIGENCE: MAINLY DEFENDANT — EAST ANGLIA
1. Kennedys Newmarket

CLINICAL NEGLIGENCE: MAINLY CLAIMANT — NORTH WEST
1. Pannone & Partners Manchester
2. Alexander Harris Altrincham
3. Jones Maidment Wilson Manchester
   - Leigh, Day & Co Manchester
   - Linder Myers Manchester

CLINICAL NEGLIGENCE: MAINLY DEFENDANT — NORTH WEST
1. Hempsons Manchester
2. Hill Dickinson Liverpool
3. George Davies Manchester

private client

Private client lawyers act for individuals, families, trusts and charities as opposed to corporate entities, and the sort of 'private client work' you'll experience will depend on the type of firm you join. In a high street firm, your client could be any member of the public, wealthy or otherwise, and could require advice on divorce, conveyancing, wills or probate. In a commercial firm, you'll focus on tax, trusts and probate advice for high net worth individuals who are prepared to pay higher fees for specialist advice and a dedicated personal service.

In this section we've concentrated on general private client lawyers who advise on the acquisition, disposal and management of the personal assets of wealthy individuals and families. The work is primarily advisory although litigation does arise from time to time.

type of work

trusts, probate and personal tax: This is not the sort of work you fall into by accident. You'll already know that you are inclined towards working with people – solving their problems and helping them manage their lives and money – and not corporate machines.

Trusts are a very popular way of holding assets and avoiding tax (rather than evading tax, which is illegal), often by holding funds in offshore jurisdictions. Trusts allow family members access to funds while also allowing the donor a degree of control over the ultimate destination of funds. The creation of trusts in other jurisdictions often means that a lawyer will have to spend time ensuring that his client understands the system of law behind the trust. A lawyer must be very careful to apprise the client of all the possible foreign law implications. As well as handling offshore trusts in conjunction with overseas lawyers and trust companies, private client lawyers find that they advise an increasing number of overseas clients seeking to invest in the UK. Offshore and private banks may also need advice about their clients' UK interests. There's clearly a lot of law involved in this type of work and if you shudder at the thought of this then private client work may not be for you. Joanna Tolhurst is a solicitor in the UK Private Client department of leading firm, Farrer & Co. She says, *"There's a lot of law involved in trusts work and it's an intellectual discipline, which you must enjoy. Most private client lawyers would probably say their favourite subject in their law degree or on the CPE was trusts."*

The solicitor is often drawn into a very detailed examination of a client's family life and finances. They have to respect the client's privacy while maintaining impartiality and giving the best possible practical advice. The solicitor must also listen to the most private details of family circumstances and finances with understanding, but without being judgemental.

You have to be naturally curious, and then the volume of personal information the client offers has to be logically sorted out in order for the client's affairs to be managed in the most tax-efficient way. Joanna says, *"Clients have to be honest with you and tell you the whole story... if you think they haven't then they need to be prompted. You might have to ask 'Are you thinking of retiring soon?' 'What are the children doing?' 'Do you like your son-in-law?' You have to be thinking all the time when they are talking to you."*

Will drafting and probate – the management of a deceased's affairs in accordance with their will (or, failing that, in accordance with the laws of intestacy) – forms a good proportion of the work of private client lawyers, especially in the early years. From the beginning a young lawyer will be able to get involved in this work. Even as a trainee you might start with ten small files of your own – new wills, a couple of probates and maybe an ongoing trust file or two. You learn how to become multi-skilled: writing and speaking to clients and researching black letter law. Perhaps the most unexpected aspect of the work is the real-life mini-dramas that you get thrown into and the practical side of the job. Joanna told us of the time when she found herself feeding Madeira cake to a tortoise and chasing a Chinchilla around a deceased client's kitchen. *"The client had left a letter saying that she wanted the tortoise fed on the cake! If the client dies without leaving any relatives, it's the solicitor who goes to the home to look for papers and start the process of disposing of the house. You learn how to do all sorts of practical things – organising house clearances and how to ship furniture."*

A private client lawyer will be consulted on a range of different issues, from immigration and employment questions through to share transactions and property deals. The most experienced individuals have the breadth of experience to give an answer to these diverse questions. In time, some private clients will get very close to you and won't do anything major without asking your advice. In a large multi-service law firm, a wise lawyer will turn to the expertise of colleagues, but he or she will always keep apprised of the advice colleagues give.

charities: This is a related area of practice where clients range from well-known national charities to low-profile, local, private charitable trusts. Work consists of charity registrations and reorganisations, Charity Commission investigations, the development of trading subsidiaries and advising charitable clients on other issues such as tax, trust or property matters. Many firms, especially the smaller ones, frequently specialise in advising particular types of charities, for example religious or environmental charities.

skills needed

…enjoy one-on-one interaction… be interested in other people's personal and family affairs… want to help people… good 'bedside manner'… good eye for detail… strong grounding in and affinity with trusts and tax… numeracy… an organised mind… naturally curious…

Joanna thinks that those in private client work *"do tend to be individualistic and quite intellectual. If your ego is huge you won't be doing it as there's less champagne and less jostling for position with colleagues."* Some would say that the reason why there are more women than men going into private client work is that certain attributes that are found quite commonly in women – an interest in getting to know people and their personal lives and understanding what they want – are the key to success.

career options

Most private client lawyers spend their entire careers in private practice, some specialising in international clients, others UK clients. Training at an established private client firm, such as Withers, Farrer & Co or Boodle Hatfield, will give the best possible start. City firms such as Allen & Overy and Macfarlanes have continued to offer these services, allowing trainees to combine private client work with a corporate training. Moves between the high street and the firms servicing wealthy individuals are not that common, but either training will set you up well for provincial practice. In the 1990s large corporate practices shed private client departments, but a few firms with clients amongst the new breed of 'e-trepreneurs' have benefited from retaining private client lawyers. In-house opportunities are limited although a few offshore trust companies and private banks do have in-house legal advisors. Banks in, say, the Bahamas, Cayman Islands and Channel Islands employ lawyers in advisory or risk control positions. Those who want to spend time in an offshore and tropical haven can pretty much do so as soon as they have built up some post-qualification experience.

For charities specialists there is less scope in terms of law firms specialising in this area, but with the opportunity to make strong contacts with clients, there is always the possibility of moving into a more general role within the sector. For details of the leading private client and charities firms, refer to *Chambers UK*.

LEADING FIRMS FROM CHAMBERS UK GUIDE 2002-2003

SPECIALIST PRACTICE AREAS — PRIVATE CLIENT

TRUSTS & PERSONAL TAX
LONDON

1
- Macfarlanes
- Withers LLP

2
- Allen & Overy
- Charles Russell
- Currey & Co
- Lawrence Graham

3
- Boodle Hatfield
- Farrer & Co
- Forsters
- Speechly Bircham
- Taylor Wessing

4
- Baker & McKenzie
- Bircham Dyson Bell
- Payne Hicks Beach

5
- Berwin Leighton Paisner
- Hunters
- Linklaters
- May, May & Merrimans
- Nicholson Graham & Jones
- Simmons & Simmons
- Wedlake Bell

6
- Dawsons
- Lee & Pembertons
- Pemberton Greenish
- RadcliffesLeBrasseur
- Rooks Rider
- Smyth Barkham
- Trowers & Hamlins

TRUSTS & PERSONAL TAX
WALES

1
- Edwards Geldard Cardiff
- Hugh James Cardiff

2
- Margraves Llandrindod Wells

TRUSTS & PERSONAL TAX
THE SOUTH

1
- Cripps Harries Hall Tunbridge Wells

2
- Adams & Remers Lewes
- Penningtons Godalming
- Stevens & Bolton Guildford
- Thomas Eggar Chichester
- Thomson Snell & Passmore Tunbridge Wells

3
- Blake Lapthorn Portsmouth
- Charles Russell Guildford
- Lester Aldridge Bournemouth
- Moore & Blatch Lymington
- Mundays Cobham
- Paris Smith & Randall Southampton
- White & Bowker Winchester

4
- Barlows Guildford
- Brachers Maidstone

5
- DMH Brighton
- George Ide, Phillips Chichester
- Godwins Winchester
- Griffith Smith Brighton
- Rawlison Butler Crawley
- Whitehead Monckton Maidstone

TRUSTS & PERSONAL TAX
SOUTH WEST

1
- Burges Salmon Bristol
- Wilsons Salisbury

2
- Osborne Clarke Bristol
- Wiggin & Co Cheltenham

3
- Bond Pearce Plymouth
- Charles Russell Cheltenham

4
- Clarke Willmott & Clarke Bristol
- Foot Anstey Sargent Plymouth
- Hooper & Wollen Torquay
- Veale Wasbrough Bristol

5
- Coodes St Austell
- Michelmores Exeter
- Rickerbys Cheltenham
- TLT Solicitors Bristol

TRUSTS & PERSONAL TAX
THAMES VALLEY

1
- Boodle Hatfield Oxford

2
- Blandy & Blandy Reading
- Boyes Turner Reading
- Henmans Oxford
- Iliffes Booth Bennett (IBB) Uxbridge

3
- BP Collins Gerrards Cross
- Matthew Arnold & Baldwin Watford

4
- Pictons Hemel Hempstead

5
- Stanley Tee Bishop's Stortford

TRUSTS & PERSONAL TAX
MIDLANDS

1
- Martineau Johnson Birmingham

2
- Browne Jacobson Nottingham
- Hewitson Becke + Shaw Northampton
- Lodders Stratford-upon-Avon

3
- Higgs & Sons Brierley Hill
- Lee Crowder Birmingham
- Pinsent Curtis Biddle Birmingham
- Wragge & Co Birmingham

4
- freethcartwright Nottingham
- Gateley Wareing Birmingham
- Shakespeares Birmingham

TRUSTS & PERSONAL TAX
EAST ANGLIA

1
- Mills & Reeve Norwich

2
- Hewitson Becke + Shaw Cambridge
- Taylor Vinters Cambridge

3
- Greene & Greene Bury St Edmunds
- Howes Percival Norwich

4
- Cozens-Hardy & Jewson Norwich
- Prettys Ipswich
- Roythorne & Co Spalding

5
- Ashton Graham Bury St Edmunds, Ipswich
- Hood Vores & Allwood Dereham
- Willcox & Lewis Norwich

SPECIALIST PRACTICE AREAS – PRIVATE CLIENT

TRUSTS & PERSONAL TAX – NORTH WEST

1
- **Halliwell Landau** Manchester

2
- **Addleshaw Booth & Co** Manchester
- **Birch Cullimore** Chester
- **Brabners Chaffe Street** Liverpool
- **Cuff Roberts** Liverpool

3
- **Cobbetts** Manchester
- **Pannone & Partners** Manchester

TRUSTS & PERSONAL TAX – NORTH EAST

1
- **Dickinson Dees** Newcastle upon Tyne
- **Wrigleys** Leeds

2
- **Addleshaw Booth & Co** Leeds

3
- **Pinsent Curtis Biddle** Leeds

4
- **Andrew M Jackson** Hull
- **Grays** York
- **Irwin Mitchell** Sheffield
- **Lupton Fawcett** Leeds
- **Rollits** Hull
- **Ward Hadaway** Newcastle upon Tyne

5
- **Brooke North** Leeds
- **Gordons Cranswick Solicitors** Leeds

CHARITIES – THE SOUTH

1
- **Blake Lapthorn** Portsmouth
- **Thomas Eggar** Chichester

2
- **Barlows** Guildford
- **Cripps Harries Hall** Tunbridge Wells
- **Griffith Smith** Brighton
- **Lester Aldridge** Bournemouth
- **Thomson Snell & Passmore** Tunbridge Wells

CHARITIES – THAMES VALLEY

1
- **BrookStreet Des Roches** Witney
- **Manches** Oxford
- **Winckworth Sherwood** Oxford

2
- **Henmans** Oxford
- **Linnells** Oxford

CHARITIES – LONDON

1
- **Bates, Wells & Braithwaite**

2
- **Farrer & Co**

3
- **Nabarro Nathanson**
- **Withers LLP**

4
- **Berwin Leighton Paisner**
- **Bircham Dyson Bell**
- **Charles Russell**
- **Sinclair Taylor & Martin**

5
- **Allen & Overy**
- **Claricoat Phillips**
- **Harbottle & Lewis**
- **Macfarlanes**
- **RadcliffesLeBrasseur**
- **Stone King**

6
- **Herbert Smith**
- **Lawrence Graham**
- **Lee Bolton & Lee**
- **Linklaters**
- **Trowers & Hamlins**
- **Winckworth Sherwood**

CHARITIES – THE SOUTH WEST

1
- **Stone King** Bath

2
- **Bond Pearce** Exeter
- **Burges Salmon** Bristol
- **Osborne Clarke** Bristol
- **Veale Wasbrough** Bristol
- **Wilsons** Salisbury

3
- **Rickerbys** Cheltenham
- **Thring Townsend** Bath
- **Tozers** Exeter

CHARITIES – WALES

1
- **Edwards Geldard** Cardiff

CHARITIES – MIDLANDS

1
- **Anthony Collins Solicitors** Birmingham
- **Martineau Johnson** Birmingham
- **Wragge & Co** Birmingham

2
- **Hewitson Becke + Shaw** Northampton
- **Lee Crowder** Birmingham

CHARITIES – EAST ANGLIA

1
- **Mills & Reeve** Norwich
- **Taylor Vinters** Cambridge

2
- **Cozens-Hardy & Jewson** Norwich
- **Greenwoods** Peterborough
- **Hewitson Becke + Shaw** Cambridge
- **Leathes Prior** Norwich

CHARITIES – NORTH WEST

1
- **Birch Cullimore** Chester
- **Brabners Chaffe Street** Liverpool

2
- **Halliwell Landau** Manchester
- **Oswald Goodier & Co** Preston
- **Pannone & Partners** Manchester

CHARITIES – NORTH EAST

1
- **Wrigleys** Leeds

2
- **Addleshaw Booth & Co** Leeds
- **Grays** York

3
- **Dickinson Dees** Newcastle upon Tyne
- **Irwin Mitchell** Sheffield
- **Rollits** York

4
- **McCormicks** Leeds

property/real estate

Let's face facts, most students find land law simply dull, dull, dull. Why on earth would anyone choose to become a property lawyer? There's one fairly simple reason: property work involves real projects – things you can actually touch and real people, who you deal with right from the get go. Forget Re: Vandervell's Trusts, think of developing a new cinema in Leicester Square or converting an old factory site into a residential complex. Property deals are big, fat and tangible and, if you like, you can go and walk around in them. As Sophie Hamilton, senior partner at leading property firm Forsters, says, *"I don't understand Eurobonds and Futures other than in an intellectual way. I can't get hold of them in my hand and I wouldn't get excited about a 90-page document dealing with them, but properties are real."*

There's another simple reason why some trainees have a Road to Damascus experience with property – you get buckets of client contact from an early stage, handle your own cases and make a real difference from the outset. It appeals to those with a sense of independence. Wragge & Co associate, Mark Chester, dispelled the dull as ditch water myth: *"Don't be frightened off by the crap you go through at university and law school. Messrs Megarry and Wade are enough to send you into a coma, but practice is different."*

type of work

Work is divided between transactional matters and one-off management advice. Sophie gave us some examples of the sort non-transactional advice clients may need: *"The owner of an investment property might ring and say 'Enron have just gone bust and we let them a large amount of office space 18 months ago. What do we do now?' Or the occupier of a small property might ring and say, 'Someone's just dumped a skip in my yard? How do I get rid of it?'"* When does the average Eurobonds lawyer ever have to deal with a skip load of anything?

Most work is transactional and the best-informed property lawyers are those who keep themselves apprised of what's going on in the industry – the movers, the shakers and the deals. They are more likely to be reading *Property Week* and *The Estates Gazette* than Megarry and Wade. In the first couple of years you'll learn how to do *"bog standard"* work – sales and purchases, leases and transfers of leases, consents for the alteration or subletting of buildings. Mark told us that it's important to learn the basics inside and out before stepping up into more specialised work. Even the deals at *"the pointy end"* strip back to the fundamentals of the basic deals you cut your teeth on.

Across the country, most property lawyers act for a wide variety of clients: homeowners, small business tenants, landlords, investors and banks. They see the property market from all angles and must be able to champion the cause of these different parties. A varied workload is part of the appeal for many, but it does mean that the lawyer must continually adapt his or her style of communication and advice to suit the client. Only in the very largest firms will the property solicitor be pigeonholed into acting for just one type of client – usually large investors or banks. For Sophie, *"The most interesting clients are the developers; entrepreneurs who are coming up with the deals and the new projects."* Mark agrees with her.

Arguably, the fundamental decision to be made is between being a litigator and a commercial lawyer. Having chosen the latter, becoming a property lawyer simply means that you chose a job where deals are centred on land and buildings instead of, say, company shares (or maybe those Eurobonds). Certainly, the property lawyer's job will touch upon various other disciplines – company law, finance, revenue law, trusts, liquor licensing, health and safety, telecommunications, environmental law, agricultural law, insolvency, project finance and planning. Pretty quickly you learn about the role of surveyors and property agents, engineers and architects; you'll interact with the Inland Revenue, local authorities, the Land Registry, Companies House, banks and mortgage lenders, brokers, designers… and the list goes on. A property lawyer will get to know most of their contemporaries in the surveying firms locally. Surveyors are more gregarious than lawyers and Friday lunchtimes see hordes of surveyors in the city bars. Brave property lawyers are genuinely welcomed and valuable contacts are often made. You'll become an integral part of the professional world of property and you'll understand that clients regard you as a business adviser not the dull academic that you feared you'd become in land law lectures at uni.

day in the life of…

9am Consider 'Things To Do' list, which has become constant companion. Calculate that, without interruptions, list can be eliminated in two days. Fat chance! Morning post has now doubled said list. Receive latest draft of complex supermarket development agreement from counterpart acting for landowner. Said counterpart has a sneaky habit of never remembering to draft clauses to reflect points agreed in negotiations. Must check document with hawk's eye and redraft where necessary. Answer half a dozen short and simple letters and turn to supermarket project.

11.30am Mortgage funds arrive for purchase of totally gorgeous Chelsea penthouse for chairman of senior partner's most important client. Quick calculation confirms that we have total purchase money in firm's account – time to complete the deal and allow a cool £1.8 million to zing across electronically to seller's solicitors. Client is excited as an eight-year old on a sugar high (bodes well for gift of flowers).

2.10pm Double espresso in world-dominating coffee franchise has added to wonderful 'edgy' feeling, which always accompanies deal completion. Call from seller's solicitor to say all money received and sale is completed. Call delighted and gushing client. (Flowers now a dead cert.)

2.45pm Start lengthy task of reading purchase contract and lease for restaurant client opening new themed eatery in old water mill. Must become expert on all matters of a watery nature, read surveyors report closely and look into the limitations imposed on listed buildings.

4pm Eyes beginning to glaze over with volume of small print. Decide to have a fast and furious 90 minutes on itty-bitty elements of 'To Do' list. Interrupted by call from client whose financially troubled tenant has missed rent payment. Look at lease and advise anxious client. Agree to draft letter to send to errant tenant.

5.15pm Sign outgoing letters. Big bouquet still not showed up. Turn attention to water mill documents.

7pm Enough is enough. Tomorrow's another day…

skills needed

good on paper… good negotiator… persuasive in argument… precision and care… respect and understanding of black letter law… the ability to multi-task… well organised mind and paperwork… lateral thought… numeracy… an interest in the property world… team player… work well alone… flexibility…

The amount of documentation to be considered and amended requires you to be well organised, calm and ready to embrace detail. Successful property lawyers combine the capacity for new ideas and clever strategy with a willingness to sit down and turn the ideas – word by word – into watertight agreements. Negotiation skills are key. In addition to being able to argue a point well, you've got to know when to push, when to dig your heels in and when to give in. In this respect, pernickety lawyers do not make the best practitioners! Skills will come (in time) from practice, common sense and a good knowledge of what the property market will allow you to get away with. It's also your job to uncover everything there is to know about a property so tenacity is important. Ideally you'll be one part private detective, one part horse trader and one part draftsman.

Your dealings with clients, other lawyers and property professionals will be both on the phone and in meetings. You'll need to express yourself clearly and confidently. Generally both sides have the same goal and so the real trick is to get the best deal for your client within the time scale that they set for you. The most successful and satisfied property lawyers actually get on very well with their opposite numbers. Sophie told us that *"It makes all the difference in a transaction... everyone comes to the party at the end of the deal."*

At times in the biggest firms, a young lawyer might be a part of the team working on just one (albeit big) project. More typically, a property lawyer will have scores of different cases on the go at any one time, so you have to be pretty adept at juggling them all. You learn early on how to prioritise tasks. And you also learn that the list of 'Things To Do' never goes away!

career options

Just as the fortunes of the property market have been cyclical, the fortunes of property lawyers rise and fall accordingly. No longer just a support for more glamorous and bigger-billing departments, deals are more sophisticated and 'corporatised' than ever before and property lawyers can hold their heads up high.

Some in-house lawyers perform much the same function as those in private practice. Clerical Medical has a large in-house legal department with specialist property lawyers handling the fund's property deals in tandem with solicitors in private practice. At Warner Bros. lawyers act more like clients, instructing firms to carry out the work for them.

Know-how jobs crop up regularly as do public sector roles, say at the Land Registry or in a local authority. Some property lawyers even turn into developers... after all, why waste all that experience?

LEADING FIRMS FROM CHAMBERS UK GUIDE 2002-2003

SPECIALIST PRACTICE AREAS — PROPERTY/REAL ESTATE

REAL ESTATE: LARGER DEALS
■ LONDON

1. Linklaters
2. Clifford Chance
3. Berwin Leighton Paisner
   Herbert Smith
   Lovells
4. Ashurst Morris Crisp
   Freshfields Bruckhaus Deringer
   Nabarro Nathanson
   SJ Berwin
5. Allen & Overy
   CMS Cameron McKenna

REAL ESTATE: MEDIUM DEALS
■ LONDON

1. Dechert
   Denton Wilde Sapte
   Lawrence Graham
   Macfarlanes
2. DJ Freeman
   Gouldens
   Norton Rose
3. Forsters
   Mayer, Brown, Rowe & Maw
   Slaughter and May
4. Eversheds
   Olswang
   Simmons & Simmons
5. Field Fisher Waterhouse
   Richards Butler

REAL ESTATE: SMALLER DEALS
■ LONDON

1. Boodle Hatfield
   Maxwell Batley
2. Manches
   Nicholson Graham & Jones
   Speechly Bircham
   Travers Smith Braithwaite
3. Finers Stephens Innocent
   Fladgate Fielder
   Julian Holy
   Trowers & Hamlins
4. Hamlins
   Mishcon de Reya
   Osborne Clarke
   Park Nelson
   Stepien Lake Gilbert & Paling
   Taylor Wessing

REAL ESTATE
■ THAMES VALLEY

1. Pitmans Reading
2. BrookStreet Des Roches Witney
   Denton Wilde Sapte Milton Keynes
3. Clarks Reading
   Harold Benjamin Littlejohn Harrow
   Iliffes Booth Bennett (IBB) Uxbridge
   Morgan Cole Oxford, Reading
4. Linnells Oxford
   Matthew Arnold & Baldwin Watford
5. Boyes Turner Reading
   BPC Business Lawyers Beaconsfield
   Fennemores Milton Keynes
   Manches Oxford
   Nabarro Nathanson Reading
   Pictons Luton
   Stanley Tee Bishop's Stortford

REAL ESTATE
■ THE SOUTH

1. Blake Lapthorn Fareham, Portsmouth, Southampton
2. Bond Pearce Southampton
   Paris Smith & Randall Southampton
   Stevens & Bolton Guildford
3. Clyde & Co Guildford
   Cripps Harries Hall Tunbridge Wells
   Thomas Eggar Chichester, Horsham, Reigate, Worthing
4. Brachers Maidstone
   DMH Brighton, Crawley
   Laytons Guildford
   Lester Aldridge Bournemouth
   Steele Raymond Bournemouth
   Thomson Snell & Passmore Tunbridge Wells
5. Coffin Mew & Clover Portsmouth, Southampton
   GCL Solicitors Guildford
   Moore & Blatch Southampton
   Penningtons Basingstoke, Godalming, Newbury
   Rawlison Butler Crawley
   Shoosmiths Fareham

REAL ESTATE
■ WALES

1. Eversheds Cardiff
2. Berry Smith Cardiff
   Edwards Geldard Cardiff
3. Morgan Cole Cardiff, Swansea
4. Hugh James Cardiff
   Palser Grossman Cardiff Bay
   Robertsons Cardiff

SPECIALIST PRACTICE AREAS — PROPERTY/REAL ESTATE

REAL ESTATE ■ SOUTH WEST

1. **Burges Salmon** Bristol
   Osborne Clarke Bristol
2. **Beachcroft Wansbroughs** Bristol
   Bevan Ashford Bristol, Exeter, Plymouth, Taunton
   Bond Pearce Bristol, Exeter, Plymouth
   Michelmores Exeter
3. **Clarke Willmott & Clarke** Bristol, Bristol
   TLT Solicitors Bristol
4. **BPE** Cheltenham
   Davies and Partners Gloucester
   Rickerbys Cheltenham
   Stephens & Scown Exeter, Liskeard, St Austell, Truro
   Veale Wasbrough Bristol
5. **Charles Russell** Cheltenham
   Clark Holt Swindon
   Davitt Jones Bould Taunton
   Foot Anstey Sargent Plymouth
   Lyons Davidson Bristol
   Thring Townsend Bath, Swindon

REAL ESTATE ■ MIDLANDS

1. **Eversheds** Birmingham, Nottingham
   Wragge & Co Birmingham
2. **Hammond Suddards Edge** Birmingham
   Pinsent Curtis Biddle Birmingham
3. **DLA** Birmingham
   Lee Crowder Birmingham
4. **Browne Jacobson** Nottingham
   Freethcartwright Leicester
   freethcartwright Nottingham
   Shoosmiths Northampton, Nottingham
5. **Edwards Geldard** Derby, Nottingham
   Harvey Ingram Owston Leicester
   Knight & Sons Newcastle-under-Lyme
   Martineau Johnson Birmingham
   Wright Hassall Leamington Spa

REAL ESTATE ■ EAST ANGLIA

1. **Eversheds** Cambridge, Norwich
   Hewitson Becke + Shaw Cambridge
   Mills & Reeve Cambridge, Norwich
2. **Taylor Vinters** Cambridge
3. **Birketts** Ipswich
4. **Ashton Graham** Bury St Edmunds, Ipswich
   Greene & Greene Bury St Edmunds
   Greenwoods Peterborough
   Prettys Ipswich
   Wollastons Chelmsford
5. **Ellisons** Colchester
   Few & Kester Cambridge

REAL ESTATE ■ NORTH WEST

1. **Addleshaw Booth & Co** Manchester
   Bullivant Jones Liverpool
   Cobbetts Manchester
   DLA Liverpool, Manchester
   Eversheds Manchester
2. **Halliwell Landau** Manchester
   Hammond Suddards Edge Manchester
3. **DWF** Liverpool
   Field Cunningham & Co Manchester
   Pannone & Partners Manchester
4. **Beachcroft Wansbroughs** Manchester
   Mace & Jones Manchester
5. **Aaron & Partners** Chester
   Brabners Chaffe Street Liverpool
   Cuff Roberts Liverpool
   Hill Dickinson Chester, Liverpool, Manchester
   Jones Maidment Wilson Altrincham, Manchester
   Walker Smith & Way Chester

REAL ESTATE ■ YORKSHIRE

1. **Addleshaw Booth & Co** Leeds
   Walker Morris Leeds
2. **DLA** Leeds, Sheffield
   Pinsent Curtis Biddle Leeds
3. **Andrew M Jackson** Hull
   Cobbetts Leeds
   Eversheds Leeds
   Hammond Suddards Edge Leeds
4. **Gordons Cranswick Solicitors** Bradford, Leeds
   Nabarro Nathanson Sheffield
5. **Denison Till** York
   Gosschalks Hull
   Irwin Mitchell Sheffield
   Rollits Hull
6. **Keeble Hawson** Sheffield
   The Frith Partnership Leeds
   Wake Smith Sheffield

REAL ESTATE ■ NORTH EAST

1. **Dickinson Dees** Newcastle upon Tyne
2. **Eversheds** Newcastle upon Tyne
3. **Robert Muckle** Newcastle upon Tyne
   Ward Hadaway Newcastle upon Tyne
   Watson Burton Newcastle upon Tyne

public interest

civil liberties and human rights

type of work

When most of us look at a case, even if it seems unfair, we are likely to resign ourselves to the fact that nothing can be done because the law is the law. Civil liberties lawyers, such as Danny Simpson, head of the criminal and civil liberties department at Howells in Sheffield, believe that *"we ought to be able to use the existing law to challenge injustices."*

This kind of work stems from an attitude of mind. Civil liberties or human rights aspects will be found in many cases if you look for them. It is fast reaching the point when almost every case, civil or criminal, will contain at least one of these elements. In the civil context, cases may involve discrimination at work, for example, where people are unfairly passed over for promotion, miss out on maternity and holiday leave, or do not receive equal, fair pay for equal work. Family law is also a growing area involving civil liberties, increasingly in the areas of child access and residency. Child access cases mainly involve separated fathers and the term 'reasonable access' – even quite recently, courts have ruled one day per month to be 'reasonable', but this is due to be appealed. The right to family life enshrined in the Human Rights Act is frequently the basis of arguments in family proceedings. Human rights concerns have also been raised in cases concerning housing tenancies, where the issue might be a gay or lesbian partner's right to succeed to a tenancy previously held by a deceased partner.

Miscarriages of criminal justice involve bringing convictions before the Criminal Cases Review Board to take them to the Court of Appeal.

The administrative law dimension involves the judicial review of decisions by public bodies. With recent case law appearing to expand the definition of a public body, it seems likely that this field of work will continue to grow. One such challenge involved a patient in a private psychiatric hospital objecting to changes in the way her ward was being run. The judge declared that the hospital was in effect exercising the powers of a public authority and was therefore susceptible to judicial review.

a day in the life...

A typical day for Danny often involves going to court for criminal proceedings. On other days he may visit people in jail to discuss their grievances over how they are being treated. In the office there's plenty of client contact and a large caseload. Danny has a habit of taking on cases that no one else will take, even if that means doing it for free, as he believes *"it's no good just letting things lie if they are morally or politically offensive."* Even junior lawyers can expect to conduct their own advocacy, attend the Coroner's Court, see clients in prison and deal with miscarriage of justice cases.

skills needed

...passion... determination... demonstrated commitment... creativity... showing initiative... communicate well with joe public and with the court... love of advocacy...

career options

If you're looking for a training contract with one of the firms that specialise in human rights and civil liberties, be aware that this is an incredibly competitive area. However, firms with criminal and family departments, which take on cases with civil liberties aspects, often find it difficult to recruit talented and committed trainees. The problem, of course, is that the work is almost entirely legally aided (or done for free if no funding is available). These firms cannot offer the salaries that attract trainees to commercial firms. A firm might create a job for you if you can-convince them that you are worth taking on. Demonstrate your passion and commitment by carrying out voluntary work and joining relevant organisations. Law centres and voluntary work are the alternatives to private practice and it is not uncommon for dedicated lawyers to move between the two.

immigration law

type of work

Immigration covers two areas: business and personal. Business immigration tends to be practised in larger firms with corporate clients that want to bring over employees and their families to live and work in the UK. There are some individual clients, for instance under the new Highly Skilled Migrants Programme, which, according to the Government, aims to tackle the current skills shortage in the UK.

Personal immigration work is summed up by Lanis Levy, a solicitor at Glazer Delmar in South London: "*A client is asking you to address one of the most fundamental issues in their life – the question of whether they will be permitted to live and work or study in the country they choose.*" For many, this will be a truly heartfelt issue, determining whether they can be together with their spouse/partner and family.

Immigration work is certainly varied and involves more than the basic assistance given to those who want to become British through the process of naturalisation. Most people are familiar with asylum work, which aims to enable those who fear persecution at home to stay in Britain. Your work might involve arranging for someone to visit relatives in the UK or for a student to come and study here. A more unusual case might see you representing a prisoner facing deportation after serving a sentence for a relatively minor conviction, even though they had lived in Britain for 20 years.

a day in the life…

There is absolutely no typical day for Lanis. In the office there are calls to be returned to clients, such as a woman with a child who has been abandoned in her flat by her partner. She has no idea how she will pay next month's rent as her immigration status does not entitle her to claim any benefits. Lanis admits, "*I like to take on cases where people have come to the end of the line.*" Another client is having difficulties in getting support from social services. Next there is an appeal hearing to rearrange because the interpreter who showed up to the last hearing didn't speak the same dialect as the client. Attendance at an appeal will then necessitate a trip out of the office, with Lanis carrying out her own advocacy. Once every couple of weeks she will visit a client in prison. Lanis is clearly passionate about her job – "*It can be the most rewarding work imaginable!*" From early on, a trainee will take instructions from clients and attend interviews at the Home Office or the Immigration Service. They will prepare statements and representations to the Home Office or chase up pending claims. With support from more senior colleagues, they will take on their own cases.

skills needed

…sensitivity… compassion and commitment… able to deal with emotional and distressed clients… tenacity… willing to question decisions by authorities… language skills may be a real boon…

career options

Practitioners are certainly not motivated by financial gain as most of the interesting and challenging work is publicly funded. In fact, working in the voluntary sector can be the most satisfying as the progress of the case is not hampered by funding constraints. This is the only real alternative to private practice. Any kind of experience you can get with law centres, refugees', women's or human rights' organisations or charities will be invaluable in helping you decide if this is the kind of work that suits you. You can also keep up to date in this fast-moving area by joining organisations like the Joint Council for the Welfare of Immigrants, or by becoming a student member of the Immigration Law Practitioners Association. Not all immigration lawyers do their own advocacy, but it means an enormous amount to the client to have the same person take their case from start to finish. If advocacy is important to you, there's plenty of opportunity to develop this skill as an immigration lawyer.

education

type of work

This is a multi-disciplinary practice area, advising educational institutions on all aspects of the law. Its distinguishing features are an underlying public law dimension and a regulatory system that is particular to educational institutions. Further and higher education institutions may also be incorporated as companies and so require the same business advice as any other corporate client. *"This has to be tempered by a recognition of the fact that they are charities and publicly funded, with a set of ethics and a keen sense of academic freedom,"* stresses John Hall, head of the education law group at Eversheds.

The work may involve advice on generating different sources of income or on buying IT equipment. Just like any business, colleges and universities need advice on all the usual aspects of their day-to-day running, such as employment, property, planning, construction and PFI/PPP. Universities also have IP-rich spin-off businesses, which require advice. Occasionally advice will be needed following a complaint from a student and a different firm will represent the student.

a day in the life…

A typical day for John might involve advising on a strategic partnership between a university and industry, followed by phone calls to the DfES to discuss regulations or clear policy issues. At lunchtime there could be an education team meeting with employment lawyers to review internal procedures at a university following a claim of discrimination. In the afternoon he might meet his main contacts at a college with a funding deficit to chat generally about how the firm might be able to advise them. Perhaps the college ought to decrease the number of campuses from five to three, which would then involve decreasing the amount of accommodation and restructuring staff. Getting governing body approval, bringing in consultants and carrying out an options feasibility study would be prerequisites and it would be likely that the college would want to invest in new IT and refurbish some of its buildings. Many different areas of law are, therefore, involved in just one meeting.

skills needed

…commercial outlook… the self confidence to 'take a view'… teamwork… pragmatism combined with common sense and ethics… multi-disciplinary approach… keeping up with changes in the sector… ability to get under the client's skin…

career options

As education is at the top of the political agenda, this area is subject to an enormous amount of change. This is especially the case with structural and funding aspects of the post-16 education system. Education law would suit a person who is interested in giving *"commercial advice with an approach driven by public sector values."* The only real alternative to training in private practice is to apply to a local authority for a training contract. This will provide a wide training in all areas of local government, after which the newly qualified could specialise in education issues. Choose a niche firm if you wish to advise children, students and parents on education issues like exclusions from school, bullying or provisions for students with special needs. *Chambers UK* identifies leading education firms by their specialism. Once qualified, there are a few opportunities to work in the Department for Education and Skills and an increasing number of opportunities to work in-house at universities.

LEADING FIRMS FROM CHAMBERS UK GUIDE 2002-2003

HUMAN RIGHTS
LONDON
1. **Bindman & Partners**
2. **Bhatt Murphy**
3. **Christian Fisher**
   Hickman & Rose
4. **Birnberg Peirce & Partners**
   Deighton Guedalla
5. **Simons Muirhead & Burton**
   Taylor Nichol
   Thanki Novy Taube
   Winstanley-Burgess
6. **Irwin Mitchell**
   Scott-Moncrieff, Harbour & Sinclair

HUMAN RIGHTS
MIDLANDS
1. **Tyndallwoods** Birmingham
2. **McGrath & Co** Birmingham

HUMAN RIGHTS
THE NORTH
1. **AS Law** Liverpool
   Harrison Bundey & Co Leeds
   Howells Sheffield
   Irwin Mitchell Sheffield
2. **David Gray Solicitors** Newcastle upon Tyne
   Robert Lizar Manchester

IMMIGRATION: PERSONAL
LONDON
1. **Bindman & Partners**
   Birnberg Peirce & Partners
   Wesley Gryk
   Winstanley-Burgess
2. **Coker Vis Partnership**
   Deighton Guedalla
3. **Bartram & Co**
   Gill & Co
   Glazer Delmar
   Luqmani Thompson
   Powell & Co
   Wilson & Co

IMMIGRATION: BUSINESS
LONDON
1. **CMS Cameron McKenna**
   Kingsley Napley
2. **Bates, Wells & Braithwaite**
   Reed Smith Warner Cranston
3. **Baker & McKenzie**
   Eversheds
   Magrath & Co
4. **Gherson & Co**
   Mishcon de Reya
   Sturtivant & Co
5. **Fox Williams**
   Gulbenkian Harris Andonian
   Harbottle & Lewis
   Lovells
   Norton Rose
   Penningtons
   Pullig & Co
6. **DJ Webb & Co**
   Taylor Wessing

IMMIGRATION
THE SOUTH, THAMES VALLEY & SOUTH WEST
1. **Bobbetts Mackan** Bristol
   Darbys Oxford
   Eric Robinson & Co Southampton

IMMIGRATION
MIDLANDS
1. **Tyndallwoods** Birmingham
2. **Nelsons** Nottingham

IMMIGRATION
EAST ANGLIA
1. **Gross & Co** Bury St Edmunds
   Leathes Prior Norwich
   Wollastons Chelmsford

IMMIGRATION
THE NORTH
1. **David Gray Solicitors** Newcastle upon Tyne
2. **AS Law** Liverpool
   Harrison Bundey & Co Leeds
   Howells Sheffield
3. **Jackson & Canter** Liverpool
   James & Co Bradford
4. **Davis Blank Furniss** Manchester
   Samuel Phillips & Co Newcastle upon Tyne
   Thornhill Ince Manchester

SPECIALIST PRACTICE AREAS — PUBLIC INTEREST

EDUCATION: INSTITUTIONS
LONDON
1. Eversheds
2. Beachcroft Wansbroughs
3. Lee Bolton & Lee
   Winckworth Sherwood
4. Farrer & Co
   Lawfords
   Reynolds Porter Chamberlain
5. Berrymans Lace Mawer

EDUCATION: INDIVIDUALS
LONDON
1. Levenes
   Teacher Stern Selby
2. Ashok Patel & Co
   Fisher Meredith
3. Coningsbys Croydon
   Gills Southall
4. John Ford Solicitors

EDUCATION: INSTITUTIONS
WALES
1. Eversheds Cardiff
2. Morgan Cole Cardiff

EDUCATION: INDIVIDUALS
WALES
1. Russell Jones & Walker Cardiff
2. Sinclairs Penarth

EDUCATION: INSTITUTIONS
THE SOUTH & SOUTH WEST
1. Stone King Bath
   Veale Wasbrough Bristol
2. Rickerbys Cheltenham
3. Bevan Ashford Bristol
   Bond Pearce Plymouth, Southampton
4. Beachcroft Wansbroughs Bristol
   DMH Brighton
   Michelmores Exeter
   Thomas Eggar Chichester
5. Osborne Clarke Bristol
   Steele Raymond Bournemouth
   Tozers Exeter

EDUCATION: INDIVIDUALS
THE SOUTH & SOUTH WEST
1. AE Smith & Son Stroud
2. Blake Lapthorn Fareham

EDUCATION: INSTITUTIONS
THAMES VALLEY
1. Manches Oxford
   Morgan Cole Oxford
   Winckworth Sherwood Oxford

EDUCATION: INSTITUTIONS
THE NORTH
1. Eversheds Leeds, Manchester, Newcastle upon Tyne
2. Pinsent Curtis Biddle Leeds
3. Addleshaw Booth & Co Manchester
4. DLA Liverpool
   Irwin Mitchell Sheffield
   Robert Muckle Newcastle upon Tyne

EDUCATION: INDIVIDUALS
THE NORTH
1. Elaine Maxwell & Co Lancaster

EDUCATION: INSTITUTIONS
MIDLANDS
1. Martineau Johnson Birmingham
2. Eversheds Birmingham, Nottingham
3. Wragge & Co Birmingham
4. Browne Jacobson Nottingham

EDUCATION: INSTITUTIONS
EAST ANGLIA
1. Mills & Reeve Cambridge, Norwich
2. Eversheds Cambridge, Norwich
3. Birkett Long Colchester
   Wollastons Chelmsford

shipping

definition of terms

P&I Club: Protection and Indemnity Club – a marine insurance club run mutually by and for ship-owners.
Charter party: a commercial instrument – essentially a contract for the hire of an entire ship for the purpose of import or export of goods.
Bill of Lading: a receipt for goods loaded given by the master of the ship, a contract of carriage between the owners of the ships and the owners of the goods and a negotiable certificate of title for the goods themselves.
Salvage: reward payable by owners of ships and goods saved at sea by 'salvors'.

Shipping. What images come to mind? Greek shipping magnates chomping cigars? 17th century West Country ne'er-do-wells scouring the high seas for treasure and thrills under the lawless (and giveaway) banner of the Jolly Roger? The reality of shipping law is that it's an area filled with variety, complexity and, depending on the strand you go into, unpredictability. As Chris Hobbs, Head of Norton Rose's Greek office, says, *"you never quite know what's going to happen during an average day, but whatever does happen is quite often exciting."* Shipping is truly international in terms of the travel potential and the people and places you deal with. Someone who likes a simple, unvarying routine and the safety of staying in their office is unlikely to be suited for a career as a shipping lawyer.

type of work

Unsurprisingly, shipping law concerns ships, and more specifically the carriage of goods or people by sea. It can be either contentious or non-contentious.

Contentious work is broken down into wet ('admiralty') work and dry ('marine') work. Unsurprisingly again, the terms 'wet' and 'dry' are key indicators to the nature of the work. Wet work concerns disputes arising from accidents or misadventure at sea, ie collision, salvage, total loss and yes, even modern-day piracy. Wet lawyers are often former naval officers or ex-mariners (in the main *sans* dead albatrosses hanging from their necks). Dry work concerns disputes over contracts made on dry land, such as charter parties, bills of lading, cargo or sale of goods contracts.

Non-contentious work is primarily ship finance and ship-building contracts, sale and purchase agreements, employment contracts for crew members, affreightment contracts, registration and re-flagging of ships. Further niche areas include yachting or fishing, which usually involve regulatory matters. As James Gosling, a partner at Holman Fenwick & Willan, states, *"You really get a good handle on the basics of contract law and drafting"* and it goes without saying that this will be invaluable to your career as a lawyer – whether or not in shipping.

Few shipping lawyers handle both contentious and non-contentious work and those that do generally work in smaller firms or overseas offices. The type of firm you train with normally pre-determines your post-qualification specialism. There are a number of specialist shipping firms in London such as Ince & Co, Holman Fenwick & Willan and Clyde & Co, where contentious work will take up the majority of the training contract. Other more general corporate firms such as Norton Rose are known predominantly for their non-contentious shipping practices (ship finance in particular) and yet maintain contentious shipping teams as well as offering a wide training in other areas of law.

a day in the life of....

The global nature of the client base means you're acutely aware of the different time zones that you're working to on any given day, and you plan your time accordingly. A wet lawyer *"might come trudging in on*

Monday thinking the world's fallen in, and the next thing you know you're on a plane to Tahiti." Not every day's as glamorous, of course, and *"you may be asked to go to some pretty unpleasant places and told to just get on with it."* James told us, *"For me at least, it sure beats conveying a house in North Finchley!"*

Many cases are high profile, attracting media interest. Think about The Marchioness, Herald of Free Enterprise, the Braer oil spillage and the Sea Empress – all have involved lawyers in various capacities. James says of wet work: *"Getting involved in casualty cases is a real adrenalin rush. You often have to get to a ship as quickly as you can to preserve evidence and make sure you get the right story from the witnesses."* You then have to get the right 'forum' – the most beneficial jurisdiction for your client – as quickly as possible. Wet lawyers need to act fast. Any delay to a ship, howsoever caused, costs money. Your client expects you to analyse problems quickly and come up with sensible answers.

As for non-contentious work, don't be under any illusions – ship finance is nowhere near as exciting as casualty work, nor does it offer the same opportunities for travel. In the main, you'll be drafting, and considering finance agreements and other standard contracts relating to ships and their crew.

It's a controversial question: how do women fare in the rather macho world of shipping? Regrettably, shipping clients from some cultures have traditionally been rather male-oriented when it comes to business. It remains true that most of the top shipping lawyers are male but things are changing. James told us, *"Virtually half the clients on the insurance side are women."* More women are making their presence known in ship finance and dry work, but it's a different story in wet work. Why? James explained: *"The plain and simple truth is you'd be asking for trouble if you sent a woman to investigate a collision between a Greek vessel and a Mexican vessel somewhere in West Africa. It's not the safest place for a man, never mind a woman."* In addition, *"a lot of masters of vessels find it difficult telling a man what they did wrong, let alone a woman."*

skills needed

dry/wet:...no place for shrinking violets... abreast of legal developments/industry trends... firm grip on contract, tort and court procedure... flexible over hours... available to travel... good communicator... sense of humour... common sense... team spirit and self motivation... **wet:** ...previous experience of life at sea helpful (but not essential)... guts/sense of adventure...

Dry lawyers need to develop a good knowledge of conflicts (as distinct from forum shopping) as well as contract and tort. As for wet lawyers, they need to be bold as they will face adversity and the unexpected. You also need to be *"an engaging person with a broad outlook on life."* You'll be interacting with a vast range of people from different cultures and different ends of the social scale; many will have been schooled in the university of life. These clients – ship owners, operators, traders and charterers through to P&I clubs, other insurers and hull underwriters – are a real mixed bag. *"Claims handlers in P&I clubs are usually English and middle class, whereas salvors are often hulking great Dutchmen who've done salvages in some of the wildest places in the world."* Clients all tend to be larger than life – as James says, *"Whether they're hull underwriters or ship owners, they're risk-takers by their very nature, and they enjoy it."*

A keen analytical mind and a commercial outlook won't go astray. Chris says that *"a lot of people write us off as a bunch of partying, rather frivolous animals but if you look at the law of contract, and to an extent the law of tort, a lot of the cases that laid down fundamental principles are shipping cases."* Other than having been a mariner or naval officer, is there any experience that can help? *"Well, if you've seen a bit and done a bit and know a bit about the world, that can help."* At the end of the day, being a good lawyer in this field is just as much about common sense as *"knowing all the legal stuff."* Oh, *"a good liver"* also comes in handy!

"Ships are quite romantic things," James told us. *"Very few people get into shipping law and then leave it*

during a mid-life crisis to go and do M&A, for example." We wondered just how romantic he was feeling when he told us: *"I've been shot at and I've been on sinking ships…"*

career options

Jobs outside London are relatively few as shipping work is limited to larger port towns. In the firms with overseas offices, assistants can work abroad for a few years or even permanently. This is generally considered a good career move, particularly with regard to partnership prospects back home. If, following qualification, you decide shipping is not for you, as a contentious shipping lawyer you'll have gained a solid grounding as a commercial litigator. If you've been doing non-contentious work, you should have little problem shifting into general finance or corporate work.

If private practice does not appeal, P&I clubs, ship owners, operators and marine insurers all have openings for specialist lawyers, but the financial rewards will be less than in private practice, as will the legal component of the position. Ship owners or operators would want you to have knowledge or experience of the industry before approaching them for an in-house position. The predominance of English law in international shipping makes it relatively easy for in-housers to walk the plank back into private practice. Alternatively, you could convey houses in North Finchley!

LEADING FIRMS FROM CHAMBERS UK GUIDE 2002-2003

SHIPPING
■ LONDON

[1] **Holman Fenwick & Willan**
Ince & Co
[2] **Clyde & Co**
[3] **Hill Taylor Dickinson**
Richards Butler
[4] **Bentleys, Stokes & Lowless**
Clifford Chance
Holmes Hardingham
More Fisher Brown
Norton Rose
Shaw and Croft
Stephenson Harwood
Waltons & Morse
[5] **Barlow Lyde & Gilbert**
Jackson Parton
Lawrence Graham
Thomas Cooper & Stibbard
[6] **Fishers**
Hill Dickinson
Middleton Potts
Watson, Farley & Williams

SHIPPING: FINANCE
■ LONDON

[1] **Norton Rose**
[2] **Stephenson Harwood**
Watson, Farley & Williams
[3] **Allen & Overy**
Clifford Chance

SHIPPING
■ THE SOUTH & SOUTH WEST

[1] **Davies, Johnson & Co** Plymouth
Foot Anstey Sargent Exeter, Plymouth
[2] **Bond Pearce** Plymouth, Southampton
Lester Aldridge Southampton

SHIPPING
■ EAST ANGLIA

[1] **Dale & Co** Felixstowe
John Weston & Co Felixstowe
[2] **Prettys** Ipswich
[3] **Birketts** Ipswich

SHIPPING
■ THE NORTH

[1] **Andrew M Jackson** Hull
Eversheds Newcastle upon Tyne
Mills & Co Newcastle upon Tyne
Rayfield Mills Newcastle upon Tyne
[2] **DLA** Liverpool, Manchester
Hill Dickinson Liverpool, Manchester

sports law

Strictly speaking, sports law is more an industry focus rather than a discipline in its own right and consequently sports lawyers practice a broad range of law. However, there is a distinct and ever-developing body of law specifically concerning sports-related issues. This is best illustrated when national law and particular sports regulations collide, such as in the Bosman case, wherein football regulations governing player transfers were at odds with European employment regulations.

Sporting regulatory bodies are increasingly being taken to court (and hit for six) for imposing rules which conflict with the prevailing laws of the land. There was no doubt in the minds of the sports lawyers we spoke to that the continuing trends of increased professionalism and the globalisation of sporting concerns will lead to more sports-related law-making, whether through legislation or judicial decisions. Further specific industry regulation is as inevitable as a dismal performance of the British Winter Olympic team (curling aside).

type of work

Lawyers entering the area can expect to become familiar with trademark issues, data protection issues, sponsorship and broadcasting agreements and general contractual law as well as more specific sports-related issues like player transfers. The work is nearly always contractual, with a strong IP bias in terms of intangible rights.

Sports law can be broken down into three main components:
- The regulatory, disciplinary, criminal and personal injury advice given to individuals, teams and ruling bodies;
- Media / sponsorship and advertising;
- Corporate and commercial advice, eg the Stock Exchange listing of a football club.

Most firms with a sports practice will have a leaning to one or other of these aspects of the work. It would be worth your while ascertaining who acts for who and what type of work each concentrates on. As usual, we recommend you use *Chambers UK* for your research.

Sportspeople being sportspeople, there is a need for advice on crime, personal injury and of course employment law. In addition, EU and competition issues are increasingly coming into play. Sports law is as wide as a Gareth Southgate penalty miss. Fraser Reid, head of Theodore Goddard's Sports Department, makes the point that *"to be lucrative, a sports practice must focus on commercial matters rather than sports governance – unless you're acting for the leading sporting bodies."* He adds: *"Commercialism has firmly taken over from administration, both in the marketplace in the roles of administrators and in law firms' sports practices."* There's so much capital injected into and generated by sport that *"there's a real need for lawyers to become involved and provide advice on the protection and exploitation of sporting commercial rights."*

It's definitely a more established and structured practice area than it used to be. Jonathan Hall, RFU Secretary and Legal Officer, remembers the early 90s: *"A few people were beginning to practise sports law, but it was more the case that IP lawyers would advise in relation to sports-related trademark work or the corporate department would advise in relation to an acquisition of a sports company, for example."* This evolution has taken place in about the last ten years, and particularly since the emergence of PayTV. Why so? *"It's tagged along with the growth in new media and technology – there are now far more ways of getting access to sport in general, and football in particular."* Indeed, the consensus is that the warming up of the sports law area has been very football-driven, with other sports having benefited off the back of both the capital and the publicity that's been injected into and generated by football. You don't need to be a sports lawyer to realise that the stratospheric rise in money and publicity associated with the industry means more rights to be looked after, more regulation and more deals. In short, more legal work! Even the current crisis in football will provide plenty of legal work.

a day in the life…

Our interviewees would have us believe that there's simply no such thing as a typical day, but one thing is clear, sports lawyers don't, as a rule, regularly spend eight hours poring over one document. True, junior lawyers can expect to spend a lot of their time drafting basic sponsorship and broadcasting agreements and giving written advice on various IP issues such as trademark and copyright, but much of the time is spent meeting and speaking with clients, and forming good relationships with them. Fraser told us: *"My career is in the law – it's what I'm qualified to do – and I love sport, so combining the two is perfect. If I wasn't a lawyer, I would want to be a sportsman and if I wasn't a sportsman I would want to be a lawyer."*

skills needed

… basic legal skills… commercial nous… good interpersonal skills… background reading (and watching)… innovation… proactivity… it's what you know and who you know…

In this industry more than most, people really do know you by your name, and personality counts for a lot. You don't necessarily need unbridled passion for sport (such as a propensity to paint your face with team colours and sing largely risible team anthems). You do need to show a genuine interest in the industry – to follow it, keep up with developments and talk enthusiastically and cogently about it. It's an embryonic market and extremely competitive to break into so you need to be technically excellent and innovative. Remember, people love to be associated with famous names – lawyers are no different, and they're generally protective of their relationships with sporting clients and guarded against new entrants.

It's not an area where you can just sit back and watch from the sidelines; you must be ahead of the game and, just as importantly, you must be seen to be ahead of it. Rights holders, sports agents and broadcasters alike will have commercial nous and they won't expect their lawyer to be without it.

career options

In private practice, sports specialists have moved into this area both by accident and design. Sports lovers often try to steer their careers in this direction, while corporate, litigation, intellectual property or personal injury lawyers who have acquired a sporting clientele may suddenly find themselves being referred to as sports lawyers. In the last couple of years, some lucky young assistants have been able to specialise on qualification and become a junior part of the few dedicated sports law teams that do exist.

There are various opportunities in the industry, in particular in the larger federated governing bodies (such as the FA, the MCC or the RFU). You could also work for a sports broadcaster negotiating rights, or as an agent for sports personalities or teams. One possible advantage of moving in-house is outlined by the RFU's Jonathan Hall. A lot of law firms may not have the variety or volume to give you a broad range of experience in the industry. Johnathan says *"a lot of them focus on a very narrow area and you'll get very good experience in that area, but that's about it."* So it's all happening in-house then? *"I certainly think so. The chances are that you will find yourself dealing with 'sports law' issues almost all of the time, although there are clearly non-sports law issues to address, as with any organisation."*

There's no doubt that sports law as a practice area is very much geared towards self-described 'sports nuts', namely people who like to combine their professional qualifications with something in which they have a strong personal interest. And how many other practice areas really offer that opportunity to combine your career with your passion? Probably about as many as the number of countries which field truly world-class rugby league teams. Anyone who doesn't know the answer to that question probably isn't cut out to be a sports lawyer!

LEADING FIRMS FROM CHAMBERS UK GUIDE 2002-2003

SPORT: COMMERCIAL/MEDIA
■ LONDON

1. Denton Wilde Sapte
2. Bird & Bird
   Hammond Suddards Edge
3. Nicholson Graham & Jones
   Olswang
   SJ Berwin
4. Freshfields Bruckhaus Deringer
   Harbottle & Lewis
   The Simkins Partnership
   Theodore Goddard
5. Ashurst Morris Crisp
   Clintons
   Collyer-Bristow
   Field Fisher Waterhouse
   Herbert Smith
6. Couchman Harrington Associates
   Memery Crystal

SPORT: REGULATORY
■ LONDON

1. Denton Wilde Sapte
2. Farrer & Co
   Hammond Suddards Edge
   Max Bitel, Greene
3. Charles Russell
   Simmons & Simmons
4. Freshfields Bruckhaus Deringer
   The Simkins Partnership

SPORT
■ THE SOUTH

1. Clarke Willmott & Clarke
   Southampton

SPORT
■ SOUTH WEST

1. Clarke Willmott & Clarke Bristol
2. Osborne Clarke Bristol

SPORT
■ WALES

1. Hugh James Cardiff

SPORT
■ MIDLANDS

1. Hammond Suddards Edge
   Birmingham

SPORT
■ THE NORTH

1. James Chapman & Co Manchester
   McCormicks Leeds
2. George Davies Manchester
3. Addleshaw Booth & Co Manchester
   Hill Dickinson Liverpool, Manchester
   Walker Morris Leeds
4. Zermansky & Partners Leeds

tax

"Nothing pleases finance directors more than saving some tax. If you give advice that saves your clients tax in the commercial world, then they're going to be very happy people." These words from Jonny Gillespie, an associate at Pinsent Curtis Biddle in Leeds, neatly summarise the immense and enduring value of corporate tax lawyers. Their primary role is to advise as to the most tax-efficient means of structuring and running business. Tax work is highly client-focused; a good deal of the work is for repeat clients who invariably want quick and commercial answers to complex questions. If you're looking to avoid dealing with people by sequestering yourself away in a tiny office with dusty statute books and dodgy lighting, don't become a tax lawyer.

type of work

The voluminous and ever-evolving nature of tax law requires constant attention to black letter law, but it's not the case that you'll be forever poring over the minutiae while your colleagues in sexier areas get to close deals and pop champagne corks. There is a wide variety of tax work on offer – transactional, contentious and general advisory – not to mention an increasingly international aspect to the transactional work in particular, where the relevant laws of a number of jurisdictions need to be considered. Tax is a crucial component of every major deal undertaken by commercial firms. Whether the matter is corporate, finance or property-related, you can be sure that tax lawyers will be among the key advisors.

Greg Sinfield, head of Indirect Taxes at Lovells, told us *"It takes a long time for young lawyers to build up the experience necessary to advise in a wide range of situations. People shouldn't think that they'll become an expert in less than four to five years."* There's a huge quantity of law relevant to the area and, when giving advice, practitioners need to take into account not only tax legislation and cases, but also other areas of law which may be relevant. While you don't need to have your eyes shifted to the side of your head, you do need to develop all round vision.

Tax law evolves at a far greater rate than the majority of other practice areas so you'll need to be constantly on the lookout for change. As Alasdair Douglas, a partner at Travers Smith Braithwaite, says, *"Other types of lawyers get their knickers in a twist if there's new legislation once every ten years. But we're used to it. There's a huge amount of new law in tax every year. Last year there was a 400 page Finance Act, and this year it will probably be just as big."* Jonny adds that *"the thing about tax is that no matter how qualified or senior you are, you will never know everything because it's changing all the time – it doesn't stand still."*

a day in the life…

You'd be forgiven for thinking that most of a tax lawyer's work involves dealing with numbers and doing mathematical calculations. But you'd be wrong. Douglas French, a partner at Clifford Chance, says, *"Tax lawyers don't do a lot of the boring stuff – we don't do compliance work, we don't file returns, we don't do due diligence or computations."* So what does a typical day involve? Researching law, advising on deals, advising on how to structure business activities… and basic fire-fighting! That said, Alasdair stresses how much corporate support work there is. *"In most commercial firms, junior tax lawyers will work on acquisitions and disposals of businesses and companies till it's coming out of their ears!"* However, he adds that *"tax law has the greatest intellectual challenge as a junior lawyer simply because it's so difficult to get your head around as an area of law. Secondly, tax lawyers are dealing with law all the day – not working out the logistics of getting a deal done or shuffling bits of paper."*

As far as the work/life balance goes, Jonny thinks

that "*it's much better than in a lot of other departments. We do work hard but we usually manage to do it within normal working hours… if you like burning the midnight oil and having lots of 4am corporate completions, then tax may not be for you.*" Why are the hours so reasonable? It's mainly the nature of the work itself that allows it to be completed within normal working hours, which links in nicely with the fact that "*tax lawyers are so in demand that firms generally treat them well.*" Another bonus of the job, according to Alasdair, is the fact that you deal with and get to know lawyers from right around the firm on a day to day basis. "*You get to work on the corporate deals, the property deals and the banking deals.*"

skills needed

… good academics… analytical mind… thinking outside the box… willing to challenge and test… clear communication… commerciality… technical excellence… great interpretation of black letter law… no anorak required!

One of the most important things you must do as a tax lawyer is to get complex messages across to your clients in a concise and understandable manner. By and large, your clients will not be tax experts and they will not want a lengthy academic discussion as to tax theory. What they will want is to know the commercial effect of the relevant legislation on their business and they will want to know it quickly.

Tax lawyers have to be commercially-minded and able to communicate really complex ideas to non-experts. But as Douglas states, "*While the vast majority of us aren't anoraks, tax law is likely to appeal to lawyers who like law – reading statutes and cases.*" The studious or academic side does need to be there but remember, it's just a part of the picture. Douglas goes on to say, "*One of the most valuable qualities a tax lawyer can have is creativity and innovation; the ability to think outside the box, to think about a set of facts from all angles and save some tax.*"

career options

It's interesting to note that some of the most respected tax barristers have only been at the Bar for a few years. It's not that they have defied the logic of everything we've said so far, it's because a number of them had already achieved a successful track record as a tax solicitor. Excellent news: this part of the Bar is known for its super-high earnings.

As for the alternatives to private practice, in a nutshell, your options are pretty clear. You can work in-house in the tax department of a large corporate or bank, or you can work for the government in Inland Revenue or Customs & Excise. Greg makes the point that "*if you go in-house at a corporate or bank, you only have the one client, which if you're lucky will give you an array of matters to deal with. If you work for the government, you get a fantastic range of matters because the government deal with all types of tax issues.*" Although the working pressures are less under a public paymaster, unfortunately so are the financial rewards. As Jonny observes, "*The flow tends to be the other way – people usually join a commercial law firm from Inland Revenue or Customs & Excise and get paid much more after getting valuable knowledge and practical experience of tax law in the civil service.*"

Some solicitors move to accountancy firms in a tax consultancy role (as distinct from working for the legal arm of an accountancy firm). While "*it's very similar to working for law firms,*" according to some there are "*certain cultural differences,*" which can make for a rather bumpy adjustment to the new job.

Overall, the skills and knowledge gained through working in private practice are portable at all levels of qualification. There's certainly no shortage of positions in private practice for those who want them, provided they're "*made of the right stuff.*" After just a few years of bedding down in the area, junior tax lawyers become a very marketable commodity. As Jonny states, "*firms are always keen to have a decent tax lawyer, and this is reflected in the salaries.*" There's just one draw back – the public image. As one of our tax lawyers said, "*When I meet a girl a party and I tell her what I do, it tends to kill conversation stone dead!*"

LEADING FIRMS FROM CHAMBERS UK GUIDE 2002-2003

TAX: CORPORATE
■ LONDON

1
- **Freshfields Bruckhaus Deringer**
- **Linklaters**
- **Slaughter and May**

2
- **Allen & Overy**
- **Clifford Chance**

3
- **Ashurst Morris Crisp**
- **Herbert Smith**
- **Norton Rose**

4
- **Berwin Leighton Paisner**
- **Denton Wilde Sapte**
- **Lovells**
- **Macfarlanes**
- **Simmons & Simmons**
- **SJ Berwin**
- **Travers Smith Braithwaite**

5
- **CMS Cameron McKenna**
- **Nabarro Nathanson**
- **Olswang**

6
- **Clyde & Co**
- **Field Fisher Waterhouse**
- **McDermott, Will & Emery**
- **Theodore Goddard**
- **Watson, Farley & Williams**

TAX: CORPORATE
■ THE SOUTH & SOUTH WEST

1
- **Burges Salmon** Bristol
- **Osborne Clarke** Bristol

2
- **Blake Lapthorn** Fareham
- **Wiggin & Co** Cheltenham

TAX: CORPORATE
■ MIDLANDS & EAST ANGLIA

1
- **Pinsent Curtis Biddle** Birmingham
- **Wragge & Co** Birmingham

2
- **DLA** Birmingham
- **Eversheds** Norwich, Nottingham

3
- **Mills & Reeve** Cambridge

TAX: CORPORATE
■ THE NORTH

1
- **Addleshaw Booth & Co** Leeds, Manchester
- **Pinsent Curtis Biddle** Leeds

2
- **Eversheds** Leeds, Manchester
- **Hammond Suddards Edge** Leeds, Manchester

3
- **Dickinson Dees** Newcastle upon Tyne
- **Walker Morris** Leeds

SPECIALIST PRACTICE AREAS

TAX

169

tmt

TMT (Technology, Media & Telecoms) is the funky new name that law firms are giving their IT, telecoms, IP, broadcasting and e-commerce practices. While the renaming of some organisations is just a bit too Emperor's New Clothesy, (think Consignia for the Post Office) it is appropriate for technology lawyers. This is an ever-changing practice area and just as the technology industry evolves with rapidity, so must the lawyers servicing it. Kim Nicholson is a TMT partner at Olswang. She says, *"You need to be a driven and questioning person – constantly asking 'what's next?'"*

Michael Chissick is the head of the IT and E-commerce Law Group at Field Fisher Waterhouse. He told us, *"It's an area of law where you have to be a bit more nimble than others. You have to keep reinventing yourself."* He started out in computer law in the late 80s and by 1996 e-commerce had arrived. In the mid-90s multi-media came and went. When digital TV hit, he and his colleagues got up to speed on that. When the dot.com bubble burst they had to adjust to the fact that the lucrative start-up market was disappearing. Michael and his team now find that 'e-government' is their hot topic, given the Government's stated aim of delivering services on-line.

so who are the clients?
- IT and telecoms suppliers and their customers;
- huge multi-nationals with offices across Europe and the US;
- small entrepreneurs or start-ups;
- local and central government and charities;
- web-based businesses, software developers, hardware suppliers and maintainers, disaster recovery suppliers;
- 23-year-olds winning and losing fortunes from their dad's garages!

The concept of 'convergence' keeps TMT lawyers on their toes these days. Telecommunications, TV and the internet are becoming so interrelated and interchangeable that lawyers in the sector must learn to master each of these media. As Michael told us, *"It's all going to come together; you'll be watching TV on your phone and sending e-mail from your TV. Will phone lines win or will Sky TV take over? It will change the way we all work. I might have to get involved in more content issues as my telecoms clients might become involved in buying in content. We will have understand all the new developments and develop all the necessary skills. We may have to become more of a one-stop shop."* Kim agrees: *"If someone's predominant field is IT contracts, they still have to understand regulatory telecoms stuff; they must know the likely hurdles. There's a necessity for lawyers to work really closely together."*

type of work

IT and internet-based work involves a lot of commercial contract drafting, for example, terms and conditions for a website, software development agreements, computer games licences or outsourcing (where outside IT specialists are brought in to set up and run a company's computer systems). Clients will seek advice on issues such as data protection compliance or cyber-squatting (domain name disputes). Lawyers are also drawn into a support role, working with their corporate colleagues on M&A transactions. Competition law rears its head, for example, where large IT suppliers are accused of abusing a dominant position in the market place.

Some matters may even lead on to litigation and, at this stage, non-contentious TMT lawyers will enlist the help of specialist TMT litigators. Richard Yates is a one-year qualified TMT lawyer in Nabarro Nathanson's Reading office. These contentious lawyers regularly handle disputes over contracts to provide IT services (hardware/software/maintenance/disaster recovery etc.).

If a piece of software simply doesn't do what the customer thought it would, their primary goal is to get to the point where the software will work. In these circumstances, lawyers need to handle matters in a way that doesn't ruin the relationship between the parties. Richard says, *"Our clients look for alternatives to traditional litigation; for many it's all about getting the next deal moving."* Then there are disputes between competitors, perhaps over intellectual property in software or the name or design of a website. Even without a customer-supplier relationship to protect, mediation, expert determination and other less formal methods of dispute resolution are very popular with TMT clients. TMT lawyers are likely to spend less time in court than ordinary commercial litigators, and more time advising clients on strategies for negotiating settlements to disputes. Major IT suppliers are often keen to avoid the publicity of litigation at a time when poor sector performance is being reported in the press. But not all cases are resolved amicably. Big multi-million pound disputes do reach the High Court and TMT litigators may be called upon to rush to court on very short notice to apply for emergency injunctions (eg to prevent ongoing breach of copyright in a client's software).

Lawyers acting for telecoms clients are additionally called upon to give advice on the regulatory regimes, which govern the sector and are designed to protect the interests of consumers. There's been so much legislation from Brussels in last few years that Kim says, *"Even at 15 years qualified I still need to bone up on new law. I need to be constantly thinking of new risks and opportunities."* There's a heavy transactional side to telecoms law and any observer will have noted the consolidation in the industry in the last couple of years. The big issue of recent times has been the 3G mobile phone licenses issued by governments across Europe and Broad Band and Wireless Local Loop are very 'now'. If these terms baffle and leave you cold, you're not destined for TMT!

a day in the life…

Michael told us that there are periods when he's involved in really big deals that occupy all his time and take him out of the office with a team of lawyers and clients. *"That's maybe three or four times a year. Usually my day is more varied though. After I've picked up my e-mails to find out what's happening in the US, there are normally a couple of small agreements around for me to advise on. It's very rare that I don't have a meeting every day, either with lawyers or a client."* 80% of the typical TMT lawyer's work is transactional in nature, be it a large M&A deal or a smaller commercial contract. Michael says, *"We are becoming more like corporate lawyers; co-ordinating other parts of the firm – employment, pensions, banking, tax, etc. IT lawyers today are what corporate lawyers were ten years ago."*

The reality is that as a TMT lawyer you exist to service the many needs of your client sector. New laws and cases appear and your job is to navigate a path through these as well as being a good all-round commercial advisor. Good news: TMT lawyers normally get the chance to go on secondment to clients. Young solicitors at Field Fisher Waterhouse enjoy spells at clients such as Colt Telecom, the BBC and Accenture.

skills needed

…general grounding in corporate and contract law… commercial… ability to be a deal-maker… understand 'hard' regulatory matters… sensitive to the needs of 'creatives'… keep up to speed with new technology… comfortable with technical jargon… industry knowledge… gut feel for the issues… be thrilled by change… innovative… knowledge of competition law and copyright matters… a sensible approach to risk…

Are you always the first of your friends to buy gadgets? Michael confesses to this; he's fascinated by technology. Having a background in the technology sector will help, but is by no means essential. If this all sounds rather boysie, rest assured that as many women go into the area as men. Kim confirms, *"The* business people are quite logically minded," and certainly the techies are that way. "*For example, software programming is a structured mental process.*" And as for the lawyers, like Michael, Kim says, "*I am quite a gadget person. Most people here do like gadgets!*"

Commercial draftsmanship is a core skill. Commonly, there are no precedents for what you're trying to achieve – there were none for 3G mobile phone licences – so you must not be put off by a blank piece of paper. You have to be innovative and come up with some 'outside the box' thinking. Richard says, "*Sometimes we need to advise our clients that there is no point in spending £5K on the perfect legal case, when a cheaper route is just as likely to achieve the right result.*" Little in this area of law is traditional. Innovative technology clients call for innovative legal advisors.

Before you start your training you can help yourself enormously by keeping up with developments in technology. Michael has a monthly legal column in *Internet Magazine* and also recommends *Computing*, *Internet World* and *Computer Weekly*. Kim recommends *New Media Age* as it gives an overview of what the main companies are doing. If you're already up to speed with the movers and shakers in the sector and how the market has shifted then when you start your training you can spend more time developing legal skills and less time grasping the basics of the sector.

What you definitely don't need to be is a nerdy no-mates. People skills are vital and you'll learn to deal with clients who are poles apart in terms of needs and temperament. Richard explained: "*Dispute management is part of everyday life for large multi-national clients and instructions come from in-house lawyers familiar with disputes. Emotions can run stronger in disputes involving smaller clients where the outcome may make or break the business, and may have a direct personal impact on the company director who is giving you instructions.*"

career options

As it's still seen as a sexy new area of law, it's quite competitive at the junior end. It's not a shrinking market, but the 25% year-on-year growth ended with the technology slump of 2000/2001. The lawyers we spoke to were adamant that if you have a passion for the sector then you should pursue your dream job. Twinning your interests with your legal training is the route to job satisfaction. Teams within law firms tend to be quite stable, but some lawyers do move in-house and often find their role becomes wider ranging than in private practice. These jobs are almost certainly going to be on the non-contentious side.

LEADING FIRMS FROM CHAMBERS UK GUIDE 2002-2003

INFORMATION TECHNOLOGY — LONDON
[1] **Baker & McKenzie**
Bird & Bird
Clifford Chance
[2] **Allen & Overy**
Lovells
Masons
Taylor Wessing
[3] **Denton Wilde Sapte**
Field Fisher Waterhouse
Olswang
Osborne Clarke
Tarlo Lyons
[4] **Freshfields Bruckhaus Deringer**
Herbert Smith
Kemp Little LLP
Linklaters
Shaw Pittman
Slaughter and May
[5] **Ashurst Morris Crisp**
Berwin Leighton Paisner
Bristows
CMS Cameron McKenna
DJ Freeman
Mayer, Brown, Rowe & Maw
Nabarro Nathanson
Simmons & Simmons
Theodore Goddard

INFORMATION TECHNOLOGY — THE SOUTH
[1] **Bond Pearce** Southampton
Clyde & Co Guildford
DMH Brighton

INFORMATION TECHNOLOGY — THAMES VALLEY
[1] **Nabarro Nathanson** Reading
Osborne Clarke Reading
The Law Offices of Marcus J O'Leary Wokingham
[2] **Manches** Oxford
Olswang Reading
[3] **Clark Holt** Swindon
Willoughby & Partners Oxford
[4] **Boyes Turner** Reading

INFORMATION TECHNOLOGY — SOUTH WEST
[1] **Osborne Clarke** Bristol
[2] **Beachcroft Wansbroughs** Bristol
Bevan Ashford Bristol
Burges Salmon Bristol
[3] **Foot Anstey Sargent** Plymouth
Laytons Bristol

INFORMATION TECHNOLOGY — WALES
[1] **Edwards Geldard** Cardiff
Eversheds Cardiff
Morgan Cole Cardiff

INFORMATION TECHNOLOGY — MIDLANDS & EAST ANGLIA
[1] **Wragge & Co** Birmingham
[2] **Eversheds** Birmingham, Nottingham
[3] **Hewitson Becke + Shaw** Cambridge, Northampton
Pinsent Curtis Biddle Birmingham
V-Lex Ltd Worksop

INFORMATION TECHNOLOGY — THE NORTH
[1] **Addleshaw Booth & Co** Leeds, Manchester
Masons Leeds, Manchester
[2] **Eversheds** Leeds
Pinsent Curtis Biddle Leeds
[3] **Halliwell Landau** Manchester
[4] **Hammond Suddards Edge** Leeds, Manchester
Irwin Mitchell Leeds

TELECOMMUNICATIONS — LONDON
[1] **Allen & Overy**
Bird & Bird
Clifford Chance
[2] **Baker & McKenzie**
Linklaters
Olswang
[3] **Denton Wilde Sapte**
Field Fisher Waterhouse
Simmons & Simmons
[4] **Ashurst Morris Crisp**
Freshfields Bruckhaus Deringer
Taylor Wessing
[5] **Charles Russell**
Mayer, Brown, Rowe & Maw
Norton Rose
Osborne Clarke

TELECOMMUNICATIONS — THE REGIONS
[1] **Eversheds** Leeds
Wragge & Co Birmingham

international firms...international locations

Several UK firms claim the title 'global law firm', having gone through international expansion and mergers. Transatlantic mergers are the latest trend: the last year has brought a US merger for Withers and, on a much larger scale, the creation of Mayer, Brown, Rowe & Maw. US firms regard London as the gateway to Europe and, consequently, we are likely to see more US/UK tie-ups. The quest for merger partners in Europe continues (most recently demonstrated by Taylor Joynson Garrett joining forces with Germany's Wessing), although it is probably fair to say that almost all the leading continental firms that are minded to merge have already done so. A few firms remain resolute in their policy of 'best friends' relationships rather than mergers; most notable among these is Slaughter and May.

Pick the right training contract and you'll effectively guarantee time in an overseas office. You can go to one of the biggest UK-based international firms or you can go to a smaller firm with foreign offices. Alternatively, you could choose to train at one of the US firms in London.

the top international players

We picked our Top 15 international firms from those featured in the *True Picture*, after consulting research from *Chambers Global 2002-2003*. We show, in brackets, the number of rankings each firm attained in that publication. Each ranking derives from recommendations from the market place in an individual practice area in a separate country or region. The scope of Chambers Global has increased to include litigation, real estate and corporate recovery and this has had the effect of altering the position of firms from the table in last year's Student Guide. For detailed information on global practice, refer to Chambers Global on www.chambersandpartners.com or consult the copy in your university's careers library or law department.

THE TRUE PICTURE GLOBAL TOP 15	
1	Clifford Chance (106)
2	Baker & McKenzie (98)
2	Freshfields Bruckhaus Deringer (98)
4	Allen & Overy (97)
5	Linklaters (excl. Netherlands) (80)
6	White & Case LLP (51)
7	Lovells (36)
8	Herbert Smith (33)
9	Denton Wilde Sapte (32)
10	Norton Rose (31)
11	Ashurst Morris Crisp (29)
12	Slaughter and May (26)
12	Simmons & Simmons (25)
14	Weil, Gotshal & Manges (25)
15	CMS Cameron McKenna (20)

Four US firms (Shearman & Sterling, Skadden Arps, Cleary Gottlieb and Latham & Watkins) have numerous rankings but do not appear in the True Picture

trainees abroad

Although time abroad gives you experience of working in another jurisdiction, you'll not normally practise foreign law. Repeatedly, trainees tell us that overseas seats are hard work – offices are generally smaller than in London and trainees shoulder greater responsibility. The trick to securing certain of the most popular overseas seats is still, to a degree, a case of waging an effective campaign of self-promotion and getting the prerequisite experience in the UK. At firms with less emphasis on overseas placements, at least half of the trainees decide against time abroad as a result of other commitments or simply a desire to spend all their seats in the UK. Some fear that six months away from the action at home might mean that they are out of sight and out of mind, and this is certainly something to bear in mind if you are posted abroad when decisions are being made about NQ jobs.

It may be hard work. It may be an eye-opener. It may even be lonely if you're in a less popular location, but the overwhelming feeling is that time abroad is an unmissable experience.

So what's on offer in the locations to which trainees are most likely to be sent? Here's what we found out.

brussels

Home of commerce, bureaucracy and Tintin, Brussels is located right in the heart of the new Europe and plays host to the headquarters of many EU institutions. 159 embassies are based there, in addition to 120 IGOs and 1,400 NGOs. Political powerhouse it may be, but it is probably fair to say that you can cram most of Brussels' attractions into a weekend. So what about spending a whole six months out there? When speaking to Brussels trainees it was hard to tell whether they had been spending too much time with the city's 2,500 diplomats or whether there just wasn't that much to reveal about the place; they proved to be hard nuts to crack. Frequent references were made to chocolate, mussels and beer, but the city's more obscure delights, including the museums of fencing, lace, trams and comic strip art, had eluded most of them.

Work: Competition for Brussels seats is *"not exactly fierce,"* as most trainees opt for warmer, more romantic climes. If you have a particular interest in EU or competition law, you want to be close to home, or the possibility of rejection makes you anxious, Brussels could be for you. Several trainees opted for the city because they spoke French and wanted to improve it, but language skills are not considered to be a particular advantage, especially since many firms will provide tuition. *"Competition law can be quite intense at times,"* but all-nighters and Saturdays in the office are *"very rare."* In addition to EU law, *"there is also a lot of quality trade work coming through the city."* A DLA trainee said her work was characterised by *"big deals, lots of research and lots of responsibility."* Much of her day was spent monitoring public affairs and reviewing EU publications and websites. Don't underestimate the volume of research-based tasks that will come your way. *"You won't get much client contact but there are a lot more conferences and seminars to attend."*

Rest and play: Baker & McKenzie provides a one-bedroom apartment affording lovely views of the office, two streets away. DLA offers a beautiful Art Nouveau flat in the centre of the city. Many trainees live in an enclave in the Schuman area near to the Commission buildings and tend to flock together; tours and events are laid on by the many firms in the city. The climate may be English but there's *"a much better quality of life and much better food"* to be had. Prices tend to be about two thirds of what you would pay in London and there's no need to force yourself onto the tube each morning. Brussels is only two and a half hours and £75 away from the UK, so persuading friends and family to visit won't prove to be a problem. *"I haven't had a weekend on my own since I got here."* Brussels is a manageable city with a pleasant pace of life. Just as New York has the Statue of Liberty and Rhodes had its Colossus, Brussels' most famous symbol is the Mannekin Pis, a small statue of a boy relieving himself into a fountain.

Best Things: Restaurants, European lifestyle, Internationalism.
Worst Things: Cobblestones in high heels, Poodles.

frankfurt

As the Florida swamps are to the American Alligator, so Frankfurt would seem to make the ideal habitat for the UK Finance Trainee. Frankfurt is the European capital of Capital, and is *"clean, cosmopolitan and friendly."* If you want an unforgettable time in a radically different environment then politely decline, but Frankfurt is a good place to live in the basic sense of the verb. *"It's the nicest place I've been for everyday living. You never get that busy feeling. There's always space."* The city is famous for its enormous airport (incorporating a nightclub and an adult cinema) and its business conventions; most of Frankfurt's visitors see little else of the place. *"If you're into culture there are better places to be."* Even though most business is done in English, being able to speak German is of real advantage in terms of *"building up a rapport with clients and locals and making the most of your time there."* The consensus was that the ski season is the best time of year to be in Frankfurt, but in the summer you can enjoy lovely parks and open-air pools. Think Tooting Lido, but clean and green and pleasant.

Work: Linklaters offers the quintessential Frankfurt experience: a capital markets seat on the 32nd floor of a skyscraper. At most firms the work is paper-intensive and it's finance all the way. A lot of work is done in English and pertains to English law, but *"you can't be afraid of German law."* A Lovells trainee described a corporate and banking seat in which they experienced a wide variety of work and the same hours, atmosphere and manners as back in London. There's not a lot of client contact and, as in other European capitals, there is a danger of getting roped into mundane translation work. Sadly, a lot of the work involves *"taking an old precedent and then changing the figures for a new transaction,"* but it was refreshing to hear that *"there is no culture where you feel you have to stay late."*

Rest and play: The *"classy"* Linklaters apartment has a balcony, is one minute from the office and located right above an English pub. *"Except for clothes, you won't need to bring anything. It's a bit like living in a hotel."* The Lovells flat is also within easy walking distance of the office which means that, compared to the London commute, *"you gain two hours every day."* All the UK trainees are clustered in the same part of town so you've a ready-made social circle, if you so desire. The best thing about the bars and clubs is that you never have to stand up or queue. *"Frankfurt's waiters have excellent memories."* If it all seems just too nice and you need to exorcise rebellious urges, it's cheap to hire a Merc and go for a cruise down the Autobahn, where the only speed limitation is your nerve.

Best Things: Standard of living, Structure.
Worst Things: Lazy shopkeepers and erratic opening hours.

hong kong

Back with the Chinese after 99 years of British rule, Hong Kong has become the boisterous love child of Chairman Mao and Ronald McDonald. A city obsessed with money, shopping and branded goods, *"when it's all lit up at night you feel like an extra from Blade Runner."* Yet despite the pace, the political contradictions, the crowds and the smog, Hong Kong residents must be doing something right since they enjoy the third highest life expectancy in the world. When the hum of money gets too much for you, you can take a free Tai Chi class in the park or visit one of the region's Buddhist temples and remote islands. September to March is mild; otherwise it gets very hot and sweaty.

Work: A Stephenson Harwood trainee spoke of his (semi-masochistic) desire to work in a *"hugely challenging"* and *"radically different"* culture. *"Much of the time you can't answer a question easily and you keep having to go back to the books."* This was not down to inattentiveness at law school apparently, but because Hong Kong operates under a totally different jurisdiction. *"There is no comfort zone."* His seat was in business technology and involved offering advice to start-up companies in a dot.com incubator, but mostly trainees will deal with general commercial work. Herbert Smith offers litigation seats and one trainee we spoke to had spent much of her time on IP law. You must be ready to master a whole new set of traditions and etiquette before you can deal effectively with clients and colleagues. Only 10% of the lawyers at Stephenson Harwood are Westerners so trainees have a chance to mix with the locals and their families. *"You are treated as a guest and are encouraged to get out and enjoy yourself."*

Rest and play: Stephenson Harwood has a large flat with a guest bedroom – rare in a city where space is at a premium. Just like the Herbert Smith apartment, it is situated on The Levels, a residential hill where your relative altitude reflects your wealth. Most trainees live halfway up with the expats, where there is a pleasant village atmosphere. In Hong Kong *"everything is do'able."* You work and party in the same area and you can be as adventurous as you like with the local food. *"When you can't stand to see another noodle you can always go for a fat steak at La Pampa."* In terms of museums and galleries the city is *"not so impressive."* *"Why does Hong Kong have a space museum?"* pondered one trainee. If you find yourself lured into the murky underworld of the karaoke clubs *"you'd better learn your song properly. Locals take it very seriously and often practice in their lunch breaks."* The Chinese Opera is another quintessential Hong Kong entertainment although one trainee confided that *"it's like nothing I've ever seen and something I never want to see again."* Travel opportunities abound. You can easily get to Shanghai and Beijing, or pop to mainland China for a round of golf or to pick up counterfeit goods. Most firms have a junk, which you can take for a spin.

Best Things: Lifestyle, Nightlife, Water-skiing and beach picnics.
Worst Things: Pollution and humidity.

madrid

Having come through a bloody civil war and spent decades languishing under Franco, Spain has played a hard game of catch-up with its neighbours, but now, according to one trainee we spoke to, *"Spain is really starting to move on the international scene… it's an exciting time to be out here."* Madrid is everything a capital city should be: vibrant, affordable and fun. *"For young, single people it is ideal."* You would be wise to avoid a summer seat, however, since Madrid can become scorching hot and the savvy locals all flee to the coast.

Work: Being a trainee solicitor is not the best way to soak up the easy-going 'mañana' ethos for which the locals are famous. Madrid is a regional commercial centre like Paris or Frankfurt, and you can expect to be handling the same kind of commercial and corporate work, with plenty of private M&A and corporate housekeeping, etc. Good Spanish is essential, since you will mostly be handling Spanish law. *"You end up working just as hard as in London, but people are less likely to come up to you and tell you that something's urgent."* SJ Berwin's offices are dress-down on Friday, but the working environment is *"smart and conservative."* *"In Madrid you generally see a lot more people wearing suits."* There is a fair bit of *"grunt work"* involving *"translation and checking, but when there's chargeable work on, it always takes priority."* A two- or three-hour siesta in the middle of the day can jar with Protestant sensibilities and, when there's a lot of work on, the long lunch break means you can be in the office until 10–11pm. *"People guard their weekends quite jealously,"* said a trainee from Linklaters. She had never to work Saturdays and had never pulled an all-nighter in Madrid.

Rest and play: SJ Berwin's apartment is smart and central. It's a 25-minute walk to the office and half an hour to the centre of town. The Linklaters apartment is allegedly *"the best by quite a long way,"* near Colon and right in the centre of things. Madrid is a real cultural oasis in the otherwise barren central plains of Spain. Bar culture figures highly and the city boasts three of

SPECIALIST PRACTICE AREAS

INTERNATIONAL

177

the best art collections in Europe: the Prado, the Reina Sofia and the Thyssen. Queues for the latest movies stretch twice around the block but tickets cost a quarter of what you would pay in the West End. Madrid is an ideal base for trips to the surrounding towns and countryside and *"you are positively encouraged to get away at weekends."* The locals are open and friendly and it is easy to immerse yourself in Spanish life. Whether you want to go to a bullfight, see some art, hang out in cafés or watch some proper football, Madrid has it all. One Linklaters trainee was so seduced by the Spanish way of doing things that *"on New Year's Eve I ate 12 grapes in front of the telly."* When in Spain…

Best Things: Food, Social life, Weather, Lifestyle.
Worst Things: Long days, Having to go out so late, Dishonest cabbies.

the middle east

The big business centres of the Middle East receive a good number of trainees each year, attracted by the guarantee of fine weather, high-profile work and exotic glitz. Oil has turned Abu Dhabi from a small fishing village into one of the richest cities in the world in just 40 years, and skyscrapers and palm trees now predominate. Trainees find that *"the city is incredibly anglicised and the culture shock is minimal,"* but life for women can be *"extremely frustrating."* *"I wasn't a feminist before I went out there, but I am now,"* said one trainee. If Abu Dhabi isn't to your liking, *"stunningly beautiful"* Muscat, the capital of Oman, offers a more authentic taste of life in the Gulf. March to September is the best time to go, although you'll be air conditioned all year round. Temperatures of up to 50°C make the summer months the quietest (and cheapest) but you won't get as many public holidays.

Work: In the Gulf *"they have a different way of doing business,"* but they still tend to do it in English.

Commercial work features highly and there is an emphasis on project and finance work. One trainee from Trowers & Hamlins found himself dealing with *"a vast range of things from enormous power stations to people worried about lost luggage."* There's plenty of client contact, and you may get PR and marketing experiences that you'd never have back in London. The typical working day runs from 8am-1pm and then 4–7pm and the lunch break is best spent *"swimming, water-skiing or taking a nap."* The week runs from Saturday to Wednesday, with some trainees required to work Thursday mornings. Because there are only three days in common with foreign offices the pressure can build up fast. *"When someone phones up and asks for something to be done by the end of the week, it often means it has to be done there and then." "Work becomes much more a part of your daily life than it is back in London,"* but then there's not much to do in Muscat once you've been to the Souk and admired the views.

Rest and play: *"Fabulous"* apartments with sea views are par for the course and come with all mod cons short of gold taps and fittings. Free memberships of swanky hotel health clubs also come as standard, as do cars and free petrol. If it's culture you're after, think twice about Abu Dhabi, since *"there isn't much."* Trainees agree that there's an *"excellent quality of life"* however, and with the Maldives, Oman and Petra all within striking distance, holidays become a major expense. The expat community and office colleagues make up a big part of a trainee's social life, which was variously described as *"lively," "rowdy"* and *"liberal."* The scene in Muscat is much smaller than in Abu Dhabi, and socialising takes place in the city's half dozen hotels. By the end of your six months *"the waiters will know exactly what you are going to drink and where you are going to sit."*

Best things: Lifestyle, Quality work, Landscape.
Worst things: Heat, Isolation, Boredom.

moscow

If you have a taste for adventure and are concerned that a lifetime of due diligence won't give you any good stories to tell the grandchildren, you may want to consider heading out to the Wild East. *"Moscow doesn't attract applicants like Singapore does. Most people in Moscow have an interesting story and a real interest in it."* With its fascinating history, stunning architecture and a metro system with more chandeliers than your average palace, Moscow is rounded off with *"an appealing edge of madness." "There's no routine, something always happens… it makes working in a law firm a bit more interesting."* As with any frontier town, there is a fair amount of crime and punishment, and things change fast. *"People have preconceptions of Moscow which are not true. You can't sell jeans and you won't have to queue for food. It is very Western. You're not going to starve."* Winter is the best time to be there if you're not out to get a tan. Expect plenty of *"fresh, crisp snow"* and temperatures of down to –30°C.

Work: Many firms offer energy work in addition to a regular diet of banking and corporate. A Denton Wilde Sapte trainee worked on a high-profile Black Sea gas pipeline case that touched on complex ownership issues and maritime law. The workload for all the trainees we spoke to was described as *"steady." "You can expect to do things that are well beyond trainee level. It gives you a lot of confidence."* English is the language of the office, but pidgin Russian is helpful, if only to get around the city and make sense of the *"mind-boggling"* Cyrillic alphabet. Levels of autonomy and interest in one Moscow office were so high that London proved a bit of a disappointment for one trainee who *"felt crushed by the full weight of the hierarchy"* on his return. Trainees of the world unite! You have nothing to lose but your contracts!

Rest and play: Most firms in Moscow provide their trainees with good-sized apartments within the Zone 1 Garden Ring, although some provide an allowance for suitable accommodation. Be aware that even in the plusher buildings, *"water and heating can go off quite sporadically."* You will never be at a loss for things to do in Moscow. *"Things happen,"* reported one trainee, mysteriously. A trainee from Norton Rose was surprised by an impromptu lingerie parade down the middle of a quiet restaurant that she was eating in. It seems that many nocturnal entertainments quickly degenerate into fashion/strip shows. Russian food is *"heavy,"* but you won't be limited to the *"greasy potato patties"* that one trainee recalled fondly from a trip in the early 90s. Travel-wise you can get as far as St. Petersburg on an overnight train and there's a circuit of picturesque towns around the city known as 'The Golden Ring'. Any final pearls of wisdom before you defect? *"There are many things that you should know before you go out there, but half the fun is discovering them for yourself."*

Best Things: Surreal social life, Anarchy.
Worst Things: Hassle from the police, Bribery, Traffic and pollution.

new york

When asked what they liked most about New York, trainees tended to give us the same answer as the Pope. "Tutti buoni," he told reporters, "everything is good." *"Manhattan life is 24-7 and people do everything for you."* Convenience comes at a price, however. *"You'll need to get used to giving away dollar bills."* Despite overseas allowances and cheap taxis, even trainees coming from London found it *"extremely expensive."* The trainees we spoke to were out in the city at a difficult time but reported that it had quickly bounced back since September 11th. The new mayor is leading the bid for the 2012 Olympic Games, whose ancient motto, 'Swifter, higher, stronger' (whatever that is in Greek), could easily be adopted by the city itself. *"New Yorkers have an amazing spirit,"* confirmed one trainee. The best time to be out there is in the fall, when the city is *"absolutely beautiful"* and you don't have to put up with intense heat or cold .

Work: New York law is reasonably similar to UK law and trainees are likely to come in contact with similar work. Project finance and banking figure highly and a lot of work from Latin America comes through the city. Clifford Chance offers its trainees a Capital Markets seat, dealing mainly with South American banks, plus one in Project Finance and one in Corporate. The atmosphere in their New York office was more formal than in the UK, with a good old-fashioned partner hierarchy dictating where people sit and the size of the office. One trainee we spoke to had regularly been in the office after midnight during a busy period, but generally, nine to eight are typical hours. *"Before I went out there I was worried that I would never see the light of day,"* admitted an Allen & Overy trainee. Any language barriers? One trainee told us: *"I find I have to speak more loudly and repeat myself."*

Rest and play: Trainees get apartments with fantastic views on the Upper East and Upper West sides but, from the sound of things, don't spend much time at home. You'll need a head for heights and a taste for concierges and marble atria. Beyond the daily cost of living, the main expense is *"jetting off for the weekend."* One trainee talked of trips to New Orleans and Bermuda, and when you tire of the *Sex and the City* lifestyle, you can do the *West Wing* and *Ally McBeal* thing in Washington and Boston. There's skiing upstate in the winter and summer weekends in the Hamptons. *"Manic"* is how one trainee described the social life. *"There are a million bars and the best restaurants in the world."* Locals eat out all the time and the good places are booked up months in advance. Culturally, New York is in a league of its own and, between them, the Whitney, the Met, the Guggenheim and the Moma contain some of the most important art of the last century. Sustained by a potent mix of caffeine and Cosmopolitans, one trainee confided to us: *"When I get back to London I'm going to sleep for a week."*

Best things: Convenience, Lifestyle, Diversity
Worst things: Tipping, Hours

paris

Get a bottle of red wine, a pack of Gauloise and some Godard movies, and ask someone with a husky voice to whisper a list of Paris' monuments and museums in your ear. If this does it for you, and you have at least a GCSE in French, then make a beeline for the capital of romance, style, art and haughty grandeur. Whether you feel more at home in the cafés of the Left Bank or on the leather sofas at the National Bank, there is everything a young bourgeois or bohemian could wish for, from haute couture to basement jazz clubs. The best time to go is March to September. In May it's not too hot and there are no tourists around; it's the perfect time to invite friends across. *"I had so many people come out to visit that I got to know the sites of Paris far better than most tour guides,"* claimed one trainee.

Work: Clifford Chance has seven seats for trainees, most of which deal with broad-based finance issues covering projects, asset finance, general banking and structured finance. There's also a fair bit of corporate and property work coming through the city. Eversheds offers a seat in Public International law. Its trainee found she was working for US and UK lawyers on arbitrations between countries and governments, which tended to be *"quite academic."* Trainees have to manage themselves far more in Paris than in London and find they are given a lot more rope. *"Long-term it's very beneficial, but there were times when you wish you could have an easier life."* The hours are varied but reasonable. *"Work won't be keeping you in every night."* One trainee from Clifford Chance found he had a couple of late nights a month and only worked two weekends while out there.

Rest and play: Clifford Chance's flats afford amazing views and are situated in the south west of the city on the 30th floor; only ten minutes walk from the office in the 15th arrondissement. Eversheds has an apartment in La Marais, right in the centre of things. If you want it, there's a ready-made e-mail social scene for the numerous UK trainees in the city. *"Some people spend every night in the Firkin." Bars are open until 2am and the club scene is of similar quality to London's. Long gone are the days when French music meant Serge Gainsbourg or Johnny Hallyday; Paris has had a revival of late, giving the locals all the more reason to be snooty to foreigners. Travel is a great temptation since *"Paris is an ideal springboard to the rest of Europe."* Depending on the time of year, you can be on the slopes or the sands within a few hours thanks to the high-speed TGV. Parisian restaurants are spectacular and dining out is likely to take care of your surplus euros. *"I tend to eat out four or five times a week,"* claimed one trainee, but with the rent taken care of and a living allowance, *"you're still onto a bit of a money-spinner."*

Best Things: Food, Wine, Romance.
Worst Things: French TV, No bacon sarnies, The attitude towards the English.

singapore

With its polyglot society, occasional drizzle, excellent transport links and general efficiency, Singapore is basically the Brussels of the Far East. The opium dens and rickshaws of the colonial past have been swept aside to make way for a brave, new civic utopia where the streets are safe and clean, everything is air-conditioned, and an automated taxi system means you'll never wait more than four minutes for a cab. *"Precision"* is what it's all about, and the city runs like a Swiss timepiece. Singapore is known as 'The Fine City' as much for its rigorously enforced penalties as for its splendour. You're liable to be fined for jaywalking, failing to flush the toilet or importing packs of chewing gum that are surplus to personal use. *"It's like living in a very nice bubble,"* admitted one trainee, *"but six months was quite long enough."* Singapore is non-seasonal, but the humidity can be a shock, and depending on whether you sweat or merely glow, *"perspiration is a problem."*

Work: The work is *"more laid-back than in London."* You'll mostly be involved in litigation, project finance and corporate work. Shipping also figures highly in the smaller niche firms, offering a variety of work that overlaps with other practice areas. A Watson, Farley & Williams trainee found herself assisting partners on a variety of tasks including taking a witness statement on a docked vessel, refinancing and restructuring shipping lines and handling a collision claim concerning a ferry disaster. Other work included drafting different shipping documents and visiting the Ship Registry to discharge and register mortgages of vessels. Some firms also deal with aviation law. A trainee from Freshfields Bruckhaus Deringer spent much of her seat out in Jakarta helping with the restructuring of a local airline. Don't be deceived by the *"efficient and relaxed atmosphere,"* however. The work can build up and a WF&W trainee mentioned that she and trainees at some other firms ended up staying in Singapore over Christmas, even though they didn't have to work on the public holidays. *"Everything in the city works,"* and that will include you.

Rest and play: The Freshfields accommodation is in a pleasant area outside the centre with a pool and tennis court, but trainees from other firms live centrally in the expat enclave. This was variously considered *"great fun"* or *"quite claustrophobic."* It's fair to say that Singapore is singularly lacking in culture, so much so that last year both Robbie Williams and Manchester United had to be imported to entertain/irritate the locals. To compensate, there is a well-established social scene amongst UK trainees and expats, and all new arrivals find themselves on an e-mail list. The main expense for trainees is *"boozing,"* largely in the city's many waterfront bars. *"Shopping is the national pastime."* Singapore is a great base for travel and trainees spend weekends away from the city taking advantage of cheap package deals to Malaysia, Thailand, Indonesia, Cambodia and the South Pacific.

Best things: Travel opportunities, Cultural difference.
Worst things: Claustrophobia, Distance from home.

tokyo

Back on its feet after earthquakes, gas attacks and financial crises, Japan has emerged from the 90s as a schizoid hybrid of Advanced Capitalism and Zen Buddhism. At some point something's got to give, but for now the tensions that run through the capital like fault lines make it a vital, edgy and exciting place to be; *"Tokyo is off the planet."* Crowded, cramped, noisy and hectic, it is the *"archetypal concrete jungle, but with a real charm to it."* It is efficient and extraordinarily expensive. *"If you count your pennies you are likely to have a heart attack. You can easily spend two or three hundred pounds in a night."* Go in September and you'll miss the rainy season and get some skiing done. March is a month of *"blue skies and cherry blossoms."*

Work: Tokyo is mainly banking work, but Denton Wilde Sapte trainees will get to have a crack at whatever comes into the office, from energy to litigation work. You need to have *"a lot of stamina."* You are likely to be handling your own cases and *"you won't feel like a trainee."* One Ashurst Morris Crisp trainee in a finance seat was involved with a local dam and tower blocks, and a methanol plant in Saudi Arabia. You're unlikely to get much client contact unless you are a master of oriental languages and etiquette, but you will be involved in marketing work. A DWS trainee admitted that *"a slow day was 12 hours and it was normal to work weekends."* Although the hours were sometimes considered to be *"excessive,"* everyone out there works hard so it's not like you'll be stuck in your office looking wistfully out the window at your carefree contemporaries. *"It seemed pretty normal."*

Rest and play: DWS has a brand new Western-style apartment while other firms provide more traditional Japanese-style accommodation complete with tatami matting. Ashursts has a central place in Hiroo, *"the Hampstead of Tokyo."* A trainee e-mail list *"gives you a good base to expand from,"* so you'll not feel isolated. Expect to go out with people from the office, but the Japanese are notoriously reserved. *"They have very distinct professional and personal personas and they are difficult to get to know."* It's easy enough to work and play in the same district, but you should make the effort to get out of Roppongi. *"All the bankers and lawyers congregate there, but it's a bit sleazy."* For traditional entertainment, *"karaoke is a must."* The Japanese do it in a booth with their friends; it's not about embarrassing yourself in front of strangers. Live Sumo wrestling is highly recommended. Apparently, *"there are lots of monks involved."* Bullet trains take you to Hiroshima, Miya Jima and Nikko for day trips and in winter you can be on the slopes in an hour and a half.

Best Things: Visual stimulation, Safety.
Worst Things: Language problems, Hard to get to know the Japanese.

who goes there?

If you're wondering which firms to apply to based on your language skills or an interest in a particular foreign culture, the following table should help. We asked law firms to tell us where they offered trainee postings. Most of the locations listed are offered at least regularly, if not at every single seat location.

OVERSEAS SEATS – WHO GOES THERE?

LOCATION	FIRM
Abu Dhabi	Denton Wilde Sapte, Richards Butler, Simmons & Simmons, Trowers & Hamlins
Amsterdam	Allen & Overy, Clifford Chance, CMS Cameron McKenna, Freshfields Bruckhaus Deringer, Herbert Smith, Linklaters, Norton Rose, Slaughter and May
Athens	Norton Rose, Richards Butler, Shadbolt & Co, Thomas Cooper & Stibbard
Australia	Baker & McKenzie, Slaughter and May
Bahrain	Norton Rose, Trowers & Hamlins
Bangkok	Allen & Overy, Linklaters, Norton Rose, Watson, Farley & Williams
Barcelona	Osborne Clarke
Berlin	Hammond Suddards Edge
Bratislava (Slovakia)	Allen & Overy, Linklaters
Brussels	Allen & Overy, Ashurst Morris Crisp, Baker & McKenzie, Blake Lapthorn, Cleary, Gottlieb, Steen & Hamilton CMS Cameron McKenna, Clifford Chance, Cobbetts, Coudert Bros, Dechert, Dickinson Dees, DLA, Eversheds, Freshfields Bruckhaus Deringer, Hammond Suddards Edge, Herbert Smith, KLegal, Linklaters, Lovells, Mayer, Brown, Rowe & Maw, Nabarro Nathanson, Norton Rose, Olswang, Osborne Clarke, Pinsent Curtis Biddle, Shearman & Sterling, Simmons & Simmons, SJ Berwin, Slaughter and May, Taylor Vinters, Taylor Wessing, Theodore Goddard, White & Case, Wragge & Co.
Bucharest	Linklaters
Budapest	Clifford Chance, CMS Cameron McKenna, Linklaters
Cairo	Denton Wilde Sapte
California	Osborne Clarke, Weil Gotshal & Manges
Chicago	Baker & McKenzie
Cologne	Linklaters
Copenhagen	Osborne Clarke, Slaughter and May
Dar es Salaam (Tanzania)	Shadbolt & Co
Dubai	Clifford Chance, Clyde & Co, Denton Wilde Sapte, Trowers & Hamlins

LOCATION	FIRM
Düsseldorf	Simmons & Simmons
Frankfurt	Allen & Overy, Ashurst Morris Crisp, Baker & McKenzie, Clifford Chance, Freshfields Bruckhaus Deringer, Linklaters, Lovells, Norton Rose, Osborne Clarke, Simmons & Simmons, SJ Berwin, Slaughter and May
Gibraltar	Denton Wilde Sapte
Hamburg	Allen & Overy, CMS Cameron McKenna
Helsinki	Osborne Clarke, Slaughter and May
Hong Kong	Allen & Overy, Baker & McKenzie, Barlow Lyde & Gilbert, Bird & Bird, Clifford Chance, Clyde & Co, CMS Cameron McKenna, Coudert Bros, DWS, Freshfields Bruckhaus Deringer, Herbert Smith, Linklaters, Lovells, Norton Rose, Richards Butler, Shadbolt & Co, Shearman & Sterling, Simmons & Simmons, Slaughter and May, Stephenson Harwood, White & Case
Lisbon	Simmons & Simmons
Luxembourg	Osborne Clarke, Slaughter and May
Madrid	Allen & Overy, Ashurst Morris Crisp, Clifford Chance, CMS Cameron McKenna, Freshfields Bruckhaus Deringer, Linklaters, Osborne Clarke, Simmons & Simmons, SJ Berwin, Slaughter and May, Stephenson Harwood
Milan	Allen & Overy, Ashurst Morris Crisp, Clifford Chance, Freshfields Bruckhaus Deringer, Hammond Suddards Edge, Herbert Smith, Linklaters, Norton Rose, Simmons & Simmons, Slaughter and May
Monaco	Berwin Leighton Paisner, Eversheds
Moscow	Allen & Overy, Baker & McKenzie, Clifford Chance, Coudert Bros, Denton Wilde Sapte, Herbert Smith, Linklaters, Norton Rose, White & Case
Munich	Ashurst Morris Crisp, Hammond Suddards Edge, Norton Rose, SJ Berwin
New York	Allen & Overy, Clifford Chance, Dechert, Freshfields Bruckhaus Deringer, Lovells, Simmons & Simmons, Slaughter and May, Weil Gotshal & Manges
Oman	Trowers & Hamlins
Oslo	Slaughter and May

SPECIALIST PRACTICE AREAS

WHO GOES THERE?

OVERSEAS SEATS – WHO GOES THERE?

LOCATION	FIRM
Paris	Allen & Overy, Ashurst Morris Crisp, Bird & Bird, Clifford Chance, CMS Cameron McKenna, DWS, Eversheds, Freshfields Bruckhaus Deringer, Hammond Suddards Edge, Herbert Smith, Holman Fenwick & Willan, Linklaters, Lovells, Norton Rose, Osborne Clarke, Richards Butler, Shadbolt & Co, Shearman & Sterling, Simmons & Simmons, Slaughter and May, SJ Berwin, Theodore Goddard, TSB, Watson, Farley & Williams, White & Case
Philadelphia	Dechert
Piraeus	Clyde & Co, Holman Fenwick & Willan, Ince & Co, Norton Rose, Stephenson Harwood, Watson, Farley & Williams
Prague	Allen & Overy, Clifford Chance, CMS Cameron McKenna, Linklaters, Lovells, White & Case
Rome	Allen & Overy, Clifford Chance, CMS Cameron McKenna, Hammond Suddards Edge, Linklaters, Simmons & Simmons
Rotterdam	Osborne Clarke, Simmons & Simmons
Sao Paolo	Clifford Chance, Linklaters, Richards Butler
Shanghai	Clifford Chance, Simmons & Simmons, Stephenson Harwood

LOCATION	FIRM
Singapore	Allen & Overy, Ashurst Morris Crisp, Clifford Chance, Denton Wilde Sapte, Freshfields Bruckhaus Deringer Bruckhaus Deringer, Herbert Smith, Linklaters, Norton Rose, Shearman & Sterling, Slaughter and May, Stephenson Harwood, Watson, Farley & Williams, White & Case
St Petersburg	Osborne Clarke
Stockholm	Linklaters, Slaughter and May
Stuttgart	CMS Cameron McKenna
Talinn (Estonia)	Osborne Clarke
Tokyo	Allen & Overy, Ashurst Morris Crisp, Clifford Chance, Denton Wilde Sapte, Freshfields Bruckhaus Deringer Bruckhaus Deringer, Herbert Smith, Linklaters, Lovells, Slaughter and May
Turin	Hammond Suddards Edge
Warsaw	Allen & Overy, Clifford Chance, CMS Cameron McKenna, Linklaters, Norton Rose, White & Case
Washington	Baker & McKenzie, Coudert Bros, Dechert

THE TRUE PICTURE

introduction 186
top 120 firms table 188
the true picture 191

a guide to training with 120 of the top firms

our methodology

This year we interviewed trainees at 120 of the top law firms in England and Wales, asking about everything from seat allocation to social life. The 'True Picture 120' firms were selected by the size of their trainee populations. By expanding the *True Picture* again this year, we've been able to cover a wider variety of firms – from City giant Linklaters to Southend-on-Sea crime specialist TMK Solicitors, which has 11 trainees. None of the *True Picture* is vetted or even seen by any of the firms we cover prior to publication.

We ask firms to provide us with complete lists of their trainees and newly qualified solicitors, and we then select a sample of individuals randomly from these lists. Most firms know by now that our first task is to work out whether or not any names have been left off the list. The remainder do themselves no favours by 'editing' the lists! We then pick names at random and interview trainees and NQs by telephone. About 98% of the time they are happy to talk to us. Our interviews average 30 minutes and our sources are guaranteed anonymity.

Once we've completed our interviews for a firm, we then look for consensus of opinion on certain topics. Some trainees' opinions differ significantly from those of their peers, but we do not hunt for sensational stories. If we refer to trainee moans in the *True Picture*, it is because the issue in question has been raised by a number of individuals.

A couple of expressions need explanation:
'grunt work' refers to administrative, yet essential, tasks like bundling and scheduling documents in litigation, and putting together completion bibles (copies of all relevant documents) or supervising visitors to data rooms in transactional departments. **'CoCo'** is the abbreviated name for company/commercial departments.

our findings

This year we found that trainees were sometimes edgy and more critical of their firms than during the past three or four years. The job market has tightened and the rose-tinted spectacles are off. We have tried to look beyond the current market when writing the *True Picture* as we recognise that things will have changed by the time our readers start their training. The massive salary hikes of recent years are over for the time being.

Every year trainees tell us that responsibility varies between departments. In property you might handle several small files. The experience in litigation depends entirely on the type of cases your firm undertakes; you may take small cases all the way through to settlement, or you may be stuck for months on documentation in larger cases. In times of plenty, corporate means long hours, which commonly climax in dreaded all-nighters. However, at the moment, some trainees find they have little to keep them busy and some corporate trainees are leaving work at 5.30pm, even in the magic circle firms.

A majority of firms offer four six-month seats, some a six by four-month rotation and others still have their own pattern. Trainees move between departments, either sharing a room and working for a partner or senior assistant, or working for a number of lawyers, perhaps in an open-plan environment.

Your choice of firm will be based partly on location, partly on size and partly on the practice areas available...then it's a matter of chemistry. Some firms are stuffier than others; some are quite pc. Some firms have a very pronounced work ethic; others are more easy-going. It's really important that you find the one that fits you and this is the very reason we spend six months putting the *True Picture* together!

During our interviews we noticed that different issues affect trainees at different types of firms:

what's new at magic circle firms?

- Salaries have stopped rising.
- At some firms, armies of paralegals mean less dross work for trainees; at others there are fewer paras. On big deals your role will be small.
- The hours can be grim when there's masses of work on, but of late there hasn't.
- The chances of going overseas are high. Campaign for a popular seat as soon as you can.
- Trainees know that the firm's name on their CV will carry them far. Many intend to stick around for just a few years post-qualification and then see what takes their fancy.

what's new at mid-sized firms?

- A wide range of work is on offer within this group of firms. If finance doesn't get you excited, you can find a firm that will allow you to skirt around the whole 'City' thing.
- You are less likely to get an overseas placement.
- Partners know who you are and you're likely to know the majority of people at the firm.
- Some firms have been tightening their belts in harsher economic conditions. A few have made redundancies; most are cautiously optimistic for the future. The technology sector is still fragile.
- A number of firms have had excellent retention rates in 2002; at others, they have been much lower than normal.

what's new at national firms?

- Some firms require trainees to move around the country; some offer the opportunity to do so; at others, movement is almost impossible.
- Salaries are usually high for the relevant region, although there may be differentials among the offices of a single firm.
- You won't always get the same work at each office. Make sure the one you choose does the work you want as well as other branches.
- The firm may be as big as City megafirms, but deals and clients aren't as likely to be blue-chip.
- You get the advantages of a more intimate atmosphere in a smaller office, with the benefits of a larger network of lawyers across the country.

what's new at regional firms?

- At the top regionals you'll find great quality work. A few compete with City firms for business…and win! Look at the success of Burges Salmon, Wragge & Co, Dickinson Dees, etc.
- Often take trainees with local connections and older trainees who have strong local roots and can bring first-career skills and contacts.
- Pay is good in Leeds, Birmingham, Manchester, etc. You'll work hard for less money, but the cost of living is lower. There are fewer rats in the race.
- A trend towards commercial work means many firms have shed private client/crime/family/PI or are in the process of doing so.

what's new in niche firms?

- Experience in other areas of work may be minimal and may limit your choices on qualification.
- Firms are vulnerable to fluctuations in the market. Eg. consolidation of NHS clinical negligence defence work into just 15 approved firms has left other defence firms looking for new work.
- Firms want applicants who bring something extra to the job, eg. industry experience, contacts
- Competition for trainee places can be fierce.

and finally…

Applicants are often self-selecting, shying away from the magic circle and focusing instead on smaller firms, assuming they will be easier to get into. But, on paper, with fewer contracts available, the odds of getting into a small regional firm are much lower than they are for the magic circle. We hope the *True Picture* will help you to find a firm that you want to work for and one that wants you. The most important thing is to understand what type of work it does and what type of place it is, because no matter how hard or how easy it is to get a training contract, you'll want to enjoy it.

THE TRUE PICTURE TOP 120 FIRMS

RANK	FIRM NAME	CITY	TOTAL TRAINEES	PAGE NUMBER TRUE PICTURE	PAGE NUMBER A-Z
1	Eversheds	London*	205	271	508
2	Clifford Chance	London	245	238	484
3	DLA	London*	151	262	504
4	Linklaters	London	290	332	544
5	Allen & Overy	London	215	193	458
6	Freshfields Bruckhaus Deringer	London	178	285	518
7	Hammond Suddards Edge	London*	97	294	523
8	Herbert Smith	London	174	299	526
9	Lovells	London	121	335	546
10	Norton Rose	London	125	361	561
11	Slaughter and May	London	158	399	582
12	CMS Cameron McKenna	London*	108	243	486
13	Denton Wilde Sapte	London*	103	255	499
14	Pinsent Curtis Biddle	Birmingham*	74	373	567
15	Ashurst Morris Crisp	London	107	200	460
16	Nabarro Nathanson	London*	60	356	559
17	Addleshaw Booth & Co	Leeds*	64	191	457
18	Simmons & Simmons	London	101	394	581
19	Berwin Leighton Paisner	London	66	209	465
20	Osborne Clarke	Bristol*	57	365	563
21	Baker & McKenzie	London	60	202	461
22	Wragge & Co	Birmingham*	46	438	606
23	SJ Berwin	London	80	397	466
24	Bevan Ashford	Bristol*	50	211	467
25	Mayer, Brown, Rowe & Maw	London	49	349	553
26	Taylor Wessing	London*	52	410	589
27	Morgan Cole	Cardiff*	36	354	558
28	Barlow Lyde & Gilbert	London*	35	204	463
29	Masons	London*	50	346	552
30	Irwin Mitchell	Sheffield*	28	313	534
31	Stephenson Harwood	London	45	406	585
32	Beachcroft Wansbroughs	London*	53	207	464
33	Bird & Bird	London	31	215	468
34	Macfarlanes	London	38	340	549
35	Bond Pearce	Plymouth*	24	219	470
36	Clyde & Co	London*	40	241	485
37	Lawrence Graham	London	34	319	538
38	Halliwell Landau	Manchester*	25	292	522
39	Field Fisher Waterhouse	London	23	276	511
40	Theodore Goddard	London	30	412	591

*Indicates branches elsewhere in England and Wales. Only head office location listed.

THE TRUE PICTURE TOP 120 FIRMS

RANK	FIRM NAME	CITY	TOTAL TRAINEES	PAGE NUMBER TRUE PICTURE	PAGE NUMBER A-Z
41	Richards Butler	London	45	385	573
42	Olswang	London*	43	363	562
43	Shoosmiths	Northampton*	26	390	579
44	Mills & Reeve	Cambridge*	37	351	556
45	Charles Russell	London*	26	234	481
46	Burges Salmon	Bristol	40	230	477
47	Hill Dickinson	Liverpool*	17	303	528
48	Dickinson Dees	Newcastle*	30	257	501
49	DWF	Liverpool*	17	266	506
50	Travers Smith Braithwaite	London	40	419	595
51	Dechert	London	30	253	497
52	Reynolds Porter Chamberlain	London	18	383	572
53	Cobbetts	Manchester*	23	245	488
54	Blake Lapthorn	Portsmouth*	14	217	469
55	Pannone & Partners	Manchester	16	369	564
56	Penningtons	London*	21	371	566
57	D J Freeman	London	26	259	503
58	Browne Jacobson	Nottingham*	21	228	476
59	Klegal	London	21	317	536
60	Trowers & Hamlins	London*	31	421	596
61	Walker Morris	Leeds	29	425	597
62	Manches	London*	17	342	550
63	Freethcartwright	Nottingham*	15	283	517
64	Holman Fenwick & Willan	London	20	306	530
65	Weil, Gotshal & Manges	London	17	432	602
66	Withers LLP	London	21	436	605
67	Ince & Co	London	23	310	533
68	Martineau Johnson	Birmingham*	25	344	551
69	Gouldens	London	32	291	521
70	Nicholson Graham & Jones	London	18	359	560
71	White & Case	London	30	434	603
72	Farrer & Co	London	14	274	509
73	Speechly Bircham	London	10	403	583
74	RadcliffesLeBrasseur	London*	16	379	570
75	Edwards Geldard	Cardiff*	24	268	507
76	Hugh James	Cardiff*	17	308	532
77	Watson, Farley & Williams	London	24	428	599
78	Ward Hadaway	Newcastle	16	427	598
79	Lewis Silkin	London	13	329	543
80	Sidley Austin Brown & Wood	London	10	393	580

*Indicates branches elsewhere in England and Wales. Only head office location listed.

THE TRUE PICTURE TOP 120 FIRMS

RANK	FIRM NAME	CITY	TOTAL TRAINEES	PAGE NUMBER TRUE PICTURE	PAGE NUMBER A-Z
81	Brabners Chaffe Street	Liverpool*	18	223	473
82	TLT Solicitors	Bristol	15	416	594
83	Cripps Harries Hall	Tunbridge Wells*	14	251	492
84	Veale Wasbrough	Bristol	13	423	n/a
85	Laytons	London*	13	322	539
86	Mace & Jones	Liverpool*	9	338	548
87	Bristows	London	17	227	475
88	Foot Antstey Sargent	Plymouth*	9	279	514
89	Lester Aldridge	Bournemouth*	9	327	542
90	Gateley Wareing	Birmingham*	11	289	519
91	Harbottle & Lewis	London	8	297	524
92	Boodle Hatfield	London*	10	221	n/a
93	Thring Townsend	Swindon*	12	414	593
94	Bircham Dyson Bell	London*	10	214	n/a
95	Finers Stephens Innocent	London	8	278	512
96	Wedlake Bell	London*	10	430	600
97	Taylor Vinters	Cambridge	10	408	587
98	Capsticks	London	12	232	480
99	DMH	Brighton*	10	265	505
100	Andrew M Jackson	Hull	11	197	n/a
101	Hodge Jones & Allen	London	10	304	529
102	Clarks	Reading	10	236	482
103	Ford & Warren	Leeds	12	281	n/a
104	LeBoeuf, Lamb, Greene & MacRae, LLP	London	9	324	540
105	Brachers	Maidstone*	13	225	474
106	Shadbolt & Co	Reigate*	9	388	577
107	Palser Grossman	Cardiff*	8	367	n/a
108	Leigh, Day & Co	London*	10	326	n/a
109	Coffin Mew & Clover	Fareham*	9	247	489
110	Pritchard Englefield	London	8	377	569
111	Prettys	Ipswich	8	376	568
112	Steele & Co	Norwich*	10	404	584
113	Russell-Cooke	London	12	387	574
114	Reed Smith Warner Cranston	London	13	381	571
115	Hextalls	London*	9	301	n/a
116	Coudert Brothers	London	8	249	490
117	Kaim Todner	London	14	315	n/a
118	Anthony Gold	London	8	198	n/a
119	TMK Solicitors	Southend*	11	417	n/a
120	Galbraith Branley	London	10	287	n/a

* Indicates branches elsewhere in England and Wales. Only head office location listed.

the true picture 120

Addleshaw Booth & Co

the facts
Location: Manchester, Leeds, London
UK ranking by size: 17
Total number of trainees: 64
Seats: 4x6 months
Alternative seats: Secondments
Extras: Manchester Legal Advice Centre

Addleshaw Booth & Co is a member of the elite of northern law firms, and it has big plans for London. To join this respected national giant, you'll need good academics and an outgoing nature as its wide range of work makes it a very popular choice.

northern roots
Back in 1997, Leeds firm Booth & Co (well respected for finance) got into bed with Manchester's Addleshaw Latham & Sons (leading in corporate). In 1998, it produced a child and packed it off to see if the streets of London really were paved with gold. Over the last four years, the London office has been pampered and nurtured, and is now expected to stand on its own two feet. Will it one day be expected to look after its parents in their old age?

As national firms go, Addleshaws is not of the Starbucks variety with branches everywhere. No one's expecting it to open up a fourth UK office or launch a string of overseas offices any time soon. Instead, Addleshaws takes a 'best friends' approach to international lawyering, forging relationships with selected firms in Europe and beyond. Be prepared for a UK-based training in Leeds, Manchester or London, although some of the current trainees have moved to London from the north (many with no intention of going back). Occasionally trainees switch between Leeds and Manchester, but are not pushed to move, although, "*it's encouraged to spend time in another office.*"

Most trainees attended northern universities or had northern roots, but the firm attracts applicants from all over. "*There's no bias to recruiting from the north,*" one trainee was adamant. Typically, they chose the firm because they wanted "*somewhere large, corporate and commercial, and with a really good reputation in the north.*" Leeds and Manchester are both big enough legal centres to provide quality work and serious clients. To illustrate this point, in July 2002 the firm completed a £750 million bond issue for one of its building society clients, Cheshire BS. That sort of work is normally the preserve of top City firms.

division of labour
A four-seat rotation will take you through the three main divisions – property, commercial and transactions. Within each, there's plenty of choice, so, for example, property litigation comes within property (as does – bizarrely – family and private client). Commercial offers the most popular seats – employment, IP, and competition work. The transactions division holds the big, gutsy corporate and banking seats.

Seat allocation works well, although "*naturally there are always going to be winners and losers.*" "*IP and employment, trade and reg, and departments where there's only one seat available are always oversubscribed.*" There are a few variations between the northern offices – if you want contentious IP or banking litigation, you'll have to do it in Leeds, and if you want private equity or corporate finance, you might prefer a seat in Manchester. If time away from the office is important to you, there are two regular client secondments near to Manchester: one with MyTravel and one with AstraZeneca. Others crop up as and when.

On the subject of responsibility and client contact, we heard plenty that allows us to simply say 'Super!' Appraisals are regular in almost all cases and the system is properly managed. Supervisors (with whom you will share a room) are usually selected after careful thought, and consequently we heard only a minimal amount of grumbling about supervisor attentiveness and feedback.

leeds: learning the alphabet

Addleshaws sits in a smart canal-side building just behind Leeds Railway Station. Predominantly white with splashes of corporate blue, it has a huge, glass atrium with a café. An outdoor, decked area adds to the cruise ship feel – you half expect Jane MacDonald to come through the doors cabaret-style, belting out a Lulu cover. The atrium is great for office socials or just lunch. *"I know the names of about 85% of the people in this office and recognise almost all the faces,"* said one trainee. As in Manchester, many trainees already knew each other before starting at the firm. *"Lots of us went to the same universities and law schools,"* confirmed one source. Indeed, it struck us that the York branch of the College of Law was almost the reception class for Addleshaws big school. One trainee told us, *"I look back fondly on my first few months at the firm, and being put with a group of people that I might have seen as my competitors and finding so many like-minded people."*

The job will demand a good chunk of your time during the week. Almost everyone we spoke to started at 8.30am and worked through until 6pm or 6.30pm most nights. In some departments, particularly in transactional areas, longer hours await you when a transaction builds up a head of steam. On Friday nights you'll probably end up in local bar Homarus. *"It's a cocktail bar that does two for one until 7.30pm… There you'll find people from different departments to mingle with."* A social committee has organised all manner of fun from horse and dog racing to trips to Alton Towers. The firm's size and geographical spread mean that Christmas parties are held separately for each office, but different divisions of the firm have cross-site away days, which one trainee described as *"team building and bouncy castles."*

manchester: hive of activity

The Manchester stronghold occupies the top half of a large office complex near the Bridgewater Hall and G-MEX. In last year's *True Picture* interviews, trainees spoke of slightly different cultures in the Manchester and Leeds offices. Manchester was previously held to be more traditional and conservative – less go ahead, less pushy perhaps. *"The perception was that Manchester was more traditional and Leeds, younger. I think Addleshaws is still slightly more traditional than DLA and some others in Manchester,"* concluded one source. But this year, trainees talked less of differences and more of similarities. *"I've noticed it getting more lively here in Manchester; I think there is more of a buzz about."* There have certainly been some changes – in summer 2002, a group of lawyers from the collapsed law firm Garretts joined the Manchester office at much the same time that, nationwide, some 11 partners were pushed from the Addleshaws partnership. The theory is that the firm is gunning for greater profitability.

But back to that buzz in Manchester… The Commonwealth Games has a lot to answer for – the firm took the role of official lawyers to the Games. It can only add to the trainees' sense that they're employed by just about the most respected firm in the city. Those we spoke to were also keen to discuss the firm's recent navel-gazing exercise – The ABC Way. Across the UK, Addleshaws folk have been focus grouping to discuss *"what defines us and what we aspire to. What we expect from ourselves and how we treat staff."* One trainee was happy to report, *"It's shown that the firm was already doing a lot of things right and most people are happy."* But, *"it's highlighted the need to ensure that all partners are accessible for staff and will listen to problems. There's been a slight perception of a them-and-us attitude with some partners, a few barriers."* The ABC Way *"shows that they will take views on board. Since it happened there have been signs that people have been making more effort."*

There's plenty of effort put into socialising: *"Most Friday nights, people will go for at least a couple, and sometimes some stay out all night."* Favourite bars include Rain Bar, Pitcher & Piano and Slice. *"We usually end up somewhere cheesy!" one trainee confessed. "On Fridays, Slice will be full of Addleshaws trainees…everyone else will be either over 50 or under 17!" Midweek, the blokes prefer "proper pubs." Well done, boys!

Some departments are better at socialising than others. 'Boo!' to the property department. 'Hurrah!' for the fun-lovin' corporate recovery team and for the transactions division lawyers who, rather like old British Rail, are 'getting there', after seeing the benefits of fun on a recent away day.

london: a capital idea

Into profit after just three years, Addleshaws' London venture is doing very nicely, thank you. The aim is to grow the office so it's the same size as the others. As one prophetic trainee concluded: "This office is the future for the whole firm; its growth will ensure the future for Leeds and Manchester." It bodes well for those looking to relocate to the capital and for students seeking an Addleshaws training but unwilling to sacrifice London life. Interestingly, senior partner Paul Lee has just made the London office his permanent home.

Trainees can choose from corporate, property, commercial or construction litigation, PFI, trade and regulatory, banking and two very popular "dogfight seats, seen as glam and trendy" – employment and TMIP (technology, media and IP). There are also secondments to financial clients. As the London office grows, so should the range of seats. "Commercial property is the biggest department," explained one trainee. "It's made up of ex-Manchester and Leeds lawyers and lateral hires from big firms in London." Being in a smaller office makes it easier to "cross borders and go into different departments." "You're certainly not sat in your department as a nameless face." Hours are described as "sensible."

There's an abundance of client contact. "I've had more in London," confirmed one source. "There are lots of marketing events: seminars and invitations to clients to come and watch sporting events in our offices. At the Wimbledon semi-finals, the champagne was flowing in the office and there was a similar thing with World Cup football and bacon butties." There's a slightly less hierarchical "all hands to the pump" mentality, but that's not to say Leeds and Manchester are any more hierarchical than any other law firm.

Nationwide, the September 2002 qualification process went smoothly and 22 of the 26 qualifiers took jobs with the firm, distributing themselves fairly evenly across the firm.

and finally…

The main reason for applying to Addleshaw Booth is still its super reputation in Leeds and Manchester, but the firm has a clear vision for London, so expect to see opportunities expanding there. If you take your career and your training seriously, this is a firm that will too.

Allen & Overy

the facts

Location: London
UK ranking by size: 5
Total number of trainees: 215
Seats: 4x6 months (see below)
Alternative seats: Overseas seats, secondments
Extras: Pro bono – Battersea Legal Centre, Privy Council death row appeals, language training

Allen & Overy is one of the five firms with a membership card for the elite magic circle. It falls into the heavyweight class for finance work, but craves proper recognition for its achievements in corporate and other areas of practice.

total eclipse

Trainees are required to spend 12 months of their training in banking and corporate groups and international capital markets (ICM). "Traditionally A&O has been seen as a finance firm, but they have been in it so long and are so far ahead with Clifford Chance that the corporate department gets eclipsed. General corporate brought in more revenue last year than banking," one trainee informed us. Both banking and corporate offer a wide variety of practice groups. Banking is divided into global loans, financial services regulatory, leveraged finance, restructuring and projects, while corporate includes M&A, equity capital markets, financial institutions, private equity, competition, communications, media and technology, energy & utilities and environmental.

Trainees must also undertake three months in a contentious area of law. The idea of a litigation seat divides trainees into two camps: those who can't get enough and those who can't wait to get out. If you know you want as much of it as possible, the good news is that you can extend your stay in the department. One trainee indicated: "*I have friends who extended to six months and I might too.*"

During the remainder of their contract, trainees choose from a good selection of other areas. Property (a practice the firm is determined to build up) allows them to run smaller files, as well as being thrown titbits on larger transactions. And then there are a number of sought-after niche seats, including private client, competition, tax and EPI (employment, pensions and incentives). These niche departments all orbit the main corporate and finance deals, providing the necessary support services. Our interviewees had their savvy hats on when discussing this aspect: "*If you're going to a specialist department, you still need general corporate experience to see how this part of the work feeds into the transaction.*" One source stressed that the spread of departments meant there was room for two types of trainee at A&O: "*Some have a general interest in law so get more exposure to hard law. Some people prefer pushing paper around and doing transactional work.*"

blind man's bluff

About a month into your training contract you'll be asked to select all your seats. "*It sounds bad, but you're not totally blind,*" said one old hand, referring to the series of information evenings laid on to assist you. Opinion was split between those who thought matters were then "*set in stone*" and those who said it was relatively easy to ask for changes. To get that coveted seat in, say, competition or employment, you play your trump card – a 'priority seat' request. This baby guarantees you the one thing you most want. Sadly, priority seat trump cards can't be traded for hard cash or sexual favours on the A&O black market.

Trainees tell us they'd be prepared to cut down a seat to just three months if they weren't getting on with their supervisor or they just found the work uninspiring. The firm acknowledges that it's a waste to keep a someone in a seat if it's not working out for them, but changing seats is not always possible, as it depends very much on the needs of different departments at any given time.

the f word

A few little birds told us that the recruitment partner sent round an e-mail instructing trainees that whenever they are representing the firm at recruitment events they were to stress that A&O doesn't just do finance work. Our sources formed two camps (what, again?) over the question of A&O's finance focus. "*It's a bit misleading to suggest otherwise…but it's why I came here,*" said one representative of the 'finance forever' group. Others staunchly defended the variety of work available: "*It's deceptive because the finance department gets so much press. The other departments have top people and do top work.*" One source said, "*My partner in corporate wouldn't be happy to be told it's just a banking firm.*" A&O is highly rated for almost everything it does by our colleagues on the *Chambers UK* and *Chambers Global* guides, but it doesn't lead in corporate or litigation or property. It's a whole other story concerning almost anything finance-related though.

One can understand why any firm hates being labelled as a one trick pony when it offers excellent lawyers and handles important work in other areas. And you don't have to be a rocket scientist or a Chambers' researcher or even a member of A&O's management board to appreciate the importance of diversification. The recruitment partner was wise to send that e-mail, but do remember that finance work is central to A&O's business and it will also be a central part of your training contract. Maybe the best thing to do is to examine what happens to trainees on qualification: of the 54 September 2002 qualifiers, 45 stayed on with the firm. 47% of those joined banking and capital markets groups, 23% went into corporate groups and the remaining 30% found homes in litigation, property and other niche areas.

corridor of death

No treatise on A&O would be complete without a mention of ICM's infamous securitisation seat. There was a time when a first-seater would rather have been tossed to an ill-tempered mutated sea bass at dinnertime than be thrown headlong into the group affectionately termed *"the corridor of death."* Luckily, none of our sources recounted horror stories to match those of their predecessors. Prevailing economic conditions mean that this department has been calmer of late but there remains an element of baptismal fire about this seat. *"You need a six-month seat in the jargon department before you can even put pen to paper,"* and *"I felt like my trainer was speaking Russian!"* But trainees can get their teeth into decent work. *"In ICM some of the deals were quite small and I was running them. In some departments, that's just not feasible, but in ICM I never felt like I was just sitting in the office, waiting for insignificant jobs."*

Chambers Global's International Banking & Finance Law Firm of the Year 2002

Many of our interviewees had experienced the long hours departments during a quieter time, so moans about hours were infrequent. Across the firm, most supervisors are reasonable human beings so the hours are totally work-dependant. One source said, *"I closed one deal, which was pretty hectic. On the worst day I went home at 5am, but we got the next day off."* Often *"things don't kick off till lunchtime. The hours would be different if they came in and pulled their finger out in the mornings. It's like they expect to be working late – it's a mind-set."* Er…isn't it also something called international time zones? If a job has a New York angle, your working day will shift back to accommodate those across the pond.

On the subject of the quality of trainee tasks, our sources pitched their tents again. From one lot – *"I've sometimes felt I've been twiddling my thumbs and at other times I've felt like I've been really useful. You can still enjoy the mundane work if it's important."* And from another – *"Support staff are amazing. In smaller firms, trainees have to do the crap themselves."* There's room for both views. Quite simply, your experience will depend on what's going down in a department when you get to it and what departments you get to.

home and away

Internationally, A&O is huge and the fourth seat is when many trainees find out just how huge. Trainees tender for overseas postings, stating why they want a particular destination, what experience they've had so far and what type of work they'd like to cover. Natural selection (love, mortgages, the local Sunday league) means that there are usually enough international seats to go round. In a nutshell, a foreign seat means *"a wicked social life,"* a free flat and more responsibility in a smaller office. The overseas offices are *"still A&O, but not."* Trainees find a different working culture, yet New Change is just an e-mail or phone call away. Back in Old Blighty, competing fourth-seat opportunities include client secondments, perhaps to investment banks such as Barclays Capital, Goldman Sachs or CSFB, or to corporate clients like Liberty or Thomson.

Trainees were adamant that even if you haven't a clue what area of law you want to qualify into, it is worth coming to A&O for the training. Quite simply, they tell us, *"It's second to none."* The PSC is not telescoped into two weeks at the start, but is delivered in smaller chunks over the whole training contract. Some told us that a new job is overwhelming enough without having to deal with the finer points of business accounts at the same time, but others would have preferred it all at the beginning. Who's got the flysheet? Additionally, there's a never-ending programme of compulsory lectures and skills seminars on everything from IT to networking.

pc world

It's not unusual for law firms to trot out the same old tosh about working in a friendly environment. Some go on about it at such length that they'd have us believe that it's actually kind words and twinkly-eyed smiles that fuel the global economy. But we'll make an exception for A&O. It's old news that this is the 'friendly face of the magic circle' and we're not about to tell you different.

A&O's culture evolved in a once ill-defined, primeval soup of niceness. We've watched it grow a couple of legs, and it now stands upright and holds a manifesto. 'Values into Action' is a firm-wide initiative to classify niceness into six core values. "*It sounds like a cheesy sound-bite but it really does work. They were probably things that were around anyway,*" thought one trainee. Another had been truly inspired: "*It definitely improves the atmosphere as I always have the values at the back of my mind – I strive for excellence.*" One trainee chuckled, "*They've added the values onto our screen savers to brainwash us every day!*" Values into Action certainly causes a few giggles: "*People will stand and hold the door open for five minutes because they're terrified of letting it slam in someone's face!*" The values have even permeated appraisal forms and trainees must now indicate the ways in which they have demonstrated them. We suspect their responses may be served with either wine or pineapple chunks.

Trainees have their own ideas about A&O culture. "*It's not stiff upper lip,*" offered one, while another told us that the full-time dress-down policy has "*done wonders.*" Of course, in such a big firm, not everyone lives up to the fluffy stereotype. "*There's one partner who's just so clever that other partners are scared of him. You've just got to be intimidated...but he's supposedly chilled out a lot recently.*" Partners are generally interested in you, but if they are up to their necks in it, don't expect an in-depth chat about the latest masterpiece you've drafted. Having said that, "*I've never felt like I was just a trainee and should go and look in the library because I dare not ask a partner for help.*"

shagadelic

You could weather a nuclear winter in One New Change. There are doctors, dentists, physios, a gym, a canteen and get this… a bar. "*It speaks volumes that we're the only firm to have a bar.*" (Er…not quite the only firm.) The obvious attraction to today's youth, lacking in get-up-and-go, is that it's on the premises – and cheap. One trainee said, "*I never expected to make so many good friends at work. At first you don't think you want it, but the size means you don't get to see them in the day so you want to meet up after work.*" The Heeltap & Bumper, a stone's throw from the office, gets plenty of custom, but "*we leave Shoeless Joe's and Balls Brothers to free drinks on the partners.*" In 2006 A&O will set up shop on one half of the old Spitalfields Market over towards Brick Lane and a shortish walk to some oh-so-trendy Shoreditch bars. Way, way back, Spitalfields was once a medieval priory and hospital but don't worry about contracting bubonic plague, you'll have corporate medical insurance.

The *Student Guide* team sent out its extensive feelers into the New Change gossip exchange. We hear tales of drunken exploits between trainees, some even fuelled by departmental drinks and dinners. We hear of e-mail flirting and trainees you dare not flirt with. And intra-office romance? In a firm this size…what do you think?

and finally…

Top-quality clients and a prestigious training is combined with a genuine interest in the well-being of staff. But remember: "*No one's running a holiday camp here*" – A&O can be an exacting place to work at times.

Andrew M Jackson

the facts
Location: Hull
UK ranking by size: 100
Total number of trainees: 11
Seats: 4x6 months
Alternative seats: None

If you've never driven along the undulating stretch of the M62 motorway that connects Humberside with the rest of the north of England, you probably don't need to continue reading. Andrew M Jackson is a healthy commercial firm that proves beyond all doubt that there's more to Hull than fish.

est. 1874

There's many a street in Hull where huge wooden props hold up the houses. Subsidence caused by mining, apparently. Think of this firm as one of the props holding up the commercial activity of the region. Imagine yourself, if you like, as a pillar of the business community. That's pretty much how Andrew M Jackson views its role and, as cheesy as it may sound, that could be you just a few years after qualification.

If you know the area, you'll know the firm's name. AMJ is looking for those who already understand the way things work in this part of the world. Folk are *"straight talking and down-to-earth; those who don't need the airs and graces a city person would need." "Giving a straight answer and talking in plain English"* is valued, and the firm wants *"hard-working people who can go out and represent the firm in the region."* It usually finds them close to home.

Trainees stress the firm's professional image. *"It prides itself on being efficient and cost-effective,"* and is determined to preserve the reputation it has built up over the last 130 or so years. If *"respectability"* and *"honour"* (how fantastic to hear that word) are printed on the firm's metaphorical doormat, then once you're inside you'll be pleased to learn that you can take off your smart shoes and put on a comfortable pair of slippers. As one trainee told us, *"It is very commercial and it tries to show a rigid image, but when you walk through the doors you realise it treats its staff well."*

fish and ships

This is a firm with a plan. *"Originally it had very strong connections with the shipping industry and then it diversified into other commercial areas."* And how. Commercial property is the biggest department now – *"perhaps twice as big as any other department"* – but litigation and shipping are important and there's a strong push being made in the corporate department. *"The firm knows where it wants to go and the type of clients it wants to attract."* And they are? *"Large national plcs right down to smaller owner-managed businesses."* The firm has some international work of the *"fish and shipping and Icelandic"* variety, but it's certainly not all maritime. Other top clients include MFI, Carpetrite, Express Dairies and Northern Foods.

Assume you'll see a seat in corporate (*"hardest to get"* at the moment, but definitely a growing department) or commercial property and you won't be far off the mark. Commercial litigation is popular (partly because this is where you may get some employment law experience), as is shipping (*"approachable partners and definitely not old school"*). Trainees prefer the commercial seats and that's just where the firm wants them to qualify. However, they do cut their teeth on private clients in conveyancing, tax and trusts and family seats, and a general litigation seat offers personal injury work and neighbour disputes. Up till now, trainees have been able to work for *"completely contrasting clients,"* from the legally aided in family, through to hardcore corporates. But our sources warn that if you're looking for a firm that can give you the high street experience then go to the high street. *"The emphasis will become even more commercial;" "the only legal aid work is in family,"* and *"PI is downscaling."*

no floundering around

The small trainee population can usually decide amongst itself how to divvy up the seats and usually people get what they want. But once in a new department they learn that the experience can differ somewhat from their last seat. Some trainees have their own rooms; others share with another trainee or paralegal; only a few share with a partner. The general consensus is that appraisals and feedback are not among the firm's strong points. Some trainees had never had an appraisal and, given the chance to be senior partner for the day, were adamant that they'd ensure a much more systematic approach. Corporate is off the hook on this one though: its partners were applauded for their efforts. We spoke to the firm and they told us of two new initiatives: training sessions for supervisors and a new mentor system whereby all new recruits will be allocated a partner to keep an eye on their progress over the two years.

Trainees gave due praise to their seniors for handing over good work. *"I don't think we ever feel like we are floundering around on our own. I've certainly never felt like I've been landed right in the middle of it."* Reports of rewarding tasks and responsibility far outweigh tales of the (inevitable) lows of more menial jobs. Advocacy experience and client handling is there for the taking and so too is a role in marketing. *"There are evening seminars for clients and they actively encourage you to go and learn how to deal with that sort of thing – the marketing side is important."*

trawlers in rough seas

The culture of the firm is a welcoming one and everyone rubs along together very nicely, but the social scene is far from kicking. Maybe it's because many of the lawyers live out of town. Maybe it's because trainees already have a life in the area and workmates aren't the be-all and end-all. The Hull Trainee Solicitors Group puts on a few jollies and there's a couple of pubs that get some business from AMJ lawyers, but it's safe to leave your party hat at home most weeks.

AMJ is located right in the heart of the older part of town, near to Whitefriargate, but *"it's not the most attractive office on the face of the earth."* Clients are treated to various paintings of *"trawlers in rough seas"* in the meeting rooms, although once you get beyond the client areas *"it's a mishmash of partitions and filing cabinets."* A few moans about insufficient computer terminals will, one hopes, be rectified soon. Salary moans have to wait until qualification before they dissipate. In September 2002, three of the four qualifiers stayed with the firm. The fourth had plans in another part of the country.

and finally…

A respected firm with plenty of decent clients on its books, this is a chance to shun the big boys of Leeds and London. If you're a City slicker looking for international finance deals, you'll be all wrong for Andrew M Jackson. On the other hand, if you're happy to deal with overworked City lawyers, while sitting pretty in one of Hull's finest firms, you'll be all right.

Anthony Gold

the facts

Location: London
UK ranking by size: 118
Total number of trainees: 8
Seats: Flexible (usually 1x12 + 2x6)
Alternative seats: None

London firm Anthony Gold was set up in 1963 to cater for both commercial clients and individuals. It's an ideal choice for trainees unwilling to choose between either type of client before they've gained any real experience…and those with an eye on a London career but no desire to get lost in a flock of sheep.

take it to the bridge

Anthony Gold has offices at both London Bridge (handling commercial work) and in Streatham, South London (where it is best known for its work in family and housing). It mixes commercial work and services to individuals with some considerable success. *"It is a progressive, open and friendly firm,"* said one of the trainees we spoke to. "*Because the London Bridge office has the commercial departments, it is more of a City-type office,*" whereas the Streatham branch "*feels more like a high street practice.*" Just to use the family departments in each office to illustrate a point, "*Streatham does legal aid and contact, children in care, domestic violence, etc. whereas London Bridge doesn't do legal aid as it doesn't pay so well – they pick and choose the things they take on.*"

golden opportunities

And what of the work? Well, if you want real responsibility and real cases with real clients, rather than tiny bits of gigantic cases for equally large and faceless corporations, forget the big City firms and go for Gold. In the London Bridge office, five commercial seats are on offer, both contentious and non-contentious. Disputes range from construction and IP cases through to general debt and contractual matters. There's a strong focus on negligence cases against solicitors, accountants, surveyors and other professionals who've dropped a clanger in the course of their work. The company/commercial department advises small businesses such as restaurants on company sales, employment issues, joint ventures and shareholder agreements.

Down in Streatham, there's a more right-on agenda. In housing, "*cases are very short-lived; they come and go very fast. My supervisor kept a close eye on what I was doing but I had a huge amount of work and was effectively running my own case load.*" One trainee said, "*You get quite a lot of responsibility early on. Within a month or two you can have your own cases.*" It's not an environment for the hesitant as, after sitting in on just a couple of client interviews, you could be going it alone. "*It's the best way to learn; you get really involved in the department, and you feel like you're needed there.*" One trainee told us, "*I'm constantly amazed at how varied things are – court, conferences, home visits to clients, working with interpreters, researching and drafting. In a firm like this you have a varied range of clients from those who may not speak English and have uncertain status in the UK, to paying private clients.*"

The hours differ across departments: in Streatham it's almost nine-to-five, but in the litigation and commercial departments at the Bridge, trainees "*get in at 8.30am and leave about 6pm.*" Not exactly killer hours, but "*if there is a big thing coming up and you have bundles to get ready you might have to work later, but no more than a couple of nights a week.*" Trainees do spend some time doing more administrative tasks like bundling and photocopying (more so in Streatham because "*there is less secretarial support*"), but they take it in their stride. "*If they have a backlog you are expected to help out,*" said one source, who also stressed that "*it is compensated for by the quality of the other stuff.*"

golden bullet

Trainees sit with partners or senior solicitors for the duration of their contract, which will be split into three or four seats of varying length. "*Supervision varies a bit from seat to seat,*" but most supervisors "*build time into their day to discuss what's happening.*" PI is "*what the firm is best known for*" and is seen by the trainees as very 'now'. You won't be forced into a seat you're not interested in and there are no compulsories beyond the Law Society's basic requirements. When it comes to allocating seats, the training honchos are "*really, really flexible.*" We even heard of one trainee who was interested in criminal law (an area which Anthony Gold doesn't practice) and was allowed to go to a different firm to get the experience she wanted. Not many firms would bite that particular bullet.

In 2002 the firm was able to offer jobs to two out of three of its qualifying trainees. Those hoping to build a family and private client practice tend to stay with the firm on qualification more commonly than those with a bent for commercial work.

headbanging

Anthony Gold is a fairly relaxed place to work. That's not to say it isn't professional; it's just that with so many staff who "*really care*" about the work they are doing, there's less need to crack the whip. "*It* has a good reputation and a better ethos than City firms," explained a source. "It's as PC as a law firm gets," said another (only half joking). Many of the people here have been involved in caring and charitable work before turning to the law. "Although it is hard to generalise, people are extremely committed."

On Friday staff take advantage of a dress-down policy and, in the evening, you're likely to find them in "the closest bar possible." Try Hitchcocks or the Thameside at London Bridge. "Streatham is not so good for social stuff as there are only two trainees and the other staff are less interested in going out," but the local Crown & Sceptre still sees a portion of trainee salaries. The firm throws Christmas and summer bashes to bring everyone together. "They're a lot of fun" and "a great way of meeting people." Partners join in too: "You just forget they are partners," said one trainee referring to a moment of karaoke carnage. "A partner and a couple of assistants did Motorhead's 'The Ace of Spades'...headbanging and stuff. It was really, really amusing." Double up or quit? Just watch your sides don't split!

and finally...

If you want both private client and commercial work, and to be treated like a real lawyer from day one, scribble the name Anthony Gold on your list.

Ashurst Morris Crisp

the facts

Location: London
UK ranking by size: 15
Total number of trainees: 107
Seats: 4x6 months
Alternative seats: Overseas seats, secondments
Extras: Pro bono – Privy Council death row appeals, Toynbee Hall & Islington Law Centres, language training

Ashurst Morris Crisp has built its reputation on its corporate expertise. It remains a respected and competitive top City firm, despite having a comparatively small number of fee earners when compared with the behemoths of the magic circle. It has a number of international offices throughout Europe and Asia, and continues to harbour transatlantic desires. Recently spotted in a cosy corner with old friends and New York M&A experts, Fried Frank Harris Shriver & Jacobson, the firm denies this necessarily means a coupling is on the horizon.

tax returns

As its website boasts, it has been "providing legal services for more than 175 years" and "consistently ranks in the top three of law firms with the highest number of clients listed on the London Stock Exchange." Corporate deals are Ashursts' lifeblood, so it's not surprising that a corporate seat is mandatory, and many trainees take it as their first assignment. The firm is particularly well regarded for its private equity practice and has had a super year in major buyouts. Over on the public side of the fence, it's also had some high profile instructions, including Railtrack Group's £7.5 billion disposal of Railtrack plc. In addition to corporate, Ashursts asks that you do two seats from property, litigation, international finance or energy, transport & infrastructure. This leaves one totally free choice – so use it wisely!

Tax remains "a very nice little department" and extremely popular. "People are falling over each other to do it." Why? "It has a youthful atmosphere – they're a nice, fun bunch of people" with "intellectually challenging work." Clearly, "if you like the people you're with, you tend to like the seat you're doing." Other popular seats include energy, transport & infrastructure, along with the "nichier seats" such as IP or employment, where there are "relatively few places and quite a high demand."

room with a view

Trainees sit with a supervisor, who is either a partner or a senior solicitor. Good news: "the trainee gets the view!" If there's a view to be had, that is. Some of the offices in the main building (Broadwalk House) overlook the building's large atrium. One trainee pointed out the virtues of building number two – Broadwalk West – where the litigation and real estate departments are housed. *"It was built a couple of years ago, it's spacious and it's got lots of natural light."*

Trainees talked about their hours: *"They've varied a lot, depending on how busy things get. I've never had any killer hours, although during the busier times I did ten- or 11-hour days, particularly leading up to corporate completions."* By all accounts, all-nighters are not a hugely regular occurrence (but the market has been flat of late). *"You expect to put in big hours when you join a corporate law firm,"* one source said matter of factly. Banking and corporate are *"more cyclical, with periods of slack and then periods of intense activity,"* but away from these, *"in real estate and planning the workflow tends to be consistent. I had a lot of little files to manage by myself, so I could manage my time and not have to stay late."*

finding a space

Trainees tell us, *"You take as much responsibility as you can, but it varies according to the department."* One interviewee explained: *"In real estate you can take a small file of your own and have as much responsibility as possible. If you're handling a lease on two car parking spaces, for example, you can learn everything there is to know about leasing. But in something like litigation they tend to be big matters, which have to be partner- or senior assistant-led, so you don't get as much responsibility there."* Although you *"mainly work for your principal, if someone comes in and asks if you can help and you're free then you do it."* Trainees have the option of requesting a mid-seat review, which will be *"really just an informal chat"* between you and your supervisor to see how you're getting on and how you can improve. One trainee commented, *"I didn't really feel I needed one...I felt the ongoing feedback I had was enough."* However, at the end of the seat there is a formal review in which you obtain written feedback.

Aside from secondments to some of the firm's big name clients, there are seats available in a number of overseas offices, namely Brussels, Frankfurt, Madrid, Milan, Paris, Singapore and Tokyo. If you want one of these slots, take note: they are highly competitive and you should make your preference known at a very early stage. Depending on the office, there'll be one or two places available every six months. Languages are *"fairly crucial"* for the European offices (with the exception of Brussels), which means that the Asian seats *"work out to be more competitive."* Fourth-seaters will take preference over other trainees. One interviewee raved about his time overseas: *"It was great! Corporate-based work mostly, but it's a seat where you'll get a very well-rounded training because you get to deal with marketing and other aspects, which you wouldn't see in the London office. There's more responsibility because it's a smaller office and of course there's a new culture to enjoy as well."*

from blue blood to blue-chip

Ashursts has had a rather blue-blooded, conservative reputation. We wondered if this image still prevails or if the firm has managed to shake it for good. *"It's an old firm, founded in eighteen-something so a sense of tradition is there, but it has a lot of vision in that there are offices popping up left right and centre. It's looking to have an international future rather than staying behind,"* one trainee said. This view is borne out by the firm's overseas expansion and its current 'liaison' with the Americans. Yet three years ago Ashursts retreated from a merger with Clifford Chance, and one can't help but wonder if there's still a side to the firm that is more comfortable with all things established.

As to why trainees were attracted to Ashursts, one source said, *"I spoke to people within the profession and they told me it was a real lawyer's firm. It's got a strong corporate reputation, blue-chip clients and a very high retention rate, not just at trainee level but later on too. I thought that was a fair indication of happiness in the workplace."* Another pointed out: *"It's not the biggest firm in the City, but looking through the business pages you often see Ashursts' clients featured along with deals we've worked on."* Presumably that trainee meant deals like the £12 billion take private of de Beers. Another said, *"Given that we're not part of the magic cir-*

cle, the amount of high-profile work we do is surprising." What came through from our interviewees was their sense that there's no need to compromise between top-quality work and an ever so slightly smaller working environment. "*You've got the large clients and deals, but it's not so huge that you feel like a faceless number – you can get to know a lot of people in the firm.*"

It's a good idea to try and get on Ashursts' summer scheme. As one trainee explained, "*Quite a lot of people in the scheme I was on eventually became trainees at the firm.*" Typically, the firm attracts plenty of applications from the very best universities, but trainees were keen to stress, "*They're moving away from the old Oxford/Cambridge tradition.*" There are also a number of 'foreign trainees', who studied in other jurisdictions then came over to the UK to train. One trainee said, "*If you're ego-driven and so competitive that you'd posture and throw your weight around to further yourself, that wouldn't go down well. It's very much all hands on deck here in that everyone works together and takes the credit together.*" Another interviewee added, "*Some people I know at college wouldn't fit in on that score.*" Which makes us wonder where those people are now…

dogs dinner
Each department has its own social events and there is an annual firm-wide quiz night with teams made up of partners, assistants, trainees and support staff. For the corporate department (and plenty of non-corporate trainees) there are 'Sundowners' every Friday night – local bar, wad of money…you figure out the rest. In the summer months, litigation and property have al fresco drinks on the terrace of Broadwalk West every Friday night. "*Ashursts tends to be quite generous about subsidising events,*" we heard. For trainees in particular, there are "*loads*" – a ball each January, "*trainee dogs nights*" (greyhound racing, in case you needed to ask), curry nights and salsa nights. One particularly hospitable partner holds a party for trainees every summer at his house in Surrey.

Ashursts continues to attract top quality graduates and has a commendably high retention rate. In September 2002, 30 of the 33 qualifiers stayed on. Just under half took corporate jobs and the rest distributed themselves around the other departments.

and finally…
Ashursts is a pukka City firm that (to use an overworn phrase) punches above its weight in fee earners, particularly in the corporate realm. For those wanting experience abroad, it has a number of international offices. In short, it has a history of excellence and an understanding of what's required in the future.

Baker & McKenzie

the facts
Location: London
UK ranking by size: 21
Total number of trainees: 60
Seats: 4x6 months
Alternative seats: Overseas seats, secondments
Extras: Pro bono – Waterloo Advice Centre, death row appeals

Starting from a single office in Chicago in 1949, Baker & McKenzie now boasts 63 offices in 35 countries, staffed by local lawyers. London is a big part of the European operation, co-ordinating many of its cross-border transactions. Baker & McKenzie is a global giant, doing great work for household name clients.

dressing up
The recruitment website feels very Mr Benn. As if by magic, you can fancy dress lawyers who've bravely offered themselves up for scrutiny. Sadly, no shopkeeper appears… Ironically, social commentators reckon Mr Benn (welded to his suit and bowler even on the weekends) was a perennial City man, who only dressed up to escape the monotony of his daily life. So is it all window dressing designed to lure students into a life of drudgery or does it reflect a genuine desire to be individual?

it's a small world

The firm earns its daily crust as *"a kind of a one-stop shop,"* fulfilling the needs of multinational companies such as Avis, Cisco, Compaq, DaimlerChrysler, ntl, Shell and Sony. One trainee told us: *"In all the work I have done, I cannot remember doing a single thing for a company that is predominantly UK-based."* That trainee also played down the US origins of the firm and stressed the worldwide nature of its business. *"It doesn't like to be considered a US firm... I can only really see the US origins through the clients."* Much of the work is of the corporate and commercial variety, and it is for this reason that all trainees are required to complete a corporate seat, *"which has a reputation due to the late nights. I've worked until 3am and on one occasion didn't sleep for almost 48 hours."* Pass that boy the Pro Plus. But the range of other seats is really impressive. Spots are available in banking and finance, dispute resolution, competition and trade, employment, projects, tax, communications and IT/IP.

Look at our parent publication *Chambers UK* and you'll find the firm leads in various areas, notably employment (2nd band), IP (3rd band), IT (1st band) and telecoms (3rd band). The IP/IT department is particularly popular with trainees and, even though there are six seats available at each seat rotation, *"if you want to do IP it's wise to tell people early on."* The team recently won plaudits for its ground breaking work, representing Levi Strauss in its battle with Tesco et al in the European Court of Justice.

one world vision

True to its international form, there are opportunities for overseas secondments at every stage of your career. Trainees go to *"all sorts of places like San Francisco, Frankfurt, Canada, Australia, Hong Kong and Russia."* Unlike some other global law firms of a similar size, Baker & McKenzie has grown entirely organically, slowly adding more and more offices to its roster. This is in contrast to those rivals that have brought local law firms into their networks and rebranded them, in the process creaming off the good stuff and dumping poorer performers. One source said, *"The firm wants to develop a quality image worldwide,"* indicating that it is ironing out the creases of inconsistency between offices. Baker & McKenzie is a firm that trades on its international capability and it is *"continually looking to find new ways to deal with clients and break new markets."*

> Chambers Global's Middle East Law Firm of the Year 2002

The firm has an interesting 'Eat What You Kill' policy, which means *"there's a share of the bills for lawyers who bring clients to the firm. It can be up to 10% of bills if a partner is solely responsible for bringing the client in!"* That's some incentive for keeping your contacts book up-to-date! Trainees are eager to, and do, stay post-qualification: in the last few years, retention rates have hovered at about 70%, and in 2002, 21 out of 30 qualifiers were offered jobs and all but one accepted.

an equal slice of the pie

It won't always be a *"mad bonkers rush"* as hours are generally quite civilised, although trainees mentioned that, at times, they worked on into the wee small hours while watching their peers in the same department leave to go home. In litigation, for example, *"some trainees were taking too much on at the same time and at the same stage of the process. When they reached court it was easy to become overloaded."* Across the firm, this is now been addressed: *"One partner per department has responsibility for trainees' work capacity, and it has certainly improved things."*

Training sessions? *"A lot – some good and some of questionable quality where a handout would suffice, but they are trying to make stuff more interactive and it perhaps allows people to learn more."* At the start of the contract there's a two-week induction course: *"It is very comprehensive (perhaps too much so) but it is nice to meet fellow trainees and spend time without the pressure of work."*

Supervision differs from seat to seat: *"Some supervisors will be quite hands-off which allows for creative input, but gives a bit of edginess, whereas others will be extremely hands-on."* Whatever the supervision style of your boss, trainees tell us that you'll never feel underused. *"You have to take responsibility, but you are not going to get lost because partners won't let you."*

mad for it

Baker Mac trainees are an active and sociable lot. *"You certainly won't find a Bakers trainee that fits the typical City mould."* We heard words like *"individuality," "confidence," "drive"* and *"openness"* on several occasions. It seems that if you're after a training contract, *"being you is the important thing."* Bless. That said, some overseas experience might enhance your chances; many from the current crop have language skills, quite a few have travelled and a few have even qualified in other jurisdictions before starting out with the firm. Considering what Baker & McKenzie does, we're hardly surprised. Top tip: investigate the firm's 12-week international clerkship programme. It's the ideal opportunity to discover what international practice is all about.

The firm's pro bono project, Making A Difference (MAD, but not in the Inspector Gadget sense), covers mostly non-legal activities, although it is keen to beef up the legal side. Having represented several universities for free, it is now turning its attention to death row cases. *"It's as interesting as hell because it is such a contrast to what you normally do,"* one trainee enthused. Cake sales (no Bakery jokes please), school visits and a riverside soup kitchen all give trainees plenty of chance to get involved. Sports teams include mixed hockey and football, and from time to time trainees compete in more varied events against other firms, such as the CARE International charity contest and the Manches Cup sailing regatta.

dancing with dinosaurs

"It sounds like a terrible cliché, but people here know how to work hard and play hard," one source told us. And by heck do they! Not only is B&M one of the few firms to have a bar in-house, but it has three balls – Christmas, spring and summer. At Christmas, trainees put on a review, which *"is essentially a big piss-take of the partners."* The recent spring ball was held at the Natural History Museum and we're led to believe that 'Sabre Tooth Tiger Feet' and T.Rex classics really got the dodgy dancers moving. Add in twice-yearly departmental parties, 'hello/goodbye' drinks at each seat rotation, a kamikaze desire for karaoke and monthly drinks in the firm's restaurant (complete with subsidised Starbucks – scary) and it starts to sound like university all over again. Throw in local haunts Brodies (*"close but not too cheap and renowned for flat lager"*), O'Neill's, St Brides Tavern and the new Evangelist in Blackfriars and it's perhaps a miracle they get any work done at all. How on earth some managed to slope off to Walthamstow dogs for a slap-up meal, a few pints and a quick flutter is anyone's guess.

and finally…

If you are looking to be a respected fish in a decent-sized UK pond, with a good chance of a swim across the sea to an overseas seat, Baker Mac really ought to be on your list.

Barlow Lyde & Gilbert

the facts
Location: London, Oxford
UK ranking by size: 28
Total number of trainees: 35
Seats: 4x6 months
Alternative seats: Secondments
Extras: St Botolph's Project

They're a chatty bunch over at Barlow Lyde & Gilbert. If you're seeking something other than a common or garden, corporate-led, City training then read on and learn a bit about this impressive litigation firm and its toe-, foot- and leghold in the insurance market. Oh, and lest we forget (and so ensuring the wrath of all concerned), we'll tell you all about its growing non-contentious practice while we're at it.

crashing your way in

Group 4 is a brilliant place to start your training. But before you get measured up for a security guard's uniform and practice sleeping on the job, be aware that this is the name given to the general insurance litigation department. You'll not snooze your way through your first six months, as it's a fast-paced seat offering all the basics an aspiring litigator could hope for. *"General insurance is a mixture of work for motor insurers in smashes and crashes, local authority work, including slips on paving stones, bullying in schools and stress at work, and then there's work for the NHSLA."* With lower value cases you can get your teeth into *"first drafts and lots of advocacy (interlocutories, extensions of time and small case management conferences)."* As you take cases from start to finish, *"six months goes fast."*

You may then move into commercial litigation or one of the professional indemnity groups. Whether you're put into a group handling accountants', solicitors', financial markets or general professional indemnity, your broad overview of the litigation process will be fine-tuned. Claims are bigger and many are international. There's always a danger that trainees can end up doing an awful lot of 'grunt work' on high-value litigation – ie document listing and bundling, but *"thankfully, that's aimed primarily at paralegals and litigation assistants."* It's fair to say that *"you can't fully escape it as a trainee, as some cases are so document heavy that even junior lawyers are doing it."* As a litigator this is how you *"earn your stripes."*

getting down to business

Say the word 'reinsurance' at BLG and you'll get all sorts in response. *"Some of the other departments have a giggle about reinsurance,"* sniggered one trainee. *"They're seen as a bit nerdy in that department,"* another added. Apparently, it's because the partners are real specialists in their field and it's quite an intellectual area of work. Yet many trainees believe reinsurance and international risk is one of the coolest departments to be in. *"It's fantastic! The work is really good, especially if you like tricky, technical pieces of research and case law interests you."* One of the matters being handled when we spoke to trainees was the Troika scheme, designed to help shore up the ailing aviation industry following September 11. It's big stuff.

So far, all we've talked about is contentious, insurance industry work, so let's switch tack. All trainees undertake a non-contentious seat and, increasingly, some do two. Corporate is the most popular of those on offer, but you can opt for banking, property, tax, employment or commercial (including IP/IT). The corporate, commercial and banking areas are expanding and a small Oxford office was opened in 2001 specifically to capture business from hi-tech clients.

Concerning the divvying up of seats, one trainee advised: *"You should be quite proactive about showing where your interests lie, although people here aren't pushy and 'me, me, me'. Actually, I was a little embarrassed when I put my case to a partner to get their backing."*

withering looks

We'll not bleat on about the usual topics of responsibility, supervision and appraisals. They are, respectively, high, high and often enough. The hours prove to be no source for complaints either, with the average day being 9am-6.30/7pm. In some seats you may do a few evenings until 8pm, but there are no nightmare stories. Trainees put decent hours down to two things: the focus on contentious work and BLG's attitude to work. Admittedly, with litigation you have a greater chance of planning your day/week and avoiding the peaks and troughs of transactions. One trainee said, *"I'll get a withering look from my supervisor at 5.40pm, and they'll say 'Don't you have a life?' You are encouraged not to be a saddo here!"* Glad to hear it.

lateral thinking

Each department has its own character. Reinsurance, you'll remember, is full of industrious boffins. *"Property is like being in a holiday camp. It's just one partner,* who's hysterical, and three senior assistants." Over in Group 4, you could be forgiven for thinking they were all suffering from football fever (well, they had just been through the World Cup when we called). Corporate is ambitious, young and "a bit laddy," and banking shares the go-getting feel of the commercial team.

Trainees tell us that BLG has suffered from a left-hand/right-hand syndrome, in that not everyone really knew what went on in other departments. Recently, the firm was paid a visit by management consultants... "Departments used to be called divisions, but the name was too... divisive, so the word is now banned." Surely the consultants came up with more than that? Indeed they did. There's a new emphasis on "cross-departmental talking" and "more mingling." Whereas "trainees got to see everyone in the firm, this didn't happen at other levels," one source explained. So, 'lateral communities' have been established to connect everybody. The trainees were already the perfect example of such a community, but now there's one for 0- to 3-year qualified lawyers, and so on up the ranks.

smile high club

There's a thing called the aeroplane test. Basically, you pass if you're the sort of person someone wouldn't mind sitting next to on a long-haul flight. So long as you pass the test and you've got enough upstairs in the brains department, you'll be attractive to BLG. Fitting in with others is so important in insurance-led firms as this type of client gives repeat work, year after year. The ability to work as part of a team of lawyers and client representatives is paramount. Top tip: a high proportion of the firm's trainees did a vac scheme or paralegalled at BLG.

Enthusiasm counts for a lot, as does a healthy interest in the law as an academic and intellectual discipline. Trainees talked about dissecting cases, devising strategies and working out reasoned answers to legal problems. One contrasted it to a period of time spent at a magic circle firm. "It was the two most boring weeks of my life; I was just reading bond issue prospectuses." A full programme of training sessions will be supplemented by a good dose of partner brain-picking. One source said, "Partners are really hot on you knowing the law inside out so you get plenty of training when you first join a department." Another confirmed this, saying, "Poorer supervisors have been weeded out," while a third told us: "I had the insurance market and how it works explained to me – and the same with stockbroking, etc."

stop! thief!

BLG has a Hong Kong office. If you were absolutely desperate to go, you might be given a plane ticket and directions, but it could never really be described as a regular secondment. Client secondments crop up as and when, but most trainees stay in the London office. Last year we described it as Denver-Carrington because of its OTT 80s marble and shoulder pads décor. We weren't berated for that description. "It's all Colonel Gaddafi's fault," said one source, "He owns the building." One of its best features was the impressive atrium. "Maybe Richards Butler were jealous, because they've now stolen our atrium by putting a floor in between the 7th and 8th storeys." Do BLG trainees know or socialise with their RB neighbours? "We keep meaning to meet up with them but we never have." Our opinion? They're well matched – maybe love could blossom!

"The office is at the last frontier of the City; if you move any further east you're in dodgy territory." Liverpool Street is just five minutes away though, and there's no shortage of pubs nearby. The Poet pubs are still drawing 'em in after work. There's The Purple Poet and The Poet and the Slug & Lettuce (which also used to have a Poet name). Confused? We are. And now, there's all that extra BLG mingling... the acres of marble floor were perfect for a recent Giant Scalextrics night. If sport is your thing then you're in the right place as there are teams for football, netball, cricket and rugby sevens. And if you play golf, "Brilliant! You'll be senior partner in no time!"

13 of the 15 September qualifiers stayed with the firm in 2002, and trainees were generally favourable in their comments on the process of offering jobs.

and finally...

Trainees recommend BLG heartily to those with an interest in litigation and a desire to avoid what they see as the treadmill of the megafirms. The corporate department may be the fastest growing department, but the contentious side of the practice still heavily outweighs it. If that suits you, apply quick smart.

Beachcroft Wansbroughs

the facts

Location: London, Bristol, Winchester, Birmingham, Leeds, Manchester
UK ranking by size: 32
Total number of trainees: 53
Seats: 4x6 months
Alternative seats: Secondments

Beachcroft Wansbroughs is a national firm offering a general commercial training with a strong emphasis on litigation, health sector and insurance work. The firm is spread across the UK and currently recruits trainees in London, Leeds, Bristol and Manchester.

rise and shine

Regardless of which office you find yourself in, the general consensus is that this is a very decent place to make a living. *"It's quite understated and not as in your face as other firms,"* reported one trainee. Beachcroft Wansbroughs is an accredited 'Investor in People', which means it has to meet certain standards in appraisal and management and keep its employees purring. Although trainees seem to agree, *"Our profile could be raised a bit,"* the firm nevertheless provides fertile ground for young lawyers to put down roots. Having gone through the stressful process of merging four years ago, it's beginning to stir and make its presence felt more often. As one trainee told us, *"The firm has been hiding its light under a bushel, but now I get the feeling that it's trying to drive forwards and compete with the larger national firms."* Apparently, there are still a few *"unresolved issues"* left over from the merger – a bit of a north/south thing – we decided not to pry.

Across the network, Beachcrofts retained a healthy 24 of its 29 September 2002 qualifying trainees

london: southern comfort

London offers the widest range of seats, and is a smart choice if you want to get a mix of contentious and corporate work. You are likely to get a go in the corporate, insurance and PFI/projects departments and you'll be lucky to avoid a seat in property, which trainees commonly wrinkle their noses at. The most popular seats, as ever, are employment, IT/IP and a secondment to Unilever. Be ready for a strong focus on insurance work, particularly on the litigation side. As a trainee you share an office with a partner, which generally works well. Concerning appraisals, often the *"I'd rather chat than fill in a form"* approach wins the day, which suits many trainees down to the ground.

The hours are *"pretty civilised:"* usually about 9am-6.30pm. *"This isn't the place for the blue-chip 3am crowd."* You do your work and then leave. *"No one bats an eyelid if I've finished my work and I'm out the door at 5.31pm."* Trainees modestly described themselves as *"quite ordinary"* and the office as stable and established – *"Change doesn't come quickly here."* For example, the 'smart casual' regulations recommend that *"ladies can wear blouses"* and *"gentlemen can wear T-shirts with collars."* It is indeed a gentlemanly place: *"No one here is considered to be a bit of a bastard."* One trainee concluded: *"It's not Tom Cruise-style.* [The Firm or Top Gun, we wondered] *You don't have to give up your life."*

In terms of socialising and jollies, there's a trainee lunch every quarter and sporadic drinks in the downstairs café. The scene is *"casual"* but *"inclusive."* Most trainees had plenty of time to lead their own lives outside of the office. *"I don't want to spend all my time with lawyers,"* reasoned one. If you're afraid that you'll get overlooked if you don't make your face known, rest assured that *"networking down the pub does you no good."* *"We have the occasional quiz night, cricket party or curry down Brick Lane,"* reported one. Should you feel the urge, round about you'll find a Hogshead and a Live Bait, or there's always the Mucky Duck beside the office, although apparently it is "*not very aesthetically pleasing.*" In contrast, the offices are "*space age.*"

Typically trainees had made a considered choice to join the firm: "*I wanted a medium-sized London practice. Training at one of the big firms is just about law firm kudos. When you're 20 you just see the big name and you don't think about the billing targets and the kind of work you'll be doing. Beachcroft Wansbroughs is about balance.*" When asked to sum the firm up, one trainee informed us: "*It's about decent people, decent hours, decent work and decent pay.*"

bristol: bones of contention

As the national centre for training and administration, Bristol is a large office with not too many trainees. It retained its prized place on the panel of the National Health Service Litigation Authority (NHSLA) and so you'll be sure to get a piece of the clinical negligence pie, if you want it. Seat allocation is pretty flexible, but expect a healthy diet of litigation, including professional indemnity, PI and commercial litigation. On the non-contentious front you might try propert, employment or CoCo. The Bristol office is considered to be less pressured than the London office. Typical hours are 9.15am until 6pm, with a mysterious hour and fifteen minutes for lunch. "*I enjoy a quiet life,*" reported one trainee. Again, "*if you want magic circle work you will be disappointed, but lots of new departments are emerging.*"

Apparently the firm is looking for people who are "*balanced, sociable, enthusiastic and with lots of varied interests.*" And if that weren't enough, like a good rally car, you've also got to be "*hard-working, flexible and responsive.*" It's dress-down all week and socially there's "*nothing too outrageous.*" Instead of prearranged gatherings and parties, "*things tend to happen as and when.*" Come Thursday and Friday nights trainees head for The Quay on the waterfront, or else you'll find them in Revolution and O'Neill's. The firm occupies "*neat*" offices in the middle of the city, with the Cattle Green park just around the corner for summer lunches.

manchester: milk, one sugar

The Manchester office is "*growing phenomenally,*" but still tends towards the contentious. "*You must want to do litigation,*" was one trainee's considered advice. The office handles a lot of work for the NHS and the public sector, but there are also expanding opportunities in corporate since a team from the now defunct firm, Garretts, boosted that side of the practice. The seat in multi-track defendant insurance litigation, deals with anything from high-level PI motor claims to public liability issues and offers the chance to run your own files, while for those who fancy time out of the office, the odd secondment crops up to clients like ICI.

You'll get a big helping of client contact and responsibility. "*I've never been made to feel like I'm at a loose end,*" said one trainee. "*I've got friends training in London firms who are working on deals so massive that they don't get the chance to get fully involved. Here I've had a good crack at the whip.*" Another trainee agreed, "*You have plenty of opportunities to get your hands dirty and prove yourself.*" There's internal training once a month and there are law updates and external lecturers to keep you on point.

The Manchester office struck us as having a more upbeat and breezy atmosphere than the others. In recent times a move has put the firm in the centre of town, which is "*a bit expensive for the girls*" since there are three shoe shops just around the corner. It overlooks St. Anne's Church and "*no one has more than a ten-minute walk to work.*" The office itself is "*cracking*" – vibrant colours, fresh flowers in reception and windows all around. It's dress-down, "*but as a trainee you may as well wear a suit,*" since you never know when you may find yourself going to a meeting with your clients. Trainees here describe themselves as "*straight,*" "*solid,*" "*consistent*" and "*persistent.*" And "*here the partners will make you a cup of tea if they're getting one, which is refreshing.*"

At the end of a hard week there are plenty of

places to unwind. There's even a bar on the 4th floor with table football and Sky TV. It's a good place to relax and have a pint with colleagues, and if you're having midmonth money blues, there's a draw for £100. Some of the other favourites are Sam's Chophouse and Tom's Chophouse, or else there's Tiger Tiger if you want to go dancing. *"There's lots to do, but you won't be forced into it. It's a good social firm."*

leeds: north square

The Leeds office absorbed the Sheffield practice in 2001, when that office closed. We were told, *"It's a pretty steady ship. There are no horrid departments."* Lots of litigation (particularly defendant clinical negligence and PI) and decent hours make for happy trainees, a number of whom have had previous careers in the health sector. One trainee discussed the office's orientation: *"The Leeds office has always been primarily litigation. There's a bit less variety than in some other offices, but it's looking to grow generally and to expand into more non-contentious areas."* One felt there was *"a brick wall between me and corporate work,"* and their advice was to *"recognise that it's an insurance-based practice and look carefully at what we do."*

You may have seen the *"very pleasant"* offices in the recent C4 drama series *'North Square'*. They occupy one of the Georgian terraced houses with a *"tardis-like"* extension out the back. The setting is lovely in the summer. To unwind trainees tend to gravitate towards the nearby Slug & Lettuce and All Bar One. *"There's a slight lack of enthusiasm, but there's a hardcore who are always up for it."* Again, in this office, *"trainees have their own lives."*

and finally…

The firm is looking to expand its commercial and corporate sides, but *"it's not going to change overnight."* Recognise, for the moment, and particularly outside London, that litigation will be a staple part of your diet. But that may well be the very thing that attracts you…

Berwin Leighton Paisner

the facts

Location: London
UK ranking by size: 19
Total number of trainees: 66
Seats: 4x6 months
Alternative seats: Overseas seats, secondments

On 1st May 2001 the legal scene experienced the confluence of Berwin Leighton and Paisner & Co. The firm has now broken into the top 20 size-wise, and is nudging its way into the games played by the big boys on larger finance and corporate transactions. Commercial property remains a mainstay and is complemented by highly successful spin-off practices in property finance and property litigation. The Paisner legacy brought in, amongst other things, an interesting TechMedia practice.

their able, winning poser

Take one look at the BLP website and you'll spot that it's a firm that's really into its branding…and its anagrams. Rumour has it that the firm even had its designers come up with a special font. Trainees confirm that BLP is going in all guns blazing on the marketing front, with the thrust being to cross-sell its services (convincing existing clients of one department that they really want to use the rest of the firm too). We're not sure how the anagrams fit in, but they do give us hours of fun. We're happy to forward anything particularly saucy and inappropriate to the good folk at BLP, just in case you are worried it might ruin your chances of getting an interview.

Various trainees described the firm as *"progressive,"* *"ambitious"* and *"no-nonsense."* One said, *"We don't think short-term. We build up a relationship and don't say bye bye to the client after just one transaction."* High-powered stuff – the firm clearly knows what it wants from partners down to trainees, but our sources didn't want to sound hard-nosed. *"We're not aggressive but we are pushing forward." "We hope we don't throw it in people's faces.*" The atmosphere behind the public face substantiates these claims that BLP isn't a firm of ruthless go-getters. There's even a full-time dress-down policy. Trainees describe the firm as "*hard-working but pleasant.*" "*The partners are easy to approach and they take an interest in you as well as trying to educate and progress you.*"

Our sources had all had a year to mull over their thoughts about the merger and spoke positively about the new firm. The first-years, of course, had only ever worked at BLP but had applied to Berwin Leighton or Paisners respectively. All of them had, therefore, applied to medium-sized firms and they recognised that the merger represented a trade-off between intimacy and quality work. "*I would liken it more to a big firm culture now. It's no longer small and cosy, but I think the transactions are bigger and we have greater capability.*" On the one hand, "*there is more diversity now as there are more departments and opportunities.*" But on the other, "*it is a bit more daunting and I now know fewer people.*" The trainees expressed a little concern that "*if it starts getting any bigger I don't know if trainees would get such good quality work. I do think the quality is good now.*"

brainpower enlisting, eh?
With such a strong reputation for its property work ("*it's our main export*"), you might expect to spend a fair amount of time in the property department. As it happens, the only compulsory seat is, in fact, some form of litigation. That said, trainees confirmed that "*they will try to get you into real estate and corporate.*" Certainly, you are likely to have some sort of interaction with property work or property clients, whether in a straight property, property finance, property litigation, planning or construction seat. While some trainees seek to avoid straight property, it is the main reason some others apply to the firm. Its top-notch reputation in the field is unquestioned.

Trainees undertake four six-month seats and from 2002, new joiners will be asked for their preferences. "*Everyone wants to do corporate,*" but that's not a problem as the corporate department is large and, if you want it, a seat there is guaranteed at some point. The same goes for property. There is greater competition for finance seats as this department is smaller, but, even then, it is just a question of when, not if. "*Projects and property finance are popular for being hard-working and having good quality work.*"

Trainees who applied to Paisners could have expected to get a general commercial or TechMedia seat, but as there are now more trainees competing for these departments, a seat is far from guaranteed. If you hanker after litigation experience, you'll be able to walk right into this department as "*there is a general reluctance to go into it.*" Neither the private client or charities seats are high up on the trainees' 'to do' lists, so you should have no trouble getting one or other of them either. If you fancy jet setting around the world, this isn't the firm to apply to, but there is a spot available in Monaco for those who aspire to hobnobbing in Casino Square or star spotting in the marina. French isn't essential but having already done a corporate seat is advantageous. Client secondments are available to Tesco (the firm is neutral on shelf-stacking experience) and construction client, Ove Arup. Other mini-secondments also crop up.

hire able winner not pigs
So is it possible to identify subspecies amongst the trainee population at BLP? "*In the past you could tell Paisners trainees from the Berwin Leighton ones, but I don't know if that still holds true,*" said a source. So what are the characteristics of a typical trainee? "*We're probably slightly more down-to-earth and relaxed than magic circle trainees.*" "*We're all hard-working and keen to please.*" As we found last year, trainees here are the safe sort. "*We'll generally tow the line. We're quite conformist and will do as we're told.*" That's not to say they're a flock of sheep: "*People are allowed to have different personalities!*"

able where not inspiring
If the trainees are a safe bet then so is the training. Most feel comfortable with the type and quantity of work they are given, which means they are stretched,

but rarely pushed to the limit. "*As a trainee you're given quite a lot of support. It's not that they expect too much of you, but they expect results.*" Another source agreed, "*I don't feel out of my depth at all, but if I did there's no stigma attached to saying this work is a bit beyond me.*" At the same time, "*it's not the place for you if you need constant supervision and patting on the head.*" In keeping with this, feedback isn't necessarily constant. "*Sometimes I can't sneeze without someone double-checking it.*" At other times, "*it would be nice for someone to say 'well done', but you're just expected to get on with it.*" In departments such as real estate, planning and property litigation, trainees get their own files to run. Even in the finance department, trainees go along to meetings and "*they're happy for me to chat to, e-mail and phone clients.*"

Each department has its own training programme to ensure that all trainees have the same level of legal knowledge. "*Whoever is in the training department obviously thinks about these things.*" And we thought they just sat there all day…

probe this genial winner

BLP is a sociable firm during working hours and is pretty relaxed after hours. The social scene is "*not massive, but it's there if you want it.*" The firm currently occupies two buildings, Adelaide House at London Bridge and Bouverie House about a mile away on Fleet Street. It is something of "*a mission*" to meet up with people based at Bouverie House, despite the shuttle bus between the two offices. In August 2003 the firm will be one happy family as it has managed to annex the building next door to Adelaide House.

The social scene starts with a bang at the beginning of the training contract, but tails off in the second year as third- and fourth-seaters get their heads down and work towards qualification. Our sources lamented the demise of the weekly free drinks at FOB, the bar under Adelaide House, but there is still the staff canteen, Alibi, for meeting and greeting. It's the venue for firm-wide drinks held several times a year. The trainees aren't a cliquey bunch, but each intake tends to socialise amongst itself. There is no pressure to join in,

but should you feel like doing so, the social life "*centres around drinking, and there's lots of sport.*" Adelaide House trainees head for the unimaginative Fine Line or Hogshead, or there's a proper pub called The Ship. When trainees organise something special, everyone will make the effort to attend, but these reliable types won't go in for anything too wild, just some "*good, old, harmless dancing on tables.*" Friday nights and the weekends belong to friends outside work so "*Thursday is the new Friday.*" So Manhattan.

fly and nail…

Although BLP is no longer a choice for those who want to work in a cosy, medium-size firm, its size means greater and better opportunities. Apply if you are a well-rounded individual with a desire to make the best of your two years as a trainee. Your experience won't be too wild and unconventional – this is a straight-down-the-line, well-organised and hard-working firm that'll do exactly what it says on the tin.

Bevan Ashford

the facts

Location: Tiverton, Taunton, Plymouth, Exeter, Bristol, London, Birmingham.
UK ranking by size: 24
Total number of trainees: 50
Seats: 4x6 months
Alternative seats: Secondments
Extras: Pro bono – legal drop-in centre (Tiverton)

The firm has a national reputation for its healthcare litigation and projects/PFI work, but Bevan Ashford can offer trainees exposure to just about any aspect of the law that takes your fancy, be it commercial, matrimonial, crime or personal injury. Having doubled in size in recent years, it now has seven offices split between two profit centres: one in the West Country (Tiverton, Taunton, Plymouth and Exeter) and the other along a Bristol-London-Birmingham axis.

west life

All eyes are on the Western front, where things are far from quiet. If you're worried that geography means that you'll miss out on all the action, don't be. Despite the relative economic disadvantages of the region, last year the West Country partnership outstripped the city folk for profitability. It also attracted some big names, including the former boss of Plymouth City Council's legal department who was brought in to head up the public sector department. A former chairman of PricewaterhouseCoopers was also recently appointed as the firm's first non-executive director, with a mission to tone its corporate/commercial practice and drive expansion in this area. Rest assured that you won't be spending two years dealing with disputes arising from cider abuse, sheep rustling or surfing accidents.

The *"friendly"* Plymouth office offers purely commercial work, and the smaller offices in *"family-orientated"* Tiverton and *"relaxed"* Taunton offer a bit of everything. If you fancy a stint in crime or family, Tiverton and Taunton may be of interest for six months. Some love it so much they stay put. In these offices you may be one of just a couple of trainees or, at times, the only one, but our sources felt the old adage about the smaller the firm, the better the training holds true at Bevan Ashford. It's not that the firm as a whole is small, just that trainees are split into pockets. *"They treat you like an individual,"* reported one.

Bevan Ashford takes its fair share of older trainees, many of whom have acquired relevant skills and knowledge in first careers or in postgraduate work. *"The personality tests they use have done a good job. Most people here have a bit of real-life experience; it's not just 22-year-olds from redbrick universities."* It's good to come across a firm that seems to positively encourage older applicants, *"just so long as you've got a few years in you before you retire!"* There is no shortage of locals applying for contracts at the West Country offices, but people head down from all round the country, eager for a piece of the action, while keen to avoid the stresses of London life.

And what a life! This year's West Country summer party had a Eurovision Song Contest theme, with every office having to pick a country and perform an appropriate song. While the main Exeter office's Italy number was memorable (Pope and four cardinals singing Mambo Italiano), the winners came from Exeter's conveyancing office. Victory was secured by a rendition of Frère Jacques and a rather exuberant ten-minute can-can. Mon dieu!

exeter: town and country

There's plenty of friendly rivalry between the Bristol and Exeter offices. Apparently Bristol attracts *"the city sort,"* whereas Exeter has more *"outdoor activity types."* Whether you prefer to keep your suit dry with an umbrella or a Gore-Tex mountain jacket should give you a pretty good idea where you'd best fit in. An Exeter trainee enthused: *"You've got the coast and the moors within easy reach. This part of the world is absolutely beautiful."* We've often heard that the typical Exeter Uni type goes down well in the office, and certainly for those graduates who can't bear to leave the place, it's a great option.

The *"heads down"* open-plan office is right on the Southernhay strip close to other Exeter firms. On the phone we heard seagulls in the background, which made a pleasant change from the sound of traffic or the raised voices of stressed associates. *"In Exeter you get a much better deal than in City firms. The partners are keen to get you running your own files."* Levels of responsibility are so high, in fact, that *"if they'd told me what I'd be doing beforehand I would probably have panicked."*

bristol: good health

Everyone we spoke to in Bristol had done a clinical negligence seat, which is the office's forte, and in some cases was the main draw to training in the office. Some trainees have requested and got two stints in this department. If you're a medical professional considering a second career then this is definitely a firm to examine. Just remember that for NHS work (be it litigation or commercial/projects) you'll want the

Bristol-London-Birmingham axis. *"There's very little grunt work,"* one source told us. *"The work we do is on a level with the assistant solicitors, but just more highly supervised. My friends at London firms only get a minor role in something big."* Another trainee agreed, *"Our training is probably a lot better than at many London firms, but we just don't have a name on the CV."*

In the Bristol office *"you wouldn't know who the partners were unless you were told."* It is commercially driven, but there's still a friendly environment. *"It's relaxed, so long as you pull your weight."* Typical hours are 9am to 5pm, but 12-hour days are not unheard of when you're handling commercial or corporate work. Rest assured though, *"if you have to work late, it will always be acknowledged."* The dress code is smart casual and once a month they enjoy total dress-down. The social life is what you make of it, but within the firm there are plenty of events and office drinks. Don't expect a web of intrigue though: *"There's never any gossip. Everyone's a bit boring really."* Many people have at least *"tenuous family links"* to the area.

The Birmingham office is the newest in the Bevan Ashford fleet and offers a variety of seats focused heavily on NHS-related work. At this time, the London office takes trainees from Bristol for a six-month seat, though the type of seat varies according to trainee preference and departmental needs.

cash on delivery

Regardless of location, trainees opt for Bevan Ashford because they are keen to work for a respected commercial firm without London stresses. *"If you want to be a part of a growing national practice with good work and good lawyers then apply here,"* said one. *"It's not cliquey and it's not pretentious, and it offers a rich variety of commercial and public sector work,"* said another.

Across the offices there's plenty of feedback and assessment. You'll have one-, three- and six-month appraisals in each seat (a bit of a *"paper exercise"* in some seats), and trainee lunches are attended by all trainees as well as the training partner and the folk from HR. If you've got any grumbles there are plenty of opportunities for them to be aired. One minor irritation in Bristol is that trainees have to deliver the mail in the mornings, *"a complete waste of time"* apparently, but then at least you'll get to put some names to faces. Another grumble concerns the salary. You may not be paying London prices, but getting on the property ladder in Exeter or Bristol is still a struggle. *"It's annoying when the partners are pressurising you to meet targets and trying to persuade you that they're poor. We read Legal Week, so we know exactly what they're on!"*

let's talk about socks

The firm offers the option of part-time training contracts over three years, the first two years simultaneous with the LPC. The trainees we spoke to about this route considered it *"a very difficult balancing act to pull off,"* especially if you value your free time or have a social life. If you take this route, you'll have to hit your targets when you're in trainee mode, just like everyone else, but you'll spend two or three days every month or so doing your LPC. The benefit of this approach is that you'll get a not unreasonable salary right from the off, which is great if you've got dependants or a mortgage to pay. In the long run though, a newly qualified lawyer is going to be considerably better off than someone in the third year of a training contract, so many feel it makes sense to let the firm sponsor you through a one-year LPC and take out a bank loan to make ends meet. The third year of the contract can feel like penance when you've worked your socks off for the past two years. Of those who worked their socks off and qualified in September 2002, 19 out of 24 stayed on with the firm.

and finally…

Bevan Ashford is a good bet, particularly if you have past experience or a particular interest in clinical negligence or the healthcare sector. Whether you'd rather lead the quiet life in Tiverton or the high life in Bristol, it's a firm that's got something for just about everybody.

Bircham Dyson Bell

the facts
Location: London, Cardiff, Edinburgh
UK ranking by size: 94
Total number of trainees: 10
Seats: 4x6 months
Alternative seats: None

An interesting Westminster firm with a reputation that's more high politics than high finance. We recommend you to read on…

jaws for the taking
Rated among the best in the country for parliamentary agency and public affairs by *Chambers UK*, other traditional strengths include charities and private client work. But change is afoot, and the corporate and property departments have sent out increasingly interesting signals since the merger with niche City practice Bower Cotton in 2000. There's a feeling that this firm is navigating the shark-infested waters of the London legal scene with considerable nous. *"The City firms chew up a lot of the work and take over a lot of smaller firms. We're constantly shoring up our practice, absorbing departments from other firms, making sure the base is strong…"* Smells like a strategy to us.

The Westminster office is the seat of power and the base for all trainees. There are no hard and fast rules as to seat allocation, but most trainees spend their first year doing two seats from private client, commercial property and litigation. Company/commercial and parliamentary are traditionally reserved for second-years. A series of judicious mergers seems to have been accompanied by a sort of permanent revolution in housekeeping. *"They're very keen on practice management standards, lots of protocols, lots of IT and library support. It's a very professional set-up."*

charity cases
Trainees had no complaints about the quality of their work. *"As soon as you walk through the door here, you start being responsible for your own output. You're in at the deep end and you either sink or swim. Partners will check your work, but they want to know that they can give a trainee a task and get something decent back."* The hours are relaxed compared to the City hothouses, but despite the absence of an all-night culture, *"in seats like property the caseload can be quite overwhelming to begin with. Most trainees will be happy to stay late a bit, until they get into a rhythm."* Your supervisor will usually be a partner, but work will come from a variety of sources. *"It's good because you get to see a much greater variety of work than if you were working under just one person. My litigation supervisor did only property litigation, but I also got general commercial experience by working with other members of the team"* There's no employment seat, but a seat in CoCo will allow you to get some experience of it. A cursory glance at the client list of the firm reveals some big names in the charities sector, and charity work will feature heavily in the private client seat.

politeness costs nothing
Not all trainees come here suffering from Westminsteritis although many are aware that *"a parliamentary seat is there if you want it."* (If only politicians had it so easy.) Most gravitate to the firm for its size and intimate feel. You'll not have stressed colleagues zoom past you as your 'hello' falls on deaf ears. *"I worked here as a paralegal and even then I wasn't intimidated by anyone, they're all just such nice people, so polite."* Yes, this is a very – how shall we put it? – civilised firm. In terms of background, the trainees are *"the most disparate bunch of people I've ever met!"* The current crop of trainees has done everything from surveying to bomb disposal. (Bet they're good in eyeball-to-eyeball negotiations!) The firm wants applicants with *"a range of experience and things to talk about;" "someone with a good academic background, who's confident thinking through a problem, who's articulate and conscientious."*

Appraisals come in the middle and at the end of every seat. In practice, the efficacy of this system will depend on which partner you are sat with, *"how busy they are and how much they've been bullied by HR."* It doesn't seem to have ruffled any feathers though. All of the September 2002 qualifiers stayed on.

broadway baby
The firm has occupied swish offices on Broadway since late 2001 and the trainees are still thrilled at the idea of air con and 24-hour news screens in reception. *"We've shed the grandfather clock image!"* they cried in delight. The facilities are good and there's a cafeteria for when it's too chilly to go and sunbathe in nearby St James's Park. 'Staff lunches' are also a regular feature of Birchams' life: a couple of partners will host a dozen or so people drawn from all levels and departments of the firm. It's an excellent opportunity to test that old adage that there's no such thing as a free lunch. When it comes to going out, Westminster isn't short of a pub or six, even if they do tend to be fusty old drinking dens packed full of scheming politicos. Trainees assure us that The Sanctuary and The Star are both utterly pleasant and full of Birchams lawyers.

and finally…
The firm is becoming a slicker, more commercially oriented operation, but it's still a great choice if you know you want to experience private client practice in London. And, although the grandfather clock in reception may have been traded in for a plasma screen, just like the two houses down the road, *"It's still a quirky, idiosyncratic place with lots of characters."*

Bird & Bird

the facts
Location: London
UK ranking by size: 33
Total number of trainees: 31
Seats: 4x6 months
Alternative seats: Overseas seats, secondments

Offering TMT, IP and much, much more, Bird & Bird is attracting the sort of graduate who wants to get a high-quality training while giving the megafirms a wide berth. Want to know more?

on target
Choosing Bird & Bird *"is not a hit-and-miss thing,"* trainees tell us. *"We're after good work for good clients and a firm with a decent reputation, but we're not after the sort of work big City firms do – securitisation and stuff, where, as a trainee, you are at the bottom of the food chain or you're in all night reading prospectuses."* The firm's strong IP/TMT orientation means it is particularly attracted to science grads. *"They do market quite aggressively to Imperial and other top science universities,"* one trainee said, but another stressed that, sciences aside, *"there's no particular university they're looking at or one single thing you've done that will make you right."* In spite of the science and TMT focus, trainees come to the firm with different ideas about what they want to achieve. Some even want to go into areas like banking or property. There are no compulsory seats, but if you want to do an IP seat, yet you don't have a science background, then doing a litigation seat beforehand will assist. *"It puts you in a much stronger position. Having litigation experience adds a gloss to what you can then do in an IP seat – you can go in at a more advanced level."* Basically, *"they want people to hit the ground running."*

Corporate and general commercial are both popular seats, as is 'Company C', which offers plenty of IT work and clients. IP and the perennial favourite, employment, never lack takers. Some trainees are attracted by the firm's sports law practice, but we were asked to stress that *"There's no seat in a separate sports department; it's a case of sitting with a partner in commercial who deals with sports cases. You'll get the flavour of it."* In September 2002, 10 of the 13 qualifying trainees stayed with the firm, spreading themselves across the firm's non-contentious departments and IP.

old birds and young 'uns
Training sessions? *"Loads,"* especially in the first year, when trainees have numerous compulsory seminars to attend. A Freshers' Week-style induction

covers everything from time-recording to information on the telecoms sector.

Our sources worked "*only rarely past 7pm.*" Some talked optimistically of shorter days in property and litigation, but all agreed that corporate entails longer hours. One trainee recalled a 1.30am departure: "*It's only natural that every once in a while there will be times when you have to roll up your sleeves.*" "*You've got to put in hours when needs be, and someone who's prepared to get on with it and get stuck in will do well here.*" The partners expect hard work and may not suffer fools gladly, but almost all our sources felt completely relaxed about asking questions of their seniors. More than that, two trainees talked about a feeling of equality in the working relationship between partners and trainees.

> Chambers Global's International Communications Law Firm of the Year 2002

Even though some partners are leaders in their field, trainees can still express opinions. "*I enjoy sitting down and having legal debates – they show a healthy respect for your intelligence.*" "*It's like I have a working relationship with someone who is my colleague (not a partner).*" As one trainee said, "*You don't have to be deferential – even us young 'uns have one or two things to offer!*" But you'll be doing grunt work from time to time. "*There is an attitude that if you get that done you'll get something better,*" an attitude that "*no one thinks they are too good to do anything like that… sometimes you're there at one photocopier and a partner's at another.*"

Trainees portray the Bird & Bird lawyer as quite quirky and slightly unusual. It's a firm of real individuals, they told us. "*There's not a moulded attitude here, we all want different experiences.*" When it comes down to it though, all trainees want good work experience. One said proudly, "*In litigation I was running a couple of smaller cases and, in general, the subject matter of cases is interesting, particularly IT and telecoms and patents.*"

sweaty disco

Generally, everybody gathers in the pub after work once a week. Underneath the building, Walkers is a bit "*narrow and dingy,*" but if you're up for it, you can brave the sweaty Friday night disco in the basement. The IP department shuns Walkers in favour of the "*cosy and crowded*" Castle. Even the partners "*get out the door quite quickly to have a drink together…but they tend to drift off earlier, maybe to go somewhere more chic!*" 'Partners' drinks' (so called because they take place in the partners' dining room) are held every three months and "*rumble on for a fair old while.*" Each week e-mails fly around concerning various sporting endeavours, such as cricket against clients or softball in Regent's Park. "*It's just for fun. We really don't take it too seriously, unlike some firms.*" Ooh! Who? "*Um, Denton Wilde Sapte.*" It'll be war next season…

extending the nest

Perhaps reminiscent of the sweaty disco at Walkers, the Fetter Lane offices can be a little cramped. There's a second office (for IP and property) in nearby Furnival Street, which renders the Fettid Lane trainees green with envy. "*It's a toss-up between a buzz and enough space,*" one told us. "*We have a good location here, but the office has drab colours – greys and beiges – and is very mid/late 80s. Furnival Street is a bit more pastelly* [soft peppermint and lilac] *and more late 90s.*" Furnival Street has nice abstract prints in the meeting rooms. In Fetter Lane, "*There are still a few venerable old Birds around.*" The trainee meant paintings of founding partners, not stuffed birds…or partners.

Established in 1846, the firm's ancient history "*feels pretty detached from us now. We've moved on in the last few years.*" It's a client-led change: "*There's a degree of informality in the way our clients work, and you have to embrace the attitudes that they espouse.*" It's a bit different from dealing with bankers all day. The firm's style tends "*towards the modern. We're not touchy-feely or anything, but we know we are doing modern areas of law with modern clients.*" The sector focus is central to the way the firm operates. "*Departments have divisions, but the sector *focus allows us all to pull in the same direction.*" You can extend this logic to the firm's overseas offices. Trainees have been monitoring the firm's expansion and so have we! "*Europe is its main target area.*" The firm has offices in Brussels, Paris, Stockholm, Hong Kong, The Hague and Düsseldorf. Good news: new overseas seats include Hong Kong and Paris and later on, once qualified, you could take advantage of the 'twinning scheme' that moves assistants around the network. For trainees, client secondments are available.

footloose

Trainees see themselves as friendly, upbeat and confident, but not pushy; they are competitive in a way, "*but you'd never not feel secure with colleagues – you'd never trample on others.*" Perhaps the perfect example of Twobirdishness came in the form of the story about a trainee who was deep in serious conversation with a partner…it was perfectly acceptable that she had no shoes on at the time. "*It's a relaxed atmosphere here; they're just not concerned about trivial things.*"

The informality of Bird & Bird cuts both ways. It helps in getting what you want from your training contract, but there are just a couple of "*minor grouses.*" It's seen as ironic that in a technology-focused firm the IT system could be better. And we did hear of a tiny minority of supervisors who are in the habit of throwing work at trainees and just expecting them to get on with it. The majority are praised: "*There are a lot of good ones around – those that have the time to look at your work and talk it over and give you feedback, who will listen to you and give thought to your career development.*"

and finally…

We're giving the thumbs up, not flicking the bird, to this training experience. Bird & Bird is growing in all directions – internationally, in London, in its reputation for non-TMT/IP work, and in its trainee population. It offers quality and often cutting-edge work combined with intellectual stimulation and a fairly hassle-free atmosphere.

Blake Lapthorn

the facts

Location: Fareham, Portsmouth, Southampton, London
UK ranking by size: 54
Total number of trainees: 14
Seats: 4x6 months
Alternative seats: Brussels, secondments

Blake Lapthorn is a broad church firm with good coverage in its South Coast heartland. Even though it's already the biggest firm in the area, it's still expanding, having merged with highly rated insolvency specialists Sherwin Oliver in November 2001.

on the couch

For trainees, the story is simple. "*I'm from the area and I remember them as a high street firm. They've really changed over the last seven years. A lot of firms that were on a par with Blake Lapthorn in the area when I was young are still at that stage and haven't moved forward.*" The transformation has been achieved, in part, by "*the younger rung of partners in their mid- to late-30s, who've come out of London. Most of them are in our company/commercial department, and they've brought a real London culture to the firm and seem to be the driving force now.*"

A psychiatrist would have a field day with all the comparisons trainees make between BL and London firms. Rivals on the South Coast do not interest them, but there's an obsession with measuring themselves against London players. For example: "*City firms take on a lot of trainees, and I questioned whether the training could be as good at a larger firm that couldn't focus on my individual needs. Being one of 12 is nice; being one of 112 wouldn't be so good.*" And: "*I wouldn't say the people here are not ambitious, but it's not the be-all and end-all here that it might be in the City.*" And: "*The size of the client is smaller and the resources are fewer than at City firms, but we're often on the other side of them in deals. It's not unusual to go up to London for a completion.*" Our shrink might conclude that, in terms of academics and CVs, a typical Blake Lapthorn trainee could have got a City job, but something in their temperament or their lifestyle kept them away.

The firm wants trainees who'll stick around after qualification. One of them explained: "*If you are local, the firm is interested to know that.*" Another enthused about how "*in the brochure they advertise that they're happy to take on people in their second careers. There's certainly a few of us like that here,*" and many have taken time out to travel. The intake of five trainees a year is half what it was just a couple of years ago – the firm says it wants quality not quantity.

more coco than cocoa

There are no compulsory seats, although "*you really can't avoid a private client seat at Blake Lapthorn – it's the way the firm is structured. It's got a strong private client base and you know that when you arrive, so you're ready for it.*" The Portsmouth-based private client practice offers seats in conveyancing, probate and trusts, although they're not that popular. "*They're seen as being fairly dreary.*" Corporate and commercial seats win the popular vote: "*This doesn't mean none of us are interested in anything else, but it's the booming part of the business and it's seen as quite dynamic.*" Indeed, five of September 2002's qualifiers took jobs in CoCo.

In most departments you sit with or near to your principal. "*It's a good system. If you're not sitting with a principal, you don't know what their work pattern is, and you don't know when it's acceptable to butt in and ask questions.*" One trainee found the training to be "*a good balance in that you're not given too much responsibility in your first seat, but it builds up,*" while another said, "*It can get very hands-on and frantic at times.*" In short, "*you're not shielded or mollycoddled as a trainee here – you really do have to pitch in.*"

a choice of toppings

Most trainees move between the different offices during their training. It's not mandatory; it's more a function of how the practice areas are spread. In addition to the bulk of the private client practice, the Portsmouth office has professional indemnity, insolvency and family, while the Southampton office deals with more of the corporate/commercial, commercial property, personal injury and employment work. Fareham ("*about 20 minutes drive from either Portsmouth or Southampton*" and on the side of the M27) includes a thriving children's law team, while the London office handles corporate/commercial, property, commercial litigation and family work (although there are no London seats at present).

Aside from practice areas, we wondered if there are any other discernible differences between the offices. "*The Portsmouth and Fareham offices look exactly the same – they look a bit like Pizza Hut with raised roofs in the centre of the building.*" Our sources report that Southampton has a younger atmosphere than the others ("*I don't think any of the older equity partners are sitting in Southampton*") and has a city centre location. During your time in Portsmouth and Fareham, forget walking down the high street at lunchtime, you'll need to get your car keys out. Youth and transport. Hmmm, it sounds disturbingly like a government department...

There's a six-month secondment up for grabs at ICI, and in the past a trainee has gone to Zurich... Zurich Insurance that is. For trainees wanting to go overseas, a three-month stint is available each year with an associated Brussels firm, Renouf & Co. By all accounts there's stiff competition for this seat, so some language ability (specifically French) will assist.

And so to the subject of clients...big name clients. Not just local companies, but nationals and multinationals. Major retail banks, South West Trains, P&O, Costa Coffee, Thomson Travel, PwC, Waitrose, BAA, RAC, Whitbread, Pizza Express...we could go on. But we won't.

treats lines and wrinkles

It's easy enough to leave work at 5.30pm if you need to, but generally trainees talk of being "*out the door by 6pm or 6.30pm.*" The longest hours tend to be in corporate, but even in that seat "*you've definitely got time* to do things in the evening that aren't work-related... It's definitely not a case of out the door and straight home because it's late – those occasions do arise, but they're rare."

One trainee said wistfully, *"When we first started we went out together a lot, but as things have gone on we don't go out so much."* Ah, the ravages of time! However, the trainees do make a point of having a get-together outside of work at least every two months or so, with venues ranging from people's houses to pubs and bars. In each office there are regular Friday night drinks, as well as interdepartmental social events, like paintball and tenpin bowling, organised by the firm's social committee.

One source said, *"Prior to my arrival, all but one of ten trainees left for London for more money."* The improved NQ remuneration package has gone down well: the 12-strong class of 2002 were all offered jobs on qualification, and all but one stayed. Bravo, Blake Lapthorn!

and finally...
In addition to having one of the top-rated corporate practices in the southern counties, the firm offers an impressive range of practice areas. As one trainee said, *"Almost any area you'd like to follow, you're likely to be able to do so here."* If you want all this and the delights of a South Coast lifestyle, you know what to do.

Bond Pearce

the facts
Location: Bristol, Exeter, Leeds, London, Plymouth, Southampton
UK ranking by size: 35
Total number of trainees: 24
Seats: 4x6 months
Alternative seats: Secondments

Through organic growth and small mergers, Bond Pearce has grown from a chilled-out regional firm into a major commercial player across the south and west of England.

four corners
Although many trainees have local connections, the firm also attracts a fair few talented 'outsiders' who could just as easily walk into training contracts in the City. As one trainee succinctly put it: *"Bond Pearce doesn't have to work hard to attract trainees."* With an ever-growing reputation in commercial work, it is a long way from being a local shop for local people. Trainees are recruited into a particular office, but from time to time ask to undertake seats in other offices. Such moves are always by request. London and Leeds do not take trainees, but don't let that put you off – there is plenty going on in each of the others. No seat is compulsory and allocation is driven by business need. The seat menu is reasonably standard across offices but some, like Plymouth, are more contentious in orientation than others, like Southampton or Bristol.

plymouth: good vibrations
The Plymouth office is the historical and spiritual home of the firm, and perhaps the swankiest of the six offices. Less than an hour from Newquay and the best surfing in the country, *"you can see the beach from the office window"* and be there with your feet in the sand sucking on a Zoom in less than two minutes. *"You meet people all the time who are into sailing, surfing, water sports and so on."* Most trainees here aren't driven by work and money, but favour the personal touch that is hard for big City firms to replicate. One source told us: *"The place is easy-going and not at all arduous – when I came for interview I immediately got a good vibe."*

"You are given lots of responsibility from day one." We're not talking the odd client meeting here or there, either. We heard of trainees running their own files from start to finish, particularly in the personal injury seat. PI *"isn't strictly compulsory, but almost everyone does it."* It makes up a large chunk of the work in Plymouth, with the firm representing some defendant clients and claimants referred by trade unions, as well as a smaller number of individuals on a conditional fee basis. There's a distinctly contentious feel to the work in Plymouth, although there

are non-contentious seats in corporate/commercial and property. *"The employment seat is currently seen as hugely sexy,"* and another hot spot is construction.

Environmental work in Plymouth often draws trainees from other branches or maybe its that they've heard about the Plymouth office's local pub, The Mount Pleasant, and its *"wicked sausage sarnies."* With just four or so trainees at any one time, you'll get to know your peers well. In September 2002, one of the two qualifiers stayed with the firm.

exeter: movement of the people

Bob Marley once asked, "Open your eyes and look within: Are you satisfied with the life you're living?" If you are likely to answer 'no' after a couple of years in London, then read on. As the smallest of the four main sites, Exeter has fewer seat options, but it still offers great work and client exposure. It also has a larger corporate/commercial department than Plymouth and a financial services seat. Much of the trainees' work is to be found in the property and PI departments, so *"nearly every trainee will go into PI for the first seat."* Two PI seats, three new trainees a year – you do the maths.

Exeter is commercially oriented; *"It doesn't advertise on the back of buses."* Indeed, the PI department handles cases for unions rather than chasing ambulances. Again, the 'real work and real responsibility' message rings out. One source told us, *"You'll get as much responsibility as you can handle. You don't have to get everything right; you just need to demonstrate that you know where to go for help if you need it."* We heard of trainees not only running their own files, but also hosting client meetings and even instructing counsel.

Again, the office atmosphere feels very Bond Pearce and is *"just like Plymouth, but smaller."* A typical working day sounds like a breeze compared to City hours. Even keen trainees *"usually leave before six,"* presumably to pop to the Southernhay Wine Bar next door. Although the town itself can be pretty sleepy, the trainees we spoke to seemed active enough, *"occasionally going paintballing or for a meal organised by the sports and social club."* You are unlikely to bump into partners on such occasions, but *"it's not because they are stand-offish – most are older with families."* The TSG in Exeter is pretty active so you'll get to know the other trainees in town quite quickly. Although there was an exodus in 2001, with qualifiers moving to other offices due to a lack of NQ jobs, all three September 2002 qualifiers were retained.

southampton: wanna be in that number?

Southampton is the home of The Saints, which could explain why trainees feel almost blessed. They are soon to be reunited in a shiny, new office building smack bang in front of the central train station, having so far been split between three separate sites. We are told Southampton is *"more akin to a London office than the Plymouth and Exeter offices, both in feel and work ethic."* Indeed, there is a *"faster pace"* in Southampton as *"the location of the office* [in a big city] *makes it a bit more commercial."* *"There is more pressure to hit targets,"* stressed one source, although no one has been pulled up for failing to meet one.

Starting out at Southampton you will discover that *"at least one of the first-years will do the property seat, and others will generally do insurance."* Not everyone enjoys the insurance seat. One source moaned, *"After a couple of months with 150 files that were all the same it was very boring."* Yet others rave about the responsibility it brings: *"Having a file that you can pretty much do what you want with is great,"* and we heard of trainees *"doing small hearings in chambers, which is something a lot of people in bigger firms don't get to do."* Too true.

Employment and commercial are the hot seats. *"They held interviews for the trainees who wanted to get into employment because it was so popular."* With the added lure of a five-month secondment to B&Q (legal department, not shelf stacking), no wonder it's a favourite. Other shorter client secondments take place on an ad hoc basis. In September 2002, half of the six qualifiers took jobs in the Southampton office.

Socially, the Soton crew had previously been hampered by being split between three sites but that should no longer pose a problem. Bar Risa is the venue of choice and partners will occasionally put up the cash for drinks. Hurrah! for the two trainees who breathed life back into the Southampton Young Lawyers Group, organising a summer ball for their peers in the city. Actually, our Chambers and Partners Recruitment colleagues sponsored the event. *"It was pretty wild!"* one of them confessed.

bristol: the pipes are calling

In 2001 the Bristol office absorbed local rival, Cartwrights (minus its insurance practice, which may have conflicted with BP's claimant/union work). One trainee told us, *"The Southampton and Bristol offices are going to grow more and faster than the others"* because the firm as a whole is *"moving away from the smaller end of the market."* Bristol as a city is going places and attracting precisely the type of businesses that the firm wants on its client roster, such as House of Fraser, a client to which some lucky Bristol trainees have been seconded. One trainee thought Bristol was *"more hard-hitting than the other offices, and trainees are probably more highly pressured, because it has big corporate clients as opposed to smaller ones."* Trainees in other offices might not agree, but it's fair to say that Bristol handles bigger clients/deals more often. Contentious and non-contentious work is evenly balanced – banking and insolvency are strong, as are property and insurance.

Here's a little-known fact – the lyrics of 'Danny Boy' were written by local barrister Frederick Weatherley in 1913. They may not be penning karaoke classics, but Bond Pearce's Bristol lawyers are *"not blinkered to work, work, work"* and are *"not overly serious."* Of colleagues, one trainee said, *"Everyone is the sort of person you want to go to the pub with."* A well-timed e-mail ensures a large group does indeed head out together to RSVP on Friday nights, and on sunny days you can catch trainees topping up their tans outside the Quay Bar on the riverside.

There is a close association with the Bristol Trainee Solicitors Group, which organises fortnightly events. And with football, golf, cricket and netball on offer, there's plenty to keep you occupied in the evenings, which is perhaps a good thing given that you'll be on your way home by 6pm most nights. Six of the eight Bristol qualifiers stayed with the firm post qualification in September 2002.

and finally…

Bond Pearce has much to offer. *"You get the quality of life you don't get in London, good-quality work, lots of responsibility and good training."* Make sure you pick the right office for you because you're unlikely to move during your training contract. Top tip: the Bond Pearce summer placement scheme is an essential part of the recruitment process, so get with the programme if you possibly can.

Boodle Hatfield

the facts
Location: London, Oxford
UK ranking by size: 92
Total number of trainees: 10
Seats: 4x6 months
Alternative seats: Secondments

Split between London's West End and Oxford, Boodle Hatfield has a particularly strong property practice, and offers commercial work. But it's the high-profile private client/financial planning work (or FP as they say in the biz) that continues to define the firm's style. Think personal, think stylish, think cultured.

the estate kids

Although all trainees work in London, the Oxford office is anything but a satellite, and is home to a number of key partners. As a trainee in the London office, you'll choose your four seats from property, private client, corporate, employment and litigation. (We've set these out in descending departmental size order.) This might not look like a massive range of seat options when compared to bigger firms, but as one trainee pointed out: *"The variety of work you'll get within any given seat is much better."* There's no danger of over-specialising, and for those of you with an interest in family work, this is likely to feature in the litigation seat. Add to this the tasty morsel of a secondment to ICI (available to most who want it and described as *"a definite highlight"*).

The only compulsory seat is property but sadly trainees seem unenthusiastic about the department. That's a shame because Boodle's top-notch team undertakes masses of work for the Grosvenor Estate and some exciting deals and developments land on its lawyers' desks. As one trainee said, *"It's not a bad place to do your first seat – you learn good skills and get a bit more autonomy…and the people are really lovely."* Litigation was described as a sure-fire winner. It's a very small but friendly department where *"they let you get out and about more, and you get to do all those lawyery things like arguing with people!"* The employment team works as a part of the corporate department, and is recognised as an up-and-coming area of the firm.

personal ads

Boodles marks itself out as a firm with a personal touch. Private client lawyers are a special breed – the work is totally people-oriented so, if faceless corporates turn you off, you'll be in your element. Clients come from around the world seeking advice on matters of personal and family wealth management. If you enjoyed your university or CPE trusts course, you'll love the emphasis on the law itself in private client work. Yet, *"financial planning is sometimes more about using your initiative than the law as such."* Sometimes clients will consult you on *"quite random"* matters. We heard of one trainee who was asked by an overseas client to help import a car into the UK.

Trainees spoke of a more forward-thinking approach, and the rise of youngish partners *"reflecting the type of client we're trying to attract – young, dynamic people rather than large corporations. They want to be known for quick turnaround, one-to-one contact and a client-friendly approach."* The firm's corporate clients are commonly of the entrepreneurial variety, smaller private companies and venture capitalists. Marketing and PR companies, pubs and drinks companies have all been the subject of recent deals.

warm glow

In terms of the training scheme itself, the consensus was that beneficial changes have been made of late. Even two years ago, trainees wouldn't have described it as a well-oiled machine, but a coherent strategy is now in evidence. The firm has listened to trainees' comments and shown a willingness to take criticisms on board. It is also planning to introduce a mentoring scheme for all staff. Trainee appraisals are held quarterly (if occasionally haphazardly), and *"no one's going to slap you down, even if major issues have to be raised. This is a safe environment to learn in and I've found it very confidence-building."*

Most days you'll get away by 6.30pm and, if you're not gone by 7pm, someone will probably bundle you through the door. Responsibility is pretty good but don't expect to be sending out letters before having them checked. We were also pleased to hear that trainees are only expected to do *"the photocopying that takes a bit of intelligence,"* and even then, not that often. *"We have a guy in the basement who's been doing the photocopying for about twenty years. He's slightly pale."*

When asked to describe the typical trainee our interviewees reeled off: *"not geeky," "not sloaney," "not megalomaniacs,"* and *"not too driven." "It's not a place to come to if you're out for world domination,"* cautioned one source. Most trainees chose Boodle Hatfield on the basis of abstract intangibles, rather than an insatiable lust for juicy clients or a particular practice area. It offers an attractive alternative to *"cold and impersonal"* City firms. One trainee lost himself happily reminiscing about the assessment day… *"It was the first interview that I actually enjoyed, where I came out with a smile on my face. I just liked the feel of the place."* Trainees are thankful that they are not expected to buy into the brand: *"No one makes unreasonable demands. They expect you to have a real life going on else-*

where." It seems to be working: three out of four trainees qualifying in September 2002 stayed with the firm. *"People may come here with a vague intention of moving off to bigger things one day, but they never do!"*

retail therapy
Although the building was described dismissively as *"a bit of a rabbit warren,"* the Mayfair location gets rave reviews. Oxford Street is on hand for when you get an urge for retail therapy, or you can spend your lunch hour lounging in nearby Grosvenor and Berkeley Squares. The refined pleasures of the neighbourhood might be a little sedate for those who secretly crave the macho Red Bull pace of the City though. On the social side, firm-wide events are organised occasionally, but you're more likely to find yourself stepping out for lunch with a couple of colleagues than joining a general stampede to the pub on a Friday night. Partners don't tend to go out with assistants and support staff: *"It's an unwritten rule. I think they do get out sometimes though."* Let's hope so.

and finally…
Private client work is part of what gives this firm its personal streak. If you want a thoroughly decent training and you want to work with thoroughly decent people, Boodle Hatfield should be on your list.

Brabners Chaffe Street

the facts
Location: Liverpool, Manchester, Preston
UK ranking by size: 81
Total number of trainees: 18
Seats: 4x6 months
Alternative seats: Secondments

Brabners Chaffe Street (that's 'Chaif', not 'Chaff') was born on 1st January 2002 out of the merger of Liverpool and Preston firm Brabners and Manchester's Chaffe Street. This new partnership now offers its full range of commercial and private client services to businesses and individuals across the North West.

before and after shots
The impetus for the merger came from Brabners' desire to expand into Manchester without having to trouble itself with opening a brand new office. Luckily for Brabners, the old Chaffe Street partnership was in the process of dissolving, so it was able to snap up six of the partners, a bunch of other lawyers and staff (including three trainees) and the Manchester city centre office building. We spoke to several lovely trainees from both the Liverpool and Manchester offices and although the merged firm is a relatively young venture for them they spoke with enthusiasm about their new, improved firm.

Liverpool is the larger office and has five departments – corporate, property, litigation, employment and private client. Manchester offers corporate, property and employment (Chaffe Street's insolvency lawyers went off to DLA and four other partners left to set up Pinsent Curtis Biddle's Manchester office) plus a little commercial litigation. Liverpool takes six trainees per year, Manchester two and Preston one. Trainees in Liverpool are assigned a seat plan when they start, which takes in four of the five departments for six months each. One trainee explained, *"If you have a real yearning to do the one you're not down to do, you can change."* In Manchester trainees have six-monthly meetings with the training partner, during which they express preferences for their next seat.

Applicants will be asked to state which office they would like to work in and will not be forced to undertake a seat in another office. On the other hand, if they fancy a jaunt around the North West to another office, they need only ask. If the tastes of current trainees are anything to go by, future trainees will be clamouring for employment seats, with corporate also high on their wish lists. A secondment to a large Mersey-based corporate client is on offer for those interested.

are your feet on the bottom?

The firm offers *"lots of responsibility and some quite complicated work."* Clients range from wealthy individuals through smaller owner-managed businesses to plcs and the roster includes Emap, Edinburgh Woollen Mills and Rage (producers of the Beckham game). Trainees help out on bigger deals by taking on component tasks of their supervisors' transactions, but they also get to run their own, smaller files in departments like property and litigation. Exposure to decent work and clients is high from day one and trainees have to learn fast. One spoke philosophically about how far they'd developed, professionally, over the two years and how much easier things had become: *"I came to a conclusion the other day. I looked around and thought 'I've got less work', but actually, I've just adjusted to it."* It's not uncommon for trainees to contribute to a meeting on a bit of law they have researched and they are continually dealing with clients. Responsibility is not forced upon them but it is there for the taking. One source said, *"I feel out of my depth all the time, but not without feeling I have back-up."*

Appraisals take place in the middle and at the end of each seat and all our sources agreed that the continual stream of feedback is excellent. *"90% of the time I hear back on my work within half an hour."* *"They'll let you know when you've made great strides."* One source is *"almost embarrassed by how much my supervisor helps me. If I ask something he's not sure of he'll go to the library and almost do me a report."* Trainees sit with a partner and take most work from them, but if you fancy a bit of variety, *"you can just go knocking on doors and ask for the sexy bits of law."*

the benny hill show

Trainees refer to *"a purely positive atmosphere."* The atmosphere isn't laid-back in a lazy sense; it's more a case of: *"We all work hard but are expected to enjoy our jobs."* There is an emphasis on teamwork and a *"mutual respect for everyone."* Trainees' contact details are given on the firm's website so why not use them to find out a bit more? *"We all look out for each other. If one of us was under huge pressure, we would be looking to help them out."* Across the board, Brabners Chaffe Street employees *"want to go the extra mile and put themselves out for people."*

Since merger there has been no Manchester-Liverpool/Preston rivalry. The firm has been working hard to integrate its staff across the three offices, with each taking turns to host visits from the other offices. By the time we spoke to them, the Liverpool and Preston trainees had all been over to Manchester for a night out in the city, courtesy of the firm. Over in Liverpool, The Living Room is a favourite venue for after work drinks; however, the Manchester trainees haven't managed to make it that far up Deansgate and prefer the safe option of the All Bar One near the office. The Liverpool trainees are often known to make a night of it on a Friday, availing themselves of the office showers to get glammed up, and after firm-wide drinks every month, some of the partners brave a night out with the youngsters. Liverpool trainees have a high profile in the Merseyside TSG, commonly occupying committee positions.

When we spoke to them, the Manchester office had yet to experience the joys of the Brabners Christmas party, when the trainees are responsible for the entertainment. *"It's like an old Benny Hill sketch where we take the piss out of the partners. They absolutely love the attention."* We bet they do!

In September 2001 six of the seven Liverpool trainees qualified into the firm. In September 2002, the figures were down, with around half of the qualifiers across the Liverpool and Manchester offices staying.

and finally…

If you want a firm with a truly North West feel, diverse work and a decent level of responsibility, Brabners Chaffe Street seems to fit the bill. If the warmth and good humour of the trainees we spoke to is a measure of anything, then it looks as if it's one heck of a nice firm to work for.

Brachers

the facts
Location: Maidstone, London
UK ranking by size: 105
Total number of trainees: 13
Seats: 4x6 months
Alternative seats: Occasionally Lille

Brachers has occupied a position as a leading Kent practice for well over 100 years. Trainees hankering after a quality firm in the South East should read on…

smells like team spirit

You can *"cover a lot of ground"* and get a *"good broad training"* at Brachers. Our sources chose the firm for many reasons, but all wanted to avoid a life of grime in the capital. For some, the attraction was clinical negligence work – Brachers retained a prized position on the NHSLA panel, which was hacked from 90-odd firms to 15. For others, it was the chance to do family and private client work for wealthier clients than your average high street operation – *"It's established farmers and middle-class/rich clients."* The firm's larger commercial departments – corporate, property, litigation and employment – are the draw for yet others.

Some want a purely commercial training; others follow the private client route. Harmony reigns. *"We all help each other out and there's no treading on each others' toes,"* said one. If there is any competition, then it's over the two employment seats in London. Six months in the City *"bolt-hole"* usually satisfies any lingering urge for a cosmopolitan existence.

in betweenies

Brachers trainees describe it as *"in between a high street firm and City firm. There's not much supervision in one and not much responsibility in the other."* We were impressed by the trainees' tasks: *"Clinical negligence is fertile ground for interesting work. I achieved settlements and handled appointments with district judges. I liked being able to see the results of my work."* In PI, too, there are good opportunities: interim hearings, settlement negotiations and conferences with counsel.

No training contract is ever a utopia, but at Brachers *"you're not slave labour. OK, some seats don't go as well as others and you do get some crummy work, but mostly you're treated as a respected part of the firm."* Some supervisors are *"not organised enough and like to fly by the seat of their pants so they can't organise their trainees either,"* but the better ones give *"lots of responsibility with proper supervision and client contact."* Depending on the confidence of different trainees and the seats they were talking about, we heard a range of views on whether you need to be tough to survive or whether you could coast along. One said, *"If anything, I got too much responsibility too soon, but when I needed help they were there."* Another agreed, *"They throw you in at the deep end, but there's someone ready to pull out the plug at the bottom!"* Another trainee felt they were idling at times: *"I was twiddling my thumbs a lot of the time. They have moved people out of a seat if it's not worked out, but they have to deal with it quite discreetly."* Of course.

exceedingly nice cakes

The corporate department handles deals for Kent businesses and a few bigger, juicier clients, but one trainee was at pains to point out: *"The issues are the same on the deals we do and deals that are ten times the size."* We heard reports of trainees writing due diligence reports and being at the partner's side at all stages of the action. There are no set rules on seating: litigation is open-plan, in corporate you share an office with a partner and elsewhere you may share with a trainee. One said, *"With your own office you have time to think and get on with the work, although you do have to make a positive effort to find people when you need help."*

'No set rules' is an expression equally applicable to the firm's culture. Its four separate buildings in Maidstone are all within minutes of each other on the London Road. *"It fragments the place a little"* and *"there's not much cross-departmental fraternising,"* our sources said. Easily fixed, we assumed: why not just hang out together more? Well, on Thursdays, anyone in the firm can defy the old adage that there's no such thing as a free lunch. With its crabsticks, jam tarts and Happy Shopper yoghurts, the event is described as "*a bad 1970s buffet,*" but the Wagon Wheels and Mr Kipling treats go down a storm though…

the maidstone debate
Departments conform to stereotype. "*Corporate is quite tense; when I walk in I feel it.*" Some of its lawyers are ex-City and the department works later than others. "*In probate most of the clients are not alive, so deadlines are less pressing and it's more relaxed.*" The London office, with about 15 staff, is "*very relaxed even though it's busy.*" It has dress-down Fridays, for example, while "*that wouldn't wash in Maidstone with our landed and agricultural clients. If everyone were walking around in khakis and trainers, they'd think they'd wandered into the wrong place. I wouldn't say it's a particularly New Age firm!*"

Many partners are the sort who've "*been at Brachers for a long time and have worked their way up.*" One trainee thought the firm was "*quite paternalistic*" and the average lawyer "*not the sharp attitude, shoulder-padded type.*" Parts of the firm remain "*quite traditional,*" yet "*employment and corporate are extremely progressive.*" It's likely that the tone is set by the clients for whom each department acts: landed gentry v Eurotunnel v RSPCA v Charlton Athletic FC. But, whoever's calling the shots, the lawyers "*set high standards for themselves and trainees.*" We always ask trainees what they'd change if they were senior partner. Trainee-partners at Brachers would drive it forward as a more cohesive unit and, perhaps, be pushier to win more business.

Ironic then that trainees describe themselves as "*steady and competent,*" and "*not overly ambitious or hard-nosed.*" Some grew up in the South East; equally as many didn't. Apparently, "*Maidstone is not the greatest place to go out and socialise. Just outside there's Yalding and Bearstead with their cricket pitches and pubs – it's real picture book stuff. I think they just scooped up all the grotty bits of Kent and chucked them into Maidstone. There's no nice old bit to the town and no favourite pub where we have a free bar on Friday nights.*" Oh dear! The best we got was: "*Maidstone's not that bad.*"

french connection
The trainee social budget gets spent in restaurants, at barn dances, concerts and dog racing. And then there's the religiously observed Friday lunchtime meet in local bar Hanrahans. Most partners will attend the annual Christmas party; a few will participate in group events (such as a recent day trip to France or a team meal); and one holds a big BBQ at his house. The type of relationship you can build with partners "*depends on the partner.*"

Brachers is part of a network called Law South (which also includes firms like Blake Lapthorn and Wilsons), through which much of the formal training is organised – "*There's always an e-mail every month indicating the availability of courses.*" Law South also runs an exchange programme with the Lille Bar Association and we heard of one trainee being seconded to a French firm for three months.

There's sponsorship for law school in the form of a £6,000 loan, which is written off if you pass all your exams and you stay with the firm for four years after qualifying. Naturally, trainees would like to see this increased and (like others in the region) they find the salary doesn't stretch as far as they'd like, although it did go up recently. To alleviate the problem of landing in a new town with a suitcase of student debt, the firm offers two first-year trainees accommodation in a house share. And then at the end of the two years, a healthy number stay. In September 2002, four out of five qualifiers stayed at Brachers and the fifth went back to the organisation she'd been seconded from.

and finally…
"*Best of both worlds*" is how trainees would sum up Brachers. It has quality work for decent clients and, for the most part, very manageable hours. Whether you're suited to private clients or corporates, you'll find something that fits.

Bristows

the facts
Location: London
UK ranking by size: 87
Total number of trainees: 17
Seats: 4x6 or 2x6 + 4x3 months
Alternative seats: Secondments

A top-ranked specialist in intellectual property, Bristows attracts similarly specialist trainees, but has a few other tricks up its sleeve.

pants on first

It's not its only field of practice, but Bristows has cornered a large portion of the market for leading edge IP work. Building on foundations laid in 1837, it has represented a diverse range of clients, including the Jockey Company during the 1940s, successfully protecting a patent on a new invention – Y-fronts! But it certainly isn't all pants now, and they are not limited to straightforward IP cases. The firm's Christmas card list is an almost endless roster of well-known innovators in the communications, media, IT, electronics, and pharmaceuticals sectors. DuPont, Ericsson, Novartis, Sony, Philips...we could go on and on.

The trainees seem well capable of complex work, with the majority having science backgrounds. If you are a science nut, expect to be treated more like a god than a geek. In fact, four of the current 14 trainees have PhDs. Although you don't have to have a doctorate to train here, *"drive, attention to detail and mental capacity"* are all necessary characteristics. That's another way of saying you have to be really bright – 250W headlight, not 20W night light. *"The firm wants independent thinkers who can quickly grasp complex new concepts and really understand the client's business."*

know-it-alls

The science and technology sector is becoming increasingly global, and Bristows' clients come from as far afield as the USA and Japan. If you find yourself working on a large project for one of these big companies, you may have a little less responsibility than you had hoped for. You can expect to work alongside some of the world's best (lawyers and scientists); one trainee told us of their frequent amazement at partners' vast knowledge, causing the reaction *"How do you know that?"* on an almost daily basis. On the other hand, if you become involved with a smaller project for one of the many start-ups that the firm represents, you could find yourself with as much responsibility as you can handle. *"It's really gratifying when you are left alone to work on a case; the responsibility is a challenge, but seeing the end result of your efforts is great."*

molecular bonding

It goes without saying that you will be expected to do a seat in IP. Most of the trainees we spoke to had completed six months in IP litigation, followed by three months working on non-contentious IP law. Not every Bristows trainee will end up as an IP lawyer, and not all training will be in IP, but it is the core of the business. *"More and more non-scientific clients are turning to the firm for representation, particularly in the commercial litigation and company law departments."* As well as seats in the other departments, which include tax, commercial property, EU/competition, employment and environmental law, it is not uncommon for final-year trainees to spend some time on secondment to one of the firm's bigger clients. Even when on secondment, the trainees remain extremely close. One trainee asked his colleagues back at base to photocopy materials he needed from the Bristows' library, only to be told by the library staff: *"Why didn't you ask us? You're still one of us!"*

This sense of team spirit, although not uncommon in firms of this size, is central to Bristows' philosophy. The special closeness is in part due to the small number of new trainees each year (most coming from similar backgrounds) and an office environment *"where you are not expected to be chained to a desk all day."* *"If you are sat there for hours, you will eventually be asked if you need help or coffee."* In a tear-jerking display of affection, one trainee told us that the lowest point of their career to date was "*when I realised that one of the other trainees would be leaving on qualification.*" In 2002 five out of seven qualifying second-years stayed with the firm.

well supported

As if wearing metaphorical Y-fronts of their own, trainees can expect to be well supported – training is structured and supervised properly, with partners overseeing meetings between trainees and their new supervisors to ensure a fluid handover. This early handholding is particularly important for those who come to IP work from a traditional legal background, as some of the information can be highly technical.

Growing from a small, family business into one of the top IP firms in the UK appears to have put pressure on the firm in a way that has yet to be addressed. The trainee intake is rising, and lateral hires of assistants and partners from other firms are more common. Based in several offices on the same road, there is a sense that some of the treasured closeness could be in peril, if the firm can't find a new home or fix its current one. The buildings vary greatly in quality and "*could all do with a bit of tarting up.*" A few more kitchens and communal areas might prevent drowned-rat sandwich-dashes during rainy lunchtimes and crumbs in the files. That said, as one trainee succinctly put it, "*I would rather eat my lunch at my desk than get lost in the machinery of a big firm.*" Don't expect to be sat on your behind at a desk all day and late into the night. Our sources think Bristows is "*not overtly competitive and there's no stay-late culture.*" "*You are not expected to surrender the rest of your life.*"

In spite of their braininess, trainees still undertake certain humbling tasks. We were told that "*photocopying and pagination end up with the trainees when there is no one else to do them,*" and "*as there is no outdoor clerk, the trainees share that work* [ie going off to issue and collect papers from court] *on a rota.*" It's not altogether bad – in the summertime there's usually an ice-cream van in Lincoln's Inn Fields, between the RCJ and the office. Just don't drip raspberry sauce on the pleadings.

where do you want to go today?

With more PhDs per square metre than anywhere else in the City, and people working on gadgets and gizmos that would leave Bond's Q puzzled, it comes as something of a surprise that the biggest problem trainees face is where to drink on a Friday! From the bank of converted homes that make up the offices, it's a short trip to the nearby George, but Bar Columbia, the Seven Stars and the Pitcher & Piano only heighten the indecision. In addition to weekly pub trips and birthday booze-ups, the firm holds monthly drinks parties and an annual dinner dance that stirs up more 'She did what?!?' e-mails than a group of tipsy 18-year-olds forced to spend a day in a room with a photocopier.

and finally…

If you are looking for a smaller, tightly-knit firm and IP is your thing, Bristows should be high on your list. If you have science qualifications or techy-boffin tendencies, you'll be particularly appreciated. Beam us up!

Browne Jacobson

the facts

Location: Nottingham, Birmingham, London
UK ranking by size: 58
Total number of trainees: 21
Seats: 4x6 months
Alternative seats: None

It's well known that Browne Jacobson is heavily geared towards insurance clients. Indeed, insurance litigation, including personal injury matters, is high on the agenda, but the firm also undertakes a significant amount of corporate/commercial work as well as private client matters.

three little pigs

You remember the story. One pig built his house from corporate deals, one rented a lovely home in the property department, and then the third little squealer won a lovely big mansion in litigation. The big bad wolf huffed and puffed, but failed to dislodge even a roof tile. Browne Jacobson's training contract is much the same; there are no compulsory seats, but *"the firm would like all its trainees to do a corporate seat, a property seat and an insurance seat."* Over in insurance there are some lovely acronyms for the different contentious groups. PIG, for example, handles professional indemnity cases, while PAG does insurance work for public authority clients. There are plenty of personal injury seats and a new one in clinical negligence (one of the firm's rapidly expanding departments). The NHS Litigation Authority handles all of the clinical defence work of the NHS and it's a solid endorsement of Browne Jacobson's work that it retained a place on the panel of just 15 firms that now act for the authority.

The corporate/commercial department is very popular with trainees. As one said, *"In corporate you get a good overview of what's going on in different areas around the firm – for every transaction there's tax support, property support and employment support."* Even seats that are not enticing at first instance turn out to offer worthwhile experiences. One trainee said, *"I didn't particularly want to do property, but it was rewarding in terms of the responsibility I was given and the breadth of experience I got from it."* The consensus is that there's plenty of trainee input into seat moves, and *"where your first-choice seat is available, you'll generally get it."*

six paces north, two east

Reflecting BJ's steady organic growth, the Nottingham office is *"a series of old buildings that have been joined at various stages, over who knows how long."* *"It's a bit of a hotchpotch of buildings…a real rabbit warren."* Hopefully it fares a bit better than the one in *Watership Down*! It takes weeks to get used to, we're told, and all new trainees need a map. *"Once you get that, you're generally OK – as long as you can read a map of course."* One trainee made the astounding statement: *"I've been here 18 months, and there are still some parts of the building where I get to and wonder 'Where do I go now?'"*

Other than during the annual (boozy) pubcrawl-cum-treasure hunt, finding their way around the city proves unproblematic for the vast majority of trainees, as most have links with Nottingham, whether personal or educational. *"A lot of us went to university or did the LPC here and liked it so much we didn't want to leave."* They reminded us what a good reputation the firm has in Nottingham and throughout the region. The firm is now the fifth biggest in the Midlands.

Nottingham is the focal point for trainee positions. However, if you want an assignment in Birmingham or London, you only need ask. When we interviewed in the summer of 2002, no one had chosen to leave the Nottingham office, but this is, apparently, unusual. Neither Birmingham nor London are full-service offices: Birmingham has seats available in either clinical negligence or insurance, while in London it's either corporate or insurance.

right royal knees-up

There's no doubt; Browne Jacobson is a sociable firm. As one trainee said, *"It's a very welcoming atmosphere. Provided they are prepared to get involved and be friendly around the office, most people will fit in here."* There are plenty of firm-wide events, which are *"especially good for trainees, as it helps us to get our faces known."* Another interviewee noted: *"It's really not a traditional, stuffy solicitors firm like some that I went to for interviews."* There's a pub next door frequented by a cross-section of the firm, from partners right down to support staff. *"There's no us and them."* The Royal Children, or as it's more affectionately known, 'The Kids', is *"a stone's throw away"* and has been *"the pub of choice since the year dot: there are partners here who went there when they were trainees."* Blimey! Maybe they should rename it 'The Getting On A Bits'… Apparently it's *"not the nicest pub* in the world (and certainly not the trendiest), but it's the company that counts."

hotel california

Prior to joining, trainees are *"taken out three times by the current trainees, usually to a restaurant or for drinks."* The rationale behind these meet and greets is *"so you'll know a few friendly faces in each department."* We tried to start a rumour regarding a secret initiation ritual involving tar and feathers…but it didn't stick. Students are also assigned a mentor (a trainee in the year above them) who sticks with them throughout the course of their training contract. *"You can contact them even before you start if you've got any queries or problems."*

Trainee meetings are held on a quarterly basis, sometimes more often. At these powwows, issues are raised in relation to training and seat movements. The training partner and manager are in attendance to listen to trainees unburden themselves. One of our sources said, *"The fact that we do get on so well as a unit means we can discuss things outside meetings and speak with one voice in the meetings – we have strength in numbers and we get a lot of say."* Power to the trainees!

As one trainee put it, *"A couple of years ago retention wasn't great, but now the firm is making more of an effort to retain as many trainees as possible."* In fact, in September 2002 seven out of eight of the qualifying second-years were kept on, going into a range of departments including employment, commercial and clinical negligence. One trainee told us that he recently met a recruitment consultant at a Nottingham Law Students Society event who told him, *"We have problems with Browne Jacobson – no one ever wants to leave!"*

and finally…

A top choice in Nottingham, Browne Jacobson inspires affection and loyalty. Apply if you want the opportunity to sample plenty of litigation as well as corporate and private client work in a firm where you won't get lost in the crowd.

Burges Salmon

the facts
Location: Bristol
UK ranking by size: 46
Total number of trainees: 40
Seats: 6x4 months
Alternative seats: Secondments
Extras: Pro bono – Bristol University Law Clinic

Regarded as a top dog in Bristol, Burges Salmon is a heavyweight commercial practice. If you are looking to stay away from the big smoke but want to be involved with top-notch clients, Burges Salmon should be somewhere near the top of your list.

bourgeois salmon

The trainees of rival Bristol law firms occasionally use the moniker 'Bourgeois Salmon' to describe our current subject and there's possibly more than a little jealousy behind this. Burges Salmon is, as far as regional firms go, just that little bit more pukka than others – in the past some trainees have even suggested it is the Slaughter and May of Bristol. With clients such as FirstGroup, Orange, Honda and Reuters on its books, you could be forgiven for thinking this is a big City firm. And with such a client base, there is naturally a little of the City approach to the work. One source told us, *"It is almost Swiss in the way it runs"* and we can only assume this means practicality, efficiency, economy and design, but without the cuckoos. Everything is well run because *"if they think something is worth doing, they do it well."*

It is fair to say that in the past, the firm has portrayed a slightly stuffy image to the outside world, but just five minutes conversation with any of the current trainees will convince you this is just so old hat. One source admitted, *"It's not an elitist place, although I thought that when I came here."* To many of the current lawyers, it's all a bit of a joke: *"Stuffiness isn't part of the ethos here. People can laugh about themselves."* What you most certainly won't find are the excessive hours often associated with London work. Even though the firm is *"becoming increasingly more commercial and City-like and inevitably this means you may have to work longer, there's no one cracking the whip."* Coupled with a permanent dress-down policy, it is tough to make allegations of serious stuffiness stick. In short, the firm *"gives you everything a City firm does but without the stress."*

musical chairs

Burges Salmon's six-seat system put us in mind of the children's party game where, when the music stops, you get your bum on a seat as quickly as you can, and spend only a millisecond there before some crazed dad turns the volume back up and off you go again… The tune you might hear is the 'end-of-seat blues' – you have just enough time to get comfortable before you are unceremoniously moved on. Trainees do sometimes grumble about this, but the BS bunch seem pretty happy with it, pointing out that it is *"a double-edged sword – you get the blues more, but you don't get stuck in a department you're not interested in."* It's great for undecided trainees who get to experience 50% more of a firm than those on a four-by-six pattern.

Of the six seats, four are compulsory – company/commercial, property, then either commercial lit or APLE (agriculture, property lit and environment) and either employment/pensions or tax & trusts. Tax & trusts *"attracts a very academic type of person,"* but is generally *"not so popular with trainees as most come here with no tax knowledge and never really warm to it."* Conversely, our sources tell us, *"There is a premium on all commercial seats,"* particularly employment which, as *"a youthful and progressive department,"* is a firm favourite. Should you find the seat you wish to qualify into early on in your training, don't panic: you can 'double up' for a second run through in your final seat. In this way, you'll be sure to hit the ground running if you make the qualification grade. For those wanting to escape the office, secondments to clients such as British Aerospace and Orange may appeal. Ask about overseas seats and you'll hear the wah-wah-oops buzzer. Nothing doing. Burges Salmon has never displayed any signs of empire building. That said, a recently instituted scheme has seen qualified lawyers heading off for secondments to US firm Thompson Hine, and word on the street is that trainees may be participating in the future.

pass the binoculars

The firm looks further and further afield for its work. Long gone are the days when the commercial activity of the South West sufficed. About 75% of its business is thought to emanate from outside the region. But there's a whole swathe of other work and clients sat alongside the megadeals for national and international corporate giants. Agriculture and bloodstock specialists, for example, act for the great and good of the landed and farming communities as well as the National Trust and the Crown Estate, and there are a number of large charities on the firm's books. Thriving family and private client departments also offer opportunities for trainees. These more traditional aspects of the firm's business sit comfortably with the go-getting corporate and commercial departments.

Our sources all spoke of being given real responsibility and, wherever possible, being entrusted with their own files. The terms 'general' and 'basic' were used a lot when we asked trainees to describe their duties, but this is to be expected in a firm handling large deals. *"It's classic trainee stuff,"* quipped one source. Even where you have less responsibility *"you still do exciting things"* and *"you'll never be left in the lurch."* Trainees share the office of their supervisor, who monitors the volume and spread of work. Don't expect to be spoon-fed though. *"The supervisors aren't teachers. If you don't get what you need, you have to find it yourself"* and *"if you aren't getting the work, you have to push for it."* Trainees recommend proactivity: *"It's your career after all."* Indeed it is.

dunroamin?

We looked hard for a common denominator among trainees. Some had previous careers (and these were diverse) while others came straight from university. Some are *"very rounded,"* others *"a bit starchy."* Having said that, they do fit into a loose, indefinable Burges Salmon mould – essentially, *"they are academic and outgoing people,"* although *"really off the wall types won't fit in."* They are *"personable types who are good in all social situations,"* one source noted, vaguely. We did find one strong connection – all of our sources had some link to Bristol, be it through birth or study. This possibly says more about the attraction of the city itself: Bristol is a place that's hard to leave. With the volume and calibre of applications the firm receives, expect to be required to show your dedication to a career in Bristol.

Apparently there are trainees who don't fit this local bill; we just couldn't find them. Perhaps they were engaged in a spot of retail therapy when we called. The office is situated right on the recently redeveloped waterfront, just five minutes from Clifton (*"the posh part of Bristol"*). Decked out in a modern style, *"with a dash of the Burges Salmon pink where they can get it in,"* the firm continues to grow through the building. With *"curvy desks and black computers"* there's an abundance of clean, Ikea-esque design that would have TV's Linda Barker running for the nearest bundle of twigs. The toilets are equally free from fussiness: *"They're really space-age and pink. Real pink not Burges Salmon pink! You don't even have to touch the flush, you just wave your hand over it,"* enthused one trainee. Definitely in the running for the 'John of the Year Award.'

in the pink

The current trainees are *"very sports minded."* They go sailing four or five times a year and take part in a variety of one-off events such as the firm's golf competition. They won the area mixed hockey league last season, play touch rugby on Wednesdays, five-a-side football on Mondays, and, albeit less frequently, indulge in the odd game of cricket. When they aren't being health conscious, the bars beckon. *"Nine times out of ten"* the Pitcher & Piano plays host to a night out, but being *"slap-bang in the middle of the pubs and eateries,"* the trainees are spoilt for choice. *"On Friday an e-mail goes round about drinks,"* one trainee noted, *"and everyone including five- and six-year-qualified solicitors and the odd partner joins in."* On top of this, *"the company and commercial department has monthly drinks"* on partners' tabs. Add in a summer party, departmental Christmas parties and a firm-wide Christmas knees-up and it's easy to see why Burges Salmon trainees sound a bit smug when they talk about their quality of life. *"It really is like all the firm's literature says it is,"* insisted one trainee. And with all but one of this year's 17 trainees offered a job on qualification, well, the party just never ends.

and finally…

It is the Rolls-Royce of South West law firms, but you don't need a double-barrelled name or an old-school tie to make it here. If big-name clients float your boat, but long Tube commutes and London prices give you the willies, grab an application form post-haste.

Capsticks

the facts

Location: London
UK ranking by size: 98
Total number of trainees: 12
Seats: 6x4 months
Alternative seats: Secondments
Extras: Pro bono – Putney Law Centre

Capsticks is known for its clinical negligence expertise and fields one of the largest defence teams in the country. It also has a significant and growing practice for healthcare clients in general commercial work. Train there and you'll have six whole seats to find out that there is more to this firm than clin neg.

health and happiness

Many trainees have a pre-existing interest in matters medical or scientific, but *"they're recruiting more broadly than just for clinical negligence. They need com-*

mercially-minded people to handle things like property and employment for these clients." Interestingly, only one of September 2002's qualifiers went into clinical negligence, with the rest picking other departments.

The firm allows you to do a seat twice, and your final seat will normally be in the department that you hope to qualify into. Employment seems the most popular: *"It's a hot topic and you can do your own advocacy, which is exciting for a trainee."* But clin neg is what Capsticks is best known for; it's the dominant department in the firm (taking up at least three of the seven floors in the building) and, as one trainee put it: *"A lot of people come here with the idea that they might like to do it."* Predictably, you will have to do at least one seat there, and many end up doing two. *"Some, if they really like it, will end up doing three!"* While the standard seat involves dealing with *"straightforward"* claims, there's also the opportunity to do a general advisory seat in clinical law, where you'll field *"totally random queries from healthcare clients – anything from probate to criminal stuff, consent and confidentiality issues."*

getting a leg up
Trainees recommend you undertake a vacation placement. Four out of the five second-years did at least one, as did all of the first-years. *"A summer placement is pretty much the way to get a training contract here."* *"It's well structured and gives you the flavour of the different departments. I did three days in one department, four days in a different one, then three days in another."*

The hours are perfectly reasonable: *"Most people get in around 8.30/9am and work till 6pm."* There's an emphasis on managing your workload, being productive during the day, and not hanging around in the evening. *"If you've got your work done you can go home at 5.30pm and it won't be frowned upon."* The longest hours are found in the commercial department, particularly in relation to major PFI projects.

going into hospital
Our interviewees talked positively about responsibility. *"It's a sliding scale – you're eased in at the beginning,* but you get a lot more as you go on. You'll be treated as a newly qualified by your sixth seat." This increased responsibility *"never becomes a pressure"* as *"nothing goes out unchecked,"* so you *"never have to bite your nails as to whether you said the right thing or not."* Trainees are *"certainly not hidden away"* in terms of client exposure. *"We're really put out there – there's a real emphasis on working with clients from the beginning."*

Most trainees will be seconded to a hospital or NHS Trust, usually for one day a week, occasionally two. Such secondments can last for three weeks, a couple of months, or even (in the case of one trainee) a couple of seats. You might work in the claims management department of a hospital or your role could be *"more commercially-based, dealing with queries about property or VAT issues."* *"It can be really good fun,"* enthused one source. *"I got my own office there and I was the first point of contact for anyone at the hospital who had legal issues, whether that was a nurse or a finance director."* There is a downside: *"You're pretty much told where you're going and when – you don't really get a choice."*

on the floor
"Trainees never really do photocopying of any size – that goes to our photocopying department," although there are *"times when you've got a hearing the next day and 27 different bundles to get out."* One trainee told us of *"sitting on the floor cross-legged with my supervisor and secretary putting bundles together."* The trainees praised the firm's medical records department for its *"efficiency"* and rated the secretarial support as *"extremely good."* *"The aim is to keep administrative work away from the trainees and get you doing substantive tasks."* One trainee concluded: *"When you're on a big case, you sometimes get tasks that are less than thrilling, but they're never isolated – they're always vital to the matter and give you an idea of how to put a case together."*

Mostly, trainees sit with their supervisor but occasionally second-years will get their own offices, although this *"depends on what floor you're on and what's available."* Trainees tell us they are a resource used by different lawyers in the department, although usually the bulk of their work will come from their supervisor. *"For example, within the clinical negligence department someone might do a lot of brain-damaged baby cases – if you're working for other people as well, you won't just do that type of work."*

The office is *"not the most attractive building in the world."* *"I'd be lying if I said it's got beautiful Victorian stonework,"* said one trainee. *"It's like a council block."* Inside, however, it's a different story: *"It's got a good layout, is quite spacious and has big glass offices. There's certainly no cramping of desks in the corridor."* Everyone from a department will be based on one floor, so *"there's a real team feeling on whatever floor you're working on."* One trainee added: *"The claim to fame of the seventh floor is that you can see the London Eye."* Capsticks is blessed in terms of its location right in the heart of Putney, near to lots of pukka bars, restaurants and shops, as well as the Thames. A few of the trainees even live within walking distance, which is a *"total godsend"* when one considers the transport nightmares many City trainees experience.

all talk

Appraisals help to *"shape your training. The end-of-seat appraisal is all about what you're interested in and what you want more of."* In the absence of a trainee forum, *"issues get resolved with your supervisor at first instance."* *"The partners are relatively young, so you don't feel intimidated by approaching them."* *"We do chat amongst ourselves, particularly coming up to qualification,"* said one trainee, but *"there's not enough of us to need to co-ordinate everyone's views: we already know what our views are!"* No need to ask their views on retention. As in 2001, all the 2002 qualifiers stayed on.

There are plenty of departmental seminars on new developments in the law, plus *"we get a lot of people like doctors and dentists coming in to talk to us,"* which is good for *"getting to know expert witnesses."*

je ne regrette rien

Capsticks' trainees are a close-knit bunch. *"It's a really good social scene,"* said one. A committee organises theatre trips, comedy club nights and BBQs, etc. More informally, the local Nando's is favoured at lunchtime, particularly on Fridays, and after hours there's Le Piaf, a wine bar that's *"so close you can just roll out of Capsticks straight into it."* Although it inspires varying levels of affection, *"on Friday nights, half the workforce is in there"* and *"you'll get 20 people around a table, from someone in photocopying right through to an equity partner."* At the opposite end of the spectrum is the Prince of Wales, or as it's otherwise known, the 'Prince of Darkness'. *"It's got a slightly dark and dingy interior"* was one explanation; *"it's a smoky, old man's pub"* was another.

and finally…

Clinical negligence dominates, and yes, Capsticks is steeped in the business of the NHS, but there's plenty to show that the training spans a range of work, albeit all for health sector clients. If the health of the nation interests you, it's an obvious choice.

Charles Russell

the facts

Location: London, Cheltenham, Guildford
UK ranking by size: 45
Total number of trainees: 26
Seats: 4x6 months
Alternative seats: None
Extras: Pro bono – Bethnal Green Law Centre

Charles Russell: a medium-sized commercial firm with offices in London, Guildford and Cheltenham. But roll it over and you'll see a thriving 200-year-old private client practice. What all this means for you, dear reader, is a thoroughly broad training.

dual identity

Charles Russell has had a renaissance. It's largely due to the growth and increasing profile of the firm's media and communications group in recent years, particularly in telecoms, where trainees say the firm "*punches above its weight against bigger players.*" That's exactly what our colleagues at *Chambers UK* tell us too! "*The media/telco team is one of the driving forces of the new-look Charles Russell,*" but it's not been at the expense of private client and family work or more traditional businesses. Attaching itself to the media and technology sectors as it has (ie sufficiently but not wholly), and winning clients like Scoot.com, ITN, Hello! and Cable & Wireless, CR has turned itself from a perfectly respectable commercial practice into a darned good one. It sees success in a range of areas from employment and defamation to sport and reinsurance.

One trainee concluded: "*Charles Russell's philosophy is very much one of cross-fertilisation between the commercial side and the private client side.*" Other than doing a corporate seat and a private client or family seat, trainees have a pretty free rein to flit from one side to another. For several, "*the range of work was the attraction. When I started my training contract, I didn't know what I wanted to do. It's good because there's decent commercial work, but you've also got the opportunity to try private client.*" The firm doesn't force trainees to opt for one or other part of its business, believing that the diversity will make them better lawyers.

roped in

As to what attracted trainees to the firm, we heard: "*You don't just get lost in obscurity, because it's not the size of Linklaters or Clifford Chance.*" Also, "*because it doesn't take on many trainees, you get more involved in cases, your individual responsibility is higher and you get treated more like a fee earner.*" Wherever possible, "*you get given your own files where you're responsible for the day to day management.*" Employment is especially "*hands-on*" in this respect, whilst over in litigation, PI cases particularly lend themselves to trainees. In property, you'll be given conveyances to handle, while in private client you'll get to draft wills and trust settlements. As for client contact, "*we get quite a bit of that in all departments, whether it's over the phone, in meetings or at marketing events.*" The firm has no paralegals so there will be times when you'll need to do photocopying, bundling and the like, but "*it's not overwhelming.*"

"*An average day for trainees is probably about 9am till 6pm,*" although corporate transactions do require a bit more of their time. One interviewee told us that, after a patch of gruelling hours, there was a bottle of champagne on his desk with a note from the partner saying thank you. Formal training sessions usually take place weekly and are video linked to the Guildford and Cheltenham offices.

on the carpet

The London office is in a 1970s tower block on New Fetter Lane, which just happens to be the old Maxwell building. "*Robert Maxwell had a helipad on the roof, but I've never seen it used,*" one source said. Our editor remembers that in Bob's day, the carpet on the executive floor had big 'M's woven into it – we trust it's been replaced! And speaking of being replaced, one cheeky trainee said, "*Everything round it is being demolished, so hopefully they'll get around to us eventually!*"

The social scene is "*there if you want it, but it's not forced on you.*" There are a number of sports teams – cricket, rugby, netball, softball and tennis – and client events stretch beyond the sporting to the purely social. Recently trainees went along to an evening of computer games and giant Connect 4. Firm-wide staff drinks are held once a month, alternating between the office and a nearby pub, The Cartoonist.

guildford's pulling powers

Six trainees have gravitated to the Guildford office, attracted by its good name and "*the fact that I wouldn't have to go to London to get a good training.*" Each undertakes four seats chosen from property, family, company/commercial, litigation (with specialist units including insolvency, employment and personal injury) and private client. As in Cheltenham, commercial property is the biggest department, but litigation also features high on the agenda. We got the impression that although this is essentially a standalone office with its own client base (private clients, some plcs, but mostly private companies and partnerships), there is now more interaction with London. *"To begin with we felt a bit like a satellite office, but things have changed quite drastically since we've been getting a lot more cross-referral work. If we've got the relevant expertise, we will help them out at cheaper rates."*

The office occupies a modern building just five minutes' walk from the town centre and the riverside pubs (The George Abbott and The Whitehouse). The trainees are a close group and enjoy regular firm-wide social events, often of a gloriously provincial nature. A spot of clay pigeon shooting and a night of skittles with colleagues no doubt reminds you exactly why you bypassed London.

cheltenham's greenhouse effect

The Cheltenham office is the smallest and takes one or two trainees at most each year, offering them six months in commercial property, company/commercial, litigation and private client. One trainee told us, *"You certainly don't have City hours here – you get to live more of a normal life."* As there are so few of them, it impacts on the style of training. *"We've got fewer assistants than in London too so it means that if your partner goes on holiday, often you'll get the responsibility that assistants might have taken up in a larger office."*

It sounds like the office is growing though: *"There's a new person here every time you blink"* and, consequently, it has moved into new premises. Cheltenham is a gorgeous regency town and Charles Russell is located in one of its smartest parts. *"The penthouse"* at the top of the new building is described as an air-conditioned greenhouse and seems ideally suited to client events. *"They're really keen to make you a part of it all here...there are a lot of younger people and it's like a very big family."* A nurturing one, no doubt. And for family nights out, just a short step away is Montpellier Wine Bar, Casa and in the summer the Imperial Gardens. Shopaholics and racing buffs beware: Cheltenham may seriously damage your wealth, especially in Gold Cup week when the town goes nuts.

Sadly, the retention rate in September 2002 was not as good as usual. All the qualifiers stayed in Cheltenham and Guildford, but in London it was six out of 11. Both the family and employment departments were oversubscribed and some others got offers they simply couldn't refuse – like an in-house job at Warner Music.

and finally...

Charles Russell is a classy mid-size firm that's shaken off its old school sensibilities and turned itself into an impressive media- and telecoms-led commercial outfit. It's small enough to retain a measure of intimacy and allow you to shine, yet it's big enough to get some cracking work.

Clarks

the facts
Location: Reading
UK ranking by size: 102
Total number of trainees: 10
Seats: 4x6 months
Alternative seats: None

Very much a Reading firm, with a client base drawn from the town's burgeoning corporate and IT scene, and with a sprinkling of exciting London names for good measure. Across the Thames Valley the name Clarks brings more to mind than sensible shoes.

best buddies

What it does bring to mind is a solid and diversified practice, including a particularly enviable reputation for employment work. The employment group even has its own website at employmentbuddy.com, which features little stickmen having their HR problems solved by those clever boffins from the Clarks employment team (*"We're very into preventive medicine,"* intoned one well-primed trainee). But there's more to Clarks than employment work. An environment group has recently been established, spanning the corporate and property teams, and the firm is also going great guns in planning, construction and pensions. While the last couple of years have seen the odd huffy departure and a few fancy foot shuffles in terms of strategy, things have been looking good since 2001 and the firm has been recruiting at all levels.

We found trainees remarkably relaxed on the subject of seat allocation. No scheming and backstabbing here; it's *"open to discussion, and they juggle it so people can do what they want at some point."* Don't get the impression, however, that you'll have a dizzying array of seats on offer. Remember that the core areas of the firm's practice are corporate, employment, commercial property and commercial litigation, and these could well end up being your four seats. But it's also possible to substitute one of the above for a seat in commercial/IP/IT, and there is planning and residential property work to be had in the commercial property seat…if that's what gets you excited. It's actually incredibly refreshing to find a mid-sized firm where all trainees who want to get their hands on a *"glamorous"* employment seat can do so.

talking things over (and over)

The training is well organised and our sources were happy with the level of feedback they received throughout. Ah yes…feedback! We hope you like being appraised as you'll have 26 (count 'em!) reviews in the course of your training contract. Yep, that's one a month plus two more for good measure, and trainees swear blind that supervisors never skimp and are always *"positive and encouraging."* One said: *"In appraisals we talked about everything, including what I hadn't had a chance to try and wanted to get involved in before the end of the seat."* And, as another trainee said, *"Don't apply here if you want to spend two years sitting quietly in a room just ploughing away."*

Although *"you have to be proactive in making the appraisals work for you,"* you'll find them paying dividends as you take on more and more work when you're seen to be ready for it. *"It's all about progressing* without feeling you're being pushed too fast." "If you're feeling confident, they'll let you have a go, but it's not seen as bad if you don't want to take on too much to start with."

hi ho silver lining

The Clarks kids get on well, but they don't necessarily have loads in common, unless you count a strong desire not to work in London and a commitment to the life part of the work/life balance. Clarks encourages flexible working (even among partners) and you'll be out of the office and home well in time for the news or *Hollyoaks*, whichever takes your fancy. It comes across as a very human place: *"There's a lot of interaction between different parts of the firm. We've grown a lot in the last three years, but it's maintained that family feeling. There's room to forge friendships."*

We're pleased to report that there are no nightmare seats where you'll be camped out next to the photocopier. There's a certain amount of low-level work, yet trainees here are the sort who will pull a cloud inside out looking for the silver lining; they insist that they always feel *"part of the team,"* even when putting bundles together. The level of client exposure will vary from relatively little in corporate to stacks in residential property, employment and litigation. *"When you get taken to a meeting with a client, most fee earners will introduce you and tell them that you're the contact for day-to-day issues, so you feel involved all the time."* While some firms hold trainees back from social contact with clients, expecting them to emerge, butterfly-like, on qualification, Clarks wants you to be presentable from day one. So whether you see it as a chore or you just can't wait to get your schmoozing hat on, the advice is to *"try to go along to as many marketing and client events as possible."* Two out of the three September 2002 qualifiers stepped into Clarks NQ positions.

the man from a.c.c.o.u.n.t.s.

The South East isn't a cheap place to live with no London weighting, but trainee salaries compare reasonably well with rivals in Reading. The office was described variously as *"full of character"* and

TRUE PICTURE OUR TOP 120 FIRMS

237

"*cramped.*" A listed building, it used to be Reading's Great Western Hotel. There is talk of a move to buildings that "*fit our profile better*" in the not-too-distant future, at which point the Great Western will put its legal days firmly behind it and become a hotel once again. After work, the trainees (together with a mysterious "*guy in accounts*") are unofficially responsible for getting the troops out of the office and into the pub. Don't worry if you're not a natural-born Club 18-30 rep; a social committee organises regular tomfoolery for all staff and partners.

and finally…

Clarks has a great reputation and it wins some jolly good business from the City off the back of it. If the Thames Valley is your kinda place, and particularly if you want to work for an independent partnership that's not run from elsewhere in the country, then step on up.

Clifford Chance

the facts

Location: London
UK ranking by size: 2
Total number of trainees: 245
Seats: 4x6 months
Alternative seats: Overseas seats, secondments
Extras: Pro bono – Hackney and Tooting Advice Centres, language training

It's the largest law firm in the world. It has more overseas offices than you can shake a stick at (32 in 19 countries) and plans for continued expansion. It's big. It's bold. It's Clifford Chance.

guide me

If Clifford Chance's size gives you the willies then fear not. Before you start your training contract you'll receive your own Lonely Planet guide to the firm, which is rather inventively called 'The Guide to Groups'. Compiled by trainees, it details the work, the hours and even the social scene of the various departments. Trainees also use the guide to identify their subsequent three seat choices. But why talk about choices, this is a finance firm isn't it?

Well, not exactly. Yes, finance is the only compulsory seat, and many trainees even do two of them, but you'll certainly see plenty of corporate work too. Corporate has come on a pace in the last few years and in London it is about two thirds of the size of the finance practice. The good news is that the definition of a finance seat is broad and "*can be ticked off by doing a foreign seat or something related like insolvency.*" As one trainee put it: "*The finance focus is a selling point for many people, but you must make sure that's right for you.*"

Niche departments like ECR (European competition regulation), CMT (communications media and technology), employment and IP are much loved and "*always oversubscribed.*" If you want to get into a niche department, "*talking to partners can be helpful; it gets you known and demonstrates your interest.*" Litigation has its fans and is easily attainable, although the downside is that "*it doesn't generally take so many people on qualification.*" If you express an interest in qualifying into litigation, you'll get a six-month seat there; otherwise you'll do only three months.

hours to cherish

Opinion is divided as to whether or not there's a stay-late culture. One trainee said, "*It depends on the seat, but the general attitude is you should enjoy the quiet times and put in the hours when it's busy.*" Others said: "*Some trainees find it hard to leave when they've finished their work because they feel guilty seeing others still working.*" Without question, the least popular seat is securitisation because of the hours. "*If you hear a nightmare story of someone having a bad seat, it inevitably comes from securitisation. Everyone's desperate to avoid it like the plague.*" One trainee gave us a different perspective: "*It has a reputation for being a very hard working department, but it's untrue that they work harder. This is recognised internally and they're trying to turn around the stigma it has,* which is unfair and counterproductive for attracting NQs. I had a brilliant supervisor, lots of responsibility and client contact. People who work the longest hours are often the most fun because they're relaxed around each other, although home lives can get a bit out of kilter."

how many noughts?

You'll share an office with your supervisor, and occasionally also with another junior lawyer. Supervisors tend to be assistants rather than partners, as they're closer to trainees in both age and the type of work they do. Many trainees were *"pleasantly surprised"* by the responsibility they were given. *"You have preconceptions of big firms that you're just going to be cannon fodder, but on the whole they give you work designed to prepare you for qualification."* One said: *"It's a balance between giving trainees as much responsibility as possible and needing them to do the crap tasks sometimes."* Firms like Clifford Chance handle deals of such high value that trainees can only ever expect to play a supporting role. *"They'll never ask a trainee to chat to this bank about selling this particular company; that's not going to happen. But at the same time, within that multimillion pound deal there might be other stuff for us to do such as dealing with certain parties and organising conditions precedent."*

Trainees rave about formal training, describing CC as *"very hot"* on the topic. Each department runs an induction programme and ongoing lectures. Some sources felt that appraisals varied *"markedly"* from the *"extremely detailed"* to the *"sketchy"* depending on the supervisor. *"My best supervisors have been frank in their praise and their criticism, which helps you move on and develop,"* one interviewee added.

i ride for clifford chance!

We heard a story about a graduate who spent the summer working for a large and well-known estate agency. The company was keen to motivate staff and improve productivity. Our young hero found himself participating in a workshop during which he and his colleagues watched film clips from Laurence Olivier's epic 1944 movie, Henry V. As the session proceeded, corporate pride began to swell until, ultimately, each estate agent stood up and proclaimed: "I ride for…." Well we won't tell you the name of the company, but the point is this: Clifford Chance knows that to get the best out of its young lawyers it has to enable them to buy into the corporate dream.

> "It wants to be the first to do things, not following the herd."

In their induction trainees are made fully aware of the firm's global strategy and goals. As one put it: *"CC definitely wants to be at the top of everything. That's very clear when you hear people in management speaking."* Trainees told us: *"If something momentous happens, we'll get an e-mail or a speech telling us what we're doing and where we're going – you really feel part of the firm."* One said, *"There's a lot to be said for the brand. The name Clifford Chance causes such an immediate reaction with a lot of people. It's very thrusting and plans to be the best at everything it can possibly be."* More specifically, *"you get a sense it wants to be the first to do things, not following the herd, but leading the pack for others to follow."* In this respect, the firm has an impressive track record. It led the way across the Atlantic with its merger with New York's Rogers & Wells and next year it will lead the way out of the City and into Canary Wharf. Trainees say, *"It's very innovative, progressive and forward-looking."* One trainee suggested: *"All the other magic circle firms are keen to achieve what Clifford Chance wants, but they don't say it as loudly, so people probably don't associate them with being as aspirational."*

We've mentioned in previous editions that it's almost a mantra that 'the needs of the firm come first' and, indeed, on the firm's website, it calls itself "A truly integrated global law firm where our people believe in one approach." While there are disturbing undertones of an Orwellian collective in the words "integrated" and "one approach," none of our interviewees sounded like spirit-broken Winston Smiths.

"Yes, there is that feeling of the needs of the firm being paramount, but that's more to do with seeing ourselves as one entity and trying to achieve something together as that entity. It's a positive thing rather than a sacrifice."

common ground

Do trainees have anything in common? One interviewee exclaimed: "*In some cases, I hope not!*" Apparently, they range from "*those who keep their heads down and don't speak*" right through to "*the loud ones who are in the pub every day.*" We agree with the trainee who said, "*There's none of the snobbery you might expect at a firm this size. It doesn't matter where you're from or how you talk.*" In keeping with the firm's global outlook, "*there are a lot of lateral hires who aren't English, which is great as it really adds to the international flavour of the firm.*"

We wondered if CC was a firm that would suit absolutely every applicant. Our sources had a few answers: "*If you want control over your time, knowing what you'll be doing every night of the week, you might have problems.*" Another said: "*Work has to be your very high priority here or you'll struggle.*" Another potential stumbling block relates to the work: "*If you don't like finance, you'll struggle, but you'd be stupid to apply here and not realise that finance is the fulcrum of the firm.*" And finally: "*Don't come here expecting a guarantee of qualifying into a niche department because the numbers dictate otherwise. Go to a specialist niche firm if you're thinking that.*" The firm has a good record for retaining its NQs: in 2002, 89 out of 102 stayed on.

fitter, happier, more productive…

In 2003, CC will leave Gotham City for Canary Wharf. An internal magazine, 'In the Dock', charts the progress of the new office development and boats have ferried employees down the Thames to check it out. There's even a virtual reality tour showing what it will all look like, "*awesome new fitness centre*" and all. In true firm style, one trainee said, "*Whatever we have here is going to be bigger and better in Canary Wharf – especially the gym.*"

While the new office will be on both the Jubilee Line and the DLR, some South London trainees, or those in West London, or in fact anywhere that isn't in the vicinity of East London believe they will have a longer journey to and from work. Others take a more robust view: "*It's not that big a deal. If you want to meet friends in the City, that's ten minutes on the Tube and it's 15 minutes to the West End.*"

on a flight to self-discovery

A seat abroad is virtually guaranteed, but competition for some locations is intense. If you mentioned languages in your TC application, your proficiency will be assessed. "*If you don't reach a certain standard with the language, you won't be going to any offices where it's the native tongue.*" CC is keen to make use of your talents, so "*if you speak Russian, it's unlikely you'll get to Hong Kong!*" Breathe easy if you only speak English – some offices require nothing more than devotion to duty. There are also overseas client secondments, like Airbus in Toulouse and EADS in Paris.

Certain seats need particular prior experience – many overseas postings are for finance-related work and a London finance seat is essential before you'll be considered for, say, capital markets in New York. "*English law tends to govern finance transactions worldwide, whereas corporate clients often use local lawyers to do their deals.*" The advantage of a stint overseas (apart from the obvious travel/living abroad) is that smaller offices offer more responsibility: many trainees find they are stretched in ways they'd never expected.

Needless to say, a high proportion of the work in London will be international and an overseas posting is not mandatory. "*Some people have mortgages, or partners they don't want to leave, or they've got children, or they've had a year or two travelling the world already.*" Back in the UK, client secondments abound.

save the rhino

Socially, "*it's just like university!*" "*The firm's big enough that you're bound to find a group of trainees you like.*" The Hogshead next door to Gotham City is a handy meeting point: "*You'll often find trainees in there.*" What about assistants and partners? *"They might be in there, but it's usually too packed to tell."* There's no shortage of bars to choose from on Friday nights, particularly in nearby Farringdon and Smithfield. And as for Canary Wharf? More of that next year…

We couldn't let one aspect of the firm's cultural life pass without mention. We have it on good authority that partners were recently sold off in a slave auction to raise money for endangered white rhino. We're not sure how much one would set you back or indeed which of the two species has a thicker hide. Answers on a postcard please.

and finally…

If size matters to you, Clifford Chance wins hands down. If you want a trailblazing firm with world vision, it is exactly that. Just bear in mind that finance and corporate deals power the firm and, at times, the job will feel consuming.

Clyde & Co

the facts
Location: London, Guildford, Cardiff
UK ranking by size: 36
Total number of trainees: 40
Seats: 4x6 months
Alternative seats: Overseas seats, secondments
Extras: Language training

Clyde & Co acts for clients in over 135 countries and has offices in Athens, Paris, Caracas, Dubai, Hong Kong, Singapore and St Petersburg. With international practice strengths in shipping and insurance, you could be forgiven for thinking there's little else on offer. You'd be wrong of course.

choices choices

The majority of trainees work in the London office, with another half a dozen or so in Guildford. The firm is happy for you to move in either direction to do one seat or more. A heavy M4 corridor theme defines the Guildford office (*"Given the location of the office there's more of a focus on technology companies down here"*), but by and large, most of the seats available in London are also available. *"A lot of people think the Guildford office is the bum deal before they get there,"* one source said, *"but everyone who works there knows it's a cushy deal. It overlooks rolling hills, the interior is beautiful and it's a small office so everyone gets on really well."* Ooh tough choice!

Talking of choices, the HR mob *"work very hard to give you something you've asked for."* Officially, there are no compulsory seats, not even in the firm's core areas of shipping or insurance, but in practice most trainees end up in one or other area, if not both at some point. In London, we were told: *"Although you can avoid doing a shipping seat, inevitably you will do a seat with an insurance core to its business – it's a huge umbrella, covering medico-legal through to construction."* Another agreed: *"Some people do two types of insurance seat."*

Shipping seats are *"always popular,"* employment has become *"very trendy"* and there's considerable interest in the corporate seats. *"There's not a huge uptake for property. People get put off by the way it's taught at college."* However, *"most people who do a property seat end up liking it"* as *"you get lots of client contact and run your own files, which you get less of in litigation as the cases are generally bigger and there's more at stake."*

the lost wallet

The majority of trainees have their own offices. This is in keeping with (and perhaps even the reason for) the idea that you'll have a good deal of independence in your work. One trainee said, *"There's responsibility from the word go… They've got you case handling early on, and they want people who aren't afraid to do that."* In terms of hours, we learned that most trainees stay *"till sixish, maybe later if there's a completion or a hearing on."* Corporate was said to have extended hours on a *"sporadic"* basis – *"there's a lot of sitting around, but when a deal comes in you need to stay and do the work, particularly if the client is in another country."* Having said that, *"your work is what counts,* not how long you stay in the office." As for weekends, we were amused to hear one trainee's story: "*I've come in twice on weekends, once for work and once to collect my wallet that I'd forgotten!*" We hope they had understanding friends on Friday night…

hog-tied
We asked our interviewees to mull over the identity of the typical trainee. "*The general theme that comes across is life experience*," said one in response. "*Most of my intake have other languages or have travelled the world – there aren't many who have done the usual route of university and the LPC.*" The firm wants people who are up for a challenge. "*Sometimes there is a bit of fear, but you can go to a senior assistant or a partner to talk about things. They're conscious that they're giving you a lot of responsibility from early on and are attracted to people who want that. In this respect, the claims made in the recruitment material are genuine and this may put some people off, but those people may not be right for the firm.*"

Responsibility comes incrementally, and while you will be given your own cases in a number of seats, everything will be checked before it goes out. "*There's a good level of decision making, particularly on lower level claims. You get to discuss tactics with the partner rather than just being told what to do.*" Another commented: "*There's never been an occasion where I've been just petrified or hog-tied not knowing what to do or where to go.*"

There are six-monthly reviews and the option of a mid-seat review, although many trainees don't bother to exercise it. "*They're really good at coming up and saying 'good job' or 'what about doing it this way next time', so you've generally got a pretty good idea of how you're doing.*" We learn that tedious document management doesn't feature that much, as a rule. "*We all get bundles and photocopying to do from time to time, particularly in big cases, but Clydes is really good at getting paralegals in to do grunt work. They know trainees are too valuable to be shut in a room doing that stuff.*"

Many of our interviewees had a pre-existing interest in litigation, while others were drawn in by the firm's medium size ("*I didn't want one of the massive firms*") and "*pretty small*" trainee intake ("*it's more personal and allows you to make yourself known to people*"). And, of course, it offers international travel! Three overseas offices currently offer seats – four in Dubai (two corporate, one litigation and one secondment to an airline) and one each in Hong Kong (a corporate seat) and Piraeus (a shipping seat). The firm "*never has trouble filling the Dubai seats*" as there are apparently "*lots of perks.*" Great apartment, car, free mobile phone…no wonder they're champing at the bit. "*It's a combination of good work and a nice lifestyle.*" Back in Old Blighty, there's a regular six-month corporate secondment to a pharmaceuticals company. September 2002 retention figures were better than ever, with 19 of the 20 qualifiers being offered jobs and 18 accepting them.

ship ahoy and tup love
The consensus is that the London office building is "*not the world's most attractive office block.*" It's described as being "*retro 70s orange*" and like "*a square doughnut with a hole in the middle.*" The best bits overlook Tower Bridge, the London Eye and the Lloyd's building. There's simply no contest between the London office building and the one in Guildford. The latter is "*a very pleasant place to work. It's got leafy surroundings and a country dacha feel.*"

In London, there's a free bar in the firm's canteen every Thursday. It's open to everyone and is said to be "*very handy*" from a trainee's wallet point. One particularly appreciative trainee said, "*I didn't go last Thursday and that's the first time I've been home in the light and sober on a Thursday in all the time I've been here!*" Rather appropriately, the pub down the road is called The Ship and it's "*a bit of a favourite – but only because it's close.*" In addition to various sporting endeavours, there are events such as bowling and trips to the races.

Guildford is "*a town suited to meeting up at lunchtime.*" The venue of choice is The Tup, which is, conveniently, just over the road but there's no major evening social scene. About a year ago the regular Guildford office drinks evening went from monthly to quarterly. "*Not enough people came along and those that* did were the same people every time." The less is more principle was applied successfully and *"you see more people coming along now, from throughout the firm."*

and finally…

If you're looking for a truly international market leader in shipping and insurance, then Clyde & Co fits the bill admirably. It will give you a broad commercial training, but be prepared for lots of litigation.

CMS Cameron McKenna

the facts

Location: London, Bristol, Aberdeen
UK ranking by size: 12
Total number of trainees: 108
Seats: 4x6 months
Alternative seats: Overseas seats, secondments
Extras: Pro bono – Islington Law Centre, language training

CMS Cameron McKenna is a top ten City firm offering trainees a top-level salary, big-name clients and overseas seats. It sells itself on its 'nice place to work' reputation, but we wanted to dig a little deeper. Choosing between those top firms is tough…

smile, you're at camerons

Let's examine the caring, *"friendly and cuddly"* reputation. The trainees all talked about it: *"Most people choose it because it's a top ten firm, but on the boundaries – you get all the perks of being with a well-known firm, but can still have a life."* There's a sense that trainees want the big time, but not the really big time: *"You get paid as well as at the magic circle, but you are not expected to deliver as much."* For the second year running, Cameron McKenna won a coveted place in *The Sunday Times'* '100 Best Companies To Work For' survey and each year it conducts *"taking stock surveys"* of its own. *"There are quite a lot of surveys on attitudes,"* said one source, *"covering everything from atmosphere to work-load."* The last one has resulted in a new intranet and regular e-mails from the managing partner, each designed to promote better communication between departments. *"The marketing department has gone a bit bananas with posters all around the firm – it's really going for a community atmosphere."*

"Trainees are not the sort who'd give you a big smile and then as soon as they're round the corner would stab you in the back. We'd make boring TV if we were all on Big Brother." They admit to being competitive over the most popular seats, but are *"not underhand or cut-throat."* *"Willing to work, but not ambitious to the point of driving anyone into the ground"* sums it up. *"There's no one especially arrogant or over-confident – it's not the firm's style – it has a more restrained and pally approach."* Everyone we spoke to came across as balanced and charming; they lacked arrogance and were keen to help us with our research. In short, they were bright and thoroughly likeable…but the 'oomph' that we sense in trainees at some firms wasn't as pronounced.

We were forever hearing how everyone is *"so, so friendly,"* and that the firm's a place where you can *"just be yourself."* This laissez-faire attitude seemed slightly at odds with the firm's stated aim of pushing forwards under its CMS banner. Indeed, some trainees were so laid-back that we weren't sure if they'd grasped the idea that the CMS part of the name was integrally bound up with the firm's international strategy and business, rather than just being the logo for *"a free bag and video to do with the new image."*

a shot in the dark

Hot on the heels of the 1997 merger between Cameron Markby Hewitt and McKenna & Co, the firm undertook a programme of alliance building to boost its existing network of overseas offices. CMS means very different things to different trainees. Of the merger and then the alliance, one told us: *"The firm took two leaps in a short space of time; it tried to take on two hurdles at once. It now needs to reinforce what the CMS alliance actually is."* Those who go overseas for a spell, see the reality of the alliance much more readily than the stay-at-homes: *"Back in London we have less contact with CMS firms, but [overseas], a lot more of our work is cross-border."*

Chambers Global's International Power Law Firm of the Year 2002

The Hong Kong seat is the most competitive, as *"people see it as a bit glam."* Prague is also reasonably popular, but with places like Warsaw, Aberdeen (oil & gas/BP secondment) and even Bristol (insurance/ banking litigation/corporate recovery), *"people usually turn away in fright."* But, *"HR still has to fill the seats. They tell you politely, and you have to take it, if they have decided you're the one!"* Some of the alliance firms offer seats – Amsterdam, Rome and Paris, for example. One trainee said thoughtfully, *"We've got CMS firms throughout Europe, but we've not got the New Yorks and Singapores, etc. When students see an alliance of different law firms, they assume it's slightly different to us having offices in these places."* Another trainee wasn't convinced that the alliance affected trainees in any concrete way: *"It's got the potential to be very good in the future, but at the moment it's a marketing gimmick – free pens, shot glasses and T-shirts. From a training perspective I've not noticed a difference."* Sounds like some international strategy sessions for trainees are needed.

mighty morphin' power rangers

The lukewarm interest in overseas seats that we perceived shouldn't be taken as an indication that Cameron McKenna is a johnny-come-lately to the international game. It was the first UK firm to show any interest in Eastern Europe…years ago. But Eastern Europe, and its huge potential for (amongst other things) energy and projects work, is not at the forefront of most trainees' minds. Maybe attitudes will change as and when countries like the Czech Republic and Poland join the EU. If you have an interest in Eastern Europe or projects and energy work, make a beeline for this firm – we doubt that you'll find better. Its electricity sector work recently earned it a *Chambers Global* gong – International Power Firm 2002.

If six months abroad doesn't appeal, you can happily undertake four seats in London and cover plenty of ground. Our interviewees normally chose the firm because it offers *"opportunities to sample a good few areas at a high standard."* In past years we've hit on interviewees for whom the firm's sterling reputation in pharmaceuticals/healthcare or construction were the real draw for them, but we must have missed that breed in our random sampling this year. Although these departments were dented by some high-profile partner losses in the last two years, they remain very strong and are still market leaders.

three is the magic number

Trainees understand the firm's stated aim is to grow its corporate and finance practices. *"In past years, energy, projects and construction (EPC) has been quite strong, but banking and corporate are not far behind now."* No seat is compulsory (other than the Law Society's contentious requirement) but HR will guide you towards doing at least two or three of the main groups – corporate, banking and finance, insurance, property and commercial.

The system of seat allocation gets a fairly steady thumbs up. With a large trainee population, you're always going to get mutterings of *"winners and losers,"* and we're absolutely sure that HR plays a straight hand, but there's an indication that various departments do have influence. Some lobby hard to avoid getting first-seaters, preferring trainees with a little experience under their belts. If the department is not that popular, it can lead to seasoned trainees feeling they are kicking their heels towards the end of their contracts. One trainee's tip: *"Be vocal as to what you want from early on. Go out and put your marker on certain departments. It's a similar game to politics: negotiate a bit; say 'OK, you can send me to property, if I get what I want'."*

Trainees confirmed (again) this year that the third

seat is seen to be pivotal to the two years' training. "*A lot of emphasis is placed on seat three. It is kind of the be-all and end-all. By your third seat you have been here a year and it's naturally the one you want to qualify into. The feeling is that it is vital to get a third seat you really want.*" A very healthy 31 out of the 35 September 2002 qualifiers stayed on with the firm, spreading themselves right across all areas of practice.

near-death experiences

Getting on and getting ahead requires you to show initiative. "*If you're seen as a safe pair of hands, they will give you a go.*" Overwhelmingly, trainees believe that "*partners and seniors have been there to give up their time and are willing to explain things to you. Trainees are not there just to do the donkey work; they are there to learn.*" But, as with all firms handling high-value work, there's (sometimes mundane) document management to be taken care of. "*The lows come when you're not quite sure why you are doing something and it seems like a really tedious job, but you'll be a part of a big team and you will come out the other end into the light.*" The litigation department has paralegals, but according to our sources, corporate and property could use a few more.

However, there's absolutely no shortage of formal training sessions and HR are pretty hot on attendance: "*The training programme is compulsory and you have to justify why you're not going, if you miss one.*"

riotous behaviour

Corporate seats can bring long hours, but elsewhere 9.15am-6.30/6.45pm is fairly standard. After work there are several favourite pubs (all named after body parts and sharp implements) from the Hogshead, to the Butchers Hook & Cleaver. However, the pub that's dearest of all is the unpretentious Hand & Shears (aka 'The Handy Beers'): "*Everyone goes there from the top corporate partners down.*" Although "*quite aware of a hierarchy,*" trainees join in with team lunches (partners and all) and every couple of months 'Atrium drinks' means firm-wide "*mingling at every level.*" At the banking department's Christmas party, it's the trainees' duty to perform a skit at the partners' expense.

Cameron McKenna has its feet and hands in the same pool as the biggest City firms, and its management head is facing overseas, but we reckon its heart is still in the land of the mid-sized firm. One source concluded: "*I'd call it a young firm and it's still got a fair bit to learn. It maintains a medium-sized firm feel while doing big firm work.*" Another compared it with the giants next door: "*We're not important enough to get anti-capitalists rioting outside our front door. Clifford Chance is a totally different operation in every way, shape and form.*"

and finally…

Some students shun the magic circle, and many of them join firms like CMS Cameron McKenna. What's crucial for them is that they will 'enjoy' both their work and the community into which they walk on day one of their training contract. The firm inspires great affection in its new recruits; their message is join them if you want to stay human.

Cobbetts

the facts

Location: Manchester, Leeds
UK ranking by size: 53
Total number of trainees: 23
Seats: 4x6 months
Alternative seats: Secondments

Cobbetts is a large, independent Manchester firm that's now in Leeds, following a recent merger with Read Hind Stewart. We say 'independent' because many of the big-hitters in Manchester are branch offices of national firms. Cobbetts is best known for its property expertise, but handles plenty more besides.

corn on the cobbetts

"*It's too cheesy – when we first started all everyone said was 'it's such a friendly firm'.*" Oh puh-lease, this is the kind of corny stuff your poor *True Picture* team hear day in day out. We simply glaze over, nod politely and move swiftly on to the question about typical working hours. But with Cobbetts trainees it goes on – "*It's really friendly…it just is: it's ridiculous*"…And on… "*Everybody is really friendly and the trainees are happy and all get on together.*" OK, we get the picture. What's more, it appears to be love at first sight: "*I loved the firm on interview and was desperate to get in.*" Even trainees who had done vac schemes elsewhere were converted to Cobbetts, after just one half-day interview.

We continued along the Cobbetts path to joy to find out more about the firm. Trainees say it is quite traditional in some respects – since swallowing up part of the competition (Slater Heelis back in 1998), Cobbetts is now Manchester's oldest firm and has some "*core traditional values*" at its heart. "*It's a solid place to work: trustworthy,*" but not stuffy. Honesty and integrity are valued: "*It sounds old-fashioned, but we're expected to be respectful of each others' views and feelings.*"

But times they are a-changing and the firm it is a-growing. Nobody takes over a Leeds practice without a plan in mind, after all. However, Cobbetts seems determined to maintain its intimate feel: "*It pays a lot of attention to the people within the firm, and is trying to retain that while expanding.*" Without fail our interviewees cited the potential for growth as one of the best reasons to apply to Cobbetts. "*It energises you that the firm is expanding.*" There's a collective ambition, in the manner of The Three Musketeers (one for all, etc.) rather than one-upmanship amongst trainees. "*They're not the types to screw others to get ahead.*" No one will be applying for Big Brother 4, then…

murder on the courtroom floor

As commercial property accounts for around half of the firm's work and the property department is huge (27 partners at the last count), each trainee will do a property seat in their first year. Clients range from housing associations and house builders through to commercial developers and investment funds. If property is your bag, this firm will be heaven. Last year it was involved in Whitbread's sale of its entire public house portfolio (over 3,000 valued at £1.625 billion) and the transfer of almost 10,000 homes from the local authority in Blackburn.

Your other first-year seat will be some variety of litigation, the idea being that the Law Society's requirements can be fulfilled in the first year. There's plenty of opportunity to gain advocacy experience in the litigation seat – trainees typically go down to the County Court and do repossession hearings in front of a district judge in chambers. Cobbetts also handles agency hearings for other firms, which aren't based in Manchester. This is a real confidence booster as "*there is often a solicitor on the other side.*" "*The first time I thought I was going to die – but some DJs are quite nice and tell you what to do,*" one source said.

Second-years have a better idea of what they want, having had a year to look around. Their seats could include corporate, employment (as a part of a 12-lawyer team acting for employers and execs), the popular commercial seat (which includes IP and IT) and various other options such as private client, tax and pensions. The odd mini-secondment crops up with banks and larger corporate clients. With the advent of the Leeds office, trainees will have to be a bit more flexible as they may now be required to do a seat there. Leeds will also have its own recruits, and we understand it is looking for three per year initially.

schmoozly does it

In such an "*open and friendly*" firm (are you bored of these quotes yet?) it is not surprising that our sources felt well supported. "*We weren't just thrown to the lions and my work was checked, down to individual letters.*" The level of responsibility given to trainees depends on their particular supervisor, but it is there for the taking most of the time. "*You're allowed to run things yourself, if you want to, but if you're stuck then there's always someone to help.*" Trainees share a room with another lawyer, be it a partner or an assistant, and client contact is positively encouraged from day one. Among the firm's well known clients are Matalan, Whitbread, *The Manchester Evening News*, British Rail Property Board,

Burger King and Lancashire County Council.

It's not all work, work, work: trainees attend marketing events to schmooze with clients. There is certainly work to be done though; the hours tend to be 8.30am–5.30pm and late nights have been known in corporate and litigation, but infrequently. Apparently there is one training supervisor who doesn't believe trainees should work beyond nine to five.

all talk

Trainees receive IT training and skills seminars focusing on things like presentation, accounts and time management. Outside speakers frequently give lectures, perhaps on other disciplines, such as stockbroking, to show how the role of solicitor interlinks with others. Every month in the first year, trainees meet the training manager *"for a handholding exercise"* and to discuss their work and how they are getting on with their team. There are more substantial reviews at three- and six-month intervals, when the training supervisor fills in a form, which the trainees discuss with them, then with the training manager and the training partner. Phew! The upshot is *"you always have a point of contact and it's really reassuring."* The qualification process went well in September 2002, with ten of the 12 NQs staying at the firm.

24-hour party people

For a paltry £2 a month (deducted from your salary and then the whole fund matched by the partners), a social club ensures that the firm is wined, dined and whisked off to such glamorous destinations as Chester Races, Alton Towers and the Commonwealth Games. And at a bargain price too…a three-course meal for £5? You can't say fairer than that. Folk from all levels of the firm turn up for these events. One source said, *"Thankfully, we don't go out as much as we did when we first joined."* They didn't mean that the trainee social life is awful; au contraire, it is enthusiastically rated as *"brilliant,"* if a little full-on at the start. On a Friday night it's *"guaranteed"* that trainees and junior solicitors will make an appearance in the city centre bars across the road. *"It used to be All Bar One, but now Chez Gérard are doing two for one…"* Enough said. In fact, any night of the week you're likely to see a familiar face across the road. *"When you qualify, you shift to socialising with people in your department after work on a Friday,"* but coincidentally this often ends up across the road in Chez Gérard too. Strange.

Cobbetts' social network is strong enough to supply your whole social life if you've just moved to the area. Another bonus of being a trainee in Manchester is the city's Trainee Solicitors Group, which arranges its very own (generously sponsored) social events. And it would be plain rude not to mention Manchester's nightlife – perhaps the biggest pull of all.

and finally…

If you set on Manchester, you can't afford to neglect Cobbetts. It's known for property work, but don't let that put you off if land law is just too painful. The corporate and commercial practice is broad and expanding – you need not contemplate a life involving the District Land Registry forever. 'Balanced' sums up the firm – in terms of the quality of work, the people, your life, the universe and everything.

Coffin Mew & Clover

the facts
Location: Portsmouth, Southampton, Fareham, Gosport.
UK ranking by size: 109
Total number of trainees: 9
Seats: 6x4 months
Alternative seats: None

At the height of the Pokémon craze, thousands of Japanese schoolchildren accidentally surfed onto Coffin Mew & Clover's website. Doubtless they made little sense of it and were enormously disappointed. We trust our readers will find more to interest them. Indeed, if your heart is set on a legal career on the South Coast and you've not yet checked this firm out, now is the time to do so.

evolution

Coffin Mew & Clover has been around since the late 19th century and, until recently, it operated from a host of small offices scattered along the coast. It's now concentrated on four sites: Portsmouth, where it has a brand new home in North Harbour; Southampton, where its new premises are described as altogether "*more upmarket;*" Fareham on the side of the M27; and Gosport. One trainee confirmed our suspicions by saying, "*It's becoming a bit less High Street, if you get my drift.*" We certainly do. Actually, CM&C has been 'in the commercial way' for some time now, pushing itself forward and focusing more on corporate clients. Smart, new offices are simply the most recent step in the evolutionary process.

Its business can't be defined in a snappy four-word sentence, so you'll forgive us for listing its main practice areas: corporate/commercial, employment, commercial litigation, property, social housing, PI, clinical negligence and mental health, family, crime, trusts & probate, IP and finance/business regulation. The message here is 'opportunity'. Even if you turn up on your first day with little more than vague ideas, chances are, by the end of your contract, you'll know exactly where you want to qualify. "*You certainly get a broad training,*" said one source. After mandatory four-month spells in property, litigation and commercial, your desires will be taken into account for the remaining year. Generally, seat allocation works well: "*Even those who are focused on one thing can usually be accommodated.*" Occasionally, a seat won't be to your liking and you might "*feel like you are going backwards,*" but in any firm with a varied practice there has to be a bit of give-and-take.

costa del solent

The client base stretches from Joe Public to regional businesses and housing associations, universities and health trusts. If you can't find something to suit, you're probably looking at the wrong part of the country and the wrong career. "*Everyone comes here with different ideas,*" said one trainee. "*Some definitely want to do crime; others want to do litigation.*" We noted a corporate/commercial leaning amongst trainees; PI and private client have fewer devotees but offer responsibility. In private client, "*you get a lot of exposure to wills, tax planning, probate, charity work and some pensions.*" In a CoCo seat, you'll be more restrained in what you can do and will work closely with the partners. "*You have less client exposure but it's a really good seat – management buyouts and things like that, some employee share issues but it's more corporate than commercial.*"

You will be required to travel. Before you rush out and buy a flight bag and posh leather cover for your passport, let us clarify that you will be travelling around the south of England. Even the pile of shells known locally as the Isle of Wight doesn't yet have passport control, so keep calm. Certain seats are only on offer in one of the offices (eg, commercial lit in Southampton, crime in Portsmouth), so you may end up bouncing between the various sites during the course of your training. Additionally, trainees are sent on external courses and so, all in all, a car will certainly be handy. "*I wouldn't suggest trying to do without one,*" warned one source. You might want to invest in air con in your motor: "*There's no dress-down policy, not even on a hot day on the Costa del Solent.*"

what's cooking?

The trainee population reflects the eclectic nature of the firm's business: not all are local, some are mature and they all seem to be looking for something different. As one put it: "*The firm is a mix of different sorts of law and different sorts of clients, and all the people here are very different.*" It doesn't take a genius to work out that with all this variety, you'll pick up some pretty useful skills over the two years. In family or crime your client handling skills will be road tested daily; in PI and property you'll learn file management; in employment you'll find real life applications for the law; and in corporate you'll discover how teams bring a deal to fruition. After two years in a general practice of this type, you'll feel all plump and rounded.

Several pubs on Portsmouth's recently developed Gunwharf Quays have become regular ISPs (imbibed-spirit providers) for the Coffin crew. We also liked the sound of nights in though: *"There's a good trainee network and we have dinner at different people's houses fairly regularly."* We've pictured these trainees as a clutch of Jamies and Nigellas who love nothing better than to cook up a storm for their friends. However, we suspect that this breed of socialising may, in part, be a product of the size of trainee salaries. But there's good news: sponsorship is offered for law school so you won't have quite the same debt to haul around as trainees at smaller firms. As for the September 2002 qualifiers, two out of the three stayed on with the firm.

and finally...

When considering the work/life balance, it's clear that at Coffin Mew & Clover the scales are tipped toward life: you'll be expected to work hard, but not to bust a gut. You'll not have to choose between different types of practice until you approach qualification; so perhaps the most difficult choice will be between the red and white of The Saints and the blue and white of Pompey. Our old man said be a Pompey fan...

Coudert Brothers

the facts

Location: London
UK ranking by size: 116
Total number of trainees: 8
Seats: 4x6 months
Alternative seats: Overseas seats
Extras: Language training

This multinational partnership was started in New York in 1853 by the three sons of a French immigrant. International expansion started as early as 1879 when Coudert Frères was launched in Paris. With 31 offices in 19 countries, you can see why it prefers the tag 'multinational' to 'US' firm.

open borders

The London office opened in 1960 and handles a wide range of work, including corporate/commercial, banking and finance, competition, property and litigation. In addition to a compulsory litigation seat, trainees must complete two other seats from these core areas and there is a decent chance of seat abroad. Usually it's in Brussels (described by one trainee as *"the default overseas seat"*) although from time to time Moscow may pop up or occasionally Hong Kong or Washington when business needs arise.

Coudert's London office is part of a large network and the international aspect of the job is evident on a daily basis with trainees liaising with lawyers from all sorts of jurisdictions. As one said, *"I've forged relationships with Coudert people in different offices around the world."* Our sources also stressed the *"great deal of overlap"* between departments in terms of work. *"It's a small office environment, and because of the way the departments are arranged geographically, they're not as separate and distinct as they might be in larger firms."* One trainee explained: *"In any one seat, particularly in corporate or banking, you could get experience of three or four departments. You might be doing banking, telco, competition and corporate work all in the one seat."*

international time zones

In terms of client contact, *"you're encouraged to sit in on conference calls,"* although face to face contact is minimal at trainee level: *"It's the nature of the beast, I guess – a lot of our clients are based abroad."* Regarding hours, a typical response was that *"on an average day I'm in at 9/9.30am and I leave between 6/6.30pm. It could be earlier or later – it's swings and roundabouts."* At some point you'll hit late nights and weekends: *"The fact that we have offices globally means that quite often a major deal will involve more than one office"* and, therefore, more than one time zone. Traditionally, corporate and banking have the longest hours; one trainee said, *"When I was doing corporate, there were a couple of months when I was there till about 9pm or 10pm each evening."* However, they're not driven like slaves. *"You pull your weight when the work comes in, but you're not expected to put on a show and be here 12 hours a day if you're not needed."*

compact and bijou

The property department has more domestic clients and offers direct contact with them. We also learned of an in-house conveyancing function, which sees trainees in the property department handling their colleagues' residential conveyancing. *"You take instructions from the staff then run the files while you're doing a property seat. You learn about file management, client care and how to bill, while also getting to work on larger property deals."* The rationale is that the firm *"doesn't have too many small standalone deals"* for trainees to work on, so the scheme gives them that exposure. Trainees raved about the property department, with one interviewee stating: *"It's probably the most organised and well-run department to do a seat in."*

Property takes one trainee at a time, whereas corporate and litigation vary the numbers according to workload and *"where people want to be."* Trainees don't share offices with their supervising partner; instead they sit with an associate. In terms of responsibility, we learned that *"it's pitched at a good level."* One trainee said, *"You'll get given work by partners where they think you're the best person to do it and also where they think it will stretch you."* Another explained what he liked about Coudert: *"We don't have a massive number of trainees and the firm's pretty compact anyway, so you pretty much know everyone."* Along these lines, *"the firm's structure and size means that the work and feedback you get is probably a lot better than at some of the larger firms." "You don't just get fed scraps,"* although, of course, more menial tasks do need to be done from time to time. *"We don't have a massive team of paralegals to do all the grunt work, so it's all hands on deck."* Partners and all, apparently.

Feedback is said to be *"constant and constructive,"* while on a more formal basis there are mid-seat and end-of-seat reviews with your supervisor. Additionally, there are regular lunches with the good folk in HR so that trainees can *"bring up things they may not necessarily be happy bringing up with their supervisor."* As for formal training sessions, there are videos or talks *"officially on three Wednesdays out of four."* All carry a three-line whip.

older, wiser and multilingual

The average Coudert trainee is a little older than you might find elsewhere. *"Most have done something before coming to law, either working or travelling,"* said one source. *"You tend to get a lot of responsibility very quickly, which may be why they don't tend to take 21-year-olds just out of law degrees. They want people who'll feel comfortable calling clients and coming in to work at a certain level on a deal."* In addition, *"there's a strong international aspect"* to all the trainees in that they have *"languages coupled with life experience."* One trainee said, *"The only 'young' trainees come from an international background and speak other languages fluently, which shows experience in itself."*

As to those who'd struggle to fit in, *"it's probably not the best place for someone who expects everything to be scheduled and organised on a timetable."* In this vein, *"it's a small office, so people expect you to be proactive and take the initiative a bit more in terms of seeking out work and fixing problems yourself."* Proactivity pays off: *"When people realise you're genuinely interested in an area of work, they'll give you a lot of responsibility... as long as you show you're capable, of course!"* Of course.

no arm in it

The purpose-built office has five floors, with Coudert the sole occupant The interior is *"not extravagant"* but *"fairly modern, clean and comfortable."* Typically for a 'US' firm in London, the office is permanently dressed-down. There's just one criticism: *"The lifts are terrible."* Oh dear, how so? *"They're temperamental – they sometimes go all the way up to the top by themselves and they don't recognise an arm."* Eh? *"If you stick an arm in the closing doors, they won't open."* The office sits close to Tate Modern and the Millennium Bridge, over which *"a few core people who are real fans"* lead regular lunchtime expeditions. *"You've got enough time to walk over, have lunch, do some shopping and walk back."*

"Everyone gets on well, but different departments are on different floors." Perhaps with the intention of combating this spatial separation, drinks are laid on once a month to enable staff to *"mix as a firm."* In terms of local watering holes, many Coudert people divide their time between The Hatchet, near Mansion House and The Bell near Cannon Street. We also heard about a *"very, very good theatre organiser"* within the firm who arranges nights out for staff to see different plays and go for drinks afterwards.

and finally…

Coudert is evidently keeping its youngsters happy – three out of the four qualifiers stayed in September 2002 with the fourth moving to Brussels. As one said, *"The attraction is the quality of the work, the responsibility and the relationships you can build with everyone from IT to the partners."* If you want international work in a small City office, we suggest you find out more.

Cripps Harries Hall

the facts
Location: Tunbridge Wells, London
UK ranking by size: 83
Total number of trainees: 14
Seats: usually 6 of varying length
Alternative seats: None

Set in an area of *"outstanding natural beauty,"* this Kent firm offers a slice from many different pies. The firm celebrated its 150th anniversary in 2002 and has a proud heritage, but trainees are keen to stress that Cripps Harries Hall has moved firmly into the 21st century. According to one (who clearly had a knack for *Student Guide* sound bites), *"The firm knows where it comes from and where it is going."* We thought we'd tag along for the ride…

cripps with everything

The firm's butter is spread on several slices of bread, with about 60% of work issuing from the commercial, finance and investment departments, and the remainder split between dispute resolution and private client. Cripps has made lateral hires to strengthen its teams, and it has just taken on its first IP partner to head up a unit in the corporate department. It has a small London presence, but as a trainee you won't spend time there. Trainees consider that the firm's real strengths lie in commercial property and private client work, but with a flexible training system and plenty of departments to choose from, Cripps is an ideal place for those who want to test a variety of waters before taking the plunge at qualification.

"There is no standard trainee diet. Although you make a plan at the start, it is subject to change." People start out being pencilled in for six seats with the longest stint in commercial property and the shortest, by virtue of its popularity, tending to be employment. Check out the work areas online and you will see the firm handles just about everything from wills to whistle-blowing, neighbour disputes to PFI projects, and agriculture to data protection. If you were the MD of a newly merged company that was going belly up, and you wanted a quick divorce, and to amend your will and evict some unruly tenants, then Cripps would be your one-stop shop. *"When I was looking for a training contract I didn't know what I wanted to do so coming to a place like this is ideal. You can't avoid doing some kind of property seat, and you have to do some litigation, but beyond that you're pretty much given free rein. So long as you make your preferences known, they'll always try and put you where you want to be,"* reported one trainee.

video kids

Work-wise, *"you'll get whatever you feel you can take on,"* but rest assured that *"everything is closely monitored."* Training is taken *"very seriously"* and includes a mix of external lectures and video seminars to keep lawyers apace with developments. The IT team is also on the ball, and you can book in for training if you can't work out your spreadsheets or how to win at minesweeper. There are plenty of training sessions to fill your lunch breaks: "*Some are very helpful, some are useless, airy-fairy things like communication skills,*" said one trainee who already knew how to speak their mind. The hours are "*pretty decent,*" averaging 9am-6pm, but "*if you leave at 5.15pm you won't get shouted at.*" One trainee was keen to dispel the idea we put in last year's True Picture that you could always count on being home in time for Neighbours. Apparently, if you are a Ramsey Street aficionado you'll need to know how to programme your VCR.

The office itself is split between five separate buildings ("*all within ten yards of each other*"), which means that to speak with some of your colleagues you may have to look both ways and cross the road. Although it may be harder to get to know everyone, at least you get the chance to stretch your legs. Despite the age of the firm, the offices themselves are "*modern, clean and not at all olde worlde. They're user-friendly and a nice atmosphere in which to work.*"

tunbridge wails?

One thing that several of our sources brought up was the trainee salary, which, while not meagre, doesn't seem to take into account the price of life and property in Tunbridge Wells. On the other hand, the firm offers discretionary bursaries and interest-free loans to ease the financial burden on trainees while at law school. Also, the seat system isn't to everyone's liking: "*There is a danger of having several short seats which end up being of limited use.*" You should also think twice if you are a club fiend or an SW3 socialite, but then London is only 45 minutes away if you get a craving for cocktails or repetitive beats.

One trainee said, "*This is the largest firm in the South East which can give you a flexible training and client contact from an early stage plus a national client base. However, if you want a career in London then you probably won't be satisfied here.*" The choice is a simple one: "*It's a quality of life decision at the end of the day.*" "*In terms of ability we could all have trained at London firms, so there must have been a reason for us to come here instead.*" And that reason? "*There's no commute and you don't have to do the hours.*" One trainee broke it down like this: "*If you want to restructure Eurotunnel then there's no substitute for London, but I get the feeling that a lot of the big deals are almost done by the time they turn up. You're just filling in the gaps. On smaller deals you get to structure the whole deal and work with your client from early days.*"

casino royale

Royal Tunbridge Wells is an elegant Georgian spa-town in the heart of the Kent countryside. It was granted the 'Royal' prefix in 1909, but inspire the less formal and more descriptive adjectives of "*charming*" and "*attractive.*" This is the kind of town your Mum would like. But then it's not your Mum who's going to train here. "*It is quite provincial in some respects, although that's not always a bad thing.*" Cutting out the commute means you get more leisure time – you can play nine holes after work very easily. For anyone moving from a large city it may come as a shock to find that "*it's not very multicultural.*" Remember, we're talking about Tunbridge Wells not New York.

It is a "*family firm,*" which apparently means that most of the lawyers are married or in long-term relationships. Combine this with the fact that the town is described as "*beautiful but quiet,*" and you won't be surprised to hear that the social life is "*fun but limited.*" A lot of Cripps people end up in nearby pubs at the end of the week (Sankey's wine bar is a favourite) and there are end-of-month drinks with wine and food in the office. At the last summer ball there was a casino, a covers band and fireworks for all. To celebrate 150 years in the business, everyone was given a pair of engraved champagne flutes to toast the next 150. There are regular cricket matches against clients and mysterious beer and sausage events that happen "*as and when.*" For proper nights out, you could try Brighton or, like one of our sources, make regular pilgrimages to the capital. "*It takes 45 minutes to get there, which is the same as it takes most of my friends to commute in from where they have to live."

In terms of an identikit Cripps trainee, *"Everyone here is well educated but they're not stuffy. No one is dull or boffy. They're interesting and well-rounded."* It was also felt that you needed to put yourself around and make your desires very clear in order to avoid disappointment. *"The more confident you are the more work they'll give you,"* and thankfully, *"they realise that it's uneconomical to get you doing the dogsbodying."* The firm is clearly into hanging onto its trainees: each of the the September 2002 qualifiers were offered a job and all but one accepted.

and finally…

If you want exposure to a wide range of work, have decided on a career in the regions rather than in the City, and you prefer cream teas to the latest Cream compilation cd, then you'll want to check out Cripps Harries Hall.

Dechert

the facts

Location: London
UK ranking by size: 51
Total number of trainees: 30
Seats: 6x4 months
Alternative seats: Overseas seats, secondments
Extras: Pro bono – various law centres

When kissing cousins Titmuss Sainer Dechert and Dechert Price & Rhoads got hitched in 2000, they legitimised a transatlantic relationship of some six years' standing. Having dumped the names they didn't share, they are fully merged and increasingly 'together'…but just ask your gran what can happen when a jazzy American visitor is allowed to court a prim English rose.

under surveillance

In last year's *True Picture*, we noted that would-be Dechert trainees (and our good selves) would have to keep constant watch over developments following the merger. That still rings true, but a clearer picture is emerging. The firm is still one of the cosier of the mid-tier firms in the City, but the American influence is becoming more noticeable, not least in the turnover stakes. The London office recorded a turnover of £45.5 million for its first full financial year following the merger – an impressive 22% up on the previous year. All good news for the partners, but was this at any cost to trainees?

fine and yankee doodle dandy

Although no one could quite put their finger on it, there is a change in the air; *"there's something just a little bit different about Dechert."* Maybe it's the contact with the Americans: *"It's really interesting to listen to what the Americans are doing,"* enthused one trainee. With trainees from London swapping seats with their American counterparts and American partners frequently dropping in to say 'howdy', *"it feels like things are happening all the time."* There is *"a slightly more entrepreneurial style now, with more focus on getting the cash in"* and this has resulted in the work ethic shifting just a smidgen. Having said that, *"the office still feels very English – the atmosphere is very relaxed and open."* English? Relaxed and open? Have we missed something? It might be more accurate to say the office feels very 'Dechert', in that *"there is no unnecessary pressure; people are very low-key."* It's fair to say it is *"quite a subdued firm"* in that it has a good technical ability but *"isn't flashy about it; we're not yeehah!"*

a flying start

Six four-month seats mean *"you get a wider experience of the firm and make good contacts."* Also, *"if you are unsure of where you want to qualify, the six-seat pattern is perfect."* Some trainees have done up to three terms in the same department, getting them off to a flying start on qualification. There are no compulsories but most will do corporate and property seats as well as the required time in litigation. A programme of lunchtime lectures and seminars is *"very comprehensive and well attended…and not just by trainees!"*

The London office has a property bent, but it isn't the be-all and end-all, with thriving corporate, employment and IP practices, among others. The popularity of seats varies from year to year, but the hot seat will usually be one of this trio or one of the secondments to Brussels, Philly, Boston or Washington. With the firm representing such diverse clients as *The Telegraph*, Nike, Dixons, Tesco and the designers of the London Eye, trainees will be able to get their teeth into some juicy national and international work with plenty of client contact. *"I was sent to see a client alone to advise on a substantive issue of law. To be trusted to do that at an early stage was a really good feeling."*

orwell and good

Dechert uses the slightly scary term 'firm citizen' (a phrase that would undoubtedly send a shiver down Orwellian hero, Winston Smith's, spine) to describe the type of person they want: someone who contributes to the community vibe and is a team player. *"Anyone who is too aggressive and doesn't want to work as part of a team might not fit in."* So, if you want to make it to partner, it might be a good idea to get involved in one of the sports on offer, or to be involved with training in the role of mentor to a first-year trainee during your second year, or to pitch in with marketing, or maybe just *"nod, smile and say hello"* as often as possible.

Supervisors give regular, informal feedback and will check everything *"that might open us up to negligence actions."* Ample support is there, but you aren't monitored 24/7 either; the firm's very own George (Bernard George, director of training and former head of the College of Law) is quite unlike Big Brother. BIG BERNARD IS WATCHING YOU, but he clearly doesn't run the place like Oceana, as the trainees positively gushed about him and his team: *"Bernard's great – he'll always make time for an informal chat if you have any concerns, whatever they are about."* His 25 community points and 'Good Citizen' badge are in the post!

If you have something controversial to say, you won't be carted off to Minitrue for a dose of doublethink or vaporisation by the Thought Police – feedback is two-way *"and you're encouraged to be forthright if you have problems. There are plenty of ways to get things sorted in confidence."* This reflects the firm's desire to recruit confident, self-assured trainees. In recent years, there have been trainees who've already qualified in other jurisdictions and several starting out on second careers.

the ministry of love

Dechert lawyers are a pretty close, friendly bunch. On Valentine's Day, the trainees traditionally write sweet, little love poems to each other. (Yeuch!) Partners, on the whole, are not aloof, except that *"they have their own dining room."* Although you might find a dinosaur here and there, we are told the partners *"are relatively young and dynamic people by and large."* In a recent charity auction they were changing hands for 200 quid – a snip when you consider average City hourly rates. They sound like they're up for a laugh though; we even heard of one partner taking a trainee off to Highbury to watch the Gunners in the Champions League.

There are several regular do's, with a flagship Christmas party, quarterly drinks and trainee-organised pub outings. Don't expect a mad-for-it, in-your-face social scene here though, as *"there aren't that many trainees"* and *"many are that little bit older and have families and partners."* The Clachan (as close as can be to the office without actually being a part of it) and Ye Olde Cock are regular haunts for after-hours drink. Surprisingly, we were told that there was nothing formally organised for trainees during their first week, but then Dechert is a firm where *"you won't be fattened up so you feel obliged to work constantly."*

Having been accused of being *"somewhat overprotective of its budgets"* (in part because it cut the trainee sports budget – oh dear, no dragon boat racing for you!), *"it is now learning from the Americans to spend* money in the right places." Just as well, because although the offices are in a good location, near to both Covent Garden and Leicester Square, *"they are pretty grot – although clients are kept away from the grotty parts."* Apart from the Ikea-cum-airport departure lounge basement and the odd floors that have had the 'changing rooms' treatment, the place is a bit decrepit and could do with some sprucing up. We heard mumblings that the firm might be relocating: *"It must be looking for new offices. For the size of firm it has become, the offices are not quite good enough."*

and finally…

If you fancy being involved in a relaxed, growing firm that offers great training, overseas secondments, a diet that isn't all corporate, corporate, corporate, and you are happy to eschew a spanking new workpod in favour of offices that weren't even fashionable in 1984, you could do worse than Dechert.

Denton Wilde Sapte

the facts

Location: London, Milton Keynes
UK ranking by size: 13
Total number of trainees: 103
Seats: 4x6 months
Alternative seats: Overseas seats, secondments
Extras: Pro bono – Prince's Youth Business Trust

Denton Wilde Sapte is the product of the merger in 2000 of respected energy and media specialists Denton Hall with traditional banking firm Wilde Sapte. While retaining the strengths of both, it nevertheless continues to develop its own identity. The post-merger dust has now settled to reveal a successful City firm with offices spanning Europe, Asia and the Middle East and, depending on the outcome of current talks (or perhaps we should say occasional semaphore messages) with US firm Pillsbury Winthrop, possibly even the US…

double jeopardy

There are no compulsory seats, aside from the Law Society's requirements, which you can *"kind of wing"* by doing a *"litigation-heavy seat"* like employment or IP. This is one of the major selling points for trainees: *"You've got free rein – there's so much variety here and you don't have to do banking or corporate if you don't want to. A lot of trainees do a combination of niche seats."* Sounds very accommodating. *"If there's a lot of competition for particular seats, certain people may be asked to do something else,"* but trainees tend to get their first or second choices in their later seats. You may also be pleased to hear that Milton Keynes and its concrete cows do not feature in the training experience.

"Media [ie TMT] *is always oversubscribed. Plenty of people are attracted to the firm for its media strength"* and the fact that *"it's seen as being quite glamorous."* It is so popular, in fact, that in the past more than a few trainees applied to do the seat again. This prompted the introduction of a 'double jeopardy' rule preventing any seat being done twice. An exception is made where a seat is under-subscribed. Of course. Employment and energy are also popular, as is corporate (*"Even if you're not going to qualify into it, it's a good one for experience and for the CV"* although *"the hours can be terrible"*). Those interested in finance should take note that *"they have difficulty filling all the banking seats."* Why? *"Banking is not perceived as being as interesting as other areas and it's got longer hours."*

the wilde bunch

OK, so Denton Hall was *"a cool media firm"* and Wilde Sapte belied the first half of its name by being *"a more formal, stuffy banking firm."* How have the two managed to find common ground? The point was made that *"a number of people who were unhappy about the merger have now left and there's been a lot of lateral hires since then, all of which has added to the identity of the new firm."* We did wonder if there are residual traces of the legacy firms. Well, reminiscent of China's policy on Taiwan, there is one firm but two offices. The banking, corporate and energy departments are based in Fleet Place, while the old Denton Hall haunt in Chancery Lane houses litigation, TMT and property (the latter set to make a move to Fleet Place early in 2003). The Chancery Lane office is "*a lot older*" with "*more of a traditional feel about it;*" Fleet Place, on the other hand, is "*brand new,*" "*more spacious*" and is generally perceived to have better services – more paralegals, bigger print room, canteen, etc. Chancery Lane has "*better hours*" though. And what's the point of these comparisons? Maybe this – the DWS tie up is viewed as one of the most successful law firm mergers of recent times because the two firms offered different and not competing practices.

One trainee even ventured an opinion as to what the firm was now all about: "*It's quite a progressive firm with a drive to do whatever's best to get the work done rather than just sticking to traditional methods.*" Our suggestion that he move into the firm's marketing department was firmly, but not unkindly, rebuffed!

would like to meet

"*Personable, hard-working and there to do well*" is the type of applicant one source thought the firm was after in its new recruits. Another added: "*They want people who are ambitious but not ruthless. Even now as we're coming up to qualification, we're effectively pitted against each other but there's no backbiting. Every trainee is genuinely interested in what everyone else has done, even if we're going for the same job.*" Another said: "*I know even those who are not in my specific group of friends well enough to stop and chat to in the corridor and I know what seats they've done.*"

Trainees share an office with their supervisor, who is "*half the time a partner, half the time a senior solicitor and occasionally a younger solicitor.*" We marvelled at their shape-shifting powers. "*They make a real effort in choosing the supervisors*" so that the "*people who really want to be involved in training and are best suited to it*" get a steady influx of trainees. There is a formal appraisal at the end of six months and an optional mid-seat review – "*At least, I hope it's optional because I've never done one!*" said one trainee. There is "*no shortage*" of formal training. At the start of every new seat, departments put on department-specific lunchtime lectures "*two to three times a week for usually about five or six weeks.*" In addition, every Tuesday night trainees are invited to lectures organised for all fee earners, although these are "*not compulsory – I generally pick the ones that sound interesting.*"

In terms of hours, a fairly typical day would be 9am till 6.45pm. One trainee noted, "*I do feel a bit guilty if I leave before half six. I generally ask people who are around in the department if I can do anything for them before I go.*" Is this as a result of pressure from above? "*No, it's just a feeling I get.*" Overall, banking and corporate seem to have the longer hours, corporate on a cyclical basis ("*If a deal's coming up to completion, I might stay till midnight or later*"), banking more consistently.

Responsibility varies across the seats. One source said, "*In competition I didn't get much, but it's an incredibly tricky area of law. There I was doing mainly research-based tasks. Property was the absolute opposite. I had loads and I was managing my own files. Banking varied according to the size of the case I was working on. On the smaller ones I ran files and dealt with clients; on larger matters I was a small cog in the machine.*" Is there a lot of grunt work? "*We don't have a lot of photocopying: we've got a very efficient print room so any large photocopying goes there as a matter of course.*" However, trainees are "*not infrequently*" called on to undertake bundling duties and document listing in the litigation department and bibling tasks in the banking department. In general, interviewees thought that more paralegals "*would be nice*" to ease the burden in these seats.

two tribes?

When we interviewed them, the second-year trainees were a mix of those who applied to the two legacy firms, and we identified certain social groups amongst them. "*Those who've been into corporate and banking from the beginning tend to be friends, and those who are into litigation and media tend to hang* out together," although people do "cross over between the groups." "We don't go out en masse – there's 48 in my intake after all – but we're all mixed in terms of the Denton Hall trainees and those from Wilde Sapte."

Fleet Place seems to have the edge on Chancery Lane for places to unwind in after work. By all accounts, Chancery Lane doesn't really have a favourite pub, but as one trainee said, "There are so many places in Farringdon and Clerkenwell that it's not really a problem to find one." Fleet Place has The Old Monk, which is virtually next door, although nearest doesn't necessarily mean dearest. One trainee said, "It's a bit crap; it hasn't got a lot of character, but it is close and it serves pints." This contrasts with the Corney & Barrow "a stone's throw away," where "more senior people" from the firm are said to go. One cheeky source said, "Some trainees go there, but I don't unless someone else is paying!"

Client secondments to well-known companies are available as part of the energy and banking seats. On the DWS website, it describes itself as a "leading international firm" and certainly it offers a plethora of overseas seats. Hong Kong is the most popular posting due to the fact that it's perceived to be "very glamorous," while Singapore, Paris and Dubai are also highly sought-after. Less popular postings include Cairo ("People don't know what to expect") and Gibraltar ("People think it's going to be dull").

Many second-years felt that the process of qualification job offers is too nail-biting and could be better organised. But the good-ish news is that 42 of the 51 qualifiers were offered jobs on qualification in 2002 and each of these accepted.

and finally…

Denton Wilde Sapte is a success story. It offers trainees experience in an interesting variety of sectors and has the added attraction of being relatively free of constraints as to how they spend their two years. Borrowing the central slogan from the firm's website, our "assured advice in an uncertain world" is that you might want to apply.

Dickinson Dees

the facts

Location: Newcastle-upon-Tyne, Stockton-on-Tees
UK ranking by size: 48
Total number of trainees: 30
Seats: 4x6 months
Alternative seats: Brussels, secondments

Newcastle. What does it bring to mind? Jimmy Nail (gissa job), Alan Shearer (gissa ball), Paul Gascoigne (gissa pint)? Maybe even *Get Carter*, one of Michael Caine's greatest films (but the worst endorsement of Newcastle in the history of cinema). If you're looking to work in the North East, just remember that Dickinson Dees is one of Newcastle's proudest offerings.

the ties that bind

More than half the trainees have links of some kind to the North East, whether family or educational. One said, "I'm from Newcastle and I've never had any inkling to live elsewhere. As soon they offered me a place, I didn't bother attending any other interviews. It's the biggest and most profitable of all the firms in the region." In light of these comments, is it an official policy to hire trainees with local connections? "It's more a preference…they don't want to spend money training you just to have you disappear on qualification." It's well known that the firm hires with a view to retaining 100% of its trainees. This year 20 jobs were available for 12 qualifiers and all but one accepted. A hot romance with a soft southerner prevented the twelfth from staying. With a 20%-odd rise in profits over the year, Dickie Dees didn't need to leave anyone out in the cold. We even heard that "a trainee who was on secondment here from Enron was kept on permanently after the company went belly up." All heart…

stellar stuff

The firm's website reads, "If it's legal, we'll do it," which is laudable, not to mention broad-minded. The firm does indeed operate a full range of practice areas and although it's certainly ambitious ("*We have the North East market tied up, so we tender for work outside the region, particularly in Leeds*"), it presently has no ambition to set up any offices outside the region. There's a small branch in Stockton-on-Tees, which has now been open a year, but given that this is a mere 30 miles away, "*it's more of a satellite.*"

Being top dog in the region brings with it certain notions of establishment; notions some trainees were quick to talk down. "*We're not as traditional as people think we are – we're pretty relaxed and sociable.*" This was slightly counterbalanced by the comment: "*We're not open-plan and we don't have dress-down Fridays – we're certainly not that radical!*"

four seasons

Of your four seats, three are compulsory – property, company/commercial and litigation. This latter department is currently one of the more popular as "*you get lots of responsibility, the work's varied and you get to go out and about to conferences and courts.*" One trainee said, "*They maintain a balance between teaching you and giving you responsibility for a caseload. In corporate, there's no way I could run a £20 million deal on my own a month into my seat, but with litigation I could start with smaller debt recovery cases and work my way up.*"

The private client department gives trainees a particularly high level of responsibility. "*After only six weeks I had 30 files relating to wills and trusts, I was going to client meetings and I was taking instructions.*" At the other extreme, in corporate: "*The trainee orders pizzas on deal completions, although that's not so bad 'cos you get to choose them!*" Cheesy quips aside, our sources got decent work in that department too. In the last year it advised Parkdean Holidays on its £32 million AIM flotation and Grainger Trust on its £477 million bid with Deutsche Bank for BPT.

In all departments, Dickie Dees gets the best of business from the region and some impressive instructions from further afield. It's been appointed to advise the National Trust on all its property work in the Midlands and the North and continues to advise Govia, Thames Trains and Thameslink on a range of rail franchising and investment work worth more than £1 billion.

brolly good show

Trainees share offices with supervisors, who could be partners or associates. Supervision is high: "*Everything has to be fed through supervisors before you send it out, whether e-mails, letters or whatever, and if you're going to speak with a client you have to discuss the content with your supervisor first.*" Sounds like a firm with a reputation to protect. As far as the hours go (and if you're in corporate they tend to go later than elsewhere), trainees generally seem to be living the lyrics of the Dolly Parton classic, *Nine to Five*. "*It's a Newcastle thing!*" one trainee explained. "*The city has a slower pace than London. People walk slower, drive slower and expect to work fewer hours.*" But it's no Mickey Mouse job.

There are quarterly meetings when all trainees meet with the graduate programme officer and raise issues on an anonymous basis. "*If you want to sit and moan, you can, if you want to be constructive, you can.*" One mentioned that they asked for three days extra holiday (in line with the top Leeds firms) and got them; another achievement was business cards for trainees. Less successful were requests for more biscuits and a corporate umbrella!

well tonight, matthew…

One of the highlights of the social calendar is a firm-wide *Stars In Their Eyes* competition. This gala evening involves members of staff dressing up as various artists and performing favourite songs. "*It's mainly associates and partners who do the dressing up. Trainees tend not to because they don't want to make fools of themselves.*" Oh, go on… Last year, Queen and the Bee Gees assailed eardrums, but the winner was an Elvis performer (making us fear that by 2010, one in three staff will be Elvis impersonators).

Elvis, of course, was (or is) one of the great romantic crooners. We got to wondering if Dickie Dees trainees were big on romance. "*There's been a few cheeky* snogs in my year, but the year below tends to be a more frisky bunch," said one trainee who sounded like he wished he'd deferred a year! Along these lines, the thrice-yearly Newcastle Trainee Solicitors Group events were described as being *"good for meeting young ladies"* and are also occasions where *"trainees tend to go to town on alcohol consumption."* The TSG events are also an excellent opportunity to meet your peers at other firms. *"The Newcastle legal community is a small one and it helps to get to know people who may well be acting on the other side from you in the near future."*

The offices were described as *"one of the best things about working here."* The positively palatial six-storey building has a *"square horseshoe shape"* and a *"magnificently modern"* interior. It overlooks the river Tyne and has spectacular views of the Baltic Flour Mills (currently being developed into an art gallery, concert hall and cafés). Another aspect of its location, location, location right on the Quayside is, as one appreciative trainee explained, that it's close to all the best bars. The Pitcher & Piano is especially near and popular – *"I could throw a biro onto it from my window."* The office manager may now finally understand how the stationery cupboard empties so quickly.

chilling tales

Client secondments are available intermittently. One trainee was seconded to Nissan for a month during his litigation seat recently and someone else went to Durham City Council on an exchange during their employment seat. From January to March of each year, there is a competition seat for second-year trainees with Renouf & Co, an affiliated firm in Brussels. Trainees have to give a presentation demonstrating how the seat will benefit both them and the firm. Interested first-years were recently flown over to Brussels and put up for a weekend at the firm's expense, during which time they were shown around the office by the present incumbent. However, despite such attractions as a sauna in the basement of the Brussels flat, there wasn't much competition for the seat last time. Family commitments and a conflicting desire to do seats in other areas were cited as reasons for its relative unpopularity. One trainee mentioned, *"I didn't really want to go to Brussels – it's freezing there from January to March."* And Newcastle's subtropical at that time of year?

and finally…

Dickinson Dees sounds like a shiny, happy place, but *"that's not to say that out of 550-odd lawyers you don't have a few robo-lawyers."* Its name will carry you far in the (usually unlikely) event that you decide to move to pastures new. While trainees are paid less than their counterparts in Leeds and London, this is more than offset by the lower cost of living. For those set on a top-flight career in the region, this is one heck of a firm.

DJ Freeman

the facts

Location: London
UK ranking by size: 57
Total number of trainees: 26
Seats: 3x8 months
Alternative seats: Secondments
Extras: Language training

DJ Freeman offers a slightly different take on commercial lawyering. It's shuffled everyone around such that within each of its three departments there are lawyers of all types working for the same client sector. Its three pillars of strength are property, insurance and the newly merged technology and media department. We're a little disappointed that the firm has dropped its snooker balls logo, but we'll get over it…

the breaks

Litigation and corporate lawyers are spread round the firm on a cross-departmental basis so, for example, there are corporate bods (30 firm-wide) and litigators (90 firm-wide) working from within the property department and handling work exclusively for property clients. All this restructuring has taken place for the benefit of clients, but what does it mean for the trainees? The trainees we spoke to about the client sector approach to law knew the drill: "*We sell ourselves on the fact that our lawyers understand their client sectors better than our competition.*" That's the theory dealt with, so how does it work in practice?

Well, we thought we knew…and then the system changed! Trainees now do three seats of eight months in each of the departments, namely property, insurance and technology and media. Previously, some trainees had told us that when it came to getting the seat they wanted: "*It seemed to be a matter of who can shout the loudest*" and we got the impression that a number of them weren't always getting what they'd wanted. Note to the incoming training partner: "*I think that particular desires should be taken into account a bit more; the system seems a bit perverse at times. We have no idea what goes on behind the scenes.*" We presume the new system will bring more certainty…watch this space!

the players

The property department is regarded as "*the most friendly*" with good hours and high levels of responsibility. As well as more routine management work, which enables trainees to run files, there's some technical limited partnership fund creation going on. Last year the department acted for Capital & Regional on two such matters, together worth over £1 billion. Retail parks, shopping centres and leisure and entertainment destinations have all featured prominently.

Over in technology and media, there's a real mixed bag of work. At one end is a defamation team that's been involved in Mohamed Al Fayed's scraps with Neil Hamilton and at the other company/commercial work. Falling somewhere in the middle is media litigation ("*interesting cases and clients*") and IP. And then, lurking mysteriously amongst it all is a seat with the public international law team, which is "*a unique and amazing experience.*" The team recently represented the Nigerian Government in its eight-year-old land (plus a bit of sea) border dispute with Cameroon. Impressive stuff…and the kind of work that's only on offer in a tiny number of firms in the UK.

The insurance department came off third in the popularity stakes, but there's no shortage of decent work. The department's corporate lawyers have busied themselves with the largest capital-raising in the history of AIM. There is a seat available in insurance litigation, which includes contentious film finance work (done in conjunction with the technology and media department) as the firm acts for a number of film industry insurers.

No regular overseas postings, but we did learn of one trainee who spent time at the International Court of Justice in The Hague. A few lucky trainees get to sample life in-house – there is a regular secondment to the in-house legal department of Shell, while other one-off opportunities have included the TV production company, HatTrick. A secondment to a major TV broadcaster is currently in the pipeline.

practising your shots

"*Different departments do appraisals differently,*" but very often they take the form of "*a quick chat over coffee.*" While many trainees concede that "*seat allocation and appraisals need to be more consistent,*" the quality of training appears to satisfy. "*I can't say I've had a single boring day here,*" said one. "*The supervisors take a real interest and you feel that some of them have a real desire to see you learn. You get praised a lot.*" In terms of responsibility, one trainee reported: "*I do much less grunt work than friends at other firms. I genuinely feel that I've not had any crap work.*" Another said, "*You do as much as a junior assistant. It's not considered economical to get you doing the sh*t* work.*" Hours are described as "*fantastic:*" on average 9.30am-5.30pm.

There are oodles of workshops and seminars to keep you up to date, although we heard mixed views on the usefulness of some. We did like the sound of a session on "*how to circulate.*" For those of you who've yet to master the art, the secret is to "*remember each person's name and something interesting about each of them.*"

splitting the pack

At present the office is spread over three sites. 43 Fetter Lane is the base of operations and plays host to the firm's canteen (providing *"fresh, cheap lunches"*), the library and print room. If you find yourself working late, the canteen takes call orders and you can bring your friends in to sample its delights. 1 Fetter Lane holds the property department and, just around the corner, Newspaper House is home to technology and media. The three-way split leads to a sense of being *"isolated"* at times and it all feels like *"a bit of a mishmash."* The quest for the mythical single office goes on.

Happy 50th birthday DJ Freeman! Actually, the firm's founder, David Freeman, is more senior than that…but it would be rude to say just how much more. For the anniversary the firm had a fairground event (actual merry-go-round, helter-skelter and all) in the East End with five different restaurants and champagne flowing all night. Week by week, *"there's lots of socialising, if you want it."* Favourite pubs include The Cartoonist and The Hogshead on Fetter Lane, and The Old Cock Tavern on Fleet Street. There's a highbrow movie club, where trainees get together to watch *"French films and directors' cuts." "It's not for the Warner Village crowd; it's a bit more cerebral,"* reported one. The firm also does good deeds for charity; recently a number of staff flung themselves out of a plane in a sponsored parachute jump. All this fun aside, trainees did moan to us about their holiday entitlement – they get only 20 days, which is a little shy of the London trainee average. Poor things…

designed for living

"There are lots more female than male trainees," one source said, confirming the stats we'd worked out for ourselves. Indeed, the firm boasts a high percentage of women partners and lots of them are young. *"The firm approaches the career path of women in a sensible way. You're not going to be stopped from having children."* We salute you, DJ Freeman.

So what sort of people are these trainees? *"You need to have high academics but not take yourself too seriously."* By their own admission they are *"bright"* but *"confident rather than arrogant." "We tend to be well-rounded individuals. People are motivated and proactive,"* said one. From a second: *"We tend to be quite good fun."* A third concluded: *"We're broad-minded and unstuffy. There's a fairly flat management structure here and they're not obsessed with rankings."* In terms of its ambitions, one trainee we spoke to thought that the firm *"plods on."* So is DJ Freeman the legal equivalent of a Ford Mondeo? Maybe this is why there's a new senior partner and managing executive *"to change things and move things forward."* Maybe they'll lower the suspension and soup up the engine.

One of the real pluses of this firm is that *"they do believe in life outside of work. When you qualify you're allowed to take ten weeks' holiday before you start back."* Yesss! And DJ Freeman doesn't have the same airs and graces or ego as some firms. *"The unpretentious brochure attracted me. There were no pictures of superheroes or people with double Firsts from Oxbridge looking like they'd just walked off the catwalk. I've never felt intimidated by the people who work here,"* said one trainee.

engineered to last?

In September 2002, nine jobs were offered to 14 qualifiers. Eight applied and seven were successful. These are far from the best retenton stats that the firm has produced so, again, watch this space in next year's book.

and finally…

DJ Freeman seems to be a very pleasant place to work. The novel approach to the firm's structure threw up the odd trainee grumble during our interviews, but the latest restructuring and three-seat system may deal with these. Trainees talk about a firm that's gearing up for a bright future and they certainly have a good deal of affection for it.

DLA

the facts
Location: Birmingham, Leeds, Liverpool, London, Manchester, Sheffield, Glasgow, Edinburgh
UK ranking by size: 3
Total number of trainees: 151
Seats: 4x6 months
Alternative seats: Brussels, secondments
Extras: The Prince's Trust

This boisterous national firm dares to dream big. With nine UK offices handling quality work, and plans for further expansion abroad, the firm is gearing up for a major offensive. As all good leaders know, an army's effectiveness depends on its size, training, experience and morale, and DLA seems to offer it all.

grand designs
"*The managing partner keeps having visions.*" The latest of these is a five-year plan to become "A top five, full-service European law firm with a real presence in Asia." With increasingly sizeable deals landing on the table at home, and the D&P network of European links reaching into the continent, the firm is seriously pursuing this vision. "*DLA is really driven and really growing. It's an exciting time to be here,*" reported one trainee. If all this makes the managing partner, Nigel Knowles, sound like an unappealing cross between Napoleon and Joan of Arc, be assured that there's a heart to accompany the mouth and trousers. In this case, the small blue one given to each employee, bearing the inscription: "Take the passion and make it happen." The line comes from the movie *Flashdance*, which also provides the backing music for a specially commissioned inspirational film of "winning moments." It only seems fair to set the mantra in its proper context: "*...I can have it all/ (Bein's believin') bein's believin'/ (Take your passion, make it happen) make it happen / (What a feeling) what a feeling... (to fade)*" Who's got the office legwarmers?

Despite its expansionist tendencies and international ambitions, DLA is not the acronym for a private liberation army, but the end result of a series of mergers that swept five firms together. After a few years of fallout and consolidation, the firm is now considered to be well-integrated and able to offer a good network of expertise for lawyers at all levels to draw upon.

iron glove, velvet fist
"*DLA is very driven and ambitious at board level, but a lot more easy-going at the operational level.*" As regards the charge that DLA is aggressive, "*there's nothing wrong with being ambitious,*" one trainee replied. "*Despite the label, I was very surprised by how approachable everyone was.*" Trainees agree that the place is refreshingly down-to-earth and friendly. "*They look after you here,*" reported one. "*Rather than feeling proud to work here, you feel that the firm is proud of you,*" gushed another. But don't think you'll get off easily just because the firm cares: "*You still need to be career-focused. DLA trainees are driven – it's definitely not for those who want it easy.*"

One trainee said, "*It's about making as much money as possible in the nicest way possible.*" If such sentiments make you feel warm inside, you'll be right at home. DLA wants people who are "*confident, outgoing and bubbly.*" In law, as in life, "*there are opportunities, you just have to go out and grab them.*" Take the passion...

marching orders
There are no compulsory seats, although we noted a trend for a corporate seat, a banking seat, a litigation seat and then something like insolvency, employment/pensions or property. Seat allocation is generally considered to be clear, open and fair and there are the usual favourites: everyone wants employment and IP – "*the sexy seats.*" Property was considered "*one to avoid,*" although some did concede that it was more interesting in practice than during the LPC. "*Contentious sorts want commercial litigation seats, and the non-contentious sort want banking.*" In terms of secondments, some lucky trainees can spend time with IPC Media in London and ICI in Manchester. But for an army on the march into

Europe, it's surprising that at any one time there's only one three-month stint available out in Brussels.

The size of deals and cases will vary from office to office, but the training itself is standardised, and *"there's plenty of it."* Recently, there have been firm-wide training weekends in Amsterdam, Lisbon and Brussels. *"The firm invests an awful lot in its trainees and it's keen to retain them."* In September 2002, it offered jobs to 53 of its 59 qualifiers and they all accepted.

firm roots and healthy branches

Geographical separation hasn't dented the sense of community: *"It's only the buildings that separate us."* In the past we sensed a little snobbishness between London and the regions. Trainees tell us that's no longer the case, but there are still a few differences. For example, Sheffield and Liverpool don't have quite as wide a selection of work or plush new offices. There are strong links between Leeds and Sheffield and between Manchester and Liverpool, where trainees regularly have nights out together.

We wondered if there are any DLA trainee hallmarks. *"They definitely look for people with commercial nous,"* one source said. Apparently, *"you have to be interested in practical law rather than the academic side of things,"* and many of those we spoke to had considered careers in accountancy, business or finance. *"There's a big emphasis on commerciality, but also on people with maturity."* Another trainee considered that *"you have to be able to think laterally as well as legally and have practical as well as academic skills."*

the price is right

The Leeds office is *"one of the newest buildings in the city."* We went, we saw and we were mightily impressed. As far as the work is concerned, Leeds lawyers regularly use the D&P network, and the corporate department is, apparently, always on the phone to Spain, Amsterdam and France. It's full-service, but *"with no particular specialisms."* There are strong links between Leeds and London, since a lot of work gets shipped up from the capital to be done at the Leeds price. Beyond the office, the local Slug & Lettuce is a popular choice for R&R on a Friday night, or else there's trendy Babylon. The TSG is very active in the city and there are plenty of *"barbecues and buffets"* to attend if the fridge is empty.

mission control

The London office is *"lovely, light and airy,"* with lots of *"glass and dodgy art work."* Trainees in the London branch are the sort that want City work, but not to be one of hundreds – *"The City is anonymous enough as it is."* *"I did some work at a small regional firm, but I thought to myself, this is not what it is all about."* *"Assume you will work long hours"* and you should be just fine. *"Some of the work is mundane and doesn't test you, but you've got to expect that. There's always good work around."* There is dress-down on Fridays, but to quote one trainee: *"Sometimes you do feel like the lowest of the low and if you have to meet clients without a suit you tend to feel even lower."* If you have a social conscience, the firm does pro bono work for The Prince's Trust. You'll typically be appointed as a mentor for a start-up company. *"I was in complete control and got to see the whole picture,"* said one trainee we spoke to.

The banking department is apparently the place to be for big boozy lunches, and after hours the local All Bar One and Fine Line are firm favourites. So too are (cattle market) Nylon and the dingy City Pipe. There are *"lots of do's"* to attend, but *"no team building exercises,"* which most people we spoke to greeted with a sigh of relief.

on the docks

Liverpool is one of the smallest offices, taking only five trainees. *"They like people with ties to the area, since they're more likely to settle into working life here."* Apparently, *"demands are just as high as in London."* The office's strengths were felt to be in corporate, employment, real estate and pensions. It also has a marine insurance practice.

Liverpool is considered to be slightly more laid-back than other branches, although Friday

TRUE PICTURE OUR TOP 120 FIRMS

263

dress-down is "*more trouble than it's worth.*" Sounding a bit like the Linklaters trainee of Liverpool, one source said rather confidently, "*We know we're the best…other firms are just jealous!*" One trainee had frequently found themselves opposite an assistant solicitor on deals, but another told us, "*It is a shock to the system when you first start. Trainees tend to get a bit ignored.*" Down by the docks (we heard seagulls), the building itself leaves a lot to be desired. "*It could do with a lick of paint!*" A move is on the cards. Out of hours, trainees get to the races or go bowling and, come Friday, tend to congregate in a nice little pub nearby with a live band.

humble origins

DLA Sheffield has a "*magnetic field*" around it – "*It's hard to leave once you've been here for a couple of days.*" Must be something to do with the steel. This is the office where the DLA dream first started. Once global domination is complete, there will no doubt be a citywide public holiday and a statue of Nigel Knowles in the main square. "*There's a real sense of community. A lot of the lawyers have been here since day one.*" (Shouldn't that be Year Zero?) There's a bit of "*friendly tension*" with other firms in the city, said one source. "*Other firms are a bit in awe of us.*" So modest!

Despite a water feature ("*a rock which dribbles water*") and Sky TV in reception, the office is a "*poor relation*" in terms of its building. Trainees rarely work past 7pm and it's quite common to head home at 5.30pm. Socialising is "*informal,*" and goes on in the local Ha!Ha! or All Bar One. The end-of-year party took on an 80s theme, with many of the partners making an appearance in ridiculous costumes. "*Some people came dressed in 1880s style.*" Very clever.

loved up

Birmingham works open-plan in a modern building in the style of "*posh Ikea.*" The hours in banking can vary, but so long as you are prepared to muck in when necessary, you can often get out by 5.30pm. Downsides? "*Lots of admin to do on the big deals.*" In England, the Birmingham office is fourth in size (London comes top, with Leeds and Manchester then neck and neck).

The social scene is "*excellent.*" In the pub there's a "*trickle-down*" effect, whereby lawyers buy drinks for each other based on wage differentials. "*People notice when DLA is in the room. We're loud and we like to take a few tables!*" Trainees enjoy concerts, wine-tastings and quiz nights, and sports are big. There's five-a-side football, golf trips, and several lawyers run the NY Marathon with financial support from the firm. The office is also keen on getting its trainees mingling with local young professionals so client entertainment features highly. By all accounts, the Christmas party is "*notorious for secret snogging in the corner.*" Lawyers have met and married at the Birmingham branch, including a partner and a trainee. Based on Brum activities alone, we are happy to award DLA the title 'UK's Most Luvved-Up Law Firm'. There's been some stiff competition out there, so well done!

mad for it?

Where other offices have walls, open-plan Manchester has "*pods.*" "*It's a bit crowded.*" Hours can be long, but the office nevertheless maintains a relaxed atmosphere. "*You can take the piss out of partners here and they don't mind.*" It's a "*refreshingly normal*" place to work – "*Not too intense and not too pin-striped.*" Apparently, you've got to make the effort and be both "*driven*" and "*easy-going.*" When asked to cite an example of someone who managed this seemingly contradictory juggling act, someone suggested Jeremy Paxman. But remember, all you little Jeremys: "*If it gets to 4am, you can't be a prima donna about it. Shouting at the support staff does not go down well.*" The social scene is there if you want it. Trainees go paintballing, wine-tasting and dancing. There's also a handy Pitcher & Piano right underneath the office.

and finally…

DLA trainees were easily among the most satisfied of all of our interviewees this year. With its grand plans and enthusiastic army, the firm offers an awful lot for student hopefuls – a more intimate City experience and great quality work in the regions. Napoleon once said: "The great proof of madness is the disproportion of one's designs to one's means." When the time comes, Mr Knowles, you may borrow our ruler.

DMH

the facts
Location: Brighton, Crawley, London, Worthing
UK ranking by size: 99
Total number of trainees: 10
Seats: 4x6 months
Alternative seats: None

DMH is the largest firm in Brighton and has a strong reputation throughout the South East. There's a certain something about this firm that makes it stand out from the mass of competent regional firms. It's not just that the lime green web site all but glows in the dark and it's not just a lovingly nurtured brand…

artistic license
Donne Mileham & Haddock metamorphosed, with barely a backward glance at its slightly silly name, into slick, commercial DMH in 2000, and a London presence was achieved with the 2001 takeover of a small City firm, Fairbairn Morris. Forward-looking. Innovative. Creative. Approachable. Most law firms try to get this message across, but few pepper their websites quite as liberally with such adjectives as DMH. But it's not just talk. Modern art galleries in the Brighton and Crawley offices are "*novel and a talking point.*" Teambuilding is given high priority. One year at the AGM, a local samba band somehow managed to persuade everyone from recalcitrant secretaries to sceptical partners to stage "a co-ordinated spectacle of music, dance and colour." (website quote) Spin aside, the last few years really have seen changes.

roaming around
Brighton is the largest office, offering the greatest number of seats from crime, family and private client through to corporate, construction, commercial litigation, property and planning. The ever-growing Crawley office is home to the innovation & media department (IT/IP) and also handles employment and commercial property, one of DMH's strongest areas. The newer London office handles PI and property. DMH has worked hard on its commercial client roster and currently acts for local authorities, the University of Sussex, regional businesses, housing associations, Brighton & Hove Albion FC, national hotel chains, house builders, NHS trusts and banks.

There are no compulsory seats and the menu on offer to trainees is long. But remember, planning and property are core practice areas and it would be unusual for a trainee to not do a stint in either. It is certainly possible to steer well clear of private client seats, if they leave you cold, and we got the impression that this is how most trainees felt on the subject. It's likely that your time will be split between Brighton and Crawley, and some trainees do a stint in London. Employment is an enormously popular department, but don't just assume that you'll be one of the lucky few who manage to bag this seat. The preferences of trainees are taken into account when allocating seats, but there's little doubt that business needs come first. If there are seats you've set your heart on, be prepared to do a bit of discreet lobbying (or "*keeping in with the right partners*" as one trainee put it).

The offices are open-plan, so you'll be sitting near your supervisor but not necessarily under their nose. "*Trainees have a defined role to play. You're never just a spare part and you never feel you're doing something just for the sake of it.*" Responsibility can come quickly: "*In property litigation I had my own caseload and time pressures,*" said one source. Some seats offer more opportunities to unchain yourself from the desk: "*I did my planning seat in the summer and I spent the whole time roaming around the Sussex countryside, looking at old houses,*" one trainee enthused. We also heard reports of trainees putting their language skills to good use when dealing with a large French client.

rallying the troops

The firm's attempts to encourage interaction between the offices are in evidence in a number of work-cum-social initiatives. The firm's rag, 'Briefly Speaking', keeps the troops apprised of DMH gossip (the official version anyway), and the social committee organises trips to the London Eye, barbecues, riverboat cruises and other fun and games. Then there's the *"highlight"* of the AGM. The chairman and managing partner motivate and inspire with speeches on the firm's objectives and strategy, followed by an afternoon of exercises, quizzes and sketches, during which departments show the rest of the firm how they actually spend their days. The experience is rounded off with a dinner dance. All this bonding might sound slightly heavy-handed to the cynics among you, but trainees agree that *"it is helpful in letting everyone know what management is trying to achieve. The firm is growing quickly and this allows people from the different offices to get to know each other."*

potty animals

Trainees are often at least in their mid- to late-20s and have spent the last few years doing everything from travelling and working abroad to temping or postgrad study. Links with the area won't go amiss, if only because a bit of local knowledge helps in a firm with a considerable volume of property development work. The firm also makes much of its association with the University of Sussex. It's looking for people who *"are confident, talkative and have a lot of common sense."* And those who are likely to stay post-qualification: in 2002 four out of five second-years were offered a job and each of them accepted.

Most of the Brighton and Crawley staff live in Brighton (once you've seen Crawley you'll understand why) and decent hours allow them to make the most of the excellent location. The Brighton office is just two minutes from the station, and you might even be lucky enough to get an office with a sea view. Brighton beach… lunchtime…that's gotta be good! The firm is keen to encourage a healthy interaction between staff at all levels and younger partners will come along to meals (vindaloo fiends take note: there's a well established curry club) and trips to the pub. The Pond is a drinking establishment loved and loathed in equal measure. Its ceiling is (and we kid you not) *"covered with hanging porcelain potties."*

and finally…

Despite a rapidly evolving commercial identity, this is still a place for people who value their personal time. All eyes are trained on the commercial side of the practice, but trainees can still get experience of the private client side, if that's what they choose. Just like Brighton itself, DMH has a palpable onwards-and-upwards vibe. Enjoy!

DWF

the facts

Location: Liverpool, Manchester, Warrington
UK ranking by size: 49
Total number of trainees: 17
Seats: 2x6 + 3x4 months
Alternative seats: None

DWF is an ambitious, mid-sized firm providing a full range of services for commercial and insurance clients from its base in the North West. If its website – with orbiting moons, starry backdrop and streaking comet – is anything to go by, galactic expansion could be on the cards!

small steps and giant leaps

As an apprentice at this firm, your two years will be divided between four main departments: corporate, insurance, property, and commercial litigation. Recently the seat system was altered such that trainees now undertake a six-month seat followed by three four-month slots and then another six-month assignment in the department they hope to qualify into. It's gone down well with trainees as it ensures they get exposure to most of the firm's core business and *"the firm is fairly flexible, so long as you give them notice of what you want."*

Historically the firm's strength has been in insurance and this is still a large part of its work, but trainees tell us that *"other departments have expanded faster over the last couple of years."* One estimated that *"the firm has grown by about 100 % in three years."* In particular, corporate and banking has come on in leaps and bounds. *"The firm has an active marketing department and is apparently anxious to let people know what it's doing."* Indeed, DWF's work is now hitting the deals pages of the legal press. In July 2002, for example, the firm acted for Bank of Scotland on a £76 million finance facility for the MG Rover Group.

divine

Trainees are hard-working but don't encounter excessive hours: 8.30am to 6.30pm is about average, but be prepared for longer hours in company/commercial when there's a deal on. *"Just because you're outside London, don't expect it to be a walk in the park."* At times, *"you work all the hours God sends,"* admitted one trainee, although when we checked the client listings on the website, we found no mention of Him. The firm can, however, boast clients in the league of Rothschild, Manchester Airport, Castrol, Sega, Lloyds TSB and Royal & SunAlliance. Insurance companies provide a hefty chunk of the firm's work, but trainees state categorically: *"DWF doesn't just handle insurance."* Clearly you're not going to be *FT* front-page darlings, but *"there's lots of quality company and commercial work."*

je ne sais quoi

At the helm of Starship DWF is senior partner Jim Davies, *"a loud, lively character with a big grin on his face."* The majority of partners, we are told, are a mix of those who've trained with the firm or escapees from London. One trainee told us: *"It's a modern place with its finger on the pulse."* Someone else added: *"The firm has a good reputation as a commercial practice, but offers something a bit quirky and different to your Eversheds, etc."* One trainee described the firm as *"unstuffy and pragmatic."* Yet another considered it *"an intelligent firm that allows you to be an individual. The downside is that you can get a boss who is a bit wacko!"* Despite this interest in maintaining a certain je ne sais quoi, DWF doesn't lose sight of the fact that it is an ambitious and successful business. *"It's looking at the bottom line and it's becoming more strategic…it wants profits."*

Responsibility builds up over the course of a seat and over the two years. *"We're not just left to photocopy and make the tea. In certain departments I really did feel like a qualified solicitor,"* gushed one source. Another said proudly, *"My high point is when a file remains on my desk."* There seems no shortage of daily feedback from most supervisors, but when it came to formal end-of-seat appraisals, most of those we spoke to thought that *"a more robust system would be good."* Trainees also get at least two to three hours a month of structured training sessions, mostly spot-on but *"a bit of a mixed bag,"* according to some. Generally, trainees agreed that they were receiving *"a good solid training in a well-respected commercial practice"* but conceded that if you have your heart set on a juicy client secondment or overseas seat, you're likely to be disappointed.

top guns

The firm takes new recruits of all ages and backgrounds. Current trainees ranged from fresh-faced law school graduates to people who'd had careers in local businesses or as secretaries and electricians. During our *True Picture* interviews up and down the land, we often ask what trainees might have become had they not opted for the law. Well, it's official: a number of the DWF trainees were once aspiring fighter pilots. Despite the undeniable excitement of certain areas of the law, they did concede that they had to look elsewhere for a comparable adrenalin rush. But it struck us that they all had an enthusiasm for the law, which is pretty refreshing, given the comments we hear at some firms. So are they a completely different breed to their peers elsewhere? Doubtful. Is the firm doing something to maintain their enthusiasm? Clearly.

One tough-talking trainee told us: *"You stand out as an individual. You're very visible so you have to be brave."* Another agreed: *"Trainees need to be articulate and able to hold their own."* We have to admit to being a little thrown when yet another stressed that everyone was *"clean-looking."* The majority have close ties to the North West, be this through their upbringing or education. Part of the firm's plan is to get trainees it can hang on to, and in 2002 all seven second-years were offered NQ jobs with the firm, and only one hadn't yet decided to accept when we made our final checks.

tale of two cities

There's not much difference between the Liverpool and Manchester offices in terms of their character and the work they handle, and you'll generally spend all your time in one or the other. *"The firm's four key departments are evenly spread between the two. There's very much a collegiate feel and lots of fluidity between them."* When pressed, one trainee told us that the Manchester office is *"excellently located"* and *"much more plush"* than Liverpool's, which is *"a bit of a rabbit warren. It's been here for donkey's years."* Over in Warrington, non-legally qualified staff deal with bulk conveyancing and debt collection. The office is known as DWF Maxima and features little in the daily lives of trainees.

There's a suited and booted dress code but frequent charity dress-down days. *"We get Easter eggs each year,"* one trainee revealed. Lovely. We asked if there was much dating going on at the firm. *"A fair bit. A few of the youngsters are going out, although they may be keeping it secret!"* Oops, not any more!

manchester lights

The social scene is *"vibrant and active,"* especially for the first-years. Apparently second-years grow a touch more serious as they approach qualification. But no matter how senior you get, Manchester has a lot to offer in terms of fun and it's a good choice of city for living well. *"There's no way I could face London commuting and stress,"* admitted one source. Trainees lighten their wallets at Bar 38, Squares, Brannigan's, or if they want a classic old-man pub, The Abercrombie.

In Liverpool, some trainees have set up second homes in The Vanilla Lounge and The Living Room. *"It's a real party town,"* said one. There's a lot of money being pumped into the city at present, as evidenced by all the building work going on. Also, compared to training in London, you can easily live within walking distance of the office, and despite the lower pay than you'd get in the City, you'll find it much easier to get on the property ladder. Actually DWF has played a part in the rebirth of Liverpool, having worked for several years for a £32 million EU fund providing loans and equity to small businesses in Merseyside.

and finally…

DWF has big plans and stars in its eyes. There's a lot more going on than its traditional insurance work, so don't pigeon-hole it just because it acts for large insurance companies. One to consider if you've got the requisite enthusiasm and energy to keep up.

Edwards Geldard

the facts

Location: Cardiff, Derby, Nottingham
UK ranking by size: 75
Total number of trainees: 24
Seats: 6x4 months
Alternative seats: Secondments

A firm of two halves, Edwards Geldard offers a full range of legal services from its bases in Cardiff and the East Midlands.

six of the best

The firm has switched to a six by four-month seat pattern at the request of trainees. *"It's a great initiative,"* said one interviewee. *"It allows us to make a more considered choice before qualification, and it shows that the powers that be really listen to what we've got to say." Each office offers much the same range of departments and seats, the most popular of which seem to be employment and commercial litigation, where *"you get exposed to a variety of different disputes."* At the other end of the spectrum, residential property is *"not terribly popular with people who've come to a commercial law firm to do commercial work,"* yet it does offer a good amount of client contact.

The 8.30/9am–5.30/6pm hours were described as *"very civilised, very healthy." "Even the busiest amongst us go home at seven."* However, at peak times in the transactional seats the working day can stretch further. One trainee had a few war stories about a big deal they'd assisted with: *"It was tough, but it was a great feeling when I'd got it done."* Over in the personal injury department, trainees are *"constantly busy – you're never bored or stuck for something to do there."*

doing a ton

In terms of responsibility, one trainee summed things up neatly: *"It's always been appropriate for my level of experience. They're prepared to give you the ball and let you run with it."* Another added, *"Someone who needs to be led by the hand will struggle. They want people who are prepared to get their hands dirty and who, after a couple of months in each seat, will step up and look after files."* How about 100 debt recovery files in a commercial litigation seat? Constant supervision and feedback means that *"everything we draft, whether it's a letter to a client or a memorandum of research, gets checked, and you get taken through any changes."* On a more formal basis, there are monitoring meetings every two months with the departmental training partner. There's a bit of grunt work to be done: *"You've got to be prepared to do your share. Sometimes the support staff are busy and you'll have to do your own typing or photocopying."* However, such work is *"not the principal task of trainees."*

Client contact is there for the taking: *"I've had the opportunity to deal with everyone from Joe Bloggs off the street to the managing director of big companies,"* said one trainee. This contact extends to marketing too – trainees help with seminars, run around the football pitch and rack their brains for useless trivia at pub quizzes, all in the quest for better client relations. *"The firm is well aware that marketing's a big part of legal practice now, so the sooner they get you out meeting people, the better."*

show me yours and i'll show you mine

In each location, most trainees have a strong local connection. Indeed, at least half the Cardiff trainees have names like Davies or Evans! In each of the offices, trainees are a tightly knit group. As one Midlands trainee said, *"You're not one of 80 trainees here, you're one of four in this office. Everyone knows your name."* As far as trainees are concerned, it's not so much a case of 'never the twain shall meet' as a case of 'rarely the twain shall interact'. A Cardiff trainee explained: *"When we first start, we meet up and have a look around their offices, and then they come down and look at ours. But other than that, we don't have much contact with the East Midlands trainees."* There must be some, surely? *"If they want something from our library, they might give one of us a call, but other than that, not really."*

hanesion o gaerdydd

Cardiff offers a full range of commercial and private client seats and is thoroughly respected in the region, invariably vying with its two main rivals, Eversheds and Morgan Cole, for top dog status. Its IP and IT practices are regarded as the best in Wales, while the busy corporate department handles some pretty decent M&A work and certain transactions have an international angle to them. Among EG's major clients are S4C, the Welsh Development Agency and Admiral Insurance.

The office is described as *"very spacious," "modern and bright."* One trainee said, *"I was once told it has the highest free-standing spiral staircase in Europe, but I suspect they were having me on!"* If anyone can verify the claim, drop us a line. Welsh is spoken by many in the office but all communication with our good selves should be in English. A couple of trainees share an office with their supervisor, but most sit open-plan.

The social scene is *"thriving,"* with the Cardiff TSG a particularly lively group. *"The Cardiff legal community is a small one, and many trainees and pupil barristers went to university or law school together."* One of our sources chose the firm because of *"the enthusiasm of its trainees and the real camaraderie between them."* After work the venue of choice is Ha!Ha!, where you're likely to bump into more senior lawyers. *"We're encouraged to socialise with other levels – the senior partners themselves are very proactive on the social front."* We heard about regular team lunches and nights out and even an annual trainee skiing trip (they're out on the piste the whole time, no doubt).

our other half is in nottingham

Think of Derby and Nottingham as a single unit, if you can. *"They're trying to present the East Midlands offices as a whole rather than saying the Derby office does this and the Nottingham office does that."* One trainee told us: *"At the time I was recruited, I thought I would be mainly in Derby, but these days it's seen as an East Midlands training contract,"* with trainees *"yo-yo-ing"* back and forth between the two locations for different seats. This all ties in to the fact that, following its merger with local firm Eking Manning, the Nottingham office grew to be as big as the one in Derby. We certainly noticed a change in attitudes from when we'd last interviewed trainees in the summer of 2001. The two offices are definitely closer and there's even more of a sense that the Midlands half of the firm is on the up. *"A lot of the decision makers are still quite young; they don't come across as crusty, old partners. Many are in their 30s and 40s, which makes them that more approachable and makes the firm's outlook tally more closely with your own."*

Nottingham has a heavy insolvency element to its commercial litigation practice and also *"more of the main employment people."* In addition, it has some German lawyers and the office often wins referral work through their contacts. The Derby office's speciality is a commercial contracts department and it has *"the bulk of the debt collection disputes."* Otherwise, *"the teams are quite equal between Derby and Nottingham."* Trainees understand the logic of offering *"a larger pool of talent for East Midlands clients to choose from."* A glance at the client roster reveals banks, rail companies, power companies, Derby County FC, Derbyshire County Council, Chubb and Toyota, to name but a few.

taking pride in derby

The Derby lawyers recently moved into Pride Place, a *"swanky"* building *"on an industrial development* [we guess that should read 'business park'] *near the new football stadium."* One trainee confirmed there were a couple of pubs close by, *"but not places I'd want to go for a drink after work."* Add to this the fact that *"not as many people actually live in Derby as live in Nottingham. More of them are based in outlying villages and the Peak District, so they need a car to get in"* and it's easy to see why Nottingham is the more sociable office. *"Nottingham's a bigger and better city than Derby,"* pronounced one trainee. Sorry Derby.

One trainee who'd had experience of both East Midlands offices commented, *"The Derby office is much nicer than Nottingham,"* which is basically *"an older-style office."* Confusingly, in the latter, *"the stairs don't always take you where you want to go – people often get lost in here!"* Sounds a bit like Hogwarts! *"They're hoping to move in the near future – it's getting pretty tight in there."*

Traditionally high retention was not matched in September 2002: in the Midlands, four out of six qualifiers stayed on, while in Cardiff, it was three out of six.

and finally…

We're told that the Edwards Geldard 'pub test' we mentioned last year was spot on: *"The partners are looking for people who'll be confident and can deal with the tasks given to them, but who they can also talk to in the pub after work."* If either Wales or the East Midlands is your territory, this firm should be of interest.

Eversheds

the facts
Location: Birmingham, Cambridge, Cardiff, Ipswich, Leeds, London, Manchester, Norwich, Nottingham.
UK ranking by size: 1
Total number of trainees: 205
Seats: varies between offices
Alternative seats: Overseas seas, secondments
Extras: Pro bono – various law centres

With masses of quality clients on its books, Eversheds offers a great training. Whether you're seeking City experience or want to stay in the regions so you don't have to travel for hours to see your folks, read on…

level heads
Eversheds is experiencing "*an awakening.*" After allegations that it was really just several separate regional offices operating under a shared name, the last few years have seen greater integration. Eversheds' greatest common denominator is the people it employs – down-to-earth, outgoing and gloriously 'normal'. This is a firm filled with level heads. Eversheds, like Boots the chemists, has branches everywhere, including Paris, Monaco and Brussels, which are offered for short trainee placements. The advantages of working at an Eversheds office are that "*you get to know a lot of people in your own office*" and you get the back up of a wider network.

We found trainees to be devoid of airs and graces. There's a dress-down policy, a trend towards open-plan offices, and a drive to use plain English. Even its Oxbridge graduates are the sort who worked hard for their place, as opposed to the sort who had it all to lose from the start. Some firms are very hierarchical and trainees have little knowledge of, and even less input into, the firm's future. Not here. "*Even if you are sat with an equity partner, it's not formal; they chat with you about how things are going with the firm.*" With no compulsory seats other than the Law Society's requirements, it looks like the training is as hassle free as it gets.

London: size is everything
London is the administrative hub of the firm – the executive is based here and it just shades Birmingham as the largest site. Beyond that it is just another Eversheds office: "*It's not stuffier just because it's in the City.*" It may be a weedy 19th in the City muscle league, but Eversheds trainees have shunned the biggest City offices, saying, "*Once they get beyond a certain size there is a degree of impersonality.*" London operates a four by six-month seat pattern. Employment and IP/media regularly attract the most attention, although "*there is no department that really struggles or is the last choice for everyone.*" With a long list to choose from and no compulsories, there's something to suit everyone. If you're looking to get to the top of the billion pound mega-deals tables, this is not the firm to go to. That said, after an excellent performance in 2001/2002, our colleagues at *Chambers UK* promoted the London office to its table of firms handling mid-size corporate deals (valued in hundreds of millions of pounds).

As a trainee, you'll occasionally have to do "*more mundane tasks like bundling, indexing or scheduling,*" but "*in all seats you can take on as much responsibility as you like.*" "*There is no fear that you'll be dumped in at the deep end*" and "*there's the security that you can ask people for help.*" Socially, trainees make the most of things. With rugby sevens, hockey, cricket and a theatre group, "*the distractions are there if you want them.*" The Seahorse across the road is a popular venue.

birmingham: well endowed
Just like the London office, Birmingham runs a four-seat pattern. Trainees sit with partners and supervision is about as good as it gets. All trainees are expected to spend some time in the property department, which will provide perhaps the most responsibility. "*I always have four or five of my own files on the go at any one time,*" said one trainee. Understandably, in corporate there's less individual responsibility. Much of the work is orientated toward private equity, and as part of a team you'll be doing the standard trainee fare: "*I've done my share of

due diligence, data room work and photocopying," one source said. "But you also work with the team on BIMBOs, MBIs and some deal refinancing." Top of the seat wish list is good old employment; "it's a very popular seat," "everyone is smitten, perhaps because it is common sense, not really tough law." Trainees here work on top-level cases, "always for the respondents, top directors, human resource managers, and so on."

The office "is brand-spanking new" and the marble atrium "gives the place the feel of big-citydom." It houses a restaurant too, so if the heavens open, there's no need to get a soaking in your search for a chicken balti. Trainees are "sociable people, quick witted and quick thinking." Although, at times, work can be "a bit prosaic," "it's generally excellent and the supervisors are a good bunch." By their own admission, the Brum crew are "a bit more outgoing and raucous" than their peers at the other offices. "There aren't too many shy, retiring types," and "there is just the right number of trainees," which, in turn, makes them "very close knit – we look out for each other." After work, The Mailbox and Broad Street's bars are a target for trainees, whilst Jools Holland's Jam House pulls them in on pay day "when feeling particularly well endowed in the wallet department."

east of england: orgasmic

We'll start by assuming that readers know East Anglia from East Angular. It is nowhere near Tunisia. There are three offices in the East of England group – Cambridge, Ipswich and Norwich. "Each has the core departments, such as property, commercial, corporate and employment." Ipswich also has specialist construction and projects groups, and Cambridge houses a biosciences group. "Although not pushed to move," trainees are encouraged to shift between offices. We spoke to some who had completed seats in all three and others who'd not moved at all. If you decide to roam, six-month seats mean you'll have a chance to really experience living in each town before moving on.

You can expect typical trainee jobs on larger projects: "You do the day-to-day correspondence, with lots of e-mails and client contact by telephone, a lion's share of due diligence work, and you have a small input into the agreements," said one trainee. The corporate department was a one-time favourite, but this year's trainee group have restored employment to the top spot. "The East of England group has some of the best employment partners in the country" and is "probably the most notable of the departments."

Many of the UK largest biotech companies are to be found in East Anglia's Silicon Fen, so it is no surprise that "more and more applicants have science backgrounds." Whichever seats you choose, "they take training very seriously… They never say 'I'm too busy,' they always find time for you." Should the need arise, "they go right back to basics and get the statute out for you."

The social scene is "picking up since we have moved into the new office," one Cambridge trainee told us. The Flying Pig is favoured, although "there tend to be a few Mills & Reeve trainees in there." (Yes, and they say it's their bar!) The Ipswich office is also quite modern, "with some really good views over the town." Trainees looking for excitement head for Keo, or The Curve Bar, owned by Ipswich and Ireland footie hero Matt Holland. Just don't mention penalties, because it's a favourite with the Tractor Boys too! Norwich is "underrated as a place to live" and "surprisingly lively." Ha!Ha! is awash with local professionals and Tombland is another fave, but if you really want your night to go with a bang, head to Orgasmic.

the north: fun and games

Manchester and Leeds are closely linked and "one managing partner looks after both offices." The northern trainees know each other well – in addition to the week they spend together at the beginning of their contract, "departmental inductions are typically held with a day in Leeds and a day in Manchester."

Manchester trainees work in "a swanky, new building," although the trade off is that it is a fair way from the City centre. The Leeds office is "a mid-80s building…standard fare" but "smack in the city centre, so you can go for a wander in the shops at lunchtime." Both sites have felt the effect of the drive to standardise the regional offices. It *"feels much more like the same firm selling the same services,"* and it is now *"clearer to everyone who is dealing with what, and how it filters down."* The development of the firm's intranet has contributed to this in a big way.

the real north: losing your inhibitions

Eversheds Newcastle is hot on shipping, clinical negligence and property finance, so it attracts trainees looking for niche seats as well as the daily bread. In 2002 it moved into jaw-dropping new offices and *"everyone from equity partners to secretaries sit together open-plan,"* which means *"that nervousness you get from crossing a door threshold goes; the barriers come down."* The award-winning offices are *"funky and cool,"* have *"fantastic views of the Tyne Bridge"* and an Arabella Lennox-Boydroof garden. All ends up, you'll be hard pushed to find a better working environment.

Just like their colleagues elsewhere, the Geordie clan knows how to have a good time. Football, hockey and cricket teams play against clients and other firms. *"The hockey goalkeeper is a senior associate"* and *"the Newcastle managing partner plays on the football team."* Away from sport, vodka bar Revolution has caused one or two hangovers. Although we aren't keen on clichés, they really do have a work-hard play-hard ethic. Who said it was grim up north?

east midlands: significant others

Recently, all the lawyers in the Derby branch were shuffled over to the larger Nottingham office, so let's face it, nobody's going to fall off their chair when it closes. Nottingham has close links with Birmingham and one source confirmed *"some of the lawyers work in both offices."* All this moving about reflects the increasingly close bonds nationwide, with *"the national structure taking hold, and things being made the same across all the offices."* Trainees say there is *"regular interaction with other offices, and this has only just started to happen in a major way."* None of the four six-month seats are compulsory, but *"they do like you to do property*

as whatever department you are in there will be some connection with property." In property you'll have some of your own files, but don't panic: *"Supervision throughout is extremely good."* A trainee social club organises outings to plays and concerts and in Nottingham trainees frequent The Rotunda for post-work drinks.

cardiff: extra-curricular activities

Hot on the heels of their Geordie counterparts, the Cardiff crew recently moved to new open-plan offices. Not only is it right by the train station and therefore handy for those who live a little further away, but it has a popular café, which means you don't need to go far for lunch. Not that these trainees are likely to stray far anyway; most have a connection with south Wales, be it through study or family. Understandably, the Cardiff offices wants *"people with a connection, or at least a very strong desire to be here."*

With a strong team spirit and a good range of seats on offer, there is seldom any dispute over choices. *"Whenever the seats changed around I always got what I had asked for,"* said one source. That also applies to cash if you want to go organise a lunch or start up a sports team. If you have an interesting project and can find a few colleagues to support it, *"the firm is quite good at funding things."* And at the end of a week of decent hours, good work and good training, the Cardiff trainees like nothing better to unwind in Ha!Ha! Make all the sheep jokes you want – these *bechgyn y bachgennes* have got plenty to laugh about.

Eversheds retained all but 13 of its 93 qualifiers in 2002, and all but two were offered jobs. A few chose to qualify into other offices in the network, either for personal reasons or because the job they wanted was available there.

and finally…

Eversheds is easier to gauge now that it is one integrated partnership rather than a collection of separate profit centres. The training experience varies ever so slightly from office to office, but wherever you go, you'll feel like you're home.

Farrer & Co

the facts
Location: London
UK ranking by size: 72
Total number of trainees: 14
Seats: 6x4 months
Alternative seats: Secondments

Located in Lincoln's Inn Fields in an old Georgian town house, Farrer & Co is to other City law firms what Fortnum & Mason is to Tesco. Its royal connections and long history of private client work may not be everyone's cup of tea, but if you want a broad training with some first-class opportunities, then the firm is definitely worth a closer look.

bespoke tailoring
Farrers is ideal for trainees who don't know exactly what they want to qualify into. *"You don't get pigeon-holed straightaway,"* confirmed one source. *"I was particularly attracted by the wide spectrum of seats. I didn't know exactly what kind of law firm I wanted to practise in; I just knew that I didn't want to get absorbed into a big City firm."* If other firms offer their trainees a one-size-fits-all contract, Farrers does its best to tailor the experience to each individual. During your six seats, you'll do property (commercial, private and 'estates' options), charities/private client (domestic or international), commercial (including banking and employment) and litigation (family, media or general commercial), followed by a 'wild card', which can be used anywhere. You'll then join the department you hope to qualify into for a final seat.

good breeding
When asked about popular seats, we typically heard something about *"horses for courses,"* although clearly private client was popular. On Farrers' courses, the horses are well fed and well groomed, and will most likely end their days grazing peacefully in a meadow after years of loyal service rather than down in the knacker's yard with some of their overworked, burnt-out contemporaries. The partners are *"accommodating and friendly"* and, while you are well supervised, *"you are expected to show initiative,"* much like those horses that finish the Grand National even if they lose their riders at the first jump. When you do have to go the distance, you'll always get a sugar lump: *"People do say thank you and that makes a huge difference."* As all thoroughbred owners know, training and upkeep require a lot of time, commitment and investment. *"At the end of the day the firm wants to develop the skills and services that they can offer their clients."* To this end, Farrers encourages external language training and *"is happy to consider foreign secondments, if the proposal is sensible."*

private parts
One source had originally applied to a whole range of firms, but when asked the inevitable question: 'Why do you want to be a corporate lawyer?' he realised quite simply that he didn't. *"I didn't want to have to do three different types of banking seat."* On the other hand, *"private client work is something I really enjoy. It's fascinating to learn about how other people lead their lives. You can find yourself drawing up wills with people who have six kids by three different wives and trying to work out what should happen to the vintage Aston Martin."* The charities department works for trusts, national charities, museums and schools. Secondments are available to the London Business School and the Science Museum.

Farrers has an enhanced media and defamation practice following its 2001 merger with Crockers Oswald Hickson. At the time of our interviews, one trainee was on secondment to a TV station. For some the firm will lose appeal because it doesn't act for hordes of FTSE 100 companies and the facilities in the building aren't of the standard of the megafirms, but then big-name corporates and an on-site gym are not things that interest Farrers' current crop of trainees. They consider their style to be more understated.

"It's like working in a big family house where everyone knows each other," and trainees are invited to dine at high table rather than sent below stairs to scrub the

pots and pans. One even served up champagne to The Queen on her recent visit to the firm. How's that for client contact! Levels of responsibility are high: "*I've been sent to do important jobs, which is flattering, even though it would have been better to have an assistant to support me.*" The work culture was described as "*superb*" and being in the office past 9pm is "*an absolute rarity.*" Trainees were clearly happy with the firm as a whole: of the September 2002 qualifiers, six out of nine were offered a job and all accepted.

The vac scheme is felt to be a key part of the recruitment process, when trainees can get a feel for the place and potential suitors can be sized up by HR before they are admitted to the family. "*If you come and check it out and you like the feel of the place then you can rest assured that there are no nasty surprises.*" Just be smart when dealing with the trainees; "*they have a real say in things. People are forming impressions of you all the time.*"

true blue?

Trainees come from different backgrounds and universities. "*The stereotype of the Farrers trainee is not true. Times have changed and the firm is evolving.*" There is a good mix of people fresh out of law school and those with previous careers in journalism, banking and the armed forces, for example. According to the private client brochure, a Farrers solicitor aims to become "*a friend, an ally and a confidant – what would once have been called a 'man of affairs'.*" Quite.

We were told repeatedly to ignore the "*toffee-nosed image,*" but clearly if you are a radical republican or the illegitimate child of a country earl with a chip on your shoulder, there are probably places where you would feel more comfortable. "*We're all middle class here,*" offered one trainee. If they thought about moving into big glass offices or switching to dress-down, "*the trainees would be the first people to complain.*"

Farrers inspires great loyalty and many of the partners underwent their training at the firm. Even if they have no family name, fortune and traditions of their own to carry on, the trainees we spoke to cared about the name, fortune and traditions of the firm. Some acknowledged, however, that a continued lack of diversity might count against it. Every family needs new blood to keep the genes strong and, to that extent, it was felt that Farrers was broadening its horizons when it came to recruitment. "*My tutor at university said I'd need an injection of blue blood to get in. The reputation is still there, but there has been a massive dilution.*"

house style

The firm plays cricket against the Royal Household and numerous other clients. It has an away weekend every summer where it takes on teams fielded by bankers, Coutts and *The News of the World*. One trainee said, "*I can't remember much of the cricket,*" so closing the door on that topic. What is clear though is that no one cares too much about the final score and even though "*being discreet is part of the job,*" the words "*big,*" "*piss*" and "*up*" did slip from someone's mouth. "*As a trainee it's quite common to be in the pub with some of the more senior partners and assistants.*" Everyone agreed that the caring relationship that is fostered by private client work is one that infuses the whole firm. An annual trainee review, written by the second-years with a view to making a few jokes at the partners' expense, is performed at Christmas. "*It's taken very seriously. They even give you time off to practise!*"

Despite the stately home comparisons, there's no upstairs-downstairs mentality. "*There are no artificial barriers between people. You can chat to partners or to the support staff.*" You may find all this either "*very caring*" or "*quite claustrophobic.*" It's lucky, therefore, that you have plenty of time for a life outside work. "*I rarely have to cancel my plans,*" claimed one trainee.

and finally…

Whether you're simply looking for a mid-sized London firm that can offer you a good range of work and the personal touch, or you tend to gravitate towards National Trust properties and hanker after the good old days of the gentleman-lawyer, you should find that Farrer & Co caters to your needs.

Field Fisher Waterhouse

the facts
Location: London
UK ranking by size: 39
Total number of trainees: 23
Seats: 2x6 and 3x4 months
Alternative seats: Secondments

FFW is a medium-sized commercial firm on the edge of the City, offering trainees a grounding in traditional corporate and finance work, and exposure to more niche areas such as IP, IT and clinical negligence. The general consensus seems to be that you'll get a first-class training without the stresses and strains associated with some of the larger City firms.

no regrets
Most trainees had put a lot of thought into their choice of firm, and were typically attracted to one of the niche areas. Although the firm has a respectable corporate practice, it is not the major draw. A standard response was: *"It offered me the seats that I wanted with a competitive salary attached. It was as simple as that."* FFW has indeed got some interesting commercial practice areas and it is almost the only City firm to boast a claimant clinical negligence department. If you relish the camaraderie and adrenalin built up during regular all-nighters then you will probably go unfulfilled. FFW is marketed as a *"lifestyle firm"* and, insofar as is possible in a firm of City solicitors, it seems to take this commitment pretty seriously.

One source told us: *"When you're looking for a training contract there's always the temptation to apply for somewhere big and bold, but I am very glad I didn't do that. If you want to wear the name of your firm like a designer label and you care a great deal about the size of the deals and your place in the rankings, then this probably isn't the place for you."* What you do get here, however, are high levels of responsibility from an early stage and a more personal relationship with the people you work with. Apparently, *"you rarely pass a stranger in the corridor."*

5ive
The training programme is based around a unique five-seat system that is felt to offer *"that bit extra."* The main practice areas are corporate & finance, property, litigation and IP/IT, but the firm's only hard-and-fast requirements are that you do a contentious and a company/commercial seat. The remaining three seats are left open for you select what interests you most. You can choose your contentious seat from a range of departments, including commercial litigation, clin neg, travel & tourism, IP/IT, or within the professional regulatory group, which acts for the General Medical Council, nursing bodies and the new General Social Care Council.

When it comes to seat allocation, you are encouraged to be frank about your hopes and fears at a meeting a month before you rotate. Since there are only ten trainees in a typical intake, competition for seats is not ridiculous. The firm made a real effort to keep all its trainees in 2001 when they completed their training. Even though there was only one job available in the employment department they decided that they could stretch and take two rather than have someone go elsewhere. In 2002, eight out of the ten trainees were offered jobs, and each of them accepted. The firm has recently joined a pan-European alliance of law firms, which has opened up the possibilities for foreign secondments for qualified lawyers.

no big heads
While it may not be as trendy as some of its media-oriented competitors, many of whom still regard FFW as comparatively old school (*"more wood panels than frosted glass"*), if you're interested in striking a balance right from the off, then it continues to be a pretty good bet. There have been no great shake-ups of late, but then that's not really their style.

The graduate brochure is illustrated with colourful utopian, constructivist paintings that depict gleeful trainees with disproportionately small heads (not a physical characteristic that anyone had particularly picked up on) leaping around gleaming international cityscapes. While that may be overstating the trainee experience slightly, those we spoke to were pretty content with their lot. Certainly FFW comes nearer to a Brave New World than to the gulags of some of their Big(ger) Brothers. *"People here are defined as being lighthearted, which is a tone that's set by the partners,"* said one trainee. *"We are treated as colleagues rather than slaves."*

karen fanclub

When it comes to first impressions and actually getting in, FFW has a reputation for having one of the more difficult interviews. You don't tend to get asked specific legal questions, but they want to test your reactions. Example? *"I was asked which seven famous people I would take with me to a desert island,"* reported one. Someone else was surprised by the friendly tone of the proceedings: *"I wasn't sure if they were laughing at me or my jokes, but they offered me a job, so presumably the latter."* Our sources were unable to discern a particular type that the partners were looking for other than suggesting that *"they don't recruit arrogant people."* Apparently, *"there is a place here for everyone whether you want to build a big social life or just bury yourself in a hole. The only requirement is that you don't rub people up the wrong way."* Trainees seem to have a good idea of what they want and where they are going. *"It's definitely a vocational thing,"* said one. Not many people had just fallen into the law because they couldn't think of anything better to do, or at least they weren't admitting to it.

"You can be confident that you will be judged on your merit and not on which school or university you went to," reported one source. But if you are looking for speedy self-advancement then don't apply. You must be prepared to muck in and work as a team. These trainees are a pretty uncomplaining lot, but if you've got any moans *"from your love life upwards,"* then there's always a shoulder to cry on attached to *"Auntie Karen,"* the much-loved head of graduate recruitment.

keeping up appearances

Trainees noted a split between the more traditional departments and the newer practice areas in terms of dress code and atmosphere, but that's not to say there's any great tensions or identity crises. It's hardly tattoos and piercings versus pinstripe suits. One trainee told us: *"When we read somewhere that we were supposed to be sexy media lawyers we looked at each other and had a good laugh about that. It's considered quite wacky to wear a polo shirt, but then that's lawyers for you!"*

It's certainly refreshing to hear about lawyers not taking themselves too seriously. The Christmas pantomime last year was based on Snow White, the dwarves replaced by seven trainees who went by the names of Happy, Grumpy, Tipsy, Dopey, Skiver, Sloaney, and Crappy. Don't worry. If you don't find yourself fitting neatly into one of these profiles we're confident that Auntie Karen would be interested to hear from you anyway. Obviously the inter-departmental clothing confusion spills into playtime, since *"there was a fair bit of cross-dressing going on"* and a partner did the honours as the mirror on the wall. The Christmas party was on the theme of 'Rhinestones and Rock Stars', so there was at least one Elvis and quite a few Madonnas in attendance. Some of the partners came dressed as cowboys. We heard confused reports of water pistols being drawn.

all back to mine

Outside the festive season, socialising is still taken quite seriously. It's not unknown for a partner to put their card behind the bar or to invite trainees back to their house for a party. In terms of facilities, the firm has just built a squash court and recently opened up a coffee lounge downstairs called The Bolthole, which features a big TV and comfy sofas. If it sounds too much like Ally McBeal for your tastes, one trainee assured us: *"We don't dance to soft rock and we don't have communal toilets."* Apparently the 2,000-year-old London Wall runs through The Bolthole, so it's a bona fide tourist attraction as well as a place to eat your lunch.

If you're into sports then there are plenty of internal and inter-firm tournaments to get involved in. Touch rugby was a top choice for client entertainment, and that's Field Fisher Waterhouse just about down to a tee: active, competitive and team-focused, but without the tears and bruises that you would expect from some of the bigger, full contact firms. In addition to the in-house entertainment, there is plenty happening on the firm's doorstep. No longer on the edge of things, the area is picking up, with new bars and restaurants opening up all the time. If chain pubs don't float your boat then there are plenty of smaller, more soulful places to unwind in.

and finally…
Plenty of IP and IT clients, a general commercial training and the opportunity to sample some interesting niches: it's a great mix and it's all on offer in a firm that won't swamp you or steal your personal life.

Finers Stephens Innocent

the facts
Location: London
UK ranking by size: 95
Total number of trainees: 8
Seats: 4x6 months
Alternative seats: None

Based in the heart of the West End, Finers Stephens Innocent came into being in 1999 following the merger of general commercial and property practice Finers with media specialists Stephens Innocent. Acting for both public and private companies as well as private individuals, the firm is now 90 lawyers strong.

hot or not?
The firm is divided into six principal areas – commercial property, litigation, corporate/commercial, IP & media, private client and employment. This spread of activity is half the appeal to trainees. The other half is that it's a West End firm, not a City machine. As one interviewee said, *"I thought it would be a good opportunity to get a balanced training at a firm that was well respected*, but not a City firm where you're going to be working all the hours God sends."* Some were attracted by the media work, others by the strong property practice.

Strictly speaking, there are no compulsory seats but given the size of the litigation, property and CoCo departments, you'll do a seat in at least one of these during your two years. The media/IP seat is terribly popular: *"It has top level work and interesting characters;"* employment is regarded as *"sexy and fashionable;"* and family also has its supporters.

who's in your little black book?
In a firm of this size, trainees can be assured of getting hands-on experience but this also means *"you can't hide away."* *"You have to be proactive on your own account – even though you're supervised, you have to be able to handle the pressure of your workload and think on your feet."* With your own files in many departments, you'll get your fair share of client exposure. *"On certain matters you even have to invoice the client yourself, so you're running the whole financial side too."* One trainee told us: *"From the first day, I was dumped into things and sometimes you think 'Bloody hell!'"* but the support is there. No one could ever accuse the firm of holding trainees back. *"In my first month here, I was given* [a celebrity's] *phone number and told to contact her!"*

"If you're looking for a large City firm where you can do purely commercial work, this isn't the place for you." However, *"if people want to do some* [smaller] *corporate finance transactions, some interesting media work and varied litigation ranging from judicial review to defective cars, then they should check us out."*

the nitty-gritty
The hours are very reasonable – mostly nineish to sixish. One relieved trainee said, *"I don't feel anyone's checking me in or checking me out!"* A couple of others talked about working some very late nights in corporate, but not constantly. *"It's feast or famine,"* one said. *"For weeks you can be leaving at 5.30pm and then a deal comes in and you're staying much later."* Over in litigation it's *"more staggered – you know what the deadlines are*

from the outset so you can structure your workload and time a bit better." The commercial property department was described as "the biggest and most consistently busy department, as there's a high volume of work coming in from a large number of corporations, and it's quite labour-intensive." As for grunt work, it's definitely there, particularly in litigation, where "bundling is unavoidable if there's a big case going on." Thankfully, the general office staff do most of the big photocopying jobs.

Trainees share offices with their principal although they also receive work from others in the department to "broaden their training." The two training partners run a formal appraisal system, and regular group meetings between them and the trainees offer the chance to air issues of concern to all. As for training, external lecturers venture in to give presentations and there are internal skills seminars and departmental updates. Trainees normally attend everything that's going, "usually one and sometimes two things a week."

stars in their ears

FSI doesn't hide its light under a bushel. Its media team, and in particular Mark Stephens (who regularly appears in print and on radio and TV), does a good job of keeping the firm's profile high. "It can be a real shock to the system to wake up and hear Mark Stephens on the radio after you've seen him in the corridor the day before," one trainee said. We were also told that the trainees are actively involved in helping him research and prepare his contributions to the Radio 4 quiz show Points of Law and Jimmy Young's show on Radio 2.

The firm is split over two buildings as it has outgrown its main office on Great Portland Street. It's a great location and ideally placed for lunchtime shopping and post-work drinks. Frequently visited locals include Ha!Ha! and the more traditional Albany. Most popular of all is Villandry, a wine bar for which, we were told, "you need to raise a mortgage" in order to visit. A social committee organises regular events – a Jubilee party, a Halloween party, "give them an excuse and they'll throw a party!" Every month 'Wind Down' in the office involves "drinks and nibbles" for all staff, and every week a breakfast is laid on to chase away Monday morning blues. A dress-down policy applies every Friday and for the whole of August. No jeans or trainers though – it's not that meeja!

By now you may have a fair appreciation that FSI is a very amiable place to work. It's partly down to the size of the firm, partly down to the nature of the clients ("entrepreneurial, medium-sized businesses looking for a differentish law firm") and partly down to the fact that West End partnerships tend to be a little more chilled than their City counterparts. "It's always been a progressive law firm, not just taking on cases for financial merit, but also to develop different areas of law." We always love it when a trainee describes their firm as "exciting!"

The run-up to September 2002 was a nail-biting time for qualifiers. Sadly, 2001's high retention (seven out of eight) was not repeated and only two jobs (employment and PI) were available to the five qualifiers. In the end, only one of them stayed. As one first-year said, "Let's hope next year improves."

and finally…

If you're looking for "some interesting work, a lot of client contact, diverse roles including marketing, and you want to contribute from an early stage," you know what to do!

Foot Anstey Sargent

the facts
Location: Plymouth, Exeter
UK ranking by size: 88
Total number of trainees: 9
Seats: 4x6 months
Alternative seats: None

A fine West Country player with a successful merger two years in the bag, strong regional clients and a stated ambition to become the best business firm in the South West in five years. Foot Anstey Sargent is on a mission.

read all about it

Our interviewees were bursting with tales of cheery receptionists welcoming them by name on their first day, and people coming up to say 'hello' before they had any clue who was who. So far so happy families. The firm is modernising and implementing changes quite typical of larger firms. There is much excited talk of business plans, swanky new IT systems, and a recently expanded training scheme. As one trainee put it, *"aggressive isn't the right word, but they have a bit of a vision and there's a sense they want to go places."*

If you're interested in private clients, these can range from criminals or those in tricky family situations to dead people. On the commercial side, there are seats in company/commercial, commercial property, employment, insolvency, banking and property litigation. The plan is to beef up the commercial side of the practice by reinforcing the firm's strong regional client base and winning a few more national clients. It has been notably successful in this latter objective with banking and newspaper clients. *"Commercial property is a popular seat,"* was an oft-repeated comment. Why? *"Probably because it's one of only a handful of commercial, non-contentious seats. The trend towards commercial work is very apparent among trainees, maybe even more so than in the firm as a whole at the moment."* We suspect that the property seat's supervisor might also be part of the appeal. He doubles up as the training principal and had the balls to take up our challenge of a True Picturing in about two minutes flat. His superhero outfit is in the post.

any other business?

The trainees we spoke to had a fair level of say in where they ended up, at least in their second year. There are no compulsory seats, and *"with so few trainees, there's not too much competition. You'll usually get your first choice."* The approach to seat allocation is described as *"flexible"* and the firm has no objection to trainees spending a full year in one department, if that's what lights their fire. While the level of responsibility varies between departments, the general principle is a sort of 'guided freedom'. Trainees won't always get to run their own files, although those we spoke to claimed they *"wouldn't like to be left on their own"* anyway. All trainees sit with their supervisors but get work from other members of the team as well. Feedback and appraisals are, generally, well organised, although monthly group discussions were written-off by one trainee as *"pretty useless"* – qualified by a hasty *"but that's 'cos we have no complaints."*

feeling wanted

So what type of applicant is the firm looking for? Aside from the usual stuff – good academic record, strong personality – it really is all down to your roots. Many trainees attended university or (even better) grew up in the region. Feigning a love of cream teas and Ginsters at interview might not be enough. *"They define the region broadly though,"* one trainee assured us. Behind this preference for locals is the usual combo of touchy feely *"regional identity"* and simple irritation with qualifiers disappearing off to the Big Smoke. *"You've got to convince them you understand the realities of working for a provincial firm."* On the minus side this means *"appalling transport links to London and less than amazing nightlife."* On the plus side, there's a huge amount to be said for *"walking on Dartmoor and an all-round great quality of life."* Consider the hours for a start: you can often count on being out of the office by 5.15pm – a joy simply unheard of in City firms.

Applications from mature students are sensibly welcomed. Their existing knowledge of how to work and greater life skills are recognised. And used. *"You can't hide like you can in a big firm,"* commented one source. The recruitment procedure is *"one of the toughest down here,"* although the firm is not thought to be dogmatic about boringly perfect academic records. Trainees noted that the firm does not simply take on trainees just to put bums on seats, so if you get an offer, *"you'll know it's because they liked you and they really want you."* Everyone agreed that, given their heavy involvement in client entertainment, trainees need to be sociable and have something to say for themselves.

"I only had to do washing-up at a client event once!" commented one. Yikes! Bring your marigolds…

padded cell

The Plymouth office looks quite slick on the website – a mass of black, mirrored glass glinting menacingly in the sun. As it turns out, it used to be a TV studio, so as you toil away in your fully soundproofed office, console yourself with the thought that no one will hear if you strangle your boss. As for Exeter, hmmm… Comments ranged from the resolutely positive (*"stately and imposing, sort of Dickensian in a good way"*) to the tell-it-like-it-is (*"the most old-fashioned building you ever saw…no lift…freezing in winter"*). Fret not. New offices are in the pipeline and the Exeter gang should be happily ensconced somewhere snazzy by the time you get there.

The region's Trainee Solicitors Groups are active, particularly in Exeter, with regular booze cruises, parties and barbecues and a *"high-ish level of participation"* from the various firms in and around town. This isn't the kind of place where you can parachute into a ready-made social life though. Foot Anstey Sargent isn't chasing identikit trainees straight out of university, and this means that many already have well-established lives in the area. Trainees told us that their salaries aren't stratospheric, but we checked and they're towards the top end for the region and might even allow you to mention the 'M' word to your bank manager without him laughing in your face. The firm has a good record for retention: all this year's trainees were offered a job on qualification, and this has been the case for the last four years.

and finally…

Foot Anstey Sargent isn't looking for those who thrive on bright lights and big city life, but it does offer a varied and flexible training and an excellent work/life balance. For those committed to the West Country, it's a smart choice.

Ford & Warren

the facts
Location: Leeds
UK ranking by size: 103
Total number of trainees: 12
Seats: 6x4 months
Alternative seats: None

Ford & Warren is a mid-sized, broad-based commercial law firm in Leeds. If you prefer a single-site, organically grown firm to a rolled-out national franchise, then take a look at this one. And don't be put off by the low-tech website.

kings of the road

According to one trainee we spoke to, the firm is particularly strong in transport (one of the best in the country), employment, insurance litigation, and both claimant and defendant PI work, so if roads and what happens on them is your thing then your search is over. The firm offers seats in various departments ranging from family through to corporate.

Some trainees felt they didn't get much input into seat allocation, saying: *"You go where they need you."* Others disagreed. *"When you are offered a place on the training scheme they like to understand your strengths and weaknesses and place you accordingly. You end up getting a balance of contentious and non-contentious work."* One thought: *"It's a bit silly when you have two people in seats that they don't particularly enjoy when, if you swapped them, they would be much happier."* The message seems to be that you should make it very clear what you'd like to experience and keep sending the message to the powers that be. But with all five September 2002 qualifiers offered a job, our sources were wholly positive about the qualification process and applauded the firm for its approach: *"On qualification, they will bend over backwards to put you where you want to be."*

The firm acknowledges that certain trainees find some areas of practice less thrilling than others, and rather than force a full seat in debt collection, family or residential conveyancing, allows trainees to opt for a three-month mini-seat. *"In areas like res con, two or three months is quite enough!"* reported one source.

holding pens

The offices are *"informal"* and open-plan. Trainees sit together in *"trainee banks." "You get to chat to the other trainees and it's much better than sharing an office with a partner,"* thought one. Another told us, *"It's possibly easier to get on with the work once you've got it. If you're sat in with your principal there's always the danger that other things will get thrown at you."* We assume they were referring to files rather than staplers, hole punches and stress balls. Seniors give *"constant guidance and feedback"* and trainees understand that *"the firm wants you to develop all the fundamentals and a wide spread of legal knowledge. It doesn't want you to specialise too early."*

You'll get an end-of-seat appraisal with your supervisor, and monthly reviews where you are expected to fill in a form saying what you've done. *"Informally you get appraisals almost daily and the nice thing is that you always get thanked for the work you do. You always get praised when you do something good."* There are monthly internal training sessions for everyone in the firm. These are described as *"good and clear and you get handouts. They're not too heavyweight and they're not pitched too high."*

One trainee told us: *"Compared to other firms there's not a lot of difference in pay but the hours are much better. I don't often work more than 9am-5.30pm, I've never done a weekend and only stayed beyond 7pm on a handful of occasions."* Grunt work is kept at a minimum: *"You only have to do the dross if there's no one else around to do it."* Another said, *"Even the partners photocopy here."*

the way of the ninja

When we questioned trainees about F&W's modest marketing efforts, we were told that it is deliberate in its understatement. *"The firm is innovative but not in a way that follows standard patterns. It doesn't just jump on the bandwagon."* Another felt that it had been keeping a low profile intentionally, so as to be able to pop out of nowhere on a deal and stun the opposition with its legal prowess. *"It's all part of the game plan. People aren't aware of just how good we are."*

Having heard little about the firm, one trainee was pleasantly surprised: *"I turned up for interview at this seven-storey castle in the middle of Leeds. I had a bit of banter with the secretary and the interview was very friendly. When they made me an offer I actually dumped my contract elsewhere. There was a much better vibe here."* When asked to describe F&W's ethos and reconcile mixed reports regarding its formality, one trainee explained: *"It is formal in that you have to adhere to formal dress and behaviour codes, but the partners and associates themselves are unstuffy. It's traditional – you are expected to behave like a lawyer, but the structure of the firm is modern."*

baby boom

The firm tries to avoid jargon and waffle – *"People like to use simple English."* Described as *"quite a young firm with lots of people in their 20s,"* when we conducted our interviews, F&W was going through a period of *"baby visits."* As one of the lads said, *"When you hear all the girls cooing in the corridor you know there's a baby being pushed around."* We tried to find an identikit trainee but were told that *"they're keen to take people who have alternative backgrounds. They don't just want people straight out of law school. Half the trainees are around 30 and they like people who have taken time out and done something a little bit different."* In the words of one trainee: *"They are looking for people with drive and independence; people who can drive their own careers forward; people who can make decisions and develop the business."* Phew!

steamy

The offices, right opposite Leeds Magistrates' Court, have been refurbished recently. There's plenty of space and *"lots of plants and coffee machines around the place."* The seventh-floor staff area has been kitted out with *"suede sofas and Ikea furniture"* and there's a useful café. The only minor gripes were that it gets pretty hot in the summer, and *"bigger desks would be nice."* Want, want, want!

Most socialising is informal (*"It's really up to you to make the effort"*), although there are well-attended departmental parties and a firm-wide Christmas bash. If you are up for a night out, *"there's a hardcore group which goes out every Friday for drinks,"* and when the troops are mobilised, favourite haunts include Bar 38, Fat Cat and Henry's. We also learned of summertime dragon boat racing and trips to watch cricket.

and finally…

In summing things up, a trainee declared Ford & Warren to be *"down-to-earth, ambitious and unpretentious. Good clients but without crazy hours."* It doesn't court publicity so, if you like what you see, rest assured that you've not been duped by smoke and mirrors.

freethcartwright

the facts
Location: Nottingham, Leicester, Derby
UK ranking by size: 63
Total number of trainees: 15
Seats: 4x6 months
Alternative seats: None

Freethcartwright is one of the largest law firms in the East Midlands and boasts offices in Nottingham, Leicester and Derby. The practice is divided roughly equally between commercial property, private client, dispute resolution (in particular clinical negligence, product liability and personal injury) and corporate and commercial services.

give me a p! give me an r!

The bulk of the trainees are based in Nottingham and spread over four sites. There are no compulsory seats and trainees' requests are taken into account. Clinical negligence and personal injury are always popular, given the firm's supersonic reputation for high-profile matters including the soya breast implant class action and the MMR vaccine litigation.

"It's quite a large department and it's well respected in the claimant arena." That's a very modest assessment, we feel! Three cheers for the commercial property lawyers: somehow they've achieved the impossible and persuaded trainees that their work is sexy. *"It's a very busy area at the moment, so you can guarantee you'll get quality work coming in all the time,"* one trainee told us. *"It's very much the case that if something appropriate comes in, they're more than happy for you to have a crack at it,"* particularly sale and purchase files. Now if they ever get bored with drafting leases, we'll happily pimp these partners out to the 99% of firms who can't persuade trainees to rush into property seats.

Nottingham also offers seats in commercial services and employment. Over in Leicester, there are two positions on offer: a general comlit seat and one in clinical neg/PI. Both are well subscribed as *"it's nice to get away from Nottingham for six months"* and *"it's a fairly young office so it's an exciting time to be there as it establishes itself and expands."* One source said their time in Leicester was *"the most sociable seat I've had in terms of time and money spent on making sure the staff are well looked after."* As for Derby, one slot will be available in corporate finance from September 2002.

you're not from round here, are you?

Even if not locally born and bred, many trainees studied in Nottingham and then chose to stay put and settle down. We've been there – so we can understand why. *"You have to be able to demonstrate a commitment to Nottingham or the Midlands – the best way they can ensure retention is to hire people who want to live in the area."* There's certainly some commitment shown by one second-year trainee: we heard that he commutes into work each day from Birmingham! While a one-week vacation placement is a relatively common route into a training contract with the firm, a number of the current first- and second-years started out as freeths paralegals. Our interviewees told us why they had chosen the firm. *"We're a top three firm in the East Midlands, so it was a fairly easy decision,"* said one. Another told us: *"The breadth of work they had on offer was a real*

283

attraction. I didn't know what I wanted to do when I started, and here I could keep my options open – I could try clinical negligence and I could give commercial property a go." As for the trainees themselves: "We're a proactive bunch socially – we'll happily ask for more events and more money to put them on." Along these lines: "There's slightly more focus on making sure we enjoy ourselves than there is with the fee earners. I guess they want trainees to be happy so that they stick around after qualifying."

ch-ch-changes; steady as she goes

In past years, we've written about how the firm has been in a state of flux. This year's interviewees believed things had crystallised: "*A lot of the changes have now come into operation – the firm knows where it's going and what type of firm it is.*" One source added: "*It's more of a steady ship and it's going in the right direction.*" And that is? "*It's no secret that it's focusing more on corporate/commercial work.*" Indeed, the firm "*carved out*" and discarded family and crime from its practice and "*if you look across the firm now, commercial property is arguably the strongest, with corporate getting stronger.*" We have no doubt that the PI/clin neg work is as secure as ever: it continues to contribute "*huge fees*" and brings freeths welcome profile. The consensus is that while it has worked out its direction, freeths needs to keep pushing. "*If we want to make ourselves the number one firm in the East Midlands, we need to compete at the top level. At the end of the day, we're a business and corporate/commercial is where the money is.*"

Most of freeths' commercial clients are Midlands-based private companies and owner-managed businesses. "*It's mainly local businesses. Most of the plc work outside London is done in major commercial centres such as Birmingham, Manchester or Leeds rather than Nottingham.*" That said, the property department has a number of clients from further afield, notably "*quite a few banks.*" A note of caution from one of our sources: "*Nottingham's a nice place, but it's not a major commercial centre. If you're hugely ambitious and want to be where there's constant action, with a consistently high quality of commercial work, you might be better off elsewhere.*"

The Nottingham lawyers are split across four buildings, three of which are open-plan. Bringing everyone together in one building would "*help the firm feel like more of a united entity,*" but it's unlikely to happen any time soon, according to our sources. "*The lease doesn't end for a while yet and they're looking to see what the economy does before making any decisions.*"

now then, now then

Open-plan seating means that feedback is "*constant.*" "*I've got partners to the left, in front and behind me, so if I spin around on my chair and ask something, I'll get three answers!*" Trainees are assigned a 'guardian' in each seat in addition to their supervisor, and the appraisal system was praised for being "*useful and thorough.*" Satisfaction with the training resulted in four out of the five qualifiers staying in September 2002.

"*Everyone wants to be the best lawyer they can be, but they don't want to sacrifice their lives for it.*" In the Slug & Lettuce next door to the Low Pavement office in Nottingham, you're "*guaranteed*" to find a fair few freeths people at the end of the week. And "*if anyone knows how to have a good time, it's the Leicester people,*" who are described collectively as "*one big social animal.*" As well as trainee events (such as charity white water rafting), there are departmental and firm-wide jollies. At the Christmas party, trainees traditionally stage a short comedy show for the entertainment of the firm. They are given time to rehearse and money to buy props (mainly "*silly hats and silly costumes*") and then "*for 15 minutes on Christmas party night, everyone's fair game!*" One senior partner always joins in the revelries and, over the years, he's dressed up in a tutu, masqueraded as a Spice Girl and, at last year's party, performed as Jimmy Saville!

and finally…

Whether you're attracted by top-notch clinical negligence and class action work or you're simply looking for a Midlands firm with a growing commercial profile, check out freethcartwright. It might be able to fix it for you to become a qualified solicitor.

Freshfields Bruckhaus Deringer

the facts
Location: London
UK ranking by size: 6
Total number of trainees: 178
Seats: 3 or 6 months long
Alternative seats: Overseas seats, secondments
Extras: Pro bono – RCJ CAB, Tower Hamlets Law Centre, Privy Council/US death row appeals, language training

Freshfields Bruckhaus Deringer, proud bearer of the title 'magic circle firm', has a fantastic reputation both nationally and internationally. In every area in which it works, it is either at or near the top of the pile. Snap a Freshfields lawyer in half and you'll find 'quality' written all the way through. The training provides a skeleton key that will open any door.

bye-bye goldilocks

It's been assumed that the typical trainee was of the blues and blondes school: the "*not very nice*" Oxbridge types "*who looked down their noses at you.*" As the old public school-and-off-to-Oxbridge route into the City is challenged, "*so the recruiting department has had to be more amenable – it doesn't want to miss out on excellent candidates.*" Sure, half of its trainees (50% as at August 2002) are Oxbridge, but if you've got the right attitude and brains, you could come from any number of universities. Freshfields has recruited from over 70 different ones worldwide in the last four years.

The trainees are confident creatures: "*pretty sorted but with less strut and swagger.*" They have the self-assured stroll of bears rather than the feline prowl of some City lawyers. "*The firm is high on enthusiasm and a high-energy place, but there's no pretension.*" The Oxbridge grads we tracked were the types who had worked hard for their place and now intended to make the most of it. Sharp, enthusiastic and eager to please, "*everyone is clever, hard-working and driven.*"

out of the box

All of our sources stressed Freshfields' interest in people's inherent abilities – "*It wants to take what you are and make the best of it.*" If you have one of the recruitment packs, chances are you've already noticed the difference. "*You look at loads of application forms and they really are all the same, and then you look at the Freshfields one and there's this big blank box that says 'tell us about you'.*" The biggest plus is that "*you can just say what you want*" and "*you don't have to try to bend it all into a little box.*" There's no need to prove that you pulled off the impossible armed only with an empty bottle of Fairy and some blu-tac. The only possible downside is that after days of inventing wild stories about mountain rescues and bigging-up what they did in the Brownies, Scouts or tennis club, some people are probably too stunned to fill it in.

You don't need a deerstalker and magnifying glass to deduce that Freshfields could also be un poquito interesado en los idiomas. Not only is the London office "*seriously cosmopolitan,*" with lawyers from all over the world, but also trainees handle plenty of international work. We spoke to people who had liaised with lawyers in offices from Austria to Australia. Forget just talking on the telephone; there's a serious chance of getting a seat abroad. If you land a contract at Freshfields, your first trip after starting could be to the post office for yet more forms – this time an E111 and an SE04.

Here are a few tips to getting your overseas seat: experience in a similar seat in London will help, as will "*a really clear idea of where you want to qualify.*" Fortunately, a second language won't always be needed, and there's a list available to indicate which language skills you might need for each country. There are seats in Madrid, Frankfurt, Milan, Paris, Bangkok and similar places, but the jewels in the crown, at least if trainees' recommendations are anything to go by, are Singapore, Hong Kong, Tokyo and New York. Because these are in such demand, "*there's no guarantee you'll get your first choice.*"

the long and the short of it

Trainees mix up long and short seats of six and three months. The optimistic side of us says this is to give them greater choice, but when in half-empty glass mode, we're inclined to conclude that there aren't enough of the favourites to go around. The first seat is always a six monther and thereafter it's up to you as to how long a seat should be. Some, like IP and competition (if you can get them), are only ever short ones. In larger departments, such as finance, corporate and litigation, there's less concern: *"They are huge and sooner or later you'll get there, although you might not get the specific team you are after."* Although the repetition of the words *"oversubscribed," "no guarantee"* and *"bend over backwards"* made our ACME brochure-speak detector gently bleep itself to oblivion, we have to conclude the system is fairly effective.

> Chambers Global's South & SE Asia Law Firm of the Year 2002

In addition to the Law Society's contentious requirement, trainees do corporate and finance seats. Usually these last two add up to a minimum of nine months, but could be shorter for those hell-bent on litigation, say, or longer for those dead set on specialised finance seats or winning a popular posting like New York. If you're not interested in an overseas seat, there are regular secondments to clients such as IBM, Morgan Stanley and Goldman Sachs.

Your supervisor will always be either a partner or a senior solicitor, but you may share a room with a junior solicitor. Appraisals take place every three months. The level of responsibility you can expect to receive varies greatly depending on the time of year and from seat to seat. *"Fairly predictably, corporate doesn't have much responsibility because invariably the deals are pretty big,"* said one source. *"But then there is always the question of whether you really want all that responsibility."* With deal price tags that Oooooh so loudly, we suspect not. As a result, along with *"a bit of document management,"* corporate trainees *"tend to help on small aspects of the deal"* and *"get little pockets"* of work. It's a similar story over in the tax department, *"where, due to the nature of the advice, it could be dangerous to leave it to trainees."* You'll have plenty of accountability in property. We heard of trainees with their own *"quite difficult files." "It's good because the phone rings and it could be a client or an agent, and you just have to deal with it."* The ever-popular IP department provides trainees with a chance *"to do lots of research that you have to really think about"* and *"to draft licences as part of wider corporate transactions – it's corporate support, but not in a gimpish way."* OK, let's not delve any deeper...

how many hours, paleface?

Trainees gave mixed reports on hours. Some were lucky and caught corporate at a quiet time; the majority identified it as the main offender in the long-hours saloon. While the plucky finance seats arrived for the showdown packing well-crafted nine-to-six shooters, ol' corporate hustled into town with a fearsome nine-to-nine magnum. Scared? The colour should be draining from your face: the first nine was on Monday morning and the second on Friday night. *"It was absolutely horrific,"* uttered one recuperating trainee.

Although all-nighters are not the norm, they can happen in a department where upwards of 25 lawyers and a posse of support staff can be required for a single deal. But then, *"if you want to be stuck on your own all day, become a barrister, because this is about teamwork here"* said one source, and *"when others have been at it for weeks it's good to take a bit of the workload off them."* At least *"you won't be doing the grunt work"* because Freshfields has invested heavily in paralegals (they match the trainees man-for-man) including a night team. Apparently, you can just leave your stuff on your seat in the evening and it will all be sorted and proofed for you by the morning. Hey, can we get some of that?

In September 2002, 46 out of 47 qualifiers were offered a job and 42 accepted. We asked a number of first-years and LPC students how they felt about qualification and all of them regarded a training contract offer from Freshfields as a permanent job offer.

achy-breaky hearts

Stroll across the ironstone square and into reception and you immediately start to breathe in professionalism. The spacious offices are strangely devoid of desktop PCs – everyone has laptops. The little devil on our shoulder insists this is to squeeze every drop of work out of the day, and we aren't going to argue with him this time. The offices surround an atrium, at the bottom of which is the library. And then there's the in-house restaurant, not to be confused with the Costa Coffee shop, also on site. Another plus is the gym. Although small (and sweaty), it is reasonably well-equipped and includes a dance studio, where a six-week yoga course will cost you a piddling 20 quid. For country music aficionados, there's always the line dancing class. Yes, you did just read that.

When they get fed up with 65 Fleet Street, trainees escape to The Bank of England. The Hogshead is popular when they want to pig-out, and The Witness Box and The Tipperary are conveniently built into sides of the office. Aside from these, there are twice-monthly department drinks, the Christmas party, the summer party and the *"any excuse for a party."* As if that wasn't enough, you can join various sports clubs – football, rugby, netball and softball. Not content with the existing travel opportunities, the climbing club recently went to hang out in Spain.

and finally...

If you are looking for a high-quality City training in a big firm, Freshfields could be your legal love match. For years it's struggled with the tag of being elitist. It's also had a reputation for being the place to go for super-long hours. We didn't find these charges capable of sticking. Times have changed. OK, it's been a quiet year, but we heard plenty to convince us that trainees will be in a fine position, even when the big deals come stampeding back into town. Step on up if you're prepared to give it your best shot.

Galbraith Branley

the facts
Location: London
UK ranking by size: 120
Total number of trainees: 10
Seats: number varies
Alternative seats: None

This north London firm specialises in crime, family, PI, and mental health work, as well as actions against the police. It's on the Serious Fraud Panel and handles some fairly high-profile criminal matters. Recently it was involved in a landmark case (one of their lawyers was even on the TV news) regarding violations of the human rights of psychiatric patients.

a life of crime

Crime is what draws people in, and what better place to do it than in deep north London. You've got to come to where the crime is and *"London is the best place for it, unfortunately!"* Someone from a sheltered background may get quite a shock when they start the job: *"You're suddenly dealing with the lower echelons of society. It can be quite an education."*

Crime doesn't pay big bucks, but it does offer the *"excitement, variety and interest"* that you might lack in commercial practice. *"I like being unable to plan my week,"* said one source. *"I also get a buzz from helping people."* Someone else admitted they were a bit drained by the end of the crime seat: *"A lot of the time you're dealing with drug addicts and you don't get much thanks,"* while another said, *"dealing with endless traffic offences and shoplifting is like swimming through treacle."*

well hello, clarice

Mental health work offers an opportunity to advocate. Trainees are expected to get up on their feet at managers' meetings (where patients can appeal against being sectioned). These *"little trials"* demand plenty of preparation and nerve. *"It's very good practise,"* even though *"they start you off on cases that you're not expected to win.*" The downside of mental health work, particularly for women, is the "*sleazy men*" that you sometimes come in contact with. Think Agent Starling coming face to face with Dr Lecter. "*The guys are protective*" though, and if anyone feels uncomfortable there is always support and someone else to step in. This area of work can be truly rewarding and there are times when you'll feel very good about your part in helping someone get his or her life back on track.

The PI department (which operates on a no win, no fee basis) is felt to be really kicking off now, and the family department deals with the usual range of matrimonial and children's law matters. Remember, this is a high street practice, so don't expect too many trophy wives and offshore accounts.

We discovered a refreshing mix of noble crusaders and *LA Law* aficionados. Some were attracted to the work because of their politics; others by the thrill of dealing with clients at the 'challenging' end of society. Just to challenge our preconceptions about legal aid lawyers, one trainee told us: "*I'm not really ethically motivated. Lots of my friends think I have no morals!*" Although motivations vary, two things bind trainees pretty tightly: "*booze and football.*" After cross-examination, one trainee confessed: "*We go out for drinks between one and five times a week.*" Trainees are considered to be "*relaxed and sociable*" and must thrive on hard work and pressure and, most importantly, "*they need to have a good sense of humour.*" Apparently, there is no one with a superiority complex and everybody pulls their weight. "*Usually there's always someone who people think is a bit of a dick. Not here though.*"

needs must

The seat system is flexible to the extent that trainees sometimes end up working in whichever departments have the greatest need. You will definitely experience crime at some point but, apart from that, seat allocation is open to discussion. Most enjoyed this flexibility. "*If you know that you want to do crime work you can get stuck into that rather than have to waste your time in other departments.*"

As a criminal lawyer you will be on call 24 hours a day three times a month. This can be either "*a real buzz*" or a "*pain in the arse.*" One of our interviewees told us: "*At the beginning I was terrified about giving bad advice. You can't lose sight of the fact that this is someone's life you have in your hands.*" Colleagues and police are apparently supportive. "*So long as you're polite with the police then they are with you. At the end of the day, you're both just doing your job.*" The firm's name is held in high regard in the area. "*No one gives you any sh*t when you turn up and say that you're from Galbraith Branley.*" The cases you deal with in the early hours can vary "*from cannabis to rape and murder.*" When you're not on call, the office day usually means an 8am-6pm commitment, but some people end up staying until 7pm or 8pm. One trainee went into the office most Saturdays, "*just to keep on top of things.*" Another estimated that they did an average of a 50-60 hour week.

One bone of contention is that trainees don't get paid a percentage for their overnight efforts when they are on call. The trainee salary is higher than the Law Society minimum, especially so in the second year, and trainees do get a Christmas bonus, which goes some way to compensating for those unremunerated evenings in the police station. No complaints about retention anyway: in 2002, all four qualifiers stayed on with the firm, which is a very good hit rate. Indeed, retention is a big thing with this firm: we learned that all bar one of its solicitors trained there.

law and order

Instead of being sat in an office with a supervisor (which is the norm in most commercial firms), at Galbraith Branley the trainees sit in an open-plan area, with the senior lawyers sat around the edge in their own offices. The office itself is considered to provide a pleasant working environment. It is "*tidy and impressive,*" although "*it is getting a bit overcrowded.*" At the moment there are three people hot-desking, which is "*a real hassle*" but a good way to get to know people all over the office. "*A lot of the stuff is learned on the job, but if you're having trouble you can always turn to the partners* and other lawyers," and second-years are ideally placed to impart their wisdom to first-years. There aren't too many formal group sessions. "*Maybe there could be more intensive extra training,*" thought one source. "*If you don't get told off, you know you're doing well. It would be nice to hear praise a bit more often…a bit more feedback would be good.*" Quality of work and levels of responsibility were considered by everyone to be pretty high. "*Everyone tends to do their own photocopying, but other than that there's very little tedious stuff.*"

and finally…
Despite long hours and challenging work, our interviewees agreed: "*I may get stressed, but I'm never bored. I've never woken up and thought I don't want to do it today.*" This is a training that will allow you to hold your head high and be proud of what you've achieved in two years. Galbraith Branley, bring it on!

Gateley Wareing

the facts
Location: Birmingham, Leicester, Nottingham
UK ranking by size: 90
Total number of trainees: 11
Seats: 4x6 months
Alternative seats: None

Gateley Wareing is a trim commercial firm championing small and medium-sized Midlands businesses. It's not trying to steal any crowns from the Birmingham giants, but these firms do tend to drop smaller jewels and Gateley Wareing is quick to scoop them up.

say 'aaah'
Originally a Birmingham firm, it now has two smaller offices in Leicester and Nottingham. Each takes trainees and moves between them at trainee level are permitted. In 2003 the main office will move to Birmingham's old Ear, Nose & Throat Hospital. One trainee saw this as indicative of GW's ambitions: "*It's nice to be part of an evolving beast as you're able to play your part. The move will be a significant change – we'll have twice the amount of space.*" And scope for endless nose job jokes…

GW recently won the Birmingham Law Society's Firm of the Year award for firms under 20 partners. "*It is looking to be the dominant force in the owner-managed business sector. Eversheds, Pinsents, Wragges, etc. have grown into huge firms with big-ticket work; it's no longer possible for other firms in Birmingham to do that, and it's not necessary for us.*" Trainees are proud that the firm is "*not huge and bloated,*" believing their own contributions to be more important as a result. As one said, "*You really have a chance to make a name for yourself here.*"

tough love
Forget training by numbers, "*you're not just checking or photocopying documents, you're a part of the fee earning team.*" Supervisors take time out to sit down and explain why they are doing what they are doing. "*You get quite a lot of individual contact with your supervisor,*" one source commented. Partners are generally easy to get along with, although rumour has it that "*some should say thank you a bit more*" and "*one guy gives people a hard time; but he toughens you up and he believes that if you can learn to handle him, you can handle anyone.*"

Some trainees talked about having handled client meetings and small corporate completions on their own; another about the various court applications she'd made and another about having led negotiations on the settlement of a dispute. "*It shows they trust you to do a reasonable job and you really learn a lot... When I was in corporate I wasn't tenth down the chain of people, I was involved in everything from speaking to clients to dealing with documents and that's where I learned most.*" In short, you'll be "*allowed a lot of rein on a tiddler of a job.*" And if we heard about how Gateley lawyers "*roll their sleeves up*" once, then we heard it a dozen times…

matthew 7:7
It's not often we get biblical, but when we learnt how the trick to getting more responsibility was to simply

ask for it, we were glad that one of our number has a degree in theology and could remember the Sermon on the Mount. So, verily we say unto you, prospective trainees: "Ask, and it shall be given you; seek, and ye shall find; knock [on a partner's door], and it shall be opened unto you."

This emphasis on performance means that there's no place to hide and no room for slacking. *"If you were miles off mark or had been lazy, you'd get a flea in your ear"* and the pressure *"ramps up from your first to your fourth seat,"* but you can always talk to someone *"if things get wayward."* GW wants confident trainees with a bit of personality, those who can *"interact with clients across the board."* One source said, *"I've been encouraged to get out there, get on with things and get my face known."*

bad hair day

Every month the separate offices have their own social events and every three months there's a firm-wide do. Bowling, meals out, drinks parties, casino nights, treasure hunts (*"like Mission Impossible, haring all over the countryside"*) and quizzes – that sort of thing. Departments compete against each other and points are awarded at each event. *"Last year corporate won overall, so they got money for a night out."* As corporate is the biggest department, *"there's always a huge amount of discussion about the weighting of the scoring."* Are the stakes really that high?

Trainees organise the entertainment at the Christmas party. Last year it was a 70s disco and the year before that fancy dress. The winner had gone to an awful lot of effort to dress up as Don King. Someone in IT was Bob the Builder and the partnership secretary shaved his head to be Gandhi. *"Everyone enters into the spirit of it. Actually, people can't get enough of it."*

One source said, *"I know every single member of the firm. If I was working over in Nottingham, for example, I'd get there early and have a quick catch-up with people before I started."* The firm's intranet – Backstage – is available on the main GW website, so do check it out. Apparently, it demonstrates the firm's desire for *"a balance between the work and life outside the office…You learn a bit about your colleagues as people."* If you're a film buff or into gigs, you can air your views on Backstage. If you want a drink after work, the local bar in Birmingham is Kempsons. *"It's the first one you'll try"* in order to find your workmates.

and so, my fellow trainees

Formal training sessions range from the practical to the couch potato-esque (*"You are supposed to attend Legal Network TV twice a week"*) to the feng shui-like (which chair to sit in/making people comfortable in meetings/working a room at a marketing event). This latter type goes down well and trainees would like more of it. And what does the firm want more of? *"People who have a long-term interest in the Midlands," "those with a commercial approach"* and *"bubbly outgoing characters"* with confidence. One went so far as to say that the question applicants should ask themselves is not *"What can Gateley Wareing do for you, but what can you do for Gateley Wareing?"* Kennedy would be proud!

There's an officially appointed 'head trainee', who acts as a liaison with HR, so in a quiet moment we busied ourselves designing a nice uniform in the navy and burgundy corporate colours. Our respect went out to the guy flying a lone flag for male trainees. The firm's recruited more fellas for 2002/2003 so here's looking forward to a better performing footie team and conversations more diverse than *"dresses and shopping."* The gender balance at the top of the tree contrasts with the trainee population. Only one of the 17 partners is female, but trainees have high hopes for a clutch of senior female associates. In September 2002, three out of the six qualifying trainees were offered and took jobs at the firm.

and finally…

If the kudos of a big name on your CV and *FT* headlines are less important to you than being an active part of the Midlands' business community, then get your backstage pass. And if you're game for a laugh or you can do a mean Don King, what are you waiting for?

Gouldens

the facts
Location: London
UK ranking by size: 69
Total number of trainees: 32
Seats: Non-rotational
Alternative seats: None
Extras: Pro bono – Waterloo Legal Advice Centre

Gouldens' distinctive style and non-rotational training system set it apart from other commercial firms. Be absolutely sure that you're big and bold enough for the challenges it will throw at you. If you are, get set for a thrilling ride and a big fat bank account.

the way it works
Day one, you get your own room and a free rein. You must hunt and gather your own work from partners and assistants across the firm. Your room might be located in the property department, but most of your work could be corporate. It's your choice. Over the course of the two years you have to fulfil certain experience requirements, but there's absolutely no need to spend six months in any particular area of practice. Consequently you belong to no one and will not find yourself the pet or plaything of a power-mad partner.

In theory, you'll build up relationships with partners who do work that most interests you and you'll convince them to give you more and more of what you want. In practice, *"there's a bit of begging and then, after about six months, you'll have made contacts with those you like working with. In those first few months you have to go round and say 'I'm willing to do work'. Your very early work patterns are often set by geography…I did have to go down from my room and say: 'Can I have corporate work?'"* Some trainees move rooms after a while.

the debate
It's important to get your face known early on. *"You need to be someone who is confident."* Really confident. One trainee said they had a huge amount of sympathy for the minority who didn't take to the system. *"Most gain confidence from it, but with others it destroys it."* The message is clear: don't fall into this firm by accident. Think carefully about how you will adapt to the system and whether you have the inner strength *"to cope with sitting in an office by yourself all day, every day."* You must really enjoy responsibility. And we're not using that word 'responsibility' in the same (rather warm and fuzzy) way we do about most other firms.

An enthusiastic proponent of the 'home alone' scheme told us: *"It can be fantastic. I've learned I can cope with a lot more than I ever thought possible. If anyone could have told me what I'd be handling now, I'd never have believed them!"* From another who gave the system a thumbs-up: *"It's a leap of faith coming here. I like the concept of responsibility and I'm glad I've already done the scary bit of being out there on my own with clients, but an awful lot is dependent on who you work with."* If you work with someone who gives a lot of feedback then it's great, but some trainees bemoan the fact that you miss out on learning from a partner by continually watching and listening to them. A more circumspect trainee said: *"You're a lawyer when you come in, from day one, that's sexy and it's great, but I am actually a trainee and I want to be educated."* A few feel that partner support is a valuable commodity for which demand outstrips supply. Not everyone thrives when left to their own devices. The good news is that eight out of ten 2002 qualifying trainees were offered and accepted jobs.

game over
With all this libertarian thinking in action, we wanted to know how the firm prevents trainees from slipping through the cracks. *"For the first year we had lunchtime meetings once a month. It's done as a group – the trainees, the training partner and the training manager. That's where you bring up work issues. We didn't have one-on-ones."* While this might sound lacking to some, others think the system perfectly adequate. *"I don't feel isolated. With the vast majority of partners, you can pop into their office and talk about a work problem. I can only judge from my particular friends, but I think people tend to cope quite*

well. I happened to find myself two partners who are excellent and they give me very full-on supervision. If you can find people, then you don't feel you must run things by yourself." The point is that not everyone finds people.

Prove yourself early and you're a winner. It's a mini-version of Gouldens' 'six years' rule. By that stage (and you should regard that as a lifetime away!) you'll either make partner or leave. It's one reason why the firm's (deliberately) not grown in size and why there are fewer 'career assistants' than you need for a good game of chess. Gouldens has stayed small and extremely profitable. No flab. We're bored with that tired old *"punches above its weight"* label. Why not imagine a nippy, sharp-clawed velociraptor fighting a lumbering stegosaurus in some weird dinosaur Tekken arcade game instead? It works for us.

exactly what it says on the tin

Great news: *"On a vac scheme you get to see what it's really like here. We don't have the resources to be any other way."* Don't take that resources comment as an indication of the firm's pecuniary situation. It's indicative of the unstructured approach to the firm's existence and the fact that the scheme is not stage managed to the nth degree. There's no long hours culture. 9am to 7pm is the norm. After that you'll be ready for a drink at The Smoky Irish over the road or up on the roof of the office in the summer. (They keep them away from the edges, we hear.) *"I think we pride ourselves on not having a massive hierarchy at all,"* one source said of the relationship with partners. Chances are they've just paid for your pint. *"The firm's generous – you just order a cab at 8pm, if you've had a sh*t day."* The firm is, of course, most notably generous in the huge salaries it pays.

It's not a traditional firm. It's not that it's wacky or zany, it's just that the normal rules seem less relevant somehow. One trainee summed up the partners: *"As a group they are independent minded to a fault. You won't find them browbeating each other into a corner."* Some have likened Gouldens to barristers chambers. What comes to the fore is a commercial 'get on with it and prove yourself' culture.

and finally…

Come here if, after your first year, you want to concentrate completely on developing your niche, and if you want to feel a year qualified at NQ stage. Unless you're a tough cookie, or if you prefer to learn at your master's side, you may be better suited to a more conventional firm. *"Everyone knows it's classed as a quirky firm,"* one trainee told us. And, for the right candidate, this makes Gouldens all the more appealing!

Halliwell Landau

the facts
Location: Manchester, London, Sheffield
UK ranking by size: 38
Total number of trainees: 25
Seats: 4x5 + 1x4 months
Alternative seats: Secondments

Last year was a busy one for Manchester's Halliwell Landau. It edged closer to a multi-site strategy with a view to winning more work from London clients and it was instructed by more AIM-listed companies than any other Manchester rival. Biggest in Manchester? Yep! Ambition? You betcha! Profits? Great!

halliwell i never

With impressive growth figures, this is a firm that thinks big and looks to the future. Halliwells is fiercely proud of its roots and its independence (*"It is first and foremost a Manchester firm"*), but it competes directly with the national firms that dominate the North and is now pushing its 11-partner London outpost. Forever innovating, Halliwells has also launched its own HR consultancy arm and a fully outsourced virtual dealroom facility for its corporate clients.

When we asked trainees why they picked the firm in the first place, they typically told us that they lived or had studied in the North West and had been looking for something other than a local branch of a national firm. *"I wanted somewhere home-grown but also* ambitious. It's a small enough firm for you to know most people and there's potential to grow with it," one said. Most conceded that there was an element of truth in the firm's reputation for boldness. *"We tend to take a hard line on corporate deals and litigation. The firm is aggressive in its marketing and its pursuit of clients, but internally it's very friendly."* Another trainee thought of the firm as *"a go-getter,"* pursuing new business regardless of barriers.

halliwell and good

The firm has just put in place a new seat system whereby four seats of five months will be rounded off with a fifth, four-month seat. Trainees will do this last seat either in the same department as their fourth seat or in the department they plan to qualify into. The vast majority of assignments are Manchester-based, but there are a couple of seats in the London office handling both contentious and non-contentious commercial work. The insurance litigation office in Sheffield does not take trainees at this time. Three seats will be spent in commercial litigation, corporate and property and the fourth is down to you, but if you want a popular seat such as employment or IP then you'll have to fight for it. *"They ask for your top three choices and do their best to accommodate you."* Not only is there variety in the seats on offer, but also within a department you may be able to persuade your supervisor to slant your experience towards a particular type of work. *"The point of the training is for us to experience as much as we can so that we can find our area and then be the best we can be."* Someone had clearly scoffed a few motivation pills that morning.

A couple of trainees felt the corporate department was leading the charge forward; others stressed the importance of banking and even employment. There's bags of AIM work and the firm acts for oodles of national clients from breweries and sports concerns to insurance, engineering and good old-fashioned heavy industry. There are no overseas opportunities, but if you want a stint in London or a secondment to a big local chemicals client or a medical client in litiga-

tion, then just ask. The firm has just arranged a trainee secondment to the Commission for Racial Equality.

check mate

"The only defining feature of the trainees," said one source, *"is that they seem to be switched-on and have the ability to hit the ground running."* It's certainly not a place for wallflowers (and, according to one interviewee, *"not leery maniacs"* either!). Our sources were keen to stress that *"you are not spoon-fed or mollycoddled, so at times you can feel a bit out of your depth. This way of training may not suit everyone."* For those up to the challenge, *"trainees really get into the thick of things. There's lots of responsibility delegated to trainees. Most of the grunt work is outsourced...they don't tend to dump it on us."* The kinds of people who will thrive are those who *"like a challenge...and want to raise their profile. If you like to take things slowly and would like your training to be a careful system of checks and double checks then this isn't the place."* Potential applicants are advised to check they have the requisite levels of *"ambition and drive."*

Halliwells' lawyers are described as *"down-to-earth, dedicated, professional and personable."* The hierarchy was considered to be reasonably flat, but there was a telltale comment that *"it's good to have a structure to work within."* One trainee told us, *"I spent a long time researching the type of firm that I wanted...this is the sort of place where you can build up a reputation and climb the ladder as fast as possible."* Whoa boy!

how are you, pumpkin?

Expect an abundance of formal training sessions on *"everything from basic telephone techniques to how to do corporate transactions."* A variety of external speakers come in to educate trainees and seniors alike, supplementing the internal training. *"Each department decides what they need to focus on."* You're also encouraged to get involved in the marketing side of things. *"The firm tries for full retention of its trainees so it makes good sense to introduce us all to the clients right from the outset."* Consequently, there are sessions on networking and public speaking.

For a good part of your two years, you'll sit with a partner in their office. It's considered *"an excellent way to see how they build up a rapport with their clients."* Also, *"it's the best way to build up a relationship with your supervisor; it's easy to throw questions across the room."* Although most were very positive on the point, there were one or two minor moans about the appraisal system. *"I've never actually had an end-of-seat review,"* admitted one trainee. Day by day it is easy enough to get feedback from those you work with, though.

The hours are *"reasonable,"* but *"you won't get off lightly just because you're outside London,"* one trainee admitted. *"Generally, I'm out of the office by 7pm, maybe 8pm. Depending on how much work is coming in, it's not unknown for you to be in the office until the wrong side of midnight."* This is evidence of the firm's industrious character and its ability to win good work.

After two years of riding your shiny, new chopper bike as best you can with your supervisor running behind, *"qualification comes as a natural progression rather than like someone suddenly taking the training wheel off."* However, there was a bit of edginess and a few calls for more transparency and information about the process of getting an NQ job this year. While the firm had 100% retention in 2001, at the time of our interviews in early July 2002, some trainees were still unsure of their fate. But we got the facts in the end: seven of the ten qualifiers stayed with the firm.

putting on weight

The offices are central but *"bulging."* The partnership has had the ergonomics boffins and designers in to try and reorganise the space, but as one trainee concluded, *"if the firm keeps growing we're going to have to move pretty soon."* Look at the statistics in the firm's A-Z entry at the back of this book, particularly the one that tells you what percentage of assistants trained with the firm. What it tells you is that Halliwells is sucking in lawyers like a tornado.

The social side of firm life is considered to be *"excellent."* Apparently, *"trainees do bond very well"* and, a few years down the line as a qualified lawyer, it's likely you'll still be close and go out for drinks with each other and the newest generation of trainees. If you're a keen sportsman or woman, you'll enjoy regular cricket and football matches, and an annual, firm-wide summer barbecue is good for keeping up links with those in other departments. The favourite watering hole is the nearby Chez Gérard (or Chez Halliwell as it has become known). Close by are the Printworks and Triangle centres, which are ideal for shopping and entertainment. Actually, *"you've got the whole of Manchester on your doorstep."*

and finally…

If you find it hard to be *"ambitious, driven and enthusiastic"* when it comes to things legal, you may have a bit of a problem fitting in to this exuberant, confident and expanding practice. If you started to buzz while reading this and your palms are just a bit sweaty, it's a sign that you need an application form.

Hammond Suddards Edge

the facts

Location: Birmingham, Leeds, London, Manchester
UK ranking by size: 7
Total number of trainees: 97
Seats: 6x4 months
Alternative seats: Overseas seats, secondments
Extras: Pro bono – Paddington Law Centre, language training

As one of the larger regional firms, Hammond Suddards Edge offers a broad commercial training across its four UK offices and international outposts. Bit by bit, through a series of mergers, Hammonds has been hammering itself into a new shape.

losing its edge?

According to a June 2002 report in the legal press, the firm plans to drop the Suddards and the Edge from its name. Apparently, some clients had difficulty pronouncing it. If this is true, trainees didn't seem to know too much about it. *"I'd heard the firm was looking to change its name, but if it was as simple as changing it to Hammonds, I'm sure we would have been told by now,"* said one mystified source. *"There certainly hasn't been any official communication about it, but I'm convinced it is true,"* said another equally bemused trainee. The firm has become image-conscious: *"There's definitely a rebranding process going on but I don't think we will have a radical name like 'Monday' or 'Tuesday',"* said another source, referring to the recent PriceWaterhouseCoopers rebirth. Perhaps fears of pirate websites with dancing donkeys are the cause of all the hush. All we can conclude is that there is a chance the firm will be plain old Hammonds by the time you read this.

follow the van

Moving between the UK offices is an integral part of the Hammonds' experience and trainees must complete seats in three of the offices. *"The firm is completely inflexible on that,"* warned a source. So, listen up – you will have to move but the firm provides subsidised accommodation. *"It's £40 a week, even in London, and we only pay that so we don't get taxed,"* chirped one happy source. Properties range from *"nice but basic"* in Leeds to *"really rather good"* in Birmingham, where the trainee flats are in a luxury block with a gym, sauna and rooftop terrace. Chances are it will be a long time until you can afford to live so close to work and in such opulence again.

We heard a few grumbles over forced moves but, in fairness, recent mergers have exacerbated the problem as *"trainees recruited from elsewhere didn't really sign up for rotation."* Moving trainees around is a military exercise: *"We all have to move on the same day, so a man collects all your stuff in a van on a Saturday morning. An army of industrial cleaners go in and clean, and then you can move in to your new place on the same day."*

It's easy to be sceptical of the whole set-up. It sounds too much like a set-up, for one thing. Secondly, the very same logic that says 'if you move around you will know people in the other offices better' can also be employed to argue that 'you'll know people in the office you qualify into less well.' That may be true to an extent; *"I needed some tax advice but didn't know anyone here so I contacted someone in London,"* said a source. However, the general idea is quite exciting and most trainees seem to enjoy the experience. We'll leave you to decide whether it sounds like heaven or hell.

Still reading? Then we'll proceed on the basis that moving is cool with you and you like living away from home in a flat that isn't yours with someone you hardly know. Sound familiar? *"For two years it's like an extension of university,"* chirruped one interviewee.

are you winding me up?

Trainees are expected to complete a corporate and a property seat, as well as gain the contentious experience required by the Law Society. This still leaves three more seat options. Since the firm operates by way of national practice groups rather than autonomous regions, similar seats are offered in each office. With clients such as BP Amoco, Compass, Clear Channel Communications, clothing chain Bon Marché and Unilever Pension Fund, the firm has recently handled some pretty valuable deals.

London offers a rare seat option within the firm's commercial IP department – sports law. If sports law is your thing then you'll already have worked out what a rare opportunity this is, and you're no doubt delighted that Hammonds merged with niche sports practice, Townleys, last year. There are equally popular general IP teams around the country, where trainees are given *"a lot of responsibility for trademark portfolios and domain name disputes"* along with smaller roles on *"a few heavyweight cases on copyright issues."*

London also offers the chance to work as part of the large insolvency team, which was enhanced by the absorption of factoring specialists, Wildes, in 2001. Expect lots of individual responsibility here too – Hammonds Direct, the firm's high-volume conveyancing service up north, provides lots of work for the Winders Court (the informal name for the bankruptcy bit of the High Court). At bankruptcy hearings "there are hundreds of winding-up petitions, and you are up and down all the time when the judge calls you." High Court? Judge? Oh yes, this is about as real as it can get. "They are quite keen for you to go to court alone," said one trainee, "but even though it's scary it is a good experience."

speech marks

There's a similar "here's a document, go and draft it" approach in all the offices and in almost all departments. However, we also heard that trainees "are so spoon-fed it is unbelievable." This strange contrast stems from the support trainees receive. Every trainee has "a daily supervisor, who is either a partner or an associate," as well as a training partner for each seat. "Every fee earner and partner responsible for training has now been trained themselves." In some departments, Thursday mornings mean "mandatory training sessions that are given the same status as client meetings." Trainees select a couple of legal updates each week, and take turns to speak for an hour on a particular legal topic, while "partners chip in their knowledge." Add in rigorous drilling in everything from billing techniques to basic legal knowledge, and you have a rather effective training programme…

…which even includes language training should you desire it. And you might, particularly if you choose to pop off to Paris, Munich or Milan for a four-month stint. If the idea of conversing in anything other than The Queen's own leaves you tongue-tied, there's always the seat in Brussels. At this time there are no postings to the small Hong Kong office.

all back to mine

The standard of the offices is one of the few remaining inconsistencies of HSE. The London office is a typical glass-fronted building in Cutlers Gardens. Leeds is a smart yet standard offering, except for the quirky, Playschool-inspired triangular windows. Manchester also offers a comfortable, if rather standard, site. Birmingham, however, ("all a bit 1960s-stylee and not the best") rather lets the side down. Again, the firm isn't resting on its laurels, and "it is rumoured they are looking for a new building, although there is a shortage of office space in Birmingham."

The special nature of the training makes for a unique social scene. Think of the house parties full of random people that you attended at uni and you are on the right lines. Trainees all spend two weeks together when they first start their contract "and then they disappear off all over the country." They make a big effort to stay in touch and the 'flat-crawl' phenomenon is no small part of it. The idea is that trainees get to see their future homes. The reality is somewhat different. Essentially, trainees "decide on a city for a night out, then go around all the flats boozing, and hopefully end up in the one they are meant to be sleeping in." Messy.

More regularly, the Slug & Lettuce and Casa are popular after work with Leeds trainees and the Manchester mob head for the Ape & Apple. The Magpie and The Poet are London favourites and it's the Naked Pepper that pulls in Birmingham trainees when they really should be heading home. Generous partners will even put a credit card behind the bar on a Friday night. All the offices offer a range of sports, and all have "brilliant social committees" that organise everything from themed nights to subsidised trips to Eurodisney and other attractions.

knowing me knowing you

The merger between Hammond Suddards and Edge Ellison, and the subsequent addition of the two niche practices, Townleys and Wildes, has made for swift growth. Like any merger, there's always a sense of uncertainty: "The firm is a bit fragmented, but that isn't really its fault. There are people who are only too happy to talk about the old days, and when someone is made up to partner they say 'that's a Hammonds person' or a Townleys person, and so on." This is "even more acute in London where people have been physically thrown together," unlike in the regions "where we've been able to get to know each other gradually." Clearly it's making a full-bore effort to create one big, happy ship but there have been departures. Unfortunately some of the Wildes lawyers have exited already and, at the last count, some 16 partners are reported to have left the firm in the 12-month period leading up to September 2002.

All our interviewees were outspoken, but in no way offensive. If things seemed wrong, they told us, and unlike trainees at some firms, they didn't seem too concerned who knew. This upfront, plain-speaking attitude is Hammonds all over. In September 2002, 35 of the 42 qualifiers stayed with the firm to carry on speaking its language.

and finally…

A tough and determined national player with ambitions in the City and Europe, Hammonds will suit young, free and single applicants with a bit of spark and something to say for themselves. Those with children or in particularly clingy relationships may struggle with the tour of Britain.

Harbottle & Lewis

the facts

Location: London
UK ranking by size: 91
Total number of trainees: 8
Seats: 4x6 months
Alternative seats: Secondments

West End firm Harbottle & Lewis didn't leap onto the meeja bandwagon in the 1990s; since way back in 1955 when Laurence Harbottle opened shop with Mr Lewis, it's concentrated on film, theatre, publishing and the affairs of actors, writers, managers and producers. This remains the principal focus, although the business now incorporates practically every aspect of the media industry plus aviation and charities.

spot the talent

The client base is pretty hot – actors, celebrities, sports icons and rock stars feature right through to dot.com entrepreneurs, company directors, financiers and airline executives. Harbottles has acted in numerous high-profile matters, including the successful action brought by Virgin against BA, ground-breaking central contracts for the English cricket team and Chris Evans' £225 million sale of Ginger Media Group. One trainee explained what drives the firm: "*Laurence Harbottle established a very strong theatre practice, and his ethos is still very much part of the firm. He was very interested in getting artists up and running and putting projects together.*" Another added: "*The firm is very much about acting for the talent: the artists rather than the record labels, the aspiring producers rather than the finance houses.*" That said, it does act for both industry and artists where there is no conflict. Over in the charities department things are pretty busy and the firm boasts clients including Comic Relief, The Queen's Golden Jubilee Trust and The Diana, Princess of Wales Memorial Fund.

The key point to remember is that most of the firm's work is the same as any other commercial firm of the same size: property transactions, corporate and finance deals, and commercial disputes. Yes, the clients may be more exciting than your average widget manufacturer or insurance company, but don't expect your training to be a constant round of celeb packed parties and backstage passes.

variety show

As a trainee, you'll have compulsory seats in company/commercial, litigation and property, with the fourth seat allotted "*according to your interests.*" You'll be told at the beginning what seats you're going to do and when you're going to do them, although there is "*some room for negotiation.*" Knock us down with a feather: the most popular seats are those in IP and entertainment! "*It's exciting work, it's seen as more glamorous than other areas and it's what we're known for.*" Also flying high in the popularity stakes is a six-month secondment to Virgin Atlantic (Richard Branson's business empire is a hugely important source of work). That said, at least one trainee didn't like the idea of hiking out to Gatwick every day!

"*They try to take on a group of trainees with varied*

interests" as "*there's only ever going to be one job available in entertainment at most on qualification, so it'd be recruitment suicide for them to take on five trainees who want to be music lawyers.*" This was certainly borne out in September 2002, when of the four qualifiers, one ended up in the film/TV group, another in the IP department and a third took up a position in property. The one who left took a plum job though: an in-house position at record company BMG.

taking centre stage

Official office hours are 10am to 6pm. "*It is based on the theatre timetable*," one trainee explained. You won't always be able to slip away for a quick supper and a show though; work can drag on longer, particularly in the litigation department, when preparing for trial or case management conferences. In CoCo too: "*When completions are coming up, you can have three weeks of working from half eight till one in the morning.*" There are also some long hours to be found in the film and TV department at the end of the tax year in March when "*you can say goodbye to the whole month*" as you experience a shower of sale and leasebacks of films and television programmes. One excited trainee reported: "*I've heard it gets interesting when they're looking to complete something like 30 films in three days.*" Action!

In terms of responsibility, "*you're given as much as you want*," particularly in property and litigation, where you'll have your own files and be on the phone to clients right from the start. In CoCo, your role will usually be a supporting one, but there's still a chance to shine. One trainee proudly told us: "*On one transaction I got to do all the due diligence, write the disclosure letter and do client meetings on my own.*"

facing the critics

Trainees generally share offices with senior assistants and seem happy with the supervision and feedback they receive: "*Every letter and document gets checked and corrected and, if you're doing something wrong, someone will tell you well before appraisal stage.*" Monthly meetings with the training partner are "*really informal chats and catch-up sessions,*" and then every six months he'll conduct a formal review with "*proper forms to fill out.*"

stars in their eyes

Bear in mind that Harbottles is a modest-sized firm, with just a small number of trainees. If you want to hide away or blend into a huge team, it's not the place for you. And a note for the *Heat/Hello!* readers: "*They don't hire trainees who look like they're going to be star-struck.*" You will encounter stars whichever department you're in and you'll have to keep your feet firmly on the ground and your jaw off it. One trainee stressed this point, saying, "*Yes, you may be selling Robbie Williams' house, but at the end of the day you're still selling a house. The work is the same.*" Sure, you'll see famous people around, whether in the firm's reception or strolling around the West End, but "*it doesn't happen every five minutes and you don't really notice it after a while.*" On the slim chance that you get to talk to anyone famous, it will be "*someone D- or E-list. They're not really going to let A-list celebs speak to a trainee on the phone, particularly if it's a high-profile and sensitive matter.*"

the fans

The office is located in a "*nice period building*" in Hanover Square. "*We've got proper offices with proper walls – no Formica, collapsible, grey partition walls.*" There's just one complaint: an absence of air con in most rooms makes summertime "*particularly uncomfortable*" – one interviewee had three fans going during our interview!

And who said there's no such thing as a free lunch: all lawyers are invited to eat in the firm's dining room every day at 1pm sharp. The West End is "*not the City by any stretch of the imagination, and that's what a lot of people like about it.*" There are plenty of places to eat, drink and shop. End-of-month drinks are supplemented by impromptu gatherings of trainees and assistants in places like Mash, Match, The Loop and The Duke of York.

and finale…

You don't need to have the theatre in your blood to make a success of your training at Harbottle & Lewis, but if you are fascinated by the world of entertainment and the media generally, you will be in your element...even if you turn into a property or an aircraft finance lawyer at the end of the day.

Herbert Smith

the facts
Location: London
UK ranking by size: 8
Total number of trainees: 174
Seats: 4x6 months
Alternative seats: Overseas seats, secondments
Extras: Pro bono – Privy Council death row appeals, language training

Herbert Smith is commonly mistaken for a magic circle firm. This is understandable given its size, huge partner profits and host of blue-chip clients. Another misconception is that this is a litigation firm, with a corporate practice winning best supporting actor and other departments taking mere walk-on roles. True, the firm has a fearsome reputation for blockbuster dispute work and enough litigators to call up an army of extras for those epic battles, but the screenplay has moved on a few scenes. Cast aside misconceptions; stop obsessing about labels and read on...

on general release

Operating a four by six-month seat system, a corporate seat is compulsory, but could be satisfied by a stint in banking. A litigation seat is also required but given the firm's reputation we weren't surprised to learn that everyone's happy about this. *"It's one of the reasons I chose the firm,"* our sources usually confirmed. The litigation assignment could take the form of a contentious-heavy seat such as construction or IP, but generally the firm prefers you to do *"proper litigation"* for six months.

At each rotation there are 16 overseas seats. Far Eastophilia ensures that Hong Kong, Singapore and Tokyo are particularly prized. Six client secondments (including BSkyB, Coca-Cola, Cable & Wireless and IBM) and two placements for judicial assistants at the Court of Appeal are also heavily subscribed and there's healthy competition for the more specialist practice areas, such as employment, tax and IT/IP. The picture that emerges is one of plenty of choice. Think multiplex rather than high street Odeon.

international cast

OK, so we know what trainees are looking for (*"A proper training in litigation and corporate rather than just doing three types of banking seats"*), but what about the firm's wish list? *"Communication skills and the ability to get on with people are very important. Being a good lawyer is not just knowing everything about the law – it's also about walking into a room full of people you've never met before and being able to have a sensible conversation with them."* And where is it finding them? *"There is a high proportion of people from Oxbridge, like any City firm, but we've got people from all over the place."* Such as? *"Bristol, Swansea, Sheffield and further afield from places as diverse as Belgrade, Moscow, India and Pakistan."*

One trainee expanded further: *"We're not all boffiny academic types and we're not all sporty jocks – it's a mix."* So what does link them? *"We're all heading in the same direction, otherwise we wouldn't be here. We want City work."* Undoubtedly, the firm is making a concerted effort to recruit sufficient numbers of trainees for whom litigation is not the be-all and end-all. On qualification, the numbers have to be right or you end up with wannabe litigators pumping gas and waiting tables in the corporate department.

on the set

Trainees talked of a collegiate atmosphere. Departments are subdivided into groups and *"a surprising amount of teamwork goes on. I'm quite impressed as a trainee that you can feel part of a team."* One trainee attempted to shed light on the firm's character: "*It's quite energetic. It doesn't just sit back and admire itself or rest on its laurels – it has an aim, a direction. It's forward-looking.*" Another thought: "*It is traditional, but as law firms go, it's definitely not old-fashioned.*" We got past reception and took a tour of the set. We sniffed the air. Our impressions? Big. Solid. Sensible. Confident. Herbert Smith has a proper smell about it – one where the library smells of books and lawyers' offices smell of good honest labour.

Responding quite typically to our question on hours, one source said, "*If you averaged out all my hours, they would be 9am to 6.30/7pm.*" Then again, "*every trainee has busy periods where they're in the office till nine, ten or 11 at night, sometimes in two-week bursts, sometimes for a month.*" This is particularly the case in corporate where you might find your hours are scheduled to suit US clients, "*who often forget that 2pm their time is time to go home here!*" But when you've just finished a deal or you're in the early stages of another, you could have weeks when you're out at 5.30pm and have time to catch the early screening. Litigation is said to be "*more on an even keel*" but "*if you've got a court deadline on Monday, you may be in on the weekend.*" Most of our interviewees had weekended at some point, often "*on jobs you want to spend a bit more time on to get them just right, which is easier to do when there's no one else around.*"

...and action!

The amount of responsibility you'll get depends on the area of practice: "*Obviously there are times when you have to man a photocopier, and obviously they're not going to give a huge Baring-esque trial to a second-year trainee!*" However, "*generally your supervisor will give you responsibility to run a file or oversee aspects of a deal where they can, or allow you to develop a relationship with a client where they can.*" In corporate you're more likely to take the job of a runner than a leading role opposite the client; trainees talked of a great deal of due diligence and verification work on transactions. Over in departments like IP or property, you'll be more like the up-and-coming young director of a lower budget independent flick. One trainee told us: "*In property I had ten to 15 files that I managed day to day.*" Another trainee said, "*I've been to loads of meetings and in court with clients. I've also had my own files where I've spoken regularly with clients and built up relationships and been invited to dinner.*"

We mentioned last year that some supervisors are better than others. One trainee summed things up: "*One of my supervisors really appreciated his role, regularly updating me on what he was doing and going out of his way to find me interesting and varied work. Another one didn't have a clue what he wanted me to do and found it difficult to delegate – it was like getting blood out of a stone.*" However, "*other people in the group were aware of this, so they compensated for it by giving me good work.*" Across the firm most supervisors do a great job at directing trainees, but the charges stick a little more often in the busy corporate department. On a more positive note: "*HR are aware that certain supervisors haven't been tuned into trainees and they're addressing it.*"

Mid- and end-of-seat reviews with supervisors are supplemented by separate ones with departmental training partners and all departments run induction lectures followed by ongoing briefings at least monthly. In addition, trainees attend firm-wide seminars with external and internal speakers.

the wrap parties

The office itself is "*nice and swanky*" and slap-bang in the middle of Exchange Square, behind Liverpool Street Station. "*It's an excellent location with lots of bars,*" enthused one source. In the summer, "*it's good to step outside and eat your sandwiches on the steps watching all the people who don't have to go back to work sipping Pimm's.*" Indeed, in the summer the crowded square almost has the feel of Brighton beach...but without the pebbles, and the sea, and the pier, and the nudists.

At the start of the training contract, there are "*lots of getting-to-know-you evenings*" involving "*talks and alcohol,*" and then the Christmas parties arrive and before you know it you're de-mothing your tux for the trainee ball, and then it's the firm's summer party. *"You're not corralled into group activities too much...There's no pressure on you to go out all the time, but if you do, there's always something going on."* We like the sound of the drinks trolley tradition in various departments: every month, *"the trolley turns up with drinks in the late afternoon and everyone in the department stands around chatting and then you head to the pub."* Tax is particularly sociable: *"They're always having champagne, whether it's monthly drinks, a birthday or a leaving party."* One source who'd done a tax seat said, *"There was one fortnight in particular when I thought 'God, I can't drink any more champagne!'"*

Herbert Smith's local is Futures, *"a dangerous little greenhouse of a bar"* located a stone's throw away and *"always full to the brim"* with Herbert Smith lawyers. *"We've almost annexed Futures – it's like part of the building,"* one trainee commented, while another whispered: *"It's a real confessional."* Futures has become a *"natural stopping-off point for trainees, assistants and partners. There's a good cross-section on Friday nights and it's a good place to catch up."*

forgetting your glasses

A major criticism emerged from our interviews. In a cost-cutting measure, which our interviewees saw as *"short-sighted,"* the firm has removed the pick 'n' mix counter from its fifth floor staff restaurant. Trainees are *"devastated"* as it was *"one of the biggest selling points of the firm – it's a huge loss to trainees."* For the record, the *Student Guide* team is happy to sign any petition to bring it back. Fifty out of 52 second-years were offered a job on qualification in 2002 and 44 stayed with the firm, with about a third going into corporate, a third into litigation and a third into other departments.

and finally…

Herbert Smith has won the litigation Oscar time and time again, but recently it's been producing box office smashes in corporate and banking. Whatever your tastes, so long as they're commercial, this firm should appeal. Buy your ticket, grab some popcorn and let the action begin.

Hextalls

the facts
Location: London, Birmingham, West Sussex
UK ranking by size: 115
Total number of trainees: 9
Seats: 4x6 months
Alternative seats: None

Hextalls (rebranded from Hextall Erskine) specialises in insurance-related work. UK and international insurance companies, Lloyd's syndicates, brokers and loss adjusters will all be a part of your world as a Hextalls trainee, but while these clients account for the majority of business, Hextalls also acts for some private UK and foreign-based companies and public sector clients, such as local authorities and NHS trusts.

come again

The firm has four departments – personal injury, insurance and commercial disputes, employment, and corporate/private client. All trainees are London-based, and spend three six-month seats assisting litigation teams and six months with non-contentious teams. In practice this works out as two seats in PI and one in insurance and commercial disputes (reinsurance, professional indemnity/general litigation) or vice versa. When you go back for your second seat in PI or insurance and commercial disputes, *"you sit with a supervisor who specialises in something different to give you more variety."* For example, in PI different fee earners handle health and safety claims, medical negligence or road traffic accident work.

The fourth seat will focus on employment matters or you'll work more generally for the corporate/private client team, which handles corporate/commercial, property, wills and family work.

looking forward

"Reinsurance is the one everyone wants to go into. They've got lots of high-profile work and the cases are a lot bigger than in many of the other areas." That said, PI is the

biggest department by volume of work and number of lawyers. It is particularly well known for its sports and respiratory claims expertise. Trainees explained that Hextalls is *"trying to build up the profile of the other departments as well"* and *"extend our reputation from just being a solid PI firm."* The employment law department, in particular, is felt to be *"really up-and-coming."*

"It's a forward-looking firm," one trainee said. *"They appointed a new chief executive last year and he's really trying to move the firm forward, steer it in a new direction."* Overall, the firm is felt by trainees to be *"in a state of flux."* The PI department recently introduced a new case management IT system that helps fee earners diarise their work. *"It has lots of standard letters and reminders of when to do things – it's a bit of a shake-up to make the fee earners more efficient."* As for insurance and commercial disputes, in July 2002 the firm's good friend, Chicago-based Clausen Miller, tempted three key partners away. Unfortunately this came on the back of other departures from the department.

being heard

Trainees share a room with and get most of their work from their supervisor. Litigation generates a lot of paper, so expect your fair share of grunt work, particularly in PI. But generally, trainees were happy with the levels of responsibility they were given. One trainee talked about running professional indemnity files: *"My partner let me write all the letters, make all the phone calls and do day to day stuff on cases with him checking the whole time."* There's a fair amount of advocacy, particularly in PI: *"I had a reasonable amount of applications before a District Judge and a Master in the High Court, and I also got to run a couple of case management conferences."* As for client contact, *"we mostly deal with representatives of insurance companies,"* over the phone or face to face during conferences with counsel, trials or drinks afterwards.

Our interviewees were satisfied with the amount of day to day feedback they got on their work. *"If you draft something, whoever's given you the work will point out to you if you need to change anything and explain why you need to change it."* That said, *"with some people you have to ask 'Can you let me know what you thought about that report,' or 'Would it be possible for me to go with you to that hearing?'"* There were no complaints about hours. *"I usually get in about 9am and leave about 5.30/6pm,"* said one source. *"To be honest, it's like that throughout the firm. Certain fee earners do stay later and, when the work demands it, people will work longer hours."*

thinking for yourself

Trainees tell us Hextalls is looking for *"people who can think for themselves and think on their feet"* and *"someone who's self-confident and able to get on with what they've been given. There's a small number of people in the firm and everyone's busy, so you need the confidence to go off and do something without necessarily asking what to do every step of the way."* You don't need experience in the insurance industry, *"you just need motivation and enthusiasm to learn."* One trainee estimated that *"90% of all the trainees who've qualified or left to qualify in the past ten years have gone into insurance, either personal injury or reinsurance."* With four second-years approaching qualification in 2002, the firm offered two NQ jobs – one in employment and one in reinsurance. Loyalty to the fore, our interviewees were keen to stress that *"most of the partners and fee earners trained here."*

winding down

The firm is located in Aldgate East. *"It's great – there are seven or eight pubs within two minutes' walk,"* raved one trainee. The Marine Broker hosts Hextalls' 'After Hours' freebie drinks event *"every couple of months."* Trainees and fee earners also have a soft spot for The Dispensary.

and finally…

If you're looking for a smaller City firm that's deeply rooted in its chosen client market and one that will allow you to litigate until the cows come home, Hextalls fits the bill.

Hill Dickinson

the facts
Location: Liverpool, Manchester, Chester, London
UK ranking by size: 47
Total number of trainees: 17
Seats: 4x6 months
Alternative seats: Secondments

Established in 1810 as a niche shipping practice, Hill Dickinson now offers exposure to many areas of the law. It's one of the largest and best-known firms in the North West with litigation and insurance work accounting for around half of its business.

hillbillies
Trainees do four six-month seats and rotate between the insurance, maritime & transit, health, and commercial departments. Litigation is a major part of the firm's work and it has a prestigious place on the NHS Litigation Authority panel that handles all clinical negligence claims brought against the NHS. The firm is also instructed by several of the biggest insurance companies (among them Zurich, Norwich Union and Royal & SunAlliance) and, accordingly, all trainees will pass through the insurance department. Beyond that, they can chose from a myriad of seats, including company/commercial, shipping, property, private client, IP and construction. Seat allocation was considered to be pretty fair, although don't be surprised if you don't get much choice in your first year. There's also an opportunity to be seconded to insurance clients should you fancy a bit of time in-house.

"*Litigation is the firm's bread and butter,*" explained one trainee. "*It's likely that you'll do two seats in litigation, but you'll never find that you do two seats of the same work.*" The hours are pretty civilised by legal standards. "*I'm rarely in the office after 5.30pm,*" reported one trainee. There is no danger of getting sucked into a long-hours culture; as another trainee told us: "*It's your work that speaks and not your presence in the office.*" Responsibility levels are high, but you can't expect to escape all the ugly grunt work – it's part and parcel of almost every training contract. "*Every trainee does their fair share of it, but it is offset by good, proper work.*"

natural born commuters
Most of those we spoke to had been recruited from the local area. Liverpool is the hub of things with the Manchester and Chester offices smaller and more relaxed. Although previously heavily focused on PI litigation work, the Manchester office recently took local firm Gorna & Co under its wing to boost its commercial capabilities. One trainee concluded: "*The merger has gone very smoothly. We all settled in together very well.*" If you're not a natural born commuter and you would prefer a single-site training for personal reasons, then be aware that trainees are expected to move between the offices in the North West. London is somewhat out of the northern loop and seems to have its own way of doing things. It recruits a couple of trainees every year directly into the largely autonomous City office, and handles company/commercial, insurance litigation and goods and transit work.

Just in case you were thinking it's all insurance clients, we thought we'd sprinkle in some examples of other clients: Bank of Scotland, Camelot, FLS Aerospace, United Utilities and for those of you looking for sexy sports clients, Liverpool and Newcastle Football Clubs.

Supervision is considered to be "*excellent.*" "*When dealing with clients, one partner referred to me as their assistant rather than a trainee. I loved that!*" one trainee gloated. Our sources received useful feedback from their supervisors, or as one of them put it: "*They don't think twice about scribbling over my stuff!*" There are monthly meetings in Liverpool for all trainees, which are as much an excuse to meet and have a drink as anything else. "*More structured training would be a good thing,*" thought some trainees. Appraisals with the trainee committee come at the end of every seat. One trainee told us that the system works perfectly adequately: "*You don't tend to get any nasty surprises in appraisals. I've always known where I've stood.*"

hill's angels

One trainee felt that their favourable first impressions of the firm were pretty accurate. *"People are down-to-earth. They were genuinely helpful all the way from reception. Trainees are not seen as the dregs of the office."* The firm itself was considered to be *"forward-thinking and progressive"* in its outlook. Apparently, *"changes are embraced"* and *"communication is a big thing."* Sounds like they've just been paid a visit by the consultants. Further evidence of the business hypnotists: *"Trainees are proud to work and work hard."* Steady on. None of this starry-eyed visionary stuff seems to have put people off, anyway. In 2002 all the qualifying trainees were offered a job and all but one accepted.

"It's a youthful firm with lots of young partners. At other places it seems you have to sit out a period of time before you're made up, whereas here there's definitely a professional meritocracy." And don't worry about selling your soul. *"They respect the fact that you've got a life outside of work."* In some cases, people manage to have a life inside work. During the football World Cup you could hear whoops and groans coming from various partners' rooms. It was assumed that they were watching the games. We were warned that you have to be a *"tough nut"* to get on in the Liverpool office. *"You need to be lively and engage in Scouse banter; otherwise you'll think that they're taking the piss."* For some people *"Liverpool may come as a bit of a culture shock;"* there's lots of football rivalry and in-jokes. Something about donning the curly wigs and shell suits…

When we asked for the typical Hill Dickinson trainee profile we were told that *"most people are from the area, from redbrick universities and straight out of law school,"* but our sources hastened to add: *"If someone is good enough and can show that they'll fit in then they'll be given consideration."* Our sources assessed themselves as *"quite ambitious."* One told us: *"People are eager to push themselves forward. There is a fair bit of competition."*

hill raisers

Trainees say that the social life is *"second to nowhere."* *"People from other firms say we get out more often than them."* One trainee who was new to Liverpool said, *"I moved in on my own and it didn't take any time to settle in."* First stop on a Friday night in Liverpool is Trials, opposite the office, and then it's on to the city's many clubs and bars. The whole firm takes off for a residential weekend of lectures and fun every autumn. Apparently it all got too much for one partner who came dressed as a gladiator in a toga and leather sandals. No one could remember why precisely.

and finally…

If you want to stay in (or move to) the North West and gain exposure to a wide range of law, then Hill Dickinson should be on your list. With its litigation, insurance and non-contentious commercial work, *"if you can't find something you enjoy doing here then you are probably in the wrong career."*

Hodge Jones & Allen

the facts

Location: London
UK ranking by size: 101
Total number of trainees: 10
Seats: 4x6 months
Alternative seats: None

Based in London's gritty Camden Town, Hodge Jones & Allen provides a range of high street legal services, including 'no win, no fee' personal injury and publicly funded (legal aid) work. Beyond the ordinary, it handles sensitive, high-profile multi-party claims on issues such as MMR, the Marchioness disaster and Gulf War Syndrome. This work sits alongside a bustling commercial property department, possibly the firm's largest growth area.

home alone

Should you come to HJA as a 'normal' trainee following the typical four-seat system, you can expect to be involved in anything from criminal law, *"where you* really need to be able to pick things up quickly," through family and employment to PI, specialist clinical negligence and commercial property. It's also possible to 'double up' with two seats in a department that especially interests you. We say 'normal' trainee, because the firm has a novel scheme for some trainees. On the one hand it recruits trainees from among its own paralegals, once they have experience as police station advisors, civil litigation assistants and suchlike. But then it also has a separate training within the housing department where some stay for the whole of their contract, only nipping out to fill the gaps necessary to keep the Law Society happy. This system means that from early on *"you get a real feeling that you have had a positive effect. It's great when you hear that a client has not been evicted from their home, or that dangerous property has been repaired. It gives you a real lift."*

The training was praised by our sources. In addition to their supervisors, *"newly qualified solicitors help you see how everything really works."* With regular feedback and partners happy to field questions, trainees tell us they feel secure when left to work alone.

deeply dippy 'bout the work you've got…

The trainees are a principled bunch. We're not talking hippy-dippy, but more that they are of *"high moral fibre."* The core of the firm is not money-driven and *"your typical high-flying City type would be a fish out of water here."* Many of the trainees are already experienced volunteers, having worked in law, advice and housing centres, and so on. This is something the firm actively looks for in applicants: *"They want evidence of a genuine commitment to legal aid and this type of work."*

Operating a rota for 24-hour police station coverage, the firm encourages continued volunteering. Trainees who sign up for the Police Station Accreditation Scheme end up advising suspects in custody. *"You certainly don't get lumbered with dull jobs!"* Indeed not. At the time we went to press, Camden was undergoing a summer madness crime wave. According to the *Camden New Journal*, the murder rate was on a par with Moscow and Johannesburg. There is client contact *"right from the start,"* with plenty of opportunity to handle your own blood-and-guts cases.

Don't expect to be on the train home at 6pm every day, even though the station is right next to the office. Some departments have a *"stay late culture where it's easy to fall into doing long hours,"* and with other work, such as mental health matters, the complexity of a case may not reveal itself until you are well into it. Clients, too, *"can be difficult,"* but when you are the last line of defence, people tend to become desperate and demanding of your time. That, like it or lump it, is the nature of this work. If you're not committed, you're reading about the wrong firm.

the tides…

HJA floats its boat on a sea of publicly-funded work with such success that it draws both minnows and whales of cases into its wake. If you are to sail on this ship without falling overboard, *"you need to know the ropes."* Publicly funded work has its peaks and troughs. Our sources tell us that on the one hand it is straightforward *"because you are working from the start within a fixed budget,"* and this is controlled by the lawyer not the client. The downside is the mountain of additional paperwork that goes with it. *"It can be difficult moving from a volunteer background, where costs are never really considered, to a private legal aid firm, where you are billing and recording every cost."* Well, you could always work in the commercial property department…

…they are a-changing

… which is where we find a growing tension. The firm has previously been at pains to point out that "In housing cases, we only represent tenants and not landlords," painting a soft, pastel portrait of its right-on people politics. Although people-based cases still form the core of the firm's work, the commercial property department has moved from having a cameo to a leading role within its overall structure, with the firm as a whole becoming *"more departmentalised."* "The firm is less focused on legal aid work, and the type of trainee coming here will probably change to reflect that. It's still not totally commercially oriented; it's just trying to attract a wider range of clients." It isn't exactly an identity crisis – it's more like a 14-year-old lad who wakes one morning to find his voice is an octave lower than it was when he went to bed. It takes time to get used to the change. The adoption and promotion of a flourishing cash cow, although not welcomed by all, has been praised because it might well safeguard all the other stuff. 2002 was an unusual year for retention: the firm only offered a job to one out of four qualifying second years. The other three will doubtless find that the HJA name on their CV will stand them in good stead.

the second office

Opposite HJA is the second office, or Mac Bar, as the rest of Camden knows it. Rather like the firm, Mac Bar has undergone a transformation in the last couple of years. Once a scuzzy, sticky-carpeted, Withnail-esque affair, it now exudes Camden cool. A short way up the road, past the bookies, is the Parma Café. It's the favourite haunt of the criminal department and symbolises the no-frills, 'neighbourhood' feel of the firm.

With intrafirm marriages dotted around, HJA lawyers sound like a close-knit bunch. If you fancy hobnobbing with the partners, there are quarterly drinks in the *"neutral, efficient and workmanlike"* offices, where you can take the opportunity of offering the HJA equivalent of an apple for teacher – *"If you think someone has done a particularly outstanding job, you can nominate them for one of the monthly prizes, which range from a bottle of champers to short holidays."* During the summer months, the firm also organises outings to distant shores, such as the South Coast resort of Brighton.

and finally...

Hodge Jones & Allen is not a firm for the fainthearted. That said, if you are the big-hearted sort who doesn't mind hard graft for less money and wants to give a little back, you'll fit right in.

Holman Fenwick & Willan

the facts

Location: London
UK ranking by size: 64
Total number of trainees: 20
Seats: 4x6 months
Alternative seats: Overseas seats, secondments
Extras: Language training

Holman Fenwick & Willan was founded in 1883 by a bunch of world-weary buccaneers who decided to end their days of plundering on the high seas, get on the right side of the law and form a highly respected City shipping firm. OK, that's a lie. We'll take the Jolly Roger screen saver off our pcs and find out which way the wind really blows for HF&W trainees...

discuss

We are pleased to report that the firm has recruited discerning applicants who knew exactly what they wanted from their training. It bothers us when trainees moan that what's on offer at their firm doesn't match up to the hard sell tactics on display at law fairs and in recruitment brochures. Well done, HF&W!

Of their four six-month seats, trainees are required to do just one non-contentious seat chosen from corporate, ship finance, property, EU/competition or energy. The other three seats are usually contentious, although *"if you really want to, you can do two non-contentious seats. They do try to accommodate you, but the firm is heavily litigation-based."* Due to their small number and the fact that they chatter a lot, trainees *"usually know if everyone's going for a particular seat at the same time and so you know to try for it next time."* The message on seats is this: *"If you want something, make it known and push in the right places."* This is particularly the case in relation to a stint overseas. Foreign seats are available, but only on an *"as desired"* basis. At the time we interviewed, there was a trainee in Paris doing general comlit and one getting shippy in Piraeus.

We suggest you read the shipping feature in our Solicitors Practice Areas section of this book. Once you've done that, you'll see why admiralty work is regarded as *"exotic and glamorous."* The reinsurance department is said to be *"booming"* and *"getting good work"* at present, and so attracts its fair share of applicants too. As for less popular seats, one trainee mentioned that the non-contentious seats aren't oversubscribed. *"The non-contentious seats aren't what people generally come here to do, but there are a good variety of them and you can get some good experience."*

do you know who i am?

Trainees share offices with their supervisor, usually a partner but occasionally a senior assistant. In smaller departments, the bulk of your work will come directly from your supervisor, while *"you're more likely to freelance for other people in bigger departments."* Three-monthly appraisals alternate between the recruitment partner and another independent partner. The idea is that you have *"the chance to be assessed objectively by someone who's totally removed from your work,"* although there was some debate as to the efficacy of an appraisal with someone who hasn't seen you work. Regarding on-going feedback, our interviewees agreed that *"some people are better than others. Sometimes it's like getting work back from teachers; they say 'Well done, excellent work'. With others though, if they don't say anything and your work goes out, you assume it's good."*

In general, our interviewees were happy with the approach taken by supervisors and responsibility. *"You're judged on what you can do rather than what you can't do. When I've done well, I know it because they tell me and reinforce it. But equally, when I've made mistakes, they're sensitive about it – they explain where I've gone wrong and hope that I won't do it again!"* Regarding client contact, *"in smaller departments you're very much part of the team, and if a client can't get hold of more senior lawyers, they'll often want to talk to you."* Pleasingly, *"clients talk to us and usually at least know our names. Some of my friends at other firms don't know who the client is half the time."* Client secondments crop up on an ad hoc basis.

masterful

Trainees work from 9am to 6.30/7pm on average. *"If you're in a very busy department, or if the work is especially urgent, then yes, you'll stay later."* For example, in the event of a collision, a trainee in the admiralty department might need to go out to the scene to take witness statements, and in litigation, *"coming up to a hearing, there's always a certain amount of urgency."* Other busy departments include reinsurance, where the lawyers work consistently longer hours.

So, if not piratical, what's a typical HF&W lawyer like? *"There are a lot of big characters here – they're really looking for something extra in people."* Trainees are *"from all over the shop"* and *"a number of us have done other things"* before coming to the firm. One trainee elaborated: *"There are a couple of ex-Master Mariners, a couple from the reinsurance industry and a number who've done a Masters' degree or travelled extensively."* The ideal applicant is someone willing to take responsibility for their own work; the confident sort *"who is already their own person."* We also learned that *"they want people who can think not just in purely legal terms – a lot of our clients don't give a fig about what the law says. They're everyday people who want to know how their business will be affected and you have to be able to relate to them on a commercial level."* Languages are also said to be *"a very good asset"* (plain English included) and e-mails are often sent around the office asking, for example, *"Is there a German speaker in the house?"*

meatfeast

The international nature of the firm's work is a major attraction. *"I've rarely done any work here that didn't have an international aspect to it,"* confirmed one source. Another attraction is the firm's compact size. One trainee stressed: *"It's big enough to get meaty commercial work but, at the same time, all the partners know who I am."* HF&W is a firm with a long tradition in its specialist areas so does this mean new recruits should know their place? *"There's much less hierarchy than you'd expect. If you're working on something that requires special expertise, people will often say go and chat to part-*

ner X about it and he'll be happy to help you. It's not like the partners do one thing, the assistants do another and the trainees do something else – we're all working together."

Our interviewees estimated that more than half of the current crop had done a vacation placement or had paralegalled at the firm before being offered a training contract. One explained: *"They don't take many trainees and they want to take a jolly good look at you."* Perhaps as a direct result, HF&W has traditionally been rather successful at retaining its trainees on qualification and September 2002 proved no different: five out of the six qualifiers stayed.

wet faces

The London office is split between three buildings, two of which are *"grand old buildings with art deco frontage"* on Lloyd's Avenue. The third, a nearby, modern and spacious office, puts the *"tired-looking"* areas in the former to shame. We heard mutterings about refurbishment though…

The social scene is *"not regimented – it's not like there are a huge amount of organised things where drinks are thrown at you."* Social events are *"mainly departmental,"* with the admiralty team said to be *"the big ravers – they know how to have a good time."* This is a firm where everyone will know your name and *"If you send out an e-mail about someone's birthday drinks, you're bound to get people turning up from throughout the firm."* Chain bars feature heavily on Friday nights, with a Pitcher & Piano up one end of Lloyds' Avenue and a Slug & Lettuce guarding the other exit. Respect goes to those who venture further afield to bars with a bit more character. There is a softball team, a golf posse and sailors galore who head off to Docklands throughout the summer months.

and finally…

As one trainee put it: *"If you don't like litigation, you might want to think twice about coming here."* However, if Holman Fenwick & Willan's specialists do appeal, and you want bags of international work, we suggest you climb aboard.

Hugh James

the facts
Location: Cardiff, Merthyr Tydfil and five others in Wales, Bristol
UK ranking by size: 76
Total number of trainees: 17
Seats: 4x6 months
Alternative seats: None

Recently separated from its short-lived merger partner, West Country firm Ford Simey, Hugh James remains one of the largest and most respected firms in Wales. Its clients range from large corporates right through to individuals walking in off the high street.

merger? what merger?

Founded in 1960, Hugh James has a national reputation, particularly for contentious work. The merger and demerger with Ford Simey was tied in to an insurance client. Four years ago it hooked up with the West Country firm to safeguard work for CGNU and then, in 2002, CGNU decided all its work should be handled by the Cardiff office. The union became redundant. The demerger has had no discernable impact on trainees – all are based in Wales and they'd never had any real contact with Ford Simey anyway.

close encounters

Be prepared for a sink or swim training. *"You're given a lot of responsibility and you're expected to get on with things,"* one trainee said. Another agreed: *"It's vital that you be a self-starter here. You're certainly not spoon-fed."* This is *"part of the culture of the firm; the way it's been since it was founded."* Trainees describe the Cardiff office as *"the heart of the commercial practice,"* although it does still take some clients off the street. It is *"dominated by commercial property and business litigation,"* with other strong departments including company/commercial, family and lender services. The Merthyr Tydfil office is said to be *"claimant-dominated"* and *"somewhere in between commercial and high* street." It has *"quite a professional-looking office that gives a feel of a modern commercial firm"* and yet it acts for a high proportion of *"walk-in clients,"* particularly on family and personal injury matters. It is renowned for its miners' industrial diseases class actions.

There are no compulsory seats, although in practice you can be sure of at least one in litigation. *"It seems to be the main focus of the firm"* and offers bags and bags of advocacy. *"Very shortly after starting at the firm, I was attending court on my own. They gave me an opportunity to observe a solicitor a few times and then I was doing it myself." "You'll do a few hearings each week, although nothing too big – an awful lot of agency work and repossession hearings."* Life's quite unpredictable in this seat. *"You get a lot of people just phoning up or walking in off the street with a legal problem"* and, as the trainee, you'll often have to take the initial instructions and divert the client to the appropriate department.

Commercial property is a rewarding seat: *"I have quite a lot of my own files to run (under supervision) for clients ranging from housing associations to people off the street."* The hands-down favourite, however, is the joint employment/CoCo seat, which *"everyone fights over."* It's *"six months of a very broad range of subjects from two hot practice areas."* Without doubt, the least popular seat is lender services. *"It's the one everyone dreads and shies away from"* as it involves *"predominantly remortgaging properties."* Due to the sheer volume of work, it now takes two trainees at any one time, the more fortunate of whom will get to work directly for the managing partner. *"You'll get more variety if you work for him, he does a lot of secured lending work."*

Normally, trainees spend at least one of their seats in a branch office (which includes Merthyr Tydfil, despite it being of equivalent size to the Cardiff HQ). Working in the valleys in, perhaps, wills and probate, crime or conveyancing gives trainees firsthand exposure to high street clients. Given the high level of responsibility in the branch offices, such postings tend to be *"reserved for second-years, so you can get your first year's experience in Cardiff."*

swimming lessons

Trainee hours are generally 8.30am to 5.30pm in the valleys and slightly longer in Cardiff. The longest hours come in corporate, particularly when a big completion is due. Trainees usually have their own office, although in some seats they sit open-plan. In all seats, trainees take work from a variety of sources and not just their supervisor. *"Solicitors within a department tend to have their own areas of work, so you can get a very broad range of experience within a seat."* An end-of-seat appraisal takes place with the head of HR and one or other of the two training partners. On qualification in September 2002, four out of six trainees were offered jobs and each of them accepted.

Our sources were of the view that *"to all intents and purposes, you're treated as a fee earner."* In terms of grunt work, *"it's normally left to office juniors: it's certainly never a case of people dumping piles of documents on your desk to photocopy."* That said, trainees do undertake *"some mundane tasks that people higher up don't want to do, like bundling and filling in legal aid forms."* They're philosophical about these tasks: *"It's a trade-off."*

seismic activity

Most trainees have a link with Wales. One said, *"I was looking for a large firm that could give me a good commercial training and still offer me a wide variety of practice areas to explore. It's hard to do better than Hugh James, if you're keen to stay in Wales."* Our sources kept referring to their fellow trainees by name, telling us who was where and really giving life and personality to their accounts of training at the firm. We'll succumb to stereotyping and conclude that the Welsh just love a good natter. But it's more than that – this is a really chummy firm. Confirming our theory, one trainee said, *"They certainly don't want people who are just going to beaver away without socialising."*

"The general atmosphere is more relaxed in Merthyr than in Cardiff." Maybe it's because it is *"out of the city"* or maybe it's because *"the partners there are younger. Everyone seems close enough to your own age that you feel they can relate to you as a trainee."* In addi-

tion, because the clients tend to be smaller in Merthyr, "*you're let loose on them a lot more*" than in Cardiff, where "*the work tends to be a notch higher, so you're not given as much responsibility on files.*"

Merthyr Tydfil has "*by far the nicest building. It was purpose-built a few years ago and is smart and well furnished.*" The building is called Martin Evans House, after the original high street solicitors that Hugh James took over in the town. "*It was a marketing decision to call the building that. A lot of people in Merthyr still call us Martin Evans & Co, even though that firm hasn't existed for 15 to 20 years.*" The Cardiff office has four floors of a tower block right in the centre of the city. The branch offices out in the valleys each have a high street location. But be careful: Bargoed has a history of earthquakes!

there's no need to feel down

"*Everybody goes out,*" particularly on Friday nights, when the bars in Cardiff are said to be "*awash*" with Hugh James trainees. Proceedings will kick off in Ha!Ha! – "*It's the first place you come to, so it does a roaring trade with our lot.*" Trainees from other firms like Edwards Geldard and Eversheds end up there too, and given that many of these trainees did their LPC together in Cardiff, it can feel like a weekly law school reunion. After a few you might slope off next door into Bar Med, which is "*more of a club*" and "*a bit more lively.*" Many of the branch office trainees converge on Cardiff on Friday nights. "*A lot of Merthyr trainees live in Cardiff, so they pop home and get changed and within an hour of finishing work they're out with us in Cardiff.*"

Even though this is prime rugby territory, football seems to be the game of choice at Hugh James, with rugby played only on an ad hoc basis. The footie team is a model of egalitarian thinking, with partners, assistants, trainees and support staff all playing together against "*other law firms, barristers, councils...whoever will play us really.*"

Tragedy! At last year's Merthyr Tydfil Christmas party those scampish litigation partners did not dress up as Village People and perform their own, very special version of YMCA. How do we know this? Trainees told us they couldn't remember it happening, although they acknowledge that this is "*not necessarily a good indication of what did or did not actually happen.*" Especially as there was a hypnotist present...

and finally...

A top three Welsh firm. A massive variety of work and clients. Very high levels of responsibility. A good social life. If these things are on your wish list, apply, apply, apply...especially if you can form letters of the alphabet with your arms after a few sherbets.

Ince & Co

the facts

Location: London
UK ranking by size: 67
Total number of trainees: 23
Seats: 4x6 months
Alternative seats: Piraeus, secondments

This firm thrives on disaster – oil spills, shipwrecks, plane crashes, big fires and even piracy. When disaster strikes and a client presses the big red 'Emergency Response' button on the firm's website, an Ince & Co lawyer will be ready to zip up his pinstriped uniform, grab the recovery manual and wade in to sort things out. Sounds exciting, but will your training be one big adrenalin rush or will you be watching behind the safety barriers? Read on to find out...

steel yourself

Ince & Co has acted for the shipping and insurance industries for more than 130 years, and work for these two client sectors will dominate your training. Of their decision to pick Ince, one trainee said, "*I thought better that than an all-round firm that's larger but mediocre.*" Our sources were absolutely right to say, "*You get a lot of overseas lawyers and clients holding Ince*

& Co in very high esteem." And with world renown come plenty of interesting cases from far and wide. One trainee estimated that *"90% of the clients I come across are foreign."* For example, you might have a London-based P&I club working on behalf of a South American charterer or a Greek ship owner. In light of this, surely language skills are essential? Apparently not: language skills will rub various clients up the right way, but you don't need them as *"the accepted and common language in shipping and insurance is English."*

Chambers Global's International Shipping Firm of the Year 2002

What you will need is nerves (and maybe pants) of steel, because this is no ordinary training contract. The first thing to note is that there are no seats, at least not in the conventional sense. Every six months, you will share an office with a different partner, but you won't belong to them – think of it as renting a desk for a while. The second notable feature is that you'll carry cases with you throughout your training contract and for as long as they take. No wimping out and handing work over to the new incumbent of a seat, no farewell to the client, no respite from the odd 'lemon' of a case that you might acquire. If this is beginning to sound like an ordeal, you might not have what it takes to succeed here; but if this excites you, you'll want to know how trainees cope with the responsibility thrust upon them.

bravery rewards

In order to succeed, *"you need to be tenacious, confident, practical and streetwise."* Ince loves (and recruits) self-reliant trainees. One trainee concluded: *"It's almost like a large set of barristers' chambers here – that ethic is really encouraged."* How so? Well, you're told to treat partners like clients, you get to research and write your own opinions and you become very attached to and involved with your cases. In the main your cases will be quite small, although you'll also become involved in bigger matters in a supporting role. *"You really get to see the whole of a case, taking it on with a view to taking it to court like a barrister."* Another trainee noted: *"We're fundamentally a litigation firm, so you have to have a litigator's temperament, otherwise you won't get on here."*

Although the partner you sit with will take responsibility for you, work will come from a number of different quarters. And since many of the partners have particular specialisms, you'll get *"a good spread of experience."* After a short while, certain partners will (hopefully) take a shine to you and then *"come knocking on your door with work. If you're too busy you tell them, if not, then you take it on. It's very informal but it works fine."* We did hear that the system brings with it an air of competition between trainees, but not to the extent that it gets ugly. While this system is not unique (Gouldens scheme operates in much the same way and it's closer to how young US lawyers start out), it is rare in large UK firms. *"The way that Ince goes about its business is excellent: it confers a lot of responsibility on its solicitors, expects a lot of them and the solicitors produce good results."* Basically, you grow up fast at Ince.

nautical nautical very very nautical

Time to mention the L word: *"The training here is very, very litigation-based."* One trainee's experiences were fairly typical: dry shipping, admiralty, aviation, insurance/reinsurance and general commercial disputes as well as employment, immigration and, on the non-contentious front, basic company/commercial activities such as buying and selling companies. The firm is building up its energy practice and also handles property matters and even private client work. The variety is there if you want it, but no one's going to complain if you get stuck into dispute work and keep asking for more. All second-years can now apply for a six-month posting to the firm's Piraeus office, which is a new and *"immensely popular"* initiative. On top of this, a fair few trainees go on secondment to shipping or insurance companies, either at home or abroad. Despite the firm being *"very open"* to such secondments, there's no formal system and they tend to arise on a largely ad hoc basis.

Plenty of talks and seminars are open to trainees, usually over lunch, and first-years attend a three-month litigation skills course put on by one of the firm's partners, which *"takes you through various aspects of procedure and tactics in litigation."* When trainees join the firm, and before they start work proper, there is a two-week induction programme with lectures on various topics pertinent to the core areas of the firm's business. *"When we start, the terminology in shipping and insurance is completely new to us,"* explained one trainee. *"It's a basic introduction to the industries so we don't feel out of our depth."* A member of the training committee and the trainee principal will review your progress every six months. On an ongoing basis, *"whenever you've done some work, you can go and see the partner you've done it for, and they'll generally tell you what they think."* One trainee noted: *"The best feedback is whether people give you another case or not!"*

the merchant of venice

The fact that you retain your cases from go to whoa means that there's a cumulative effect as your workload builds up, which can mean late nights or weekends. A typical week was said to be *"from 8.30/9am till 7pm each night"* with *"the odd blip when there's a lot of stuff happening on different cases at the same time."* But, *"there's not this mindless culture to be seen to be in the office late no matter what your workload. Everyone knows it's swings and roundabouts, so when the work comes in you give your pound of flesh."*

Despite trainees' praise for the Ince Way, some thought the firm to be *"traditional and old-fashioned – they've been using this method ever since the firm came into existence and it's one of the oldest firms in the City."* Other comments were that *"it's very male-dominated and quite hierarchical,"* with *"lots of pinstripe suits from public school backgrounds."* Yet our trainee interviewees also concluded: *"We went to lots of different universities."*

And what of the office itself? *"It's practical,"* was the diplomatic assessment of one trainee. *"It's a concrete block with a 1970s look,"* and *"it could do with being knocked down and rebuilt from the ground up,"* were the less diplomatic assessments of others. These stark appraisals might have something to do with the fact that the building is *"blatantly on a site bombed during the war,"* although it is *"in the middle of some glorious old pre-war buildings"* right opposite the Tower of London. It is *"respectable enough – neither pretentious nor ultra-modern"* and we're delighted to report that the walls are appropriately adorned with pictures of sinking vessels and fires aboard ships. One trainee took the opportunity to tell tales out of school: *"They could do with some windows or extractor fans in the men's toilets… It's a no smoking office and lots of people* [hopefully men] *go in there to smoke, which doesn't do much for the aroma."*

evil child catcher

Last summer trainees had a truly scrumptious night out at the West End production of Chitty Chitty Bang Bang. A sports and social committee organises annual cricket matches, and rugby and football games as well as trips to polo matches. There's an All Bar One literally 20 yards away, which seems to be the first port of call for any after-work social gatherings. As one candid interviewee said, *"It's not adventurous, but it's local,"* and *"you're guaranteed to find a good core of people there to detox the week with on Friday nights."* There's also a monthly firm-wide get-together in Foxtrot Oscars, which apparently has *"the air of a gentlemen's club,"* but isn't one. On the second Thursday of every month there are free drinks from 5.31pm onwards till the budget runs out, generally at about 7.30-8pm. Smart trainees socialise with partners at every opportunity. *"Yes, you can have a jolly with them, be charming and impress them, but the hierarchy doesn't dissolve."*

The firm definitely hires its trainees with a view to retaining them. However, there's no quota system: *"It's not like they think they have to keep on a specific percentage every year and then turf out the rest. Either you make the grade here or you don't, and if you do they'll keep* you on. Sometimes they keep 100%; sometimes it's 50%." In September 2002, six out of the seven qualifiers stayed with the firm (two others had already left beforehand).

and finally…
Train at Ince & Co and you'll be a part of a thoroughly respected firm. You'll get masses of responsibility and learn a huge amount by running your own cases from start to finish. And that big red Emergency Response button on the firm's home page, how cool is that? Adventurous types should climb aboard.

Irwin Mitchell

the facts
Location: Sheffield, Leeds, Birmingham, London
UK ranking by size: 30
Total number of trainees: 28
Seats: 4x6 months
Alternative seats: None
Extras: Pro bono – Free Legal Information Service

Sheffield-born Irwin Mitchell now counts Birmingham, Leeds and London among its conquests. It built its name on personal injury and clinical negligence work but it also offers an extensive range of corporate and commercial services. In 2002 turnover was up by almost 17% and it recorded the second highest partner profit increase in the country.

when disaster strikes
Its specialist PI work remains one of the most popular options for trainees. Hardly surprising, given Irwin Mitchell's reputation for high-profile cases pertaining to disasters such as The Marchioness, Piper Alpha and the Kings Cross Fire plus group actions like vCJD, children's organ retention, and miners' disease claims. This top-level PI and clin neg practice is set against a backdrop of wide-ranging commercial work. *"They do a bit of everything,"* said one of our sources.

One interviewee mentioned that its image as a *"northern firm"* appealed to him, although of course *"it has expanded beyond that now."* Trainees also note: *"There's a real mix of people here – from the old redbricks right down to the old polys."* Another hinted at the firm's attitude towards more mature applicants, saying, *"There are very few people that have just gone straight from university and the LPC into the firm and there are plenty who've had years out and done exciting things with their lives."* One trainee opined: *"The firm ranges from personal injury right through to corporate, so you need different types of personalities."* However, there is at least one common feature: *"There's none of us just sat here quietly; we're all very sociable and we're all quite loud."*

juggling act
Strictly speaking, there are no compulsory seats. However, as is made clear to trainees at the outset, you must be prepared to be *"relocated"* throughout your contract, if necessary. As one trainee said, *"It's easy to say that's not a problem at your interview, but when it comes down to it, it can be a hassle to up sticks and move cities."* Before each seat rotation, you'll be asked to give your three preferred department and office destinations. Apparently, graduate recruitment manager and *"Angel of the North,"* Sue Lenkowski, has *"a hard job trying to place us all"* in that she has to consider not only seats, but location as well. The consensus is that *"you'll never go lower than your second choice"* in terms of office. Notably, *"a lot of people do their fourth seats in the department they want to qualify into"* and even if trainees have already done a particular seat, the firm is generally happy for them to repeat it.

Our interviewees were generally happy with the tasks they were asked to perform. One told us: *"Your responsibility will build up through each seat. As your skills develop and your confidence grows you get to go see clients and handle matters on your own."* Some grunt work is *"par for the course"* as litigation, in particular, can be document heavy. When there's a backlog in lower level tasks, trainees have to pitch in. One trainee moaned: *"I spent six months doing photocopying* and bundling in personal injury." However, she also said, "*If they give you crappy work, they always apologise and they do encourage you to delegate wherever possible.*"

You'll have your own supervisor, but you'll also work for other fee earners in the department. It's your responsibility to organise three-monthly reviews, but trainees spoke of having sufficient ongoing feedback. As one said, "*They're not going to wait three months to tell you if you're rubbish at something!*" On hours, one trainee's answer was typical: "*There's not the emphasis on working massive hours that there might be in City firms – it's very much a nine to five firm.*" Apparently, in most departments, "*if you worked till 7.30pm, you'd walk away and moan that you'd had a late night!*" And even in corporate, "*if you've been there till two or three in the morning, it's expected you'll come in to work at two or so in the afternoon to give you a lie-in.*"

Traditionally IM has had a good retention rate on qualification and September 2002 saw all but one of the 15 qualifiers stay with the firm.

sheffield: who's the daddy?

The Sheffield office is the "*great granddaddy*" of the firm. It's where it all started 80 years ago and still plays host to IM's core PI business, including the alarmingly-named Catastrophic Injuries team. It also offers a full range of services including corporate, property, insurance, private client and trainee hot spot, business crime. All initial training contract assessments take place there, regardless of which office trainees end up in, but subsequent interviews could be in any one of the offices. Continued expansion has led to the opening of a second office in the city, now home to the insurance and probate departments. However, we were left in no doubt that the main office building is "*at best described as functional,*" "*a bit 80s*" and "*could do with some sprucing up.*" It has a good location in the centre of the city, but other IM offices are felt to be "*nicer because they're newer.*" Many trainees have their own room, but it's just as likely that you'll share with another trainee or paralegal or sit at an open-plan workstation. Support services are reputedly "*second to none – Sheffield has more of them because it's the main office.*"

Sheffield's Trainee Solicitors Group is "*overwhelmed*" by Irwin Mitchell people, who constitute almost half the organisation. The firm socialises in local bars, most recently venturing regularly to the new Bar Sola. With its "*concrete floor and plastic furniture,*" it's "*too trendy for its own good!*"

checking out new leeds

Opened just four years ago, the Leeds office offers plenty of variety. Leeds is the commercial hub of the North so unsurprisingly this office has concentrated on that type of client. Trainees tell us that IM is "*building up a Yorkshire emphasis.*" One explained more clearly: "*While it's always been a Sheffield-centred firm, the Leeds office has now built up to such an extent that it's a major player in the Leeds market.*" Through the endeavours of IM's Leeds lawyers, "*the firm is showing that it can offer more to regional clients.*" Indeed, the client roster is stuffed with industrial and commercial concerns from the region.

As newer office, "*there's a bit more space than there is in Birmingham or Sheffield*" and trainees are "*virtually guaranteed to get their own offices.*" One of the firm's self-styled "*gypsy*" trainees said, "*The Leeds and Birmingham offices tend to have younger crowds than Sheffield*" and "*a later hours culture.*" Additionally, "*Leeds is the most organised in terms of going out.*" Trainees often head to Babylon, which by all accounts is not as gloriously civilised as its biblical namesake, but nevertheless is "*always a good laugh*" and filled with young lawyers from a number of Leeds firms.

the Birmingham connection

Founded in 1989 to handle insurance litigation work, the Birmingham office also undertakes claimant personal injury, legal expenses work and IM Business (that's corporate services to those not programmed in IM-speak), and has a burgeoning private client practice to boot. It offers at least two commercial seats, and there have been as many as eight trainees working there at any one time. *"The trainees who choose Birmingham tend to have some kind of pre-existing connection with it, which isn't so much the case with Sheffield or Leeds."* Along these lines, another trainee told us, *"Birmingham never seems to be very popular with people who don't have a connection with the city."* To be fair, it's actually *"probably the swankiest of all of them"* and certainly one trainee liked it better than the Sheffield HQ: *"I thought Birmingham would be an industrial black hole, but it's actually a great city. Sheffield on the other hand really is an industrial black hole!"* If trainees feel like letting their hair down after work, the fave spot nearby is The Trocadero.

london calling

The 11-partner London office was set up in 1995 to undertake claimant personal injury and employment work. While these remain its chief strengths, it has also developed some commercial and debt recovery work, which continues to expand. One seat in personal injury two years ago is now six seats in various practice areas (personal injury, commercial litigation, business crime, corporate/commercial, clinical negligence and most recently a three-month stint in employment). Some think *"because London is the smallest office, Sheffield, Birmingham and Leeds tend to think of it as being more of a satellite"* and *"talk to each other more than they do to London."* But in London they told us: *"We're getting more respect as the office grows."* There is still one issue where the trainees would like even more respect though – money. *"Salaries go further up North than they do in London."* However, one trainee did make the point that *"we're not paid a fantastic amount compared with the big London firms, but we've got a better quality of life in terms of hours. Proportionately it works out about even."* Swings. Roundabouts.

London is open-plan and being smaller than the others has its advantages: *"It's nice because we tend to do things as an office rather than individual departments."* Favourite after work haunts for the FNPC (Friday Night Pub Club) include Livebait, Harley's and The Gate, while the wine bar Holborn Colony is a popular mid-week destination for the HDC (Heavy Drinkers Club) and makes one trainee feel *"very Ally McBeal when we're in there – it's at the bottom of our office block, so it feels very much like our bar!"*

and finally…

IM's protecting an awesome reputation in its PI and clin neg specialisms in the North, but it's also expanding in all directions. As one trainee put it, *"there aren't many firms this size where you get the chance to do corporate, personal injury and private client work in your training contract."* If all this appeals and you're prepared to take an office move in your stride, then get Irwin Mitchell on your shortlist.

Kaim Todner

the facts

Location: London
UK ranking by size: 117
Total number of trainees: 14
Seats: usually 3
Alternative seats: None

From offices in the City, Islington, Caledonian Road and Elephant & Castle, Kaim Todner provides legal assistance to London's residents.

dedication is what you need

The key areas in Kaim Todner's general practice are family, crime, mental health, medical negligence, personal injury and prisoners' rights. *"It has a Legal Aid certificate,"* and has earned itself a *"good reputation in the legal aid world."* Trainees generally undertake three seats and *"almost invariably you'll do a criminal seat as this is the main part of the firm's business."* You can then choose *"to a certain degree"* which two of the other areas you would like to experience. The distribution of the firm's work means that you will probably spend time in two or more of the offices during your training contract. *"It is really quite flexible,"* said one source. You could even do "*two areas of law at the same time.*" We heard of trainees spending three days a week in one department and two in another. And why not? Variety is the spice of life, after all.

That variety is carried over into the people at Kaim Todner. It has "*a multiracial staff, which is reflective of London itself.*" One source added: "*Trainees here tend not to be the traditional type; they usually have a bit of work experience behind them. They've had some sort of similar career, or have worked for another firm as a paralegal.*" The benefits are clear. "*Because you have all these people from different careers, ex-social workers, police officers, etc. in terms of incidental support it is really good.*"

In the week that we interviewed at Kaim Todner, our researcher was also speaking with trainees at a City megafirm. He noticed the differences between the two firms immediately: Kaim Todner is a very matter-of-fact, no-nonsense place. "*It is practical, progressive and brisk; that's the nature of legal aid work – it has to be, otherwise it becomes impossible to do,*" explained one trainee. This is not the sort of firm you just fall into by accident. You won't normally find it on the random hit lists of those students using the scattergun technique to getting a training contract. The trainees who come here are "*dedicated to Kaim Todner and often have some knowledge of it beforehand.*"

nice and terrifying

Because trainees begin on a three-month trial period, "*you stay in that first seat* [where you have spent the trial] *after you get the training contract.*" Although a trial period is not the norm in commercial practice, it is more common in high street firms – they don't want to waste resources on those who are not up to the job or not in the right job at all. It cuts both ways. As one trainee put it: "*It means that if people don't like the place they don't waste any more of their time.*"

Trainees take on serious levels of responsibility within a short space of time. "*There's always a lot of work in legal aid firms, so they allow you to get really involved. You get your own caseload fairly quickly.*" In mental health work, for example, "*you start out shadowing solicitors, then going to see clients on your own, and then you move up to the mental health review tribunals.*" Thankfully, responsibility doesn't come all at once. "*They give you increasing responsibility to fit you. I saw my first client, alone, after a few weeks and did my first tribunal after about five months*" said one source. Trainees start with "*quite basic and informal hearings, then civil tribunals and then criminal tribunals.*" "*It's bloody terrifying but really good,*" said a rather chuffed trainee.

out and about

The "*very busy but pretty organised*" criminal department provides ample opportunities to get your hands dirty. The firm handles a huge volume of work, but each case needs individual attention. "*Obviously it is a business, but that isn't the primary concern of the file administrators – it's all about the clients.*" The work can involve a lot of time away from the office, be it prison visits or trips to police stations under the Police Station Accreditation programme. Trainees are required to sign up to the programme and, once qualified, "*go onto a monthly rota and do one weekend and a couple of evenings per month.*" Unlike some firms, "*they pay you for it, too.*"

Before panic sets in, be reassured that all this responsibility comes with a good level of support. The offices ("*not flashy but practical*") are generally open-plan, although "*supervisors have their own offices.*" Open-plan working allows trainees to get advice quickly. "*You can discuss things more easily and you feel less isolated,*" said one source. Although trainees are assigned supervisors, they aren't tied to them for support. "*We sort of flit around depending on who we want to discuss things with,*" one interviewee explained. Appraisals "*are regularly spaced, every three or four months*" and "*you go through the files you have and discuss where your strengths and weaknesses lie.*" This approach is "*less formal*" and "*much quicker,*" but isn't perceived by trainees to be less effective than the more regimented appraisal systems at some firms. The firm is keen to hang on to its qualifiers and all four second-years were offered a job in September 2002.

fabrication

After hours goings-on say much about the social structure of the firm. *"You get supervisors, receptionists and lawyers coming out; it's everybody together,"* said a source. *"Because there are so many of us, there is always something going on." "We generally invite barristers from the chambers on our approved list along too."* Challenging our hard-fought inclination to stereotype, one trainee told us how they'd recently had a night out with a bunch of barristers at super-cool, Farringdon super-club Fabric. Robes? Wigs? Drum n Bass? Naah…

For regular nights out, *"all the offices have a dodgy, old pub over the road."* Trainees have *"loads of favourites,"* but on the most-frequently-mentioned-pubometer, The Melton Mowbray in Chancery Lane just edges it.

and finally…

If you are interested in either standard high street work or specialist fields such as prisoners' rights and mental health appeals, Kaim Todner is one of the largest London firms of this type. You'll probably need to back up your application with a bit of relevant experience, but if you're right for this firm, chances are you've already got it by the lorryload.

KLegal

the facts
Location: London
UK ranking by size: 59
Total number of trainees: 21
Seats: 4x6 months.
Alternative seats: Brussels, secondments
Extras: Language training

KLegal is a relative newcomer to the UK market although KLegal International has over 3,000 lawyers in 50 different jurisdictions. It set up shop in London in 1999 as the tied law firm of accountancy giant KPMG and, like the washing-up pile in a student house at exam time, it's grown fast.

rub-a-dub-dub…

…three men in a tub: an accountant, a lawyer, and a financial advisor…each rowing in the same direction. For many people, the concept of the MDP is entirely novel, yet it is the beating heart of the KLegal philosophy. The acronym stands for 'multidisciplinary practice' and, according to the firm's trainees, *"it is definitely the way forward."* If you don't yet know much about the MDP principle, then we suggest you start mugging up now. Simply put, an MDP involves different professionals, such as accountants and lawyers, entering into partnership together and offering their services to shared clients.

According to its website, KLegal is "pioneering the MDP principle through close association with KPMG." We couldn't have put it better ourselves, and we'd like to point out that in the UK, this particular pioneer has travelled considerably further along the trail than any of its rivals. After the Enron catastrophe, the wheels fell off Andersen's Garretts wagon and it was broken up for spare parts. PwC's Landwell wagon, with fewer horses pulling the load, appears to be some distance behind KLegal and Ernst & Young's tiny Tite & Lewis poses no real threat.

Yet a barrier lies in the path of full integration – professional regulations presently forbid it. At the moment, by operating a system of Chinese walls, *"the firm is as close to KPMG as it can be without upsetting the Law Society."* A rule change that would have allowed them to get even closer seemed good to go in England and Wales until the Law Society's plans to relax the extent of the ban were held up by parliamentary timetabling.

And then came the Andersen/Enron affair. Resultant industry panic has thrown the debate wide open again. The European Court of Justice ruled (on a Dutch case) that a ban on MDPs between lawyers and accountants is anti-competitive, but could be justified. The European Commission called for tougher restrictions on multidisciplinary practice, and over in the US, the American Bar Association and most state bar associations take a restrictive

317

stance. It's impossible for us to take the debate far here, so we won't. But you should follow up on the topic and ask the firm's representatives to explain its current progress and opinions on the matter. Sadly, our attempts to do this were met with some suspicion during trainee interviews, but they've no reason to suspect your motives. MDP is a hot potato, so don't feel stupid about asking for information.

over the wall

After it began trading in 1999, KLegal started drawing well-respected lawyers away from established City firms. The prospect of a fresh challenge in a tradition-free environment must have been attractive. And then in March 2002 KLegal merged with Scottish giant McGrigor Donald. Not since the days of Hadrian had such a daring raid been carried out north of the border (except, maybe, when Edward I pinched the Stone of Scone). Trainees explained: *"McGrigors had a mid-sized London office, but was much, much bigger in Scotland. It wanted more international reach as there was a feeling it had gone as far as it could."* The result? The merger of the London office in its entirety, and the welcoming of McGrigor Donald in Scotland and Northern Ireland to the KLegal international fold. Our sources tell us that *"due to rules in Scotland and Ireland, McGrigors has had to keep the name."* We suspect the McGrigors brand was so strong in Scotland and NI that there was no way it was going to drop it!

Things have changed since the merger, and its not been confined to minor irrelevancies such as the renaming of departments into 'clusters' or moving all staff into the offices KLegal shares with KPMG in Dorset Rise. The McGrigor Donald merger injected several important new clients and the new improved client roster is indeed impressive, including big names like Airtours, Fiat UK, Bank of Scotland, BP Energy, Sony Music and EMI.

taste the difference

The moment you bite into this firm, you'll notice a very different flavour. Much of the firm's business feeds through from KPMG – not surprising given that the firm is *"in the same building and on the same computer system* [as KPMG] *– the branding and the culture are quite similar too."* If ever you wanted to find out if lawyers and accountants are alike then this is the place to do it. KLegal has even adopted the KPMG 'Values Charter'.

Just like many of their common or garden peers at conventional firms, KLegal trainees sit with their supervisors (either partners or senior associates) on a typical four by six-month seat rotation. As well as the contentious experience required by the Law Society, trainees must do a stint in corporate. Beyond that they can express their preferences for the remaining seats. The employment, IP and corporate seats are currently the most popular, with property and banking also featuring highly on the 'best seat in the house' chart. A competition seat in Brussels offers time away from the office and we heard of trainees popping off to Europe for the odd day or two. The hours sound pretty reasonable, with most trainees getting away by 6.30pm and rarely needing to stay beyond 8pm, even in the transactional seats.

One trainee said, *"Having a fair bit of responsibility, and lots of opportunities to experience things like submissions in the courts and dealing with clients directly"* was a real high point of the training. There's a sense of real enthusiasm: *"Partners will say, 'Hi, we have a meeting tomorrow, d'ya wanna come?'"* Trainees are keen to stress: *"Because of the MDP idea, you're able to get involved in transactions from an earlier stage."* One trainee remarked: *"You get involved in deal negotiations, rather than just dotting the i's and crossing the t's."*

piggyback rides

The freshness of the firm is not lost on trainees. *"There's a sense that it is new, growing, exciting and so on, and you can be a part of it."* Through KPMG, our sources said they got a level of training and resources that you wouldn't normally expect from such a young firm. They receive additional training from KPMG professionals that *"would be invaluable to a* trainee at any firm, and is certainly useful here." Other pluses are the well-established KPMG pro bono scheme, dubbed 'community broking', and the various KPMG sports teams, which include rugby, football, hockey and netball. This year, KLegal established its own teams, so a bit of in-house competition could well be on the way.

Trainees feel fully involved in the business. We were told that *"being listened to is one of the best things. You feel like you can speak up in meetings."* We also heard that *"there is no strict structure, with partners on a higher level. There is a team atmosphere and you feel like your ideas are as valuable as those of the partners."* This carries over into social events. *"Partners socialise with us a lot and get very involved."* The Evangelist plays host to KLegal lawyers when they're not sampling the delights of the *"spit and sawdust"* pubs around Bow Lane.

KPMcGLegal

It would be remiss of us not to report on some of the more curious findings of our interviews. For example, in London, trainees refer to themselves or other trainees as alternately McGrigor Donald or KLegal trainees. When we called KLegal's main number, receptionists were just as likely to answer the phone with the words *"Hello, KPMG!"* When we interviewed, ex-McGrigor Donald trainees in London were receiving training via video conferencing facilities from Glasgow and trainees at KLegal's Dorset Rise HQ knew the KPMG trainees better than their peers who were still over at the old McGrigors building. It was hard to see the precise relationship between all the pieces of the jigsaw.

And then came news of redundancies. 62 staff from across the KLegal UK network were to be shed, 20 of them lawyers from London. The reason given was the slowdown in transactional work. Be aware that KLegal was not the only City firm to announce redundancies or, indeed, to ask LPC students if they would defer the start of their training contracts. For those completing their training, the retention rate in London in September 2002 was eight out of 12.

and finally…

As trainees told us: *"If you want to be a part of this, you have to be aware that there is a different kind of attitude. If this isn't what you are looking for, then you really wouldn't fit in."* If you're looking to get in at the beginning with a young, ambitious and standard-challenging firm, then KLegal could be of interest.

Lawrence Graham

the facts
Location: London
UK ranking by size: 37
Total number of trainees: 34
Seats: 4x6 months
Alternative seats: None

Lawrence Graham is a full-service, mid-sized commercial firm, prowling at the better end of the London legal scene. It's particularly hot on property and environmental work, and has a top-notch private client department that has been entrusted with the administration of the Estate of Princess Diana.

lg knows best

The firm's calm and collected nature actually gives our editor a bit of a headache. No matter how many trainees we interview, nothing sensational or headline-grabbing ever comes to the fore. And we're never quite sure whether that's a good or a bad thing. The absence of major criticisms in interviews and the reasonably high retention rates on qualification (11 out of 15 in September 2002) are testament to a firm that keeps its trainees happy. But we still don't feel we know the place…and this is our sixth edition.

The firm is split between two sites. Its main Strand office handles property, private client, commercial litigation, insolvency and corporate, and a smaller City office at St Mary's Axe does shipping, insurance and reinsurance work. Trainees tend to do a seat in litigation, one in property, one in corporate and a fourth seat of their choice. *"I'd rather be trained generally than be trained as a rocket scientist,"* said one source of the over-specialised training of some firms. As trainees know they will all go through the three main departments, there's no rumpus or squabbling. However, a few implied that the seat allocation wasn't particularly transparent. *"You get the feeling that a lot more is going on behind the scenes,"* thought one trainee.

live a lotto

We went looking for the firm's strengths. The considered opinion of one insider was that it was *"good on property and in cross-selling from that department."* The corporate/commercial department may not handle the fattest deals in the City, but it does do well in the medium-ticket market. The firm's name is not going to be splashed across the front page of the *FT* on a regular basis, but on the plus side, you're more likely to be away with the fairies (or your friends) when the first edition hits the stands, not slumped in a data room. We heard of ample opportunities to experience work in interesting niche areas of law. For example, the firm does *"lots of gaming and gambling"* as part of its work for the National Lottery.

We're always interested in the views of trainees on different areas of work. In property, *"you sit [open-plan] in the middle of the floor in your own pen,"* and it's a great seat *"if you like to dive in and get on with things."* The private client department (a rarity in big London firms) is, for some, *"much more interesting than property,"* with plenty of drafting and research and international clients. *"It's an intense environment with more dominant individuals."* Employment and comm/tech (with its IT/IP work) are hot seats. Oil & Gas isn't. Commercial litigation involves lots of research and writing attendance notes, but *"not many trainees have to go to the courts and stand up before a master."* *"I'd rather die than advocate!"* exclaimed one trainee. Steady on. And what of reinsurance? *"Most people don't want to go to St Mary's Axe – they think they might feel a bit out of it – but once they get there they love it."*

Doubtless some trainees will disagree with the above comments, but this only serves to emphasise the inconsistency we encountered in our interviews. The low points for a couple of trainees were the times when they felt they were underworked. *"In the corporate tax seat there wasn't much work for me and it was a bit depressing,"* said one, whilst another moaned about not being given enough to do in litigation. But then others felt that pressure during busy periods was the worst thing about the job. Some of the trainees we spoke to had, at times, had two supervising partners and were getting work from four or five people: *"I could be concentrating on one set of urgent work and then get chased up by other people."* Another trainee sighed: *"Sometimes you get lots of work put on you because everyone is busy. You're trying to turn things around and there'll be work coming at you from every angle."* Thankfully, everybody talked enthusiastically about the high points – the times when they had responsibility and were able to feel like *"actual lawyers."*

Some felt the appraisal system was *"a bit one-way"* and that certain partners were reluctant to fill in the required form. Others said it was a brilliant system and *"very two-way."* Generally, *"supervising partners are adept at listening to you and what your needs are. They try to give you as good work as possible without compromising the assistants,"* who are, in turn, *"approachable and helpful."* Across the departments, trainees talked of being able to *"demonstrate potential and ability within the realms of reality."* (What!?) One testified: *"We're treated like colleagues, not like a resource. I have my own files to run – it's quality stuff, it's not just photocopying and carrying things up and down stairs."* Hard-working, but not slavishly so is how they sum up LG.

bear essentials

To dispel a rumour, we are assured that the firm is *"established rather than conservative."* *"The firm is less staid and more receptive to external influences. It is becoming more media- and market-friendly,"* concluded one trainee. There are temporary art exhibitions in the windows of the Strand office and *"strange drinks* evenings when the art changes…you get lawyers and artists in different corners of the room." When quizzed about the artwork and this aspect of the firm's character, one trainee concluded: *"There is an absurd edge to the firm. They try and be a bit zany."*

Perhaps this is the inspiration for the graduate recruitment brochures. Rather than the standard glossy offering, with images of happy, young, international execs, Lawrence Graham's recent material has taken a surprisingly surreal approach. In its own words: "Graduates join us to be trained as superior solicitors, not party animals." The brochure pack bears the confusing legend: "Car Tyres, Containers and Career Opportunities" and features images of sculptures and installations by the contemporary artist David Mach.

We went onto Mr Mach's website. Of his more lawyer-friendly oeuvres Mach says, "I'm obsessed with the idea of individuality, especially in our mad, weird, bizarre, dangerous world. It's just a relentless barrage of stuff which we have to pick our way through, wrestle with and, if we can, get in a half-nelson." And then, alongside the now familiar images of car tyres and containers, we found a sadly overlooked series of sculptures – demonic teddy bears (customised with plastic fangs and tongues from a taxidermist). We pondered on all this for some time, but we're still no closer to understanding how it relates to an LG training.

harmonious chords

At times, the flood of self-effacing comments did worry us – *"We need to be more hard-nosed; other firms probably think we're a bit soft."* *"I'm not sure if many people have heard about us!"* and *"we're not taken as seriously as other firms."* But LG is said to be firming up, flexing its muscles and raising billing targets. In spite of this, the tone remains unwavering and melodious. *"We are spoilt rotten,"* gloated one trainee. *"It doesn't forget about the people who work here."* And who are they exactly? In contrast to the comments of a couple of years ago, *"trainees all seem to be aged 23 and from universities like Bristol and Warwick."* They are also quite sure of what they want: *"When you choose a medium-sized firm you are automatically saying 'I'm not going to work every hour that God sends'."* Size is one of the firm's winning features – it's all about getting the balance between *"the big firms where you work all night and the small ones where there's no money."* Staying late is actively discouraged, but Monday evenings mean training lectures. There are also workshops on skills and IT topics.

"People enjoy the mentality here. In some departments it's dress-down all week long which makes for a good bit of office banter." Such as? *"What are those disgusting cords you're wearing?!"* The office is a bit crowded, but we were told that the firm is looking to buy a new building. Even though it may look like a *"concrete box"* from the outside, inside we heard that it's *"perfectly comfortable."* One trainee took a harsher view of things: *"The office is minging. It's a grey monstrosity circa 1972."*

back to the garden

For the crew at 190 Strand, Daley's wine bar is the only place to hang out. It's virtually an annexe of the firm and is *"haunted by partners."* The office is just two minutes' walk from Covent Garden and yet there is a *"magnetic force field"* that keeps people in Daley's. The social committee organises quiz nights, bowling trips and wine-tastings and every summer there's a ball and a soiree on the roof of the office. At last year's bash, the managing partner must have thought he was back at Woodstock, as apparently he went round painting flowers on people's faces. We are stardust, we are golden…

and finally…

We're certain that you'll get a rock solid training, responsibility and lots of client contact at Lawrence Graham, but we're still somewhat confused by the firm. We've decided therefore, to give the last word to one of the trainees. He simply said, *"I wouldn't want to be anywhere else."*

Laytons

the facts
Location: Bristol, Guildford, London, Manchester
UK ranking by size: 85
Total number of trainees: 13
Seats: 4x6 months (Guildford: 1x12 + 2x6)
Alternative seats: None

With distinct specialist practice areas and a fair bit of geography separating them, Laytons' four offices each have their own feel.

the slice is right

Like the ingredients that go into a pizza, Laytons' four offices are each mouth-watering prospects in their own right; you don't have to mix them together to make it work. The autonomy extends to recruitment too, so if you want to work in London, apply to London, and so on. Trainees also indicate that, beyond London, the offices commonly recruit those with local connections. The result is a firm *"with strong loyalties – there is a very personal element to the relationship between the solicitors and their clients."*

Yet there's also a good working relationship between the four sites. Trainees talked about interaction with colleagues in other offices, and are aware of the connectivity. When an office takes on a really big or specialist matter, expertise is often called in from other offices and *"there's quite clever use of technology to co-ordinate teams."* One trainee told us that a colleague in the City had said, *"Drop by if you are ever in London."*

london: troop movements

London is not the main office, as such, but it is a hub for much of the firm's higher value corporate work, and it picks up valuable private clients and complex tax or trusts matters. Corporate is the biggest department, and with several large plcs on its books, there's an international aspect to some of the work. Property is also a fair size, but neither of these departments wins out as a clear favourite with the trainees. *"There's no 'corporate is best' attitude; you just go where you will enjoy the work,"* one of them explained. The system of seat allocation runs as smoothly as silk. With so few trainees, *"they know your preferences and your skills."* Ask for what you want and usually you'll get it. Trainees get responsibility early on and lots of face to face client contact, but *"because we're small, there's no army of paralegals to do all the admin."* Hours are reasonable. One trainee spoke of *"a couple of midnight to one o'clock jobs,"* but *"this was actually an exciting rarity."* It seems to be the case that *"if you are there at 10pm, you either have time management problems or you have been given too much to do"* and associates will say, *"Hey, you're a trainee, go home!"*

"It's a personal training," we heard. *"In a smaller firm there is less need for formality as people work and talk together all the time."* The flip side is that *"they don't want people who are going to upset the balance."* One source informed us: *"The trainees are all from different backgrounds,"* but what they do have in common is that all are *"very stable and together."* *"We're confident but not loud-confident; it's a quiet confidence with quiet efficiency."* Indeed, all the Laytons trainees, across all the offices, appear to have this 'quiet, confident efficiency'. And maybe that's why the firm tries to hang on to its trainees when they qualify. In 2002, eight of the ten second-years were offered jobs and six accepted.

Housed on the upper floors of the Carmelite building on Victoria Embankment, the office has *"great views over London."* Subtlety and neatness are to the fore. Strangest of all, annexed to the library you will find the chillingly named 'War Room'. Senior partners shoving model lawyers around a giant map of London? No, it's just where folk go to prepare for court *"because it's spacious and quiet."* Sadly, there's no secret bunker either. Nor a canteen...but they do have *"a tuck shop"* for those essential rations. Impromptu nights out start in The Harrow, and The Bell is popular for special occasions. Partners may pop along – *"They aren't untouchable!"*

guildford: buzzing

Despite its proximity to London, the Guildford office is no satellite and undertakes a wide range of work. Since its 2001 merger with Lochners Technology Solicitors (rated by our big-momma publication, *Chambers UK*, as the best IP practice in the South), the IP and IT practices have charged ahead. The firm represents large clients such as Nokia, Harley-Davidson, and, perhaps most notably, Remington in its successful ECJ challenge of the Philips' shape trademark (a case sure to be familiar to all aspiring IP lawyers – if not, give up now). *"IP is the new buzz area,"* noted one trainee, clearly oblivious to the shaver gag.

On the property side, much of the work is for house builders, *"covering all aspects from the purchase of brownfield sites through the planning stage to plot sales."* Guildford wannabes take note: *"The first seat is a year long, otherwise you wouldn't get anything out of it… during the first three months you're learning about the admin and the people."* The length of the first seat means *"they don't want to place you just anywhere; you choose your first seat at the initial interview."* Trainees then complete two six-month seats.

One trainee mulled over the benefits of training in Guildford: *"It has a good client list but not London hours, so trainees get the best of both worlds."* The brand new office is *"welcoming and looks quite spacey* [!]*"* The businesslike atmosphere of the London office travels the hour (or less) that it takes to get to Guildford, but *"from senior partners to juniors, no one feels too grand to do anything. You'll see senior partners* [copying and colouring] *their own plans* [in property]*."*

Trainees *"need to be pretty intelligent, but clued-up rather than intellectual."* *"Most are fairly confident,"* which is a good thing as they must look after their own files and see them through from start to finish. The work ethic is all about *"looking after Laytons and not just number one."* Trainees aren't single-minded about work though; four of them were attempting to restart the Young Surrey Lawyers Group when we telephoned. Amongst themselves they organise bowling and cinema nights, and *"the firm all mixes and goes out for drinks in the evening."* Old Orleans is popular for food, as is The Star Inn in Quarry Street, but Yates and similar chain pubs are preferred for drinks. *"There is no stay late culture,"* and with the town centre only three minutes' walk away, you can *"nip to Sainsbury's for your weekly shopping in the lunch break."*

bristol: cloak and stagger

The Bristol office handles the same basic areas as the others (commercial property, employment, insolvency, private client and company/commercial) and has a thriving construction group. Trainees report *"responsibility without feeling a huge burden or pressure,"* although they had an idea that *"Bristol isn't so relaxed as the other offices."* But it is a supportive environment, where you will be *"trusted to manage your own files properly and to get on with things."*

On the site of the old St. Bartholomew's Hospital, the office is filled with *"lots of big, green, leafy plants"* and paintings by Bristol artists rather than nasty portraits of crusty, old partners or insipid watercolours. Lending an air of grandeur to the square outside is the Cloaked Horseman, by local sculptor David Backhouse. There's an active social committee, organising everything from family fun days to BBQs and bowling. On a less formal front, e-mails will go out, *"always on a Friday and potentially any other day,"* encouraging people to visit The Three Sugar Loaves. All Bar One and the bars and restaurants along Corn Street are also easy targets.

manchester: a family affair

Manchester is home to a well-respected matrimonial team, with corporate as the other main department. Expect *"enough responsibility to meet your needs,"* *"a lot of client contact"* and *"a good level of constructive feedback."* Even in the smaller employment, property and litigation departments, you will be involved in client meetings and given good work. *"There's no sense of 'Oh, you're just a trainee fit to do the crappy bits no one else is interested in'."* By all accounts, *"it's a relaxed atmosphere, with people laughing and joking a lot. You'll be able to* have a natter with people during the course of the day," chuckled one happy soul. Another source put it rather more bluntly: *"It's a friendly firm, the work's varied and you don't come in thinking, 'Oh sh*t, that place again'."*

Laytons Manchester is situated *"on a busy street off a main thoroughfare, surrounded by traditional businesses."* The meeting rooms and reception are *"substantial, elegant and sophisticated."* There is a Christmas party open to all, and a meal and drinks at the expense of the partnership every couple of months. Trainees are not averse to the odd night out as a group, and *"there tends to be a session in the pub* [Bar 38] *every week or two."* Just behind the office, El Rincon is popular for lunchtime tapas, and the Australian pub, Walkabout, occasionally gets a visit. The firm runs a five-a-side footie team in the local league. Red or blue, we wonder? Perhaps the office décor will give you a clue…

and finally…

Each of Laytons' offices must compete with its local peers for your attention. Good clients, flexible training, a sense of humour, a hard working ethos and a wide range of practice areas…there's five pretty good reasons why you may want to apply.

LeBoeuf, Lamb, Greene & MacRae

the facts
Location: London
UK ranking by size: 104
Total number of trainees: 9
Seats: 4x6 months
Alternative seats: None

US law firm LeBoeuf, Lamb, Greene & MacRae was founded in 1829 and since then it has developed a fearsome global reputation for legal services to the insurance and energy industries. Its London office opened in 1995 and now has around 55 qualified English and American lawyers.

gas, ghana and platform shoes

The firm's website states that its London practice has "a distinctly English and European flavour", with its work "often multinational in character, whether for UK clients seeking legal assistance with worldwide operations or for US and European clients using London as a key operating base." Sounds like a fair assessment. This international dimension is also reflected in the make-up of the trainee population: *"There are a lot of trainees who speak at least two languages"* and *"throughout the firm there are a lot of people from other European countries and further afield."*

The largest departments are litigation and corporate, and trainees must spend time in each. A third seat can be taken in project finance, property or tax, and then the fourth will be a return visit to the department into which you hope to qualify. As one source said, *"The firm is renowned for its insurance litigation, so a lot of trainees want to get involved with that."* Don't expect low level claims: the cases are often of enormous importance and tackle issues with widespread impact. For example, the firm acts for NFU Mutual Insurance on all matters relating to Foot and Mouth, and its reputation in the insurance sector generally has led to its involvement in a number of matters arising out of September 11. It also acted for Royal & SunAlliance in the litigation brought by Elton John against his former manager. The insurance industry additionally feeds corporate work to the London lawyers.

The energy team advised the Kingdom of Saudi Arabia on one of the largest oil and gas projects in the world – the $100 billion 'Natural Gas Initiative', which saw the restructuring and privatisation of the Kingdom's gas assets. And despite a couple of high-level London partner defections at the end of 2001, the project finance team is active in advising clients in Africa, the Middle East and Eastern Europe. Recently it had a hand in the Maputo ports project in Mozambique and the Ghanaian Volta River Authority's negotiations with Shell/Chevron concerning gas transportation. Big stuff. As you can imagine, your role as a trainee will be small but, undoubtedly, it will be interesting.

up close and personal

"You hear about American firms being sweatshops, but it's not like that here," one source was keen to stress. *"It's up to you how you structure your day, as long as the work's done."* We heard of one trainee who came in from 8.30am till 6.30pm and worked through lunch while others started at 9.30am, took lunch and stayed till 8.30pm. Even busy departments have welcome lulls. On responsibility: *"You won't stagnate as a trainee. You find yourself being trusted more and given more responsibility"* and *"they like you to use your initiative and be flexible."* Being flexible also extends to the inevitable – grunt work. The litigation seat in particular involves a touch more than is ideal and photocopying and bundling tasks prompted a few moans. Trainees think that more paralegals would improve their lot.

The size of the office has its pluses though: *"It's small so you're more likely to assist with good work and deal directly with clients."* One source said, *"You have to be quite proactive – you can't just sit there and expect things to happen without doing anything. If you're interested in doing some particular type of work, you often have to go looking for it – it won't just come to you."*

There was comment that *"it's a bit male-dominated up at the top,"* but then we heard a familiar message: *"It's an American firm in London, so it's not as staid as some City firms."* Trainees also enjoyed the feeling of not being on a production line that churns out scores of newly qualifieds each year. Unfortunately, only one out of five second-years stayed on in September 2002, qualifying into tax.

keep your passport handy

End-of-seat appraisals take place with the managing partner and one other. *"They work well,"* although there was comment that a mid-seat appraisal might be helpful. In terms of informal feedback, we heard that *"some supervisors operate on a no news is good news basis."* This was supported by comment that *"you have to ask if you want specific feedback on a piece of work, otherwise they'll just take it and use it,"* although *"they might say 'good job!'"*

There are internal training sessions *"about once a month,"* some of which are just for trainees, some for seniors too. A firm-wide induction programme involving a trip to New York (the head office) awaited the lucky first-years who started in September 2002. At the moment, there are no secondments to any of the firm's other 24 offices; however, *"the work in London is international, so you're quite likely to travel as a result of that,"* particularly once qualified.

american gothic

The office is a *"nice Gothicy building"* with high ceilings and *"lots of huge windows which give a lot of light."* Strangely, the floors occupied by LeBoeuf are each three floors apart: the sixth floor houses the corporate department, the project finance and tax teams take up part of the ninth, and the litigation department is on the twelfth and highest floor, which offers *"great views over London."* In keeping with most US firms in the City, there is a permanent business casual dress code, breached only when meeting clients or going to court.

Trainees often meet up at lunchtime for coffee and in the evening for drinks. Poon's, a Chinese restaurant underneath the building, is ideal for meals when working late. If you have a thirst to quench, there are quite a few pubs nearby, although the key patrons of these establishments seem to be associates, trainees and support staff, with partners making an appearance *"every now and then."* The number of bars mentioned implies that the firm is rather sociable. A newly refurbished and *"bigger and better"* Balls Brothers sits at the bottom of the building, but any number of other regular haunts play host.

and finally…

One trainee summarised training at LeBoeuf: *"It's quite a young firm, we're well-paid and it's generally interesting work."* Another added: *"It's a small office so you get to know everyone very quickly, but at the same time you've got the resources of a large firm."* If the idea of being a nameless face in the crowd appals you, but you want meaty international work, you know what to do.

Leigh, Day & Co

the facts
Location: London, Manchester
UK ranking by size: 108
Total number of trainees: 10
Seats: 2x12 months
Alternative seats: Secondments

Conceived in 1987 as a clinical negligence firm with an additional practice in immigration work, Leigh, Day & Co has retained its focus. Clin neg still accounts for about a third of its work, but it now also specialises in all aspects of personal injury law and human rights. All of its ten trainees are based in London.

injury time
Leigh, Day's website states: "The firm is committed to representing those who have been injured." Indeed, over the years the firm has represented many claimants in landmark cases, including the Sellafield Leukaemia children, Diane Blood, Japanese prisoners of war, Docklands residents, Mull of Kintyre Chinook crash victims and asbestos workers in southern Africa and India. It has also pioneered claims for children who suffer cerebral palsy as a result of birth trauma and other catastrophic injury cases.

You will do two seats, each of one year's duration. While there was comment that *"a couple of us voiced a preference and that was taken into account,"* none of our interviewees had been consulted at length about seat choices. Instead, *"you're generally just assigned."* Many trainees will do a year in clinical negligence and then a year in either the human rights department, PI or the complex claims department, which handles large multiparty actions. The work of this latter department encompasses everything from environmental claims to judicial review work. Bear in mind that this is a niche firm and, while the contentious/con-contentious balance will vary from seat to seat, non-contentious experience is likely to be minimal.

"The office hours are 9.30am until 5.30pm and you're not expected to stay much past that unless there's something big on." Generally, working late is *"very rare,"* but in the busiest department, complex claims, trainees *"have spates of coming in early and leaving late,"* especially when close to trial, mediation or settlement. This is largely due to the fact that in multiparty claims there are often a lot of claimants' cases to coordinate and the judicial review work is often of an urgent nature. People are really committed to their jobs though and we'd bet next month's salary that they are only too happy to put in the extra effort.

witnessing the experts
One trainee remarked that the firm has a high proportion of partners to other staff, particularly in the clinical negligence department, where each partner has just one assistant or one trainee working for them. This is thought to be useful as *"you get a one-to-one relationship with a partner."* Trainees seem delighted with the responsibility they are given: *"You get to know everything on a case from beginning to end, so you're confident when you graduate. It's not like there are some jobs for partners and assistants and then there are trainee jobs – you get to have a bash at everything."* One trainee said, *"Increasingly I've been given lead responsibility on matters; I've picked experts, instructed counsel and sifted through records."* That said, everything's supervised heavily.

You'll generally share an office with another trainee or a paralegal, never your supervisor – *"God! That would be a nightmare!"* exclaimed one interviewee. However, trainees are happy with the feedback they receive. *"I pass work over to my supervisor to check. She'll come in and tell me if I've done it right or wrong, and how to improve it. That happens almost every day."* On a more formal basis, there are six-monthly appraisals.

liberal outlook, life experience
Leigh, Day is not media-shy. Its work, lawyers and its stance on various issues are all well known. On this latter point, trainees said, *"It's a highly politicised, quite*

radical and left wing firm." It's also "*a socially responsible firm*" which "*tries to knock down barriers. When other firms won't touch things, Leigh, Day will.*" For example? The Japanese POW case and southern African asbestos claims. There are occasional opportunities to travel abroad and liaise with injured parties. We heard about two trainees who flew to Kenya to help take statements from Masai and Samburu people who'd been injured by discarded MoD landmines. We also heard of a trainee who flew to Bangladesh to help gather information about a poisoned water supply.

Trainees told us the firm is looking for those with a demonstrable commitment to its work. Quite commonly, "*they take mature students – people who have worked here as paralegals or who have had other careers.*" A couple of the current trainees were previously doctors, another was a research scientist and one was a social worker. There is also a trainee on secondment from the World Wildlife Fund, who is working for a partner handling environmental claims. And in a relatively new arrangement, one trainee spends a year in the firm's clinical negligence department and a year on exchange with a trainee from mental health law specialists Scott-Moncrieff, Harbour & Sinclair.

the last of the mojitos; grin and bear it

The London office is described as "*a kind of 1960s monster stuck on to a 15th century gate*" (St John's Gate in Farringdon). It's a good location – close to the High Court and there are cool bars, clubs and eateries nearby. In line with the firm's down-to-earth atmosphere, the dress code is "*anything you like bar jeans and trainers,*" although you need to be "*suited up*" if you're meeting a client or going to court.

Friday drinks involve wine, beer, nibbles, the boardroom and plenty of chitchat. Occasionally proceedings are themed – a Greek night involved a lot of Greek food, a Jamaican night involved a lot of Jamaican rum, and a Cuban night involved an awful lot of mojitos! The firm's local is The Bear, described as close by and "*very incestuous.*" In keeping with the ursine theme, "*if people are feeling a bit broke*" there's always The White Bear on St John's Street, a relatively cheap taxi drivers' hang-out.

The training partner takes everyone out for dinner at the beginning of the year and throws a barbecue at her house in the summer. On a firm-wide basis, there's a team-building summer outing: "*Everyone's invited and I think it's compulsory to attend,*" said one source. Another concurred: "*Nobody's supposed to be in the office that day. If people don't want to go, they have to take a day's leave.*" The firm also seems to be rather keen on Christmas, organising a seemingly endless round of festive lunches and parties.

you know the score

Of the five qualifying trainees in 2002, only one stayed on. "*You pretty much know the score when you get here. They made it clear that there'd be a limited number of jobs available.*" If someone stays on, "*it's more about being in the right place at the right time. It's not about competing with trainees the whole way through.*" Our interviewees believed that the firm's reputation will carry them far. And it probably will.

and finally…

Quite simply, Leigh, Day & Co is every idealistic young lawyer's dream.

Lester Aldridge

the facts

Location: Bournemouth, Southampton, Bournemouth
UK ranking by size: 89
Total number of trainees: 9
Seats: 4x6 months
Alternative seats: Occasional secondments

Bournemouth beauty Lester Aldridge has now tucked Southampton into her bikini bottoms and continues her promenade along the South Coast attracting attention as she goes. If you want to walk down to the beach at lunchtime and five hours later catch the sun as it sinks slowly into France, read on…

i say, i say, i say

As one trainee said, "*I wasn't interested in the City lifestyle, but I still wanted good work at a decent sized commercial firm, and this gave me an opportunity to combine that with a lifestyle I enjoy.*" Clients range from private individuals and small, local businesses to large banks and corporations. The Southampton office has done much to assist in winning bigger clients and deals. But it's not all commercial work: LA has top-notch private client and family practices.

The employment, corporate, property development and asset finance and banking practices are split between Southampton and Bournemouth, while fast-track and residential property is handled in an office at Bournemouth International Airport. The trusts, tax and wills departments are solely Bournemouth-based. Trainees are encouraged to move between the three offices, and seat allocation will depend on the workflow and the interests of the trainees.

As in most firms, second-years get priority and first-years fill in the gaps, which makes them sound rather like polyfilla. One source spoke of a bit of a sweetener: "*We knew what our first seat would be a week before we started when we got invited to a night at a comedy club by the current trainees.*" We trust that the seating information wasn't part of the stand-up routine.

king of your own sandcastle

"*Trainees are at the disposal of any fee earner in the department.*" (Not in every sense we trust!) What happens is that a number of partners and assistants will give you work, but there's no supervisor sitting in the room with you. Approximately half of Lester Aldridge's trainees share with another trainee, while half have their own rooms. There are two exceptions to this general rule: fast-track and residential property, which position their trainees in an open-plan part of the department.

Fast-track is "*the one that'll wear you down the quickest – it's fast and furious and people tend to talk about it with a little bit of fear in their voices.*" Although worked very hard, trainees feel that it's a good learning experience. The hours are reputed to be "*the worst – generally you'll be there from 8.30am till 7.30pm in the evening.*" However, hours in other seats don't appear to be anywhere near as bad. One interviewee typified the general response: "*I tend to be out of the office by 5.30pm or 6pm most days. If something needs to be done, then people will do it and work later, but there's no expectation that you graft into the early hours just for the sake of it.*" With all the potential for fun and healthy activities like sailing in the area, we're both unsurprised and rather envious.

catch of the day

Client exposure is good. "*We're introduced to clients fairly early on when we join a team,*" one trainee told us. "*It's so they know who we are and what our role is.*" Another said, "*We become points of contact; we're not hidden from anybody, which is good because the best way to learn is to be involved in dealing with clients.*" There were no moans about grunt work. "*There's none of that for trainees. Every team has administrative assistants and any photocopying and bundling will be done by them.*" Bliss!

As for formal training, every team has regular sessions, either fortnightly or once a month, depending on the team. There are firm-wide seminars and trainees are also encouraged to look out for external courses run by the Bournemouth Law Society or other providers. "*If you express an interest, they'll generally let you attend.*" But there's always a catch, isn't there? You'll generally have to give a presentation about the course to your team afterwards. Oh well, look at it as an opportunity to improve your stand-up routine.

Around half the trainees are from the area and we wondered if there was a typical trainee in any other sense? "*We're all pretty outgoing.*" Apparently, "*you can't really exist in your own little shell, it's important for you to be able to interact well with your team and with clients.*" One trainee said, "*As a whole we're a pretty tight-knit group with similar interests – we all appreciate what the area has to offer,"* although he recognised that *"if you're just after the money you may view it differently."*

on the sniff

"If you want to become involved on a social level, it's all laid on for you. It's just a question of whether you take advantage of what's on offer." Monthly firm-wide events peel off a social calendar that's drawn up at the beginning of the year. The firm makes an effort to ensure staff get to know each other outside the work context. Everyone is invited to these events, *"from partners right down to post room people, and often people's partners as well."* There are happy hours in the seventh floor boardroom on the last Friday of every month. Apparently, *"there's a hard core of party animals you can rely on to be there at 5.30pm on the nose."* When they receive heavy hints that they should leave (for the evening, not for good) they then adjourn to the pub. Downes is two minutes' walk from the front door, *"or one minute's run if you're desperate!"* And on Friday nights, *"some of us go into Bournemouth and usually end up at the nightclub Jumping Jack's. It's a bit cheesy, but it's fun."* Apparently the cheese stems from the intermittently duelling pianos. Don't ask – we certainly didn't.

And what news of Sparkle, the famed pet pooch that roams freely around the fifth floor? *"She's still around – she's just had a haircut so she's a bit less shabby."* Since unearthing her in last year's *True Picture*, we've managed to get Sparkle column inches in *The Guardian* and *Legal Week*. Patience darling, Hollywood beckons... Apparently the newly shorn Sparkle spends her time sleeping in the vicinity of the photocopier and *"going on the sniff"* for sandwiches or chocolate. *"I'm wise to her tricks now. If she comes into my office and pesters me for a bite of my sandwich, I just push her out the door."* Despite Sparkle's canine contribution to the firm's open-door policy, LA is currently restricted to one dog and there is no truth in the rumour that the property department is being moved to make way for a petting zoo.

The office building is *"dark brown." "It's nothing much to look at, but we're opposite the Inland Revenue and it's a lot better looking than their building."* Anyone else care to comment? *"The carpet tiles are a bit old and the office could do with a bit of revamping, particularly when you compare it to the office in Southampton."* To prevent the Bournemouth trainees from attempting a midnight furniture raid on the Southampton office, the Bournemouth office is currently being *"done up."*

The firm has taken steps to address the drain of newly qualifieds to London. As one trainee put it: *"Three or four years ago it certainly used to be the case that many trainees would stay on for a year after qualification and then move to the City for the salaries. However, they've now made salaries as competitive as they can be for the South and a lot fewer people are leaving."* Five out of the six September 2002 qualifiers stayed with the firm. *"We were all jumping up and down in February wanting to know what's happening. They said they'd let us know by the end of March, and they did."*

and finally…

South Coast living, great regional work, good-humoured colleagues. What more could you want…other than a celebrity pooch, of course! Enjoy.

Lewis Silkin

the facts

Location: London
UK ranking by size: 79
Total number of trainees: 13
Seats: 4x6 months
Alternative seats: None

Lewis Silkin claims to offer a more irreverent take on commercial law and looks for a certain mythical quality in its trainees that it calls Silkiness. Not so long ago it moved from Westminster into new offices on the fringes of the City, so we thought we'd see if the x factor had survived the journey.

the third way

Lewis Silkin was set up by a Labour MP (who lent his name) and, in the past, it was associated with lefty-liberal values and a commitment to clients in Peckham as well as Pimlico. In recent years it has moved away from its old image, so much so that many trainees were hard-pressed to tell us who Lewis Silkin was. *"We're not a political firm. At the end of the day we're a commercial law firm and we're here to make money,"* said one. The firm has real niche strengths in advertising and marketing law, a burgeoning employment practice and some pretty cool clients. Its social housing group is one of the leading teams in the country and its continued existence is perhaps confirmation that the partnership still values its original ethics.

As a first-year trainee, you'll most likely complete a seat in property, and either general litigation or corporate, followed in your second year by a stint in two of the other main areas – employment, IP, media, construction and property lit. In the past, graduates were attracted by the firm's commitment to social causes. Today, they are more likely to be drawn by the cutting edge Marketing Services Group (*"The glamorous side of the firm where you get to deal with creative people"*) and the super-sexy employment department, which now accounts for almost a quarter of the firm. That said, there still seems to be a commitment to the concept of 'welfare' in its widest sense. The partners are apparently *"a caring bunch"* and, we were told, *"trainees tend to help each other out. There's no room for selfishness and putting other people down."*

the golden mean

Aristotle had a theory that the good life was achieved by choosing the path between two extremes, and trainees seemed to be doing an excellent job of steering a course between the excesses and deficiencies to which other firms might fall prey. Just in case your Aristotle is a touch rusty, it basically boils down to 'moderation in all things'. Trainees told us that if you were *"very shy"* or a *"City Boy,"* then you'd be more comfortable elsewhere.

When it comes to recruitment, the first- and second-years help pick future trainees – those with the x factor. Unfortunately, those we spoke to weren't much help in defining Silkiness. The best we got was: *"It's a gut instinct. You know when someone will fit in or not."* So our researcher took a trip over to the firm's new offices in a quiet square alongside Samuel Johnson's house. *"You get the impression that the firm has arrived after years in the wilderness,"* said one trainee of the new location. At last, all the departments are now under one roof, which, apparently, has brought the firm closer together and *"increased the Silkiness."* Our researcher asked the receptionist about the Silkiness, and then he asked a partner he met in the lift. No one could help. Perhaps it's in the water? Possibly. The evidence is in the meeting rooms: unbranded, designer bottles – blue stopper for still, green for sparkling…

the third tap

…and then we learned that in the kitchens on every floor there are mysterious third taps that deliver sparkling water.

the silk road

Trainees are, for the main part, content with the level of responsibility and quality of work they receive, and appreciate that *"you've got to take the rough with the smooth."* You won't escape menial tasks, but people will take note if you've spent all day at the photocopier. While some firms may have more paralegals and office support on hand, one trainee reassured us: *"I never felt that all I'd done was photocopy, paginate, fax and shred."* *"Today's photocopying will be tomorrow's big trial,"* said another pragmatically. On the inevitable occasions when you are required to put in that little bit extra, *"it's appreciated – like you really have done something above and beyond the call of duty."*

One trainee reported: *"I've never felt like I've got too much work to do."* And another concluded: *"It's all about enthusiasm without being boring. You'd just get ridiculed if you stayed until midnight."* When you have to work late in the office, *"it's like sitting around with your friends,"* which is *"bizarre, but good."* At the end of a deal there's always champagne and long lunches. And then we heard a whisper of what might be the Silkiness…a trainee told us how people could always be themselves: *"So long as you work hard and get the job done they don't mind what you do."* If it works well and is in harmony with the firm's aims, your style is unimportant.

Perhaps Silkiness is a philosophy and not a character trait after all. Each to his own. You do it your way and I'll do it mine. Different strokes, etc. Lewis Silkin is not a firm for etiquette and tradition. Having moved on from its Labour roots, it has rebranded itself as silkily as, well, New Labour; occupying the middle ground, flirting with the City, supporting social housing and hanging out with cool meeja types.

the prozac theory

The system of seat allocation is considered to have room for improvement. Some of our sources didn't seem to get much of a choice at all, but that said, several trainees were pleasantly surprised to find that their second choice seats were far more enjoyable than they'd imagined. *"I was put off property by the lectures at law school, but it is actually pretty interesting. It's a good first seat, especially as you can get a good handle on the firm's style."* The department has a *"superb atmosphere."*

There are three-monthly assessments and plenty of meetings with the training partner to make sure you're getting on OK, but the emphasis is on *"ongoing appraisal and not letting the problem fester."* *"As a trainee you shouldn't be afraid to ask questions. You're here to learn,"* a source stressed. Another trainee agreed: *"There are no demotivating tendencies…you're treated as the future of the firm."* In September 2002, Lewis Silkin boasted 100% retention of qualifying trainees.

The dress code is smart casual, but Lewis Silkin lawyers are sensitive to clients' needs and try to mirror their style. Make sure you have a wardrobe that stretches in all directions as you move around the firm. At the end of the day though, *"we wear whatever feels comfortable."* By now you should know that means not too smart, not too informal…

We can only conclude that Lewis Silkiness is a prescription – the legal equivalent of Prozac. *"I can't really give you any highs or lows. Things tend to be steady,"* said one trainee. *"If you don't have a smile on your face people will ask what's wrong,"* confirmed another. *"I'd had an offer from a magic circle firm and I came to the interview here feeling a bit cocky, but I left with a huge smile on my face. The partners were relaxed and wearing jeans. It was all quite laid-back and fun and I knew that it was the firm for me."* At another interview: *"The partners didn't ask me about law. They wanted to know what I thought about the situation in Kosovo. They wanted to see if I had an opinion and could express it well."*

plastic fangs

There's informal Friday night socialising down the pub – Groucho Club for corporate; Hodgsons wine bar for others – and the social committee is *"very active."* Apparently the firm was the Corporation of London's only applicant for a Golden Jubilee road closure order. As one trainee said, *"We don't need much of an excuse to put up a marquee and throw a party!"* The social committee is made up of partners and staff from all levels of the firm, so they come up with things with the broadest possible appeal. Nothing too boisterous, nothing too quiet. Just right. In the last year there have been trips on the Thames, a Blues party, and a spontaneous visit to Edinburgh. Fancy dress at last year's Halloween party was, however, limited to *"plastic fangs."* *"It's easy to make friends and get settled,"* we were told. *"Everyone knows everybody."*

and finally…

Lewis Silkin is a confident, well-packaged, mid-sized firm. If you want interesting clients and a balanced life, this is definitely one to check out. Unless you're hung up on formality and tradition.

Linklaters

the facts
Location: London
UK ranking by size: 4
Total number of trainees: 290
Seats: 4x6 months
Alternative seats: Pro bono – Disability Law Service, Liberty, Mary Ward, Toynbee Hall and Southward Law Centres, Privy Council death row appeals, language training

Having passed the online 'test yourself' section of Linklaters' excellent website, we've again been invited to apply for a training contract. If you are interested in a truly top-notch City firm, why not take up the offer on our behalf?

absolutely wizard
Linklaters is one of the quintet of firms forming the magic circle. It's not a top five firm for nothing: it has a pile of awards for its corporate endeavours, including a Queen's Award for International Enterprise. One trainee, giddy with delight at the firm's achievements, told us: *"You can't beat Linklaters"* because *"it has always got its eye on the competition and is always looking for ways it can be better."* The firm continues to handle some of the highest profile work for a roster of clients that includes names such as Shell, Vodafone, Hewlett Packard, BA, Merrill Lynch and BT. In place of herbology, broomsticks, satchels and strange blue potions, Harrys and Hermiones at Linkaters get fat wallets, blue-chip clients and a real chance to travel, as well as some long hours and rigorous schooling.

Perhaps the hardest task for those students set on a high broomstick-flying career in the City is spotting the difference between the big firms. Even trainees struggle: *"I'm still trying to work out what distinguishes us from the other magic circle firms,"* said one candid source. The problems is, you see these firms everywhere. They have attractive stalls at all the Law Fairs, they turn up at your uni on the milk round, they advertise in your Law Soc rag, and their partners stare at you from the front pages of the legal press, all the while burning their names into your sub-conscious. Linklaters, by the way, has just undergone a rebranding exercise, dropping the '& Alliance' from its global moniker to make it easier to identify. These top firms are all of such high repute that many students resort to outdated stereotypes to split the difference, or simply fill out all five application forms and sit back and wait for the replies to land on the doormat.

A good starting point is to consider the size and orientation of the firm you want to work for. Linklaters is second biggest of the five magic circle firms and its focus is primarily corporate, as opposed to financial. That's not to say that business is limited to corporate work, just that it's facing that direction. Size matters: it will affect the way you work and the way you are trained. Of the big five, Linklaters' London trainee population is about 20% bigger than Clifford Chance's and more than 50% bigger than Freshfields'.

better all the time
You have to be quick to keep abreast of the ever-changing training scheme at Linklaters: it's constantly looking for ways in which the scheme can be improved. Until quite recently, trainees were required to do six seats of four months, but this has switched to a four by six-month pattern *"because trainees were complaining that they didn't have enough time to settle in* [to a seat], *get going and wind down."* This move has limited the dreaded end-of-seat blues, but there's now less chance to fly around between different departments.

The benefits that trainees are entitled to at various stages of qualification have been drastically modified. They are now invited to take a six to 12-month sabbatical after the LPC or on qualification *"to go and do something constructive like a language course."* Dubbed as a 'personal development plan', the deal also sees the firm paying 20% of the salary you would have received during the same period. *"It was changed after we asked for a month of unpaid leave when we qualified,"* said one trainee. We have to admit; we did wonder if the scheme was designed to cope with an oversupply of trainees and NQs, but we're willing to be convinced. If the scheme is still in full swing in three years' time, we'll eat our keyboards. And anyway, think about it… all that money, all that free time. Blimey, we'd take it in a flash…but then, we're worn out old hacks who need a very long holiday! Interestingly, only one of the September 2002 qualifiers took up the offer to defer their NQ job.

> Chambers UK Law Firm of the Year 2001

Linklaters has always prided itself on the quality of its training and it has now introduced a week-long pre-LPC business foundation course run by Manchester Business School. Your vacation may be cut short by a week but the course will doubtless be a useful primer for the City LPC. Trainees are asked to have some idea as to where they want to qualify before the training contract starts; the idea is that a seat plan can be built around what's needed to achieve the end goal. That might sound a bit scary, and not everyone does feel able to make a choice, but Linklaters really goes to town on pre-training contract contact and so you'll have a fair amount of info about the work involved in each area of practice.

early bids
The firm has three main divisions: corporate, global finance & projects and commercial (which includes things like IP, IT, real estate and tax). A seat in each of the three departments is 'sort of compulsory' in as much as the trainees we spoke to thought they were and graduate recruitment said they were not. *"It is a good basic seat pattern for those who don't have a clear idea of what they want to do,"* we were told. For the remaining seat, trainees have a free choice *"between a specialist seat in London or a core seat overseas."* The majority of trainees eventually get the opportunity to sit where they most desire, but as for popular niche seats, *"if you say right at the beginning what your particular interests are, you will probably get the seat, but if you change your mind later, it's unlikely to work out."*

being the best i can be
There is perhaps a grain or two of truth in each of the magic circle firms' hackneyed stereotypes. *"Generally speaking, trainees here are enthusiastic; the type of people who want to do well,"* said one source. *"We're very confident people,"* said another. They are also out to impress, and they need to be quite tough and savvy to achieve this. *"It's a friendly place, but at the end of the day we are in competition with each other and want to make a good impression."* Think of a football squad – all of the players have to work together in training sessions, but ultimately only 11 of the 22 will make the final team. The trainees do care about their peers, the firm and the clients, but ultimately we sensed that they care most of all about their own careers. Just like the firm, *"which is always looking for ways it can be better than it is,"* these trainees won't settle for the reserve bench.

hooked
Starting out at any large City firm can be a bit of a culture shock, and it's no different at Linklaters. *"People are approachable, but it is sometimes difficult to tell where you are in the scheme of things and you have very little control."* Not only that, *"the firm has a desire for accuracy; it wants perfection and it looks to give the best and most detailed advice it can provide in the shortest time."* As a result, in the middle of a big deal the atmosphere can be *"intense and all consuming."* The firm doesn't hide the level of commitment it is looking for – read between the lines of the recruitment brochure and website and the message is as plain as the nose on your face. *"Don't come to Linklaters if you aren't willing, or don't want, to take responsibility and make a commitment. You've got to be willing to make sacrifices and be flexible with your life if you want to succeed here – big deals are not going to be predictable and give you a nice, easy life."* We heard of trainees working punishing schedules in

several departments, particularly corporate and banking. *"The long hours can be a pain, but then you are being paid to do it."* It all sounded quite depressing until one trainee quipped: *"I can count the number of times I have left early on the fingers of Captain Hook's bad hand."* You know the deal: important transactions, long hours, effort required. But then, you also know that a Linklaters training is your passport to anywhere.

staple diet

Trainees get a fair amount of responsibility, but the size of deals dictates they get less than their peers at smaller firms. *"I got fairly decent stuff from my associate in corporate, but I didn't have any client contact,"* admitted one source, while another said *"I felt completely involved and got a nice letter of thanks from the client."* *"I did lots of note taking at meetings and would facilitate requests. They need someone who can go off and won't be missed that much,"* said a third. As much as you'd all love to negotiate a headline deal, the paperclips and staples end of corporate work needs to be handled by someone who'll get things right, and working on document management, proof reading and a bit of photocopying is all part of the learning curve. However, we were surprised to discover that the firm has just three paralegals and 26 legal support assistants. This may go some way to explaining why it can support many more trainees than magic circle rivals.

In the property department it's a different story on the responsibility front: trainees get their own lower-value files and are often the primary contact for the client. *"It is great preparation for qualification as you get a lot of your own smaller matters, and although you are still supervised, you are the responsible person."* At the same time they will also *"assist on property issues that arise in other big deals."* Corporate support work crops up across many departments because of the huge transactional emphasis of Linklaters' business. Many trainees spend only four weeks on a litigation 'mini-seat' sandwiched into a seat elsewhere. This is great news for those who only put 'experience in mooting competitions' on their application forms to fill space.

For those of a different persuasion, full six-month litigation seats are available.

tongue-tied

Should you take advantage of one of the many overseas seats on offer, you could find yourself with more responsibility than you'd ever anticipated. In an overseas seat, *"the pool of trainees is so much smaller so when it is busy the trainee work is spread more thickly,"* and *"you're seen as a bigger part of the team."* Linklaters boasts a huge number of overseas seats and many trainees see this as one of the best reasons for choosing the firm. Trainees must apply for the particular office they want and are then interviewed before being offered options. There are enough seats abroad for everyone who wants one – indeed, some 90% of trainees go overseas or take a client secondment.

Although a foreign language isn't always necessary, having one could greatly improve your chances of getting your first choice – so long as it's the right language of course. Similarly, experience in the relevant practice area will help: if you're going for a corporate posting, having done a previous seat in corporate or finance will improve your chances. As we found over at Clifford Chance and in some other firms, your foreign tongue could very well tie you to a seat whether you like it or not. Although the firm *"won't force you to go abroad if you really don't want to,"* we spoke with trainees who had been sent to entirely different offices from any they had requested apparently because they had a basic knowledge of the host language. *"I did it when I was 16 and couldn't remember a word of it, but the firm was good in providing extra language lessons before I went."* An overseas seat, wherever located, will be an unforgettable experience giving you a high level of responsibility as well as the novelty of living abroad for six months.

linkstars

A brief scan of the trophy cupboard and notice boards in the corridors around Silks, the in-house restaurant, confirms an abundance of sporting and social distractions. Although there are the usual round of department drinks, Christmas and summer balls and the infamous Friday night sessions, *"the social side is, in all fairness, a take-it-or-leave-it thing."* When trainees do break away from the office, the King's Head and St. Pauls are favoured pubs. Budding Dariuses will be delighted to learn that the firm has just completed its in-house search for a superstar – a karaoke mutant called LinksIdol. Well, we've always said that a good shout after a hard day can be a very cleansing and calming experience…

The Silk Street offices are opposite the Barbican and ideal for culture vultures. Once you've negotiated your way past the extra-nippy security guards and made your way into reception, you'll notice a collection of clocks displaying different international times that serve to remind visitors of the international nature of the firm. It's a bit Anna Ryder-Richardson-meets-upper-crust-Ikea-meets-BUPA-hospital on a luxury scale. Cool, calm and collected: serene even. The 24-hour restaurant, *"which is really a trendy canteen,"* serves subsidised food and Starbucks coffee (no conspiracy theories please). *"I'd only eat this well if I was at home and my mum was cooking for me,"* one trainee told us. Bless! Buy the man a Delia book. As well as good discounts at two local gyms, trainees also get the use of the well-equipped in-house gym. Small as it is, it smells a good deal fresher than its equivalent over at Freshfields.

Of the 49 second-years who qualified in September 2002, 44 took jobs and started immediately, one took time out for 'personal development' and four left the firm.

and finally…

Linklaters takes its training responsibilities incredibly seriously and it pioneers new ideas in an effort to improve the scheme. Who knows, the personal development programme may turn out to be a roaring success and become adopted by other firms. We certainly look forward to finding out. Now, where's that online test thing…

Lovells

the facts

Location: London
UK ranking by size: 9
Total number of trainees: 121
Seats: 4x6 months
Alternative seats: Overseas seats, secondments
Extras: Pro bono – The Prince's Trust, Community Links, language training

Lovells is a top-flight, broad-church, corporate and commercial firm that's long been known as a pleasant place to work. Has it now set its sights on gatecrashing the magic circle party? Read on if you're looking for an ambitious but amiable employer.

giant steps are what you take

Despite its size, we've always described Lovells as a friendly firm; a Dahlian BFG of the legal world if you will. This opinion survives another round of trainee interviews unscathed. With a serious international capacity, a fantastic client roster and top-notch work, Lovells is more than capable of blowing a dream or two through the open windows of impressionable would-be lawyers. But don't be fooled: just as Dahl's giant could kidnap a child when the need arose (although he didn't eat her), Lovells doesn't sacrifice profits and firm management for sweetness and light.

Some trainees are concerned that the well-worn phrase 'friendly firm' implies that Lovells is too cosy and somehow *"less professional."* One went so far as to say, *"it sounds trite and glib to say Lovells is known for its friendliness."* Although some of the more acerbic members of the *Student Guide* team sit with sharpened HBs, ever-ready to burst mythical bubbles, we can't say Lovells is a ruthless and miserable place, because it isn't. In stark contrast, another source gushed, *"It is quite proud of being the friendly firm of the City. It compares itself to the magic circle, but likes to be seen as more down-to-earth."* Proof, if ever it were needed, that there really is no pleasing everyone. Oh well…

The giant has spent the last few years striding across the globe, picking up overseas offices through a series of mergers and lateral hires, particularly in Europe. According to its own blurb, its 26 offices and 1,500 lawyers worldwide make it the eighth largest law firm on the planet. "*The aim is to get into the magic circle, and this is probably going to happen soon,*" a confident (and optimistic) source told us. We're not sure if this idea is on- or off-message at Lovells, but that's what some of our sources thought. A giant-sized net won't guarantee the big prize, but it will make it easier to catch dream clients. Lovells acts on huge deals (last year the £940 million demerger of TI Automotive from Smiths) and cases (the £1 billion BCCI action against The Bank of England, almost a decade old).

> Chambers Global's Western Europe Law Firm of the Year 2002

With the growth of the London office, its old building was full to bursting. In July 2002 Lovells relocated to new offices of which it is justifiably proud. We took the tour and particularly liked the Oriental-themed client floors (complete with Zen garden) at the top of the building. There's "*a canteen with discounted dinners,*" so you can stuff yourself silly, and "*a gym with a pool room*" (balls-type, not swimming-type) so you can work it off afterwards or unwind with a few frames. The Lovells giant has even got an American friend called Starbucks in to make the coffee.

moon on a stick

One of the reasons trainees seem so content is the quality of training they receive. "*It is so good, it is almost overkill.*" There are around 15 special sessions relevant to each seat: "*In property there are courses on land registration and doing searches, and a case example of a lease or of a purchase – whatever is relevant to the seat.*" All in all, "*the training is incredibly comprehensive.*"

Trainees believe they are "*heavily supervised.*" Mid- and end-of-seat reviews are supplemented by "*almost constant feedback – so you don't get any shocks.*" Recently the format of feedback forms was changed at the trainees' request, "*so you get an overall grade rather than several grades for separate areas.*" To cap it all, "*you also get a bit of praise when you need it.*" Trainees do have some formal direct contact with partners; each is assigned to a contact partner on arrival, usually in a different department to the one they start in. "*If you have a serious problem, you can talk to them as they are more independent.*"

A compulsory corporate seat will see trainees working on "*anything from M&A to capital markets.*" As for subsequent seat choices, "*they do try to accommodate you, but you are more likely to get what you want in your second or third seat.*" Due to the nature of the work, responsibility varies enormously from seat to seat. "*On my first day with the firm I went into the property department and was handed over 60 files,*" enthused one trainee. "*I was doing all manner of conveyancing, drafting of licences from beginning to end and general property work.*" Conversely, "*as part of a team in the corporate department, you are constantly involved but have far less responsibility overall.*" To some, responsibility is the be-all and end-all, but you can't have it all the time; "*I'm trying to avoid any big cases because they need people to do photocopying,*" said one source, only half joking. But that's just the way it goes in a department where "*one phone call can have you there all night, unlike property where you have a deadline of sometime next month.*"

bad dreams?

Working hours vary from seat to seat, and as with any other City firm the longest are found in the corporate department. On the upside, "*if you work past eight pm, you get a free dinner, and if you work past nine pm, you get a free taxi all the way home.*" Carrot anyone? Trainees told us their average hours run from 9am to 6pm, with the odd 8pm finish now and again. In comparison to some of the other top twenty firms and the *Student Guide* team, this seems positively part-time.

IP is *"the most popular seat by far,"* and competition runs a close second. *"Although some trainees are scared of corporate, there really are no nightmare seats."* The good news is that Lovells offers more seats in niche departments than almost any other firm of comparable size. As one trainee put it, *"The broad scope of the firm's work gives you good opportunities. If you aren't sure what you want to do, this puts it slightly ahead of the competition."*

find some space

There is, as yet, no permanent colony on the moon, but as soon as one is established and needs lawyers, Lovells will probably be there. It offers secondments and overseas seats for those with an urge to roam. Ever wondered how in-house lawyers do it? Six months with Barclays, BAT, Esso, Prudential or Merck should satisfy your inquisitive mind. *"It's a charmed life on secondment,"* quipped one trainee, *"on some you even get a car for six months."* No matter what drives you, you can find it; some trainees love their time at BAT because of the bowl full of free cigarettes in reception. In all cases, *"it's good to escape from the firm for six months, and it's a chance to get a different view of things."*

Brussels, Frankfurt, Hong Kong, Moscow, New York, Paris, Prague and Tokyo all offer seats, but be aware: they are all sought after – *"Hong Kong and New York are clear favourites."* None have specific language requirements except those in Germany (pretty good) and France (enough to get by). Lovells has won awards in the past for pro bono work and trainees are encouraged to get involved, but with an increasing workload, for most, *"the ability to keep it up decreases."* E-mails are sent around inviting trainees to get involved: take one up and you're likely to get an awful lot of responsibility to boot. It's yet another chance to shine in a firm where trainees love to do just that.

dear diary

When you come here, you won't be expected to change beyond recognition to fit some corporate trainee mould – *"They are just looking for confident individuals."* *"There is a liberal sprinkling of Oxbridge graduates"* working alongside trainees from other respected institutions, and *"a few older graduates."* We've always had a sense with Lovells trainees that they are the sort who are eager to please and easily pleased. That's not meant as a slight, just a comment on the collective attitude and outlook. Just think about the lowest maintenance girl/boyfriend you've ever had and then remember the bunny boiler in *Fatal Attraction*. *"There are no muppets here,"* noted one trainee *"unlike at school or university where you meet people and sometimes think 'how the hell did they get here?'"*

These people aren't slouches; they have one of the busiest social calendars we've come across. The standout favourite watering hole on Thursday and Friday nights is the Bottlescrue. *"Everyone who ever talks about Lovells goes 'Ooh, the Bottlescrue,'"* said one (accurate) source. When they fancy a change, Mr David's Sports Bar or The Old Monk are likely targets, with trainees moving on afterwards to the trendier surrounds of Clerkenwell or Smithfield. *"There's a meritocracy down the pub,"* so *"you can sit with your supervisor and have a bit of a laugh."* *"It's pretty good as the supervisors like to buy you drinks."*

Lovells had a big fancy dress bash in May 2002, themed on couples from history. *"The senior partner dressed as Batman and did a bit of a skit"* and there were prizes for the best outfits, including a weekend for two in Paris. There are also Christmas and summer parties exclusively for trainees. *"A Christmas ball for the whole firm would be nice too,"* said one party animal who clearly gets out too much. If, like her, all this isn't enough for you, there's softball and other team sports, greyhound racing, archery, go-karting and plenty more to fill any remaining pages in your diary.

and finally…

If you're looking for a lively, energetic and expanding firm, Lovells could be it. The training is good, the clients top-drawer and the work/life balance not at all bad. And, despite some trainees trying to persuade us otherwise, they are a friendly bunch. Just don't forget that you'll have to work pretty darn hard.

Mace & Jones

the facts
Location: Liverpool, Manchester, Huyton, Knutsford
UK ranking by size: 86
Total number of trainees: 9
Seats: 4x6 months
Alternative seats: none

Mace & Jones is a North West firm with a nationally recognised employment law practice and strengths in family, commercial and property work. If it's a smaller commercial firm in the NW you're after, then Mace & Jones has your name written all over it.

my kind of people
Trainees tend to be *"down-to-earth, hard-working, but game for a laugh." "We're all very supportive of each other and get on very well."* Those we spoke to thought that the firm was *"looking for more than just good legal minds. They want people who can promote the firm in a positive light."* Mace & Jones does seem to favour applicants with a sense of humour (and a knowledge of pop culture). One trainee confessed that during the training contract interview, *"I got into a conversation about Michael Barrymore, and I thought that I had blown it."* Obviously not. The firm is also attracted to those with a bit of life experience. One trainee ran a bar for years before taking the legal plunge, another had been a legal secretary, and one of the partners was a nurse in a former incarnation. Whatever their background, the urge to get involved with some of the firm's top-notch employment work is a common theme.

M&J, at least on the surface, is *"very strict and professional. We don't have dress-down, and the firm is keen to preserve its corporate image."* One source considered it *"a straitlaced, clean-cut place that values its professional image very highly."* Another said, *"Before I came here, what I knew about Mace & Jones is that other lawyers use them. We're lawyers' lawyers."* Perhaps picking up on the evolution of the firm, one trainee surmised that M&J was *"a mix of traditional old school lawyers and modern proactive lawyers. There is a split but it works well."* Trainees all agreed that the firm is a pleasant place to work. *"Underneath there's a strong sense of people looking out for each other."*

finding your feet
"Compared to some other firms there's very little structured legal training. You just learn on the job," said one trainee. Some took to this system like ducks to water; others considered that the formal programme was *"a bit poor."* This said, there is a comprehensive induction when you start, as well as IT skills training. Perhaps to compensate for the absence of formal seminars, etc. trainees get involved in things like writing commercial updates for clients. *"You also help in researching seminars for clients,"* and this certainly keeps you up to scratch on important and developing issues.

The appraisal system also yielded a few moans. One trainee thought the appraisal form would be better suited to the director of ICI. *"It's so complicated and irrelevant for the things that trainees do."* Given the chance to be senior partner for the day, one trainee pledged to develop *"a much more structured system. I would give trainees a clear outline of the kind of work they should expect from a seat. It's often quite hard to find your feet when you start in a new one."* But the really good news is that there are *"a broad range of seats, and you are likely to get the ones you want."* In 2002, the firm retained four out of five of its qualifying second-years.

The firm is split between main offices in Liverpool and Manchester, with small offices in Huyton and Knutsford. *"The atmosphere is very different from office to office,"* reported one trainee. *"Liverpool is more happening; Manchester a bit more elite."* While they may all share the same name, the consensus was that the offices are very separate. *"At present they don't feel well-connected."* Things are changing though: *"The offices have become more integrated since we took on HR people. Alison in Liverpool is a good contact point; someone to speak to if you have a situation."* In all offices except Huyton, trainees share a room with a partner.

liverpool: fab four

This is the biggest office in the firm, and it takes six of the nine trainees. It allows them to choose four seats from corporate, commercial litigation, property, employment and family, and although trainees are *"encouraged to do commercial areas,"* there's work to suit all tastes. One trainee had opted for M&J because *"I wanted to stay in the area and do PI and employment work. I like the court side of law. I was attracted by the whole Ally McBeal thing!"* If non-contentious work is your bag, you might well have beaten a path to the door of the partner who handled a job for Cavern City Tours concerning the development of the Beatles Hotel, due to open in 2003.

The office is *"very sociable."* There are table football tournaments and an annual golf day. Or how about the annual bowling challenge with local accountants (wonder who keeps score)? Last summer the invites to the 50s themed party came with a compilation CD of tracks by the Beach Boys and tunes like 'Hippy Hippy Shake'. At the previous year's Christmas bash, the lawyers rewrote the lyrics of 'The Twelve Days of Christmas', so there was *"a partner in a toupee in the place of a partridge in a pear tree"* and *"seven trainees training, etc…"* Thanks, we get the picture.

"Trainees go out for lunch as often as we can. We have drinks after work at places like Havana, Baa Bar [shooters for £1 Monday through Thursday] *and Revolution."* Apparently it's not unusual for partners to show their faces for an hour or two. There's a strong football theme to the office – they're all mad for it. There are also plenty of events organised by the Young Professionals Group where you can build up your contacts with local accountants, surveyors, potential clients and so on.

the little 'uns

The nearby Huyton office specialises in personal injury work and takes one of the Liverpool trainees for a seat. It's said to be *"even more of a laugh"* than the bigger Liverpool office, but that doesn't mean you'll be slacking off – you'll have your own caseload so you'll be pretty busy. The office is *"a rabbit warren"* and is housed in a block of converted flats. *"Terrible offices, pleasant atmosphere"* was the consensus. The Knutsford branch is of the high street ilk, handling wills, probate and conveyancing work for local moneyed clients. At present it doesn't take trainees.

manchester: fat wallets

The Manchester branch is driven very much by its corporate and commercial work, and is home to three trainees. The office built up its construction law capability earlier in 2002 by seducing a team from rival firm Kirk Jackson. It is divided between three buildings located around a single courtyard. It's a little cramped and *"sometimes you don't see people for a week or two because of the way things are laid out."* As far as the atmosphere goes, *"people appreciate it when you are enthusiastic about things."* *"It is far more relaxed up here than in London. Here no one will bat an eye if I'm in at nine and out by five."* Clients may not be listed in the FTSE 100, but you deal with names that are big in the region. *"You're not selling electricity to Azerbaijan for $50 million, but you can see clients in town – they'll be firms you've heard of and people you've seen around."*

On the first Friday of every month everyone piles into Rain Bar and the partners put up the money for drinks. Bowing to the inevitable last summer, the firm even hired out a bar for England's World Cup efforts. Everyone gets on swimmingly, and according to one trainee, *"The only way you can tell who the partners are is by the size of their wallets."*

and finally…

This is a well-regarded commercial firm offering a broad range of seats and good clients. So if you can hang on until qualification for bigger bucks, then take a look. You may have to go knocking on the door since, at the time of writing, there was no recruitment brochure or recruitment info on the website. This is clearly a word-of-mouth kind of place. Spread the word.

Macfarlanes

the facts
Location: London
UK ranking by size: 34
Total number of trainees: 38
Seats: 4x6 months
Alternative seats: Secondments
Extras: Language training

As City firms go, Macfarlanes sits very high in the first division, just underneath the magic circle premiership. With a smaller squad and intensive training, this firm is *"the choice of the more discerning trainee."*

double espresso
Macfarlanes is a corporate firm, and *"to an extent, the other departments are there for support."* Think of it as the strong dark espresso shot at the bottom of your latte. A raw corporate seat will get you buzzing, but will keep you up. *"Corporate work is the real draw. We regularly find ourselves acting against firms from the magic circle."* The hours are just what you'd expect in the City: *"Most people have done a couple of weekends and all-nighters, but it's corporate that's the killer."* In this kind of environment, *"ivory tower academics wouldn't get on so well. It is high pressure and you need to be robust. A lot is expected of you and, the later it gets, the less forgiving they tend to be."* If you want decaf or soothing herbal tea then you shouldn't be looking in the City anyway.

like a rolling stone
Trainees will typically complete seats in litigation, property and corporate, with the fourth seat a choice between private client or a more specialised area of corporate law; for example competition or tax. Employment and IP litigation are on the top of most trainees' wish lists, and the advice is that *"if you have a particular interest in one of the departments you must express it early. Don't leave it until the last moment."* In terms of seat allocation, *"you can't always get what you want,"* but in terms of decent exposure and a rounded training, you will find that you get what you need. And that includes *"bucket-loads of responsibility."*

There are no overseas seats, but should you so desire, you could spend half of your litigation seat in the Court of Appeal working as an assistant to a judge. Wanted: *"Research boffin in dusty room with no windows...excellent hours."* There's also a secondment to the legal department of venture capitalist 3i. Private client work is an attraction for some trainees. It's something that sets the firm apart from most others of a similar size and corporate orientation, although it appears to be something that you either love or you hate. *"It depends on whether you like dealing with people with trust funds, and doing meticulous wills and trusts work,"* said one trainee, clearly unconvinced.

take your partner by the hand
"I feel like the firm is actually investing in me. I wanted lots of attention and I get plenty," gloated one trainee. Supervision is seen to be uniformly good – *"If someone is pants, they get weeded out pretty quickly."* To supplement the supervisor-trainee osmosis, there's also lots of structured training. *"I've got trainee seminars coming out of my ears,"* said one satisfied customer. When you first start a seat, *"you don't get many lunch breaks,"* as there are lectures every week for the first ten. For early bird linguists wanting to catch the würm, there are German and French classes at 8.15am on Tuesday mornings.

Supervisors were praised for taking a *"paternal interest in your work."* And when you start, you'll also be allocated a mentor partner as well as a buddy from amongst the second-year trainees. *"It's good to have someone watch over you,"* we heard. They'll be there for you through the good times (completion dinners) and the bad (paginating and the data room).

conserve and protect
The firm was described by one insider as *"fluffy and blue-blooded,"* but other trainees preferred the more prosaic *"hard-nosed but friendly."* Either way it seems a difficult (if not downright bizarre) balance to strike.

"Middle class, well-rounded individuals" won't have trouble fitting in. The firm has a reputation for being more conservative than some of its peers...and it hates it, hence the way it markets itself to students. Beanie Man (the character who graces the website, brochure, law fair stand and even the bookmark in this book) has taken up the challenge on Macfarlanes' behalf for three years now. Bottom line: Macfarlanes is what it is: respectable, reputable, established and oozing quality. *"They've found a way of doing things and it works. I suppose to that extent it is conservative,"* suggested one trainee. If that's how the steady ship Macfarlanes is kept afloat on the sea of high profits, *"why fix it?"* asked one trainee. *"It's a no-frills place, but we're proud of that. We're not looking to take over the world."* Glad we got that one cleared up.

Although many of the trainees we spoke with had received and considered offers from the magic circle, most were swung by the pleasant atmosphere at this smaller firm. *"The first time I came, people were charming and polite from the receptionist to the senior partner."* The firm definitely fills a gap in the legal market: *"If you don't want to be part of a huge intake, but want corporate work of incredibly good quality with quality clients then there's not much choice but to come here,"* thought one.

when a plan comes together
"I've heard us being referred to as Macfastlanes. People think that we are very keen to prove ourselves." This image was put down to the efforts of Charles Martin and his team in the corporate department, who are renowned across the City for working like dogs. One trainee told us, *"I think the firm takes different people on for different reasons. You need the brainiacs, but you also need client handlers. There seems to be a broad cross-section."* Apparently, you'll find everything from aggression to eccentricity amongst the new recruits here. If the bigger firms have amassed entire armies of trainees, Macfarlanes goes for the 'A-Team' approach. After all, it would be unreasonable to expect one guy to drive the van, get the ladies, fly the plane, and make the plans!

shabitat
In terms of its offices, the firm *"could try harder."* *"It looks like my gran decorated it!"* one trainee despaired. Macfarlanes is spread accross five buildings on Chancery Lane. *"The firm is prudent. It wants to save money,"* explained one trainee, clearly forgetting that the firm is the 4th most profitable in the country. *"Don't come here for the offices. You won't find atria, gyms, fountains and hairdressers."* The meeting rooms are *"plush"* with some well chosen art, but the lawyers' offices themselves contain *"more MDF than you'd find in MFI."* Café 5 (billed as the *"hub of the firm"*) serves up decent canteen fare. *"I'm pretty fussy,"* admitted one trainee, *"and I eat there!"*

Fridays are dress-down. *"I love it. It gives you the psychological edge,"* said one trainee mysteriously, leaving us to only imagine what they had hanging in the wardrobe. Never leave a lawyer with a term like smart casual. The limits are constantly being tested. *"What is the difference between a skate shoe and a trainer?"* pondered one trainee. Generally though, *"dress-down means dress like a Sloane. Most of us have had to buy special Macfarlanes outfits."* Cords and blouses seem to go down well.

the (not so) hidden fortress
"Trainees hang out together all the time," Last year a group went to Paris for a weekend and spent a day at Ascot races. There's an annual sailing weekend and masses of sport, if that's your game. In line with the the firm's ethos, the social scene is kept nice and simple. It's rare for trainees to make it past The Castle on the corner. *"If it wasn't for us, the place would probably go bust,"* one trainee joked. Actually, we think you'll find that quite often it's the partners who buy the drinks.

and finally…
If you want City work in a more intimate environment, then step right up. One trainee summed Macfarlanes up like this: *"Its strengths are the quality of work and training. Its weaknesses are the premises and the football team."* Well, you can't have it all…

Manches

the facts
Location: London, Oxford
UK ranking by size: 62
Total number of trainees: 17
Seats: 4x6 months
Alternative seats: None

With offices in London and Oxford, Manches offers a good grounding in commercial work combined with a prestigious family law department.

enjoy your stay
Reputation and location are key factors for those opting for a Manches training. The London office has a prime spot in the heart of the West End. Its distinguished neighbours include the BBC, the LSE, the Law Courts, Covent Garden, and some of the capital's top theatres and hotels. Students and tourists give the area a buzz that's missing inside the *"soulless"* Square Mile. *"It's not just the City rat pack with their suits and umbrellas,"* said one trainee. *"It's traditional on the outside, modern on the inside…you're made to feel very welcome."* It sounds more like the nearby Savoy Hotel than other law firms.

While the *"jewel in the firm's crown"* is a renowned family practice, our interviewees were keen to point out that Manches has a healthy reputation for its corporate and property work and, as a trainee, you'll spend most of your time in these commercial areas. Manches has a stated aim to focus on technology, property, construction and retail clients. Among its clients are well-known names like WHSmith, Argos, Reuters, Nestlé, Jigsaw and Liberty. Its IP and e-commerce work is attracting a lot of attention, with these lawyers acting for clients like Condé Nast, Marks & Spencer and Royal & SunAlliance.

family rooms
The family department offers its clients a five-star service, and if they prove themselves, trainees can get involved in all aspects of divorce, children's residence, contact, schooling and maintenance issues, domestic violence injunctions and even surrogacy. This is an area with lots of breaking law, and Manches is likely to be at the forefront of it. True, you'll be dealing with 'top end' clients, but you'll get to meet all sorts of people. *"It's not all millionaires with money to throw around. Some people are prepared to make sacrifices to get the best legal advice, in the same way that some people are prepared to give up a lot to privately educate their kids."* Nevertheless, some trainees suggested that the family department has *"a certain reputation"* and *"you have to have the sort of face that fits."* Those whose style was not suited to the department felt like *"observers"* rather than active participants, but those who fitted in sensed an *"electric buzz"* to the place and told us: *"You've got to have no problem with working non-stop."*

noisy guests
Manches trainees see themselves as *"go-getters"* and *"high-flyers,"* and when asked what other lawyers might say about them, they conceded that the stereotypical Manches lawyer is *"noisy and not afraid to voice an opinion."* Our interviewees said: *"You need to show a lot of commitment, but they're not after you body and soul."* Because they can't compete with the megafirms in terms of size, the firm looks for people with a bit of bark. *"The place attracts characters rather than clones."*

The vacation scheme is thought to be an integral part of the recruitment process, and is designed to give you a real taste of what the place is like. *"They won't take you on a bus tour or show you round the Houses of Parliament."* One trainee sat in with a senior assistant and was let loose on a client to sort out an affidavit. *"You are treated like a lawyer from day one,"* and in this case, well before that. In terms of perks and facilities, this hotel is *"no-frills,"* but who needs a minibar and soothing music when the bed is comfortable and the linen is fresh. One trainee told us: *"A lot of people I know were wooed by big firms with expensive dinners and free stationery, without properly investigating what they'd end up doing there."* Still, they'll have plenty of time to fondle their branded stress balls when they're locked in the data room on a big corporate deal.

every room is different

There is no dress-down in the London office, and that's just how trainees like it. They take themselves as seriously as their work, and the consensus was that *"smart casual does not inspire confidence."* After all, you wouldn't expect the doorman at the Savoy to wear jeans.

In terms of feedback and appraisals, *"the firm takes criticism very well and positively encourages you to suggest improvements."* How could we improve your stay? Well, people thought that there should be more structure to the training and more contact with the training partner: *"Sometimes it's very stressful being a trainee."* Apparently there's some inconsistency between seats in terms of induction. *"Some departments could make life easier when you first get into them,"* sighed one trainee. The partners and assistants are *"idiosyncratic in the way they train trainees,"* so you won't feel like you're being turned out of a mould. Nevertheless, *"there are some people you certainly wouldn't want to train with."* Ouch! You're not going to get the standardised Holiday Inn experience in each department; each will have its own unique view and style. The checking out figures aren't too bad anyway: out of eight September 2002 qualifiers, five stayed with the firm.

upstairs, downstairs

Like good hotel staff, you'll need impeccable manners and presentation when dealing with clients, and you must be prepared to polish the cutlery at times. *"A bit of photocopying is good for your humility,"* apparently. Hours can be long, especially in the family and corporate departments, but *"won't kill you."* The pace is probably more like a workout with a personal trainer than a walk in the park. *"There are no social hermits here, but at the same time there's no atmosphere of forced jollity."* While your social life won't be hijacked by the firm, *"you need to play the game. It is wise to get involved and make yourself known."*

This is a firm that you can check in and out of, rather than the Hotel California-esque homes away from home that some bigger London firms have become. *"Everyone has something outside work,"* we learned. Amongst the trainees there's an opera singer, someone who's undertaking a course in sports law in their own time, and someone who makes R&B music. We can only wonder what the old guard (some of the Manches family still head departments) would make of sharing their offices with Puff Daddy and Pavarotti. So long as they don't make a scene and don't keep the other residents up, they probably all get along swimmingly. Unfortunately, it seems that not all the partners were getting along together swimmingly. Just before we went to press, we read one or two interesting press items about musical differences in the property department. It seems that in the last year, five partners in the hit-making line-up have left the firm.

On out-of-hours socialising, we were told, *"it happens,"* but clearly it isn't *"happening."* The Strand's wine bars are preferred haunts and tastes are markedly highbrow. Trainees turned their noses up at the mention of annual Christmas pantomimes that feature at some other firms. No doubt they considered it to be the kind of ghastly activity you'd be press-ganged into on a cheap package holiday. *"I recently had a nightmare involving a firm pantomime,"* confessed one trainee. The consensus was that such frippery would be unnecessarily *"time-consuming"* and *"a bit sad." "There's great potential to make a fool of yourself at an office pantomime,"* considered one trainee, and we certainly wouldn't want that now, would we? The Manches Cup is an annual firm-sponsored sailing regatta, but no one we spoke to could confirm its charms or, for that matter, its existence. You're not forced to participate: as one source put it, *"Being out on the Solent wearing a nasty kagoul is not really my kind of thing."*

country retreat

If the London office is a stately hotel, then the Oxford branch (which services publishing concerns, hi- and biotechnology clients plus other local businesses and individuals) is an affiliated B&B. It offers the same kind of work as in London but on a smaller scale, at a slower pace and in a smart casual kind of way. All in all, it's a nice, relaxed place to be; the kind of establishment where no one would mind too much if you nick the soap or the hand towels and the reception wouldn't get shirty if you miss check-out time.

There's no movement of trainees between the London and Oxford offices; too bad if you decide London's just become too much for you and you fancy six months of dreaming spires and punting. Four trainees are based in this 18-partner office, and the range of seats covers everything from family to IP/IT, with the staple company/commercial and property offerings in between. Not surprisingly given its proximity to techie Thames Valley clients, IP/IT is seen as a real strength of this office.

and finally...

One of the UK's best firms for family law, it also offers a good general commercial training. If Oxford is your target, you'll definitely want to apply, and if the idea of two years at a London megafirm leaves you cold, then hurry up and make a reservation at Manches.

Martineau Johnson

the facts

Location: Birmingham, London
UK ranking by size: 68
Total number of trainees: 25
Seats: 6x4 months
Alternative seats: None

Martineau Johnson is Birmingham's second largest independent. It sits very nicely, thank you, on a long-held and sturdy reputation for commercial work. But there's more...it also sits high in the Midlands rankings for charities law, private client, education, IP, energy and public law. If you've got Birmingham firms in mind then Martineaus should be one of them.

laugh? i did the seat again

The firm offers its trainees six seats of four months and the menu is a long one. All experience a corporate-related seat (which includes straight corporate, banking or trade & utilities), a property seat, and a contentious seat (general commercial disputes, employment and IP) and one of either private client or education. The firm is *"happy for you to double up if you find your niche."* We heard of one trainee, for example, who loved corporate so much that they grabbed *"a full twelve months of corporatish work."* That corporate department, while we're on the point, has an average M&A deal value of £14.4 million and has built up a tidy roster of venture capital clients.

Doubling up in the most popular departments may prove harder to achieve. Don't fall off your chair, but among the most popular seats is employment. As we all know by now, *"it's a very sexy topic"* and, at this firm, *"it's a very trainee-friendly department... employment is good at using trainees properly, getting the most out of them and making them part of the team."* Private client leaves the more commercially minded trainees a bit cold as they think it's all going to be *"dusty papers."* One less rigid in their views explained its appeal though: *"It acts for the most landed gentry in the region,"* with different teams dealing with *"new and old money – actually, it's quite interesting work."* There are many charities on the firm's books and you may also be interested to learn that Martineaus acts for loads of universities (including seven in the region) and the College of Law. Whatever your bag, there's a lot to choose from and, from time to time, that includes short client secondments.

Most interviewees spoke of working from 8.30/8.45am until 5.30pm/sixish. One trainee summed it up like this: *"I've never done a weekend and I don't intend to start now."* Another said, *"We know that work is work and that there are other things in life. That doesn't mean we're not committed to the firm...we work* hard when we have to." Corporate and banking rack up the longest hours along with the construction department, which is not only "*very, very busy*" and high on responsibility, but where "*they'll get you involved in marketing quite a lot, particularly client seminars.*"

30 minutes of fame

Trainees will share an office with their supervisor, who is usually the primary source of their work. In general, our interviewees thought they received decent attention and feedback: "*Everything gets checked before you send stuff out, and as you progress you find more and more stuff going out the door is your own work.*" One trainee told us he'd run some client meetings himself, "*usually small completions or taking down instructions,*" while another had been "*the first point of contact*" for a few clients in the corporate department. We were most amused to hear of one trainee's experience: "*I took a call for my supervisor when he wasn't around and it was a client. The client said 'You'll do' and put me on a conference call for half an hour. I took down notes and tried to sound like I knew what I was talking about.*" What about the supervisor? "*He walked in just as I finished the call.*" And was no doubt very proud indeed.

However, there have been occasions where some very hard-working partners weren't able to get trainees involved enough. This is not in the least bit unusual in any firm, but nevertheless, trainees raised the issue at one of their periodic meetings with the training honchos. It sparked an initiative designed to "*identify the supervisors who've been doing it for years, but aren't necessarily the best people to do it anymore.*" One trainee opined: "*It's been more about putting forward younger associates who haven't previously been considered.*" In addition, trainees also proposed that a "*guidance note*" be written on how to train them "*in today's world.*" Now don't start imagining some sort of Cultural Revolution in which 23-year-olds start running the firm; it was more a case of management taking the kids' views on board. As one of them said, "*You really feel you can open your mouth if necessary.*"

goodnight grandpa

"*Martineaus likes enthusiastic, lively people.*" Although there's no official policy, "*they don't like people who've been rejected by London firms seeing Birmingham as a second option.*" With most trainees the Brum connection is clear: "*A lot of us have been to Birmingham University or one in the surrounding area…Others grew up here or have family in the region.*" But what about the old perception of Birmingham as being dreary with "*horrible buildings from the 60s and 70s?*" One trainee was particularly keen to dispel the myth: "*There's been lots of development in Birmingham in recent years. A lot of money's been ploughed into the city and you can't go anywhere without seeing a construction site or a new club.*" Speaking of which, apparently several lap dancing clubs have opened up in Birmingham lately, including the now notorious Spearmint Rhino. We should perhaps stress that Martineau Johnson, unlike a certain firm in London, has never had its name splashed over the national press vis-à-vis this establishment.

Indeed, the firm was once described in the legal press as being 'Waltonesque'. Luckily, the firm isn't nearly as sleep-inducing as an average episode of the show, but it does have "*a real family-type atmosphere.*" Accordingly, "*you know whoever you're in the lift with, and everyone mingles together down at the pub – trainees, secretaries, associates, partners. There's no division.*"

Martineaus is "*a well-respected old player – it's the oldest commercial firm in Birmingham.*" Old firm, yes. Pensionable, no. "*There are lots of assistants in their late twenties who qualified here and partners in their early 30s*" as well as a senior partner who is "*exceedingly young for a firm our size.*" He – IP lawyer Bill Barker – is 42 and a very nice man by all accounts. However, some trainees thought Martineaus was "*quite traditional.*" In this vein, there was comment that "*a few things need shaking up a bit, such as our approach to marketing and pressing for fees – we're not as aggressive as some of our peers in Birmingham.*" Another trainee agreed: "*We're seen as being more laid-back, and while I wouldn't want to lose that general feeling, I think we should work out what type of clients we're going after and really make a big push* in that direction." Then again, others said, *"marketing is an area we're working on a lot – we're concentrating on finding our place in the market and we're developing cross-departmental referral."* Ooh, make up your minds…

old joint stock posse
Every Friday, there's a charge over to the Old Joint Stock, which *"tends to be full of lawyers, accountants and surveyors."* (Dante's seventh circle of hell comes to mind.) *"Martineaus has a corner at the back of the bar."* Confirming the favourable reports from other Brum firms, Martineaus trainees are *"very active"* in the Birmingham Trainee Solicitors Society. BTSS stages regular events – recently a wine-tasting evening. *"It was allegedly very good,"* one sauce said. *"I remember the beginning, but the wine flowed very freely and I'm hazy on the rest!"* The final word on the Birmingham social scene also encased a dig at London: *"You can stay out till 2am and you won't have to pay 30 quid to get a cab south of the river because the Tube has closed!"* The truth of the matter is that Martineaus does, in fact, love London. Its office in the capital was originally set up to handle banking work and has now expanded to encompass employment, education, corporate and property work. There is currently one trainee seat there in banking litigation. And if that trainee ever feels lonely on a Friday night, they can come and sit in our corner of Ye Olde Red Cow in Smithfield.

The office is split between two buildings on either side of St Philip's Square, but in 2004 everyone will come together in a new office that is currently under construction. It's billed as being *"more hi-tech – there's even talk of having desks moving up and down depending on whether you want to sit or stand."* Nine of the 13 qualifying trainees were kept on in September 2002, eager for the arrival of the wondrous new office furniture.

and finally…
Yet again, we got a sense that Martineau Johnson is pretty much spot-on when it comes to training matters. And yet again, its trainees came across as clued up, highly motivated and articulate.

Masons

the facts
Location: London, Bristol, Leeds, Manchester, Glasgow, Edinburgh
UK ranking by size: 29
Total number of trainees: 50
Seats: 4x6 months
Alternative seats: Secondments

No, this is not a report on secret rituals in ancient, dusty lodges. In fact, it's no secret that Masons is the leading law firm serving the construction and engineering industry. However, there is more to Masons than just construction. Its IT practice is regarded highly as are its projects and energy practices, and packed around these departments are a host of smaller commercial groups. We report here on the training in Masons' four English offices.

london life
The firm has recently undergone a restructuring. In London, this has meant the end of its former six by four-month seating system so that it is now in line with the other offices in offering four six-month seats. Firm-wide, the restructuring has meant the end of the old CEIPA department (construction, energy, infrastructure and projects). The departments are now organised into four divisions: international & energy; UK construction & engineering; capital projects; and technology & business services. This latter division incorporates areas such as dispute resolution, property, corporate/commercial, employment, tax, health & safety, facilities management, insolvency and pensions. Trainees must do one seat in either the international & energy group or the UK construction & engineering group, but otherwise, they have a choice as to the remaining seats. We will be able to report on how the new system is received by trainees in next year's *True Picture*, but we suspect that those who moaned to us about the old double helping of CEIPA would have welcomed the change. While a

few trainees have engineering degrees, and a couple of others have prior experience of the construction industry, many arrive with *"no interest in construction at all,"* attracted simply by the firm's medium size and its *"excellent reputation for training."* Our advice: do enough research so that you understand the nature of Masons' business and its client base.

Corporate/commercial is a particularly favoured seat: *"You should have general commercial experience to balance out construction and property. It gives you a broader training and makes you more attractive."* In addition, *"it's known for being a really friendly department with really nice people."* The projects seat is also popular: *"It's seen as an up and coming area of law,"* plus *"they have a different way of working there, which really appeals."* The department is nicknamed 'Club Lounge' because of a hot-desking system whereby *"you get a laptop, mobile and trolley and sit at whatever desk you feel like for the day, then just pack up at the end of the day."* One trainee said, *"You work as a team more efficiently, and you get to know everybody as opposed to just your room-mate."* Time will tell if other department heads will adopt hot-desking. In terms of responsibility, employment is popular as trainees get to run some of their own files, although it is described as *"incredibly hard-working."*

According to our sources, the least popular seat was in energy. Aside from the usual gripes about late hours, our interviewees explained that *"all the cases there are huge, involving hundreds of millions of pounds, and many of them go on for six or seven years."* This means trainees *"can only ever come in at a very low level."* One convert to the delights of the tax seat said, *"People try to avoid it because they think the work's going to be boring, but most people who do it find it rewarding."*

building up responsibility

Trainees usually share an office with their supervisor, who is either a partner or a senior associate. As for responsibility, apparently it depends on the supervisor and the nature of their work: *"Some are good at letting you work on your own cases, some aren't."* In terms of feedback, again: *"It depends on who you're working for."* Parts of the old CEIPA group came in for some flak: *"Some of the supervisors in construction aren't suitable either because of their character or because they're so busy that they don't have time to explain things to you. They tend to leave you to it."* This was compared with the old PPE group (property, planning and environment), which *"really sets the standard"* in terms of *"people who are friendly, open and willing to answer questions and spend time with you."* Mid- and end-of-seat appraisals are scheduled in addition to a six-monthly appraisal with the two training managers.

On the subject of hours, London trainees tell us they are in the office from 9am until 6.30/7pm on average. However, later hours can crop up in construction, where trainees *"worked till eight or nine at night a lot,"* employment, and company/commercial *"when there's a deal coming up."* Client secondments offer high levels of responsibility, and are encouraged by the firm. Aside from ad hoc secondments (such as one to HBG Construction three days a week), there is a regular six-month slot available at the Construction Federation. It's popular, although a previous seat in construction is required as you'll be *"on the phone to construction companies that want advice as to claims and contracts, and if you've not got some experience, you'll flounder."*

While, *"there's definitely a huge construction theme linking the departments"* in terms of both the clients and the work, trainees stress that *"the public perception that we are a construction firm detracts from other departments such as information technology, and projects & finance. They are great departments in their own right, but get overshadowed."*

bringing the house down

Trainees were particularly clear about the sort of applicant that would be right for Masons. *"Those who are more introverted might not fit in."* One trainee explained: *"If you're quiet, they'll mistake it for lack of confidence. The firm likes its trainees to be outspoken."* Another commented: *"If you like working on your own, you shouldn't apply. You really need to be able to work as* part of a team as we handle a lot of big cases that require teams of five or six people. People who are academically good but don't mix well with others will have problems." In addition: "You've got to be prepared to knuckle down and put the hours in." Along these lines, another trainee said: "They're not slow at telling you you're not doing something well or when you need to pull your finger out."

The highlight of the social calendar is the trainee revue at the Christmas party. The revue itself goes on for about an hour and consists of "Harry Enfield-type sketches" written and performed by trainees for the benefit of the other staff and partners. "The way we do it is we find someone who can sound or look like a personality from the firm and dress them up accordingly. Alternatively, we pick a trainee who doesn't look at all like one of the personalities and dress them up!" The script itself is passed to a partner for approval, although by all accounts "she basically rubberstamps whatever we want to put on." There are five or six "distinctive partners" who are sent up every year, particularly "one bloke who curses non-stop and plays a lot of cricket – we just dress someone up in cricket overalls and get them to swear a lot and it brings the house down." Any "scandal" from the previous 12 months will be faithfully re-enacted: "A van got stolen and we took the piss out of the postroom person for leaving it unattended." A fringe benefit of the revue is that "it's a good way for the first-years to get to know the second-years very quickly, because we've generally just arrived at the firm and there are a lot of meetings and rehearsals." We trust our invite is in the post for the 2002 performance.

northern: taking the biscuit

The firm's offices in Leeds and Manchester have recently united, with the resulting entity called Masons Northern. Trainees in both offices are now encouraged to spend one of their seats on the other side of the Pennines. The new approach has been well received, as employment, pensions, property and environment seats are available in Manchester but not Leeds. "*Manchester trainees historically had a wider range of seats to choose from,*" said one Leeds trainee, "*but now we can share in the benefit of that.*" In Leeds there is also a one-month secondment to the North Yorkshire County Council, which is "*really useful if you're going to do projects or private finance work*" as "*you'll see the inner workings of government on projects.*" As in London, the client roster is rich with construction clients.

We paid a visit to the Leeds office one day...we were just passing. For the record, Masons was the only Leeds firm we visited to give us biscuits with our tea (although we make no assumptions about relative profitability on this basis). It's a more intimate affair than the London office; it has a cosy feel, despite acres of space for staff to run around in. It exudes a calm and professional atmosphere, but has a funky eating area where folk can gather for lunch or coffee. Leeds shares an entertainment committee with Manchester and trainees from both offices socialise together "*quite a bit.*" In Leeds the trainees' favourite pub is Wharf Street, while in Manchester it's the Pitcher & Piano.

bristol: four square meals

All trainees experience a construction-related seat plus commercial property, projects & finance (much of it facilities management), and property litigation (offering lots of client exposure). "*They are good at spotting when you are confident enough to take on responsibility,*" one source said. Moves to another office for a seat are possible, but you'd have to present a good case. The office occupies "*a nice building with Georgian frontage and lots of space*" and is located in "*a very picturesque square,*" albeit not in Bristol's best neighbourhood. Among the English offices it is the only one to dress-down on the last Friday of every month. One trainee told us: "*The guy in charge here is very laid-back and that permeates down.*"

Sadly, only six out of the 13 London qualifiers stayed with the firm in September 2002, although the picture was slightly better in the regions, with four out of six staying – two in Manchester, and one apiece in Leeds and Bristol. As one trainee said, "*A lot of the offers that have been made were in areas which trainees didn't want to qualify into.*"

and finally…

If construction, engineering, IT, energy or large international projects are your bag, you'll not find better than this market leader. Opportunities certainly exist in other areas of practice and for clients unrelated to the construction industry, but do your homework. Bottom line: you'll get good quality training at a firm that's well respected by the profession.

Mayer, Brown, Rowe & Maw

the facts
Location: London
UK ranking by size: 25
Total number of trainees: 49
Seats: 4x6 months
Alternative seats: Brussels, secondments
Extras: Pro bono – RCJ CAB

Very British Rowe & Maw recently joined forces with Chicago powerhouse Mayer, Brown & Platt. It's now something like the tenth largest international firm and has 13 offices worldwide. From our point of view, the new global entity is certainly a far cry from the Rowe & Maw that we wrote about last year. Well, sort of. Read on…

pistols at dawn

In the London office, trainees undertake four six-month seats. A stint in corporate is compulsory, as is one in litigation (which can be satisfied by any number of contentious areas of work). Aside from that, it's up to you how you spend your remaining 12 months. The two IP seats are among the most popular as it's *"a young and well-regarded group"* and *"it's a really interesting subject at university so a lot of people want to see what it's like in practice."* Consequently, *"there's a lot of duelling over it."* The same rings true for employment: *"The people who go there always enjoy it because it makes a real effort to get them involved."* Along these lines, one trainee said, *"You get to dismiss a couple of directors in the first couple of months, which is always fun."* Public law is another small department that is *"always competitive to get into."* Spotted the pattern yet?

But there's more. The Lloyd's insurance litigation seat (so-called because of its location) is *"half seen as a secondment"* and has its fans. *"You generally get a lot of responsibility and high-quality, interesting work."* One trainee made the point that *"it makes a change from the general litigation seat where some of the cases go on for years. In insurance litigation, many of the cases aren't on nearly such a long-term basis so trainees can get a tilt at them from start to finish during a seat there."*

try us, trust us

Trainees share offices with their supervisors and mid- and end-of-seat appraisals are followed by an informal chat with the training co-ordinator *"to see how you're getting on generally."* In terms of hours, you'll be gone by 6.30/7pm most nights, but *"there are times when you have to work late."* No prizes for guessing that it is corporate where you're likely to stay longest. One trainee said, *"2am is the latest I've stayed, with a few midnights and a couple of 10pms."*

Many of our interviewees felt that the corporate department gave its trainees very little responsibility compared with other departments. We've held back on most of the negative comments; suffice to say the overriding sentiment amongst our interviewees was that *"they could definitely make better use of the trainees."* One trainee said, *"They don't trust us with anything major… Nor do we get much client contact. It's very much like the trainees should be seen and not heard."* We were astounded to learn that the corporate department, the biggest department in the firm, doesn't have any paralegals. *"Not even one! They've got 12 trainees, which is far too many. They could just have six trainees and six paralegals."* There was some saving comment that as you get more experienced and prove yourself, the tasks become more interesting. However, most interviewees thought that the corporate department *"need to try their trainees out a bit more, involve them a bit more in their work and not play their cards so close to their chest."*

Over in the litigation department we're very pleased to report that there's a keenness to give trainees responsibility. "*In litigation they'll often say what they want and leave you to use your nous and figure it out, particularly in relation to drafting.*" Ironically, last year it was the litigation department on the receiving end of sharp trainee tongues. There are good reports from property, where "*you get more hands-on work*" and "*a lot of opportunity to run your own files.*" One trainee told us, "*I had 10 to 15 of my own files which I did all the day to day stuff on under supervision, and I also had involvement with other people's larger matters.*"

There is an opening in Brussels every six months (for which proficiency in French is "*pretty much a necessity*"), but currently there are no firm plans for any more overseas seats. Client secondments – to Unilever, AstraZeneca, Marsh & McLennan and Reuters – involve general corporate/commercial work and trainees normally need to have done a corporate seat before being considered. The secondments are popular because "*you get a lot of responsibility and autonomy*" and "*you're a bit like a commercial counsel, advising and drafting and all kinds of good things that will be good practice for qualification.*"

slow and bore loses the race…

Last year we mentioned that Rowe & Maw had a bit of an identity crisis that was slowly being resolved in favour of the younger and more go-ahead partners as opposed to the more traditional elements of the firm. Surely the merger with US behemoth Mayer, Brown & Platt has put paid to this argument once and for all? Well, yes and no. From the perspective of the self-described "*heritage Rowe & Maw trainees,*" the merger hadn't had a huge impact on the firm as yet. "*The Mayer Brown people have really blended in – there weren't that many of them compared to us. A few Americans have come into the corporate and finance departments, but you don't really notice them until they open their mouths!*" One source said, "*We haven't really noticed any significant effects of the merger yet at trainee level – I'm sure it's impacting further up the food chain though.*" (We'd bet it is.) Along these lines: "*On paper it's a very different firm – it sounds more impressive and probably gets more work in as a result of the global connection – but the culture and atmosphere in the London office is still very much the same as it was before.*"

R&M trainees typically wanted a medium-sized City firm which would give them broad-based experience and good grounding in City work, but one with a good work/life balance. Even after merger, that's exactly what they've got. For MB trainees, however, the merger has had a greater impact – "*We've been subsumed into the Rowe & Maw training system.*" Despite the size of the Mayer Brown Empire worldwide, the firm's London office prior to the merger was "*a small office with six trainees in total. Now I'm one of 24 trainees in my year alone. It's had repercussions in terms of the work we do. There's a lot more form-filling and hierarchy in such a big office.*" As one said, "*I specifically joined Mayer Brown because it was a small firm where I could get some interesting finance work. I felt like I was treated like a lawyer there, but here the hierarchy means I'm very much bottom of the pile and don't get as much hands-on work.*"

Trainees think the Mayer Brown influence is going to become much stronger, particularly in terms of giving it "*more of an American-style service culture*" and "*an international flavour.*" One trainee said, "*For a firm I thought might be amazingly traditional, it's quite forward-thinking – it surprised a lot of people with the merger!*"

you say tomato, i say tomato

There's a difference between the trainees from Mayer Brown and those from Rowe & Maw. "*We're more outspoken than the Rowe & Maw trainees,*" said an MB source, which was entirely accurate if our interviews were anything to go by. "*They're lovely people, but they're not boat-rockers – they're more willing to accept their lot and get more responsibility when they qualify.*" It's common across US firms in London for trainees to be treated like grown-up lawyers from a very early stage, so we weren't surprised to hear this. The dress code is also an issue. The MB London office had a permanent business casual dress code, while R&M only abandoned suits on Fridays. *"The issue was brought up in the merger negotiations, but Rowe & Mawe said they wouldn't consider it, so we now have to wear suits."*

Despite the shock of merger, Mayer Brown trainees are delighted by the seat choices now available to them. As for formal training sessions, this was said to be *"much better"* than what was on offer at Mayer Brown, with firm-wide, departmental and trainee-specific programmes all winning plaudits for being *"really well structured."* There are *"What we do in…"* sessions presented by each department every couple of months, so that *"you have an idea of every department"* by the end of your training. *"Corporate takes training sessions especially seriously. We have seminars every Wednesday morning in relation to corporate transactions as well as things like maximising profitability and reading corporate accounts."*

praise the lord

Just prior to the merger, Rowe & Maw moved to *"bright, swanky"* new offices in Pilgrim Street. *"They've really gone for it with the colours: some of the walls are bright green, some orange, some yellow,"* said one delighted trainee. We especially like the sweep of glass staircase in reception and have had to restrain ourselves from launching into a tap routine on our visits. The Mayer Brown folk moved in with their briefcases of tricky finance deals at the beginning of March 2002.

Trainees socialise *"all the way down Carter Lane,"* but the two most popular establishments bear no relation to their names. In The Evangelist no one's especially vocal about their religious beliefs and the staff in The Booksellers don't peddle anything of a literary nature. *"Some departments are better at formal social functions than others."* Top marks to corporate, who *"really get into the work they're doing and this enthusiasm carries over into the pub."*

In September 2002, 16 of the 20 qualifiers stayed on. We learned that over-subscription for litigation jobs was largely responsible for the four departures.

and finally…

In a few years this report will look like one of those Blue Peter time capsules that get dug up by accident, so revealing quaint and awkward gizmos from the past. Future trainees will be hired by Mayer, Brown, Rowe & Maw, not by either legacy firm. When the London office feels the full effect of the rest of the Mayer Brown international network, change will be inevitable, but we suspect that the best of Rowe & Maw culture will survive. The final word goes to the trainee who said, *"I'm taking bets on how long they keep such a long name!"* So are we, as it happens!

Mills & Reeve

the facts
Location: Cambridge, Norwich, Birmingham, London
UK ranking by size: 44
Total number of trainees: 37
Seats: 6x4 months
Alternative seats: None

No longer just the largest firm in East Anglia, Mills & Reeve has spread from Norwich and Cambridge to Birmingham and, more recently, has established a London outpost. This fine filly has a marvellous pedigree and healthy ambition.

airbrushed to perfection

Mills & Reeve trainees (and partners) eschew London in favour of *"a large and respected regional firm with lots of variety in the workload."* One said, *"One of the reasons I wanted to work outside London was that regional firms are more flexible. Mills & Reeve has high-quality work but at the same time offers a decent work/life balance."* Another told us clearly and bluntly: *"I went to Cambridge University and I wanted to stay in the area, but at the same time I didn't want to be stuck in some high street, rubbishy firm, so Mills & Reeve was by far the best option."* It's simple: a Mills & Reeve trainee is the sort who could have gone to a leading City firm, but chose not to. And the sort who wouldn't fit in? "*Anyone who enjoyed working on their own, or a maverick who wanted to go out on a limb, probably wouldn't be very happy. It's a very team-oriented atmosphere.*"

Perhaps to demonstrate its openness (nothing to hide here, nothing to hide!), or perhaps to give a few clues as to what it's looking for, the firm posts its trainees' photos and biogs on the website, although one said, "*I wish I'd gotten the chance to airbrush mine – it's horrible!*" We saw her photo and it's not that bad! Don't worry if you can't bring glamour to the firm; it's actually after perky, bright, well-rounded grads. Our interviewees were certainly lively, if occasionally guarded, in their responses.

the patter of tiny feet

There is a six by four-month seating system, with trainees usually returning in their final seat to the department they hope to qualify into. Eight months of their preferred area of work is felt to be the ideal gestation period for newly qualified solicitors. One source said, "*You do actually feel you're earning your money. As you move through your seats you start feeling less like a trainee and more like a lawyer.*" Responsibility is there for those who want it: "*They give you as much as you can cope with. Everything is supervised and checked carefully, and if you're wrong, you're told you're wrong.*" As for client exposure: "*We get a great deal of it. If there's a meeting, we'll go along – how else can you become a good lawyer?*"

Moves between the offices are certainly possible, although not required. One trainee told us: "*If you have a specific reason for wanting to move, such as there being a department based in one of the other offices, they will encourage you and do everything they can to assist you.*" Apparently the firm isn't too bothered whether or not applicants have a regional connection, but "*you do need to demonstrate a commitment to the firm. The last thing they want is for you to bugger off to London straight after qualification.*" All bar two of the 16 September 2002 qualifiers stayed.

norwich: knowing me, knowing you

Norwich. It's in a very flat county and it's the home of the Norwich City Canaries, Colman's Mustard and Alan Partridge. The fair cathedral city was the genesis for the Mills & Reeve family of offices, founded in 1880 to serve the landed and moneyed folk of the region. The Norwich office still undertakes a large amount of private client work and its agriculture practice is widely regarded as being the strongest in the region. However, these days the mainstay is corporate/commercial for regional businesses.

One trainee told us: "*The Norwich office is slightly more traditional than Cambridge, which is partly because of its private client base, whereas Cambridge is geographically and culturally closer to London.*" Another observed: "*Norwich people tend to start earlier and leave earlier than Cambridge people.*" This can't be down to different time zones, surely? The firm has regular Monday night drinks in a new wine bar that's just opened across the road, but the trainees' trusty local is The Hogshead.

The firm's due to take up residence in "*brand spanking new*" premises in June 2003 (hot on the heels of the Birmingham office's recent move). "*We need the space. We've occupied our current building for a long time and it's a bit antiquated.*" You can see an artist's impression of the new building on M&R's website, as well as details of the current state of development. When we looked, this amounted to a photo of a building site and four cheerful-looking blokes in hard hats. Strangely, there are no pictures of the several skeletons (ancient ones) that have been unearthed!

cambridge: tales of the city

Located in 'Silicon Fen' – a hub for the hi- and biotech industries – the Cambridge office has expanded its expertise beyond traditional private clients and conventional commercial work to encompass top-notch IP and venture capital work. There's a good deal of valuable business to be had on the Cambridge Science

Park and spinning out from the University. As one trainee put it: "*It was the variety of work that attracted me more than the location. I was so impressed with the firm that I would have relocated anywhere.*" Perhaps saluting the city's theatrical tradition, another trainee told us: "*We're close to London, so we're waiting in the wings for all the clients who get sick of paying City fees.*"

Socially, The Flying Pig remains **the** place. It's described as "*snug*" with "*standing room only on Friday nights.*" Our researcher went up to Cambridge and had a lovely, long chat with the landlord. In the interests of discretion, his findings will remain locked in a filing cabinet until our 2033 edition. As for the pub next door, "*It never attracts anybody in general…Who knows how it stays in business?*" The additional implication was "*Who cares?*" And why not – when you find a good Pig, stick to it! Which leads us to a bit of a problem…Eversheds has recently moved its Cambridge office to the same street. While some trainees were worried that their beloved Pig would be "*colonised*" by Eversheds, others boasted: "*They don't have a multi-storey car park like us!*" This might sound trivial, but parking is much sought after in Cambridge. As for M&R's parking etiquette, it's first come, first served, which is, as one trainee said, "*forward thinking and the best way of thinking, especially if you're at the bottom of the pile!*"

It all sounds lovely, but there is a slight drawback. It seems that the local hospital is five minutes down the road, which means that ambulances frequently drive past, sirens blaring. Speeding past almost as frequently (and also headed towards the hospital) are fire engines with sirens blaring. But that's a whole other story involving the nurses' home and an over sensitive fire alarm. Maybe you could ask about it at interview…or in the Pig!

birmingham: getting fired up

Noted for its healthcare work in particular, the new Birmingham office building is said to be a "*vast improvement – if you saw the last office, you'd know why!*" We pressed for further information…"*It looked like a 1960s tax office.*" The new office is in a modern tower block with "*three spacious floors and excellent catering.*" One floor is devoted to client meetings and keep-fit classes (!) held in the boardroom. From having been the social scene ugly sister of Cambridge and Norwich last year, the Birmingham office appears to have lifted its game. It now offers quizzes every month (held in the amazingly versatile boardroom), as well as trips to the theatre and bowling. On the last Friday of every month there's an office get-together in the firm's favourite hostelry, Horts.

One trainee made the point that most people who apply to the Birmingham office tend to have links with the Midlands, so they're not as keen to move between offices as they might be in East Anglia. We also learned that Birmingham is less intense than Cambridge. How so? "*Cambridge is a more conventional office; here we're open-plan. It's a more trendy and cosmopolitan office – we share the building with loads of different people and it's quite interesting to meet them all when we have a fire drill.*" What is it with this firm and fire alarms??

Quality of life was emphasised by our interviewees. In Birmingham, besides open-plan seating ("*good for the free flow of ideas*"), trainees also have the benefit of flexitime, with core hours of 10am to 4pm. As one source said, "*I work hard and I play hard. I have lots of time-consuming hobbies and I don't want to get fat by being stuck behind a desk.*" So wise, so young…

and finally…

Mills & Reeve is a super firm. One of the very best of its kind, in fact. There's plenty on offer in terms of general commercial work plus some excellent niche areas, but be aware that specialist departments are popular and, as such, have the potential for posing supply/demand problems for those looking to qualify into them. Pick an office in a location that appeals to you, with the knowledge that you can move if you need to.

Morgan Cole

the facts
Location: Cardiff, Swansea, Oxford, Reading, London, Croydon
UK ranking by size: 27
Total number of trainees: 36
Seats: 4x6 months
Alternative seats: Secondments

Morgan Cole has the clout to pull in clients like BPAmoco, ICI, Sony, Xerox and top insurance companies. According to its recruitment material, over the next few years the firm aims to become a top five insurance and employment practice and to double its profitability. That's the plan. What's the story so far?

the vision
In 1998 leading Welsh firm Morgan Bruce merged with Thames Valley partnership Cole & Cole. Even before the dust had settled, it had absorbed niche London insurance firm Fishburn Boxer. In 2000 a Croydon branch was added. What with the shift towards insurance work and a string of high-profile defections in the years following the mergers, one trainee opined, *"the firm has yet to form a stable character."* Nevertheless, Morgan Cole does have a clear strategy for the future and the senior bods talk about their *"visions, values and goals."* It's moving towards a market sector approach, targeting health, insurance, energy and technology.

new kids on the block
What about that website! It claims that Morgan Cole lawyers are made of "The Right Stuff" and features fighter pilots and astronauts from the epic 80s movie of the same name. *"It's a bit like your Dad trying to be trendy,"* suggested one source. Especially when amongst the youngest generation at the firm, The Right Stuff is more likely to conjure up images of Jordan Knight, Donny Wahlberg and friends sporting acid-wash jeans and bandanas. Nevertheless, as one trainee said, *"The firm is open-minded and progressive."*

The regional groupings are *"pretty autonomous,"* althoughthere are initiatives to better integrate the firm. Each region handles broadly the same work, but each office has particular areas of expertise. Reading is strong in insurance and PI work, Oxford has a top family division, Swansea is big on PI and Cardiff has particular talents in IP/IT. Yet most trainees choose their office for its geography and not its specialisms. When we asked what had led them to the door of Morgan Cole, many spoke of wanting to work for a firm that was *"large, commercial and regional."*

Concerning seat allocation, *"everyone gets what they want to an extent. The system is pretty fair."* Trainees sit down together to resolve any *"occasional squabbles"* and a couple of secondments are available to leading clients. Morgan Cole clearly takes the training process seriously and aims to recruit to retain. One trainee thought: *"They are keen on developing their trainees. Recruitment is an expensive process and they don't want to lose anybody."* In September 2002, the firm was able to offer 15 jobs to the batch of 19 qualifiers and 12 of them accepted.

in for the long haul
While we heard that *"everyone is very committed to making a success of their careers"* and *"we all want to do business here,"* this isn't the firm for your champagne-quaffing city slicker. But take heed of the trainee who said, *"I have enjoyed my training far more than friends at magic circle firms. People here enjoy their jobs. Some people treat their training contract as a two-year stint; here it's long term."* Another said, *"You should come to Morgan Cole if you're not vain about the name on your CV, if you want a measure of geographical flexibility and if you want a firm at the beginning of its expansion rather than one that's an established behemoth."*

In terms of clients and deals, *"rather than billion pound megadeals, we often get involved at an early stage for smaller clients who have potential, and then help them all the way through to the IPO stage. That's really satisfying."* Another advantage over training at a megafirm is that you're more likely to have the time for friends and fun outside the office. According to one source: "*Just because we know there's a balance to be struck doesn't mean we're not serious players.*" To get on at Morgan Cole you must "*want to succeed and take part in the firm. It's not just a job. It is something that is important.*" Wow! Is this another firm with a motivational video, we wonder?

thames valley: hi-tech and hoe-downs

The firm is well positioned to target the IT industry and emerging biotech clients in what has become the UK's answer to Silicon Valley. As a TV trainee you are expected to work in either Reading or Oxford and the firm will pay for your train ticket between them. On the whole the trainees usually live in Oxford and commute to Reading from there.

There are differences between the offices: "*People find it more relaxed in Reading. The Oxford office takes itself more seriously.*" Reading is in the middle of town, whereas the Oxford office is a fair walk from the city centre and on the fringes so people tend to drive into work. Reading is divided between the swish Apex Plaza and a 60s block in Friar Street. On the sartorial front, it's dress-down all week. Oxford has dress-down only on Fridays. While the Reading trainees exploit the town's many pubs and bars, the Oxford trainees enjoy occasional country pub lunches and, this year, a barn dance in one of the partner's barns.

wales: sun, sea, sand and sex

The Welsh offices are in Swansea and Cardiff, with Cardiff boasting more specialised corporate and commercial departments. Swansea offers exposure to the three main areas of work (property, litigation and business services) and Cardiff can supply seats in all of the above plus insurance, employment, banking and property litigation. The Cardiff and Swansea offices are closely linked, but you'll be unlikely to travel between the two on a very regular basis. The typical diet for the Welsh trainee would likely be two seats of litigation as a main course with a starter of property and a dessert of commercial work. One told us: "*I wanted a small office atmosphere with proper work to do. People I spoke to in London knew the name and said it was a good firm...and I can see the beach from my office, which is something that you can't do from Liverpool Street!*" In Wales "*people are real team players. Partners will be alongside you doing the photocopying to make the deadlines.*" Trainees tend to be a little older than average, and nearly everyone has either taken time off to travel or has had a previous career – Cardiff has an ex-lifeguard, a one-time rally driver and several ex-NHS employees. One trainee concluded: "*They are concerned with your personality and ability. If you get stuck in you can get as much out of your training as you want.*"

We learned that the Swansea office building left a bit to be desired, but the firm was shortly on the move to swish purpose-built offices complete with balconies and sea views. On the social front there are regular curry club and quiz nights and the quizmaster in the Swansea office is famed for his impersonations and trivia knowledge. There are plenty of opportunities to take on your clients at golf, although the firm's record is not great, apparently, since "*clients get to spend more time on the course!*" You won't find yourself chained to your desk late into the night: "*Partners come around at 5.30pm and ask why you're still here.*"

The open-plan Cardiff office has a balance of English and Welsh lawyers and is bang in the city centre. Nearby there are lots of "*lawyer pubs*" – trainee favourites include Ha!Ha! and Henry's. The subsidised social scene includes trips to theme parks, balls and go-karting. Dating in the Cardiff office is, apparently, "*rife*" and "*there's always a scandal going around!*" One trainee put the number of couples at seven, which places the firm very high in our 'Most Luvved-Up Law Firms' league table.

london: 1001 insurance claims

There are only eight trainees in London, but they do the PSC alongside the Thames Valley trainees so they all get to meet up. If you want the full variety of seats, then you might opt for the Thames Valley or Wales, but if you want a London experience, three separate offices around the capital offer several options. Fishburn Morgan Cole is a specialist insurance division that handles professional indemnity work and mainstream insurance and reinsurance. Croydon (which no longer takes trainees) handles motor claims, *"trips and slips"* and the like. The third office in Fleet Street is the real hub of things and offers trainees a taste of property, commercial litigation, property litigation and employment. During the day, there's little mixing as *"everyone's on different floors and there are no communal spaces."* But, *"there's lots of drinking and meals out. We're encouraged to have a life outside of work."* There are monthly curry nights in Brick Lane, and the various pubs on Fleet Street beckon to trainees. At last year's Christmas do the theme was Arabian Nights, with belly dancers providing the entertainment. *"They weren't from the firm though."*

and finally…

Whether your pop culture references involve bold fighter pilots or fresh-faced popstars, Morgan Cole would appear to offer something for everyone, once it's decided that you're made of the right stuff. One trainee told us, *"This is a firm where you are expected to take part and encouraged to succeed. You're Morgan Cole from the day you join."* If you're keen to do business (and you don't mind friends and colleagues calling you Morgan), then you know what to do.

Nabarro Nathanson

the facts
Location: London, Reading, Sheffield
UK ranking by size: 16
Total number of trainees: 60
Seats: 6x4 months
Alternative seats: Brussels, secondments
Extras: Language training

A large and well-established firm offering trainees a winning combination of good clients and a very satisfactory work/life balance. With offices in London, Reading and Sheffield, it continues to diversify from its core property practice.

what's on the menu?

Trainees are keen to debunk the image of Nabarros as a property firm, but we get the impression that they've swallowed the marketing spiel and forgotten that a fair whack of the business in all departments comes from property clients. It's a heritage they should be proud of. The firm increasingly offers quality work in a variety of departments, but if you have a pathological aversion to landlords, developers and property investors, just remember that you can run but you can't hide.

The big news this year is that Nabarros has embarked on a six by four-month seat system. Trainees welcome the move. *"If you're not certain what you want to qualify into it's ideal. It also means you're more likely to have a go at the most popular seats."* The only snag is that there's less time to sink your teeth into a particular discipline, but to counterbalance this, your last seat will be taken in the department into which you hope to qualify. And while on that subject, 24 of the 26 September 2002 qualifiers stayed on, distributing themselves across the firm – five into property groups, nine into corporate groups and ten into litigation and more specialist departments.

Once you've completed mandatory spells in litigation and property, you'll have a choice as to what you cover. There's a full range of commercial options back home and a competition seat in Brussels. The rule of thumb for getting what you want is to push for it. *"Someone got out to Barcelona for six months on qualification…it's just a matter of asking."* From the London base, it's also pretty easy to move around nationally, so if you hanker after a seat in Reading or Sheffield, that's always a possibility.

building blocks

Before being admitted into this trainee wonderland, you must prove you can revert to childhood. We heard disturbing reports from Sheffield of trainee hopefuls being asked to build and then deconstruct towers of Lego – presumably to prove how well they worked in groups (and perhaps how well they understood construction clients' needs). If you enjoy that kind of thing, the vac scheme is to be recommended. One trainee agreed with us: *"They are prepared to put a fair whack of time and money into the scheme,"* and the HR department seems keen to find trainees that way. Once you've started your training, be assured that you'll continue to be noticed and nurtured. *"This is a good place to stay and to continue a career. There are opportunities for early promotion. It's a good place to get noticed."*

So what is Nabarros after? Think about how a burger tastes better with all the trimmings. *"They are looking to make you into a good lawyer and they want you to be able to handle all aspects of the work. It's no good being a genius at the technical side if you can't chat to clients."* Lunchtime seminars will keep you up to speed with developments in the law and shine up your nascent lawyering skills, and you can practice networking through a longstanding and successful initiative called ContactNN – a group organised by trainees and NQs with the aim of building links with other young professionals/clients.

whips and intimidation

Although it is expanding its corporate business and works for household names (eg Oracle, Siemans, Body Shop, HSBC), Nabarros is not up there with the premier league on international megadeals. It does exceedingly well in the AIM market though. Our interviewees had no problem with Nabarros' position in the corporate law food chain: *"We're not trying to be something we're not. We don't go for the really top clients; if you want to work for Clifford Chance then this isn't the place for you. Here, though, you can keep your life!"* Just to make that crystal clear: *"At Nabarros you get high-quality work without sacrificing your social life."* This doesn't mean you can just flip the cruise control switch. *"If you just want to get through two years and then qualify you won't get on here. You can't just sit in the corner and wait for the work to come to you. At bigger firms you may be able to coast along and let the other trainees take the glory or the flak. Here you have to get stuck in."*

Trainees say they're treated like fee earners. *"We get a fair crack of the whip and plenty of decent work."* One trainee pitched us her views on the benefits of the training: *"I've had a much better experience than friends at some of the bigger London firms. I'm not stuck in a data room all day. Most of my friends at magic circle firms don't know how to be lawyers yet."* We're told Nabarros looks for *"independent thinkers"* and takes on a high proportion of non-law graduates. It seems to help if you are *"assertive and friendly."* *"Having a smile and offering help goes a long way."* Jolly good…but we were a little dubious about the claim that *"your enthusiasm is appreciated even more than your ability."*

One issue that came out in last year's *True Picture* interviews was whether or not trainees are supervised by sufficiently senior lawyers. They share offices, not with partners but with assistant solictors, some of whom may only have had a couple of years of post-qualification experience. This year, trainees were eager to emphasise the benefits of this approach. *"We get more leeway to speak our minds and ask questions. You can get first-hand experience of the kind of work you'll be doing on qualification and, in any case, the partners are approachable and always keeping an eye on things."* One trainee stressed: *"They give praise where praise is due."*

monday, tuesday, happy days

The London office is by far the biggest with about 250 lawyers on site. It's considered to be young and progressive in its outlook – it has a full-time dress-down policy and the senior partner has only recently come to terms with the misery of reaching 40. One trainee considered that *"the senior people here are open to new ideas and new ways of communication."* In the words of others: *"The emphasis is on balance"* and *"everyone here is personable and hardworking and enthusiastic."* It made us feel like we'd just stepped onto the set of faux-50s TV show *Happy Days*, where the kids are all healthy, happy, hardworking and keen to please the grown-ups. If the trainees are the legal world's answer to Richie, Ralph, Joanie and Potsie, we suppose that makes senior partner, Simon Johnston, The Fonz, and managing partner, Nicole Paradise, the firm's very own Mrs Cunningham. Actually, she'd probably prefer to be the Suzi Quatro character…

The smart offices in Holborn are bright and spacious. When the pressure's off, you can always flip a few coins into the proverbial juke-box in the informal meeting area, aka 'Breakout', where you can get a cup of coffee and, if you time your training right, watch World Cup football. Nabarros' local pubs are The Perseverance and The Enterprise. How motivational!

sheffield: matching shoes and bags

In Sheffield, trainees can't escape property since it's the biggest department on offer. They also choose from the standard mix of commercial, construction, litigation and pensions, with corporate and employment seats being perennially popular. Sheffield has a nice little earner in its PI practice, a legacy from the days when many of the lawyers worked together as the in-house legal team of British Coal. The client base of the Sheffield office has a very industrial feel to it, mirroring the economy of the region. According to one of our sources: "*In Sheffield you get quality work. It's not just a satellite of London, whatever people may think.*"

Next to the canal, the "*light and airy*" open-plan offices come equipped with a subsidised canteen, a dry-cleaning service and even a car washing service, if you're prepared to part with your keys and your money. Plenty of trainee and departmental socials supplement firm-wide summer and Christmas bashes. There's also no shortage of bars to sample after work, especially on West and Division Streets, which are the trendy up-and-come areas. In addition, "*you're encouraged to go to breakfast seminars and client barbecues, and to mix with as many people as possible.*" Sheffield trainees are also active in their own version of ContactNN and have put on events including a treasure hunt around the city, a spring ball, and an 'Image and Style' evening where they listened attentively to a fashion guru from the House of Fraser. We've cancelled our subscription to *Vogue* and will henceforth rely entirely on Nabarros' recruitment brochure for style advice.

reading: six long hours by camel

Reading has four trainees and can expose them to corporate, property, employment, IP/IT, charities and litigation. Set up to cater to hi-tech clients, it is perceived to be the best place for IT work. Described as "*friendly and innovative,*" it's a comparatively small but modern office and home to around 30 lawyers. Not only does it compete for local work, it handles a lot of referral work from London and lawyers from each office travel between them to deal with clients. "*You get exposure to clients from day one,*" one source told us. "*They're definitely not afraid to expose you to them…they put their trust in you.*" Trainees feel that the size of the office and working in small teams is the real reason why they get responsibility. "*In this office you are treated as a bona fide fee earner. You get London quality work, but without the hassles of London life,*" one enthused.

Reading hours are much the same as those in London. "*I've come in on six or seven weekends over the last two years,*" confessed one. After hours, trainees tend to head for the Oracle Centre. Trainees have also been known to indulge in giant Scalextrics games and camel racing with clients ("*not real camels, but like Donkey Derby*"). What with the different departments and offices, "*Last year I ended up going to about four different Christmas parties*" boasted one interviewee.

and finally…

Judging by the fond way in which trainees spoke of the firm, training at Nabarros sounded to us a bit like hanging out in Arnold's Diner, just with a bit more homework to do and a few pesky clients to handle. Of course, the offices are of a much higher standard. If our memories serve us correctly, Fonzie used to operate out of a toilet. Coolamundo!

Nicholson Graham & Jones

the facts
Location: London
UK ranking by size: 70
Total number of trainees: 18
Seats: 4x6 months
Alternative seats: Occasional secondments
Extras: Pro bono – Battersea Law Centre, language training

You want a medium size firm because you don't want the cut-throat atmosphere or death-defying hours of the top ten. You want to get to know everyone in your firm, or at least recognise their faces. You want to get some hands-on experience and a bit of responsibility as a trainee. So far so good, keep reading.

the clapham omnibus
NGJ is a broad-based commercial practice. So if it doesn't have a particular niche, how do we distinguish it from other medium-sized firms? The answer is that it's hard to do that. The training system is typical, the atmosphere warm and the range of work not slanted in any particular direction. This is 'Everyfirm', the commercial firm on the Clapham omnibus.

Each trainee sits with a partner, who could even be head of a department. They feel they are *"used well."* *"They are good at gauging what you are capable of doing without throwing you in at the deep end."* There will be the obligatory photocopying and trial bundle preparation from time to time, but *"the person who gives it to you will apologise and tell you how it fits into the bigger picture."* Partners are not proprietorial with their trainees so you can seek work from others in the department if you want to try something a little different. Trainees show up around 9am, but beware: some training lectures start at 8.30am. It is rare to leave after 7pm, unless you are in the corporate department. There's no 'work all night' attitude, but *"we have our moments."* Actually, one of our sources had the dubious honour of being the only trainee to have stayed all night.

all sorts
At NGJ, trainees spend at least one seat in each of the company, property and litigation departments. *"You don't so much ask for a seat as talk about which one you would like next."* But trainees are expected to justify their choices, so *"you can't just pick a department because it's trendy or the partner's a good laugh."* The most popular seats are IP and employment, and the firm will consider splitting a six-month seat into two lots of three months if it is oversubscribed. There may also be the possibility of a secondment to a client.

There really is a variety of work on offer here. In corporate it does well with AIM-listed companies and small and medium-sized enterprises. Construction and PFI deals contrast with private client and charities work. Clients come from across the globe. Last year, for example, the firm handled an electricity project in Lagos and a deal involving Dutch dustcarts. There are some top names in IT/e-commerce on the firm's books, as well as sports clients such as Ryder Cup Ltd, Wasps RFC, Leeds Utd, and Frank Warren. Holiday companies and London Boroughs sit side by side with The British Film Institute, The Press Association and Dame Shirley Porter. We suspect client parties are interesting affairs.

crazy, crazy nights
This year we think we've managed to pick out something really different about Nicholson Graham & Jones. By joining, you'll be letting yourself in for group bonding and general merry-making at an annual weekend away at a converted country house. Some are sceptical about this kind of thing: *"It's the thing that almost put me off joining,"* was the drastic response of one source. *"It's team-building where they say 'build a coffee machine with a piece of string and some matchsticks'."* However, the typical NGJ type won't sneer from the sidelines, they'll get stuck in. *"It's a bit cheesy, but everyone buys into it and has a go."*

The true horrors of the weekend are revealed at Saturday night's themed party. *"It was horrific, just horrific,"* whimpered one scarred survivor. *"It would *just terrify you,"* sobbed another. Yes, we are talking about four senior partners (three from company, one from litigation, but we weren't able to elicit names) dressed up as KISS *"with full-on face paint; the works."* Prepare yourselves…last year they dressed as the Spice Girls and their photos now adorn the walls of the company department. We tried to get someone to scan them and pop them on an e-mail, but no one was game enough. Come on NGJ, you know you want to! It is worth mentioning another partner (female this time) who appeared in a *"revealing little lacy basque,"* and a trainee who dressed as Marilyn Manson.

At least these grotesque tales make a welcome break from bland quotes about friendly atmosphere, open door policy, approachable partners…yawn. The weekend away does highlight the aspects of the culture at NGJ that prompted many trainees to accept their training contract offer. Teamwork is the key and if you're unsure of anything, you must talk to your seniors. *"All the old fogies are approachable!"* one trainee quipped. Our sources felt that the partners weren't just approachable because of their individual personalities, but because the firm encourages it. NGJ could be likened to a rare orchid. It blossoms once a year at the weekend party when the fun rains down, but hunkers down sensibly and quietly for the rest of the year. Trainees found the atmosphere *"very much like the clichés, I was expecting it to be much like it is."* One source took the job because *"I didn't think other medium firms would be radically different so I took my first offer."* And there's a good chance you'll still be there two years later: in September 2002 all ten qualifying trainees were offered a job and eight accepted.

bubbling along

Trainees seem confident; *"not loud, but not shrinking violets."* *"We all get on really well, it's incredibly boring really."* They range in ages and backgrounds, and it is not uncommon for them to have had other careers before law. NGJ seems to make an impression from just a one-day interview, when associates and partners take the time to talk to applicants when they are shown around. The trainees socialise as a group quite a bit, beginning at the beginning *"when the newly-qualifieds and second-years take you out, get you drunk and tell you how things work."* They meet up for drinks after work and at weekends, and every month or so a big effort is made to arrange a special night out. Favourite haunts include The Fine Line and All Bar One, *"more for convenience than excitement."* It has been known for partners to take trainees and assistants out for a few beers, if there's an occasion like a completion or a birthday – *"They know their obligation!"*

soft sell

Trainees are happy; the only real complaint concerns NGJ's image. Last year we reported on its rebranding as 'A Better Partnership'. One source told us of a marketing committee, to which everyone is encouraged to contribute ideas. Yet, another trainee had *"no idea what the strategy is"* and felt that someone needed to get stuck in and sort out NGJ's image. *"I'm very aware that, despite our size and work, we still have a relatively low profile and people haven't heard of us."*

Something else that could do with sorting out is the dress code. It's so complicated that at least one trainee had lost track of it completely. *"I can't work out the detail of what I can and can't wear!"* Once upon a time only Fridays were dress-down, then it was the whole week, but then things got *"out of hand"* (we are conjuring up images of Gene Simmons), and then an incredibly complex e-mail was circulated with stipulations such as 'no heavily logoed T-shirts'. The end result is that it's easiest to just wear your suit and leave the tie in your desk drawer.

and finally…

It's cuddly, supportive and a thoroughly nice place to work. The trade-off for not working for big clients every day is that you might well get more responsibility. NGJ trainees work hard but are not particularly stressed and are certainly not required to give up their social life. Applications are especially welcomed from those with a well-stocked fancy dress wardrobe.

Norton Rose

the facts
Location: London
UK ranking by size: 10
Total number of trainees: 125
Seats: 6x4 months
Alternative seats: Overseas seats, secondments
Extras: Pro bono – Tower Hamlets Law Centre, language training

Top ten London firm Norton Rose is best known in the corporate, finance and shipping fields. It handles big-ticket work for a wealth of equally big clients and a majority of the work has an international dimension. So, as a student, how do you distinguish it from its seven bedfellows in the consortium of eight megafirms behind the City LPC?

too hot to care
The firm has an innovative six-seat training system, but it isn't the number of seats that is special. In a bizarre twist of fate, for the second year running, we are writing this on a hot and humid Friday afternoon and, frankly, life is still far too short to spend it detailing the intricacies of the seat pattern. It's got more twists than Olga Corbett so look at the Norton Rose A-Z profile at the back of this book for the full skinny.

…Great, you're back. Let's run through the three compulsory seats. Stop number one is corporate. Handling *"big-ticket work for big corporations,"* there's often little individual responsibility on offer, particularly at the start. *"You pick up more as you go along"* though. After building up his supervisor's trust, one trainee reported being *"given stuff to draft alone."* One trainee told it differently: *"I was thrown in at the deep end in corporate, but it was brilliant."* The conclusion we reached is that the difference between the teams within a department can make a huge difference to your experiences. Corporate 3 was this year's winner, and many trainees were eager for another visit.

Over in litigation, as well as *"lots of legal research"* trainees get hands-on experience. *"I did an application hearing in chambers in front of a Deputy Master,"* enthused a source. *"I had lots of responsibility, liaising with counsel and that type of thing,"* said another. Sure, *"there's always a bit of photocopying, but generally what I was doing was fairly interesting."* As for banking, there's less enthusiasm, unfortunately. *"It's a good introductory seat,"* but the work *"can be quite same-ish at trainee level."* We don't wish to sound like harbingers of doom (you'll have read about it in the legal press anyway), but the acquisition finance team suffered some key partner losses in 2002. But finance work is the beating heart of Norton Rose and it's inconceivable that it won't take steps to redress this loss.

Beyond the compulsories, niche seats await. The environmental department has plenty to offer. We heard of a trainee being given a mini-client to look after on a planning enquiry. They even got to lead some meetings. Tax, too, is worthy of praise: *"It is more technical, so there's more research and it is a bit more academic,"* said one happy customer. Essentially, *"you'll get the responsibility when they feel you can handle it."* If you want to be fully stretched on a much more regular basis, a good idea would be to disappear off to one of the smaller overseas offices. Norton Rose doesn't offer overseas seats to those in their first or second seat, so you won't need your passport for a while. It's all change from your third seat though; you could take a trip to Amsterdam, Athens, Bahrain, Bangkok, Brussels, Cologne, Frankfurt, Hong Kong, London, Milan, Moscow, Munich, Paris, Piraeus, Singapore or Warsaw. Phileas Fogg eat your heart out. There is also a range of juicy client secondments on offer.

v norton rose
You'll be hard-pushed to find a typical trainee. *"It takes all sorts and that is its strength."* Although one trainee claimed: *"There are only three or four trainees from Oxbridge,"* in reality the number is around one in three. From one source we heard that, at the start of the contract, *"when we introduced ourselves, I realised we are from all over."* *"There are people here from Ten-*

nessee to Prague," proclaimed another. Several trainees pointed to the subdivision of departments into distinct groups with their own identities. To us it suggests the firm won't try to hammer you into a new shape. "They are happy to take you as you are," and "you'll find a team where you fit in," said a source. As a result, you should be able to "play to your strengths."

Despite their protestations, we did find common traits amongst those we spoke to. They are mostly "strong minded," "confident, opinionated and outgoing." "Pretty much everyone in my intake is a very strong person," said one source. That's not to say Norton Rose trainees are bullies: quite the contrary, they're a supportive bunch. We even heard stories of people tempering their standby requests for qualification jobs based on the first preferences of others. "We all avoided one group for our second and third choices because we knew someone desperate to qualify there. We didn't want to spoil their chances." How refreshing. "It's not like some firms where you don't dare show weakness because you know people are prepared to exploit it." Apparently, the difference is apparent even before you get to the firm. "Norton Rose trainees at law school were so much more laid-back than the others." Yep, we heard that too. The camaraderie looks set to continue: 50 out of 54 qualifiers took a job on qualification in September 2002.

split personality
Late nights are on the cards, mainly due to the size and volume of deals in transactional groups and corporate support work in other areas. Looking particularly shifty in the ID parade are the usual long hours suspects, banking and corporate, whilst sidekicks property and tax sit outside in the Cortina with the engine running. "I worked a weekend after a week of late nights," said a source, "but afterwards the partner came round, thanked and took us all out. It was nice because I had just thought it was expected." It is expected, but it's also appreciated, particularly when "at times you are sitting there on your own in the office at 1am and you think 'What the hell am I doing with my life?' but you kinda know you're gonna feel like that sometimes." Do ya?

Perhaps one reason why departments feel so different from each other is that they are "split between six or seven buildings," (even the trainees don't know). Whilst newly refurbished Staines House (no Ali G jokes, please) is on the doorstep of the larger twins, Kempson and Bishops House, Moorgate is "otherwise known as Margate because it is so far away." Rumours abound as to the future: "The leases run out in four or five years so they are looking for somewhere else," one trainee speculated. "They have just got planning permission for building on top of Kempson," claimed another source. "I can't believe they are going to build on top!" exclaimed one interviewee. "It will look like a giant lipstick."

trainees that lunch
Trainees spoke rather casually about formal training. "There are lunchtime seminars where people talk you through deals and things" and "little workshops and lecture things in each of the departments." The firm is certainly keen to get trainees up to speed. Responsibility lies, in the first instance, with the trainee's supervisor. In addition, each of them is assigned a mentor "who is usually someone who went to the same university, or has something else in common with you." "Mentors often take their trainees out to lunch, just to see how they are getting on." However, "not all mentors are so good," moaned one unhappy soul. "Some of them aren't that keen, and it would be better if they offered themselves for the role rather than being appointed to do it."

absolutely minking
On the social front, "there's a lot on…almost too much!" "There's a brilliant social committee," and "there are lots of sporty-type things to do," be it playing softball in Regent's Park on a Tuesday night ("which is fielding with a beer in your hand, as far as I can see") or rugby, football, women's football, hockey or netball. A trainee bar on Monday nights is always well attended. "Most trainees go," one source informed us. "It is in one of the conference rooms and a good chance to have a few drinks and catch up with people." Exchange Square, Clerkenwell, Shoreditch and Brick Lane were all men-

tioned, but the hands-down favourite pub is The Old Monk, or rather "*the Old Mink because it smells like one.*" Although it is "*a bit of a dive*" and "*dark and damp because it is underground,*" "*you can fall out of work and into the Monk.*" Perfect. And for dinner? "*We go to Pizza Pomadoro, which has a live band and ends up with people dancing on tables.*" According to one source, there are "*a couple of trainee couples*" in the most recent intake. Apparently, "*this is the nature of big law firms.*" They've been watching too much Ally McDoolally, we reckon.

and finally…

For those in search of a big international firm, Norton Rose makes a good alternative to the magic circle. With similar work, clients and ethos, it provides a good grounding in lawyering…and it sounds as if there are some jolly nice people there.

Olswang

the facts

Location: London, Reading
UK ranking by size: 42
Total number of trainees: 43
Seats: 4x6 months
Alternative seats: Brussels, secondments
Extras: Pro bono – Toynbee Hall Law Centre, Tower Hamlets

This young London firm has an excellent reputation for telecommunications, media and defamation work, and in recent times has been one of the fastest growing firms in the capital. At law fairs, you'll spot Olswang trainees wearing combat trousers while their peers look sheepish in their suits. The nature of the firm's work and its relaxed image appear to get the youth vote; last year the firm received more applications than most of the big City players despite only offering a fraction of the places. With MTV in reception and bossa nova hold music, if you're into oak panelling, cigars and port, then look away now.

breaking rank

The training contract at Olswang is sliced up into the traditional four six-month seats. While there are no compulsories, you will divide your time between company/commercial, entertainment, litigation and property. It's done exceedingly well in winning the sort of clients it set out to – BBC Worldwide, Granada, Carphone Warehouse; the list goes on and on. And its business has diversified, ensuring top rankings in core areas (TMT, sports, defamation, etc.), and an admirable performance across the league tables, particularly in private equity, mid-size corporate deals, employment, property and corporate tax.

A new development that's had a mixed reception from trainees is the introduction of 'Know How' – a three month period of research/admin work within one of the six-month seats. Rather like the onset of puberty, you know it will happen, it's just a case of when. Depending on which department you're in, you may find yourself writing legal updates, looking for breaking law or amending precedents. Some see the benefits of Know How; others are less than thrilled to be taken away from client work. It does look suspiciously like it's designed to keep a bulging trainee population occupied during a time of fewer deals.

Trainees also have the option of being seconded to one of the firm's high-profile clients and get to see what goes on inside Viacom, BSkyB, the BBC and *The Mirror*. There's also an office out in Brussels, but apparently "*if you don't speak French, you don't stand a chance of getting sent there.*" In May 2002, Olswang took over the Reading operation of now defunct firm Garretts. Given the M4 corridor location, it comes as no surprise that the office has a focus on IT business. It offers three training contracts and there are four seats available, namely litigation, MCT (media, communications & technology), property and corporate.

logan's run

Work is considered to be interesting and of a high quality. Trainees are given excellent levels of responsibility, and many were concerned that if they

TRUE PICTURE — OUR TOP 120 FIRMS

weren't kept on they would probably have to go somewhere bigger and slip down a few rungs. If you prove that you've got what it takes, there's no stifling hierarchy to hold you back. The chief executive is in his thirties, and there are "*lots of women with lots of power.*" (By that they meant top-ranked lawyers, not whips and stilettos.) The firm is young and progressive, in fact so much so, that there was some anxious speculation about what happens when Olswang lawyers started to go grey? Someone suggested that there was "*a pit in the basement.*" We wonder if that's what happened to recently 'retired' chairman, Simon Olswang.

We'd like to baffle you with statistics for a moment. These stats will be new to the head honchos at Olswang too, so we hope they're concentrating… Our parent publication *Chambers UK* has come up with a new way of ranking firms, which involves taking the number of individual lawyers that are ranked in *Chambers UK* as leading lawyers in their field and dividing it by the total number of lawyers in the firm. Well whaddya know, Olswang has the highest 'density' of ranked lawyers of any London firm. 30 of its 178 lawyers (16.85%) attained *Chambers UK* rankings.

totally rad

Much has been made of the firm's image as a trendy media firm, and it certainly seems to have been a big draw for the trainees we spoke with. A comment was: "*I chose Olswang because it was booming and had that happening media edge. I though it was a bit cool.*" If you're hoping to go to Olswang for this reason, please be aware that you're not going to be skateboarding around the office and playing pinball with your supervisor all day. It may look more *Smash Hits* than *Legal Week*, but this is marketing of the Trojan horse school. The people, the work and the levels of responsibility are "*fantastic,*" but "*it's not all media luvvies and dot.com entrepreneurs.*" You're going to be earning your pennies as a lawyer, not as a TV exec or an adman and "*you are not going to be hanging out with the stars or jetting off to LA.*" The general advice for trainees is to do your research and look beyond the brochure. Maybe Olswang is trying too hard with its image. There's certainly an edge to the place that is akin to finding a Britney Spears CD and a baseball cap in your Dad's glovebox.

star trekking

While the firm's name may sound like a warlike tribe from a sci-fi series (identified by their wrap-around shades and boom boxes), apparently there is no house style for trainees. The firm looks for "*go-getters,*" but there's no typical route in, and many have avoided the direct line straight out of uni and through law school. Trainees have diverse backgrounds and aspirations, yet everyone is apparently "*friendly and caring*" (bleuch!). Someone compared the atmosphere to being back at school when everyone pitches in and helps out when you miss a lesson or are late with your homework. Yet again, we heard that some teachers are not as diligent as others when marking homework – appraisals differ in quality from seat to seat.

Be warned though, "*if you are an awkward git, your reputation will spread like wildfire.*" Shy, retiring types may also have a rough time of it. "*You must be very outgoing in order to get yourself known. You've got to be able to put yourself around a bit and know how to promote yourself.*" But it's not a cut-throat place and at the end of the week everyone goes out drinking together. "*There's no need for a forced atmosphere of jollity. It happens anyway.*" On the fun front, trainees get involved with wine-tasting, ski trips, horse racing and "*lots of do's in marquees.*" With offices in Covent Garden, there'd be something wrong if there wasn't a top social scene!

no logo

Since winning the Chambers and Partners *Law Firm of the Year* award in 2000, the firm has had something of a rough ride through the economic downturn, a problem faced by all firms when times are hard in their particular field of expertise or client sector. The firm has been propelling itself through troubled waters like a jellyfish, expanding and contracting in line with the hi-tech market. Like a jellyfish, it may be beautiful and unnervingly graceful, but there is a sting in the tail. Having been sucked in, some trainees we spoke to were anxious about being spat out again. Its poor 2001 trainee retention acted like a Lutine Bell to the profession. One chime: bad times ahead for trainees everywhere. For the second consecutive year, Olswang has only had jobs for about half of its qualifying trainees. This year 10 out of 19 stayed post-qualification in September 2002.

Admittedly trainees were talking to us at a time when tension and anxiety over qualification was running high, but we heard that *"the place is run as a very successful business and it is not tolerant of people who are not up to scratch."* With hindsight it's easy to point the finger and say that the firm over-recruited in recent times, but just a couple of years back Olswang lawyers were working their behinds off. Sure, there have been redundancies lately, but who saw the tech slump coming? There's no doubt that cutbacks and a drop in profits have had a negative impact on morale. *"Sometimes you feel that they care more about their image than the people who work here,"* said one trainee. But in spite of all of this, most trainees want to stay with the firm after qualifying, although one sighed: *"Making it to partnership looks pretty tough from where I'm standing."* That special Olswang feeling may be on vacation during these leaner times, but with new offices and (hopefully) an improving market, we look forward to its first day back at work.

and finally…

Olswang is definitely a firm out of the mould. True, it gains and sheds lawyers like Luther Vandross gains and loses weight, but that's not to say that those managing the firm don't know what they're up to. Olswang is as outthere as law firms get, if you want to be outthere too, just remember, so do several thousand other applicants.

Osborne Clarke

the facts

Location: Bristol, London, Reading
UK ranking by size: 20
Total number of trainees: 57
Seats: 4x6 months
Alternative seats: Overseas seats, secondments
Extras: Language training

Osborne Clarke has strong links to the technology sector and continues to impress on the general corporate/commercial side. Not satisfied with three UK offices, the firm has been busy consolidating its network in Europe and California. The Big Cat (the firm's hitherto unspeciated logo – now identified as a tiger) is increasing its hunting ground…

prowling the M4

OC's original lair, Bristol, has 31 trainees, and, sizewise, is closely pursued by London, with 21. The smaller Reading office has just five. *"Movement is encouraged. They like people in the three offices to get to know each other,"* although, unless you state a preference, you will almost always get a seat in the city you live in. A London source said, *"If you expressed a desire to go to Bristol, they'd try to get you there because they think it's a good idea to have us move around. But they don't try and persuade you to move unless they are pushed; say, if there were more trainees than seats in London."*

There are no compulsory seats, but *"they encourage you to get broad experience."* It's generally accepted that as a trainee you should do some background research, *"so you can pick the team (and lead partner) you like the sound of."* We heard favourable reports on practically every seat bar a couple: as if it were a hazardous military mission, *"they're always searching for volunteers to fill the property seat."* Private client is also unpopular. *"Before you get to the firm, you completely overlook the fact that it has a private client department – it tends to be promoted as being corporate/commercial, IT and IP."* "Private client has this dry, depressing aura," said one source who'd avoided it. We heard that a few trainees choose to do a three-month litigation seat rather than the full six months. As one trainee explained: "[Second-years] *who aren't sure what they want to do can get split seats to give them exposure to more things.*" Most trainees know exactly what they want, though – solid commercial training with the chance to get stuck into decent work. Across the network, 11 out of the 17 September 2002 qualifiers stayed with the firm.

the big orange boat

"*Leslie Perrin wants the firm to be more like a rowing eight rather than a slave ship,*" one trainee told us. We smiled, knowing that this comment is just **so** Mr P. He's the firm's senior partner and one of the most well-known senior figures in the profession. We've no doubt that OC's place in *The Sunday Times'* '100 Best Companies to Work For' rankings is, in no small part, down to his vision for the firm. Trainee comments on the firm's ethos are certainly heart-warming: "*The Orange Pages list everybody in the firm by first name, which is a nice touch. It confirmed my earlier impression that the firm is very inclusive, with a feeling that you're really working for a team.*" What else? "*It's very down-to-earth – without the airs and graces that you can get at big City firms. It has always had a good sense of direction and it hasn't lost it.*"

Just like a rowing crew, your fellow trainees will stick by you when you find yourself in choppy waters. "*If you're stuck or you're late with a piece of work, you can send round an e-mail to the other trainees and they would help out.*" We presume the same goes for the more mundane grunt work: "*The majority of paralegals are in the Bristol office, so in London you have more of what paralegals would otherwise get.*"

Our sources recommend quiet, shy, academic types to steer clear of OC. "*It suits people who are bright and independent. I certainly wouldn't think it was a firm for someone who doesn't like the limelight or giving presentations at team seminars in front of everyone including partners.*" If you only remember one thing after reading this: "*It's not a firm for miseries!*"

pushing the boat out further

OC's overseas network is a mixture of its own foreign offices and associated firms. For a while, it called itself Osborne Clarke OWA, to reinforce the concept of the alliance, but the tail dropped off the name after a bust-up with a major player in the alliance, Germany's Graf Von Westphalen. OC has six overseas offices of its own (Germany, Spain, Denmark and California) and associations with firms in Brussels, Paris, the Netherlands and the Baltic region. Trainees do feel a part of something international, and they talked about how some of their work had a cross-border element to it. "*Often lawyers and inwardly seconded 'trainees' from associated offices come over and it's good to meet them.*" "*It's becoming more and more a factor of working here,*" one trainee told us. "*International work is definitely on the increase; we're always getting opinions from foreign lawyers on, say, corporate or banking deals.*"

Although only the firm's Frankfurt, Cologne and California offices take trainees on a regular basis, potentially, overseas seats are available in all of the offices in the network. If you do an overseas seat, you'll be expected to pledge allegiance to the firm. "*It's probably because it's an extra expense and they want to reap the benefit of their investment. It's a back-door pledge to say you will stay with the firm on qualification – you sell your soul to OC!*" We're not sure what part of your body you have to sell to get a client secondment, but in the past trainees have spent time with clients such as Equitable Life and Imperial Tobacco.

bristol: cat's cradle

The firm recently moved its HQ into a new building that's been set up on an open-plan basis. Reflecting the inclusive atmosphere, which the building was intended to inspire, decisions as to furniture and food for the new cafeteria were handed over to the firm's general populace. There was even a committee responsible for selecting the artwork (no rotting Damien Hirst animal carcasses, we trust). As with most committees, "*there have been differences of opinion*" and the firm will be "*hanging on to some of its old pieces* that have been around for hundreds of years." We presume they mean paintings, not rotten old partners. Every month, on 'First Friday' nights, the partners shout all the staff a drink (or two, to be more specific). Little vouchers are handed out beforehand and *"everyone goes along to the pub with their two Tiger Tokens!"*

london: eyes down

Although it has recently experienced a number of partner-level departures, the London office has grown quite rapidly in the last few years, and a full house means that the large IT department must occupy a building just down the road. *"As soon as we have more space in the main building we will get everyone under one roof,"* reported one trainee. If you do a banking seat, be careful: *"The eighth floor looks right across St Paul's to the London Eye – it's quite distracting!"* After work, there's always someone coaxing people down to the pub – quite often the Magpie & Stump. What, no First Friday? *"We had something similar called Second Wednesday. It died off at the end of last summer, although there's always talk of reviving it."* Oh go on, you know you want to.

reading: your future?

The Reading office is still very much the baby brother of Bristol and London, but it has a certain appeal: *"People tend to go there because it's a much smaller office than the other two and you can get a better idea of working in a smaller, close-knit firm. Sometimes there's a reluctance to go there, but many that do go want to stay there."* Its Thames Valley location ensures plenty of IT and e-commerce work as well as a smaller (but still healthy) range of other seats.

fancy dress

A firm-wide dress-down policy is in keeping with the firm's unstuffy character, although one trainee said, *"If you go to a client meeting then you have to wear a suit and so it can be a bit of a bore to keep getting changed."* Doubtless they're happy to have the opportunity to do so though. *"It's one of the things that they are very good at. Even if you are not working with a particular client, often the partners will say 'Come and pop in to the client meeting; it might be good experience'."*

When it comes to Christmas parties, there's an awful lot of dressing-up. The last party had a Hollywood theme, with one entire team dressing as Harry Potter characters. This obsession with costumes is, we suspect, all of Mr P's doing – in a former life he was an actor.

and finally…

It really came as no surprise to us that our sources were really happy with their lot in life. They had chosen Osborne Clarke in the hope of getting a good quality training from a firm that's known for its pleasant atmosphere. And by the sounds of it, that's exactly what they've got.

Palser Grossman

the facts

Location: Cardiff, Birmingham, Bristol, Southampton
UK ranking by size: 107
Total number of trainees: 8
Seats: 4x6 months
Alternative seats: None

Celebrating its tenth birthday in 2002, Palser Grossman started life in Cardiff and has branched out into England. The commercial side is growing steadily, but only the foolhardy will ignore the fact that a hefty 60% of this firm's work is insurance-related, mainly defendant insurance litigation. As a trainee this will be reflected in your experiences.

injury time

Interested in personal injury work? Hopefully so. Your first, and quite possibly second, seat will be in this department. Give or take the occasional sigh of resignation, trainees told us that PI makes for an excellent starting point. "*It's a big department and there's a high volume of files so you do get responsibility. The procedural nature of the work actually helps you settle in and find your feet. You develop a rhythm because you see the same kinds of issues come up again and again.*" A second PI seat tends to allow you more autonomy as you are able to put the skills and knowledge learned in your first seat to good use.

The preferences of second-years are taken into account in seat allocation and this leads to a run on commercial litigation, commercial property and corporate. Commercial property in particular is viewed as an up-and-coming area. There's *"a huge upswing in the work – it's really booming. We've taken on a few really good people too."* In commercial litigation, the nature of the beast means that the quality of trainee tasks can be more hit-and-miss as there are a few giant cases to assist on. *"One case involved 18 lever arch files of documents, so preparing the bundles was a big job."* Another agreed: *"There are some really high-value files that a trainee will get involved with when they arrive in the department. It's like a rite of passage; you can't qualify until you've done your time on this file!"* But one trainee described a high level of responsibility from early on: *"My supervisor asked me to take a look at a small claim and tell him if I thought we had a case. I said I thought we did, and he told me to run with it. I ended up doing the whole thing from start to finish, all the advocacy and everything."*

When it comes to hours, you'll work by *"big boys' rules."* No one will be watching to see when you come back from lunch, but when there's work to be done you must be happy to stick around for a couple of extra hours to get it out of the way. With the exception of a few seats, trainees will share an office with a fee earner who will act as their supervisor. Work will come from various members of the team, which keeps trainees busy. Perhaps this is why formal appraisals were felt to be slightly haphazard. On the other hand, trainees were happy with the level of informal feedback and praise they received. *"I just ask my supervisor if we can get together and go through things over a pint, and they're always happy to do that."* A committee composed of a trainee, a newly qualified lawyer and a few partners acts as a forum through which trainees can communicate any concerns. The only gripe that we came across was that trainee salaries don't quite match up to the image of the firm. Having said that, the cost of living is very reasonable in South Wales and we reckon any trainee salary that will enable you to get a mortgage sounds pretty good. On the other hand, with law school debts to pay...

anything you can do...

The Cardiff office handles commercial work and PI, and the three smaller, English offices are entirely devoted to PI. All the trainees are recruited for Cardiff, but many will spend six months in the Bristol office. *"There's quite a bit of light-hearted us and them-ism between the commercial and the PI sides of the firm,"* one trainee revealed. *"It comes out in football matches and daft e-mails."* *"But two out of three of the founding partners came from the PI side, and you do sometimes get the feeling that in decision making, PI has two votes to commercial's one..."*

Trainees described a firm where everyone is *"young in age or at least heart"* and one that has shown itself to be open to new ideas and is willing to move with the times. There's a sense of camaraderie amongst staff – first-year trainees, unsure of their real-life lawyering skills, aired these concerns to young fee earners in the pub. Before long the fee earners had organised a series of informal seminars and presentations to help build their confidence.

baywatch

The firm likes to see itself as the *"trendy younger brother"* of its local competitors – national giant Eversheds and regional firms Morgan Cole and Edwards Geldard. *"The feeling here is that we're doing a similar level of work to those firms, that we do the job well and we have fun doing it."* So how can you spot the Palser Grossman posse among Cardiff's hordes of trainees? *"We're scruffier! We dress-down every day. It's partly 'cos* we're down in the bay and it's quite trendy there with all the bars and cafes and such. The other firms are up in the town, so they like to strut about a bit!"

Trainees tell us that the firm is looking for people who have seen a bit of life and are likely to interact well with clients. *"You have to be alright academically but not a whiz-kid or anything. No back-room boys!"* Socially, there's usually something going on. Big nights on the razzle will invariably start in the partner-owned bar in the basement (*"It's very Ally McBeal"* and yes, some of the partners do actually own it!!). Spontaneous bouts of socialising, trips to the cinema and bowling sessions are soon to be formalised through the creation of a social committee with a budget and a mandate to make merry. Good luck chaps!

and finally...

The challenge of staking out their territory alongside larger and longer established competitors gives Palser Grossman trainees a strong sense of identity. They don't live to work but they're into their jobs. Don't come here if you want a hard-boiled, corporate training, but do check the firm out if you're after a varied mix of contentious and non-contentious work.

Pannone & Partners

the facts
Location: Manchester
UK ranking by size: 55
Total number of trainees: 16
Seats: 4x6 months
Alternative seats: None

Not an Italian sandwich shop but one of the largest and most respected firms in Manchester. Pannones has been doing the business since 1851, boasts a thriving commercial practice and is nationally respected for its personal injury and clinical law expertise. Impressive stuff.

schizophrenia

Pannones covers everything under the sun from corporate deals and business crime to wills and probate. Clients range from individuals wanting compensation for slips and trips to those in the most remarkable of situations (the firm acted for Saudi nurse Deborah Parry, Asil Nadir and conjoined twins Mary and Jodie). Major organisations and companies such as Texaco, Manchester Airport, Nike and the Rugby Football Union also come to the firm. You don't need to be schizophrenic to apply here, but *"the split between private client and commercial gives enormous potential to experience different things."*

Even though personal injury is one of the firm's major strengths, one trainee reassured us: *"I didn't feel like I was expected to do a PI seat and the firm didn't mind at all that I didn't want to."* But if you have no particular aims, you will probably end up there at some stage during your training contract as it is the firm's largest department, and it takes three or four trainees every six months. PI is a prerequisite for those who want one of the highly sought-after clinical negligence seats, and each year we discover that a number of trainees join the firm because of its achievements in this latter field. If you have a medical background, this is an excellent firm to choose. Yet trainees are at liberty to focus on purely commercial seats. According to one trainee at least, sampling a non-commercial seat may simply confirm your worst fears: *"It helps when you've done one private client seat as you know you don't ever want to do it again!"* Perhaps the most popular of all assignments is a stint in the employment department because of its blend of applicant and respondent work.

anything to add?

The trainee experience varies from seat to seat. You might run your own small debt claims in litigation, seeing them through from start to finish, or you could find yourself opposite Ashursts or Freshfields lawyers on a large corporate transaction. PI, in particular, is *"definitely a proving ground. From day one you get your* own caseload." Client contact is par for the course and, even on the larger cases, supervisors make the effort to take trainees along to hearings and meetings. *"I am always asked for my opinion at the end of a client interview, and whether I have anything to add,"* said one source.

Pannones has a high partner to assistant ratio and, consequently, *"partners have time to train you like you are still at university."* You may be impressed to learn that around one third of the partners are women. Generally, partners are relaxed (many of them are quite young and many more are Pannones born and bred), and our sources agreed that they placed a heavy emphasis on feedback. *"I was in with my partner for one and a half hours recently, while she went over my work, suggested tactics and told me why she would do certain things."* Each department has a designated training partner and each trainee undergoes a mid-seat review as well as an end-of-seat appraisal. Trainees are universally happy with the system and feel able to talk to their supervisor, the head of training or another fee earner with whom they have built up a rapport. *"There isn't a blame culture here. If something does go wrong we are encouraged to be open with problems and resolve them."*

fingers on buzzers

You'll either get your own office or you'll share with other trainees. This isn't a licence to mess around as, *"although you never feel like the partners are looking over your shoulder, they expect you to get on with it."* The trainee network provides support: *"You can just e-mail the trainees as a group if you need help and then there's a race to see who can find the answer – it's a bit sad really!"* Sounds pretty good to us.

We reckon any one of the youngsters at Pannones could have talked for England at Manchester's recent Commonwealth Games. *"If you get a room full of our trainees for a seminar or something, we have to be told to shut up all the time."* The firm employs sociable and down-to-earth people and most trainees are from Manchester or the North West. *"There is no one poncing around thinking they are particularly special."* Indeed, *"there's no point acting like you're better than the secretaries as they usually know more than you!"* *"We are a Northern firm with a Northern sense of humour,"* and, in true Northern style, they are not afraid of hard work. *"We are ambitious, but not particularly competitive, and we wouldn't stab anyone in the back to get ahead."*

romanchester

If a roomful of trainees is a handful, we pity the rest of Manchester when school is out. *"People expect you to have a life and see your friends."* Standard hours hover around 8.30am to 5.30pm. September sees *"the start of the really big social binge."* Second-years take the new first-years out for a meal and there are plenty of big groups out for lunches and evening drinks. Friday jeans-and-trainers dress-down makes the end of week celebrations all the easier – Manchester is their oyster. There's the Printworks, Deansgate Locks and Walkabout, but *"the closer to the office the better."* The Hogshead just across the road and The Old Monk with its *"bottles of wine for £5"* always draw them in. *"If we're being classy with the newly qualifieds then we go to The Restaurant Bar and Grill."*

And there's more... for a tiny £2-a-month subscription to the social club, you can enjoy an event a month. Past successes include go-karting, pool competitions and pub quizzes. But beware of those litigators – *"There is fierce competition between departments and the litigators are pretty sharp at quizzes."* The Manchester Trainee Solicitors Group plays an important role. The firm pays for membership for all its trainees and several of them have been elected to the management committee. Associates and partners are not afraid to strut their stuff either. Firm-wide events always seem to bring out the best in folk, such as the IT department drunk on the dance floor, or all those who are married to someone in the firm being hauled up on stage. *"There was a stage full of people – lots of people have found love at Pannones."* Bless! A final tip from those in the know: when you start in September, find out when the MTSG Christmas Ball will be and book the next morning off work. *"It's a tradition that partners try and make* you work the next day – but they also go along, so it's fun to see what state they are in the following morning."

p&pstars

There are two important figureheads at Pannones. The senior partner, Mr Pannone himself, is by all accounts a man with his fingers in all the right pies (see his profile on the P&P website). The other star is managing partner, Joy Kingsley. It's still unusual for a large commercial firm to have a female managing partner and she does a jolly good job of keeping the firm's profile high in Manchester and beyond. Trainees are star-struck by what their management has achieved. *"A lot of hard work has gone into making everything go well, but it all comes dead naturally to them."* This is a firm that has grown steadily over the past few years and yet has hung onto its feel-good factor.

Pannones' office is situated in the heart of Manchester on Deansgate. It is three buildings for the price of one, joined together in a rather higgledy-piggledy manner. It's a standing joke that when trainees join they are given a map of the buildings. They all connect…just not on the same floor. There's a bit of up, down, in, out and shaking it all about before you can make a smooth transition from one building to the next. *"At first it's better just to go downstairs, out through reception and back in next door."* A lucky corporate trainee occupies one of the most prized rooms – the view out of one of the two walls of windows on the sixth floor is of Old Trafford itself. We have no idea if qualification also brings the promise of a better room for trainees, but in September 2002 seven out of 11 qualifying trainees stayed to find out.

and finally…

As a trainee you can do almost anything as long as it's legal. If you have already set your heart on claimant personal injury or clinical negligence work, then you can't ignore this nationally renowned specialist. You won't earn the biggest pay cheque in Manchester; however, we doubt that you'll care.

Penningtons

the facts

Location: London, Basingstoke, Godalming, Newbury
UK ranking by size: 56
Total number of trainees: 21
Seats: 4x6 months
Alternative seats: None

Spread across four offices, Penningtons gives trainees the chance to test plenty of water before deciding which pool to dive into. Expect everything from solid commercial work to claimant PI, family and private client. Because the offices are all based in the South, there is more integration than you'd find at some of the larger national practices. This is a firm with a London presence and an intimate feel.

foot and mouth

We spoke to trainees in all four offices but the general message was the same: *"I chose Penningtons because I wanted a first-rate training and a broad variety of work."* Beyond that, either you want to be in London, in which case you won't have to do the silly hours that some of your peers in the City end up doing, or you want to stay well clear of the capital, in which case you have the choice of three towns in three different counties. In terms of the typical trainee, *"the recruitment lady appears to go for slightly eccentric types with unusual backgrounds."* People here have studied everything from English to engineering, *"but we are all capable of thinking on our feet and are not afraid of speaking our minds."*

Over the course of your training contract, Penningtons prefers you to experience a litigation seat (possibly PI or clin neg, especially in regional offices) and a seat in its biggest practice area, property, where you might work for one of its two biggest clients, CGNU and Berkeley Homes. The firm then tries to accommodate your needs and desires for the remaining 12 months. The private client department is hot (three of the four office's senior/lead partners are private client lawyers) and *"lots of people want to do IP, but there's always too many after it."* There's decent corporate work on offer, but it was felt that if you want to carve a career acting for FTSE 100 clients, *"you should definitely be looking at the big City firms."* Having said that, *"there are lots of interesting clients from shipping companies to political parties."* While the firm might be one of the smaller fish in the big London legal sea, trainees nevertheless find themselves opposite lawyers from the bigger firms on deals. *"There is no pretence here. What we do, we do well."*

penningtonssss...

The London office is the hub of the firm and has been serving clients for over two centuries. *"It is quite a conservative place,"* according to our sources; for example, *"personal e-mailing is frowned upon."* But in the last few years the firm has abandoned its traditional 'buckle' logo in a rebranding exercise. Instead, it's opted for a big bold 'P' that looks like it has been lifted from the dying moments of a mobile phone 'Snake' game. Get your Nokia out and make the comparison.

Conveniently located deep in the City, between Cannon Street and Mansion House Tube stations, the office occupies *"a large anonymous block."* Most trainees share an office with a partner, while some draw the long/short straw (depending on your view) and share with a newly qualified lawyer. *"You get to look things up together!"* one told us. The London office hosts monthly 'First Monday' training lectures, when trainees from the provincial offices come together for schooling. Once class is out, it gives trainees *"a chance to catch up and have a drink."* Unwinding in London tends to be *"quite conventional"* and there's *"no funny stuff."* (!) Socialising generally goes on in local branded wine bars and a sports and social committee subsidises trips to events like the new Queen musical 'We Will Rock You'. There is a firm-wide quiz night in December, which is usually won by the London office, since *"they're the kings of trivia."* There's also an inter-office rounders tournament, which is usually won by the cross-firm IT team. We don't know why though.

Penningtons trainees are as concerned about their blood pressure as the size of their deals and describe their hours as *"extremely civilised."* The London office is a safe bet if *"you want to work in the City on a decent salary but without having to slog your guts out."* One trainee took the view that *"you should come here if you want to see what law is really like. You'll get a good overview of the whole process."*

oh godalming!

If you want to stay put in the Home Counties, the smart Surrey town of Godalming is situated midway between London and the South Coast and offers trainees a taste of the good life. The office only takes two trainees each year and exposes them to a mixture of private client, property, litigation (including top-level claimant personal injury and clinical negligence) and corporate/commercial work. One trainee said, *"I chose the firm because I was interested in PI and clinical negligence work, basically the individual client contact side of law rather than the commercial side."*

One trainee who had previously worked as a paralegal in the capital felt that *"in the big London firms there are fewer opportunities to be noticed and to be an individual."* In Godalming you get *"good levels of responsibility without the pressure."* Another trainee told us: *"There's a hard-working environment and a relaxed social side. Get-togethers are positively encouraged."* On the social front there are monthly events ranging from wine-tasting evenings to trips to the races. Or you could go star-spotting – among Godalming's famous local residents are Chris and Billie, and Anthea Turner.

amazingstoke

The Basingstoke office takes one or two trainees a year and since there are only four departments (company/commercial, litigation, property and private client), there'll be no surprises as far as seat allocation is concerned. It offers the same range of seats as Godalming – it's just that it's in a different county and attracts those keen to stay in Hampshire. One trainee asked us: *"Why would you want to relocate to Basingstoke?"* We couldn't answer. The ethos is *"young and relaxed, although you would struggle to call it trendy."* When our researcher suggested that Basingstoke was a bit out of the main action, one trainee countered by saying, *"Some students think that if you want to work on decent commercial deals then you have to go to London, but that's not the case."* In property, there are plenty of house builder clients, and technology companies instruct the corporate team. By way of contrast, the PI and clinical negligence teams act for claimants.

The hours are as you'd expect in the regions. *"A couple of weeks ago I did a 46-hour shift, but that's almost unheard of. Usually I'm in at 9am and out by 6pm."* Lawyers all work open-plan in a new office that's described as *"plush."* As we reported last year, levels of responsibility are *"somewhere between enough and nearly enough."* One trainee told us, *"I've been fairly sheltered and for a long time I was heavily supervised."* The social scene is, at best, ad hoc: there are plenty of pubs, but not many trainees to go in 'em.

newbury: little havana

Lovely Newbury is the jewel of Berkshire, famous for a racecourse, a bypass and Swampy's mates. Like Basingstoke and Godalming, it is closely linked to the London mothership. As a trainee you'll do the standard mix of property, litigation, CoCo and private client. Commercial property is the biggest department and the employment side is on the up. The kind of people who thrive in the Newbury branch are those who are *"up for anything and keen to learn."* They are the sort of people who get involved in sports and social events outside the office. The local watering hole is Bar Cuba, and partners and associates come out quite regularly. We got a sense that the office has more of a buzz than the other regional branches.

The office is right in the centre of town at the end of the high street. It is *"quite traditional,"* but largely open-plan. Friday, as in the rest of the firm, is dress-down, and casual means *"no ripped jeans."* You're unlikely to bust a blood vessel here on the work front, but be aware that *"a partner views your chargeable units each day to see what you've been up to."* No slacking! If this particular part of the country is where you want to live and work, you're unlikely to be able to do better than secure a Penningtons training contract. And there's pretty good news on retention: across the offices, seven out of ten trainees were offered and accepted a job on qualification in 2002.

and finally…

An established reputation, a good work/life balance, an interesting range of work, increasing commerciality and a choice of offices outside the capital makes Penningtons an attractive option for anyone looking for something slightly out of the ordinary and slightly out of the pressure cooker.

Pinsent Curtis Biddle

the facts
Location: Birmingham, Leeds, London, Manchester
UK ranking by size: 14
Total number of trainees: 74
Seats: 4x6 months
Alternative seats: Brussels, secondments
Extras: Language training

Pinsent Curtis Biddle was born out of a merger in February 2001 between national firm Pinsent Curtis and City boutique Biddle. This year it didn't so much merge with as throw a lifeline to the beleaguered Birmingham office of the law firm formerly known as Garretts. This classy firm has never been as mouthy or aggressively expansionist as some of its national peers, particularly as regards its (deliberate?) lack of focus on Europe. However, Pinsents remains a force to be reckoned with on a national basis, which just goes to show that its traditional qualities of polish, panache and gentility haven't prevented it from making its way in the world.

finding your vocation in life

Trainees are under no obligation to move offices, although the option is there. *"They try to accommodate people from Birmingham or Leeds who want to come down to London,"* but by all accounts, most London trainees tend to stay put. In 2002 the firm opened up in Manchester and at the time of publication, three trainees were in that office, all doing corporate work.

There are no compulsory seats, although the powers that be have mooted the idea of making corporate mandatory: *"They nudge you in the direction of doing one."* One trainee didn't like the idea of a compulsory seat in anything: *"I think the opportunity to do as many seats as possible and find your niche is one of the selling points of the firm."* Supply and demand permitting, *"you'll definitely get your first choice for at least one of your four seats."* In London, CTTM (commercial, trade, technology and media) is one of the most popular. *"It sounds very sexy with advertising and media on the one hand and standard IT/IP work on the other."* This reflects the fact that Biddle had a large and reputable media team (although bits of it fell off during the merger). Northern trainees said, *"obviously eyes flashed at the prospect of doing media in London after Biddle joined,"* with the corollary that *"there's not much of that stuff done up north."* Other popular seats include employment and corporate. *"We're very corporate-led and they are the real money-runners of the firm."* Property is a key area and takes a large number of trainees.

friends in high places

"Pinsents is more independent-minded than a lot of firms." Is there a typical Pinsents trainee? Apparently not. *"We have all types from Sloaney and ambitious to bookish and academic."* One source said, *"There's a niche for pretty much everyone; it's just a question of finding it."* The consensus is that you'll be OK as long as you're prepared to work hard and pitch in. *"It's a team-focused firm and you're encouraged to get involved in non-work activities too."* Along these lines, trainees organise a lot of their own social outings and there are also events organised *"from up above"* (although we find it hard to believe that He has the time to organise parties, even for a firm as well-respected as Pinsents!)

One trainee sounded very much like the late John Wayne when he pronounced: *"I've got files to manage, deadlines to meet and no mistakes to make."* There are three-monthly reviews, although *"you'll know long before your review whether anything's wrong. No one's backward about coming forward."* As for grunt work, one source said, *"The photocopier and I have not become best friends"* while another noted: *"there's not much in the way of photocopying but there's a hell of a lot of proofing!"*

save the trainee

Hours tend to be *"pretty much 9am to 6ish"* with *"occasional periods of panic."* Painting a Hammer Horror picture, one trainee told us: *"When I was in corporate, I worked on a deal that went on for four months with not many earlyish nights. I was doing a lot of paper shuffling and leaving at eleven most nights."* Over in major projects and PFI, people *"put in very heavy time."* A few trainees called for extra paralegals and support staff.

However, trainees don't feel late nights are ingrained in the culture: *"You take it as the workload finds you – when you've got a lot to do, you just have to get your head down and do it."* In terms of client contact, supervisors are generally *"very good at introducing you – there's never a meeting I'm at where the client doesn't know who I am,"* although that trainee went on to say, *"there's plenty where I don't know who they are!"* A regular secondment is available to ALSTOM, with others (including Transco and CGNU) arising as and when. There's also one four-month seat available in Brussels at an affiliated firm Renouf & Co. A *"workable level of French"* is required.

Friday dress-down means smart casual, although this has many interpretations across the offices. The strictest is in London, where no jeans or trainers are allowed, although an exception is made for May Day when *"you can wear whatever you like so you don't get beaten up"* (by anti-capitalist protesters, we presume). One interviewee told us she was patriotically sitting in her England shirt when we called on the Friday of the historic England World Cup win against Argentina.

There's a twice-yearly event called National Trainee Day, which takes place in April and December (and sounds vaguely like a charitable fund-raiser). Trainees converge on one of the offices for seminars, with the wider brief of *"getting to know each other."*

london: old biddle weds new beau

One of our interviewees said, *"What really appealed to me about Pinsent Curtis was that the London office had just been set up and had an amazing atmosphere. They were aiming to double their size within two years."* Another commented: *"I wanted to be in London, somewhere that was well-respected in corporate/commercial and all the other work you need for a decent training, but with a non-magic circle mentality."* After the Biddle merger, the London office was apparently *"top-heavy"* with trainees in comparison with the other offices, although one trainee opined: *"Give it another intake and that will be rectified."* Trainees view London as being *"more pressurised"* than Leeds or Birmingham, saying, *"In the London culture, clients' expectations are higher."*

The old Biddle office is described as *"up a winding set of stairs"* with a *"quaint, bookish atmosphere,"* while the old Pinsent Curtis office has a very nice view over Liverpool Street with *"stylish"* client meeting rooms, although the rest is *"practical rather than luxurious."* The trainees' watering holes are One of 2 and Bangers, which is *"more of a junior hangout."*

birmingham: bulging

The Birmingham office is said to be *"open-planish"* with an *"air of temporary."* It is a *"mishmash of partitions"* and in a *"perpetual state of flux with people constantly coming in, so walls have to be removed and departments shifted."* Most recently, the office *"accommodated"* Garretts (which is a terribly polite euphemism for the rescue operation). *"It was a mild shock. We made the offer to Garretts and they quickly accepted; then we got told they were coming into the office the next day."* We learned that the trainees have had very little to do with the Birmingham TSG. *"It's very full of people who are very full of themselves."* Miaow! Hold us down and smack us for stirring, but other Birmingham trainees think that Pinsents are *"a bit quirky and a law unto themselves."* So there you are… More enthusiasm is shown for the local All Bar One, which is where Friday night revelries kick off. Other prime locations include Primitivo.

leeds: the importance of being earnest

The Leeds office building is just a couple of years old and is *"very open-plan"* with *"plenty of glass and typing."* Trainees think it has a *"more business-like atmosphere"* than the other two offices and an air of being *"earnest and young."* (Aren't they one of the big four accountants?) Trainees sit *"next to, behind or just over from"* their supervisors in *"pods"* of four desks with one- and two-year qualifieds taking up the remaining seats. According to our interviewees, these seating arrangements reflect the fact that *"you're not just your supervisor's property – you're a team asset."* The open-plan structure, intended to promote more of a team ethos in the office, seems to be doing its job well: *"It's easier to bounce ideas off people in your team and build relationships with them if you're all sitting together."* The official office bar is the Slug & Lettuce, just *"15 paces away."* It's the meeting point for Friday night trainee adventures. Well, this is Leeds after all…

As for retention statistics, in terms of the Pinsents trainees, 32 out of the 38 September 2002 qualifiers were retained. However, the Garretts trainees who joined the firm in May were not so lucky; out of five September 2002 qualifiers, only one stayed on.

and finally…

If you want a good supply of corporate/commercial work for good quality clients, 'Pinsent Courteous' will offer you exactly this. It's stayed true to its regional origins while pumping resources into London, but it's not become caught up in the scramble for European offices.

Prettys

the facts
Location: Ipswich
UK ranking by size: 111
Total number of trainees: 8
Seats: 4x6 months
Alternative seats: None

Prettys has grown steadily over the last ten years and now has over 135 staff, including 16 partners, working from its offices in Ipswich. The firm is well regarded in the region for both its commercial and private client work. Conventional wisdom has it that the work divvies up three-ways between private client, insurance-related work and the commercial practice. But things are changing and the commercial department is arguably the fastest growing at the moment.

medal, medal
"Mutley, you snickering, floppy eared hound. When courage is needed, you're never around. Those medals you wear on your moth-eaten chest should be there for bungling at which you are best. So, stop that pigeon, stop that pigeon…" Dick Dastardly. We love a firm that takes a novel approach to marketing. If you've not yet checked out Prettys' website then do look at it…maybe you can tell us where all the origami birds and off-the-wall quotes fit in!

look before you leap
The firm is extremely active in defendant PI work, and there are also claimant injury (commonly 'no win, no fee') and overseas litigation teams. *"You see some absolutely corking cases in claimant PI – people getting drunk and jumping in the shallow end of swimming pools, that sort of thing,"* one trainee told us. But don't knock it – this is a seat where you'll be actively involved in the work of the department, and might even find yourself using your languages talking to foreign agents and law firms associated with Prettys through the European 'Galexy' network. In PI, you'll also have numerous opportunities to interview clients and effectively run a case from the outset. *"You're even able to do your own court hearings, which helps you get your confidence up."*

The rural property and estates department acts for local farming clients, and a seat in this area will let you get your teeth into *"really diverse work and loads of client contact."* The firm's continuing commitment to its private client practice provides good work for trainees. *"Private client is a seat where you really do get to meet with clients yourself, draft basic wills, do small probates and help out on bigger probates, as well as getting some matrimonial experience."* A niche French property practice and high-profile National Farmers' Union work add variety to a client base of wealthy individuals.

bootiful!
Seats are available in CoCo, employment, property, IT/IP, commercial litigation and shipping and transport. And for a small firm there are some pretty big-name clients on the books, including Citibank International, the MOD, Ipswich Town Football Club and best of all, Bernard Matthews. Competition can be tough for the popular seats, but the small trainee population means it's never too much of a headache. At a mid-seat review with the personnel manager, trainees make their seat preferences clear and then sit back and wait with fingers crossed.

The hours you chalk up depend on the department and its workload, but usually, turning out time is 5.30pm. That said, *"they like people who show willing. If you do a little bit extra they appreciate it, but you're really left to manage your own time."* All trainees underlined the fact that across the departments, tedious admin work is simply not a part of the job description: *"It all goes straight down to the postroom."*

chillin' with the tractor boys
What do you think of when you think of Ipswich? If you don't know the place already, you may draw a blank at that question. Suffolk is a hidden gem and no

doubt many want to keep it that way. Prettys' trainees assured us that Ipswich isn't a no-place, and were generally very positive about the town and the firm's centrally located offices. "*You really do slow down when you come here from a big city. It's great because you're getting good work and that can bring its own pressures, but then you can just head out and take your full lunch break in the sun.*" The offices are part open-plan and pleasant to work in. There's an interesting theory that the building itself is one of the reasons why the size and nature of the firm are so often misinterpreted – "*From the front it looks like an old house and at the back it's quite a big modern office block.*"

Not everyone hails from East Anglia, although there's little doubt that local links can only work in your favour. Regional firms like to feel confident that trainees will stay post-qualification and not rush off for high-paying jobs in London at the first opportunity. Other than that, Prettys is looking for "*people who can do things off their own bat, who aren't too dependent on seniors.*" "*More important than a brilliant academic record is a willingness to participate in marketing and promoting the firm outside the office. They want people who can get on with people.*" In 2002, four out of five trainees were offered a job on qualification and three accepted.

The firm actively fosters the social scene, and there are regular cricket and football matches, and even an annual walking holiday (in past years they've been to the Yorkshire Dales and the Peak District, and Ireland is the hot favourite for next year.) One trainee mused on the "*maleness*" of the firm: the male-dominated partnership, the endless dissection of cricket matches in the pub… It's doubtless true, but hardly exceptional. Everyone from partners to trainees is to be found in Prettys' local, Mannings, on a Friday night. "*It's a really old, dark pub. We all complain, but we always go! It's become a tradition.*" The local Trainee Solicitors Group is a busy one and Prettys trainees have, by their own admission, shown a tendency to dominate the committee every year.

and finally…

As East Anglian firms go, this is among the best in terms of growth and reputation. In the course of a two-year training contract you'll get involved in some high quality work, and probably at closer quarters than you might in a larger firm. Our interviewees saw training in Ipswich as a healthy option: you're an hour from the pleasures of London when you want them, but you don't have to live with the constant roar of the city. You'll know if this firm is right for you.

Pritchard Englefield

the facts
Location: London
UK ranking by size: 110
Total number of trainees: 8
Seats: 4x6 months
Alternative seats: None

Pritchard Englefield is a medium-sized City firm with a predominantly corporate/commercial focus. There are plenty of firms that fit that bill; this one is unusual in that just over half of its clients are German or French. If you want to train here, you need to be proficient in one of these languages or you'll have to bring something pretty remarkable to the party.

continental breakfast

There are no compulsory seats and second-years get first dibs at each rotation. The firm gets trainees to "*work things out between themselves*" with the training partner acting as final arbiter in any dispute. CoCo is by far the most popular seat, not just because "*many trainees join the firm because they want to qualify into corporate law,*" but "*as CoCo probably has the most German and French clients, you've got more opportunity to use your second language. That really sells it.*" Commercial lit is popular for the same reason. Trainees are less likely to gun for private client, personal injury or clinical negligence, simply by dint of personal preferences.

In some departments, trainees share an office with another trainee, while in others they sit with their supervisor. On hours, one trainee said, quite typically, "*I usually come in at 9am and leave anywhere between 6pm and 8pm.*" The longest hours are to be found in CoCo, where on the very odd occasion you could be there to greet the dawn. "*Thank God they had a canteen!*" one source said. Unsurprisingly, the department handles plenty of cross-border transactions, particularly those with a European aspect.

someone to watch over me

A hands-on approach is evident in the training, reflecting the firm's desire to give trainees responsibility at an early stage. One talked of appearances before masters in the High Court; another mentioned running files in commercial property and "*babysitting*" a vacationing fee earner's files in CoCo. We also heard from a trainee who'd run a number of files in clinical negligence. "*I got to write all the letters, make all the phone calls, do file reviews and work out the next step on a number of matters. My supervisor would look over my shoulder and would discuss the files with me.*" On this point, the trainees were happy with feedback. "*The general rule is that if you want more responsibility, you can ask for it. But it's a good firm in terms of supervision. Nothing goes out without someone seeing it.*"

Alongside these challenges there will be some grunt work, whether that's photocopying, bundling or other "*horrible things.*" This is particularly the case in personal injury or commercial litigation. "*When there are trials coming up, you might be photocopying and putting trial bundles together for four or five hours a day.*" In light of this, we were told: "*It might be good to have a few more junior people*" (ie paralegals) to help out with "*general office work.*" However, our interviewees were also keen to stress that "*it's not a big part of the job*" and "*you get less of it the nearer you get to qualification.*"

all talk

"*The French side of the business has a very young and dynamic feel, whereas the German side is run in a more traditional way.*" While this may reflect the "*different styles*" of the people running each component, it may also reflect the fact that "*we're longer established on the German side than the French side.*" It may also have something to do with the fact that in Germany business is often conducted in quite a formal manner.

Trainees talk of drafting letters on English law for French or German clients: "*It might be something relatively simple in English, but difficult to translate. For example, explaining to a German company the difference between a limited company and a plc in England.*" You'll need to find the right balance because "*there's a big difference between business German and everyday German, and it's the same with French.*" Over in the personal injury department you might have to deal with a German tourist who's injured himself and wants a native German speaker to represent him. "*You've just got to make sure you explain things clearly in their language. But as a lawyer you've got to do that anyway.*"

we are familie

Aside from a number of dually qualified lawyers, there is also a German speakers' group and a French speakers' group comprising staff from "*bilingual secretaries*" right through to senior partners. As well as meeting about once a month to keep up with who's working on what, the groups host social events for clients, including chocolate tasting, pétanqe and croquet. Fee earners without a second language are firmly in the minority…perhaps they need a support group of their own!

Languages aside, trainees were attracted by the size of the firm: "*I didn't want to go to a large firm where I'd be one of 100 trainees,*" said one, while another added: "*I like being able to walk into the building and know everybody – it's got a real community feel.*" Although only one of the firm's four qualifiers stayed with the firm in September 2002, the others are following quite varied career paths, heading off to the EC in Brussels, a law firm in Germany and a specialist clinical negligence practice. One interviewee made a salient point: "*Many of the trainees* who've left here in the past have gone on to big international firms. The training here is respected and they've been constantly able to use their other languages, so they're marketable commodities."

bare essentials

The office overlooks Liverpool Street Station and our interviewees raved about its location on the corner of Spitalfields. Staff get to dress down (*"no bare legs, no bare feet, no shorts and nothing transparent or more suited to pole-dancing venues"*) every Friday and throughout August. Recent firm-wide activities have included a picnic and softball in Hyde Park, a treasure hunt and a quiz night. As for local pubs, Dirty Dick's is favoured for birthdays and organised events, while Hamilton Hall, The Old Monk and The Magpie are all popular with trainees and assistants.

and finally…

So long as your interests and skills fit with Pritchard Englefield's business, you're made. The firm isn't looking for many trainees, just the right ones, so if you've got what it takes and you want to get up close and personal, you'd be mad not to investigate further.

RadcliffesLeBrasseur
the facts

Location: London, Leeds, Cardiff
UK ranking by size: 74
Total number of trainees: 16
Seats: 4x6 months (London), 2x12 months (Leeds)
Alternative seats: None
Extras: Pro bono – Battersea Legal Advice Centre

Housed in the maze of small streets around Parliament Square and Westminster Abbey, SW1 old boy Radcliffes, best known for its private client and charity work, has added to its name and been for a quick botox session. Its appearance has improved and there's a renewed sparkle in the eye.

come together

RadcliffesLeBrasseur has undergone a number of changes over the past couple of years, mostly through a series of small-scale mergers. First, a specialist property firm, Jay Benning & Peltz, was added to Radcliffes in 2000 and then came medical law specialists Le Brasseur J. Tickle (stop laughing) in December 2001. This latter merger ensures the firm a toehold in the north of England in the shape of a small Leeds office and one in Cardiff (which does not currently take trainees). More than a quarter of the merged firm's work is now in the healthcare sector (acting for health authorities, GPs, private sector providers, insurers and medical charities), with the remainder made up of corporate, charities (over 140 of them), property and tax/private client. Leeds, London and Cardiff still feel *"very separate." "There's little contact with the London office,"* said a spotter in the north. *"We share resources,"* but *"we've got different clients and it is like a different firm."* It's by no means all negative though; there are some enormous pluses, and not just from the perceived security that comes from the weight of numbers and the support that different departments can offer. *"It is now a younger firm,"* said a source. Above all, *"it feels more progressive."*

But it also feels *"quite top-heavy and there seem to be more partners than assistants."* As one source put it: *"As with any merger, someone needs to ask, 'Do we need all these fee earners? Do we need more?' It's still finding its feet."* Given that there have been departures from the firm, it is clear that someone has been asking these questions. And then, just before we went to press, the firm's charismatic chief exec left quite abruptly and the conductor's baton was handed back to the senior partner. Everything pointed to musical differences.

finding your niche

RadcliffesLeBrasseur trainees in London complete four seats of six months each. Although *"they would like you to do property,"* there are no compulsory seats. It is a very different story in Leeds, where trainees currently sit in just two departments, for a year each. If you're looking at Leeds, be sure that the firm offers exactly what you want; otherwise you could have a very dull time. The Leeds office takes on property and healthcare work, as well as a healthy dose of company/commercial. Although the specialist healthcare seat was once the darling of the London office, it has slipped from popularity this year, to be replaced by the national favourite – employment. "*Everyone wants to do employment, but it wasn't like this before; people found their own niche and it was more of a mixed bag.*" Tax and personal injury are very popular too, again because of their niche value. All in all, "*since the mergers, trainees have so many more opportunities.*"

raw deal

In the matrimonial department "*so many of the skills are transferable*" that the gulf you may have perceived between commercial and private client is significantly narrowed. "*To deal with a divorce you have to look at different areas of law, including property and tax.*" "*It isn't high street stuff; it's big,*" said a source. "*It's under the private client department and, as it is litigation, the forms are similar…and the amounts of money involved can be as high as in some commercial deals.*" Above all, because you will be "*dealing with people at their rawest*" you'll be well prepared to "*deal with any awkward clients.*"

Conversely, trainees can get less responsibility over in commercial litigation: "*At the beginning of the seat I was paginating documents,*" said one. "*I've worked until 10pm, midnight, even two in the morning, paginating documents,*" said another, but these hours only crop up when a big case builds up a head of steam. Since the merger with Jay Benning, the property department has expanded and "*there's more work going through it now.*" In the Leeds office, the property department handles both commercial and residential work and is generally home to first-years. "*There is scope for doing lots of different bits and pieces in property,*" one source said. You could even be called upon to help do research for the corporate department, or be asked to draft a partnership agreement.

still plucky

RadcliffesLeBrasseur is "*looking for something different*" in its trainees. Last year, we were told of a required level of "*pluckiness.*" We heard the same again this year, which either proves that it's true or that even trainees read this book! So, as one 2002 interviewee saw it: "*You've got to have balls – a pluckiness – but without being obnoxious and arrogant.*" Another source said, "*You are given a lot of responsibility, and naturally it is scary, but you just deal with it.*" The firm is looking for the assured confidence that comes with knowing who you are and what you are all about. "*It isn't a case of 'this is our house style'. They allow individuality…they won't clone you.*" In 2002 the firm offered jobs to nine out of the 11 qualifying second-years, and all but one accepted.

No one's pretending that the firm handles the biggest deals in the City, but trainees know that a deal's a deal irrespective of how many noughts are on the price tag. Smaller deals and smaller teams mean trainees get closer to the front line. There's a generalist nature to many of the seats on offer, which has the effect of making sure trainees don't over specialise and do receive a rounded training. You'll have an appraisal in the middle of each seat with your supervisor and the training partner. Partners also oversee everything that trainees do and give regular feedback. "*You learn so much just from listening to them on the phone,*" said a source. "*They take you to meetings and you can see how they capture a room.*"

frogmen of sw1

Throughout our interviews, we heard that RadcliffesLeBrasseur employees are a sociable bunch, wherever they are in the country. Things are a little less hectic in Leeds, largely due to the smaller size of the office, yet "*if anyone wants to go for a drink, be it secretaries, fee earners or office juniors, everyone goes out.*" Ad hoc works. In London, things are more organised: a social committee (originally started by trainees) has *"captured the imagination of the firm,"* reported a source, tongue firmly in cheek. Certain activities are far removed from run-of-the-mill dinners and theatre trips (although these are on offer too). *"We've had wine-tasting and frog tours,"* said one trainee. Frog tours? *"You get in amphibious vehicles and do the tour of London thing, then go down by the side of the MI6 building into the Thames, a bit like Chitty Chitty Bang Bang."* Rather spoils the James Bond illusion, doesn't it?

The social committee recently embarked on a new project: monthly breakfasts. These informal events offer orange juice, bacon sarnies and, importantly, *"a good opportunity to drop in and meet people."* And after work, The Marquis of Grandby, just around the corner from the office, is a popular haunt for all levels of the firm, partners and all.

and finally…

RadcliffesLeBrasseur has even more to offer than in the past. If you crave massive deal after massive deal and foreign travel, it's probably not the place for you, but if the idea of decent work and early responsibility appeals, then dust off your frogman suit.

Reed Smith Warner Cranston

the facts

Location: London, Coventry
UK ranking by size: 114
Total number of trainees: 13
Seats: 4x6 months
Alternative seats: None

In January 2001, London and Midlands firm, Warner Cranston, a self-styled "City boutique law firm" took on a transatlantic twist by merging with American firm, Reed Smith. No partners have left, more have been hired, and the UK partnership's turnover has increased.

a tale of two cities

The London office is the larger of the two in the UK and takes eight trainees. Coventry has been a full-service office (and hence able to take its own trainees) for two years now, and currently has three of them. Coventry may seem an odd location, but it is not a regional offshoot handling purely Midlands work. It has clients from all over the UK, France and the US. Work is divided between the two offices, not according to the client's location, but according to the expertise of the partners. Consequently, trainees in both offices should be exposed to high-quality work. Training is managed centrally, and there are some shared training sessions. These are often cleverly patched through by conference phone or on powerpoint, but Coventry trainees sometimes go to London for workshops. Since the firm tries to recruit people who are committed to either London or Coventry, the issue of moving offices never really comes up.

In London, there are four main departments. Trainees spend a year in the business and finance department, then six months in litigation and six months in either property or employment. In the future, there may be some scope for doing a stint in either tax or company secretarial within the business and finance year. Coventr trainees do six months in each of the four departments – commercial property, corporate/commercial, employment and commercial litigation. It's not the biggest firm in the UK (which, naturally, is why many of you are reading this feature) and so the seat choice isn't huge, but the different departments offer a wide range of work. If you want to take a more generalist approach to commercial law, then small- and medium-sized firms win hands down. Two out of three of the September 2002 qualifiers chose to stay on with the firm.

Warner Cranston attracted some large and prestigious clients even before its merger, but with the American backup, it can flex a bit more muscle. Of late, it has acted on large deals for Eurostar and the sale of the Aroma chain of coffee shops by its client McDonald's. Other significant clients include Barclays and Swiss Re.

flat-packed

All our sources told us how flat the firm is. They didn't mean that everyone has a personality like a wet Monday; rather that everyone's pretty much on a level. Trainees feel a part of the team from day one and find that they can *"talk to the managing partner in the same way as they can with the other trainees and support staff."* Everyone knows and talks to everyone, even if they've been sent to (or were always in) Coventry. *"You get to take the mickey out of the partners and they like it because they can be rude back without feeling like they've upset you."* When asked if the atmosphere in this firm marked Warner Cranston out from other firms of its size, the reply was: *"It marks it out from most firms of any size!"* The firm's working style is a practical one. *"We never bombard people with the law; it's more about practical commercial solutions."* So would it suit trainees looking for a less academic approach? *"I feel more like a business advisor as I have great client relations, and we're instantly taught to explain things in layman's terms."*

tales from the deep

"If you're someone who needs to feel appreciated and not like pond life, then you'll like it here." Be ready to take on responsibility though: *"When you've done something once, they'll leave you to get on with it next time. It can be unnerving, but there's always someone to ask."* Trainees are supervised by a partner, who will generally involve them as much as possible in transactions. At meetings, they are introduced to clients as junior lawyers, and they instantly become a point of contact for them. *"Clients know who I am and I speak to them on the phone and via e-mail,"* confirmed one source. There are *"no silly hours"* and it's perfectly acceptable to come in at 9.30am and leave at 5.30pm if you really aren't busy. In Coventry, they actually lock the office doors at 7pm and only partners have keys. Shame!

"There isn't a type of person that you think would be fine here or one that wouldn't," was the rather unhelpful answer we got to our question about who'd fit in at the firm. *"You have to be commercially oriented, or at least have a willingness to learn,"* one offered, eventually. If those we chatted to are anything to go by, then trainees are generally confident and chatty. The current Coventry trainees seemed to be older than the norm, having had previous careers. Apparently, *"the firm doesn't judge too much on what university you went to; it just wants someone capable."*

show me the money

In London, the firm has just moved to from one funky premises into another on the south bank of the Thames, doubling its floor space in the process. Apparently, most of the partners are quite young and venture out of the office for drinks along with everyone else. Sometimes they even pay. *"That's the only reason we want them there,"* one trainee said, surely joking. In London, Thursdays and Fridays see excursions to The Mughouse, The Anchor or over the river at Shoeless Joe's. The Wine Wharf is another firm favourite, but it's pricey, *"so we don't go there unless there's a credit card around"* – don't you mean a partner? If sport is your thing then you'll be able to join the London 'US firms' softball league, or play football (our type not their type) or cricket against clients. Does Ronald know how to play cricket?

The Coventry social scene is *"very much at the embryonic stage"* but the office is expanding. Trainees from both offices enjoyed a weekend in Baltimore in 2002, which enabled them to meet up with some of their US peers.

and finally…

Quality of work, quality of work and quality of work are the reasons trainees are drawn to Reed Smith Warner Cranston. Oh…and a pretty good bunch of colleagues.

Reynolds Porter Chamberlain

the facts
Location: London
UK ranking by size: 52
Total number of trainees: 18
Seats: 4x6 months
Alternative seats: None

RPC has one of the largest and most respected insurance and reinsurance practices in the country. Besides its Holborn office, it also has a second 'City' office located in the thick of things near Lloyd's of London. The firm labels itself as 'an exceptional law firm' so we thought we'd find out just how exceptional it was.

up in court
Seat allocation works well. "*You generally get two, maybe three of the seats you choose.*" "*They don't say you have to do particular seats, but the reality is you will have to do at least one insurance seat.*" The seat could be in solid insurance/reinsurance, or professional liability, or healthcare (NHSLA clinical negligence). Away from the bread-and-butter activity, there is a lot of competition for corporate seats. One trainee explained: "*Basically there are only two non-contentious seat options – corporate and property – and a lot of people don't want property.*" And just in case you haven't already checked, our parent publication, *Chambers UK*, ranks the firm for its work in defamation, education and family; each takes a trainee, as does employment.

You'll definitely get a chance to hone your advocacy skills at RPC. "*I've got a fair amount of advocacy experience – most of us have, given the nature of the firm.*" In your first year, you'll have to assist the outdoor clerks (on a rota system), which involves both court appearances and agency work. Fear not, most advocacy will be "*applications before a District Judge or a Master – they won't give trainees anything too difficult.*"

tales of the city
The 'City' office is "*hugely busy and getting busier*" and is renowned for being tough on trainees. Our sources told us: "*It's hard work there, you're really thrown in at the deep end,*" and "*trainees there do much longer hours than in our main office.*" That said, you will get "*fantastic legal training*" and if you want to qualify into insurance, the work is of an incredibly high standard. There are two insurance seats available in the City office, although, according to some of our interviewees, "*it would be easier on the trainees if there were three.*"

After you join a department, you'll receive work from several partners. One will become your supervisor and monitor your work. Responsibility "*varies from seat to seat…I've done everything from bundling right up to going out and taking witness statements from people and running my own files. That's what being a trainee should be about – a wide range of stuff.*" Hear! Hear! Another trainee said, "*We have a paralegal team but I would be lying if I said I hadn't done bundling before. However, I've never heard any trainee complain that they're doing too much of it or too much photocopying.*"

talking points
Trainees are automatically invited to any talk or seminar put on within the firm and many of these carry a three-line whip. In terms of raising issues, there are "*four points of contact if you have a problem.*" There is a minder system (no, not like Arfur and Tel – ask your parents) whereby, if you have any queries, you can consult a partner from the training committee. Then there's your supervisor or HR, and finally, for first-years, there's a 'buddy system', whereby a second-year is appointed to look after each newbie and answer "*basic questions.*"

So is there any room for improvement in the training? One source said, "*The review system could be slightly improved…I've never had any horrendously bad reviews, they're always a nice chat.*" So what's the problem? "*I've never had any really good constructive criticism – I've had to raise any problems rather than have them raise it with me.*" Another trainee confirmed this: "*I've never had anyone take me aside for ten minutes and chat about work – it's just something they haven't thought of doing." Anything else? "Closer relations between the City and Holborn offices. The City office is almost a separate entity and I don't really know what's going on over there."

getting in the door…

The Holborn office is "a 1960s block – the client meeting rooms are lovely, but I'm not being unprofessional when I say we have a pretty appalling staffroom." Oh dear. "It's basically two tables, a really old sofa and a drinks machine with a copy of The Times and The Daily Mail. Nobody goes there – well, only a handful." Another trainee concurred: "I've never worked anywhere where there's nowhere to have a break – most of us go out for lunch or eat a sandwich at our desks." On a positive note, the corporate floor has recently been refurbished "to a high standard," and the other floors are likely to follow suit in the near future.

Those we spoke to were all clear about why they chose RPC. "The majority of trainees don't want to work in the top ten. They chose this firm specifically because there's more emphasis on a life outside the office. In addition, because it's a litigation firm, I'd say we all probably wanted to do some kind of litigation ultimately." Another trainee noted: "From the bigger firms you hear stories about trainees not getting home and having to stay all night, where the law really is your life." Four of the six qualifying trainees stayed with the firm in September 2002.

One trainee explained to us that RPC, like all medium-sized firms, is looking for academic ability and committed, hard-working trainees. "But they also want people with a CV showing an interest in life outside of law." Another interviewee confirmed this, explaining that the firm wants above average all-rounders. "If you're very straight with no personality, even if you're super bright, you're not the person they're looking for. They'd rather have people with personalities, especially given our heavy client contact." And this is exactly the point. Insurance clients give a lot of repeat business, year after year. The ability to get on with others and forge relationships with these clients is key. Interestingly, the interviewees all stressed the importance of "fitting in." "You must be involved as much as possible – being a team player is encouraged." Another trainee commented: "You couldn't just go through and keep your life outside work totally separate. You're never just encouraged to go and do work by yourself. It's important to get on with everyone."

…and out the door

RPC doesn't have a long-hours culture. "If you averaged my entire training contract, they'd probably work out to about 9.00am to 6.30pm with an hour for lunch." Another trainee pointed out, "If the work's in and you've got to get it done, they wouldn't be very happy if you left early. However, in a week when the work's under control, you can leave earlier." The trainees in the City office work longer hours; "often from 8am till 8pm each day."

Our sources were keen to stress the social side of RPC. "The culture here is both work and play – the firm is very good on social events." On the first Thursday of every month there are firm-wide drinks in a local pub, The Three Cups. First Thursday drinks seemed to have fallen from favour, when we interviewed, however. "It's not all that well-attended these days," one trainee admitted. The pub closed down for a while for renovations and the occasion has "yet to be fully revived." Leaving aside the recuperating First Thursday, there are four firm-wide parties a year. The Christmas party is "a big dress-up affair" and the summer party is always fancy dress. "Last year it was an Oscars party, this year it's rumoured to be school disco." And that's when we decided to change the conversation… We later found out it had a plain old Jubilee theme.

and finally…

If billion pound corporate deals are your thing, this is not be the place for you. But if you're keen to get hands-on contentious work, it's got your name written all over it. As one source said, "It's a big enough firm to get high-quality work but small enough to know exactly who everyone else is…our reputation is high even though our size isn't the biggest." Well, size isn't everything!

Richards Butler

the facts
Location: London
UK ranking by size: 41
Total number of trainees: 45
Seats: 4x6 or 3x6+2x3 months
Alternative seats: Overseas seats, secondments
Extras: Pro bono – St Botolph's Project, Liberty; language training

Renowned for its work in shipping and media, Richards Butler is a charming medium-sized commercial firm that's rich in international offices, interesting work and characterful lawyers.

we are amused
Over 60% of the London office's revenue is generated from overseas clients, which in 2002 earned the firm a Queen's Award For Enterprise in International Trade. With dual-qualified lawyers from across the globe, several 'foreign' trainees, and a handful of British polyglots, the offices are *"really rather cosmopolitan."*

You'll be laughing all the way to the end of the week with the variety of seats on offer. Insolvency, planning, banking, corporate, employment, shipping, media and more…For those drawn to foreign shores, there are postings in Athens, Piraeus, Abu Dhabi, Hong Kong and Paris. Some trainees jump at the chance of a client secondment, and with big names such as MTV, the BBC and Rank to choose from, who'd blame them? As you'd expect, the competition for the sexiest positions is stiff, but *"with a comparatively small intake you are almost guaranteed to get at least two of the seats you want."* Is this a trainee utopia?

Well, no doubt this very question is hotly debated by the Trainee Solicitors Committee. With each intake, two new trainees are elected to represent their peers in meetings with the senior partner and the head of HR. Up and down the country such forums are used to discuss things like seat allocation, social budgets and biscuit rations. And it's no different at Richards Butler. When the basic training format recently changed from five seats of varying length to four seats of six months each, it was only after a lengthy consultation process through this channel.

not drowning but waving
Secondments and overseas placements aside, the most popular seats are litigation, where *"trainees are absolutely loving it"* and media, *"which is really popular, yet inexplicably only has room for a single trainee."* Other niche seats include IP and employment, generally reserved for second-years. There are no compulsory seats, but most trainees can expect to do a stint in corporate and either shipping or general litigation.

Don't expect to be able to touch the bottom all the time: *"Partners trust you enough to get stuck in. You are not there just to answer the phone and take messages."* You could be running your own small files in property and finance seats, advising UK-based clients on the law in other jurisdictions in employment, or applying your new skills in a shipping office overseas. We heard of one trainee who had only been at the firm for three months when she was sent to Macedonia and then Piraeus on a due diligence exercise. For another, fear turned to elation when given a file to manage involving the sale of a ship. *"When you realise that you have finished something you didn't think you could possibly do, it is a real high."* We bet it is. If you are a wimpy intellectual swimmer, you had best bring your orange armbands and float along to work.

For the doggy paddlers, lifeguard and swim-coach support in the form of trainer and supervisor will not only give feedback at the end of a seat, but will talk technique mid-stream. With a personal fitness coach (or 'mentor') to help with the dry-side training, you should cruise through your training contract.

shiny happy people
We hate such clichés but the firm has a *"work hard, play hard"* take on daily life. You'll work the odd late night (sometimes very late) and the odd weekend, but none of our sources thought this was out of the

ordinary or much of a bind. As one trainee told us: "*I had to do a weekend's work, but I would feel guilty complaining about it – it was in Athens, after all!*" Another said, "*If you are the kind of person who wants to go to the biggest firm, which generates the most revenue, and you want to work till midnight because it makes you feel good, then don't come here!*" Our sources pointed to mature trainees who'd crossed over to the law from diverse sectors of industry. "*The firm doesn't discriminate on grounds of age or background; it is interested in what you have done with your life and where you are headed.*"

Our researcher was keen to get to the bottom of the general happiness felt by trainees, so he dug for dirt…and found more joy. "*People make an effort to show appreciation for the work you have done. They are very polite, and there isn't an aggressive, consciously 'corporate' way of doing things, just a serious attitude to work.*" The regularity of 'happy quotes' became quite sickening, convincing us that it is either true, or that all the trainees brains are linked (à la *The Simpsons*) to an electrical device delivering body-convulsing shocks to anyone uttering treacherous words. In past years we've always noted how realistic and pragmatic RB trainees were about their lot in life, so making this year's happyheads all the more convincing. And the happiness looks set to continue: in September 2002, 11 out of the 12 qualifiers were offered jobs and all accepted.

the big heist

Situated in an imposing building with "*an archway bigger than Marble Arch,*" the firm is currently expanding its existing office space into the atrium on the ninth and tenth floors. Aha! We come to RB's side of Barlow Lyde & Gilbert's 'Richards Butler stole our atrium' story. Interested parties may wish to cross-refer to the feature we've written about this neighbouring firm. The building (owned by Colonel Gaddafi, we're informed) is home to the centrepiece of the firm's social scene. Existing long before Ms McBeal and her tuneful colleagues, the 531 Club (so named because it begins as soon after knocking-off time as possible) serves up a monthly supply of free booze and a large function room – The Dome – plays host to the Christmas fancy dress party. Everyone attends the larger do's, from trainees right up to the chairman.

"*People are laid-back and easy to get on with and not at all snotty like you might find at some of the biggest firms. They tend to be unique individuals with distinct personalities.*" On summer days, staff (only some of them barking) lounge in the midday sun on the roof terrace, or in the neat little gardens fronting the building. With dress-down Fridays, the atmosphere sounds distinctly chilled. In last year's *True Picture*, we described Richards Butler trainees as the kids at school who got on with everyone and didn't care that they weren't wearing the 'right' trainers. We stand by that comment; the firm in general is "*not over the top towards image.*" They certainly seem to be a sociable and genuinely supportive bunch of individuals though.

pure poetry

Although Aldgate East is the wild frontier of the City, on a weekly basis trainees, fee earners and support staff alike venture forth to one or other of the three nearby Poet pubs. Perhaps in an effort to limit confusion, the Slug & Lettuce chain has consumed one of the three Poets, although "*it is exactly the same as it always was.*" For those not keen on gastropods, two Poets remain – The Poet and The New Poet. It seems the trainees are a little more inventive than the publicans of the area, and they have renamed these The Green Poet and The Purple Poet. Our researcher tried to work out which was which and then had to go and lie down in a darkened room.

and finally…

If you are uncertain of the field in which you'd like to specialise, but don't want to get lost in a sea of new faces at a megafirm, Richards Butler ought to appeal. We must confess that these trainees refresh the parts of us that others rarely reach.

Russell-Cooke

the facts
Location: London
UK ranking by size: 113
Total number of trainees: 12
Seats: 4x6months
Alternative seats: None

A smaller but well-respected practice with three offices in and around London, Russell-Cooke offers a varied training in surroundings to suit.

balancing act
This is the sort of place that people come to in search of a manageable balance between work and life. In the firm's own words, the kind of trainee they want is "independent-minded." In return they promise a "humane, sensible working environment." Everything our interviewees said reinforced this point. *"The firm is relaxed and straightforward,"* one said, quite simply. Another expanded, saying: *"The atmosphere depends very much on the department that you're in. The partners in the more established areas tend to be more traditional."* The firm has Investors In People accreditation.

Russell-Cooke is also the sort of place you might come to if you want to sample various areas of work before taking the plunge and specialising on qualification. If you've known since the age of ten that corporate tax or high-value M&A deals are for you, then Russell-Cooke won't suit, but for those of you not yet ready to choose between corporate or private clients, it has much to offer. *"I came here for the good reputation and the diverse work,"* confirmed one source. Another told us that the training lets you keep your options open.

it's all in the mix
The largest branch – Putney – is described as *"the unofficial head office"* and is where many of the administrative functions are performed. It can offer trainees seats in personal injury, crime, commercial property, private client, non-legally aided family, company/commercial, employment and residential conveyancing. Its lower overheads mean that work for individuals is financially viable. Depending on who we spoke to, Putney is split into three, four, five or even six buildings (the official word is that there are actually just three!). *"It's a real rabbit warren,"* said source and in this sense, it can feel a little *"disparate."*

The Bedford Row office, in the legal heart of the capital, deals primarily with commercial and contentious property work, criminal and professional regulatory matters. In the main, its clients are corporate and it plays host to two trainees at any one time. It's a considerably smaller office, but *"there are some decent people there and you're in town so you get to go out all the time."* *"The hours are generally excellent,"* said one source, adding that the commercial litigation seat is a touch more demanding on that score.

The third office in Kingston upon Thames is just a few miles further south west from Putney. Acting for local authority clients it is well regarded for its children's law cases as well as legally aided family work plus crime and residential conveyancing. Bringing home the point that you need to pick the right office for any particular speciaslism, one interviewee stated: *"If you want to concentrate on legally aided family work you have to work in Kingston."*

speak up
Trainees move between the offices during their training. Most spend at least a year in Putney, usually taking in one other office, and occasionally both. The first seat is allotted by the firm and then you'll have a say in the next three. It is described as *"accommodating and flexible"* over seat allocation but the advice of one trainee was: *"You've got to be vocal in order to get what you want."* We were also told that *"you should expect to do at least one seat that is property-related."*

Some trainees are hell-bent on working for the private clients in family, crime or PI, while others clearly favour the commercial departments. A number of our sources indicated a drive to promote the commercial side of the practice: *"They are trying to aim towards 50/50 commercial/private client. About 40-45% of the clients are corporate clients at the moment. The thing is, we are so well established in Putney that the community expects a strong private client practice from us. I think that's a good thing though."* Bottom line? The broad spread of clients looks set to continue.

oomph!

In practice trainees sit where there is space – several actually have offices of their own. By all accounts there's not a huge amount of internal training sessions but *"they always encourage you to go on external courses."* The approach seems to be that you *"get on with it and ask questions on the job."* Responsibility is high and trainees take an active role in running files, but when there's photocopying and the inevitable grunt work to be done, everyone chips in. *"It wouldn't be fair to be sat at your desk doing nothing to help out."*

"They are looking for people with a bit of oomph, people with their own minds." But, remember, oomph needs to be combined with a willingness to try different things in different locations. Of the good relationships that can be built with colleagues, one of our interviewees said, *"Job satisfaction is 50% what you are doing and 50% who you're doing it with."* Too true! All of the September 2002 qualifiers stayed with the firm.

tales of the riverbank

Sat right next to Putney Bridge, on the main shopping street, there's plenty of hustle and bustle going on all around Russell-Cooke's HQ. After work, favourite haunts include The Fox, Le Piaf (rubbing shoulders with Capsticks' lawyers) and the local Slug & Lettuce. There is a firm-wide summer party held in Kingston every year and an annual *"dressy"* Christmas party. And as if these weren't enough, there's an annual conference where everyone heads off to a smart hotel for speeches, brainstorming and entertainment. Sports are a big thing too with golf, cricket, netball, and sailing all on the agenda. Although small, Bedford Row is thought to be the most sociable of all three offices and Kingston is believed to be the most laid-back of the three. It is in a lovely location right next to the river so many staff go out together for pub lunches.

If you're a devotee of south west London then you'll agree that Putney is a superb location. One such convert said, *"I didn't want to be in the City. City firms are rigid in the way you are expected to behave and do your work."* But if you're not really a fan then *"the location is a bit of a pain."* The debate should be easy to resolve. Why not simply check out SW15 before applying?

and finally…

If you want to sidestep the whole City thing and train with a London firm that's got a style of its own, Russell-Cooke may be just what you're looking for.

Shadbolt & Co

the facts

Location: London, Reigate
UK ranking by size: 106
Total number of trainees: 9
Seats: 4x6 months
Alternative seats: Overseas seats, secondments

At first glance, this firm looks like a niche construction practice, and that's how many in the profession will describe it. Actually, it offers trainees a wider variety of work over its two UK offices in Reigate and London. There are further outposts in Paris, Hong Kong and now Athens and Tanzania.

short cut

The seat system is the standard four by six-month affair, and although trainees don't choose their seats, the impression we get is that the HR department is quite accommodating. There is scope for varying the length of seats, and the fact that so many trainees have previous experience means that, at times, the Law Society permits certain trainees to qualify early. Be prepared to move between the two UK offices, but as Reigate and London are so close, this will be unproblematic. Reigate is the HQ and trainees love it: "*It's London quality work, and London is nearby, but it's not London.*" Reigate is home to construction lawyers and those in various other commercial practice areas; the St Paul's office in the City carries out both contentious and non-contentious construction work. Up until recently, the firm had a second City office in The Minories, which was home to an aviation and marine insurance group. However, these lawyers have now left the firm to become a separate partnership.

poles apart

"*You should definitely expect a seat in contentious construction work as it's the firm's main area, its biggest department and our prime income.*" We understand it accounts for some 40% of turnover. Thankfully, good old-fashioned litigation is no longer the only way to resolve disputes. Arbitration, adjudication, conciliation and mediation are becoming the accepted by the construction and engineering industry and, as a market-leading firm, Shadbolts will ensure that you'll become well-versed in all these methods. Our sources assured us that even if you don't know anything about construction at first, you are likely to find it interesting. "*People think they are going to be spending all their time researching the Scaffolding Act or something but you get a broad grounding in dispute resolution.*"

The construction and engineering industry is a truly international one and the law of choice is usually English. Consequently, an enormous amount of Shadbolts' work is international, allowing trainees to pursue interests in multi-jurisdictional matters. The London office has a great deal of involvement in ICC arbitration and trainees may find themselves acting in a rapporteur role. At every seat rotation, there is a seat offered in Paris (it helps if you speak French), while there is also the possibility of doing a six-month seat in any of the overseas offices. These offices have their own local clients but also advise English clients, and Paris is particularly hot on international arbitration.

drafty rooms

Non-contentious construction work is responsible for about 30% of the firm's turnover and provides trainees with some constructive work of their own. Rather than picking up the pieces after a project has gone wrong, this seat will teach you how to draft the contracts that enable projects to proceed. There are seats in other non-contentious areas like PFI, corporate/commercial and property. Shadbolts also handles contentious work that's unrelated to construction. Following a recent restructuring, commercial litigation is now part of the contentious construction group, and is popular with trainees as it allows them to gain broad experience. Employment law is now practised in a standalone group.

With 26 partners and just 9 trainees, expect a lot of partner involvement in your training. In a smaller firm like this, trainees tend to be given as much responsibility as they can handle. There may not always be the opportunity to run your own files, especially since construction claims can be worth millions of pounds, but you'll feel that your input is valued. "*My research and first draft go a big way towards the final product,*" said one source proudly. Of course, "*no trainee is immune from the curse of the photocopier, but not at the expense of training.*" Client contact is encouraged and trainees are always introduced as a part of the team and a point of contact for clients. Trainees have formal appraisals every six months (with less formal appraisals occurring mid-seat), during which they are expected to evaluate their own performance as well as the quality of the training.

who's dick?

This is a "*high quality firm without being too in-your-face.*" There are no "*namby-pamby mission statements*" and the atmosphere is much more down-to-earth. We must give founding father, Dick Shadbolt, an award for being the partner most frequently mentioned by trainees in this year's *True Picture* research. Don't worry, Dick, it was all positive!

Though each office has a slightly different feel, the firm is *"compact, even across the three offices:"* and *"friendly yet very professional."* As one put it, *"There are no great barriers between the ranks."* This is a place *"where everyone feels valued."* Standard hours hover around 9.30am to 5.30pm and one source hadn't *"been home after 6pm for ages."* At times you'll work later, but when there is work to be done it is a *"team effort"* and *"all hands on deck."* In September 2002, five of the eight qualifiers stayed on deck and remained with the firm.

"Mature self starters… with outside interests" is how the firm describes its dream applicants. We reckon that's just what it's got in its current trainees. They are slightly older than their peers at other firms and they bring a range of experiences with them. Some have worked in construction or engineering, while others are linguists or have worked or grown up overseas. *"Perhaps less than 20% have done the 'straight from university to law school to training contract route'."* Trainees share *"a bent towards international law"* and an *"international outlook."* Personalities are equally as diverse but all seem mature and practical with *"a lack of pretentiousness and a hands-on mentality."*

They're sociable but *"not absolutely mad for it every Friday as many have families."* Those who do want to share a drink after work head over to The Venture, across the road from the Reigate office. *"It used to be the Desert Rat…then went all up market!"* By all accounts, Reigate is *"pretty good for restaurants"* and trainees will go out for lunches or dinners from time to time. The Shadbolts cricket team is *"excellent."* Alas, its football team could do with *"some inspired signings."* *"We play like a bunch of lawyers!"*

and finally…

In *Chambers* parlance, this firm punches above its weight in its areas of expertise. Those looking for an international twist to a construction-heavy commercial training would be well advised to apply to Shadbolt & Co.

Shoosmiths

the facts

Location: Northampton, Nottingham, Reading, Solent, Milton Keynes, Basingstoke
UK ranking by size: 43
Total number of trainees: 26
Seats: 4x6 months
Alternative seats: Secondments

Shoosmiths is a rare beast: a national firm with offices spreading from the South Coast right up to the Midlands, and yet none in London. Sounds perfect for those who still want quality work but aren't prepared for London's sky-high housing prices and the daily horrors of the Tube.

burning desire

Shoosmiths has undergone a strategic review and condensed its divisions from three into two – commercial services and personal injury. There are no compulsory seats, although most time is spent in commercial services. For those who want them, there are also occasional secondments to clients such as Abbey National, Daimler Chrysler and Hogg Robinson.

Northampton has the largest number of departments and the largest selection of seats while at the other end of the scale Nottingham has just four seats to offer. Movements between the offices can be arranged. As one Nottingham trainee told us: *"If I'd had a burning desire to do financial litigation or PFI, for example, there might have been room for me to move down to Northampton."* In practice, most stay the full two years in the office into which they were recruited.

satisfaction guaranteed

In September 2002, eight out of ten qualifying trainees said they preferred Shoosmiths NQ positions. From this we can only conclude that the firm is doing right by its youngsters. Certainly, decent hours are one of its selling points. For most an average day means 8.45/9am until 5.30/6pm. *"If you're busy, you wouldn't* expect to walk out the door at half-five, but there's no long hours culture. I've been here once till 9pm and I've been in once at seven in the morning, but I've never done a weekend." As for late hours on Fridays, forget it: most people knock off at 5.15pm. The highlight of the trainee social calendar in 2002 came when the firm paid for them all to go to London, stay in a hotel and attend a dinner at the Atlantic Bar & Grill. Why? *"To get us all together and say 'thanks for all your hard work.'"* We've no doubt that it was like a big, alcohol-fuelled school trip. Trainees enjoy their time together as a group but even when apart, they keep in touch. Proof that some long-distance relationships can work out!

Formal appraisals are supplemented by a good flow of info from your boss or bosses. *"As many of us work near our principal in an open-plan setting, it's easy to get feedback."* Sitting open-plan is great from a trainee's viewpoint as *"you get to hear conversations on the phone and if you've got a problem you can just swing your chair around and shout and everyone can chip in."*

intercity training

As for responsibility and client contact, *"I have some clients I deal with directly and I've done a number of minor applications in the County Court by myself. If you're not ready to get involved quickly, this might not be the place for you."* One trainee sensibly stressed: *"It depends on the department – you won't get a high level of responsibility in corporate, because you can't take on a deal by yourself."* However, in employment or property, *"you get to run files on your own from start to finish"* and *"many clients ring up to speak to you specifically."* As one trainee said, *"They don't just dump you in it and expect you to do everything but they don't mollycoddle you either – the responsibility you're given reflects your abilities, your confidence and your understanding of the work."*

There is a firm-wide trainee Training Day every two months, usually in Northampton but occasionally in Nottingham or Reading. These involve talks from partners and assistants in the morning and after lunch, more practical, interactive soft skills sessions (eg negotiation or stress management).

Training Days are *"good for catching up with trainees from other offices – the firm's very keen on us all interacting."* While on the subject of talking, we heard that *"all the major changes happening in the firm are communicated quite quickly to all staff – they like to keep us informed, even at trainee level."*

balancing act

If there is anything that links trainees, it is a desire to work outside of London. This doesn't mean they are anti-London; on the contrary, one interviewee said, *"I love London but I hate its long hours and fast-paced culture."* While our sources all wanted to join a regional law firm, they didn't want to compromise on the work that would be available to them. As to what the firm wants of its recruits: *"They're looking for people who are confident – able to pick up different tasks and not necessarily get fazed." "The common link is that we're all energetic, enthusiastic and able to use our initiative."* To promote that elusive concept – a healthy work/life balance – a law firm needs to employ staff who value both in equal measure. Shoosmiths' trainees tell us they fit that bill: *"We're all proficient and hard-working, but we're sociable and well-rounded."* As for who might not fit in so well, we understand that *"really bookwormy people wouldn't have the best of times – you really do need a personality and you need to be practical."*

A point to note: the firm has a permanent dress-down policy across all its offices, except for Northampton, where it's just Thursdays and Fridays. The slogan for this policy – "act smart, dress casual" – is even printed on Shoosmiths' sweatshirts. In a moment of enlightenment the powers that be decided dress-down should mean just that so even jeans are acceptable. The picture that emerges is a straightforward practical attitude to getting the job done. No airs and graces, no divas or demons, no slavery or martyrdom. Investors In People award? Duh… of course!

We wondered if life at Shoosmiths was the same across the country. From what we can gather, local accents and slight variations in clients and work aside, the answer is yes.

391

northampton: shooworld

Based in a business park just off the M1, the firm's HQ is known as The Lakes. "*It's a bit of a nature corner*" with "*lots of water, fountains and birds out the back*" and a tennis court in the carpark. The office goes against the national trend in that a number of departments have not gone open-plan. The work is primarily commercial, and while there is a small personal injury department, by far the bulk of the firm's PI work is done in the serious injuries unit in Basingstoke. The dozen trainees hang out together a fair bit. Every Friday there's a drinks party open to all staff, although "*it's mainly the same diehards who turn up every week, so the firm is trying to publicise the event a bit more widely.*" Shoosmiths' annual summer party is also held in Northampton, as is the firm-wide pub quiz (which is no doubt a hotly contested affair). There are two local pubs – Lakeside is "*a short hop away*" and "*good for a quick drink*" while the Britannia is "*just round the corner*" and described as "*a lively place that lots of Shoosmiths go to for lunch, particularly on Fridays.*"

nottingham: loctite

Located centrally in a modern building next to the canal in Nottingham, it's described as "*a laid-back, down-to-earth office where everyone gets on and everyone knows everyone.*" The three trainees experience commercial litigation, corporate/commercial, employment and commercial property, with their only choice being the order in which they do them. After work, a number of bars beckon, but the two most popular are Via Fossa and the Lock & Lace. One trainee said, "*It's a really friendly office – it's not really a case of secretaries, fee earners and partners going to different bars; we all go together.*"

reading: it means business

This is another out of town office just five or six minutes' walk from The Oracle – "*a big shopping centre with cafés and bars that are handy for lunchtimes.*" There's a fair bit of IT work kicking around, reflecting the Thames Valley's leaning towards technology business. There are four trainees in the office at any one time and seats are available in corporate/commercial, property and employment. Personal injury is available in the firm's special injuries unit in Basingstoke should a trainee wish to go there. Staff generally make merry on Friday nights, and invariably this means a trip to The Turks. Recently its social committee organised a skittles evening and a trip to Ascot.

solent: coasting along nicely

The Solent office is also "*on a business park,*" this one at Fareham on the side of the M27. Spurning the open-plan plan, its two trainees share offices with their principals. The key departments are litigation, commercial property and corporate/commercial, with employment, landlord and tenant and construction also present. "*The Solent office has quite a lot of young people*" and is of a size that means the whole mob tend to go out together as an office. The core group is made up of "*five- to six-year qualifieds right down to first-year trainees.*" If you're looking to neck a quick drink, The Parson's Collar will suffice but, as one source put it: "*If we want to go out properly, we tend to go to Southampton, which is only seven miles away.*" Near the office are a shopping centre, a sandwich bar and a gym.

milton keynes: around and about

MK is just 16 miles from Northampton so a number of fee earners split their time between these branches. It's a reasonably small and "*quite intimate*" office, with "*something like 30-35 desks in total.*" It offers seats in corporate/commercial, property and employment. The five trainees frequent the local Wetherspoons hostelry for pub lunches and, on a Friday, most make the trek to the drinks party in-house up at The Lakes.

and finally…

Shoosmiths is a thoroughly decent firm with clients and work to match. It's clearly been busily recruiting and retaining some particularly level-headed and down-to-earth trainees in the last few years. You just might want to become one of them.

Sidley Austin Brown & Wood

the facts
Location: London
UK ranking by size: 80
Total number of trainees: 10
Seats: 4x6 months
Alternative seats: None

Sidley Austin Brown & Wood came together in 2001 as the product of the merger of two US firms – Sidley & Austin and Brown & Wood. It's a huge international organisation, but a London training contract will provide a distinctive and intimate English experience.

time lords
The London office has a strong finance focus and particular strength in capital markets. As one trainee said quite bluntly: *"You would be pretty stupid to apply without knowing this. You probably wouldn't even get past the interview."* If mainstream/corporate finance and specialised structures leave you cold then look elsewhere. The international finance group (IFG) and the corporate departments power this office, and it is these departments that offer the majority of post-qualification opportunities. There are two other departments – tax and property – but trainees estimate that around 80% of the work in these are by way of support for corporate and finance transactions. In July 2002 the property department received a boost with the arrival of two partners from Denton Wilde Sapte.

The firm operates a four by six-month seat system, but it is possible to bend or stretch time according to your particular interests or to ease the pressure in departments with a particularly full-on workload.

parlez-vous finance?
All trainees begin with a seat in IFG – it needs the most trainees. As a first seat, it's a challenge. *"Law school just can't prepare you,"* our sources said. *"Some of the stuff is totally deal-based and you just can't teach it."* First you need to get your head around the jargon. *"I thought, people are going to pay me money to sit here and do this work and I have no idea what they are talking about!"* But sooner than you think, you start to speak their language: *"Although there is only so much time supervisors can devote to a trainee when they are busy, it's amazing how much you pick up by being immersed in it."*

The other seats are done in the three remaining departments. Corporate is small and popular, but growing (although it relies heavily on the IFG and other offices of the firm, particularly the US offices, for much of its work and clients). The bulk of the corporate team came from Sidley & Austin as Brown & Wood was so finance-oriented. The merged firm set about building up the corporate practice and, quite recently, following the arrival of a big cheese from Pinsent Curtis Biddle, an insolvency group was set up.

course proceedings
Sharper readers may have noticed that there is no litigation department. So how do trainees get the required contentious experience? The answer is simple: a course run over four weekends at Nottingham Law School's London outpost. *"I quite enjoyed the course as it was good to get the trainees together, but there is no substitute for practical experience,"* thought one source. But it's fair to say that none of our sources were interested in becoming litigators. *"If you're going to stay with us on qualification, there's not much point knowing about litigation because if it gets to that stage then we haven't been doing our job properly."*

For those who have made a decision to work in a City firm but aren't sure if a focus on finance is really what they're after, one trainee's words may assist: *"Finance is actually very interesting here. It's not just negotiating loan agreements – we do lots of cross-border transactions involving different elements of law."*

across the pond life
One of the key reasons trainees apply to the firm is its US origins. As one said, *"I knew very little about international finance but I quite liked all things American."*

The firm has six US offices and four more in Asia but trainees don't undertake overseas placements. London was Sidleys' only European outpost until it recently nabbed a small Geneva office from a rival. In last year's book we reported on merger talks with a German firm, von Boetticher Hasse Lohmann, but these were put on ice in the spring of 2002. Most London-based lawyers are English but this did not disappoint our sources: "*Lots of our clients are from the States and we interact with lots of our American colleagues. We dial internally to go through to Chicago.*"

snooze you lose

In finance, "*the hours aren't desperately good,*" but that goes for any firm handling this calibre of work. Clients like Morgan Stanley, Lehman Brothers and Deutsche Bank don't expect their lawyers to work Sleepyville hours. The average trainee day in IFG runs from 9am to 6.30/7pm, but at the height of a transaction you'll see much more of the office. "*I worked until about 11pm two to three times a week for a couple of weeks and then up until 5am on one night,*" recalled one source. With only a dozen trainees and more than enough work to go round, your role in a deal will be crucial. "*I've always sat down at the beginning and had the whole transaction explained to me,*" one reported. Of course trainees do find themselves photocopying or proofing on occasions, but when that happens, "*I understand why. Partners are aware that you are on a training contract, not a cheap labour contract, and they take their training responsibilities seriously.*" There were a few moans about formal appraisals, in that they could be more regular, but we understand the training head honcho has taken this on board.

Hi-de-hi!

Trainees gushed about the firm's atmosphere. "*We are serious when we have to be, but not at all when we don't.*" It is small enough for everyone to know each other, despite being in two separate offices (a throwback to the pre-merger days). The trainees are a mixed bag. A few are straight out of university; others have had careers (often finance-related) before turning to law. Above all, they are "*very ambitious, very conscientious, enthusiastic, motivated, and up for a laugh.*" And they plan to stay...in 2002 five out of six qualifiers were offered a job and each accepted.

Partners will show up for firm soirees, but don't expect any of them to slip on a holiday rep's jacket and lead you on a pubcrawl. "*They work very hard but understand assistants and trainees have lives outside the office.*" When drinks are suggested, trainees sensibly spend their time "*avoiding the Pitcher & Piano and the Slug & Lettuce!*" A social committee organises go-karting, bingo and bowling and there was recently a "*posh*" barbeque in Gray's Inn and a Christmas party at Claridge's. On occasion, lawyers can be found sharing drinks up on the balcony of the Threadneedle Street office, enjoying the views over the City.

and finally…

This isn't a broad training contract, but for the right applicant it's a great experience that's ripe for the picking. True to most US firms in London, it's a hugely well-paid and challenging job, but the majority of your colleagues will be as English as a fry-up.

Simmons & Simmons

the facts

Location: London
UK ranking by size: 18
Total number of trainees: 101
Seats: 4x6 months
Alternative seats: Overseas seats, secondments
Extras: Pro bono – Battersea Legal Advice Centre, RCJ CAB, language training

Simmons has been a respected name in the City forever. Its main thrust is corporate and financial, and it has some extremely good specialist departments – employment and IP to be more specific. Recent merger talks with Watson, Farley & Williams promised an interesting new dimension to the finance side of the practice and a smattering of new overseas offices. But the deal is off, implying that Simmons is happy enough with who it is already.

a lot of wedge

Trainees select seats from three groups. Two seats must come from the group containing corporate/financial markets, one must be contentious (IP and employment each fall into this category, so you can't do both) and the third group contains departments such as tax, property, environment and private client. This system has been in place for a little over a year, *"so seat choice is not as free as it once was."* There's a preference for getting your core seat at either the second or third rotation, when you are a little less green, but before the point at which you will want to apply for your NQ position. Overall, seat allocation (always hard in a big firm) works well, although *"it feels like it gets more hairy towards the end as you run out of time."* Almost all get to do their number one choice of seat and *"it's very rare you will be sent somewhere against your will."*

Corporate and financial markets are *"bringing in a lot of wedge"* to the firm, but IP and employment are so good that it's easy to fall into the trap of regarding them as the firm's raison d'être. Mistake. *"A fair number choose the firm because of employment and IP… they are only support departments at the end of the day, but they are a draw."* Bottom line: it's a corporate firm and *"you wouldn't get through an interview if you just say you're into IP and employment."* The rest apply to Simmons because it is a City practice with all the benefits that come with it – a great salary, the chance to work overseas, and deals and clients to be proud of.

fire and brimstone

Trainees see themselves as different to their magic circle counterparts, *"but not different in a worse way."* Those with the snobbish view on the point simply need not apply. One trainee explained: *"I applied to the magic circle and then I walked away from my Simmons interview thinking, 'I don't think any other law firm can give me more'."* Another said, *"I was expecting fire and brimstone, but it was a great day."*

Simmons' trainees talked about what they saw as the firm's cultural advantages over bigger rivals: they believe it offers a better working environment. Simmons is *"justifiably proud of its reputation for being an extra nice place to work,"* and the fact that it won 48th place in *The Sunday Times'* '100 Best Companies to Work For' survey for 2002.

riders on the storm

And what of that atmosphere? *"Egalitarian is probably not the right word as the atmosphere differs between departments,"* one source said. Some, such as corporate, have a *"looser"* and less formal feel to them with extremely approachable partners, whereas IP, for example, was identified as having a strong hierarchy with more *"clear partner types."* As one trainee put it: *"Some have been here a long time, since a time when partners were partners and there was none of this team thing."* Another said, *"With older partners you know who they are and you won't stop and chat to them, but the younger ones you have a laugh with."*

Mostly trainees get the impression that *"there's a lot of pride taken in being open to change, especially given what's happened in the last few years. The firm's not stuck in a rut."* This reference to 'the last few years' concerned the period in the late 90s when Simmons' profitability and reputation suffered a dent due to partner defections. It must have been an uncomfortable period for the firm – it was lambasted by the legal press and Simmons-kicking was almost a national sport. Hats off to the firm for riding the storm. Trainees who had an opinion on the subject felt that the difficult years were partly responsible for the way Simmons feels now. There's a sense that it still has something to prove to the outside world. *"I think it is quite driven,"* said one trainee. *"It was driven before, but it was being driven in the wrong direction. I feel now that the partnership feels it's going in the right direction."* Another said, *"It was trying to be something it's* not – it was trying to grow and force its way into the magic circle. We now know we are good at what we do, and so we continue at what we are good at."

naked ambition
If determination is a trait of the firm as a whole, it's especially noticeable in trainees. Ambition is also immediately apparent – they **really** want to do well. When asked to describe the typical trainee, one said, "*Most people are easy to get on with, although not everyone is laid-back or the type I'd immediately be friends with. People are outwardly confident and self-assured...some are very driven. But trainees never come into conflict with each other.*"

It is so important to trainees that the firm be recognised for what it is and what it has achieved. We wondered if the much talked about art on display around the firm was part and parcel of the need to be noticed. You'd be forgiven for mistaking the CityPoint offices for the Tate Modern, what with the Damien Hirst ("*single-handedly kept in business by Simmons*") pieces in the restaurant and the 'inner ear/urinal piece' on the wall of reception. If you get a choice of venue for your interview, ask for meeting room 16 – it's home to 'naked running man'.

rise to the challenge
A good supervisor can make all the difference when you're a trainee, and it seems that HR picks them out with a bit of thought. "*They look at the workload of solicitors and give trainees out that way.*" Responsibility "*completely depends on who you're sitting with. In some I had to rise to the challenge; in another the work wasn't desperately interesting.*" The best are "*completely fantastic and give a lot of thought to what work their trainee is receiving; others (either through being very busy or stressed) didn't give that much thought to training.*"

Our sources discussed the best and worst of being a trainee. "*Using my mind*" ranked highly: "*I've done quite a low level of grunt work. Most of what I've done has involved thought, although obviously there are occasions when you end up photocopying.*" But the desire to be a part of a firm that's going somewhere means trainees seem happy to "*assist in any way you can.*" A gold star for the property department: our sources raved about their time there. Corporate, too, was praised for allowing trainees to get stuck in. Low points include "*exhaustion – heading home at 4am.*" As for formal training sessions, "*there's more than we know what to do with!*"

seeing in the dark
There's a danger in regaling stories about trainees working killer hours, if only because the reality of how hard trainees work depends on the department they're in and the strength of the market. This year's all-nighter could be next year's night in the pub. Or vice versa. Suffice to say that none of our sources had been under the lash and "*hours are not the predominant topic in the pub.*" "*You go home when the job gets done*" and "*pressure comes from yourself.*"

Certain perks have a carrot-like effect though: "*If I finish at or before 7pm then that's it. But if it's 7.30pm I wait for free dinner at 8pm, and after 9pm we get free taxis home.*" The personal ambition of some trainees comes through. "*People are really trying to impress in the departments they want to qualify into. You're thinking, 'What will they remember of me?'*" The fact that there are sought-after seats/NQ jobs means that for those with an eye on them, "*it is competitive.*" Hardly surprising when you consider the fact that the firm has London's top employment team and stomps over most of the competition in IP and certain other areas.

herding cats
It's a big firm so the Corney & Barrow below the office is an important place. The trainee social scene starts strong, "*but tails off and becomes less frequent as you get into the two years.*" This is understandable – corralling 45 of your intake for a night out is a "*logistical nightmare.*" Departmental socials become more important and there are some very quaint traditions at the firm. Tea parties are very much in vogue – Fri-

day afternoons see tables groaning with cakes in IP and the commercial department has regular Friday 5pm drinks.

And this is a firm that loves to love. *"Simmons is quite big on romance. Some of the partners are married to each other, and there are several assistant couples and trainee couples. The only day it's absolutely empty after 6pm is Valentine's Day!"*

see-through

The move to CityPoint last year had a positive effect on the firm. *"It definitely helps with cohesion,"* and the *"swanky"* canteen's a great meeting place. In the same time frame, [goddess] Janet Gaymer has become senior partner. *"She's making a conscious effort towards transparency…you have an awareness of what's actually going on."* Trainees are buoyant and optimistic about the new-look Simmons; one said, *"Simmons used to be quite traditional, but in the year-and-a-half I've been here it has moved on a bit."* It's standard suits Monday through Thursday and then on Fridays and for three months in the summer it's the standard *"City uniform of chinos and a blue shirt."*

For a peek at life as an in-house lawyer you might try for a secondment to one of the firm's clients. Those craving foreign food and the added responsibility of time in an overseas office have plenty to choose from as well, although the usual glamour spots – New York, Paris, Hong Kong, etc – are heavily subscribed. Poor old Düsseldorf on the other hand…

In terms of retention, the firm made 27 offers to the 35 September 2002 qualifiers; all but three accepted.

and finally…

The well-promoted 'nice place to work' label is the genuine article and corporate pride is huge. Applications are welcomed from the intellectually snappy as well as the happy clappy. Do show up to the right place for interview though – if you're sat in reception looking out the window at a wobbly bridge, then you've ended up in the real Tate Modern.

SJ Berwin

the facts
Location: London
UK ranking by size: 23
Total number of trainees: 80
Seats: 4x6 months
Alternative seats: Overseas seats

Having celebrated its 21st birthday in 2002, SJ Berwin barged its way into London's top twenty, unafraid of the older playground bullies. Offering a heady corporate-and-Redbull cocktail, it looks at what you can achieve rather than where you come from. With oodles of energy, its star remains in the ascendant.

work it a little…

"If you aren't prepared to work hard, or you want to blend into the background, don't come here," was the sound advice of one trainee. The firm doesn't make a secret of its 'push it' ethos, and this doesn't stop people applying for, accepting and enjoying training contracts here. Why? *"Because there is good work and you get treated well."* As we highlighted in last year's *True Picture*, there's no evidence of slavery or drudgery, but it aims for fast turnaround times on client requests because *"if we don't, Linklaters will."* SJB is a tough little scrapper of a firm, which has climbed into the ring with the big boys, taken the best body blows thrown at it, grinned and had one hell of a good go back.

Trainees tell us that the firm has *"a nicely balanced hierarchy. It's entrepreneurial and it's definitely not cliquey or stuffy or anything like that."* If you're hunting for a firm with a dynamic, go-ahead style, trainees suggest you plump for SJB. *"It's vibrant, young, ambitious, hard-working, forward thinking and expanding very quickly."*

go team!

Some students work their socks off but leave university with a 2:2 and go on to make great lawyers. Some slack, laze about and drink too much but end up

TRUE PICTURE — OUR TOP 120 FIRMS

with a 2:1 and are appalling at the job. Although it probably doesn't shout about it, SJB realises this. It takes the trouble to find out what you are capable of, rather than assuming 2:1 = great solicitor. *"You get a chance to prove yourself,"* said a proud holder of a lower second class degree. Your Alma Mater is also unimportant. There is *"quite a diverse range of uni backgrounds,"* confirmed one trainee. *"They don't look at your CV and go 'Oh, you're not Oxbridge'."*

We hunted for SJB trainee hallmarks. One insisted, *"We are all slightly barking,"* but the others thought, *"There is absolutely no set type."* We beg to differ. If you hadn't already realised, *"you have to be ambitious, energetic and driven"* to work here. *"If you are more of a conservative, country squire person, it just isn't gonna work."* It is, however, *"a supportive, environment,"* *"so if you send out an e-mail saying 'I've got to do this and haven't a clue', someone will come and say 'You need to do this, this and this'."* Just like on TV's *Catchphrase*, at SJB, 'if you see it, say it': *"They don't think 'He's a trainee and should just sit in meetings and listen';"* you will be expected to give your opinion on matters, both work- and non-work-related. In terms of the latter, *"you can take things to the management without fear, they don't discourage talking."* And usually, *"problems get sorted out quick smart."* The management is always aware of what the competition is up to: *"A little while ago a trainee said, 'Hey, trainees at other firms get more holiday', and the management committee gave us more."* Trainees feel *"well looked after."*

push it for two...

The seat rotation is a four by six-month affair, with enormous differences between seats. Two seats are taken in the corporate division, where there are *"lots of characters."* (Nicely put.) You'll meet with a few who are *"full of themselves…a bit 'We Are The Corporate Department',"* but SJB didn't get where it is today without that type of lawyer. Corporate is split into three departments. Corporate 3 is the successful private equity group (PEG). SJB was one of the first firms to get into this field, and it now sees itself as *"the sexiest department ever."* *"They tend to put first-years in private equity,"* so get ready to doggy-paddle! One trainee said, *"They talk in their own language and you have no idea what it means so initially it is quite scary."* *"It's all very different here,"* another said. *"You get files thrown at you [not literally] and you get to see nuggets of bigger deals."* You'll find the longest hours here too: *"You could be in for two weeks until 11pm and then be expected to do an all-nighter."* Who's got the Pro Plus?

Corporate 1 has a more international feel, involving a little private equity plus M&A, investments and corporate recovery. Expect *"a fair amount of responsibility and some late nights."* Again trainees tell us the late nights are no problem. *"You just get used to it, and you're not fiddling around, so the time just goes. It's only when you stop that you realise you are quite tired."* In Corporate 2 expect to be doing *"research for flotations and rights issues"* for plcs. Trainees here spoke of the odd all-nighter, but *"they let you go home at noon the day after – you aren't expected to do a full day."* On average, our sources left this department at 8pm. *"You don't feel that you can walk out at 6.30pm,"* said one trainee frankly.

hold it for two...

Away from corporate, banking is popular as *"two new partners are bringing in more work and the department is expanding."* It can get a bit hectic there: *"When things are escalating, you can feel like you are losing control, but there are people to bring you back."* In short, *"it can be a bit seat-of-the-pants!"* Employment is hugely popular and hard to get into. *"When you have been to private equity and worked until 2am, and then you go to employment and at 7.30pm they ask what you are still doing in the office, it's a real eye-opener."* Property is *"a very good, cuddly team that everyone wants to get into,"* gushed one trainee. *"Being encouraged every day and patted on the back for the work you've done is brilliant."*

There's a temptation to pull out all the stops and be super-trainee if you win a prized seat in a smaller department that you're eyeing up for qualification. This can turn a very full-on 12 months into a very full-on 18 months. Also, regarding niche seats, *"don't* expect the moon on a stick," as *"sometimes you do have to fight for seats – you have to be realistic about it." "Don't expect niche seats all the way through because it ain't gonna happen,"* warned one interviewee. We heard a few grumbles about seat allocation, with trainee A getting the seat trainee B had asked for and vice versa. *"The person responsible for seat allocation will try to give you the seats you want,"* but make sure they know what you want. And if you fancy a change of scenery, one of the overseas placements to Brussels, Paris, Munich, Frankfurt or Madrid may have you reaching for your passport. Speaking of change of scenery, in September 2002 eight of the 40 qualifiers went looking for pastures new, while 32 stayed with the firm.

and relax!

Although it's a bit of a cliché, there is *"a real feeling of work hard, play hard."* When they hit the tiles, trainees invariably end up in Centro. *"We should buy that bar and make it our own,"* quipped one regular. *"Trevor McDonald is in there most nights, and Channel Five news are there too…and Ant and Dec and the occasional boy band, so it's good for the girls!"* PJ and Duncan? Oh, please! It's just as well SJB pays a top salary as a large glass of wine will set you back close on six quid! The Russian vodka bar, Potemkin, and The Blue Lion are alternative venues, although *"The Lion is just not so nice."* Its saving grace is that it has a late licence.

Trainees lunch together, and will often get invited out by assistants. If you don't want to venture past the front door, the firm has its own dining facilities and all meals are free. On the last Friday of the month there are drinks in the boardroom, and afterwards trainees generally nip off elsewhere for a few. There's no need to take extra glad rags because the firm operates a smart casual policy every Friday. There are occasional departmental socials too, such as Scalextrics evenings, to which entire teams, including secretaries and established clients, are invited. On top of this there are trainee parties at Christmas and in the summer, and a range of sports teams to join.

"The ITN building is fantastic!" SJB's property department enjoys its seventh floor and, with a massive atrium in the middle, it is *"very warm, like a greenhouse."* In contrast, most of the firm lives in the main '222' building, reproduced on much of the firm's literature. It's *"very 1960s"* and *"definitely not Canary Wharf."* During a recent refurbishment, the old 'work pods' were removed, so *"it is looking a hell of a lot better."* Following a trend amongst law firms, there are new 'breakout areas' – *"part of the office with very groovy chairs where you can go and relax and chill." "The original chairs were very yellow and bright; now they are black leather, very meeja!"* boasted one excited trainee, before muttering in Oliver Twist-like tones: *"But we don't actually get to sit and chill there. We don't have the time."*

and finally...

SJ Berwin is nitro-fuelled and loaded with character. If you have more get up and go than the average applicant, you'll fit right in. Trainees work hard, right enough, but just try shifting the smiles from their faces. If you're looking for a challenge, get your skates on. Can we go and lie down now?

Slaughter and May

the facts

Location: London
UK ranking by size: 11
Total number of trainees: 158
Seats: 4x6 months
Alternative seats: Overseas seats
Extras: Pro bono – Islington Law Centre, language training

One of the most profitable law firms in the universe, the inner workings of Slaughter and May are somewhat shrouded in mystery and most often judged on hearsay. It steadfastly refuses to play by other firm's rules and you won't find its representatives standing around at law fairs trying to woo you with freebie stationery, stress toys or chocolates. The recruitment brochure is minimalist and high-ply and it avoids the ubiquitous, cheesy photos of young execs having the time of their lives. This is a highly successful law firm, not a holiday camp.

general selection

You can read up about sky-high partner profits and supersonic corporate deals in the legal press – and we recommend that you do. Once digested, you'll understand why the firm's work is held in such high regard and why its partners are loaded. But the two things we really wanted to know were how exactly the firm differs from others in the magic circle, and where certain ideas of frostiness come from.

Slaughters' generalist approach to law seems to distinguish it from its peers. As a corporate lawyer you'll get exposure to a broad range of work, rather than being required to narrow your field of vision. *"Here you are first and foremost a corporate lawyer not, for example, an oil and gas lawyer."* We're not saying that Slaughters doesn't have specialists, just that, as a youngster, you won't be pushed into becoming one. This is a real bonus when starting out, especially if you have little idea about what you want to practise. *"When I had my interview I was studying literature and didn't know the first thing about law,"* admitted one. *"I'm useless at making decisions,"* confessed another. To take on this generalist approach, *"you've got to be versed in many different areas of law, which may be a bit more stressful but it makes it less boring."* To an extent *"it's a philosophical difference about what makes a good lawyer,"* and you don't have to be a genius to realise that it takes a lot of work to keep all your bases covered.

For many, the initial appeal is Slaughters' no-nonsense request for a CV and covering letter, rather than an extended essay on leadership and courage in times of adversity. At interview you won't get grilled on the technicalities of cross-border M&A, you'll just have a relaxed chat with a partner to see if you get on with them. And the secret to succeeding at interview? *"Just be honest and be yourself. If you want to get a training contract at any cost, you can prepare answers to all the usual silly questions, but, at the end of the day, if you manage to get through without being honest you're unlikely to enjoy working there,"* advised one trainee. We learn something new every day researching this book: apparently, *"honesty is the key to happiness."* In the same way, you won't get wooed, wined or dined by the firm in its attempt to capture your attention on a vac scheme. *"It's not out to be overly friendly and give you a false impression of what the work is all about."*

prime cuts

Another thing that makes Slaughters that bit different is its international strategy. Rather than rolling out the same brand across the world, Slaughters has only half a dozen offices in the main commercial centres, and combines these with a network of 'best friends'. *"The policy here is to do what we do best, which is English law. If we need expertise in German law then we use German lawyers."* It's the delicatessen approach to the law. Nowadays you can get perfectly good olives and salami in Tesco, but if you want the best, you've got to know where to look. Trainees would have you believe it's the same with these lawyers. *"Clients don't come to Slaughters if they just want to get the job done. There are plenty of places around that will charge less. People come here to get things done in a different way."* The Slaughters way.

There's an emphasis on individualism. *"Even though you work in a team, ultimately you are on the line. They are keen to emphasise that it's all about individual judgement. It's very hands-off in terms of management; they let you do the work the way you want to do it."* Another trainee agreed: *"They care about the quality of the work not the approach you take to it."* The upside is that *"this isn't just a lawyer factory."* The downside is that things might get *"a bit chaotic at times."* You may have heard the expression that managing lawyers is like herding cats. Well, we get the impression it's particularly true at this firm.

After deep thought, one trainee explained their attraction to a life in the law: *"I like using Dictaphones."* For most, it was a more considered choice.

The firm undertakes to train you from scratch in everything, but expects you to arrive with a good grasp of the fundamental principles of law, so pay attention to your studies now. Many trainees admit that commercial nous was not something they'd started off with. "*I still don't read the FT as much as I should,*" one confessed. Rather than hard-nosed commerciality, what trainees bring to the firm is a problem-solving ability. In a spot check you'd be more likely to find a chess set or a crossword than a Monopoly board (let alone a PlayStation) hidden in a desk drawer.

As befits a corporate-driven firm, trainees will typically spend 12 months in corporate seats, a seat in something contentious and then a seat in something more niche, like property, pensions and employment, IP or tax, for example. "*People are generally keen to do corporate work. When you come to a good firm you want to do the work it excels at.*"

If spending time abroad is a priority then Slaughters is still worth considering. One trainee told us, "*Everyone who wants to go abroad gets to go. There are always more seats than takers.*" Six-month secondments are offered by each of the firm's overseas offices and with best friends firms, many of which are among the best in their countries (eg Spain's Uría y Menéndez).

bare-knuckle fighting

Trainees at medium-sized firms voice concerns about the megafirms, saying that they don't much like the idea of being a small cog in a big machine. Imagine, if you will, those little birds that hang around hippopotamuses picking the food from their teeth. Slaughters trainees say, "*You've just got to be realistic.*" If you aspire to the biggest and best deals, you've got to start at the bottom of the food chain. "*You get to see how decisions are made and how things are done. You learn how to be responsible and how to organise yourself.*" It's like being a runner on a film set and watching how the director brings things together. As a trainee your name won't be up in lights, but you'll probably find it in the credits.

Hours are extremely variable and can be very long. An average would be 9am-7pm, but you're highly likely to be called in for the odd weekend and all-nighter. Hours are "*up and down*" and "*the gloves come off on qualification,*" but we kept hearing that there is no pressure to stay late if there's nothing on. Although current trainees had started out at a quieter time economically, they did stress that if you want a quiet life (and at busy times, any life at all), then you shouldn't be looking at the magic circle. "*Of course, hours can be hardcore. That comes with the territory,*" one trainee spoke plainly.

dear trainee

You won't have billing targets as a trainee or as an assistant. "*It's part of the firm's culture not to aim for targets, but to get the job done. You do what you have to do.*" This also adds to an atmosphere of solidarity amongst the people you work with. One source said, "*I was amazed by how co-operative people were and how little competition there was between trainees.*"

There are all manner of seminars and workshops to attend, but your day-to-day training will be dependent on your supervisor and the chemistry between you. All the partners are "*highly impressive from an intellectual point of view, but some of them are almost the mad professor type.*" We heard about one trainee whose supervisor instructed them by e-mail even though they shared an office. Supervisors range from "*the good to the bad*" and from "*the honest to the overly honest,*" which, we suppose, ought to make them overly happy. While the atmosphere is regarded as friendly, "*it is very hierarchical.*" One trainee said, "*Partners are different creatures from the rest of us!*"

new school ties

Trainees elsewhere sometimes assume that the simple application procedure is a cover for Masonic handshaking and old school ties. "*Don't come here if you want to meet fellow old Etonians. There aren't any,*" said one of our interviewees. Another agreed: "*I expected it to be a lot worse. I thought there'd be a lot more* arrogant, condescending sh*ts." There is an *"Oxbridge bias,"* but only to the extent that *"the best people will have been at the best universities."* There are people from all over – *"family ties won't get you anywhere"* and *"you won't find those public school types who are arrogant without being bright."* During our interviews we came across names and accents from around the world. *"It is an international place,"* confirmed one trainee.

Slaughters seems to attract less of the loud, sporty types and more of the cerebral types. One trainee thought, *"You've got a better chance of fitting in here if you are a bit quirky and off the wall."* Another told us that a friend at a different magic circle firm had, during their induction, been told to *"Live the brand."* *"If conformity is what you like then you might not be so good here."* By all accounts the firm is a refuge for *"talented and creative people who may find it harder to fit in at other firms."*

retention issues

Is Slaughter and May a byword for arrogance? *"We are perfectionists. That is not the same as being arrogant,"* one trainee retorted. *"I think there is an element of jealousy,"* another added. *"We're more anal about getting things done really well. We charge more because we strive for perfection. Maybe sometimes we don't hesitate in telling lawyers on the other side what they've done wrong. If you've done it right it's annoying having to stay in the office dealing with other people's rubbish."* Er…OK.

Trainees describe themselves as *"friendly, enthusiastic and polite."* One trainee quoted a supervisor who told them: *"In a big corporate firm like this your clients can sometimes be very demanding, so the least we can do is make life pleasant for each other in the office."* There is a real sense of camaraderie: *"I was amazed by how uncompetitive it is. I assumed it would be about people jostling for position and getting in with the right partners."*

Trainees are pragmatic about their training and realistic about their futures. In September 2002, all but one of the 45 qualifying trainees were offered a job and 42 chose to accept.

mind your step

After years in terrible offices, Slaughters recently moved to a *"beautiful," "airy"* and *"plush"* new building in Bunhill Row. Just like the lawyers, the offices are *"classy and understated."* There is a *"first-rate"* restaurant and a coffee shop on site (think Whittard's rather than Starbucks), but don't expect the mini village that you might find at Clifford Chance – you're expected to step into the outside world should you need to buy toiletries or rent videos. Apparently they keep pairs of black socks at the front desk should any visiting clients accidentally step in the floor level water feature in reception. Seeing as you don't get free Slaughters stress balls or stationery at law fairs, you might try for a free pair of socks if yours are wearing a bit thin.

finger on the button

"I hate organised fun," said one trainee, who also had a rant about chain bars, restaurants and coffee bars. *"Why go to a soulless All Bar One when there are individual, traditional pubs?"* Quite. Socialising is purely voluntary, though well subsidised by the firm. Locals include The Vault, All Bar One (clearly not everyone has a problem) and the King's Head. There's a big annual do in The Grosvenor, and this summer the firm hired a funfair for a party. It was *"a cross between a village fête and a big piss-up!"* The dress code for the latter, in typical Slaughters' style, was *"as you feel comfortable."* The firm is a patron of the nearby Barbican Centre so discounts and freebies are available. *"Some partners have tickets coming out of their ears. E-mails will go round but you've got to be quick and reply within 30 seconds to stand a chance."*

and finally…

Many countries qualify for the World Cup, but some keep coming up with the goods year in, year out. Slaughter and May is as dependable as the Germans but has the added flair of Brazil. To say *"this firm is the best"* may be immodest, but, in terms of superior lawyering and big profits, it is possibly true. All you've got to work out is whether it's the best for you.

Speechly Bircham

the facts
Location: London
UK ranking by size: 73
Total number of trainees: 10
Seats: 4x6 months
Alternative seats: None

Speechly Bircham is a well-balanced, mid-sized firm that has undergone a revamp in recent times. Although most business is of a commercial nature, it is held in particularly high regard for its private client work.

bending minds…

The firm's approach to training guarantees that *"people are aware of your ability and you get a level of responsibility that suits you. It's not piled on so you can't cope."* With only five trainees taken on each year, *"the firm is the right size for you to be able to get noticed and get in amongst it all."* As with other London firms of the same size, Speechly Bircham has a high partner to assistant ratio. *"People apply to the firm because it gives the best of both worlds, being a City firm with City clients, but without the typical City work environment."* It knocks about with some respectable clients, including Cable & Wireless, The Royal Bank of Scotland, MORI, and the RSPB. The quality of work is there and *"people work hard, but there is an air of relaxation about the place; they know there is more to life."*

At first glance, it doesn't appear an overly ambitious firm, and although it *"isn't old-fashioned,"* according to trainees, it is *"stuck in its ways."* Ultimately, it is happy with who it is and not desperate to be something it isn't. The rebranding of two years ago was more like a fresh coat of a fashionable shade than a full-blown makeover. Speechlys doesn't go in for fads like dress-down or art-house brochures with over-exposed photos, so if you are the sort of person who likes the idea of stability, security and consistency, then this firm should appeal. But never underestimate the importance of a small streak of weirdness. Imagine the mind of the partner who, during a phone interview, tried to hypnotise one of the researchers on our parent publication *Chambers UK*.

It would be wrong to say that the firm doesn't care about its image; it's just that loud and jazzy have all been rejected in favour of subtle, clear and functional (and, after what we learned about the resident hypnotist, maybe subliminal). Take a look at the smart but simple trainee brochure or the firm's website if you don't believe us. This no-fripperies (but watch the pendulum) ethos carries over into the office space. Spread over five floors in St Andrew Street, it is the antithesis of their old offices. *"Very bright, with lots of glass and plenty of meeting rooms."* For simplicity, *"all the floors have almost identical layouts"* and for clarity they all have different colour schemes so *"when you get out of the lift on the wrong floor everything is yellow when it should be mauve."* The whole office is quite modern, but the only really fanciful indulgence is the collection of *"slightly arty paintings"* scattered about the place.

…and stretching seats

"The popularity of seats changes from year to year," although the commercial seat is generally favoured. In the property department, expect *"lots of matters to deal with from start to finish."* Likewise, the popular employment seat provides an opportunity to *"see the whole picture, because files are not normally open for more than a few months,"* and it's *"a 50:50 split between acting for employers on disciplinary matters, and individual appointments and redundancies,"* so you will be able to see both sides of the coin. In fact, employment proved so popular that in 2002 all five second-years decided they wanted to qualify into it. In the end two trainees stayed with the firm, one in employment and one in construction. The flagship private capital (private client to you and us) department attracts applicants. *"It has some amazing clients all around the world, so you get a pretty broad variety of work."* There are some limitations on what you can do and when, for example, corporate is generally reserved for sec-

ond-years as *"the firm feels you should have more experience…and so you hit the ground running. The nature of the work means you are likely to be stretched."*

The duration of a seat is generally six months, but we heard of trainees staying longer to finish up cases, and others tailoring their seat options to suit their interests; *"they want you to get a broad range of seats, but they really take in the wishes of the trainee."* The variety of work was mentioned by every trainee we spoke to, as was the changeable work schedule. Our sources spoke of occasional early starts and late finishes *"in emergencies"* across the spectrum of seat options.

Common to most firms, each interviewee insisted there was no typical trainee. The most we could glean from our sources was that Speechlys was *"looking for people with initiative"* who are *"understated."* Certainly *"as a group they complement each other well."* These guys 'n' gals are clever, collectively sensible, serious in work, keen to help out, friendly and outgoing. They want to be noticed and appreciated, but can't be bothered to jump up and down shouting loudly in order to achieve that. Apparently, *"there aren't any bombastic characters."* *"We are all quite open and outgoing people who are easy to get on with. There's no one who sits in the corner and doesn't speak,"* ventured the only trainee brave enough to climb into a pigeon-hole. We concur.

the way to a trainees heart

In contrast to the picture of serenity and calm painted within the office, the Speechly Bircham trainees don't sit in some Zen garden when its time to unwind – they like to party. *"On Friday evenings we tend to head for The Bottlescrue or The Hoop & Grapes,"* said one source. Walkabout and The Hogshead will occasionally get a visit, but with *"loads of pubs in Chancery Lane and Holborn"* the trainees are a bit spoilt for choice.

Monthly drinks evenings are open to all and *"bring people together and help them stay in touch."* Several partners get involved in these events, particularly the younger ones, and at the annual Christmas and summer firm-wide parties you'll find them all on the razz. *"Quite a lot of the senior partners are a good laugh and you can safely sit and have a joke with them,"* one trainee informed us. The firm holds a monthly assistant solicitors' lunch *"and the in-house chef is very good and a really nice guy."* On the days when chef isn't serving up free gourmet dishes, trainees might well be found in the local greasy spoon, Poppins, *"particularly if they have been out on the tiles the night before."*

Trainees are encouraged to get involved in presentations and client entertainment, and they aren't too proud to loiter for the free canapés and booze. They also get out and socialise with clients and other trainees through the firm's sports teams. *"There is something going on almost every week, be it netball, hockey, cricket or football,"* and these too carry the promise of committee dinners and pub discussion lunches.

and finally…

There are many reasons why you might feel drawn to Speechly Bircham – good clients, a healthy work attitude and a more intimate environment. Just ignore the fact that its name makes it sound like an accomplice of Penelope Pitstop baddie Sylvester Sneekly!

Steele & Co

the facts

Location: Norwich, London, Diss
UK ranking by size: 112
Total number of trainees: 10
Seats: 4x6 months
Alternative seats: None
Extras: Pro bono – Citizens Advice Bureaux

Steele & Co once had a string of offices in small towns, but in the last few years it's turned into a more focused commercial outfit concentrating on higher value work for increasingly larger clients. From its stronghold in Norwich and outposts in London and Diss, Steele & Co services regional and national corporates and its roster of local authorities is particularly impressive.

you decide

The different offices have different functions. What used to be the Steele & Co Thetford office is now a separate LLP specialising in criminal work, but there is a crime seat up for grabs there if you want it. The Diss office is also seen as quite remote from the training experience although the links to business in Norwich are obvious. The London office in Vauxhall concentrates on services to London local authority clients, while the office in Holborn is building up work for corporate clients and operates an interesting joint venture with a Cheltenham-based firm, BPE.

The Norwich office serves corporate and private clients plus local authorities. With all this variety on offer, we weren't in the least bit surprised to hear trainees say, *"Within logistical constraints, you can pretty much say how you want to spend your two years."* It would be possible to lean your four-seat training towards non-corporate seats – family, personal injury and civil litigation. Or, if corporate clients were your bag, you could steer away from private clients altogether. Some trainees had spent two years on mostly contentious work; others had done the opposite.

bootiful

"More and more, trainees are spending time in more than one office," one trainee told us. *"It helps us understand the scope of the firm and increases the ambit of experience that trainees get."* Gaining London experience is high on the agenda for many trainees, particularly as they aren't all Norfolk born and bred. That said, *"quite a few of us are from UEA. And though I never thought I'd say it, Norwich has got a pull. Life is a bit slower here… but it's a lovely area to live in and easy to get to London to see your mates."* Another had us dreaming when she said, *"We're not far from the coast so you can just pop up to Cromer on a Saturday afternoon and loll on the beach."*

Whether it's the delights of the Norfolk countryside, historic Norwich or the attractions of Steele & Co itself is hard to tell, but the firm has a good record on retention. For the last three years all trainees have been offered a job on qualification: All of the 2001 qualifiers and three of the four in 2002 chose to stay on. All those we spoke to had been impressed with the firm's outlook and ambition. *"You should emphasise that this is a young firm,"* one trainee encouraged us. *"Very few solicitors are grey-haired or dinosaurs, they are relatively young and that's the result of growth, both organic and through lateral hires. It really shows at firm-wide events when you actually get to see the demographics."*

adventures

Trainees think Steele & Co is progressive. This is demonstrated by various spin-off ventures – a human resources consultancy, and e-business consultancy and the BPE/Steele & Co co-operation designed to win corporate clients and deals in London. *"It's not the majority of our work,"* stressed one trainee, indicating that we shouldn't overemphasise these aspects of the firm's business, but it does at least show a willingness to try new things. All trainees work in open-plan offices, surrounded by more senior members of their team. *"I really like that about Steele & Co,"* one said. *"Things are kept very informal so it's easy to approach your team leader. Of course it's daunting at first when you have to give advice over the phone as everyone can hear you, but you also get tips and ideas from hearing others speak."*

Trainees say the ideal applicant is a law grad with legal work experience behind them and a desire to get stuck in. Local authority work will see you handling your own cases and making applications in court regularly. The positive attitude of trainees really came through in interviews: *"They encourage ambition here,"* said one source of the new title of associate partner. *"It gives you something to strive for."*

the fun bus

Steele & Co sits in a business park on the outskirts of Norwich. *"It's in need of a makeover as it's all a bit dull and magnolia,"* several trainees agreed. The out of town location is not ideal either as it limits what you can get up to at lunchtimes (there's a McDonald's and a Homebase with a Costa Coffee shop, and on Thursdays a free 'fun bus' transports staff to and from the city centre.) A car gives greater freedom: "*You can drive to a pub or to Dunston Hall which is 5-10 minutes away, but after work, most people make their way straight home.*"

When trainees do gather in town for an end-of-week drink, you'll find them in the Slug & Lettuce or Orgasmic, distinguishable from other Norwich trainees by the fact that they've been home and changed. One little bird said we could also tell them apart from Mills & Reeve and Eversheds because they wouldn't be found "*stood in a corner drinking champagne or thinking we are a cut above everyone else.*" When pressed as to the reason for this, our little bird said, "*There's a lack of pretension and competition between us. We don't feel like we've got to prove anything.*"

and finally...

A forward thinking firm with particularly well-respected practices in employment, corporate and litigation and in its services to local authorities. If Norfolk appeals, this is definitely one to consider.

Stephenson Harwood

the facts
Location: London
UK ranking by size: 31
Total number of trainees: 45
Seats: 4x6 months
Alternative seats: Overseas seats
Extras: Pro bono – Hoxton Law Centre, Language training

If you are after a broad training in a mid-sized City firm then this is one to add to your list. It recently underwent a merger with shipping firm Sinclair Roche & Temperley but kept its name (which will tell you something about the merger). With plenty of new crew to help her sail, this is a new era for the firm. We thought we'd climb aboard and have a look around.

the seven seas

The firm focuses on five principal legal disciplines: corporate law, commercial litigation, shipping, property and private capital. It targets these at four key business sectors: the financial sphere, the IT world, property players and maritime services. One trainee explained the strategy: "*We can't get the big deals and compete with the big boys on manpower so we saw the need to be strategic and focused.*" Think stealthy ninja versus chunky sumo.

The firm operates a four by six-month seat system, and nothing is compulsory other than the satisfaction of the Law Society's minimum requirements for both contentious and non-contentious work. You need to "*put yourself around*" if you want to get the hot seats (which vary from year to year but generally include ship finance, employment and corporate). "*There's a lot of competition for the best seats so you should get to know the personalities involved and find out where the good work is,*" said one strategist. We were pleasantly surprised to hear that Stephenson Harwood trainees buck the trend of most law firms – "*Property is pretty popular!*" The merger with SRT means that it now has one of the largest shipping practices around. This fact hadn't been lost on the trainees, one of whom told us: "*If you want shipping then come here.*"

SH offers trainees opportunities all over the globe. If you want to stick to Europe, head for Madrid or Piraeus. Or if you fancy somewhere a bit more exotic you could up and move to Hong Kong, Singapore or Shanghai. Fear not, there isn't an excessive amount of competition between trainees for overseas seats. "*People suddenly find themselves with mortgages and boyfriends or girlfriends, and suddenly six months in Piraeus doesn't seem so appealing.*" You old romantics!

rocking the boat

"*There is a preconception that Stephenson Harwood is very traditional when, in fact, there's quite a young set of people at the place.*" Is it not possible to be young and traditional then? (The debate on that one raged all afternoon.) One trainee told us: "*I came here because it struck me as being quite friendly and paternalistic. It's not as intimidating as other firms. It's not a sink or swim environment…they nurture you." Another agreed: "*There are some great people here. Generally the culture is very relaxed and a bit old school. The negative side of that is that it isn't as forward-looking as other firms. It is a nice place to work though.*" It might be a little unfair to describe a firm as 'not forward-looking' when it's had the nerve to go through the changes Stephenson Harwood has.

Just to fill you in on recent history, quite a number of partners were tossed overboard when a new three-year plan was announced back in 1999. Since then the firm has been re-hulled and has set a new course – hence the focus we discussed at the head of this report. The merger with SRT in May 2002 bulked up the business, but left a salty taste in some mouths as it involved axing a few of the crew, but, as one trainee said, "*It's difficult for any firm to undergo a merger.*" Concerning SH's decision to take on SRT, one source said, "*It is a bit of a gamble, but I think that long-term it will benefit both firms.*" The two legacy firms are seen to complement each other in that they have "*similar strengths and goals in maritime and asset finance.*" Now the mission is for the newly merged entity to "*find its feet, consolidate and work out where it wants to go…*"

the crew

The trainee profile is predominantly redbrick and Oxbridge with a pretty even split between law and non-law grads. After a considerable pause, one trainee told us: "*It's a difficult firm to tie down as far as the people are concerned. They're well spread in terms of background.*" Someone else added: "*People here get on really well and no one takes themselves too seriously. No one is overly keen and there's no raw ambition oozing out of people.*" The hours are considered to be very good, although one cynic suggested that "*maybe if they achieved what they wanted to in departments like corporate then hours would be a lot worse.*" Your average day will be 9.30am-7pm and as a trainee you have billing targets, but these are not set in stone. The trainees we spoke to had "*never known of someone being called in for not hitting targets. So long as you are productive, whether doing billable work or not, there's no fuss.*"

Most departments hold weekly or fortnightly talks for trainees. "*Property and litigation are very strong on training and talks tend to be done by someone who has done bundling and pagination in their recent memories.*" As a trainee you sit in an office with a partner or an assistant who is at least three or more years qualified. There is an official appraisal system in place but, in practice, the amount of constructive feedback you receive depends on the supervisor. You'll get all the responsibility you could wish for in most seats, although it was felt that on occasion the work wasn't delegated to the lowest level possible in all departments. Most of our sources were happy though, saying, "*because we do smaller deals we get more hands-on experience. You do have a bit of grunt work to do but it can still be interesting.*" We're pleased to report that the partners are always approachable. "*You can talk to them just like you'd talk to anybody. I appreciate not being treated like some kind of scum.*"

The retention rate for September 2002 qualifiers wasn't great at 13 out of 21, but to be fair, 12 months before it was 93% and in March 2002 it was 75%. The qualifiers distributed themselves across the firm and one went out to Singapore on a three-year posting.

party of five

The office is right in front of St Paul's Cathedral. "*The view is actually quite inspiring,*" punned one trainee. "*It's a nice spot compared to the concrete jungle up the road.*" There's even a gym and an on-site Au Bon Pain. After work, trainees frequent Shaws Booksellers and The Evangelist (neither sells books nor religion; both sell booze) and the nearby Rising Sun (for Thai food). On a Friday night it's not uncommon to share a table in the pub with a partner or a secretary. Trainees see themselves as "*a decent bunch*" and there's an obvious bond between them. Once a year they organise a big event for "*up to five friends each*" from various City companies and institutions, so a new generation of young professionals can mix and misplace each other's business cards. In the last few years they've had a casino and a race night. The party scene took a dent at the end of 2001 as the Christmas party was cancelled in a belt-tightening exercise. The Grinch had left the building within six months though, and in 2002 the firm enjoyed its annual summer bash.

There's a permanent business casual dress code, and fortunately there's a Gap just down the road enabling you to stock up on khakis and twill shirts quite easily. It's advisable to keep a suit in the office though, just in case the clients come calling. When asked to explain business casual one trainee told us that it is *"Alan Partridge-style."* Aha!

and finally…

We asked trainees what should inspire students to apply to Stephenson Harwood. One told us: *"It is potentially a new type of firm and that's very exciting."* Another trainee (a self-proclaimed *"easily pleased little bugger"*) said, *"You've just got to want the firm as it is. If you really want to do the massive M&A work then you're not going to do it here."* On the other hand, if you want to hang onto your own life and to focus on what Stephenson Harwood does best, then get that application form.

Taylor Vinters

the facts

Location: Cambridge
UK ranking by size: 97
Total number of trainees: 10
Seats: 4x6 months
Alternative seats: Brussels

Taylor Vinters is almost two firms in one. The commercial lawyers provide a range of services to start-up technology enterprises, priding themselves on staying with clients as they grow. Flip the firm over and you'll see its private client origins. It's long been advisor to farmers and wealthy individuals in East Anglia, and the rural business and private client sides of the firm are still going strong.

soft centres and tough nuts

Taylor Vinters' excellent reputation in Cambridge certainly hadn't escaped trainees: all our sources had applied to the firm on the back of it, although not all have a long connection to the place. They appreciate the fact that the reputation applies to the whole of the firm's broad range of practice areas – rural business (including bloodstock and equestrian services), matrimonial, personal injury, employment, IP, property and corporate.

First-years start with a seat in either PI or property. PI is *"liked throughout"* as *"it's a good, soft, friendly seat to start in"* although you'll be out of the stalls and running your own files quite quickly. Property is less popular but *"pretty much guaranteed"* because of the volume of work. There are three seats on offer in the property department – rural, commercial property & planning, and construction & development. Recently the trainees moaned about finding some of the department's work boring so the firm switched around supervisors, who are now described as *"younger and more vibrant and more willing to teach."*

Individual preferences are taken into account for the second seat and beyond. In the past, the IP and employment departments have been too small to take trainees routinely, but *"if you say 'I really want to do this seat', they will try and make room, even if they haven't had a trainee there before."* Trainees in corporate need to be attentive, enthusiastic and plucky as the supervisor keeps them on their toes: *"If you are quiet and sensitive or just not that interested in corporate work then it can be a nightmare seat."* If you've got what it takes though, you'll love it and you can also ask to gain a bit of IP experience. Each year there's a three-month secondment to Brussels firm, Renouf & Co. and there may soon be a permanent seat in the recently expanded employment department.

the bigger picture

"I want to be a corporate lawyer but not just a specialist," said one trainee, intent on extolling the virtues of smaller regional firms. *"Train here and you'll get to see*

the bigger picture." Taylor Vinter's deals may have considerably lower price tags than those of City firms, but our sources believe their experience of transactional work helps them become more rounded. "*My friends in the City just do share sale agreements whereas I've drafted shareholder agreements, transferred businesses, tailored shelf companies to clients' needs and done a group restructuring.*" It's probably important to remember that this is not just any old regional firm; it's slap-bang in the middle of Silicon Fen, with all its hi-tech and biotech activity. Also, clients such as the University of Cambridge (and a number of its colleges) put novel and interesting work the firm's way.

It was good to hear trainees singing out in support of the private client practice too. "*Trainees generally have the opinion that they are not as interested in private clients,*" but it seems that there are a few rising in the ranks who are hoping to qualify into the area.

foot in the past, eye on the future

So if some lawyers are hanging onto the firm's roots and others are sniffing out the future does that make for a divided feel to the firm? Apparently not. Everyone's under the one roof and gets on swimmingly. One trainee told us, "*They are modernising all the time – I've seen drastic changes since I've been here.*" There's a swanky, new IT system and new conference rooms with "*all mod cons.*" In terms of personnel, "*they seem to be recruiting more younger and techie people.*" With this outlook comes a permanent dress-down policy and open-plan working in most parts of the firm.

"*There isn't a work-till-you-drop ethic but I wouldn't say it's laid-back,*" one source said. Though you are likely to be "*aware of their presence*" when an equity partner is around, "*there is a pretty flat hierarchy.*" The firm works in teams and it is "*a good firm for involving you in things and letting everyone know what's going on.*" Typically, lawyers are "*not hugely ambitious, just good at the job without the big ego.*" Of the new recruits, "*you could never say 'There goes a Taylor Vinters trainee' like you could with some other Cambridge firms.*" There may not be a typical trainee, but "*the firm seems to know what it is looking for.*" Unfortunately, only two of the five qualifiers stayed on with the firm in September 2002, one in PI and the other in corporate.

officially secret acts

Trainees described "*absolutely fantastic*" levels of responsibility. Of course, it varies from department to department, but generally we heard: "*I've done valid work and have had day to day control of certain matters.*" One source said, "*I've been given important roles in big transactions, while heavily supervised, and I've enjoyed it.*" Trainees talk to clients on the phone or communicate via e-mail and, particularly in private client, they get to conduct meetings on their own. They are also happy with the level of feedback, and for some it comes on a daily basis. Trainees are able to voice their opinions: "*Most of us feel the managing partner is very open and would be happy to speak to her about anything.*" Recently there was even a firm-wide review of partners and how well they teach junior lawyers. All the (anonymous) responses were shredded afterwards!

Overlooking the Science Park, TV suffers from a basic problem: "*We can't stumble out of the office into the pub as people always drive to work*" and the bar across the road in the Q.ton forum closes quite early. Groups of younger staff make the effort to rectify the problem and head over to bars in the centre of Cambridge, and a social committee organises monthly events including trips to the Newmarket races, bowling and karaoke. On the sports front, a netball team awaits a new lease of life just as soon as someone masterminds its comeback. Curiously, when we interviewed, the cricket team was preparing to go on tour to…Amsterdam!? We didn't dare ask…

The coolest thing about Taylor Vinters is the group of lawyers that have their own clandestine beer fridge – you know who you are! The fridge is in a top-secret location: "*I can't tell you where or people have to die.*" It comes into its own at about 5pm, normally on a Friday, but it could be any night – you never know when it's going to strike. "*I'll be working away and I'll hear the fridge open…it makes me laugh when I hear it.*" And if this is news to the rest of the firm, then it's because *"we have to drink up before we leave the* [CENSORED] *department. It's all very cloak-and-dagger!"*

and finally…

If Cambridge is your thing, you don't have to leave. Taylor Vinters is a smart firm with a game plan and plenty of diverse business. And there are some sneaky so-and-sos with a fridge full of beer. Perfection!

Taylor Wessing

the facts

Location: London, Cambridge
UK ranking by size: 26
Total number of trainees: 52
Seats: 4x6 months
Alternative seats: Brussels, secondments
Extras: Language training

We'd like to thank Taylor Joynson Garrett for kindly merging with Germany's Wessing before we went to press. We just hate missing out on exciting new developments and, by any measure, this merger is an exciting development. And just in case you were wondering, Wessing is pronounced with a 'v' as in vest.

the story so far…

IP work is at the heart of TW's reputation: it's a top player in both hard and soft IP matters. Surrounding this are some large and respected mainstream departments, which enables it to hold its head high as a full-service firm of particular interest to companies in the TMT and life sciences sectors. For years TJG had been telling everyone who'd listen that its success rested on its breadth of practice; that clients were drawn to its door because it could handle their corporate finance as well as their copyright. Have we all got the message? Good. We understand from our colleagues on *Chambers Global* that it's been much the same story over in Germany with Wessing. And so now, the two firms are going to test the theory that two plus two equals more than four.

The firm is always keen to recruit trainees with science backgrounds, particularly those with science degrees, but it most certainly doesn't limit its attentions to the lab boffins. Even if IP or IT leaves you cold, you'll be satisfied with the work on offer. We suspect that European languages will stand you in good stead now that it's all eyes on Europe.

Of the four seats, up till now, only litigation was compulsory. A mandatory spell in corporate is now in the pipeline. Thus far, trainees have been consulted about which department and which supervisor they'd like to work with. *"I got to choose all my seats,"* one satisfied customer told us. Another said, *"They've got it down to a fine art; if you don't get your first choice, you will get it next time."* We weren't in the least surprised to learn that the most popular seats are based around IP and IT/e-commerce. Science grads fare well in the hard IP seats, working on tricky patent matters, while those with no 'previous form' find the softer work easier to get their heads around. There's no need to scrap with your peers to get a seat; these departments always need plenty of bodies. In employment it's a different story: *"It's people-oriented and very popular,"* but there is only room for a couple of trainees. Private client is *"one of TJG's best-kept secrets."*

going up to Cambridge

Up until July, we thought the biggest news would be the firm's acquisition of an office in Cambridge. Well before the Enron/Andersen fiasco, TJG absorbed the Silicon Fen operation of the now-defunct law firm Garretts. The move was a smart one for TJG; it acquired a host of technology venture capitalist clients and reinforced its brand image – a firm that's serious about science and technology. It currently offers the opportunity for one trainee to do half of a corporate seat there every three months.

Back in January 2002, when the Cambridge office 'opened', it struck us that TJG was putting into practice Richard Dawkins' selfish gene theory. Shared surname, shared business focus…QED shared DNA. The move made perfect sense. The Cambridge lawyers must have impressed the big cheeses in London because when things went totally tits up for Garretts, TJG rescued some teams from its London office. Who said chivalry was dead? (Besides Liz Hurley to Steve Bing, of course.)

making a name for yourself

We asked trainees to explain the firm's appeal. Their answers went right back to the selection process: *"It wasn't aggressive and there was no psychometric testing. People talked to me like they really wanted to know who I was, as opposed to just what I could do."* One decided he would go to TJG even if he received an offer from a magic circle firm: *"I'm more suited to a mid-size firm. In big firms there's so much competition and getting your name known is difficult. Here I'm already known by three quarters of the firm after doing three seats and working on every floor."* Presumably such exposure is helpful in getting the seats that you want? *"It certainly is."*

We suspect that the Wessing tie-up will make the firm even more appealing to students, although at this stage the international opportunities for trainees are still limited. There's one posting to the firm's Brussels office for a competition seat every six months and a number of trainees get to go on shorter business trips to assist on deals taking place in Europe or the US. The American connection is particularly noticeable in corporate and IP work. One of our interviewees made the point that *"it feels like an international firm even though we don't have many international offices."* While it is likely that trainees will be able to take up a six-month posting in Germany at some point, nothing is available yet.

which button do i press?

In most seats there's a high degree of client contact; you will be asked for your opinion in meetings and made to feel part of the team. As one trainee said, *"It's a fast learning curve but it's a great one, which prepares you for the wider world after qualification."* Sure, *"there are times when you get overworked and the hours bunch together, and occasionally your interest can go to the wall."* But, *"you don't just feel like you're at a photocopier pushing the big green button all day."* The highs are there for the taking. *"When you are given responsibility, you can feel on top of the world. A corporate partner let me finalise a deal of £3 million when an associate went on holiday – he said he thought the experience was important and that I could handle it."* Tempering this enthusiasm, another remarked: *"Sometimes we have to do the grunt work – litigation is bad for lots of bundling as sometimes paralegals can't do all the work themselves."*

Sadly, the respectable retention rates of the last few years were not matched this year, with only 12 of the 20 September 2002 qualifiers staying on with the firm. For a firm busy growing, it was a surprising and disappointing tally.

no quack pots

We almost suggested that one trainee go head-to-head with Anna Ryder Richardson on *Changing Rooms* when she described the office to us. *"There's a lot of modern art, there's a lot of light coming in and I like the colour scheme – teal and terracotta. If you're looking to be at a firm for a long time, you want to like the environment you're working in."* OK, so that's the look of the place, what of the feel? *"Down-to-earth,"* according to our interviewees; no one is super-ruthless and no one is super-zany. *"Broad-minded,"* was another typical answer. One trainee made the point that *"all the trainees are genuinely nice."* Hmmm, we've heard that before. *"Yes, you do have to compete for seats, but there's the sense that we're friends competing as opposed to stabbing people in the back." "We were really pleased for the person who got the last Brussels seat, and people congratulated me for getting a* [certain] *seat even though they'd been competing for it and hadn't got it themselves."*

"In by 9.30am and out by 6.30-7pm," seems to be reasonably standard for trainees. Although hours do vary from department to department, it's very much the case that if you've finished your work you go home. After hours, the local pub, the Witness Box,

could tell a tale or two about life at the firm. However, The Evangelist on Blackfriars Lane has also been preaching to the converted since it opened. *"The Evangelist is livelier – but the Witness Box is closer!"* Ooh, tough choice!

and finally…
Taylor Wessing has switched into empire-building mode after several years of organic growth as TJG. With firm foundations in the UK and Germany, healthy links to the US and optimism among staff, we suspect this is a good time to get on board.

Theodore Goddard

the facts
Location: London
UK ranking by size: 40
Total number of trainees: 30
Seats: 4x6 months
Alternative seats: Overseas seats, secondments

An established City presence, Theodore Goddard attracts clients across the board from the media to the City's big financial institutions. The trainees we spoke to were drawn in by quality work and the utterly civilised nature of the firm. As one trainee informed us, *"It's a very convivial place to be."*

please be seated
The seat system is a standard four by six-month model. It is possible, in some cases, to split one seat between three months in London and three in either Paris or Brussels or on a secondment to a client. These occur on an ad hoc basis to large corporates or music or film companies. Expect to spend time in corporate or finance as well as the litigation department which, in addition to general commercial cases, covers work in the banking and insurance sectors plus employment, medical negligence and white-collar crime. Property, construction, media, defamation and IP will all attempt to distract you. The last trainee manager did a great job of making the seat system more transparent and now *"everyone seems to have had all the seats they wanted."*

In past years we've heard more about the sexy media work in the firm's entertainment department, but the trainees we spoke to this year felt that TG was shifting focus onto more straight-up City work. One trainee said, *"The media department has been quieter of late"* and another added: *"It may sound glamorous, but at the end of the day it's still law."* If you are determined to make it as a media lawyer, but don't stretch to a Hoxton fin and the right Nikes then this would be a good place to ply your trade. As one of our interviewees put it: *"This is not Olswang!"* Just to hammer home the message, another interviewee warned: *"Don't expect it to be glamorous just because the clients are."* Indeed, one trainee's considered opinion was that banking is now the new hot seat. TG recruit trainees with a spread of aspirations, consequently not everyone will be queuing up for the meeja work. In addition to clients like Sony, Universal and Warner as well as a whole host of pop stars, the firm also acts for airlines, numerous banks, big telecoms companies and a range of plcs. So if it's a pure corporate/commercial training you're after, don't be afraid to say so.

little britain
For some students, the firm will fall down on its lack of international presence. *"Many of our peers can offer their trainees more opportunities,"* sighed one source. Too true. If you're desperate for at least six months in some far-flung location then the firm you want is two doors down the road in a building we call Gotham City. In 2001, TG was in merger talks with international firm Salans, and since those talks fell through after September 11, eight of the firm's partners jumped ship to other City practices. When we asked trainees why this had happened and what implications it had for the firm, they were keen to stress that the place was *"far from being in meltdown."* It was considered that the defectors had just felt limited by the

firm's lack of international capacity that the merger would have remedied. *"The process has come to a close. The departures were mostly announced together it's just that people have chosen to leave at different times."* We obviously touched a bit of a nerve. *"It's no secret that we're considering a merger. Getting an international outlook is one of our priorities."* Watch this space.

getting dirty

Responsibility is good. *"Even in my first seat I went to meetings and took instructions over the phone. I was never just sitting around like a spare part."* Another trainee told us: *"It's great to get your hands dirty."* On high-value cases and transactions, trainees will find themselves managing the inevitable mountain of documents, but that's par for the course in City firms. Tedious work is kept to a bearable minimum: *"There aren't enough trainees to have them doing crap."* Generally trainees sit with partners, but don't worry about the firm running out of partners before you get there because, apparently, *"sitting with an associate is much more useful. You can ask a lot more questions."* Some supervisors are only three- to four-years qualified, but *"the younger ones are keen to prove themselves as managers so they take the job seriously."*

the chattering classes

"The firm does err towards the conservative," thought one trainee. *"After all, there aren't many firms around that still have the name that they started off with!"* Well put. At the same time, there is plenty of youthful vigour to balance any conservative tendencies. *"Some of the big-hitters are in their mid-30s which makes a big difference. The firm is good at promoting people who have new energy."* And anyway, there's nothing wrong with a bit of old school; *"There's still a gentlemanly approach. It's nice having doors held open for you."* One trainee told us: *"It's a very talkative firm. Everywhere you go you ending up chatting to someone. It's like a hive."*

There is good internal training (*"about three hours each month, which is just right"*). As well as legal updates, you'll have courses on everything from drafting to presentation skills. Trainees report plenty of *"ad hoc"* but *"useful"* feedback from supervisors, as they are generally aware that you need *"guidance and reassurance."* The emphasis is on informal appraisal, but you'll get the full works at the end of each seat.

The firm tends to take on a good number of older trainees who have gained some experience beforehand. *"The firm values people who have had a bit more time to make the decision,"* thought one source. Many have been on the road with a backpack; most have something going on outside of work and *"the confidence that come from experience"*. TG people are *"normal and down-to-earth."* One of them said, *"You're not going to find a lot of public school toffs."* Someone else thought that the firm was looking for *"people who haven't got an over-inflated sense of their own importance."* There's certainly nothing over-inflated about the latest set of retention figures. In September 2002, 11 out of the 12 qualifiers stayed on with the firm.

cowboys

They say you should never judge a firm by its building, which in TG's case is fortunate since it was roundly described as *"brown"* and *"not as glamorous as it might be."* There's a good restaurant downstairs and decent coffee vending machines on each floor but *"the offices aren't hi-tech, although they do the job."* Work hours average out at 9am to 7pm, although it can get *"intense"* in corporate. We were reassured that *"if you've done your work you can go home at a reasonable hour."* All-nighters are rare and you are *"extremely discouraged"* from working at weekends.

There are bags of organised sports should you care to flex a few muscles. The firm has annual softball and touch rugby tournaments. Partners are considered to be *"a friendly bunch,"* and it's not unusual to find one of them at the bar with their credit card. *"If you want a social life, it is there. There's always someone around to buy you a drink,"* said one trainee. Favourite haunts include the local sports bar, Extra Time, and one of the best pubs on the planet, Ye Olde Red Cow (where you may also find our own good selves most days).

and finally...

There are a lot of mid-sized fish in the City's legal pond so you'll want to choose carefully. This one may not yet have much of an international dimension, but there is every likelihood that it will see a set of merger talks through to a successful conclusion (at some stage). Theodore Goddard can give you a wide range of decent City work and, if you want it, some sexy meeja stuff. And all this without having to train at a megafirm and be one of a hundred or more trainees. As one of them said, *"If I stay in London, I won't want to be anywhere else."*

Thring Townsend

the facts
Location: Bath, Swindon, Frome, Newbury
UK ranking by size: 93
Total number of trainees: 12
Seats: 4x6 months
Alternative seats: Secondments

One of the larger law firms in southern England, Thring Townsend provides a range of both commercial and private client services. The firm recruits trainees into its Bath and Swindon offices.

thrings ain't what they used to be

Thring Townsend is the product of a merger between Thrings & Long and Townsends in 2000. Since then it's been doing the business for subsidiaries of multinational companies, government bodies, charities and family-owned enterprises, as well as private clients. The firm has achieved Investors In People accreditation and also has a Community Legal Service franchise for personal injury and family work. *"A lot of people have been waiting for big changes, and now they're happening,"* reported one interviewee.

After pausing for breath post-merger, it is all go again – trainees pointed to a new graduate recruitment team (*"Sean, the new guy, is excellent"*) and new thinking. *"There's been a review of the firm, and of the trainee scheme in particular,"* said a source. The identity of supervisors, the benefits package and a trainee forum have all been examined in the quest for greater transparency and flawless training. *"They've realised that trainees are the future of the firm,"* one concluded. Indeed, four out of the five September 2002 qualifiers stayed on with the firm.

ticky boxes

Trainees generally complete four seats, although it can vary. There are no compulsories beyond the contentious requirement imposed by the Law Society, although the busy conveyancing department *"often ends up being a first seat."* From the second seat onwards, Thrings tries hard to cater to trainee requests and will consider making positions available in other offices, if necessary. This is particularly the case on qualification. We heard of three qualifiers who all wanted to go to the same department – *"Somehow they organised it!"*

Although based in either Bath or Swindon, you must be flexible about where you work. One reported doing part of a seat in Newbury; *"It's nice to be in a different office for a while,"* they said. Full seat moves aside, a Swindon trainee may end up spending time in Bath, for example, for *"a week here or there if they needed a bit of extra support."* Many of the teams work across the offices, although Swindon is especially hot for company/commercial and PI, taking on high-value claims, particularly in relation to head and spinal injuries. Bath has larger litigation teams and Newbury is well respected in commercial property.

Bath and Swindon are open-plan and trainees sit next to their supervisors, who will *"go through things with you and are very patient."* A *"ticky-box system"* is used for reviews, and there are more formal appraisals with the head of HR and the training partner. *"They groom you for the future and try to find out what is best for you. They nurture you, I suppose,"* said one satisfied source. We're assured that trainees aren't just the recipients of other people's boring chores: *"There is stuff you do as a trainee that's not very exciting, but not that much."* Apparently, *"in conveyancing, everyone does their own photocopying, even the partners."* The hours are good, and only in CoCo is there any real likelihood that you'll have to burn the midnight oil.

full of beans

The identity of the most popular seat chops and changes, but the private client department always has its fans as its work is so varied. *"Drafting wills, seeing clients, dealing with probate, gifts and transfers of land, initiation of trusts, life tenancies; it is a constantly changing field,"* reported one former tenant. *"The department is quite young,"* said one source, *"and the older people who are there are quite full of beans."*

Everyone who does it really enjoys the PI seat and the same goes for construction litigation. The current favourite is corporate/commercial, so get your elbows at the ready if you want to secure a seat there. *"It's seen as glamorous – closing deals and stuff,"* said one interviewee. *"I liked the variety of the work and the team,"* said another. *"You have a lot on your plate and, as you get work from everyone, you have to juggle,"* added a third.

"Many people choose family as a later seat." While some partners handle fee-paying private clients and do more ancillary relief matters, others work for legally aided clients on childcare and contact cases. The department also receives instructions from Wiltshire County Council. Although it's a very busy team, the training is hands-on and supervision is tight. *"I did divorce petitions, went to court and saw clients on my own, and sat behind counsel a lot, but I also went with my supervisor wherever he went."*

lapping it up

We generally ban use of the word 'friendly' in interviews, but had we done so with this lot they'd have struggled to finish a sentence. That's not to suggest trainees here are monotonous or samey: *"The oldest is in her 50s and we have trainees straight out of college."*

"All the trainees are friendly," said another source, inadvertently incurring a 50p fine for the f-word. While *"they are quite happy to do whatever work there is,"* Thring Townsend trainees are not doormats, but they do seem quite easily pleased – not a bad word cropped up in our interviews. They are also supportive of each other: when the fan and the proverbial collide, you'll probably get a trainee shoulder to cry on. *"Sometimes all you want is someone to say 'I'm on your side, it's okay.'"* Yuck!

Over in Swindon, one trainee raised the possibility of a happy hour at a meeting with the chief exec, and both permission and a budget were immediately extended. Since then, 'Brass Nights' in the local brasserie have been a regular fixture every other Friday. There's plenty going on in Bath too as many of the staff are young and up for socialising. Both Bath and Swindon trainees have good links with their local TSGs and the firm itself has a decent social calendar with a Christmas ball, BBQs, derby nights and pub quizzes. For those of a sporting persuasion, there's football, cricket, *"the odd golf thing"* and, recently, a charity swimathon.

The Swindon branch recently moved into a new building. It's slightly out of town on a business park, but is well designed with *"a big tree in reception that goes right up through the whole of the building. It's really nice and really professional for when you bring in your clients, particularly commercial clients."* On Thursdays there's a free bus into town so staff can do their shopping or go to the pub during an extended 75-minute lunch break. The trial dress-down period seems to have metamorphosed into a permanent policy, adding to *"the congenial atmosphere"* fostered by the firm.

and finally…

Thring Townsend seems to take training and the views of its trainees seriously, and it is working hard to mould its slightly far-flung battalions into one formidable force. If this part of the country is in your sights, we suggest you take a closer look.

TLT Solicitors

the facts
Location: Bristol
UK ranking by size: 82
Total number of trainees: 15
Seats: 4x6 months
Alternative seats: None

TLT was born out of the merger between two Bristol firms, Trumps and Lawrence Tucketts in 2000. The two biggest firms in Bristol have taken their eye off the South West ball, and TLT has been swift and savvy enough to jump up and grab it.

great leap forward
Why do people choose this firm? Well, one trainee sounded as if she'd been involved in strategic policy formulation when she told us: *"Because of the merger it's very focused on where it wants to go and what it wants to achieve. It's obviously looking to expand further and put itself on a level with Osborne Clarke and Burges Salmon in Bristol."* You've got to hand it to these trainees; they know what the game plan is! They were also really keen to talk quite simply about the basic appeal of TLT: *"They were a good-sized Bristol practice that did both commercial and private client work, which was great because I was unsure which way I was going to go,"* one trainee admitted. Another said, *"They came across as being interested in me as a person and my all-round qualities."* For one devoted Bristolian, the firm was the natural choice: *"TLT offers great quality work without the expectation of City hours. It's a better quality of life here."*

Our sources described TLT as *"quite dynamic," "young-thinking,"* and *"forward-looking."* It is apparently *"taking on larger clients all the time"* and has divided into five practice groups in order to pursue its goals. These practice groups are banking and lender services, commercial services, property, employment, and services to individual clients. *"It's early days yet, but we've had a lot of positive feedback from clients and good turnover figures."* Clients include high street banks and six of the top ten mortgage lenders, Wallace & Gromit's creators Aardman Animations, Imperial Tobacco, UWE and the University of Bath. There's still room for the little guy (whether he's wearing the right or wrong trousers) – both the family and private client departments are going as strong as ever.

chase me!
By all accounts, *"the corporate and commercial litigation seats are always popular – a lot of trainees here are looking to go into those areas or get a good commercial awareness."* As in every firm across the land, employment is also popular. One trainee pointed out: *"There's a lot of family and private client work here too, so they tend to recruit people with different interests so there's a bit of a spread across the firm."* The lender services department tends to only take first-seat trainees, as *"they do a lot of bulk litigation and remortgaging work and it's not an area many trainees would like to qualify into."* There are no compulsory seats save for the fact that *"they like to see you do some type of property, which can either be residential property or investment/corporate support."*

You'll usually share an office with your supervisor, who could either be a partner or an assistant, but in a couple of departments you'll work open-plan. Wherever you sit, the training offers a steep learning curve and the responsibility builds up *"as your knowledge and confidence grows." "There's an element of photocopying and the like, but there's a lot of secretarial and admin support so you certainly don't get bogged down. The emphasis is there for you to be a fee earner and while you're not made to feel like you have targets, they want you to feel like you're contributing to the team."*

There are two-monthly reviews whereby each trainee sits down with their supervisor and discusses *"areas deserving of praise and areas that need to be worked on – you tell them how you think you're doing, and they tell you how they think you're doing."* Sounds like a lot of talking! While supervisors generally adhere to the timing of the review system, sometimes it requires you to be proactive, *"chasing them and pinning them down."* Ooh er! On a more informal basis, interviewees tell us that *"you generally get feedback on each piece of work you're doing, whether the amendments are just written on the work or whether they come and talk about it."*

when two become one

At the moment, the trainee profile is quite varied. *"The firm likes to have a cross-section of people."* By all accounts, it's a fairly even split between *"students who began their training contracts straight from university and law school, and mature people doing law as a second career."* Most have connections with the South West: *"It's a factor in recruiting, as they'd like to know whether you're applying to TLT in particular or just blanket applying across the country."* However, *"it wouldn't count against you if you're not from the South West – one trainee actually moved their family from London to do the training contract."* We'll bet a fiver they won't be going back. Three out of the five qualifiers stayed on with the firm in September 2002.

TLT has two offices *"left over from the merger."* The aim is to move the entire firm into one of them this autumn, and we understand that it's going to be the office in Redcliffe Street. It's *"a really modern building, spacious and airy and really handy for town and Broadmead."* It sounds like TLT's played its Trump card as the building has *"fantastic views of Bristol," "a Starbucks across the street"* and a location *"right by the water."*

greyhounds in the slips

Average hours work out at a respectable 9am-6pm. As one source said, *"It's not a culture where you're expected to work crazy hours. But when there's work to be done, you stay a bit later (especially in the corporate department)."* Weekends? *"God no – we try to avoid them!"* and *"we're too busy with social things."* And what of the social scene? We hear that *"there's always someone you can go out for a drink with."* In something out of the Twilight Zone, the local pub for each of the offices is called The Shakespeare, the Redcliffe Street version of which also gets *"invaded"* (à la Henry V) by Burges Salmon lawyers on Friday nights. There are regular quiz and karaoke nights, and there's plenty going on with the local Trainee Solicitors Group. *"Most trainees in Bristol studied the LPC here, so we know lots of people outside the firm as well – it's a close-knit, friendly community."* And so too, you'll be pleased to hear, is the grown-up legal community. The firm also fields various sporting teams (such as netball, football and hockey) that compete against local solicitors and accountants. Trainees at TLT see themselves as slightly less grand and more down-to-earth than their peers at the BS and OC, but we're assured that on the playing field everything's level.

and finally…

TLT is a firm on a mission. It wants to be up with the big boys in Bristol, and on all the evidence, it's not doing too badly. Do you want to be converted?

TMK Solicitors

the facts

Location: Southend, Basildon, Chelmsford
UK ranking by size: 119
Total number of trainees: 11
Seats: 3x4 + 1x12 months
Alternative seats: None

TMK is the largest firm in Essex. The recently refurbished main office in Southend is a short stroll from the Golden Mile and the pier.

the place to be

Before we go into any detail about the firm, let's clear a couple of things up. Southend, favoured seaside holiday resort of TV's *Eastenders*, is on the Essex coast at the mouth of the Thames Estuary. Originally a fishing village, it is popular with commuters; with two rail lines to London and the M25 only 30 minutes away, the infrastructure is good, and it has its own airport. It is the largest town in the county, with a population of around 176,000. Of these, only a small proportion are called Kevin or Sharon, even less wear white stilettos these days, and although there are a lot of Ford cars around, not all of them are Escorts. It's a lively, bustling, no-nonsense place and with Southend people, you know where you stand. *"It can be a bit of a culture shock, a bit tough to settle in,"* thought one trainee, so if you can't handle people being up-front with you, then stop reading now.

a house of repute

Founded in 1981, TMK's roots are in criminal work. It has built an excellent reputation, attracting a wealth of referrals from local firms and CABs, existing clients, the mags court, and through the free advice line it runs. *"If we get a call from the CAB, a new client in reception or a caller on the advice line, we try to see them straight away."* More recently, family and civil litigation departments have joined crime as the firm's mainstays, with growing PI, general litigation, employment, housing, mental health and immigration departments coming along on their coat-tails.

"TMK is very business-minded, both as a firm and its individuals" and because *"at least half of the work is public funded,"* *"the focus is on efficiency – you can't afford to waste time."* The firm believes that *"if you work files properly and organise your time, you can make money from publicly funded work."* And to enable it to continue to do so, it is looking for *"confident, articulate people who can handle things themselves, on the spot."*

Turn away if you're squeamish because *"there's some gruesome stuff, like looking at photos of bad injuries and post-mortems."* Above all, you'll need good people skills to cope with everyone from distraught family members through business people to hardened criminals. You *"can't be a shrinking violet,"* particularly as you'll have to speak plainly to clients. *"If someone is going to prison, we'll tell them that, we won't try and make it sound better than it is. We won't say 'we can get you off', if we can't. We don't give people bullshit."*

spelling bee

Trainees spend their first year doing three seats of four months in crime, family and civil litigation. *"You have to learn fast. I saw a client on my own on the first day,"* enthused one interviewee. Typically, the whole of the second year is spent in one seat, usually where the trainee has already 'done time' (pardon the pun). The Chelmsford office now takes a second-year trainee. You will need to decide what you want to do early on, as the firm *"asks new trainees what they want to specialise into in two years' time."* But don't let that scare you off. *"At the end of your training you'll be well prepared and there will be nothing that will frighten you."*

You'll get your own clients and files in civil lit – housing issues, basic contract disputes, harassment matters, neighbour disputes and the like. You are well supervised, but *"partners won't interfere unless you ask for help."* *"If you show initiative you'll be given the opportunity to take on bigger stuff on your own."* Although you won't get your own clients in crime straight away, you'll be encouraged to join the Police Station Accreditation Scheme and go on a rota of lawyers called (at any time day or night) to the cells. *"You learn so much when you start doing the police work on your own,"* one source said.

Trainees are assigned to partners and have regular Monday morning meetings with them plus *"15 minutes or so of feedback every day, when supervisors set aside their work and check yours."* There are meetings every three months, with presentations to trainees on important legal developments, and (we were delighted to hear) *"a spelling test for words like 'committal' and 'defendant'."* It might sound stupid, but do you really want the magistrates to laugh at you?

last orders

Perhaps due to its size and the continued involvement of the founding partners, the firm is *"very hierarchical, and always has been."* Not that the senior partners send down commands from on high – Patrick Musters, for example, takes a very active role in the whole training process, and he regularly *"goes around making sure the people at the bottom are happy."* Good teamwork is important, but the firm isn't particularly democratic – *"But then you don't need that to organise things properly."*

The only thing that the senior partners might not do as frequently as the assistants and trainees, is *"turn out of bed at 3am to go down to the station for a client interview. But at their time of life you can't expect that – they've earned their stripes."* When the trainees come up to qualification, they need to pass muster. Trainees told us that TMK traditionally retains about 50% of its qualifiers, although this year this rose to 75%, with two going into crime and one into civil litigation.

A social committee organises quiz nights, the Christmas party and sports events. There are loads of bars conveniently placed within stumbling distance, but trainees eschew the The Last Post in favour of the slightly more upmarket Inane, Churchill's or Clarence Yard. It's not because they are snobby, but because *"you are more than likely to run into clients in The Post!"*

and finally…
If you are looking for a regional firm specialising in crime, family or other high street work, you really need look no further than TMK. Make sure the location suits you and make sure you're game enough to handle this well-established and energetic firm.

Travers Smith Braithwaite
the facts
Location: London
UK ranking by size: 50
Total number of trainees: 40
Seats: 4x6 months
Alternative seats: Overseas seats
Extras: Language training

A corporate-driven firm with a more pleasant, understated atmosphere than you'd normally expect of the City. Offering big deals, but without big egos, year after year Travers Smith Braithwaite manages to attract some of the best trainees. It wants to be seen as a premium brand firm: an alternative to the law factories. And in our book, it's getting what it wants.

people like us
The firm's own brochure recommends: *"peacocks need not apply"* (presumably meaning that they don't like show-offs). To stick to this avian metaphor, Travers Smith Braithwaite trainees, with their poise, good breeding and quiet competence probably see themselves more like kestrels, especially when compared to the eagles and hawks at some of their City neighbours. Trainees come across as contented, quietly confident and calm, and they all think they're onto a good thing compared to the megafirms. *"It's a lawyer's law firm. When you speak to people at other firms they tell you that you've done well to get in here."*

Each year we scour for clues as to what type of applicant different firms go for. The TSB website helpfully sets out the biogs of its current trainees. As in previous years, it shows that a high proportion of trainees come from just a few universities. Oxbridge, Exeter and Durham seem to have been the clear favourites of the recruitment team recently. When we put it to one trainee that it seemed a little narrow-minded to take 70% of trainees from just four universities, they countered that the firm was just interested in the best applicants, not in the university that applicants had attended. *"It just turns out that the best applicants come from the best universities."* But to claim that *"the university you went to is utterly irrelevant"* didn't do much for one witness' credibility.

The bottom line seems to be that *"trainees are exclusively middle class, but there's no attitude of filling the place with old Etonian and Harrow boys. I think they're looking for articulate people who can show that they have a life outside the firm."* One trainee did concede that the firm did have an *"old school"* and *"traditional"* side, which went some way to explaining the recruitment from the more establishment institutions. Despite this, trainees were keen to stress that *"at the end of the day I think they are just looking for people they would like to work with,"* and *"you're given every chance to prosper and you are judged on your merits."* One told us: *"We are not overly serious, and not overly ambitious."*

To apply you won't need to tell any porkies about

how you once rescued a mountain goat with a twisted ankle from the upper reaches of the Himalayas; a letter and CV is all that is required in the first instance. *"They assume that if you've got a good degree from a decent university and can make it through an interview then you've got what it takes,"* said one trainee. With no flaming hoops to jump through, recruitment is straightforward and sensible – rather like the firm.

are we doing a deal?
Successful applicants attend drinks and presentations at the firm during the Easter vacation before they start, and make their seat choices then. The selection is not set in stone though – if you feel the need to change, the firm is pretty accommodating. Six months of corporate (including banking), property and litigation will be followed by a free choice from the remaining departments, which include employment, pensions, tax, corporate recovery and financial services. For those with wanderlust, there's a seat in Paris and there have been discussions about creating a six-month posting to the recently acquired Berlin office.

Property is a very good seat to start with since you are likely to get *"small deals to cut your teeth on."* The employment team *"has an excellent reputation"* and offers *"a one-to-one training with a good mix of contentious and non-contentious work."* You are more likely to get bogged down with admin tasks in the company department because the deals involve so much documentation and are worth so much money, but even then, said one source, *"I got to draft a contract."* In 2001, the department handled around 90 M&A transactions with a total value of £5.8 billion, and private equity work is high on the agenda, with the firm acting for both venture capitalists and management teams.

In terms of training, the smaller, more intimate ethos of TSB means that you're more likely to get more individual attention. *"There are fewer fee earners here than at other firms so they have to rely on trainees a lot more,"* said one source. You'll be sat in an office with a partner and an assistant, which is thought to be *"an ideal way of learning"* and means that *"you can bounce silly questions off the assistant rather than the partner."* Each department gives internal seminars on *"really useful stuff that you need to know."* This side of training takes the form of two lunchtime sessions each week.

staying power
As one source said, *"I just wanted a place where I felt comfortable, could do quality work, and where they recruit to retain."* In a recent survey of attrition rates in the legal press (to monitor which firms lost most employees to other firms or professions) TSB scored very highly for holding on to its lawyers. Several of the trainees we spoke with thought they'd have a hard time finding a better working environment in London. *"If you can't get on with people here you'll have difficulties getting on with people anywhere."*

The office itself has recently been extended and refurbished and for the first time in a decade the whole firm is now under one roof. The staff restaurant serves up subsidised meals and you even get a £5-a-week allowance, which goes a long way. There's also a Starbucks coffee machine. (Blimey – they get everywhere!) *"After 6.30pm you have unlimited access to junk food and you get free dinner between 7pm and 9pm,"* enthused one trainee, clearly oblivious to the carrot-like effect such perks have. One other notable and telling freebie is the leather briefcase that mark trainees' first 12 months with the firm and comes embossed with their initials. *"A nice gesture,"* thought one trainee. Unfortunately you don't get a matching umbrella at the end of your second year. Nine out of 13 September 2002 qualifiers stayed on with the firm.

roman orgy?
The offices are close to super-trendy Smithfield, which is considered to be a pleasanter place to work than most parts of the City. When it comes to unwinding after hours, the Bishop's Finger is the traditional trainee haunt. Socialising is encouraged, *"just so long as you maintain the balance and don't come in steaming mid-week!"* There is an annual Christmas

party. Last year it was a *"highbrow, black-tie affair at the Dorchester with excellent food and wine."* Don't be deceived though. The year before there were tales of power-lifting gladiators and lawyers dressed in togas attending a Bacchanalian knees-up at Vinopolis. Trainees noted the *"sportiness"* of the place. There are teams for rugby sevens, hockey, football, softball, cricket and golf, where the firm takes on other law firms and clients. TSB organises a half marathon in Paris each year, but *"if you go you have to run;"* it's not an excuse for shopping and lounging around in pavement cafés!

Alas, we must report that Travers has lost its crown as the most luvved-up firm in the UK. For two years running we heard tales of drunken fumbles and blossoming romance amongst trainees, but the love well has run dry. As one trainee told us: *"People have realised there are other fish in the sea."*

and finally...

Despite a recent strategy review, TSB will most likely continue down the same well-trodden path. It may not be as cutting edge as some of the big(ger) boys, but if you're on to something good, it seems wise to conserve it. A heartily recommended training.

Trowers & Hamlins

the facts

Location: London, Manchester, Exeter
UK ranking by size: 60
Total number of trainees: 31
Seats: 4x6 seats
Alternative seats: Overseas seats

Trowers & Hamlins has an unrivalled practice in social housing, which is closely linked to its burgeoning construction practice. It is also dominant in the Middle East, with offices in Oman, Abu Dhabi, Bahrain, Cairo and Dubai concentrating on large-scale projects and general corporate work.

public seating

If you like the sound of combining either or both of Trowers' strongest suits with a more general commercial training, then quite simply, you'll not find a better place. Fear not; you'll not be forced into one or other specialism for the majority of your training. Indeed, the consensus among trainees is that, with a bit of luck, *"you'll get every seat you ask for,"* and at worst you'll have *"a fairly good run."* Property is inevitable and trainees are made aware that *"it would be good"* if they did a corporate/commercial seat. Having said that, some trainees are deemed to have satisfied this by having done a public sector seat, which is *"effectively half corporate and half property."* The construction department also sets pulses racing. As for the housing and public sector departments, *"because of their size and the nature of the firm, every trainee tends to spend time in at least one of them."* The housing department acts for over 250 social landlords plus banks and building societies lending large sums to them.

A couple of trainee positions are available in Manchester every two years and applicants tend to be recruited locally. The Manchester office is much smaller and has less to offer in the way of seat options so its trainees are given the choice of six months of London corporate work, should they want it. Reversing the flow of traffic, some London trainees go up north for property litigation.

gulf balls

The Abu Dhabi office takes a trainee every six months and Oman opens its doors to two. Bahrain and Dubai have also recently started offering seats. One trainee extolled the virtues of the Abu Dhabi office: *"There's the prestige in being at the largest firm in the Middle East and the lifestyle is fantastic. It's got an enormous expat population and you get a great package in terms of living and travel expenses."* Fabulous! But of course, there's a catch: *"The official office hours in the Middle East are 8am-7pm every day and you're expected to work a five and a half-day week."* It follows that *"the office is a bigger part of your life in the Middle East than in*

London." Another trainee, who'd been out to Muscat, was thrilled to have had major international clients use them as the first point of contact. *"My involvement was of a level that I probably wouldn't have got in London. I was treated like I was a qualified rather than just a trainee and I came back to London with a huge amount of confidence and a range of good commercial experience."*

In the first week, almost every trainee claims to want time in the Gulf offices but, over time, the numbers drop off as girlfriends/boyfriends/spouses and mortgages exert more influence. (Duh?!) With five seats on offer every six months and just 15 new trainees taken on each year, the chances of securing a posting are high. One trainee offered this advice: *"Just open your mouth on day one and express interest, and every so often keep mentioning it."*

sinking your teeth in

Levels of responsibility depend heavily on the seat you're in. One trainee told us: *"In some departments you get more back-up in terms of support staff. In property I was running my own files so I had secretarial help, but in corporate it was more a case of me assisting other people with their work rather than producing my own work."* Another said, *"In property I got a massive amount of responsibility. I was given conveyances in the handover from the previous trainee and had to field calls from clients from day one."* Overall, interviewees agreed that *"it's tricky being thrown in the deep end, but you have to get used to it."*

"If you do something wrong, you'll be told in a constructive way. You're not a solicitor yet. You're a trainee – you're there to make mistakes and there is a safety net." With training lunches every third Monday, involving speakers (usually from the firm, but sometimes external) giving lectures on various topics, there's plenty to digest other than the sandwiches. *"It's a good way to get to know what those departments are all about and what work they do,"* one source said. Another added: *"They're a good opportunity for trainees to get together. It's social as well as educational."* It's an easy, relaxed approach to training – *"You don't take notes. You just listen and hope it sinks in!"* Back to student days then!

electric blue pants

To fit in at Trowers you need to be *"individual, amiable and reasonably ambitious – but not overly so."* When pressed, our sources confirmed that the firm has a team atmosphere, and so *"if you're aggressive and out to make it as the big boy who wears the braces and the electric blue pants, it's not the place for you."* Another trainee added: *"You must have character…they're not interested in people who try to hide their light under a bushel."* Hide? We're not sure there are any hiding places. It's not that big a firm, and you're closely supervised and reviewed every three months, so *"everyone will know who you are and what you're up to."* The managing partner makes an effort to get to know all the trainees and will have a meal with each new intake at the beginning of their training contracts. Ooh! It doesn't bear thinking about…too much cutlery…tricky bits of fish…all those nervous, shaky hands.

The office is a *"unique"* tower in the shape of an equilateral triangle, which *"takes some getting used to"* so put a protractor in your pencil case on day one. On two sides there are *"awesome"* views of Tower Bridge and the Tower of London, which *"gobsmacked"* one of our interviewees for eight months. He was less moved by the other side, which has *"no view at all."*

winged beasts

"There are social activities all the time," raved one trainee, who went on to tell us about two-monthly drinks up on the top (ie sixth) floor at the end of every billing drive and firm-wide pub quizzes and karaoke evenings. These events enable trainees to get to know people from other departments and catch up with those they already know. Trainees socialise most regularly with those in their own intake, and the new Bar 38 on The Minories has become quite popular. Bottom line: *"You can have as much or as little of a social life as you want, but there's always someone going out for drinks after work – and someone who makes the mistake of carrying on!"*

One trainee encapsulated it beautifully when he said, *"I'd love to stay on a long-term basis, but if it pans out that I can't, I've got my options open – I feel well trained and* confident that I've got wings if I want to use them." We were heartened to learn that in September 2002 there were more NQ jobs available than there were qualifiers to fill them. 13 out of the 14 stayed on with the firm, with three going to the Gulf.

and finally…

If social responsibility is important to you, but you want to work at the decision making end of housing, then make a beeline straight for Trowers & Hamlins. If you're interested in the Middle East, this is **the** firm to go for. If you're not quite sure what moves you, consider the firm for its general commercial training.

Veale Wasbrough

the facts

Location: Bristol
UK ranking by size: 84
Total number of trainees: 13
Seats: 4x6 months
Alternative seats: None
Extras: Bristol Law Centre

A Bristol firm that targets its broad range of services at medium-sized businesses, public sector clients and the not-for-profit sector, Veale Wasbrough is a decent sized partnership (third largest single-site Bristol independent) without a big, brash mentality.

heinz 57 varieties

A former president of the Bristol Law Society once intimated to one interviewee that VW was a good place to train because it had the potential to offer such a broad range of work. There aren't many firms where you could be working on a £50 million commercial contract one week and then change seat to run 50 of your own low-value PI claims the next.

Trainees tend to spend at least one seat in the commercial property department (one of the firm's core strengths), a period in some variety of litigation and a seat in CoCo (*"That's company/commercial – I hate that shortening"*). Other seats can be found in employment and construction. Departments such as schools, family, and estates and tax planning do not regularly take trainees, *"but if you really wanted a seat there, they would make every effort to accommodate you."* While *"there isn't one duff seat,"* *"no one actually wants to do PI."* It can turn out to be a blessing in disguise – running your own files brings bags of responsibility and client exposure.

all talk

About 18 months ago VW employed a dedicated training manager. Part of their duties is to act as an intermediary between trainees and partners, and training-wise, things have looked up ever since. Previously held feelings that there was no one to talk to and problems in securing the right amount of the right sort of work seem to have dissipated. *"They are making a genuine effort to make it a bit more structured and give you something to aim for,"* confirmed one satisfied customer. Appraisals take place in the middle and at the end of each seat and there are detailed checklists of skills and experiences to tick off in between. The mid-seat review is also the time to lay claim to the seat you want next. One source said, *"They now make strenuous efforts to make sure you get your first choice."* Prior to each seat rotation you can find out exactly what you've let yourself in for. *"We have a meeting just for trainees and we talk frankly about how the seats really are."* And there's more: VW has a buddy system that pairs up each new trainee with an existing one when they join the firm. Talk? We can almost see the cows from here.

It might be something to do with having an open-plan office, but there's no need to feel isolated at this firm. *"You never feel like you're intruding, and you can hear everything else that goes on around you."* Trainees learn to seek advice from more senior colleagues from early on as they participate in a scheme whereby the firm offers a free half-hour of legal advice to the members of one of their union clients. *"These people phone up with all manner of strange problems and I have to ask people to help me from all over the firm."*

early impressionists

VW makes an impression on its future trainees in just a one-day interview. *"There are no airs and graces. All firms' recruitment brochures say their firm is friendly, but this one's claim has been backed up in my experience."* Many of its applicants have studied in Bristol and want to stay in the city. The relaxed attitude of the firm seems to be another part of the appeal. *"They don't do the hard sell...their attitude is 'If you like it, this is what it is'."* We were relieved to hear that the VW trainees have good common sense as well as good academics. Those we spoke to judged most to be *"quite independent and strong characters (but not brash), quite outgoing (but not in a bad way) and all just normal."*

Each trainee sits with a partner, gets to know their cases and takes calls from their clients. Responsibility varies with the type of deal or case. On a larger deal in CoCo, one source found it *"good on overall training, but the work didn't involve as much responsibility."* Other trainees have led client meetings, with the partner just there to bail them out. *"You have to be able to say 'no' to work sometimes,"* as almost anyone in the department may try and grab you to assist them. Outside office work, trainees advise at the Bristol Law Centre and the firm also participates in the Young Enterprise scheme, enabling trainees to lord about as business managers once a week in local schools.

home comforts

The hours are really rather civilised. Quite simply, *"you do your work and then go home or to the pub."* The typical day is 9am to 5.30/6pm but, on Fridays, folk are out of the door by 5pm. One lucky trainee spent a nightmare couple of weeks in corporate, culminating in a 5am finish one Sunday morning. Fortunately, we hear, they got some time off to recover afterwards.

The firm occupies a Listed wall of a big old warehouse. There is a whole building behind this wall...just not the original one. The social life of the firm starts in the office, or more precisely in the canteen (*"top floor...lovely views"*). *"It's a nice focal point that other firms don't have. You don't have to go up for lunch with anyone, you can just chat to anyone who's there."* Added home comforts include tea and toast in the morning. The food by all accounts is decent, but the downside is *"we have to pay for tea and coffee."* Oh dear! But it gets worse...*"We don't have a mug angel."* A what? *"Other firms have a mug angel who washes mugs overnight."* So remember, don't forget to pack your Marigolds in that nice briefcase your Mum's going to buy you before you start your training contract. As for those completing their training, two out of the three September 2002 qualifiers stayed with the firm.

encore une fois

VW lawyers just keep going back to Encore, their local pub. There is no pressure to join the fun, but if trainees want it (and we get the impression they usually do), there's enough going on to provide a good social life, even if you've just moved to Bristol. A sports and social committee organises monthly events, and be prepared for the Christmas and summer parties. Recent themes have included the 1970s and heroes and villains. We didn't dare ask about the costumes...

Apparently, the firm has a bit of a reputation in Bristol...but it's all good. *"We're known for being a sociable firm. You can always rely on us to turn up."* VW encourages its trainees to get involved in the Bristol Trainee Solicitors Group and is even happy for them to give up work time for the cause. But this isn't just a CV filler: *"I thought it would be a chore, but it gives you a really wide range of friends."* The TSG seems to be the perfect forum for trainee 'exploits' because *"if the gossip was internal it would be bad as your partner would know what you had been up to!"* The Bristol legal community is just the right size for word to get around easily. *"There's always salacious gossip that pops out after events, but our firm isn't a major source."* Shame.

and finally...

If you are undecided about which Bristol firm is for you, consider an application to Veale Wasbrough. It offers a Third Way, being neither hardcore corporate nor high street.

Walker Morris

the facts
Location: Leeds
UK ranking by size: 61
Total number of trainees: 29
Seats: 6x4 months
Alternative seats: None

Walker Morris is proud of its heritage. Unlike many of its peers in Leeds, it has not established offices elsewhere, nor does it have any discernible plans to do so. However, it continues to forge relationships with clients outside the region and the single-site strategy is certainly paying dividends, literally. Turnover and partner profits have shown a healthy increase despite a sluggish economy. Its website may come across as a real Jimi Hendrix experience, but the real Walker Morris is rather less freaky. Some firms are solid, grounded and sorted, and this is one of them.

the good, the bad and the ugly

As a trainee, you will do six seats, three of which will be in the mainstays of corporate, property and litigation. You may end up with something more than the plain vanilla version of each; for example, property litigation counts as a property seat, employment counts as a contentious seat and PFI comes under the banner of corporate. In practice, trainees will normally be allocated these 'compulsoryish' seats during their first year. Second-years then adopt a fairly unorthodox method of seat allocation, divvying up the choice spots amongst themselves and taking the outcome to the training partner for approval or rejigging in the event that agreement cannot be reached. *"Generally everyone gets what they want eventually,"* although sometimes there are *"Mexican stand-offs over seats!"* Doubtless this method enables trainees to hone negotiation skills.

There were a number of new seats on offer this year, namely in environmental law and public sector/PFI. We also heard there was a private client seat available *"if someone wants it – but it's rarely taken up."* Trailing in last place in the popularity stakes is retail property, which is *"probably a legacy of conveyancing and landlord and tenant at college."*

the good life

Our interviewees were attracted to the firm for a variety of reasons. One was impressed by the interview: *"It wasn't about getting your back up and seeing if you had the mettle to fight back, but about seeing whether you're a person they'd like to have around."* Another liked its single-site policy: *"It's centrally managed and not splintered into offices around the country, so if you need to talk to someone, they're not someone alien. They'll be someone you've seen walking in the corridor."*

The Leeds factor should never be underestimated: *"If you're not someone who wants to stay in Leeds, Walker Morris is not for you."* That said, proving your credentials will not be too difficult. *"They're not looking for you to have x amount of relatives in Yorkshire or anything like that."* Indeed, our interviewees came from any number of places, *"some north, some south."* The bottom line is that the firm *"focuses on people who have a real desire to be in the North and are not looking to bugger off to London after qualification."* On the contrary, a desire to stay away from London is a common theme. *"We're not a bunch of flat-capped, whippet-keeping Yorkshire people; we just want different things out of life."* And the final word on Leeds v London? *"I don't like getting a cattle-train to work and paying a fortune for a dilapidated flat. It's a quality of life issue. Leeds is a big financial hub and a lively place, it's close to the Yorkshire Dales and the moors, it's near the coast and it's got good country pubs."* Hmmm…they've got a point. We took a pre-6am train to Leeds one day last summer and we watched lawyers arriving for work. Easy? Like a London Sunday morning!

boomerangs and balls

As a trainee, you will share an office with your principal, who is usually a partner. One of our sources said, *"Sitting with a partner is great, because they work at the highest level so they can give you higher quality work than* you'd get if you were sitting with someone more junior." Client secondments arise on an ad hoc basis. When we interviewed, one trainee was away for four months at BUPA. We understood they were in good health.

While hours vary from department to department, trainees indicate the working day runs from 8.45/9am until sixish. Corporate has *"spurts of longer hours"* and *"if you're working on a big completion it will take you into the night."* Formal appraisals take place at the end of each seat as well as a more informal (and optional) mid-seat review, commonly of the *"lunch or a beer and a chat"* variety. While our interviewees were happy about appraisals, some were less ecstatic about day by day feedback. One trainee said, *"I think I'd make some of the more senior partners go on a course in communication skills. Some of them aren't very good at talking to you."* Another added: *"Feedback varies from principal to principal – some are better than others and some you actually have to chase if you want specific feedback."* That said, your work *"never just disappears – it always comes back with corrections."*

Trainees are given as much responsibility as they can handle. *"You're expected to do the job and get on with it calmly and professionally."* So, *"if you're looking to have your hand held,"* forget it. Particularly in the property and litigation seats you'll get to run small files from pretty early on and attend client meetings. One trainee told us: *"a couple of times I was sent to client meetings on my own, which was quite frightening, but a good experience."* The consensus is that *"to be a trainee here, you need to be very determined and have a pretty strong personality."* One trainee said, *"It's a dynamic firm, very driven and very ambitious. They require a big level of commitment and hard work from their staff."*

going to the dogs

Leeds is stacked with bars and pubs, but there are two that have a magnetic pull. Wharf Street is *"a 60-second stumble"* from the back door of the office and tucked down an alleyway. It's particularly popular on Friday nights when it's *"Walker Morris-dominated,"* from partners through to support staff. Then there's Sous Le Nez – *"handy for client brunches"* or just *"grabbing a bite at lunchtime."* There are firm-wide drinks evenings on the last Thursday of every month, but trainees have their own social budget, which is spent on things like go-karting, paintballing and *"going to the dogs."* We assume this means greyhound racing, not massive binges in Wharf Street. The Leeds Trainee Solicitors Group events are *"a good laugh"* and you'll invariably hook up with all your friends from law school who've distributed themselves around Leeds firms.

The office is right in the centre of Leeds, *"handy for court"* and *"three minutes' walk from the train station."* In recent times, the firm has expanded to such an extent that *"it doesn't fit the building anymore"* and the insurance litigation department has been relocated in office space across the road. The firm's dress code means you'll be suited and booted all week long.

film critics

All trainees are invited to attend a series of training videos about various areas of law. They are produced by the College of Law and put on *"about once a week in batches."* Opinion as to the merits of the videos was split. One trainee explained: *"The College of Law collates all the latest cases and gets people to talk about them. But by the time they've produced it, put it on tape and released it, it's about six months behind."* In addition, *"the people they get on tend not to be particularly photogenic or particularly polished for TV."* Oh dear! We did hear some counterbalancing comment, though: *"Even if the area in question doesn't interest you, it's a good idea to attend, because you might pick up something that's useful – it's a good way of becoming well-rounded."* In September 2002, eight out of the 11 second-years stayed on at the firm after qualifying.

and finally…

Do you want a career in Leeds? Are you prepared to be challenged? Do you want to work in an office that's top (and only) dog rather than one of several branches? If you answered yes to these questions, Walker Morris is going to be your preferred option.

Ward Hadaway

the facts
Location: Newcastle-upon-Tyne
UK ranking by size: 78
Total number of trainees: 16
Seats: 4x6 months
Alternative seats: None

Sited a stone's throw from the Millennium Bridge on Newcastle's recently redeveloped Quayside, Ward Hadaway is thriving. Not only does it have the best commercial litigation department in the region, it's brave enough to put real lawyers in its brochure…

no rest for the WHicked
In last year's *True Picture*, we reported that Ward Hadaway had merged with Keenlyside & Forster from across the river in Gateshead. Although it doesn't yet have quite the presence of a certain local rival, it is well on the way after several similarly ambitious mergers and take-overs. And there are rumoured to be more to come. *"That's the whole thing about the firm, it is constantly growing and changing,"* said one source. With the ability to poach senior partners from the likes of Eversheds and Pinsent Curtis Biddle, in the last dozen years Ward Hadaway has grown in excess of 1000%. The firm draws on a respectable pool of local, national and international clients, so trainees can be assured of a good quality work. WH won't rest on its laurels – *"The firm is energetic and enthusiastic for the work, and always out to provide new services and get new clients."*

mighty meaty
Stepping into a four seat system, new trainees are asked if there are specific areas they would consider for qualification and the training is built around their answers. If you are undecided, the training is flexible enough to allow for this. In any case, you won't be asked to make a final decision about where you want to qualify until well into your last seat, giving you at least 18 months to get your head on the right way.

Trainees are expected to do *"one commercial, one property and one litigation seat, but can chose within those areas."* IP and IT are popular, but the departments are relatively small, so think carefully if this is your only motivation for applying. The planning department features more frequently on trainee wish lists because *"you have your own files and immediate responsibility for your workload"* and *"the work turns around quicker so you get to follow your own cases all the way through to the end."* Not only that, *"you get client contact all the time, over the phone and at on-site meetings. The supervisor comes with you, but you're left to ask most of the questions."*

The firm is renowned for its healthcare team, and as an NHS Litigation Authority panel member, it conducts a lot of clinical negligence defence work. It's a big attraction for trainees and *"a department that people really enjoy as it is so specialist,"* although *"the content of the cases can be quite depressing at times."* *"The work is normally quite meaty,"* so trainees understand that they won't always get complete responsibility for cases.

wahoo!
Trainees typically sit with partners or senior associates and receive *"constant support and supervision."* *"For the first six weeks or so you are heavily supervised while they work out how you will cope,"* but once supervisors have ascertained your abilities, *"they give you work and just let you get on with it."* Trainees say, *"The firm has got the balance just right."* The best bit, gushed one, is *"when you get the first document back without red pen on it. You go 'Wahoo! That can go straight out!'"* Bless!

Many supervisors offer a 15- to 20-minute feedback session each morning, *"so they know what you are up to and how you are getting on."* These supplement official reviews in the middle and at the end of each seat. They certainly sound prepared to go the extra mile to make the training experience a good one. We heard of partners dropping in on trainees who had sat with them in earlier seats for a chat and to see how they were finding their new home. In fact, the only grumble we heard was over the system for airing grumbles!

painting a pitcher

The firm is housed in two buildings, back-to-back on Newcastle's quayside. The older of these, Sandgate, is still less than ten years old and has *"normal little box offices that you share with a partner,"* unlike the open-plan layout of the brand new Keel Row. *"Work-wise the open-plan offices are better because you are surrounded by your team, but you have absolutely no privacy,"* said one source. The top floor meeting rooms have fantastic views of the Tyne and Millennium Bridges, and the walls are adorned with paintings and pictures of the same – *"Just in case you have your back to them and can't be bothered to turn around."* Generally, *"the offices are pretty simple and have everything you need,"* including a staff room, so you can pop off to eat your sangers out of the Newcastle rain. Watch out hay fever sufferers: the firm is *"big on flower arrangements,"* and agoraphobics ought to be aware that *"the amount of glass and windows make it really light and airy."*

Should you find yourself in need of some liquid refreshment, stroll on over to the Pitcher & Piano, favoured alehouse of the trainees. *"It's almost a religious experience,"* whispered one, devoutly. *"People try to finish bang on five on a Friday."* Find that in London and we'll eat our keyboards! Stereo, a new bar tucked away behind the offices, is increasingly pulling them in, as is Waterline. But the most diverse of the trainees' destinations is Live Theatre – a theatre at night and a café by day. On the subject of food, WH trainees are sure to be found lunching together every Friday; it's a collective thing. Just look at the Newcastle United fans after any game and you'll see what we mean. In terms of retention, five out of the eight September 2002 qualifiers stayed on with the firm.

and finally…

Ward Hadaway sponsors The Fastest Fifty, a scheme for up-and-coming businesses in the region, and is investing in itself by investing time in these ventures. So if you want to be a part of a team that looks after its own and values its regional roots, head on past the Angel and look for the curvy bridge.

Watson, Farley & Williams

the facts

Location: London
UK ranking by size: 77
Total number of trainees: 24
Seats: 6x4 months
Alternative seats: Overseas seats
Extras: Language training

Watson, Farley & Williams started life in 1982 as a niche shipping practice. Matters nautical remain core business, but it has expertise in many other corporate and commercial areas, and a particularly strong asset finance practice.

wake up call

The firm operates a six-seat system, which includes three compulsory seats – finance (either 'pure' or ship finance), litigation and corporate. Then you'll choose between property, IP, employment, tax or EU law or return visits to the main departments. Judging by trainees' comments, you'll usually get a reasonable amount of say in seat allocation: *"There aren't enough of us to cause any real headaches, and they're generally pretty flexible."* An overseas seat is offered to all trainees and *"rarely not taken up,"* particularly in light of the fact that any of the compulsories can be done abroad.

An average day is *"about 9.20am to 6.15pm,"* although *"everyone goes through busy periods."* In terms of late nights, *"the shipping team has some of the latest hours, particularly when they're closing finance."* The work is so international that this may impact on your hours: *"You might find you have to wake up at a certain time to co-ordinate a transaction between Hong Kong, Australia and Surinam."* Sounds complicated!

thrown a lifeline

Each trainee shares an office with their supervisor, who tends to be either a partner or an assistant who is *"senior by quite a few years, not just a few years qualified."* The responsibility given to trainees is generally high.

One said, "*They throw you in at the deep end, but you're not just left to drown – there's always support there.*" While some trainees mentioned that they would have liked more client contact, others said, "*From the word go I've been given my own files to work on, and I've had a lot of interaction with clients.*" Along these lines, one trainee reported: "*I've had a number of client meetings where it was just me and the client in the meeting room dealing with things.*" By all accounts, responsibility is higher still in the overseas offices. "*The teams there are generally smaller. You'll get absorbed into the team pretty quickly and they'll require you to get involved from day one.*" One trainee told us of attending a meeting in a foreign country by himself as the representative of one of the firm's clients. "*It was a business transaction relating to taking delivery of a new vessel. There were Russians and Germans on either side of the table yabbering away to themselves, while I was there to make sure all the delivery documentation was up to scratch and the conditions precedent for the loan satisfied. After I'd done that, I handed over US$15 million.*" That sure beats proof-reading!

Sounds great – but what about grunt work? "*We do our fair share, but we're certainly not chained to a photocopier and putting bundles together all the time.*" It seems that it all balances out.

talking points

All trainees have mid- and end-of-seat reviews as well as an annual one. The mid-seat review is "*more an informal chat*" with your supervisor, possibly over lunch. While most interviewees were happy with the system, there was some comment that the reviews "*don't always go according to plan.*" "*Sometimes they've been late, or they haven't happened, because my supervisor's been too busy and has kept putting it off.*" As for ongoing feedback from supervisors, we heard mixed reports. Some are brilliant, others not. We learn that HR has bought itself a whip and isn't afraid to use it.

"*There are in-house lectures from different specialists within the firm,*" as well as a variety of external speakers. Departmental seminars and lunchtime meetings have, on occasion, even involved trainees making the presentation. "*I'm glad I did it, but I'm also glad I don't have to do it again!*" said one source.

You may have heard that the firm spent much of 2002 in merger talks with Simmons & Simmons. The talks died a death in the early summer, but it raises the question of whether or not WF&W is determined to find a partner. Funnily enough, this is exactly what we wrote 12 months ago in last year's *True Picture* after cancelled talks with a US firm. To repeat the salient bit again: firms merge when they think it makes good business sense. Will WF&W try again?

international firm of mystery

"*It originally started as a shipping finance practice, so over the years, irrespective of what department you go into, you tend to find banking clients.*" In addition to banks, there are a lot of ship owners and "*companies wanting to enter into lease transactions.*" Trainees stressed that "*a lot of the work is interlinked with the shipping aspect – the litigation department does a lot of wet and dry maritime litigation and our international finance group encompasses both shipping and pure finance, so the deals tend to cross over.*"

The prevailing feeling was that the firm is "*youthful and progressive – it's only 20 years old, so it's certainly not stuffy or old-fashioned. There are a number of heads of department who are in their mid- to late-30s.*" "*Although they're quite a young bunch, that's not to say they're not experienced. A lot of partners trained here and rose through the ranks.*" Pretty much everything you work on has an international flavour to it, even at trainee level. One trainee elaborated on this point: "*It's one of the aspects I've really grown to love here – working with clients and lawyers from all over the world. You have to think about time zone aspects and knock-on effects in other jurisdictions, which involves liaising with a lot of foreign counsel.*"

All trainees get the chance to spend a seat abroad, but "*if you don't want to go, they won't press you to.*" That said, if for example you're a fluent French speaker, "*they might think about trying to persuade you to go to Paris.*" That raises an interesting point. Are languages a determining factor in where you can go? Yes and no, it seems. *"Most of the clients you deal with in shipping will be speaking English,"* however, some seats are really only suitable for those with the relevant language.

mind-blowing decisions

"I wanted some international work and overseas experience," said one trainee, explaining their reason for choosing WF&W. *"With a large firm you can get that, but you also get swallowed up."* The size of the firm is important to trainees. *"I wanted decent commercial experience but I also wanted to be able to recognise everyone in the building in a short period of time."* And as for the shipping theme, one told us: *"I didn't know anything about shipping when I joined. My impression was 'God, that must be a bit dry!' However, the shipping seat really blew my mind. It's phenomenally interesting and the responsibility you get there is fantastic."*

"The firm offers other areas, but a lot of trainees come here specifically for shipping. The norm is that people do one shipping seat, maybe even two." In addition, we were told: *"If you've got no interest in going abroad or doing international work, there's not much point coming here."* It comes as no surprise that quite a few trainees are from international or slightly unusual backgrounds. In the current crop, there are Russian, Danish, German and Greek Cypriot trainees, as well as a number of people who had worked or studied abroad for a year as part of a language degree.

ship shape

Although there is a permanent dress-down policy, *"some people feel more comfortable dressing up all the time."* The firm occupies a *"flash"* building with a central atrium. We're told that *"the upstairs corridors look very much like a ship."* You don't say! The fourth floor canteen is said to have improved since getting a new chef in 2001. *"It's very sociable"* at trainee level, with regular drinks evenings and frequent group lunches. Beneath the building there's an All Bar One (*"our very own Ally McBeal Bar"*) where people from the firm *"hang out quite a lot,"* which according to a couple of the confirmed chain-bar haters we encountered is *"unfortunate."* Thankfully, there are plenty of decent bars in Hoxton and Shoreditch where trainees arrange to meet up with younger assistants.

Contrasting with the previous year's figures, only five out of the 12 qualifiers stayed with the firm in September 2002. Trainees said, *"A lot of departments simply weren't taking on anyone, full stop."* *"It became very competitive this year, particularly in relation to finance and shipping, which is a shame."* Indeed.

and finally…

There is more to WF&W than shipping. The firm's asset finance practice is particularly highly regarded, and there are a variety of other practice areas on offer in this *"driven and dynamic"* environment.

Wedlake Bell

the facts
Location: London
UK ranking by size: 96
Total number of trainees: 10
Seats: 4x6 months
Alternative seats: None

Set in the delightful surrounds of Covent Garden and Guernsey, Wedlake Bell's lawyers make their mark in areas as diverse as corporate and banking right through to employment, education and private client.

mapping out the future

Our interviewees were drawn to the firm for fairly similar reasons. *"You get to know everyone fairly quickly and it's a good atmosphere – you feel like you're really making a difference as part of a team."* Actually, there's parity between the number of partners and assistants at Wedlake Bell so the front line is within reach, even for trainees. Most simply didn't want to work in a huge City firm – *"The attitude here is really geared towards quality of life; it's not just work, work, work."* And it's certainly not work, work, work for just one type of client. *"The variety really appeals to me,"* one of our sources explained. *"You could be dealing with wealthy individuals or multinational companies, private client work through to corporate takeovers."*

Commercial property is described as a *"stronghold"* of the firm and trainees must do a seat there as well as one in litigation. Employment is particularly popular as it is *"a hot topic, a growth area and a good department."* We were told: *"They try and do what they can to accommodate your interests,"* although as one trainee pointed out: *"It's a small firm and there aren't that many of us to fight about seats."* We learned that new trainees now have all of their seats mapped out for them soon after starting their training contract. One first-year told us: *"I had input at my initial interview; they asked me what areas I was interested in and then about two months before the end of my first seat they told me what my seats would be for the rest of my contract. Two of them are areas I'd expressed interest in, so I'm happy…it's nice to have the certainty."*

the art of conversation

The prevailing feeling was that Wedlake Bell is *"fairly traditional in its roots,"* but nevertheless is *"moving forward"* and *"becoming a lot more modern and keeping up with the times."* Trainees put this down to a progressive management board. As one source said, *"There's an increasing number of young partners here and they are the driving force for modernisation."* Some were more cautious in their assessment of the firm's evolution: *"We're an excellent firm, but we could be even better. We need more of a corporate vision and long-term strategy – we've been around for ages and we've got so much to offer, but we're just plodding along at the moment."*

Wedlake Bell has character. *"There are a lot of personalities floating around here,"* laughed one source, while another commented: *"They like their trainees to be outgoing and socially confident. They stress the importance of forging good relationships with clients and we often go out with them, so you have to be able to hold your own in terms of conversation and getting on with people."* One trainee went even further: *"If you don't have social skills, you're*

absolutely buggered here!" The client roster is stuffed full of smaller corporates, family businesses and SMEs. There's a good deal of crossover between the private client and commercial sides of the firm, with different departments handling the personal and business interests of the same clients. The small satellite office in Guernsey is also an important part of the equation, offering advice about offshore trusts, etc.

The London office is currently situated right in the centre of Covent Garden, split between two buildings, with the private client department, probate and *"some sort of conveyancing"* situated across the road from the main building. However, plans are afoot to bring everyone under one roof in High Holborn in 2004. *"They've been very good in terms of showing us plans of the building and how it's all going to fit together."* In addition, *"there are individuals from each team providing feedback as to how the building should develop – we're getting real input into it."* No disrespect to our interviewees, but we trust that their advice was limited to the layout of the offices and nothing more technical.

working the room

You will share an office with your supervisor and the bulk of your work will be for them with *"bits and bobs"* being done for others in the department. *"Because the teams here are fairly small, with about a dozen lawyers in each, a lot of people will come to you to give you work."* Those we spoke to were impressed with the balance between supervision and responsibility. *"You want responsibility, but at the same time you want someone there to make sure you're doing the job right, and you've got that the whole time here. Your work never just disappears into the ether."* Eventually, *"it gets to the point where they don't check every letter you send out."* While the consensus was that the firm throws its trainees *"in at the deep end,"* it plays it such that *"you develop professionally at the level of your own confidence – if you didn't feel comfortable doing something, they wouldn't make you."* Presumably still thinking in swimming pool metaphors, one trainee said, *"You don't get your hand held, but they never let you get out of your depth."*

"Where they can give you files of your own, they will," although this is said to be easier in departments like commercial property, where there are smaller matters available, as opposed to somewhere like litigation, where cases "can drag on for years." And the more menial side of things? "We're not training to be photocopier technicians – they very much discourage that." It goes without saying that Wedlake Bell wants its trainees to interact with clients: "You get to sit in on meetings and you're not expected to keep your mouth shut. Once you've had contact with a client, they encourage you to keep that contact." In addition, the firm puts on various client seminars and trainees must play their part and network. In bigger firms you might be able to hide behind a partner or senior associate, but here you're often going to be one-on-one with clients. "That's why social skills are important."

Formal appraisals take place every six months with HR and a couple of partners from the training committee, and you'll have "casual" monthly meetings with your supervisor, if you feel you need it. Many don't as they find the ongoing free flow of information quite sufficient.

like lambs to the boozer

The hours are certainly one of the selling points of this firm: 9.15am to 5.30/6pm was the average workday of our interviewees and "no one works on weekends." As one trainee said, "Our salaries aren't as high as City firms, but I didn't want to work all the hours God sent me like they do in the magic circle. I'd rather have a pay cut and a life." Even in the busiest departments, "it's never till sun-up – we're not that insane!" As far as the corporate department goes, we were told that the partner in charge has time management down to a fine art and plans ahead such that "even when we're ready for completion, the hours are only half eight to half seven or eight." Quick, someone find him a *Student Guide* merit badge.

Aside from firm-wide quarterly drinks and the Christmas and end-of-year parties, there are also regular departmental jollies. And, of course, there are Friday nights…"It's a good-humoured and fun firm to be in." The traditional pub of choice is The Lamb & Flag, where "people have gone since the year dot out of habit," although some trainees were "trying to shake it off for somewhere a bit more modern." Who knows where they'll get to after the office move. Of the six September 2002 qualifiers, four stayed with the firm.

and finally…

Do you want a West End offering "challenging work" but "not 16 hours a day?" Do you have social skills coming out of your ears? If you answered yes to these questions, Wedlake Bell should be on your list.

Weil, Gotshal & Manges

the facts

Location: London
UK ranking by size: 65
Total number of trainees: 17
Seats: 4x6 months
Alternative seats: Overseas seats

Just to clear up a few things before we start, we should point out that Weil, Gotshal & Manges are not fungal infections or luxury watches and Manges rhymes with the river Ganges. The firm was founded 70-odd years ago in New York, and the London office has been doing the business since 1996.

call of the weil

The firm bridges the gap between US and UK corporate and finance law and is the main player in the restructuring of Enron, Global Crossing and WorldCom. Even if you've never touched an *FT* in your life, you'll still have heard about these clients. If you're not interested in big transactions, and words like merger, acquisition and structured finance leave you cold, then turn the page now. Trainees pass through the corporate and finance departments at least once, spend three or six months in litigation, and then spend the rest of their time in areas like property, tax, insolvency or the US group. Despite its reach, just two of the foreign offices are available to trainees at present: New York and Silicon Valley.

money talks

When we mentioned US firms to trainees at other places the first things that came to mind were fat wallets, casual clothes and killer hours. We put that to the kids at Weil Gotshal. *"We work no longer hours than the magic circle firms, but it's true that we get paid a bit more."* Trainees here considered that *"big UK law firms are stuffy and you end up being just a number. Here they don't look down on you and you are treated as a lawyer from the outset."* The logic of Weil Gotshal trainees is that *"people choose magic circle firms because they are an institution. They're like redbrick universities."* If you are seeking high-end corporate and finance deals, then the choice between magic circle and US firms is a bit like going to a university that your parents approve of or going somewhere non-establishment that offers exactly the course you want. Trainees here are the kind of people who will try something new. Of course, the remuneration package plays no small part in the courtship.

> Chambers Global's Insolvency/Corporate Recovery Law Firm of the Year 2002

staying for another?

We asked one interviewee what their peers say about Weil Gotshal when they meet them down the pub. *"The usual thing that people bring up is the salary. When you tell them where you work you'll get a response like 'drinks on you then'."* And to counter an idea that seems to be doing the rounds amongst students: *"We are firmly seated in London and the firm's policy is based on permanence rather than setting up shop to make a quick buck. The firm is not going to pull out during the next downturn because the services we offer mean we're well poised for the economy going either way."*

Although the London office handles UK law, trainees believe that the knowledge they acquire of US law gives them a real advantage. *"Lots of acquisition structures and institutional finance rely on US law nowadays,"* one explained. They believe that their skills and experience will stand them in good stead in the event of any future career move. For the moment, though, no one's moving anywhere: all five qualifiers stayed with the firm in September 2002.

the clash of civilisations

US firms in London deal with their mixed roots quite differently. Some consider the US tag to be a misnomer and talk of themselves as the UK office of an international firm; others are surprised every time they step out of door to find that the cabs are black instead of yellow. At Weil Gotshal, they like to celebrate both aspects of the firm. *"This year we celebrated the Jubilee and the 4th of July,"* one trainee reported with pride. Each year the firm holds a retreat for its European lawyers. In 2002 the London contingent headed down to Barcelona for the conference talk and cava. *"Events like that remind you that you are part of a big network. I was surprised to meet so many characters I'd dealt with on transactions."* Everyone enjoyed quad biking and sailing in between the business. Retreat, consolidate, attack. Somebody's been reading their Sun Tzu.

value added

The social side of the firm is excellent. *"Everyone goes out together."* Trainees liked being part of a big global network but working out of a more intimate office. One told us: *"I don't get the feeling of a hierarchy. I've shared a cab with the senior partner and talked about holiday plans."* Mr Francies was also having everyone back to his during the summer for a party. *"He must have a massive place,"* speculated one trainee. Another said, *"You need people who can add value to a situation. You need someone who will be as chirpy at midnight as at nine in the morning."* Aha! So there's the catch. You need to be able to keep a big, all-American smile on your face when 'have a nice day' slides towards having a not so pleasant night. *"You have to work hard, but the hours are no worse than at the magic circle."* 9am - 7pm is average, but if there's work to do, you'll have to scrap your plans. Trainees gave us the impression that, compared to the City megafirms, you will be more like a trout in a pond than a minnow in a lake. *"I am given as much responsibility as I can handle and want to handle,"* said one trainee. *"During one transaction I had an integral role in the process. On the other side there were one- or two-year qualifieds doing the same thing as I was."*

What of the training? The firm hasn't been in London that long, but we were told that any teething problems were now firmly resolved. However, it's not become overly systematic: *"I felt that it might have become very anglicised since the training principals are all ex-magic circle. Because of that they are well aware of the work that you need to do, but they came to a US firm presumably because they wanted a change of style."* Trainees get an hour or two of training sessions each week and assessed the feedback and appraisals as both fair and useful. *"There is definitely no lack of training. The partners are well aware of their responsibilities towards trainees."* One trainee sobbed: *"I'm proud to have trained here."* Group hug everyone.

weil you were sleeping

The office itself is *"excellently located"* and *"immaculate."* Apparently it's a bit tight in litigation (*"the desk size halved when I started there"*), but other than that there's plenty of legroom. There's an on-site Starbucks but no McDonald's. Instead, a chef will rustle something up for you if you're still around and feeling peckish from 7pm onwards. *"There's only one bed in the building and I've only used it once when I had a hangover,"* said one trainee. *"It's very comfortable,"* said another.

Smart casual is the order of the day. But don't let down your guard. There are some sharp minds hiding in those slacks and chambray shirts. You'd be forgiven for mistaking Weil's recruitment brochure for a Marks & Sparks catalogue since it's made no effort to airbrush out the famous green letters on the cover and all the trainees sport lambswool and brushed cotton.

weil things

No sympathy from us for the trainee who said, *"My partner* [huggy-kissy type not boss type] *gets pissed off because there is a lot of socialising."* While you won't be blacklisted if you don't attend functions, *"you won't get the full Weil Gotshal experience."* One of the associates left to set up the nearby Sosho Match, which now gets a fair bit of custom from old colleagues. A recent party took a cowboys and indians theme, so *"there were a lot of Pocahontases running around."* Maybe he got his wires crossed, but one partner turned up in full drag – *"fishnet stockings and the works."*

and finally…

Weil, Gotshal & Manges will suit you if you want to work for big blue-chip companies, both domestic and international, but you don't want to be a part of a trainee army. Be prepared for the long hours and great expectations that will come with the job.

White & Case

the facts

Location: London
UK ranking by size: 71
Total number of trainees: 30
Seats: 4x6 months
Alternative seats: Overseas seats, secondments
Extras: Language training

White & Case is a global player with 40 offices. It started out in New York in 1901 and set up in London in 1971. If you've been monitoring White & Case's progress over the past few years, you'll have seen that its UK training scheme has grown enormously…just like the London office as a whole.

where everybody knows your name

Some US firms have the sort of London office that is worn on the arm like a trophy girlfriend; others have succeeded by focusing on a very narrow range of work, usually particular strands of finance; others still are really beginning to flourish in London, hiring top lawyers and paying them handsomely for what they bring to the firm. White & Case falls into this last category. "It started out as a flag-flying office for the firm, but is now becoming a London firm in its own right," said one trainee. "The partners here are committed to the place. It's not like they're going to suddenly pull out and head back to the States." Actually, there are only a handful of US lawyers in the London office and, after 30-odd years, the firm has solid roots here.

The appeal is a heady cocktail of foreign offices, huge salaries and top-class deals, served up in an intimate office "where everyone knows each other." W&C started taking trainees in 1996, and in the early years there was a sense that it was finding its feet when it came to training sessions, etc. For some of the partners, having one of the small army of trainees in their offices is a bit of a novelty, but our sources said, "The training has definitely improved. There are more sessions geared towards trainees and we have plenty of firm-wide know-how seminars." One said, "Sometimes I wish I had a more formal training structure," but others felt 'flexibility' was no bad thing. "It's ideal if you want commercial work in a firm that is a bit individual and in the process of growth." There is still a heavy emphasis on finance and projects work, but there are plenty of other seats, such as litigation, property, tax and IP. Overall, White & Case offers the largest and perhaps also the broadest training programme of the US firms in London.

wanderlust

The opportunities for travel are "fantastic." Everyone does a foreign seat; indeed, it would be an odd choice of firm if you didn't want six months overseas. The placement is neither a subsidised holiday nor compensation for 18 months of drudgery back in London. The firm clearly wants to integrate its youngsters into the worldwide White & Case network and infect them with legal wanderlust while they're still young. There's a chance of going to Singapore, Hong Kong, Warsaw, Paris, Brussels, Moscow, Prague…basically any place where deals are done and there's money to be made. Back in London you'll handle international work on a daily basis. With clients like ABN AMRO, BNP Paribas, Barclays Capital, CSFB, Deutsche Bank, Morgan Stanley and loads of others, you'll understand why finance – both structured and project – is going to feature highly.

Rumours abound about the long hours culture of US firms. Why else would they pay such huge salaries? However, trainees reassured us that the extra cash didn't mean unnecessarily long hours: "We are very busy, but not overworked. You'd struggle to find 50% of people here at 9 o'clock." The hours are generally 9.30am-7pm, and people do take lunch. Basically, the hours and attitudes are what you'd expect of a busy City firm, and "if you enjoy finance work, you're not going to have any problems." "There was a period of a couple of weeks when I was only getting a few hours sleep each night," said one trainee, but that's not typical, and you always get "downtime" at the end of big transactions. In terms of grunt work, "you'll be the one responsible for the photocopying rather than actually having to do it."

Chambers Global's Eastern Europe Law Firm of the Year 2002

If you want a predictable, quiet life then clearly you'd be suited to a different town and a different area of practice. "I was attracted to the finance side of things. I liked the way you put deals together and I like to work on things that are different every time. I wasn't interested in other areas of the law; I suppose I'm not a particularly compassionate person." Come on…you're not that awful!

Proponents of 'US firms' in London say they allow greater independence and are more meritocratic than traditional City players. Our sources subscribed to this theory. Although the firm is currently split over several sites in the heart of the City, all are within a few minutes of each other. With its continued expansion, the firm plans to move to new premises in 2003. The smart casual dress code and various human touches around the office pull the firm away from the hard edge of City work. For example, in the library there's a section given over to novels. Just make sure you don't get caught reading Jilly Cooper when you're supposed to be researching high yield debts.

onwards and upwards

There are plenty of Oxbridge and top redbrick grads, plus others from unis that are seen as 'on the up'. The training partner told us: *"Trainees have got to be fun to work with. Arrogance can be knocked out of people over two years, but it would be harder for the quiet, retiring type. Transactional work is team-based. You need to get along with people."* One trainee thought that *"they're looking for commercial acumen, common sense and confidence."*

So, will we ever hear White & Case referred to as a top tier London firm? *"We don't see ourselves as inferior to the magic circle,"* said one. *"In terms of the work we do, they're not up on us." "There is a certain snobbery at City firms. People sometimes ask why I didn't go to the magic circle, but I think I'm happier here than I would be elsewhere."* Trainees buy into the onwards and upwards mentality. All three of the September 2002 qualifiers accepted jobs; two staying in London and one refusing to be parted from a beloved secondment to Singapore.

the pursuit of happiness

The social scene is *"far too active…I seem to be out with people from work every night."* There's a Corney & Barrow right on the doorstep, where everyone from partners to secretaries ends up on a Thursday night. Indeed, on a summer's day, the noise from the bar filters up into the offices from lunchtime onwards. In terms of organised jollies, there's an annual boat trip and an (inappropriately named) 'retreat' involving paintball and treasure hunts. In true Manhattan style, you'll get to put on your cocktail wear for the Christmas bash and in March 2002, there was a ski weekend with the Prague office – *"An e-mail went out and off we went."* Closer to home there's Dragon Boat racing in Docklands, wine-tasting and ten pin bowling.

and finally…

Big deals, smaller office, guaranteed opportunities for foreign travel. The formula is a simple one, so if working with magic circle firms, rather than working for them, is what appeals, look no further.

Withers LLP

the facts
Location: London
UK ranking by size: 66
Total number of trainees: 21
Seats: 4x6 months
Alternative seats: None

Withers built its reputation on private client and family law. In the last few years the firm has moved, merged, become an LLP and stepped up its marketing. It seems there are exciting times ahead.

atlantic sound

On 1 January 2002 Withers merged with New York private client firm Bergman Horowitz & Reynolds, forming a transatlantic Limited Liability Partnership (which in Ladybird book terms means that, in exchange for going public with the sums, partners limit personal liability). As one trainee explained, *"private client work in the US is much wider than in the UK. It's not just trusts and wills. They look after all their clients' business needs too, which tend to be substantial companies and family holdings."* Actually, that sounds very much like what Withers has been doing all along. LLPs are going to feature more commonly, so full marks to the firm for being ahead of the game.

rich pickings

Withers is organised into five main departments: corporate, family, litigation, private client and property. Much of their work draws on cross-departmental expertise. Around 40% of the firm's UK revenue comes from its lucrative private client and charities work, and these prove to be popular areas for trainees. While they still deal with high net worth individuals (known to the firm as "sophisticated global citizens"), everyone we spoke to was keen to stress that the client base has diversified considerably from the green welly brigade that put the food on the table in the past. *"It's not just aristocrats and rich landowners. If you have money, you need advice; it doesn't matter if you are a farmer or a dot.com entrepreneur."* The firm acts for around 15% of *The Sunday Times* rich list, so we're talking about some seriously loaded clients with considerable business interests.

Withers also has one of the best family departments in the country and this acts as a big draw to applicants. Forget about Mr and Mrs Average fighting over the semi in Ealing, we're talking about tricky financial settlements, international issues and the need to be terribly discreet about everything. Because of its enviable reputation and high-profile customers, the family department is not perceived as being quite so willing to let trainees have a totally free rein. *"They're very cautious about letting you loose on the clients,"* one trainee cautioned. All in good time…

You'll be allocated your first seat and then have *"varying amounts"* of input into the other three. As one trainee said: *"You've got to be realistic. A little more flexibility in seat length would be nice but it is hard to run a business and give people everything that they want."* There are plenty of *"contemporary, upbeat departments"* to neutralise any notion of old-school stuffiness exuding from parts of the private client wing. Employment and corporate are both described as *"small and young"* and are therefore popular with trainees. Although there are no foreign seats, there are offices in New York, New Haven and Milan, and plans for LA and Switzerland. We told you things were getting exciting!

looking after your own

Many trainees chose Withers because of the interesting range of work on offer, and also, if they were being honest, because they didn't have a clue about what area of law to practice. One trainee advised: *"If you suspect that you want corporate and finance work, then one of the bigger City firms would be better. If you know you want private client and family, then this is just about the best place you could come, and if you're not sure what you want to practice, here you can get a balanced training and good exposure to all the areas."* Clearly the firm takes training very seriously and is keen to hear trainees' comments and suggestions. External mentors come in to make sure everyone is happy and to make a confidential report to the firm on areas for improvement. This is an enlightened and unusual step.

No grumbles over trainee tasks: *"You're not expected to run around and do the crap jobs. In order for the departments to be profitable they need to use the trainees profitably."* One source said, *"If they feel you can handle it, you'll get as much responsibility as you want. I was handling clients and playing important roles on deals from an early stage."* Working hours are regular and civilised, with 9.30am to 6.30pm a firm-wide average. *"You have to put in more hours in corporate and family when there are big deals and cases on,"* confirmed one trainee.

are you with us?

"The firm has become more international and more commercial in the broadest sense." Despite the old image, trainees assured us that *"it's not that traditional…you won't find any oak panelling here."* As a mark of its progressive attitudes, Withers was the first firm in the City to appoint a female senior partner. Another thing our interviewees begged us to stress was the absence of billing pressure. *"There's never been any pressure on the trainees to bill chargeable hours. You can get on with training. It's quite an enlightened attitude. You don't feel you have to bill, bill, bill. You feel like you're here to learn."* *"The firm is very genuine. They respect individuals and treat you like human beings. The other day one of my supervisors told me to slow down and not burn myself out,"* one interviewee confided. Trainees seemed to think that opting for a place like Withers was a lifestyle choice rather than a career move. *"At a firm of this size it is possible to strike the balance."* One trainee gloated: *"I have a life outside the office and I get paid a decent salary. It's a win win situation. I've got friends in the*

437

magic circle who I simply don't see anymore." Apparently the merger has had little effect on the day-to-day lives of trainees. *"People were enthusiastic about it, and because it was with a foreign firm, we haven't had to squeeze into the same offices or have lots of redundancies."*

One trainee made the extravagant claim: *"I can walk into the head of department's office whenever I like and say what I like."* The doors may be well off their hinges when it come to office policy, but telling your supervisor exactly what you think of his tie while he's in the middle of a client meeting probably won't do too much for your qualification chances. While we're on the subject of dress, *"I think we have dress-down,"* one trainee said, a little unsure of the policy.

the italian job

"A lot of people have foreign languages, particularly Italian," we heard. Apparently the firm actively recruits those with an Italian background since it has a lot of clients who are based in Italy and it boasts a Milan office. Generally though, *"they are very much focused on personality. If you can argue your side and if they like you, then they'll take you on."* Most people were seen to be *"good team players"* and one trainee told us that *"individualists might have a tough time."* *"Probably around 50% of us are Oxbridge and the rest tend to be from the more traditional universities."* We were also informed by someone whose alma mater was more *"grey concrete than red brick"* that the firm does not discriminate against less traditional universities.

get yer skates on

The firm now receives visitors in a state of the art office block right opposite the Old Bailey. The inside is characterised by *"big desks and big cupboards."* The standard adjectives came thick and fast – *"modern…light… airy…nice."* One trainee boasted, *"It's a fabulous, modern building with an old façade. It is in a V-shape with left and right trouser legs."* Blimey!

There are regular departmental outings to bowling alleys, comedy clubs and ice-skating trips. Last year at the Somerset House rink on The Strand, there were plenty of partners with their skates on. Trainees also took part in a pub-style quiz in one of the firm's conference rooms where they were served with fish and chips. Hope they opened the windows before the next day's client meetings. Favourite trainee pubs include The Old Monk and the Corney & Barrow. For the traditionalists and local historians, The Magpie & Stump is right next door. Apparently, it used to be possible to witness executions in the Old Bailey from up on the top floor. There was nothing too gory about trainee retention in September 2002. Seven out of the ten qualifiers stayed with the firm.

and finally…

After all the glowing reports and superlatives (one trainee assured us *"no thumb screws were applied"*) the last words go to the realists: *"It's not perfect, but nothing ever is. Compared to other firms this place is paradise."* One trainee added: *"It's not a sailboat on the Med, but it could be a lot worse."* Too right. Well done, Withers.

Wragge & Co

the facts

Location: Birmingham, London
UK ranking by size: 22
Total number of trainees: 46
Seats: 4x6 months
Alternative seats: Brussels, secondments
Extras: Language training

Darling of the Midlands, Wragge & Co basks in a glorious reputation. This beefy regional firm competes for juicy deals with leading London players and wins the hearts and minds of its trainees. Success is a word invented by Wragges, and you'll have to impress if you want to be a part of it.

one nation under a groove

If, as far as you're concerned, working in London isn't the be-all and end-all, then consider this firm seriously. It has a small London office, concentrating mainly on IP and technology work, but the main action is up in Birmingham. With around 1,200 staff, Wragges has hogged a fair chunk of the region's work and pulls in clients from all over the UK. Settling for 'best friend' alliances with foreign firms, it's never developed an overseas network of its own, but has its share of cross-border work. Securing the one overseas seat (competition in Brussels) is not high on the agenda of the majority of its trainees. So what is?

Almost all those we spoke to confirmed it was Wragges' kick-ass reputation that attracted them. It's not just that it sits at the top of the rankings for the work it handles; it's because it pays at the top of the scale for Birmingham and it's become known as one of the best places to work in the country. Nothing we've heard leads us to doubt that it has earned its reputation fair and square. "*Its relaxed informality makes going to work enjoyable, but more than anything it's a sense of belonging. It's not a firm that has a chip on its shoulder about being regional.*"

Two years ago we described the firm as a legal Disneyland. One trainee (probably referring to us) said, "*Some of the descriptions of life at Wragges are over the top,*" but he still believed that "*as far as trainees go, we're in a pretty privileged position. Talk to a first-seat trainee and they'll be blown away by this place.*" Wide-eyed, gushing enthusiasm turns into respect for "*management who make good business decisions*" and a satisfaction that this is possibly as good as it gets.

doing the rounds

Expect to be rotated around the firm to experience a range of work types. Every trainee must do a corporate/commercial seat, a property seat and a contentious seat. As everyone knows they will move through these areas, there's a reasonably low level of campaigning for specific seats, although the most likely top options are IP and employment and, currently, project finance. The fact that no one particular area of work draws applicants to the firm adds to the general sense of satisfaction with seat allocation. Just as personality clashes with supervisors are rare, grumbles over who gets what are few. Client secondments at trainee level do arise, largely ad hoc.

"*The key is to demonstrate that you'll have a go at things and not say 'I'm only a trainee'. You'll go far if you try.*" But the financial pressures are taken away from trainees. "*As much as you want to get into billing and targets, etc. you know you are on the sidelines from that. Partners make that clear to you.*" Maybe it's a Birmingham thing, but people do go home at 5.30pm. "*There's no macho hang-up about hours.*" Clearly there are times when you'll see more of the office than you'd like, but, as you may find yourself living just 15 minutes away from the office, it's not a big problem.

little birds, big nest

Just five years ago, Wragges was a fraction of the size it is today. Despite measures to reclaim office space in their Colmore Row HQ, it's still a tight squeeze and two nearby buildings are also full. Open-plan working has taken over from individual offices, with partners, assistants, trainees and secretaries sitting together. "*You almost always sit next to a supervisor. It's like being a little bird – 'feed me, feed me, feed me.' You need their attention.*" Bless! This 'all in it together' ethos is at the heart of the Wragges culture. Some trainees worried that the different departments are becoming little firms of their own. One source prayed the firm wouldn't "*go the way of the top five [ouch!] accountancy firms, where you sit at your desk – if you have one – do your chargeable hours, lob them into the system and go home.*" The management is apparently alive to these concerns, and there seems little chance the office will become the sort of place where there's "*a deadly silence except for the whirr of the photocopier.*"

atmospheric conditions

Central to the 'Wragges Way' is the preoccupation with seeking feedback from staff. Committees spring up from all over the firm. Call it navel-gazing or call it good sense, but the management team (learn the names John Crabtree and Quentin Poole – they have been key to everything) invests a considerable amount of time and effort into getting to know the workforce. The 'Gusto' committee focuses on drawing out and implementing bright ideas, while the 'People First' Committee concentrates on communication. *"It's as a result of the committees that they got highest placed law firm in The Sunday Times' 100 Best Companies to Work For survey,"* one source told us. Then again, one or two others regarded the frequent questionnaires as *"all a bit culty...a waste of time."*

All this could smack of a firm that's self-absorbed and a little pretentious, but Wragges isn't living in rarefied atmospheric conditions. The phrase we heard repeated in interviews (to the point of tedium), was *"down-to-earth."* Trainees are definitely breathing the same air as the rest of us. There's a healthy feel about the firm and the task now is to protect it in the years to come. Perhaps one way of doing that is to ensure that even the most junior of lawyers gets involved in managing the firm. Departmental business plans are widely available, and trainees can add their two pennies' worth. *"A friend at Slaughters said she didn't think there was a business plan, and if there was it was no concern of the rank and file! Here we have involvement in business decisions; the plan is prepared by lawyers at all levels. It means you learn commercial awareness."* 13 out of the 15 September 2002 qualifiers stayed on with the firm.

the witness protection programme

Many regional firms recruit trainees with a local connection. Wragges has moved beyond that and a large number of trainees started a new life when they joined the firm. Some had never been to Birmingham before. Ever wondered what it might be like on a witness protection programme – new name, new city, new job, new friends? We're thinking about recommending the firm to intelligence agencies worldwide. One Brum newbie said, *"It's been a really pleasant surprise, although I'd be lying to say it's a world-class city. There's a very tight professional community here; I can walk down the street and meet people I know. If you really, really love London you might not like it, but it is a much* healthier place to work."

The firm-wide social club organises tickets for musicals (Chicago, Riverdance, etc. – if that's your bag), theatre (proper), concerts (eg. Madonna) and trips to things like 'The Good Homes Show' (no comment). The Christmas party at the ICC brings everyone together, so presumably the queue for the bouncy castle is really long. Trainees have their own social scene in Brindleyplace, at the Metro, B3, Bushwackers (*"they've tried to go a bit upper class but it's not working; it's still a bit mirrored and seedy"*), All Bar One and sometimes round the back of the office at Hotel du Vin. The Birmingham Trainee Solicitors Society got a mention from all our interviews – almost everyone attends the events. Not everyone attends gigs thrown by the Wragges assistants' band, Platinum Sponge, but they're good for a laugh.

blockbuster

Even out of work, you can't escape the scene or your 1,200 colleagues. The two most popular neighbourhoods are Moseley and Harborne. 'The Harborne Syndrome' means that no matter where you go – the supermarket or the video store – you'll bump into your workmates. You'll probably catch the 'school bus' into work with them, and you may even live with them. *"It's almost like an extension of uni and law school, although slightly nicer, of course!"* Of course.

We know they're not clones, but generally *"trainees come here because they are people people."* *"The firm will make a genuine effort to make you feel included – you will be dragged kicking and screaming out of your shell, but you won't be frogmarched down the pub."*

and finally…

It's not Disneyland, but you'll certainly have fun. It's a much sought-after training, so take your application very seriously – Wragges can afford to pick and choose. One source summed it up by saying, *"The firm has a conservative business plan and generally seems to have done things quite carefully. The people steering the ship know what they are doing."* They certainly do.

A-Zs

universities and law schools A-Z 442
barristers A-Z 453
solicitors A-Z 457

Cardiff Law School

Centre For Professional Legal Studies, PO Box 294, Cardiff CF10 3UX
Tel: (029) 2087 4964 Fax: (029) 2087 4984
Email: Brookfield@Cardiff.ac.uk
Website: www.cardiff.ac.uk/claws/cpls

contact
Mr Ian C Brookfield
Tel: (029) 2087 4941

university profile

Cardiff Law School is long established, well-resourced and enjoys an international reputation for its teaching and research. In the most recent assessment of research quality conducted by the Higher Education Funding Council, Cardiff achieved a grade 5 rating, placing it in the top law schools in the country. Cardiff offers opportunities for students to pursue postgraduate study by research leading to the degrees of M.Phil and Ph.D. In addition, taught Masters degrees in the areas of canon, commercial, marine affairs and medical law are offered in full and part-time mode.

legal practice course and bar vocational course

Within the Law School, the Centre for Professional Legal Studies is validated to offer both the Legal Practice Course and the Bar Vocational Course. Students are taught by experienced solicitors and barristers who have been specifically recruited for this purpose. All students pursuing the vocational courses are guaranteed placements with solicitors' firms or sets of chambers, while students studying the Bar Vocational Course additionally enjoy a one week placement with a Circuit or District Judge. Cardiff's Legal Practice Course has three times been rated 'Excellent' by the Law Society; one of only three out of the 31 providers of this course to hold the top ranking.

facilities

Recent developments within the Law School include extensive IT provision together with dedicated accommodation for the vocational courses which house a practitioner library, courtroom facilities, and fixed and movable audio visual equipment for recording interactive practitioner skills activities. In addition, the main law library contains one of the largest collections of primary and secondary material within the UK. The Law School is housed in its own building at the heart of the campus, itself located in one of the finest civic centres in Britain and only a short walk from the main shopping area. The University has its own postgraduate centre, together with a full range of sporting and social facilities.

University of Central England in Birmingham

School of Law, Franchise Street, Perry Barr, Birmingham B42 2SU
Tel: (0121) 331 6600 Fax: (0121) 331 6622
Email: lss@uce.ac.uk
Website: www.uce.ac.uk

contact
Please apply to:
Admissions Officer,
School of Law, Franchise Street, Perry Barr,
Birmingham B42 2SU

Tel: (0121) 331 6600
Fax: (0121) 331 6622
Email: lss@uce.ac.uk
Website: www.uce.ac.uk

college profile
The School of Law at UCE Birmingham has been a major centre for legal education and training in the city for over thirty years. Its close links to the city's burgeoning legal community ensure that its courses reflect the modern needs of the profession. A wide range of law courses is taught by experienced and well-qualified staff, in a law school noted for its friendly and approachable atmosphere in which students are treated as individuals. Facilities include a legal practice resource centre, fully-equipped IT workrooms and a court room and solicitor's office, both with audio-visual recording.

lpc / postgraduate diploma in legal practice (full or part-time)
Students on the LPC benefit from the extensive and varied practice experience of the teaching team. A programme of guest speakers provides further specialist input. Interactive teaching and learning methods replicate typical transactions you will encounter in practice and develop the self-sufficiency and confidence necessary when embarking on your training contract.

cpe / postgraduate diploma in legal studies (full or part-time)
The CPE places emphasis on the development of legal skills through the use of interactive teaching methods and problem solving techniques. The small class sizes and 'open door' policy ensure that every student receives full support from course staff to reach their full potential.

pgdip / llm international human rights (full or part-time)
Focusing on European law or the death penalty in the USA. USA study includes a semester in the USA with funding available.

pgdip / llm european legal studies (full or part-time)
European law in its political and business contexts.

pgdip/ ma immigration policy, law and practice (part-time)
The implications of current law and practice in the UK.

City University, London - Institute of Law

City University, Institute of Law, Northampton Square, London EC1V 0HB
Tel: Dept of Law: (020) 7040 8301   ICSL: (020) 7404 5787
Fax: Dept of Law: (020) 7040 8578   ICSL: (020) 7831 4188
Email: Dept of Law: cpe@city.ac.uk   ICSL: ICSLcourses@city.ac.uk
Website: www.city.ac.uk/law

college profile

Law has been taught at City since 1977. In 2001, the portfolio of law activity was significantly enhanced when the Inns of Court School of Law (ICSL) became part of the University, joining the established Department of Law to form a new Institute of Law. This formalised a long-standing relationship between the University and the School, and made City the first university in London to offer courses for both branches of the profession and for students and practitioners at all stages of legal education.

The Department of Law is best known for its CPE (Common Professional Examination) course which is one of the largest and most respected CPE courses in the UK, with a long-standing reputation with the Bar and a strong and growing reputation amongst City law firms. Its graduate entry LLB programme is also well established. There is a growing LLM (Master of Laws) modular programme which contains a number of distinct pathways leading to the award of a specialist LLM degree.

The Inns of Court School of Law is a leading provider of postgraduate legal training for both solicitors and barristers and offers a unique LLM in Criminal Litigation, a well-established CPD programme which includes the PSC for trainee solicitors and Higher Rights training. Its successful Pro Bono project gives vocational course students the opportunity to work with live clients at the School's Advice Clinic or to work with a voluntary partner.

courses offered

cpe/diploma in Law (Department of Law - full or part-time).
graduate entry llb (hons) (Department of Law - two years full-time).
bar vocational course (ICSL - full or part-time).
legal practice course (ICSL - full-time). Rated Very Good by the Law Society.
llm programme (Department of Law and the ICSL - full or part-time).
- Anglo-American Law
- Criminal Litigation (contact the ICSL)
- Environmental Law
- Human Rights
- International Law

contact
Full course brochures are available from the Department of Law or ICSL as appropriate

department of law
Tel: (020) 7040 8301
Fax (020) 7040 8578
Email: cpe@city.ac.uk

icsl
Tel: (020) 7404 5787
Fax: (020) 7831 4188
Email: ICSLcourses@city.ac.uk

City University London

Inns of Court School of Law

The College of Law

Braboeuf Manor, Portsmouth Road, Guildford GU3 1HA
Tel: (0800) 328 0153 Fax: (01483) 460460
Email: info@lawcol.co.uk
Website: www.college-of-law.co.uk

contact
Freephone:
(0800) 328 0153
Email: info@lawcol.co.uk

college profile
The College of Law, the largest legal training establishment in Europe, has branches in Birmingham, Chester, Guildford, London and York. The College has an excellent reputation with law firms and chambers, and its teaching staff are professionally qualified as solicitors or barristers. The College's Careers Advisory Service uses its specialist knowledge and extensive contacts to help students gain training contracts and pupillages. It offers the following courses:

graduate diploma in law (full-time, part-time or distance learning)
The GDL is the law conversion course for graduates of disciplines other than law who wish to become solicitors or barristers. Students will receive in-depth tuition in seven foundation subjects from tutors with a proven track record in providing legal education. Successful students receive a Diploma in Law and are guaranteed a place on the College's Legal Practice Course.

legal practice course (full-time, part-time, or block learning)
The LPC is the vocational stage of training for prospective solicitors. The College's LPC has been developed in consultation with both City and provincial firms to address the real needs of today's legal profession, and ensure the course meets the demands of life in practice.

bar vocational course (full-time)
The BVC is the vocational stage of training for prospective barristers and is available at the College in London. It has been developed in conjunction with practising barristers to prepare students for life in their early years at the Bar. Practitioners from highly respected sets of chambers also contribute to the delivery of the course.

For further information about courses at any of the College's branches please contact Admissions.

The College of Law
of England and Wales

London Metropolitan University

Department of Law, Governance and International Relations,
London City campus, 84 Moorgate, London EC3M 6SQ
Tel: (020) 7320 1616 Fax: (020) 7320 1163
Email: enqs@lgu.ac.uk
Website: www.londonmet.ac.uk

university profile

London Metropolitan University was created on 1 August following the merger of London Guildhall University and the University of North London. The University offers a wide range of professional law courses available in full-time and part-time day and evening modes. The teaching style of these courses is considered to be one of the friendliest and most thorough available. The University prides itself on giving students personal and individual attention; it is committed to keeping class numbers low; and its IT facilities include a number of the software programmes that are found in practice. Students receive training that is relevant, professional and geared towards ensuring success. There is easy access to underground and mainline stations.

legal practice course (full-time or part-time day and evening)

Many of the teaching staff are either recently out of practice, or still in practice, and therefore the emphasis is on the provision of professional training. Welfare and commercial electives are offered, including some rare subjects such as immigration and international trade.
Class sizes are deliberately limited and skills training is provided in smaller groups to ensure personal and individual attention. Computers are utilised within the classrooms along with video cameras to ensure that all the latest training and practitioner tools are made available to students. A unique (to London) part-time day course is offered to provide flexibility in training modes. The part-time day and evening mode is also run in collaboration with South Bank University.

common professional examination/postgraduate diploma in Law (full-time or part-time day or evening)

Training is both by lectures and tutorials with an emphasis on the seven foundations of legal knowledge. The course prides itself on an intimate atmosphere with personal and individual attention offered to all students. A variety of teaching and assessment methods are utilised including research assignments, case and statute analysis, and oral presentations. Fee assistance is provided to those students wishing to continue with the LPC at London Metropolitan University. The University also offers a flexible mode of study, which enables students from a wide range of backgrounds to undertake the course.

Manchester Metropolitan University

School of Law, Elizabeth Gaskell Campus, Hathersage Road, Manchester M13 OJA
Tel: (0161) 247 3050 Fax: (0161) 247 6309
Email: law@mmu.ac.uk

contact
Contact the Admissions Tutor for the relevant course

college profile
The School of Law is one of the largest providers of legal education in the UK, and enjoys an excellent reputation for the quality and range of its courses. The School's courses are well designed and taught, combining rigorous academic standards with practical application.

bar vocational course (full-time)
This course provides the vocational stage of training for intending practising barristers. Adopting a Syndicate Group approach, the BVC is activity based and interactive. Extensive IT and audio visual facilities combine with dedicated, well equipped premises to provide an enjoyable and stimulating experience. Excellent student support is provided including mentoring by practising barristers and an Additional Professional Programme which is designed to bridge the gap betweeen student and professional life.

legal practice course (full-time or part-time)
This course is for those wishing to qualify as a solicitor. Offering a full range of commercial and private client electives the Legal Practice Course, taught by professionally qualified staff, prepares you for every day practice. There is a dedicated Resource Centre and an excellent pastoral care programme for LPC students. Consistently recognised by the Law Society for its high quality.

postgraduate diploma in law/cpe (full-time or part-time)
An increasing number of graduates enter the legal profession this way, with employers attracted by the applicant's maturity and transferable skills. The course places emphasis on the acquisition of legal research and other relevant legal skills. Subject to successful completion of the PgDL, the school guarantees a place on the MMU LPC or BVC, provided that Law Society and Bar entry requirements are met.

Middlesex University

Middlesex University Business School, The Burroughs, Hendon, London NW4 4BT
Tel: (020) 8411 5090 Fax: (020) 8411 6069
Email: headmissions@mdx.ac.uk
Website: www.mubs.mdx.ac.uk

college profile
Middlesex University Business School (MUBS) is the largest business school in London and is located at the Hendon campus, within 30 minutes of Central London by underground rail. The law group has been offering both undergraduate and postgraduate programmes for over 25 years and hosts the Centre for Research in Industrial and Commercial Law, with current projects in Employment Law (Whistleblowing), Environmental Law and European Law.

undergraduate programmes
The University offers three qualifying law degrees which provide exemption from the first stage of professional legal education for those seeking a professional career in law. Those are: the LLB (Hons), BA (Hons) Business Law and BA (Hons) Law and Criminal Justice. A combined honours, non-qualifying degree is also offered in Legal Studies.

postgraduate programmes - llm
A flexible programme for law graduates or practitioners who wish to specialise in a particular area. The University specialises in international trade, competition and the regulation of new electronic technologies.

llm in employment law
Designed for practising lawyers, human resource practitioners, trade union officials and advice workers. Applications from students with a non-law background are welcomed. Students who have not practised law previously will undertake a pre-course block on legal principles and methods.

pg diploma in law/cpe (full-time and distance learning)
Designed for non-law graduates who wish to pursue a career in law. The programmes are recognised by the Law Society and the General Bar Council, while the CPE board approves the CPE programmes. The Pg Diploma is studied one year full-time, whilst the CPE is offered as a two year distance learning course. The programmes provide the academic stage to your legal education that leads to qualification as a barrister or solicitor. Students who successfully pass the programme have a guaranteed place on the full-time LPC at the College of Law.

contact
Campus Admissions,
Middlesex University
Business School,
The Burroughs,
London NW4 4BT

Tel: (020) 8411 5090
Fax: (020) 8411 6069
Email:
headmissions@mdx.ac.uk
Website:
www.mubs.mdx.ac.uk

Northumbria University

School of Law, Northumbria University, Sutherland Building,
Newcastle-upon-Tyne NE1 8ST
Tel: (0191) 227 4494
Fax: (0191) 227 4557
Website: http://law.northumbria.ac.uk

contact

School of Law Admissions Office
Tel: (0191) 227 4494
Fax: (0191) 227 4557
Email: la.information@northumbria.ac.uk

college profile

The School of Law at Northumbria University is known for its excellence in the provision of academic and professional legal education. Situated in central Newcastle, the School has over 60 full-time teaching staff and is one of the largest departments in the University. Full-time, part-time and distance learning modes of study are available. The School is validated to run the Bar Vocational Course, the Legal Practice Course and the Common Professional Examination/Diploma in Law Course. It also offers the Professional Skills Course and an extensive LLM programme, including courses in Mental Health Law, Medical Law, Commercial Law, European Law, International Trade Law and Commercial Property. The Law School has dedicated lecture and workshop accommodation together with its own Law Skills Centre which includes a large practitioner library, court room and offices with full CCTV facilities plus open access IT equipment.

lpc (full-time or part-time)
- the vocational training course for students who wish to qualify as solicitors
- a wide range of corporate and private client electives
- practical workshops

bvc (full-time)
- the vocational training course for students who wish to qualify as barristers
- practical skills training in dedicated accommodation
- strong practitioner participation

cpe (full-time or distance learning)
- the academic stage of training for non-law graduates who wish to qualify as solicitors or barristers
- structured study materials
- opportunity to obtain a law degree with an additional study programme
- guaranteed places for successful students on the Legal Practice Course

northumbria UNIVERSITY
great *learning* great *experience* great *future*

Nottingham Law School

Nottingham Law School, Belgrave Centre, Nottingham NG1 5LP
Tel: (0115) 848 6871 Fax: (0115) 848 6878

contact
Nottingham Law School,
Belgrave Centre,
Chaucer Street,
Nottingham NG1 5LP

bar vocational course

Nottingham Law School has designed its BVC to develop to a high standard a range of core practical skills, and to equip students to succeed in the fast-changing environment of practice at the Bar. Particular emphasis is placed on the skill of advocacy. Advocacy sessions are conducted in groups of six and the School uses the Guildhall courtrooms for most sessions. The BVC is taught entirely by recently practising barristers, and utilises the same integrated and interactive teaching methods as all of the School's other professional courses. Essentially, students learn by doing and Nottingham Law School provides a risk-free environment in which students are encouraged to realise, through practice and feedback, their full potential.

legal practice course

The LPC is offered by full-time and part-time block study. This course has been designed to be challenging and stimulating for students and responsive to the needs of firms, varying from large commercial to smaller high street practices.

Nottingham Law School's LPC features: integration of the transactions and skills, so that each advances the other, whilst ensuring the transferability of skills between different subject areas. Carefully structured interactive group work which develops an ability to handle skills and legal transactions effectively, and in an integrated way. A rigorous assessment process that nevertheless avoids 'assessment overload', to maintain a teaching and learning emphasis to the course. A professionally qualified team, retaining substantial links with practice. An excellent rating from The Law Society's Assessment Panel in every year of its operation.

the graduate diploma in law (full-time)

The Nottingham Law School GDL is a one year conversion course designed for any non-law graduate who intends to become a solicitor or barrister in the UK. The intensive course effectively covers the seven core subjects of an undergraduate law degree in one go. It is the stepping stone to the LPC or the BVC at Nottingham Law School, and a legal career thereafter. It is a graduate Diploma (Dip Law) in its own right and operates on a similar basis to the LPC (see above), though inevitably it has a more academic basis.

University of the West of England, Bristol

Faculty of Law, Frenchay Campus, Coldharbour Lane, Bristol BS16 1QY
Tel: (0117) 344 2604 Fax: (0117) 344 2268
Email: law@uwe.ac.uk
Website: www.uwe.ac.uk

contact

Gabriel Fallon
Tel: (0117) 344 3769
Fax: (0117) 976 3841
Email:
gabriel.fallon@uwe.ac.uk

college profile
The Bristol Institute of Legal Practice, which is part of the Faculty of Law at the University of the West of England, Bristol, is one of the largest providers of professional legal education in the United Kingdom. The Law Society has recognised the quality of its Legal Practice Courses by awarding them an 'Excellent' rating. It is also proud to be one of only seven providers outside London to be validated by the Bar Council to run the Bar Vocational Course. Moreover, the Higher Education Funding Council for England and Wales rated teaching across the Faculty as a whole as 'Excellent'.

courses
The Bristol Institute of Legal Practice offers the following courses:

legal practice course - lpc (full-time and part-time) The Institute's Legal Practice Courses have a national reputation for quality, which has been recognised by the Law Society with its award of an 'Excellent' rating. Moreover, it currently offers more elective subjects (13) than any other provider in the country. The Faculty has very good links with both local and national firms of solicitors.

bar vocational course - bvc (full-time) In 1996 the UWE Faculty of Law was successfully validated by the Bar Council to run the Bar Vocational Course. When validating the course the Chairman of the Bar Council remarked among other factors taken into account was 'the standard of the facilities to be made available for the Course and the strength of support from the local Bar'.

common professional examination (full-time and part-time) The Faculty has run CPE courses for over 20 years. Both the full-time and part-time versions of the course are recognised nationally as being high quality. They are also very popular and highly respected by the Legal Profession. The courses have very high pass rates and, on the successful completion of the Bristol CPE, students also receive a Postgraduate Diploma in Law.

University of Wolverhampton

School of Law, Molineux Street, Wolverhampton WV1 1SB
Tel: (01902) 321000 Fax: (01902) 321570

college profile
Based in Wolverhampton and offers courses for students intending to become solicitors. The law school has been offering these courses for over 20 years. Its LPC programme has had consistently good ratings. The lecturers are drawn from experienced solicitors, barristers, academics and individuals from business and industry. There are excellent IT facilities, a well-stocked library and a sports centre.

legal practice course (full/part-time)
The vocational training course for those intending to practise as solicitors. The core subjects of Business, Litigation and Conveyancing are taught, together with a range of commercial and private client options. Professional skills courses, practical workshops and seminars are all part of the training. Close links with local practitioners, mentoring and CV distribution. Purpose built courtroom. Exclusive LPC resources room. Group social activities.

common professional examination (full/part-time)
The academic stage of training for non-law graduates wishing to become solicitors or barristers. A full programme of lectures and tutorials is offered on this demanding course. Students are taught by experienced practitioners. Places on the LPC are guaranteed for successful students. Flexible studying choices are under review.

contact
Ms Loraine Houlton
Head of Corporate & Professional Division
Tel: (01902) 321999
Fax: (01902) 321567

UNIVERSITY OF WOLVERHAMPTON

Blackstone Chambers (P Baxendale QC and C Flint QC)

Blackstone House, Temple, London EC4Y 9BW   DX: 281
Tel: (020) 7583 1770   Fax: (020) 7822 7350
Email: clerks@blackstonechambers.com
Website: www.blackstonechambers.com

No of Silks	28
No of Juniors	34
No of Pupils	4 (current)

contact
Ms Julia Hornor
Practice Manager

method of application
OLPAS

pupillages (p.a.)
12 months 4
Required degree grade
Minimum 2:1
(law or non-law)

income
Award £30,000
Earnings not included

tenancies
Junior tenancies offered
in last 3 years 100%
No of tenants of 5 years
call or under 7

chambers profile
Blackstone Chambers occupies modern, fully networked premises in the Temple.

type of work undertaken
Chambers' formidable strengths lie in three principal areas of practice: commercial, employment and public law. Commercial law includes financial/business law, international trade, conflicts, sport, media and entertainment, intellectual property and professional negligence. All aspects of employment law, including discrimination, are covered by chambers' extensive employment law practice. Public law incorporates judicial review, acting both for and against central and local government agencies and other regulatory authorities, human rights and other aspects of administrative law. Chambers recognises the increasingly important role which mediation has to play in dispute resolution. Two members are CEDR accredited mediators.

pupil profile
Chambers looks for articulate and intelligent applicants who are able to work well under pressure and demonstrate high intellectual ability. Successful candidates usually have at least a 2:1 honours degree, although not necessarily in law.

pupillage
Chambers offers four (or exceptionally five) 12 month pupillages to those wishing to practise full-time at the Bar, normally commencing in October each year. Pupillage is divided into three or four sections and every effort is made to ensure that pupils receive a broad training. The environment is a friendly one; pupils attend an induction week introducing them to the chambers working environment. Chambers prefers to recruit new tenants from pupils wherever possible. Chambers subscribes to OLPAS; applications should be made for the summer season.

mini pupillages
Assessed mini pupillages are available and are an important part of the application procedure. Applications for mini pupillages must be made by 30 April; earlier applications are strongly advised and are preferred in the year before pupillage commences.

funding
Awards of £30,000 per annum are available. The pupillage committee has a discretion to consider applications for up to £7,500 of the pupillage award to be advanced during the BVC year.

4 Essex Court (Nigel Teare QC)

4 Essex Court, Temple, London EC4Y 9AJ
DX: 292 London (Chancery Lane)
Tel: (020) 7653 5653   Fax: (020) 7653 5654
Email: pupillage@4sx.co.uk
Website: www.4sx.co.uk

chambers profile
4 Essex Court is one of the leading commercial chambers. Chambers offers a wide range of services to its clients within the commercial sphere specialising particularly in maritime and aviation law. 4 Essex Court is placed in the first rank in both specialisms by *Chambers Guide to the Legal Profession 2001-2002*. In shipping law seven silks and nine juniors were selected by *Chambers* as leaders in their field; in aviation *Chambers* concluded that "these highly commercial barristers are at the forefront of the aviation field". In both these areas the set had more 'leaders in their field' selected than any other set of chambers. Chambers advises on domestic and international commercial litigation and acts as advocates in Court, abitration and inquiries in England and abroad.

type of work undertaken
The challenging and rewarding work of chambers encompasses the broad range of commercial disputes embracing arbitration, aviation, banking, shipping, international trade, insurance and reinsurance, professional negligence, entertainment and media, environmental and construction law. Over 70% of chambers' work involves international clients.

pupil profile
4 Essex Court seeks high calibre pupils with good academic qualifications (at least a 2:1 degree) who exhibit good written and oral skills.

pupillage
Chambers offers a maximum of four funded pupillages of 12 months duration (reviewable at six months). Pupils are moved amongst several members of chambers and will experience a wide range of high quality commercial work. Outstanding pupils are likely to be offered a tenancy at the end of their pupillage. Further information can be found on the website.

mini pupillages
Mini pupillages are encouraged in order that potential pupils may experience the work of chambers before committing themselves to an application for full pupillage.

funding
Awards of £30,000 p.a. are available for each funded pupillage - part of which may be forwarded during the BVC, at the Pupillage Committee's discretion.

No of Silks 8
No of Juniors 31

contact
Secretary to Pupillage Committee

method of application
Chambers' application form

pupillages (p.a.)
1st 6 months 4
2nd 6 months 4
12 months
(Reviewed at 6 months)
Required degree
Good 2:1+

income
1st 6 months
£15,000
2nd 6 months
£15,000
Earnings not included

tenancies
Current tenants who served pupillage in chambers 21
Junior tenancies offered in last 3 years 6
No of tenants of 5 years call or under 7
Income (1st year)
c. £40,000

St Philip's Chambers

55 Temple Row, Birmingham B2 5LS
Tel: (0121) 246 7000   Fax: (0121) 246 7001
Email: clerks@st-philips.co.uk
Website: www.st-philips.co.uk

chambers profile
St Philip's Chambers is one of the largest barristers chambers in the country. Since formation in 1998 it has quickly gained a reputation for innovative change and has become a leading player at the regional and national bar. The recent relocation to state of the art facilities at the heart of Birmingham's commercial centre has underlined St Philip's continuing desire to remain on the front foot as legislative and competitive pressures increase.

type of work undertaken
St Philip's is a multidisciplinary chambers. Its individual specialisations are focused around six practice groups - commercial, crime, employment, family, public law, and personal injury and clinical negligence.

pupil profile
The set is looking for exceptional and well-rounded individuals with good intellectual ability and a practical approach to problem solving. It is more interested in potential than background.

pupillage
The set expects to offer three 12 month pupillages to commence in October 2003. All pupillages are offered with a view to a tenancy and attract funding of £10,000 for the first six months and an income guarantee for the second six. Pupils gain experience in the work of all of the practice groups.

mini pupillages
Mini pupillages are available by agreement. Please contact Elizabeth Hodgetts.

funding
See under pupillage.

No of Silks	10
No of Juniors	126
No of Pupils	5

contact
John de Waal
Tel: (0121) 246 7000

method of application
On chambers' own application form - please don't send CVs

pupillages (p.a.)
Three 12 month pupillages offered every year

tenancies
Pupils are selected with a view to tenancy

annexes
None

St Philips

3 Verulam Buildings (Christopher Symons QC/John Jarvis QC)

3 Verulam Buildings, Gray's Inn, London WC1R 5NT DX: LDE 331
Tel: (020) 7831 8441 Fax: (020) 7831 8479
Email: chambers@3vb.com
Website: www.3vb.com

chambers profile
3 Verulam Buildings is a large commercial set with a history of expansion by recruitment of tenants from amongst pupils. Over the past 10 years two of its pupils have become tenants every year. Chambers occupies recently refurbished, spacious offices overlooking Gray's Inn Walks with all modern IT and library facilities. Chambers prides itself on a pleasant, friendly and relaxed atmosphere.

type of work undertaken
A wide range of commercial work, in particular banking and financial services, insurance and reinsurance, commercial fraud, professional negligence, company law, entertainment, insolvency, public international law, EU law, arbitration/ADR, building and construction as well as other general commercial work. Members of chambers regularly appear in high profile cases and a substantial amount of chambers' work is international.

pupil profile
Chambers looks for intelligent and ambitious candidates with strong powers of analysis and reasoning, who are self confident and get on well with others. Candidates should normally have at least a 2:1 grade in an honours subject which need not be law.

pupillage
Chambers seeks to recruit four funded 12 months pupils every year through OLPAS. Each pupil spends three months with four different members of chambers to gain experience of different types of work. Chambers also offers pupillages to pupils who do not intend to practise at the Bar of England and Wales.

mini pupillages
Mini pupillages are available for one week at a time for university, CPE or Bar students who are interested in finding out more about chambers' work. Chambers considers mini pupillage to be an important part of the recruitment process. Candidates should have, or expect to obtain, the minimum requirements for a funded 12 month pupillage. Applications are accepted throughout the year and should be addressed to David Head.

funding
In the year 2003-04 the annual award will be at least £32,000 payable monthly.

No of Silks 18
No of Juniors 33
No of Pupils 4

contact
Mr Peter Ratcliffe
(Pupillage)
Mr David Head
(Mini pupillage)
Pupillage Committee

method of application
OLPAS, or for unfunded pupillage & mini pupillage CV & covering letter stating dates of availability

pupillages (p.a.)
12 months 4
Required degree grade 2:1

income
At least £32,000 per annum.
Earnings not included

tenancies
Current tenants who served pupillage in chambers 31
Junior tenancies offered in last 3 years 4
No of tenants of 5 years call or under 8

Addleshaw Booth & Co

Sovereign House, PO Box 8, Sovereign Street, Leeds LS1 1HQ
Tel: (0113) 209 2000 Fax: (0113) 209 2060
100 Barbirolli Square, Manchester M2 3AB
Tel: (0161) 934 6000 Fax: (0161) 934 6060
25 Cannon Street, London EC4M 5TB
Tel: (020) 7788 5000 Fax: (020) 7788 5060
Email: grad@addleshawbooth.com
Website: www.addleshawbooth.com

firm profile
Addleshaw Booth & Co is more than just a leading UK law firm, it is a national player with an international reputation. The firm's client portfolio features a spectrum of high profile companies including J Sainsbury plc, the Rugby Football League and AstraZeneca. The firm is particularly proud of its involvement as lawyers and official sponsors of the XVII Commonwealth Games (Manchester 2002). Over 60 fee-earners have advised on different aspects of the Commonwealth Games, building up expertise unique within the UK legal profession. The firm has a strong focus on client relationships and in recognition of its achievements the firm was awarded the Daily Telegraph/energis Customer Service Award 2000.

main areas of work
Banking and financial services; commercial property; corporate finance; commercial services; litigation and dispute resolution; enact (housing); private client.

trainee profile
Graduates who are capable of achieving a 2:1 and can demonstrate commercial awareness, motivation and enthusiasm. Applications from law and non-law graduates are welcomed, as are applications from mature students who may be considering a change of direction.

training environment
During each six month seat, there will be regular two-way performance reviews with the supervising partner or solicitor. Trainees have the opportunity to spend a seat in one of the other offices and there are also a number of secondments to clients. Trainees are seated with a qualified solicitor or partner and work as part of a team, enabling them to develop the professional skills necessary to deal with the demanding and challenging work the firm carries out for its clients. Practical training is complemented by high quality training courses provided by the in-house team and the College of Law.

sponsorship & benefits
CPE and LPC fees are paid, plus a maintenance grant of £2,500 and £4,500. Benefits include corporate gym membership, season ticket loan, subsidised restaurant.

vacation placements
Places for 2003: 40; Duration: 2 weeks; Apply by 14 February 2003.

Partners 123
Assistant Solicitors 562
Total Trainees 65

contact
Mrs Simran Foote
Graduate Manager

method of application
See website

selection procedure
Interview, assessment centre

closing date for 2005
31 July 2003

application
Training contracts p.a. 40
Applications p.a. 2,300
% interviewed p.a. 10%
Required degree grade 2:1

training
Salary
1st year (2001)
£20,000-£20,500
(Manchester & Leeds)
£28,000-£28,500 (London)
2nd year (2001)
£21,000-£21,500
(Manchester & Leeds)
£29,000-£29,500 (London)
Holiday entitlement
25 days
% of trainees with
a non-law degree p.a.
45%

post-qualification
Salary (2001)
£32,000
(Manchester & Leeds)
£48,000 (London)
% of trainees offered job
on qualification (2002) 85%

other offices
Leeds, London, Manchester

Allen & Overy

One New Change, London EC4M 9QQ
Tel: (020) 7330 3000 Fax: (020) 7330 9999
Email: graduate.recruitment@allenovery.com
Website: www.allenovery.com

firm profile
Allen & Overy is one of the world's premier international law firms, with major strengths in banking, corporate work and international capital markets. All departments work closely together to meet the needs of clients which include governments, financial institutions, businesses and private individuals.

main areas of work
Corporate; banking; international capital markets; litigation; real estate; private client; tax; employment and related areas.

trainee profile
Intellectual ability is a prerequisite but as Allen & Overy is a commercial firm it also looks for people with a good level of business understanding. The firm looks for creative, problem solving people who can quickly identify salient points without losing sight of detail. You will need to be highly motivated, demonstrate initiative and the ability to alternate between leading and being part of a team.

training environment
Within a highly pressurised environment, trainees obtain a balance of practical and formal tuition. You will experience at least four different areas of work, but will spend a significant amount of time in at least two of the following departments: banking, corporate and international capital markets. Your preferences will be balanced with the firm's needs. Seminars provide practical advice and an introduction to each area of law. Overseas placements are available. A positive, open and co-operative culture is encouraged both professionally and socially. A range of sporting activities are available.

benefits
Private healthcare scheme, private medical insurance, season ticket loans, subsidised restaurant, gym membership, six weeks unpaid leave on qualification.

vacation placements
Places for 2003: 90; Duration: 3 weeks; Remuneration: £250 p.w.; Closing Date: 31 January 2003. Places available in London, Brussels, Frankfurt and Paris.

sponsorship & awards
CPE and LPC fees and £5,000 maintenance p.a. (£4,500 outside London, Oxford and Guildford).

Partners 416*
Associates 1,376*
Total Trainees 456*
denotes world-wide figures

contact
Graduate Recruitment

method of application
Application form & online

selection procedure
Interview

closing date for 2005
CPE candidates
End Feb 03
Law students End Aug 03

application
Training contracts p.a. 120
Applications p.a. 4,000
% interviewed p.a. 10%
Required degree grade: 2:1

training
Salary
1st year (2001) £28,000
2nd year (2001) £32,000
Holiday entitlement
25 days
% of trainees with a
non-law degree p.a. 40%
No. of seats available
in international offices
31 seats twice a year

post-qualification
Salary (2002) £50,000
% of trainees offered job
on qualification (as at
31/3/02) 93%
% of partners (as at
31/1/02) who joined as
trainees 49%

international offices
Amsterdam, Antwerp, Bangkok, Beijing, Brussels, Bratislava, Budapest, Dubai, Frankfurt, Hamburg, Hong Kong, Luxembourg, Madrid, Milan, Moscow, New York, Paris, Prague, Rome, Shanghai, Singapore, Tirana, Tokyo, Turin, Warsaw

Arnold & Porter

Tower 42, 25 Old Broad Street, London EC2N 1HQ
Tel: (020) 7786 6100 Fax: (020) 7786 6299
Email: graduates@aporter.com
Website: www.arnoldporter.com

Partners	12
Assistant Solicitors	23
Total Trainees	0

contact
Graduate Recruitment

method of application
Application on firm's application form

selection procedure
Interviews & assessed by exercise

closing date for 2005
15 August 2003

application
Training contracts p.a. 3-5
Required degree grade 2:1

training
Salary minimum £30,000
Holiday entitlement 25 days

post-qualification
Salary £59,000

overseas/regional offices
Washington DC, New York, Denver, Los Angeles, Century City, Northern Virginia

firm profile

With seven offices and almost 700 lawyers worldwide practising in over 25 practice and industry areas Arnold & Porter is able to bring clients a sophisticated understanding of changing environments at the intersection of business, law and public policy. The firm was established in Washington DC in 1946 and the London office was initially opened in 1997, but has grown rapidly over the past two years. As of mid-2002 there are almost 40 lawyers in the London office.

main areas of work

Arnold & Porter is a full service law firm providing legal services worldwide. In the London office the practice areas include litigation, telecommunications, information technology, intellectual property, competition, corporate, life sciences, pharmaceutical regulatory, product liability and healthcare. The firm's clients include multinationals, UK and European concerns ranging from start-ups to Fortune 500 companies. Chambers and Partners presented the firm with the Chambers Global 2001-2002 'Antitrust Law Firm of the Year in North America' Award.

trainee profile

The firm's commitment to excellence means that it expects its trainees to be well-rounded individuals with an outstanding academic background.

training environment

The London office reflects the environment of the firm generally. It has a collegial and informal atmosphere which is enhanced by twice-weekly informal social gatherings and other events, a casual dress policy and team-based assignment policies. Trainees will be expected to work on several matters at once and to assume responsibility quickly. The office emphasises teamwork and trainees will be quickly exposed to working for a variety of partners and fee-earners throughout the office and the firm. In the US, the firm is rated as the number one choice for new associates. The London office offered training contracts for the first time last year, to commence in 2004.

sponsorship & benefits

Sponsorship is provided for CPE/LPC. Private health insurance, a season ticket loan and life assurance are amongst the benefits offered by the firm.

vacation placements

Summer vacation scheme, applications on the firm's application form to be received by 14 February 2003.

Ashurst Morris Crisp

Broadwalk House, 5 Appold St, London EC2A 2HA
Tel: (020) 7638 1111 Fax: (020) 7859 1800
Email: gradrec@ashursts.com
Website: www.ashursts.com

firm profile
An international City practice, smaller than its principal competitors, yet consistently ranked amongst the top few firms in terms of the work in which it is involved and clients for whom it acts.

main areas of work
Company/commercial, real estate, litigation, international finance, tax and energy, transport and infrastructure, with specialist groups in competition; construction; employment, incentives and pensions; environment; insolvency; insurance and reinsurance; intellectual property; life sciences; planning; product liability; property litigation; sport; and technology, media and telecommunications.

trainee profile
Candidates should want to be involved in the highest quality work that a City firm can offer. The firm is looking for high achievers academically as the work is intellectually challenging. Candidates should show common sense, good judgement, a willingness to take on responsibility, a sense of humour and an outgoing nature.

training environment
The training contract consists of four six month seats, one of which is a general corporate seat. Two seats are then spent in any two of the remaining main areas of practice. This will typically leave trainees with six months to choose one other department or specialist area of law in which they would like to gain experience. Trainees also have the opportunity to spend one of their seats abroad or in-house with a major client.

benefits
Benefits include private health insurance, pension, life assurance, interest-free season ticket loan, gym membership and 25 days holiday per year during training.

vacation placements
Places for 2003: 2 week Easter placement scheme primarily aimed at final year non-law undergraduates and all graduates. Two 3 week summer placement schemes primarily aimed at penultimate year law undergraduates. Remuneration £250 p.w. Closing date 31 January 2003.

sponsorship & awards
CPE and LPC funding, plus £5,000 maintenance allowance p.a. (£4,500 outside London and Guildford). LPC Distinction award of £500. Language tuition bursaries.

Partners 140
Assistant Solicitors 448
Total Trainees 104

contact
Stephen Trowbridge
Graduate Recruitment

method of application
Online

selection procedure
Interview with 1 assistant followed by interview with 2 partners

closing date for 2005
31 July 2003

application
Training contracts p.a. 50
Applications p.a. 2,500
% interviewed p.a. 20%
Required degree grade 2:1

training
(2001)
First six months
£28,000
Second six months
£29,000
Third six months
£31,000
Fourth six months
£32,000
Holiday entitlement
25 days
% of trainees with a non-law degree p.a. 45-50%
Number of seats abroad available p.a. 12

post-qualification
Salary £48,000
% of trainees offered job on qualification 97%

overseas offices
Brussels, Frankfurt, Madrid, Milan, Munich, New Delhi, New York, Paris, Singapore, Tokyo

Baker & McKenzie

100 New Bridge Street, London EC4V 6JA
Tel: (020) 7919 1000 Fax: (020) 7919 1999
Email: london.graduate.recruit@bakernet.com
Website: www.ukgraduates.bakernet.com

firm profile
Baker & McKenzie is a leading global law firm with more than 60 offices in 35 jurisdictions. In London, Baker & McKenzie is an established City firm of solicitors with a strong domestic and foreign client base providing legal services to multinational and domestic corporations, financial institutions, governments and entrepreneurs.

main areas of work
Corporate; commercial; dispute resolution; banking and finance; EC, competition and trade; employment; intellectual property and information technology; pensions; tax; projects; property. In addition the firm has cross-departmental practice groups, such as e-commerce and communications, insurance and reinsurance, business recovery and environmental law.

trainee profile
The firm is looking for trainee solicitors who are stimulated by intellectual challenge and want to be 'the best' at what they do. Effective communication together with the ability to be creative but practical problem solvers, team players and to have a sense of humour are qualities which will help them stand out from the crowd. Language and IT skills are also valued.

training environment
Four six month seats which include corporate and a contentious seat, usually within the firm's highly regarded dispute resolution department, together with the possibility of a secondment abroad or with a client. During each seat you will have formal and informal reviews to discuss your progress as well as subsequent seat preferences. Your training contract commences with a highly interactive and practical induction programme which focuses on key skills including practical problem solving, interviewing, presenting and the application of information technology. The firm's training programmes include important components on management and other business skills, as well as seminars and workshops on key legal topics for each practice area. There is a Trainee Solicitor Liaison Committee which acts as a forum for any new ideas or problems which may occur during the training contract. Trainees are actively encouraged to participate in a variety of pro bono issues and outside office hours there is a varied sporting and social life.

benefits
Permanent health insurance, life insurance, private medical insurance, group personal pension, subsidised gym membership, season ticket loan, subsidised staff restaurant and bar.

Partners	73
Assistant Solicitors	222
Total Trainees	60

contact
Natalie McGourty

method of application
Letter & application form. Online applications also welcome

selection procedure
Candidates to give a short oral presentation based on the facts of a typical client problem, interview with 2 partners, meeting with a trainee

closing date for 2005
Non-law 18 Feb 2003
Law 28 July 2003

application
Training contracts p.a. **30**
Applications p.a. **2,000**
% interviewed p.a. **10%**
Required degree grade **2:1**

training
Salary
1st year (2002) **£28,000 + £3,000 'golden hello'**
2nd year (2002) **£32,000**
Holiday entitlement
25 days
% of trainees with a non-law degree p.a.
Approx 50%
No. of seats available abroad p.a. **Variable**

post-qualification
Salary (2002)
£50,000–£52,000
% of trainees offered job on qualification (2002) **65%**
% of partners (as at 1/9/02) who joined as trainees **40%**

Baker & McKenzie continued

vacation placements
London Summer Placement - Places for 2003: 30; Duration: 3 weeks; Remuneration: £250 p.w.; Closing date: 31 January 2003.
International Summer Placement - Places for 2003: 3-5; Duration: 6-12 weeks divided between London and an overseas office; Remuneration: £250 p.w.; Closing date: 31 January 2003.

sponsorship & awards
CPE funding: fees paid plus £5,000 maintenance
LPC funding: fees paid plus £5,000 maintenance and choice to receive either an additional £2,000 or a laptop computer

additional information
As mentioned, trainees have the opportunity to spend three months working in one of the firm's overseas offices. Trainees have already been seconded to its offices in Sydney, Hong Kong, Frankfurt, Chicago, Riyadh, Washington, Brussels and Moscow. In addition, the firm also operates an Associate Training Programme which enables lawyers with 18-24 months pqe to spend between 6-24 months working in an overseas office.

trainee comments
"During my training contract I have undertaken work of an excellent quality at both national and international levels. I have had a high level of responsibility which has been backed up by strong supervision and support. This has all been coupled with a friendly and relaxed atmosphere where no question is too trivial, and a social life which involves every level of the firm. It has been a challenging and rewarding experience." (Julia Hemmings, 3rd seat trainee, University of Birmingham)

"My confidence has grown immensely as a result of the first class training I have received at Baker & McKenzie, and the global reach of the firm has proved to be a stimulating and exciting forum in which to work. The varied challenges have certainly kept me busy, but at the same time the amiable and 'open door' environment has meant that there is always somebody available and willing to point me in the right direction." (Fraser Bennett, 1st seat trainee, University of Durham)

"From day one at Baker & McKenzie I felt a valued part of the team. Even though most of our clients are high profile, I was still given a lot of responsibility and spent my first few months regularly on the telephone to overseas clients. It's not all work though! With trainee, departmental and firm-wide events, there's plenty of life outside the office." (Jastine Barrett, 2nd seat trainee, Heriott-Watt University)

overseas offices
Almaty, Amsterdam, Bahrain, Baku, Bangkok, Barcelona, Beijing, Berlin, Bogotá, Bologna, Brasilia, Brussels, Budapest, Buenos Aires, Cairo, Calgary, Caracas, Chicago, Dallas, Düsseldorf, Frankfurt, Geneva, Guadalarjara, Hanoi, Ho Chi Minh City, Hong Kong, Houston, Hsinchu, Juarez, Kyiv, Madrid, Manila, Melbourne, Mexico City, Miami, Milan, Monterrey, Moscow, Munich, New York, Palo Alto, Paris, Porto Alegre, Prague, Rio de Janeiro, Riyadh, Rome, St Petersburg, San Diego, San Francisco, Santiago, São Paulo, Singapore, Stockholm, Sydney, Taipei, Tijuana, Tokyo, Toronto, Valencia, Warsaw, Washington DC, Zürich

Barlow Lyde & Gilbert

Beaufort House, 15 St Botolph Street, London EC3A 7NJ
Tel: (020) 7247 2277 Fax: (020) 7643 8500
Email: grad.recruit@blg.co.uk
Website: www.blg.co.uk

firm profile

Barlow Lyde & Gilbert is a leading international business law firm with more than 300 lawyers and 72 partners. The firm's principal office in the UK is in Aldgate in the City of London. BLG is particularly well known for its expertise in insurance law having first started to practise in this area in the 19th century. The firm has long been recognised as pre-eminent in all aspects of this field and it has formed the bedrock from which the firm has expanded into virtually all areas of business law. Today BLG is widely-based with strong practices in corporate, financial and commercial law, as well as in all kinds of commercial litigation. The firm also has highly rated aviation, shipping, information technology and employment teams.

trainee profile

BLG recruits 16-18 trainees each year and looks for intelligent and motivated graduates with good academic qualifications and with the social skills that will enable them to communicate effectively and get along with their colleagues and clients.

training environment

During your training contract you will have six month seats in four different areas of the firm. The firm will always try to accommodate a trainee's preference for a particular type of work and there may be opportunities to spend time in its other offices, on secondment with clients or on exchange programmes with overseas law firms. A capable trainee will be given responsibility from an early stage in his or her training, subject of course to supervision, and will have to deal regularly with clients. Social activities play an important role for BLG and successful candidates can look forward to a variety of sporting and social events which ensure that people in different parts of the firm have a chance to meet and stay in contact with each other. Trainees are also encouraged to participate in the firm's various pro bono activities.

vacation placements

An increasing number of BLG's trainees come to the firm through its vacation schemes. Whether you are a law or non-law student the firm will introduce you to a City practice. You will be given the opportunity to become really involved and you can even choose which department you want to spend time in. The closing date for applications is 28 February. The firm also runs open days and drop in days throughout the year. Application is by way of a covering letter and application form.

sponsorship & awards

Full payment of fees and a maintenance grant are provided.

Partners 72
Assistant Solicitors 185
Total Trainees 35

contact
Caroline Walsh
Graduate Recruitment & Development Manager

method of application
Application form & covering letter

selection procedure
Interview day

closing date for 2005
31 July 2003

application
Training contracts p.a.
16-18
Applications p.a. 2,000
% interviewed p.a. 10%

training
Salary
1st year £28,000
2nd year £30,000
Holiday entitlement
5 weeks

post-qualification
Salary £47,000
% of trainees offered job on qualification (2002) 86%

other offices
Hong Kong, Shanghai, Oxford

Beachcroft Wansbroughs

100 Fetter Lane, London EC4A 1BN
Tel: (020) 7831 6630 Fax: (020) 7242 1011
Email: bwtrainee@bwlaw.co.uk
Website: www.bwlawfutures.com

firm profile
Beachcroft Wansbroughs is a dynamic and progressive commercial law firm currently employing 1,200 staff across seven locations with ambitious plans for future growth. The firm is committed to developing a consistent performance culture for each individual to reach their full potential.

main areas of work
Employment; corporate services; commercial property; insolvency; professional indemnity; clinical medical negligence; personal injury; construction; insurance litigation; special projects.

trainee profile
The firm looks for outgoing, commercially minded people with 2:1 honours degree in any subject. You'll need to be an excellent team player, possess a mind capable of analysing, interpreting and applying complex points of law.

training environment
Training takes place over a two year period, during which time you'll pursue a demanding study programme, whilst occupying four six months seats in some of the key areas of commercial law. Responsibility will come early and the firm provides the supervision and support to enable you to develop and grow. The firm also runs an in-house training schedule open to trainees to attend which provides additional skills training to the PSC.

benefits
The firm operates a flexible benefits scheme, allowing you to buy and sell certain aspects of your benefits package, including holiday, pension and private health care. This gives you individual choice, depending on your current needs and circumstances.

sponsorship & awards
Beachcroft Wansbroughs provides payment for LPC and £3000 bursary.

Partners 128
Assistant Solicitors 375
Total Trainees 60

contact
Naomi Birch
Graduate Recruitment & Development Officer
Admin Centre
One Redcliff Street
Bristol BS1 6NP

method of application
Apply online for an application form

selection procedure
Assessment centre & panel interview

closing date for 2005
1 August 2003

application
Training contracts 25-30
Required degree grade 2:1 preferred

training
Salary
1st year
£24,750 (London)
£17,500 (Regions)
2nd year
£26,750 (London)
£19,500 (Regions)

offices
Birmingham, Bristol, Brussels, Leeds, London, Manchester, Winchester.

Berwin Leighton Paisner

Adelaide House, London Bridge, London EC4R 9HA
Tel: (020) 7760 1000 Fax: (020) 7760 1111
Email: traineerecruit@blplaw.com
Website: www.blplaw.com

firm profile
Berwin Leighton Paisner is a top 15 City practice. It is a commercial law firm with expertise in many major industry and service sectors. The firm is a modern growing practice that puts a premium on commercial, as well as technical advice, client relations and transactional care. The firm is entrepreneurial and innovative.

main areas of work
Corporate finance; tech media; commercial; employment; commercial property; planning; environment; regulatory; construction and engineering; banking and capital markets; property finance; PFI/projects; and litigation and dispute resolution.

trainee profile
The firm is looking for intelligent, energetic, positive and hard working team players who have an interest in business and gain a sense of achievement from finding solutions.

training environment
Training starts with an induction covering all the practical aspects of working in a law firm from billing to client care. Comprehensive technical education programmes have been developed for each department and trainees attend weekly seminars supplemented by trainee lunches and skills sessions. You will undertake a tailor-made Professional Skills Course which is run in-house. Trainees spend six months in four seats and your progress will be reviewed every three months. The office environment is relaxed and friendly and trainees can enjoy early responsibility secure in the knowledge that they are fully supervised.

benefits
Flexible benefits package including permanent health insurance, private medical insurance, subsidised conveyancing, subsidised gym membership, 25 days holiday a year.

vacation placements
Places for 2003: Open Days held during the Easter Vacation, application by CV and covering letter before 28 February 2003. Attendance at an Open Day could lead to a one week placement in the Summer Vacation. There are 180 places on the Open Days and 60 places on the summer placement scheme.

sponsorship & awards
CPE/PgDL and LPC fees paid and £4,500 maintenance p.a.

Partners 120
Assistant Solicitors 212
Total Trainees 67

contact
Claire Benson

method of application
Firm application form

selection procedure
Assessment day & partner interview

closing date for 2005
31 July 2003

application
Training contracts p.a. **35**
Applications p.a. **2,000**
% interviewed p.a. **5%**
Required degree grade **2:1**

training
Salary
1st year (2000) **£28,000**
2nd year (2000) **£32,000**
Holiday entitlement
25 days
% of trainees with a non-law degree p.a. **30%**
No. of seats available abroad p.a. **4**

post-qualification
Salary (2002) **£48,000**
% of trainees offered job on qualification **83%**
% of assistants who joined as trainees **35%**
% of partners who joined as trainees **19%**

european offices
Brussels, associated office in Paris

SJ Berwin

222 Gray's Inn Road, London WC1X 8XF
Tel: (020) 7533 2268 Fax: (020) 7533 2000
Email: graduate.recruitment@sjberwin.com
Website: www.sjberwin.com

firm profile
Since its formation in 1982, SJ Berwin has established a strong reputation in corporate finance. It also has a number of niche specialisms in areas such as film finance and private equity. Much work is international and clients range from major multinational business corporations and financial institutions to high net worth individuals.

main areas of work
Corporate 45%; property 20%; litigation 17%; EU and competition 8%; commercial media and IP 7%; tax 3%.

trainee profile
The firm wants ambitious, commercially-minded individuals who seek a high level of involvement from day one. Candidates must be bright and determined to succeed. They should be likely to achieve a 2:1 or first.

training environment
Four seats of six months each will be completed, and the seats are set, ideally, to the needs of the trainee. Two seats will be in the corporate finance arena, which includes Frankfurt and Madrid. The firm has a dedicated training department and weekly training schedules coupled with training designed specifically for trainees allow a good grounding in legal and non-legal skills and knowledge. Overseas seats are available in Paris, Frankfurt, Brussels and Madrid.

benefits
Corporate sports membership, free lunch, health insurance.

vacation placements
Places for 2003: 60; Duration: 2 weeks; Remuneration: £225 p.w.; Closing Date: 31 January 2003.

sponsorship & awards
CPE and LPC fees paid and £4,500 maintenance p.a.(£5,000 in London).

Partners 120
Assistant Solicitors 270
Total Trainees 80

contact
Graduate Recruitment Team

method of application
Check website

selection procedure
2 interviews (early September)

closing date for 2005
31 July 2003

application
Training contracts p.a. 40
Applications p.a. 3,000
% interviewed p.a. 10%
Required degree grade 2:1

training
Salary
1st year (2001) £28,000
2nd year (2001) £32,000
Holiday entitlement
50 days over 2 years
% of trainees with a non-law degree p.a. 40%
No. of seats available abroad p.a. 8

post-qualification
Salary (2001) £50,000
% of trainees offered job on qualification (2001) 80%
% of assistants (as at 1/9/01) who joined as trainees 26%
% of partners (as at 1/9/01) who joined as trainees 12%

overseas offices
Brussels, Frankfurt, Madrid, Berlin, Paris, Munich

Bevan Ashford

35 Colston Avenue, Bristol BS1 4TT
Tel: (0117) 918 3050 Fax: (0117) 918 8954
Email: hr.training@bevanashford.co.uk
Website: www.bevanashford.co.uk and www.bevan-ashford.com

firm profile
Bevan Ashford is one of the highest regarded national practices in the UK with a network of seven offices in Bristol, Birmingham, Exeter, London, Plymouth, Taunton and Tiverton. With 87 experienced partners, each of whom is a specialist in their field, and a total staff of over 700, the firm is able to provide clients with an efficient, professional and cost-effective service. Its national reputation means that the firm's client base ranges from multinational corporations and institutions through to smaller businesses, partnerships and individuals. Its success in attracting and keeping quality clients is achieved by the firm's complete commitment to total client care. By recruiting, training and keeping top quality personnel the firm believes it can continue its culture of client care and offer its clients the individual standards of service they require.

main areas of work
Healthcare 27%; commercial property 20%; commercial litigation 15%; company and commercial 16%; private client 17%; other work 5%.

trainee profile
Bevan Ashford is only as strong as its people. The firm's success is achieved by attracting and keeping enthusiastic, bright people with sound common sense, plenty of energy and the ability to work and communicate well with others plus a sense of humour! Language and IT skills are also desirable.

training environment
The core of your training will be practical work experience in conjunction with an extensive education programme consisting of talks, lectures and a residential weekend seminar to back-up the practical work. The training is aimed at developing attitudes, skills and legal and commercial knowledge essential for your career success. Your practical work experience will be reviewed on a regular basis by your supervising partner and you will be encouraged to take on as much work, and responsibility, as you wish. The firm is friendly with an open door policy with a wide range of social, sporting and cultural activities plus an active social club.

vacation placements
Places for 2003: 80. Closing Date: 31 March 2003.

sponsorship & awards
Available for LPC and in some cases PgDL (CPE).

Partners 87
Assistant Solicitors 158
Total Trainees 42

contact
HR and Training
(0117) 918 3050

method of application
Application form (available from the firm's website) & covering letter

closing date for 2005
31 July 2003

application
Training contracts p.a. 25
Required degree grade 2:1

post-qualification
% of trainees offered job on qualification (2002) **95%**

other offices
Birmingham, Bristol, Exeter, London, Plymouth, Taunton, Tiverton

Bird & Bird

90 Fetter Lane, London EC4A 1JP
Tel: (020) 7415 6000 Fax: (020) 7415 6111
Website: www.twobirds.com

firm profile
Bird & Bird is a 100 partner international law firm, employing approximately 530 staff including 30 trainees with offices in Brussels, Dussseldorf, Hong Kong, London, Paris, Stockholm and The Hague. The firm's size ensures a friendly but stimulating environment where legal, business and inter-personal skills can be developed and recognised. The firm has a clear business focus to provide a full range of legal services to specific industry sectors: communications, IP, IT, life sciences, media, sports, e-commerce and banking and financial services. The firm's international ability and strong sector focus will enable you to work across borders and industry sectors.

main areas of work
Company 56%; intellectual property 23%; litigation 12%; property 8%; private client 1%.

trainee profile
The firm looks for high calibre recruits – confident individuals capable of developing expert legal skills and commercial sense.

training environment
Following an introduction course, you will undertake four seats of six months, three of which are spent in company, litigation and property. The choice of final seat is yours. You will share an office with a partner or senior assistant who will guide and advise you. You will hone drafting and legal research skills and gain familiarity with legal procedures. The firm encourages you to make an early contribution to case work and to meet clients immediately. Internal seminars and external lectures are arranged to cover the PSC. Trainees are welcome to join the number of sports teams at the firm and to attend various social events and outings.

benefits
BUPA, season ticket loan, subsidised sports club membership, life cover, PHI, pension.

vacation placements
Places for 2003: 24; Duration: 3 weeks; Remuneration: £220 p.w.; Closing Date: 14 February 2003.

sponsorship & awards
LPC and CPE fees paid and a yearly maintenance grant of £3,500.

Partners 100*
Assistant Solicitors 200*
Total Trainees 30*
denotes worldwide figures

contact
Lynne Walters
lynne.walters@twobirds.com

method of application
Online application form

selection procedure
Assessment mornings

closing date for 2005
31 July 2003

application
Training contracts p.a. 14
Applications p.a. **1,500**
% interviewed p.a. **10%**
Required degree grade **2:1**

training
Salary
1st year (2003) £26,500
2nd year (2003) £28,500
Holiday entitlement
25 days
% of trainees with
a non-law degree p.a.
Varies

post-qualification
Salary (2001) £46,000
% of trainees offered job on qualification (2000) **100%**
% of assistants (as at 1/9/00) who joined as trainees **20%**
% of partners (as at 1/9/00) who joined as trainees **17%**

overseas offices
Brussels, Dusseldorf, Hong Kong, Paris, Sweden, Stockholm, The Hague

Blake Lapthorn

Harbour Court, Compass Road, North Harbour, Portsmouth PO6 4ST
Tel: (023) 9222 1122 Fax: (023) 9222 1123
Website: www.blakelapthorn.co.uk

firm profile
Established in 1869, and currently with almost 60 partners, 210 solicitors and executives and a total of 460 staff, Blake Lapthorn is one of the largest law firms based in the South of England with offices in Fareham, Portsmouth, Southampton and London. Many solicitors who joined the firm as trainees are now partners. They have been joined by others who have brought City experience to the firm. The resulting mix allows the firm to be a leader in its region and to compete with most City-based firms. The firm acts for a wide variety of clients, both commercial and private. The recent growth in its commercial client base has attracted clients nationally and internationally. The firm also acts for many major commercial household names, as well as for a number of local authorities, educational establishments, government agencies and various other public bodies. The breadth of the firm's business offers trainees all the challenges and opportunities of a big City firm, yet with all the advantages of a regional firm.

main areas of work
Company/commercial; commercial property; litigation; private client.

trainee profile
In addition to excellent academic achievements, the firm values previous experience, which has developed maturity and a wider perspective. Commercial awareness, team-working and well-developed communication skills are also an advantage as well as familiarity with the use of IT.

training environment
Five to seven trainees are recruited each year and have a minimum of four placements lasting three or six months. Trainees' preferences are taken into account as far as possible, but the firm believes in providing well-rounded training supplemented with in-house education and regular appraisals and reviews with the Training Principal. Trainees are also allocated a 'mentor', normally a senior solicitor.

sponsorship & awards
LPC: Fees of up to £6,000; bursary of £4,000.

Partners 60
Assistant Solicitors 210
Total Trainees 15

contact
Alan Burnhams
HR Director

method of application
Firm's application form

selection procedure
Interview + presentation & group exercise

closing date for 2005
31 July 2003

application
Training contracts p.a. **5-7**
Applications p.a. **500**
% interviewed p.a. **10%**
Required degree grade **2:1**

training
Salary
1st year (2002) **£16,000**
2nd year (2002) **£18,000**
Holiday entitlement
22 days

post-qualification
Salary (2002) **£28,500**
% of trainees offered job on qualification (2002)
100%

Bond Pearce

Ballard House, West Hoe Road, Plymouth PL1 3AE
Tel: (01752) 266633 Fax: (01752) 225350
Email: thosken@bondpearce.com

firm profile
Bond Pearce is one of the UK's leading commercial law firms and one of the fastest growing with over 60 partners with a total staff in excess of 600.

main areas of work
The size of Bond Pearce and the full range of legal services provided ensures trainee solicitors gain unrivalled experience with training in four separate specialist seats. Specialist groups within Bond Pearce, backed up by effective support services, provide the highest quality of services to a broad range of clients: commercial group (corporate, banking and insolvency, commercial litigation); insurance group; property group (commercial property, planning and environment, private client); and personal injury.

trainee profile
Successful candidates may come from various backgrounds and enjoy a wide range of interests, but will have in common the desire to excel at their work and get the most out of life. Personal qualities are paramount. The firm looks for bright and enthusiastic individuals who can demonstrate commercial focus, intellectual ability and flexibility/adaptability.

training environment
Trainee solicitors have their own desks in the same office as the partner, associate or senior solicitor with whom they are working. They become an integral part of each team, closely involved in the diversity of their work and whilst fully supervised, trainees are encouraged to take on as much responsibility as possible. Technology plays a vital role in Bond Pearce. The firm's offices are linked by a networked computer system, the accounts and time recording systems are fully computerised and all staff, including trainee solicitors, are equipped with a fully networked PC on their desks. There are close links between the firm's offices and trainee solicitors join together in all training and many social activities. Bond Pearce has a thriving sports and social club.

vacation placements
Closing Date: Deadline for summer placement scheme is 31 March 2003.

sponsorship & awards
LPC financial assistance.

Partners 63
Assistant Solicitors 160
Total Trainees 40

contact
Tina Hosken

method of application
Application form & CV

selection procedure
Interviews & vacation placement scheme

closing date for 2005
31 July 2002

application
Training contracts p.a. 10-15
Applications p.a. 500
% interviewed p.a. 10%

training
Salary
1st year (2000)
Depending on location up to £16,250
Holiday entitlement 20 days
% of trainees with a non-law degree p.a. 25%

post-qualification
Salary (2000)
Depending on location up to £28,000
% of trainees offered job on qualification (2000) 93%
% of assistants (as at 1/9/00) who joined as trainees 38%
% of partners (as at 1/9/00) who joined as trainees 37%

Boyes Turner

Abbots House, Abbey Street, Reading RG1 3BD
Tel: (0118) 959 7711 Fax: (0118) 957 3357
Email: hbarnett@boyesturner.com/lcassar@boyesturner.com
Website: www.boyesturner.com

firm profile
Boyes Turner is a leading Thames Valley practice, renowned for its insolvency and medical negligence work and well respected for corporate and commercial, commercial property, intellectual property, employment, personal injury, family law and private client. While the focus for growth has been commercial work, the firm retains a commitment to its private clients.

main areas of work
Company/commercial (including employment) 20%; commercial property 20%; medical negligence/personal injury 20%; litigation 15%; insolvency 10%; family 5%; private client 10%.

trainee profile
Boyes Turner regards its trainees of today as its assistant solicitors and beyond of tomorrow and expects a high level of commitment, hard work and resourcefulness. Trainees must be responsive to the firm's mission to provide an excellent quality of service to both commercial and individual clients and also contribute to the team-working philosophy.

training environment
Training seats are currently organised into four six month seats; trainees gain experience in both commercial and private client practice areas. Work covers both individual and commercial clients, with as much client contact as possible, supervised by a partner or a senior solicitor. The Training Principal and HR Manager oversee all aspects of the programme, while each trainee is assigned a tutor (one of the partners) who reviews their progress monthly. This is on two levels – first in assessing how the trainee is developing as a lawyer and secondly how the trainee is developing as an individual, including communication and negotiating skills.

benefits
Firm pension scheme, life assurance, 25 days holiday.

sponsorship & awards
LPC loan of £3,000 and only one loan per applicant. Interest free and repaid over training contract.

Partners 22
Assistant Solicitors 15
Total Trainees 8

contact
Helen Barnett
Lisa Cassar

method of application
Letter & CV

selection procedure
2 interviews & 1 week work placement

closing date for 2005
31 July 2003

application
Training contracts p.a. **4**
% interviewed p.a. **1%+**
Required degree grade **2:2**

training
Salary
1st year (2002) **£17,000**
2nd year (2002) **£18,000**
Holiday entitlement
25 days
% of trainees with
a non-law degree p.a.
Varies

post-qualification
% of trainees offered job on qualification (2002)
100%
% of assistants (as at 1/9/02) who joined as trainees **30%**
% of partners (as at 1/9/02) who joined as trainees
19%

B P Collins

Collins House, 32-38 Station Road, Gerrards Cross SL9 8EL
Tel: (01753) 889995 Fax: (01753) 889851
Email: jacqui.symons@bpcollins.co.uk
Website: www.bpcollins.co.uk

firm profile
B P Collins was established in 1965, and has expanded significantly to become one of the largest and best known legal practices at the London end of the M4/M40 corridors. At its main office in Gerrards Cross, the emphasis is on commercial work, with particular strengths being company/commercial work of all types, commercial conveyancing and general commercial litigation. Alongside this there is a highly respected private client department specialising in tax planning, trusts, charities, wills and probates, and an equally successful family law team.

main areas of work
Company/commercial, employment, IT/IP, civil and commercial litigation, commercial conveyancing, property development, private client and family law.

trainee profile
Most of the partners and other fee-earners have worked in London at one time or another but, tired of commuting, have opted to work in more congenial surroundings and enjoy a higher quality lifestyle. Gerrards Cross is not only a very pleasant town with a large number of high net worth private clients but it is also a convenient location for serving the extremely active business community at the eastern end of the Thames Valley including West London, Heathrow, Uxbridge, Slough and Windsor. The firm therefore looks for trainees who are likely to respond to this challenging environment.

training environment
The firm aims to have six trainee solicitors at different stages of their training contracts at all times. Trainees serve five months in four separate departments of their choice. The final four months is spent in the department handling the sort of work in which the trainee intends specialising. The firm has a training partner with overall responsibility for all trainees and each department has its own training principal who is responsible for day to day supervision. There are regular meetings between the training principal and the trainee to monitor progress and a review meeting with the training partner midway and at the end of each departmental seat. The firm also involves its trainees in social and marketing events including golf and cricket matches, go-karting and racing and other sporting and non-sporting activities and has its own six-a-side football team.

sponsorship & awards
50% LPC costs refunded once trainee starts contract.

Partners 17
Assistant Solicitors 20
Total Trainees 6

contact
Jackie J Symons

method of application
Handwritten covering letter & CV

selection procedure
Screening interview & selection day

training
Salary
1st year £17,000
2nd year £18,000

Brabners Chaffe Street

1 Dale St, Liverpool L2 2ET
Tel: (0151) 600 3000 Fax: (0151) 227 3185
Brook House, 77 Fountain Street, Manchester M2 2EE
Tel: (0161) 236 5800 Fax: (0161) 228 6862
7-8 Chapel Street, Preston PR1 8AN
Tel: (01772) 823921 Fax: (01772) 201918
Email: Trainees@brabnerschaffestreet.com
Website: www.brabnerschaffestreet.com

firm profile
One of the top North West commercial firms, Brabners Chaffe Street, in Liverpool, Manchester and Preston, has the experience, talent and prestige of a firm that has a 200-plus-year history. Brabners Chaffe Street is a dynamic, client-led specialist in the provision of excellent legal services to clients ranging from large plcs to private individuals.

main areas of work
The firm carries out a wide range of specialist legal services and Brabners Chaffe Street's client base includes plcs, public sector bodies, banks and other commercial, corporate and professional businesses. Brabners Chaffe Street is organised into five client-focused departments: corporate (including commercial law); employment; litigation (including media); property (including housing association and construction); private client.

trainee profile
Graduates and those undertaking CPE or LPC, who can demonstrate intelligence, intuition, humour, approachability and commitment.

training environment
The firm is one of the few law firms that holds Investor in People status and has a comprehensive training and development programme. Trainees are given a high degree of responsibility and are an integral part of the culture of the firm. Seats are available in the firm's five departments and each trainee will have partner level supervision. Personal development appraisals are conducted at six monthly intervals to ensure that trainee progress is valuable and informed. The training programme is overseen by the firm's Director of Training, Dr Tony Harvey, and each centre has a designated Trainee Partner. It is not all hard work and the firm has an excellent social programme.

sponsorship & awards
Partial sponsorship may be available for the LPC.

Partners 39
Assistant Solicitors 45
Total Trainees 18

contact
Liverpool office:
Dr Tony Harvey
Director of Training

method of application
Application form

selection procedure
Interview & assessment day

closing date for 2005
Apply by 31 August 2003 for training contracts commencing in September 2005

application
Required degree grade
2:1 or higher, or postgraduate degree

training
Holiday entitlement
25 days

offices
Liverpool, Manchester, Preston

Brachers

Somerfield House, 59 London Road, Maidstone ME16 8JH
Tel: (01622) 690691 Fax: (01622) 681410
Email: info@brachers.co.uk
Website: www.brachers.co.uk

firm profile
Brachers is a leading firm in the South East with an established City office. The firm is principally involved in corporate and commercial work although it has a niche private client practice. The firm has a leading healthcare team, one of 14 on the NHSLA panel.

main areas of work
Company/commercial, general litigation, medical negligence, commercial property, employment, private client and family.

trainee profile
Candidates need to have a strong academic background, common sense and be team players. Both graduates in law and non-law subjects are considered as well as more mature candidates.

training environment
Trainees have four six-month seats out of company/commercial, property, general civil litigation, defendant insurance, medical negligence, family, employment, and private client. Trainees have two appraisals in each seat. The firm has an open door policy and is committed to developing a long term career structure. Social events are organised.

sponsorship & awards
LPC/CPE £6,000 discretionary award.

Partners	22
Assistant Solicitors	26
Total Trainees	13

contact
Mary Raymont

method of application
Handwritten letter & CV

selection procedure
Interview day with partners

closing date for 2005
31 July 2003

application
Training contracts p.a. 6
Applications p.a. 400
% interviewed p.a. 7.5%
Required degree grade 2:1

training
Salary:
1st year (2005) TBA
(2002) £16,000
2nd year (2006) TBA
(2002) £17,500
Holiday entitlement
20 days

post-qualification
Salary (2002) £27,500-£30,000
% of trainees offered job on qualification 100%

regional offices
Maidstone & London only

Bristows

3 Lincoln's Inn Fields, London WC2A 3AA
Tel: (020) 7400 8000 Fax: (020) 7400 8050
Email: info@bristows.com
Website: www.bristows.com

firm profile
Bristows specialises in providing legal services to businesses with interests in technology or intellectual property. The firm acts for some of the largest companies in the world and helps protect some of the most famous brands. Its work reaches beyond intellectual property law to corporate and commercial law, property, tax, employment law and litigation.

main areas of work
Intellectual property 54%; company/corporate finance/commercial 15%; IT 16%; commercial litigation (including employment) 10%; commercial property (including environmental) 5%.

trainee profile
Bristows is looking for applicants with outstanding intellects, with strong analytical skills and engaging personalities. It is also looking for people who will contribute to the ethos of the firm. Bristows is a very friendly firm and believes that you get the best from people if they are in a happy and supportive working environment.

training environment
The firm's training programme gives you the knowledge and skills to build on the extensive hands-on experience you will gain in each of its main departments. You will be working closely with partners, which will accelerate your training. Part of this training may also involve a secondment to one of a number of leading clients. With the international spread of its clients, the probability of overseas travel is high, especially upon qualification.

benefits
Excellent career prospects, a competitive package, firm pension scheme, life assurance and health insurance.

vacation placements
Schemes are run for one week during Christmas and Easter breaks, two weeks during the Summer break. Remuneration: £200 p.w.; Closing Date: Christmas –29 November; Easter/Summer – 28 February.

sponsorship & awards
CPE/LPC fees plus £5,000 maintenance grant for each.

Partners 28
Assistant Solicitors 47
Total Trainees 17

contact
Graduate Recruitment Officer

method of application
Application form

selection procedure
2 individual interviews

closing date for 2005
31 January 2003 for February interviews,
31 August 2003 for September interviews

application
Training contracts p.a. **Up to 10**
Applications p.a. **3,500**
% interviewed p.a. **6%**
Required degree grade **2:1 (preferred)**

training
Salary
1st year (2002) £26,000
2nd year (2002) £28,000
Holiday entitlement
4 weeks
% of trainees with a non-law degree p.a. **71%**

post-qualification
Salary (2002) **£43,000**
% of trainees offered job on qualification (2002) **71%**
% of assistants (as at 1/9/01) who joined as trainees **41%**
% of partners (as at 1/9/01) who joined as trainees **53%**

Browne Jacobson

44 Castle Gate, Nottingham NG1 7BJ
Tel: (0115) 976 6000 Fax: (0115) 947 5246
Aldwych House, 81 Aldwych, London WC2B 4HN
Tel: (020) 7404 1546 Fax: (020) 7836 3882
102 Colmore Row, Birmingham B3 3AG
Tel: (0121) 237 3900 Fax: (0121) 236 1291
Email: info@brownej.co.uk
Website: www.brownej.co.uk

firm profile
Browne Jacobson is a substantial business and insurance services law firm, which has a practical approach providing a first class client service. Already acknowledged as a leading regional practice offering a comprehensive range of services, the firm has continued to develop a nationwide reputation for quality and has a growing international presence. It operates from Nottingham, London and Birmingham. International development is driven primarily through London and Paris where the firm has an associated office and through key relationships with selected US law firms.

main areas of work
Insurance Services: Personal injury litigation; professional indemnity; public authority and defendant medical negligence.
Business Services: Corporate and commercial; tax and financial planning; commercial property; commercial litigation and employment.

trainee profile
The firm's trainees are bright, have high academic ability and bring enthusiasm and commitment to its practice. Personable and practical, they are able to demonstrate an appropriate sense of humour and work as part of a team whilst accepting individual responsibility.

training environment
Training at Browne Jacobson is practical and structured. You will spend four periods of six months working in all practice areas of the firm to obtain an overview and experience many new challenges. The firm aims to develop rather than control its trainees; you will have a programme of skills training during which you will be strongly supported by Browne Jacobson's training team.

sponsorship & awards
PgDL, LPC.

Partners 43
Assistant Solicitors 89

contact
Carol King
Training Manager

method of application
CV & covering letter to Carol King, or via website

selection procedure
Assessment Centre

closing date for 2005
31 July 2003

application
Training contracts p.a. **8**
Applications p.a. **1,500**
% interviewed p.a. **5%**
Required degree grade **2:1**

training
Salary **£18,000**
Holiday entitlement
20 days
% of trainees with a non-law degree p.a. **5%**

post-qualification
Salary **Regional variations**
Holiday entitlement
5 weeks

Burges Salmon

Narrow Quay House, Narrow Quay, Bristol BS1 4AH
Tel: (0117) 902 2766 (brochure) (0117) 902 7733 (enquiries) Fax: (0117) 902 4400
Email: alexandra.van-hattum@burges-salmon.com
Website: www.burges-salmon.com

firm profile
Based in Bristol, with a facility in London, Burges Salmon is one of the UK's leading law firms which offers an exceptional quality of life combined with a reputation normally regarded as the preserve of the City firms. More than 75% of its top 100 clients are based outside the South West, and the firm is consistently ranked amongst the UK's most profitable. Burges Salmon's success is based on a simple strategy: a focus on quality people, a breadth of practice areas and a single site approach. This ensures a cohesive culture combining professionalism, enthusiasm and a sense of humour which attracts and retains staff and clients alike.

main areas of work
Burges Salmon provides national and international clients with a full commercial service through five main departments: company commercial, property, tax and trusts, commercial litigation, and agriculture, property litigation and environment (APLE). Specialist areas include: banking, EU and competition, corporate finance, environment, employment, IP and technology, and transport.

training environment
The Law Society monitor recently accredited the firm with six points of good practice where the previous maximum in visits to other firms had been two. This underlines Burges Salmon's reputation for having one of the best training programmes in the country. Training is personalised to suit each individual, and the six seat structure means that you will not be restricted in the practice areas you are able to experience before qualification. This dedication to trainees is highlighted by an extremely high retention rate, which is well above the industry average. Trainees are given early responsibility balanced with an open door policy for advice and guidance. There are many opportunities for trainees to take an active role in cases involving high profile clients including Orange, Honda, Ministry of Defence, Reuters, Coca Cola HBC and EMI, as well as running their own files on smaller cases.

benefits
Annually reviewed competitive salary, annual bonus, pension scheme and mobile phone.

vacation placements
Places for 2003: 32; Duration: 2 weeks, Remuneration: £150 p.w., Closing Date: 21 February 2003.

sponsorship & awards
PgDL/LPC fees plus maintenance of £4,500 (LPC) or £5,000 (PgDL and LPC (£2,500 p.a.)).

Partners 50
Assistant Solicitors 150
Total Trainees 40

contact
Alexandra Van-Hattum
Graduate Recruitment Officer

method of application
Employer's application form available on website

selection procedure
Penultimate year law students, final year non-law students, recent graduates or mature candidates are considered for open days, vacation placements &/or training contracts

closing date for 2005
8 August 2003

application
Training contracts p.a.
20-25
Applications p.a. **1,500**
% interviewed p.a. **10%**
Required degree grade **2:1**

training
Salary
1st year (2002) **£20,000**
2nd year (2002) **£21,000**
Holiday entitlement
24 days
% of trainees with a non-law degree p.a. **40%**

post-qualification
Salary (2001) **£34,000**
% of trainees offered job on qualification (2002) **94%**
% of assistants who joined as trainees (2002) **50%**
% of partners who joined as trainees (2002) **30%**

Cadwalader, Wickersham & Taft

265 Strand, London WC2R 1BH
Tel: (020) 7170 8700 Fax: (020) 7170 8600
Email: hrdept@cwt-uk.com
Website: www.cadwalader.com

firm profile
Cadwalader, Wickersham & Taft is a major New York based law firm, recognised for its innovative approach to legal and commercial matters. The London office, established in September 1997, is renowned for its expertise in capital markets, financial restructuring, corporate, project finance, litigation and real estate. The office services clients interested in capitalising on the European and worldwide markets, as well as those seeking US-style investment banking services and access to American capital markets.

main areas of work
Capital markets, financial restructuring, project finance, corporate, litigation, real estate and banking and finance.

trainee profile
Candidates need to demonstrate that they are intellectually bright and ambitious, have good communications skills and a commitment to the law. The firm looks for well-rounded individuals with a desire to succeed and a robust and resilient personality.

training environment
Training consists of four six month seats taking into account trainees' preferences. Responsibility and exposure to client meetings will take place at an early stage. Trainees share an office with a partner or associate, who supervise, review performance and provide feedback on a regular basis. Formal reviews will be carried out every six months. Elements of the PSC will occur at the start of the training contract; the remainder will take place over the following two years. The firm is friendly and supportive with an open door policy, operating a business casual dress down code all year round. There is also a varied sporting and social calendar.

benefits
Permanent health insurance, season ticket loan, BUPA (dental and health) and life assurance.

sponsorship & awards
CPE Funding: Fees paid plus £4,500 maintenance.
LPC Funding: Fees paid plus £4,500 maintenance.

Partners 7
Assistant Solicitors 45
Total Trainees 7

contact
HR Department

method of application
CV & covering letter

selection procedure
2 interviews

closing date for 2005
31 August 2003

application
Training contracts p.a. 4-6
Applications p.a. 500
% interviewed p.a. 10%
Required degree grade 2:1

training
Salary
1st year (2001) £30,000
2nd year (2001) £33,600
Holiday entitlement
24 days

post-qualification
Salary (2001) £65,000
% of trainees offered job on qualification (2002) 67%

overseas offices
New York, Washington, Charlotte

Campbell Hooper

35 Old Queen St, London SW1H 9JD
Tel: (020) 7222 9070 Fax: (020) 7222 5591
Email: humanresources@campbellhooper.com
Website: www.campbellhooper.com

Partners	21
Assistant Solicitors	31
Total Trainees	8

contact
Annette Fritze-Shanks

method of application
CV with covering letter

selection procedure
Interviews

closing date for 2005
31 July 2003

application
Training contracts p.a. 3-4
Applications p.a. c.1,500
% interviewed p.a. 3-4%
Required degree grade
2:1 any discipline

training
Salary
1st year (2002)
£21,000-£22,000 p.a.
2nd year (2002)
£23,000-£24,500 p.a.
Holiday entitlement
25 days

firm profile
With over 200 years experience, Campbell Hooper is well equipped to face the requirements of today's ever changing market and adopts a modern and dynamic management style with high investment in IT, knowledge management and training. The firm's clients are involved in a variety of industries including information technology, telecoms, banking, advertising, construction, property investment and development, media, manufacturing, a number of service industries and local government and government departments. Membership of Proteus, a European network of independent law firms, provides an invaluable international aspect to the firm.

main areas of work
High standards of client service are delivered through four departments: company/commercial; commercial property; construction; private client. The principal areas of work are charities; company; construction; defamation; domestic conveyancing; employment; environmental; European; family; immigration; insurance; litigation; media; planning; property; rating; tax; trust and estate planning and wills and probate.

trainee profile
Applications are welcomed from those with a keen commercial focus complemented by a solid academic history. Motivation, enthusiasm and professional commitment are equally important.

training environment
You will develop your commercial acumen and legal flair through exposure in each of the four departments. Equal emphasis is placed on providing you with both professional and personal career support. This is facilitated through day to day coaching from either a partner or solicitor, constructive feedback on performance through mid and end of seat reviews and mentoring from the trainee partner who will take a personal interest in your professional development. In addition the firm is committed to continuous development and you will be encouraged to attend client seminars, be actively involved in practice development initiatives as well as participating in other training and development activities including the compulsory professional skills course.

sponsorship & benefits
LPC and CPE fees paid. Benefits include private medical insurance, pension scheme, life assurance, permanent health insurance and season ticket loan.

Capsticks

77-83 Upper Richmond Road, London SW15 2TT
Tel: (020) 8780 2211 Fax: (020) 8780 4811
Email: career@capsticks.co.uk
Website: www.capsticks.com

Partners	28
Assistant Solicitors	42
Total Trainees	12
Other Fee-earners	8

firm profile
Rated as the country's leading healthcare law firm by the Chambers Guide and other leading directories, CAPSTICKS handles litigation, administrative law, commercial and property work for a wide range of healthcare bodies, including over 150 NHS Trusts, PCTs and Health Authorities, and healthcare-related charities and regulatory bodies.

main areas of work
Clinical law 54%; commercial 6%; commercial property 15%; dispute resolution 7%; employment law 18%.

trainee profile
Successful candidates possess intellectual agility, good interpersonal skills and are capable of taking initiative.

training environment
Six four-month seats, which may include clinical negligence/personal injury; commercial property; contract and commercial; employment law and commercial/property litigation. Trainees take responsibility for their own caseload and are involved in client meetings from an early stage. There are also opportunities to contribute to the firm's marketing and management processes. There are numerous in-house lectures for all fee earners. There is an open door policy, and trainees receive informal feedback and supervision as well as regular appraisals. Despite the firm's rapid expansion, it has retained a friendly atmosphere and a relaxed working environment. There are numerous informal social and sporting activities.

benefits
Bonus scheme, pension, PHI, death in service cover, interest-free season ticket loan.

vacation placements
Places for 2003: Yes; Duration: 2 weeks; Closing Date: 28 February 2003.

sponsorship & awards
Scholarship contributions to CPE and LPC courses.

contact
Sue Laundy

method of application
Application form

selection procedure
Candidates are encouraged to participate in the firm's summer placement scheme. Final selection is by interview with the Training Principal & other partners

closing date for 2005
31 July 2003

application
Training contracts p.a. **6-8**
Applications p.a. **c.200**
% interviewed p.a. **c.19%**
Required degree grade
2:1 or above

training
Salary
1st year TBA
2nd year TBA
Holiday entitlement
22 days p.a. (increased by 1 day p.a. to max 25 days)
% of trainees with a non-law degree p.a. **41%**

post-qualification
Salary (2002) **£40,000 + benefits**
% of trainees offered job on qualification (2002) **100%**
% of assistants (as at 1/9/02) who joined as trainees **45%**
% of partners (as at 1/9/02) who joined as trainees **7%**

Charles Russell

8–10 New Fetter Lane, London EC4A 1RS
Tel: (020) 7203 5000 Fax: (020) 7203 5307
Graduate Recruitment Line: (020) 7203 5353
Website: www.cr-law.com

firm profile
Charles Russell is a progressive City law firm with regional offices in Cheltenham and Guildford and a network of close professional contacts throughout the world. It continues to grow, offering a wide range of legal services for both corporate and private clients. The firm recruits a small number of trainees for a firm of its size. This enables trainees to undergo the best possible training. The firm is committed to its clients and their demands. It also respects the fact that its staff need to have a life of their own. This ethos fosters a strong team spirit throughout the firm.

main areas of work
Whilst the commercial division offers the opportunity for involvement in major corporate transactions, the firm's commitment to private clients and charities remains unshaken. The firm has five core areas spreading across the commercial and private sectors: media-comms, employment, charities, private client and family. The services of other practice areas also highly regarded in their own right and include corporate/commercial, litigation, commercial property and insurance.

trainee profile
Trainees should be balanced, rounded achievers with a solid academic background. Outside interests are fundamental.

training environment
Trainees spend six months in four of the following training seats – litigation, company/commercial, property, private client, family, employment and intellectual property. Wherever possible the firm will accommodate individual preference. You will be seated with a partner/ senior solicitor. Regular appraisals are held to discuss progress and direction. Trainees are encouraged to attend the extensive in-house training courses. The PSC is taught both internally and externally. All trainees are expected to take on as much responsibility as possible. A social committee organises a range of activities from quiz nights through to sporting events.

benefits
BUPA immediately, PHI and life assurance after six months service.

sponsorship & awards
CPE and LPC fees paid and annual maintenance of £4,500 (under review) to London trainees. One-off grants in the LPC year are paid to Cheltenham and Guildford trainees.

Partners 80
Associates 21
Assistant Solicitors 140
Total Trainees 30

contact
Eileen Moran
Graduate Recruitment
Line: (020) 7203 5353

method of application
Handwritten letter & application form

selection procedure
Assessment days to include an interview & other exercises designed to assess identified performance criteria

closing date for 2005
31 July 2003

application
Training contracts p.a.
10–12
Applications p.a. **Approx 2,000**
% interviewed p.a. **3%**
Required degree grade **2:1**

training
Salary
1st year (2002) £27,000
2nd year (2002) £29,500
Holiday entitlement
25 days

post-qualification
Salary (2002) **£45,000**

regional offices
Also offers training contracts in its Cheltenham & Guildford offices. Applications are dealt with by the London office

Clarks

Great Western House, Station Rd, Reading RG1 1JX
Tel: (0118) 958 5321 Fax: (0118) 960 4611
Email: inmail@clarks-solicitors.co.uk
Website: www.clarks-solicitors.co.uk

firm profile
Founded in 1913, Clarks is a commercial law firm with a proven track record across the UK and overseas (with 15 partners and 11 associates). Clients range from small to medium sized enterprises to multinational companies. Clarks is particularly recognised for the number of international FTSE 250 clients who have chosen to use its services. Based in Reading, Clarks has taken full advantage of the rapid commercial and professional expansion of this thriving 'capital' of the Thames Valley.

main areas of work
Commercial property; corporate and technology; litigation; employment; planning; insolvency; private client; environmental and energy.

trainee profile
Candidates must have a consistently good academic record and should have effective interpersonal skills. Language skills are an advantage.

training environment
On joining Clarks, trainees will receive a full induction programme. Trainees immediately become part of a team and are encouraged to have direct involvement with clients and to play a part in building long-term relationships with them. Training usually consists of seats of six months in four of the following teams: property, corporate, litigation, employment and IP/IT. Within each seat you will have a mentor (a partner or an associate) who will have responsibility for guiding and encouraging you through that seat. In addition to training within a workgroup you are also encouraged to attend the firm's in-house weekly seminars. Clarks also supports you in your professional skills courses. Clarks is a classic yet innovative firm with an open, friendly culture. It retains a high number of trainees upon qualification and a significant number have progressed through the firm to become associates or partners.

benefits
Pension, free conveyancing.

vacation placements
Places for 2003: On application.

Partners 15
Assistant Solicitors 42
Total Trainees 10

contact
Sarah Moore
HR Manager

method of application
Application form (from brochure or website) or letter and CV

selection procedure
Open day/interview & second interview (with limited written tests)

closing date for 2005
No closing date

application
Training contracts p.a. 5-6
Applications p.a. 500-600
% interviewed p.a. 10%
Required degree grade
Usually 2:1 or above (but will consider lower grade subject to explanation)

training
Salary
1st year (2000) £17,000
2nd year (2000) £18,500
Holiday entitlement
20 days

post-qualification
% of trainees offered job on qualification (2002) 75%
% of assistants (as at 1/9/00) who joined as trainees 35%
% of partners (as at 1/9/00) who joined as trainees 40%

overseas offices
Affiliated to TagLaw worldwide - ability to second to foreign office possible, subject to appropriate language skills

Cleary, Gottlieb, Steen & Hamilton

City Place House, 55 Basinghall Street, London EC2V 5EH
Tel: (020) 7614 2200 Fax: (020) 7600 1698
Website: www.clearygottlieb.com

firm profile
Founded in the United States in 1946, from its inception the firm has maintained a strong international presence. It now has over 700 lawyers in 11 offices worldwide with more than 250 lawyers in Europe, with offices in Paris (opened 1949), Brussels (1960), Frankfurt (1991) and Rome (1998) in addition to London (1971). It is common for lawyers to spend time in offices other than their home office.

main areas of work
Mergers and acquisitions (takeovers, cross-border mergers, joint ventures), securities (equity offerings, debt offerings, bond issues, privatisations, global offerings, private placements), banking and finance, tax, EU and competition law.

trainee profile
Candidates must have an excellent academic background including at least a 2:1 law degree from a top UK university and have an open and outgoing personality. IT and language skills are an advantage.

training environment
There are no departments. Trainees sit with partners and senior solicitors and will do a mix of M&A, capital markets, tax and regulatory work. Seats change every six months. One seat will be in Brussels and there will be opportunities to travel and work in other offices. Ongoing legal training is provided by regular training talks covering all areas of law practised at the firm. Trainees will be required to take the New York bar exam. Assistance will be given with this. Trainees will work on a wide range of matters, many governed by laws other than English law. Trainees will in most respects be fulfilling the same roles as first year lawyers do in its other offices.

benefits
Pension, health insurance, long-term disability insurance, health club, employee assistance programme.

sponsorship & awards
LPC Funding: Fees paid plus £4,500 maintenance award.

Partners 13
Assistants 44
Total Trainees 4

contact
Melanie Driffill

method of application
Letter & CV

selection procedure
2 interviews

closing date for 2005
30 Sept 2003

application
Training contracts p.a.
Up to 4
Required degree grade **2:1**

training
Salary
1st year (2000) £33,000
2nd year (2000) £39,000
Holiday entitlement
20 days

post-qualification
Salary varies from office to office

overseas offices
Brussels, Frankfurt, Hong Kong, Milan, Moscow, New York, Paris, Rome, Tokyo, Washington DC

Clifford Chance

200 Aldersgate Street, London EC1A 4JJ
Tel: (020) 7600 1000 Fax: (020) 7600 5555
Email: graduate.recruitment@cliffordchance.com
Website: www.cliffordchance.com/grads

firm profile
Clifford Chance is the world's first fully integrated law firm with 32 offices throughout Europe, Asia and America. It delivers legal services to powerful and influential businesses and financial institutions around the globe, working across international borders to shape the deals that make the news. As a trainee this means you will gain breadth and depth in your experiences.

main areas of work
Banking and finance; capital markets; corporate; litigation and dispute resolution; real estate; tax, pensions and employment.

trainee profile
Consistently strong academic profile (minimum 2:1 degree), a broad range of interpersonal skills and extra curricular activities and interests.

training environment
The Clifford Chance training contract has been devised to provide you with the technical skills and experience you need to contribute to the firm's success on a day-to-day basis, to achieve your professional qualification and to progress to a rewarding career. Your two year training contract consists of four six month seats. Most trainees will spend a seat on a secondment at an international office or with a client. In each seat you will be working alongside senior lawyers. Trainees are encouraged to use initiative to make the most of expertise and resources available to the firm. Three-monthly appraisals and monitoring in each seat ensure trainees gain a range of work and experience.

benefits
Prize for first class degrees and distinction in LPC, interest-free loan, private health insurance, subsidised restaurant, fitness centre, life assurance, occupational health service, and permanent health assurance.

vacation placements
Places for 2002-2003: Christmas, Easter and summer break. There is a strong social element to the programme; Duration: 2 weeks; Remuneration: £270 pw; Closing Date: 8 November 2002 for Christmas scheme; 31 January 2003 for other schemes.

sponsorship & awards
CPE and LPC fees paid and currently £5,000 maintenance p.a. for London, Guildford and Oxford, £4,500 p.a. elsewhere.

London office
Partners 230
Lawyers 835
Trainees 245

contact
Louise McMunn
Graduate Recruitment

method of application
Application form.
Preferably apply online

selection procedure
Assessment day comprising an interview with a partner & senior solicitor, a group exercise & a verbal reasoning test

application
Training contracts p.a. 130
Applications p.a. 2,000
% interviewed p.a. 25%
Required degree grade 2:1

training
Salary
1st year £28,500
(Aug 2002)
2nd year £32,000
Holiday entitlement
25 days
% of trainees with
a non-law degree p.a. 35%
No. of seats available
abroad p.a. 84

post-qualification
Salary (Aug 2002) £50,000
% of trainees offered job
on qualification (2002) 95%

overseas offices
Amsterdam, Bangkok, Barcelona, Beijing, Berlin, Brussels, Budapest, Dubai, Düsseldorf, Frankfurt, Hong Kong, Los Angeles, Luxembourg, Madrid, Milan, Moscow, Munich, New York, Padua, Palo Alto, Paris, Prague, Rome, San Diego, San Francisco, São Paulo, Shanghai, Singapore, Tokyo, Warsaw, Washington DC

Clyde & Co

51 Eastcheap, London EC3M 1JP
Tel: (020) 7648 1580 Fax: (020) 7623 5427
Email: careers@clyde.co.uk
Website: www.clydeco.com

firm profile
A major international commercial firm with over 700 personnel worldwide and a client base spanning more than 100 countries. It is a leading practice in international trade, insurance, reinsurance, shipping and energy, and has experienced a high level of growth in corporate and finance. UK offices are in London, Guildford and Cardiff, with trainee solicitors recruited for London and Guildford.

main areas of work
Insurance/reinsurance; banking, corporate commercial and tax; marine and transport; general commercial litigation; property; employment.

trainee profile
The firm has no stereotypical trainee. Non-law graduates are welcome, especially those with modern languages or science degrees. The firm places as much importance on finding candidates with an outgoing, interesting personality as it does on academic credentials.

training environment
Trainees are immediately given as much responsibility as they can handle, and usually have their own office. They are also encouraged to take on as much client contact as possible, and are involved in developing business relationships. The PSC is run in-house and there is a full programme of lectures, seminars, courses, workshops and educational visits.

benefits
Subsidised sports club, interest free ticket loan, staff restaurant and weekly free bar.

legal work experience
The firm runs Legal Training Assessment Days during the Easter holidays and a Summer Vacation Placement scheme for 2 weeks in July. Closing Date: 28 February 2003.

sponsorship & awards
CPE and LPC fees paid and maintenance grant. Sponsorship provided where no LEA funding available.

Partners 120
Fee-earners 424
Total Trainees 41

contact
Georgia de Saram
Graduate Recruitment Manager

method of application
Application form & covering letter

selection procedure
Individual interview with Graduate Recruitment followed by interview with 2 partners

closing date for 2005
15 August 2003

application
Training contracts p.a. **20**
Applications p.a. **3,000 +**
% interviewed p.a. **6%**
Required degree grade **2:1**

training
Salary
1st year (2002) **£27,000**
2nd year (2002) **£30,000**
Holiday entitlement
25 days
% of trainees with
a non-law degree p.a. **50%**
No. of seats available
abroad p.a. (2002) **5**

post-qualification
Salary (2002) **£46,000**
% of trainees offered job
on qualification (2002) **95%**

overseas offices
Belgrade, Caracas, Dubai, Hong Kong, Nantes, Paris, Piraeus, Singapore, St Petersburg*
* Associated office

CMS Cameron McKenna

Mitre House, 160 Aldersgate Street, London EC1A 4DD
Tel: (020) 7367 3000 Fax: (020) 7367 2000
Email: gradrec@cmck.com
Website: www.law-now.com

firm profile
CMS Cameron McKenna is a major full service UK and international commercial law firm advising businesses and governments on transactions and projects particularly in the UK, continental Europe, the Asia Pacific region, North America and Southern Africa. It has particular strengths in a number of industry sectors such as banking and international finance, corporate, construction, projects, energy, healthcare, bioscience, insurance and real estate. The firm is modern, entrepreneurial and innovative and is strong on achievement.

main areas of work
Banking; corporate; insurance; energy; projects and construction; real estate; commercial.

trainee profile
The firm looks for high-achieving team players with good communication, analytical and organisational skills. You will need to show initiative and be able to accept personal responsibility, not only for your own work, but also for your career development. You will need to be resilient and focused on achieving results.

training environment
The firm is friendly and supportive and puts no limits on a trainee's progress. It offers four six month seats, three of which will be in the firm's main area of practice. In addition you may gain experience of a specialist area or opt for a secondment to national or international clients. In each seat you will be allocated high quality work on substantial transactions for a range of government and blue-chip clients. Regular appraisals will be held with your seat supervisor to assess your progress, skills and development needs. The three compulsory modules of the PSC will be completed before joining, allowing trainees to become effective and participate on a practical level as soon as possible. The Professional Skills Course is complemented by a comprehensive in-house training programme that continues up to qualification and beyond.

vacation placements
Places for 2003: 55; Duration: 2 weeks; Remuneration: £225 p.w.

sponsorship & awards
PgDL and LPC Funding: Fees paid and a maintenance grant of £5,000 (London, Guildford and Oxford), £4,500 (elsewhere).

Partners 180
Assistant Solicitors 460
Total Trainees 110

contact
Graduate Recruitment Team (0845) 3000 491

method of application
Online application form
www.law-now.com

selection procedure
2 stage selection procedure. Initial interview followed by assessment centre

closing date
31 July 2003

application
Training contracts p.a. **80**
Applications p.a. **1,500**
% interviewed p.a. **27%**
Required degree grade **2:1**

training
Salary
1st year (2001) **£28,000**
2nd year (2001) **£32,000**
Holiday entitlement
25 days + option of flexible holiday
% of trainees with a non-law degree p.a. **40%**
No. of seats available abroad p.a. **Currently 15**

post-qualification
Salary (2002) **£50,000**
% of trainees offered job on qualification (2002) **90%**

CMS Cameron McKenna continued

additional information
Every trainee has a PC on their desk with email connection and access to legal and business databases. The firm financially supports trainees who wish to learn or improve a foreign language. There will be the opportunity to become involved in a number of sporting and social events.

trainee comments
"The firm has an incredibly wide base of areas to choose from, varying from healthcare and biotechnology to energy, projects and construction to the more traditional areas of banking, corporate and litigation. You'll find yourself in a pleasant and down to earth working environment where you'll be offered a variety of different opportunities, both in and out of work." (Trainee solicitor, Property).

"Compared to other firms where I have friends it's very friendly and unstuffy here. It has retained the smaller firm environment even though we're now a top ten firm. Some firms pay lip service to the 'open door' idea but it really happens here. My best moment so far was helping the team who pitched against four of the top ten City firms for one of two places to do work for the Post Office - and we were appointed." (Trainee solicitor, Commercial).

"The most rewarding thing about the international opportunities here, whether it's before or after qualification, is the sheer scope the firm can offer you. There is no doubt that an international perspective is a massive selling point for law firms. Clients don't want to be dealing with one firm in London and any number of others overseas. And that's great news when you're a trainee because you have more chance to travel during your training contract, and then after qualification. My overseas experience was an invaluable part of my contract. I completed a seat in Hong Kong in our Corporate Recovery Group and worked in Orissa, India on the restructuring of the electricity industry. I doubt I'd get those kind of opportunities elsewhere." (Solicitor, Corporate).

branch offices
Visit www.law-now for further information

C/M/S/ Cameron McKenna

Cobbetts

Ship Canal House, King Street, Manchester M2 4WB
Tel: (0161) 833 3333 Fax: (0161) 833 3030
Email: lawyers@cobbetts.co.uk
Website: www.cobbetts.co.uk

firm profile
The new look Cobbetts now boasts offices on both sides of the Pennines following its merger in May 2002. The firm continues to place high quality and long term relationship building with clients at the forefront of its strategy for success – a strategy which resulted in controlled sustained growth of around 20% p.a. This has been achieved through good management, and an emphasis on the needs of the clients, intermediaries and the firm's own personnel. Cobbetts believes in relationships, quality of environment and job satisfaction for all. Job satisfaction for trainees is shown by its trainee policy 'Recruit -Train - Retain'. Those three words say it all.

main areas of work
Cobbetts operates through a number of flexible service teams based on work type and managed within two divisions – corporate and property.

trainee profile
Law and non-law graduates.

training environment
Four six month seats are available. Typically these include one property, one litigation and one commercial/corporate seat. There is an opportunity for one trainee each year to spend three months in Brussels.

benefits
Social club and LA Fitness pool and gym.

vacation placements
Places for 2003: 24 placements are available during July and August.

sponsorship & awards
CPE and LPC grant available.

trainee comments
"Life at Cobbetts is busy, challenging and varied."
"I would highly recommend Cobbetts as a firm to train with if you are looking for a challenging but enjoyable work environment together with a fun social life."
"Large enough and commercial enough to be one of the big players in the business, but yet relaxed enough and personal enough to make that difference to your training contract."
"...you work hard but there's always someone to help if you're unsure."

Partners	74
Fee-earners	92
Total Trainees	22

contact
Richard Webb
Trainee Partner

method of application
Application form (available on request/via Internet)

selection procedure
Half day assessments

closing date for 2005
31 July 2003

application
Training contracts p.a.
12-14
Applications p.a. **700**
% interviewed p.a. **10%**
Required degree grade **2:1**

training
Salary
1st year Competitive rate
2nd year Reviewed each year
Holiday entitlement
20 days
% of trainees with
a non-law degree p.a. **30%**
No. of seats available
abroad p.a. **1**

post-qualification
% of trainees offered job on qualification (2001)
100%
% of assistants (as at 1/9/00) who joined as trainees **75%**
% of partners (as at 1/9/01) who joined as trainees **60%**

overseas offices
Brussels

Coffin Mew & Clover

Fareham Point, Wickham Road, Fareham PO16 7AU
Tel: (01329) 825617 Fax: (01329) 825619
Email: saralloyd@coffinmew.co.uk
Website: www.coffinmew.co.uk

firm profile
Founded more than a century ago, the firm has grown to become one of the larger legal practices in the South East with major offices located in the cities of Portsmouth and Southampton and just off the M27 Motorway at Fareham. The firm is in the enviable position of operating a balanced practice offering private client and business services in approximately equal volume and is particularly noted for a number of niche practices with national reputations.

main areas of work
The firm is structured through eight core departments: corporate/commercial; employment; commercial litigation; personal injury; commercial property; family/crime; residential property; trust/probate. Niche practices include intellectual property; finance and business regulation; social housing; medical negligence and mental health.

trainee profile
The firm encourages applications from candidates with very good academic ability who seek a broad-based training contract in a highly progressive and demanding but friendly and pleasant environment.

training environment
The training contract is divided into six seats of four months each which will include a property department, a litigation department and a commercial department. The remainder of the training contract will be allocated after discussion with the trainee concerned. The firm aims to ensure that the trainee spends the final four months of his or her training contract in the department in which he or she hopes to work after qualification.

benefits
CPE and LPC funding available by discussion with candidates.

vacation placements
Open week in July each year; application as per training contract.

Partners 20
Assistant Solicitors 25
Total Trainees 9

contact
Sara Lloyd
Director of HR & Administration

method of application
CV & covering letter

selection procedure
Interview

closing date for 2005
31 July 2003

application
Training contracts p.a. **4-5**
Applications p.a. **400+**
% interviewed p.a. **5%**
Required degree grade **2:1 (save in exceptional circumstances)**

training
Salary
1st year
Competitive market rate
2nd year
Competitive market rate
Holiday entitlement **20 days**
% of trainees with a non-law degree p.a. **25%**

post-qualification
Salary (2002) **£24,500**
% of trainees offered job on qualification (2001) **100%**
% of assistants who joined as trainees **25%**
% of partners who joined as trainees **50%**

Coudert Brothers

60 Cannon Street, London EC4N 6JP
Tel: (020) 7248 3000 Fax: (020) 7248 3001
Email: info@london.coudert.com
Website: www.coudert.com

Partners	9
Assistant Solicitors	23
Total Trainees	8

contact
Simon Cockshutt

firm profile
Founded in 1853, Coudert Brothers is a global partnership with 31 offices in 18 countries worldwide. In London the firm was one of the first English multinational partnerships of English solicitors and registered foreign lawyers. The firm advises on all aspects of national and international business law.

method of application
Letter & CV

selection procedure
2 interviews with partners

closing date for 2005
31 July 2003

trainee profile
The quality and complexity of legal work undertaken by the firm demands that it recruits only individuals of the highest calibre. It is essential that trainees are enthusiastic, confident and outward going individuals, able to perform in a fast-moving and challenging environment. Early responsibility is routine and broad-based experience guaranteed. Coudert Brothers accepts law and non-law graduates. Applicants should have at least three A-level passes at grades A and B and a 2:1 degree. In view of the international nature of the firm's work and clients, language skills are an advantage, but not essential.

application
Training contracts p.a. 4
Required degree grade 2:1

training
Salary (Subject to review)
1st year (2002) £28,000
2nd year (2002) £32,000
Holiday entitlement
20 days

training environment
The training at Coudert Brothers comprises four six month placements. Three of these will be with the firm's core practices: corporate and commercial, banking and finance, litigation and property. The fourth will be drawn from one of the firm's other disciplines: energy and utilities, telecommunications, tax and funds and competition law. There is an opportunity for a secondment to one of the firm's overseas offices, usually Brussels. Partners and senior assistants ensure that trainees gain practical experience in research, drafting, procedural and client-related skills by working closely with them during each placement. There are regular appraisals during the two year training contract. Legal and professional training is provided through an in-house training programme and external conferences.

post-qualification
Prospects are good as the firm only takes a small number of trainees each year

overseas offices
Almaty, Antwerp, Bangkok, Beijing, Berlin, Brussels, Frankfurt, Ghent, Hong Kong, Jakarta, Los Angeles, Milan, Moscow, Munich, New York, Palo Alto, Paris, Rome, San Francisco, San José, Singapore, Stockholm, St Petersburg, Sydney, Tokyo, Washington DC

benefits
Pension, health insurance, subsidised gym membership, season ticket loan, private medical and dental care.

associated offices
Budapest, Prague, Mexico City, Shanghai

sponsorship & awards
CPE Funding: Fees paid plus £4,000 p.a. maintenance (discretionary).
LPC Funding: Fees paid plus £4,000 p.a. maintenance (discretionary).

Covington & Burling

265 Strand, London WC2R 1BH
Tel: (020) 7067 2000 Fax: (020) 7067 2222
Email: graduate@cov.com
Website: www.cov.com

firm profile
Covington & Burling is a leading international law firm, founded in Washington in 1919, with over 500 lawyers and offices in London, Washington, New York, San Francisco and Brussels. The firm's London office was established in 1988 and is growing at a steady rate. It is known for its expertise in cutting-edge fields, including information technology and e commerce, software, telecommunications, healthcare and life sciences and, in such work, the firm represents many household names.

main areas of work
The major practice areas include corporate and commercial work such as mergers and acquisitions, venture capital and private equity transactions, securities and finance, licensing and strategic alliances, intellectual property, information technology, competition, food and drug regulatory law, employment, litigation and arbitration, insurance and tax. There is no formal demarcation between practice areas and, at a firm level, practice areas spread across offices.

trainee profile
The firm is looking for outstanding students who are committed to providing quality legal advice in an imaginative way. In this way the firm will be able to maintain its ability to respond to the evolving needs and expectations of its clients. The firm obviously looks for team players, but above all else it also looks for intellectual distinction, imagination and integrity. In return the firm believes that the future will bring even more challenging and dynamic opportunities for Covington lawyers.

training environment
Trainees will spend six months in each of corporate, IT/IP and litigation practice areas. The fourth seat will be spent within the food and drug or the tax practice areas. The firm encourages junior members to take responsibility at an early stage of their career.

benefits
Pension, permanent health insurance, private health cover, life assurance and season ticket loan.

vacation placements
16 places during summer vacation. Closing date for applications 28 February 2003.

sponsorship & awards
CPE, PgDL and LPC fees paid. Maintenance grant of £5,000 per annum.

Partners: 156*
Associate Lawyers &
Other Fee-earners: 345*
Total Trainees: 4 (2004)
* denotes worldwide figures

contact
Graduate Recruitment Manager
(020) 7067 2091
graduate@cov.com

method of application
Application form & covering letter

selection procedure
1st & 2nd interview

closing date for 2005
31 July 2003

application
Training contracts p.a. 4
Required degree grade 2:1

training
Salary:
1st year £28,000
2nd year £32,000
(subject to review)

overseas offices
Brussels, New York, San Francisco, Washington

COVINGTON & BURLING

Cripps Harries Hall

Wallside House, 12 Mount Ephraim Road, Tunbridge Wells TN1 1EG
Tel: (01892) 506006 Fax: (01892) 506360
Email: aol@crippslaw.com
Website: www.crippslaw.com

firm profile
Established almost 150 years ago, Cripps Harries Hall has progressed steadily towards being regarded as the leading law firm in the South East outside London. It is an innovative and young firm; most of the partners are in their thirties or forties and the atmosphere is friendly and outgoing. The firm achieved the Lexcel quality mark in January 1999, the first 'Top 100' firm to do so. In addition to its headquarters in Tunbridge Wells, there is an office in central London.

main areas of work
Commercial 42%; dispute resolution 31%; private client 27%. Financial services are provided by the firm's associated company Cripps Portfolio.

trainee profile
Cripps Harries Hall is looking for talented, confident, capable people who want to make a contribution during their period of training and who will want to stay with the firm as assistant solicitors and potential partners. You will be expected to integrate expert legal advice with a highly developed use of information technology.

training environment
The two year training contract is divided into six periods, spent in different departments where you receive a thorough grounding in the relevant practice and have frequent one-to-one reviews of your progress. You will usually share a room with a partner, and work as an integral member of a small team. The Director of Education will arrange your continuing education to include seminars, courses and training in business, presentation, IT and marketing skills.

sponsorship & awards
Discretionary LPC Funding: Fees – 50% interest free loan, 50% bursary.

Partners 34
Assistant Solicitors 39
Total Trainees 13

contact
Annabelle Lawrence
Head of Human Resources

method of application
Handwritten letter & firm's application form available on website or directly via the website

selection procedure
1 interview with Managing Partner & Head of Human Resources

closing date for 2005
31 July 2003

application
Training contracts p.a. 8
Applications p.a. **Up to 750**
% interviewed p.a. 6%
Required degree grade **2:1**

training
Salary
1st year (2002) £16,000
2nd year (2002) £18,000
Holiday entitlement
25 days
% of trainees with
a non-law degree p.a. **10%**

post-qualification
Salary (2002) £30,000
% of trainees offered job on qualification (2002) **90%**
% of assistants/associates (as at 1/5/02) who joined as trainees **35%**
% of partners (as at 1/5/02) who joined as trainees **20%**

associated firms
A network of independent law firms in 18 European countries
Cripps Portfolio

Cumberland Ellis Peirs

Columbia House, 69 Aldwych, London WC2B 4RW
Tel: (020) 7242 0422 Fax: (020) 7831 9381
Email: rogerhollinshead@cep-law.co.uk
Website: www.cep-law.co.uk

Partners	11
Assistant Solicitor	10
Total Trainees	4

contact
Roger Hollinshead

method of application
Letter & covering CV (adding reference to 'Chambers')

selection procedure
2 interviews with partners

closing date for 2005
30 September 2003

application
Training contracts p.a. **2**
Applications p.a. **300**
% interviewed p.a. **4%**
Required degree grade **2:1**

training
Holiday entitlement
20 days

firm profile
A central London firm of solicitors with a varied practice. The firm has a broad base of commercial and institutional clients including those involved in the media and information technology, quasi government councils, sporting associations, charities, City Livery companies, housing associations and landed estates, as well as having an established reputation for its private client services.

main areas of work
Company/commercial; commercial property; litigation and private client.

trainee profile
Law and non-law graduates who have a consistently strong academic record. Individuals who can work with and relate well to others; who are commercially aware, with an ability to think creatively and to make a contribution to the firm. The firm is looking for candidates who have presence and enthusiasm, who are outgoing and articulate and who have a broad range of outside interests. IT skills are important.

training environment
Trainees spend six months in each of the company commercial, litigation, private client and property departments under the supervision of a partner or senior assistant. Trainees are fully involved in all aspects of the work of the department. Client contact and early responsibility for handling your own caseload are encouraged, subject to necessary guidance and supervision. There are a number of social, sporting and marketing activities going on during the course of the year and life outside the office is encouraged. An open door policy applies and the firm has a friendly and informal environment. Where possible the firm aims to recruit its trainees at the end of the training contract. The PSC is taught externally at the College of Law.

benefits
Season ticket loan, luncheon vouchers.

sponsorship & awards
It is not the firm's policy to offer vacation placements or sponsorship.

Davenport Lyons

1 Old Burlington Street, London W1S 3NL
Tel: (020) 7468 2600 Fax: (020) 7437 8216
Email: dl@davenportlyons.com
Website: www.davenportlyons.com

firm profile
Davenport Lyons is a leading entertainment and media law practice and combines this work with strong company/commercial (including IP/IT), litigation, property and private client departments. The firm adopts a keen commercial and practical partner-led approach and builds on long-term partnership with its clients.

main areas of work
Media/entertainment, music; litigation (defamation/IP/IT/contentious/property/general commercial/dispute resolution/insolvency/entertainment licensing); company and commercial (IP/IT); commercial/residential property; tax and trust; matrimonial; employment.

trainee profile
2:1 or above; interesting background; business acumen; practical with breadth of interests; sociable; knowledge of foreign languages an advantage.

training environment
Four seats of six months each. Three-monthly assessments. Supervision from within departments. Ongoing programme of in-house lectures and professional skills training. Davenport Lyons offers interesting hands-on training. Trainees are treated as junior fee-earners and are encouraged to develop their own client relationships and to handle their own matters under appropriate supervision.

benefits
Season ticket loan; client introduction bonus; contribution to gym membership; discretionary bonus; 23 days holiday.

vacation placements
Places for 2003: 10; Duration: 2 weeks; Remuneration: £175 p.w.; Closing Date: January 2003.

sponsorship & awards
The firm does not normally offer financial assistance.

Partners 30
Assistant Solicitors 46
Total Trainees 10

contact
Ann Goldie
HR/Training Manager
Michael Hatchwell
Training Partner

method of application
CV & covering letter

selection procedure
Interviews

closing dates
Closing date for 2003
August 2002
Closing date for 2004
February 2003

application
Training contracts p.a. **5**
Applications p.a. **1,500**
% interviewed p.a. **2%**
Required degree grade **2:1**

training
Salary
1st year (2002) **£25,500**
2nd year (2002) **£27,500**
Holiday entitlement
23 days
% of trainees with a
non-law degree p.a. **40%**

post-qualification
% of trainees offered job
on qualification (2001) **75%**
% of assistants (as at 2002) who joined as trainees **15%**
% of partners (as at 2002) who joined as trainees **3%**

DAVENPORT LYONS

Davies Arnold Cooper

6–8 Bouverie Street, London EC4Y 8DD
Tel: (020) 7936 2222 Fax: (020) 7936 2020
Email: daclon@dac.co.uk
Website: www.dac.co.uk

Partners	47
Total Fee-earners	175
Total Trainees	14
Total Staff	334

firm profile

Davies Arnold Cooper is a leading law firm based in the City of London with offices in Manchester and Madrid. The firm consists of 47 partners and 175 lawyers. The firm's core strengths are insurance, product liability, construction and energy, property and property finance and transport and competition. Its lawyers regularly feature in the leading legal reference directories as acknowledged leaders in their particular field of expertise. The firm looks at future issues and has recently been at the forefront of matters such as transnational litigation, personal injury, rehabilitation, corporate governance and corporate accountability, project development, risk financing and health and safety. The firm's clients are major British and international companies, large UK and international insurers and re-insurers, Lloyd's and quoted property companies. The firm also acts for a number of banks, financial institutions and professional partnerships.

trainee programme

For further information on the firm and its training contracts, please visit the website www.dac.co.uk

Dawsons

2 New Square Lincoln's Inn, London WC2A 3RZ
Tel: (020) 7421 4800 Fax: (020) 7421 4848
Email: info@dawsons-legal.com
Website: www.dawsons-legal.com

Partners:	22
Assistant Solicitors:	18
Total Trainees:	8

contact
Philippa Heppenstall
p.heppenstall@dawsons-legal.com

method of application
Application form & covering letter or CV & covering letter

closing date for 2005
Subject to availability, there is no closing date for applications

application
Minimum degree grade 2:1 & As & Bs at A-level

firm profile
A partnership of lawyers set in the heart of legal London with a solid reputation for high professional standards and a personal, partner-led service. It is the firm's aim to combine the most effective and efficient service with the quality of advice and personal approach which has been the hallmark of the firm since its foundation in the early 18th century.

main areas of work
The firm is organised into five departments: corporate commercial; family; litigation; private client; property.

trainee profile
Second-year law students and final year non-law students with excellent A-level grades who are expecting to achieve at least a 2:1 degree. Applications are also welcomed from candidates who are currently on, or have recently completed, the PgDL or LPC course.

training environment
Dawsons has a very good reputation for providing extremely high quality training, with all trainees assigned to a partner, conducting matters on their own under that partner's supervision and assisting the partner with his or her other work. This allows the trainees to learn and develop under expert guidance and supervision and at the same time provide a valuable contribution to the busy practitioner. Training consists of four six-month seats in at least three of the following departments: property; private client; corporate and commercial; litigation; family. The final seat is usually intended to be in the department in which you will hope to work after qualification, subject to the availability of places.

vacation placements
The firm offers a number of vacation placements each year for either one or two weeks during the Easter and Summer vacations. These placements are designed to give you a flavour of what it might be like to be a trainee at Dawsons.

DAWSONS
SOLICITORS

Dechert

2 Serjeants' Inn, London EC4Y 1LT
Tel: (020) 7583 5353 Fax: (020) 7775 7322
Email: application@dechert.com
Website: www.dechert.com

firm profile
Dechert is an international law firm with 13 offices throughout the UK, US and continental Europe. The City of London office practices in a wide spectrum of business, commercial property and litigation specialisations. For example, the firm has particular strengths in banking and securitisation, construction, customs and excise, defamation, employment, financial services, intellectual property, insurance, investigations, property finance and tax. With a total staff of over 1,520 worldwide Dechert competes sucessfully in the national and international arenas. The firm invests heavily in training with trainees having the opportunity to work on high profile national and cross-jurisdictional projects. The offices in order of size are: Philadelphia, London, New York, Washington, Boston, Paris, Brussels, Princeton, Hartford, Newport Beach, Luxembourg, Harrisburg and Frankfurt.

main areas of work – London
Business law (including areas such as corporate, financial services, banking, securitisation and IP) 52%, litigation 25% and property 23%.

trainee profile
Candidates should be able to empathise with a wide range of people, as their clients come from all walks of life. Dechert looks for enthusiasm, intelligence, an ability to find a practical solution to a problem and for powers of expression and persuasion. Also wanted are those with a desire and ability to promote the firm's business at every opportunity. Dechert wants people who will remain on qualifying and make their careers with the firm.

training environment
Unusually training is divided into six four-monthly periods, giving trainees the chance to sample a wide range of work. Your supervisor will participate with you and a Trainee Panel Partner (who will be responsible for your well-being throughout your training contract) in a formal oral and written assessment of your work towards the end of each seat. Trainees have the opportunity to spend four months in the firm's office in Brussels and some trainees may now spend a period in their second year in one of the US offices. The greater number of seats makes it easier to fit in with any special requests to work in specific areas of the firm. The London office was the first English firm to appoint a training director in the early 1980s and their most recent appointee is the former director of the College of Law in London. The PSC is provided in a tailored format by the firm, with some modules taking place in-house. That apart there is an extensive training programme in which trainees are encouraged to participate (numerous aspects being particularly aimed at trainees).

Partners (London) 48
Assistant Solicitors (London) 91
Total Trainees (London) 28

contact
Lynn Muncey

method of application
Application form

selection procedure
Communication exercises & interviews with partners & assistant solicitors

closing date for 2005
31 July 2003

application
Training contracts p.a. 20
Applications p.a. Over 1,500
% interviewed p.a. Approx 9%
Required degree grade 2:1 (or capability of attaining a 2:1)

training
Salary
1st year (2002) £28,000
2nd year (2002) £32,000
(to be reviewed in September 2003)
Holiday entitlement 20 days
% of trainees with a non-law degree p.a. Varies
No. of seats available abroad p.a. 3 (plus shorter secondments to US offices)

post-qualification
Salary (2002) c.£50,000
(to be reviewed July 2003)
% of trainees offered job on qualification (2001) 100%
% of partners (as at 1/7/02) who joined as trainees 30%

Dechert continued

benefits
Free permanent health and life assurance, subsidised membership of local gym and interest-free season ticket loans.

vacation placements - 2 programmes
Date: 7 to 18 July 2003 and 21 July to 1 August 2003; Places for 2003: 16 (8 on each programme); Remuneration: no less than £225 p.w.; Closing Date: 28 February 2003.
Open days: Dates: 4 April 2003 and 3 July 2003; Number of places: 20-30 on each.

sponsorship & awards
CPE/PgDL and LPC fees paid and £4,500 maintenance p.a. (where local authority grants unavailable).

trainee comments
"The relatively small number of training contracts offered each year reflects the emphasis on the individual needs and wants of each trainee at Dechert. The four-month rotation system allows the opportunity to sample up to six areas of law, with seats in the US offices being the most sought after. A truly open door policy and willingness to dedicate time to supervision means trainees undertake challenging work. The atmosphere is relaxed and Dechert's retention rate on qualification remains high (all but one in 2001)." (Charmian Averty, newly qualified solicitor, read law at King's.)

"The training I've received at Dechert has been absolutely first-rate. The quality of the supervisors is the key - they're all so well-trained that you never feel like you've been imposed on them. The result is you get lots of responsibility, client contact, your own files and a feeling that you're being taught as well as learning by experience. I was surprised to find, particularly in the litigation seats, just how many matters I was given to run myself, even doing applications before judges or hosting client meetings myself. The quality of the training is also very high, thanks to Bernard George, with feedback always acted on, while the seat rotation genuinely felt like it was geared towards meeting my career plan rather than just fitting in with whatever the firm had to offer." (Stuart Goldberg, newly qualified solicitor, read Law at New College, Oxford.)

"I feel that my training at Dechert has prepared me well for life post-qualification. Trainees are given all the support they need and are encouraged to take on responsibility for their own files from the start which develops the confidence that comes from dealing with clients and other lawyers on a daily basis. The training contract is flexible and well-organised. Bernard George does a fantastic job. He listens to what you have to say and seems to have a sixth sense for knowing where your strengths lie and which departments will bring the best out of you. (Andrew Harrow, read Geography at St John's College, Oxford.)

overseas offices
Boston, Brussels, Frankfurt, Harrisburg, Hartford, London, Luxembourg, Newport Beach, New York, Paris, Philadelphia, Princeton, Washington

Denton Wilde Sapte.

Five Chancery Lane, Clifford's Inn, London EC4A 1BU
Tel: (020) 7242 1212 Fax: (020) 7320 6555
Email: trainingcontracts@dentonwildesapte.com
Website: www.dentonwildesapte.com

firm profile
Denton Wilde Sapte is a large international law firm with particular strengths in banking and finance, corporate, energy and infrastructure, technology, media and telecommunications, real estate and dispute resolution: the firm's practice areas are as strong and diverse as its client list. The firm has offices in Europe, the Middle East, Asia and the CIS. In addition, the firm is a founder member of Denton International, a network of leading law firms that covers 23 jurisdictions.

main areas of work
Corporate 35% (including tax, media, energy, employment and pensions); dispute resolution 25%; banking and finance 23%; real estate 18%.

trainee profile
The firm looks for candidates from any degree discipline with a strong academic and extra curricular record of achievement who are good team players. They should also have excellent interpersonal skills and the flexibility to grow with the firm. Languages are an advantage, but not essential.

training environment
Four six month seats, one of which may be spent in one of the firm's international offices. Two week induction at the beginning of contract including PSC core modules completed by October. Remaining electives should be completed by the end of the first year. The firm works to maintain a collegiate and open working environment where ideas are shared and people work together to achieve goals.

benefits
Holiday entitlement commences at 23 days, meal away from home allowance, private health cover, season ticket loan, subsidised sports club membership, permanent health insurance, life assurance.

vacation placements
Places for 2003: Approximately 50 places available on information weeks/open days during summer. Closing date for vacation placements is 14 March 2003 with interviews taking place during March/April 2003. Closing date for 2005 training contracts is 8 August 2003.

sponsorship & awards
CPE and LPC tuition fees covered plus £4,500 maintenance grant for each year of study, £5,000 if studying in London.

Partners 200
Fee-earners 696
Total Trainees 110

contact
Emma Hooper

method of application
Application form

selection procedure
First interview; selection test; second interview

closing date for 2005
8 August 2003

application
Training contracts p.a. **45**
Applications p.a. **2,000**
% interviewed p.a. **10-15%**
Required degree grade **2:1**

training
Salary
1st year **£27,000-£28,000**
2nd year **£30,000-£31,000**
Holiday entitlement **23 days**
% of trainees with a non-law degree p.a. **40%**
No. of seats available abroad p.a. **Currently 10**

post-qualification
Salary (2002) **£48,000**
(**£50,000 after 6 months**)
% of trainees offered job on qualification (2002) **80%**

overseas offices
Abu Dhabi, Almaty, Beijing, Cairo, Dubai, Gibraltar, Hong Kong, Istanbul, Moscow, Muscat, Paris, Singapore, Tashkent, Tokyo

associated offices
Barcelona, Berlin, Budapest, Chemnitz, Cologne, Copenhagen, Czech Republic, Dar es Salaam, Düsseldorf, Frankfurt, Gothenburg, Hamburg, Lusaka, Madrid, Malmö, Potsdam, Stockholm, Vienna

Devonshires

Salisbury House London Wall London EC2M 5QY
Tel: (020) 7628 7576 Fax: (020) 7256 7318
Email: trainee-recruitment@devonshires.co.uk
Website: www.devonshires.com

firm profile
Devonshires has been in the City of London for more than 150 years. The firm prides itself on its reputation for providing all its clients - who are based throughout England, Wales and the Channel Islands - with expert, cost-effective advice. The firm is a recognised leader in the social housing market and currently advises over 220 registered social landlords. The firm also advises financial institutions and stock exchange listed debt issuers; charities; corporations; government - domestic and international; insolvency practitioners; NHS trusts; private clients; professional service providers; property developers and investors - including financial institutions.

main areas of work
Property 30%; litigation 25%; banking and corporate 20%; PPP/PFI 10%; construction 5%; employment 5%; religious charities 5%.

trainee profile
The firm recruits high calibre trainees who are all-rounders. You don't have to be a law graduate - the firm welcomes applications from all disciplines and all universities. What you must have are keen commercial and technical qualities and proven academic abilities. You will also be able to show a demonstrable interest in a legal career and have a wide range of interests outside the office.

training environment
Training usually involves four seats of six months each, working with partners and senior staff in departments such as banking (company and commercial), church/charity, construction, employment, family/matrimonial, housing management litigation, litigation/dispute resolution, PFI and property. You will be required to cover a minimum of three practice areas and have a minimum of three months contentious experience.

benefits
Interest-free season ticket loans, healthcare scheme membership, subsidised health-club membership, dress down Fridays.

sponsorship & awards
Consideration for LPC funding.

Partners 15
Total Number of Fee-earners 71
Total Trainees 6

contact
Angela Hall
Human Resources Manager
(020) 7628 7576

method of application
Online application form at www.devonshires.com
(from 2003)

application
Training contracts p.a. 6
Applications p.a. 400
% interviewed p.a. 5%
Required degree grade
2:1 and higher

training
salary for each year of training **£ market rate**
holiday entitlement
22 days

post-qualification
Salary negotiable
% of trainees offered job on qualification **75%**

regional offices
Manchester

Dickinson Dees

St. Ann's Wharf, 112 Quayside, Newcastle upon Tyne NE99 1SB
Tel: (0191) 279 9000 Fax: (0191) 279 9100
Email: law@dickinson-dees.com
Website: www.dickinson-dees.com

firm profile
The largest firm in the North East, Dickinson Dees has developed a national reputation for both commercial and private client services. The firm has new premises on Newcastle's Quayside and in the Tees Valley. The firm has an associated office in Brussels with opportunities for trainees to spend time on secondment there.

main areas of work
Corporate 30%; property 30%; private client 20%; litigation 20%.

trainee profile
Good academic and analytical ability. Good commercial and business sense. Confident, personable and adaptable with good communication skills. Able to fit into a team.

training environment
Trainees are relatively few for the size of the practice. You are fully integrated into the firm and involved in all aspects of firm business. The training contract consists of four seats. One seat is spent in each of the commercial property, company/commercial and litigation departments. You are able to specialise for the fourth seat. This is encouraged so that personnel rise through the firm rather than being recruited from outside. Trainees sit with partners or associates and training is reviewed every three months. The firm has its own Training Manager. There are in-house induction courses on each move of department and opportunities for trainees to get involved in the in-house training programme. The firm offers a tailored in-house Professional Skills Course which is run in conjunction with the College of Law. The working environment is supportive and friendly. You will lead a busy life with sporting and social events organised by the office.

vacation placements
Places for 2003: 36; Duration: 1 week; Remuneration: £125 p.w.; Closing Date: 28 February 2003. Application forms are available.

open days
Open days will be held in the Christmas vacation 2002, and the Easter and Summer vacations 2003. Application forms are available on request. Closing date: 15 November 2002 for Christmas Open Day, 28 February 2003 for Easter and 30 April 2003 for Summer Open Days.

Partners 62
Total Fee-earners 279
Total Trainees 30

contact
Jamie Pass

method of application
Application form & letter

selection procedure
Interview & in-tray exercise

closing date for 2005
31 July 2003

application
Training contracts p.a. **15**
Applications p.a. **700**
% interviewed p.a. **10%**
Required degree grade **2:1**

training
Salary
1st year (2002) **£18,000**
2nd year (2002) **£19,500**
Holiday entitlement
23 days
% of trainees with
a non-law degree p.a. **50%**
No. of seats available
abroad p.a. **1**

post-qualification
Salary (2002) **£30,000**
% of trainees offered job
on qualification (2002)
100%
% of assistants (as at
1/9/02) who joined as
trainees **60%**
% of partners (as at
1/9/02) who joined as
trainees **34%**

other offices
Tees Valley, Brussels

Dickinson Dees continued

sponsorship & awards
CPE/LPC fees paid and £4,000 interest free loan.

trainee comments
"I wanted to work for a firm which combined the level and breadth of work of a leading City practice with the convenience and lifestyle of living here in Newcastle. In Dickinson Dees I found what I was looking for." (David Bawn, first year trainee in 2001/2002, read Law at Leicester University.)

"Dickinson Dees offers a unique combination of outstanding training, unprecedented trainee support and top quality work, all within a dynamic yet remarkably friendly and relaxed culture. A fantastic firm with which to start and fully develop a first class legal career." (Paul Newton, first year trainee in 2001/2002, read Law at Sheffield University.)

"I was impressed at how everyone treated me as an important member of the team from the start, rather than just an extra pair of hands." (Mihoko Hirano, first year trainee in 2001/2002, read Japanese Law at Chuo University, Tokyo.)

"Right from my very first visit I knew I had found the firm where I wanted to complete my training; Dickinson Dees has the strength and depth in its commercial practice areas to match most backgrounds and aspirations plus a genuine commitment to your training, great clients and informal, friendly colleagues - what else do you need?!" (Nicholas Payne, first year trainee in 2001/2002, read Zoology at Oxford University.)

"I wanted to work at a law firm which was going to allow me to have hands on experience from the beginning. Dickinson Dees certainly encourages trainees to be involved in quality work from day one." (Claire Brawn, second year trainee in 2001/2002, read Law at Newcastle University.)

D J Freeman

43 Fetter Lane, London EC4A 1JU
Tel: (020) 7583 4055 Fax: (020) 7353 7377
Email: graduaterecruitment@djfreeman.com
Website: www.djfreeman.com

firm profile
D J Freeman is an innovative firm whose lawyers work in multidisciplinary teams concentrating on specific business sectors. It is one of the leading firms in the property services, insurance and technology and media industries, and is highly regarded for commercial litigation work done both for sector and non-sector clients.

main areas of work
Property services 42%; insurance services 29%; commercial litigation 14%; technology and media 15%.

trainee profile
Clear and creative thinkers who work well under pressure and as part of a team.

training environment
Trainees spend six months in the firm's major practice areas, and once a month are able to discuss their progress in each seat with a partner. Believing supervised experience to be the best training, the firm soon gives trainees the chance to meet clients, be responsible for their own work and join in marketing and client development activities. Regular workshops in each seat help develop basic skills in the different departments. Any suggestions or concerns can be voiced at a trainee solicitors' committee. The firm has an active social committee which organises events from quiz evenings to wine tasting, as well as a theatre club.

benefits
Subsidised meals in staff restaurant; BUPA after three months; a variety of social and sporting events.

vacation placements
A summer vacation scheme is offered for law students who are about to start their last year at university and students in other disciplines who are about to commence the law conversion course. Applications should be made on the firm's application form. Places for 2003: 18; Duration: 3 weeks; Remuneration: £200 p.w.; Closing Date: end of February 2003.

sponsorship & awards
CPE and LPC funding.

Partners 50
Assistant Solicitors 80
Total Trainees 28

contact
Graduate Recruitment
(020) 7556 4181

method of application
Application form

selection procedure
Interview

closing date for 2005
31 July 2003

application
Training contracts p.a.
12–15
Applications p.a. 800
% interviewed p.a. 10%
Required degree grade 2:1

training
Salary (2001)
1st six months £26,000
2nd six months £27,000
3rd six months £28,000
4th six months £29,000
Holiday entitlement
20 days

post-qualification
Salary (2002) £48,000

DLA

3 Noble Street, London EC2V 7EE
Tel: (020) 7796 6677 Fax: (0121) 262 5793
Email: recruitment.graduate@dla.com
Website: www.dla.com

firm profile
DLA is an ambitious and forward thinking firm with modern values and a clear strategy for the future. The firm has offices in Birmingham, Edinburgh, Glasgow, Leeds, Liverpool, London, Manchester and Sheffield, and the fee income for the previous financial year topped £200 million. In 2002 DLA was named 'Law Firm of the Year' at *The Lawyer* awards, and has also recently achieved the 'Investor in People' standard.

main areas of work
DLA has 10 main practice groups. They are as follows: banking; business support and restructuring; commercial and projects; corporate; human resources; insurance; litigation; marine, aviation and reinsurance; real estate; technology, media and communications.

trainee profile
The firm wants exceptional people as good academic ability alone is no longer sufficient. DLA values individuality and wants to recruit people from different backgrounds with a wide range of skills. Successful candidates will believe in themselves, relate well to other people, have an appetite for life and a desire to succeed in business.

training environment
The firm deliberately takes on a relatively small number of trainees. This enables it to offer a broad range of experience, a high level of responsibility and excellent prospects on qualification. During their training contract, trainees complete four six month seats in different commercial areas, learning through observation and practice. Through-the-job training is complemented by an ongoing commercial skills training programme and by the Professional Skills Course, which is run in-house.

benefits
Contributory pension scheme, health insurance, life assurance, 25 days holiday, good sports and social facilities and car scheme.

vacation placements
Places for 2003: 200; Duration: 1 week; Remuneration (2002 figures): £210 per week (London), £155 per week (Regions and Scotland); Closing Date: 28 February 2003.

sponsorship & awards
Payment of full fees during the PgDL and LPC years, plus a maintenance grant in both years.

Partners 304
Associates 179
Assistant Solicitors 390
Total Trainees 151

contact
Sally Carthy
National Graduate Recruitment Manager

method of application
Application form

selection procedure
First interview, second interview, assessment afternoon

closing date for 2005
31 July 2003

application
Training contracts p.a. 85+
Applications p.a. 2,000
% interviewed p.a. 15-20%
Required degree grade 2:1

training
Salary
1st year £28,000 (London)
£20,000 (Regions)
£16,000 (Scotland)
2nd year £31,000 (London)
£22,000 (Regions)
£18,000 (Scotland)
% of trainees with a non-law degree p.a. 40%

post-qualification
Salary
£48,000 (London)
£33,000 (Birmingham)
£32,500 (Other regional offices)
£30,000 (Scotland)
% of trainees offered job on qualification 90%

overseas offices
Brussels, Hong Kong, Singapore, plus a network of associated European offices

DMH

100 Queens Road, Brighton BN1 3YB
Tel: (01273) 329833 Fax: (01273) 747500
Email: jean.clack@dmh.co.uk
Website: www.dmh.co.uk

firm profile
DMH is an approachable and innovative firm with an open culture which encourages personal development and provides its personnel with a high level of support in order to achieve this. The firm offers expertise and service comparable to City firms to a range of commercial organisations, non-profit institutions and individual clients. By focusing on the client's needs DMH provides practical and creative solutions. DMH operates from offices in Brighton, Crawley, London and Worthing.

main areas of work
Corporate/commercial; commercial property, planning and environmental; employment, intellectual property/IT; litigation; residential conveyancing; personal injury; private client.

trainee profile
The firm welcomes applications from motivated graduates from all backgrounds and age groups. Enthusiasm, a mature outlook and commercial awareness are as prized as academic ability, and good communication skills are a must. Ideal applicants are those with the potential to become effective managers or strong marketeers.

training environment
Usually four six month seats taken from the following areas: employment, intellectual property/IT, corporate/commercial, planning and environmental, commercial property, commercial litigation, property litigation, personal injury, civil litigation, residential conveyancing and private client work. Trainees are closely supervised by the partner to whom they are attached but have every opportunity to work as part of a team and deal directly with clients. The majority of seats are in the Brighton and Crawley offices.

vacation placements
Places for 2003: Priority given to trainee interviewees with a limited number of unpaid places; Duration: 1-2 weeks; Closing Date: 31 January 2003.

Partners 35
Assistant Solicitors 20
Total Trainees 10

contact
Jean Clack

method of application
CV & covering letter

closing date for 2004
December 2002

application
Training contracts p.a. 4-6
Applications p.a. 400
% interviewed p.a. 3%
Required degree grade 2:1

training
Salary
1st year (2002) £16,500
2nd year (2002) £19,000
Holiday entitlement 23 days
% of trainees with a non-law degree p.a. 50%

post-qualification
Salary (2002) £28,000
% of trainees offered job on qualification (2002) 80%
% of assistants (as at 1/7/02) who joined as trainees 40%
% of partners (as at 1/7/02) who joined as trainees 40%

DWF

5 Castle Street, Liverpool L2 4XE
Tel: (0151) 236 6226 Fax: (0151) 236 3088
Email: trainees@dwf-law.com
Website: www.dwf.co.uk

firm profile
Davies Wallis Foyster is one of the leading law firms in the North West, providing a full range of services for corporate and commercial clients and insurance clients. Over the years, the firm has recruited market leaders in all its service areas and has built substantial, multi-skilled teams around them. It is, therefore, capable of delivering a menu of world-class services to help clients achieve a competitive edge. The firm has a reputation for the quality, style and energy of its people and its willingness to provide client references. DWF is a member of EU-LEX International Practice Group, a well respected network of international law firms handling cross-border work.

main areas of work
Services for corporate and commercial clients 65%; Services for insurance clients 35%.

trainee profile
DWF wants trainees to play a part in building on its success. The firm is looking for trainees who enjoy working as part of a busy team, who respond positively to a challenge and think they have what it takes to deliver results for clients. The firm is looking for its partners of the future.

training environment
All trainees commence life at DWF with a welcome programme designed to provide a clear picture of the firm and its services before moving to their first seat. The firm provides a flexible seat rotation including corporate, property, commercial litigation and insurance with agreed options which focus on post-qualification aspirations. This is supplemented by general training as well as specific training relevant to the particular seat which may be run in-house or using external courses. Appraisals are carried out during each seat to review progress and development. Trainees will have the opportunity to join in the busy social life within the office and with local trainee solicitors' groups.

benefits
Life Assurance, pension scheme.

vacation placements
Open day events at each office.

sponsorship & awards
LPC funding for tuition fees.

Partners 53
Assistant Solicitors 91
Total Trainees 17

contact
Carol Stead
HR Officer (Manchester address)

method of application
Handwritten letter & CV or DWF application form

selection procedure
2 stage interview/selection process

closing date for 2005
4 August 2003

application
Training contracts p.a. 8
Applications p.a. c.1000
% interviewed p.a. 5%
Required degree grade 2:1 in any subject preferred

training
Salary:
1st year (2002) £16,750
Holiday entitlement
23 days p.a. minimum

post-qualification
% of trainees offered job on qualification (2002) 100%

Edwards Geldard

Dumfries House, Dumfries Place, Cardiff CF10 3ZF
Tel: (029) 2023 8239 Fax: (029) 2023 7368
Email: info@geldard.com
Website: www.geldards.com

firm profile
Edwards Geldard is one of the leading regional law firms. In the United Kingdom the firm's offices are located in Cardiff, Derby and Nottingham. Whilst continuing to expand the traditional areas of work in the company and commercial, commercial property, dispute resolution and private client departments, the firm has acquired particular expertise in a variety of 'niche' areas of legal work. These include mergers and acquisitions, corporate finance and banking, intellectual property, public law, planning and environmental law, energy law, rail and transport law, construction contracts and building arbitration, employment law, insolvency, trusts and tax, secured lending, property litigation and clinical negligence. The firm's growth in recent years has been characterised by an expansion of its work for major Stock Exchange listed clients and for City of London based organisations and by the growing reputation of its work for public sector bodies.

main areas of work
Company/commercial 40%; property 25%; litigation 20%; other 15%.

trainee profile
Candidates should be motivated and hardworking with a strong academic background. A sense of humour is essential, as is involvement in extra curricular activities and interests which show evidence of a balanced and well-rounded individual.

training environment
Training is divided into six four month seats in the firm's main practice areas. Trainees are allocated to a particular team and are supervised by the lead partner or senior solicitors working within the team. An 'open door' policy applies and trainees are regarded very much as an integral part of the team to which they have been allocated. A dedicated partner within each office has responsibility for the trainees in that office. A senior partner monitors consistency, progress and development across the three offices. Training is reviewed every three months. Your formal training will be a combination of external courses and internal seminars. Early contact with clients is encouraged in both work and social environments, as is the acceptance of responsibility. The atmosphere is friendly and the firm encourages its own social and sporting functions outside the office.

benefits
Life assurance at three times salary, 23 days holiday entitlement per annum.

sponsorship & awards
£5,000 towards the LPC and £2,000 towards the CPE.

Partners	42
Assistant Solicitors	63
Total Trainees	24

contact
Owen Golding
Human Resources Manager

method of application
Application form

selection procedure
Interview

closing date for 2005
For summer placements end of February 2003, otherwise end of July 2003

application
Training contracts p.a. **12**
Applications p.a. **400**
% interviewed p.a. **20%**
Required degree grade **2:1 desirable**

training
Salary
1st year (2001) **£15,500**
2nd year (2001) **£16,500**
Holiday entitlement
23 days
% of trainees with a non-law degree p.a. **Varies**

post-qualification
Salary (2002) **Under review**
% of trainees retained (2002) **75%**

Eversheds

Senator House, 85 Queen Victoria Street, London EC4V 4JL
Tel: (020) 7919 4761 Fax: (020) 7919 4919
Application Form Hotline: (Freephone) (0500) 994500
Email: gradrec@eversheds.com
Website: www.eversheds.com

firm profile
A European law firm with offices in Asia, Eversheds has over 2,500 legal and business advisers based in 20 locations. Its distinctive approach gives clients access to a large team of lawyers who combine local market knowledge with an international perspective.

main areas of work
Corporate, commercial, litigation and dispute management, commercial property, human resources (employment and pensions) and commoditised services. In addition to these core areas each office provides expertise in a further 30 business and industry sectors.

trainee profile
Eversheds' people are valued for being straightforward, enterprising and effective. The firm listens to its clients. It likes to simplify rather than complicate. It expects trainees to be business-like, unstuffy and down-to-earth. You will need to display commercial acumen, imagination and drive and, above all, you will need to be results-driven. As a trainee you will get as much responsibility as you can handle and will benefit from the 'hands on, learning by doing' philosophy. The firm takes your training very seriously but expects it to be fun too.

training environment
You will be encouraged to play a major part in the direction your training and development takes, with advice and supervision always available. In each department you will sit with a partner or a senior assistant and participate from an early stage in varied, complex and high-value work. Eversheds aims to retain as many trainees as possible on qualifying and many of the partners were trainees with the firm. A steep learning curve begins with a week of basic training followed by departmental seats – three of which will cover the firm's main practice areas. During your training you will also complete an Eversheds designed Professional Skills Course and, on qualification, follow a progressive career structure.

benefits
Regional variations.

vacation placements
Places for 2003: 130; Duration: 2 weeks; Remuneration: regional variations; Closing Date: 31 January 2003.

sponsorship & awards
CPE/LPC fees and maintenance grants.

Partners 402
Assistant Solicitors 2046
Total Trainees 205

contact
Andrew M Looney
Graduate Recruitment Officer

method of application
EAF to be returned to London office, specifying the region you wish to work in

selection procedure
Selection days include group & written exercises, presentations & interview

closing date for 2005
31 July 2003

application
Training contracts p.a. **100**
Applications p.a. **4,000**
% interviewed p.a. **15%**
Required degree grade **2:1**

training
Salary
1st year London (2001) £28,000
2nd year London (2001) £30,000
Holiday entitlement **23 days**
% of trainees with a non-law degree p.a. **45%**
No. of seats available abroad p.a. **Up to 12**

post-qualification
Salary London (2002) £48,000
% of trainees offered job on qualification (2002) **98%**

offices
Birmingham, Brussels, Cambridge, Cardiff, Copenhagen*, Hong Kong*, Ipswich, Kuala Lumpur*, Leeds, London, Manchester, Milan*, Monaco, Newcastle, Norwich, Nottingham, Paris, Rome*, Singapore*, Sofia*
* *Associated office*

Farrer & Co

66 Lincoln's Inn Fields, London WC2A 3LH
Tel: (020) 7242 2022 Fax: (020) 7242 9897
Email: trainees@farrer.co.uk
Website: www.farrer.co.uk

firm profile
Farrer & Co is one of the UK's leading law practices. It provides a range of specialist advice to private, institutional and corporate clients.

main areas of work
The firm's breadth of expertise is reflected by the fact that it has an outstanding reputation in fields as diverse as matrimonial law, offshore tax planning, employment, heritage work, charity law and defamation.

trainee profile
Trainees are expected to be highly motivated individuals with keen intellects and interesting and engaging personalities. Those applicants who appear to break the mould – as shown by their initiative for organisation, leadership, exploration, or enterprise – are far more likely to get an interview than the erudite, but otherwise unimpressive, student.

training environment
The training programme involves each trainee in the widest range of cases, clients and issues possible in a single law firm taking full advantage of the wide range of practice areas at Farrer & Co by offering six seats, rather than the more usual four. This provides a broad foundation of knowledge and experience and the opportunity to make an informed choice about the area of law in which to specialise. A high degree of involvement is encouraged under the direct supervision of solicitors and partners. Trainees attend an induction programme and regular internal lectures. The training principal reviews trainees' progress at the end of each seat and extensive feedback is given. The firm has a very friendly atmosphere and regular sporting and social events.

benefits
Health and life insurance, subsidised gym membership, season ticket loan.

vacation placements
Places for 2003: 18; Duration: 2 weeks at Easter, 3 weeks in summer; Remuneration: £220 p.w.; Closing Date: 31 January 2003.

sponsorship & awards
CPE Funding: Fees paid plus £4,500 maintenance. LPC Funding: Fees paid plus £4,500 maintenance.

Partners	55
Assistant Solicitors	58
Total Trainees	14

contact
Graduate Recruitment Manager

method of application
Firm's application form & covering letter

selection procedure
Interviews with Graduate Recruitment Manager & partners

closing date for 2005
31 July 2003

application
Training contracts p.a. 6-8
Applications p.a. 1,500
% interviewed p.a. 2.5%
Required degree grade 2:1

training
Salary
1st year (2002) £26,000
2nd year (2002) £28,000
Holiday entitlement
22 days
% of trainees with
non-law degrees p.a. 42%

post-qualification
Salary (2002) £40,000
trainees offered job
on qualification (2002)
90%
% of assistants (as at 1/9/01) who joined as trainees 72%
% of partners (as at 1/9/01) who joined as trainees 70%

Fenners

15 New Bridge Street, London EC4V 6AU
Tel: (020) 7936 8000 Fax: (020) 7936 8100
Email: info@fenners.com

firm profile
Fenners is a City based firm specialising in company/commercial law, corporate finance, technology law, commercial property, town planning and banking law. The firm has a broad client base, including listed and unquoted companies, financial advisers, brokers, banks and other institutions.

main areas of work
Commercial property 40%; corporate/commercial 40%; banking 20%.

trainee profile
Candidates will demonstrate academic excellence combined with commitment and motivation to pursuing a career in a specialist City firm. In addition, extra curricular activities and interests are highly regarded as evidence of a balanced and well rounded candidate.

training environment
Training consists of seats within the firm's commercial property and corporate/commercial departments, with an option for a further contentious seat. You will sit with a partner or an experienced solicitor who will provide you with daily tasks and support. In addition, you will have an opportunity to receive feedback and discuss your progress with your training principal every three months. Fenners' trainees are highly valued and their development within the firm is encouraged by providing a challenging, supportive and enjoyable environment in which to work.

benefits
Health insurance, season ticket loan.

vacation placements
Places for 2003: 6; Duration: 2 weeks; Remuneration: competitive rates; Closing Date: 30 April 2003.

sponsorship & awards
CPE and LPC funding to be discussed with candidates.

Partners 6
Assistant Solicitors 3
Total Trainees 6

contact
Robert Fenner

method of application
Handwritten letter & CV. Brochures available on request

selection procedure
2 interviews with partners. The firm does not require completion of an application form. Candidates should submit CVs

closing date for 2005
Applications should preferably be received by 1 September 2003

application
Training contracts p.a. **2**
Applications p.a. **1,200**
% interviewed p.a. **2%**
Required degree grade **2:1**

training
Salary
1st year Market for City
2nd year Market for City
Holiday entitlement
22 days
% of trainees with a non-law degree p.a.
Variable

post-qualification
Salary Market for City

Field Fisher Waterhouse

35 Vine Street, London EC3N 2AA
Tel: (020) 7861 4000 Fax: (020) 7488 0084
Email: kmd@ffwlaw.com
Website: www.ffwlaw.com

Partners	77
Assistant Solicitors	110
Total Trainees	23

contact
Karen Danker

method of application
Firm's own application form & covering letter

selection procedure
Interview

closing date for 2005
31 August 2003

application
Training contracts p.a. **10-12**
Applications p.a. **2,000**
Required degree grade **2:1**

training
Salary
1st year (2002) £26,000
2nd year (2002) £29,120
Holiday entitlement
25 days
% of trainees with a
non-law degree p.a. **50%**

post-qualification
Salary (2002) **£45,000**
% of trainees offered job on qualification (2002) **80%**
% of assistants (as at 1/9/02) who joined as trainees **40%**
% of partners (as at 1/9/02) who joined as trainees **40%**

firm profile

Field Fisher Waterhouse is a City law firm with a reputation for providing a quality service to an impressive list of UK and international clients. It recently formed The European Legal Alliance with four other European law firms, giving it a presence in 12 European cities. The firm has particular strengths in its core practice areas of finance; corporate; commercial property and brands, technology, media and telecommunications. It is also highly regarded for its expertise in commercial litigation, medical negligence and personal injury, aviation travel and tourism, employment and professional regulation. The firm prides itself on its collegiate atmosphere, its creative and commercial approach to the law and its constructive approach to career development.

main areas of work

IP/IT 25%; property 21%; corporate 16%; litigation 13%; banking, finance and commercial 14%; professional regulation 7%; employment 3%; other 1%.

trainee profile

The firm is looking to recruit ambitious individuals with ability, enthusiasm and determination, who will be able to respond creatively and commercially to its clients' needs. It values strong personal qualities as well as academic achievement and welcomes applications from both law and non-law students.

training environment

Training will be split into five seats to enable you to gain the widest possible exposure to the firm's broad range of practice areas. In each seat you will work with several partners and assistants to gain a wide experience of the department. Feedback is ongoing and you will participate in a formal assessment at the end of each seat. The firm aims to develop your grasp of legal principles and to foster your commercial awareness. Your training will combine practical hands on experience and a comprehensive training programme of in-house lectures and external seminars. Staff enjoy the benefits of a busy sports and social committee, a 'Bolt Hole' lounge and dining area and squash courts.

sponsorship & benefits

Tuition fees and maintenance grant paid for CPE/PgDL and LPC. 25 days annual holiday, interest free season ticket loan, private medical insurance and life assurance.

vacation placements

Places for 2003: A summer vacation scheme will be run during July 2003. Application by CV and covering letter, between 1 February 2003 and 28 February 2003.

Finers Stephens Innocent

179 Great Portland St, London W1N 6LS
Tel: (020) 7323 4000 Fax: (020) 7580 7069
Email: gradrecruitment@fsilaw.co.uk
Website: www.fsilaw.co.uk

firm profile
Finers Stephens Innocent is an expanding practice based in Central London providing a range of high quality legal services to corporate and commercial clients. The firm offers a range of services focused to meet the requirements of its primarily commercial client base. The firm's philosophy includes close partner involvement and a commercial approach in all client matters. Dedicated teams create services that are supplied in a cost effective manner with a working style which is personable, client supportive and informal. The firm is a member of the Network of Leading Law Firms and of Meritas.

main areas of work
Commercial property; litigation; media; employment; family; defamation; company/commercial; private client. See the firm's website for further details.

trainee profile
The firm looks for academic excellence in applicants. It also looks for maturity, an interesting personality, strong communication skills, ability to think like a lawyer and an indefinable 'it' which shows that you have the potential to become a long-term member of the firm's team. Mature applicants are especially encouraged.

training environment
After your induction programme, you will complete four six month seats, sharing a room with either a Partner or Senior Assistant. The firm has two Training Partners who keep a close eye on the welfare and progress of trainees. There are regular group meetings of trainees and an appraisal process which enables you to know how you are progressing as well as giving you a chance to provide feedback on your view of your training.

benefits
20 days holiday, pension, private medical insurance, life insurance, long-term disability insurance, subsidised gym membership, season ticket loan.

vacation placements
Places for 2003: 12; Duration: 2 weeks during Summer; Closing Date: 30 March 2003.

sponsorship & awards
LPC and CPE course fees.

Partners 33
Assistant Solicitors 34
Total Trainees 8

contact
Personnel Department

method of application
CV & covering letter

selection procedure
2 interviews with the Training Partners

closing date for 2005
31 July 2003

application
Training contracts p.a. 4
Applications p.a. 500
% interviewed p.a. 5%
Required degree grade 2:1

training
Salary
1st year
Highly competitive
2nd year
Highly competitive
Holiday entitlement
20 days
% of trainees with
a non-law degree p.a.
0-33%

post-qualification
Salary
Highly competitive
% of trainees offered job on qualification (2001)
90%

Fladgate Fielder

25 North Row, London W1K 6DJ
Graduate Recruitment Line: (020) 7462 2299 Fax: (020) 7629 4414
Email: gradrec@fladgate.com
Website: www.fladgate.com

firm profile
Fladgate Fielder is an innovative, progressive and thriving law firm based in the heart of London's West End. The firm's business covers the whole spectrum of commercial activities. It provides a full range of legal services to a client base drawn from all sectors of commerce and industry in the UK and overseas, including multinationals, major institutions and listed companies, clearing banks, lenders and entrepreneurs.

main areas of work
The firm's four main departments comprise property, corporate, litigation and tax. These are complemented by cross-departmental units focusing on sports, media and technology, employment and benefits, intellectual property and insolvency.

trainee profile
In addition to a strong academic record, your extra-curricular activities and personal qualities are important to us; the firm's trainees will have commercial acumen, enthusiasm, leadership potential, excellent interpersonal skills and a genuine interest in the law. Fladgate Fielder is keen to attract candidates with developed language skills, particularly French, German and Italian.

training environment
You will normally be given the opportunity to complete six months in each of the firm's main departments: corporate, litigation, property and tax. In each seat you will sit with and be supervised by a partner or senior solicitor. In addition to on-the-job training and the PSC (undertaken externally), your career development will be encouraged through a number of activities. Each department runs a programme of talks and seminars covering legal and skills training; cross-departmental sessions are held on a regular basis. There is also the opportunity to attend sessions covering such topics as networking and time management.

benefits
Pension, permanent health insurance, life assurance, season ticket loan, sports club loan, bonus scheme.

Partners	32
Assistant Solicitors	36
Total Trainees	6

contact
Sharon Xenophontos

method of application
Application form & covering letter

selection procedure
Selection morning including interview and other exercises

closing date for 2005
31 July 2003

application
Training contracts p.a. 3
Applications 500
% interviewed 6%
Required degree grade 2:1

training
Salary for each year of training £23,000-£25,000
Holiday entitlement 20-21 days

post-qualification
Salary To be confirmed
% of trainees offered job on qualification 100%

FLADGATE FIELDER
SOLICITORS

Foot Anstey Sargent

21 Derry's Cross, Plymouth PL1 2SW
Tel: (01752) 675000 Fax: (01752) 671802
Email: training@foot-ansteys.co.uk
Website: www.foot-ansteys.co.uk

firm profile
Foot Anstey Sargent has fast become one of the leading regional law firms in the Westcountry. It is recognised nationally for its expertise in many sectors, including the niche areas of banking, employment, insolvency, media and shipping. The firm, its partners and associates have a strong reputation and are well known within the region.

main areas of work
Commercial property, company and commercial, criminal advocates, family and childcare, property litigation, and private client in addition to the niche areas as noted above.

trainee profile
The firm welcomes applications from confident positive law and non-law graduates with strong academic backgrounds and established communication skills. A strong team ethos is paramount to the firm. Trainees can expect to be welcomed into a challenging (but rewarding!) environment and must be committed to achieving high standards. A good sense of humour is essential.

training environment
The wide range of legal services provided by the firm offers trainees opportunities in many areas of the law in either the Exeter or Plymouth offices. Trainee solicitors undertake four seats of six months. Whenever possible (with the exception of the first seat) trainees are able to select their seats. All trainees attend an induction course. Individual monthly meetings are held with supervisors and a group meeting with the training manager. Appraisals are conducted quarterly by supervisors. A non-partner acts as a confidential and objective counsellor. Regular communication between the trainees and supervisors ensure an open and friendly atmosphere. The PSC is taught externally.

benefits
Contributory pension, 25 days holiday.

vacation placements
The deadline for the summer placement scheme is 31 March 2003.

Partners 28
Assistant Solicitors 45
Total Trainees 16

contact
Richard Sutton
(01752) 675000

method of application
Handwritten letter & CV, or online at
www.foot-ansteys.co.uk

selection procedure
Interview & assessment day

application
Training contracts p.a. 8

post-qualification
Salary (2001) £27,825
% of trainees offered job on qualification (2001) 100%

Forbes

Marsden House, 28-32 Wellington Street (St. Johns), Blackburn BB1 8DA
Tel: (01254) 662831 Fax: (01254) 681104
Email: siobhan.hardy@forbessolicitors.co.uk

firm profile
A leading North West practice with nine offices, including an office recently established in Leeds, and over 300 staff, Forbes is progressive and forward looking in all aspects of its business. Underlying the practice is the strongest commitment to quality, both in its service to clients and as an employer, with strong emphasis being placed on staff training and career development – a fact confirmed by Forbes being one of the first firms to be recognised as an Investor in People. Offering a wide range of legal expertise, Forbes is noted, in particular, for excellence in company/commercial, civil litigation, defendant insurer, crime, family and employment services. Three partners are qualified Higher Court Advocates and the firm holds many Legal Aid franchises as well as ISO 9001 accreditation.

main areas of work
Company/commercial, civil litigation, defendant insurer, crime, family and employment services.

trainee profile
Forbes looks for high-calibre recruits with strong local connections and good academic records, who are keen team players.

training environment
A tailored training programme involves six months in four of the following: crime, civil litigation, defendant insurer, matrimonial, and non-contentious/company commercial.

Partners 22
Assistant Solicitors 44
Total Trainees 8

contact
Siobhan Hardy

method of application
Handwritten letter & CV

selection procedure
Interview with partners

closing date for 2005
31 July 2003

application
Training contracts p.a. **3**
Applications p.a. **350**
% interviewed p.a. **Varies**
Required degree grade **2:1**

training
Salary
1st year At least Law Society minimum
Holiday entitlement
20 days

post-qualification
Salary (2002)
Highly competitive
% of trainees offered job on qualification (2001)
Usually 100%

Forsters

67 Grosvenor Street, London W1K 3JN
Tel: (020) 7863 8333 Fax: (020) 7863 8444
Email: ajfairchild@forsters.co.uk
Website: www.forsters.co.uk

firm profile
Forsters opened for business in 1998 with 11 of the 22 founding partners previously being partners of Frere Chomley Bischoff. It is a progressive law firm with a strong reputation for its property and private client work as well as thriving commercial and litigation practices. The working atmosphere of the firm is friendly and informal, yet highly professional. A social committee organises a range of activities from quiz nights to sporting events as Forsters actively encourages all its staff to have a life outside of work!

main areas of work
The firm has a strong reputation for all aspects of commercial and residential property work. The groups handle investment funding; development; planning; construction; landlord and tenant; property taxation and residential investment and development. Forsters is also recognised as one of the leading proponents of private client work in London with a client base comprising a broad range of individuals and trusts in the UK and elsewhere. The firm's commercial practice specialises in acquisitions and financing for technology, communication and media companies whilst its litigation group conducts commercial litigation and arbitration and advises on a broad spectrum of matters.

trainee profile
Successful candidates will have a strong academic background and either have attained or be expected to achieve a good second class degree. The firm considers that factors alongside academic achievements are also important. The firm is looking for individuals who give a real indication of being interested in a career in law and who the firm feels would readily accept and work well in its team environment.

training environment
The first year of training is split into three seats of four months in three of the following departments: commercial property, private client, company commercial or litigation. In the second year the four month pattern still applies, but the firm discusses with you whether you have developed an area of particular interest and tries to accommodate this. The training is very 'hands on' as you share an office with a partner or assistant who will give you real responsibility alongside supervision. At the end of each seat your progress and performance will be reviewed by way of an appraisal with a partner from the relevant department.

sponsorship & benefits
22 days holiday p.a., season ticket loan, permanent health insurance, life insurance, subsidised gym membership. No sponsorship for CPE or LPC courses is currently provided.

Partners 22
Assistant Solicitors 40
Total Trainees 6

contact
Alison Fairchild

method of application
Application form

selection procedure
First interview with HR Manager & Graduate Recruitment Partner; second interview with 2 partners

training
Salary
1st year (2002) £24,000
2nd year (2002) £26,000
Holiday entitlement
22 days

post-qualification
Salary (2002) £41,000
% of trainees offered job on qualification **100%**

freethcartwright

Willoughby House, 20 Low Pavement, Nottingham NG1 7EA
Tel: (0115) 936 9369 Fax: (0115) 859 9603
Email: carole.wigley@freethcartwright.co.uk
Website: www.freethcartwright.co.uk

Partners	49
Assistant Solicitors	67
Total Trainees	13

contact
Carole Wigley

method of application
Application form

selection procedure
Interview & selection day

closing date for 2005
31 July 2003

training
Starting salary (2002)
£15,800

branch offices
Nottingham, Leicester, Derby

firm profile
Tracing its origins back to 1805, freethcartwright became Nottingham's largest firm in 1994 with successful offices now established in Derby and Leicester. Whilst freethcartwright is a heavyweight commercial firm, serving a wide variety of corporate and institutional clients, there is also a commitment to a range of legal services, which includes a substantial private client element. This enables it to give a breadth of experience in training which is not always available in firms of a similar size.

main areas of work
Property and construction, commercial services, private client and personal litigation.

trainee profile
freethcartwright looks for people to bring their own perspective and individuality to the firm. The firm needs people who can cope with the intellectual demands of life as a lawyer and who possess the wider personal skills which are needed in its diverse practice.

training environment
freethcartwright is committed to providing comprehensive training for all its staff. The firm's training programme is based on in-house training covering technical matters and personal skills, supplemented with external courses where appropriate. The firm endeavours to give the best possible experience during the training period, as it believes that informal training on-the-job is the most effective means of encouraging the skills required in a qualified solicitor. One of the firm's senior partners takes responsibility for all its trainees and their personal development, overseeing their progress through the firm and discussing performance based on feedback. Normally, the training contract will consist of four six month seats in different departments, most of which are available in the firm's Nottingham offices, although it is possible for trainees to spend at least one seat in another location.

Freshfields Bruckhaus Deringer

65 Fleet Street, London EC4Y 1HS
Tel: (020) 7936 4000 Fax: (020) 7832 7001
Email: graduaterecruitment@freshfields.com
Website: www.freshfields.com

firm profile
Freshfields Bruckhaus Deringer is a leading international firm with a network of 29 offices in 19 countries. The firm provides first-rate legal services to corporations, financial institutions and governments around the world.

main areas of work
Corporate; mergers and acquisitions; banking; dispute resolution; joint ventures; employment, pensions and benefits; asset finance; real estate; tax; capital markets; intellectual property and information technology; project finance; private finance initiative; US securities; EC/competition and trade; communications and media; construction and engineering; energy; environment; financial services; restructuring and insolvency; insurance; international tax; investment funds.

trainee profile
Good academic qualifications, good record of achievement in other areas, common sense and creative thinking. Language and computer skills are also an advantage.

training environment
The firm's trainees receive a thorough professional training in a very broad range of practice areas, an excellent personal development programme and the chance to work in one of the firm's international offices or on secondment with a client in the UK or abroad. It provides the professional, technical and pastoral support necessary to ensure that you enjoy and make the most of the opportunities on offer – during your training contract and beyond.

benefits
Life assurance; permanent health insurance; group personal pension; interest-free loan; interest-free loan for a season travel ticket; free membership of the firm's private medical insurance scheme; subsidised staff restaurant; gym.

vacation placements
Places for 2003: 100; Duration: 2 weeks; Remuneration: £500; Closing Date: 14 February 2003 but apply as quickly as possible after 1 December 2002 as there may not be places left by the deadline.

sponsorship & awards
CPE and LPC fees paid and £5,000 maintenance p.a. for those studying in London and Oxford and £4,500 p.a. for those studying elsewhere.

Partners 505
Asst Solicitors 1,664
Total Trainees 184
(London-based)

contact
Maia Lawson

method of application
Application form

selection procedure
1 interview with 2 partners & written test

closing date for 2005
24 July 03 (non-law graduates)
24 August 03 (law graduates)

application
Training contracts p.a. **100**
Applications p.a. **c.2,500**
% interviewed p.a. **c.10%**
Required degree grade **2:1**

training
Salary
1st year (2002) £28,000
2nd year (2002) £32,000
Holiday entitlement **25 days**
% of trainees with a non-law degree p.a. **c.40%**
No. of seats available abroad p.a. **c.48**

post-qualification
Salary (2002) **£50,000**
% of trainees offered job on qualification (02) **99%**

overseas offices
Amsterdam, Bangkok, Barcelona, Beijing, Berlin, Bratislava, Brussels, Budapest, Cologne, Düsseldorf, Frankfurt, Hamburg, Hanoi, Ho Chi Minh City, Hong Kong, Madrid, Milan, Moscow, Munich, New York, Paris, Prague, Rome, Shanghai, Singapore, Tokyo, Vienna, Washington DC

Gateley Wareing

Windsor House, 3 Temple Row, Birmingham B2 5JR
Tel: (0121) 234 0121 Fax: (0121) 234 0079
Email: www.gateleywareing.com
Website: wwarburton@gateleywareing.com

firm profile
A 20-partner, Midlands-based practice with an excellent reputation for general commercial work and particular expertise in corporate, commercial, employment, property, commercial dispute resolution, construction, insolvency and banking. The firm is expanding (165 staff) and offers a highly practical, commercial and fast-paced environment. The firm prides itself on its entrepreneurial style and its work hard/play hard reputation. The firm focuses on owner-led businesses, but also counts some household names and internationals amongst its clients.

trainee profile
Applications are invited from second year law students and final year non-law students. Applicants should have (or be heading for) a minimum 2.1 degree, and should have at least three Bs (or equivalent) at A-level. Individuals should be hardworking team players capable of using initiative and demonstrating commercial awareness.

training environment
Four seats of six months each with ongoing supervision and appraisals every three months. PSC taken internally. In-house courses on skills such as time management, negotiation, IT, drafting, business skills, marketing, presentation and writing in plain English.

benefits
Bonus scheme (up to 10% of salary), a current trainee offered as a 'buddy' - a point of contact within the firm, library available, invitation to summer party prior to joining.

vacation placements
12 two week placements over the summer. Deadline for vacation placement scheme is 14 February 2003 and for training contracts is 31 July 2003. Apply immediately by requesting an application form or online at www.gateleywareing.com

sponsorship & awards
LPC with maintenance grant of £3,500: CPE.

Partners 20
Vacancies 6
Total Trainees 12
Total Staff 165

contact
Mrs Wendy Warburton
HR Manager

closing date for 2005
Vacation placements:
14 February 2003
Training contracts:
31 July 2003

training
Salary
1st year £17,500
2nd year £19,500

post-qualification
Salary £31,000

offices
Birmingham, Leicester, Nottingham

GATELEY WAREING
SOLICITORS

Goodman Derrick

90 Fetter Lane, London EC4A 1PT
Tel: (020) 7404 0606 Fax: (020) 7831 6407
Email: mail@gdlaw.co.uk
Website: www.gdlaw.co.uk

firm profile
Founded in 1954 by Lord Goodman, the firm now has a broad commercial practice and is well known for its media and defamation work, particularly relating to television.

main areas of work
Media 24%; commercial and general litigation 18%; corporate 31%; property 15%; charities/private client 4%; employment 8%.

trainee profile
Candidates must show that they will quickly be able to handle responsibility and deal directly with clients. They must be suited to the firm's work environment, present themselves confidently and be quick thinking and practically-minded.

training environment
Training at the firm is based on direct and active involvement with the work of the practice. The PSC is partly carried out at the start of the training contract, with some courses taking place over the following two years, coupled with the firm's general training programme. Trainees are in addition expected to initiate personal research if specialist knowledge needs to be gained for a particular piece of work. Periods of six months are spent in four of the following departments: company/commercial, media, property, litigation, employment and private client. Work groups within these main departments allow trainees to experience further specialist fields. Trainees' own preferences and aptitude will be monitored by the supervising partner and discussed at monthly meetings and at three-monthly appraisals. The firm has a very friendly and informal environment.

benefits
Medical health insurance, season ticket loan, pension scheme.

sponsorship & awards
LPC fees plus maintenance grant.

Partners	21
Assistant Solicitors	7
Total Trainees	7

contact
Nicholas Armstrong

method of application
CV & covering letter

selection procedure
2 interviews

closing date for 2005
End of July 2003

application
Training contracts p.a. 3/4
Applications p.a. 900
% interviewed p.a. 3%
Required degree grade
Min. 2:1

training
Salary
1st year (2002) £23,000
2nd year (2002) £24,500
Holiday entitlement
25 days
% of trainees with a
non-law degree p.a. 60%

post-qualification
% of trainees offered job
on qualification (2002) 66%
% of assistants (as at
1/9/02) who joined as
trainees 66%
% of partners (as at 1/9/02)
who joined as trainees
24%

Gouldens

10 Old Bailey, London EC4M 7NG
Tel: (020) 7583 7777 Fax: (020) 7583 6777
Brochure request hotline: (0800) 0856 750
Email: recruit@gouldens.com
Website: www.gouldens.com/recruit

firm profile
Gouldens is a leading commercial firm based in the City of London. It provides a full range of legal services to major commercial clients from the UK and overseas.

main areas of work
Company/commercial (including tax) 43%; property (including planning) 25%; litigation (including IP) 20%; banking/capital markets 12%.

trainee profile
Candidates should have obtained or be predicted a 2:1 degree in any discipline. They should be willing to accept the challenge of responsibility in an atmosphere where not only technical expertise but flair, originality and enthusiasm are rewarded.

training environment
The firm operates a unique non-rotational system of training and trainees receive work simultaneously from all departments in the firm. The training is designed to provide freedom, flexibility and responsibility from the start. Trainees have their own office and are encouraged to assume their own workload which allows early responsibility, a faster development of potential and the opportunity to compare and contrast the different disciplines alongside one another. Work will vary from small cases which the trainee may handle alone (under the supervision of a senior lawyer as a mentor) to larger matters where they will assist a partner or an assistant solicitor. The firm runs a structured training programme with weekly seminars to support the thorough practical training and regular feedback trainees receive from the assistants and partners they work with. The firm looks to retain all trainees on qualification.

benefits
BUPA, season ticket loan, subsidised sports club membership, group life cover.

vacation placements
Places for 2002/2003:
Christmas (non-law): 16; 2 weeks; £250; Closing Date 31 October.
Easter (non-law): 16; 2 weeks; £250; Closing Date 28 February;
Summer (law): 40; 2 weeks; £250; Closing Date 28 February.

sponsorship & awards
CPE and LPC fees paid and £5,000 maintenance p.a.

Partners 41
Assistant Solicitors 57
Total Trainees 32

contact
Lisa Holmes

method of application
CV and letter online at www.gouldens.com/recruit

selection procedure
2 interviews with partners

closing date for 2005
31 October 2003. Please apply by the end of July to ensure an early interview slot

application
Training contracts p.a. 20
Applications p.a. 2,000
% interviewed p.a. 10%
Required degree grade 2:1

training
Salary
1st year (2002) £32,000
2nd year (2002) £36,000
Holiday entitlement
5 weeks
% of trainees with
a non-law degree p.a. 45%

post-qualification
Salary (2002) £55,000
% of trainees offered job on qualification (2002) 90%
% of assistants (as at 1/9/02) who joined as trainees 64%
% of partners (as at 1/9/02) who joined as trainees 61%

Halliwell Landau

St. James's Court, Brown St, Manchester M2 2JF
Tel: (0161) 835 3003 Fax: (0161) 835 2994
Email: pmrose@halliwells.com

firm profile
Halliwell Landau is the largest independent commercial law firm in the North West. Over the last few years the firm has increased substantially in both size and turnover and now has in excess of 200 fee-earners and 60 partners. This development leads to a continuing requirement for solicitors and has given rise to more internal promotions to partnerships.

main areas of work
Corporate/banking 24%; commercial litigation 20%; commercial property 17%; insolvency 12%; insurance litigation 12%; planning/environmental law 4%; trust and estate planning 4%; intellectual property 4%; employment 3%.

trainee profile
Candidates need to show a good academic ability but do not necessarily need to have studied law at university. They should demonstrate an ability to fit into a hardworking team. In particular Halliwell Landau is looking for candidates who will develop with the firm after their initial training.

training environment
Each trainee will spend six months in at least three separate departments. These will usually include commercial litigation, corporate and property. So far as possible if an individual trainee has a particular request for experience in one of the more specialist departments then that will be accommodated. In each department the trainee will work as a member of one of the teams within that department as well as being able to assist other teams. Specific training appropriate to each department will be given and in addition trainees are strongly encouraged to attend the firm's regular seminars on legal and related subjects. There is also a specific training programme for trainees. Each trainee will be assessed both mid-seat and at the end of each seat.

benefits
A subsidised gym membership is available.

vacation placements
Places for 2003: 24; Duration: 2 weeks; Remuneration: £100 p.w.; Closing Date: 31 March 2003.

sponsorship & awards
CPE and LPC fees will be paid in full.

Partners 67
Assistant Solicitors 94
Total Trainees 19

contact
Paul Rose

method of application
CV & application form.
Online application preferred

selection procedure
Open days or summer placements

closing date for 2005
31 July 2003

application
Training contracts p.a. **10**
Applications p.a. **1,000**
% interviewed p.a. **5%**
Required degree grade **2:1**

training
Salary
1st year (2002) £19,500
2nd year (2002) £20,500

post-qualification
Salary (2000)
£26,000-£28,000
% of trainees offered job on qualification (2001) **100%**
% of assistants (as at 1/9/00) who joined as trainees **12%**
% of partners (as at 1/6/01) who joined as trainees **5%**

Hammond Suddards Edge

7 Devonshire Square, Cutlers Gardens, London EC2M 4YH
2 Park Lane, Leeds LS3 1ES
Trinity Court, 16 Dalton Street, Manchester M60 8HS
Rutland House, 148 Edmund Street, Birmingham B3 2JR
Tel: (020) 7655 1000 Fax: (020) 7655 1001
Website: www.hammondsuddardsedge.com

firm profile
Hammond Suddards Edge is one of the top 10 leading commercial law firms in the UK, with offices in London, Birmingham, Leeds, Manchester, Brussels, Paris, Berlin, Munich, Rome, Milan, Turin and Hong Kong. The firm has nearly 2,000 staff, including 200 partners, 589 solicitors and 97 trainees, and is regarded as innovative, opportunistic and highly successful in the markets in which it operates.

main areas of work
Corporate; commercial dispute resolution and commercial insurance; construction; employment; EU and competition; finance law (includes banking); intellectual property and commercial; media/IT; pensions; property; sports law; tax.

trainee profile
Hammond Suddards Edge seeks applications from all disciplines for both vacation work and training contracts. It looks for three characteristics: strong academic performance, work experience in the legal sector and significant achievement in non-academic pursuits.

training environment
Around 40 trainee solicitors are recruited each year who each carry out six four month seats during their training contract. All trainees are required to move around a minimum of three offices during their training and subsidised trainee accommodation is provided in all locations to facilitate this process. Trainees can choose their seats as they progress through the training contract.

benefits
Subsidised accommodation in all locations. Flexible benefits scheme which allows trainees to choose their own benefits from a range of options.

vacation placements
Places for 2003: 60; Duration: 3 weeks; Remuneration: £230 p.w. (London), £180 p.w. (Leeds, Manchester, Birmingham); Closing Date: 28 February 2003.

sponsorship & awards
CPE and LPC fees paid and maintenance grant of £4,500 p.a.

Partners 200
Assistant Solicitors 589
Total Trainees 97

contact
The Graduate Recruitment Team

method of application
Online application form

selection procedure
2 interviews

closing date for 2005
31 July 2003

application
Training contracts p.a. 40
Applications p.a. 2,000
% interviewed p.a. 3%
Required degree grade 2:1

training
Salary
1st year (2000) £20,500+ subsidised accommodation
2nd year (2000) £23,000+ subsidised accommodation
Holiday entitlement
23 days
% of trainees with a non-law degree p.a. 25%
No. of seats available abroad p.a. 9

post-qualification
Salary (2002)
London £47,500
Other £33,000-£34,000
% of trainees accepting job on qualification (2002) 85%

overseas offices
Brussels, Paris, Berlin, Munich, Rome, Milan, Turin, Hong Kong

Harbottle & Lewis

Hanover House, 14 Hanover Square, London W1S 1HP
Tel: (020) 7667 5000 Fax: (020) 7667 5100
Email: kathy.beilby@harbottle.com
Website: www.harbottle.com

firm profile
Harbottle & Lewis is recognised for the unique breadth of its practice in the entertainment, media, travel (including aviation) and leisure industries. It undertakes significant corporate commercial and contentious work for clients within these industries including newer industries such as digital mixed media.

main areas of work
Music, film and television production, theatre, broadcasting, computer games and publishing, sport, sponsorship and advertising, aviation, property investment and leisure.

trainee profile
Trainees will have demonstrated the high academic abilities, commercial awareness, and initiative necessary to become part of a team advising clients in dynamic and demanding industries.

training environment
The two year training contract is divided into four six month seats where trainees will be given experience in a variety of legal skills including company commercial, litigation, intellectual property and real property, working within teams focused on the firm's core industries. The firm has a policy of accepting a small number of trainees to ensure they are given relevant and challenging work and are exposed to and have responsibility for a full range of legal tasks. The firm has its own lecture and seminars programme in both legal topics and industry know-how. An open door policy and a pragmatic entrepreneurial approach to legal practice provides a stimulating working environment.

benefits
Lunch provided; season ticket loans.

sponsorship & awards
LPC fees paid and interest-free loans towards maintenance.

Partners 19
Assistant Solicitors 51
Total Trainees 6

contact
Kathy Beilby

method of application
CV & letter

selection procedure
Interview

closing date for 2005
31 July 2003

application
Training contracts p.a. 3
Applications p.a. 800
% interviewed p.a. 5%
Required degree grade 2:1

training
Salary
1st year (2002) £23,500
2nd year (2002) £24,500
Holiday entitlement
in the first year 23 days
in the second year 26 days
% of trainees with
a non-law degree p.a. 40%

post-qualification
Salary (2002) £41,000
% of trainees offered job
on qualification (2002) 50%

Henmans

116 St. Aldates, Oxford OX1 1HA
Tel: (01865) 722181 Fax: (01865) 792376
Email: welcome@henmans.co.uk
Website: www.henmans.co.uk

firm profile
Henmans is a well-established Oxfordshire based practice with a strong national reputation, serving both corporate and private clients. Henmans' philosophy is to be extremely client focused to deliver exceptional levels of service. The firm achieves this through an emphasis on teamwork to ensure clients always have access to a specific partner with specialist support, and through an ongoing program of recruitment and training to guarantee clients optimum advice and guidance. Henmans has invested heavily in IT and has implemented a case management system to enhance services and client care. Henmans' policy of bespoke services and controlled costs ensure that both corporate and private clients benefit from City level litigation standards at competitive regional prices. The firm is now accredited as an Investor in People

main areas of work
The firm's core service of litigation is nationally recognised. The personal injury and clinical negligence litigation is strong, as is professional negligence work. Professional negligence and commercial litigation: 29%; personal injury: 26%; property: 17%; private client (including family)/charities/trusts: 16%; corporate/employment: 12%.

trainee profile
Commercial awareness, sound academic accomplishment, intellectual capability, IT literate, teamworking, good communication skills.

training environment
Trainees are introduced to the firm with a detailed induction and overview of the client base. Experience is likely to be within the PI. Property, family, professional negligence/commercial litigation and private client departments. The firm values commitment and enthusiasm both professionally and socially as an integral part of its culture. The firm provides an ongoing programme of in-house education and regular appraisals within its supportive friendly environment.

Partners 21
Assistant Solicitors 34
Total Trainees 6

contact
Viv J Matthews (Mrs) MA FCIPD
Human Resources Manager

method of application
Application form on website

selection procedure
Interview with HR Manager & partners

closing date for 2005
30 June 2003

application
Training contracts p.a. 3
Applications p.a. 450

training
Salary
1st year (2002) £15,500
2nd year (2002) £17,000
Holiday entitlement
20 days
% of trainees with a non-law degree p.a. 30%

post-qualification
Salary (2000) £26,000
% of assistants (as at 1/7/02) who joined as trainees 30%
% of partners (as at 1/7/02) who joined as trainees 15%

Herbert Smith

Exchange House, Primrose Street, London EC2A 2HS
Tel: (020) 7374 8000 Fax: (020) 7374 0888
Email: graduate.recruitment@herbertsmith.com
Website: www.herbertsmith.com

firm profile
Herbert Smith is an international broad-based law firm with a network of offices in Europe and Asia. It is renowned for the strength of its profile in international M&A, corporate finance and international projects, and is widely recognised to be pre-eminent in litigation and arbitration. The working environment is strongly team-orientated, friendly and informal. Herbert Smith has a formal alliance with the German firm, Gleiss Lutz, and the Dutch and Belgian firm, Stibbe.

main areas of work
International mergers and acquisitions; corporate finance and banking (including capital markets); energy; projects and project finance; competition; real estate; international litigation and arbitration, tax; employment and pensions; construction and engineering; insurance; investment funds; IP and IT; US securities.

trainee profile
Trainees need strong academic records, common sense, self-confidence and intelligence to make their own way in a large firm. They are typically high-achieving and creative thinking – language skills are an advantage.

training environment
Structured training and supervision are designed to allow experience of a unique range of contentious and non-contentious work. You will be encouraged to take on responsibilities as soon as you join the firm. You will work within partner-led teams and have your own role. Individual strengths will be monitored, developed and utilised. On-the-job training will be divided into four six-month seats. One seat will be in the corporate division, one in the litigation division and you have a choice of specialists seats such as IP/IT or EU and competition, as well as an opportunity to go on secondment to a client or an overseas office. Great emphasis is placed on professional and personal development and the firm runs its own legal development programme. There are good social and sporting activities.

sponsorship & benefits
CPE and LPC fees paid and £5,000 maintenance p.a. Benefits include profit share, permanent health insurance, private medical insurance, season ticket loan, life assurance, gym, group personal accident insurance and matched contributory pension scheme.

vacation placements
Places for 2003: 115. Christmas (non-law students only), Easter (law and non-law students). Closing Date: 22 November 2002 for Christmas scheme; 31 January 2003 for Easter and Summer scheme. Opportunities in some of the firm's European offices.

Partners 194
Fee-earners 713
Total Trainees 203

contact
Kate Quail

method of application
Application form

selection procedure
Interview

closing date for 2005
31 August 2003

application
Training contracts p.a. **100**
Applications p.a. **1,750**
% interviewed p.a. **20%**
Required degree grade **2:1**

training
Salary
1st year **£28,500**
2nd year **£32,000**
Holiday entitlement
25 days, rising to 27 on qualification
% of trainees with a non-law degree p.a.
c.40% plus

post-qualification
Salary (2002) **£50,000**
% of trainees offered job on qualification (2002) **95%**

overseas offices
Bangkok, Beijing, Brussels, Hong Kong, Moscow, Paris, Singapore, Tokyo

associated offices
Amsterdam, Berlin, Frankfurt, Jakarta, Munich, New York, Prague, Shanghai, Stuttgart, Warsaw

Hewitson Becke + Shaw

42 Newmarket Road, Cambridge CB5 8EP
Tel: (01604) 233233 Fax: (01223) 316511
Email: mail@hewitsons.com (for all offices)
Website: www.hbslaw.co.uk (for all offices)

firm profile
Established in 1865, the firm handles mostly company and commercial work, but has a growing body of public sector clients. The firm has three offices: Cambridge, Northampton and Saffron Walden.

main areas of work
Three sections: corporate technology, property and private client.

trainee profile
The firm is interested in applications from candidates who have achieved a high degree of success in academic studies and who are bright, personable and able to take the initiative.

training environment
The firm offers four six month seats.

benefits
The PSC is provided during the first year of the training contract. This is coupled with an extensive programme of Trainee Solicitor Seminars provided by specialist in-house lawyers.

vacation placements
Places for 2002: A few placements are available, application is by way of letter and CV to Caroline Lewis; Duration: 1 week.

sponsorship & awards
Funding for the CPE and/or LPC is not provided.

Partners	48
Assistant Solicitors	47
Total Trainees	16

contact
Caroline Lewis
7 Spencer Parade
Northampton NN1 5AB

method of application
Firm's application form

selection procedure
Interview

closing date for 2005
End of August 2003

application
Training contracts p.a. **15**
Applications p.a. **1,400**
% interviewed p.a. **10%**
Required degree grade **2:1 min**

training
Salary
1st year (2002) £17,000
2nd year (2002) £18,000
Holiday entitlement **22 days**
% of trainees with a non-law degree p.a. **50%**

post-qualification
Salary (2001) **Under review**
% of trainees offered job on qualification (2001) **60%**
% of assistants (as at 1/9/01) who joined as trainees **47%**
% of partners (as at 1/9/01) who joined as trainees **20%**

Hill Dickinson

Pearl Assurance House, 2 Derby Square, Liverpool L2 9XL
Tel: (0151) 236 5400 Fax: (0151) 236 2175
Email: law@hilldicks.com
Website: www.hilldickinson.com

firm profile

Hill Dickinson is one of the leading commercial law firms in the UK, providing legal advice to both the domestic and international markets from each of its four offices in London, Liverpool, Manchester and Chester. Delivering a highly professional and added value service the firm is alert to the ever changing and increasing demands being placed upon different markets and is well positioned to support its clients in all aspects of their legal requirements.

main areas of work

With a wealth of specialists, the firm advises a range of clients including corporates, the private sector, individuals and the public sector and is structured into four specialist groups: commercial, insurance and litigation, health, and marine and transit. Specialisms include sport and media, corporate law, European law, employment, pensions, PFI, intellectual property and technology, private client, professional indemnity, fraud and policy and regulation, clinical negligence, mental health, shipping, goods in transit and yachting, to name a few.

trainee profile

Commercial awareness and academic ability are the key factors, together with a desire to succeed. Trainees are viewed as the partners of the future and the firm is looking for personable individuals with whom it wants to work.

training environment

Trainees spend six months in each of the four departments (commercial, insurance and litigation, health and marine and transit) and will be given the chance to specialise in specific areas. You will be given the opportunity to learn and develop communication and presentation skills, legal research, drafting, interviewing and advising, negotiations and advocacy. Trainees are encouraged to accept responsibility and are expected to act with initiative. The practice has an active social committee and a larger than usual selection of competitive sporting teams.

vacation placements

One week structured scheme with places available for 2003. Apply by CV and covering letter to Carla Emery (Partner) by 30 April 2003.

sponsorship & awards

LPC funding provided. Further funding and maintenance awards are under review.

Partners 85
Assistant Solicitors 82
Total Trainees 20

contact
Ruth Lawrence
Partner
rjl@hilldicks.com

method of application
CV & passport-sized photograph with supporting letter

selection procedure
Assessment day

closing date for 2005
End of August 2003

training
Salary
1st year (2001) £16,500
2nd year (2001) £18,000
Salaries are currently under review
Holiday entitlement
4 weeks

post-qualification
% of trainees offered job on qualification (2000)
100%

offices
Chester, Liverpool, London, Manchester

Hodge Jones & Allen

31-39 Camden Road, London NW1 9LR
Tel: (020) 7482 1974 Fax: (020) 7267 3376
Email: hja@hodgejonesallen.co.uk
Website: www.hodgejonesallen.co.uk

firm profile
Hodge Jones & Allen was established in 1977, and has expanded rapidly, especially since moving to new premises in September 1997. The firm is led by one of the founding partners, Patrick Allen. It has been involved in a number of high profile cases including the King's Cross fire, Broadwater Farm, Greenham Common, the Marchioness disaster, the Sheep Dip litigation, MMR and Gulf War Syndrome. Good management and IT systems have played an important role in the firm's growth.

main areas of work
Personal injury and clinical negligence 33%; crime 27%; family 18%; housing 10%; property 6%; employment and mental health 6%.

trainee profile
Ideally candidates should have strong IT skills together with a proven commitment to and/or experience of working in Legal Aid/Advice sectors.

training environment
Trainees have a full induction on joining HJA covering the work of the firm's main departments, procedural matters and professional conduct. Training consists of four six month seats and trainees normally share an office with a partner who assists them and formally reviews their progress at least once during each seat.

benefits
Pension, life assurance, permanent health insurance, quarterly drinks, summer outing, Christmas party.

Partners	18
Assistant Solicitors	34
Total Trainees	11

contact
Sarah Firth
Personnel Manager

method of application
By application form only, 1 year in advance

selection procedure
Interview & selection tests in previous autumn

closing date for 2005
September 2004

application
Required degree grade
2:1 degree preferred

Holman Fenwick & Willan

Marlow House, Lloyds Avenue, London EC3N 3AL
Tel: (020) 7488 2300 Fax: (020) 7481 0316
Email: grad.recruitment@hfw.co.uk

firm profile
Holman Fenwick & Willan is an international law firm and one of the world's leading specialists in maritime transportation, insurance, reinsurance and trade. The firm is a leader in the field of commercial litigation and arbitration and also offers comprehensive commercial and financial advice. Founded in 1883, the firm is one of the largest operating in its chosen fields with a team of over 200 lawyers worldwide, and a reputation for excellence and innovation.

main areas of work
The firm's range of services include marine, admiralty and crisis management, insurance and reinsurance, commercial litigation and arbitration, international trade and commodities, energy, corporate and financial.

trainee profile
Applications are invited from commercially minded undergraduates and graduates of all disciplines with good A levels and who have, or expect to receive, a 2:1 degree. Good foreign languages or a scientific or maritime background are an advantage.

training environment
During your training period the firm will ensure that you gain valuable experience in a wide range of areas. It also organises formal training supplemented by a programme of in-house seminars and ship visits in addition to the PSC. Your training development as an effective lawyer will be managed by the Recruitment and Training Partner, Ottilie Sefton, who will ensure that your training is both successful and enjoyable.

benefits
Private medical insurance, permanent health and accident insurance, subsidised gym membership, season ticket loan.

vacation placements
Places for 2003: 16; Duration: 2 weeks. Dates: 23 June - 4 July / 14 July - 25 July; Remuneration (2002): £250 p.w.; Closing Date: Applications accepted 1 Jan - 14 Feb 2003.

sponsorship & awards
PgDL Funding: Fees paid plus £5,000 maintenance; LPC Funding: Fees paid plus £5,000 maintenance.

Partners 80+
Other Solicitors & Fee-earners 120+
Total Trainees 20

contact
Graduate Recruitment Officer

method of application
Handwritten letter & typed CV

selection procedure
2 interviews with partners & written exercise

closing date for 2005
31 July 2003

application
Training contracts p.a. 8
Applications p.a. 1,200
% interviewed p.a. 5%
Required degree grade 2:1

training
Salary (Sept 2002)
1st year £28,000
2nd year £30,000
Holiday entitlement 22 days
% of trainees with a non-law degree p.a. 50%

post-qualification
Salary (2002) £50,000
% of trainees offered job on qualification (Sept 2001) 100%

overseas offices
Hong Kong, Nantes, Paris, Piraeus, Rouen, Shanghai, Singapore

Howes Percival

Oxford House, Cliftonville, Northampton NN1 5PN
Tel: (01604) 230400 Fax: (01604) 620956
Email: law@howes-percival.co.uk
Website: www.howes-percival.co.uk

firm profile
Howes Percival is a 34 partner commercial law firm with offices in Leicester, Milton Keynes, Northampton and Norwich. The firm's working environment is young, progressive and highly professional and its corporate structure means that fee-earners are rewarded on merit and can progress to associate or partner status quickly. The type and high value of the work that the firm does places it in a position whereby it is recognised as being a regional firm by location only. The firm has the expertise, resources, and partner reputation that match a city firm.

main areas of work
The practice is departmentalised and the breakdown of its work is as follows: corporate 30%; commercial property 25%; commercial litigation 20%; insolvency 10%; employment 10%; private client 5%.

trainee profile
The firm is looking for six well-educated, focused, enthusiastic, commercially aware graduates with a minimum 2:1 degree in any discipline. Howes Percival welcomes confident communicators with strong interpersonal skills who share the firm's desire to be the best.

training environment
Trainees complete four six month seats, each one in a different department. Trainees joining the Norwich office will remain at Norwich for the duration of their training contract. Trainees in the East Midlands will, where possible, complete a seat in each of the three East Midlands offices. Trainees report direct to a partner and after three months and again towards the end of each seat they will be formally assessed by the partner training them. Trainees will be given every assistance by the fee-earners in their department to develop quickly and will be given responsibility as soon as they are ready.

benefits
Contributory pension scheme. Private health insurance. LPC funding. The firm owns brand new accommodation in the Northampton area that is rented out to trainees.

vacation placements
Vacation placements are available in July and August. Please apply to Miss Katy Pattle at the above address for further details.

Partners	34
Assistant Solicitors	25
Total Trainees	10

contact
Miss Katy Pattle
HR Assistant

method of application
Letter, CV & firm's application form

selection procedure
Assessment centres including second interview with training principal & partner

closing date for 2005
31 July 2003

application
Training contracts p.a. 6
Applications p.a. 300
% interviewed p.a. 10%
Required degree grade 2:1

training
Salary
1st year (2002) £18,750
2nd year (2002) £20,000
Holiday entitlement
23 days p.a.

post-qualification
% of trainees offered job on qualification (2002) 75%
% of assistants (as at 1/9/01) who joined as trainees 30%
% of partners (as at 1/9/01) who joined as trainees 7.5%

Hugh James

Arlbee House, Greyfriars Rd, Cardiff CF10 3QB
Tel: (029) 2022 4871 Fax: (029) 2038 8222
Email: training@hughjames.com
Website: www.hughjames.com

firm profile
Hugh James is one of the UK's leading regional law firms and has experienced phenomenal growth and success since it was formed in 1960. It has for many years been one of only a handful of firms to dominate the legal scene in Wales. Hugh James is placed high in the table of the top 100 law firms in the UK. The firm offers its clients a comprehensive service covering the whole of South Wales through its seven offices.

main areas of work
The practice is divided up into four divisions: business litigation (26%); business services (30%); claimant litigation (28%); public funded (16%). Specialist teams have been established to service niche areas of the law and the firm has a multidisciplinary approach to the provision of legal services.

trainee profile
Hugh James welcomes applications from law and non-law undergraduates with a good class degree. Candidates must exhibit first class legal and practice skills and good interpersonal and IT skills are essential. The majority of trainees are retained upon qualification and are seen as an integral part of the future of the firm. Hugh James is proud of the fact that most of its present partners were trained at the firm.

training environment
Trainees generally undertake four seats of not less than six months which may be in any of the firm's offices. Broadly, experience will be gained in all four main work categories. The breadth of work dealt with by the firm enables it to ensure that over-specialisation is avoided.

benefits
Company contribution to stakeholder pension scheme.

vacation placements
Places for 2003 available.

Partners 44
Assistant Solicitors 51
Total Trainees 14

contact
Jane O'Rourke
HR Director

method of application
Application form available from HR Manager

selection procedure
Assessment day

closing date for 2005
31 June 2003

application
Training contracts p.a. 7
Applications p.a. 350
% interviewed p.a. 30%
Required degree grade 2:2

training
Salary
Competitive & reviewed annually

other offices
Merthyr Tydfil, Bargoed, Blackwood, Talbot Green, Treharris, Pontlottyn

Ince & Co

Knollys House, 11 Byward Street, London EC3R 5EN
Tel: (020) 7623 2011 Fax: (020) 7623 3225
Email: claire.kendall@ince.co.uk

firm profile
Since its foundation in 1870, Ince & Co has specialised in international commercial law and is best known for its shipping and insurance work.

main areas of work
Shipping and aviation 38%; insurance/reinsurance/professional indemnity 27%; energy/construction/environment/pollution/personal injury 17%; Business and Finance Group including corporate/private client/property 7%; international trade/commodities 7%; sale and purchase 4%.

trainee profile
Hard working competitive individuals with initiative who relish challenge and responsibility within a team environment. Academic achievements, positions of responsibility, sport and travel are all taken into account.

training environment
Trainees sit with four different partners for six months at a time throughout their training. Under close supervision, they are encouraged from an early stage to meet and visit clients, interview witnesses, liaise with counsel, deal with technical experts and handle opposing lawyers. They will quickly build up a portfolio of cases from a number of partners involved in a cross-section of the firm's practice and will see their cases through from start to finish. In the second year of their training contract there is the opportunity of a seat in the Piraeus office. They will also attend in-house and external lectures, conferences and seminars on practical and legal topics.

benefits
STL, corporate health cover, PHI, contributory pension scheme.

vacation placements
Places for 2003: 21; Duration: 2 weeks; Remuneration: £250 p.w.; Closing Date: 14 February 2003.

sponsorship & awards
LPC fees, £4,750 grant for study in London, £4,000 grant for study elsewhere. Discretionary sponsorship for CPE.

Partners 64*
Assistant Solicitors 83*
Total Trainees 24*
* denotes worldwide figures

contact
Claire Kendall

method of application
Typed/handwritten letter & CV with contact details of 2 academic referees

selection procedure
Interview with HR professional & interview with 2 partners from Recruitment Committee & a written test

closing date for 2005
31 July 2003

application
Training contracts p.a. 8
Applications p.a. 2,500
% interviewed p.a. 5%
Required degree grade 2:1

training
Salary
1st year (2001) £27,000
2nd year (2001) £30,000
Holiday entitlement
22 days
% of trainees with a non-law degree p.a. 55%

post-qualification
Salary (2002) £47,000
% of trainees offered job on qualification (2002) 83.3%. 83.3% accepted!
% of assistants (as at 2002) who joined as trainees 44.6%
% of partners (as at 2002) who joined as trainees 62.5%

overseas offices
Hamburg, Hong Kong, Le Havre, Paris, Piraeus, Shanghai, Singapore

Irwin Mitchell

St. Peter's House, Hartshead, Sheffield S1 2EL
Recruitment Line: (0114) 274 4580
Email: enquiries@irwinmitchell.co.uk
Website: imonline.co.uk

firm profile
Irwin Mitchell is a rapidly expanding national practice with 80 partners and over 1,500 employees with offices in Birmingham, Leeds, London and Sheffield. It is particularly well known for commercial law, commercial litigation, insurance law, business crime and claimant personal injury litigation. The firm's strong reputation for dealing with novel and complex areas of law and handling developmental cases such as the vibration white finger, CJD and the Matrix-Churchill 'arms to Iraq' affair means that it can offer a broad range of experience within each of its specialist departments, giving trainees a high standard of training.

main areas of work
Corporate services 27%; claimant personal injury 27%; insurance litigation 35%; private client 11%.

trainee profile
The firm is looking for ambitious, well motivated individuals with a real commitment to the law and who can demonstrate a positive approach to a work life balance. It recruits law and non-law graduates. Foreign languages and IT skills are an asset. Irwin Mitchell believes trainees to be an investment for the future and endeavour to retain trainees upon qualification.

training environment
The two year training contract consists of four seats. The firm's trainees also benefit from a structured induction programme, monthly training events and the Professional Skills Course which is run in-house and financed by the firm. Each trainee has a quarterly review with their supervising partner to focus on performance and development ensuring progress is on track.

vacation placements
Places for 2003: 50; Duration: 1 week; Remuneration: £75 p.w.; Closing Date: 1 March.

sponsorship & awards
Payment of PgDL and LPC fees plus a £3,000 maintenance grant.

Partners 80
Assistant Solicitors 181
Total Trainees 27

contact
Sue Lenkowski

method of application
Firm's application form & covering letter. Call the recruitment line between 1 April & 31 July

selection procedure
Assessment centre & interview during September. Successful candidates invited to attend second interview

closing date for 2005
31 July 2003

application
Training contracts p.a. **15**
Applications p.a. **1,000**
% interviewed p.a. **7%**

training
Salary
1st year £17,000
2nd year £19,000
(outside London)
reviewed annually
Holiday entitlement
24.5 days
% of trainees with a non-law degree p.a. **25%**

post-qualification
% of trainees offered job on qualification **95%**
% of assistants who joined as trainees **41%**
% of partners (2002) who joined as trainees **22%**

Keoghs

2 The Parklands, Bolton BL6 4SE
Tel: (01204) 677000 Fax: (01204) 677111
Email: info@keoghs.co.uk

firm profile
Keoghs is one of the UK's leading insurance litigation firms offering national coverage to clients and acts for most of the UK's major insurance companies. The company and commercial team specialise in commercial business advice serving a client base ranging from the private individual to small growing businesses and national blue chip organisations. The high standard of service given to new and existing clients has enabled the firm to achieve ISO 9001 accreditation.

main areas of work
The main practice areas are personal injury litigation, commercial litigation and company commercial (which includes corporate, employment, intellectual property commercial property and private client).

trainee profile
The firm is looking to recruit the partners of the future and indeed many current partners and assistant solicitors joined the firm as trainees. Applicants should be able to demonstrate a high academic standard (at least a 2:1 degree but not necessarily in law), an ability to work in a team, and good communication and decision making skills. The firm welcomes commercially aware, enthusiastic and self motivated candidates with good IT skills and a sense of humour.

training environment
Trainees undertake a flexible programme of six month periods in each of the firm's three main practice areas of defendant personal injury litigation, commercial litigation and company commercial work. A final six months can then be spent in the department of the trainee's choice. The trainee will work as part of a specialist team, receiving specific training from their departmental supervisor. The supervisor will also assess the trainee during and at the end of their placement to review progress and development of their drafting, research, communication, advocacy and negotiation skills. The firm's Training and Development department runs a comprehensive programme of in-house training designed to complement the compulsory Professional Skills Course.

Partners	29
Trainees	8
Total Staff	354

contact
Mrs Frances Cross
Director of HR

method of application
Apply by sending a CV & covering letter

selection procedure
By 2 stage interview

closing date for 2005
August 2003

application
Training contracts p.a. **3 in Bolton, 1 in Coventry**
Applications p.a. **800**
% interviewed p.a. **3.5%**
Required degree grade **2:1**

training
Salary for each year of training
Currently under review (in excess of Law Society minimum)
Holiday entitlement
25 days + 8 statutory days

post-qualification
Salary **£26,800**
% of trainees offered job on qualification **The firm aims for 100%**

regional offices
Bolton, Coventry

KLegal

1-2 Dorset Rise, London EC4Y 8AE
Tel: (020) 7694 2500 Fax: (020) 7694 2501
Website: www.klegaltrainees.co.uk

firm profile
Founded in July 1999, KLegal is the UK associated law firm of KPMG. Since its formation, KLegal has grown to be one of the top 30 law firms in the UK.

main areas of work
The firm's focus is on developing its legal expertise in practice areas that complement the services offered by KPMG. These include banking and finance; corporate; dispute resolution; e-business and digital media; employment; intellectual property; IT and telecommunications; private equity; projects/PPP; real estate; tax litigation.

trainee profile
KLegal is looking for outstanding candidates with ambition who share the firm's vision and who are capable of helping the firm achieve this. The firm is a constantly changing environment and is looking to those who see the opportunities this provides both for themselves as individuals and for their colleagues in general.

training environment
KLegal's training is based upon a conventional rotation of seats of six months in four main practice areas. The firm provides opportunities for its trainees to learn their legal skills as part of multidisciplinary teams enabling them to become among the best commercially minded lawyers in the City. Secondment opportunities within KPMG may also be available. The firm's personal development training is second to none. Its commitment is to provide an enjoyable experience, allowing individuals to maximise both their own personal and professional development.

benefits
Flextra, the firm's flexible benefit scheme, allows staff the opportunity to shape their own reward package by indicating their preferences. Benefits include life assurance, pension, a daily lunch allowance and 25 days holiday.

vacation placements
Places for 2003: 12; Duration: 5 weeks; Remuneration: £250 p.w.; Closing Date: 21 February 2003.

sponsorship & awards
CPE Funding: Fees paid plus maintenance of £4,500.
LPC Funding: Fees paid plus maintenance of £4,500.

Partners 72
Assistant Solicitors 300
Total Trainees 80

contact
Graduate Recruitment Officer

method of application
Online application via website

selection procedure
2 interviews & assessment exercises

closing date for 2005
31 July 2003

application
Training contracts p.a. 30
Applications p.a. c.750
Required degree grade 2:1

training
Salary (Reviewed annually)
1st year £28,000
2nd year £32,000

post-qualification
Salary £50,000

overseas offices
Member of KLegal International

Landwell

Southwark Towers, 32 London Bridge Street, London SE1 9AE
Tel: (020) 7212 1990 Fax: (020) 7212 1570
Website: www.landwell.co.uk

Partners	21
Trainees	20
Total Staff	145

contact
Joanne Cox
Graduate Recruitment

method of application
Apply via
www.landwell.co.uk

closing date for 2005
31 July 2003

application
Training contracts p.a. 8
Required degree grade
You should have, or
expect to obtain, a 2:1
degree in any subject

training
Salary Competitive and
in line with market rates

overseas offices
Landwell, and its network,
offer legal services across
the world. The firm works
with 2,700 business
lawyers in over 40
countries

firm profile

Landwell is a multinational, multidisciplinary legal practice providing business oriented legal advice on domestic and cross-border deals. With 2,700 specialist lawyers in over 40 countries, the firm works with PricewaterhouseCoopers to provide seamless legal, tax and consultancy expertise. Here in the UK, Landwell advises a range of large national and multinational companies, governments and financial institutions. The firm works both on a stand-alone basis, often with other lawyers in the Landwell international network, and with consultants and other advisers in PricewaterhouseCoopers as part of a multi-disciplinary team. Its international network specialises in delivering national and international solutions to complex business problems. Acting for a large range of multinational and international clients, Landwell has dedicated cross-border client service teams in the areas of M&A, corporate restructuring, intellectual property, financial services, e-business, employment and global mobility. The firm's approach ensures that global teams are assembled quickly and effectively and that they work with the client through a single point of contact and to a single common standard.

main areas of work

The key areas of specialisation at Landwell in the UK are M&A transactions, IPOs and private equity work, corporate restructuring, e-business, intellectual property, IT, employment, immigration, financial services, banking, real estate and tax litigation.

trainee profile

Landwell wants to see applicants with a genuine interest in business law and the ambition to be a part of a new model of legal practice. In return, the firm offers you something unique. The speed of its growth, its relationship with PricewaterhouseCoopers, its global reach and its philosophy all serve to differentiate it from the majority of existing law firms. While the quality of the firm's work and the excellence of its training can match that of any traditional law firm, it spends more time than most out there in the real business world, alongside its clients, reaching out into new ground.

sponsorship & awards

Trainee lawyers joining the firm are eligible to apply for a scholarship award to assist with the costs of the CPE/Diploma in Law course and the Legal Practice Course. If successful, you will receive the total cost of the tuition and examination fees (from the date of signing your contract) and also a significant contribution towards your living expenses.

Lawrence Graham

190 Strand, London WC2R 1JN
Tel: (020) 7759 6694 Fax: (020) 7379 6854
Email: graduate@lawgram.com
Website: www.lawgram.com

firm profile
Lawrence Graham is a growing firm with a broad client base, which includes many UK and international public and private companies, pension funds, financial institutions, shipping companies, small businesses and private individuals. The firm's business is divided into four main practice areas: commercial property, company and commercial, litigation and tax and financial management. Each of the four main practice areas is organised into specialised teams. The firm has associations with many law firms throughout the world, including North America, Europe and the Far East. It also has an office in the Ukraine where the firm has had clients since the 1920s.

main areas of work
Property 35%; company and commercial 29%; litigation (including shipping) 23%; tax and financial management 13%.

trainee profile
The firm purposely recruits a small number of trainees for its size to enable comprehensive, hands on training. Candidates, who are normally of 2:1 calibre, should demonstrate strong technical and interpersonal skills, the ability to understand a client's commercial priorities and objectives and the judgement to deal with complex problems.

training environment
Trainees are given the opportunity to learn both formally and practically. Seminars are regularly held throughout the two years. Training consists of four six month seats including a seat in each of the company and commercial, litigation and property departments. The fourth seat can be in either tax and financial management or back to one of the main departments. Each trainee is assigned a mentor. All work is supervised but independence and responsibility increase with experience. Social and sporting events are also organised.

benefits
Season ticket loan, on-site gym.

vacation placements
Places for 2003: 40; Duration: 2 weeks during Easter break and 4 x 2 weeks between June and August; Remuneration: £225 p.w.; Closing Date: 31 January 2003.

sponsorship & awards
CPE Funding: Course fees and £4,000 maintenance grant.
LPC Funding: Course fees and £4,000 maintenance grant.

Partners 85
Assistant Solicitors 103
Total Trainees 33

contact
Human Resources Officer

method of application
Firm's application form.
For law After 2nd year results
For non-law After final results

selection procedure
Interview

closing date for 2005
31 July 2003

application
Training contracts **18**
Applications p.a. **1,000**
Required degree grade **2:1**

training
Salary
1st year (2001) **£28,000**
2nd year (2001) **£32,000**
% of trainees with a non-law degree p.a. **40%**

post-qualification
Salary (2001) **£48,000**
% of trainees offered job on qualification (2001) **98%**
% of assistants (as at 1/9/01) who joined as trainees **42%**
% of partners (as at 1/9/01) who joined as trainees **32%**

Laytons

Carmelite, 50 Victoria Embankment, Blackfriars, London EC4Y 0LS
Tel: (020) 7842 8000 Fax: (020) 7842 8080
Email: london@laytons.com
Website: www.laytons.com

firm profile
Laytons assigns a core legal team to each client who knows its business and can advise directly or by deploying the specialist skills of colleagues. The approach to legal issues is practical, creative and energetic, providing high quality advice founded on a range of complementary specialist skills relevant to the firm's primary fields of focus. The firm is a single national team operating through its four offices, each of which draws on the strengths of the whole with the benefit of excellent IT and communications.

main areas of work
Company/commercial 45%; commercial property/land development 17%; general litigation 13%; employment 10%; trusts, private client and private tax 5%; technology and media 10%.

trainee profile
All trainees have contact with clients from an early stage, working on a wide variety of transactions. Trainees will soon be responsible for their own files, although they are always supported and have regular appraisals throughout the training contract. The firm recruits with a view to retaining trainees to assistant level. Trainees are also encouraged to participate in the firm's business development activities.

training environment
Trainees are placed in four six month seats in each of the firm's principal departments: company commercial, property, litigation and private client.

vacation placements
Places for 2003: 6; Duration: 1 week; Closing Date: 31 March 2003.

sponsorship & awards
CPE Funding: Yes; LPC Funding: Yes.

Partners 38
Assistant Solicitors 42
Total Trainees 18

contact
Ian Burman

method of application
Application form

selection procedure
2 interviews

closing date for 2005
31 August 2003

application
Training contracts p.a. **8**
Applications p.a. **2,000**
% interviewed p.a. **5%**
Required degree grade
1 or 2:1

training
Salary
1st year (2002) **Market rate**
2nd year (2002) **Market rate**
Holiday entitlement
22 days

post-qualification
Salary (2002) **Market rate**
% of trainees offered job on qualification (2000) **80%**
% of assistants (as at 1/9/00) who joined as trainees **90%**
% of partners (as at 1/9/00) who joined as trainees **20%**

LeBoeuf, Lamb, Greene & MacRae

1 Minster Court, Mincing Lane, London EC3R 7AA
Tel: (020) 7459 5000 Fax: (020) 7459 5099
Email: traineelondon@llgm.com
Website: www.llgm.com

firm profile
LeBoeuf, Lamb, Greene & MacRae is an international law firm with some 750 lawyers worldwide in offices across Europe, the US, Africa and the Middle East. The London office, established as a multinational partnership in 1995 employs almost 60 lawyers and is the hub office for the firm's European and international practice. The London office handles varied, interesting work and will suit people who want early responsibility in a relaxed but hard working environment.

main areas of work
General corporate, litigation, energy, corporate finance, project finance, capital markets, private equity, insurance, insolvency, property, tax, intellectual property.

trainee profile
Leboeuf, Lamb, Greene & MacRae is looking for outstanding people in the broadest possible sense. The firm welcomes applications from varied, non-traditional backgrounds. Inter-personal skills are very important: the firm likes bright, engaging people. Linguistic skills are useful (but not crucial). The firm wants proactive people who will contribute from day one.

training environment
Trainees spend six months in four seats. The firm's training programme is comprehensive and covers an induction programme, participation in internal seminars and training sessions and attendance at external courses, including the Professional Skills Course. You will be encouraged to act on your own initiative from an early stage. Trainees sit with a senior lawyer, often a partner, who can give ongoing feed back and guidance and progress is reviewed every six months.

benefits
Private medical insurance, season ticket loan, subsidised restaurant.

sponsorship & awards
Full payment of CPE/LPC fees and maintenance grant of £4,500 provided.

Partners 12
Counsel 6
Assistant Solicitors 30
Total Trainees 8

contact
Andrew Terry

method of application
CV & covering letter

selection procedure
2 interviews

closing date for 2005
31 August 2003

application
Training contracts p.a. 4
Applications p.a. 1,000
% interviewed p.a. 3%

training
Salary
1st year (2002) £33,000
2nd year (2003) £37,000
Holiday entitlement
20 days
% of trainees with a
non-law degree p.a. 50%

post-qualification
Salary (2002) £65,000

overseas offices
Albany, Almaty, Beijing, Bishkek, Boston, Brussels, Denver, Harrisburg, Hartford, Houston, Jacksonville, Johannesburg, Los Angeles, Moscow, New York, Newark, Paris, Pittsburgh, Riyadh, Salt Lake City, San Francisco, Tashkent, Washington

Lee Bolton & Lee

1 The Sanctuary, Westminster, London SW1P 3JT
Tel: (020) 7222 5381 Fax: (020) 7222 7502
Email: enquiries@1thesanctuary.com
Website: www.leeboltonlee.com

firm profile
Founded in 1855, Lee Bolton & Lee is a successful medium-sized firm based in Westminster. It is closely associated with parliamentary agents and solicitors, Rees and Freres, who provide a specialist service in parliamentary, public and administrative law.

main areas of work
Commercial; property; private client; litigation; charity; education work.

trainee profile
The firm seeks to recruit trainees with a good degree (2:1 or above), first class communication skills, motivation, professionalism, initiative, enthusiasm, and a sense of humour.

training environment
Trainees spend six months in each of four seats: private client, property, litigation and commercial property, sitting with either a senior solicitor or a partner. Training is comprehensive and covers a full induction programme, participation in internal seminars and training sessions and attendance at external courses, including the Professional Skills Course. Trainees are given responsibility for their own files from the beginning, and whilst this might at first seem daunting, the firm operates an open door policy and help is never far away. Progress is reviewed monthly by your elected Supervisor and every three months by the Training Principal. There are various sporting and social events.

benefits
Season ticket loan, non-guaranteed bonus.

sponsorship & awards
A contribution towards LPC funding but dependent upon being offered a training contract.

Partners	14
Assistant Solicitors	10
Total Trainees	4

contact
Susie Hust

method of application
Letter & CV

selection procedure
Panel interview

closing date for 2005
End July 2003

application
Training contracts p.a. 2
Applications p.a. 800
% interviewed p.a. 3%
Required degree grade 2:1

training
Salary (2001)
1st year £19,000
2nd year £20,000
Holiday entitlement
22 days
% of trainees with a
 non-law degree p.a. 50%

post-qualification
Salary (2001) £29,000
% of trainees offered job
on qualification (2001) 50%
% of assistants (as at 1/9/00) who joined as trainees 40%
% of partners (as at 1/9/00) who joined as trainees 15%

Lester Aldridge

Russell House, Oxford Road, Bournemouth BH8 8EX
Tel: (01202) 786161 Fax: (01202) 786110
6 Enterprise Way, Aviation Park West, Christchurch BH23 6EW
Tel: (01202) 597700
Alleyn House, Carlton Crescent, Southampton SO15 2EU
Tel: (023) 8082 0400 Fax: (023) 8082 0410
Email: juliet.milne@lester-aldridge.co.uk
Website: www.lester-aldridge.co.uk

firm profile
LA is a dynamic business, providing both commercial and private client services. Based on the south coast (in Southampton and Bournemouth), it operates predominantly within central southern England, although it offers a number of services on a national and international basis, including LA Marine and Asset Finance and Banking. LA is run as a business with a corporate-style management structure. The firm's vision is to be recognised as the best law firm within its region.

main areas of work
Litigation 20%; corporate, banking and finance 36%; private client services 24%; commercial property 21%.

trainee profile
Candidates should have strong intellectual capabilities, be commercially aware, resourceful and able to relate easily to other people. IT skills and a team approach are also required.

training environment
Trainees receive an extended version of the firm's induction procedure which covers the firm's aims, values and structure, marketing, administration and support services. Training consists of four six month seats across the firm. About halfway through each seat, trainees discuss their preferences for the next seat and every attempt is made to match aspirations to the needs of the firm. Trainees have a training principal for the duration of the contract who will discuss progress every month. They receive a comprehensive formal appraisal from their team leader towards the end of each seat, and the managing partner meets all trainees as a group every three months.

benefits
Life assurance and pension schemes.

vacation placements
Places for 2003: 8; Duration: 2 weeks; Remuneration: £75 p.w.; Closing Date: 31 March 2003.

sponsorship & awards
Discretionary.

Partners 33
Assistant Solicitors 22
Total Trainees 12

contact
Juliet Milne

method of application
Letter, CV & completed application form

selection procedure
Interview by a panel of partners

closing date for 2005
16 August 2003

application
Training contracts p.a. 5
Applications p.a. 300
% interviewed p.a. 5%
Required degree grade 2:1

training
Salary
1st year (2001) £16,500
2nd year (2001) £18,000
Holiday entitlement
22 days
% of trainees with
a non-law degree p.a. **20%**

post-qualification
Salary (2001) **£29,000**
% of trainees offered job on qualification (2001) **100%**
% of assistants (as at 1/9/01) who joined as trainees **30%**
% of partners (as at 1/9/01) who joined as trainees **25%**

Lewis Silkin

12 Gough Square, London EC4A 3DW
Tel: (020) 7074 8000 Fax: (020) 7832 1200
Email: train@lewissilkin.com

firm profile
Lewis Silkin places the highest priority on its relationship with clients, excellent technical ability and the commercial thinking of its lawyers. As a result, it is a profitable and distinctive firm, with a friendly and lively style.

main areas of work
The firm has a wide range of corporate clients and provides services through four main departments: corporate, employment, litigation and property. The major work areas are: construction; corporate services, which includes company, commercial and corporate finance; commercial litigation and dispute resolution; employment; housing and project finance; marketing services, embracing advertising and marketing law; property; technology and communications, which includes IT, media and telecommunications.

trainee profile
The firm looks for trainees with keen minds and personality, who will fit into a professional but informal team. Law and non-law degrees considered.

training environment
Lewis Silkin provides a comprehensive induction and training programme, with practical 'hands-on' experience in four six month seats. At least three of these seats will be in one of the main departments. The fourth seat can be in one of the specialist areas. Trainees usually sit with a partner who can give ongoing feedback and guidance and progress is formally reviewed every three months. Trainees have the opportunity to get involved in the firm's social and marketing events and also to represent the firm at local trainee solicitors' groups and Law Centres.

benefits
Life assurance, critical illness cover, health insurance, season ticket loan, group pension plan.

vacation placements
Places for 2003: None.

sponsorship & awards
Full fees paid for LPC.

Partners 38
Assistant Solicitors 48
Total Trainees 13

contact
Ruth Willis
Head of Human Resources

method of application
Application form

selection procedure
Assessment day, including an interview with 2 partners & an analytical exercise

closing date for 2005
31 July 2003

application
Training contracts p.a. **6**
Applications p.a. **1,000**
Required degree grade **2:1**

training
Salary
1st year £26,000
2nd year £28,000
Holiday entitlement
25 days

post-qualification
Salary (2002) **£42,000**

Linklaters

One Silk Street, London EC2Y 8HQ
Tel: (020) 7456 2000 Fax: (020) 7456 2222
Email: graduate.recruitment@linklaters.com
Website: www.linklaters.com

firm profile
Linklaters advises the world's leading companies, financial institutions and governments on their most challenging transactions and assignments. With offices in major business and financial centres, it delivers an outstanding service to its clients anywhere in the world.

main areas of work
The firm's clients fall into three core areas of work: corporate, finance and projects, and commercial. Within these core areas, the firm has over 20 practices in which trainees have the opportunity to gain experience, such as M&A, capital markets, banking, projects, asset finance, real estate, litigation, intellectual property, EU and competition and tax.

trainee profile
Linklaters recruits those who enjoy challenges, are creative, have an ability to solve problems and strive to do the best work possible. In return trainees get the best training and opportunities. You benefit from working in a firm with a strong coaching and supportive ethos. You learn from working with colleagues at the top of their profession, from different cultures and countries. The firm's open door policy ensures that you are never left to fend for yourself because Linklaters prides itself on its strong teamwork both within the firm and with its clients.

training environment
You will have the opportunity to learn cutting-edge legal skills. You will also get a great insight into the firm's clients, whether they are FTSE 100 corporates or the global investment banks. You will learn about their businesses and how Linklaters helps them achieve their goals around the world. You may be asked to go on secondment to a client, or work in one of the international offices during your training. The firm is able to do this by giving you a seat plan, tailored to your specific strengths and interests, which is focused towards your qualification.

sponsorship & benefits
PgDL and LPC fees are paid in full, plus a maintenance grant of £4,500-£5,000 p.a. Personal Development Programme - 20% of salary paid for constructive time off (c. 6-12 months) after the LPC or on qualification. PPP medical insurance, life assurance, pension, season ticket loan, in-house gym and corporate membership of Holmes Place, in-house dentist, doctor and physio, 24 hour subsidised restaurant.

vacation placements
Places for 2003: 120 at Christmas, Easter and Summer. Opportunity for some summer students to spend some time in one of the European offices. Remuneration: £250 p.w.

Partners 490
Associates +1,500
Trainees +400
(Worldwide)

contact
Dominique Eisinger

method of application
Application form (available online)

selection procedure
2 interviews (same day)

application
Training contracts p.a. 150
Applications p.a. 2,500
% interviewed p.a. 20%
Required degree grade 2:1

training
Salary
1st year £28,500
2nd year £32,000
Holiday entitlement 25 days
% of trainees with a non-law degree p.a. 33%
No. of seats available abroad p.a. 90-100

post-qualification
Salary £50,000 + bonus
% of trainees retained on qualification Approx 90%

offices
Alicante, Amsterdam, Antwerp, Bangkok, Beijing, Berlin, Bratislava, Brussels, Bucharest, Budapest, Cologne, Frankfurt, Hong Kong, Lisbon, London, Luxembourg, Madrid, Malmö, Milan, Moscow, Munich, New York, Paris, Prague, Rome, São Paulo, Shanghai, Singapore, Stockholm, Tokyo, Warsaw

Linnells

Greyfriars Court, Paradise Square, Oxford OX1 1BB
Tel: (01865) 248607 Fax: (01865) 728445
Email: law@linnells.co.uk
Website: www.linnells.co.uk

firm profile
A progressive and expanding South East practice, specialising in property and commercial law. Areas of niche expertise include publishing, education, IT/e-commerce, ADR, asset finance litigation, construction, clinical negligence and charity law. Offers a highly personalised service for businesses and individuals.

main areas of work
Residential property/development 25%; commercial property 16%; corporate/commercial 24%; commercial dispute resolution 18%; private client 17%.

trainee profile
High achievers who are confident with good communication, writing and interpersonal skills as the firm's trainees are given early responsibility and interesting work, including meeting clients, preparing correspondence and attending court.

training environment
Trainees spend six months in four departments. Recent seats have included property/development; company/commercial; commercial litigation, media and technology; personal injury/clinical negligence; probate/tax/trusts. Supervision is given by departmental partners with regular appraisals. Trainees attend advocacy courses and other external and in-house training sessions. They are encouraged to give short presentations to internal teams to feedback knowledge gained on external courses, and to participate in the firm's staff and social committees. There are opportunities to be seconded to overseas firms and client in-house departments.

benefits
Social event subsidies; discounted legal services. Oxford is an attractive city, offering many social and cultural attractions, and just an hour from London. The firm has a lively sports and social programme.

vacation placements
Places for 2003: on application.

Partners	22
Assistant Solicitors	20
Total Trainees	6

contact
Lynn Ford
HR & Training Manager
(01865) 254250

method of application
Cover letter with application form (request via website)

selection procedure
Assessment centre followed by interviews with HR & Training Manager & two partners

closing date for 2005
31 July 2003

application
Training contracts p.a. 3
Applications p.a. 2,000
% interviewed p.a. 2%
Required degree grade 2:1

training
Salary:
1st year (2002) £16,000
2nd year (2002) £17,000
Holiday entitlement
20 days

post-qualification
Starting salary (2002)
£30,000
Holiday entitlement
22 days
% of trainees offered job on qualification (2002)
66%

Lovells

Atlantic House, Holborn Viaduct, London EC1A 2FG
Tel: (020) 7296 2000 Fax: (020) 7296 2001
Email: recruit@lovells.com
Website: www.lovells.com

firm profile
Lovells is one of the world's leading international law firms based in the City of London, with offices in Asia, Europe and North America. The firm's strength across a wide range of practice areas sets it apart from most of its competitors.

main areas of work
The firm's core areas of practice are corporate, litigation, commercial property and specialist groups (including EU/competition, intellectual property, media and telecommunications, employment, tax).

trainee profile
High calibre candidates who can demonstrate intelligence, lateral thinking, commercial awareness and personality.

training environment
Trainees spend six months in four different areas of the practice to gain as much experience as possible. They have the option of spending their third seat in an international office or on secondment to the in-house legal department of a major client. A comprehensive programme of skills training is run for trainees both in-house and externally, placing a particular emphasis on advocacy and communication. Trainees are offered as much responsibility as they can handle as well as regular reviews, six monthly appraisals and support when they need it.

benefits
PPP medical insurance, life assurance, PHI, season ticket loan, in-house gym, staff restaurant, in-house dentist, doctor and physiotherapist, discounts at local retailers.

vacation placements
Places for 2002: 90. Placements available at Christmas 2002 (closing date 15 November), Easter and Summer 2003 (closing date 14 February).

sponsorship & awards
CPE and LPC course fees are paid, and a maintenance grant is also provided of £5,000 for London, Guildford and Oxford and £4,500 elsewhere. In addition, £500 bonus on joining the firm; £1,000 advance in salary on joining; £500 prize for a First Class degree result.

Partners 336
Assistant Solicitors 800
Total Trainees 172

contact
Clare Harris
Recruitment Manager

method of application
Online application form

selection procedure
Assessment day: critical thinking test, group exercise, interview

closing date for 2005
31 August 2003

application
Training contracts p.a. **75**
Applications p.a. **1,500**
% interviewed p.a. **18%**
Required degree grade **2:1**

training
Salary
1st year (2002) £28,000
2nd year (2002) £32,000
Holiday entitlement
25 days
% of trainees with a non-law degree p.a. **40%**
No. of seats available abroad p.a. **18**

post-qualification
Salary
(2002) £50,000

international offices
Alicante, Amsterdam, Beijing, Berlin, Brussels, Budapest, Chicago, Düsseldorf, Frankfurt, Hamburg, Ho Chi Minh City, Hong Kong, London, Milan, Moscow, Munich, New York, Paris, Prague, Rome, Singapore, Tokyo, Vienna, Warsaw, Washington DC, Zagreb

Lupton Fawcett

Yorkshire House Greek Street Leeds LS1 5SX
Tel: (0113) 280 2000 Fax: (0113) 245 6782
Email: elizabeth.brown@luptonfawcett.com
Website: www.luptonfawcett.co.uk

Partners	29
Assistant Solicitors	31
Total Trainees	5

contact
Paul Forster
(0113) 280 2134 or
Liz Brown
(0113) 280 2251

method of application
Employer's application form & handwritten letter

selection procedure
Interviews & Assessment Days

closing date for 2005
31 July 2003

application
Training contracts p.a. 4
Applications p.a. 300
% interviewed p.a. 10
Required degree grade 2:1 preferred

training
Salary
Competitive with similar size/type firms
Holiday entitlement 20 days

post-qualification
Salary Competitive with similar size/type firms
% of trainees offered job on qualification 100%

firm profile

Lupton Fawcett is a well established yet dynamic and integrated practice. The firm offers a full range of legal services to both commercial and private clients alike on a quality-driven and client-led basis with the emphasis on providing first-class cost-effective and practical solutions which exceed the clients expectations. The firm was one of the first in Leeds to hold both Investors in People and the Law Society's Lexcel quality standard.

main areas of work

The commercial division offers the chance to gain experience in corporate, commercial property, employment, intellectual property, insolvency and commercial and chancery litigation. On the private client side, opportunities are available in financial services, trusts and probate, family and specialist personal injury. Further specialist areas of the firm include licensing and advocacy, IT and e-commerce, sports law, debt recovery and insurance litigation.

trainee profile

Although strong academic achievements are required, the firm places a high value on previous experience and interests which have developed commercial awareness, maturity and character. Trainees will also be able to demonstrate enthusiasm, confidence, good interpersonal and team skills, humour, initiative, commitment and common sense.

training environment

Training at Lupton Fawcett is normally split into four six month seats. Trainees office share with the partner or associate with whom they are working and are an integral part of the team, assuming a high degree of responsibility. Appraisals following each seat take place to ensure that progress is monitored effectively. A full in-house training program enables continual development as well as from training gained from excellent hands-on experience. Trainees will have the chance to meet clients and be responsible for their own work, as well as being involved in and actively encouraged to join in marketing and practice development initiatives. There is a full social programme in which the trainees are encouraged to participate as well as sporting events organised by the office and an excellent informal social culture.

benefits

Health insurance, season ticket loans, interest free loans towards LPC funding available by discussion with candidates.

Mace & Jones

19 Water Street, Liverpool L2 0RP
Tel: (0151) 236 8989 Fax: (0151) 227 5010
Email: donal.bannon@maceandjones.co.uk
14 Oxford Court, Bishopsgate, Manchester M2 3WQ
Tel: (0161) 236 2244 Fax: (0161) 228 7285
Website: www.maceandjones.co.uk

firm profile
Mace & Jones is a leading regional practice in the North West and remains a full service firm while enjoying a national reputation for its commercial expertise, especially in employment, litigation/insolvency, corporate and property. The firm's clients range from national and multinational companies and public sector bodies to owner managed businesses and private individuals, reflecting the broad nature of the work undertaken. Sound practical advice is given always on a value for money basis.

main areas of work
Commercial litigation/insolvency 15%; commercial property 15%; company/commercial 15%; employment 35%; personal injury/private client/family 20%.

trainee profile
The firm seeks to recruit highly motivated trainees with above average ability and the determination to succeed. The right calibre of trainee will assume responsibility early in their career. The firm provides a comprehensive internal and external training programme.

training environment
Trainees complete an induction course to familiarise themselves with the work carried out by the firm's main departments, administration and professional conduct. Training consists of four six month seats in the following departments: company/commercial, employment, commercial litigation/personal injury litigation, property law, family law. Strenuous efforts are made to ensure that trainees are able to select the training seat of their choice. A trainee will normally be required to share an office with a partner who will supervise their work and review the trainee's progress at the end of the seat. The PSC is taught externally. The firm operates an open door policy and has various social events.

Partners	34
Assistant Solicitors	43
Total Trainees	9

contact
Donal Bannon
Liverpool Office

method of application
Covering letter & typed CV which should indicate individual degree subject results

selection procedure
Interview with partners

closing date for 2005
31 March 2004

application
Training contracts p.a. **9**
Applications p.a. **1,500**
% interviewed p.a. **2%**
Required degree grade **2:1**

training
Salary
1st year (2001) **£13,000**
2nd year (2001) **£13,500**
Holiday entitlement
20 days
% of trainees with a non-law degree p.a. **40%**

post-qualification
Salary (2002) **Negotiable**
% of trainees offered job on qualification (2001) **100%**
% of assistants (as at 1/7/02) who joined as trainees **50%**
% of partners (as at 1/9/02) who joined as trainees **40%**

Macfarlanes

10 Norwich Street, London EC4A 1BD
Tel: (020) 7831 9222 Fax: (020) 7831 9607
Email: gradrec@macfarlanes.com
Website: www.macfarlanes.com

Partners	58
Assistant Solicitors	125
Total Trainees	38

contact
Graham Stoddart

firm profile
A leading City firm serving national and international commercial, industrial, financial and private clients.

method of application
Online via website

main areas of work
Corporate 49%; property 25%; litigation 13%; private client 13%.

selection procedure
Assessment day

trainee profile
Any degree discipline. Actual or predicted 2:1 or better.

closing date for 2005
31 July 2003

training environment
Macfarlanes divides the training contract into four six month periods. You will usually spend time in each of the firm's four main departments (corporate; litigation; property; private client). There is an extensive in-house training programme. Trainees have responsibility for real work and make a contribution that is acknowledged and appreciated.

application
Training contracts p.a. 25
Applications p.a. **1,500**
% interviewed p.a. 15%
Required degree grade **2:1**

training
Salary
1st year (2002) **£28,000**
2nd year (2002) **£32,000**
Holiday entitlement
21 days
% of trainees with a
non-law degree p.a. **40%**

benefits
21 working days holiday in each calendar year (rising to 26 days upon qualification); interest free season ticket loan; pension; free permanent health insurance*; free private medical insurance*; subsidised conveyancing; subsidised health club/gym membership; subsidised firm restaurant; subscription paid to the City of London Law Society or the London Trainee Solicitors' Group.

*After 12 months service.

post-qualification
Salary (2001) **£50,000**
% of trainees offered job on qualification (2001)
95%
% of assistants (as at 1/9/01) who joined as trainees **60%**
% of partners (as at 1/9/01) who joined as trainees **65%**

vacation placements
Places for 2003: 40; Duration: 2 weeks; Remuneration: £250 p.w.; Closing Date: 28 February 2003 but applications considered and places offered from the beginning of January 2003.

sponsorship & awards
CPE and LPC fees paid in full and a £5,000 maintenance allowance for courses studied in London, Guildford and Oxford and £4,500 for courses studied elsewhere. Prizes for those gaining distinction or commendation for the LPC.

Manches

Aldwych House, 81 Aldwych, London WC2B 4RP
Tel: (020) 7404 4433 Fax: (020) 7430 1133
Email: sheona.boldero@manches.co.uk
Website: www.manches.com

Partners	48
Assistant Solicitors	62
Total Trainees	20

firm profile
Manches is a highly focused London and Oxford-based commercial firm with strengths across a range of services and industry sectors. The firm's current strategy has seen a greater concentration and focus on the firm's core commercial industry sectors of technology, property and construction, while continuing to be market leaders in family law. The firm offers 10 trainee places each September.

main areas of work
Industry Sectors: Technology, property and construction.
Legal Groups: Corporate finance (emphasis in technology); commercial property; environment and planning; commercial litigation; construction; family; trusts and estates (Oxford office only); employment; intellectual property; information technology; biotechnology (Oxford office only).

trainee profile
Manches looks for candidates with a consistently good academic record who are enthusiastic, committed and with an outgoing engaging personality. They should display a strong sense of commercial awareness, the ability to think for themselves and excellent interpersonal/social skills.

training environment
The firm provides high quality, individual training. Trainees generally sit in four different seats for six months at a time (one of which is usually in a niche practice area). The firm's comprehensive in-house training programme enables them to take responsibility from an early stage, ensuring that they become confident and competent solicitors. Trainees have the opportunity to actively participate in departmental meetings and briefings and receive regular appraisals on their progress.

benefits
Season ticket loan, BUPA after six months, permanent health insurance, life insurance, pension after three months.

vacation placements
Places for 2003: 24 approx.; Duration: 1 week; Remuneration: Under review.; Closing Date: 31 January 2003.

sponsorship & awards
CPE/PgDL and LPC fees are paid in full together with an annual maintenance allowance (currently £4,000 p.a. - under review).

contact
Sheona Boldero
Tel: (020) 7872 8690
(Graduate Recruitment line)

method of application
Application form

selection procedure
Interview with 2 partners. Possible second interview & assessments

closing date for 2005
31 July 2003

application
Training contracts p.a. **10**
Applications p.a. **1,000**
% interviewed p.a. **5%**
Required degree grade **2:1**

training
Salary (Under review)
1st year (2002)
London **£26,500**
2nd year (2002)
London **£30,000**
Holiday entitlement
22 days

post-qualification
Salary (Under review)
London **£40,250 (2002)**
% of trainees offered job on qualification (2002)
70%

Martineau Johnson

St. Philips House, St. Philips Place, Birmingham B3 2PP
Tel: (0121) 678 1418 Fax: (0121) 633 7433
Email: emily.dean@martjohn.co.uk
Website: www.graduates4law.co.uk

firm profile
Martineau Johnson combines a dynamic and commercial approach with a traditional and caring attitude. It is set to move to the most prestigious offices in Birmingham city centre, where there will be room for the expansion planned by the firm and where staff will benefit from the latest working methods. And it also has growth plans for its London office too. Its vision is built on matching legal know-how to clients' needs through building partnerships with them and based on detailed understanding and knowledge of their businesses.

main areas of work
Corporate 15%; property 16%; litigation 19%; private client 14%; education, employment and pensions 11%; intellectual property 7%; banking and insolvency 9%; trade and energy 9%.

trainee profile
Trainees are vital to Martineau Johnson's future and no effort is spared to give the best possible experience and support to them, whilst treating them as individuals. There is a very high retention rate at the end of training contracts, when trainees are generally offered roles in their preferred departments and specialisms.

training environment
Martineau Johnson's aim is to work in partnership with trainees, providing them with mentoring, supervision, support and an exposure to the key areas of the firm's practice. Trainees are actively encouraged to be an integral part of the team delivering legal solutions to its clients whilst benefiting from quality work, flexible seat rotation in a small and friendly team environment. Generally, the firm's trainees are given experience in four main areas – education/private client, commercial litigation, commercial property and corporate – and they are then given the opportunity to carry out further work in areas of their choice and specialism, which are outside the 'core' areas. There are opportunities for Birmingham-based trainees to be exposed to the London scene. Trainees benefit from a structured career training programme tailored to their personal development needs – and it covers not only legal technical matters, but also a business and commercial approach which have never been more central to successful professional careers. In giving training and offering experience that matches the best city firms, Martineau Johnson offers a rare opportunity for trainees to lay great foundations for their legal career in a fast moving, ever changing but caring environment.

Partners 46
Assistant Solicitors 110
Total Trainees 25

contact
Emily Dean

method of application
Online application form
www.graduates4law.co.uk

selection procedure
Assessment centre - half day

closing date for 2005
31 July 2003

application
Training contracts p.a. 14
Applications p.a. 500
% interviewed p.a. 10%
Required degree grade 2:1

training
Salary
1st year (2002) £18,000
2nd year (2002) £19,500
Holiday entitlement
23 days
% of trainees with a non-law degree (2002) 40%

post-qualification
Salary (2002) £33,000
% of trainees offered job on qualification (2002) 90%
% of assistants (as at 1/9/02) who joined as trainees 66%
% of partners (as at 1/9/02) who joined as trainees 42%

Masons

30 Aylesbury Street, London EC1R 0ER
Tel: (020) 7490 4000 Fax: (020) 7490 2545
Email: graduate.recruitment@masons.com
Website: www.masons.com and www.out-law.com

firm profile
Masons is one of the most highly regarded specialist law firms in Europe and the Asia Pacific region. The firm's aim is to be recognised as pre-eminent advisers providing a complete range of legal services to businesses operating in the construction and engineering, projects, energy and infrastructure industries and to users and suppliers of information and technology.

main areas of work
Masons provides a complete legal service to clients operating in the construction and engineering, projects, energy and infrastructure industries and to users and suppliers of information and technology. Its lawyers provide a comprehensive service in these sectors, as well as to other clients, in the areas of: capital projects; commercial property and development, construction and engineering; corporate and commercial, e-commerce/new media; employment, data protection, dispute resolution (property and commercial), environment, facilities management, freedom of information; health and safety; information technology, insolvency, pensions, planning, project finance and taxation.

trainee profile
Applications are welcome from both law and non-law students with a minimum 2:1 degree and 24 UCAS points. Please apply online at www.masons.com/graduaterecruitment.

training environment
After induction, your two year training contract will be divided into a number of 'seats'. Each seat will involve sharing an office with a partner or solicitor selected from one of the practice areas outlined above. Your rotation throughout the firm will ensure that you are exposed to a range of areas of law and to a variety of approaches. Wherever possible the firm tries to tailor the arrangement to meet individual needs.

benefits
Life assurance, private health care (all offices), subsidised restaurant and season ticket loan (London).

vacation placements
Places for 2002: Approx 18 in London, approx 5 in Manchester; Duration: 2 weeks between mid-June and the end of August; Closing Date: 21 February 2003.

sponsorship & awards
Fees are paid for CPE and LPC courses and maintenance grants.

Partners 98
Assistant Solicitors 230
Total Trainees 62
denotes worldwide figures

contact
Julie Lester

method of application
Apply online EAF

selection procedure
Assessment day & an interview

closing date for 2005
31 July 2003

application
Training contracts p.a. 18
Applications p.a. **1,800**
% interviewed p.a. 5%
Required degree grade **2:1**

training
Salary
£26,000-£30,000 in London. Please note that salaries & benefits vary throughout UK offices
Holiday entitlement
23 days (1st year), 24 days (2nd year)

post-qualification
Salary £47,000 in London

overseas offices
Brussels, Dublin, Guangzhou (PRC), Hong Kong, Singapore

UK offices
Bristol, Edinburgh (LSS), Glasgow (LSS), Leeds, London, Manchester

Mayer, Brown, Rowe & Maw

11 Pilgrim Street, London EC4V 6RW
Tel: (020) 7248 4282 Fax: (020) 7782 8790
Email: london@eu.mayerbrownrowe.com
Website: www.mayerbrownrowe.com

firm profile
Mayer, Brown, Rowe & Maw is the tenth largest law firm in the world, both in terms of number of lawyers and turnover (£400m). The firm has a reputation for delivering pragmatic commercial advice, and is praised for its professionalism. Mayer, Brown, Rowe & Maw has 13 offices worldwide, including representation in the world's major financial centres: London, Paris, Frankfurt and New York.

main areas of work
Construction; competition and trade; corporate and securities; employment; environment; finance and banking; insurance and reinsurance; intellectual property; litigation and arbitration; oil and gas; pensions; real estate; regulated industries; securitisation and tax.

trainee profile
The firm is interested in motivated students with a good academic record and a strong commitment to law. Commercial awareness gained through legal or business work experience is an advantage.

training environment
If you are looking for a leading international law firm that offers exposure to a multitude of blue chip companies and a wide range of international work, combined with the confidence of knowing you have a place in its future, the firm would like to hear from you. Trainees will participate in a lively, energetic and positive business culture, spending time in four six-month seats including the corporate and litigation departments. The firm's culture of getting immersed in a client's business means that there are excellent secondment opportunities. In addition to the Professional Skills Course, the firm offers an individual professional development and training programme. Three monthly apppraisals assist trainees in reaching their true potential.

benefits
Benefits include 25 days holiday per annum, interest free season ticket loan, subsidised sports club membership and private health scheme.

vacation placements
Places for 2003: 25; Duration: 2 weeks during Easter and summer vacations. Experience in two of the principal work groups plus a programme of seminars, visits and social events.

sponsorship & awards
CPE and LPC fees, plus a maintenance grant of £4,500 (£5,000 for London and Guildford).

Partners 91
Assistant Solicitors 300+
Total Trainees 48

contact
Sophie Wood

method of application
Online application form

selection procedure
Selection workshops including an interview, a business analysis exercise & a group exercise

closing date for 2005
31 July 2003

application
Training contracts p.a. **Approx 25-30**
Applications p.a. **1,000**
% interviewed p.a. **7%**
Required degree grade **2:1**

training
Starting salary (2002) **£28,000**
Holiday entitlement **25 days**
% of trainees with a non-law degree p.a. **50%**
No. of seats available abroad p.a. **2**

post-qualification
Salary (2002) **£50,000**
% of trainees offered job on qualification (2002) **85%**
% of partners who joined as trainees **35%**

overseas offices
Brussels, Charlotte, Chicago, Cologne, Frankfurt, Houston, London, Los Angeles, Manchester, New York, Palo Alto, Paris, Washington DC

McCormicks

Britannia Chambers, 4 Oxford Place, Leeds LS1 3AX
Tel: (0113) 246 0622 Fax: (0113) 246 7488
Wharfedale House 37 East Parade Harrogate HG1 5LQ
Tel: (01423) 530630 Fax: (01423) 530709
Email: enquiries@mccormicks-solicitors.com
Website: www.mccormicks-solicitors.com

firm profile
McCormicks is a unique legal practice at the heart of a vibrant commercial region. With core traditional values of integrity, technical excellence and hard work, the firm is committed to deliver an unrivalled quality of service and innovation to its clients and quality of life to its people. McCormicks combines the full range and depth of skills across its entire practice with the firm's renowned fearlessness and ability to punch above its weight in order to deliver the best possible result.

main areas of work
With a diverse range of clients from private individuals to high profile international organisations its work is never dull. Trainees are exposed to all its practice areas including sports law, media and entertainment law, corporate and commercial, commercial property, commercial litigation, charity work, family, clinical negligence, corporate crime, insolvency and intellectual property.

trainee profile
Intellectual achievement, ambition, a sense of humour and commitment to hard work are crucial qualities of a McCormicks trainee. The firm will challenge you but support you at every step of the way.

training environment
Trainees are assigned to one of five departments and supervised throughout by a mentor. The firm's training work will develop skills, knowledge and ambition within a friendly, progressive and supportive environment. Your development will be reviewed regularly by the mentor, team supervisor and the training partner. There is an open door policy and a great team spirit.

vacation placements
Places for 2003: Available in summer vacation. Closing Date: Application forms by 28 February 2003.

Partners 12
Assistant Solicitors 12
Total Trainees 7

contact
Linda Jackson

method of application
Application form

selection procedure
Selection day & interview with Training Partner

closing date for 2005
31 July 2003

application
Training contracts p.a. **4**
Applications p.a. **1,000**
% interviewed p.a. **10%**
Required degree grade **2:1**

training
Salary
1st year (2001)
Highly competitive

post-qualification
Salary (2001)
Highly competitive
% of trainees offered job on qualification (2001)
50%
% of partners (as at 1/9/99) who joined as trainees
60%

McDermott, Will & Emery

7 Bishopsgate, London EC2N 3AR
Tel: (020) 7577 6900 Fax: (020) 7577 6950
Website: www.mwe.com/london
Email: graduate.recruitment@europe.mwe.com

Partners	532*
	21 (London)
Associate Lawyers &	
Other Fee-earners	375*
	49 (London)
Total Trainees	2 in 2001
	5 in 2003

*denotes worldwide figures

method of application
CV & covering letter

closing date for 2005
31 August 2003

training
Salary
1st year (2002) £30,000

firm profile
McDermott, Will & Emery is a leading international law firm with offices in Boston, Chicago, Düsseldorf, London, Los Angeles, Miami, Munich, New York, Orange County, Silicon Valley and Washington, DC. The firm's client base includes some of the world's leading financial institutions, largest corporations, mid-cap businesses, and individuals. The firm represents more than 75 of the companies in the Fortune 100 in addition to clients in the FTSE 100 and FTSE 250. Rated as one of the leading firms in The American Lawyer's Top 100, by a number of indicators, including gross revenues and profits per Partner.
London Office: The London office was founded less than four years ago. It is already recognised as being in the top 10 of the 100 US law firms operating in London by the legal media and has grown to more than 70 lawyers in total, almost all of whom are English-qualified. The firm provides business oriented legal advice to multinational and national corporates, financial institutions, investment banks and private clients. Most of the firm's partners were head of practice at their former firms and are recognised as leaders in their respective fields by the most respected professional directories and market commentators.

main areas of work
Banking and finance; corporate, including international corporate finance and M&A; EU/competition; employment; IP, IT and e-business; litigation and arbitration; pensions and employee benefits; taxation; telecoms and US securities. London is the hub for the firm's European expansions. The firm opened its continental European offices in January 2002 in Munich, Düsseldorf in September 2002 and more will follow.

trainee profile
The firm is looking for the brightest, best and most entrepreneurial trainees. You will need to convince the firm that you have made a deliberate choice.

training environment
The primary focus is to provide a practical foundation for your career with the firm. You will experience between four and six seats over the two year period and the deliberately small number of trainees means that the firm is able to provide a degree of flexibility in tailoring seats to the individual. Trainees get regular support and regular feedback.

benefits
Private medical and dental insurance, life assurance, permanent health insurance, season ticket loan, subsidised gym membership, employee assistance programme.

sponsorship & awards
CPE and LPC funding and mainenance grant.

McDermott, Will & Emery

Mills & Reeve

112 Hills Road, Cambridge CB2 1PH
Tel: (01223) 222336 Fax: (01223) 335848
Email: graduate.recruitment@mills-reeve.com
Website: www.mills-reeve.com

firm profile
Mills & Reeve is one of the largest UK commercial law firms and works for a range of household names. It operates throughout England and Wales from offices in Birmingham, Cambridge, London and Norwich.

main areas of work
The firm offers a full range of corporate, commercial, property, litigation and private client services to a mix of regional and national businesses. The firm is a regional leader in corporate and commercial work and a national specialist in the insurance, higher education, health, agriculture and hi-tech and bio-tech industries.

trainee profile
The firm seeks trainees with a strong academic background, maturity, energy and initiative. Strong candidates will be willing to accept responsibility and drive the business forward.

training environment
Trainees are based in the Birmingham, Cambridge or Norwich office. The firm seeks to give its trainees experience in a broad range of practice areas, in as many different parts of the business as possible. Subject to the overriding needs of the business, the firm seeks to ensure that its trainees undertake seats in the work areas in which they are most interested. The firm is happy for those trainees with a desire to undertake a seat not practised in their base office to temporarily move to another office, including London, and supports the move with an accommodation allowance. During each seat, trainees sit with a partner or experienced solicitor and their performance is reviewed via a mix of formal and informal appraisals. Staff at all levels are friendly and approachable and excellent support services allow trainees to concentrate on high quality work. A full induction integrates trainees quickly into the firm and ongoing in-house lectures and training by Professional Support Lawyers support the PSC.

benefits
Life assurance at two times pensionable salary, a contributory pension scheme and 25 days holiday.

vacation placements
Applications for two week placements during the summer must be received by 1 March.

sponsorship & awards
The firm pays the full costs of the LPC fees and offers a maintenance grant for the LPC year. Funding for the CPE is discretionary.

Partners 60
Assistant Solicitors 176
Total Trainees 37

contact
Graduate Recruitment

method of application
Firm's application form

selection procedure
Normally one day assessment centre

closing date for 2005
15 August 2003 for training contracts
1st March 2003 for work placements

application
Training contracts p.a. 20-25
Applications p.a. Approx 500
% interviewed p.a. 13%
Required degree grade 2:1

training
Salary
1st year (2002) £17,000
2nd year (2002) £18,000
Holiday entitlement 25 days p.a.
% of trainees with a non-law degree 26%

post-qualification
Salary (2002) £31,500-£32,500
% of trainees offered job on qualification 93%
% of assistants (as at 1/9/02) who joined as trainees 48%
% of partners (as at 1/9/01) who joined as trainees 28%

Mishcon de Reya

Summit House, 12 Red Lion Square, London WDC1R 4QD
Tel: (020) 7440 7198 Fax: (020) 7404 5982
Email: graduate.recruitment@mishcon.co.uk
Website: www.mishcon.co.uk

firm profile
Mishcon de Reya is an unconventional commercial law firm, run by lawyers who understand business. It is an energetic and innovative practice committed to providing intelligent and creative legal advice.

main areas of work
Organised internally into litigation (32%), corporate and commercial (32%), property (27%) and family (9%) departments, the firm has also developed specialist groups to meet the demands and opportunities of a constantly evolving commercial world

trainee profile
Those who read nothing but law books are probably not the right trainees for this firm. The firm wants people who can meet the highest intellectual and business standards, while maintaining outside interests. Candidates should be cheerful, enterprising and ambitious – they should see themselves as future partners.

training environment
Trainees have four six month seats. Three of these are usually in the litigation, property and company commercial departments, with an opportunity to specialise in the fourth seat. Trainees share a room with an assistant solicitor or a partner and the firm style is friendly and informal. Computer literacy is encouraged and access to online legal and business databases is available. Trainees are encouraged to participate in voluntary work at Law Centres.

benefits
Medical cover, subsidised gym membership, season ticket loan, permanent health insurance, life assurance and pension

vacation placements
Places for 2003:12; Duration: 2 weeks; Expenses: £200 p.w.; Closing Date: 17 March 2003.

sponsorship & awards
CPE and LPC funding with bursary.

Partners 36
Assistant Solicitors 37
Total Trainees 16

contact
Human Resources Department

method of application
Application form

closing date for 2005
31 July 2003

application
Training contracts p.a. **8**
Applications p.a. **800+**
% interviewed p.a. **6%**
Required degree grade **2:1**

training
Salary
1st year **£25,000**
2nd year **£27,000**
Holiday entitlement
25 days p.a.
No. of seats available abroad p.a. **Occasional** secondments available

post-qualification
% of trainees retained 2001 **75%**
% of assistants who joined as trainees **46%**
% of partners (as at 1/8/01) who joined as trainees **19%**

Morgan Cole

Buxton Court, 3 West Way, Oxford OX2 0SZ
Tel: (01865) 262699 Fax: (01865) 262670
Email: recruitment@morgan-cole.com
Website: www.morgan-cole.com

Partners	83
Lawyers	261
Total Trainees	36

contact
Guy Constant
Training Principal

method of application
Apply online at
www.morgan-cole.com/careers

selection procedure
Assessment Centre & interview

closing date for 2005
31 July 2003

application
Required degree grade
Preferably 2:1

training
Salary
1st & 2nd year (2002)
Competitive for the London, Thames Valley and South Wales regions which are reviewed annually in line with market trends

other offices
Cardiff, Croydon, London, Reading, Swansea

firm profile
Morgan Cole is one of the leading commercial law practices in the country, providing a comprehensive service to both individual and corporate clients in both the public and private sectors. The firm has a reputation for excellence and therefore attracts the highest quality of staff from all fields. The firm enjoys strong connections throughout the UK and the USA and is a founder member of the Association of European Lawyers, one of five leading UK law firms responsible for establishing a network of English speaking lawyers throughout Europe. The firm's areas of work are acquisitions and disposals; commercial; corporate finance; employment; energy, European and competition; information technology; insolvency; intellectual property; joint ventures; management buyouts and buyins; PFI; sports law; agricultural and commercial property; construction; environment/planning/health and safety; medical negligence; personal injury; professional indemnity; commercial litigation; licensing; family; alternate dispute resolution. As a modern practice, it strives to meet the legal needs of clients in all sectors of industry and commerce.

trainee profile
Successful candidates should be commercially aware, self motivated individuals with drive and initiative who are able to apply a logical and common-sense approach to solving client problems. The firm is seeking applications from graduates/undergraduates in both law and non-law subjects, preferably with at least a 2:1 degree.

training environment
Trainees spend not less than six months in at least three different divisions, and since each division handles a wide variety of work within its constituent teams, there is no danger of over-specialisation. Trainees also have the opportunity to be seconded to some of the firm's major clients for one of their business services seats.

open days
Six in total: two in London, two in Oxford and two in Cardiff. Applications to be made online before 31 March 2003.

sponsorship & awards
The firm offers full funding of fees for attendance on the CPE/PgDL and LPC as well as making a contribution towards maintenance.

Nabarro Nathanson

Lacon House, Theobald's Road, London WC1X 8RW
Tel: (0800) 056 4021 Fax: (020) 7524 6324
Email: graduateinfo@nabarro.com
Website: www.nabarro.com

firm profile
One of the UK's leading commercial law firms with offices in London, Reading and Sheffield. The firm is known for having an open but highly professional culture and expects its lawyers to have a life outside work.

main areas of work
Company and commercial law; commercial property; planning; pensions and employment; corporate finance; IP/IT; commercial litigation; construction; PFI; environmental law.

trainee profile
Nabarro Nathanson welcomes applications from law and non law undergraduates. Candidates will usually be expecting a minimum 2:1 degree. As well as strong intellectual ability graduates need exceptional qualities. These include: enthusiasm, drive and initiative, common sense, strong interpersonal skills and teamworking skills.

training environment
Trainees undertake six four-month seats which ensures maximum exposure to the firm's core practice areas (company commercial, commercial property and litigation). The firm aims to retain all trainees on qualification. In addition to the core seats, trainees have the opportunity to gain further experience by spending time in specialist areas (eg pensions, IP/IT, tax, employment), possibly in Germany or Brussels, or completing a further seat in a core area. In most cases trainees will return to the seat they wish to qualify into for the remaining four months of their contract. This ensures a smooth transition from trainee to qualified solicitor.

benefits
Trainees are given private medical insurance, pension, 25 days holiday entitlement per annum, a season ticket loan, access to a subsidised restaurant and subsidised corporate gym membership. Trainee salaries are reviewed annually.

vacation placements
Places for 2003: 60; Duration: 3 weeks between mid-June and end of August; Closing Date: 28 February 2003.

sponsorship & awards
Full fees paid for CPE and LPC and a maintenance grant (London and Guildford: £5,000; elsewhere: £4,500).

Partners 107
Assistant Solicitors 219
Total Trainees 63

contact
Sally Bridges

method of application
Application form

selection procedure
Interview & assessment day

closing date for 2005
31 July 2003

application
Training contracts p.a. **30**
Applications p.a. **1,500**
Required degree grade **2:1**

training
Salary
1st year (2002)
London & Reading **£28,000**
Sheffield **£20,000**
2nd year (2002)
London & Reading **£32,000**
Sheffield **£22,000**
Holiday entitlement
25 days

post-qualification
Salary (2002)
London **£48,000**
Sheffield **£31,000**
(reviewed annually)

overseas offices
Brussels

Nicholson Graham & Jones

110 Cannon Street, London EC4N 6AR
Tel: (020) 7648 9000 Fax: (020) 7648 9001
Email: info@ngj.co.uk
Website: www.ngj.co.uk

firm profile
A successful mid-sized practice, offering strength across a number of key disciplines to a broad range of corporate clients.

main areas of work
Company; commercial; litigation; property; construction and engineering; banking and insolvency; private client; intellectual property; planning and environmental; employment; sport; travel.

trainee profile
The firm recruits both law and non-law graduates with strong academic backgrounds and a practical approach.

training environment
Training is broad-based with six months in each of the main departments: company/commercial, litigation and property and a six month seat of your choice. The emphasis is on-the-job training with personal supervision from partners. There is also a comprehensive induction and in-house training programnme for each department and on a firmwide basis. The firm encourages individual development through early responsibility and client contact. Trainees participate in all activities including business development and marketing. The atmosphere is genuinely friendly and supportive and trainees' contributions are valued.

benefits
Life assurance, season ticket loan, subsidised gym membership, BUPA, 25 days holiday a year, salaries reviewed every year.

vacation placements
Eight 2 week placements during July 2003; Remuneration: £210 p.w.; Closing Date: 10 March 2003.

sponsorship & awards
CPE and LPC fees paid in full plus £4,000 maintenance allowance for each (2002).

Partners 52
Assistant Solicitors 61
Total Trainees 19

contact
Tina Two

method of application
Application form

selection procedure
Interview & assessment

closing date for 2005
31 July 2003

application
Training contracts p.a. **10**
Applications p.a. **1,000**
% interviewed p.a. **10%**
Required degree grade **2:1**

training
Salary
1st year (2002) **£28,000**
2nd year (2002) **£31,000**
Holiday entitlement
25 days
% of trainees with a
non-law degree p.a. **Varies**

post-qualification
Salary (2000) **£48,000**
% of trainees offered job
on qualification (2002)
100%

overseas offices
Brussels

Norton Rose

Kempson House, Camomile Street, London EC3A 7AN
Tel: (020) 7283 6000 Fax: (020) 7283 6500
Email: grad.recruitment@nortonrose.com
Website: www.nortonrose.com

firm profile
A leading City and international law firm specialising in large-scale corporate and financial transactions. Strong in asset, project and ship finance. More than two thirds of the firm's work has an international element.

main areas of work
Corporate finance; banking; litigation; property, planning and environmental; taxation; competition; employment, pensions and incentives; intellectual property and technology.

trainee profile
Successful candidates will be commercially aware, focused, ambitious and team-orientated. High intellect and international awareness are a priority, and language skills are appreciated.

training environment
Norton Rose's seat system is innovative. In the first 16 months of the 24 month training contract, trainees will have a seat in each of the core departments of banking, commercial litigation and corporate finance, plus one in a more specialist area. The remaining time can be spent in one of three ways: all eight months in one chosen seat; or four months in one department and four months in the department in which they want to qualify; or four months abroad and four in their chosen department. In-the-field experience is considered as important as formal training at Norton Rose, and trainees are expected to learn by observing experienced lawyers at work, interacting with clients and solicitors, handling sensitive issues and organising their time as well as attending external courses. Internal competition among trainees is discouraged, as great store is placed on team-working.

benefits
Life assurance (21+), private health insurance (optional), season ticket loan, subsidised gym membership.

vacation placements
Places for 2003: 45 Summer, 15 Christmas; Duration: Summer: Three weeks, Christmas: Two weeks; Remuneration: £250 p.w.; Closing Date: 31 January 2003 for Summer, 1 November 2002 for Christmas. Five or six open days per year are also held.

sponsorship & awards
£1,000 travel scholarship, £800 loan on arrival, four weeks unpaid leave on qualification.

Partners 206*
Assistant Solicitors 600*
Total Trainees 120
* denotes worldwide figures

contact
Brendan Monaghan

method of application
Employer's application form

selection procedure
Interview & group exercise

closing date for 2005
1 August 2003

application
Training contracts p.a. **80-90**
Applications p.a. **2,500+**
% interviewed p.a. **10%**
Required degree grade **2:1**

training
Salary
1st year (2002) **£28,500**
2nd year (2002) **£32,000**
Holiday entitlement **25 days**
% of trainees with a non-law degree p.a. **40%**
No. of seats available abroad p.a. **15 (per seat move)**

post-qualification
Salary (2002) **£50,000**
% of trainees offered job on qualification (2002) **97%**

overseas offices
Amsterdam, Athens, Bahrain, Bangkok, Beijing,* Brussels, Cologne, Frankfurt, Greece, Hong Kong, Jakarta,* London, Milan, Moscow, Munich, Paris, Piraeus, Prague,* Singapore, Warsaw
* Associated office

Olswang

90 Long Acre, London WC2E 9TT
Tel: (020) 7208 8888 Fax: (020) 7208 8800
Email: ecp@olswang.com
Website: www.olswang.com

firm profile
Forward thinking and progressive, Olswang is about realising the potential of its clients, of all of its people and the potential within every situation in which its clients find themselves. The firm's aim is simple. To be the preferred law firm of leading companies in the technology, media and telecommunications sectors. Olswang knows the players, knows the business and above all, understands the issues. This has brought rapid growth. Olswang is a 450+ strong team committed to providing innovative solutions through legal excellence.

main areas of work
Advertising; banking; bio-sciences; commercial litigation; corporate and commercial; defamation; e-commerce; employment; EU and competition; film and TV (finance / production); information technology; intellectual property; music; private equity; property; sponsorship; sport; tax; telecommunications; TV/broadcasting.

trainee profile
Being a trainee at Olswang is both demanding and rewarding. The firm is interested in hearing from individuals with a 2:1 degree and above, exceptional drive and relevant commercial experience. In addition, it is absolutely critical that trainees fit well into the Olswang environment which is challenging, busy, energetic, individualistic, meritocratic and fun.

training environment
Olswang wants to help trainees match their expectations and needs with those of the firm. Training consists of four six month seats in the company, media and communications, litigation or property groups. You will be assigned a mentor, usually a partner, to assist and advise you throughout your training contract. In-house lectures supplement general training and six monthly appraisals assess development. Regular social events with the other trainees not only encourage strong relationship building but adds to the fun of work.

benefits
After six months: pension contributions, medical cover, life cover, dental scheme, season ticket loan, subsidised gym membership. After 12 months: PHI.

vacation placements
Places for 2003: June, July, August; Duration: 2 weeks; Remuneration: £250 p.w.; 15 students per scheme; Closing Date: 1 March 2003.

Partners: 58
Assistant Solicitors: 117
Total Trainees: 43

contact
Emma Price
Graduate Recruitment & Training Manager

method of application
CV & covering letter

selection procedure
Business case scenario, interview, psychometric test

closing date for 2005
28 July 2003

application
Training contracts p.a.
Up to 20
Applications p.a. **1,500**
% interviewed p.a. **6%**
Required degree grade **2:1**

training
Salary:
1st year (2002) £26,500
2nd year (2002) £30,000
Holiday entitlement
24 days
% of trainees with a non-law degree p.a. 33%

post-qualification
Salary (2002) £46,000

overseas offices
Brussels

Osborne Clarke

2 Temple Back East, Temple Quay, Bristol BS1 6EG
26 Old Bailey, London EC4M 7HW
Apex Plaza, Forbury Road, Reading RG1 1AX
Tel: (0117) 302 7178
Email: recruitment@osborneclarke.com
Website: www.osborneclarke.com

firm profile
Osborne Clarke will challenge your preconceptions about law firms. Described by its clients as dynamic, informal, straightforward and professional, the culture of the firm sets it apart from others as a great place to work. With around 500 lawyers spread around London, Bristol, Reading, Cologne, Frankfurt and Silicon Valley, USA, the firm has more than doubled its size in three years. In addition its close alliance of firms across Europe - Osborne Clarke Alliance - and its presence in Silicon Valley gives the firm an extensive international reach.

main areas of work
Corporate (corporate finance, mergers and acquisitions, venture capital), technology, media and telecoms, banking, real estate and construction, commercial, employment, pensions and incentives, litigation, tax.

trainee profile
Take it as read that candidates should have intelligence, commercial focus and strong communication skills. To succeed at Osborne Clarke they should also be down to earth, open minded and able to think outside the box.

training environment
Trainees can expect early responsibility. The firm takes an individual approach to ensure training is relevant to each trainee and offers a well structured programme. Trainees are encouraged to spend time in at least two of the firm's UK offices, in addition to which international opportunities in Europe and the US and client secondments are available.

benefits
Holiday entitlement of 25 days, employer's pension contributions, private healthcare cover, season ticket loan, permanent health insurance, group life assurance cover.

vacation placements
Places for 2003: 25-30 1 week placements during Easter or summer; Closing Date: 31 January 2003; Remuneration: £175-200 p.w. depending on location.

sponsorship & awards
CPE: Course fees paid plus maintenance grant of £3,000. LPC: Course fees paid and maintenance grant of £3,000. Some conditions apply.

Partners	113
Solicitors	250
Trainee Solicitors	55
Total Staff	880

contact
Graduate Recruitment Team

method of application
Employer's application form. Available on request or through the firm's website www.oc4jobs.com

selection procedure
Individual interviews, group exercises, selection testing

closing date for 2005
31 July 2003

application
Training contracts p.a. 25-30
Applications p.a. 1,000-1,200
% interviewed p.a. 10%
Required degree grade 2:1 preferred

training
Salary (2002)
1st year £25,000 London & Thames Valley, £19,000 Bristol
Holiday entitlement 25 days
% of trainees with a non-law degree p.a. Approx 40%
No. of seats available abroad p.a. 6

post-qualification
Salary (2002)
£34,000 Bristol, £47,500 London, £43,000 Thames Valley
% of trainees offered job on qualification (2001) 89%

overseas offices
Barcelona, Brussels, Cologne, Copenhagen, Frankfurt, Helsinki, Madrid, Paris, Rotterdam, St Petersburg, Silicon Valley, Tallinn

Pannone & Partners

123 Deansgate, Manchester M3 2BU
Tel: (0161) 909 3000 Fax: (0161) 909 4444
Email: julia.jessop@pannone.co.uk
Website: www.pannone.com

firm profile
A high profile Manchester firm continuing to undergo rapid growth. The firm prides itself on offering a full range of legal services to a diverse client base which is split almost equally between personal and commercial clients. The firm was the first to be awarded the quality standard ISO 9001 and is a founder member of Pannone Law Group – Europe's first integrated international law group.

main areas of work
Commercial litigation 16%; personal injury 29%; corporate 11%; commercial property 7%; family 10%; clinical negligence 9%; private client 11%; employment 4%.

trainee profile
Selection criteria include a high level of academic achievement, teamwork, organisation and communication skills, a wide range of interests and a connection with the North West.

training environment
An induction course helps trainees adjust to working life, and covers the firm's quality procedures and good practice. Regular trainee seminars cover the work of other departments within the firm, legal developments and practice. Additional departmental training sessions focus in more detail on legal and procedural matters in that department. Four seats of six months are spent in various departments and trainees' progress is monitored regularly. Trainees have easy access to support and guidance on any matters of concern. Work is tackled with gusto here, but so are the many social gatherings that take place.

vacation placements
Places for 2003: 50; Duration: 1 week; Remuneration: None; Closing Date: 28 February 2003.

sponsorship & awards
LPC fees paid.

Partners 63
Assistant Solicitors 67
Total Trainees 16

contact
Julia Jessop

method of application
Application form & CV

selection procedure
Individual interview, second interview comprises a tour of the firm & informal lunch

closing date for 2005
1 August 2003

application
Training contracts p.a. **8**
Applications p.a. **650**
% interviewed p.a. **9%**
Required degree grade **2:2**

training
Salary
1st year (2002) **£17,000**
2nd year (2002) **£19,000**
Holiday entitlement
20 days
% of trainees with a non-law degree p.a. **30%**

post-qualification
Salary (2002) **£29,000**
% of trainees offered job on qualification (2002) **70%**
% of assistants who joined as trainees **35%**
% of partners who joined as trainees **33%**

Payne Hicks Beach

10 New Square, Lincoln's Inn, London WC2A 3QG
Tel: (020) 7465 4300 Fax: (020) 7465 4400
Email: apalmer@paynehicksbeach.co.uk
Website: www.paynehicksbeach.co.uk

firm profile
Payne Hicks Beach is a medium-sized firm based in Lincoln's Inn. It provides specialist tax, trusts and probate advice and also specialises in matrimonial, commercial litigation, property and corporate and commercial work.

main areas of work
Private client 41%; matrimonial 22%; property 17%; commercial litigation 13%; corporate and commercial 7%.

trainee profile
The firm looks for law and non-law graduates with a good academic record, a practical ability to solve problems, enthusiasm and an ability to work hard and deal appropriately with their colleagues and the firm's clients.

training environment
Following an initial induction course, trainees usually spend six months in four of the firm's departments. Working with a partner, they are involved in the day to day activities of the department, including attending conferences with clients, counsel and other professional advisers. Assessment is continuous and trainees will be given responsibility as they demonstrate ability and aptitude. To complement the PSC, the firm runs a formal training system for trainees and requires them to attend lectures and seminars on various topics.

benefits
Season travel ticket loan, life assurance 4 x salary, permanent health insurance, contribution to personal pension plan.

sponsorship & awards
Fees for the CPE and LPC are paid.

Partners 26
Assistant Solicitors 18
Total Trainees 5

contact
Mrs Alice Palmer

method of application
Handwritten letter & CV

selection procedure
Interview

closing date for 2005
1 August 2003

application
Training contracts p.a. 3
Applications p.a. **1,000**
% interviewed p.a. **3%**
Required degree grade **2:1**

training
Salary
1st year (2002) **£25,000**
2nd year (2002) **£27,500**
Holiday entitlement
4 weeks
% of trainees with a
non-law degree p.a. **50%**

post-qualification
Salary (2002) **£43,000**
% of trainees offered job
on qualification (2002)
100%
% of assistants (as at
1/9/01) who joined as
trainees **35%**
% of partners (as at 1/9/01)
who joined as trainees
20%

Penningtons

Bucklersbury House, 83 Cannon Street, London EC4N 8PE
Tel: (020) 7457 3000 Fax: (020) 7457 3240
Website: www.penningtons.co.uk

firm profile
A London and South East law firm, with offices in the City, Basingstoke, Godalming, Newbury and Paris. There are four main departments. Specialist units cover industry sectors and key overseas jurisdictions, including North America, South Africa, Italy, France and India.

main areas of work
Property 37%; litigation 28%; corporate/commercial 21%; private client 14%.

trainee profile
Penningtons is looking for bright, enthusiastic, highly motivated and well rounded individuals with a keen interest in the practice of law.

training environment
Six month seats are provided in three or four of the following departments: corporate/commercial, property, litigation, and private client. Individual preference is usually accommodated in the second year. Trainees are given a thorough grounding in the law. International opportunities do arise. There are in-house lectures and reviews and appraisals occur regularly. The firm aims to utilise trainees' talents to their full, but is careful not to overburden them. All staff are supportive and the atmosphere is both professional and informal.

benefits
Subsidised sports and social club, life assurance, private medical, season ticket loan.

vacation placements
Places for 2003: 60 on London open days at Easter; Remuneration: Expenses; Closing Date: 15 February 2003. Some summer vacation placements out of London, closing date 15 April 2003.

sponsorship & awards
LPC funding is available. Awards are given for commendation or distinction in LPC.

Partners 57*
Assistant Solicitors 80*
Total Trainees 21
denotes worldwide figures

contact
Lesley Lintott

method of application
Covering letter, CV & application form

selection procedure
1 interview with a partner & director of studies

closing date for 2005
15 August 2003

application
Training contracts p.a. **10/11**
Applications p.a. **2,000**
% interviewed p.a. **5%**
Required degree grade **2:1**

training
Salary
1st year (2002)
£24,500 (London)
2nd year (2002)
£26,500 (London)
Holiday entitlement
23 days
% of trainees with a non-law degree p.a. **40%**

post-qualification
Salary (2001)
£38,000 (London)
% of trainees offered job on qualification (2002) **80%**
% of assistants (as at 1/9/01) who joined as trainees **45%**
% of partners (as at 1/9/01) who joined as trainees **49%**

overseas offices
Paris

Pinsent Curtis Biddle

Dashwood House, 69 Old Broad Street, London EC2M 1NR
Tel: (020) 7418 7097 Fax: (020) 7418 7050
3 Colmore Circus, Birmingham B4 6BH
1 Park Row, Leeds LS1 5AB
The Chancery, 58 Spring Gardens, Manchester M216 1EW
Email: gradrecruiting@pinsents.com
Website: www.pinsents.com

Partners	175
Assistant Solicitors	294
Total Trainees	70

contact
Ms Maxine Jayes
Recruitment Hotline:
(0845) 300 3232

firm profile
Pinsent Curtis Biddle is an award winning corporate firm with a first class reputation for the quality of its work and client satisfaction. The firm is ranked in the top 10 of named legal advisers to UK listed companies, acting for a substantial range of FTSE 100, Fortune 500 and AIM quoted organisations.

method of application
Online application form

selection procedure
Assessment centre including interview

main areas of work
Corporate; dispute resolution and litigation; employment; insurance and reinsurance; pensions; projects and commercial; property; tax.

closing date for 2005
31 July 2003

application
Training contracts p.a. **35**
Applications p.a. **2,000**
Required degree grade **2:1**

trainee profile
The firm welcomes applications from both law and non-law graduates with a good honours degree. In addition to a strong academic background the firm is looking for problem solvers with a sharp commercial acumen, who as committed team players can use their initiative and common sense to get to the heart of the clients' business and legal needs.

training
Salary
1st year (2002) £28,000
2nd year (2002) £30,000
Holiday entitlement
25 days

training environment
Trainees sit in four seats of six months across the practice groups with supervision by partners or associates. There are also opportunities for trainees to be seconded to clients. There is a supportive team structure where hands-on experience is an essential part of the learning process, with early responsibility and contact with clients encouraged. In addition to the PSC the firm has a structured development programme designed to broaden trainee business and legal knowledge. This is the first stage of the firm's focused legal management development programme that supports individuals through to partnership. The firm has an open-door policy and informal atmosphere with a positive focus on work life balance.

post-qualification
Salary (2002)
Approx **£48,000**
% of trainees offered job on qualification (2002) **80%**

summer vacation placements
Places for 2003: 90; Duration: 2 weeks; Closing Date: 28 February 2003.

sponsorship & awards
CPE/ LPC fees are paid. In addition to this, maintenance grants of £3,000 for CPE and £5,000 for LPC are offered.

Prettys

Elm House, 25 Elm Street, Ipswich IP1 2AD
Tel: (01473) 232121 Fax: (01473) 230002
Email: agage@prettys.co.uk
Website: www.prettys.co.uk

| Partners | 16 |
| Total Trainees | 8-10 |

contact
Angela Gage

method of application
Application letter & CV

closing date for 2005
Apply by the end of August 2003 to begin 2005

application
Training contracts p.a. **4-5**
Required degree grade **2:1** preferred in law or other relevant subject.
Good A Levels

training
Salary
Above Law Society guidelines

firm profile
Prettys is one of the largest and most successful legal practices in East Anglia. The firm is located in the centre of the East Anglian business community, with the expanding hi-tech corridor between Ipswich and Cambridge to the west, Felixstowe to the east and the City of London 60 minutes away to the south. The firm's lawyers are approachable and pragmatic. It provides expert advice to national and regional businesses – in particular owner managed enterprises. As members of Galexy (a network of European firms) the firm has a recognised niche speciality, providing legal assistance to corporate and private clients travelling or doing business abroad.

main areas of work
Prettys' broad-based practice allows it to offer a full service to all its clients. Business law services: company, commercial, shipping, transport, construction, intellectual property, information technology, property, employment, commercial litigation, insurance, professional indemnity and health and safety. Personal law services: French property, personal injury, clinical negligence, financial services, estates, agriculture, conveyancing and family.

trainee profile
Prettys' trainees are the future of the firm. Applicants should be able to demonstrate a desire to pursue a career in East Anglia. Trainees are given considerable responsibility early on and the firm is therefore looking for candidates who are well motivated, enthusiastic and have a good common sense approach. Good IT skills are essential.

training environment
A two week induction programme will introduce you to the firm. You will receive continuous supervision and three monthly reviews. Training is in four six-month seats with some choice in your second year and the possibility of remaining in the same department for two seats. Trainees work closely with a partner, meeting clients and becoming involved in all aspects of the department's work. Frequent training seminars are provided in-house. The PSC is taken externally.

additional information
One day placements are available (apply to Angela Gage). A trainee brochure is available on request or online. Apply by the end of August 2003 to begin 2005.

sponsorship & awards
Discretionary.

Pritchard Englefield

14 New St, London EC2M 4HE
Tel: (020) 7972 9720 Fax: (020) 7972 9722
Email: po@pritchardenglefield.eu.com
Website: www.pritchardenglefield.eu.com

firm profile
A medium-sized City firm practising a mix of general commercial and non-commercial law with many German and French clients. Despite its strong commercial departments, the firm still undertakes family and private client work and is known for its clinical negligence and PI practice and its strong international flavour.

main areas of work
All main areas of commercial practice including litigation, company/commercial (UK, German and French) and employment, also estate and trusts, personal injury, clinical negligence and family.

trainee profile
Normally only high academic achievers with a second European language (especially German and French) are considered. However, a lower second degree coupled with exceptional subsequent education or experience could suffice.

training environment
An induction course acquaints trainees with the computer network, library and administrative procedures and there is a formal in-house training programme. Four six month seats make up most of your training. You can usually choose some departments, and you could spend two six month periods in the same seat. Over two years, you learn advocacy, negotiating, drafting and interviewing, attend court, use your language skills and meet clients. Occasional talks and seminars explain the work of the firm, and you can air concerns over bi-monthly lunches with the partners comprising the Trainee Panel. PSC is taken externally over two years. Quarterly drinks parties, musical evenings and ten-pin bowling number amongst popular social events.

benefits
Some subsidised training, luncheon vouchers.

sponsorship & awards
Full funding for LPC fees.

Partners	24
Assistant Solicitors	16
Total Trainees	6

contact
Graduate Recruitment

method of application
Standard application form available from Graduate Recruitment or online

selection procedure
1 interview only in September

closing date for 2005
31 July 2003

application
Training contracts p.a. 3
Applications p.a. 300–400
% interviewed p.a. 10%
Required degree grade
Generally 2:1

training
Salary
1st year (2002) £20,750
2nd year (2002) £21,250
Holiday entitlement
25 days
% of trainees with a non-law degree p.a.
Approx 50%

post-qualification
Salary (2002)
Approx £34,000
% of trainees offered job on qualification (2002) 50%
% of assistants (as at 1/9/02) who joined as trainees 50%
% of partners (as at 1/9/02) who joined as trainees 50%

overseas offices
Hong Kong

RadcliffesLeBrasseur

5 Great College Street, Westminster, London SW1P 3SJ
Tel: (020) 7222 7040 Fax: (020) 7222 6208
Email: gradrec@radleb.com
Website: www.rlb-law.com

firm profile
From its offices in the heart of Westminster, RadcliffesLeBrasseur combines traditional values of integrity and prompt response with a client focused approach to everything that it does. It has a wide and varied client base which includes healthcare services providers, public and private companies, property companies, charities, banks, institutions, public authorities and private individuals.

main areas of work
The firm is organised into departments and experts within them integrate their knowledge in the firm's specialist market facing groups, health, corporate (including litigation), property, charities, tax and private client.

trainee profile
Its aim is to recruit trainee solicitors who have a real prospect of becoming future partners. The firm seeks not just academic but also extra curricular activities, self-confidence, determination and a sense of humour.

training environment
Trainees are introduced to the firm with a full induction week.

benefits
Health insurance, season ticket loan, life assurance, PHI.

vacation placements
Places for 2003: 20; Duration: 2 weeks; Remuneration: £200 p.w.; Closing Date: 28 March 2003.

sponsorship & awards
LPC fees paid and £4,000 subsistence.

trainee comments
"From day one, after the induction week, you have your own files and actually do the work."
"It's a thoroughly commercial firm, so it's no good being academically brilliant but financially naive."
"I liked the way people worked together to get jobs done, rather than working all hours on their own to make some kind of individual point."

Partners 59
Assistant Solicitors 40
Total Trainees 17

contact
Graduate Recruitment

method of application
CV & covering letter or application form

selection procedure
2 Interviews with partners

closing date for 2005
31 July 2003

application
Training contracts p.a. **6**
(London 5; Leeds 1)
Applications p.a. **1,000**
% interviewed p.a. **9%**
Preferred degree grade **2:1**

training
Salary
1st year (2002)
£23,500 (London)
£15,000 (Leeds)
2nd year (2002)
£26,000 (London)
£16,500 (Leeds)

post-qualification
Salary (2002) **£38,000**
% of trainees offered job on qualification (2001-02) **80%**
% of assistants (as at 1/9/02) who joined as trainees **50%**

Reed Smith Warner Cranston

Minerva House, 5 Montague Close SE1 9BB
Tel: (020) 7403 2900 Fax: (020) 7403 4221
Email: tclaxton@reedsmith.com.uk
Website: www.reedsmith.co.uk

firm profile
Reed Smith Warner Cranston is a transatlantic law firm with two UK offices located in London and Coventry and a significant US presence. The UK is known for its international work and handles all types of commercial transactions for well-known clients.

main areas of work
The firm is divided into four core departments: business and finance; international litigation; real estate; employment.

trainee profile
Enthusiastic, proactive, bright, commercially-minded graduates who want to work in a friendly atmosphere where personality, a sense of humour and a hands-on approach are encouraged.

training environment
To help trainees build a strong career, the firm invests heavily in training (approximately one training session per week) covering a range of skills including advocacy, drafting and marketing. The firm provides an informal but fast-paced working environment where trainees are immediately given access to clients and fulfilling work, often with an international bias. Trainees who are fluent French speakers will be given opportunities to develop these skills. The firm has four seats available in business and finance, international litigation, real estate and employment. Progress is reviewed regularly by a Senior Partner.

benefits
BUPA, IFSTL, life assurance, permanent health insurance, pension contributions (after qualifying period).

vacation placements
Places for Summer 2003: 12; Duration: 4 weeks (London), 2 weeks (Midlands); Remuneration: £800 (London), £300 (Midlands); Closing Date: 31 January 2003.

sponsorship & awards
CPE/LPC fees and maintenance grant plus interest-free loan.

Partners 31
Assistant Solicitors 34
Total Trainees 12

contact
Tassy Claxton
Recruitment Co-ordinator

method of application
Application form & covering letter

selection procedure
Assessment day:
2 interviews, aptitude test & presentation

closing date for 2005
31 July 2003

application
Training contracts p.a.
6 (London 4, Coventry 2)
Applications p.a. 1000
% interviewed p.a. 3%
Required degree grade 2:1

training
Salary
1st year (2001) £27,000
2nd year (2001) £31,000
Holiday entitlement
25 days
% of trainees with
a non-law degree 25%

post-qualification
Salary (2002) £48,000

Reynolds Porter Chamberlain

Chichester House, 278-282 High Holborn, London WC1V 7HA
Tel: (020) 7973 9270 Fax: (020) 7242 1431
Email: rpc@rpc.co.uk
Website: www.rpc.co.uk

Partners	54
Assistant Solicitors	155
Total Trainees	20

firm profile
Reynolds Porter Chamberlain is a leading commercial law firm with approximately 200 lawyers. In addition to its main offices in Holborn, the firm has an expanding office at Leadenhall Street in the City which serves its insurance clients. Best known as a major litigation practice, particularly in the field of professional negligence, RPC also has thriving corporate, commercial property, private client and construction departments. Another rapidly expanding part of the firm is its media and technology practice. This handles major defamation actions and has dealt with some of the biggest internet deals to date.

main areas of work
Litigation 60%; corporate 10%; commercial property 10%; construction 10%; media and technology 5%; family/private client 5%.

trainee profile
The firm appoints ten trainees each year from law and non-law backgrounds. Although proven academic ability is important (the firm requires a 2:1 or above), RPC also values flair, energy, business sense, commitment and the ability to communicate and relate well to others.

training environment
As a trainee you will receive first rate training in a supportive working environment. You will work closely with a partner and be given real responsibility as soon as you are ready to handle it. At least six months will be spent in each of the three main areas of the practice and the firm encourages trainees to express a preference for their seats. This provides a thorough grounding and the chance to develop confidence as you see matters through to their conclusion. In addition to the externally provided Professional Skills Course the firm provides a complimentary programme of in-house training.

benefits
Four weeks holiday, bonus schemes, private medical insurance, income protection benefits, season ticket loan, subsidised gym membership, active social calendar.

vacation placements
Places for July 2003: 12; Duration: 2 weeks; Remuneration: £200 p.w.; Closing Date: 28 February 2003.

sponsorship & awards
CPE/PgDL Funding: Fees paid plus £4,000 maintenance; LPC Funding: Fees paid plus £4,000 maintenance.

---

contact
Sally Andrews
Human Resources Director

method of application
Handwritten covering letter & application form

selection procedure
Assessment days held in September

closing date for 2005
15 August 2003

application
Training contracts p.a. 10
Applications p.a. **1,200**
% interviewed p.a. **4%**
Required degree grade **2:1**

training
Salary
1st year (2001) **£27,000**
2nd year (2001) **£29,000**
Holiday entitlement
20 days
% of trainees with a non-law degree p.a.
Approx **25%**

post-qualification
Salary (2002) **£45,000**
% of trainees offered job on qualification (2001) **66%**
% of assistants (as at 1/9/01) who joined as trainees **55%**
% of partners (as at 1/9/01) who joined as trainees **40%**

Richards Butler

Beaufort House, 15 St. Botolph Street, London EC3A 7EE
Tel: (020) 7247 6555 Fax: (020) 7247 5091
Email: gradrecruit@richardsbutler.com

firm profile
Established in 1920, Richards Butler is noted for the exceptional variety of its work. It has acknowledged strengths in commercial disputes, commodities, competition, corporate finance, energy law, insurance, media/entertainment, property and shipping, in each of which it has international prominence. The firm is proud to announce that a Queen's Award for Enterprise 2002 for International Trade has been awarded to the firm. This accolade was conferred as it has been 'judged to be among the best of UK companies' because of its achievements in the international market.

main areas of work
Banking/commercial/corporate/finance 32%; insurance/international trade and commodities/shipping 29%; commercial disputes 23%; commercial property 16%.

trainee profile
Candidates should be players rather than onlookers, work well under pressure and be happy to operate as a team member or team leader as circumstances dictate. Candidates from diverse backgrounds are welcome, including mature students with commercial experience and management skills.

training environment
Four or five seat rotations enable Richards Butler to provide practical experience across as wide a spectrum of the law as possible. Trainees can also apply for secondment to one of the firm's overseas offices, Hong Kong, Paris, Abu Dhabi, São Paulo, Piraeus or to one of their client in-house legal teams.

benefits
Performance related bonus, life insurance, BUPA, interest-free season ticket loan, subsidised staff restaurant, staff conveyancing allowance.

vacation placements
Places for 2003: 20; Duration: 3 weeks; Remuneration: £200 p.w.; Closing Date: 15 February 2003. In addition, the firm offers overseas scholarships to Paris, Hong Kong, Abu Dhabi and Athens. The scholarship consists of a return airfare, accomodation, living expenses and two weeks of work experience.

sponsorship & awards
CPE Funding: Fees paid plus £5,000 maintenance.
LPC Funding: Fees paid plus £5,000 maintenance.

Partners 112*
Fee-earners 436*
Total Trainees 68*
* denotes worldwide figures

contact
Jaqueline Senior

method of application
Online application form

selection procedure
Selection exercise & interview

closing date for 2006
31 July 2003

application
Training contracts p.a. **20**
Applications p.a. **2,000**
% interviewed p.a. **5%**
Required degree grade **2:1**

training
Salary
1st year (2002) **£28,000**
2nd year (2002) **£31,000**
Holiday entitlement
25 days
% of trainees with a non-law degree p.a. **33%**
No. of seats available abroad p.a. **10**

post-qualification
Salary (2001)
£48,000 plus bonus
% of assistants who joined as trainees **59%**
% of partners who joined as trainees **54%**

overseas offices
Abu Dhabi, Beijing, Brussels, Doha*, Hong Kong, Muscat*, Paris, Piraeus, São Paulo
* Associated office

Russell-Cooke

2 Putney Hill, London SW15 6AB
Tel: (020) 8789 9111 Fax: (020) 8788 1656
Email: traineeapplications@russell-cooke.co.uk
Website: www.russell-cooke.co.uk

firm profile
A medium-sized practice with three offices in the London area. The City office deals primarily with commercial and contentious property. The Putney office has a range of specialist departments including company/commercial, crime, judicial review, commercial and construction litigation, matrimonial, French property and tax, domestic and commercial conveyancing, personal injury litigation, private client and trusts. The Kingston-upon-Thames office runs a specialist childcare department plus matrimonial, domestic conveyancing and crime.

main areas of work
Commercial property 20%; company commercial 10%; commercial litigation 15%; public law 10%; private client 10%; domestic conveyancing 10%; matrimonial 10%; crime 10%; personal injury 5%.

trainee profile
Trainees will need at least two A grades and a B grade at A Level and a 2:1 degree, though not necessarily in law. You will also need to be good at the practical business of advising and representing clients. Intellectual rigour, adaptability and the ability, under pressure, to handle a diverse range of people and issues efficiently and cost-effectively are vital attributes.

training environment
Trainees are usually offered four seats lasting six months each. Photocopying and researching points of law will not take up all your time in the firm. You will have the chance to manage your own case work and deal directly with clients, with supervision suited to your needs and the needs of the department and clients. Internal training and an annual executive staff conference supplement the externally provided PSC. Social events include quiz nights, wine tasting, summer and Christmas parties and thriving cricket and netball teams.

sponsorship & awards
A grant to cover LPC course fees may be available.

Partners 30
Assistant Solicitors 37
Total Trainees 9

contact
Lisa Howard

method of application
CV & covering letter

selection procedure
First & second interviews

closing date for 2005
8 August 2003

application
Training contracts p.a. **4**
Applications p.a. **500**
% interviewed p.a. **7%**
Required degree grade **2:1**

training
Salary
1st year (2002) **£20,500**
2nd year (2002) **£22,000**
Holiday entitlement
22 days
% of trainees with a
non-law degree p.a. **50%**

post-qualification
Salary (2000) **Market**
% of trainees offered job
on qualification (2000)
100%
% of assistants (as at
1/9/00) who joined as
trainees **40%**
% of partners (as at 1/9/00)
who joined as trainees
50%

Russell Jones & Walker

Swinton House, 324 Gray's Inn Road, London WC1X 8DH
Tel: (020) 7837 2808 Fax: (020) 7837 2941
Email: enquiries@rjw.co.uk
Website: www.rjw.co.uk

firm profile
Russell Jones & Walker was founded in London in the 1920s but has expanded in recent years to become one of the largest litigation practices in the country with more than 600 lawyers and support staff and offices in London, Leeds, Birmingham, Bristol, Manchester, Sheffield, Newcastle upon Tyne, Cardiff, Edinburgh and Northampton.

main areas of work
Personal injury/clinical negligence; criminal; commercial litigation; employment; family/probate; commercial and domestic conveyancing.

trainee profile
Russell Jones & Walker are looking for candidates who are motivated and hard-working with a sense of humour and the ability and confidence to accept responsibility in fee-earning work and client care.

training environment
Each trainee will spend six months in four different departments under the supervision of a partner or senior solicitor. Your supervisor will conduct a three-month assessment and six-month review. A full induction programme and IT training is provided, together with a comprehensive in-house education timetable. The training partner supervises all aspects of the training contract. The firm is extremely sociable and trainees are encouraged to participate in social and sporting events.

benefits
Season ticket loan, pension, private healthcare or gym membership, group life assurance, all subject to qualifying periods.

vacation placements
Unfortunately the firm does not offer vacation placements.

sponsorship & award
LPC Funding: Interest-free loan provided to assist with fees available.

Partners 55
Assistant Solicitors 98
Total Trainees 16
(London and regional)

contact
HR Officer (Recruitment)

method of application
Application form – available from 1 April 2003

closing date for 2005
31 July 2003

application
Training contracts p.a. **10**
Applications p.a. **1,000**
% interviewed p.a. **5%**
Required degree grade **2:1**

training
Salary (in London)
1st year (2002) Approx **£20,000**
2nd year (2002) Approx **£21,500**
Holiday entitlement **4 weeks**
% of trainees with a non-law degree p.a. **25%**

post-qualification
Salary (2002) Approx **£32,000 (London)**
% of trainees offered job on qualification (2002) **50%**
% of assistants (as at 1/9/02) who joined as trainees **Approx 11%**
% of partners (as at 1/9/02) who joined as trainees **13%**

Salans

Clements House, 14-18 Gresham Street, London EC2V 7NN
Tel: (020) 7509 6000 Fax: (020) 7726 6191
Email: london@salans.com

firm profile
Salans is a multinational law firm with full-service offices in the City of London, Paris and New York, together with further offices in Moscow, St Petersburg, Warsaw, Kyiv, Almaty and Baku. The firm currently has over 450 fee-earners, including over 110 partners.

main areas of work
London Office: Banking and finance/corporate 50%; litigation 25%; employment 15%; commercial property 10%.

trainee profile
Candidates need to have high academic qualifications and the ability to approach complex problems in a practical and commercial way. The firm looks to recruit those who demonstrate an ability and a willingness to assume responsibility at an early stage, possess common sense and good judgement. Language skills are also valued.

training environment
Trainees at Salans are an integral part of the team. Over the course of two years trainees spend six months in four seats, chosen from the banking and finance, corporate, property, commercial litigation and employment departments. Because the firm knows how much commercial experience matters to its clients, trainees may choose to request six months on secondment with a client instead of a seat in one department. In addition to the in-house training scheme, trainees are offered the opportunity to attend external courses wherever possible. As trainees gain experience they are given increasing responsibility to deal with matters without constant supervision. Where possible the firm seeks to recruit its trainees at the end of the training period.

benefits
Private healthcare, pension, season ticket loan.

sponsorship & awards
LPC tuition fees paid.

Partners 112
Assistant Solicitors
(Worldwide) 224
Total Trainees
(London) 7

contact
Debbie Nicholls
HR Manager

method of application
Handwritten letter & CV

selection procedure
2 interviews with partners

closing date for 2005
31 July 2003

application
Training contracts p.a.
3 or 4
Applications p.a. **500+**
% interviewed p.a. **5%**
Required degree grade **2:1**

training
Salary
1st year (2000) **£24,500**
2nd year (2000) **£25,500**
Holiday entitlement
25 days
% of trainees with a
non-law degree p.a.
Variable
No. of seats available
abroad p.a. **None at present**

post-qualification
Salary (2001) **Variable**
% of trainees offered job
on qualification (2001)
75%

overseas offices
Almaty, Baku, Kyiv, Moscow, New York, Paris, St Petersburg, Warsaw

Shadbolt & Co

Chatham Court, Lesbourne Road, Reigate RH2 7LD
Tel: (01737) 226277 Fax: (01737) 226165
Email: mail@shadboltlaw.co.uk
Website: www.shadboltlaw.co.uk

firm profile
Established in 1991, Shadbolt & Co is an award winning dynamic, progressive firm committed to high quality work and excellence both in the UK and internationally. The atmosphere at the firm is friendly, relaxed and informal and there are various social and sporting activities for staff. The firm's qualified staff have a high level of experience and industry knowledge and some are widely regarded as leading practitioners in their field.

main areas of work
The firm is well known for its strengths in major projects, construction and engineering and dispute resolution and litigation with expansion into corporate and commercial, employment, commercial property and IT and e-commerce. The firm's client list includes some of the world's best known names in the construction and engineering industries.

trainee profile
Applicants must demonstrate that they are mature self-starters with a strong academic background and outside interests. Leadership, ambition, initiative, enthusiasm and good interpersonal skills are essential as is the ability to play an active role in the future of the firm. Linguists are particularly welcome as are those with supporting professional qualifications. The firm welcomes non-law graduates.

training
Four six month seats from construction and commercial litigation, arbitration and dispute resolution, major projects and construction, employment, corporate and commercial and commercial property. Where possible individual preference is noted. Work has an international bias. There are opportunities for secondment to major clients and work in the overseas offices. Trainees are treated as valued members of the firm, expected to take early responsibility and encouraged to participate in all the firm's activities, including practice development.

sponsorship & benefits
Optional private healthcare, permanent health insurance, group life assurance, paid study leave, season ticket loan, discretionary annual bonus, paid professional memberships and subscriptions, 50% refund of LPC upon commencement of training contract, PSC fees paid.

vacation placements
Places for 2003: 6; Duration: 2 weeks; Remuneration (2002): £170 p.w.; Closing Date: 16 March 2003; Interviews: April 2003.

Partners 22
Assistant Solicitors 23
Total Trainees 9
Total Staff 112

contact
Timony Kidd or Andrea Pickett

method of application
Application form

selection procedure
Interview & written assessment

closing date for 2005
31 August 2003 (interviews September 2003)

application
Training contracts p.a. 4
Applications p.a. 200
% interviewed p.a. 6%
Required degree grade 2:1 (occasional exceptions)

training
Salary
1st year (2002) £22,000
2nd year (2002) £27,000
Holiday entitlement
20 days rising to 25 on qualification
% of trainees with a non-law degree p.a. 50%
No. of seats available abroad p.a. 2

post-qualification
Salary (2002) £35,000
% of trainees offered job on qualification (2002) 80%
% of assistants (2002) who joined as trainees 52%
% of partners (2002) who joined as trainees 0%

other offices
Reigate, City of London, Hong Kong, Paris, Dar es Salaam, Athens

Shearman & Sterling

Broadgate West, 9 Appold Street, London EC2A 2AP
Tel: (020) 7655 5000 Fax: (020) 7655 5500

firm profile
Shearman & Sterling is one of New York's oldest legal partnerships, which has transformed from a New York-based firm focused on banking into a diversified global institution. Recognised throughout the world, the firm's reputation, skills and expertise are second to none in its field. The London office, established in 1972, has become a leading practice covering all aspects of English and European corporate and finance law. The firm employs over 130 English and US trained legal staff in London and has more than 1,000 lawyers in 18 offices worldwide.

main areas of work
Banking, leveraged finance and securitisation (primary and secondary structured debt, bridging facilities, debt trading and financial restructuring). Project finance (all aspects, in the power, oil, gas, telecommunications, mining and transport infrastructure sectors). M&A (public and private cross-border transactions on a pan-European scale). Global capital markets (structuring and execution of high-yield debt and equity-linked financing). International arbitration and litigation (international commercial law on a global scale). Tax (all direct and indirect tax aspects of structured finance and securitisations, domestic and international banking, capital markets issues, M&A and reorganisations). EU and competition (cross-border and UK M&A transactions, restrictive practices and abuse of dominance, competition litigation, state aid, public procurement and utility regulation).

trainee profile
The firm's successful future development calls for people who will relish the hard work and intellectual challenge of today's commercial world. You will be a self-starter, keen to assume professional responsibility early in your career and determined to become a first-class lawyer in a first-class firm. The firm's two year training programme will equip you with all the skills needed to become a successful commercial lawyer. You will spend six months in each of four practice areas, with an opportunity to spend six months in Hong Kong or Singapore. You will be an integral part of the London team from the outset, with your own laptop and mobile phone. The firm will expect you to contribute creatively to all the transactions you are involved in. The firm has an informal yet professional atmosphere. Your enthusiasm, intellect and energy will be more important than what you wear to work. The firm will provide you with a mentor, arrange personal and professional development courses and give you early responsibility. The firm wants to recruit people who will stay with it; people who want to become partners in its continuing success story.

sponsorship & awards
Sponsorship for the CPE and LPC courses, together with a maintenance grant of £4,500.

Partners	22
Assistant Solicitors	102
Total Trainees	4

contact
Kirsten Davies
Tel: (020) 7655 5082

method of application
Application form

selection procedure
Interviews

closing date for 2005
31 July 2003

application
Training contracts p.a. 6
Required degree grade 2:1

training
Salary
1st year £30,000
2nd year £34,000
Holiday entitlement 24 days p.a.
% of trainees with non-law degree p.a. 50%
No of seats available abroad 2

post-qualification
Salary £55,000
% of trainees offered job on qualification 80%

overseas offices
Abu Dhabi, Beijing, Brussels, Düsseldorf, Frankfurt, Hong Kong, Mannheim, Menlo Park, Munich, New York, Paris, Rome, San Francisco, Singapore, Tokyo, Toronto, Washington DC

Shoosmiths

The Lakes, Bedford Road, Northampton NN4 7SH
Tel: (01604) 543223 Fax: (01604) 543430
Email: join.us@shoosmiths.co.uk
Website: www.shoosmiths.co.uk

Partners	69
Assistant Solicitors	106
Total Trainees	23

contact
Claire Lewis

method of application
Application form

selection procedure
Selection centre - half day

closing date for 2005
31 July 2003

application
Training contracts p.a. **10**
Applications p.a. **1,000**
% interviewed p.a. **10%**
Required degree grade **2:1**

training
Salary
1st year (2001) £17,000
2nd year (2001) £18,000
Holiday entitlement
23 days + option to flex

post-qualification
Salary (2001) **Market rate**

offices
Northampton, Nottingham, Reading, Fareham, Milton Keynes, Basingstoke

firm profile
Growing steadily, with six offices across the country, 69 partners and 1,100 staff, Shoosmiths is one of the big players outside of London. By joining the firm you can expect to experience a full range of interesting and challenging commercial work. In a demanding legal market, Shoosmiths has developed exciting, even radical, services helping it to exceed the highest expectations of its clients. The firm supports and encourages its people to develop exhilarating, balanced careers. Shoosmiths' workplace culture offers a stimulating environment, time for family and the opportunity to put something back into the community.

main areas of work
Corporate/commercial; dispute resolution; employment; planning; commercial property; private client/family; personal injury; banking; financial institutions.

trainee profile
You will be confident, motivated and articulate with natural intelligence and the drive to succeed, thereby making a real contribution to the firm's commercial success. You will want to be a part of a winning team and will care about the kind of service you give to your clients, both internal and external.

training environment
You will be involved in 'real' work from day one of your training contract. Sitting with a partner who will oversee your training and career development, you will have direct contact with clients and will draft your own letters and documents. Your experience will build through your daily, practical, workload complemented by the training you would expect from a leading national law firm. In addition to the compulsory Professional Skills Course, the firm offers a comprehensive internal training programme that includes managerial, legal and IT training as standard. Over the course of two years, you will complete four seats of six month duration, to help you decide which area you would like to qualify into.

benefits
Life assurance, pension after 3 months, various staff discounts, Christmas Party, various social events.

vacation placements
Places for 2002: 30; Duration: 2 weeks; Remuneration: £155 p.w.; Closing Date: 28 Feb 2003.

sponsorship & awards
LPC funding: £12,500 – split between fees and maintenance.

Sidley Austin Brown & Wood

1 Threadneedle Street, London EC2R 8AW
Princes Court, 7 Princes Street, London EC2R 8AQ
Tel: (020) 7360 3600 Fax: (020) 7626 7937
Email: idrummond@sidley.com
Website: www.sidley.com

firm profile
Sidley Austin Brown & Wood is one of the world's largest full-service law firms combining the strengths of two exceptional law firms. With more than 1,300 lawyers practising in 13 offices on three continents (North America, Europe and Asia), the firm provides a broad range of integrated services to meet the needs of its clients across a multitude of industries. The firm has over 100 lawyers in London and is expanding fast.

main areas of work
Corporate securities; corporate finance; investment funds; tax; banking regulation; securitisation and structured finance; corporate reconstruction; property and property finance.

trainee profile
Sidley Austin Brown & Wood is looking for focused, intelligent and enthusiastic individuals with personality and humour who have a real interest in practising law in the commercial world. Trainees should have a 2:1 degree (not necessarily in law) and three A levels at A and B grades. Trainees would normally be expected to pass the CPE (if required) and the LPC at the first attempt.

training environment
Sidley Austin Brown & Wood is looking to recruit six to eight trainee solicitors to start in September 2005/March 2006. The firm is not a typical City firm and it is not a 'legal factory' so there is no risk of you being just a number. The team in London is young, dynamic and collegiate. Everyone is encouraged to be proactive and to create their own niche when they are ready to do so. Trainees spend a period of time in the firm's specialist groups: international finance, corporate securities, corporate commercial, tax and property. Sidley Austin Brown & Wood in London does not have a separate litigation department, although some litigation work is undertaken. The firm does, however, organise external litigation training for all trainees. In each group you will sit with a partner or senior associate to ensure that you receive individual training that is both effective and based on a real caseload. In addition, there is a structured timetable of training on a cross-section of subjects and an annual training weekend.

benefits
Healthcare, disability cover, life assurance, contribution to gym membership, interest-free season ticket loan.

sponsorship & awards
CPE and LPC fees paid and maintenance p.a.

Partners 30
Assistant Solicitors 57
Total Trainees 10

contact
Isabel Drummond

method of application
Covering letter & employee application form - please call (0800) 731 5015

selection procedure
Interview(s)

closing date for 2005
25 July 2003

application
Training contracts p.a. 6-8
Applications p.a. 500
% interviewed p.a. 15
Required degree grade 2:1

training
Salary
1st year (2002) £28,500
2nd year (2002) £32,000
Holiday entitlement
25 days
% of trainees with a non-law degree p.a. 50%

overseas offices
Beijing, Chicago, Dallas, Geneva, Hong Kong, London, Los Angeles, New York, San Francisco, Shanghai, Singapore, Tokyo, Washington DC

Simmons & Simmons

CityPoint, One Ropemaker Street, London EC2Y 9SS
Tel: (020) 7628 2020 Fax: (020) 7628 2070
Email: recruitment@simmons-simmons.com
Website: www.simmons-simmons.com

firm profile
Simmons & Simmons is a world class law firm providing advice to financial institutions, corporates, public and international bodies and private individuals through its international network of offices. It provides a comprehensive range of legal services with strength and depth. The ability to provide technically excellent, commercial and high quality advice is expected of leading law firms. Simmons & Simmons aims to provide an additional dimension by focusing on the way it works with its clients and by shaping its services to fit the clients' needs.

main areas of work
Corporate (corporate finance, M&A, private equity); finance (capital markets, structured securities, financial services); dispute resolution; competition and trade; employment; IP; major projects; real estate; tax; private capital. Main industry sector focus: construction aerospace and defence; consumer products; energy and utilities; financial markets; pharmaceuticals and biotechnology; real estate; transport; TMT.

trainee profile
While a good academic record and sound commercial judgement is important, strength of character and outside interests are also taken into consideration.

training environment
Trainees sit with a partner or senior lawyer and are given the best work to help them become world class lawyers. Whilst the firm has its requirements, it places great emphasis on trainees being able to discuss their progress and develop their professional interests. As well as having a supervisor and dedicated personnel professional they are assigned a principal who acts as mentor and provides advice on developing as a lawyer in a City law firm.

benefits
Season ticket loan, fitness loan, group travel insurance, group accident insurance, death in service, medical cover, staff restaurant.

vacation placements
Places for 2003: 40–50; Duration: 2-4 weeks; Remuneration: £250 p.w.; Closing date: 21 February 2003.

sponsorship & awards
In the absence of local authority funding LPC fees and PgDL/CPE fees are paid, plus a maintenance grant of £5,000 for London, Oxford or Guildford and £4,500 elsewhere.

Partners 203
Assistant Solicitors 449
Total Trainees 179

contact
Vickie Chamberlain

method of application
Application form, CV & covering letter or online application

selection procedure
Assessment day: Document exercise, interview & written exercise

closing date for 2005
15 August 2003

application
Training contracts p.a. 50-60
Applications p.a. 2,700
% interviewed p.a. 15%
Required degree grade 2:1

training
Salary
1st year (2002) £28,000
2nd year (2002) £32,000
Holiday entitlement 25 days
% of trainees with a non-law degree p.a. 50%
No. of seats available abroad p.a. 24

post-qualification
Salary (2002) £50,000
% of trainees offered job on qualification (2002) 80-95%

overseas offices
Abú Dhabi, Brussels, Düsseldorf, Frankfurt, Hong Kong, Lisbon, London, Madrid, Milan, New York, Paris, Rome, Rotterdam, Padua, Shanghai, Tokyo

Slaughter and May

One Bunhill Row, London EC1Y 8YY
Tel: (020) 7600 1200 Fax: (020) 7090 5000
Website: www.slaughterandmay.com

firm profile
One of the leading law firms in the world, Slaughter and May enjoys a reputation for quality and expertise. The corporate and financial practice is particularly strong and lawyers are known for their business acumen and technical excellence. Much of the firm's work spans the globe with transactions involving not only the firm's overseas offices but also leading independent law firms in other jurisdictions. No London partner has ever left the firm to join a competing practice.

main areas of work
Corporate and financial 66%; commercial litigation 11%; tax 7%; property (commercial) 6%; pensions and employment 5%; competition 3%; intellectual property 2%.

trainee profile
The work is demanding and the firm looks for intellectual agility and the ability to work with people from different countries and walks of life. Common sense, a mature outlook and the willingness to accept responsibility are all essential. The firm expects to provide training in everything except the fundamental principles of law, so does not expect applicants to know much of commercial life. Trainees are expected to remain with the firm on qualification.

training environment
Four or five seats of three or six months duration. Two seats will be in the corporate and financial department with an option to choose a posting overseas, competition or financial regulation, a property seat is optional, and one seat in either litigation, intellectual property, tax or pensions and employment. In each seat a partner is responsible for monitoring your progress and reviewing your work. There is an extensive training programme which includes the PSC. There are also discussion groups covering general and specialised legal topics.

benefits
BUPA, STL, pension scheme, subsidised membership of health club, 24 hour accident cover.

vacation placements - summer 2003
Places: 60; Duration: 2 weeks; Remuneration: £250 p.w.; Closing Date: 7 February 2003 for penultimate year (of first degree) students only.

sponsorship & awards
CPE and LPC fees and maintenance grants are paid.

Partners 123
Associates 460
Total Trainees 158

contact
Graduate Recruitment

method of application
Covering letter & CV to include full details of all examination results

selection procedure
Interview

application
Training contracts p.a.
Approx 85
Applications p.a. **2,500+**
% interviewed p.a. **20%**
Required standard
Good 2:1 ability

training
Salary (May 2002)
1st year £29,000
2nd year £32,500
Holiday entitlement
25 days p.a.
% of trainees with a non-law degree **50%**
No. of seats available abroad p.a. **Approx 35**

post-qualification
Salary (May 2002) **£50,000**
% of trainees offered job on qualification **95%+**

overseas offices
Paris, Brussels, Singapore, Hong Kong, New York

Speechly Bircham

6 St Andrew Street, London EC4A 3LX
Tel: (020) 7427 6400 Fax: (020) 7427 6600
Email: trainingcontracts@speechlys.com
Website: www.speechlys.com

firm profile
Speechly Bircham is a mid-sized City law firm with an excellent client base. Its strong commercial focus is complemented by a highly regarded private client practice. The firm handles major transactions as well as commercial disputes and has a good reputation for several specialist advisory areas, notably personal and corporate tax. Speechly Bircham's strengths lie in the synergy of the relationships between its four main departments, private capital, corporate and tax, litigation and property.

main areas of work
Corporate and tax 25%; property 25%; litigation 25%; private capital 25%.

trainee profile
Both law and non-law graduates who are capable of achieving a 2:1. The firm seeks intellectually dynamic individuals who enjoy a collaborative working environment where they can make an impact.

training environment
Speechly Bircham divides the training contract into four six month seats. Emphasis is given to early responsibility and supervised client contact providing trainees with a practical learning environment.

benefits
Season ticket loan, private medical insurance, life assurance.

vacation placements
Places for 2003: 12. The firm's summer placement scheme for students gives them the chance to experience a City legal practice. In a three-practice placement, students will be asked to research and present on a legal issue at the end of their placement; Duration: 3 weeks; Remuneration: £250 p.w.; Closing Date: 14 February 2003.

sponsorship & awards
CPE and LPC tuition fees are paid in full plus a maintenance grant of £4,000 (£4,500 for London/Guildford) p.a.

Partners 40
Assistant Solicitors 60
Total Trainees 10

contact
Nicola Swann
Human Resources Director

method of application
Application form (available by request or online)

selection procedure
Interview

closing date for 2005
31 July 2003

application
Training contracts p.a. **5**
Applications p.a. **1,000**
% interviewed p.a. **5%**
Required degree grade **2:1**

training
Salary
1st year (2002) **£26,000-£27,000**
2nd year (2002) **£28,000-£29,000**
Holiday entitlement **20 days**
% of trainees with a non-law degree p.a. **50%**

post-qualification
Salary (2002) **£45,000**

Steele & Co

2 Norwich Business Park, Whiting Rd, Norwich NR4 6DJ
Tel: (01603) 274700 Fax: (01603) 274728
Email: personnel@steele.co.uk
Website: www.steele.co.uk

firm profile
Steele & Co is an innovative and progressive commercial firm with a growing national client base. It is recognised in particular for the strength of its employment and commercial practitioners and for the range and quality of its services to local authorities and business.

main areas of work
The firm offers a full range of corporate, property, litigation and public sector services. The firm is dedicated to delivering high quality value for money services to its clients regardless of location.

trainee profile
Candidates will be highly motivated, commercially astute, with a strong academic record and previous relevant experience.

training environment
The aim is to ensure that every trainee will wish to continue their career with the firm. The training programme consists of four six month seats in the following departments: company commercial, commercial property, civil litigation, commercial disputes, employment, family and public sector. You will have some choice in the order of your seats. Trainees are encouraged to take on as much responsibility as possible with considerable client contact early on in their training contract. Bi-monthly meetings provide a forum for discussion of topical issues. The offices are open-plan, providing a supportive and learning environment which reflects the firm's accreditation to both ISO 9001 and Investor in People. Trainee solicitors are appraised at the end of each seat and are included in the firm's mentor scheme. There is an active sports and social life.

benefits
Pension, accident insurance, legal services, interest-free season ticket loan, gym membership loan.

vacation placements
Places for 2003: Places offered throughout the Summer vacation.

Partners 12
Assistant Solicitors 20
Total Trainees 10

contact
Ann Chancellor
Human Resources Manager

method of application
Online or CV & covering letter

selection procedure
Interview

application
Training contracts p.a. **6**
Applications p.a. **300-400**
Required degree grade **2:1**

post-qualification
% of trainees offered job on qualification (2001)
100%

Stephenson Harwood

One St Paul's Churchyard, London EC4M 8SH
Tel: (020) 7329 4422 Fax: (020) 7606 0822
Email: graduate.recruitment@shlegal.com

firm profile
Established in the City of London in 1828, Stephenson Harwood has developed into a large international practice, with a commercial focus and a wide client base. In May 2002 the firm combined with Sinclair Roche & Temperley to form the new Stephenson Harwood.

main areas of work
Corporate (including corporate finance, funds, corporate tax, business technology); employment, pensions and benefits; banking and asset finance; dry and wet shipping litigation; commercial litigation; property; and private capital.

trainee profile
The firm looks for high calibre graduates with excellent academic records and an outgoing personality.

training environment
As the graduate intake is relatively small, the firm gives trainees individual attention, coaching and monitoring. Your structured and challenging programme involves four six month seats in areas of the firm covering contentious and non-contentious areas, across any department within our practice groups. It may also involve a secondment to one of the overseas offices or to a client in London. These seats include 'on the job' training, sharing an office and working with a partner or senior solicitor. In-house lectures complement your training and there is continuous review of your career development. You will have the opportunity to spend six months abroad and have free language tuition where appropriate. You will be given your own caseload and as much responsibility as you can shoulder. The firm plays a range of team sports, has its own gym, subsidised membership of a City health club (or a health club of your choice) and has privileged seats for concerts at the Royal Albert Hall and the London Coliseum and access to private views at the Tate Gallery.

benefits
Subsidised membership of health clubs, private health insurance, BUPA membership, season ticket loan and 25 days paid holiday per year.

vacation placements
Places for 2003: 16; Duration: 2 weeks; Remuneration: £250 p.w.; Closing Date: 21 February 2003.

sponsorship & awards
Fees paid for CPE and LPC and maintenance awards.

Partners 100*
Assistant Solicitors 358*
Total Trainees 46
denotes world-wide figures

contact
Graduate Recruitment

method of application
Application form only

selection procedure
Interview with 2 partners

closing date for September 2005/ March 2006
31 July 2003

application
Training contracts p.a. **16-18**
% interviewed p.a. **10%**
Required degree grade **2:1**

training
Salary
1st year (2002) **£26,000**
2nd year (2002) **£29,000**
Holiday entitlement
25 days
% of trainees with a non-law degree p.a. **46%**
No. of seats available abroad p.a. **10-12**

post-qualification
Salary (2002) **£48,000**
% of trainees offered job on qualification (2002) **75%**
% of assistants (as at 1/9/01) who joined as trainees **37%**
% of partners (as at 1/9/01) who joined as trainees **46%**

overseas offices
Bucharest, Madrid, Paris, Piraeus, Singapore and, in the People's Republic of China, in Guangzhou and Hong Kong, with an associated office in Shanghai

Tarlo Lyons

Watchmaker Court, 33 St John's Lane, London EC1M 4DB
Tel: (020) 7405 2000 Fax: (020) 7814 9421
Email: trainee.recruitment@tarlolyons.com
Website: www.tarlolyons.com

firm profile
Tarlo Lyons is recognised as one of the leading law firms in the country for its expertise in information technology and related areas. The firm has expanded at 30% per annum over the past three years and nearly two-thirds of the firm's turnover now derives from IT, telecommunications and Internet-related projects and advice, including e-commerce. The firm holds Investors in People accreditation.

main areas of work
Technology and communications; media; company and commercial; commercial property; dispute resolution; employment.

trainee profile
Applicants should have a sound academic record and a natural inquisitiveness and intellectual curiosity. An interest or background in information technology or commercial ventures is an advantage, as is a gap year or work undertaken outside of law. Applicants should also have common sense, resourcefulness and a good sense of humour.

training environment
Trainees will gain work experience in all the main areas of the practice. The PSC is taught externally and trainees also attend internal seminars. Trainees meet regularly with both a supervisor and the Training Partner and formal reviews are conducted every two months. The firm has a friendly, open-door policy and trainees are encouraged to take part in a wide range of marketing, sporting and social events.

benefits
Tarlo Lyons offers competitive compensation and salary may be enhanced by an annual discretionary bonus. The firm offers membership of a private health scheme, participation in a pension plan and subsidised membership of a nearby health club.

sponsorship & awards
LPC fees paid.

Partners 29
Assistant Solicitors 33
Total Trainees 6

contact
Trainee Recruitment Co-ordinator

method of application
Application form available from website

selection procedure
2 interviews with partners & skills assessment

closing date for 2005
11 August 2003

application
Training contracts p.a. **3**
Applications p.a. **500**
% interviewed p.a. **5%**
Required degree grade **2:1**

training
Salary
1st year (2001) £24,000 on average
2nd year (2001) £26,000 on average
Holiday entitlement
25 days
% of trainees with a non-law degree p.a. **50%**

post-qualification
Salary (2001) **£42,000**
(Salary levels may increase subject to market conditions)

Taylor Vinters

Merlin Place, Milton Rd, Cambridge CB4 0DP
Tel: (01223) 225220 Fax: (01223) 426523
Email: jo.douglas@taylorvinters.com
Website: www.taylorvinters.com

firm profile
One of the largest firms in East Anglia, based in the university city of Cambridge. The largest single office firm in Cambridge.

main areas of work
Company commercial; commercial litigation; commercial property; claimant personal injury; private client.

trainee profile
Candidates should have energy, enthusiasm, intelligence, common sense, a friendly nature and a good sense of humour. Non-law degree graduates are welcomed.

training environment
The training contract comprises four seats: commercial, property/planning, claimant personal injury and commercial litigation. Opportunities exist for exchanges with European Network firms. Trainees' progress is reviewed and assessed every three months. There is an extensive in-house training programme within all departments and firmwide. The PSC is also organised in-house.

benefits
Benefits include private medical insurance, life insurance and pension. Many social activities are actively encouraged, from a theatre club to karaoke. Cambridge of course now has the largest pub in Europe.

vacation placements
Places for 2003: Places available; Duration: 1 week; Closing Date: 31 March 2003.

Partners 26
Assistant Solicitors 52
Total Trainees 10

contact
Paul Tapner/Jo Douglas

method of application
Application form

selection procedure
Single interview with 1 partner & the HR Manager

closing date for 2005
31 August 2003

application
Training contracts p.a. 5
Applications p.a. 300
Required degree grade 2:2

training
Salary
1st year (2002) £16,000
2nd year (2002) £17,650
Holiday entitlement
25 days
% of trainees with a non-law degree p.a. 40%

post-qualification
Salary (2002) £31,500 + benefits

Taylor Walton

28-44 Alma Street, Luton LU1 2PL
Tel: (01582) 731161 Fax: (01582) 457900
Email: luton@taylorwalton.co.uk
Website: www.taylorwalton.co.uk

firm profile
Strategically located in Luton, Harpenden, St Albans and Hemel Hempstead, Taylor Walton is a major regional law practice advising both businesses and private clients. Its strengths are in commercial property, corporate work and commercial litigation, whilst maintaining a strong private client side to the practice. It has a progressive outlook both in its partners and staff and in its systems, training and IT.

main areas of work
Company/commercial 15%; commercial property 20%; commercial litigation 15%; employment 5%; personal injury 5%; family 5%; private client 10%; residential property 20%; direct conveyancing 5%.

trainee profile
Candidates need to show excellent intellectual capabilities, coupled with an engaging personality so as to show that they can engage and interact with the firm's clients as the practice of law involves the practice of the art of communication. Taylor Walton sees its partners and staff as business advisers involved in clients' businesses, not merely stand-alone legal advisers.

training environment
The training consists of four six month seats. The training partner oversees the structural training alongside a supervisor who will be a partner or senior solicitor in each department. The firm does try to take trainees' own wishes in relation to seats into account. In a regional law practice like Taylor Walton you will find client contact and responsibility coupled with supervision, management and training. There is an in-house training programme for all fee-earning members of staff. At the end of each seat there is a post seat appraisal conducted by the training partner, the trainee and the supervisor. The PSC is taught externally. The firm is friendly with an open door policy and there are various sporting and social events.

vacation placements
Places for 2003: 8; Duration: Up to 4 weeks; Remuneration: Agreed with trainee; Closing Date: 30 April 2003.

Partners	25
Assistant Solicitors	44
Total Trainees	10

contact
Jim Wrigglesworth

method of application
CV with covering letter

selection procedure
First & second interview with opportunity to meet other partners

closing date for 2005
30 September 2003

application
Required degree grade 2:1 or above

Taylor Wessing

Carmelite, 50 Victoria Embankment, Blackfriars
London EC4Y 0DX
Tel: (020) 7300 7000 Fax: (020) 7300 7100
Website: www.taylorwessing.com

firm profile
Taylor Wessing was launched on 1 September 2002 with a combination of the practices of Taylor Joynson Garrett and German law firm Wessing to provide European legal services in the two largest economies in Europe. Taylor Wessing provides a full range of legal services to major corporations and growing enterprises, with a particularly strong track record in serving knowledge-based businesses in sectors such as technology, life sciences and financial services. A market leader in many of its practice areas such as intellectual property, corporate finance and inward investment from the US, Taylor Wessing offers constructive, commercial advice offered through a partner-led service with a total, long-term commitment to its clients around the world.

main areas of work
Corporate 26%; intellectual property 19%; dispute resolution 17%; commercial property 13%; finance and projects 11%; private client 7%; employment 7%.

trainee profile
Academic achievement is high on the firm's list of priorities, and a 2:1 or better is expected. It wants individuals who have good communication skills and will flourish in a competitive environment. Strength of character, determination and the ability to think laterally are also important.

training environment
Trainees will have six month seats in four different departments, with the possibility of a placement in other offices. You will be supervised by a partner or senior assistant and appraised both three months into and at the end of each seat. There will be plenty of opportunity to take early responsibility. The firm works closely with external training providers to meet the needs of the PSC. The course is tailored to suit the firm's needs, and most of the training is conducted in-house. A full sports and social calendar is available.

benefits
Private medical care, permanent health insurance, STL, subsidised staff restaurant, non-contributory pension scheme.

vacation placements
Places for 2003: 28; Duration: 2 weeks; Remuneration: £200 p.w.; Closing date: 21 February 2003.

sponsorship & awards
CPE and LPC fees paid and £4,000 maintenance p.a.

Partners 181
Fee-earners 307
Trainees 52 (UK)

contact
Graduate Recruitment Department

method of application
Firm's application form

selection procedure
2 interviews, 1 with a partner

closing date for 2005
8 August 2003

application
Training contracts p.a. **25**
Applications p.a. **1,600**
% interviewed p.a. **10%**
Required degree grade **2:1**

training
Salary
1st year (2002) **£26,000**
2nd year (2002) **£29,000**
Holiday entitlement
25 days
% of trainees with a
non-law degree p.a. **40%**

post-qualification
Salary (2001) **£48,000**
% of trainees offered job
on qualification (2001) **96%**

overseas offices
Berlin, Brussels, Dusseldorf, Frankfurt, Hamburg, Munich, and representative offices in Alicante and Shanghai

Teacher Stern Selby

37-41 Bedford Row, London WC1R 4JH
Tel: (020) 7242 3191 Fax: (020) 7242 1156
Email: r.raphael@tsslaw.com
Website: www.tsslaw.com

firm profile
A central London-based general commercial firm, with clientele and caseload normally attributable to larger firms. It has a wide range of contacts overseas.

main areas of work
Commercial litigation 25%; commercial property 38%; company and commercial 16%; secured lending 12%; private client 4%; clinical negligence/education/judicial review 5%.

trainee profile
Emphasis falls equally on academic excellence and personality. The firm looks for flexible and motivated individuals, who have outside interests and who have demonstrated responsibility in the past. Languages an advantage.

training environment
Trainees spend six months in three departments (company commercial, litigation and property) with, where possible, an option to return to a preferred department in the final six months. Most trainees are assigned to actively assist a partner who monitors and supports them. Trainees are fully involved in departmental work and encouraged to take early responsibility. Trainees are expected to attend in-house seminars and lectures for continuing education. The atmosphere is relaxed and informal.

vacation placements
Places for 2003: Possibly to those that have accepted or applied for training contracts.

sponsorship & awards
CPE Funding: None; LPC Funding: Possible.

Partners 17
Assistant Solicitors 21
Total Trainees 6

contact
Russell Raphael

method of application
Letter & application form

selection procedure
2 interviews

closing date for 2005
31 October 2003

application
Training contracts p.a. **6**
Applications p.a. **1,000**
% interviewed p.a. **5%**
Required degree grade
2:1 (not absolute)

training
Salary
1st year (2005) **£23,000**
Holiday entitlement
4 weeks
% of trainees with a
non-law degree p.a. **50%**

post-qualification
Salary (2002) **£33,000**
% of trainees offered job
on qualification (2002) **66%**
% of assistants (as at 1/5/02) who joined as trainees **48%**
% of partners (as at 1/5/02) who joined as trainees **41%**

Theodore Goddard

150 Aldersgate Street, London EC1A 4EJ
Tel: (020) 7606 8855 Fax: (020) 7606 4390
Email: recruitment@theodoregoddard.co.uk
Website: www.theogoddard.com

firm profile
Theodore Goddard is a long-established City firm which supports clients not only in the traditional legal specialisations expected of a City firm but also in the media and communications sector. It is distinctive in that it punches above its weight in the size of the transactions it handles. With a reputation for having a friendly, unstuffy atmosphere, trainees are given early responsibility and are viewed as an integral part of the firm from day one.

main areas of work
Corporate, corporate finance and corporate tax; banking; PFI; commercial litigation; commercial property; employment; intellectual property and music; film; audio-visual; e-commerce; advertising; sport.

trainee profile
The firm seeks graduates from all disciplines who can demonstrate academic excellence. In an increasingly global, technology-driven market, the firm is looking for those who think they will enjoy a fast-paced, intellectually demanding working environment.

training environment
Theodore Goddard's training is exceptional; it has won five awards both from within the legal profession and across all sectors of employment. Trainees spend six months in four practice areas with the option of three months in Brussels or on secondment with a client. All trainees are consulted about seat preferences.

benefits
Pension, profit-related bonus, permanent health insurance, private medical insurance, subsidised health and fitness club membership and firm restaurant.

vacation placements
Places for 2003: 20 in the Summer vacation (70 open day places in the Easter vacation); Duration: 2 weeks; Remuneration: £200 p.w.; Closing Date: For summer placements and Easter open days – end of February 2003.

sponsorship & awards
CPE and LPC fees paid in full. £4,500 maintenance paid for London and South East, £4,000 elsewhere.

Partners 68
Total Fee-earners 190
Total Trainees 30

contact
Recruitment Manager

method of application
Firm's online application form

selection procedure
Initial interview followed by second interview

closing date for 2005
31 July 2003

application
Training contracts p.a. **20**
Applications p.a. **3,000**
% interviewed p.a. **5-10%**
Required degree grade **2:1+**

training
Salary
1st year £27,500 (2002)
2nd year £30,000 (2002)
Holiday entitlement
25 days
% of trainees with a non-law degree p.a. **40%**
No. of seats available abroad p.a. **4**

post-qualification
Salary (2001) £48,000
% of trainees offered job on qualification (2002) **100%**

overseas offices
Brussels (associated offices worldwide)

Thomson Snell & Passmore

3 Lonsdale Gardens, Tunbridge Wells TN1 1NX
Tel: (01892) 510000 Fax: (01892) 549884
Email: solicitors@ts-p.co.uk
Website: www.ts-p.co.uk

firm profile
Established in 1570, Thomson Snell & Passmore continues to be regarded as one of the premier law firms in the South East. The firm has a reputation for quality and a commitment to deliver precise and clear advice which is recognised and respected both by its clients and professional contacts. It has held the Lexcel quality mark since January 1999. The firm is vibrant and progressive and enjoys an extremely friendly atmosphere. Its offices are located in the centre of Tunbridge Wells and attract clients locally, nationally and internationally.

main areas of work
Commercial litigation 25%; corporate and commercial property 17%; private client 21%; personal injury/clinical negligence 15%; residential property 14%; family 8%.

trainee profile
Thomson Snell & Passmore regards its trainees from the outset as future assistants, associates and partners. The firm is looking for people not only with strong intellectual ability, but enthusiasm, drive, initiative, strong interpersonal and team-working skills, together with good IT skills.

training environment
The firm's induction course will help you to adjust to working life. As a founder member of Law South your training is provided in-house with trainees from other Law South member firms. Your two year training contract is divided into four periods of six months each. You will receive a thorough grounding and responsibility with early client exposure. You will be monitored regularly, receive advice and assistance throughout and appraisals every three months. The Training Partner will co-ordinate your continuing education in the law, procedure, commerce, marketing, IT and presentation skills. Trainees enjoy an active social life which is encouraged and supported.

sponsorship & awards
Grant and interest free loan available for LPC.

Partners 35
Assistant Solicitors 35
Total Trainees 8

contact
Pauline Tobin
Personnel Manager
Tel: (01892) 510000

method of application
Handwritten letter & firm's application form available from website

selection procedure
1 interview with Training Partner & 1 other partner

closing date for 2005
31 July 2003

application
Training contracts p.a. **4**
Applications p.a. **Approximately 500**
% interviewed p.a. **5%**
Required degree grade **2:1 (any discipline)**

training
Salary for each year of training
1st year **£15,750 (Sept 2002)**
2nd year **£16,750 (Sept 2002)**
Holiday entitlement **20 days**

post-qualification
Salary **£24,750 (Sept 2002)**
% of trainees offered job on qualification **75-100%**

overseas/regional offices
Network of independent law firms throughout Europe and founding member of Law South

Thring Townsend

6 Drakes Meadow, Penny Lane, Swindon SN3 3LL
Tel: (01793) 410800 Fax: (01793) 616294
Email: solicitors@ttuk.com
Website: www.ttuk.com

firm profile

Thring Townsend is one of central southern England's leading law firms, providing a focused range of commercial and private client services. With 270 staff, and offices in Swindon, Bath and Newbury, the current practice resulted from the merger of Thrings & Long and Townsends in November 2000. The firm is committed to building on its established and excellent reputation for commercial work. Company and commercial, commercial property, agriculture, employment and commercial litigation work are particular strengths and areas targeted for further growth. The client base is impressive ranging from major national companies and local subsidiaries of multinational companies, to government bodies, charities and family owned enterprises through to internet start-ups and entrepreneurs. The firm is committed to providing excellent client service and its commitment to quality and continuous improvement has been recognised by achieving IIP accreditation, the highly regarded 'Lexcel' award and the Community Legal Service Franchise for personal injury and family work.

trainee profile

Trainees will be given a broad range of experience by doing four six month seats in a variety of teams spread across the three business units. Areas covered include company commercial; commercial property; commercial litigation; property and construction litigation; personal injury; family; employment, wills and probate; conveyancing.

training environment

Trainees find the working environment is both friendly and supportive. Partners and support staff are approachable and a sense of humour is regarded as an asset. The firm has a strong sporting ethos and an active Sports and Social Committee organises events to suit everyone's tastes.

benefits

Immediate life assurance, pension and private medical insurance after a period of 12 months. 20 days holiday in the first year rising to 25 days in the second year.

Partners 36
Assistant Solicitors 27
Total Trainees 12

contact
Sean Whittle
Head of HR & Training
Tel: (01793) 412502

method of application
Request for application form

selection procedure
Assessment centre

closing date for 2005
31 August 2003

application
Training contracts p.a. 6
Applications p.a. 300
% interviewed p.a. 10%
Required degree grade 2:1 if straight from university. If a mature student with business experience, consider a 2:2

training
Salary
1st year £13,500
2nd year £17,000
Holiday entitlement
20 days

post-qualification
Salary £25,000-£30,000
% of trainees offered job on qualification 80%

other offices
Bath, Newbury

TLT Solicitors

One Redcliff St, Bristol BS99 7JZ
Tel: (0117) 917 7777 Fax: (0117) 917 7778
Email: lbevan@TLTsolicitors.com
Website: www.TLTsolicitors.com

firm profile
TLT is the third largest firm in Bristol and one of the top 100 in the country. The firm has around 100 lawyers, a total compliment of approximately 300 people and a turnover of over £13 million.

main areas of work
Corporate, including corporate finance, acquisitions, disposals, JVs, stock exchange and a substantial amount of AIM and OFEX work; Banking, including corporate lending, all types of banking litigation, mortgage documentation, insolvency, in addition to volume recoveries and conveyancing; Employment, including strategic employment work, HR consultancy services, specialist pensions expertise and management training; Property, including secured lending, development, planning, landlord and tenant, dispute resolution, management of property portfolios and estates; Dispute resolution, including handling a wide range of heavyweight domestic and international litigation, as well as a substantial amount of ADR work, particularly mediation and arbitration. TLT's client list also includes high net worth individuals whom it advises on family matters, tax and trusts. The firm's family team is widely regarded as the best in the region.

trainee profile
A strong academic background is preferred and a resourceful personality is also a consideration.

training environment
Training is administered by the training principal and the trainee supervisor. It is divided into four six month periods. Wherever possible, the seats are settled in consultation with the trainee, preference being given to second year trainees. All trainees sit with another lawyer but in every case the work will be drawn from all parts of the team giving the widest experience. Monitoring meetings are held bi-monthly.

benefits
Pension, subsidised health insurance, subsidised sports and health club facility, life assurance.

vacation placements
Eight summer placements available, each lasting one week.

sponsorship & awards
LPC fees paid plus maintenance grant.

Partners 32
Assistant Solicitors 36
Total Trainees 16

contact
Liz Bevan
Human Resources

method of application
Firm's application form

selection procedure
Assessment day

closing date for 2005
16 August 2003

application
Training contracts p.a. 8
Applications p.a. 750
% interviewed p.a. 5%
Required degree grade N/A

training
Holiday entitlement
25 days
% of trainees with a
non-law degree p.a. 50%

post-qualification
Salary (2001) Market rate

Travers Smith Braithwaite

10 Snow Hill, London EC1A 2AL
Tel: (020) 7295 3000 Fax: (020) 7295 3500
Email: graduate.recruitment@traverssmith.com
Website: www.traverssmith.com

firm profile
A leading medium-sized corporate, financial and commercial law firm with the capability to advise on a wide range of business activities. The practice offers small, closely-knit teams providing consistent service to clients.

main areas of work
Corporate; dispute resolution; property; banking; tax; pensions; employment.

trainee profile
Applications are welcome from both law and non-law graduates. The firm looks for people who combine academic excellence with plain common sense; who are articulate - on their feet and on paper; who are determined, self-motivated and have a healthy dose of humour.

training environment
Training consists of four six month seats taken from the corporate, commercial, banking, corporate recovery, employment, dispute resolution, property, pensions, financial services and corporate tax departments. There is no crowd to get lost in; trainees quickly get to know each other and everyone else in the firm. You are treated as an individual and given immediate responsibility for handling deals and clients. Formal training includes a comprehensive programme of in-house training and seminars. Trainees sit with partners. Social and sporting activities are enjoyed by the whole firm. The firm also offers a range of pro bono opportunities within individual departments and on a firm wide basis.

benefits
Private health insurance, permanent sickness cover, life assurance cover, season ticket loans, refreshment credit, subsidised sports club membership.

vacation placements
Places for 2003: 60 places for Summer 2003; Duration: 2 weeks; Remuneration: £250; Closing Date: 31 January 2003. The firm also offers Christmas and Easter vacation placements.

sponsorship & awards
LPC and CPE fees paid and between £4,500 and £5,000 maintenance p.a.

Partners 53
Assistant Solicitors 110
Total Trainees 37

contact
Germaine VanGeyzel

method of application
Handwritten letter & CV

selection procedure
Interviews

closing date for 2005
September 2003

application
Training contracts p.a. 25
Applications p.a. **1,800**
% interviewed p.a. **25%**
Required degree grade **2:1**

training
Salary
1st year (2001) £28,000
2nd year (2001) £32,000
Holiday entitlement
20 days
% of trainees with a non-law degree p.a.
Approx 50%

post-qualification
Salary (2002) **£50,000**
% of trainees offered job on qualification (2002) **80%**
% of assistants (as at 1/9/01) who joined as trainees **57%**
% of partners (as at 1/9/01) who joined as trainees **65%**

Trowers & Hamlins

Sceptre Court, 40 Tower Hill, London EC3N 4DX
Tel: (020) 7423 8000 Fax: (020) 7423 8001
Email: gradrecruitment@trowers.com
Website: www.trowers.com

firm profile
Trowers & Hamlins is a substantial international firm. A leader in housing and public sector law, the firm also has a strong commercial side. The firm has regional offices in the UK, offices in the Middle East and links with Jordan, Yemen, Singapore, USA and Europe.

main areas of work
Property (housing, public sector, commercial) 40%; company and commercial/construction 29%; litigation 24%; private client 7%.

trainee profile
Personable, enthusiastic candidates with a good academic record and wide-ranging outside interests. The ability to work under pressure and with others, combined with versatility, are essential characteristics.

training environment
Trainees will gain experience in four seats from: company/commercial, construction, property, international, litigation, employment and private client. Trainees are encouraged to learn from direct contact with clients and to assume responsibility. The training programme is flexible and, with reviews held every three months, individual preferences will be considered. A training officer assists partners with the training programme and in-house lectures and seminars are held regularly. There are opportunities to work in Manchester and the Middle East. The firm encourages a relaxed atmosphere and blends traditional qualities with contemporary attitudes. Activities are organised outside working hours.

benefits
Season ticket loan, private healthcare after six months service, Employee Assistance Programme and discretionary bonus, Death in Service.

vacation placements
Places for 2003: 25-30; Duration: 2 weeks; Remuneration: £200 p.w.; Closing Date: 1 March (Summer). Open Day: June/July.

sponsorship & awards
CPE and LPC fees paid and £4,250-£4,500 maintenance p.a.

Partners 65
Assistant Solicitors 90
Total Trainees 30

contact
Graduate Recruitment Office

method of application
Letter, application form & CV

selection procedure
Interview(s), essay & practical test

closing date for 2005
1 August 2003

application
Training contracts p.a. **12–15**
Applications p.a. **1,600**
% interviewed p.a. **4%**
Required degree grade **2:1+**

training
Salary
1st year (2000) **£25,500**
2nd year (2000) **£27,250**
Holiday entitlement
20 days (1st year)
22 days (2nd year)
% of trainees with a non-law degree p.a. **40%**
No. of seats available abroad p.a. **Between 4 and 6**

post-qualification
Salary (2002) **£43,500**
% of trainees offered job on qualification (2002) **90%**
% of assistants (as at 1/9/01) who joined as trainees **40%**
% of partners (as at 1/9/01) who joined as trainees **45%**

overseas offices
Abu Dhabi, Dubai, Oman, Bahrain, Cairo

Walker Morris

Kings Court, 12 King Street, Leeds LS1 2HL
Tel: (0113) 283 2500 Fax: (0113) 245 9412
Email: traineerecruit@walkermorris.co.uk
Website: www.walkermorris.co.uk

firm profile
Based in Leeds, Walker Morris is one of the largest commercial law firms in the North, providing a full range of legal services to commercial and private clients. It is increasingly gaining an international reputation.

main areas of work
Commercial litigation 30%; commercial property 25%; company and commercial 25%; building societies 16%; private clients 2%; tax 2%.

trainee profile
Bright, articulate, highly motivated individuals who will thrive on early responsibility in a demanding yet friendly environment.

training environment
Trainees commence with an induction programme, before spending four months in each main department (commercial property, corporate and commercial litigation). Trainees can choose in which departments they wish to spend their second year. Formal training will include interactive role plays, interactive video, lectures, workshops and seminars. The PSC covers personal work management, advocacy and professional conduct. Individual IT training is provided. Opportunities can also arise for secondments to some of the firm's major clients. Emphasis is placed on teamwork, inside and outside the office. The firm's social and sporting activities are an important part of its culture and are organised by a committee drawn from all levels of the firm. A trainee solicitors' committee also organises events and liaises with the Leeds Trainee Solicitors Group.

vacation placements
Places for 2003: 45 over 3 weeks; Duration: 1 week; Remuneration: £150 p.w.; Closing Date: 28 February 2003.

sponsorship & awards
PgDL and LPC fees plus maintenance of £3,500 per year (PgDL and LPC) or £4,000 (LPC only).

Partners 40
Assistant Solicitors 86
Total Trainees 29

contact
Nick Cannon

method of application
Application form

selection procedure
Telephone & face-to-face interviews

closing date for 2005
31 July 2003

application
Training contracts p.a. **15**
Applications p.a.
Approx. 600
% interviewed p.a.
Telephone **16%**
Face to face **8%**
Required degree grade **2:1**

training
Salary
1st year (2001) **£20,000**
2nd year (2001) **£22,000**
Holiday entitlement
24 days
% of trainees with a non-law degree p.a.
30% on average

post-qualification
Salary (2002) **£32,000**
% of trainees offered job on qualification (2001) **60%**
% of assistants (as at 1/9/00) who joined as trainees **60%**
% of partners (as at 1/9/00) who joined as trainees **47%**

Ward Hadaway

Sandgate House, 102 Quayside, Newcastle upon Tyne NE1 3DX
Tel: (0191) 204 4000 Fax: (0191) 204 4001
Email: personnel@wardhadaway.com
Website: www.wardhadaway.com

firm profile
Ward Hadaway is one of the most progressive commercial law firms in the North of England. The firm is firmly established as one of the North East region's legal heavyweights.

main areas of work
Litigation 37%; property 31%; company/commercial 26%; private client 6%.

trainee profile
The usual academic and professional qualifications are sought. Sound commercial and business awareness are essential as is the need to demonstrate strong communication skills, enthusiasm and flexibility. Candidates will be able to demonstrate excellent inter-personal and analytical skills.

training environment
The training contract is structured around four seats (property, company/commercial, litigation and private client) each of six months duration. At regular intervals, and each time you are due to change seat, you will have the opportunity to discuss the experience you would like to gain during your training contract. The firm will always try to give high priority to your preferences. You will share a room with a partner or associate which will enable you to learn how to deal with different situations. Your practical experience will also be complemented by an extensive programme of seminars and lectures. All trainees are allocated a 'buddy', usually a second year trainee or newly qualified solicitor, who can provide as much practical advice and guidance as possible during your training. The firm has an active Social Committee and offers a full range of sporting and social events.

benefits
23 days holiday (26 after five years service), death in service insurance, pension.

vacation placements
Applications for summer vacation placements should be received by 30 April 2003. Duration 1 week.

sponsorship & awards
LPC fees paid and £2,000 interest-free loan.

Partners 45
Total Trainees 16

contact
Carol Todner
Human Resources Manager

method of application
Application form & handwritten letter

selection procedure
Interview

closing date for 2005
31 July 2003

application
Training contracts p.a. 10
Applications p.a. 400
% interviewed p.a. 10%
Required degree grade 2:1

training
Salary
1st year (2001) £17,000
2nd year (2001) £18,000
Holiday entitlement
23 days
% of trainees with a non-law degree p.a. **Varies**

post-qualification
Salary (2002) £27,500 minimum

Watson, Farley & Williams

15 Appold Street, London EC2A 2HB
Tel: (020) 7814 8000 Fax: (020) 7814 8017
Email: graduates@wfw.com
Website: www.wfw.com

firm profile
Established in 1982, Watson, Farley & Williams has its strengths in corporate, banking and asset finance, particularly ship and aircraft finance. The firm aims to provide a superior service in specialist areas and to build long-lasting relationships with its clients.

main areas of work
Shipping; ship finance; aviation; banking; asset finance; corporate; litigation; e-commerce; intellectual property; EC and competition; taxation; property; insolvency; telecoms; project finance.

trainee profile
Outgoing graduates who exhibit energy, ambition, self-assurance, initiative and intellectual flair.

training environment
Trainees are introduced to the firm with a comprehensive induction course covering legal topics and practical instruction. Seats are available in at least four of the firm's main areas, aiming to provide trainees with a solid commercial grounding. There is also the opportunity to spend time abroad, working on cross-border transactions. Operating in an informal, friendly and energetic atmosphere, trainees will receive support whenever necessary. You will be encouraged to take on early responsibility and play an active role alongside a partner at each stage of your training. The practice encourages continuous learning for all employees and works closely with a number of law lecturers, producing a widely-read 'digest' of legal developments, to which trainees are encouraged to contribute. All modules of the PSC are held in-house. The firm has its own sports teams and organises a variety of social functions.

benefits
Life assurance, PHI, BUPA, STL, pension, subsidised gym membership.

vacation placements
Places for 2003: 30; Duration: 2 weeks; Remuneration: £200 p.w.; Closing Date: 2 March 2003.

sponsorship & awards
CPE and LPC fees paid and £4,500 maintenance p.a. (£4,000 outside London).

Partners 56
Assistant Solicitors 150
Total Trainees 24

contact
Graduate Recruitment Manager

method of application
Online application

selection procedure
Assessment centre & interview

closing date for 2005
27 July 2003

application
Training contracts p.a. 12
Applications p.a. **1,000**
% interviewed p.a. **5%**
Required degree grade
Minimum 2:1 & 24 UCAS points or above

training
Salary
1st year (2001) £28,500
2nd year (2001) £32,500
Holiday entitlement
22 days
% of trainees with a non-law degree p.a.
50%
No. of seats available abroad p.a. 12

post-qualification
Salary (2002) **Not less than £50,000 at the time of writing**
% of trainees offered job on qualification (2001)
80%
% of assistants (as at 1/9/01) who joined as trainees 40%
% of partners (as at 1/9/01) who joined as trainees 4%

overseas offices
New York, Paris, Piraeus, Singapore, Bangkok

Wedlake Bell

16 Bedford Street, Covent Garden, London WC2E 9HF
Tel: (020) 7395 3000 Fax: (020) 7836 9966
Email: recruitment@wedlakebell.com
Website: www.wedlakebell.com

firm profile
Wedlake Bell is a medium-sized law firm providing legal advice to businesses and high net worth individuals from around the world. The firm's services are based on a high degree of partner involvement, extensive business and commercial experience and strong technical expertise. The firm has over 80 lawyers in central London and Guernsey, and affiliations with law firms throughout Europe and in the United States.

main areas of work
For the firm's business clients: Banking and asset finance; corporate finance; commercial property; media, IP and commercial; internet and e-business; employment services; pensions and share schemes; construction; litigation and dispute resolution.
For private individuals: Tax, trusts and wealth protection; offshore services.

trainee profile
In addition to academic excellence, Wedlake Bell looks for commercial aptitude, flexibility, enthusiasm, a personable nature, confidence, mental agility and computer literacy in its candidates. Languages are not crucial.

training environment
Trainees have four seats of six months across the following areas: corporate finance, banking, construction, media and IP/IT, employment, litigation, property and private client. As a trainee the firm encourages you to have direct contact and involvement with clients from an early stage. You will work within highly specialised teams and have a high degree of responsibility. You will be closely supervised by a partner or senior solicitor and become involved in high quality and varied work. The firm is committed to the training and career development of its lawyers and many of its trainees continue their careers with the firm often through to partnership. Wedlake Bell has an informal, creative and co-operative culture with a balanced approach to life.

sponsorship & benefits
LPC and CPE fees paid and £2,000 maintenance grant where local authority grant not available. During training contract: pension, travel loans, subsidised gym membership. On qualification: 25 days holiday, life assurance, medical insurance and PHI.

vacation placements
Places for 2003: 6; Duration: 3 weeks in July; Remuneration: £150 p.w.; Closing Date: End of February.

Partners 33
Assistant Solicitors 34
Total Trainees 10

contact
Natalie King

method of application
CV & covering letter

selection procedure
Interviews in September

closing date for 2005
End August 2003

application
Training contracts p.a.
4 or 6
Applications p.a. **800**
% interviewed p.a. **3%**
Required degree grade **2:1**

training
Holiday entitlement
20 days
% of trainees with a non-law degree p.a. **25%**

post-qualification
% of trainees offered job on qualification (2001)
50%
% of assistants (as at 1/9/00) who joined as trainees **50%**

overseas offices
Guernsey

Weightman Vizards

India Buildings, Water Street, Liverpool L2 0GA
Tel: (0870) 241 3512 Fax: (0151) 227 3223
Email: HR@weightmanvizards.com
Website: www.weightmanvizards.com

Partners	73
Assistant Solicitors	96
Trainees p.a.	12

contact
Sarah Gant
HR Adviser
Bill Radcliffe
Training Principal

method of application
Application forms & brochures are available from HR Department in Liverpool

closing date for 2005
31 July 2003

other offices
Birmingham, Leicester, London, Manchester

firm profile
Weightman Vizards is a successful and progressive UK law firm, committed to its clients and values. The firm has 73 partners heading a total of more than 560 trained and dedicated people all of whom share the sense of commitment and purpose needed to meet the firm's clients' most challenging legal requirements. With an established presence in Birmingham, Leicester, Liverpool, London and Manchester, the firm is perfectly placed to help its clients achieve their business objectives. Weightman Vizards has an established and expanding commercial practice with unrivalled presence in the insurance, litigation and public sector markets. Throughout your two-year training contract, you will have the opportunity to experience these varied work types. And you will be able to enjoy hands-on client contact from day one.

main areas of work
The firm's areas of commercial expertise include company commercial, commercial litigation, property, employment, licensing, construction, intellectual property and IT. Litigation expertise includes workplace, transport and large loss claims. Specialist teams within the firm service the healthcare, professional indemnity, public sector and police markets.

trainee profile
Weightman Vizards is a friendly firm, with a strong commitment to a team environment and a culture that encourages early, decisive and effective action from all its staff. The firm is looking for enterprising commercially-minded people, who share its commitment to client service and will contribute to the spirit of the firm by demonstrating their support for its values. Applications from a wide variety of academic backgrounds are considered. Those with a track record that demonstrates an ability to study with discipline and common sense to achieve results will have a distinct advantage. The firm believes in rewarding all of its people well. It pays a highly competitive salary that is reviewed annually. The firm offers a benefits package, which includes a pension, health cover and life assurance. If you are offered a Training Contract, the firm will pay all course/study fees for LPC and CPE study.

training environment
Weightman Vizards' expects its trainees to make a positive contribution from the outset. Four 6-month seats, with focused training and regular review meetings, provide a progressive learning environment for our young lawyers.

Weil, Gotshal & Manges

One South Place, London EC2M 2WG
Tel: (020) 7903 1074 Fax: (020) 7903 0990
Email: uktrainingcontracts@weil.com
Website: www.weil.com

firm profile
Weil, Gotshal & Manges was founded in New York in 1931. The London office, established in 1996, has grown rapidly to become the second largest office of the firm and is now the hub of the European practice. With more than 120 lawyers, it is one of the largest US-based international law firms in London, with one of the widest ranging practices. The London office provides its clients with full dual capability in US and UK law.

main areas of work
The firm advises some of the world's leading international corporations and financial institutions. Its practice bridges the traditional divide between US and UK corporate and finance law and encompasses acquisition finance, asset finance and leasing, banking, biotechnology and pharmaceuticals, commercial litigation and arbitration, competition, corporate restructurings and workouts, derivatives, environmental, financial services, mergers and acquisitions, pensions, private equity, real estate, restructuring, securitisation, structured finance, taxation and technology.

trainee profile
The firm is looking for trainees with the commercial acumen and energy to become legal experts providing high quality client service and advice to complex international transactions. It needs people who have a genuine contribution to make to the continued success in the development of the London office. It aims to recruit down-to-earth people with the intelligence, personality and drive to be happy and successful in an entrepreneurial environment.

training environment
Trainees who join the firm in 2005 will usually complete four six month seats, one of which may be in an overseas office. In order to ensure its trainees receive adequate support and on-the-job training, they each work closely with a senior associate or partner. The practical experience gained through exposure to client work is enhanced by regular internal seminars. Legal staff are also assisted by an excellent team of support staff. The firm aims to keep all trainees on qualification.

benefits
Pension, permanent health insurance, private health cover, life assurance, subsidised gym membership, season ticket loan. The firm will pay tuition fees and a maintenance allowance for CPE and LPC.

vacation placements
Places for 2003: 12 in summer vacation. Closing date for applications by EAF: 14 February 2003.

Partners 27
Assistant Solicitors 76
Total Trainees 18

contact
Cathy McDonagh
Graduate Recruitment Assistant

method of application
Employer's application form

closing date for 2005
31 July 2003

application
Training contracts p.a. 12
Required degree grade 2:1

training
Salary
1st year (2001) £35,000
Holiday entitlement
23 days

overseas offices
Brussels, Budapest, Dallas, Frankfurt, Houston, Silicon Valley, Miami, New York, Prague, Singapore, Warsaw, Washington DC

affiliated offices
Paris, Cairo

White & Case

7-11 Moorgate, London EC2R 6HH
Tel: (020) 7600 7300 Fax: (020) 7600 7030
Email: trainee@whitecase.com
Website: www.whitecase.com

firm profile
White & Case is a law firm with over 1,600 lawyers in 40 offices worldwide. The London office has been open for over 30 years and boasts over 100 UK and US qualified lawyers who work with financial institutions, multinational corporations and governments on major international corporate and financial transactions and complex disputes.

main areas of work
In the London office: acquisition finance; asset finance; banking, capital markets; corporate finance, construction; dispute resolution; employment; intellectual property; M&A; project finance; securitisation; tax; telecommunications, media and technology.

trainee profile
Trainees should be enthusiastic, be able to show initiative and have a desire to be involved with innovative and high profile legal matters. You should have an understanding of international commercial issues.

training environment
The firm's trainees are important and valued members of the London office and frequently work on multijurisdictional matters requiring close co-operation with lawyers throughout the firm's established global network. You will spend six months in each seat and cover the majority of work dealt with in the London office during the course of your training contract. You will sit with an associate or partner and hands-on experience will be supplemented by formal internal training sessions. You are encouraged to spend six months in one of the firm's overseas offices to gain a fuller understanding of the global network.

benefits
BUPA, gym membership contribution, life insurance, pension scheme, permanent health scheme, season ticket loan, discretionary bonus scheme.

vacation placements
Places for 2003: 40-50; Duration: 2 weeks; Remuneration: £250; Closing Date: End of February 2003.

sponsorship & awards
CPE and LPC fees paid and £5,500 maintenance p.a. Prizes for commendation and distinction for LPC.

Partners 31
Assistant Solicitors 70
Total Trainees 30

contact
Ms Emma Falder

method of application
Online application via firm website

selection procedure
Interview

closing date for 2005
31 July 2003

application
Training contracts p.a.
20-25
Applications p.a. **1,500**
Required degree grade **2:1**

training
Salary
1st year (2002) £33,000, rising by £1,500 every 6 months
Holiday entitlement
25 days

All trainees are encouraged to spend a seat abroad

post-qualification
Salary (2002) £60,000

overseas offices
Almaty, Ankhara, Bahrain, Bangkok, Berlin, Bombay, Bratislava, Brussels, Budapest, Dresden, Düsseldorf, Frankfurt, Hamburg, Helsinki, Ho Chi Minh City, Hong Kong, Istanbul, Jakarta, Jeddah, Johannesburg, London, Los Angeles, Mexico City, Miami, Milan, Moscow, New York, Palo Alto, Paris, Prague, Riyadh, Rome, San Francisco, São Paulo, Singapore, Shanghai, Stockholm, Tokyo, Warsaw, Washington DC

Wiggin and Co

95 The Promenade, Cheltenham GL50 1WG
Tel: (01242) 224114 Fax: (01242) 224223
Email: law@wiggin.co.uk

firm profile
Based in Cheltenham, with offices in London and Los Angeles, Wiggin and Co is a 'city-type' niche practice. It specialises in private client (particularly in international tax planning for the super-rich individual), non-contentious and contentious media law (with particular emphasis on broadcast media and entertainment) and the company/commercial fields.

main areas of work
Private client 27%; media and entertainment 37%; corporate 18%; litigation 11%; property 7%.

trainee profile
Candidates will have a strong academic background, be personable and show a willingness to work hard individually or as part of a team.

training environment
The training is divided into six 'seats'. Trainees will spend time in all five departments, namely the company/commercial, private client, media (two 'seats'), litigation and property departments. Trainees are encouraged to take an active role in transactions, assume responsibility and deal directly with clients. In-house lectures and seminars are held regularly and training reviews are held every four months. The firm offers the attraction of Cheltenham combined with technical ability and experience akin to a large City firm. Its relatively small size encourages a personal approach towards staff and client relations.

benefits
Life assurance, private health cover, pension scheme, permanent health insurance.

sponsorship & awards
CPE and LPC fees and £3,000 maintenance p.a. Brochure available on request.

Partners 13
Assistant Solicitors 11
Total Trainees 6

contact
Simon Baggs

method of application
CV

selection procedure
2 interviews

closing date for 2005
21 August 2003

application
Training contracts p.a. 3
Applications p.a. 300
% interviewed p.a. 8%
Required degree grade 2:1

training
Salary
1st year (2001) £21,900
2nd year (2001) £28,000
Holiday entitlement
20 days
% of trainees with a non-law degree p.a. 20%

post-qualification
Salary (2001) £40,000
% of trainees offered job on qualification (2002) 66%
% of assistants (as at 2001) who joined as trainees 67%
% of partners (as at 2001) who joined as trainees 23%

overseas office
Los Angeles

Withers LLP

16 Old Bailey, London EC4M 7EG
Tel: (020) 7597 6000 Fax: (020) 7597 6543
Email: ashley.napier@withersworldwide.com
Website: www.withersworldwide.com

Partners	67
Legal Staff	211
Total Trainees	22

contact
Ashley Napier
Human Resources Assistant

method of application
Application form & covering letter

selection procedure
2 interviews

closing date for 2005
31 July 2003

application
Training contracts p.a. 12
Applications p.a. 1,500
% interviewed p.a. 10%
Required degree grade 2:1

training
Salary
1st year (2002) £27,000
2nd year (2002) £29,500
Holiday entitlement
23 days
% of trainees with a non-law degree p.a. 50%

post-qualification
Salary (2001) £45,000

overseas offices
Milan, New York, New Haven

firm profile

Withers' transatlantic merger with US firm Bergman, Horowitz & Reynolds has created the first international law firm dedicated to the business, personal and philanthropic interests of successful people, their families and advisers. The firm provides integrated answers to the US, UK and international legal and tax needs of its clients whether this means restructuring their own assets, buying or selling businesses and properties, coping with divorce, termination of their employment or setting up charitable foundations. The exciting mix of work creates a diverse and interesting training for the small number of trainees employed. Withers LLP has the largest team of specialist private client lawyers in Europe and more Italian speakers than any other City law firm. This year the firm has extended its presence in Milan, opening a new office there.

main areas of work

Private client and charities 38%; family 15%; litigation 20%; corporate, company and commercial 14%; property 13%.

training environment

Trainees spend six months in four of the firm's five departments (family, property, private client, corporate and litigation). On the job training is supplemented by the firm's departmental and trainee-specific training. Buddy and mentor systems ensure that trainees are fully supported from the outset.

benefits

Interest-free season ticket loan, private medical insurance, life assurance, Christmas bonus, social events, subsidised café facilities.

vacation placements

Easter and Summer vacation placements are available. Students spend two weeks in two different departments. The closing date for applications is 7 February 2003. The firm has 24 places available during Summer and six at Easter.

sponsorship & awards

CPE/PgDL and LPC fees and £4,500 maintenance p.a. are paid. A cash prize is awarded for a distinction or commendation in the CPE/PgDL and/or LPC.

withers LLP

Wragge & Co

55 Colmore Row, Birmingham B3 2AS
Tel: Freephone (0800) 096 9610
Email: gradmail@wragge.com
Website: www.wragge.com/graduate

firm profile
Wragge & Co is a major UK law firm based in Birmingham with a substantial national and international client base including over 250 listed companies and 60 local authorities. Over 70% of the firm's turnover is generated from outside the Midlands. Wragge & Co has built its business on four strategic building blocks – clients, quality, people and profits – a focus which has fuelled the firm's national profile and growth. There is real strength and depth across a fully comprehensive range of services combined with the development of leading practices. Investment in IT has maximised efficiency while a focus on 'people culture' has secured staff retention and high profile appointments. And always there is devotion to providing the highest quality work and client service – Wragge & Co prides itself on being a 'relationship' firm. In recognition of the firm's progressive personnel policies the firm was placed 19th in *The Sunday Times* 100 Best Companies to Work For 2002, the highest placed law firm, was 'Best in the Land' according to a leading legal publication's 2001 Assistant Survey and was voted 'the law firm with best training environment' at the Trainee Solicitor Awards 2001. And in recognition of the firm's commitment to the community, Wragge & Co has a dedicated pro-bono and community support co-ordinator.

main areas of work
The firm enjoys a national reputation in areas such as corporate, dispute resolution, employment, tax, information technology, media, EU/competition, transport and utilities, project finance and banking. It has also built the UK's third largest property group, a leading UK construction practice and a top UK IP practice. Other 'top five' areas include EU and competition, public law and regulation and pensions. The quality of work is reflected in the organisations included in the firm's client list – 3i, AT&T, Royal Bank of Scotland, BMW, Boots, British Airways, Cadbury Schweppes, Cap Gemini, Ernst & Young, Carlton Communications, DaimlerBenz, GKN, H J Heinz, HP Foods, HSBC, KPMG, Land Rover, Lloyds TSB, Marks and Spencer, McDonald's, Powergen, Peugeot Motor Company, Royal & Sun Alliance, Severn Trent, Transco and Vodafone. Whilst Wragge & Co's base remains in Birmingham, the firm also has offices in Brussels, supporting the EU/competition team, and in London dealing with intellectual property and property development. As a trainee you will be given the opportunity to spend six months in either of these offices. The firm has a substantial number of international connections, regularly represents UK clients doing business overseas and acts as project managers on international transactions. It frequently works with professional advisers in foreign jurisdictions, in addition to acting for overseas clients in the UK and elsewhere. More than 25% of its work is international.

Partners 108
Assistant Solicitors 305
Total Trainees 46

contact
Julie Caudle
Graduate Recruitment & Training Manager

method of application
Applications are made online at www.wragge.com/graduate (paper application form available on request)

selection procedure
Telephone discussion & assessment day

closing date for September 2005/March 2006
31 July 2003. If you are a non-law student, please return your form as soon as possible, as the firm will be running assessment days over the forthcoming year

application
Training contracts p.a. **25**
Applications p.a. **1,300**
% interviewed p.a. **15%**
Required degree grade **2:1**

training
Salary (Sept 2002)
1st year **£21,000**
2nd year **£24,000**
Holiday entitlement
23 days
% of trainees with a non-law degree p.a. **Varies**

post-qualification
Salary (2002) **£33,000**
% of trainees offered job on qualification (2002) **90%**
% of assistants (as at 1/5/02) who joined as trainees **50%**
% of partners (as at 1/5/02) who joined as trainees **47%**

Wragge & Co continued

trainee profile
Wragge & Co are looking for graduates who are of a 2:1 standard at degree level, with some legal and/or commercial work experience gained either via holiday jobs or a previous career. Candidates should be practical with a common sense and problem solving approach to work and be able to show adaptability, enthusiasm and ambition.

training environment
Wragge & Co places considerable emphasis on transforming trainees into high quality, commercially-minded lawyers. You will spend six months in four different practice areas which usually are property, corporate and litigation, with a chance to specialise in a seat of your choice. From day one, you will work on live files with direct contact with clients, other solicitors and also be responsible for the management of the transaction and its ultimate billing. The more aptitude you show, the greater the responsibility you will be given. You will be supported by the Graduate Recruitment Team, a Partner who acts as a mentor to you throughout your training contract and a Supervisor who will co-ordinate your work and give you weekly feedback. Introductory courses are provided at the start of each seat in addition to the Professional Skills Course training requirements. This formal training complements 'on the job' learning and it is more than likely the firm's commitment to your development will extend well past the number of days recommended by the Law Society. Some of the courses will be residential, allowing you to reflect on your work practices away from the office environment and forge relationships and compare notes with your colleagues without the disturbances of your daily work.

benefits
Benefits include a prize for 1st class degree and LPC distinction, £1,000 interest free loan, pension scheme, life assurance, permanent health insurance, 23 days holiday p.a., travel schemes, travel desk, access to private medical insurance, sports and social club, independent financial advice and a Christmas gift.

sponsorship & awards
Wragge & Co will provide your tuition fees for LPC and PgDL (where relevant) and a maintenance grant of £4,500 for each year of study for LPC and PgDL.

vacation placements
Easter and Summer vacation placements are run at Wragge & Co. As part of the firm's scheme, you will get the opportunity to experience different areas of the firm, attend client meetings and get involved in real files. There are also organised social events with its current trainees. Applications are made online at www.wragge.com/graduate (paper application form available on request). Closing date for applications is 31 January 2003.

notes